Encyclopedia
of
Matchbox® Toys

Revised & Expanded 2nd Edition

Schiffer Publishing Ltd®

4880 Lower Valley Road, Atglen, PA 19310 USA

Charlie Mack

Acknowledgments

Thanks to Frank Veres for his wonderful photography and to Bob Parker for his assistance during hours of picture taking. Thanks to the following persons who reviewed and corrected text and advised some of the pricing—Art Cox, Dayle Friedman, Jim and Shawn Gallegos, Sonny Hendel, Alan Wank, Chris Getz, and Hardy Ristau. A special thanks to Christian Falkensteiner for his proofreading skills! Thanks to Peter and Nancy Schiffer for once again giving me the opportunity to write yet another book about a subject that I love!

MB4-D/43H35 1957 Chevy "1 of 750 Winner Car"

Title page photo: MB38E437 Model A Ford Van reissued as MW76 in 1998

Library of Congress Cataloging-in-Publication Data

Mack, Charles.
Encyclopedia of Matchbox toys/Charlie Mack. -- Rev. & expanded
2nd ed.
p.   cm.
ISBN: 0-7643-0866-1
1. Matchbox toys--Collectors and collecting. 2. Matchbox toys
Catalogs. I. Title.
TL237.2.M3297   1999
688.7'2'075--dc21   99-32455
CIP

Revised price guide: 1999
Copyright © 1997 & 1999 by Charlie Mack

Designed by Bonnie M. Hensley
Layout by Tammy Ward & Randy L. Hensley

ISBN: 0-7643-0866-1
Printed in China
1 2 3 4

Published by Schiffer Publishing Ltd.
4880 Lower Valley Road
Atglen, PA 19310
Phone: (610) 593-1777; Fax: (610) 593-2002
E-mail: schifferbk@aol.com
Please write for a free catalog.
This book may be purchased from the publisher.
Please include $3.95 for shipping.
Try your bookstore first.

We are interested in hearing from authors
with book ideas on related subjects.

Table of Contents

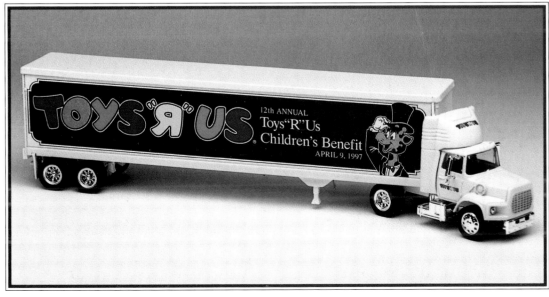

Gold Collection Rig- "Toys R Us Children's Benefit"

Introduction

The toys pictured and listed in this book represent the immense volume of items produced from 1947 through 1996, fifty years of toys. The "Matchbox" brand includes not only their popular diecast toys, but innumerable products including play sets, dolls, plastic kits, robots, and ephemera. All these, though not all pictured, are included in this massive volume.

The international scope of Matchbox toys is quite apparent as one encounters catalogs, boxes, and labels on toys printed in a dozen languages. Certain toys have been made for sale in specific countries or to promote specific companies or products. The number system on miniatures changed in 1982, when different numbering systems were introduced for worldwide and United States distribution. The result of all these variables is a fascinating and infinite variety of Matchbox toys.

The public's consistent enthusiasm and the long-term interest of children and adults alike have provided the necessary ingredients for Matchbox toys to become ideal collectible items. The old toys are becoming scarcer and variations of both old and new toys challenge collectors on a quest to own each one. Collectors seek both models and their associated packaging, as well as printed material such as catalogs and displays. Collectors are drawn by their common goals and many join organized clubs, a current list of which is included at the end of this book. Collectors clubs provide up-to-date details on current and future models as well as updating collectors on toy shows and gatherings.

A Word on Variations

In addition to the major variations listed in this text, there are countless casting, window, tire, and base variations not listed. These changes occurred as tooling became worn or parts for a certain model were exhausted and available parts from other models were used to finish production runs. Different shades of color are inevitable since different paints became mixed or were bought from different suppliers.

Certain models have interchangeable parts which can make for unauthorized variations. Replacement parts and decals have been made over the years including tires, treads, and parts that tend to break off. It is important to realize that almost all collectors and dealers are honest, but learning to recognize a restored model is your best safeguard against paying too much.

A Word on Pricing

Generally, the price noted in this book is for a mint *and* boxed model. Occasionally, some models never get boxed and may only be available blisterpacked. Current Matchbox Collectible items are only packed in Styrofoam with a white mailer box, so these could be referred to as mint only. Blisterpacks generally add little to the price of a model, sometimes as little as two percent. However, rare style blisterpacks, such as pre-1970 ones can realize ten to twenty-five percent of a premium to your model. Certain boxes can add a premium price to your model. It is suggested that you read the chapter on boxes in this book to familiarize yourself with some of the rarer boxes which command many more times the price of the model itself! The local market usually determines the price of a model. Yesteryear toys usually command a higher price in Europe and casting changes command a premium among some Yesteryear enthusiasts. A model in less-than-mint condition generally commands a price far less than a mint piece. A model that is seventy-five percent mint is valued likewise. A very chipped or broken model usually commands little or no value except in extreme cases when the model is so rare, a premium can still be added. For instance, a model priced at $1,000 that is fifty percent chipped can still command $100 if rare enough. This book is by no means perfect in its price evaluations. This is merely a guideline. You may find some items much higher or lower than those listed. A (+) sign designation for models indicates that the model is so rare that it has no high value and can command whatever the market or one's pocketbook can bear.

20-C1 Chevrolet Taxi with GRAY plastic wheels- Auctioned off in 1998 at $6600

History

Leslie Smith and Rodney Smith were school friends who reunited by chance in 1940 when they both served in the English Royal Navy. They each shared an ambition of one day having their own engineering factory and discussed joining each other once World War II was over. They eventually formed a partnership and began "Lesney Products" on June 19, 1947. This was a composite of their first names, and the word "Products" seemed appropriate because they had not decided what they would make. Leslie Smith was also employed by the J. Raymond Wilson Company which confirmed overseas orders; a position he held for several years. He worked in the evenings keeping Lesney's financial records until the company grew sufficiently to support him full-time. Rodney Smith found employment with the engineering firm of Diecast and Machine Tools in London.

With about six hundred British pounds in combined revenue, the pair bought the old tavern, Rifleman, at Edmonton, London, and some government surplus die-casting machinery. They were determined to make pressure die-casting products for industrial use.

Another employee at Diecast and Machine Tools was John W. Odell, always referred to as Jack. He contributed his particular casting skill and joined into the Lesney venture. As subcontractors for industry, the three began producing small diecast components. They were among many such firms in London contributing to the rebuilding of the city.

The English custom of taking stock inventory for taxation purposes on the first of January led to reduced orders for component suppliers during the last two months of the year. Therefore, the few Lesney employees were not kept busy producing diecastings during those months and the founders considered alternate products. Some of the other small diecast firms had made a few toys and the Lesney team experimented with this as well. In 1948, the first of these toys was produced and sold locally in London in small shops. The first toy was a large-scale Road Roller. By 1952, Lesney was supplying a few toys to some of the Woolworth stores in London for the Christmas season.

The London toy distributors considered these little toys "Christmas cracker trash" and were not enthusiastic about handling them. Children, however, loved them, so the shopkeepers needed more. By Christmas 1953, Lesney recognized that there was a market for their toys but the founders were not interested at this time in developing a sales force, storage facilities, and marketing techniques to distribute toys for a few months a year. They turned instead to agents who specialized in marketing to handle their toys. In the east end of London there were established agents long before the war. The one they contacted was Moko.

Moses Kohnstam was a German agent from Nuremberg who came to England in about 1900 to develop the toy industry. He specialized in packaging, storing, distributing, and financial backing for many small toy manufacturers. For this he received a percentage of the selling price. Moses Kohnstam's company name was Moko and the toys they distributed carried his company's name, no matter what various small firm made them. Some Moko-distributed products that had no association with Lesney included a merry-go-round, a mechanical mouse, a plastic penguin, a gantry crane, and a scooter, amongst others.

When Lesney Products began manufacturing diecast metal toys in 1948, it started with the Aveling Barford diesel road roller.

By 1953, seventeen other toys joined the Lesney line. The variety of toys in this group reflect the uncertain direction of this branch of the company. Mechanical animals, vehicles with wheels, horse-drawn items, and even a fishing novelty gadget were all tried before the success of wheeled vehicles eclipsed efforts in other directions.

Between 1950 and 1952, the British government restricted the use of zinc for non-essential products during the Korean War and therefore no diecast toys could be made. Only the tin "Jumbo the Elephant" was made by Lesney during this period.

During 1953, Jack Odell began designing smaller-scale toys. The first were smaller versions of the original Lesney toys. These small toys were enormously successful and were continued to become the 1-75 series, a concept unchanged to this day! With the growing success of the small series, the larger toys were phased out by 1954.

Each of the early Lesney toys was packaged in a cardboard box which was printed with a picture of the toy, its name, and, in some cases, Moko. From a collector's standpoint, the toy is more interesting with its original box and some have made a science of collecting boxes!

In 1953, Moses Kohnstam's successor, Richard Kohnstam, was in charge of Moko. Lesney Products and Richard Kohnstam entered into an agreement whereby Moko would package and distribute the toys. Eventually, Moko became the worldwide distributor. The year 1953 was also the beginning of the 1-75 series and "Matchbox" received its name.

In 1954, Lesney produced eighteen toys which were distributed by Moko. The trademark "Matchbox" had been registered in 1953 and belonged fifty percent to Moko which continued to provide services and financial backing for the toys. Rodney Smith had by now moved to Australia and left Lesney, leaving Leslie Smith and Jack Odell to manage the company.

During 1958, Leslie Smith felt there was potential for the toys in Asia, particularly Japan. But Richard Kohnstam disagreed. In order to open up the market, Lesney realized it had to go off on its own marketing course. It had to buy out Moko's fifty percent interest in Lesney Products. In 1959, this agreement was concluded and the company's first catalog of toys was produced. Richard Kohnstam later founded his own firm—Riko. In 1959, a second catalog was produced including the new Models of Yesteryear catalog. In 1954, distribution of Lesney toys to the United States was conducted by a salesman from New York named Fred Bronner. He became the sole U.S. importer during the late 1950's. In 1964, Lesney Products (USA) was formed as a division of the English parent company. Lesney acquired all of Fred Bronner's stock and Bronner became the first president of Lesney Products (USA).

It was in 1969 that the Fred Bronner Corporation became the Lesney Products Corporation in the United States. It was also in this year that Lesney Products faced their biggest competition, as it was in the late 1960's that Mattel introduced their Hot Wheels cars. Unlike their new competitors, Matchbox cars didn't move fast and it was a do-or-die situation for the miniatures giant. This is an earmark event in Lesney history. Lesney Products scrambled to create their own frictionless axles for their cars and in the second edition of their 1969 pocket catalog they introduced "Superfast" models. By 1970, and into 1971, the entire miniature range was converted over into Superfast style wheels. Even the King-Size range was redesigned and called "Superkings."

Matchbox Models

Taco Bell- 1962 Corvette

Taco Bell- Firebird Formula

Taco Bell- Humvee

Taco Bell- Volkswagen Concept 1

MB11G/34H9 Chrysler Atlantic- "Color Comp Inc." Christmas promotional

Chumblies preproduction Elephant

Bulgarian issue- Boat with Trailer

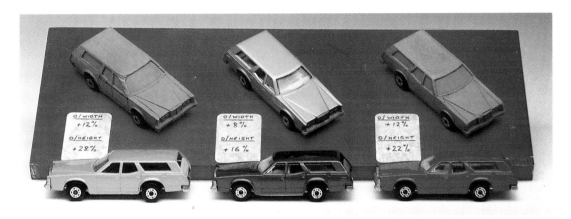

Modeling Clay Prototypes of MB74C Cougar Villager on plaque with three different Bulgarian versions of the same model.

SP12-B5 Chevrolet Lumina- "Wintech" Promotional from Hong Kong

WHEEL TYPES

1. Five Spoke

2. Four Spoke

3. Maltese Cross

4. Spiro

5. Five Arch

6. Five Crown

7. Dot Dash

8. Five Spoke Center Cut

9. Five Spoke Star

10. Eight Spoke

11. Eight Dot

12a. Racing Special (chromed)

12b. Racing Special (unchromed)

13. Starburst

14. Laser

15a. Disc with spiral— rubber tires

15b. Disc with rays— rubber tires

15c. Disc with white walls—rubber tires

16. Six Spoke

17. Goodyear slicks

18. Nine-spokeGoodyear slicks

23. Four Arch

Large Aveling Barford Road Roller

19. Six Spoke Ringed

24. Six Spoke Spiral

20. Lightning

25. Solid Disc

Large Cement Mixer

21. Goodyear Rubber

26. Four Dot Ringed

22. Hoosier Rubber

27. Five Spoke Concave Star

Large Caterpillar Tractor

Large Caterpillar Bulldozer

Soap Box Racer (MICA copy shown)

Large Horse Drawn Milk Float

Large Prime Mover Set

Rag and Bone Cart

Jumbo the Elephant

Large Ruston Bucyrus Excavator

Muffin The Mule

Large Coronation Coach

Large Massey Harris Tractor

Bread Bait Press with box

Small Coronation Coach

Covered Wagon

Souvenir Letter Opener

1-A1 Aveling Barford Road Roller

2-D1 Mercedes Trailer

4-D2 Dodge Stake Truck

1-B1 & 1-C2 Road Rollers

3-A1 Cement Mixer

5-A1 & 5-B3 London Buses

1-D Road Roller

3-B2 Bedford Tipper

5-C7 London Bus

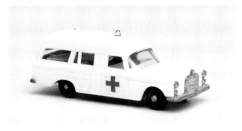

3-C2 Mercedes Benz 'Binz' Ambulance

1-E1 Mercedes Truck

5-D3 London Bus

2-A1 & 2B-2 Dumpers

4-A1 & 4-B1 Massey Harris Tractors

6-A1 Quarry Tuck

2-C1 Muir Hill Dumper

4-C2 Triumph Motorcycle & Sidecar

6-B2 Quarry Truck

6-C2 Euclid Quarry Truck

8-C3 & 8-D1 Caterpillar Tractors

10-B2 Mechanical Horse & Trailer

6-D1 Ford Pickup

8-E1 Ford Mustang Fastback

10-C2 Sugar Container Truck

7-A2 Horse Drawn Milk Float

9-A1 & 9-B2 Dennis Fire Escapes

10-D2 Pipe Truck

7-B3 Ford Anglia

9-C3 Merryweather Marquis Fire Engine

11-A4 Road Tanker

7-C1 Ford Refuse Truck

9-D2 Boat & Trailer

11-B2 Road Tanker

8-A1 & 8-B1 Caterpillar Tractors

10-A1 Mechanical Horse & Trailer

11-C1 Jumbo Crane

11-D1 Scaffold Truck

14-A1 & 14-B3 Daimler Ambulances

15-D1 Volkswagen 1500 Saloon

12-A1 & 12-B2 Land Rovers

14-C3 Bedford Ambulance

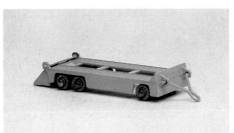

16-A1 Atlantic Trailer

12-C3 Safari Land Rover

14-D1 Iso Grifo

16-B3 Atlantic Trailer

13-A1 & 13-B1 Bedford Wreck Trucks

15-A1 Prime Mover

16-C2 Scammell Mountaineer Snowplow

13-C3 Thames Wreck Truck

15-B2 Atlantic Prime Mover

16-D1 Case Bulldozer

13-D5 Dodge Wreck Truck

15-C3 Refuse Truck

17-A4 & 17-B2 Bedford Removals Vans

17-C2 Austin Taxi Cab

18-E3 Field Car

20-B3 ERF 686 Truck

17-D1 Hoveringham Tipper

19-A1 MG TD Sports Car

20-C4 Chevrolet Impala Taxi Cab

17-E1 Horse Box

19-B4 MGA Sports Car

21-A1 & 21-B2 Long Distance Coaches

18-A1 Caterpillar Bulldozer

19-C5 Aston Martin Racing Car

21-C8 Commer Milk Float

18-B1 & 18-C3 Caterpillar Bulldozers

19-D3 Lotus Racing Car

21-D1 Foden Concrete Truck

18-D2 Caterpillar Bulldozer

20-A5 Stake Truck

22-A1 Vauxhall Cresta

22-B10 1958 Vauxhall Cresta

24-A1 & 24-B1 Weatherhill Hydraulic Excavators

26-A2 Concrete Truck

22-C2 Pontiac Grand Prix Sports Coupe

24-C1 Rolls Royce Silver Shadow

26-B2 Foden Concrete Truck

23-A1 Berkeley Cavalier Trailer

25-A1 Dunlop Van

26-C1 G.M.C. Tipper Truck

23-B3 Berkeley Cavalier Trailer

25-B3 Volkswagen 1200 Sedan

27-A2 & 27-B3 Bedford Lowloaders

23-C3 Bluebird Dauphine Trailer

25-C2 Petrol Tanker

27-C8 Cadillac Sixty Special

23-D1 Trailer Caravan

25-D1 Ford Cortina

27-D1 Mercedes Benz 230SL

28-A1 Bedford Compressor Truck

29-C2 Fire Pumper

31-C2 Lincoln Continental

28-B2 Thames Compressor Truck

30-A2 Ford Prefect

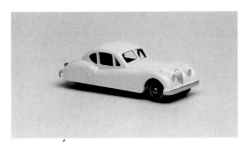

32-A2 Jaguar XK140 Coupe

28-C2 Mark 10 Jaguar

30-B7 Magiruz-Deutz 6 Wheel Crane

32-B1 Jaguar XKE

28-D1 Mack Dump Truck

30-C3 Eight Wheel Crane Truck

32-C2 Leyland Petrol Tanker

29-A2 Bedford Milk Delivery Van

31-A1 Ford Station Wagon

33-A9 Ford Zodiac MkII Sedan

29-B1 Austin A55 Cambridge Sedan

31-B9 Ford Fairlane Station Wagon

33-B4 Ford Zephyr 6 MkIII

33-C2 Lamborghini Miura

35-B2 Snow Tractor

37-B3 Coca Cola Lorry

34-A2 Volkswagen Microvan

36-A2 Austin A50

37-C2 Dodge Cattle Truck

34-B2 Volkswagen Camper

36-B2 Lambretta Scooter & Sidecar

38-A4 Karrier Ruse Collector

34-C1 Volkswagen Camper

36-C2 Opel Diplomat

38-B1 Vauxhall Victor Estate Car

34-D1 Volkswagen Camper

37-A1 Coca Cola Lorry (uneven load)

38-C4 Honda Motorcycle & Trailer

35-A4 Marshall Horse Box

37-A2 Coca Cola Lorry

39-A3 Ford Zodiac Convertible

21

39-B9 Pontiac Convertible

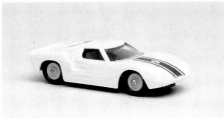

41-C6 Ford GT

43-C1 Pony Trailer

39-C2 Ford Tractor

42-A3 Bedford Evening News Van

44-A1 Rolls Royce Silver Cloud

40-A1 Bedford Tipper Truck

42-B1 Studebaker Lark Wagonaire

44-B5 Rolls Royce Phantom V

40-B3 Leyland Royal Tiger Coach

42-C1 Iron Fairy Crane

44-C1 Refrigerator Truck

40-C1 Hay Trailer

43-A3 Hillman Minx

45-A7 Vauxhall Victor

41-A1 & 41-B1 D Type Jaguars

43-B3 Aveling Barford Tractor Shovel

45-B3 Ford Corsair with boat

46-A4 Morris Minor 1000

48-A2 Meteor Boat & Trailer

50-B2 John Deere Tractor

46-B5 Pickfords Removal Van

48-B7 Sports Boat & Trailer

50-C3 Ford Kennel Truck

46-C2 Mercedes Benz 300SE

48-C1 Dodge Dumper Truck

51-A4 Albion Chieftan

47-A1 1 Ton Trojan Van

49-A5 M3 Personnel Carrier

51-B1 John Deere Trailer

47-B5 Commer Ice Cream Canteen

49-B1 Mercedes Unimog

51-C1 Eight Wheel Tipper

47-C2 DAF Tipper Container Truck

50-A1 Commer Pickup

52-A5 Maserati 4CLT Racer

23

52-B1 BRM Racing Car

55-A3 D.U.K.W.

57-A3 Wolseley 1500

53-A2 Aston Martin

55-B4 Ford Fairlane Police Car

57-B6 Chevrolet Impala

53-B5 Mercedes Benz 220 SE

55-C2 Ford Galaxie Police Car

57-C2 Land Rover Fire Engine

53-C1 Ford Zodiac MK IV

55-D2 Mercury Police Car

58-A3 BEA Coach

54-A1 Saracen Personnel Carrier

56-A5 London Trolley Bus

58-B3 Drott Excavator

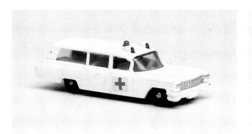

54-B1 S&S Cadillac Ambulance

56-B2 Fiat 1500

58-C1 DAF Girder Truck

 59-A2 Ford Thames Van

 61-B2 Alvis Stalwart

 63-C1 Dodge Crane Truck

 59-B1 Ford Fairlane Fire Chief Car

 62-A1 General Service Lorry

 64-A3 Scammell Breakdown Truck

 59-C1 Ford Galaxie Fire Chief Car

 62-B4 TV Service Van

 64-B1 MG 1100

 60-A5 Morris J2 Pickup

 62-C2 Mercury Cougar

 65-A1 Jaguar 3.4 Litre Sedan

 60-B1 Site Hut Truck

 63-A1 Ford Service Ambulance

65-B4 Jaguar 3.4 Litre Sedan

 61-A1 Ferret Scout Car

 63-B2 Foamite Crash Tender

 65-C1 Claas Combine Harvester

66-A1 Citroen DS19

68-B2 Mercedes Coach

71-B2 Jeep Gladiator Pickup

66-B1 Harley-Davidson Motorcycle & Sidecar

69-A3 Commer 30 CWT Van

71-C1 Ford Heavy Wreck Truck

66-C3 Greyhound Bus

69-B1 Hatra Tractor Shovel

72-A5 Fordson Tractor

67-A1 Saladin Armored Car

70-A6 Ford Thames Estate Car

72-B1 Standard Jeep

67-B1 Volkswagen 1600TL

70-B1 Ford Grit Spreader

73-A1 10 Ton Pressure Refueller

68-A1 Austin MKII Radio Truck

71-A1 Austin 200 Gallon Water Truck

73-B2 Ferrari F1 Racing Car

73-C1 Mercury Station Wagon

74-A9 Mobile Refreshment Canteen

74-B3 Daimler Bus

75-A5 Ford Thunderbird

75-B4 Ferrari Berlinetta

14-D Iso Grifo

14-D Iso Grifo

25-D Ford Cortina

26-C G.M.C. Tipper Truck

MB35-A Fire Engine

47-C DAF Tipper Container Truck

53-C Ford Zodiac MK IV

56-B Fiat 1500

61-B Alvis Stalwart

75-B Ferrari Berlinetta

RARE REGULAR WHEELS

4-D1 Dodge Stake Truck

12-C5 Safari Land Rover

22-B6 1958 Vauxhall Cresta

5-C5 London Bus

13-D1 Dodge Wreck Truck

23-B4 Berkeley Cavalier Trailer

6-B1 Quarry Truck

15B1 Atlantic Prime Mover

23-C1 Bluebird Dauphine Trailer

8-E2 Ford Mustang Fastback

17A1 Bedford Removals Van

25-C1 Petrol Tanker

11-A1 Road Tanker

17A3 Bedford Removals Van

26-B1 Foden Concrete Truck

12-C4 Safari Land Rover

18-E1 Field Car

27-A1 Bedford Lowloader

27-C1 Cadillac Sixty Special

43-A1 Hillman Minx

56-A1 London Trolley Bus

30-B2 Magiruz-Deutz 6 Wheel Crane

46-A1 Morris Minor 1000

57-C1 Land Rover Fire Engine

31-C3 Lincoln Continental

46-B9 Pickfords Removal Van

62-C3 Mercury Cougar

36-C3 Opel Diplomat

50-A6 Commer Pickup

67-B3 Volkswagen 1600TL

41-B5 D Type Jaguar

53-A3 Aston Martin

74-A4 Mobile Refreshment Canteen

41-C1 Ford GT

55-B1 Ford Galaxie Police Car

75-B5 Ferrari Berlinetta

MINIATURES 1-75

MB1-A4 Mercedes Truck

MB2-A2 Mercedes Trailer

MB2-G/15-G1 1965 Corvette Grand Sport

MB1-B1 Mod Rod

MB2-B3 Jeep Hot Rod

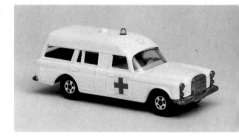

MB3-A1 Mercedes Benz "Binz" Ambulance

MB1-C2 Dodge Challenger

MB2-C11 Hovercraft

MB3-B1 Monteverdi Hai

MB1-D2 Dodge Challenger

MB2-D2 S.2 Jet

MB3-C5 Porsche Turbo

MB1-F2 Jaguar XJ6 Police Car

MB2 Mazda RX7 (Japan)

MB3-D1 Hummer

MB1-G/35K7 Dodge Viper GTS Coupe

MB2-E Pontiac Fiero

MB3-E1 Alfa Romeo SZ

MB4-A2 Dodge Stake Truck

MB5-A4 Lotus Europa

MB6-B Mercedes Tourer

MB4-B2 Gruesome Twosome

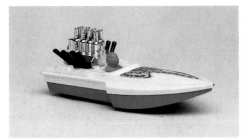

MB5-B1 Seafire

MB6-C/7-E1 I.M.S.A. Mazda

MB4-C1 Pontiac Firebird

MB5-C1 U.S. Mail Truck

MB6-E72-H2 Ford Supervan II

MB4-D43/-H2 '57 Chevy

MB5 Datsun 280Z (Japan)

MB7-A1 Ford Refuse Truck

MB4-E1 London Taxi

MB5D/56-F18 4 X 4 Jeep

MB7-B13 Hairy Hustler

MB4-F1 1997 Corvette

MB6-A Ford Pickup

MB7-C6 V.W. Golf

31

MB7-D3 Rompin Rabbit

MB8-D4 Rover 3500

MB8-I/24-I1 Airport Tender

MB7-F/51-I Porsche 959

MB8-D9 Rover 3500 (Police)

MB8-J/54-I1 Mazda RX7

MB7-G/39-H58 Ford Thunderbird

MB8-E1 Greased Lighning

MB9-A5 Boat & Trailer

MB8-A5 Ford Mustang Fastback

MB8-F/71-E3 Scania T142

MB9-B2-AMX Javelin

MB8-B10 Wildcat Dragster

MB8-G4 Vauxhall Astra Police Car

MB9-C1 Ford Escort RS2000

MB8-C7 Detomasso Pantera

MB8-H/39-F1 Mack CH800 Aerodyne

MB9-D/74-E4 Fiat Abarth

MB9-F/74-G1 Toyota MR2

MB10-F/12-J1 Dodge Viper

MB11-G/34H1 Chrysler Atlantic

MB9-H/53-E1 Faun Dump Truck

MB11-A1 Scaffold Truck

MB12-A2 Safari Land Rover

MB10-A4 Pipe Truck

MB11-B1 Flying Bug

MB12-B2 Setra Coach

MB10-B2 Piston Popper

MB11-C26 Car Transporter

MB12-C1 Big Bull

MB10-C2 Plymouth Gran Fury Police Car

MB11-D3 Boss Mustang

MB12-D10 Citroen CX

MB10-D9 Buick Le Sabre

MB11-E/67-E2 I.M.S.A. Mustang

MB12-D24 Citroen CX (Ambulance)

MB12-E/51-E2 Pontiac Firebird SE

MB13-D/63-F15 4 X 4 Open Back Truck

MB14-D3 Leyland Tanker

MB12-H/33-H1 Mercedes 500SL Convertible

MB13-F/28-M1 The Buster

MB14-E/69-E1 1983/84 Corvette

MB12-K/31-K1 Audi Avus Quattro

MB13-G1 Kenworth T2000

MB14-E/69-E11 1983/84 Corvette (Roadblaster)

MB13-A2 Dodge Wreck Truck

MB14-A7 Iso Grifo

MB14-G/28-G1 1987 Corvette

MB13-B2 Baja Buggy

MB14-B10 Mini Ha Ha
MB14-C1 Rallye Royale

MB15-A5 Volkswagen 1500 Sedan

MB13-C3 Snorkel Fire Engine

MB15-B12 Fork Lift Truck

MB15-C1 Hi Ho Silver

MB15-J/28-K1 Mustang Mach III

MB17-A5 Horse Box

MB15-D/55-E6 Ford Sierra XR4i

MB15-K1 Ford Transit

MB17-B1 The Londoner

MB15-E2/25-G9 Peugeot 205 Turbo

MB16-A14 Badger

MB17-C/51-F/28-F London Bus

MB15-F/22-F1 Saab 9000 Turbo

MB16-B1 Pontiac Firebird

MB17-D/9-E3 AMX Prostocker

MB15-H/6-G4 Alfa Romeo

MB16-D/6-D1 F.1 Racer

MB17-E/37-G4 Ford Escort Cabriolet

MB15-I/41-I1 Sunburner

MB16-E/51-H1 Ford LTD Police Car

MB17-F/50-F2 Dodge Dakota

35

MB17-G/41-J1 Ferrari 456GT

MB18-A17 Field Car

MB18-B1 Hondarora

MB18-C4 Fire Engine

MB19-A1 Lotus Racer

MB19-B12 Road Dragster

36

MB19-C1 Cement Truck

MB19-D3 Peterbilt Cement Truck

MB20-A1 Lamborgini Marzal

MB20-B22 Police Patrol

MB20-C/14-F1 4 X 4 Jeep

MB20-D/23-G/62-I30 Volvo Container Truck

MB20-E8 Volkswagen Transporter

MB20-F/66H3 Pontiac Firebird Ram Air

MB21-A1 Foden Concrete Truck

MB21-B2 Rod Roller

MB21-C5 Renault 5TL

MB21-D1 Corvette Pace Car

MB21-E/53-F1 Chevy Breakdown Van

MB22-E1 Jaguar XK120

MB23-C1 GT350

MB21-F/71-F15 GMC Wrecker

MB22-G/41-G1 Vectra Cavalier Gsi 2000

MB23-D/25-F1 Audi Quattro

MB22-A2 Pontiac Grand Prix

MB22-H/49-F1 Lamborghini Diablo

MB23-F1 Honda ATC

MB22-B4 Freeman Intercity Commuter

MB23-A2 Volkswagen Camper

MB24-A1 Rolls Royce Silver Shadow

MB22-C3 Blaze Buster

MB23-A9 Volkswagen Dormobile

MB24-B7 Team Matchbox

MB22-D/35-E1 4 X 4 Mini Pickup

MB23-B1 Atlas

MB24-C1 Shunter

MB24-D1 Datsun 280ZX

MB25-B2 Mod Tractor

MB26-A2 G.M.C. Tipper Truck

MB24-E2 Datsun 280ZX

MB25-C1 Flat Car & Container

MB26-B1 Big Banger

MB24-E10 Datsun 280ZX (Roadblaster)

MB25-D4 Celica GT

MB26-C2 Site Dumper

MB24-F1 Nissan 300ZX

MB25-D6 Celica GT

MB26-D/41-H2 Cosmic Blues

MB24-H/70-F1 Ferrari F40

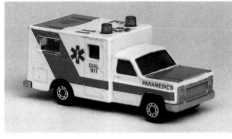

MB25-E3 Ambulance

MB26-E3 Cable Truck

MB25-A3 Ford Cortina

38

MB25J/61H1 BMW Z3

MB26-F/49-G2 Volvo Tilt Truck

MB26-G/31-H1 BMW 5 Series

MB28-A2 Mack Dump truck

MB28-H/61F5 Forklift Truck

MB27-A4 Mercedes 230SL

MB28-B1 Stoat

MB28-L/22-J1 Mitsubishi Spyder

MB27-B40 Lamborghini Countach

MB28-C1 Lincoln Continental MK V

MB29-A1 Fire Pumper

MB27-C1 Swept Wing Jet

MB28-D4 Formula 5000

MB29-B1 Racing Mini

MB27-D/73-F/51-J4 Jeep Cherokee

MB28-E1 Dodge Daytona

MB29-C1 Tractor Shovel

MB27-F1 Tailgator

MB28-E11 Dodge Daytona (Roadblaster)

MB30-A2 Eight Wheel Crane

39

MB30-B2 Beach Buggy

MB30-I3 Chevy Tahoe Police

MB31-G/2-F1 Rover Sterling

MB30-C1 Swamp Rat

MB31-A2 Lincoln Continental

MB31-I/21-G5 Nissan Prairie

MB30-D1 Leyland Articulated Truck

MB31-B1 Volksdragon

MB31-J/26-I1 Jaguar XJ220

MB30-E/23-E12 Peterbilt Quarry Truck

MB31-C1 Caravan

MB31-L1 1957 Chevy Bel Air Hardtop

MB30-F1 Mercedes G Wagon

MB31-D1 Mazda RX7

MB32-A3 Leyland Tanker

MB30-G/60-I1 Toyota Supra

MB31-E1 Mazda RX7

MB32-B2 Maserati Bora

MB32-C2 Field Car

MB33-C1 Police Motorcycle

MB34-B4 Vantastic

MB32-D/6-F14 Atlas Excavator

MB33-D/56-E/63-G1 Volkswagen Golf Gti

MB34-C12 Chevy Prostocker

MB32-E/12G1 Modified Racer

MB33-F/43-F4 Renault 11

MB34-C14 Chevy Prostocker

MB32-G1 1970 Chevy El Camino

MB33-G/74-I13 Utility Truck

MB34-D7 Ford RS200

MB33-A2 Lamborghini Miura

MB34-A2 Formula 1

MB34-E/72-J1 Sprint Racer

MB33-B1 Datsun 126X

MB34-B3 Vantastic

MB34-G/6-H1 Plymouth Prowler

41

MB39-I1 1971 Camaro Z28

MB40-G/33-I1 Ford Mondeo

MB41-D3 Kenworth Aerodyne

MB40-A1 Vauxhall Guildsman

MB40-H2 1968 Camaro Z28

MB41-F/1-E1 Jaguar XJ6

MB40-B14 Horse Box

MB40-I/282A4 FJ Holden Van

MB42-A4 Iron Fairy Crane

MB40-C/62-E/58-F1 Corvette T-Roof

MB41-A4 Ford GT

MB42-B2 Tyre Fryer

MB40-D/MB60-H1 Rocket Transporter

MB41-B2 Siva Spyder

MB42-C18 Mercedes Truck

MB40-F/68-H1 Road Roller

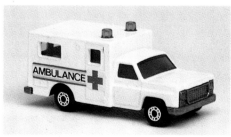

MB41-C1 Ambulance

MB42-D1 1957 Ford Thunderbird

44

MB42-E1 Faun Crane Truck

MB43-G/24-G1 Lincoln Town Car

MB44-D/68-D/26-H/10-E5 4 X 4 Chevy Van

MB43-A3 Pony Trailer

MB43-I1 Camaro Z28

MB44-E9 Citroen CV15

MB43-B2 Dragon Wheels

MB44-A2 Refrigerator Truck

MB44-F1 Datsun 280ZX Police Car

MB43-C1 0-4-0 Loco

MB44-B1 Boss Mustang

MB44-G1 Skoda LR

MB43-D1 Peterbilt Conventional

MB44-C1 Passenger Coach

MB44-C21 Passenger Coach

MB44-H1 1921 Model T Ford Van

MB43-E12 AMG Mercedes 500SEC

MB44-I5 Ford Probe

45

MB45-A17 Ford Group 6

MB46-C1 Ford Tractor

MB47-C1 Pannier Loco

MB45-B10 BMW 3.0 CSL

MB46-D1 Hot Chocolate/ Beetle Streaker

MB47-D1 Jaguar SS 100

MB45-C8 Kenworth Aerodyne

MB46-F/57-F17 Mission Helicopter

MB47-E1 School Bus

MB45-E/69-G1 Highway Maintenance Vehicle

MB46-H1 Chevy Tahoe

MB47-G1 M2 Bradley Tank

MB46-A4 Mercedes 300SE

MB47-A DAF Tipper Container Truck

MB48-A4 Dodge Dump Truck

MB46-B 1 Stretcha Fetcha

MB47-B2 Beach Hopper

MB48-B2 Pi-Eyed Piper

46

MB48-C8 Sambron Jacklift

MB49-B3 Chop Suey

MB49-I/58-G1 Volkswagen Concept 1

MB48-D1 Red Rider

MB49-C2 Crane Truck

MB50-A9 Kennel Truck

MB48-E2 Unimog with plow

MB49-D1 Sand Digger

MB50-B1 Articulated Dump Truck

MB48-F2 Vauxhall Astra/ Opel Kadette

MB49-E/72-M1 Peugeot Quasar

MB50-C1 Articulated Trailer

MB48-H7 1956 Ford Pickup

MB49-E/72-M5 Peugeot Quasar (Roadblaster)

MB50-D Harley Davidson Motorcycle

MB49-A5 Unimog

MB49-H/2-H1 BMW 850i

MB50-E1 Chevy Blazer

47

MB50-H8 Harley Davidson Chopper

MB51-D1 Midnight Magic

MB52-D1 BMW M1

MB50-I8 Harley Davidson Electraglide

MB51-G/68-F1 Camaro IROC-Z

MB52-E1 Isuzu Amigo

MB50-J1 1997 Ford F150 Pickup

MB51-K/17H6 Ford Ambulance

MB52-F2 Ford Escort Cosworth

MB51-A1 Eight Wheel Tipper

MB52-A1 Dodge Charger

MB53-A6 Ford Zodiac

MB51-B2 Citroen S.M.

MB52-B1 Police Launch

MB53-B1 Tanzara

MB51-C1 Combine Harvester

MB52-C1 BMW M1

MB53-C1 Jeep CJ6

48

MB53-D/55-J2 Flareside Pickup

MB54-D12 Mobile Home

MB54-K/38-J1 Crown Victoria Police Car

MB53-G/56-G1 Ford LTD Taxi

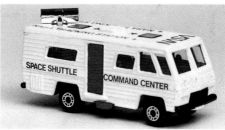

MB54-E1 NASA Tracking Vehicle

MB54-L/64-H13 Holden Commodore

MB53-H/24-J1 Rhino Rod

MB54-F1 Command Vehicle

MB55-A1 Mercury Police Car

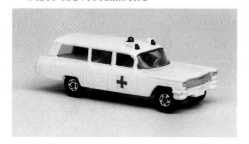

MB54-A2 S&S Cadillac Ambulance

MB54-G4 Chevy Lumina

MB55-B3 Mercury Police Commuter

MB54-B2 Ford Capri

MB54-H9 Chevy Lumina

MB55-C1 Hellraiser

MB54-C2 Personnel Carrier

MB54-J/61-G1 Abrams Tank

MB55-D1 Ford Cortina

MB61-A9 Blue Shark

MB61-B13 Wreck Truck

MB61-C5 Peterbilt Wreck Truck

MB61-E/37-H20 Nissan 300ZX

MB62-A1 Mercury Cougar

MB62-B4 Cougar Dragster

MB62-C1 Renault 17TL

MB62-D2 Chevrolet Corvette

MB62-F/31-F2 Rolls Royce Silver Cloud

MB62-G1 Volvo 760

MB62-H/64-F1 Oldsmobile Aerotech

MB62-J/72-N1 Street Streak

MB63-A1 Dodge Crane Truck

MB63-B2 Freeway Gas Tanker

MB63-C2 Freeway Gas Trailer

MB63-D3 Dodge Challenger

MB63-E/13-E9 Snorkel

MB63-J/68-K1 Ford Falcon

MB64-A3 MG 1100

MB65-C5 Bandag Bandit

MB66-D2 Super Boss

MB64-B1 Slingshot Dragster

MB65-D1 F.1 Racer

MB66-D13 Super Boss (Roadblaster)

MB64-C3 Fire Chief Car

MB65-G2 Ford F150 Pickup

MB66-E/46-E2 Sauber Group C Racer

MB64-D/9-G1 Caterpillar Bulldozer

MB66-A1 Greyhound Bus

MB66-E/46-E9 Sauber Group C Racer (Roadblaster)

MB65-A1 Saab Sonnet

MB66-B9 Mazda RX500

MB66-F/55-H2 Rolls Royce Silver Spirit

MB65-B4 Airport Coach

MB66-C1 Ford Transit

MB66-G/46G4 Opel Calibra

53

MB66-H1 MGF

MB67-G1 Ikarus Coach

MB68-G/73-D1 TV News Truck

MB67-A6 Volkswagen 1600TL

MB67-H1 Ford Expedition

MB68-I1 Stinger

MB67-B1 Hot Rocker

MB68-A3 Porsche 910

MB68-J/58I1 Porsche 911 GT1

MB67-C1 Datsun 260Z

MB68-B2 Cosmobile

MB69-A1 Rolls Royce Silver Shadow Coupe

MB67-D1 Flame Out

MB68-C2 Chevy Van

MB69-B1 Turbo Fury

MB67-F/11-F1 Lamborghini Countach

MB68-E/64-E2 Dodge Caravan

MB69-C3 Armored Truck

54

MB69-D9 '33 Willys

MB70-D1 Ferrari 308 GTB

MB71-C1 Cattle Truck

MB69-F2 Volvo 480ES

MB70-E/45-D4 Ford Cargo Skip Truck

MB71-D/32-F/72-L4 1962 Corvette

MB69-H/20-G8 1968 Ford Mustang Fastback

MB70-H/64-G1 1970 Pontiac GTO

MB71-G/59-E8 Porsche 944 Turbo

MB70-A1 Grit Spreader

MB70-I1 Mercedes E Class

MB71-H/43-J1 Mustang Cobra

MB70-B1 Dodge Dragster

MB71-A1 Ford Heavy Wreck Truck

MB71-I1 Jaguar XK8

MB70-C2 Self Propelled Gun

MB71-B1 Jumbo Jet

MB72-A1 Jeep

MB72-B2 SRN6 Hovercraft

MB72-I/65-F1 Cadillac Allante

MB73-E/27-E4 Mercedes Tractor

MB72-C2 Bomag Rad Roller

MB72-K1 Dodge Zoo Truck

MB73-H/47-F1 Rotwheeler

MB72-D2 Maxi Taxi

MB72-O1 Chevy K-1500 Pickup

MB74-A3 Daimler Bus

MB72-E27 Dodge Delivery Van

MB73-A2 Mercury Commuter

MB74-B4 Toe Joe

MB72-F1 Sand Racer

MB73-B/70-G1 Weasel

MB74-C7 Cougar Villager

MB72-G/65-E1 Plane Transporter

MB73-C/55-I/25-H2 Model A Ford

MB74-D1 Orange Peel

MB74-F2 Mustang GT

MB75-D1 Helicopter

MB79-A3 Galant Eterna

MB74-H/14-H1 Grand Prix Racer

MB75-E1 Ferrari Testarossa

MB215-A1 Chevy Panel Van

MB74-J/246-11 Formula 1 Racer

MB75-G/21-H1 Ferrari F50

MB217-A1 D.I.R.T. Modified

MB75-A3 Ferrari Berlinetta

MB76-A4 Mazda RX7

MB236 Ford Tractor

MB75-B1 Alfa Carabo

MB75-C4 Seasprite Helicopter

MB77-A2 Toyota Celica XX

MB78-A1 Fairlady Z

MB237 Tractor Shovel

MB262 Chrysler Voyager

57

MB267-A1 Chevy Lumina

MB315A1 Volvo Stake Truck

MB345A1 Bulldozer

MB268-A4 Ford Thunderbird

MB317A1 Ford Skip Truck

MB346A1 Front Loader

MB269-A1 Pontiac Grand Prix

MB338A1 Dodge Airflow

MB347A1 Road Roller

MB283-A3 Chevy Monte Carlo

MB339A2 Mack Junior

MB348A1 Scraper

MB284-A1 Chevy Super Truck

MB343A1 Excavator

MB350A1 Road Grader

MB285A1 Ice Maker

MB344A1 Dump Truck

MB351A1 Challenger Tractor

MB352A1 Trailer

MB712 Seeder

MB794A1 Glider Trailer

MB353A1 Backhoe

MB713 Rotovator

FS001-A36 Ford F800 Delivery Van

MB354A1 Soil Compactor

MB720A1 Side Tipper

FS002-A1 Ford F800 Delivery Van

MB388A1 Peterbilt Dump Truck with Plow

MB791A Motorcycle Trailer

FST Ford Super Truck

MB710 Tipping Trailer

MB792A Cattle Trailer

WRP01-A2 1996 Pontiac Grand Prix

WRP02-A7 1996 Ford Thunderbird

MB711 Hay Trailer

MB793A Inflatable Raft

59

Dodge Caravan- Las Vegas

Dodge Daytona- Las Vegas

J-21 Toyota Celica XX

J-22 Galant Eterna

Harley Davidson Springer Soft Tail

1939 Harley Davidson Knucklehead

I-A3 Silver Streak

II-A1 Sleet-N-Snow

III-A1 White Lightning

IV-A1 Flying Beetle

V-A6 Hot Smoker

VI-A2 Lady Bug

VII-A8 Brown Sugar

VIII-A2 Black Widow

IX-A1 Flamin Manta

X-A3 Golden X

MB4-F7 1997 Corvette

MB4-F18 1997 Corvette

MB10-F/12-J33 Dodge Viper

MB4-F14 1997 Corvette

MB4-F21 1997 Corvette

MB15-K58 Ford Transit

MB4-F16 1997 Corvette

MB10-F/12-J25 Dodge Viper

MB15-K63 Ford Transit

MB4-F17 1997 Corvette

MB10-F/12-J27 Dodge Viper

MB17-C/51-F/28-F51 London Bus

MB38-E438 Model A Ford Van

MB47-E30 School Bus

MB54-K11 Crown Victoria Police Car

MB44-D/68-D/26-H/10-E30 4 X 4 Chevy Van

MB54-H98 Chevy Lumina

MB68-C39 Chevy Van

MB47-E23 School Bus

MB54-H99 Chevy Lumina

MB68-C45 Chevy Van

MB47-E28 School Bus

MB54-K/38-J7 Crown Victoria Police Car

MB74-J/246-23 Formula 1 Racer

PROMOTIONAL MINIATURES

MB15-K46 Ford Transit

MB38-F12 Ford Courier

MB65-B34 Airport Coach

MB17-B7 The Londoner

MB40-I/282-6 FJ Holden Van

MB72-E14 Dodge Delivery Van

MB17-C/51-F/28F37 London Bus

MB44-H121 1921 Model T Ford Van

MB215-A1 Chevy Panel Van

MB20-D/23-G/62-I39 Volvo Container Truck

MB58-H/245-6 Chevy Panel Van

MB267A34 Chevy Lumina

MB38-E423 Model A Ford Van

MB60-G/57-G51 Ford Transit

FS001/WR002-A37 Ford F800 Delivery Van

RARE MINIATURES

MB8-A3 Ford Mustang Fastback

MB17-B48 The Londoner

MB29-C3 Tractor Shovel

MB10-B4 Piston Popper

MB18-A11 Field Car

MB30-A1 Eight Wheel Crane

MB10-F/12-J-3 Dodge Viper

MB22-C1 Blaze Buster

MB32-A4 Leyland Tanker

MB12-A1 Safari Land Rover

MB24-B1 Team Matchbox

MB32-A5 Leyland Tanker

MB14-G/28-G19 1987 Corvette

MB17-B5 The Londoner

MB24-B3 Team Matchbox

MB25-A1 Ford Cortina

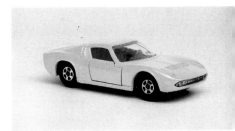

MB33-A1 Lamborghini Miura

MB34-B10 Vantastic

MB352A1 Trailer

MB38-E27 Model A Ford Van

MB45-A1 Ford Group 6

MB37-B8 Soopa Coopa

MB38-F5 Ford Courier

MB45-B13 BMW 3.0 CSL

MB37-C10 Skip Truck

MB42-A1 Iron Fairy Crane

MB48-B3 Pi-Eyed Piper

MB38-B1 Stingeroo

MB42-B7 Tyre Fryer

MB48-C5 Sambron Jacklift

MB38-C11 Jeep

MB44-H56 1921 Model T Ford Van

MB44-H60 1921 Model T Ford Van

MB49-B1 Chop Suey

MB38-E10 Model A Ford Van

MB49-C1 Crane Truck

LONG HAULS

TP 2-C1 Articulated Petrol Tanker

TP22-A2 Double Container Truck

TP23-A2 Covered Truck

TP24-A5 Container Truck

TP25-A3 Pipe Truck

TP26-A2 Boat Transporter

CY-1-A5 Kenworth Car Transporter

CY-2-A2 Kenworth Rocket Transporter

CY-3-A4 Peterbilt Double Container Truck

CY-3-B1 Kenworth Box Truck

CY-4-A1 Kenworth Boat Transporter

CY-4-B2 Scania Box Truck

CY-5A1 Peterbilt Covered Truck

CY-6A2 Kenworth Horse Box

CY-7-A1 Peterbilt Tanker

CY-7B2 Ford Aeromax Tanker

CY-8-A20 Kenworth Box Truck

CY-9-A29 Kenworth Box Truck

CY-10-A1 Tyrone Malone Team

CY-11-A1 Kenworth Helicopter Transporter

CY-12-A3 Kenworth Aircraft Transporter

CY-13-A3 Kenworth Fire Engine

CY-14-A1 Kenworth Boat Transporter

CY-15-A3 Peterbilt Tracking Vehicle

CY-16-A2 Scania Box Truck

CY-17-A1 Scania Tanker

CY-18-A5 Scania Double Container Truck

CY-18-B1 Ford Aeromax Double Container

CY-19-A1 Peterbilt Container Truck

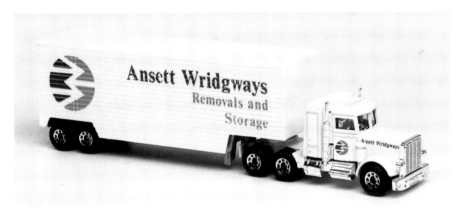

CY-20-A6 Articulated Tipper

CY-21-A1 DAF Aircraft Transporter

CY-32-A1 Mack Shovel Transporter

CY-32-B1 Peterbilt Lowloader with Bulldozer

CY-33-A4 Mack Helicopter Transporter

CY-34-A1 Peterbilt Emergency Center

CY-35-A2 Mack Tanker

CY-36-A3 Kenworth Transporter

CY-37-A1 Ford Aeromax Transporter

CY-38-A1 Kenworth Transporter

CY-39-A4 Ford Aeromax Box Truck

CY-104-A8 Kenworth Superstar Transporter

CY-104-B5 Scania Box Transporter

CY-105-A1 Kenworth Tanker

CY-106-A1 Peterbilt Articulated Tipper

CY-106-B2 Peterbilt Box Truck

CY-107-A10 Mack Superstar Transporter

CY-108-A1 DAF Aircraft Transporter

CY-109-A51 Ford Aeromax Superstar

CY-110-A3 Kenworth Superstar Transporter

CY-111-A23 Team Transporter

CY-112-A4 Kenworth T600 Superstar Transporter

CY-113-A1 Ford Aeromax Superstar Transporter

CY-203-A1 Construction Lowloader

CY-803-A1 Scania Lowloader with Dodge Truck

TC-60-A1 Team Pennzoil

ADT01 Kenworth Racing Transporter

CCY01-1 Peterbilt Box Truck

CCY02-1 Ford Aeromax Box Truck

CCY03-1 Kenworth Box Truck

CCY04-1 Kenworth Box Truck

CCY05-2 Mack Box Truck

85

CY-39-A18 Ford Aeromax Box Truck

CY-39-A22 Ford Aeromax Box Truck

CY-39-A36 Ford Aeromax Box Truck

CY-39-A38 Ford Aeromax Box Truck

CY-39-A48 Ford Aeromax Box Truck

CY-3-A9 Kenworth Double Container Truck

CY-3-A17 Kenworth Double Container Truck

CY-8-A11 Kenworth Box Truck

CY-9-A14 Kenworth Box Truck

CY-9-A15 Kenworth Box Truck

Y-1-A2 1925 Allchin Traction Engine

Y-6-A2 1916 A.E.C. "Y" Type Lorry

Y-11-A5 1920 Aveling Porter Steam Roller

Y-2-A1 1911 "B" Type Bus

Y-7-A3 1914 7 Ton Leyland Van

Y-12-A2 1899 London Horse Drawn Bus

Y-3-A2 1907 London 'E' Class Tram Car

Y-8-A3 Morris Cowley "Bullnose"

Y-13-A2 1862 Santa Fe Locomotive

Y-4-A1 Sentinel Steam Wagon

Y-9-A1 Fowler Showman's Engine

Y-14-A1 1903 Duke of Connaught Locomotive

Y-5-A4 1929 LeMans Bentley

Y-10-A6 1908 Grand Prix Mercedes

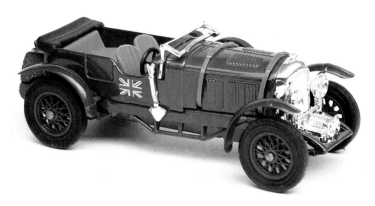

Y-2-D1 1930 Bentley 2-1/2 Litre

Y-1-B2 1911 Model T Ford

Y-1-C2 1936 Jaguar SS100

Y-3-B1 1910 Benz Limousine

Y-3-C1 1934 Riley MPH

Y-2-B2 1911 Renault Two Seater

Y-3-D12 1912 Model T Ford Tanker

Y-2-C1 1914 Prince Henry Vauxhall

Y-3-E1 1912 Model T Ford Tanker

Y-5-B6 1929 4-1/2 Litre Bentley

Y-4-B8 Shand Mason Horse Drawn Fire Engine

Y-5-C1 1907 Peugeot

Y-4-C8 1909 Opel Coupe

Y-5-D2 1927 Talbot Van

Y-4-D9 1930 Model "J" Duesenberg

Y-5-E1 1929 Leyland Titan

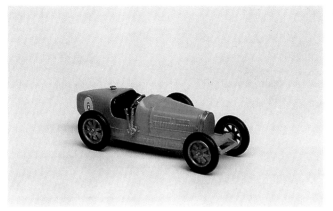

Y-6-B2 1926 Type 35 Bugatti

Y-7-B2 1913 Mercer Raceabout

Y-6-C8 1913 Cadillac

Y-7-C2 1912 Rolls Royce

Y-6-D3 1920 Rolls Royce Fire Engine

Y-7-D1 1930 Model A Wreck Truck

Y-6-E1 1932 Mercedes Lorry

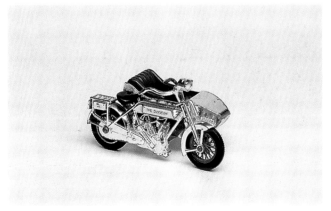

Y-8-B3 1914 Sunbeam Motorcycle & Sidecar

Y-12-E1 Stephenson's Rocket

Y-13-C9 1918 Crossley

Y-12-F4 1937 GMC Van

Y-14-B1 1911 Maxwell Roadster

Y-13-B2 1911 Daimler

Y-14-C4 1931 Stutz Bearcat

Y-13-C1 1918 Crossley

Y-14-D2 1935 E.R.A.

Y-15A1 1907 Rolls Royce Silver Ghost

Y-16-A5 1904 Spyker

Y-15-B1 1930 Packard Victoria

Y-16-B1 1928 Mercedes Benz SS

Y-15-C5 Preston Type Tramcar

Y-16-C1 1960 Ferrari Dino 246/V16

Y-16-D1 1922 Scania Vabis Postbus

97

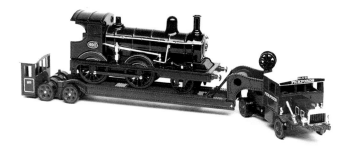

Y-16-E1 Scammel 100 Ton Transporter with Class 2-4-0 Loco

Y-17-A4 1938 Hispano Suiza

Y-18-C1 1918 Atkinson Steam Lorry

Y-18-A5 1937 Cord

Y-18-D1 1918 Atkinson D-Type Steam Lorry

Y-18-B1 1918 Atkinson Steam Lorry

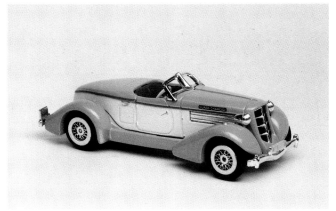

Y-19-A8 1935 Auburn 851 Supercharged Roadster

Y-19-B2 Fowler B6 Showman's Engine

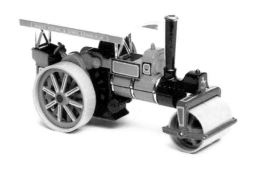

Y-21-B2 1920 Aveling-Porter Steam Roller

Y-19-C1 1929 Morris Light Van

Y-21-C1 1957 BMW 507

Y-20-A7 1937 Mercedes Benz 540K

Y-21-D2 Ford Model TT Ford Van

Y-21-A1 1930 Model A Ford "Woody Wagon"

Y-22-A7 1930 Ford Model A Ford Van

Y-23-A1 1922 AEC 'S' Type Bus

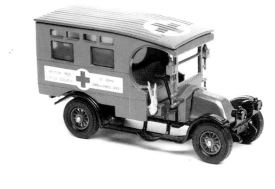

Y-25-B1 1910 Renault Type AG Ambulance

Y-23-B1 Mack Petrol Tanker

Y-26-A2 1913 Crossley Beer Lorry

Y-24-A6 1928 Bugatti Type 44

Y-27-A1 1922 Foden Steam Wagon

Y-25-A1 1910 Renault Type AG Van

Y-27-B1 1922 Foden Steam Wagon & Trailer

Y-28-A1 1907 Unic Taxi

Y-31-A1 1931 Morris Pantechincon

Y-29-A2 Walker Electric Van

Y-32-A1 1917 Yorkshire Steam Wagon

Y-30-A1 1920 Mack Model AC Truck

Y-34-A1 1933 Cadillac V-16

Y-30-B1 1920 Mack Canvasback Truck

Y-35-A1 1930 Model A Ford Pickup

Y-36-A1 1926 Rolls Royce Phantom I

Y-40-A1 1931 Mercedes Benz Type 770

Y-37-A2 1931 Garrett Steam Wagon

Y-41-A1 1932 Mercedes Truck

Y-38-A1 Rolls Royce Armored Car

Y-42-A1 Albion CX27

Y-39-A1 1820 English Stage Coach

Y-43-A1 1905 Bush Steam Fire Engine

Y-44-A1 1910 Renault Bus

Y-61-A1 1933 Cadillac Fire Engine

Y-45-A1 1930 Bugatti Royale

Y-62-A1 1932 Ford AA Truck

Y-46-A1 1868 Merryweather Fire Engine

Y-63-A1 1939 Bedford Truck

Y-47-A1 1929 Morris Light Van

Y-64-A2 1938 Lincoln Zephyr

 Y-65-A1 Austin 7/BMW/Rosengart Set

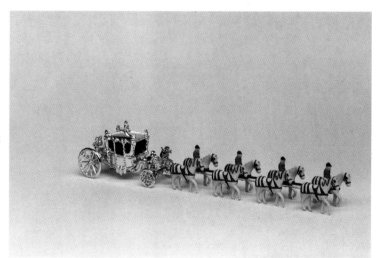

Y-66-A1 Gold State Coach

 Y-901-A Jaguar SS100—Pewter

YTF01 Citroen Van

YHS01 Gypsy Caravan

YHS02 London Omnibus

YSH03 Wells Fargo Stage Coac

YFE10 GMC Rescue Squad Vehicle

YFE11 Mack AC Tanker

YFE14 1953 Ford Fire Truck

YFE12 Model A Ford Battlion Fire Chief

YFE15 1935 Mack Pumper

YFE13 Citroen H-Type Integral Van Fire Engine

YFE16 Dodge Route Van Canteen

YFE17 1939 Bedford Fire Truck

YFE21 1907 Seagrave AC53

YFE18 1950 Ford E.83.W Van & Support Trailer

YFE22 1916 Model T Fire Engine

YFE19 1904 Merryweather Fire Engine

YFE23 1906 Waterous S/P Pumper

YFE20 1912 Benz Motorspritze Fire engine

YFE24 1911 Mack Pumper

YAS07 Fowler B6 Showman's Engine with Crane

YAS10 1918 Atkinson Steam Wagon

YAS08 1912 Burrel Traction Engine

YAS11 1917 Yorkshire Steam Wagon

YAS09 1929 Garrett Steam Wagon

YAS12 1922 Foden Steam Wagon

YYM36791 Horse Drawn Wagon

YMS01 1971 Chevelle

YMS05 1970 Boss Mustang

YMS02 1971 Cuda 440 6-Pack

YMS06 1968 Camaro SS 396

YMS03 1967 Pontiac GTO

YMS07 1970 Plymouth GTX

YMS04 1970 Road Runner Hemi

YMS08 1966 Chevelle SS396

113

YRS01 1955 Chevy Wreck Truck

YRS04 1954 Chevy Snow Plow

YRS02 1953 Ford Pickup

YRS05-1 1957 Chevrolet 3100 Pickup

YRS03 1956 Chevy Pickup

YRS05-2 1957 Chevrolet 3100 Pickup

YRS06-1 1955 Ford F150 Pickup

YIS01 1955 Chevrolet 3100 Pickup

YIS04 1957 Chevrolet Pickup

YIS02 1955 Ford F150 Pickup

YIS05 1954 Ford F100 Pickup

YIS03 1956 Chevrolet Pickup

YIS06 1953 Ford F150 Pickup

DY-9A1 1949 Land Rover Series 1.80

DY-13-A1 1955 Bentley 'R' Type Continental

DY-10-A1 1950 Mercedes Benz Konfernez Type Omnibus

DY-14-A1 1946 Delahaye 145 Chapron

DY-11-A1 1948 Tucker Torpedo

DY-15-A2 1952 Austin A40 GV4 10-CWT Van

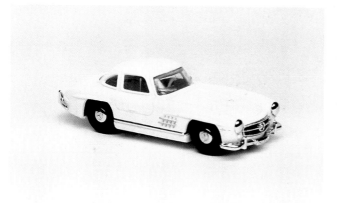

DY-12-A 1955 Mercedes 300SL

DY-16-A3 1967 Ford Mustang Fastback 2+2

DY-17-A1 1939 Triumph Dolomite

DY-21-A1 1964 Austin Mini Cooper 'S'

DY-18-A1 1967 Series 1-1/2 E Type Jaguar
Convertible

DY-22-A1 1952 Citroen 15CV 6 CYL

DY-19-A1 1973 MGB-GT V8

DY-23-A2 1956 Chevrolet Corvette

DY-20-A1 1965 Triumph TR4A-IRS

DY-24-A1 1973 Ferrari Dino 246 GTS

DYG12-A1 1956 Ford Fairlane

DYG-16A1 1955 Chevrolet Bel Air

DYG13-A1 1953 Cadillac Eldorado

VEM01 1949 Volkswagen Cabrio

DYG14-A1 1948 Desoto

VEM02 1959 Austin Seven

DYG15-A1 1958 Nash Metropolitan

VEM03 1949 Citroen 2CV

VEM04 1955 Messerschmidt KR 200

DYB01 Triumph TR8

VEM05 1962 Wolseley Hornet

DYB03 1955 Morgan

VEM06 1966 Fiat 500

DYB05 MGB

VEM07 1962 Renault 4L

DYB06 1960 Aston Martin DB4

M-1-A1   Caterpillar   Earth   Scraper

M-3-A3   Thornycraft   Antar   &   Centurion   Tank

M-1-B1   BP   Autotanker

M-4-A2   Ruston   Bucyrus

M-2-A2   Bedford   Ice   Cream   Truck

M-4-B1   or   K-4-B1   GMC   Tractor   &   Freuhof
Hopper   Train

M-2-B1   Bedford   Truck   &   York   Trailer

M-5-A1   Massey   Ferguson   Combine   Harvester

M-6-A2 Pickfords 200 Ton Transporter

M-6-B1 or K-5-B1 Racing Car Transporter

M-8-B1 Guy Warrior Car Transporter

M-7-A1 Jennings Cattle Truck

M-9-A4 Interstate Double Freighter

M-8-A1 Mobilgas Petrol Tanker

M-10-A1 Dinkum Dumper

K-1-A1   Weatherhill   Hydraulic   Shovel

K-2-B1 K.W. Dump Truck

K-1-B1   Hoveringham   Tipper

K-2-C3 Scammell Heavy Wreck Truck

K-1-C1 O & K Excavator

K-2-D11 Car Recovery Vehicle

K-2-A2 Muir Hill Dumper

K-3-A1   Caterpillar   Bulldozer

K-3-B1 Hatra Tractor Shovel

K-4-A4   International   Tractor

K-3-C1 Massey Ferguson Tractor & Trailer

K-4-C2   Leyland   Tipper

K-3-D2   Mod   Tractor   &   Trailer

K-4-D8   Big   Tipper

K-3-E1   Grain   Transporter

K-5-A2   Foden   Tipper   Truck

K-5-C-3   Muir   Hill   Tractor   &   Trailer

K-6-D1   Motorcycle   Transporter

K-6-A1   Allis-Chalmers   Earth   Scraper

K-7-A1   Curtis   Wright   Rear   Dumper

K-6-B1   Mercedes   Benz   'Binz'   Ambulance

K-7-B1   Refuse   Truck

K-6-C2   Cement   Truck

K-7-C10   Racing   Car   Transporter

K-8-A2 Prime Mover & Caterpillar Tractor

K-8-E1 Ferrari F40

K-8-B4 Guy Warrior Car Transporter

K-9-A2 Diesel Road Roller

K-8-C5 Caterpillar Traxcavator

K-9-B4 Claas Combine Harvester

K-8-D1 Animal Transporter

K-9-C2 Fire Tender

K-10-A1 Aveling Barford Tractor Shovel

K-11-A4 Fordson Tractor & Trailer

K-10-B1 Pipe Truck

K-11-B1 DAF Car Transporter

K-10-C2 Car Transporter

K-11-C1 Breakdown Truck

K-10-D1 Bedford Car Transporter

K-11-D1 Dodge Delivery Van

K-12-A1 Heavy Breakdown Wreck Truck

K-13-B3   Building   Transporter

K-12-B1   Scammell   Crane   Truck

K-13-C8   Aircraft   Transporter

K-12-C1   Hercules   Mobile   Truck

K-14-A1 Taylor Jumbo Crane

K-13-A1   Readymix   Concrete   Truck

K-14-B1   Freight   Truck

K-14-C2 Heavy Breakdown Truck

K-16-B7   Petrol   Tanker

K-15-A1   Merryweather   Fire   Engine

K-17-A2 Low Loader with Bulldozer

K-15-B2 The Londoner

K-17-B10   Articulated   Container   Truck

K-15-C1 The Londoner

K-18-A1   Articulated   Horse   Box

K-16-A1 Dodge Tractor with Twin Tippers

K-18-B7   Articulated   Dump   truck

K-20-B1 Cargo Hauler

K-19-A1   Scammell   Tipper   Truck

K-20-C7   Peterbilt   Wrecker

K-19-B2   Security   Truck

K-21-A2   Mercury   Cougar

K-20-A1 Tractor Transporter

K-21-B2   Cougar   Dragster

K-28-A3 Drag Pack

K-30-A5 Mercedes C.111

K-28-B1 Skip Truck

K-30-B1 Unimog & Compressor

K-29-A Lamborghini Seaburst Set

K-31-A1 Bertone Runabout

K-29-B2 Ford Delivery Van

K-31-B13 Peterbilt Refrigerator Truck

K-32-A3 Shovel Nose

K-34-A3 Thunderclap

K-32-B1 Farm Unimog & Trailer

K-34-B1 Pallet Truck

K-33-A1 Citroen S.M.

K-35-A2 Lightning

K-33-B1 Cargo Hauler

K-35-B1 Massey Ferguson Tractor & Trailer

145

K-36-A2 Bandalero

K-38-A4 Gus's Gulper

K-36-B1 Construction Transporter

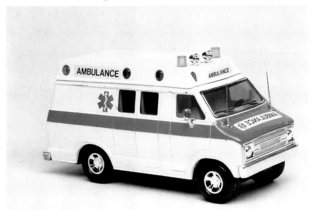

K-38-B1 Dodge Ambulance

K-37-A1 Sand Cat

K-39-A1 Milligan's Mill

K-37-B1 Leyland Tipper

K-39-B1 Snorkel Fire Engine

K-40-A4 Blaze Trailer

K-41-C1 JCB Excavator

K-40-B Delivery Truck

K-42-A1 Nissan 270X

K-41-A8 Fuzz Buggy

K-42-B1 Traxcavator Road Ripper

K-41-B1 Brabham BT 44B

K-43-A4 Cambuster

K-43-B1 Log Transporter

K-45-A7 Marauder

K-44-A2 Bazooka

K-46-A4 Racing Car Pack

K-44-B1 Surtees Formula 1

K-47-A1 Easy Rider

K-44-C1 Bridge Layer

K-48-A1 Mercedes 350 SLC

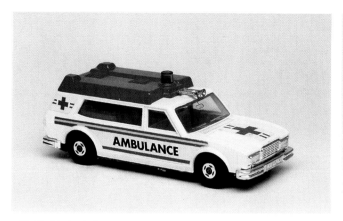

K-49-A1 Ambulance

K-53-A1 Hot Fire Engine

K-50-A2 Street Rod

K-54-A3 AMX Javelin

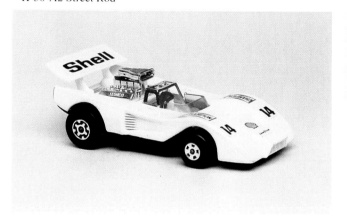

K-51-A10 Barracuda

K-55-A3 Corvette Caper Cart

K-52-A1 Datsun 240Z

K-56-A1 Maserati Bora

K-102-B1 Race Support Set

K-106-B1 Kenworth Aircraft Transporter

K-103-B3 Peterbilt Tanker

K-107-B1 Powerboat Transporter

K-104-B1 Rancho Rescue Set

K-108-B1 Peterbilt Digger Transporter

K-105-B2 Peterbilt Tipper

K-109-B1 Iveco Tanker

K-110-B1 Fire Engine

K-117-B1 Scania Bulldozer Transporter

K-111-B1 Peterbilt Refuse Truck

K-118-B1 Road Construction Set

K-114-B1 Crane Truck

K-119-A1 Fire Rescue Set

K-115-B1 Mercedes Benz 190E

K-120-A3 Car Transporter

K-160-A1 Racing Car Transporter

K-164-A1 Range Rover

K-161A1 Rolls Royce Silver Spirit

K-165-A2 Range Rover Police Car

K-162-A1 Sierra RS500 Cosworth

K-166-A1 Mercedes Benz 190E Taxi

K-163-A1 Unimog Snow Plow

K-167-A2 Ford Transit

K-168-A1 Porsche 911 Carrera

K-173-A1 Lamborghini Diablo

K-169-A1 Ford Transit Ambulance

K-179-A1 Suzuki Santana

K-171-A1 Toyota Hi-Lux

Ford Escort Cosworth

K-172-A1 Mercedes Benz 500SL

Mazda RX7

163

K-186-A1 Peterbilt Container Truck

K-190-A1 Freightliner Container Truck

K-187-A1 Freightliner Container Truck

K-192-A1 Peterbilt Lowloader

K-188-A1 Kenworth Cabover

K-193-A1 Peterbilt 359 Cabover

K-194-A1 Kenworth W900 Cab

K-189-A1 Peterbilt Container Truck

EM-13-A1 Helicopter

FM-3-A1 Massey Ferguson Tractor

EM-14-A1 Suzuki Santana

FM-5-A1 Muir Hill Tractor & Trailer

1939 Harley-Davidson Knucklehead

EM-15-A1 Mercedes Benz 190E Police Car

CS-5-A1 Unimog Tar Sprayer

Harley-Davidson Springer Soft Tail

K-108-A4 M3A1 Half Track

K-110-A1 Recovery Vehicle

K-109-A1 M551 Sheridan

K-111-A1 Missile Launcher

K-112-A1 DAF Ambulance

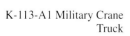

K-113-A1 Military Crane
Truck

K-114-A1 Army
Aircraft Transporter

K-115-A1 Army Petrol Tanker

K-116-A1 Troop Carrier
& Howitzer

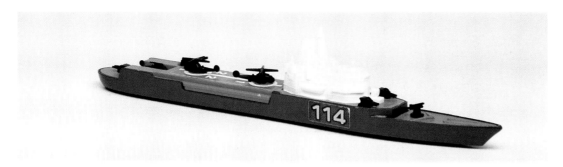

K-307-A1 Helicopter
Carrier

K-308-A1 Guided Missile
Destroyer

K-309-A1 Submarine

K-310-A1 Anti-Aircraft
Cruiser

K-311 Tanker (never issued)

K-312 Container Ship
(never issued)

ADVENTURE 2000

K-2001-A1 Raider
Command

K-2002-A1 Flight Hunter

K-2004-A2 Rocket Striker

K-2003-A1 Crusader

K-2006-A1 Shuttle Launcher

SPECIALS

SP1/2-A8 Kremer Porsche

SP9/10-B1 Jaguar XJ220

SP3/4-A7 Ferrari 512B

SP11/12-A6 Chevrolet Camaro

SP5/6-A1 Lancia Rallye

SP11-B1 Chevy Lumina

SP7/8-A7 Zakspeed Mustang

SP12-B1 Ford Thunderbird

SP9/10-A2 Chevy Prostocker

SP13/14-A12 Porsche 959

SKYBUSTERS

SB-1-A4 Lear Jet

SB-4-A6 Mirage F1

SB-2-A2 Corsair A7D

SB-5-A2 Starfighter

SB-3-A6 A300 Airbus

SB-3-B2 NASA Space Shuttle

SB-6-A3 MIG 21

SB-7-A1 Junkers

SB8-A2 Spitfire

SB-12-A3 Skyhawk A4-F

SB-9-A14 Cessna 402

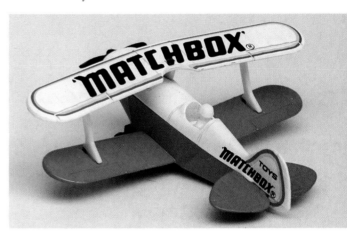

SB-12-B3 Pitts Special

SB-10-A14 Boeing 747

SB-13-A6 DC.10

SB-14-A4 Cessna 210

SB-11-A2 Alpha Jet

SB-15-A2 Phantom F4E

SB-19-A3 Piper Commance

SB-16-A2 Corsair F4U-5N

SB-20-A3 Helicopter

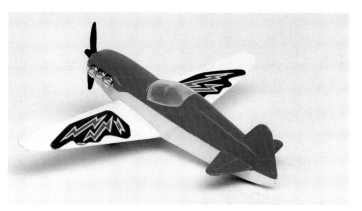

SB-17-A1 Ram Rod

SB-21-A1 Lightning
SB-22-A4 Tornado

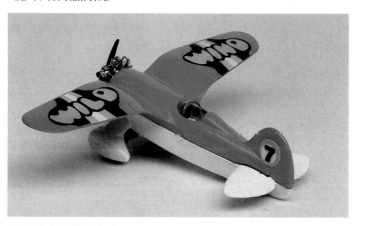

SB-18-A1 Wild Wind

SB-23-A5 Supersonic Transport

SB-27-A4 Harrier Jet

SB-24-A3 F.16 Fighter Jet

SB-28-A9 A.300 Airbus

SB-25-A1 Rescue Helicopter

SB-29-A1 SR.71 Blackbird

SB-26-A6 Cessna Float Plane

SB-30-A1 Grumman F-14 Tomcat

SB-31-A2 Boeing 747-400

SB-32-A1 Fairchild A-10 Thunderbolt

SB-34-A1 C-130 Hercules

SB-33-A1 Bell Jet Ranger

SB-35-A1 MiL M-24 Hind-D

SB-36-A1 Lockheed F-117A (Stealth)

SB-37-A1 Hawk

SB-38-A1 BaE 146

SB-39-A2 Boeing Stearman

SB-40-A1 Boeing 737-300

SB-41-A1 Boeing 777-400

WD-1-A3 Mickey Mouse Fire Engine

WD-4-A1 Minnie Mouse Lincoln

WD-2-A1 Donald Duck Beach Buggy

WD-5-A1 Mickey Mouse Jeep

WD-3-A1 Goofy's Beetle

WD-6-A1 Donald Duck Jeep

WD-7-A1 Pinnocchio's Traveling Theater

WD-10-A1 Goofy's Train

WD-8-A2 Jiminy Cricket's Old Timer

WD-11-A1 Donald Duck's Ice Cream Van

WD-9-A2 Goofy's Sports Car

WD-12-A1 Mickey Mouse Corvette

Bugs Bunny's Lumina

Wile E. Coyote's Lumina

Road Runner's Dragster

Tasmanian Devil's Sprint Car

CS-13-A1 Popeye's Spinach
Wagon

Bugs Bunny's Group C Racer

CS-14-A1 Bluto's Road Roller

Daffy Duck's Pickup

CS-15-A1 Olive Oyl's Sports
Car

183

Big Bird's Fire Engine

Bert's Tow Truck

Ernie's Taxi

Ernie's Police Car

Cookie Monster's School Bus

Zoe's Sports Car

Big Bird's Dune Buggy

Ernie's Dump Truck

Oscar's Garbage Truck

Big Bird's Delivery Van- "30th Anniversary"

Elmo's Cement Truck

Elmo's Sports Car

Cookie Monster's Airplane

Ernie's Dune Buggy

Elmo's Helicopter

Elmo's Dump Truck

Ernie's Cement Truck

Telly's Front Loader

Busy Bear's Dune Buggy

Big Bird's Mail Van

Ernie's Car Carrier with Elmo's Race Car
& Cookie Monster's Truck

HAUNTED HAULERS

Ghoul Bus

Neck Wrecker

Drac Bike

SC01-A1 Big Foot

SC04-A1 Rollin Thunder

SC02-A1 USA-1

SC05-A1 Flyin Hi

SC03-A1 Taurus

SC06-A1 Awesome Kong II

SC07-A1 Mad Dog II

SC10-A3 Toad

SC08-A1 Hawk

SC11-A4 Mud Ruler

SC09-A1 So High

SC12-A1 Bog Buster

SC13-A3 Hog

SC-16-A1 Doc Crush

SC-14A1 Mud Monster

SC-17-A1 Mud Slinger II

SC-15-A2 Big Pete

SC-18-A1 `57 Chevy

SC-19-A1 Drag-On

SC-22-A1 Showtime

SC-20-A1 Voo Doo

SC-23-A1 Checkmate

SC-21-A1 Hot Stuff

SC-24-A1 12 Pac

MW-01-A1 Carolina Crusher

MW-04-A1 Invader

MW-02-A1 Equalizer

MW-05-A1 Predator

MW-03-A1 Grave Digger

MW-06-A1 Taurus

YSTS01 Holiday Express

YSTS02 Matchbox Railroad

VMM01 Hummer

LS001 Lamborghini Diablo

VMM02 Military Jeep 4 X 4

LS002 Porsche 911 Cabriolet

LS003 Jaguar XJ220

92088 Chevy Nomad

ART112 Lamborghini Diablo

ART213 1993 Corvette

ART150 Ferrari F40

ART232 Mercedes Benz 320SL Soft Top

ART173 Jaguar XJ220

196

ULTRA CLASS CORVETTES

CCV01 1969 Chevrolet Corvette

CCV04 1997 Corvette

CCV02 1993 40ᵗʰ Anniversary Corvette

CCV05 1963 Corvette Stingray

CCV03 1957 Chevrolet Corvette

CCV06 1953 Corvette

197

SUPERFAST MINIS

'57 Chevy & Camaro Z28

Ford LTD Police Car & Lamborghini Countach

Corvette Grand Sport & Chevy Lumina

Ferrari F40 & T-Bird Turbo Coupe

Porsche 959 & BMW M1
Lamborghini Countach & Jaguar XJ6

TURBO 2

AM-2601 Pontiac Fiero

AM-2602 Peugeot 205 Turbo

AM-2606 Sauber Group C Racer

AM-2609 Ford Supervan II

AM-2610 Racing Porsche
AM-2611 Toyota MR2

SWOP TOPS

FT001 Mercedes Benz

FT002 Corvette

FT003 Ferrari Testarossa

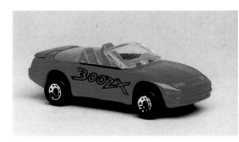

FT004 Nissan 300ZX

FT005 Porsche 968
FT006 Ford Mustang

TRS9 Ford Falcon 25th Anniversary Set

TR11 Charger

TR4 Ford Falcon GTHO Phase 3

TRS1 FJ Holden 40th Anniversary Set

TR8 Torana

TR2 FJ Holden Van

TRS10 Ford Falcon XC Hardtop Set

Garbage Truck

Garbage Truck

Police Car- Sheriff

Police Car- Metro Police

Tow Truck

Tow Truck

UFO   UFO

LSV Recon

A-Tak Hornet

Water Dragon

Humvee

Sky Scorcher

Sand Tiger

POCKET CATALOGS

1957

1959

1959—2nd edition

1960

1961

1962

1963

1964

1965

1966

1967

1968

1969

1969 2nd Edition

1970

1971

1972

1973

1974

1975

1976

1977

1978

1979/80

1980/81

1981/82

1982/83

1983

1984

1985

1986

1987

1988

1989

1990

1991

1992

1993 (GR)

1993 (UK)

1994 (Toys R Us)

1994 (UK)

1994 (US)

Early Lesney Toys

When Lesney Products was first founded in 1947, toys were only a sideline to a manufacturing business run by Leslie Smith, Rodney Smith, and Jack Odell. It was Jack Odell who first came up with the idea to make toys in 1948. At this time, these toys were not called "Matchbox". This name didn't transpire until 1953, when the first miniature models were released. From 1948 through 1955, fifteen items were released and are known as "Early Lesney Toys," the only classification prior to the release of Matchbox miniatures. Some of these models were later scaled down into miniatures while others were not. One, the Bread Bait Press, is not a toy but belongs in a fisherman's tackle box! Another item is a souvenir letter opener with a sliding inner sleeve that reveals a hidden tiny Matchbox box! As these are made by Lesney, they best fit in this category.

Aveling Barford Road Roller 1948
Cement Mixer 1948
Caterpillar Tractor 1948
Caterpillar Bulldozer 1948
Horse Drawn Milk Float 1949
Rag & Bone Cart 1949
Soap Box Racer 1949
Jumbo the Elephant 1950
Prime Mover with Trailer & Bulldozer 1950
Ruston Bucyrus Shovel 1950
Muffin the Mule 1951
Large Coronation Coach 1952
Small Coronation Coach 1953
Massey Harris Tractor 1954
Bread Bait Press 1954
Covered Wagon 1955
Souvenir Letter Opener 1962

Variations

AVELING BARFORD ROAD ROLLER, issued 1948
1. dark green body, red painted wheels, yellow flywheel cast ($700-1,000)
2. dark green body, unpainted wheels, no driver or flywheel cast ($500-750)
3. dark green body, unpainted wheels, with driver, no flywheel cast ($500-750)

4. light green body, red wheels, no driver or flywheel cast ($600-800)
5. gray-brown body, red wheels, no driver or flywheel cast ($700-1,000)
6. red body, green wheels, no driver or flywheel cast ($700-1,000)

CEMENT MIXER, issued 1948
1. pale green body, red barrel & handle, red wheels ($350-500)
2. dark green body, red barrel & handle, red wheels ($350-500)
3. dark green body, red barrel & handle, yellow wheels ($350-500)
4. dark green body, green barrel & handle, green wheels ($350-500)
5. dark green body, green barrel & handle, red wheels ($350-500)
6. red body, dark green barrel & handle, green wheels ($350-500)
7. red body, dark green barrel & handle, yellow wheels ($350-500)

CATERPILLAR TRACTOR, issued 1948
1. green body and rollers ($700-1,000)
2. dark yellow body and rollers ($600-800)
3. orange body and rollers ($600-800)

CATERPILLAR BULLDOZER, issued 1948
1. pale green body, rollers and blade ($800-1,200)
2. orange body, rollers and blade ($500-750)
3. dark yellow body, red rollers and blade ($500-750)

HORSE DRAWN MILK FLOAT, issued 1949
1. orange body ($1200-1800)
2. blue body ($2,000-3500)

RAG AND BONE CART, issued 1949
1. yellow body with red wheels ($2,000-3,500)
2. green body with red wheels ($3,000-4,500)

SOAP BOX RACER, issued 1949
1. gold body, brown driver, metal wheels ($2,000-3,500)

JUMBO THE ELEPHANT, issued 1950
1. light gray body with windup key ($800-1,200)

PRIME MOVERP WITH TRAILER & BULLDOZER, issued 1950
1. orange mover, orange trailer, all green bulldozer ($1,800-2,500)

2. orange mover, blue trailer, all orange bulldozer ($1,200-1,800)
3. orange mover, blue trailer, yellow dozer with red blade ($850-1,200)

RUSTON BUCYRUS SHOVEL, issued 1950
1. yellow & maroon body, green shovel & base ($750-1,200)

MUFFIN THE MULE, issued 1951
1. cream body with painted features, puppet strings ($450-600)

LARGE CORONATION COACH, issued 1952
1. gold painted body, king & queen cast inside ($1,000-1,500)
2. gold painted body, queen only cast inside ($400-650)
3. gold plated body, queen only cast inside ($500-750)
4. silver plated body, queen only cast inside ($650-1,000)

SMALL CORONATION COACH, issued 1953
1. silver plated body ($125-175)
2. gold painted body ($200-300)

MASSEY HARRIS TRACTOR, issued 1954
1. red body, beige wheels with black rubber tires ($850-1,200)

BREAD BAIT PRESS, issued 1954
1. red body, green wingnut & inner fixture, "Lesney Milbro" cast ($100-125)
2. red body, unpainted wingnut, green inner fixture, "Lesney" cast ($80-120)
3. red body, unpainted wingnut & inner fixture, "Lesney" cast ($75-100)
NOTE: "Milbro" was a distribution agent like Moko.

COVERED WAGON, issued 1955
1. dark green body, white cover, brown horses, no barrels cast ($150-200)
2. dark green body, white cover, brown horses, red barrels cast ($150-200)

SOUVENIR LETTER OPENER, issued 1962
1. black handle, silver blade, Lesney UK address on silver band ($175-250)
2. black handle, silver blade, Fred Bronner address on silver band ($175-250)

Regular Wheel Matchbox Series 1-75

The extraordinary success of the small Coronation Coach in 1953 encouraged Lesney Products to proceed with plans to make small-sized toys for 1953. They began to make scaled-down versions of seven of their earlier toys in this order: Diesel Road Roller, Dumper, Cement Mixer, Massey Harris Tractor, Quarry Truck, Horse Drawn Milk Float, and Caterpillar Bulldozer. The 5A London Bus was especially designed for the smaller series. The Quarry Truck was produced as a prototype of a larger toy but never issued and only a few examples survived. The Dumper design on which the 2A was based upon never made it past the drawing board for the early larger series, however the MICA club introduced a "replica" of what this would have looked like in the early 1990s. These

toys were immediately successful with children and more new toys were made each successive year.

When the personnel gathered to design a box for the new small toys, they struck on the idea of using a style resembling a match box. This was not a new thought, for in the early 1900s, toys from Germany were made with this style box. The 1940s even saw prewar toys packed this way and called "Matchbox toys." The Lesney team registered the name "Matchbox" for this series and that name has identified their toys since. Lesney Products was then using the distribution and packaging facilities of Moko for its toys, and Moko had a significant financial interest in the new series.

The actual design of the box printing is similar to a Scandinavian matchbox cover for Norvic Safety Matches. From this design, the Lesney and Moko names were substituted for the first Matchbox box design. The front and back are yellow with red letters "Matchbox Series" in an arch above a black and red drawing of each toy inside. On both sides of the drawing, the number of the toy is situated. Below the drawing, a scroll with the lettering "A Moko Lesney" appears. The word "Product" is in a small arch below the scroll. For this original design, the word "Moko" is written in script lettering. This box design was used only for the first seven toys in the series for 1953 and 1954.

Basic Model List (1953-1969)

1A Diesel Road Roller 1953
1B Road Roller (2-1/4") 1955
1C Road Roller (2-3/8") 1958
1D Aveling Barford Road Roller (3") 1962
1E Mercedes Benz Lorry 1968

2A Dumper (1-5/8") 1953
2B Dumper (1-7/8") 1957
2C Muir Hill Dumper 1961
2D Mercedes Trailer 1968

3A Cement Mixer 1953
3B Bedford Tipper 1961
3C Mercedes Benz "Binz" Ambulance 1968

4A Massey Harris Tractor (no fenders) 1954
4B Massey Harris Tractor (with fenders) 1957
4C Triumph Motorcycle & Sidecar 1960
4D Dodge Stake Truck 1967

5A London Bus (2") 1954
5B London Bus (2-1/4") 1957
5C London Bus (2-9/16") 1961
5D London Bus (2-3/4") 1965

6A Quarry Truck (2-1/8") 1954
6B Quarry Truck (2-1/2") 1957

6C Euclid Quarry Truck 1964
6D Ford Pickup 1968

7A Horse Drawn Milk Float 1954
7B Ford Anglia 1961
7C Ford Refuse Truck 1966

8A Caterpillar Tractor (1-1/2") 1955
8B Caterpillar Tractor (1-5/8") 1959
8C Caterpillar Tractor (1-7/8") 1961
8D Caterpillar Tractor (2") 1964
8E Ford Mustang Fastback 1966

9A Dennis Fire Escape (2-1/4") 1955
9B Dennis Fire Escape (2-3/8") 1957
9C Merryweather Marquis Fire Engine 1959
9D Boat & Trailer 1966

10A Mechanical Horse & Trailer (2-3/8") 1955
10B Mechanical Horse & Trailer (2-15/16") 1958
10C Sugar Container Truck 1961
10D Pipe Truck 1966

11A Road Tanker (2") 1955
11B Road Tanker (2-1/2") 1958
11C Jumbo Crane 1965
11D Scaffold Truck 1969

12A Land Rover (1-3/4") 1955

12B Land Rover (2-1/4") 1959
12C Safari Land Rover 1965

13A Bedford Wreck Truck (2") 1955
13B Bedford Wreck Truck (2-1/8") 1958
13C Thames Wreck Truck 1961
13D Dodge Wreck Truck 1965

14A Daimler Ambulance (1-7/8") 1956
14B Daimler Ambulance (2-5/8") 1958
14C Bedford Ambulance 1962
14D Iso Grifo 1968

15A Prime Mover 1956
15B Atlantic Prime Mover 1959
15C Refuse Truck 1963
15D Volkswagen 1500 Saloon 1968

16A Atlantic Trailer (3-1/8") 1956
16B Atlantic Trailer (3-1/4") 1959
16C Scammell Mountaineer Snowplow 1964
16D Case Bulldozer 1969

17A Bedford Removals Van (no base #) 1956
17B Bedford Removals Van (with base #) 1958
17C Austin Taxi Cab 1960
17D Hoveringham Tipper 1963
17E Horse Box 1969

18A Caterpillar Bulldozer (1-7/8") 1956
18B Caterpillar Bulldozer (2") 1958
18C Caterpillar Bulldozer (2-1/4") 1961
18D Caterpillar Bulldozer (2-3/8") 1964
18E Field Car 1969

19A MG TD Sports Car (2") 1956
19B MGA Sports Car (2-1/4") 1958
19C Aston Martin Racing Car 1961
19D Lotus Racing Car 1966

20A Stake Truck 1956
20B ERF 68G Truck 1959
20C Chevrolet Impala Taxi Cab 1965

21A Long Distance Coach (2-1/4") 1956
21B Long Distance Coach (2-5/8") 1958
21C Commer Milk Float 1961
21D Foden Concrete Truck 1968

22A Vauxhall Cresta 1956
22B 1958 Vauxhall Cresta 1958
22C Pontiac Grand Prix Sports Coupe 1964

23A Berkeley Cavalier Trailer (no base #) 1956
23B Berkeley Cavalier Trailer (with base #) 1958
23B Bluebird Dauphine Trailer 1960
23D Trailer Caravan 1965

24A Weatherill Hydraulic Excavator (2-3/8") 1956
24B Weatherill Hydraulic Excavator (2-5/8") 1959
24C Rolls Royce Silver Shadow 1967

25A Dunlop Van 1956
25B Volkswagen 1200 Sedan 1960
25C Petrol Tanker 1964
25D Ford Cortina 1968

26A Concrete Truck 1956
26B Foden Concrete Truck 1961
26C G.M.C. Tipper Truck 1968

27A Bedford Lowloader (3-/18") 1956
27B Bedford Lowloader (3-3/4") 1959
27C Cadillac Sixty Special 1960
27D Mercedes Benz 230SL 1966

28A Bedford Compressor Truck 1956
28B Thames Compressor Truck 1959
28C Mark 10 Jaguar 1964
28D Mack Dump Truck 1968

29A Bedford Milk Delivery Van 1956
29B Austin A55 Cambridge Sedan 1961
29C Fire Pumper 1966

30A Ford Prefect 1956
30B Magirus-Deutz 6 Wheel Crane Truck 1961
30C Eight Wheel Crane Truck 1965

31A Ford Station Wagon 1957
31B Ford Fairlane Station Wagon 1960
31C Lincoln Continental 1964

32A Jaguar XK140 Coupe 1957
32B Jaguar XKE 1962
32C Leyland Petrol Tanker 1968

33A Ford Zodiac MKII Sedan 1957
33B Ford Zephyr 6 MKIII 1963
33C Lamborghini Miura 1969

34A Volkswagen Microvan 1957
34B Volkswagen Camper (2-3/5") 1962
34C Volkswagen Camper (raised roof) 1967
34D Volkswagen Camper (flat roof) 1968

35A Marshall Horse Box 1957
35B Snow Trac Tractor 1964

36A Austin A50 1957
36B Lambretta Scooter & Sidecar 1961
36C Opel Diplomat 1966

37A Coca Cola Lorry (no base) 1956
37B Coca Cola Lorry (with base) 1960
37C Dodge Cattle Truck 1966

38A Karrier Refuse Collector 1957
38B Vauxhall Victor Estate Car 1963
38C Honda Motorcycle & Trailer 1967

39A Ford Zodiac Convertible 1957
39B Pontiac Convertible 1962
39C Ford Tractor 1967

40A Bedford Tipper Truck 1957
40B Leyland Royal Tiger Coach 1961
40C Hay Trailer 1967

41A D Type Jaguar (2-3/16") 1957
41B D Type Jaguar (2-7/16") 1960
41C Ford GT 1965

42A Bedford Evening News Van 1957
42B Studebaker Lark Wagonaire 1965
42C Iron Fairy Crane 1969

43A Hillman Minx 1958
43B Aveling Barford Tractor Shovel 1962
43C Pony Trailer 1968

44A Rolls Royce Silver Cloud 1958
44B Rolls Royce Phantom V 1964
44C G.M.C. Refrigerator Truck 1967

45A Vauxhall Victor 1958
45B Ford Corsair with boat 1965

46A Morris Minor 1000 1958
46B Pickfords Removal Van 1960
46C Mercedes Benz 300SE 1968

47A 1 Ton Trojan Van 1958
47B Commer Ice Cream Canteen 1963
47C DAF Tipper Container Truck 1968

48A Meteor Sports Boat & Trailer 1958
48B Sports Boat & Trailer 1961
48C Dodge Dumper Truck 1966

49A M3 Personnel Carrier 1958
49B Mercedes Unimog 1967

50A Commer Pickup 1958
50B John Deere Tractor 1964
50C Ford Kennel Truck 1969

51A Albion Chieftain 1958
51B John Deere Trailer 1964
51C 8 Wheel Tipper 1969

52A Maserati 4CLT Racer 1958
52B BRM Racing Car 1965

53A Aston Martin 1958
53B Mercedes Benz 220 SE 1963
53C Ford Zodiac MK IV 1968

54A Saracen Personnel Carrier 1958
54B S&S Cadillac Ambulance 1965

55A D.U.K.W. 1958
55B Ford Fairlane Police Car 1963
55C Ford Galaxie Police Car 1966
55D Mercury Police Car 1968

56A London Trolley Bus 1958
56B Fiat 1500 1965

57A Wolseley 1500 1958
57B Chevrolet Impala 1961
57C Land Rover Fire Engine 1966

58A BEA Coach 1958
58B Drott Excavator 1962
58C DAF Girder Truck 1968

59A Ford Thames Van 1958
59B Ford Fairlane Fire Chief Car 1963
59C Ford Galaxie Fire Chief Car 1966

60A Morris 12 Pickup 1958
60B Site Hut Truck 1966

61A Ferret Scout Car 1959
61B Alvis Stalwart 1966

62A General Service Lorry 1959
62B TV Service Van 1963
62C Mercury Cougar 1968

63A Ford Service Ambulance 1959
63B Foamite Crash Tender 1964
63C Dodge Crane Truck 1968

64A Scammell Breakdown Truck 1959
64B MG 1100 1966

65A Jaguar 3.4 Litre Saloon (2-1/2") 1959
65B Jaguar 3.4 Litre Saloon (2-5/8") 1962
65C Claas Combine Harvester 1967

66A Citroen DS19 1959
66B Harley-Davidson Motorcycle & Sidecar 1962
66C Greyhound Bus 1967

67A Saladin Armored Car 1959
67B Volkswagen 1600 TL 1967

68A Austin MKII Radio Truck 1959
68B Mercedes Coach 1965

69A Commer 30 CWT Van 1959
69B Hatra Tractor Shovel 1965

70A Ford Thames Estate Car 1959
70B Ford Grit Spreader 1966

71A Austin 200 Gallon Water Truck 1959
71B Jeep Gladiator Pickup 1964
71C Ford Heavy Wreck Truck 1968

72A Fordson Tractor 1959
72B Standard Jeep 1966

73A 10 Ton Pressure Refueller 1959
73B Ferrari F1 Racing Car 1962
73C Mercury Station Wagon 1968

74A Mobile Refreshment Canteen 1959
74B Daimler Bus 1966

75A Ford Thunderbird 1960
75B Ferrari Berlinetta 1965

Variations

1A DIESEL ROAD ROLLER, issued 1953
1. dark green body, red metal wheels ($100-125)
2. light green body, red metal wheels ($175-200)

1B ROAD ROLLER, issued 1955
1. light green body, red metal wheels, dark tan driver ($75-90)
2. light green body, red metal wheels, light tan driver ($75-90)

1C ROAD ROLLER, issued 1958
1. light green body, red metal wheels ($110-135)
2. dark green body, red metal wheels ($85-100)

1D AVELING BARFORD ROAD ROLLER, issued 1962
1. dark green body, red plastic rollers ($30-35)

1E MERCEDES BENZ LORRY, issued 1968
1. mint green body, orange canopy ($10-12)
2. mint green body, yellow canopy ($15-18)

2A DUMPER, issued 1953
1. green body, red dump, green metal wheels ($175-225)
2. green body, red dump, unpainted metal wheels ($60-85)

2B DUMPER, issued 1957
1. green body, red dump, unpainted metal wheels, no.2 cast ($50-75)
2. green body, red dump, gray plastic wheels, no. 2 cast ($65-80)

2C MUIR HILL DUMPER, issued 1961
1. red cab, green dump, black plastic wheels, "Laing" decals ($18-25)
2. red cab, green dump, black plastic wheels, "Muir Hill" decals ($100-150)

2D MERCEDES TRAILER, issued 1968
1. mint green body, orange canopy ($8-12)
2. mint green body, yellow canopy ($15-18)

3A CEMENT MIXER, issued 1953
1. blue body & barrel, orange metal wheels ($50-75)
2. blue body & barrel, gray plastic wheels ($75-90)

3B BEDFORD TIPPER, issued 1961
1. gray cab, maroon dump, gray plastic wheels ($250-300)
2. gray cab, red dump, gray plastic wheels ($60-75)
3. gray cab, maroon dump, black plastic wheels ($35-50)
4. gray cab, red dump, black plastic wheels ($30-45)

3C MERCEDES BENZ "BINZ" AMBULANCE, issued 1968
1. off white body, red cross decals ($15-20)
2. off white body, red cross labels ($15-20)
3. cream body, red cross decals ($15-20)
4. cream body, red cross labels ($15-20)

4A MASSEY HARRIS TRACTOR, issued 1954
1. red body, rear fenders cast, metal wheels ($75-90)

4B MASSEY HARRIS TRACTOR, issued 1957
1. red body, no fenders cast, no. 4 cast, metal wheels ($60-75)
2. red body, no fenders cast, no. 4 cast, gray plastic wheels ($75-90)

4C TRIUMPH MOTORCYCLE & SIDECAR, issued 1960

1. light silver blue body, black plastic tires ($85-110)
2. dark silver blue body, black plastic tires ($85-110)
3. metallic bronze body, black plastic tires ($2000+)

4D DODGE STAKE TRUCK, issued 1967
1. yellow cab, blue-green stakes ($150-200)
2. yellow cab, green stakes ($10-15)

5A LONDON BUS, issued 1954
1. red body, "Buy Matchbox Series" labels, metal wheels ($75-90)

5B LONDON BUS, issued 1957
1. red body, "Buy Matchbox Series" decals, metal wheels ($75-100)
2. red body, "Buy Matchbox Series" decals, gray plastic wheels ($110-135)
3. red body, "Players Please" decals, gray plastic wheels ($175-200)
4. red body, "Visco Static" decals, gray plastic wheels ($400-600)

5C LONDON BUS, issued 1961
1. red body, "Players Please" decals, gray plastic wheels ($225-250)
2. red body, "Visco Static" decals, gray plastic wheels ($85-100)
3. red body, "Drink Peardrax" decals, gray plastic wheels ($400-600)
4. red body, "Drink Peardrax" decals, black plastic wheels ($300-350)
5. red body, "Baron of Beef" decals, gray plastic wheels ($500-600)
6. red body, "Baron of Beef" decals, black plastic wheels ($500-600)
7. red body, "Visco Static" decals, black plastic wheels ($95-110)

5D LONDON BUS, issued 1965
1. red body, "Longlife" decals, black plastic wheels ($20-35)
2. red body, "Visco Static" decals, black plastic wheels ($25-40)
3. red body, "Visco Static" labels, black plastic wheels ($20-30)
4. red body, "Baron of Beef" decals, black plastic wheels ($400-600)
5. red body, "Pegram Shopfitters" labels, black plastic wheels ($400-600)(C2)

6A QUARRY TRUCK, issued 1954
1. orange cab, gray dump, metal wheels ($50-75)
2. orange cab, gray dump, gray plastic wheels ($750-1,000)

6B QUARRY TRUCK, issued 1957
1. yellow body, gray plastic wheels ($750-1,000)
2. yellow body, black plastic wheels ($40-60)

6C EUCLID QUARRY TRUCK, issued 1964
1. yellow body, recessed rear tires ($18-25)
2. yellow body, solid rear tires ($18-25)

6D FORD PICKUP TRUCK, issued 1968
1. red body, white canopy, black plastic wheels, white grille ($15-20)
2. red body, white canopy, black plastic wheels, silver grille ($20-25)

7A HORSE DRAWN MILK FLOAT, issued 1954
1. orange body, silver painted bottle load, metal wheels ($250-300)
2. orange body, orange or white bottle load, metal wheels ($75-100)
3. orange body, orange or white bottle load, gray plastic wheels ($125-150)

7B FORD ANGLIA, issued 1961
1. light blue body, gray plastic wheels ($75-90)
2. light blue body, silver plastic wheels ($45-55)
3. light blue body, black plastic wheels ($30-40)

7C FORD REFUSE TRUCK, issued 1966
1. orange cab & chassis, , silver - gray metal loader, gray plastic dump ($10-15)

8A CATERPILLAR TRACTOR, issued 1955
1. orange body ($150-200)
2. light yellow body, red driver ($200-250)
3. dark yellow body ($65-80)

8B CATERPILLAR TRACTOR, issued 1959
1. yellow body, metal rollers, yellow driver ($75-100)

8C CATERPILLAR TRACTOR, issued 1961
1. yellow body, metal rollers ($65-80)
2. yellow body, silver plastic rollers ($85-100)
3. yellow body, black plastic rollers ($50-60)

8D CATERPILLAR TRACTOR, issued 1964
1. yellow body, black plastic rollers ($18-25)
2. yellow-orange body, black plastic rollers ($18-25)

8E FORD MUSTANG FASTBACK, issued 1966
1. white body, red interior, black plastic tires ($25-30)
2. orange -red body, red interior, black plastic tires ($350-400)

9A DENNIS FIRE ESCAPE, issued 1955
1. red body, no front bumper or number cast,, metal wheels ($75-90)

9B DENNIS FIRE ESCAPE, issued 1957
1. red body, front bumper cast, no. 9 cast, metal wheels ($85-100)
2. red body, front bumper cast, no. 9 cast, gray plastic wheels ($350-500)

9C MERRYWEATHER MARQUIS FIRE ENGINE, issued 1959
1. red body, tan ladder, gray plastic wheels ($50-75)
2. red body, gold ladder, gray plastic wheels ($50-75)
3. red body, gold ladder, black plastic wheels ($35-50)
4. red body, silver ladder, black plastic wheels ($50-75)
5. red body, tan ladder, black plastic wheels ($50-75)

9D BOAT & TRAILER, issued 1966
1. dull blue deck, white hull, dark blue trailer ($25-35)
2. bright blue deck, white hull, dark blue trailer ($10-15)

10A MECHANICAL HORSE & TRAILER, issued 1955
1. red cab, gray trailer, metal wheels ($65-90)

10B MECHANICAL HORSE & TRAILER, issued 1958
1. red cab, light tan trailer, silver grille, metal wheels ($65-80)
2. red cab, dark tan trailer, silver grille, gray plastic wheels ($100-125)
3. red cab, dark tan trailer, gold grille, gray plastic wheels ($150-175)

10C SUGAR CONTAINER TRUCK, issued 1961
1. dark blue body, crown decal on rear, gray plastic wheels ($150-200)
2. dark blue body, no crown decal at rear, gray plastic wheels ($45-60)
3. dark blue body, silver plastic wheels ($100-125)
4. dark blue body, black plastic wheels ($45-60)

10D PIPE TRUCK, issued 1966
1. red body, gray pipes, black plastic wheels, silver grille ($10-15)
2. red body, gray pipes, black plastic wheels, white grille ($18-25)

11A ROAD TANKER, issued 1955
1. green body, metal wheels ($1200+)
2. butterscotch body, metal wheels ($150-175)
3. yellow body, metal wheels ($100-125)
4. red body, metal wheels, small "Esso" decal at rear ($75-90)
5. red body, metal wheels, large "Esso" decal at rear ($80-95)
6. dull red body, metal wheels, "Esso" decal at rear ($75-90)
7. red body, metal wheels, "Esso" decals on sides ($300-350)

11B ROAD TANKER, issued 1958
1. red body, "Esso" decal, gold trim, metal wheels ($150-200)
2. red body, "Esso" decal, silver trim, metal wheels ($100-125)
3. red body, "Esso" decal, gray plastic wheels ($80-100)
4. red body, "Esso" decal, silver plastic wheels ($1,000+)
5. red body, "Esso" decal, black plastic wheels ($150-175)

11C JUMBO CRANE, issued 1965
1. yellow body, yellow weight box , red hook ($25-40)
2. yellow body, red weight box, red hook ($18-25)

11D SCAFFOLD TRUCK, issued 1969
1. silver- gray body, yellow scaffolding ($10-15)

12A LAND ROVER, issued 1955
1. olive green body, metal wheels ($50-75)

12B LAND ROVER, issued 1959
1. olive green body, gray plastic wheels ($250-350)
2. olive green body, black plastic wheels ($40-60)

12C SAFARI LAND ROVER, issued 1965
1. green body, brown luggage ($15-20)
2. blue body, brown luggage ($15-20)
3. blue body, tan luggage ($15-20)
4. gold body, tan luggage ($1,500+)
5. silver body, tan luggage ($1,500+) *

** originally thought to be a "fake", it is thought that this model is a legitimate factory variation. The silver is an undercoat paint that missed the final gold second coat.*

13A BEDFORD WRECK TRUCK, issued 1955
1. tan body, red boom, metal wheels, no number cast ($65-80)

13B BEDFORD WRECK TRUCK, issued 1958
1. tan body, red boom, no. 13 cast, metal wheels ($65-80)
2. tan body, red boom, no. 13 cast, gray plastic wheels ($75-100)

13C THAMES WRECK TRUCK, issued 1961
1. red body, red metal hook, gray plastic wheels ($100-125)
2. red body, silver metal hook, gray plastic wheels ($100-125)
3. red body, silver metal hook, black plastic wheels ($65-80)
4. red body, gray plastic hook, black plastic wheels ($65-80)

13D DODGE WRECK TRUCK, issued 1965
1. green cab, yellow body, thin boom casting, gray hook, decals ($1,500+)
2. yellow cab, green body, gray hook, decals ($25-40)
3. yellow cab, green body, red hook, decals ($20-30)
4. yellow cab, green body, red hook, labels ($12-15)
5. yellow cab, green body, yellow hook, labels ($35-50)
6. green cab, yellow body, red hook, labels ($1,500+)

NOTE: Models with green cab, yellow boom, thick boom casting, red hook, red or amber dome light and crimped axles were made in 1970 after the Superfast version was produced, but were never issued on the market.

14A DAIMLER AMBULANCE, issued 1956
1. cream body, with red cross decal on roof, metal wheels ($65-80)
2. cream body, without red cross decal on roof, metal wheels ($50-75)

14B DAIMLER AMBULANCE, issued 1958
1. cream body, metal wheels ($65-80)
2. off white body, metal wheels ($65-80)
3. cream body, gray plastic wheels ($75-100)
4. off white body, gray plastic wheels (75-100)
5. off white body, silver plastic wheels ($250-325)

14C BEDFORD AMBULANCE, issued 1962
1. white body, gray plastic wheels ($300-350)
2. white body, silver plastic wheels ($300-350)
3. white body, black plastic wheels ($30-40)

14D ISO GRIFO, issued 1968
1. dark blue body, light blue interior, black plastic tires ($12-15)

15A PRIME MOVER, issued 1956
1. yellow body, metal wheels ($1,000+)
2. orange body, metal wheels ($50-75)
3. orange body, 10 gray plastic wheels ($600-800)

15B ATLANTIC PRIME MOVER, issued 1959
1. orange body, gray plastic wheels ($1,000+)
2. orange body, black plastic wheels ($50-75)

15C REFUSE TRUCK, issued 1963
1. dark blue body, gray dump, decals, no peep hole cast ($150-200)
2. dark blue body, gray dump, decals ($20-35)
3. dark blue body, gray dump, labels ($30-35)

15D VOLKSWAGEN 1500 SALOON, issued 1968
1. off white body, "137" decals ($12-15)
2. off white body, "137" labels ($12-15)
3. red body, "137" labels ($2000+)

16A ATLANTIC TRAILER, issued 1956
1. tan body, metal wheels ($50-75)

16B ATLANTIC TRAILER, issued 1959
1. tan body & towbar, gray plastic wheels ($90-110)
2. orange body, black towbar, gray plastic wheels ($500-750)
3. orange body, black towbar, black plastic wheels ($35-50)
4. orange body, unpainted towbar, black plastic wheels ($35-50)
5. orange body & towbar, black plastic wheels ($50-75)

16C SCAMMELL MOUNTAINEER SNOWPLOW, issued 1964
1. gray cab, orange dump, gray plastic wheels ($150-200)
2. gray cab, orange dump, black plastic wheels ($45-60)

NOTE: models can come with orange & white or red & white plow decals.

16D CASE BULLDOZER, issued 1969
1. red body, yellow blade, yellow canopy, green treads ($15-18)
2. bright red body, yellow blade, yellow canopy, green treads ($15-18)
3. dark red body, yellow blade, yellow canopy, black treads ($30-45)
4. olive green body, black blade, no canopy, black treads ($8-12)(TP)
5. olive drab body, black blade, no canopy, black treads ($75-100)(TP)

17A BEDFORD REMOVALS VAN, issued 1956
1. maroon body, gold trim, metal wheels, no # cast ($300-400)
2. maroon body, silver trim, metal wheels, no # cast ($350-450)
3. blue body, metal wheels, no # cast ($300-400)
4. green body, metal wheels, no # cast, solid lettered decals ($75-100)
5. green body, metal wheels, no # cast, outlined lettered decals ($100-150)

17B BEDFORD REMOVALS VAN, issued 1958
1. light green body, metal wheels, solid lettered decals, no. 17 cast ($75-100)
2. light green body, metal wheels, outlined lettered decals, no. 17 cast ($125-175)
3. light green body, gray plastic wheels, outlined lettered decals, no. 17 cast ($125-175)
4. dark green body, gray plastic wheels, outlined lettered decals, no. 17 cast ($125-175)

17C AUSTIN TAXI CAB, issued 1960
1. maroon body, light gray interior & base, gray plastic wheels ($65-80)
2. maroon body, light gray interior & base, silver plastic wheels ($85-125)
3. maroon body, dark gray interior & base, silver plastic wheels ($85-125)

17D HOVERINGHAM TIPPER, issued 1963
1. red cab, orange tipper, black baseplate ($20-35)
2. red cab, orange tipper, red baseplate ($20-35)

17E HORSE BOX, issued 1969
1. red cab, green plastic box, black plastic wheels ($15-20)

18A CATERPILLAR BULLDOZER, issued 1956
1. yellow body, red blade , metal rollers, green treads ($75-100)

18B CATERPILLAR BULLDOZER, issued 1958
1. yellow body & blade , metal rollers, green treads ($75-100)

18C CATERPILLAR BULLDOZER, issued 1961
1. yellow body & blade, metal rollers, green treads ($60-85)
2. yellow body & blade, silver plastic rollers , green treads ($150-200)
3. yellow body & blade, black plastic rollers ($60-85)

18D CATERPILLAR BULLDOZER, issued 1964
1. yellow body & blade, silver plastic rollers , green treads ($200-250)
2. yellow body & blade, black plastic rollers , green treads ($25-40)

18E FIELD CAR, issued 1969
1. yellow body, red-brown roof, black base, green wheels ($750-1,000)
2. yellow body, red-brown roof, unpainted base, green wheels ($750-1,000)
3. yellow body, red-brown roof, unpainted base, red wheels ($10-15)
4. yellow body, red-brown roof, black base, red wheels ($12-18)

19A MG TD SPORTS CAR, issued 1956
1. cream body, metal wheels ($75-100)
2. white body, metal wheels ($150-200)

19B MGA SPORTS CAR, issued 1958
1. white body, metal wheels, gold grille ($350-500)
2. white body, metal wheels, silver grille ($85-110)
3. white body, gray plastic wheels ($125-150)
4. white body, silver plastic wheels ($250-325)

19C ASTON MARTIN RACING CAR, issued 1961
1. metallic green body, gray driver, #52 decal ($125-150)
2. metallic green body, gray driver, #41 decal ($125-150)
3. metallic green body, gray driver, #5 decal ($125-150)
4. metallic green body, gray driver, #19 decal ($60-75)
5. metallic green body, white driver, #19 decal ($60-75)
6. metallic green body, white driver, #3 decal ($150-200)
7. metallic green body, white driver, #52 decal ($125-150)

19D LOTUS RACING CAR, issued 1966
1. orange body, black plastic tires, decals ($25-40)(GS)
2. orange body, black plastic tires, labels ($25-40)(GS)
3. green body, black plastic tires, decals ($18-25)
4. green body, black plastic tires, labels ($18-25)

20A STAKE TRUCK, issued 1956
1. maroon body, gold grille & tanks, metal wheels ($150-200)
2. maroon body, silver grille & tanks, metal wheels ($60-75)
3. maroon body, silver grille & tanks, gray plastic wheels ($200-225)
4. maroon body, maroon grille & tanks, metal wheels ($60-75)
5. dark red body, silver grille & tanks, metal wheels ($60-75)
6. dark red body, dark red grille & tanks, gray plastic wheels ($200-225)

20B ERF 68G TRUCK, issued 1959
1. blue body, gray plastic wheels ($60-85)
2. blue body, silver plastic wheels ($200-250)
3. blue body, black plastic wheels ($50-75)

20C CHEVROLET IMPALA TAXI, issued 1965
1. orange body, ivory interior, unpainted base, gray plastic wheels ($1000+)
2. orange body, ivory interior, silver-gray base, black plastic wheels ($35-50)
3. orange body, ivory interior, unpainted base, black plastic wheels ($25-40)
4. orange body, red interior, unpainted base, black plastic wheels ($25-40)
5. yellow body, red interior, unpainted base, black plastic wheels ($25-40)
6. yellow body, ivory interior, unpainted base, black plastic wheels ($250-350)
NOTE: version 1-3 with decals, version 4 with decals or labels, version 5 & 6 with labels

21A LONG DISTANCE COACH, issued 1956
1. light green body, metal wheels, "London to Glasgow" decals ($75-90)

21B LONG DISTANCE COACH, issued 1958
1. light green body, metal wheels, "London to Glasgow" decals ($60-85)
2. light green body, gray plastic wheels, "London to Glasgow" decals ($75-90)
3. dark green body, gray plastic wheels, "London to Glasgow" decals ($150-175)

21C COMMER MILK FLOAT, issued 1961
NOTE: all models with pale green body & black base
1. clear windows, silver plastic wheels, bottle decal, white load ($50-65)
2. clear windows, silver plastic wheels, bottle decal, cream load ($50-65)
3. green windows, silver plastic wheels, bottle decal, cream load ($40-60)
4. green windows, silver plastic wheels, bottle decal, white load ($40-60)
5. green windows, silver plastic wheels, cow decal, cream load ($40-60)
6. green windows, silver plastic wheels, cow decal, white load ($40-60)
7. green windows, gray plastic wheels, cow decal, cream load ($350-500)
8. green windows, black plastic wheels, cow decal, cream load ($20-30)
9. green windows, black plastic wheels, bottle decal, cream load ($20-30)

21D FODEN CONCRETE TRUCK, issued 1968
1. orange-yellow body & barrel, red chassis ($15-20)

22A VAUXHALL CRESTA, issued 1956
1. red body, cream roof, metal wheels ($50-75)
2. red body, white roof, metal wheels ($50-75)

22B 1958 VAUXHALL CRESTA, issued 1958
1. pinkish cream body, no windows, metal wheels ($500-750)
2. pinkish cream body, no windows, gray plastic wheels ($135-160)
3. pinkish cream body, green windows, gray plastic wheels ($135-160)
4. cream body, no windows, gray plastic wheels ($85-110)
5. cream body, green windows, gray plastic wheels ($125-150)
6. pinkish cream & turquoise body, green windows, gray plastic wheels ($1,000+)
7. dull bronze & turquoise body, green windows, gray plastic wheels ($250-300)
8. bright bronze & turquoise body, green windows, gray plastic wheels ($250-300)
9. gray & pink body, green windows, gray plastic wheels ($165-185)
10. gray & pink body, green windows, silver plastic wheels ($150-175)
11. gold body, green windows, gray plastic wheels ($175-200)
12. gold body, green windows, silver plastic wheels ($150-175)
13. copper body, green windows, gray plastic wheels ($150-175)
14. copper body, green windows, silver plastic wheels ($150-175)
15. copper body, green windows, black plastic wheels ($150-175)

22C PONTIAC GRAND PRIX SPORTS COUPE, issued 1964
1. orange-red body, black plastic wheels ($250-400)
2. red body, black plastic wheels ($20-25)

23A BERKELEY CAVALIER TRAILER, issued 1956
1. pale blue body, metal wheels, faint door outline, no # cast ($50-75)

23B BERKELEY CAVALIER TRAILER, issued 1958
1. pale blue body, metal wheels, heavy door outline, no. 23 cast ($50-75)
2. lime green body, metal wheels ($90-125)
3. lime green body, gray plastic wheels ($90-125)
4. metallic green body, gray plastic wheels ($750-1,000)

23C BLUEBIRD DAUPHINE TRAILER, issued 1960
1. metallic green body, base & door, gray plastic wheels ($750-1,000)
2. metallic tan body, base & door, gray plastic wheels ($65-80)
3. metallic tan body, base & door, silver plastic wheels ($65-80)
4. metallic tan body, base & door, black plastic wheels ($350-500)
5. metallic tan body, maroon base, black door, gray plastic wheels ($2000+)

23D TRAILER CARAVAN, issued 1965
1. yellow body, white roof, gray plastic wheels ($1500+)
2. yellow body, white roof, black plastic wheels ($30-35)
3. pink body, white roof, black plastic wheels ($20-25)

24A WEATHERILL HYDRAULIC EXCAVATOR, issued 1956
1. orange body, metal wheels ($50-75)
2. yellow body, metal wheels ($75-90)

24B WEATHERILL HYDRAULIC EXCAVATOR, issued 1959
1. yellow body, gray plastic wheels ($40-60)
2. yellow body, black plastic wheels ($30-45)

24C ROLLS ROYCE SILVER SHADOW, issued 1967
1. metallic red body, black plastic tires ($10-15)

25A DUNLOP VAN, issued 1956
1. dark blue body, "Dunlop" decals, metal wheels ($50-75)
2. dark blue body, "Dunlop" decals, gray plastic wheels ($60-85)
3. dark blue body, "Dunlop" decals, black plastic wheels ($500-750)

25B VOLKSWAGEN 1200 SEDAN, issued 1960
1. silver blue body, clear windows, gray plastic wheels ($75-85)
2. silver blue body, green windows, gray plastic wheels ($75-85)
3. silver blue body, green windows, silver plastic wheels ($90-125)
4. silver blue body, green windows, black plastic wheels ($350-500)

25C PETROL TANKER, issued 1964
1. yellow cab, green chassis, "BP" decals, gray plastic wheels ($350-500)
2. yellow cab, green chassis, "BP" decals, black plastic wheels ($20-35)
3. dark blue cab & chassis, "Aral" decals, black plastic wheels ($200-250)

25D FORD CORTINA, issued 1968
1. light brown body, black plastic wheels, no roof rack ($10-15)
2. light brown body, black plastic wheels, yellow roof rack ($25-35)(GS)

26A CONCRETE TRUCK, issued 1956
1. orange body, metal wheels, gold grille ($200-250)
2. orange body, metal wheels, silver grille ($50-75)
3. orange body, gray plastic wheels ($65-80)
4. orange body, silver plastic wheels ($250-325)

26B FODEN CONCRETE TRUCK, issued 1961
1. orange body, gray barrel, gray plastic wheels ($1,000+)
2. orange body & barrel, gray plastic wheels ($35-50)
3. orange body & barrel, silver plastic wheels ($1,000+)
4. orange body & barrel, black plastic wheels ($20-35)

26C G.M.C. TIPPER TRUCK, issued 1968
1. red cab, green chassis, silver gray dump, black plastic wheels ($10-15)

27A BEDFORD LOW LOADER, issued 1956
1. light blue cab, dark blue trailer, metal wheels ($1,500+)
2. dark green cab, tan trailer, metal wheels ($60-85)

27B BEDFORD LOW LOADER, issued 1959
1. light green cab, tan trailer, metal wheels ($75-90)
2. light green cab, tan trailer, gray plastic wheels ($75-100)
3. dark green cab, tan trailer, gray plastic wheels ($125-150)

27C CADILLAC SIXTY SPECIAL, issued 1960
1. green body, white roof, silver plastic wheels, red base, clear windows ($500-750)
2. silver-gray body, white roof, silver plastic wheels, red base, clear windows ($75-90)
3. silver-gray body, pink roof, silver plastic wheels, red base, clear windows ($65-85)
4. silver-gray body, pink roof, silver plastic wheels, red base, green windows ($65-85)
5. lilac body, pink roof, silver plastic wheels, red base, green windows ($65-85)
6. lilac body, pink roof, silver plastic wheels, black base, green windows ($75-100)
7. lilac body, pink roof, gray plastic wheels, black base, green windows ($75-90)
8. lilac body, pink roof, black plastic wheels, black base, green windows ($75-90)

27D MERCEDES BENZ 230SL, issued 1966
1. cream body, black plastic wheels ($10-15)
2. white body, black plastic wheels ($15-18)

28A BEDFORD COMPRESSOR TRUCK, issued 1956
1. orange body, metal wheels ($50-75)
2. yellow body, metal wheels ($50-75)

28B THAMES COMPRESSOR TRUCK, issued 1959
1. yellow body, gray plastic wheels ($450-650)
2. yellow body, black plastic wheels ($40-65)

28C MK.10 JAGUAR, issued 1964
1. light brown body & motor, gray plastic wheels ($1,500+)
2. light brown body & motor, black plastic wheels ($25-35)
3. light brown body, unpainted motor, black plastic wheels ($18-25)

28D MACK DUMP TRUCK, issued 1968
1. orange body, red plastic wheels with black tires ($20-30)
2. orange body, yellow plastic wheels with black tires ($15-20)

29A BEDFORD MILK DELIVERY VAN, issued 1956
1. tan body, metal wheels ($50-75)
2. tan body, gray plastic wheels ($60-85)

29B AUSTIN A55 CAMBRIDGE SEDAN, issued 1961
1. two-tone green body, gray plastic wheels ($50-75)
2. two-tone green body, silver plastic wheels ($40-50)
3. two-tone green body, black plastic wheels ($30-45)

29C FIRE PUMPER, issued 1966
1. red body, "Denver" decals, black plastic wheels ($15-20)
2. red body, no labels, black plastic wheels ($12-18)

30A FORD PREFECT, issued 1956
1. gray-brown body, metal wheels ($60-75)
2. olive brown body, gray plastic wheels ($65-80)
3. light blue body, gray plastic wheels ($200-350)

30B MAGIRUS-DEUTZ 6 WHEEL CRANE TRUCK, issued 1961
1. tan body, red boom, gray plastic wheels ($2,000+)
2. tan body, orange boom, gray plastic wheels ($2,000+)
3. silver -gray body, orange boom, gray plastic wheels, orange metal hook ($60-75)
4. silver -gray body, orange boom, gray plastic wheels, silver metal hook ($60-75)
5. silver-gay body, orange boom, gray plastic wheels, gray plastic hook ($60-75)
6. silver -gray body, orange boom, silver plastic wheels, silver metal hook ($60-75)
7. silver-gray body, orange boom, black plastic wheels, silver metal hook ($50-65)
8. silver -gray body, orange boom, black plastic wheels, gray plastic hook ($50-75)

30C EIGHT WHEEL CRANE, issued 1965
1. mint green body, orange boom, yellow hook, black plastic wheels ($2,000+)
2. dark green body, orange boom, yellow hook, black plastic wheels ($10-15)
3. dark green body, orange boom, red hook, black plastic wheels ($18-25)

31A FORD STATION WAGON, issued 1957
1. yellow body, metal wheels ($60-80)
2. yellow body, gray plastic wheels ($65-85)

31B FORD FAIRLANE STATION WAGON, issued 1960
1. yellow body, red base, clear windows, silver plastic wheels ($250-350)
2. yellow body, black base, clear windows, silver plastic wheels ($250-350)
3. yellow body, black base, no windows, silver plastic wheels ($250-350)
4. yellow body, black base, green windows, silver plastic wheels ($250-350)
5. yellow body, red base, no windows, silver plastic wheels ($250-350)
6. yellow body, red base, green windows, silver plastic wheels ($250-350)
7. green body with pink roof, red base, clear windows, silver plastic wheels ($50-75)
8. green body with pink roof, red base, green windows, silver plastic wheels ($50-75)
9. green body with pink roof, black base, green windows, silver plastic wheels ($50-75)
10. green body with pink roof, black base, green windows, gray plastic wheels ($75-100)
11. green body with pink roof, black base, green windows, black plastic wheels ($200-250)

31C LINCOLN CONTINENTAL, issued 1964
1. metallic blue body, black plastic wheels ($15-20)
2. mint green body, black plastic wheels ($15-20)
3. metallic lime body, black plastic wheels ($1,200+)

32A JAGUAR XK140 COUPE, issued 1957
1. cream body, metal wheels ($60-75)
2. cream body, gray plastic wheels ($60-75)
3. red body, gray plastic wheels ($150-200)

32B JAGUAR XKE, issued 1962
1. metallic red body, clear windows, gray plastic tires ($100-125)
2. metallic red body, green windows, gray plastic tires ($75-100)
3. metallic red body, clear windows, black plastic tires ($50-75)
4. metallic bronze body, clear windows, black plastic tires ($60-85)

32C LEYLAND PETROL TANKER, issued 1968
1. green cab & chassis, white tank, "BP" decals, silver grille ($12-15)
2. green cab & chassis, white tank, "BP" labels, silver grille ($10-15)
3. green cab & chassis, white tank, "BP" labels, white grille ($18-25)
4. dark blue cab & chassis, white tank, "Aral" labels, silver grille ($125-150)

33A FORD ZODIAC MKII SEDAN, issued 1957
1.blue body, no windows, metal wheels ($750-1,000)
2. turquoise blue body, no windows, metal wheels ($90-110)
3. turquoise blue body, no windows, gray plastic wheels ($110-135)
4. dark green body, no windows, metal wheels ($60-75)
5. dark green body, no windows, gray plastic wheels ($60-75)
6. H. blue-green, no windows, gray plastic wheels ($110-135)
7. silver-gray & orange body, no windows, gray plastic wheels ($150-175)
8. tan & light orange body, no windows, gray plastic wheels ($150-175)
9. tan & orange body, no windows, gray plastic wheels ($150-175)
10. tan & orange body, green windows, gray plastic wheels ($175-200)
11. tan & orange body, green windows, silver plastic wheels ($125-150)

33B FORD ZEPHYR 6 MKIII, issued 1963
1. blue-green body, gray plastic wheels ($35-50)
2. blue-green body, silver plastic wheels ($35-50)
3. blue-green body, black plastic wheels ($15-25)
4. light blue-green body, black plastic wheels ($15-25)

33C LAMBORGHINI MIURA, issued 1969
1. yellow body, ivory interior, black plastic tires ($250-300)
2. yellow body, red interior, black plastic tires ($10-15)
3. gold body, ivory interior, black plastic tires ($175-225)

34A VOLKSWAGEN MICROVAN, issued 1957
1. blue body, metal wheels ($75-90)
2. blue body, gray plastic wheels ($75-90)
3. blue body, silver plastic wheels ($225-350)
4. blue body, black plastic wheels ($1200+)

34B VOLKSWAGEN CAMPER, issued 1962
1. light green body, silver plastic wheels ($1000+)
2. light green body, gray plastic wheels ($65-85)
3. light green body, black plastic wheels ($65-85)

34C VOLKSWAGEN CAMPER, issued 1967
1. silver-gray body, raised roof with six windows ($35-50)

34D VOLKSWAGEN CAMPER, issued 1968
1. silver-gray body, short raised roof without windows ($25-40)

35A MARSHALL HORSE BOX, issued 1957
1. red cab, brown box, metal wheels ($60-75)
2. red cab, brown box, gray plastic wheels ($60-75)
3. red cab, brown box, silver plastic wheels ($175-200)
4. red cab, brown box, black plastic wheels ($125-150)

35B SNOW TRAC TRACTOR, issued 1964
1. red body, white treads, "Snow Trac" decals ($25-40)
2. red body, white treads, plain sides ($25-40)
3. red body, white treads, "Snow Trac" cast on sides ($25-40)
4. red body, gray treads, "Snow Trac" cast on sides ($45-65)

36A AUSTIN A50, issued 1957
1. blue-green body, metal wheels ($50-75)
2. blue-green body, gray plastic wheels ($60-80)

36B LAMBRETTA SCOOTER & SIDECAR, issued 1961
1. dark metallic green, black plastic wheels ($85-110)
2. light metallic green, black plastic wheels ($85-110)

36C OPEL DIPLOMAT, issued 1966
1. gold body, silver plastic motor, black metal base ($10-15)
2. gold body, gray plastic motor, black metal base ($10-15)
3. sea green body, gray plastic motor, gray plastic base ($2,000+)

37A COCA COLA LORRY, issued 1956
1. orange body, no baseplate, uneven cast load, metal wheels ($125-175)
2. orange body, no baseplate, even cast load, metal wheels ($85-110)
3. orange body, no baseplate, even cast load, gray plastic wheels ($125-150)

37B COCA COLA LORRY, issued 1960
1. yellow body, black base, gray plastic wheels ($75-100)
2. yellow body, black base, silver plastic wheels ($1,000+)
3. yellow body, black base, black plastic wheels ($65-90)

37C DODGE CATTLE TRUCK, issued 1966
1. yellow body, gray box, silver plastic base ($18-25)
2. yellow body, gray box, unpainted metal base ($10-15)

38A KARRIER REFUSE COLLECTOR, issued 1957
1. gray-brown body, metal wheels ($350-500)
2. dark gray body, metal wheels ($50-75)
3. dark gray body, gray plastic wheels ($50-75)
4. silver-gray body, gray plastic wheels ($90-125)
5. silver-gray body, silver plastic wheels ($500-750)

38B VAUXHALL VICTOR ESTATE CAR, issued 1963
1. yellow body, green interior, gray plastic wheels ($45-60)
2. yellow body, red interior, gray plastic wheels ($45-60)
3. yellow body, green interior, silver plastic wheels ($35-50)
4. yellow body, green interior, black plastic wheels ($30-45)
5. yellow body, red interior, silver plastic wheels ($35-50)
6. yellow body, red interior, black plastic wheels ($30-45)

38C HONDA MOTORCYCLE & TRAILER, issued 1967
1. blue-green cycle, orange trailer, no decals ($20-30)
2. blue-green cycle, orange trailer, "Honda" decals ($35-50)
3. blue-green cycle, yellow trailer, "Honda" decals ($25-30)
4. blue-green cycle, yellow trailer, "Honda" labels ($25-30)

39A FORD ZODIAC CONVERTIBLE, issued 1957
1. pink body, tan interior & base, metal wheels ($350-500)
2. pink body, turquoise interior & base, metal wheels ($75-90)
3. pink body, turquoise interior & base, gray plastic wheels ($85-110)
4. pink body, turquoise interior & base, silver plastic wheels ($150-200)
NOTE: Pink bodies vary in shades from light to dark

39B PONTIAC CONVERTIBLE, issued 1962
1. purple body, red steering wheel, red base, silver plastic wheels ($125-175)
2. purple body, red steering wheel, red base, gray plastic wheels ($1,000+)
3. yellow body, red steering wheel, red base, silver plastic wheels ($75-100)
4. yellow body, red steering wheel, red base, gray plastic wheels ($75-90)
5. yellow body, ivory steering wheel, red base, silver plastic wheels ($75-90)
6. yellow body, ivory steering wheel, red base, gray plastic wheels ($75-90)
7. yellow body, ivory steering wheel, black base, silver plastic wheels ($85-95)
8. yellow body, ivory steering wheel, black base, gray plastic wheels ($75-100)
9. yellow body, ivory steering wheel, black base, black plastic wheels ($45-60)

39C FORD TRACTOR, issued 1967
1. dark blue body, yellow hood, black plastic tires ($12-18)
2. dark blue body & hood, black plastic tires ($18-25)
3. light blue body & yellow hood, black plastic tires ($18-25)
4. orange body & hood, black plastic tires ($80-100)(MX)

40A BEDFORD TIPPER TRUCK, issued 1957
1. red cab & chassis, tan dump, metal wheels ($60-75)
2. red cab & chassis, tan dump, gray plastic wheels ($60-75)
3. red cab & chassis, dark tan dump, gray plastic wheels ($60-75)

40B LEYLAND ROYAL TIGER COACH, issued 1961
1. silver-blue body, gray plastic wheels ($50-65)
2. silver-blue body, silver plastic wheels ($50-65)
3. silver-blue body, black plastic wheels ($25-35)

40C HAY TRAILER, issued 1967
NOTE: All models made in England unless noted.
1. blue body, yellow stakes, black plastic tires with yellow wheels ($10-15)
2. yellow body, no stakes, solid black wheels ($5-8)(TP)
3. beige body, black stakes, solid black wheels ($150-200)(TP)
4. blue body, black stakes, solid black wheels ($5-8)(TP)
5. red body, black stakes, solid black wheels ($5-8)(TP)
6. red body, black stakes, solid black wheels, Macau ($5-8)(TP)
7. yellow body, black stakes, solid black wheels, no origin cast ($5-8)(TP)

41A D-TYPE JAGUAR, issued 1957
1. green body, metal wheels, "41" decal ($65-90)
2. green body, gray plastic wheels, "41" decal ($125-150)

41B D-TYPE JAGUAR, issued 1960
1. green body, gray plastic wheels, "41" decal ($65-90)
2. green body, silver plastic wheels, "19" decal ($350-500)
3. green body, black plastic tires & spoke wheels, "41" decal ($65-90)
4. green body, black plastic tires & spoke wheels, "5" decal ($150-200)
5. green body, black plastic tires & red wheels, "41" decal ($350-500)

41C FORD GT, issued 1965
1. white body, red wheels, "6" decal ($300-400)
2. white body, yellow wheels, "6" decal ($12-15)
3. white body, yellow wheels, "9" decal ($15-20)
4. yellow body, yellow wheels, "6" decal ($150-200)(GS)
5. white body, yellow wheels, "6" label ($10-15)
6. white body, yellow wheels, "9" label ($12-15)

42A BEDFORD EVENING NEWS VAN, issued 1957
1. yellow-orange body, metal wheels ($75-90)
2. yellow-orange body, gray plastic wheels ($90-120)
3. yellow-orange body, black plastic wheels ($100-125)

42B STUDEBAKER LARK WAGONAIRE, issued 1965
1. blue body, blue rear sliding roof, black plastic wheels ($35-45)
2. blue body, powder blue sliding roof, black plastic wheels ($35-45)
3. blue body, unpainted sliding roof, black plastic wheels ($85-110)
4. light blue body, powder blue sliding roof, black plastic wheels ($75-90)

42C IRON FAIRY CRANE, issued 1969
1. red body, orange-yellow boom, black plastic wheels ($12-15)

43A HILLMAN MINX, issued 1958
1. green body, metal wheels ($350-500)
2. bluish gray body with gray roof, metal wheels ($80-100)
3. bluish gray body with gray roof, gray plastic wheels ($60-75)
4. turquoise body with cream roof, gray plastic wheels ($60-75)

43B AVELING BARFORD TRACTOR SHOVEL, issued 1962
1. yellow body, yellow shovel, yellow base, yellow driver ($100-125)
2. yellow body, yellow shovel, red base, red driver ($45-60)
3. yellow body, red shovel, yellow base, yellow driver ($45-60)
4. yellow body, red shovel, red base, red driver ($100-125)

43C PONY TRAILER, issued 1968
1. yellow body, tan base, black plastic wheels ($12-15)
2. yellow body, dark green base, black plastic wheels ($12-15)

44A ROLLS ROYCE SILVER CLOUD, issued 1958
1. metallic blue body, metal wheels ($60-85)
2. metallic blue body, gray plastic wheels ($65-85)
3. metallic blue body, silver plastic wheels ($75-90)

44B ROLLS ROYCE PHANTOM V, issued 1964
1. metallic tan body, gray plastic wheels ($350-500)
2. metallic gray body, black plastic wheels ($65-80)
3. metallic silver-gray body, black plastic wheels ($65-80)
4. metallic silver-gray body, silver plastic wheels ($1,000+)
5. metallic tan body, black plastic wheels ($18-25)

44C REFRIGERATOR TRUCK, issued 1967
1. red cab & chassis, turquoise container, black plastic wheels ($12-15)

45A VAUXHALL VICTOR, issued 1958
1. red body, no windows, metal wheels ($2,000+)
2. yellow body, no windows, metal wheels ($50-75)
3. yellow body, no windows, gray plastic wheels ($50-75)
4. yellow body, green windows, gray plastic wheels ($50-75)
5. yellow body, clear windows, gray plastic wheels ($50-75)
6. yellow body, green windows, silver plastic wheels ($65-85)
7. yellow body, green windows, black plastic wheels ($50-75)

45B FORD CORSAIR & BOAT, issued 1965
1. pale yellow body, gray plastic wheels, unpainted base ($50-75)
2. pale yellow body, black plastic wheels, unpainted base ($18-25)
3. pale yellow body, black plastic wheels, silver-gray base ($50-75)

46A MORRIS MINOR 1000, issued 1958
1. light tan body, metal wheels ($2,000+)
2. dark green body, metal wheels ($65-90)
3. dark green body, gray plastic wheels ($125-175)
4. dark blue body, gray plastic wheels ($150-200)

46B PICKFORDS REMOVALS VAN, issued 1960
1. dark blue body, 2 line "Pickfords" decals, gray plastic wheels ($150-200)
2. dark blue body, 2 line "Pickfords" decals, silver plastic wheels ($350-500)
3. dark blue body, 3 line "Pickfords" decals, gray plastic wheels ($100-125)
4. dark blue body, 3 line "Pickfords" decals, silver plastic wheels ($150-175)
5. green body, 3 line "Pickfords" decals, gray plastic wheels ($75-90)
6. green body, 3 line "Pickfords" decals, silver plastic wheels ($85-100)
7. green body, 3 line "Pickfords" decals, black plastic wheels ($45-60)
8. green body, 2 line "Pickfords" decals, black plastic wheels ($175-225)
9. tan body, "Beales Bealeesons" decals, black plastic wheels ($850-1,200)

46C MERCEDES BENZ 300SE, issued 1968
1. green body, black plastic wheels ($15-20)
2. blue body, black plastic wheels ($25-35)

47A 1 TON TROJAN VAN, issued 1958
1. red body, "Brooke Bond" decals, metal wheels ($65-85)
2. red body, "Brooke Bond" decals, gray plastic wheels ($75-90)

47B COMMER ICE CREAM CANTEEN, issued 1963
1. blue body, square roof decal, striped side decal, gray plastic wheels ($350-500)
2. blue body, square roof decal, striped roof decal, black plastic wheels ($45-60)
3. blue body, oval roof decal, plain side decal, black plastic wheels ($40-60)
4. metallic blue body, square roof decal, striped side decal, black plastic wheels ($250-400)
5. cream body, square roof decal, striped side decal, black plastic wheels ($150-200)
6. cream body, oval roof decal, plain sides decal, black plastic wheels ($50-75)

47C DAF TIPPER CONTAINER TRUCK, issued 1968
1. aqua blue cab & chassis, yellow container, light gray roof ($25-30)
2. silver-gray cab & chassis, yellow container, light gray roof ($12-15)
3. silver-gray cab & chassis, yellow container, dark gray roof ($12-15)

48A METEOR SPORTS BOAT & TRAILER, issued 1958
1. tan deck, blue hull, black trailer, metal wheels ($60-85)
2. tan deck, blue hull, black trailer, gray plastic wheels ($65-90)
3. tan deck, blue hull, black trailer, silver plastic wheels ($250-400)

48B SPORTS BOAT & TRAILER, issued 1961
1. white deck, red hull, silver motor, dark blue trailer, gray plastic wheels ($150-200)
2. white deck, red hull, silver motor, dark blue trailer, black plastic wheels ($50-75)
3. white deck, red hull, gold motor, dark blue trailer, black plastic wheels ($50-75)
4. white deck, red hull, gold motor, light blue trailer, black plastic wheels ($50-75)
5. red deck, white hull, silver motor, dark blue trailer, black plastic wheels ($50-75)
6. red deck, white hull, gold motor, dark blue trailer, black plastic wheels ($50-75)
7. red deck, white hull, gold motor, light blue trailer, black plastic wheels ($50-75)

48C DODGE DUMPER TRUCK, issued 1966
1. red body, base runs full length of body ($12-15)
2. red body, base runs three-quarter length of body ($12-15)

49A M3 PERSONNEL CARRIER, issued 1958
1. olive body, metal front wheels, metal rollers ($50-75)
2. olive body, gray plastic front wheels, metal rollers ($65-85)
3. olive body, gray plastic front wheels, gray plastic rollers ($350-500)
4. olive body, gray plastic front wheels, silver plastic rollers ($75-100)
5. olive body, black plastic front wheels, black plastic rollers ($35-50)

49B MERCEDES UNIMOG, issued 1967
1. tan cab & bed, turquoise chassis, black plastic tires ($15-20)
2. blue cab & bed, red chassis, black plastic tires ($15-20)

50A COMMER PICKUP, issued 1958
1. dark tan body, metal wheels ($60-85)
2. light tan body, metal wheels ($60-85)
3. light tan body, gray plastic wheels ($65-90)
4. dark tan body, gray plastic wheels ($65-90)
5. dark tan body, silver plastic wheels ($100-150)
6. red and white body, silver plastic wheels ($650-900)
7. red & gray body, silver plastic wheels ($150-200)
8. red & gray body, gray plastic wheels ($100-150)
9. red & gray body, black plastic wheels ($100-150)

50B JOHN DEERE TRACTOR, issued 1964
1. green body, gray plastic tires ($50-65)
2. green body, black plastic tires ($25-40)

50C FORD KENNEL TRUCK, issued 1969
1. green body, tinted canopy, white grille ($15-20)
2. green body, clear canopy, white grille ($15-20)
3. green body, clear canopy, silver grille ($20-25)
4. green body, tinted canopy, silver grille ($20-25)

51A ALBION CHIEFTAIN, issued 1958
1. yellow body, "Portland Cement" decals, metal wheels ($75-90)
2. yellow body, "Blue Circle Portland Cement" decals, metal wheels ($60-75)
3. yellow body, "Blue Circle Portland Cement" decals, gray plastic wheels ($60-75)
4. yellow body, "Blue Circle Portland Cement" decals, silver plastic wheels ($250-325)
5. yellow body, "Blue Circle Portland Cement" decals, black plastic wheels, ($350-400)

51B JOHN DEERE TRAILER, issued 1964
1. green body & towbar, gray plastic tires ($35-45)
2. green body & towbar, black plastic tires ($20-30)

51C 8-WHEEL TIPPER, issued 1969
1. orange cab, white grille, "Douglas" labels ($150-200)
2. orange cab, silver grille, "Douglas" labels ($35-50)
3. yellow cab, silver grille, "Douglas" labels ($25-40)
4. yellow cab, silver grille, "Pointer" labels ($12-18)

52A MASERATI 4CLT RACER, issued 1958
1. red body, black plastic wheels, no decals ($60-75)
2. red body, black plastic wheels, "52" decals ($75-100)
3. red body, black plastic tires with spokes, no decals ($300-400)
4. yellow body, black plastic tires with spokes, "5" decals ($125-150)
5. yellow body, black plastic tires with spokes, "52" decals ($100-125)
6. yellow body, black plastic tires with spokes, "3" decals ($125-150)

52B BRM RACING CAR, issued 1965
1. blue body, "5" decal, black plastic tires ($15-20)
2. blue body, "3" decal, black plastic tires ($60-85)
3. blue body, "5" label, black plastic tires ($15-20)
4. red body, "5" decal, black plastic tires ($35-50)
5. red body, "5" label, black plastic tires ($35-50)
6. dark blue body, "5" label, black plastic tires ($35-50)

53A ASTON MARTIN, issued 1958
1. metallic light green body, metal wheels ($50-75)
2. metallic light green body, gray plastic wheels ($60-80)
3. metallic red body, gray plastic wheels ($300-350)
4. metallic red body, black plastic wheels ($250-300)

53B MERCEDES BENZ 220SE, issued 1963
1. maroon body, gray plastic wheels ($35-50)

2. maroon body, silver plastic wheels ($35-50)
3. maroon body, black plastic wheels ($20-35)
4. red body, gray plastic wheels ($60-75)
5. red body, black plastic wheels ($20-35)

53C FORD ZODIAC MK IV, issued 1968
1. metallic silver blue body, black plastic wheels ($10-15)
2. light metallic green body, black plastic wheels ($1,000+)

54A SARACEN PERSONNEL CARRIER, issued 1958
1. olive body, black plastic wheels ($20-25)

54B S&S CADILLAC AMBULANCE, issued 1965
1. white body, red cross decal, black plastic wheels ($25-35)
2. white body, red cross label, black plastic wheels ($25-35)

55A D.U.K.W., issued 1958
1. olive body, metal wheels ($50-75)
2. olive body, gray plastic wheels ($60-85)
3. olive body, black plastic wheels ($60-85)

55B FORD FAIRLANE POLICE CAR, issued 1963
1. dark blue body, black plastic wheels ($250-400)
2. light blue body, gray plastic wheels ($750+)
3. light blue body, silver plastic wheels ($750+)
4. light blue body, black plastic wheels ($75-100)

55C FORD GALAXIE POLICE CAR, issued 1966
1. white body, blue dome light, decals, black plastic wheels ($200-250)
2. white body, red dome light, decals, black plastic wheels ($35-50)
3. white body, red dome light, labels, black plastic wheels ($35-50)

55D MERCURY POLICE CAR, issued 1968
1. white body, black plastic tires, red dome light ($250-300)
2. white body, black plastic tires, blue dome light ($30-45)

56A LONDON TROLLEY BUS, issued 1958
1. red body, black trolley poles, "Drink Peardrax" decals, metal wheels ($300-450)
2. red body, red trolley poles, "Drink Peardrax" decals, metal wheels ($65-80)
3. red body, black trolley poles, "Drink Peardrax" decals, gray plastic wheels ($300-450)
4. red body, red trolley poles, "Drink Peardrax" decals, gray plastic wheels ($75-90)
5. red body, black trolley ples, "Drink Peardrox" decals, gray plastic wheels ($350-500)
6. red body, red trolley poles, "Drink Peardrax" decals, silver plastic wheels ($175-250)
7. red body, red trolley poles, "Drink Peardrax" decals, black plastic wheels ($75-90)
8. red body, red trolley poles, "Visco Static" decals, black plastic wheels ($1000+)

56B FIAT 1500, issued 1965
1. turquoise body, brown luggage, black plastic wheels ($12-18)
2. turquoise body, tan luggage, black plastic wheels ($12-18)
3. red body, tan luggage, black plastic wheels ($125-150)(GS)

57A WOLSELEY 1500, issued 1958
1. pale yellow-green body, gold grille, gray plastic wheels ($150-200)
2. pale yellow-green body, silver grille, gray plastic wheels ($60-75)
3. pale green body, silver grille, gray plastic wheels ($60-75)
4. pale gray body, silver grille, gray plastic wheels ($175-225)

57B CHEVROLET IMPALA, issued 1961
1. metallic blue body, blue roof, black base, gray plastic wheels ($125-175)
2. metallic blue body, blue roof, black base, silver plastic wheels ($75-90)
3. metallic blue body, blue roof, dark blue base, silver plastic wheels ($75-90)
4. metallic blue body, blue roof, light blue base, silver plastic wheels ($75-90)
5. metallic blue body, blue roof, powder blue base, silver plastic wheels ($85-100)
6. metallic blue body, blue roof, black base, black plastic wheels ($75-90)

57C LAND ROVER FIRE ENGINE, issued 1966
1. red body, decals, gray plastic wheels ($350-500)
2. red body, decals, black plastic wheels ($30-40)
3. red body, labels, black plastic wheels ($30-40)

58A BEA COACH, issued 1958
1. blue body, "British European Airways" decals, gray plastic wheels ($85-110)
2. blue body, "BEA" decals, gray plastic wheels ($65-90)
3. blue body, "BEA" decals, silver plastic wheels ($250-400)
4. blue body, "BEA" decals, black plastic wheels ($500-750)

58B DROTT EXCAVATOR, issued 1962
1. red body, silver-gray motor & base, metal rollers ($65-80)
2. red body, silver-gray motor & base, silver plastic rollers ($175-250)
3. red body, silver-gray motor & base, black plastic rollers ($65-80)
4. orange body, silver—gray motor & base, black plastic rollers ($50-75)
5. orange body, orange motor & base, black plastic rollers ($50-75)

58C DAF GIRDER TRUCK, issued 1968
1. cream body, red plastic girders ($12-15)

59A FORD THAMES VAN, issued 1958
1. light green body, gray plastic wheels ($75-90)
2. light green body, silver plastic wheels ($250-300)
3. dark Kelly green body, gray plastic wheels ($200-250)
4. dark Kelly green body, silver plastic wheels ($300-350)

59B FORD FAIRLANE FIRE CHIEF CAR, issued 1963
1. red body, gray plastic wheels ($175-250)
2. red body, silver plastic wheels ($350-400)
3. red body, black plastic wheels ($60-75)

59C FORD GALAXIE FIRE CHIEF CAR, issued 1966
1. red body, decal on hood & sides, black plastic wheels, blue dome light ($25-35)
2. red body, decal on hood, labels on sides, black plastic wheels, blue dome light ($25-35)
3. red body, label on hood & sides, black plastic wheels, blue dome light ($25-35)
4. red body, decal on hood & sides, black plastic wheels, red dome light ($250-400)

60A MORRIS J2 PICKUP, issued 1958
1. blue body, red & black decal, rear window cast, gray plastic wheels ($75-90)
2. blue body, red & black decal, rear window cast, silver plastic wheels ($90-110)
3. blue body, red & white decal, rear window cast, gray plastic wheels ($50-75)
4. blue body, red & white decal, rear window cast, silver plastic wheels ($75-90)
5. blue body, red & white decal, rear window cast, black plastic wheels ($50-75)
6. blue body, red & white decal, without rear window cast, black plastic wheels ($50-75)

60B SITE HUT TRUCK, issued 1966
1. blue body, yellow plastic hut with green roof, black plastic wheels ($10-15)

61A FERRET SCOUT CAR, issued 1959
1. olive green body, black plastic wheels ($15-20)

61B ALVIS STALWART, issued 1966
1. white body, yellow roof, green windows, black plastic tires with green wheels, "BP" decals ($18-25)
2. white body, yellow roof, green windows, black plastic tires with green wheels, "BP" labels ($18-25)
3. white body, yellow roof, green windows, black plastic tires with yellow wheels, "BP" labels ($50-75)
4. olive green body, no roof, green windows, solid black wheels, "3LGS64" labels ($7-10)(TP)
5. olive green body, no roof, blue-green windows, solid black wheels, "3LGS64" labels ($7-10)(TP)

62A GENERAL SERVICE LORRY, issued 1959
1. olive green body, black plastic wheels ($75-90)

62B TV SERVICE VAN, issued 1963
1. cream body, gray plastic wheels, "Rentaset" decals ($400-500)
2. cream body, black plastic wheels, "Rentaset" decals ($45-60)
3. cream body, gray plastic wheels, "Radio Rentals" decals ($750-1000)
4. cream body, black plastic wheels, "Radio Rentals" decals ($45-60)

62C MERCURY COUGAR, issued 1968
1. pale yellow body, ivory interior, black plastic tires ($1,500+)
2. metallic lime green body, red interior, black plastic tires ($12-15)

63A FORD SERVICE AMBULANCE, issued 1959
1. olive green body, black plastic wheels ($75-90)

63B FOAMITE CRASH TENDER, issued 1964
1. red body, silver nozzle, black plastic wheels ($100-150)
2. red body, gold nozzle, black plastic wheels ($25-45)

63C DODGE CRANE TRUCK, issued 1968
1. yellow body, red hook, black plastic wheels ($12-15)
2. yellow body, yellow hook, black plastic wheels ($12-15)

64A SCAMMELL BREAKDOWN TRUCK, issued 1959
1. olive green body, green metal hook, black plastic wheels ($65-80)
2. olive green body, silver metal hook, black plastic wheels ($65-80)
3. olive green body, gray plastic hook, black plastic wheels ($65-80)

64B MG 1100, issued 1966
1. green body, black plastic wheels ($15-20)

65A JAGUAR 3.4 LITRE SALOON, issued 1959
1. metallic blue body, gray plastic wheels ($150-200)
2. blue body, gray plastic wheels ($60-75)

65B JAGUAR 3.4 LITRE SALOON, issued 1962
1. red body, gray plastic wheels ($50-75)
2. red body, silver plastic wheels ($50-75)
3. metallic red body, silver plastic wheels ($50-75)
4. red body, black plastic wheels ($35-50)

65C CLAAS COMBINE HARVESTER, issued 1967
1. red body, yellow rotating blades, yellow plastic front wheels with black plastic tires, plastic rear wheels ($12-18)

66A CITROEN DS19, issued 1959
1. yellow body, gray plastic wheels ($50-75)
2. yellow body, silver plastic wheels ($150-200)

66B HARLEY-DAVIDSON MOTORCYCLE, issued 1962
1. metallic bronze body, black plastic tires ($150-200)

66C GREYHOUND BUS, issued 1967
1. silver-gray body, blue decal, clear windows ($150-200)
2. silver-gray body, blue decal, amber windows ($20-25)
3. silver-gray body, gray label, amber windows ($20-25)

67A SALADIN ARMORED CAR, issued 1959
1. olive body, black plastic wheels ($25-35)

67B VOLKSWAGEN 1600TL, issued 1967
1. red body, no roof rack, black plastic tires ($15-20)
2. red body, maroon roof rack, black plastic tires ($30-40)(GS)
3. purple body, no roof rack, black plastic tires ($275-350)

68A AUSTIN MKII RADIO TRUCK, issued 1959
1. olive green body, black plastic wheels ($60-85)

68B MERCEDES COACH, issued 1965
1. turquoise body & base, white roof & interior, black plastic wheels ($150-200)
2. orange body & base, white roof & interior, black plastic wheels ($15-20)

69A COMMER 30 CWT VAN, issued 1959
1. maroon body, gray plastic wheels ($75-100)
2. dark red body, gray plastic wheels ($75-100)
3. red body, gray plastic wheels ($100-150)
4. red body, silver plastic wheels ($1000+)

69B HATRA TRACTOR SHOVEL, issued 1965
1. orange body & shovel, orange wheels with gray plastic tires ($50-75)
2. orange body & shovel, red wheels with black plastic tires ($75-100)
3. orange body & shovel, yellow wheels with black plastic tires ($25-35)
4. yellow body & shovel, red wheels with black plastic tires ($250-300)
5. yellow body & shovel, yellow wheels with black plastic tires ($18-25)
6. orange body, yellow shovel, orange wheels with black plastic tires ($500-750)
NOTE: version #6 was originally thought to be a preproduction.

70A FORD THAMES ESTATE CAR, issued 1959
1. yellow & turquoise body, no windows, gray plastic wheels ($65-85)
2. yellow & turquoise body, clear windows, gray plastic wheels ($65-85)
3. yellow & turquoise body, green windows, gray plastic wheels ($65-85)
4. yellow & turquoise body, clear windows, silver plastic wheels ($60-80)
5. yellow & turquoise body, green windows, silver plastic wheels ($60-80)
6. yellow & turquoise body, green windows, black plastic wheels ($50-75)

70B FORD GRIT SPREADER TRUCK, issued 1966
1. red cab, light yellow dump, black plastic pull ($10-15)
2. red cab, light yellow dump, gray plastic pull ($10-15)
3. red cab, dark yellow dump, gray plastic pull ($25-35)
4. red cab, dark yellow dump, black plastic pull ($25-35)

71A AUSTIN 200 GALLON WATER TRUCK, issued 1959
1. olive green body, black plastic wheels ($60-75)

71B JEEP GLADIATOR PICKUP, issued 1964
1. red body, green interior, black plastic wheels ($150-200)
2. red body, white interior, black plastic wheels ($20-35)

71C FORD HEAVY WRECK TRUCK, issued 1968
1. red cab, white body & chassis, amber windows, red hook ($250-400)
2. red cab, white body & chassis, amber windows, yellow hook ($250-400)
3. red cab, white body & chassis, green windows, red hook ($25-30)
4. red cab, white body & chassis, green windows, yellow hook ($25-30)

72A FORDSON TRACTOR, issued 1959
1. blue body, gray plastic front wheels, gray plastic rear tires with orange wheels ($65-80)
2. blue body, black plastic front wheels, black plastic rear tires with orange wheels ($60-80)
3. blue body, gray plastic rear & front tires with orange wheels ($60-75)
4. blue body, gray plastic front & rear tires with yellow wheels ($350-400)
5. blue body, black plastic front & rear tires with yellow wheels ($1000+)
6. blue body, black plastic front & rear tires with orange wheels ($60-80)

72B STANDARD JEEP, issued 1966
1. yellow body, red interior, yellow wheels with black plastic tires ($12-18)
2. yellow body, white interior, yellow wheels with black plastic tires ($1000+)

73A 10 TON PRESSURE REFUELLER, issued 1959
1. blue-gray body, gray plastic wheels ($65-80)
2. blue-gray body, black plastic wheels ($1000+)

73B FERRARI F1 RACING CAR, issued 1962
1. red body, gray driver ($30-45)
2. red body, white driver ($30-45)

73C MERCURY STATION WAGON, issued 1968
1. metallic lime green body, black plastic tires ($12-18)

74A MOBILE REFRESHMENT CANTEEN, issued 1959
1. white body, blue base & interior, gray plastic wheels ($500-750)
2. pink body, light blue base & interior, gray plastic wheels ($1,000-1,250)
3. pinkish cream body, blue base & interior, gray plastic wheels ($500-750)
4. cream body, blue base & interior, gray plastic wheels ($450-600)
5. silver-gray body, blue base & interior, gray plastic wheels ($65-90)
6. silver-gray body, aqua base & interior, gray plastic wheels ($75-100)
7. silver-gray body, blue base & interior, silver plastic wheels ($65-90)
8. silver-gray body, aqua base & interior, silver plastic wheels ($75-100)
9. silver-gray body, pale blue base & interior, gray plastic wheels ($75-100)
10. silver-gray body, dark blue base & interior, gray plastic wheels ($250-300)

74B DAIMLER BUS, issued 1966
1. cream body, "Esso Extra Petrol" decals, black plastic wheels ($18-25)
2. cream body, "Esso Extra Petrol" labels, black plastic wheels ($15-20)
3. green body, "Esso Extra Petrol" labels, black plastic wheels ($12-18)
4. red body, "Esso Extra Petrol" labels, black plastic wheels ($12-18)

75A FORD THUNDERBIRD, issued 1960
1. cream & pink body, black base, gray plastic wheels ($125-150)
2. cream & pink body, black base, silver plastic wheels ($85-110)
3. cream & pink body, dark blue base, silver plastic wheels ($85-110)
4. cream & pink body, blue-green base, silver plastic wheels ($85-110)
5. cream & pink body, black base, black plastic wheels ($200-275)
NOTE: Pink body panels can vary from light to dark on most versions

75B FERRARI BERLINETTA, issued 1965
1. metallic light blue-green body, unpainted base, spoked wheels ($150-200)
2. light green body, unpainted base, spoked wheels ($15-20)
3. light green body, silver-gray base, spoked wheels ($60-75)
4. dark green body, unpainted base, disc wheels ($15-20)
5. red body, unpainted base, disc wheels ($1,000+)

Superfast/ Miniatures 1-75

When Mattel introduced their Hot Wheels series, Lesney Products had to revamp their entire 1-75 line to have frictionless wheels. These models were introduced in mid-1969 as the "Superfast" series. The name "Superfast" was used to describe the 1-75 series until 1980, when the 1-75 line was simply termed "Miniatures". Early models were denoted as SF and later MB, but for the sake of conformity, all 1-75 models made from mid-1969 onwards will be denoted with the "MB" designation. The sequencing of models will begin again with the letter "A," rather than to continue with the lettering sequence from the Regular Wheels.

Many miniatures in post-1969 were not available as single releases or were issued as limited editions or in special sets. By 1982, the miniature range began to diversify in such a manner that models in the standard range were modified or issued in specialized miniature categories. These special ranges are denoted with prefixes and are based on the charting below. Certain models were only sold in certain countries and these are also noted by a special notation.

Promotionals

AU—Australia	IR—Ireland
AS—Austria	IT—Italy
BE—Belgium	JP—Japan
BR—Brazil (Manaus)	SA—South Africa
CHI—China	SC—Scotland
CN—Canada	SD- Sweden
DK- Denmark	SP—Spain
DU—Dutch (Holland)	SU—Saudi Arabia
FR—French	SW—Switzerland
GK—Greece	UK—United Kingdom
GR—Germany	US—United States
HK—Hong Kong	WL—Wales
HU- Hungary	

Sub- Category Listings

AP—Action Pack
AS- Action System Pack
ASAP- Short Run Premiums
AV—Adventure 2000
BS—Brroomstick
C2—Code 2
CC—Collectors Choice
CH—75 Challenge
CL—Collectibles
CM—Commando
CR—Code Red

CP- Corvette Premieres
CT- Caterpillar
CY—Convoy
DM—Dream Machines
DT—Days of Thunder
DY—Dinky
EM—Emergency Packs
FE- First Edition
F1—Formula 1
FM—Farming Series
GC—Gold Collection
GS—Gift Set
GT—Graffic Traffic
GW—Gift Ware
HD—Harley-Davidson
HS—Hot Stocks
IC—Intercom City
IN—Indy 500
IG- Inaugural
JB—James Bond
JC- JC Penney
JR- Jurassic Park
KP—King-Size Special
KS—King-Size
LD—Limited Run
LE—Limited Edition
LL—Live N Learn (preschool)
LS—Light & Sound
LT—Lightning Wheels
LW—Laser Wheels
MB1-3—Micro Brewery
MC—Motor City
MN—Nigel Mansell
MP—Multi Pack
MT—Matchcaps
MX—Big M-X
MW- Mattel Wheels 1998 model no.
NBA- National Basketball League
NM—Nutmeg promotional
OP—On pack offer
PC1-21 —Premiere Collection
PL—Parlor City Collectibles
PS—Play set
RB—Road Blasters
RN—Roman Numeral
RT- Real Talkin'
SB—Skybuster
SC—Super Color Changer
SC1-5 Select Class
SF—Superfast
SP—Sports Pack
SR—Siren Force/Rescue 911
SS—Show Stoppers
ST—Super Trucks
STR- Star Car
TC—Team Convoy
TH—Triple Heat
TM—Team Matchbox
TP—Two Pack
TRU- Toys R Us
UC—Ultra Class
VG—Vegas models
WC—World Class
WP—Whales Project
WR—White Rose Collectibles
YST—Collectibles Train Set

The earliest subdivision of miniatures was from gift sets. This idea developed from the late 1950s and continues today. It took years for the miniatures to break into a new sub category. One of the first was the Brroomstick series issued in 1970. An orange plastic handle had string attached in which a sticker could be adhered to the front of the model so as to "drive" the model by string power.

In 1978, Lesney Products took ten models from the standard range including discontinued molds and reissued them in new colors with new names with Roman numerals on the baseplates. Some tough-to-find variations include crossover baseplates from the standard range.

In 1981, Lesney Products received a television license for Code Red in which seven miniatures and one Skybuster were issued in special colors and packaging.

In 1983, Matchbox introduced two models at the Dodge Las Vegas convention. There were only five thousand models of the Dodge Caravan and Dodge Daytona made with sealed castings, therefore no opening parts. The models were retooled to have opening parts and put into the standard line. One thousand of the special Vegas models were put on a signed plinth. The remaining four thousand were placed in special boxes.

The name "Superfast" was originally introduced in 1969 by Lesney Products to counter the marketing of Mattel's Hot Wheels. By 1980, this name was gradually phased out. The Superfast name was reborn in 1986 with twenty-five selected miniatures with specially designed, low-friction wheels and new twenty-four spoke wheel hubs. These were for the United States market only. In 1987, the United Kingdom introduced a similar set of models called "Laser Wheels" which featured an iridescent design.

Roadblasters were introduced in 1987. These miniatures featured clip-on armament to make them into battle machines. Some models even had the main casting modified including windows replaced by battle ornamentation. The series included twelve Turbo Force "good guys" and twelve Motor Lord "bad guys."

In 1988, Matchbox Toys acquired the Dinky trademark. As no new castings were made, six miniatures were re-colored and placed on Dinky blistercards so as not to lose the licensed trademark.

In 1989, Super Color Changers were introduced. These models changed color when exposed to changes in temperature, namely by dipping the model in water. The Skybuster series also included color changing.

Also in 1989, the World Class series debuted at more than twice the price of a standard miniature. The models featured gray wheels with rubber tires and chrome windows. The series was dropped in 1993 in favor of the Premiere Collection.

A series of army vehicles was introduced in 1989 in the United States called Commando. These include Strike Team "good guys" and Dagger Force "bad guys". Two Convoys were included in the series.

In 1990, Matchbox introduced a preschool range from the Live 'N Learn series. The models were done in primary colors with preschool decorations and wheels to match. Lasertronics, termed Siren Force in the United States, were also introduced in 1990. Twelve selected models (four castings in three liveries each) featured press-down front axles which activated working lights and sirens. The series was resurrected in 1991 for the "Rescue 911" TV series and again in 1996 for the Action System Light & Sound series.

Car & Driver series was a flop in 1990 as twelve cars, although issued with trading cards, were never produced in special colors. To commemorate the release of the Paramount Pictures "Days of Thunder," Matchbox introduced miniatures, Convoys, and Team Matchbox in 1990.

The debut of Lightning Wheels was in 1991. These "fastest cars on the market" featured bright colors with specially designed axles to feature extra speed on the track. The wheel hubs even featured lightning bolts.

Also in 1991, a series of all-white models called Graffic Traffic was introduced. Each model came in two and three packs and was issued with sets of water resistant marking pens and label sheets, so that children could make and decorate their own special model. Of course, decorating these yourself puts the value to "zero" on the collectors market! Action Packs also were introduced in 1991. The models included extra play accessories with a specially colored variation.

To commemorate the seventy-fifth anniversary of the Indianapolis 500, Matchbox introduced its Indy 500 in 1991. The seventy-sixth and seventy-seventh Indys also received special attention until the line ended for 1993.

Hot Stocks, similar to Action Packs, were released in 1992. The series included only six pieces—all Chevy Luminas. Triple Heat debuted in 1992. The set of six included a three pack of a miniature, a Superfast Mini and a World's Smallest.

The Harley-Davidson series included miniatures, Superking, Convoy, and large plastic motorcycles. The range, introduced in 1992, runs through 1996.

The final 1992 release was Intercom City. The highly revolutionary idea features electronic bar codes on the bases of the models. When the bar code runs over another bar code on the play environment, it sets up a play in which spoken messages are given and in turn further play is continued as suggested by the message.

Showstoppers were introduced in 1993. Called Motor Show in Europe, the series paired manufacturer models with a mirror display stand. Super Trucks also debuted. Like the Hot Stocks series, this time with six trucks. A farming series was issued in 1993 which included retooled models along with newly cast trailers.

Licenses for Formula 1 and Nigel Mansell race teams were introduced in 1994. Collector's Choice also debuted in which twenty-four vehicles were realistically painted for more "collectible" appeal.

In 1994, Matchbox in the United Kingdom decided to offer very short-run promotionals on a selected set of models. As few as three- to five-hundred models could be specially ordered using "blanks" sent from the Orient and these were tampo printed in England. A similar program was set up in the United States in 1996 with a private company called ASAP in which as few as one hundred and forty-four models could be ordered. These are Code 2 releases, and due to tight controls by Tyco, none have been released to the collectors market and no one knows what exists outside the company doing the printing. Twelve all-white models were used.

The year 1996 saw the release of the much-heralded Premiere Collection. Similar to World Class but better, the models still had rubber tires but featured chrome wheels and normal clear windows. This was extended upon in late 1996 with the Gold Collection, a five-thousand piece premiere edition issued with a gold coin.

Matchbox Collectibles, normally associated with the Yesteryear and Dinky range, issued special miniatures with two different train sets as well as a Micro Brewery set in 1996.

Although listed as a 1997 edition on the package, the 75 Challenge cars were released by November 1996. All seventy-five of the 1997 range will be available as a ten-thousand-piece run in metallic gold and issued with a collector box. These are mixed in with standard release models. By year's end, nearly twenty of the seventy-five were already reported!

White Rose & Nutmeg Collectibles

White Rose Collectibles has become a driving force in the Matchbox company since business began in 1989. As much as ten to fifteen percent or more of Matchbox's business comes by way of White Rose Collectibles. The original introductions by White Rose included four Nascar transporters, but it wasn't until 1990 that the market really began to take off on the Nascar scene. By 1995, however, with many competing companies in Nascar related items, White Rose has been branching out even further from its original ventures.

White Rose has produced Sports Collectibles since 1990 with the introduction of its Major League baseball sets which continue today. This was followed by successful licenses for the NFL, NHL, college teams, and, most recently, trucking companies.

White Rose has developed some of its own miniatures with Matchbox that are exclusive to White Rose and offered nowhere else. These include different racing vehicles as well as an F800 Ford Delivery Van. White Rose even makes its own diecast line. In fact, White Rose "married" some Matchbox to Ertl and Winross models in a special gift box promotion.

Nutmeg Collectibles, founded by Mark Daddio, covers the Sprint and Modified Racing licenses but this ended in 1994, when Nutmeg decided to deal exclusively with the Ertl toy company.

A new company, Parlor City Collectibles, tried to venture into the Modified and Sprint markets after Nutmeg left the scene but after only a few ventures, the company folded.

ASAP Promotionals

In September of 1996, Tyco Toys went into a contractual agreement with a company called Advertising Specialties and Premiums- ASAP for short. ASAP would be supplied blank models from Tyco and later Mattel Toys to produce short run production models from as few as 96 or 144 up to several thousand. These models would be produced as "authorized by Matchbox" and therefore fit into the category of code 2. Early on in the program, ASAP used existing stock models such as the red no. 4 1997 Corvette or the no. 25 red BMW amongst others if a company required other than the white colored blank supplied through ASAP as manufactured by Matchbox. These short runs are very rare as Matchbox and ASAP do not supply any reference lists to what has been made. There are models made early on they we as collectors may never know about! These items come in white generic boxes clearly marked "Special Limited Edition! Matchbox" on the sides. Many of these have turned up on the internet, tag sales, toy shows or by someone who may have worked at the company that ordered the model. The following models are used as standard stock models as promotionals and all are supplied in white only unless otherwise noted.

MB 4 1997 Corvette
MB10 Dodge Viper RT/10 (red only)
MB15 Ford Transit Van
MB17 Leyland Titan (red or white)
MB20 Volvo Container Truck
MB21 GMC Wrecker
MB25 Ambulance (orange stripe)
MB27 Jeep Cherokee (white or black)
MB33 Utility Truck
MB36 Refuse Truck
MB38 Model A Ford Van
MB47 School Bus (orange-yellow)
MB54 Chevy Lumina
MB54 Crown Victoria Police Car
MB56 Peterbilt Tanker
MB57 Auxiliary Power Truck (red)
MB63 Snorkel Fire Engine
MB67 Ikarus Coach
MB68 TV News Truck
MB68 Chevy Van
MB74 Grand Prix Racer
CY7 Ford Aeromax Gas Tanker
CY39 Ford Aeromax Box Truck

On-pack Models

As a category, on-pack offers are unusual. Many on-pack models overlap into the promotional category. The model's promotional offering was through a direct mail-in offer based on sending in tokens, proofs of purchase, and sometimes a sum of money. Most of the offers were from the United Kingdom., Australia, or the United States. Some models are actually in-pack and offered by buying a product which includes the special model directly attached in some fashion to the package. These will be included in this category.

Miniatures 1-75 Basic Listing

NOTE: In 1998, Mattel restructured the entire Matchbox 75 line. When doing so, all but 3 models were renumbered according to "series" themes. This has made a mass confusion for cataloging the Matchbox miniatures. To alleviate the problem, only new 1998 model castings will be designated with current 1998 numbers. All older editions will be listed according to their model release number. Following the description, a "MW" (Mattel Wheel) number will be designated to indicate what that model was in the 1998 lineup.

HOW TO FIND 1998 MODELS IN THIS BOOK:

When Mattel introduced the 1998 model line, the entire series was restructured into "series" groupings by theme. In doing so, nearly every model in the line was renumbered from the previous year. This was done in both the USA & ROW markets. So as not to give models in this book as many as 4 or more identification numbers it was decided to basically "ignore" the 1998 series numbers except for 1998 releases. To facilitate you finding a 1998 model in this book, go to the first column. Then go to the second column for the USA model number. This is the number that the model will be cataloged under. If there is no USA number, move to the third column for the ROW (rest of world) number to find the model listed. The fourth column gives the model name. This chart does not include any reintroduction numbers.

Mattel Wheel No.	USA No.	ROW No.	Model Name
MW1 (USA)	MB1-G	MB35-K	Dodge Viper GTS
MW1 (ROW)	MB23-G	MB20-D	Volvo Container truck
MW2 (USA)	MB38-I	MB38-I	Corvette Stingray III
MW2 (ROW)	-	MB67-G	Ikarus Coach
MW3 (USA)	MB2-G	MB15-G	Corvette Grand Sport
MW3 (ROW)	MB68-G	MB73-D	TV News Truck
MW4 (USA)	MB15-J	MB28-K	Mustang Mach III
MW4 (ROW)	MB36-D	MB36-D	Refuse Truck
MW5 (USA)	MB25-J	MB61-H	BMW Z-3
MW5 (ROW)	-	MB15-K	Ford Transit Van
MW6	MB32-D	MB32-D	Excavator
MW7	MB36-D	MB36-D	Refuse Truck
MW8	MB19-D	MB19-D	Peterbilt Cement Truck
MW9	MB33-I	MB43-F	Utility Truck
MW10	MB30-E	MB23-E	Peterbilt Quarry Truck
MW11	MB45-E	MB69-G	Highway Maintenance Truck
MW12	MB47-E	MB47-E	School Bus
MW13	MB29-C	MB29-C	Tractor Shovel
MW14	MB64-D	MB64-D	Caterpillar Bulldozer
MW15	MB42-E	MB42-E	Faun Crane Truck
MW16	MB62-J	MB72-N	Street Streak
MW17	MB49-I	MB58-G	Volkswagen Concept I
MW18 (USA)	MB34-G	MB 6-H	Plymouth Prowler
MW18 (ROW)	MB12-K	MB31-K	Audi Avus Quattro
MW19	MB11-G	MB34-H	Chrysler Atlantic
MW20	MB13-F	MB28-M	The Buster
MW21	MB57-H	MB50-G	Auxiliary Power Truck
MW22	MB50-E	MB50-E	Chevy Blazer
MW23	MB18-C	MB18-C	Fire Engine
MW24 (USA)	MB16-E	MB51-H	Ford LTD Police Car
MW24 (ROW)	-	MB8-G	Vauxhall Astra Police
MW25	MB51-K	MB17-H	Ford Ambulance
MW26	MB63-E	MB13-E	Snorkel
MW27	MB59-H	MB56-J	Camaro Police Pursuit
MW28	MB54-K	MB38-J	Crown Victoria Police
MW29	MB75-D	MB75-D	Helicopter
MW30	MB30-I	MB30-I	Chevy Tahoe Police
MW31	MB31-L	MB31-L	'57 Chevy Bel Air Convertible
MW32	MB32-G	MB32-G	1970 El Camino
MW33	MB40-H	MB40-H	1969 Camaro SS396
MW34	MB34-H	MB34-H	'33 Ford Coupe
MW35	MB48-H	MB48-H	1956 Ford Pickup
MW36	MB36-E	MB36-E	'57 Chevy Bel Air
MW37	MB37-I	MB37-I	1970 Boss Mustang
MW38	MB70-H	MB64-G	1970 Pontiac GTO
MW39	MB39-I	MB39-I	1971 Camaro Z-28
MW40 (USA)	MB69-H	MB20-G	1968 Mustang Cobra Jet
MW40 (ROW)	-	MB40-I	FJ Holden Van
MW41 (USA)	MB68-I	MB68-I	Stinger
MW41 (ROW)	MB8-J	MB54-I	Mazda RX7
MW42 (USA)	MB73-H	MB47-F	Rotwheeler
MW42 (ROW)	MB28-L	MB22-J	Mitsubishi Spyder
MW43 (USA)	MB53-H	MB24-J	Rhino Rod
MW43 (ROW)	MB61-E	MB61-E	Nissan 300ZX
MW44 (USA)	MB23-G	MB20-D	Volvo Container Truck
MW44 (ROW)	MB30-G	MB30-G	Toyota Supra
MW45 (USA)	MB27-F	MB27-F	Tailgator
MW45 (ROW)	MB31-I	MB21-G	Nissan Prairie
MW46	MB46-H	MB46-H	Chevy Tahoe
MW47	MB47-G	MB47-G	M-2 Bradley Tank
MW48	MB3-D	M3-D	Hummer
MW49	MB46-F	MB57-F	Mission Helicopter
MW50	MB50-H	MB50-H	1997 Ford F150 Pickup
MW51	MB39-E	MB35-G	Ford Bronco II
MW52	MB37-F	MB25-I	Jeep 4X4
MW53 (USA)	MB65-G	MB65-G	Ford F150 Pickup
MW53 (ROW)	MB35-F	MB16-F	Land Rover 90
MW54	MB72-O	-	Chevy K-1500 Pickup
MW55 (USA)	MB53-D	MB53-D	Ford Flareside Pickup
MW55 (ROW)	MB56-I	MB59-I	Isuzu Amigo/ Vauxhall Frontera
MW56 (USA)	MB10-F	MB12-J	Dodge Viper RT/10
MW56 (ROW)	MB7-F	MB7-F	Porsche 959
MW57	MB24-H	MB70-F	Ferrari F40
MW58 (USA)	MB4-F	MB4-F	1997 Chevy Corvette
MW58 (ROW)	MB68-J	MB58-I	Porsche 911 GT1
MW59	MB73-G	MB21-H	Ferrari F50
MW60	MB67-F	MB11-F	Lamborghini Countach
MW61	MB74-J	-	Formula 1 Racer
MW62	MB3-E	MB3-E	Alfa Romeo 155
MW63	MB21-F	MB71-F	GMC Wrecker
MW64 (USA)	MB7-G	MB39-H	Ford Thunderbird
MW64 (ROW)	-	MB54-L	Holden Commodore
MW65	MB66-G	MB46-G	Opel Calibra
MW66	MB66-I	MB66-I	MGF
MW67 (USA)	MB8-J	MB54-I	Mazda RX7
MW67 (ROW)	MB10-F	MB12-J	Dodge Viper RT/10
MW68 (USA)	MB68-J	MB58-I	Porsche 911 GT1
MW68 (ROW)	-	MB63-J	Ford Falcon
MW69	MB28-L	MB22-J	Mitsubishi Spyder
MW70	MB70-I	MB70-I	Mercedes E Class
MW71	MB71-I	MB71-I	Jaguar XK8
MW72 (USA)	MB20-F	MB66-H	Firebird Ram Air
MW72 (ROW)	MB25-J	MB61-H	BMW Z3
MW73 (USA)	MB71-H	MB43-J	Mustang Cobra
MW73 (ROW)	MB49-H	MB 2-H	BMW 850I

MB31-H BMW 5 Series (ROW)	1989
MB31-I Nissan Prairie (USA)	1991
MB31-J Jaguar XJ220 (USA)	1993
MB31-K Audi Avus Quattro (ROW)	1995
MB31-L 1957 Chevy Bel Air	1998

MB32-A Leyland Tanker — 1970
MB32-B Maserati Bora — 1972
MB32-C Field Gun — 1978
MB32-D Atlas Excavator — 1981
MB32-E Modified Racer (USA) — 1988
MB32-F 1962 Corvette (USA reintro) — 1994
MB32-G 1970 El Camino — 1998

MB33-A Lamborghini Miura — 1969
MB33-B Datsun 126X — 1973
MB33-C Police Motorcycle — 1977
MB33-D Volkswagen Golf GTi (USA) — 1985
MB33-E Renault 11 (ROW) — 1986
MB33-F Mercury Sable Wagon (ROW) — 1989
MB33-G Utility Truck (USA) — 1989
MB33-H Mercedes 500SL Convertible (ROW) — 1990
MB33-I Ford Mondeo (ROW) — 1995

MB34-A Formula 1 — 1971
MB34-B Vantastic — 1975
MB34-C Chevy Prostocker — 1981
MB34-D Ford RS200 — 1987
MB34-E Sprint Racer (USA) — 1990
MB34-F Dodge Challenger (ROW reintro) — 1991
MB34-G Plymouth Prowler (USA) — 1995
MB34-H Chrysler Atlantic (ROW) — 1997
MB34-I 1933 Ford Street Rod — 1998

MB35-A Merryweather Fire Engine — 1970
MB35-B Fandango — 1975
MB35-C Pontiac T-Roof (USA) — 1982
MB35-D Zoo Truck (ROW) — 1982
MB35-E 4 X 4 Mini Pickup (ROW) — 1986
MB35-F Land Rover Ninety (USA) — 1987
MB35-G Ford Bronco II (ROW) — 1988
MB35-H Pontiac Grand Prix (USA) — 1992
MB35-I Pontiac Stock Car (USA) — 1993
MB35-J AMG Mercedes C Class (USA) — 1996
MB35-K Dodge Viper GTS (ROW) — 1997

MB36-A Opel Diplomat — 1970
MB36-B Hot Rod Draguar — 1970
MB36-C Formula 5000 — 1975
MB36-D Refuse Truck — 1980
MB36-E 1957 Chevy Bel Air Convertible — 1998

MB37-A Cattle Truck — 1970
MB37-B Soopa Coopa — 1972
MB37-C Skip Truck — 1976
MB37-D Sunburner (USA) — 1981
MB37-E Matra Rancho (ROW) — 1982
MB37-F Jeep 4 X 4 (USA) — 1984
MB37-G Ford Escort Cabriolet (ROW) — 1985
MB37-H Nissan 300ZX (ROW) — 1990
MB37-I 1970 Boss Mustang — 1998

MB38-A Honda Motorcycle & Trailer — 1970
MB38-B Stingeroo — 1972
MB38-C Jeep — 1976
MB38-D Ford Camper — 1980
MB38-E Model A Ford Van — 1982
MB38-F Ford Courier (ROW) — 1992
MB38-G Ford Courrier (ROW) — 1992
MB38-H Mercedes 600 SEL (USA) — 1992
MB38-I Corvette Stingray III — 1994
MB38-J Crown Victoria Police Car (ROW) — 1997

MB39-A Clipper — 1973
MB39-B Rolls Royce Silver Shadow — 1979
MB39-C Toyota Supra (USA) — 1983
MB39-D BMW Cabriolet — 1985
MB39-E Ford Bronco II (USA) — 1987
MB39-F Mack CH600 Aerodyne (ROW) — 1990
MB39-G Mercedes 600 SEL (ROW) — 1992
MB39-H Ford Thunderbird (ROW) — 1995
MB39-I 1971 Camaro Z-28 — 1998

MB40-A Vauxhall Guildsman — 1971
MB40-B Horse Box — 1977
MB40-C Corvette T-Roof (USA) — 1982
MB40-D Rocket Transporter (ROW) — 1985
MB40-E Ford Sierra (USA reintro) — 1990
MB40-F Road Roller (USA) — 1991
MB40-G Ford Mondeo (USA) — 1995

MB40-H 1969 Camaro Roadster — 1997
MB40-I FJ Holden Van (ROW) — 1995

MB41-A Ford GT — 1970
MB41-B Siva Spyder — 1972
MB41-C Ambulance — 1977
MB41-D Kenworth Aerodyne (USA) — 1982
MB41-E Racing Porsche (ROW) — 1983
MB41-F Jaguar XJ6 (USA) — 1987
MB41-G Vectra Cavalier Gsi 2000 (ROW) — 1990
MB41-H Cosmic Blues (USA reintro) — 1991
MB41-I Sunburner (ROW) — 1992
MB41-J Ferrari 456GT (ROW) — 1994

MB42-A Iron Fairy Crane — 1970
MB42-B Tyre Fryer — 1972
MB42-C Mercedes Container Truck — 1977
MB42-D 1957 Ford Thunderbird — 1982
MB42-E Faun Crane Truck (ROW) — 1984
MB42-E Faun Crane Truck (USA) — 1987

MB43-A Pony Trailer — 1970
MB43-B Dragon Wheels — 1972
MB43-C 0-4-0 Loco — 1978
MB43-D Peterbilt Conventional (USA) — 1982
MB43-E AMG Mercedes 500SEC — 1984
MB43-F Renault 11 (USA) — 1987
MB43-G Lincoln Town Car (USA) — 1989
MB43-H '57 Chevy (ROW reintro) — 1990
MB43-I Camaro Z28 (USA) — 1994
MB43-J Mustang Cobra (ROW) — 1995

MB44-A Refrigerator Truck — 1970
MB44-B Boss Mustang — 1972
MB44-C Passenger Coach — 1978
MB44-D 4 X 4 Chevy Van (USA) — 1982
MB44-E Citroen 15CV (ROW) — 1983
MB44-F Datsun 280ZX Police Car (Japan) — 1987
MB44-G Skoda 130LR (ROW) — 1987
MB44-H 1921 Model T Ford — 1990
MB44-I Ford Probe — 1994

MB45-A Ford Group 6 — 1970
MB45-B BMW 3.0 CSL — 1976
MB45-C Kenworth Aerodyne — 1982
MB45-D Ford Cargo Skip Truck (ROW) — 1987
MB45-E Highway Maintenance Vehicle (USA) — 1990

MB46-A Mercedes 300SE — 1970
MB46-B Stretcha Fetcha — 1972
MB46-C Ford Tractor — 1978
MB46-D Hot Chocolate/ Beetle Streaker (USA) — 1981
MB46-E Sauber Group C Racer (ROW) — 1984
MB46-F Mission Helicopter (USA) — 1985
MB46-G Opel Calibra (ROW) — 1997
MB46-H Chevy Tahoe Police — 1998

MB47-A DAF Tipper Truck — 1970
MB47-B Beach Hopper — 1974
MB47-C Pannier Loco — 1979
MB47-D Jaguar SS 100 — 1982
MB47-E School Bus (USA) — 1985
MB47-E School Bus (ROW) — 1987
MB47-F Rotwheeler (ROW) — 1995
MB47-G M2 Bradley Tank — 1998

MB48-A Dodge Dump Truck — 1970
MB48-B Pi-Eyed Piper — 1972
MB48-C Sambron Jacklift — 1977
MB48-D Red Rider (USA) — 1981
MB48-E Unimog with plow (ROW) — 1983
MB48-F Vauxhall Astra/ Opel Kadett (ROW) — 1986
MB48-G Pontiac Firebird Racer (USA) — 1993
MB48-G Pontiac Firebird Racer (ROW) — 1994
MB48-H 1956 Ford Pickup — 1997

MB49-A Unimog — 1970
MB49-B Chop Suey — 1973
MB49-C Crane Truck — 1976
MB49-D Sand Digger — 1983
MB49-E Peugeot Quasar — 1986
MB49-F Lamborghini Diablo (ROW) — 1992
MB49-G Volvo 480ES — 1990
MB49-H BMW 850I (USA) — 1993
MB49-I Volkswagen Concept 1 (USA) — 1996

MB50-A Kennel Truck — 1970
MB50-B Articulated Truck — 1973
MB50-C Articulated Trailer (TP) — 1980
MB50-D Harley-Davidson Motorcycle — 1980

MB50-E Chevy Blazer — 1984
MB50-F Dodge Dakota (ROW) — 1990
MB50-G Auxiliary Power Truck (ROW) — 1991
MB50-H Harley-Davidson Chopper (HD) — 1994
MB50-I Harley-Davidson Electraglide (HD) — 1994
MB50-J 1997 Ford F150 — 1998

MB51-A Eight Wheel Tipper — 1970
MB51-B Citroen S.M. — 1972
MB51-C Combine Harvester — 1978
MB51-D Midnight Magic (USA) — 1981
MB51-E Pontiac Firebird SE (ROW) — 1982
MB51-F London Bus (USA reintro) — 1985
MB51-G Camaro IROC-Z (USA) — 1986
MB51-H Ford LTD Police Car (ROW) — 1987
MB51-I Porsche 959 (USA reintro) — 1994
MB51-J Jeep Cherokee (ROW reintro) — 1996

MB52-A Dodge Charger — 1970
MB52-B Police Launch — 1976
MB52-C BMW M1 — 1981
MB52-D BMW M1 — 1983
MB52-E Isuzu Amigo — 1991
MB52-F Ford Escort Cosworth — 1994

MB53-A Ford Zodiac — 1970
MB53-B Tanzara — 1972
MB53-C Jeep CJ6 — 1977
MB53-D Flareside Pickup — 1982
MB53-E Faun Dump Truck (ROW) — 1989
MB53-F Chevy Breakdown Van (USA reintro) — 1990
MB53-G Ford LTD Taxi (USA) — 1992
MB53-H Rhino Rod (USA) — 1994

MB54-A S&S Cadillac Ambulance — 1970
MB54-B Ford Capri — 1971
MB54-C Personnel Carrier — 1976
MB54-D Mobile Home — 1980
MB54-E NASA Tracking Vehicle — 1982
MB54-F Command Vehicle — 1984
MB54-G Chevy Lumina (DT) — 1989
MB54-H Chevy Lumina — 1990
MB54-I Mazda RX7 (ROW) — 1994
MB54-J Abrams Tank (USA) — 1995
MB54-K Crown Victoria Police Car (USA) — 1997
MB54-L Holden Commodore (AU) — 1996

MB55-A Mercury Police Car — 1970
MB55-B Mercury Police Commuter — 1971
MB55-C Hellraiser — 1975
MB55-D Ford Cortina — 1979
MB55-E Ford Sierra (ROW) — 1983
MB55-F Racing Porsche (USA) — 1983
MB55-G Mercury Sable Wagon (USA) — 1987
MB55-H Rolls Royce Silver Spirit (USA) — 1990
MB55-I Model A Ford (USA reintro) — 1991
MB55-J Flareside Pickup (reintro) — 1994
MB55-K Flareside with load (WR) — 1994

MB56-A BMC Pininfarina — 1969
MB56-B Hi-Tailer — 1974
MB56-C Mercedes 450SEL — 1979
MB56-D Peterbilt Tanker (USA) — 1982
MB56-E Volkswagen Golf Gti (ROW) — 1985
MB56-F 4 X 4 Jeep (ROW reintro) — 1990
MB56-G Ford LTD Taxi (ROW) — 1992
MB56-H Camaro Z28 (ROW) — 1995
MB56-I Isuzu Rodeo (USA) — 1995
MB56-J Camaro Z28 Police Car (ROW) — 1995

MB57-A Land Rover Fire Engine — 1970
MB57-B Eccles Caravan — 1970
MB57-C Wildlife Truck — 1973
MB57-D 4 X 4 Mini Pickup (USA) — 1982
MB57-E Carmichael Commando (ROW) — 1982
MB57-F Mission Helicopter (ROW) — 1985
MB57-G Ford Transit (USA) — 1990
MB57-H Auxiliary Power Truck (USA) — 1991

MB58-A DAF Girder Truck — 1970
MB58-B Woosh-N-Push — 1972
MB58-C Faun Dump Truck — 1976
MB58-D Ruff Trek — 1983
MB58-E Mercedes 300E — 1986
MB58-F Corvette T-Roof (USA reintro) — 1991
MB58-G Volkswagen Concept 1 (ROW) — 1996
MB58-H 1939 Chevy Sedan Delivery (AU) — 1997
MB58-I Porsche 911 GT1 (ROW) — 1998

MB59-A Ford Galaxie Fire Chief Car — 1970

MB59-B Mercury Fire Chief Car	1971	MB68-D 4 X 4 Chevy Van (ROW)	1983	MB245 Chevy Panel Van (WR)	1992
MB59-C Planet Scout	1975	MB68-E Dodge Caravan (USA)	1984	MB246 Formula One Racer (NM)	1994
MB59-D Porsche 928	1980	MB68-F Camaro Z28 (ROW)	1987	MB262 Chrysler Voyager (BE)	1994
MB59-E Porsche 944 (ROW)	1987	MB68-G TV News Truck (USA)	1989	MB267 Chevy Lumina (WR)	1994
MB59-F T-Bird Turbo Coupe (USA)	1987	MB68-H Road Roller (ROW)	1991	MB268 Ford Thunderbird (WR)	1994
MB59-G Aston Martin DB-7 (USA)	1994	MB68-I Stinger	1995	MB269 Pontiac Grand Prix (WR)	1994
MB59-H Camaro Z28 Police Car (USA)	1995	MB68-J Porsche 911 GT1 (USA)	1998	MB283 Chevy Monte Carlo (WR)	1995
MB59-I Vauxhall Frontera (ROW)	1995	MB68-K Ford Falcon (ROW)	1998	MB284 Chevrolet Super Truck (WR)	1996
				MB285 Ice Maker (WR)	1996
MB60-A Site Hut Truck	1970	MB69-A Rolls Royce Silver Shadow Coupe	1969	MB315 Volvo Truck (AP)	1998
MB60-B Lotus Super Seven	1971	MB69-B Turbo Fury	1973	MB319 Mercedes AAV (with bucket)(JR)	1997
MB60-C Holden Pickup	1977	MB69-C Armored Truck	1978	MB337 Mercedes AAV (with roof load)(JR)	1997
MB60-D Piston Popper (USA)	1982	MB69-D '33 Willys Street Rod (USA)	1982	MB338 1938 Dodge Airflow Van (CL)	1998
MB60-E Toyota Supra (ROW)	1983	MB69-E 1983/84 Corvette (ROW)	1983	MB339 1937 Mack Junior Van (CL)	1998
MB60-F Pontiac Firebird Racer (USA)	1985	MB69-F Volvo 480ES (ROW)	1988	MB343 Excavator (CT)	1998
MB60-G Ford Transit	1986	MB69-G Highway Maintenance Vehicle (ROW)	1990	MB344 Dump Truck (CT)	1998
MB60-H Rocket Transporter (USA)	1990			MB345 Bulldozer (CT)	1998
MB60-I Toyota Supra (ROW)	1995	MB70-A Grit Spreader	1970	MB346 Front Loader (CT)	1998
MB60-J Helicopter (USA reintro)	1997	MB70-B Dodge Dragster	1971	MB347 Road Roller (CT)	1998
		MB70-C Self Propelled Gun	1976	MB348 Scraper (CT)	1998
MB61-A Blue Shark	1971	MB70-D Ferrari 308 GTB	1981	MB350 Road Grader (CT)	1998
MB61-B Wreck Truck	1978	MB70-E Ford Cargo Skip Truck (USA)	1989	MB388 Peterbilt Dump with Plow (PS)	1998
MB61-C Peterbilt Wreck Truck	1982	MB70-F Ferrari F40 (ROW)	1989	MB710 Tipping Trailer (FM)	1993
MB61-D T-Bird Turbo Coupe (ROW)	1987	MB70-G Weasel (USA reintro)	1993	MB711 Farm Trailer (FM)	1993
MB61-E Nissan 300ZX (USA)	1990	MB70-H 1970 Pontiac GTO (USA)	1996	MB712 Seeder (FM)	1993
MB61-F Forklift Truck (ROW)	1991	MB70-I Mercedes E Class	1998	MB713 Rotovator (FM)	1993
MB61-G Abrams M1 Tank (ROW)	1995			MB720 Side Tipper (TP)	1977
MB61-H BMW Z3 (ROW)	1997	MB71-A Ford Heavy Wreck Truck	1970	MB791 Motorcycle Trailer (TP)	1979
		MB71-B Jumbo Jet	1973	MB792 Cattle Trailer (TP)	1979
MB62-A Mercury Cougar	1970	MB71-C Cattle Truck	1976	MB793 Inflatable on Trailer (TP)	1984
MB62-B Mercury Cougar Dragster	1970	MB71-D 1962 Corvette (USA)	1982	MB794 Glider Transporter (TP)	1976
MB62-C Renault 17TL	1974	MB71-E Scania T142 (ROW)	1985		
MB62-D Chevrolet Corvette	1979	MB71-F GMC Wrecker (ROW)	1988	MB 2 Savannah RX7 (JP)	1979
MB62-E Corvette T-Roof (ROW)	1982	MB71-G Porsche 944 (USA)	1989	MB 5 Datsun 280Z (JP)	1979
MB62-F Rolls Royce Silver Cloud (USA)	1986	MB71-H Mustang Cobra (USA)	1995	MB J-21 Toyota Celica XX (JP)	1979
MB62-G Volvo 760 (ROW)	1986	MB71-I 1997 Jaguar XK8	1998	MBJ-22 Galant Eterna (JP)	1979
MB62-H Oldsmobile Aerotech (USA)	1989				
MB62-I Volvo Container Truck (ROW reintro)	1991	MB72-A Jeep	1970	MB— 1983 Dodge Daytona Turbo Z (VG)	1983
MB62-J Street Streak (USA)	1996	MB72-B SRN6 Hovercraft	1972	MB— 1983 Dodge Caravan (VG)	1983
		MB72-C Bomag Road Roller	1979		
MB63-A Dodge Crane Truck	1970	MB72-D Maxi Taxi (USA)	1981	WR002 Ford F800 Delivery Van (WR)	1995
MB63-B Freeway Gas Tanker	1973	MB72-E Dodge Delivery Van (ROW)	1982	FS002 Ford F800 Delivery Van (WR)	1996
MB63-C Freeway Gas Trailer (TP)	1978	MB72-F Sand Racer (USA)	1984	FST Ford Super Truck (WR)	1996
MB63-D Dodge Challenger (USA)	1981	MB72-G Plane Transporter (USA)	1985	WRP01 1996 Pontiac Grand Prix (WR)	1996
MB63-E Snorkel	1982	MB72-H Ford Supervan II (ROW)	1986	WRP02 1996 Ford Thunderbird (WR)	1996
MB63-F 4 X 4 Open Back Truck (ROW)	1982	MB72-I Cadillac Allante (USA)	1987	Harley Davidson Springer Softtail (HD)	1995
MB63-G Volkswagen Golf GTi (ROW reintro)	1990	MB72-J Sprint Racer (ROW)	1990	1939 Harley Davidson Knucklehead (HD)	1995
MB63-H 0-4-0 Loco (ROW reintro)	1991	MB72-K Dodge Zoo Truck (ROW)	1992		
MB63-I Aston Martin (ROW)	1994	MB72-L 1962 Corvette (ROW)	1994	MB I Silver Streak (USA)	1978
MB63-J Ford Falcon (AU)	1996	MB72-M Peugeot Quasar (USA reintro)	1995	MBII Sleet-N-Snow (USA)	1978
		MB72-N Street Streak (ROW)	1996	MBIII White Lightning (USA)	1978
MB64-A MG 1100	1970	MB72-O Chevy K-1500 Pickup (USA)	1996	MBIV Flying Beetle (USA)	1978
MB64-B Slingshot Dragster	1971			MB V Hot Smoker (USA)	1978
MB64-C Fire Chief Car	1976	MB73-A Mercury Commuter	1970	MBVI Lady Bug (USA)	1978
MB64-D Caterpillar Bulldozer	1979	MB73-B Weasel	1974	MBVII Brown Sugar (USA)	1978
MB64-E Dodge Caravan (ROW)	1984	MB73-C Model A Ford	1979	MBVIII Black Widow (USA)	1978
MB64-F Oldsmobile Aerotech (ROW)	1989	MB73-D TV News Truck (ROW)	1989	MBIX Flamin Manta (USA)	1978
MB64-G 1970 Pontiac GTO (ROW)	1996	MB73-E Mercedes Tractor (ROW)	1990	MBX Golden X (USA)	1978
MB64-H Holden Commodore (ROW)	1998	MB73-F Jeep Cherokee (USA reintro)	1994		
		MB73-G Rolls Royce Silver Spirit (USA reintro)	1995		
MB65-A Saab Sonnet	1973	MB73-H Rotwheeler (USA)	1995		

Variations

MB 1-A MERCEDES TRUCK, issued 1970

1. gold body, orange canopy, blue windows, 5 spoke wheels, no labels ($18-25)

2. gold body, orange canopy, blue windows, 4 spoke wheels, no labels ($18-25)

3. gold body, yellow canopy, blue windows, 5 spoke whelps, no labels ($15-18)

4. gold body, yellow canopy, blue windows, 4 spoke wheels, no labels ($15-18)

5. red body, yellow canopy, blue windows, 4 spoke wheels, "Transcontinental Haulage" labels ($5-6)(TP)

6. red body, orange-yellow canopy, blue windows, 4 spoke wheels, "Transcontinental Haulage" labels ($5-6)(TP)

7. olive body, tan canopy, blue windows, 4 spoke wheels, "USA48350" labels ($8-12)(TP)

8. olive body, tan canopy, blue windows, 4 spoke wheels, "4TS 702K" labels ($6-8)(TP)

9. olive body, tan canopy, blue windows, 5 spoke wheels, "4TS 702K" labels ($6-8)(TP)

10. olive drab body, tan canopy, blue windows, 4 spoke wheels, "USA48350" labels ($65-80)(TP)

11. blue body, orange-yellow canopy, blue windows, 4 spoke wheels, "IMS" labels ($15-20)(TP)

12. blue body, orange-yellow canopy, purple windows, 4 spoke wheels, "IMS" labels ($20-30)(TP)

MB 1-B MOD ROD, issued 1971

1. yellow body, orange interior, unpainted base, red wheels, wildcat head label ($25-40)

2. yellow body, orange interior, unpainted base, black wheels, wildcat

head label ($15-18)
3. yellow body, orange interior, unpainted base, black wheels, flower label ($15-18)
4. yellow body, orange interior, unpainted base, black wheels, spotted cat label ($15-18)
5. yellow body, red interior, unpainted base, black wheels, spotted cat label ($15-18)
6. yellow body, red interior, silver-gray base, black wheels, spotted cat label ($18-25)
7. yellow body, orange interior, silver-gray base, black wheels, spotted cab label ($18-25)
8. yellow body, orange interior, unpainted base, black wheels, scorpion label ($25-40)
9. yellow body, orange interior, silver-gray base, black wheels, scorpion label ($25-40)
10. silver plated body, orange interior, unpainted base, black wheels, stripes tempa ($50-75)(RN)

MB 1-C DODGE CHALLENGER, issued 1976
1. red body, chrome interior, clear windows, dot dash wheels ($5-7)
2. red body, chrome interior, clear windows, 5 arch wheels ($3-4)
3. red body, white interior, clear windows, 5 arch wheels ($4-6)
4. red body, red interior, clear windows, 5 arch wheels ($7-10)
5. blue body, red interior, clear windows, 5 arch wheels ($4-6)
6. dark blue body, red interior, clear windows, 5 arch wheels ($4-6)

MB 1-D DODGE CHALLENGER, issued 1982
MB34-F DODGE CHALLENGER, reissued 1991 (ROW)
NOTE: All models with clear windows & dot dash rear wheels unless noted otherwise. Versions 1 to 4 with 5 arch front wheels.
1. orange body, unpainted base, blue roof, black interior, cast engine, "Revin Rebel" tempa, England casting ($4-6)
2. orange body, silver-gray base, blue roof, black interior, cast engine, "Revin Rebel" tempa, England casting ($4-6)
3. orange body, silver-gray base, white roof, black interior, cast engine, "Revin Rebel" tempa, England casting ($7-10)
4. orange body, silver-gray base, blue roof, black interior, cast engine, no tempa, England casting ($7-10)
NOTE: below models with plastic engine cast through hood opening.
5. yellow body, silver-gray base, black roof, red interior, 5 arch front wheels, "Toyman" tempa, England casting ($15-20)
6. yellow body, pearly silver base, black roof, red interior, 5 arch front wheels, "Toyman" tempa, Macau casting ($2-3)
7. yellow body, pearly silver base, black roof, red interior, dot dash front wheels, "Toyman" tempa, Macau casting ($2-3)
8. yellow body, pearly silver base, black roof, red interior, dot dash front wheels, "Toyman" tempa, China casting ($1-2)
9. lemon body, pearly silver base, black roof, red interior, dot dash front wheels, "Toyman" tempa, China casting ($1-2)
10. orange-yellow body, pearly silver base, black roof, red interior, dot dash front wheels, "Toyman" tempa, China casting ($1-2)
11. white body, white base, white roof, blue interior, dot dash front wheels, blue windows, no tempa, China casting ($10-15)(GF)
12. powder blue body, silver-gray base, black roof, white interior, dot dash front wheels, "Challenger" tempa, China casting ($8-10)(AP)
13. yellow body, yellow base, black roof, red interior, dot dash front wheels, no tempa, China casting ($8-12)(GS)(GR)
14. white body, silver-gray base, black roof, red interior, dot dash front wheels, "Toyman" tempa, China casting ($8-12)
15. dark blue body, silver-gray metal base, white roof, black interior, dot dash front wheels, clear windows, "Hemi" & white stripes tempa, China casting ($1-2)
16.fluorescent yellow body, gray plastic base, black roof, pink interior, gold 6-spoke spiral front & rear wheels, clear windows, black squiggly lines tempa, Thailand casting ($1-2)
17. dark purple body, gray plastic base, black roof, neon yellow interior, silver 6-spoke spiral front & rear wheels, yellow zigzag tempa , Thailand casting ($1-2)(MP)
18. florescent yellow body, gray plastic base, black roof, pink interior, silver 6-spoke spiral front & rear wheels, clear windows, black squiggly lines tempa, Thailand casting ($1-2)
19. florescent lime body, gray plastic base, black roof, black interior, silver 6-spoke spiral front & rear wheels, clear windows, black stripes tempa, China casting ($1-2)(MP)
20. white body, gray plastic base, black roof, purple interior, silver 6-spoke spiral front & rear wheels, clear windows, purple squiggly lines tempa, China casting ($2-3)
21. white body, gray plastic base, black roof, purple interior, 5 spoke concave star front & rear wheels, clear windows, purple squiggly lines tempa, China casting ($3-5)(CY)
22. dark purple body, chrome plastic base, black roof, black & white interior, chrome disc w/ rubber tires, clear windows, white stripes tempa, China casting ($3-5)(PC9)
23. dark purple body, gray plastic base, black roof, black & white interior, 5 spoke concave front & rear wheels, clear windows, white stripes tempa, China casting ($50+)(CHI)
24. red body, chrome plastic base, black roof, chrome disc with rubber tires, clear windows, yellow & orange flames tempa, China casting ($3-5)(PC11)
25. red body, gray plastic base, black roof, 5 spoke concave star front & rear wheels, yellow & orange flames tempa, China casting ($50+)(CHI)

MB1-F JAGUAR XJ6 POLICE CAR, issued 1991 (ROW)
1. white body, tan interior, blue windows & dome lights, 8 dot wheels, "Police" with blue & yellow stripes tempa, Thailand casting ($3-5)
2. white body, tan interior, blue windows & dome lights, 8 dot wheels, "Police" with checkers & stripes tempa, Thailand casting ($3-5)

MB1-G DODGE VIPER GTS, issued 1997 (USA)
MB35-K DODGE VIPER GTS, issued 1997 (ROW)
NOTE: All models with clear windows & black base unless otherwise noted.
1. metallic blue body, gray & black interior, chrome disc with rubber tires, dual white stripes tempa, Thailand casting ($4-6)(IG)
2. unpainted body, gray interior, chrome disc with rubber tires, no tempa, Thailand casting ($4-6)(IG)
3. metallic blue body, gray interior, 5 spoke concave star wheels, dual white stripes tempa, Thailand casting ($1-2)
4. black body, orange interior, chrome disc with rubber tires, orange stripes & "Matchbox Convention" tempa, China casting ($12-15)(US)
5. red body, black interior, chrome disc with rubber tires, dual white stripes tempa, Thailand casting ($4-6)(PC14)
6. red body, black interior, 5 spoke concave star wheels, dual white stripes tempa, Thailand casting ($50+)(PC14)
7. white body, dark blue interior, 5 spoke concave star wheels, dual blue stripes tempa, Thailand casting ($1-2)(MW1)
8. white body, dark blue interior, 5 spoke concave star wheels, dual blue stripes tempa, China casting ($1-2)(MW1)
9. metallic gold body, black interior, 5 spoke concave star wheels, no tempa, China casting ($5-10)(CH)
10. bright blue body, white & gray interior, chrome disc with rubber tires, dual white stripes tempa, China casting ($3-5)(GS-Chrysler)
11. blue body, black interior, 5 spoke concave star wheels, white stripe & "New York Knicks" tempa, China casting ($4-6)(NBA)
12. powder blue body, white interior, 5 spoke concave star wheels, "Utah Jazz" tempa, China casting ($4-6)(NBA)
13. teal blue body, black interior, 5 spoke concave star wheels, black stripe & "Detroit Pistons" tempa, China casting ($4-6)(NBA)
14. lavender & white body, white interior, 5 spoke concave star wheels, "Los Angeles Lakers" tempa, China casting ($4-6)(NBA)
15. black body, gray interior, 5 spoke concave star wheels, "Orlando Magic" tempa, China casting ($4-6)(NBA)
16. black & white body, red interior, 5 spoke concave star wheels, "Chicago Bulls" tempa, China casting ($4-6)(NBA)
17. orange & black body, red-orange interior, 5 spoke concave star wheels, "Atlanta Hawks" tempa, China casting ($4-6)(NBA)
18. red body, white interior, 5 spoke concave star wheels, "Houston Rockets" tempa, China casting ($4-6)(NBA)

MB2-A MERCEDES TRAILER, issued 1970
1. gold body, orange canopy, 4 spoke wheels, no labels ($18-25)
2. gold body, yellow canopy, 4 spoke wheels, no labels ($15-18)
3. red body, yellow canopy, 4 spoke wheels, "Transcontinental Haulage" label s ($4-6)(TP)
4. red body, orange-yellow canopy, 4 spoke wheels, "Transcontinental Haulage" labels ($4-6)(TP)
5. olive body, tan canopy, 4 spoke wheels, "USA48350" labels ($8-12)(TP)
6. olive body, tan canopy, 4 spoke wheels, "4TS 702K" labels ($8-12)(TP)
7. olive body, tan canopy, 5 spoke wheels, "4TS 702K" labels ($8-12)(TP)
8. olive drab body, tan canopy, 5 spoke wheels, "USA48350" labels ($65-80)(TP)
9. olive drab body, tan canopy, 5 spoke wheels, "4TS 702K" labels ($65-80)(TP)
10. blue body, yellow-orange canopy, 5 spoke wheels, "IMS" labels ($15-18)(TP)
11. yellow body, white canopy, 5 crown wheels, "Alpine Rescue" labels ($3-5)(TP)
12. yellow body, no canopy, 5 crown wheels, no tempa ($5-7)
NOTE: above models with England casting.
13. yellow body, white canopy, 5 crown wheels, "Alpine Rescue" tempa , Macau casting ($3-5)(TP)
14. yellow body, white canopy, 5 crown wheels, "Alpine Rescue" tempa ($3-5)(TP)
15. red body, white canopy, 5 crown wheels, "Unfall Rettung" tempa ($3-5)(TP)
16. white body, orange canopy, 5 crown wheels, "C & S" tempa ($3-5)(TP)
17. red body, white canopy, dot dash wheels, "Big Top Circus" tempa ($4-6)(TP)

MB 2-B JEEP HOT ROD, issued 1971
1. pink body, light green base, cream interior, 4 spoke wheels, with engine ($15 18)
2. pink body, dark green base, cream interior, 4 spoke wheels, with engine ($15-18)
3. orchid body, light green base, cream interior, 4 spoke wheels, with engine ($18-25)
4. orchid body, dark green base, cream interior, 4 spoke wheels, with engine ($18-25)
5. pink body, dark green base, yellow interior, 4 spoke wheels, with engine ($15-18)
6. pink body, dark green base, white interior, 4 spoke wheels, with engine ($15-18)
7. pink body, dark green base, cream interior, 5 spoke wheels, with engine ($15-18)
8. pink body, white base, cream interior, 4 spoke wheels, with engine ($18-25)
9. red body, dark green base, cream interior, 4 spoke wheels, with engine ($18-25)
10. red body, dark green base, ivory interior, 4 spoke wheels, with engine ($18-25)
11. red body, white base, cream interior, 4 spoke wheels, with engine ($15-18)
12. red body, white base, cream interior, 5 spoke wheels, with engine ($15-18)
13. red body, white base, cream interior, maltese cross wheels, with engine ($18-25)
14. olive body, black base, black interior, 4 spoke wheels, hood label ($8-12)(TP)
15. olive drab body, black base, black interior, 4 spoke wheels, hood label ($65-80)(TP)

MB 2-C HOVERCRAFT, issued 1976
1. light green body, tan hull, chrome scoop, amber windows, "Rescue" labels ($4-6)
2. light lime body, tan hull, chrome scoop, amber windows, "Rescue" labels ($4-6)
3. light lime body, beige hull, chrome scoop, amber windows, "Rescue" labels ($4-6)
4. dark lime body, tan hull, chrome scoop, amber windows, "Rescue" labels ($4-6)
5. light lime body, tan hull, chrome scoop, red windows, "Rescue" labels ($4-6)
6. dark lime body, tan hull, chrome scoop, red windows, "Rescue" labels ($4-6)
7. avocado body, tan hull, chrome scoop, amber windows, no labels ($7-10)
8. avocado body, tan hull, chrome scoop, amber windows, "Rescue" labels ($7-10)
9. avocado body, black hull, chrome scoop, purple windows, "Rescue" labels ($7-10)
10. avocado body, black hull, chrome scoop, purple windows, "2000" labels ($7-10)
11. avocado body, black hull, red scoop, purple windows, "2000" labels ($7-10)
12. dark lime body, tan hull, red scoop, amber windows, "Rescue" labels ($5-8)
13. dark lime body, tan hull, red scoop, purple windows, "Rescue" labels ($5-8)
14. dark lime body, tan hull, chrome scoop, purple windows, "Rescue" labels ($4-6)
15. dark lime body, beige hull, chrome scoop, amber windows, "Rescue" labels ($4-6)
16. dark lime body, black hull, chrome scoop, amber windows, "Rescue" labels ($4-6)
17. dark lime body, beige hull, chrome scoop, amber windows, "Rescue" labels ($4-6)

MB 2-D S.2 JET, issued 1981
1. black body, yellow base, yellow wings, amber windows, no tempa, England casting ($3-5)
2. black body, yellow base, yellow wings, red windows, no tempa, England casting ($3-5)
3. light blue body, white base, white wings, clear windows, no tempa, England casting ($2-4)
4. light blue body, white base, white wings, clear windows, "Viper" tempa, England casting ($2-4)
5. light blue body, white base, gray wings, clear windows, "Viper" tempa, England casting ($2-4)
6. light blue body, white base, gray wings, clear windows, no tempa, England casting ($2-4)
7. dark blue body, white base, white wings, clear windows, "Viper" tempa, Macau casting ($2-4)
8. dark blue body, white base, white wings, clear windows, "Viper" tempa, Hong Kong casting ($20-25)
9. dark blue body, white base, white wings, clear windows, "Viper" tempa, China casting ($2-4)
10. olive green body, black base, olive green wings, clear windows, "AC152" & tan camouflage tempa, Macau casting ($4-6)(CM)

MB 2-E PONTIAC FIERO, issued 1985
1. white upper body, dark blue lower body, 8 dot silver wheels, "Goodyear 85" tempa, Macau casting ($2-4)
2. white upper body, dark blue lower body, 8 dot gold wheels, "Goodyear 85" tempa, Macau casting ($5-8)
3. white upper body, dark blue lower body, dot dash wheels, "Goodyear 85" tempa, Macau casting ($4-6)
4. yellow upper body, orange lower body, starburst wheels, "Protech 16" tempa, Macau casting ($3-5)(SF)
5. yellow upper body, orange lower body, 8 dot silver wheels, "Protech 16" tempa, Macau casting ($50-75)
6. white upper body, red lower body, 8 dot silver wheels, "GT Fiero" tempa, Macau casting ($2-4)
7. yellow upper body, metallic gold lower body, laser wheels, "Protech 16" tempa, Macau casting ($3-5)(LW)
8. black upper body, red lower body, 8 dot silver wheels, "2 Dog Racing Team" tempa, Macau casting ($8-12)(HK)
9. white body, red lower body, 8 dot silver wheels, "GT Fiero" tempa, China casting ($2-4)
10. fluorescent orange body, black lower body, starburst wheels, black flames, and "Turbo" tempa, China casting ($4-6)(PS)
NOTE: Above models all have black base insert, clear windows, silver-gray interior

MB 2-G 1965 CORVETTE GRAND SPORT, issued 1990 (USA)
MB15-G 1965 CORVETTE GRAND SPORT, issued 1990(ROW)
NOTE: Following models have 5 arch front & 5 crown rear wheels unless otherwise noted.

1. metallic blue body, clear windows, chrome interior, white stripes & small '15" on doors tempa, black base, Macau casting ($2-3)
2. metallic blue body, clear windows, chrome interior, white stripes & larger "15" on doors tempa, black base, Macau casting ($2-3)
3. metallic red body, chrome windows, black interior, white stripes & "63" tempa, black base, gray disc with rubber tires, Macau casting ($15-20)
4. metallic red body, chrome windows, black interior, white stripes & "63" tempa, chrome base, gray disc with rubber tires, Macau casting ($5-8)
5. metallic blue body, clear windows, chrome interior, white stripes & larger "15" on doors tempa, black base, Thailand casting ($2-3)
6. metallic blue body, clear windows, chrome interior, white stripes & larger "15" on doors tempa, black base, China casting ($2-3)
7. metallic blue body, clear windows, chrome interior, "Heinz 57" tempa, black base, China casting ($20-25)(US)
8. metallic blue body, clear windows, chrome interior, white stripes & "Corvette" on doors tempa, black base, Thailand casting ($2-3)
9. white & blue body, clear windows, black interior, "9" & red stripes tempa, white disc with rubber tires, white base, Thailand casting ($5-7)(WP)
10. white body, clear windows, chrome interior, red striping & "Corvette" tempa, black base, Thailand casting ($1-2)
11. bright yellow body, clear windows, chrome interior, purple & black design tempa, dark gray base, Thailand casting ($1-2)(MP)
12. metallic blue body, clear windows, black interior, white stripes & "2" tempa, chrome base, Thailand casting ($2-3)(GS)
13. dark orange body, clear windows, dark blue interior, black tire tread tempa, black base, gold 6 spoke spiral wheels, Thailand casting ($1-2)
14. chrome plated body, amber windows, white interior, no tempa, white base, gold 6 spoke spiral wheels, Thailand casting ($2-4)(GF)
15. metallic blue body, clear windows, chrome interior, green flames tempa, black base, silver 6 spoke spiral wheels, Thailand casting ($1-2)(MP)
16. white body, pink windows, chrome interior, orange "The Widow" & web with spider tempa, silver 6-spoke spiral wheels, black base, Thailand casting ($1-2)
17. white body, pink windows, white interior, red outlined "The Widow" & web with spider tempa, silver 6-spoke spiral wheels, black base, Thailand casting ($2-3)
18. silver body, red windows, white interior, blue stripes tempa, silver 6-spoke spiral wheels, black base, Thailand casting ($4-5)(MT)
19. dark purple body, clear windows, chrome interior, orange flames tempa, silver 6-spoke spiral; wheels, black base, China casting ($1-2)(MP)
20. light metallic blue body, clear windows, light gray/black interior, "50" & white stripes tempa, chrome disc with rubber tires, black base, China casting ($4-5)(PC2)
21. black body, red windows, white interior, red "The Widow" with Web & spider tempa, silver 6-spoke spiral wheels, black base, China casting($2-4)
22. metallic gray body, clear windows, ivory/black interior, "50" & white stripes tempa, chrome disc with rubber tires, black base, China casting ($3-5)(PC5)
23. metallic gold body, clear windows, chrome interior, no tempa, silver 6 spoke spiral wheels, black base, China casting ($5-10)(CH)
24. white body, clear windows, dark blue & black interior, "4" with black stripes tempa, chrome disc with rubber tires, black base, China casting ($3-5)(SC3)
25. white body, red windows, white interior, "The Widow" (outlined) with web with spider tempa, silver 6 spoke spiral wheels, black base, China casting ($2-4)(Corvette Cologne)
26. dark charcoal body, clear windows, gray interior, detailed trim tempa, chrome disc with rubber tires, black base, China casting ($3-5)(CP)
27. blue body, clear windows, gray interior, detailed trim tempa, chrome disc with rubber tires, black base, China casting ($3-5)(CP)
28. black body, red windows, white interior, "The Widow" & web with spider tempa, 5 spoke concave star wheels, black base, China casting ($2-4)
29. white body, clear windows, blue & gray interior, yellow & orange flames tempa, chrome disc with rubber tires, black base, China casting ($3-5)(PC11)
30. Lemon body, clear windows, black & gray interior, detailed trim tempa, chrome disc with rubber tires, black base, China casting ($3-5)(CP)
31. gold body, clear windows, black & gray interior, detailed trim tempa, chrome disc with rubber tires, black base, China casting ($3-5)(CP)
32. metallic green body, clear windows, gray & black interior, detailed trim tempa, chrome disc with rubber tires, black base, China casting ($3-5)(CP)
33. black body, clear windows, gray & black interior, detailed trim tempa, chrome disc with rubber tires, black base, China casting ($3-5)(CP)
34. red body, clear windows, chrome interior, white band tempa, 5 spoke concave star wheels, black base, China casting ($2-4)
35. black body, clear windows, gray & black interior, detailed trim tempa, gold 6 spoke spiral wheels, black base, China casting ($50+)(CHI)
36. gold body, clear windows, gray & black interior, detailed trim tempa, gold 6 spoke spiral wheels, black base, China casting ($50+)(CHI)
37. blue body, clear windows, chrome interior, white band tempa, 5 spoke concave star wheels, black base, China casting ($1-2)(MW3)

MB 3-A MERCEDES BENZ "BINZ" AMBULANCE, issued 1970

1. cream body, blue windows, rear door opens, 5 spoke wheels ($18-25)
2. off white body, blue windows, rear door opens, 5 spoke wheels ($18-25)
3. off white body, dark blue windows, rear door opens, 5 spoke wheels ($18-25)
4. off white body, dark blue windows, rear door cast shut, dot dash wheels ($7-10)(TP)
5. olive body, dark blue windows, rear door cast shut, dot dash wheels-silver hubs ($7-10)(TP)
6. olive body, dark blue windows, rear door cast shut, dot dash wheels-black hubs ($7-10)(TP)

MB3-B MONTEVERDI HAI, issued 1973

1. orange body, unpainted base, ivory interior, blue windows, "3" label ($10-15)
2. orange body, silver-gray base, ivory interior, blue windows, "3" label ($15-20)
3. orange body, unpainted base, light yellow interior, blue windows, "3" label ($10-15)
4. orange body, unpainted base, light yellow interior, blue windows, no label ($10-15)
5. orange body, unpainted base, ivory interior, blue windows, "3" label ($10-15)
6. orange body, unpainted base, ivory interior, blue windows, "16" label ($15-20)
7. orange body, unpainted base, ivory interior, dark blue windows, "3" label ($10-15)
8. orange body, black base, ivory interior, blue windows, "3" label ($10-15)
9. orange body, black base, ivory interior, blue windows, "6" label ($15-20)

MB 3-C PORSCHE TURBO, issued 1979

NOTE: Following models with England casting & 5 arch wheels unless otherwise noted.

1. brown body, cream interior, unpainted base, clear windows, no tempa ($15-20)
2. brown body, cream interior, black base, clear windows, no tempa ($7-10)
3. silver-gray body, cream interior, black base, clear windows, no tempa ($6-8)
4. silver-gray body, cream interior, charcoal base, clear windows, no tempa ($6-8)
5. silver-gray body, red interior, black base, clear windows, no tempa ($3-5)
6. silver-gray body, red interior, brown base, clear windows, no tempa ($7-10)
7. silver-gray body, red interior, charcoal base, clear windows, no tempa ($3-5)
8. silver-gray body, tan interior, brown base, clear windows, no tempa ($7-10)
9. silver-gray body, tan interior, black base, clear windows, no tempa ($4-8)
10. silver-gray body, tan interior, charcoal base, clear windows, no tempa ($4-8)
11. matt gray body, red interior, brown base, clear windows, no tempa ($7-10)
12. matt gray body, red interior, charcoal base, clear windows, no tempa ($7-10)
13. green body, cream interior, charcoal base, clear windows, no tempa ($7-10)
14. green body, red interior, charcoal base, clear windows, no tempa ($7-10)
15. green body, red interior, black base, clear windows, no tempa ($7-10)
16. green body, orange-yellow interior, charcoal base, clear windows, no tempa ($3-5)
17. green body, orange-yellow interior, black base, clear windows, no tempa ($3-5)
18. green body, orange-yellow interior, blue-gray base, clear windows, no tempa ($5-8)
19. green body, orange-yellow interior, unpainted base, clear windows, no tempa ($5-8)
20. red body, tan interior, black base, clear windows, "Porsche 90 Turbo" tempa ($3-5)
21. red body, tan interior, blue-gray base, clear windows, "Porsche 90 Turbo" tempa ($3-5)
22. red body, tan interior, charcoal base, clear windows, "Porsche 90 Turbo" tempa ($3-5)
23. red body, white interior, charcoal base, clear windows, "Porsche 90 Turbo" tempa ($3-5)
24. red body, white interior, black base, clear windows, "Porsche 90 Turbo" tempa ($3-5)
25. orange-red body, white interior, black base, clear windows, "Porsche 90 Turbo" tempa ($5-8)
26. red body, tan interior, black base, opaque windows, "Porsche 90 Turbo" tempa ($10-15)
27. red body, tan interior, black base, clear windows, no tempa ($3-5)

NOTE: Following models with Macau casting

28. red body, brown interior, black base, clear windows, "Porsche 90 Turbo" tempa ($2-4)
29. black body, tan interior, black base, amber windows, "Porsche 90 Turbo" tempa ($2-4)
30. red body, tan interior, black base, clear windows, black edged tempa ($8-12)(JP)
31. white body, tan interior, black base, clear windows, "Boss 14" tempa ($8-12)(JP)
32. dark blue body, white interior, black base, clear windows, "Wrangler 47" tempa ($8-12)(UK)
33. white body, tan interior, black base, clear windows "Porsche" & "3" tempa ($8-12)
34. black body, tan interior, black base, clear windows, "Porsche" without side design tempa ($8-12)
35. white body, tan interior, black base, clear windows, "Boss 14" with "14" inside square tempa ($3-5)
36. white body, blue interior, black base, clear windows, "Boss 14" with "14" inside square tempa ($3-5)
37. black body, black interior, black base, clear windows, "90 Porsche Turbo" & "BP" tempa ($8-12)(DU)
38. red body, blue interior, black base, clear windows, "8 Dragon Racing Team" tempa ($8-12)(HK)
39. robin egg blue body, blue interior, black base, clear windows, "Boss 14" with "14" in square tempa ($3-5)(MP)
40. dark blue body, tan interior, black base, clear windows, "Porsche" & yellow stripes tempa ($2-3)
41. red body, tan interior, black base, clear windows, "Porsche" & "Porsche 911" tempa ($1-2)
42. black body, tan interior, black base, clear windows, "Porsche" & "Porsche 911" tempa ($2-4)(MP)

NOTE: Following models with Thailand casting unless noted otherwise.

43. red body, tan interior, black base, clear windows, "Porsche" & "Porsche 911" tempa ($1-2)
44. dark blue body, tan interior, black base, clear windows, "Porsche" & yellow stripes tempa ($1-2)
45. yellow body, tan interior, black base, clear windows, "Porsche" logo tempa ($3-5)(GS)
46. robin egg blue body, blue interior, black base, clear windows, "Boss 14" with "14" in square tempa ($3-5)(MP)
47. black body, tan interior, black base, clear windows, "Porsche 90 Turbo" tempa, Manaus casting ($20-35)(BR)
48. lemon body, black interior, black base, clear windows, spatter design & "Porsche" tempa ($2-3)(TP)
49. black body, tan interior, black base, clear windows, "Porsche 90 Turbo" tempa, 8 dot gold wheels, Manaus casting ($20-35)(BR)
50. red body, tan interior, black base, clear windows, "Porsche 90 Turbo" tempa, 8 dot gold wheels, Manaus casting ($20-35)(BR)
51. white body, red interior, black base, clear windows, small "Porsche" logo tempa, Thailand casting ($2-3)(SS)
52. white body, lt. tan interior, black base, clear windows, "Matchbox Fun Club" tempa, Thailand casting ($8-12)(UK)
53. black body, peach interior, black base, clear windows, gold "Porsche" tempa, Thailand casting ($2-3)(SP)
54. white body, blue interior, black base, clear windows, "Boss 14" with "14" inside square tempa, Thailand casting ($2-3)(SP)

MB3-D HUMMER, issued 1994

NOTE: All models with opaque black windows & 8 spoke wheels with black hubs unless otherwise noted.

1. khaki gray body, tan gun, brown & white camouflage & pink cross tempa, khaki gray base, China casting ($1-2)
2. pink-tan body, tan gun, green & brown camouflage tempa, pink-tan base, Thailand casting ($1-2)(MP)
3. dark beige body, tan gun, brown & white camouflage & pink stripe tempa, beige base, Thailand casting ($1-2)
4. olive body, black gun, "A-4873-2" & star tempa, black base, Thailand casting ($1-2)
5. green body, black gun, brown & black camouflage tempa, green base, Thailand casting ($1-2)(MP)
6. white body, black gun, blue with "Police Unit 7" tempa, black base, Thailand casting ($1-2)(MP)
7. beige body, black gun, brown camouflage tempa, black base, Thailand casting ($1-2)(MP)
8. white body, gray gun, gray & olive camouflage tempa, gray base, Thailand casting ($1-2)(MP)
9. olive body, black gun,, "Gen IV", small "8" & "The Lost World" logo tempa, black base, Thailand casting ($3-5)(JR)(PS)
10. matt olive body, black gun, "Gen IV", small "17" & "The Lost World" logo tempa, black base, Thailand casting, gray armament attachment ($3-5)(JR)
11. khaki tan body, black gun, "A4873-2" & star tempa, black base, Thailand casting ($1-2)(MW48)
12. black body, brown gun, green & brown camouflage tempa, brown base, Thailand casting ($1-2)(MP)
13. black body, brown gun, green & brown camouflage tempa, brown base, China casting ($1-2)(MP)
14. khaki tan, black gun, "A4873-2" & star tempa, black base, China casting ($1-2)(MW48)
15. beige body, black gun, brown camouflage tempa, black base, China casting ($1-2)(PS)
16. olive body, black gun, "Unit 5 Communications" tempa, black base, China casting ($1-2)(RT)

MB 3-E ALFA ROMEO 155, issued 1997

NOTE: below models with clear windows, black interior & black base unless otherwise noted.

1. red body, "7" with cross & snake design tempa, chrome disc with rubber tires, China casting ($4-6)(IG)
2. unpainted body, no tempa, chrome disc with rubber tires, China casting ($4-6)(IG)
3. red body, "8" with cross & snake design tempa, 5 spoke concave star wheels, China casting ($1-2)
4. red body, "7" with cross & snake design tempa, 5 spoke concave star wheels, China casting ($30+)(CHI)
5. white body, "8" with cross & snake design tempa, 5 spoke concave star wheels, China casting ($1-2)(MW62)
6. metallic gold body, no tempa, 5 spoke concave star wheels, China casting ($5-10)(CH)

MB 4-A DODGE STAKE TRUCK, issued 1970

1. orange-yellow body, green stakes, 4 spoke front & rear wheels ($18-25)
2. orange-yellow body, green stakes, spiro front & rear wheels ($18-25)
3. orange-yellow body, green stakes, spiro front & 4 spoke rear wheels ($18-25)
4. yellow body, green stakes, 4 spoke wheels ($75-100)

MB 4-B GRUESOME TWOSOME, issued 1971

1. gold body, unpainted base, amber windows, cream interior ($100-150)
2. gold body, unpainted base, purple windows, cream interior ($12-15)
3. gold body, unpainted base, purple windows, yellow interior ($12-15)

4. gold body, silver-gray base, purple windows, yellow interior ($12-15)
5. gold body, unpainted base, purple windows, white interior ($12-15)
6. gold body, silver-gray base, purple windows, cream interior ($12-15)
7. gold body, silver-gray base, purple windows, white interior ($12-15)
8. red body, unpainted base, purple windows, cream interior ($15-18)
9. red body, unpainted base, purple windows, yellow interior ($15-18)
10. red body, silver-gray base, purple windows, yellow interior ($15-18)
11. orange-gold body, unpainted base, purple windows, cream interior ($12-15)

MB 4-C PONTIAC FIREBIRD issued 1975
1. light blue body, unpainted base, amber windows, dot dash wheels ($5-7)
2. light blue body, unpainted base, amber windows, maltese cross wheels ($5-7)
3. light blue body, unpainted base, amber windows, 5 arch wheels ($5-7)
4. dark blue body, unpainted base, amber windows, dot dash wheels ($5-7)

MB 4-D '57 CHEVY, issued 1979
MB43-H '57 CHEVY, reissued 1990 (ROW)
NOTE: Following models with chrome interior, clear windows, 5 arch front & 5 crown rear wheels unless otherwise noted.
1. light purple body & hood, unpainted base, no tempa, England casting ($5-7)
2. red body & hood, unpainted base, "Cherry Bomb" tempa with painted hood, England casting ($2-4)
3. red body & hood, silver-gray base, "Cherry Bomb" tempa with painted hood, England casting ($2-4)
4. red body & hood, silver-gray base, "Cherry Bomb" tempa with plain hood, England casting ($2-4)
5. red body & hood, black base, "Cherry Bomb" tempa with plain hood, England casting ($50-75)
6. black body, red hood, pearly silver base, flames tempa, Macau casting ($1-2)
7. black body, red hood, pearly silver base, flames tempa, China casting ($1-2)
8. pink body, red hood, pearly silver base, flames tempa, Macau casting ($3-4)(SC)
9. light pea green body, red hood, pearly silver base, flames tempa, Macau casting ($3-4)(SC)
10. light peach body, red hood, pearly silver base, flames tempa, Macau casting ($3-4)(SC)
11. rose red body, red hood, pearly silver base, flames tempa, Macau casting ($3-4)(SC)
12. dark purple body, red hood, pearly silver base, flames tempa, Macau casting ($3-4)(SC)
13. red body & hood, pearly silver base, "Heinz 57 Chevy" tempa, Macau casting ($15-20)(US)
14. bluish purple body & hood, pearly silver base, "Milky Way" tempa, Macau casting ($15-20)(UK)(OP)
15. bluish purple body & hood, pearly silver base, "Milky Way" tempa, China casting ($15-20)(UK)(OP)
16. black body, dark red hood, pearly silver base, flames tempa, Thailand casting ($1-2)
17. black body, dark red hood, pearly silver base, flames tempa, China casting ($1-2)
18. metallic red body & hood, pearly silver base, silver stripe tempa, chrome windows, gray disc with rubber tires, China casting ($5-8)(WC)
19. yellow body & hood, pearly silver base, blue & red stripes & "57" tempa, black windows, Thailand casting ($3-5)(TH)
20. black body, dark red hood, black base, flames tempa, Thailand casting ($1-2)
21. red body, red hood, silver-gray base, flames & silver flash tempa, Thailand casting ($1-2)
22. black body, black hood, silver-gray base, yellow tempa, Thailand casting ($1-2)(MP)
23. metallic blue body, metallic blue hood, black base, silver sides tempa, Thailand casting ($2-3)(CC)
24. red body, red hood, silver—gray base, flames & silver flash & "Chubby's Diner" tempa, Thailand casting ($7-10)(US)
25. white body, pink hood, silver-gray base, pink flames tempa, Thailand casting ($1-2)(MP)
26. black body, yellow hood, steel gray base, yellow flames tempa, China casting ($1-2)(MP)
27. iridescent white body & hood, pearly silver base, pink & blue tempa, China casting ($1-2)
NOTE: All above models with chrome interior. PC & SC models with chrome disc & rubber tires.
28. gunmetal gray body & hood, red & white interior, black base, white roof & silver flash tempa, China casting ($3-4)(PC3)
29. black body & hood, red & white interior, black base, white roof & silver flash tempa, China casting ($3-4)(PC6)
30. red body & hood, chrome interior, pearly silver base, yellow flames & silver side flash only tempa (plain hood), Thailand casting ($2-4)
31. red body & hood, red & white interior, black base, white roof & silver flash tempa, China casting ($10-15)(YST)
32. dark maroon body & hood, red & white interior, black base, white roof & silver flash tempa, China casting ($3-5)(SC3)
33. red body, yellow hood, black & chrome interior, black base, orange flames tempa, China casting ($3-5)(PC9)
34. black body & base, chrome interior, pearly silver base, "Night Stalker" & flames tempa, China casting ($2-4)(AU)
35. black body, red hood, red & chrome interior, pearly silver base, yellow flames tempa, China casting ($3-5)(PC11)
34. red body & hood, black & chrome interior, black base, yellow flames tempa, chrome disc with rubber tires, China casting ($10-15)(US- Hot August Nights)
35. metallic gold body & base, black & chrome interior, black base, silver flash tempa, chrome disc with rubber tires, China casting ($175-250)(CH-Winner car)

MB 4-E TAXI FX4R, issued 1987
NOTE: All models with black wheels with silver hubs unless otherwise noted.
1. black body, unpainted base, gray interior, no tempa, Macau casting ($2-4)
2. black body, unpainted base, gray interior, "Great Taxi Ride London to Sydney" tempa, Macau casting ($5-7)(AU)
3. yellow body, unpainted base, blue interior, "ABC Taxi" tempa, red wheels with yellow hubs, Macau casting ($4-6)(LL)
4. black body, unpainted base, gray interior, no tempa, China casting ($2-4)
5. black body, silver-gray base, gray interior, no tempa, China casting ($2-4)
6. black body, unpainted base, gray interior, "London Taxi" & British flag tempa (left side only), China casting ($2-4)
7. yellow body, unpainted base, blue interior, "ABC Taxi" tempa, all red wheels, China casting ($4-6)(LL)
8. black body, unpainted base, gray interior, "Old Eight" & British flag tempa, China casting ($75-100)(BR)

MB 4-F 1997 CORVETTE, issued 1997
NOTE: All models with clear windows & black base, China casting unless otherwise noted.
1. red body, black interior, 5 spoke concave star wheels, "Launch Commemorative Jan. 6th, 1997" tempa ($150-200)(US)
2. metallic blue body, gray & black interior, chrome disc with rubber tires, detailed trim tempa ($4-6)(IG)
3. unpainted body, black interior, chrome disc with rubber wheels, no tempa ($4-6)(IG)
4. red body, black interior, 5 spoke concave star wheels, "Corvette" on windshield tempa ($1-2)
5. red body, gray & black interior, chrome disc with rubber tires, detailed trim tempa ($3-5)(CP)
6. white body, red & black interior, chrome disc with rubber wheels, detailed trim tempa ($3-5)(CP)
7. red body, black interior, 5 spoke concave star wheels, "Fiery Driven" tempa ($100+)(ASAP)
8. red body, black interior, chrome disc with rubber tires, "Corvette Cologne" tempa ($25-40)(US)
9. black body, red & black interior, chrome disc with rubber tires, detailed trim tempa ($3-5)(CP)
10. silver-gray body, gray & black interior, chrome disc with rubber tires, detailed trim tempa ($3-5)(CP)
11. metallic red body, gray & black interior, chrome disc with rubber tires, detailed trim tempa ($3-5)(CP)
12. green body, gray & black interior, chrome disc with rubber tires, detailed trim tempa ($3-5)(CP)
13. blue body, gray interior, 5 spoke concave star wheels, "Corvette" on windshield tempa ($1-2)(MW58)
14. white body, black interior, 5 spoke concave star wheels, "Lucent Technologies" with red "Gigaspeed" tempa ($100+)(ASAP)
15. white body, black interior, 5 spoke concave star wheels, "Lucent Technologies" with black "Gigaspeed/ Optispeed" tempa ($20-40)(ASAP)
16. white body, black interior, 5 spoke concave star wheels, "Route 66 Promotions" tempa ($20-40)(ASAP)
17. white body, black interior, 5 spoke concave star wheels, "Progress Pit Crew" tempa ($100+)(ASAP)
18. white body, black interior, 5 spoke concave star wheels, "Sandvik Coromant" tempa ($100+)(ASAP)
19. metallic gold body, black interior, 5 spoke concave star wheels, no tempa ($5-10)(CH)
20. white body, black interior, 5 spoke concave star wheels, no tempa ($20-40)(ASAP blank)
21. white body, black interior, 5 spoke concave star wheels, "Cisco Systems" tempa ($100+)(ASAP)
22. red body, black interior, 5 spoke concave star wheels, "Mid Town Bank" tempa ($100+)(ASAP)
23. charcoal body, red & black interior, chrome disc with rubber tires, detailed trim tempa ($3-5)(GS-TRU)

MB 5-A LOTUS EUROPA, issued 1969
1. blue body, unpainted base (NO "Superfast" cast), ivory interior, no labels, 5 spoke wheels ($75-90)
2. blue body, unpainted base, ivory interior, no labels, 5 spoke wheels ($10-15)
3. blue body, unpainted base, ivory interior, "20" labels, 5 spoke wheels ($15-18)(GS)
4. pink body, unpainted base, ivory interior, no labels, 5 spoke wheels ($10-15)
5. pink body, unpainted base, ivory interior, "20" labels, 5 spoke wheels ($15-18)(GS)
6. pink body, silver-gray base, ivory interior, no labels, 5 spoke wheels ($10-15)
7. black body, unpainted base, ivory interior, "JPS" tempa, 5 spoke wheels ($18-25)(JP)
8. black body, unpainted base, ivory interior, no labels, 5 spoke wheels ($15-20)(TP)
9. black body, unpainted base, ivory interior, no labels, dot dash wheels ($15-20)(TP)
NOTE: Available as a Bulgarian casting- assorted colors available ($35-50 each)

MB 5-B SEAFIRE, issued 1975
NOTE: Following models with "Seafire" labels and England casting unless otherwise noted.
1. white deck, blue hull, black exhausts, blue driver, no trailer ($10-15)
2. white deck, blue hull, red exhausts, blue driver, no trailer ($10-15)
3. white deck, blue hull, red exhausts, orange-yellow driver, no trailer ($10-15)
4. white deck, blue hull, black exhausts, orange-yellow driver, no trailer ($10-15)
5. white deck, blue hull, red exhausts, lemon driver, no trailer ($10-15)
6. white deck, blue hull, red exhausts, orange-yellow driver, black trailer ($10-15)(TP)
7. red deck, white hull, red exhausts, orange-yellow driver, black trailer ($8-12)(TP)
8. red deck, white hull, red exhausts, lemon driver, black trailer ($8-12)
9. red deck, blue hull, red exhausts, lemon driver, no trailer ($25-40)
10. white deck, brown hull, red exhausts, orange-yellow driver, no trailer ($85-110)
11. white deck, brown hull, red exhausts, orange-yellow driver, black trailer ($85-110)(TP)
12. white deck, brown hull, red exhausts, lemon driver, no trailer ($85-110)
13. white deck, brown hull, red exhausts, lemon driver, black trailer ($85-110)(TP)
14. red deck, yellow hull, red exhausts, red driver, black trailer ($35-50)(TP)
15. black deck, yellow hull, red exhausts, red driver, black trailer ($8-12)(TP)
16. white deck, white hull, white exhausts, no driver cast, white metal trailer (from MB9-A), "Bacardi" tempa , no origin cast ($10-15)(TP)(OP)
17. red deck, white hull, black exhausts, no driver cast, white plastic trailer, "Surf Rider" & silver stripes tempa , no origin cast ($2-3)(TP)
18. yellow deck, blue hull, no driver cast, black plastic trailer, "460" tempa, no origin cast ($3-5)(TP)
19. white deck, red hull, no driver cast, black plastic trailer, red & black design tempa , no origin cast($3-5)(TP)
20. white deck, florescent orange hull, no driver cast, black plastic trailer, no origin cast ($1-2)(MP)
21. white deck, florescent orange hull, no driver cast, black plastic trailer (China), no origin cast ($1-2)(MP)
22. navy blue body, green hull, no driver cast, black plastic trailer (China), no origin cast ($1-2)(MP)

MB 5-C U.S. MAIL TRUCK, issued 1978
1. blue body, white base, white roof with small window, silver hubs, "U.S. Mail" tempa ($4-6)
2. blue body, white base, white roof with small window, black hubs, "U.S. Mail" tempa ($5-7)
3. yellow body, black base, no roof, silver hubs, "Gliding Club" labels ($8-12)(TP)
4. yellow body, black base, no roof, black hubs, "Gliding Club" labels ($8-12)(TP)
5. yellow body, blue-gray base, no roof, silver hubs, "Gliding Club" labels ($8-12)(TP)
6. yellow body, white base, no roof, silver hubs, "Gliding Club" labels ($8-12)(TP)
7. blue body, white base, white roof with large window, silver hubs, "U.S. Mail" tempa ($5-8)
8. blue body, black base, white roof with large window, silver hubs, "U.S. Mail" tempa ($5-8)
9. olive body, charcoal base, gun cast, black hubs, "21 * 11" labels ($15-20)
10. olive body, charcoal base, gun cast, black hubs, no labels ($15-20)
11. red body, black base, "Gliding Club" labels, no gun or roof cast, silver hubs ($350-450)(TP)
NOTE: all models listed here have "No.5 U.S. Mail Truck" cast on base.

MB 5-D 4 X 4 JEEP, issued 1982 (USA)
MB56-F 4 X 4 JEEP, issued 1990 (ROW)
NOTE: Following models with black- right drive interior unless noted otherwise
1. light tan body, black metal base, "Golden Eagle" tempa, England casting ($3-5)
2. dark tan body, black metal base, "Golden Eagle" tempa, England casting ($3-5)
3. brown body, black metal base, "Golden Eagle" tempa, Macau casting ($2-4)
4. red body, black metal base, "Golden Eagle" tempa, Macau casting ($2-4)
5. olive body, black metal base, red, yellow & blue tempa, Macau casting, includes plastic armament ($6-8)(RB)
6. red body, black plastic base, "Golden Eagle" tempa, Macau casting ($1-2)
7. red body, black plastic base, "Golden Eagle" tempa, Thailand casting ($1-2)
8. yellow body, black plastic base, "50th Anniversary Jeep" tempa, Thailand casting ($12-18)(PS)
9. hot pink body, black plastic base, white bolt tempa, white interior, Thailand casting ($2-4)(DM)
10. dark met. blue body, black plastic base, pink/white/yellow tempa, right hand drive, Thailand casting ($1-2)(MP)
11. dark met. blue body, black plastic base, pink/white/yellow tempa, left hand drive, Thailand casting ($1-2)(MP)
12. turquoise body, black plastic base, "Jeep" tempa, left hand drive, Thailand casting ($2-3)(CC)
13. red body, black plastic base, white headlamp tempa, left hand drive, Thailand casting ($15-18)(BE)
14. red body, black plastic base, "Golden Eagle" tempa, left hand drive, Thailand casting ($1-2)
15. red body, black plastic base, "Wolff Systems" tempa, left hand drive, Thailand casting ($15-25)(US)

16. white body, black plastic base, black cow patches tempa, left hand drive, Thailand casting ($1-2)(MP)
17. dark purple body, turquoise interior, black plastic base, "Bad To The Bone" on hood with side tempa, left hand drive, Thailand casting ($1-2)
18. dark purple body, turquoise interior, black plastic base, "Bad To The Bone" on hood without side tempa, left hand drive, Thailand casting ($1-2)
19. charcoal body, black interior, black plastic base, "Bad To The Bone" on hood without side tempa. left hand drive, Thailand casting ($2-4)
20. metallic gold body, black interior, black plastic base, no tempa, left hand drive, Thailand casting ($10-15)(CH)
21. metallic blue body, yellow interior, black plastic base, pink & yellow hood design tempa, Thailand casting ($2-4)

MB 6-A FORD PICKUP, issued 1970
1. red body, white canopy, unpainted base, chrome grille ($35-50)
2. red body, white canopy, black base, chrome grille ($35-50)
3. red body, white canopy, green base, chrome grille ($35-50)
4. red body, white canopy, metallic green base, chrome grille ($35-50)
5. red body, white canopy, charcoal base, chrome grille ($35-50)
6. red body, white canopy, gray base, chrome grille ($35-50)
7. red body, white canopy, green base, white grille ($35-50)
8. red body, white canopy, charcoal base, white grille ($35-50)
9. red body, white canopy, gray base, white grille ($35-50)
10. red body, white canopy, black base, white grille ($35-50)
11. red body, white canopy, unpainted base, white grille ($35-50)

MB 6-B MERCEDES TOURER, issued 1973
NOTE: Following models with England casting unless otherwise noted.
1. orange body, black roof, unpainted base, clear windows, light yellow interior, 5 arch wheels ($7-10)
2. orange body, black roof, unpainted base, amber windows, light yellow interior, 5 arch wheels ($7-10)
3. orange body, black roof, unpainted base, amber windows, light yellow interior, 5 spoke wheels ($7-10)
4. orange body, black roof, unpainted base, amber windows, ivory interior, 5 arch wheels ($7-10)
5. orange body, black roof, unpainted base, clear windows, light yellów interior, 5 spoke wheels ($7-10)
6. yellow body, black roof, unpainted base, amber windows, light yellow interior, 5 arch wheels ($6-8)
7. yellow body, black roof, unpainted base, clear windows, light yellow interior, 5 arch wheels ($6-8)
8. silver-gray body, black roof, unpainted base, amber windows, light yellow interior, 5 arch wheels ($25-40)
9. silver-gray body, black roof, unpainted base, amber windows, light yellow interior, 5 arch wheels, "Rennservice" labels ($35-45)(GR)
10. bronze body, black roof, unpainted base, amber windows, light yellow interior, 5 arch wheels ($8-12)
11. bronze body, white roof, unpainted base, amber windows, light yellow interior, 5 arch wheels ($5-8)
12. bronze body, white roof, unpainted base, amber windows, cream interior, 5 arch wheels ($5-8)
13. maroon body, white roof, unpainted base, amber windows, light yellow interior, 5 arch wheels ($7-10)
14. cherry body, white roof, unpainted base, clear windows, light yellow interior, 5 arch wheels ($5-8)
15. cherry body, white roof, unpainted base, amber windows, light yellow interior, 5 arch wheels ($5-8)
16. blue body, no roof, unpainted base, clear windows, white interior, 5 arch wheels ($5-8)
17. blue body, no roof, unpainted base, clear windows, white interior, 5 arch wheels, silver stripe tempa ($5-8)
18. blue body, no roof, silver-gray base, clear windows, white interior, 5 arch wheels, silver stripe tempa ($5-8)
19. blue body, no roof, silver-gray base, clear windows, white interior, maltese cross wheels, silver stripe tempa ($5-8)
20. plum body, no roof, silver-gray base, clear windows, white interior, 5 arch wheels ($7-10)
21. plum body, no roof, black base, clear windows, white interior, 5 arch wheels ($7-10)
22. plum body, no roof, black base, clear windows, white interior, dot dash wheels ($7-10)
23. plum body, no roof, unpainted base, clear windows, white interior, dot dash wheels ($7-10)
24. plum body, no roof, unpainted base, clear windows, white interior, 5 arch wheels ($7-10)
25. white body, no roof, silver-gray base, clear windows, translucent red interior, 5 arch wheels, China casting ($8-12)(MP)
26. pale gray body, no roof, black plastic base, clear windows, translucent white interior, 4 arch wheels, Manaus casting ($35-50)(BR)
27. beige body, no roof, black plastic base, clear windows, translucent white interior, 4 arch wheels, Manaus casting ($35-50)(BR)
28. red body, no roof, black plastic base, clear windows, translucent white interior, 4 arch wheels, Manaus casting ($35-50)(BR)
29. black body, no roof, black plastic base, clear windows, white interior, 8 dot wheels, Manaus casting ($35-50)(BR)
NOTE: Available as a Bulgarian casting with "Dinky" cast on base. Assorted colors available ($15-25 each)

MB 6-C I.M.S.A. MAZDA, issued 1983 (USA)
MB 7-E I.M.S.A. MAZDA, issued 1983 (ROW)
1. dark blue body, red interior, 5 arch wheels, white & orange tempa, Macau casting ($2-4)
2. dark blue body, red interior, dot dash wheels, white & orange tempa, Macau casting ($2-4)
3. dark blue body, red interior, dot dash wheels, white & stripes tempa, Manaus casting ($35-50)(BR)

MB 6-E FORD SUPERVAN II, issued 1986 (USA)
MB72-H FORD SUPERVAN II, issued 1986 (ROW)
1. white body, black metal base, dark gray windows, no dome lights, dark blue "Ford Supervan" tempa, Macau casting ($2-4)
2. white body, black metal base, dark gray windows, no dome lights, light blue "Ford Supervan" tempa, Macau casting ($2-4)
3. dark blue body, black metal base, dark gray windows, no dome lights, "Duckhams QXR Engine Oils" tempa, Macau casting ($4-6)(TC)
4. dark gray body, black metal base, dark gray windows, no dome lights, "High Explosive/ Heavy Load" tempa, Macau casting, includes plastic armament ($6-8)(RB)
5. white body, black metal base, dark gray windows, no dome lights, "Starfire" tempa, Macau casting ($3-5)
6. white body, black metal base, dark gray windows, no dome lights, "Fuji Racing Team" tempa, Macau casting ($3-5)(TC)
7. bright yellow body, black metal base, dark gray windows, no dome lights, "Service Car BP Oil" tempa, Macau casting ($10-15)(DU)
8. red body, black metal base, dark gray windows, no dome lights, "Tizer Flavoured Soft Drink" tempa, Macau casting ($3-5)(TC)
9. yellow body, black metal base, dark gray windows, no dome lights, "Goodyear Pit Stop" tempa, Macau casting ($3-5)(GS)
10. white body, black plastic base, dark gray windows, no dome lights, light blue "Ford Supervan" tempa, Macau casting ($2-4)
11. white body, black plastic base, dark gray windows, no dome lights, "Fuji Racing Team" tempa, Macau casting ($3-5)(TC)
12. red body, black plastic base, dark gray windows, no dome lights, "Tizer Flavoured Soft Drink" tempa, Macau casting ($3-5)(TC)
13. red body, black plastic base, black windows, amber dome lights, "Fire Observer" tempa, Macau casting ($12-15)(SR)
14. red body, black plastic base, black windows, greenish yellow dome lights, "Fire Observer" tempa, Macau casting ($12-15)(SR)
15. white body, black plastic base, black windows, red dome lights, "Ambulance" tempa, Macau casting ($12-15)(SR)
16. dark blue body, black plastic base, black windows, red dome lights, "Police Control Unit" tempa, Macau casting ($12-15)(SR)
17. white body, black plastic base, dark gray windows, no dome lights, "Starfire" tempa, Macau casting ($3-5)
18. yellow body, black plastic base, dark gray windows, no dome lights, "Goodyear Pit Stop" tempa, Thailand casting ($3-5)(GS)
19. red body, black plastic base, black windows, amber dome lights, "Fire Observer/ Rescue 911" tempa, China casting ($12-15)(SR)
20. white body, black plastic base, black windows, red dome lights, "Ambulance/ Rescue 911" tempa, China casting ($12-15)(SR)
21. dark blue body, black plastic base, black windows, red dome lights, "Police Control Unit/ Rescue 911" tempa, China casting ($12-15)(SR)
22. white body, black plastic base, black windows, no dome lights, no tempa, China casting ($10-15)(GF)
23. white body, black plastic base, dark gray windows, no dome lights, light blue "Ford Supervan" tempa, Thailand casting ($3-5)
24. light gray body, black plastic base, dark gray windows, no dome lights, "Danger High Explosive/ Heavy Load" tempa, China casting ($15-20)(JP-Tomy box)
25. white body, black plastic base, black windows, red dome lights, "EMS" & orange band tempa, China casting ($3-5)(LS)
26. dark blue body, black plastic base, black windows, red dome lights, "S.W.A.T. Police Emergency" tempa, China casting ($3-5)(LS)
27. black body, black plastic base, black windows, red dome lights, "S.W.A.T. Police Emergency" tempa, China casting ($3-5)(LS)
28. bright yellow body, black plastic base, black windows, amber dome lights, "EMS" & orange band tempa, China casting ($3-5)(LS)
29. silver-gray body, black plastic base, black windows, red dome lights, "Flight Team" with purple & dark pink flames tempa, China casting ($4-6)(LS)(Avon)

MB 7-A FORD REFUSE TRUCK, issued 1970
1. red-orange cab & chassis, black axle covers ($20-35)
2. orange cab & chassis, black axle covers ($20-35)
3. orange cab & chassis, red axle covers ($20-35)

MB 7-B HAIRY HUSTLER, issued 1971
NOTE: all models with chrome interior, 5 spoke front & maltese cross wheels. Some versions may have the wheel combination reversed.
1. bronze body, black base, purple windows, "5" yellow side labels, square "5" hood label ($100-150)
2. bronze body, light gray base, purple windows, "5" yellow side labels, square "5" hood label ($100-150)
3. bronze body, black base, amber windows, "5" yellow side labels, square "5" hood label ($15-20)
4. bronze body, light gray base, amber windows, "5" yellow side labels, square "5" hood label ($15-20)
5. bronze body, gray base, amber windows, "5" yellow side labels, square "5" hood label ($15-20)
6. bronze body, black base, amber windows, "5" blue side labels, square "5" hood label ($15-20)
7. bronze body, unpainted base, amber windows, "5" blue side labels, square "5" hood label ($15-20)
8. bronze body, black base, amber windows, square "5" side labels, scorpion hood label ($25-40)
9. bronze body, green base, amber windows, "5" blue side labels, square "5" hood label ($15-20)
10. bronze body, green base, amber windows, no side labels, square "5" hood label ($15-20)
11. bronze body, black base, amber windows, round "3" side labels, scorpion hood label ($25-40)
12. bronze body, green base, amber windows, round "3" side labels, scorpion hood label ($25-40)
13. bronze body, black base, amber windows, square "137" side labels, scorpion hood label ($25-40)
14. bronze body, black base, amber windows, no side labels, square "5" hood label ($15-20)
15. bronze body, green base, amber windows, round "3" side labels, square "5" hood label ($15-20)
16. bronze body, green base, amber windows, square "137" side labels, scorpion hood label ($25-40)
17. bronze body, green base, amber windows, square "5" side labels, scorpion hood label ($25-40)
18. white body, charcoal base, amber windows, no labels ($50-75)
19. white body, black base, amber windows, checkers & stripes tempa ($15-18)
20. yellow body, black base (cast #7), amber windows, flames tempa ($85-110)(RN)

MB 7-C V.W. GOLF, issued 1976
NOTE: All models with England casting unless otherwise noted.
1. lime body, black base, yellow interior, amber windows, roof rack, no labels ($5-7)
2. green body, black base, yellow interior, amber windows, roof rack, no labels ($5-7)
3. yellow body, black base, yellow interior, amber windows, antennae cast, "ADAC" labels ($30-45)(GR)(JP)
4. dark green body, black base, yellow interior, amber windows, roof rack, no labels ($5-7)
5. dark green body, charcoal base, yellow interior, amber windows, roof rack, no labels ($5-7)
6. dark green body, charcoal base, lemon interior, amber windows, roof rack, no labels ($5-7)
7. dark green body, charcoal base, lemon interior, orange windows, roof rack, no labels ($5-7)
8. dark green body, charcoal base, red interior, amber windows, roof rack, no labels ($8-12)
9. dark green body, black base, yellow interior, orange windows, roof rack, no labels (5-7)
10. mustard body, charcoal base, red interior, clear windows, roof rack, no labels ($5-7)
11. mustard body, black base, red interior, clear windows, roof rack, no labels ($5-7)
12. mustard body, blue- gray base, red interior, clear windows, roof rack, no labels ($5-7)
13. mustard body, gray- brown base, red interior, clear windows, roof rack, no labels ($5-7)
14. red body, black base, yellow interior, amber windows, roof rack, no labels ($5-7)
15. red body, black base, yellow interior, clear windows, roof rack, no labels ($5-7)
16. red body, black base, red interior, clear windows, roof rack, no labels ($10-15)
17. red body, black base, lemon interior, amber windows, roof rack, no labels ($5-7)
18. silver-gray body, black base, red interior, clear windows, no roof rack, green side tempa ($4-6)
19. silver-gray body, charcoal base, red interior, clear windows, no roof rack, green side tempa ($4-6)
20. silver-gray body, black base, tan interior, clear windows, no roof rack, green side tempa ($25-35)
21. silver-gray body, black base, blue interior, clear windows, no roof rack, green stripe tempa ($250-400)
22. black body, black base, red interior, clear windows, no roof rack, red stripe tempa, without tow hook cast, Macau casting ($5-7)(JP)
23. black body, black base, red interior, clear windows, no roof rack, red stripe tempa, Macau casting ($3-5)(TP)
24. black body, black base, red interior, clear windows, no roof rack, red & orange stripes with "9" tempa, Macau casting ($8-12)(DY)
NOTE: Available as a Bulgarian casting. Assorted colors available ($15-25)

MB 7-D ROMPIN RABBIT, issued 1982
1. white body, red interior, "Rompin Rabbit" with brown stripe tempa, England casting ($5-7)
2. white body, red interior, "Rompin Rabbit" without brown stripe tempa, England casting ($5-7)
3. white body, tan interior, "Rompin Rabbit" with brown stripe tempa, England casting ($5-7)
4. white body, tan interior, "Rompin Rabbit" without brown stripe tempa, England casting ($5-7)
NOTE: On below variations, rabbit on hood can face left or right.
5. yellow body, blue interior, "Ruff Rabbit" tempa, with tow hook, Macau casting ($3-5)
6. yellow body, blue interior, "Ruff Rabbit" tempa, with tow hook, Hong Kong casting ($3-5)
7. yellow body, blue interior, "Ruff Rabbit" tempa, without tow hook, Hong Kong casting ($3-5)
8. yellow body, blue interior, "Ruff Rabbit" tempa, without tow hook, Macau casting ($3-5)
9. yellow body, red interior, "Ruff Rabbit" tempa, without tow hook, Macau casting ($3-5)
10. yellow body, red interior, "Ruff Rabbit" tempa, with tow hook, Macau casting ($3-5)

MB 7-F PORSCHE 959, issued 1986
MB51-I PORSCHE 959, reissued 1994 (USA)
NOTE: All models with red interior, clear windows and black base unless

otherwise noted.

1. pearly silver body, 5 arch silver wheels, "Porsche" on doors tempa, Macau casting ($2-3)
2. pearly gray body, 5 arch silver wheels, "Porsche" on doors tempa, Macau casting ($2-3)
3. pearly silver body, 8 dot silver wheels, "Porsche" on doors tempa, Macau casting ($2-3)
4. white body, 5 arch white wheels, "Porsche" on doors tempa, Macau casting ($3-5)
5. white body, 8 dot silver wheels, "Porsche" on doors tempa, Macau casting ($2-4)
6. white body, 5 arch silver wheels, "Porsche" on doors tempa, Macau casting ($2-4)
7. white body, 8 dot white wheels, "Porsche" on doors tempa, Macau casting ($3-5)
8. white body, 8 dot silver wheels, "Porsche" on doors tempa, China casting ($2-4)
9. white body, 5 arch silver wheels, "Porsche" on doors tempa, China casting ($2-4)
10. charcoal gray body, 5 arch silver wheels, "Porsche 959" tempa, Macau casting ($2-4)
11. white body, 5 arch silver wheels, "Porsche 959" with red/yellow/black stripes tempa, Macau casting ($6-8)(KS)
12. pink body, 5 arch silver wheels, "Porsche 959" tempa, Macau casting ($3-4)(SC)
13. dark purple body, 5 arch silver wheels, "Porsche 959" tempa, Macau casting ($3-4)(SC)
14. white body, 5 arch silver wheels, "Redoxon" tempa, Macau casting ($20-35)(HK)
15. white body, 5 arch silver wheels, "Pace Car/ Shell" tempa, Macau casting ($3-5)(GS)
16. white body, 5 arch silver wheels, "313 Pirelli Gripping Stuff' tempa, Macau casting ($3-5)(TC)
17. silver-gray body, gray disc with rubber tires, chrome windows, "Porsche" tempa, Macau casting ($5-8)(WC)
18. black body, 5 arch silver wheels, "Porsche" logo tempa, Macau casting ($4-6)(MP)
19. white body, 5 arch silver wheels, "Pace Car/ Shell" tempa, Thailand casting ($3-5)(GS)
20. charcoal gray body, 5 arch silver wheels, "Porsche 959" tempa, Thailand casting ($2-3)
21. chrome plated body, 5 arch silver wheels, no tempa, Macau casting ($12-18)(C2)
22. white body, 5 arch silver wheels, "Porsche" logo tempa, Thailand casting ($3-5)(GS)
23. silver-gray body, gray disc with rubber tires, chrome windows, "Porsche" tempa, Thailand casting ($5-8)(WC)
24. white body, 5 arch silver wheels, red windows, no tempa, Thailand casting ($10-15)(GF)
25. silver-gray body, 5 arch silver wheels, black windows, checkers & red stripes with "959" tempa, Thailand casting ($3-5)(TH)
26. white body, 5 arch silver wheels, "Lloyds" tempa, Thailand casting ($8-12)(UK)
27. charcoal gray body, 5 arch silver wheels, "Porsche 959" (all red) tempa, Thailand casting ($1-2)
28. dark blue body, white interior, 5 arch silver wheels, small "Porsche" logo tempa, Thailand casting ($2-3)(SS)
29 silver—g-ray body, red interior, 5 arch silver wheels, "Porsche 959" (red only) tempa, Intercom City base, Thailand casting ($35-50)(IC)
30. silver-gray body, red interior, gold 6-spoke spiral wheels, "Porsche 959" (red only) tempa, Thailand casting ($2-3)
31. dark fluorescent pink body, black interior, gold 6-spoke spiral wheels, black design & "Rage" tempa, Thailand casting ($1-2)
32. chrome plated body, white interior, gold 6-spoke spiral wheels, no tempa, white base, Thailand casting ($2-4)(GF)
33. white body, red interior, gold 6-spoke spiral wheels, "Pace Car" & checkers tempa, Thailand casting ($3-5)(Fl)
34. dark florescent pink body, black interior, silver 6-spoke spiral wheels, black design with "Rage" on sides tempa, Thailand casting ($1-2)
35. dark florescent pink body, black interior, silver 6-spoke spiral wheels, black design without "Rage" on sides tempa, Thailand casting ($2-4)
36. silver body, red interior, silver 6-spoke spiral wheels, yellow & orange stripe design tempa, Thailand casting ($2-4)
37. florescent lime body, black interior, silver 6-spoke spiral wheels, black design without "Rage" on sides tempa, Thailand casting ($1-2)
38. florescent lime body, black interior, silver 6 spoke spiral wheels, black design without "Rage" on sides tempa, China casting ($1-2)
39. white body, red interior, silver 6 spoke spiral wheels, black checkers & "Pace Car" tempa, China casting ($1-2)(F1)
40. bright blue body, gray interior, 5 spoke concave star wheels, "Go Roos! 1997" tempa, China casting ($3-5)(AU)
41. dark blue body, gray & black, chrome disc with rubber wheels, detailed trim tempa, China casting ($8-12)(UC)
42. dark blue body, red interior, gold 6 spoke spiral wheels, detailed trim tempa, China casting ($100+)(CHI)
43. white body, dark red interior, 5 spoke concave star wheels, "Porsche" logo tempa, China casting ($1-2)
44. red body, tan interior, 5 spoke concave star wheels, "Porsche" and small logo tempa, China casting ($1-2)(MW56-ROW)
45. red body, black & red interior, chrome disc with rubber tires, detailed trim tempa, China casting ($15-20)(GC)

MB 7-G FORD THUNDERBIRD, issued 1994 (USA)
MB39-H FORD THUNDERBIRD, issued 1995 (ROW)

NOTE: Models below with Goodyear slicks - white lettered unless noted. Versions 1 to 18 with China casting.

1. red body, red interior, "Motorcraft Quality Parts 15" tempa ($3-5)(WR)
2. black body, silver-gray interior, "Havoline/ Texaco 28" tempa ($3-5)(WR)
3. yellow body, red interior, "Matchbox 92" with assorted logos tempa ($20-25)(US)
4. white & orange-red body, black interior, "Hooters 7" tempa ($5-8)(WR)
5. dark red body, black interior, "Philips 66/ Trop Artic" tempa ($3-5)(WR)
6. bright red body, black interior, "Phillips 66/ Trop Artic" tempa ($3-5)(WR)
7. blue body, black interior, "Maxwell House 22" tempa ($3-5)(WR)
8. bright red body, black interior, "White Rose Collectibles 92" tempa ($15-25)(WR)
9. red body, black interior, "Motorcraft Quality Parts" without Morgan Shephard tempa ($3-5)(WR)
10. black body, silver-gray interior, "Havoline/ Texaco 28" without "MAC" tempa ($3-5)(WR)
11. black body, gray interior, "Phillips 66/ Trop Artic" tempa ($3-5)(WR)
12. red body, red interior, "Bill Elliot 11" tempa ($3-5)(WR)
13. white body, silver-gray interior, "Baby Ruth 1" (orange) tempa ($4-6)(WR)
14. white body, silver-gray interior, "Baby Ruth 1" (red) tempa ($4-6)(WR)
15. white body, black interior, "Hooters 7" without "Classic/Naturally Fresh" tempa ($7-10)(WR)
16. brown & red body, silver-gray interior, "Snickers 8" tempa ($3-5)(WR)
17. red body, red interior, black disc with rubber tires, "Bill Elliot 11" tempa (WR)(TC)($4-6)
18. red & white body, black interior, "Melling 9" tempa ($3-5)(WR)
19. green body, black interior, "Quaker State 26" tempa, Thailand casting ($3-5)(WR)
20. white & orange body, black interior, "Hooters 7" tempa, black disc with rubber tires, Thailand casting ($12-15)(WR)(TC)
21.gray body, black interior, "Hooters 7" tempa, Thailand casting ($7-10)(WR)(TC)
22. black body, red interior, "Texaco/Havoline 28" (bright orange) tempa, Thailand casting ($8-12)(WR)
23.black body, red interior, "Texaco/Havoline 28" (bright orange) tempa, black disc with rubber tires tempa, Thailand casting ($8-12)(WR) (TC)
24.matt black body, red interior, "Texaco 28" tempa, Thailand casting ($7-10)(WR)(TC)
25.white body, black interior, "Maui 17" tempa, Thailand casting ($3-5)
26. white body, black interior, "Ford 1" & checkered flag tempa, Thailand casting ($2-4) (SS)
27. dark blue body, gray interior, "Racetech Radios" tempa, Thailand casting ($1-2)(MP)

NOTE: Following models with Goodyear slicks- yellow lettered unless noted.

28. bright blue body, red interior, "Purex 83" tempa, China casting ($3-5)(WR)
29. white & red body, red interior, "Citgo 21" tempa, China casting ($3-5)(WR)
30. white body, red interior, "Baby Ruth 8" tempa, China casting ($3-5)(WR)
31. blue body, dark gray interior, "Maxwell House 22" tempa, China casting ($3-5)(WR)
32. metallic blue body, red interior, "Raybestos 8" tempa, China casting ($3-5)(WR)
33. white body, black interior, "Bojangles/Easter Seals 7" tempa, China casting ($18-25) (WR)
34. white body, black interior, "Hanes 7" tempa, China casting ($18-25)(WR)
35. white body, black interior, "Matchbox/White Rose 7" tempa, China casting ($10-15)(WR)
36. black body, silver—gray interior, "Cappio 48" tempa, China casting ($3-5)(WR)
37. fluorescent yellow body, black interior, "Country Time 68" tempa, Thailand casting ($3-5)(WR)(TC)
38. fluorescent pink body, black interior, "Country Time 68" tempa, Thailand casting ($3-5)(WR)(TC)
39. white body, red interior, "Matchbox/White Rose 1" tempa, China casting ($3-5)(WR)
40. black body, red interior, "Meineke 12" tempa, China casting ($3-5)(WR)
41. yellow body, gray interior, "Bojangles 98" tempa, China casting ($3-5)(WR)
42. white body, red interior, "Luxaire 1" tempa, plain black slicks, China casting ($12-15)(WR)
43. white body, gray interior, "Family Channel 7" tempa, China casting ($12-15)(WR)
44. white body, gray interior, "Matchbox/USA Bobsled 7" tempa, Thailand casting ($12-15)(WR)
45. red body, red interior, "Budweiser 11" tempa, black disc rubber tires, Thailand casting ($25-35)(WR)(Ertl set)
46. flat black body, red interior, "Bud 11" tempa, black disc rubber tires, Thailand casting ($25-35)(WR)(Ertl set)
47. white, red & dark blue body, gray interior, "Valvoline 6" tempa, China casting ($3-5)(WR)
48. white body, gray interior, "USA Bobsled Project 7" tempa, China casting ($12-15)(WR)
49. yellow body, gray interior, "Bojangles 98" tempa, black disc rubber tires, China casting ($4-6)(WR)(TC)
50. black body, gray interior, "Bojangles 98" tempa, black disc rubber tires, China casting ($4-6)(WR)(TC)
51. bright blue & white body, red interior, "Naturally Fresh 37" tempa, China casting ($5-8)(WR)
52. black body, black interior, "TIC Financial 0" tempa, China casting ($5-8)(WR)
53. black & red body, silver-gray interior, "Cellular One 7" tempa, China casting ($5-8)(WR)
54. blue body, gray interior, yellow lettered "Racetech Radios 16" tempa, gold 6-spoke spiral wheels, Thailand casting ($1-2)
55. white body, lime interior, no tempa, white base, gold 6-spoke spiral wheels, Thailand casting ($2-4)(GF)
56. yellow body, gray interior, "Nationwise Auto Parts" tempa, Thailand casting ($20-35) (US)
57. blue body, gray interior, white lettered "Racetech Radios 16" tempa, gold 6-spoke spiral wheels, Thailand casting ($4-6) (Aquafresh promo)
58. pink body, black interior, "Radical Cams 10" tempa, silver 6-spoke spiral wheels, Thailand casting ($1-2)
59. pink body, black interior, "Radical Cams 10" tempa, silver 6-spoke spiral wheels, China casting ($1-2)
60. blue body, black interior, "Mitre 10/ Stanley" tempa, silver 6-spoke spiral wheels, China casting ($5-7)(AU)
61. black body, lime interior, "12 Joltage Batteries" tempa, silver 6-spoke spiral wheels, China casting ($1-2)(MP)
62. dark blue body, black interior, "Wieder Racing 7" tempa, silver 6-spoke spiral wheels, China casting ($1-2)
63. black body, red interior, "Carr Auto Care 4" tempa, 5 spoke concave star wheels, China casting ($1-2)
64. red body, gray interior, "Peterson Pistons 17" tempa, 5 spoke concave star wheels, China casting ($1-2)(MP)
65. metallic gold body, black interior, no tempa, silver 6 spoke spiral wheels, China casting ($5-10)(CH)
66. dark blue body, black interior, "Wieder Racing 7" tempa, 5 spoke concave star wheels, China casting ($2-4)
67. blue body, red interior, "Carr Auto Care 4" tempa, 5 spoke concave star wheels, China casting ($3-5)(PS)
68. green body, black interior, "BP Car Care 25" tempa, 5 spoke concave star wheels, China casting ($20-25)(AU)
69. blue body, gray interior, "Peterson Pistons 17" tempa, 5 spoke concave star wheels, China casting ($1-2)(MW64)

MB 8-A FORD MUSTANG FASTBACK, issued 1970

1. white body, red interior ($50-75)
2. red body, red interior ($250-350)
3. red-orange body, red interior ($250-350)
4. red body, ivory interior ($35-50)
5. red-orange body, ivory interior ($35-50)

MB 8-B WILDCAT DRAGSTER, issued 1971

NOTE: body colors range in shades of light to dark pinkish orange on all versions.

1. unpainted base, black & orange "Wildcat" labels ($18-25)
2. black base, black & orange "Wildcat" labels ($18-25)
3. dark yellow base, black & orange "Wildcat" labels ($18-25)
4. light yellow base, black & orange "Wildcat" labels ($18-25)
5. orange base, black & orange "Wildcat" labels ($18-25)
6. charcoal base, black & orange "Wildcat" labels ($18-25)
7. charcoal base, yellow & orange "Wildcat" labels ($18-25)
8. dark gray base, yellow & orange "Wildcat" labels ($18-25)
9. light gray base, yellow & orange "Wildcat" labels ($18-25)
10. black base, yellow & orange "Wildcat" labels ($18-25)
11. unpainted base, yellow & orange "Wildcat" labels ($18-25)
12. green base, yellow & orange "Wildcat" labels ($18-25)
13. black base, "Rat Rod" labels ($25-40)
14. black base, sailboat labels ($25-40)
15. black base, no labels ($18-25)

MB 8-C DE TOMASO PANTERA, issued 1975

NOTE: Versions 1 to 10 with England casting. Versions 12 & 13 with Hong Kong casting.

1. white body, blue base, "8" hood label, with side labels, light orange interior ($7-10)
2. white body, unpainted base, "8" hood label, with side labels, light orange interior ($7-10)
3. white body, blue base, "8" hood label, with side labels, dark orange interior ($7-10)
4. white body, blue base, "8" hood label, no side labels, dark orange interior ($7-10)
5. white body, blue base, "8" hood label, no side labels, light orange interior ($7-10)
6. white body, unpainted base, "8" hood label, no side labels, light orange interior ($7-10)
7. white body, blue base, "8" hood label, no side labels, red interior ($7-10)
8. white body, blue base, "9" hood label, no side labels, light orange interior ($12-18)
9. white body, blue base, sunburst hood label, no side labels, light orange interior ($18-25)
10. white body, blue base, sunburst hood label, no side labels, dark orange interior ($18-25)
11. white body, lavender base, "8" hood label, with side labels, light orange interior ($50-75)(BR)
12. blue body, black base, tempa without "Pantera" on hood, black interior ($3-5)
13. blue body, black base, tempa with "Pantera" on hood, black interior ($3-5)

NOTE: Many versions have intermixing of front and rear wheels.

MB 8-D ROVER 3500, issued 1982 (ROW)

NOTE: All models with dot dash wheels unless otherwise noted.

1. bronze body, light tan interior, clear windows, no dome lights, England casting ($2-4)

2. bronze body, dark tan interior, clear windows, no dome lights, England casting ($2-4)
3. bronze body, white interior, clear windows, no dome lights, England casting ($2-4)
4. bronze body, white interior, clear windows, no dome lights, small maltese cross wheels, England casting ($5-8)
5. white body, light tan interior, blue windows & dome lights, chrome beacon, blue & yellow "Police" tempa, England casting ($2-4)
6. white body, light tan interior, clear windows & dome lights, chrome beacon, blue & yellow "Police" tempa, England casting ($2-4)
7. white body, light tan interior, blue windows & dome lights, chrome beacon, no tempa, England casting ($2-4)
8. white body, black interior, blue windows & dome lights, chrome beacon, no tempa, England casting ($2-4)
9. white body, black interior, blue windows & dome lights, chrome beacon, blue & yellow "Police" tempa, England casting ($2-4)
10. white body, black interior, blue windows & dome lights, black beacon, black & yellow "Police" tempa, England casting ($2-4)
11. white body, light tan interior, blue windows & dome lights, black beacon, black & yellow "Police" tempa, England casting ($2-4)
12. white body, light tan interior, blue windows & dome lights, black beacon, blue & yellow "Police" tempa, Macau casting ($2-4)
13. white body, light tan interior, blue windows & dome lights, black beacon, blue & red "Police" tempa, Macau casting ($2-4)
14. white body, light tan interior, blue windows & dome lights, black beacon, blue & red "Police" tempa, China casting ($3-5)
15. white body, translucent tan interior, blue windows & dome lights, black beacon, blue & red "Police" tempa, China casting ($3-5)
16. white body, orange-yellow interior, blue windows & dome lights, black beacon, blue & yellow "Police" tempa, Manaus casting ($25-40)(BR)

MB 8-E GREASED LIGHTNING, issued 1983 (USA)
NOTE: all models with maltese cross front & five spoke rear wheels but other combinations can occur.
1. red body, white base, black interior, Macau casting ($5-8)
2. red body, white base, black interior, Hong Kong casting ($5-8)

MB 8-F SCANIA T142, issued 1985 (USA)
MB71-E SCANIA T142, issued 1985 (ROW)
NOTE: This model was used as a component for Convoy models. Only models released as single issues will be cataloged.
1. white body, red chassis, chrome base, red/orange/yellow stripes tempa, Macau casting ($2-4)
2. blue body, white chassis, chrome base, red/orange/yellow stripes tempa, Macau casting ($2-4)
3. blue body, white chassis, black base, red/orange/yellow stripes tempa, Macau casting ($2-4)

MB 8-G VAUXHALL ASTRA POLICE CAR, issued 1987 (ROW)
NOTE: All models listed have white interior, blue windows & dome lights unless otherwise noted.
1. white body, black base, 8 dot white wheels, "Police" with red & blue stripes tempa, Macau casting ($3-5)
2. white & dark green body, black base, 8 dot white wheels, "Polizei" tempa, Macau casting ($3-5)
3. white & dark green body, black base, 8 dot silver wheels, "Polizei" tempa, Macau casting ($3-5)
4. white body, black base, 8 dot silver wheels, "Police" with red & blue stripes tempa, Macau casting ($2-4)
5. white body, black base, 8 dot silver wheels, "Police" with red & blue stripes tempa, China casting ($2-4)
6. white & dark green body, black base, 8 dot silver wheels, "Polizei" tempa, China casting ($3-5)
7. white body, white base, blue 8 dot wheels with yellow, hubs, "Police" with orange & blue stripes & face on hood tempa, China casting ($3-5)(LL)
8. white body, white base, blue 8 dot wheels (plain hubs), "Police" with orange & blue stripes & face on hood tempa, China casting ($3-5)(LL)
9. white body, white base, 8 dot silver wheels, no tempa, China casting ($10-15)(GF)
10. white body, white base, 8 dot silver wheels, "Police" with orange & yellow stripes & orange dot on roof tempa, China casting ($1-2)
11. white body, white base, 8 dot silver wheels, "Police" with orange & yellow stripes without dot on roof tempa, China casting ($1-2)
12. white body, white base, 8 dot silver wheels, "Police" with peach & yellow stripes without roof dot tempa, China casting ($1-2)
13. white body, white base, 8 dot silver wheels, yellow & black checkers & "59" in shield tempa, China casting ($1-2)(MP)
14. white body, white base, 8 dot silver wheels, "Police/ Hertfordshire" tempa, China casting ($1-2)
15. black body, black base, gray interior, 8 dot silver wheels, "Police" & Commando emblem tempa, China casting ($15-20)(CHI)(MP)
16. black body, black base, gray interior, 5 arch black wheels, "Police" & Commando emblem tempa, China casting ($15-20)(CHI)(MP)
17. white body, white base, red windows, 8 dot silver wheels, "World Cup Security/ France 98" tempa, China casting ($1-2)(MP)
18. silver-gray body, black base, 8 dot silver wheels, "Police" with red & blue stripes tempa ($1-2)(MW24-ROW)

MB 8-H MACK CH600 AERODYNE, issued 1990 (USA)
MB39-F MACK CH600 AERODYNE, issued 1990 (ROW)
NOTE: This model was used as a component for Convoy models. Only models released as singles will be listed here.
1. white body, black chassis, gray base, black & red stripes tempa, 8 spoke wheels, Macau casting ($1-2)
2. white body, black chassis, gray base, black & red stripes tempa, 8 spoke wheels, Thailand casting ($1-2)
3. red & white body, black chassis, black base, "Coke" tempa, chrome disc with rubber tires, China casting ($4-6)(PC)

MB 8-I AIRPORT TENDER, issued 1992 (USA)
MB24-I AIRPORT TENDER, issued 1992 (ROW)
NOTE: All models with dark blue windows & China casting unless otherwise noted.
1. fluorescent orange body, white ladder, silver-gray interior, 8 dot wheels, "Fire Airport Fire Rescue" tempa ($1-2)
2. fluorescent orange body, white ladder, silver-gray interior, 8 dot wheels, "Fire Airport Fire "Rescue" & "IC" logo tempa, Intercom City base ($35-50)(IC)
3. white & red body, silver-gray ladder, black interior, 8 dot wheels, "Fire Dept." with gold crest & star tempa ($1-2)(MP)
4. red body, white ladder, silver-gray interior, 8 dot wheels, "Matchbox Fire Dept." & white band tempa ($1-2)(MP)
5. florescent yellow body, silver-gray ladder, chrome disc with rubber wheels, black interior, "Westford Airport Fire Rescue" tempa ($3-5)(PC7)
6. yellow body, gray ladder, 8 dot wheels, black interior, "Matchbox Fire Dept." tempa ($1-2)(MP)
7. lemon body, red ladder, 8 dot wheels, red interior, "Airways Fire & Rescue" tempa ($1-2)(MP)
8. yellow body, white ladder, chrome disc with rubber tires, "Newfield Airport Fire Rescue" tempa ($3-5)(PC21)

MB 8-J MAZDA RX7, issued 1994(USA)
MB54-I MAZDA RX7, issued 1994 (ROW)
1. fluorescent orange body, black interior, clear windows, gold 6-spoke spiral wheels, "Matchbox Get In The Fast Lane- Toy Fair 1994" tempa, Thailand casting ($35-50)(US/GR)
2. yellow-orange body, gray interior, smoke windows, gold 6-spoke spiral wheels, black & pink hood & sides design tempa, Thailand casting ($1-2)
3. black body, orange interior, chrome windows, gray disc rubber tires, no tempa, Thailand casting ($2-4)(WC)
4. yellow-orange body, gray interior, smoke windows, gold 6-spoke spiral wheels, black & pink design tempa & "Nationwise Auto Parts" roof label, Thailand casting ($20-35)(US)
5. yellow-orange body, gray interior, smoke windows, gold 6-spoke spiral wheels, black & pink side design only tempa, Thailand casting ($4-6)(Aquafresh promo)
6. red body, gray interior, smoke windows, silver 6-spoke spiral wheels, black & yellow hood & roof tempa, Thailand casting ($1-2)
7. silver body, white interior, blue windows, silver 6-spoke spiral wheels, red blotches tempa, Thailand casting ($3-4)(MT)
8. red body, gray interior, smoke windows, silver 6-spoke wheels, black & yellow hood design tempa, Thailand casting ($2-4)
9. gold & metallic red body, gray interior, smoke windows, silver 6-spoke spiral wheels, no tempa, Thailand casting ($1-2)
10. red body, clear windows, chrome disc with rubber tires, detailed trim tempa, Thailand casting ($3-4)(PC1)
11. silver-gray body, clear windows, chrome disc with rubber tires, detailed trim tempa, Thailand casting ($3-4)(SC1)
12. metallic green body, clear windows, chrome disc with rubber tires, detailed trim tempa, Thailand casting ($3-5)(PC)(JC)
13. lemon body, clear windows, chrome disc with rubber tires, detailed trim tempa, Thailand casting ($3-5)(PC4)
NOTE: premiere & select editions have 2 tone interiors
14. metallic gold body, black interior, clear windows, silver 6-spoke spiral wheels, no tempa, Thailand casting ($10-15)(CH)
15. lavender chrome body, white interior, blue windows, 5 spoke concave star wheels, yellow & blue tempa, Thailand casting ($1-2)(MP)
16. blue body, tan & black interior, clear windows, chrome disc with rubber tires, detailed trim tempa, Thailand casting ($15-20)(GC)
17. gold & metallic red body, gray interior, smoke windows, 5 spoke concave star wheels, no tempa, Thailand casting ($2-4)
18. red body, gray interior, smoke windows, 5 spoke concave star wheels, "Go Bombers! 1997" tempa, Thailand casting ($3-5)(AU)
19. red body, black & brown interior, clear windows, chrome disc with rubber tires, detailed trim with additional brown stripe at rear tempa, Thailand casting ($4-6)(PC1)
20. green & black body, gray interior, clear windows, 5 spoke concave star wheels, no tempa, Thailand casting ($1-2)
21. dark lavender chrome body, white interior, blue windows, 5 spoke concave star wheels, yellow & blue tempa, Thailand casting ($1-2)(MP)
22. purple chrome body, white interior, blue windows, 5 spoke concave star wheels, yellow & orange tempa, Thailand casting ($1-2)(MP)
23. dark purple chrome body, white interior, blue windows, 5 spoke concave star wheels, yellow & orange tempa, Thailand casting ($1-2)(MP)
24. metallic bronze & black body, gray interior, smoke windows, 5 spoke concave star wheels, no tempa, Thailand casting ($1-2)(MW67)
NOTE: Version 24 comes in various shades of metallic gold
25. metallic orange & black body, gray interior, smoke windows, 5 spoke concave star wheels, no tempa, China casting ($1-2) (MW67)
26. dark purple chrome body, white interior, blue windows, 5 spoke concave star wheels, yellow & orange tempa, China casting ($1-2)(MP)

MB 9-A BOAT AND TRAILER, issued 1970
NOTE: Following models with England casting & white interior unless otherwise noted.
1. blue deck, white hull, light blue trailer, no label, 5 spoke wheels ($18-25)
2. blue deck, white hull, dark blue trailer, no label, 5 spoke wheels ($18-25)
3. blue deck, white hull, dark blue trailer, no label, 5 spoke center cut wheels ($3-5)(TP)
4. black deck, white hull, dark blue trailer, no label, 5 spoke center cut wheels ($65-80)(TP)
5. blue deck, white hull, dark blue trailer, "8" label, dot dash wheels ($12-15)(TP)
6. white deck, blue hull, dark blue trailer, "8" label, dot dash wheels ($12-15)(TP)
7. blue deck, white hull, dark blue trailer, no label, dot dash wheels ($3-5)(TP)
8. white deck, blue hull, orange trailer, "8" label, dot dash wheels ($5-8)(TP)
9. white deck, white hull, orange trailer, "8" label, dot dash wheels ($7-10)(TP)
10. blue deck, white hull, orange trailer, no label, dot dash wheels ($5-8)(TP)
11. milk white deck, blue hull, white interior, orange trailer, "8" tempa, dot dash wheels, no origin cast($3-5)(TP)
12. white deck, white hull, gray interior, black trailer, "Seaspray" tempa, dot dash wheels, no origin cast ($3-5)(TP)
13. white deck, white hull, gray interior, dark metallic blue trailer, yellow dashes tempa, dot dash wheels, no origin cast ($3-5)(TP)
14. blue deck, blue hull, gray interior, black trailer, white & orange spatter tempa, dot dash wheels, no origin cast ($3-5)(TP)

MB 9-B AMX JAVELIN, issued 1972
NOTE: All models listed with black air scoop unless noted. Versions 17 & 18 in USA as Limited Edition "Cam Cracker".
1. lime body, lemon interior, unpainted base, doors open, 5 spoke wheels, chrome scoop ($10-15)
2. lime body, lemon interior, unpainted base, doors open, 5 spoke wheels ($5-8)
3. lime body, lemon interior, silver-gray base, doors open, 5 arch wheels ($5-8)
4. lime body, orange interior, unpainted base, doors open, 5 arch wheels ($12-15)
5. lime body, orange interior, silver-gray base, doors open, 5 arch wheels ($12-15)
6. lime body, orange interior, unpainted base, doors open, maltese cross wheels ($12-15)
7. lime body, lemon interior, unpainted base, doors open, maltese cross wheels ($5-8)
8. lime body, white interior, unpainted base, doors open, 5 spoke wheels ($50-75)
9. lime body, blue interior, unpainted base, doors open, 5 arch wheels ($100-150)
10. lime body, yellow-orange interior, unpainted base, doors open, 5 arch wheels ($5-8)
11. lime body, yellow-orange interior, silver-gray base, doors open, 5 arch wheels ($5-8)
12. metallic blue body, lemon interior, unpainted base, doors open, 5 spoke wheels ($5-8)(TP)
13. metallic blue body, yellow-orange interior, unpainted base, doors open, 5 arch wheels ($5-8)(TP)
14. metallic blue body, yellow-orange interior, silver-gray base, doors open, 5 arch wheels ($5-8)(TP)
15. metallic blue body, yellow-orange interior, unpainted base, doors cast, 5 arch wheels ($5-8)(TP)
16. green body, yellow-orange interior, silver-gray base, doors open, 5 arch wheels ($5-8)(TP)
17. blue body, yellow-orange interior, silver-gray base, doors cast, 5 arch wheels, white tempa ($5-8)(LE)
18. blue body, yellow-orange interior, unpainted base, doors cast, 5 arch wheels, white tempa ($5-8)(LE)
19. blue body, yellow-orange interior, unpainted base, doors cast, 5 arch wheels ($5-8)(TP)
20. green body, yellow-orange interior, unpainted base, doors cast, 5 arch wheels ($5-8)(TP)
21. green body, yellow-orange interior, silver-gray base, doors cast, 5 arch wheels ($5-8)(TP)
22. red body, yellow-orange interior, unpainted base, doors cast, 5 arch wheels ($35-50)(TP)
23. red-orange body, yellow-orange interior, unpainted base, doors cast, 5 arch wheels ($35-50)(TP)

MB 9-C FORD ESCORT RS2000, issued 1978
1. white body, black base, tan interior, clear windows, "Dunlop" labels ($3-5)
2. white body, black base, tan interior, amber windows, "Dunlop" labels ($3-5)
3. white body, charcoal base, tan interior, clear windows, "Dunlop" labels ($3-5)
4. white body, charcoal base, tan interior, amber windows, "Dunlop" labels ($3-5)
5. white body, black base, tan interior, clear windows, "Phantom" labels ($7-10)(TP)
6. blue body, black base, tan interior, clear windows, "Phantom" labels ($3-5)(TP)
7. blue body, charcoal base, tan interior, clear windows, "Phantom" labels ($3-5)(TP)
8. blue body, blue-gray base, tan interior, clear windows, "Phantom" labels ($3-5)(TP)
9. white body, black base, red interior, clear windows, "Dunlop" labels ($125-175)
10. green body, charcoal base, tan interior, clear windows, "Seagull" labels ($3-5)(TP)
11. green body, black base, tan interior, clear windows, "Seagull" labels ($3-5)(TP)
12. green body, black base, white interior, clear windows, "Seagull" labels ($3-5)(TP)
13. green body, black base, red interior, clear windows, "Seagull" labels

($125-175)(TP)
14. white body, gray base, pink-tan interior, clear windows, "Dunlop" labels ($3-5)
15. white body, gray-brown base, tan interior, clear windows, "Dunlop" labels ($3-5)
16. dark green body, black base, tan interior, clear windows, "Seagull" labels ($3-5)(TP)

MB 9-D FIAT ABARTH, issued 1982 (USA)
MB74-E FIAT ABARTH, issued 1982 (ROW)
NOTE: All models with clear windows, 5 arch wheels & black base unless otherwise noted.
1. white body, red interior, brown & orange "Matchbox" tempa, England casting ($2-4)
2. white body, red interior, red & orange "Matchbox" tempa, charcoal base, England casting ($2-4)
3. white body, red interior, maroon & orange "Matchbox" tempa, England casting ($2-4)
4. white body, red interior, red & orange "Matchbox" tempa, England casting ($2-4)
5. white body, black interior, red & orange "Matchbox" tempa, England casting ($150-200)
6. white body, red interior, red & orange "Matchbox" tempa, Macau casting ($2-4)
7. white body, red interior, red & orange "Matchbox" tempa, very light amber windows, Macau casting ($2-4)
8. white body, red interior, purple & orange "Matchbox" tempa, Macau casting ($2-4)
9. white body, red interior, purple & orange "Matchbox" tempa, amber windows, Macau casting ($2-4)
10. white body, red interior, green & red "Alitalia" tempa, Macau casting ($3-5)
11. white body, red interior, dark green & red "Alitalia" tempa, charcoal base, amber windows, Macau casting ($3-5)
12. white body, red interior, green & red "Alitalia" tempa, amber windows, Macau casting ($3-5)
13. white body, red interior, dark green & red "Alitalia" tempa, amber windows, Macau casting ($3-5)
14. white body, red interior, red/orange/yellow stripes tempa, Macau casting ($8-12)(DY)
15. white body, red interior, "Matchbox 11" tempa, 4 arch wheels, Manaus casting ($35-50)(BR)
16. white body, red interior, "Matchbox 11" tempa, 8 spoke wheels, Manaus casting ($35-50)(BR)
17. blue body, black base, red interior, clear windows, "Matchbox 16/ Superfast MB" & yellow spatter tempa, Manaus casting ($35-50)(BR)
NOTE: Available as a Bulgarian casting. Assorted colors available ($15-25)

MB 9-F TOYOTA MR2, issued 1986 (USA)
MB74-G TOYOTA MR2, issued 1986 (ROW)
NOTE: All models with white lower body, white base insert, black interior, clear windows & Macau casting
1. white body, 8 dot wheels, "MR2 Pace Car" tempa ($2-4)
2. dark blue body, starburst wheels, "MR2" & pink stripe tempa ($3-5)(SF)
3. metallic dark blue body, laser wheels, "MR2" & pink stripe tempa ($3-5)(LW)
4. green body, 8 dot wheels, "7 Snake Racing Team" tempa ($8-12)(HK)

MB 9-H FAUN DUMP TRUCK, issued 1990 (USA)
MB53-E FAUN DUMP TRUCK, issued 1990 (ROW)
1. yellow body, pearly silver dump, maltese cross wheels, orange stripes tempa, Macau casting ($2-3)
2. yellow body, pearly silver dump, maltese cross wheels, orange stripes tempa, China casting ($2-3)
3. blue body, yellow dump, red maltese cross wheels with yellow hubs, orange stripes & tools tempa, China casting ($3-5)(LL)
4. orange-yellow body, orange-yellow dump, maltese cross wheels, orange stripes tempa, China casting ($2-3)(AP)
5. orange-yellow body, red dump, maltese cross wheels, no tempa, China casting ($1-2)
6. blue body, yellow dump, red maltese cross wheels (plain hubs), orange stripes & tolls tempa, China casting ($3-5)(LL)
7. florescent orange body, silver- gray dump, maltese cross wheels, no tempa, China casting ($1-2)(MP)
8. florescent orange body, black dump, maltese cross wheels, no tempa, China casting ($1-2)
9. met. gold body & dump, maltese cross wheels, no tempa, China casting ($10-15)(CH)

MB10-A PIPE TRUCK, issued 1970
1. red body, chrome base, gray pipes ($30-45)
2. orange body, chrome base, yellow pipes ($18-25)
3. orange body, chrome base, gray pipes ($18-25)
4. orange body, gray base, gray pipes ($18-25)
5. orange body, gray base, yellow pipes ($18-25)

MB10-B PISTON POPPER, issued 1973
1. blue body, unpainted base, no tempa, "Superfast" cast on base ($75-100)
2. blue body, unpainted base, no tempa, "Rola-Matics" cast on base ($7-10)
3. blue body, silver-gray base, no tempa ($8-12)
4. white body, unpainted base, no tempa ($250-300)(MP)
5. yellow body, unpainted base, flames tempa ($5-7)(LE) (issued in USA as "Hot Popper")

MB10-C GRAN FURY POLICE CAR, issued 1979
NOTE: All models with white interior and dot dash wheels unless otherwise noted.
1. white body, unpainted base, amber windows, opaque blue dome lights, "Police" with shield tempa, England casting ($2-4)
2. white body, unpainted base, amber windows, blue dome lights, "Police" with shield tempa, England casting ($2-4)
3. white body, unpainted base, blue windows & dome lights, "Police" with shield tempa, England casting ($2-4)
4. white body, unpainted base, blue windows & dome lights, "Metro" tempa, England casting ($2-4)
5. white body, silver-gray base, blue windows & dome lights, "Metro" tempa, England casting ($2-4)
6. white body, silver-gray base, dark gray windows & dome lights, "Metro" tempa, England casting ($3-5)
7. white body, unpainted base, dark gray windows & dome lights, "Metro" tempa, England casting ($3-5)
8. white body, pearly silver base, dark blue windows & dome lights, "Metro" tempa, Macau casting ($3-5)
9. white body, light gray base, blue windows & dome lights, blue "Police" tempa, Macau casting ($2-4)
10. white body, pearly silver base, blue windows & dome lights, blue "Police" tempa, Macau casting ($2-4)
11. white body, pearly silver base, blue windows & dome lights, blue "Police" tempa, 8 dot wheels, Macau casting ($3-5)
12. white body, pearly silver base, dark blue windows & dome lights, "Police SFPD" tempa, Macau casting ($2-4)
13. white body, pearly silver base, dark blue windows & dome lights, "Sheriff SP-5" tempa, Macau casting ($2-4)(MP)
14. white body, pearly silver base, green windows & dome lights, "Police SFPD" tempa, Macau casting ($75-100)
15. white body, pearly silver base, dark blue windows & dome lights, "Police SFPD" tempa, Thailand casting ($2-4)
16. black & white body, pearly silver base, clear windows, opaque red dome lights, "Adam-12/ Police" tempa, China casting ($4-6)(STR)

MB10-D BUICK LE SABRE, issued 1987
1. black body, white base, red interior, 8 dot wheels, "4" & "355 CID" tempa, Macau casting ($2-4)
2. grape & white body, white base, gray interior, laser wheels, "Ken Wells/ Quicksilver" tempa, white airscoop cast on hood, Macau casting ($5-8)(LW)
3. light pea green body, white base, red interior, 8 dot wheels, "4" & "355 CID" tempa, Macau casting ($3-4)(SC)
4. light brown body, white base, red interior, 8 dot wheels, "4" & "355 CID" tempa, Macau casting ($3-4)(SC)
5. orange body, white base, red interior, 8 dot wheels, "4" & "355 CID" tempa, Macau casting ($3-4)(SC)
6. rose red body, white base, red interior, 8 dot wheels, "4" & "355 CID" tempa, Macau casting ($3-4)(SC)
7. yellow body, red base, gray interior, 8 dot wheels, "10 Shell/ Marshall" tempa, Macau casting (2-3)
8. bright yellow body, red base, gray interior, 8 dot wheels "10 Shell/ Marshall" tempa, Thailand casting ($2-3)
9. bright yellow body, red base, gray interior, 8 dot wheels, "10 Shell/ Marshall" tempa, Thailand casting, large rear side window casting ($25-40)
10. white body, red base, gray interior, 8 dot wheels, "10 Shell/ Marshall" tempa, Thailand casting ($3-5)
11. red body, white base, silver—gray interior, 8 dot wheels, "Total Racing 07 " tempa, Thailand casting ($1-2)(MP)

MB10-F DODGE VIPER, issued 1994 (USA)
MB12-J DODGE VIPER, issued 1994 (ROW)
1. red body, black interior, clear windshield, no tempa, gold 6-spoke spiral wheels, Thailand casting ($1-2)
2. red body, black interior, chrome windshield, detailed trim tempa, gray disc rubber tires, Thailand casting ($2-4)(WC)
3. black body, gray interior, chrome windshield, "Matchbox 1995 Line Preview" tempa, gray disc with rubber tires, Thailand casting ($250-350)(US)
4. red body, black interior, clear windows, no tempa, silver 6-spoke spiral wheels, Thailand casting ($1-2)
5. red body, black interior, smoke windows, no tempa, silver 6-spoke spiral wheels, Thailand casting ($1-2)
6. black body, tan interior, clear windows, no tempa, silver 6-spoke spiral wheels, Thailand casting ($1-2)(MP)
7. yellow body, black/gray interior, clear windows, detailed trim tempa, chrome disc w/rubber tires , Thailand casting ($7-10)(PC1)
8. yellow body, black interior, chrome windows, "California Viper's Club" tempa, gray disc with rubber tires, Thailand casting ($12-18)(US)
9. white body, black interior, clear windows, "69th Shenandoah Apple Blossom Festival 1996" tempa, silver 6-spoke spiral wheels, Thailand casting ($10-12)(US)
10. metallic green body, black/gray interior, clear windows, detailed trim tempa, chrome disc w/rubber tires, Thailand casting ($8-12)(SC1)
11. red body, black/brown interior, clear windows, detailed trim tempa, chrome disc with rubber tires, Thailand casting ($3-5)(PC4)
12. charcoal body, black/gray interior, clear windows, detailed trim tempa, chrome disc with rubber tires, Thailand casting ($7-10)(PC1)(AU)
13. metallic gold body, black interior, clear windows, no tempa, silver 6-spoke spiral wheels, Thailand casting ($10-15)(CH)
14. red body, black & gray interior, clear windows, dual yellow stripes tempa, chrome disc with rubber tires wheels, Thailand casting ($25-50)(GC)
15. red body, black interior, smoke windows, no tempa, 5 spoke concave star wheels with yellow hubs, Thailand casting ($1-2)(MP)
16. red body, black interior, clear windows, "16th Annual Matchbox USA Convention 1997" decals, silver 6 spoke spiral wheels, Thailand casting ($10-15)(C2)
15. red body, black interior, clear windows, no tempa, 5 spoke concave star wheels, Thailand casting ($15-20)
16. green body, tan interior, smoke windows, no tempa, 5 spoke concave star wheels, Thailand casting ($2-3)
17. green body, gray & black interior, clear windows, dual white stripes tempa, chrome disc with rubber tires, Thailand casting ($3-5)(PC12)
18. metallic blue body, black & gray interior, clear windows, dual white stripes tempa, chrome disc with rubber tires, Thailand casting ($3-5)(PC14)
19. black body, black & gray interior, clear windows, dual silver stripes tempa, chrome disc with rubber tires, Thailand casting ($3-5)(SC4)
20. red body, black interior, smoke windows, "Hope Spring Cancer Support Center 1997" tempa, silver 6 spoke wheels, Thailand casting ($15-20)(C2)
21. green body, tan interior, smoke windows, "Hope Spring Cancer Support Center 1997" tempa, 5 spoke concave star wheels, Thailand casting ($85-110)(C2)
22. white body, black interior, clear windows, "Merry Christmas Ad-Ventures" tempa, silver 6 spoke spiral wheels, Thailand casting ($20-25)(C2)
23. yellow body, black interior, smoke windows, no tempa, 5 spoke concave star wheels, Thailand casting ($1-2)(MW56)
24. white body, black & gray interior, clear windows, dual red stripes tempa, chrome disc with rubber tires, Thailand casting ($3-5)(SC5)
25. red body, black interior, clear windows, "Lucent Technologies" tempa, 5 spoke concave star wheels, China casting ($20-40)(ASAP)
26. red body, black interior, smoke windows, no tempa, 5 spoke concave star wheels with yellow hubs, China casting ($1-2)(MP)
27. red body, black interior, clear windows, "A-Pix Entertainment" & "Drive" tempa, 5 spoke concave star wheels, China casting ($100+)(ASAP)
28. yellow body, black interior, smoke windows, no tempa, 5 spoke concave star wheels, China casting ($1-2)(MW56)
29. yellow body, black interior, smoke windows, "Matchbox Forum 1998/ First Shot" tempa, 5 spoke concave star wheels, Thailand casting ($20-25)(C2)
30. white body, black interior, clear windows, "98 White's Guide" tempa, silver 6 spoke spiral wheels, Thailand casting ($25-35)(C2)
31. red body, black interior, smoke windows, "Fiery Driven" tempa, silver 6 spoke spiral wheels, Thailand casting ($100+)(ASAP)
32. red body, black interior, clear windows, no tempa, 5 spoke concave star wheels, China casting ($20-35)(ASAP-blank)
33. red body, black interior, clear windows, "1998 Sales Meeting" tempa, 5 spoke concave star wheels, China casting ($100+)(ASAP)

MB11-A SCAFFOLD TRUCK, issued 1970
1. silver-gray body, red base, green windows, yellow scaffolding ($20-30)

MB11-B FLYING BUG, issued 1972
1. red body, unpainted base, gray windows, squared hood label, 5 spoke front wheels ($15-20)
2. red body, unpainted base, gray windows, heart-shaped hood label, 5 spoke front wheels ($15-20)
3. red body, silver-gray base, gray windows, heart-shaped hood label, 5 spoke front wheels ($18-25)
4. red body, unpainted base, gray windows, heart-shaped hood label, 4 spoke front wheels ($15-20)
5. red body, unpainted base, blue windows, heart-shaped hood label, 5 spoke front wheels ($50-75)

MB11-C CAR TRANSPORTER, issued 1976
NOTE: Cars are listed as front top car, rear top car, bottom car
1. orange body, beige carrier, black base, red/yellow/blue cars, blue windows ($4-6)
2. orange body, beige carrier, black base, red/yellow/dark blue cars, blue windows ($4-6)
3. orange body, beige carrier, black base, yellow/red/blue cars, blue windows ($4-6)
4. orange body, bone white carrier, black base, red/blue/blue cars, blue windows ($7-10)
5. orange body, bone white carrier, black base, red/yellow/blue cars, blue windows ($4-6)
6. orange body, beige carrier, black base, red/yellow/blue cars, blue windows, black hubs ($4-6)
7. orange body, beige carrier, black base, red/yellow/blue cars, green windows ($4-6)
8. orange body, bone white carrier, black base, yellow/yellow/red cars, blue windows ($7-10)
9. orange body, bone white carrier, black base, yellow/yellow/blue cars, blue windows ($7-10)
10. orange body, beige carrier, black base, red/blue/blue cars, blue windows ($7-10)
11. orange body, beige carrier, charcoal base, red/orange-yellow/blue cars, blue windows ($4-6)
12. orange body, beige carrier, charcoal base, red/yellow/blue cars, green windows ($4-6)
13. orange body, beige carrier, black base, red/orange-yellow/blue cars, purple windows ($4-6)
14. orange body, beige carrier, unpainted base, red/orange-yellow/blue cars, purple windows ($4-6)
15. orange body, beige carrier, black base, red/orange-yellow/blue cars, blue-green windows ($4-6)
16. orange body, beige carrier, black base, blue/blue/blue cars, blue windows ($10-15)
17. orange body, beige carrier, black base, yellow/yellow/yellow cars, blue windows ($10-15)

18. orange body, beige carrier, black base, all yellow-orange cars, blue windows ($10-15)
19. orange body, beige carrier, black base, red/red/red cars, blue windows ($10-15)
20. red body, beige carrier, unpainted base, red/orange-yellow/blue cars, blue windows ($4-6)
21. red body, beige carrier, unpainted base, red/orange/blue cars, blue windows ($4-6)
22. red body, beige carrier, unpainted base, red/yellow/dark blue cars, blue windows ($4-6)
23. red body, beige carrier, silver-gray base, red/orange/blue cars, blue windows ($4-6)
24. red body, beige carrier, unpainted base, red/orange/blue cars, purple windows ($4-6)
25. red body, beige carrier, silver-gray base, red/yellow/blue cars, purple windows ($4-6)
26. red body, beige carrier, silver-gray base, red/yellow/blue cars, blue windows ($4-6)
27. red body, beige carrier, silver-gray base, red/yellow/dark blue cars, blue windows ($4-6)
28. red body, beige carrier, black base, red/yellow/dark blue cars, blue windows ($4-6)
29. red body, beige carrier, black base, red/orange-yellow/red cars, blue windows ($7-10)
30. red body, beige carrier, unpainted base, red/yellow/blue cars, purple windows ($4-6)
31. red body, gray carrier, black base, orange-yellow/red/blue cars, blue windows ($4-6)
32. red body, gray carrier, unpainted base, red/red/red cars, blue windows ($10-15)
33. red-orange body, gray carrier, black base, yellow/blue/blue cars, blue windows ($7-10)
34. red-orange body, gray carrier, black base, yellow/red/blue cars, blue windows ($4-6)
35. red-orange body, gray carrier, black base, red/yellow/blue cars, blue windows ($4-6)
36. red-orange body, gray carrier, black base, yellow/red/red cars, blue windows ($7-10)
37. red-orange body, gray carrier, black base, red/yellow/red cars, blue windows ($7-10)
38. red-orange body, gray carrier, black base, red/yellow/dark blue cars, blue windows ($4-6)
39. red-orange body, gray carrier, black base, yellow/red/dark blue cars, blue windows ($4-6)
40. red-orange body, gray carrier, black base, blue/yellow/dark blue cars, blue windows ($7-10)
41. red-orange body, gray carrier, black base, blue/blue/red cars, blue windows ($7-10)
42. orange body, gray carrier, pearly silver base, blue/red/yellow cars, blue windows, Macau casting ($7-10)

MB11-D BOSS MUSTANG, issued 1982 (USA)
1. orange body, outlined "Boss" side tempa ($6-8)
2. orange body, black "Boss" side tempa ($6-8)
3. orange body, white "Boss" side tempa ($6-8)
4. orange body, no side tempa ($6-8)
5. dark orange body, white "Boss" tempa ($6-8)

MB11-E I.M.S.A. MUSTANG, issued 1983 (USA)
MB67-E I.M.S.A. MUSTANG, issued 1983 (ROW)
NOTE: All models with amber windows, chrome interior, dot dash rear wheels unless otherwise noted.
1. black body, black metal base, 5 spoke front wheels, red/white stripes & "Mustang Ford" tempa, Macau casting ($2-3)
2. black body, black metal base, 5 arch front wheels, red/white stripes & "Mustang Ford" tempa, Macau casting ($2-3)
3. black body, black metal base, 5 arch front wheels, yellow & green flames tempa, Macau casting ($1-2)
4. black body, black metal base, 5 spoke front wheels, yellow & green flames tempa, Macau casting ($1-2)
5. black body, black metal base, 5 arch front wheels, yellow & green flames tempa, China casting ($1-2)
6. yellow body, black metal base, 5 arch front wheels, black/red stripes & "47" tempa, China casting ($3-5)(AP)
7. red body, red metal base, 5 arch front wheels, no tempa, China casting ($8-12)(GR)(GS)
8. black body, greenish black metal base, 5 arch front wheels, yellow & green stripes tempa, China casting ($1-2)
9. dark orange body, black metal base, 5 arch front wheels, yellow & blue flames tempa, China casting ($1-2)
10. dark fluorescent orange body, black plastic base, gold 6-spoke spiral front & rear wheels, black squiggly lines tempa, China casting ($1-2)
11. dark florescent orange body, black plastic base, silver 6-spoke spiral front & rear wheels, black squiggly lines tempa , China casting ($1-2)
12. dark florescent orange body, black metal base, 5 arch front & dot dash rear wheels, black squiggly lines tempa, China casting ($15-25)(HU)

MB11-G CHRYSLER ATLANTIC, issued 1997 (USA)
MB34-H CHRYSLER ATLANTIC, issued 1997 (ROW)
NOTE: All models with clear windows & black base unless otherwise noted.
1. metallic tan body, tan interior, 5 spoke concave star wheels, no tempa, Thailand casting ($2-3)
2. metallic tan body, brown interior, 5 spoke concave star wheels, no tempa, Thailand casting ($1-2)(MW19)
3. metallic tan body, brown interior, chrome disc with rubber tires, "Matchbox" and "www.matchboxtoys.com" tempa, Thailand casting ($8-12)
4. metallic tan body, brown interior, chrome disc with rubber tires, detailed trim tempa, China casting ($3-5)(GS)
5. metallic tan body, brown interior, 5 spoke concave star wheels, no tempa, China casting ($1-2)(MW19)
6. metallic gold body, black interior, 5 spoke concave star wheels, no tempa, China casting ($5-10)(CH)
7. metallic gold body, black interior, 5 spoke concave star wheels with black hubs, no tempa, China casting ($25-40)(CH)
8. metallic tan body, brown & tan interior, chrome disc with rubber tires, detailed trim tempa, China casting ($3-5)(GS Chrysler)
9. metallic tan body, tan interior, 5 spoke concave star wheels, "Happy Holidays 1997 from Color Comp Inc." tempa, China casting ($250+)

MB12-A LAND ROVER SAFARI, issued 1970
1. bright blue body, tan roof luggage ($1,000+)
2. gold body, tan roof luggage ($20-35)

MB12-B SETRA COACH, issued 1970
1. gold body, tan roof, clear windows ($18-25)
2. gold body, white roof, clear windows ($15-18)
3. yellow body, white roof, clear windows ($12-15)
4. burgundy body, white roof, clear windows ($12-15)
5. burgundy body, white roof, green windows ($12-15)
6. purple body, white roof, green windows ($12-15)

MB12-C BIG BULL, issued 1975
1. orange body, green blade & base,, orange rollers ($4-6)
2. orange body, green blade & base, yellow rollers ($4-6)
3. orange body, green blade & base, black rollers ($35-50)

MB12-D CITROEN CX, issued 1979
NOTE: All models below with England casting unless otherwise noted.
1. light blue body, cream interior, silver-gray base, blue windows, no tempa ($12-15)
2. light blue body, cream interior, silver-gray base, clear windows, no tempa ($5-8)
3. light blue body, light yellow interior, silver-gray base, clear windows, no tempa ($5-8)
4. light blue body, ivory interior, silver-gray base, clear windows, no tempa ($5-8)
5. light blue body, cream interior, unpainted base, clear windows, no tempa ($5-8)
6. light blue body, cream interior, black base, clear windows, no tempa ($5-8)
7. light blue body, cream interior, charcoal base, clear windows, no tempa ($5-8)
8. light blue body, tan interior, silver-gray base, clear windows, no tempa ($5-8)
9. dark blue body, cream interior, silver-gray base, clear windows, no tempa ($5-8)
10. dark blue body, light yellow interior, silver-gray base, clear windows, no tempa ($5-8)
11. dark blue body, dark yellow interior, silver-gray base, clear windows, no tempa ($5-8)
12. dark blue body, red interior, silver-gray base, clear windows, no tempa ($175-250)
13. metallic blue body, yellow interior, silver-gray base, blue windows, no tempa ($8-12)
14. yellow body, red interior, black base, clear windows, no tempa ($5-8)
15. yellow body, red interior, charcoal base, clear windows, no tempa ($ 5-8)
16. yellow body, red interior, black base, clear windows, blue "Team" tempa ($4-6)(TP)
17. yellow body, red interior, black base, clear windows, black "Team" tempa ($4-6)(TP)
18. yellow body, red interior, charcoal base, clear windows, blue "Team" tempa ($4-6)
19. yellow body, red interior, black base, blue windows, black "Team" tempa ($4-6)(TP)
20. yellow body, red interior, black base, blue windows, no tempa ($5-8)(TP)
21. yellow body, red interior, silver-gray base, clear windows, no tempa ($5-8)(TP)
NOTE: The models below have the rear side windows deleted from the casting.
22. white body, red interior, silver-gray base, blue windows, "Ambulance" tempa ($2-4)
23. white body, red interior, black base, blue windows, "Ambulance" tempa ($2-4)
24. white body, red interior, unpainted base, blue windows, "Ambulance" tempa ($2-4)
25. white body, red interior, silver-gray base, blue windows, "Marine Division" tempa ($2-4)(TP)
26. white body, red interior, unpainted base, blue windows, "Marine Division" tempa ($2-4)(TP)
27. white body, red interior, pearly silver base, blue windows, "Marine Division" tempa, Macau casting ($4-6)(TP)

MB12-E PONTIAC FIREBIRD SE, issued 1982 (USA)
MB51-E PONTIAC FIREBIRD SE, issued 1982 (ROW)
1. dark red body, tan interior, clear windows, 5 arch silver wheels, no tempa, silver-gray base, England casting ($3-5)
2. dark red body, tan interior, amber windows, 5 arch silver wheels, no tempa, silver-gray base, England base ($4-6)
3. dark red body, yellow interior, clear windows, 5 arch silver wheels, no tempa, silver-gray base, England casting ($3-5)
4. dark red body, yellow interior, amber windows, 5 arch silver wheels, no tempa, silver-gray base, England casting ($4-6)
5. dark red body, tan interior, clear windows, dot dash wheels, no tempa, silver-gray base, England casting ($4-6)
6. rose red body, tan interior, clear windows, 5 arch silver wheels, "Firebird" tempa, pearly silver base, Macau casting ($4-6)
7. dark red body, tan interior, clear windows, 5 arch silver wheels, no tempa, pearly silver base, Macau casting ($3-5)
8. black body, tan interior, clear windows, 5 arch silver wheels, "Firebird" tempa, pearly silver base, Macau casting ($3-5)
9. black body, red interior, clear windows, 5 arch silver wheels, "Firebird" tempa, pearly silver base, Macau casting ($2-4)
10. black body, gray interior, clear windows, starburst wheels, "Haley's Comet" tempa, black base, Macau casting ($8-10)(MP)(US)
11. black body, red interior, opaque glow windows, 5 arch gold wheels, "Firebird" tempa, pearly silver base, Macau casting ($10-15)(PS)
12. black body, red interior, clear windows, 5 arch gold wheels, "Firebird" tempa, pearly silver base, Macau casting ($5-8)
13. black body, red interior, opaque glow windows, 5 arch silver wheels, "Firebird" tempa, pearly silver base, Macau casting ($10-15)(PS)
14. blue body, white interior, blue windows, starburst wheels, red/orange/yellow stripes tempa, black base, Macau casting ($8-12)(SF)
15. blue body, white interior, blue windows, starburst wheels, red/orange/yellow stripes tempa, white base, Macau casting ($3-5)(SF)
16. red body, red interior, clear windows, 5 arch silver wheels, "Maaco" labels, pearly silver base, Macau casting ($7-10)(US)
17. metallic blue body, white interior, blue windows, laser wheels, red/orange/yellow stripes tempa, white base, Macau casting ($3-5)(LW)
18. powder blue body, red interior, clear windows, 5 arch silver wheels, green/yellow/white stripes tempa, pearly silver base, Macau casting ($10-15)(DY)
19. purple body, red interior, clear windows, 5 arch silver wheels, "Firebird" tempa, pearly silver base, Macau casting ($3-4)(SC)
20. black body, red interior, clear windows, 5 arch silver wheels, "Firebird" tempa, dark gray plastic base, Macau casting ($3-4)
21. blue body, white interior, blue windows, starburst wheels, red/orange/yellow stripes tempa, white plastic base, Macau casting ($4-6)(SF)
22. black body, dark red interior, clear windows, dot dash wheels, "Firebird" tempa, dark gray plastic base, China casting ($3-5)(MP)
23. black body, dark red interior, clear windows, starburst wheels, "Firebird" tempa, dark gray plastic base, China casting ($3-5)(MP)

MB12-H MERCEDES 500SL CONVERTIBLE, issued 1990 (USA)
MB33-H MERCEDES 500SL CONVERTIBLE, issued 1990 (ROW)
1. silver—gray body, gray base, clear windshield, dark blue interior/tonneau, no tempa, 8 dot wheels, Macau casting ($1-2)
2. silver—gray body, gray base, clear windshield, dark blue tonneau, no tempa, 8 dot wheels, China casting ($1-2)
3. black body, metallic charcoal base, chrome windshield, dark gray interior/tonneau, detailed trim tempa, gray disc with rubber tires, China casting ($5-8)(WC)
4. white body, gray base, clear windshield, brown interior/tonneau, "500SL" tempa, 8 dot wheels, China casting ($1-2)
5. silver-gray body, gray base, chrome windshield, maroon interior/tonneau, detailed trim tempa, gray disc with rubber tires, China casting ($5-8)(WC)
6. silver/gray body, gray base, clear windshield, dark blue interior/tonneau, none tempa, 8 dot wheels, Thailand casting ($1-2)(SP)
7. white body, gray base, clear windshield, brown interior/tonneau, "500SL" tempa, 8 dot wheels, Thailand casting ($1-2)
8. red body, gray base, clear windshield, white interior/tonneau, none tempa, 8 dot wheels, Thailand casting ($2-3)(SS)
9. black body, white base, clear windshield, gray interior/ tonneau, pink & white tempa, 8 dot wheels, Thailand casting ($1-2)(MP)
10. white body, white base, clear windshield, maroon & black interior, black tonneau, detailed trim tempa, chrome disc with rubber tires, China casting ($12-18)(GC)
11. red body, red base, clear windshield, gray & black interior, black tonneau, detailed trim tempa, chrome disc with rubber tires, Thailand casting ($3-5)(PC10)
12. black body, black painted base, clear windshield, brown & black interior, black tonneau, detailed trim tempa, chrome disc with rubber wheels, Thailand base ($3-5)(PC12)
13. dark blue body, dark blue painted base, clear windshield, light & dark gray interior, gray tonneau, detailed trim tempa, chrome disc with rubber tires, Thailand casting ($3-5)(PC16)
14. black body, white base, clear windshield, gray interior/ tonneau , pink & white tempa, 8 dot wheels, China casting ($1-2)(MP)

MB12-K AUDI AVUS QUATTRO, issued 1995 (USA)
MB31-K AUDI AVUS QUATTRO, issued 1995 (ROW)
1. silver body, red interior, clear windows, silver 6-spoke spiral wheels, none tempa, Thailand casting ($1-2)
2. silver body, red/black interior, clear windows, chrome disc w/rubber tires, "Audi Avus" tempa, Thailand casting ($3-4)(PC1)
NOTE: Above model can be found with several wheel patterns including mixed)
3. iridescent white body, red interior, smoke windows, silver 6-spoke spiral wheels, "Avus Quattro" tempa, Thailand casting ($1-2)(MP)
4. iridescent white body, red/black interior, clear windows, chrome disc with rubber tires, "Audi Avus" tempa, Thailand casting ($3-4)(PC4)
5. red body, red/black interior, clear windows, chrome disc with rubber tires, "Audi Avus" tempa, Thailand casting ($3-4)(SC1)
6. copper body, red/black interior, clear windows, chrome disc w/rubber

tires, "Audi Avus" tempa, Thailand casting ($3-4)(PC1)(AU)
7. red chrome body, black interior, smoke windows, 5 spoke concave star wheels, "OOOO Avus" tempa, Thailand casting ($1-2)
8. purple-red chrome body, black interior, smoke windows, 5 spoke concave star wheels, "OOOO Avus" tempa, Thailand casting ($1-2)
9. gold chrome body, black interior, smoke windows, 5 spoke concave star wheels, "OOOO Avus" tempa, Thailand casting ($1-2)(MP)
10. metallic gold body, black interior, clear windows, silver 6 spoke spiral wheels, no tempa, Thailand casting ($5-10)(CH)
11. green chrome body, black interior, smoke windows, 5 spoke concave star wheels, "OOOO Avus" tempa, Thailand casting ($1-2)(MW18-ROW)
12. green chrome body, black interior, smoke windows, 5 spoke concave star wheels, "OOOO Avus" tempa, China casting ($1-2)(MW18-ROW)

MB13-A DODGE WRECK TRUCK, issued 1970
1. pale yellow cab, green rear body, red hook, "BP" labels ($50-65)
2. bright yellow cab, green rear body, red hook, "BP" labels ($50-65)

MB13-B BAJA BUGGY, issued 1971
1. pale green body, orange interior, black exhausts, red flower label ($10-15)
2. pale green body, orange interior, red exhausts, red flower label ($10-15)
3. pale green body, orange interior, black exhausts, orange flower label ($10-15)
4. pale green body, light orange interior, black exhausts, orange flower label ($10-15)
5. pale green body, orange interior, red exhausts, orange flower label ($10-15)
6. pale green body, orange interior, red exhausts, police shield label ($25-40)
7. pale green body, red interior, red exhausts, police shield label ($25-40)
8. pale green body, red interior, red exhausts, orange flower label ($10-15)
9. pale green body, orange interior (from MB47B), red exhausts, orange flower label ($25-40)
10. pale green body, orange interior, red exhausts, no label ($10-15)
11. dark green body, orange interior, red exhausts, orange flower label ($10-15)
12. dark green body, light orange interior, red exhausts, orange flower label ($10-15)
13. dark green body, orange interior, red exhausts, sunburst label ($20-35)
14. lime green body, orange interior, red exhausts, orange flower label ($350-500)(BR)

MB13-C SNORKEL, issued 1977
1. red body, unpainted base, blue windows, yellow boom & bucket ($5-8)
2. red body, silver-gray base, blue windows, yellow boom & bucket ($5-8)
3. red body, unpainted base, amber windows, yellow boom & bucket ($10-15)
4. dark red body, unpainted base, blue windows, yellow boom & bucket ($5-8)
5. dark red body, silver-gray base, blue windows, yellow boom & bucket ($5-8)
6. dark red body, unpainted base, blue windows, white boom & bucket ($5-8)
7. dark red body, unpainted base, blue windows, white boom, yellow bucket ($8-10)
8. dark red body, unpainted base, blue windows, yellow boom, white bucket ($8-10)
9. dark red body, silver-gray base, blue windows, white boom & bucket ($5-8)
10. dark red body, silver-gray base, blue windows, yellow boom, white bucket ($8-10)
11. dark red body, gray base, blue windows, yellow boom & bucket ($50-75)(BR)

MB13-D 4 X 4 OPEN BACK TRUCK, issued 1982 (USA)
MB63-F 4 X 4 OPEN BACK TRUCK, issued 1982 (ROW)
1. orange body, unpainted metal base, light purple windows, "FWD" tempa, England casting ($3-5)
2. orange body, unpainted metal base, orange windows, "FWD" tempa, England casting ($3-5)
3. orange body, unpainted metal base, red windows, "FWD" tempa, England casting ($3-5)
4. yellow body, unpainted metal base, red windows, "4X4" tempa, England casting ($3-5)
5. yellow body, silver-gray metal base, red windows, "4X4" tempa, England casting ($3-5)
6. yellow body, pearly silver metal base, red windows, "4X4 Goodyear" tempa, Macau casting ($2-4)
7. yellow body, pearly silver metal base, red windows, "4X4 Goodrich" tempa, Macau casting ($2-4)
8. white body, pearly silver metal base, red windows, "Bob Jane T-Mart" tempa, Macau casting ($10-15)(AU)
9. white body, black metal base, red windows, "63" & stripes tempa, Macau casting (1-2)
10. white body, black plastic base, red windows, "63" & stripes tempa, Macau casting ($1-2)
11. white body, black plastic base, red windows, "63" & stripes tempa, Thailand casting ($1-2)
12. red body, chrome plastic base, chrome windows, black roll bar, white & black splash & yellow zigzag tempa, Thailand casting ($2-4)(ST)
13. white body, chrome plastic base, chrome windows, pink roll bar, blue & pink design tempa, Thailand casting ($2-4)(ST)
14. metallic blue body, black plastic base, red windows, pink roll bar, pink design tempa, Thailand base ($1-2)(MP)
15. white body, red plastic base, red windows, red roll bar, bat design & dripping blood tempa, Thailand base ($1-2)
NOTE: Some versions issued in #76 Blisterpack as an error ($1-2)
16. metallic purple body, black plastic base, red windows, orange roll bar, skeleton & "Triceratops" tempa, Thailand casting ($1-2)(MP)
17. metallic purple body, black plastic base, red windows, orange roll bar, skeleton & "Triceratops" tempa, China casting ($1-2)(MP)

MB13-F THE BUSTER, issued 1996 (USA)
MB28-M THE BUSTER, issued 1996 (ROW)
NOTE: All models listed with black windows & base unless otherwise noted.
1. metallic blue body, 6-spoke spiral wheels, yellow design tempa, China casting ($1-2)
2. metallic gold body, 6-spoke spiral wheels, no tempa, China casting ($10-15)(CH)
3. purple-maroon body, 5 spoke concave star wheels, yellow & white design tempa, China casting ($1-2)
4. metallic blue body, 6 spoke spiral wheels, yellow design & "American Iron Cruise 97" tempa, China casting ($15-20)(C2)
5. raspberry body, 5 spoke concave star wheels, yellow & white design tempa, China casting ($1-2)
6. metallic green body, 5 spoke concave star wheels, yellow & white design tempa, China casting ($1-2)(MW20)
7. light metallic green body, 5 spoke concave star wheels, yellow & white design tempa, China casting ($1-2)(MW20)

MB13-G KENWORTH T2000, issued 1999
1. metallic red body, clear windows, chrome base, no tempa, chrome disc with rubber tires, China casting ($4-5)(FE)
2. unpainted body, clear windows, chrome base, no tempa, chrome dissce with rubber tires, China casting ($4-5)(FE)

MB14-A ISO GRIFO, issued 1969
1. dark blue body, light blue interior, 5 spoke wheels, unpainted base ($18-25)
2. dark blue body, dark blue interior, 5 spoke wheels, unpainted base ($18-25)
3. dark blue body, white interior, 5 spoke wheels, unpainted base ($18-25)
4. metallic dark blue body, white interior, 5 spoke wheels, unpainted base ($18-25)
5. light blue body, white interior, 5 spoke wheels, unpainted base ($18-25)
6. medium blue body, white interior, 5 spoke wheels, unpainted base ($18-25)
7. medium blue body, white interior, 5 spoke wheels, silver-gray base ($18-25)
8. powder blue body, white interior, 5 spoke wheels, unpainted base ($18-25)(JP)
9. powder blue body, white interior, dot dash wheels, unpainted base ($18-25)(JP)

MB14-B MINI HA HA, issued 1975
1. light blue windows, flesh driver, brown helmet, 4 color labels, maltese cross front wheels ($15-18)
2. light blue windows, flesh driver, brown helmet, 2 color labels, maltese cross wheels front wheels ($15-18)
3. light blue windows, pink driver, brown helmet, 2 color labels, maltese cross front wheels ($15-18)
4. light blue windows, pink driver, brown helmet, 4 color labels, maltese cross front wheels ($15-18)
5. light blue windows, flesh driver, brown helmet, 2 color labels, dot dash front wheels ($15-18)
6. light blue windows, flesh driver, brown helmet, 4 color labels, dot dash front wheels ($15-18)
7. light blue windows, purple driver, brown helmet, 4 color labels, maltese cross front wheels ($15-18)
8. light blue windows, purple driver, chocolate helmet, 4 color labels, maltese cross front wheels ($15-18)
9. light blue windows, flesh driver, chocolate helmet, 4 color labels, maltese cross front wheels ($15-18)
10. dark blue windows, purple driver, brown helmet, 4 color labels, maltese cross front wheels ($15-18)
11. dark blue windows, flesh driver, brown helmet, 4 color labels, maltese cross front wheels ($15-18)
12. dark blue windows, flesh driver, chocolate helmet, 4 color labels, maltese cross front wheels ($15-18)

MB14-C RALLYE ROYALE, issued 1981 (USA)
1. pearly silver body, black base, blue "14" tempa ($7-10)
2. white body, black base, blue & orange "8" tempa ($7-10)

MB14-D LEYLAND TANKER, issued 1982 (ROW)
NOTE: versions 1 to 4 & 6 white cab base & red windows. Version 5 & 7 with black cab base & amber windows.
1. red cab & tank base, white tank, "Elf" labels, England casting ($2-4)
2. red cab & tank base, white tank, "Elf" tempa with red stripe, England casting ($2-4)
3. red cab & tank base, white tank, "Elf" tempa with maroon stripe, England casting ($2-4)
4. red cab & tank base, white tank, "Elf" tempa with brown stripe, England casting ($2-4)
5. yellow cab & tank base, white tank, "Shell" tempa, England casting ($7-10)(JP)
6. red cab & tank base, white tank, "Shell" tempa, England casting ($60-85)
7. black cab & tank, gray tank base, "Gas" tempa, Macau casting ($4-5)(CM)

MB14-E 1983/84 CORVETTE, issued 1983 (USA)
MB69-E 1983/84 CORVETTE, issued 1983 (ROW)
NOTE: Early models cast "1983 Corvette" with later models cast "1984 Corvette"
1. pearly silver upper & lower body, red interior, dot dash wheels, "83 Vette" tempa, Macau casting ($3-5)
2. pearly silver upper & lower body, red interior, 8 dot wheels, "83 Vette" tempa, Macau casting ($3-5)
3. red upper body, light gray lower body, black interior, dot dash wheels, "Vette" & silver/ black stripes tempa, Macau casting ($2-4)
4. red upper body, light gray lower body, black interior, 8 dot wheels, "Vette" & silver/ black stripes tempa, Macau casting ($2-4)
5. red upper body, light gray lower body, black interior, 5 arch wheels, "Vette" & silver/ black stripes tempa, Macau casting ($2-4)
6. red & white upper body, red lower body, black interior, starburst wheels, "350 CID" tempa, Macau casting ($2-4)(SF)
7. red & white upper body, red lower body, black interior, starburst wheels, "350 CID" tempa with "Chef Boyardee" label, Macau casting ($12-18)(US)(OP)
8. red & white upper body, red lower body, black interior, laser wheels, "350 CID" tempa with "Chef Boyardee" label, Macau casting ($75-90)(US)(OP)
9. red & white upper body, red lower body, black interior, laser wheels, "350 CID" tempa, Macau casting ($3-5)(LW)
10. gray upper body, bluish purple lower body, no interior- replaced with light gold plated window armament, starburst wheels, stripes & stars tempa, Macau casting, includes plastic armament ($6-8)(RB)
11. gray upper body, bluish purple lower body, no interior- replaced with dark gold plated window armament, starburst wheels, stripes & stars tempa, Macau casting, includes plastic armament ($6-8)(RB)
12. red upper body, pearly silver lower body, black interior, 8 dot wheels, blue & silver tempa , Macau casting ($8-12)(DY)

MB14-G 1987 CORVETTE, issued 1987 (USA)
MB28-G 1987 CORVETTE, issued 1990 (ROW)
1. yellow upper & lower body, black interior, clear windshield, 8 dot wheels, "Corvette" & logo tempa, Macau casting ($2-3)
2. white & red upper body, red lower body, black interior, clear windshield, laser wheels, "350 CID" tempa, Macau casting ($3-5)(LW)
3. white & red upper body, red lower body, black interior, clear windshield, starburst wheels, "350 CID" tempa, Macau casting ($3-5)(SF)
4. rose red upper & silver-gray lower body, black interior, clear windshield, 8 dot wheels, "Corvette" & logo tempa, Macau casting ($3-4)(SC)
5. orange upper & silver-gray lower body, black interior, clear windshield, 8 dot wheels, "Corvette" & logo tempa, Macau casting ($3-4)(SC)
6. lemon upper & lower body, black interior, clear windshield, 8 dot wheels, "Corvette" & logo tempa, Macau casting ($1-2)
7. metallic blue upper & lower body, black & gray interior, chrome windshield, gray disc with rubber tires, "Corvette" tempa, Macau casting ($5-8)(WC)
8. red upper & lower body, black interior, clear windshield, 8 dot wheels, flames tempa, Macau casting ($7-10)(US)(OP)
9. orange-yellow upper & lower body, black interior, clear windshield, 8 dot wheels, "Corvette" & logo tempa, Thailand casting ($1-2)
10. orange-yellow upper & lower body, black interior, clear windshield, 6-spoke ringed wheels, "Corvette" & logo tempa, Thailand casting ($60-85)
11. white upper & lower body, dark pink interior, clear windshield, 8 dot wheels, stripes & zigzags tempa, Thailand casting ($2-4)(DM)
12. lime upper & lower body, black interior, clear windshield, gray disc with rubber tires, "Rally Official- Joe Bulgin" tempa, Thailand casting ($6-8)(WP)
13. red upper & lower body, black interior, clear windshield, 8 dot wheels, "Corvette" & Chevy logo tempa, Thailand casting ($1-2)
14. blue-green upper & lower body, black interior, clear windshield, 8 dot wheels, "Corvette" tempa, Thailand casting ($2-4)(SS)
15. white upper & lower body, maroon interior, chrome windshield, gray disc rubber tires, detailed trim tempa, Thailand casting ($2-4)(WC)
16. purplish upper & lower body, black interior, clear windshield, 8 dot wheels, "Corvette" tempa, Thailand casting ($2-4)(GS)
17. black upper & lower body, neon yellow interior, clear windshield, gold 6-spoke spiral wheels, pink & yellow design tempa, Thailand casting ($1-2)
18. black upper & lower body, red interior & base insert , clear windshield, silver 6-spoke spiral wheels, detailed trim tempa, Thailand casting ($2-4)(CC)
19. red upper & lower body, black interior, clear windshield, 8 dot wheels, "Corvette" & "Matchbox Line Preview 1994" tempa, Thailand casting ($250-350)(US)
20. black upper & lower body, neon yellow interior, clear windshield, silver 6-spoke spiral wheels, pink & yellow design tempa, China casting ($1-2)
21. white upper & lower body, blue interior, clear windshield, silver 6-spoke spiral wheels, orange & blue design tempa, China casting ($1-2)
22. metallic lavender upper & lower body, orange interior, clear windshield, 5 spoke concave star wheels, white design tempa, China casting ($1-2)
23. red upper & lower body, black & red interior, clear windshield, chrome disc with rubber tires, detailed trim tempa, China casting ($8-12)(UC)
24. bright green upper & lower body, white interior with pink side molding, clear windshield, 5 spoke concave star wheels, "70th Shenandoah Apple Blossom Festival 1997" tempa, China casting ($12-15)(US)
25. black upper & lower body, red & black interior, clear windshield, chrome disc with rubber tires, "Corvette Cologne" tempa, China casting ($10-15)(US)
26. black upper & lower body, red & black interior, clear windshield, chrome disc with rubber wheels, detailed trim tempa, China casting ($3-5)(CP)
27. yellow upper & lower body, black & gray interior, clear windshield, chrome disc with rubber wheels, detailed trim tempa, China casting ($3-5)(CP)
28. metallic gold upper & lower body, black interior, clear windshield, 5

spoke concave star wheels, no tempa, China casting ($5-10)(CH)
29. dark green upper & lower body, black & gray interior, clear windshield, chrome disc with rubber tires, detailed trim tempa, China casting ($3-5)(CP)
30. green-gold upper & lower body, gray & black interior, clear windshield, chrome disc with rubber tires, detailed trim tempa, China casting ($3-5)(CP)
31. purple upper & lower body, gray & black interior, clear windshield, chrome disc with rubber tires, detailed trim tempa, China casting ($3-5)(CP)
32. metallic light bronze upper & lower body, gray & black interior, clear windshield, chrome disc with rubber tires, detailed trim tempa, China casting ($3-5)(CP)
33. metallic red upper & lower body, gray & black interior, clear windshield, chrome disc with rubber tires, detailed trim tempa, China casting ($3-5)(CP)
34. bright blue upper & lower body, black & red interior, clear windshield, black disc with rubber tires, white stripes tempa, China casting ($3-5)(PC15)
35. black upper body, green-gold lower body, gray & black interior, clear windshield, gold 6 spoke spiral wheels, no tempa, China casting ($100+)(CHI)
34. metallic light bronze upper & lower body, neon yellow interior, clear windshield, gold 6 spoke spiral wheels, no tempa, China casting ($100+)(CHI)

MB15-A VOLKSWAGEN 1500, issued 1969
1. cream body, "137" decals on sides, front bumper with decal ($18-25)
2. cream body, "137" labels on sides, front bumper with decal ($18-25)
3. off white body, "137" decals on sides, front bumper with decal ($18-25)
4. off white body, "137" labels on sides, front bumper with decal ($18-25)
5. red body, "137" labels on sides, front bumper with decals ($20-35)
6. red body, "137" labels on sides, front bumper with cast design ($20-35)
7. off white body, "137" labels on sides, front bumper with cast design ($7-10)(JP)

MB15-B FORK LIFT TRUCK, issued 1972
NOTE: Casting A with plastic steering wheel, Casting B with steering wheel cast to body, Casting C with roof cast
1. red body, casting A, black base, gray forks, yellow hoist, "Lansing" labels ($10-15)
2. red body, casting A, unpainted base, gray forks, yellow hoist, "Lansing" labels ($10-15)
3. red body, casting A, green base, gray forks, yellow hoist, "Lansing" labels ($10-15)
4. red body, casting A, charcoal base, gray forks, yellow hoist, "Lansing" labels ($10-15)
5. red body, casting A, unpainted base, gray forks, yellow hoist, "T6AD" labels ($250-400)(BR)
NOTE: Above models with spiro front wheels and five spoke rear wheels. All others except version 6 with dot dash front and rear wheels.
6. red body, casting A, black base, gray forks, yellow hoist, "Lansing" labels, spiro front wheels, dot dash rear wheels ($10-15)
7. red body, casting A, black base, gray forks, yellow hoist, "Lansing" labels ($10-15)
8. red body, casting A, unpainted base, gray forks, yellow hoist, "Lansing" labels ($10-15)
9. red body, casting A, charcoal base, yellow forks, unpainted hoist, "Lansing" labels ($10-15)
10. red body, casting A, black base, yellow forks, unpainted hoist, "Lansing" labels ($10-15)
11. red body, casting B, black base, yellow forks, unpainted hoist, "Lansing" labels ($10-15)
12. red body, casting B, black base, gray forks, unpainted hoist, "Lansing" labels ($10-15)
13. red body, casting B, black base, red long forks, unpainted hoist, "Lansing" labels ($18-25)(KS)
14. red body, casting B, unpainted base, red long forks, unpainted hoist, "Lansing" labels ($18-25)(KS)
15. red body, casting B, unpainted base, black forks, unpainted hoist, "Lansing" labels ($10-15)
16. red body, casting C, black base, black forks, unpainted hoist, "Hi Lift" labels, black roof ($10-15)
17. orange body, casting C, unpainted base, black forks, unpainted hoist,, "Hi Lift" labels, black roof ($10-15)
18. orange body, casting C, silver-gray base, black long forks, unpainted hoist, "Hi Lift" labels ($18-25)(KS)
19. orange body, casting C (roof omitted), black base, black forks, unpainted hoist,, "Hi Lift" labels, black roof ($10-15)
20. orange body, casting C, silver-gray base, black forks, unpainted hoist, "Hi Lift" labels, black roof ($10-15)
21. pink-orange body, casting C, black base, black forks, unpainted hoist,, "Hi Lift" labels, black roof ($10-15)

MB15-C HI HO SILVER, issued 1981 (USA)
1. pearly silver body, black base, red interior, "Hi Ho Silver" tempa, Hong Kong casting ($7-10)

MB15-D FORD SIERRA, issued 1983 (USA)
MB55-E FORD SIERRA, issued 1983 (ROW)
MB40-E FORD SIERRA, reissued 1990 (USA)
1. white body, dark gray lower body, clear windows, gray metal base, white interior, gray hatch, black door posts, 8 dot silver wheels, England casting ($85-100)
2. white body, dark gray lower body, clear windows, gray metal base, red interior, gray hatch, black door posts, 8 dot silver wheels, England casting ($3-5)
3. white body, dark gray lower body, clear windows, gray metal base, red interior, gray hatch, plain door posts, 8 dot silver wheels, England casting ($3-5)
4. white body, dark gray lower body, clear windows, gray metal base, red interior, white hatch, black door posts, 8 dot silver wheels, England casting ($3-5)
5. white body, dark gray lower body, clear windows, gray metal base, red interior, white hatch, plain door posts, 8 dot silver wheels, England casting ($3-5)
6. silver—gray body, dark gray lower body, clear windows, gray metal base, red interior, gray hatch, "Ford XRi Sport" tempa, 8 dot silver wheels, England casting ($3-5)
7. silver—gray body, dark gray lower body, clear windows, gray metal base, red interior, gray hatch, "Ford XRi Sport" tempa, 5 crown wheels, Macau casting ($2-3)
8. pearly silver body, dark gray lower body, amber windows, gray metal base, red interior, gray hatch, "Ford XRi Sport" tempa, dot dash wheels, Macau casting ($2-3)
9. black body, dark gray lower body, clear windows, gray metal base, black interior, black hatch, white & green stripes with "85" tempa, starburst wheels, Macau casting ($3-4)(SF)
10. yellow body, black lower body, clear windows, black metal base, black interior, black hatch, "XR 4X4" tempa, 8 dot gold wheels, Macau casting ($5-8)
11. yellow body, black lower body, clear windows, black metal base, black interior, black hatch, "XR 4X4" tempa, 8 dot silver wheels, Macau casting ($5-8)
12. yellow body, dark gray lower body, clear windows, black metal base, red interior, gray hatch, "XR 4X4" tempa, 8 dot gold wheels, Macau casting ($35-50)
13. yellow body, dark gray lower body, clear windows, dark gray metal base, red interior, gray hatch, "XR 4X4" tempa, 8 dot silver wheels, Macau casting ($35-50)
14. yellow body, dark gray lower body, clear windows, dark gray metal base, red interior, gray hatch, "XR 4X4" tempa, 8 dot gold wheels, Macau casting ($35-50)
15. yellow body, dark gray lower body, clear windows, dark gray metal base, red interior, gray hatch, "XR 4X4" tempa, dot dash wheels, Macau casting ($35-50)
16. cream body, dark gray lower body, clear windows, dark gray metal base, black interior, black hatch, "55" & black band tempa, 8 dot silver wheels, Macau casting ($8-12)
17. metallic green body, dark gray lower body, clear windows, dark gray metal base, black interior, black hatch, white & gold stripe tempa, laser wheels, Macau casting ($3-4)(LW)
18. dark blue body, black lower body, clear windows, black metal base, black interior, black hatch, "Duckham's Race Team" tempa, 8 dot silver wheels, Macau casting ($3-5)(TC)
19. white body, red lower body, clear windows, red metal base, red interior, red hatch, "Virgin Atlantic" tempa, 8 dot silver wheels, Macau casting ($3-5)(GS)
20. yellow body, dark gray lower body, amber windows, gray metal base, gray hatch, "XR 4X4" tempa, 8 dot silver wheels, Macau casting ($35-50)
21. black body, black lower body, clear windows, black metal base, red interior, black hatch, "Texaco 6/ Pirelli" tempa, 8 dot silver wheels, Macau casting ($2-3)
22. red body, black lower body, clear windows, black metal base, black interior, black hatch, "Tizer The Appetizer" tempa, 8 dot silver wheels, Macau casting ($3-5)(TC)
23. red body, black lower body, clear windows, black plastic base, black interior, black hatch, "Tizer The Appetizer" tempa, 8 dot silver wheels, Macau casting ($3-5)(TC)
24. red body, black lower body, black windows, black plastic base, no interior, black hatch, "Fire Dept." tempa, 8 dot silver wheels, amber dome lights, Macau casting ($8-12)(SR)
25. red body, black lower body, black windows, black plastic base, no interior, black hatch, "Fire Dept." tempa, 8 dot silver wheels, greenish yellow dome lights, Macau casting ($8-12)(SR)
26. yellow-orange body, black lower body, black windows, black plastic base, no interior, black hatch, "Airport Security" tempa, 8 dot silver wheels, red dome lights, Macau casting ($8-12)(SR)
27. yellow-orange body, black lower body, black windows, black plastic base, no interior, black hatch, "Airport Security" tempa, 8 dot silver wheels, green dome lights, Macau casting ($18-25)(SR)
28. white body, white lower body, black windows, black plastic base, no interior, white hatch, "Sheriff" tempa, 8 dot silver wheels, red dome lights, Macau casting ($8-12)(SR)
29. black body, black lower body, clear windows, black plastic base, red interior, black hatch, "Texaco 6/ Pirelli" tempa, 8 dot silver wheels, Macau casting ($2-3)
30. white body, red lower body, clear windows, red plastic base, black interior, red hatch, "Virgin Atlantic" tempa, 8 dot wheels, Macau casting ($3-5)
31. metallic green body, dark gray lower body, clear windows, black plastic base, black interior, black hatch, white & gold stripes tempa, laser wheels, Macau casting ($3-5)(LW)
32. metallic green body, dark gray lower body, clear windows, black plastic base, black interior, black hatch, white & gold stripes tempa, starburst wheels, Macau casting ($8-12)(SF)
33. black body, black lower body, clear windows, red interior, black plastic base, black hatch, "Texaco 6/ Pirelli" tempa, 8 dot silver wheels, Thailand casting ($1-2)
34. red body, yellow lower body, clear windows, black plastic base, blue hatch, 3 faces & lion head tempa, 8 dot red wheels, Thailand casting ($15-18)(LL)
35. white body, red lower body, clear windows, red plastic base, black interior, red hatch, "Virgin Atlantic" tempa, 8 dot silver wheels, Thailand casting ($2-3)
36. black body, dark gray lower body, clear windows, gray plastic base, black interior, black hatch, white & green stripes with "85" tempa, starburst wheels, Macau casting ($3-4)(SF)
37. black body, dark gray lower body, amber windows, gray plastic base, black interior, black hatch, white & green stripes with "85" tempa, starburst wheels, Macau casting ($3-4)(SF)
38. white body, black lower body, clear window, black plastic base, red interior, black hatch, "Gemini/ N. Cooper/ 1" tempa, Thailand casting ($2-3)
39. white body, red lower body, red plastic base, red interior, clear windows, red hatch, 8 dot silver wheels, "Virgin Atlantic" tempa, Thailand casting ($12-15)
40. white body, black lower body, black plastic base, no interior, black windows, black hatch, 8 dot silver wheels, red dome lights, "Police" tempa, China casting ($1-2)(LS)
41. yellow body, black lower body, black plastic base, no interior, black windows, black hatch, 8 dot silver wheels, greenish yellow dome lights, "Matchbox Taxi Co. 555-7800" tempa, China casting ($3-5)(LS)

MB15-E PEUGEOT 205 TURBO, issued 1984 (ROW)
MB25-G PEUGEOT 205 TURBO, reissued 1991 (ROW)
NOTE: All models with clear windows, silver-gray interior & 8 spoke wheels unless noted otherwise.
1. white body, white base, red "205" with stripes tempa, Macau casting ($2-4)
2. white body, white base, black "205" with stripes tempa, Macau casting ($2-4)
3. white body, white base, dark purple "205" with stripes tempa, Macau casting ($2-4)
4. white body, white base, purple "205" with stripes tempa, China casting ($2-4)
5. white body, white base, black "205" & "Matchbox 11" tempa, Manaus casting ($35-40)(BR)
6. white body, white base, black "205" tempa, Manaus casting ($25-40)(BR)
7. orange-red body, dark gray base, "48 Michelin/ Bilstein" tempa, China casting ($2-4)
8. green body, dark gray base, no tempa, China casting ($8-12)(GR)(GS)
9. yellow body, dark gray base, "Peugeot 205/ 48 Bilstein" tempa, China casting ($2-4)
10. dark gray body, dark gray base, "Shell 37" pink & yellow design tempa, Manaus casting ($35-45)(BR)

MB15-F SAAB 9000, issued 1988 (USA)
MB22-F SAAB 9000, issued 1988 (ROW)
1. metallic red body, brown interior, black base, 8 dot wheels, no tempa, Macau casting ($1-2)
2. metallic blue body, gray interior, black base, laser wheels, "Saab Turbo" & stripes tempa, Macau casting ($7-10)(LW)
3. metallic red body, brown interior, black base, 8 dot wheels, no tempa, China casting ($1-2)
4. metallic pink-red body, brown interior, black base, 8 dot wheels, no tempa, China casting ($1-2)
5. white body, brown interior, white base, 8 dot wheels, "Saab 22" & stripes tempa, China casting ($2-4)
6. dark blue body, brown interior, dark blue base, 8 dot wheels, no tempa, China casting ($8-12)(GR)(GS)
7. silver-gray body, brown interior, white base, 8 dot wheels, "Saab 22" & stripes tempa, China casting ($8-10)(GS)
8. dark cream body, yellow & brown interior, black base, chrome disc with rubber tires, detailed trim tempa, China casting ($8-12)(UC)

MB15-H ALFA ROMEO SZ, issued 1991 (USA)
MB 6-G ALFA ROMEO SZ, issued 1991 (ROW)
NOTE: All models with black base, tan interior, smoke gray windows & 8 dot wheels.
1. red body, black painted roof, China casting ($2-3)
2. dull red body, black painted roof, China casting ($2-3)
3. red body, plain roof, China casting ($8-12)(GR)(GS)
4. red body, black painted roof, "Alfa Romeo" tempa, China casting ($1-2)
5. red body, plain roof, "Alfa Romeo" tempa, China casting ($1-2)
6. lime body, plain roof, "Alfa Romeo" tempa, China casting ($8-10)(GS)
7. blue body, "Go Eagles! 1997" tempa, China casting ($3-5)(AU)

MB15-I SUNBURNER, issued 1992 (USA)
MB41-I SUNBURNER, issued 1992 (ROW)
1. florescent yellow body, black interior, sun & flames tempa, China casting ($2-4)
2. white body, black interior, sun & flames tempa, China casting ($8-10)(GS)
3. blue body, black interior, white stripes tempa, China casting ($2-4)

MB15-J MUSTANG MACH III, issued 1994 (USA)
MB28-K MUSTANG MACH III, issued 1994 (ROW)
NOTE: All models with black painted windshield unless otherwise noted.
1. red body, red hood, black interior, gold 6-spoke spiral wheels, dark blue/white/black design tempa, Thailand casting ($1-2)
2. red body, red hood, black interior, gold 6-spoke spiral wheels, light blue/white/ black design tempa, Thailand casting ($1-2)
3. red body, red hood, black interior, gray disc with rubber tires, detailed trim tempa, Thailand casting ($2-4)(WC)
4. yellow body, yellow hood, black interior, gold 6-spoke spiral wheels, "Nationwise Auto Parts" tempa ($15-25)(US)
5. iridescent white body & hood, black interior, silver 6-spoke spiral wheels, "Ice Crusher" tempa, Thailand casting ($7-10)(PS)

6. red body & hood, black interior, silver 6-spoke spiral wheels, light blue/ white & black design tempa, Thailand casting ($1-2)
7. metallic red body & hood, black interior, silver 6-spoke spiral wheels, "Mach III" tempa, Thailand casting ($1-2)(MP)
8. dark purple body & hood, orange interior, silver 6-spoke spiral wheels, green stripes & silver windshield tempa, gray base, Thailand casting ($1-2)(MP)
9. black body & hood, red interior, silver 6-spoke spiral wheels, dark blue/ white & black design tempa, Thailand casting ($1-2)
10. white body, blue hood, black interior,, 5 spoke concave star wheels, red stripes & blue stars tempa, Thailand casting ($1-2)
11. metallic gold body & hood, black interior, silver 6 spoke spiral wheels, no tempa, Thailand casting ($5-10)(CH)
12. powder blue body & hood, black interior, 5 spoke concave star wheels, dark orange stripe tempa, Thailand casting ($1-2)(MP)
13. metallic green body & hood, light tan & brown interior, chrome disc with rubber tires, silver-gray windshield, detailed trim & "Mach III" tempa, Thailand casting ($3-5)(PC2-ROW)
14. metallic blue body & hood, ivory & blue interior, chrome disc with rubber tires, silver-gray windshield, detailed trim & "Mach III" tempa, Thailand casting ($3-5)(PC12)
15. yellow body & hood, black & blue interior, chrome disc with rubber tires, detailed trim tempa, Thailand casting ($15-20)(GC)
16. white body, red hood, red interior, 5 spoke concave star wheels, blue stripes & white stars tempa, Thailand casting ($1-2)(MW4)
17. white body, red hood, red interior, 5 spoke concave star wheels, blue stripes & white stars tempa, China casting ($1-2)(MW4)

MB15-K FORD TRANSIT VAN, issued 1995 (ROW)

NOTE: All models listed with gray interior & China casting unless noted

1. white body, gray base, "Fastway Couriers" tempa ($5-7)(AU)
2. light blue body, gray base, surfing scene tempa ($2-3)
3. white body, gray base, "Parcel Post" tempa ($4-6)(AU)
4. white body, black base, "SLP Engineering Ltd." (both sides) tempa ($12-18)(LD)(UK)
5. white body, black base, "SLP Engineering Ltd./ Lowestoft" tempa ($12-18)(LD)(UK)
6. white body, black base, "Evening Gazette" tempa ($12-18)(LD)(UK)
7. white & orange body, black base, "Grafi Press" tempa ($15-18)(DU)
8. white body, black base, "Scooter's Snowboard Shoppe" tempa ($12-18)(LD)(US)
9. black body with red roof, red base, "North Sydney Bears" tempa ($10-15)(AU)
10. black body with red roof, red base, "Balmain Tigers" tempa ($10-15)(AU)
11. black body with red roof, red base, "Gold Coast Seagulls" tempa ($10-15)(AU)
12. black body with dark blue roof, dark blue base, "Canterbury- Bankstown Bulldogs" tempa ($10-15)(AU)
13. black body with light blue roof, light blue base, "Cronulla Sharks" tempa ($10-15)(AU)
14. bright blue body with red roof, red base, "Eastern Suburbs Roosters" tempa ($10-15)(AU)
15. bright blue body with yellow roof, yellow base, "Parramatta Eels" tempa ($10-15)(AU)
16. dark gray body with white roof, dark blue base, "North Queensland Cowboys" tempa ($10-15)(AU)
17. green body with red roof, red base, "South Sydney Rabbitohs" tempa ($10-15)(AU)
18. green body with blue roof, blue base, "Auckland Warriors" tempa ($10-15)(AU)
19. lime body with yellow roof, yellow base, "Canberra Raiders" tempa ($10-15)(AU)
20. lemon body with red roof, red base, "Penrith Panthers" tempa ($10-15)(AU)
21. light yellow body with purple roof, purple base, "Brisbane Broncos" tempa ($10-15)(AU)
22. red body with yellow roof, yellow base, "Western Reds" tempa ($10-15)(AU)
23. red body with gold roof, gold base, "South Queensland Crushers" tempa ($10-15)(AU)
24. plum body with white roof, white base, "Manly Sea Eagles" tempa ($10-15)(AU)
25. white body, black base, "Western Suburbs Magpies" tempa ($10-15)(AU)
26. white body, orange base, "Illawarra Steelers" tempa ($10-15)(AU)
27. white body with red roof, black base, "St. George Dragons" tempa ($10-15)(AU)
28. white body with bright blue roof, black base, "Newcastle Knights" tempa ($10-15)(AU)
29. white body, black base, "Rentokil Initial" tempa ($12-15)(UK)(LD)
30. white body, black base, "Hannant's" tempa ($12-15)(UK)(LD)
31. white body, black base, "Coldseal" tempa ($12-15)(UK)(LD)
32. white body, black base, "NSVA Van Nationals Billing Northampton" tempa ($15-20)(UK)(LD)
33. white body, black base, "NSVA Van 23 Years on the Road Members Van" tempa ($25-40)(UK)(LD)
34. white body, black base, "NSVA Van 23 Years on the Road Committee Van" tempa ($100-150)(UK)(LD)
35. white body, black base, "NGK- The World's Only" tempa ($50-75)(UK)(LD)
36. white body, black base, "Phoenix Natural Gas" tempa ($12-15)(UK)(LD)
37. white body, black base, "Starlec" tempa ($12-15)(UK)(LD)
38. white body, black base, "Ultra Link" tempa ($125-175)(UK)(LD)
39. white body, black base, "Euro Dollar" tempa ($12-15)(UK)(LD)
40. white body, black base, "EFI Disc Brakes" tempa ($12-15)(UK)(LD)
41. white body, black base, "Morgan Lovell" tempa ($12-15)(UK)(LD)
42. white body, black base, "Standish Van Hire" tempa ($12-15)(UK)(LD)
43. white body, black base, "Windscreen Auto" tempa ($100-150)(UK)(LD)
44. white body, black base, "Abbey Stainless" tempa ($12-15)(UK)(LD)
45. white body, white interior, black base, no tempa ($20-25)(ASAP-blank)
46. white body, black base, "Rotamole/ Pitmole" tempa ($100-175)(UK)(LD)
47. white body, black base, "Envelopes UK" tempa ($12-15)(UK)(LD)
48. white body, black base, "NSVA 25th Anniversary- Committee Van" tempa ($100-150)(UK)(LD)
49. white body, black base, "NSVA- 25 Years of Vanning" tempa ($15-20)(UK)(LD)
50. white body, black base, "National Windscreens" tempa ($12-15)(UK)(LD)
51. white body, black base, "Poltransplant Navartis" tempa ($85-110)(Poland)(LD)
52. white body, black base, "Panasonic Colin Smith" tempa ($12-15)(UK)(LD)
53. white body, blue base, surfing scene tempa ($1-2)(MW5-ROW)
54. white body, black base, "Hankook Tyres" with black roof logo tempa ($15-20)(Malta)(LD)
55. white body, black base, "Hankook Tyres" with blue roof logo tempa ($15-20)(Malta)(LD)
56. white body, black base, "Hankook Tyres" with red roof logo tempa ($100-150)(Malta)(LD)
57. white body, black base, "Hankook Tyres" with orange roof logo tempa ($100-150)(Malta)(LD)
58. white body, white interior, black base, "Smith Kline Beecham" tempa ($50+)(ASAP)
59. white body, white interior, black base, "American International Recovery" tempa ($100+)(ASAP)
60. black body, white interior, silver-gray base, blue windows, "Stegosaurus" & skeleton tempa ($1-2)(MP)
61. white body, black base, "Eurolines" tempa ($12-15)(UK)(LD)
62. white body, white interior, black base, "Lincare" tempa ($100+)(ASAP)
63. white body, white interior, black base, "Precision Cargo" tempa, China casting ($75+)(ASAP)

MB16-A BADGER, issued 1974

1. bronze body, silver-gray base insert, green windows, chrome antennae ($8-10)
2. bronze body, light gray base insert, green windows, cream antennae ($4-6)
3. olive drab body, light gray base insert, green windows, cream antennae ($65-80)(TP)
4. olive body, light gray base insert, green windows, cream antennae ($5-7)(TP)
5. bronze body, dark gray base insert, green windows, cream antennae ($4-6)
6. bronze body, dark gray base insert, blue-green windows, cream antennae ($4-6)
7. bronze body, black base insert, blue-green windows, cream antennae ($4-6)
8. bronze body, black base insert, green windows, cream antennae ($4-6)
9. bronze body, black base insert, green windows, ivory antennae ($4-6)
10. bronze body, dark gray base insert, green windows, ivory antennae ($4-6)
11. bronze body, dark gray base insert, blue-green windows, black antennae ($4-6)
12. bronze body, dark gray base insert, green windows, black antennae ($4-6)
13. bronze body, black base insert, green windows, black antennae ($4-6)
14. bronze body, black base insert, purple windows, black antennae ($5-8)

MB16-B PONTIAC, issued 1979

1. tan body, unpainted base, dark tan hood label, dot dash wheels ($5-8)
2. tan body, unpainted base, brown hood label, dot dash wheels ($5-8)
3. light tan body, unpainted base, olive hood label, dot dash wheels ($5-8)
4. metallic tan body. unpainted base, chocolate hood label, dot dash wheels ($5-8)
5. green-gold body, unpainted base, olive hood label, dot dash wheels ($5-8)
6. green-gold body, unpainted base, olive hood label, 5 crown wheels ($5-8)
7. green-gold body, unpainted base, olive hood label, 5 arch wheels ($5-8)
8. green-gold body, unpainted base, no hood label, dot dash wheels ($5-8)
9. green-gold body, unpainted base, chocolate hood label, dot dash wheels ($5-8)
10. green-gold body, unpainted base, brown hood label, dot dash wheels ($5-8)
11. dark gold body, unpainted base, chocolate hood label, dot dash wheels ($5-8)
12 dark gold body, unpainted base, chocolate hood label, 5 arch wheels ($5-8)
13. dark gold body, unpainted base, olive hood label, 5 arch wheels ($5-8)
14. dark gold body, unpainted base, brown hood label, dot dash wheels ($5-8)
15. dark gold body, unpainted base, olive hood tempa, dot dash wheels ($5-8)
16. white body, unpainted base, blue hood tempa, dot dash wheels ($4-6)
17. white body, unpainted base, purple hood tempa, dot dash wheels ($4-6)
18. white body, unpainted base, no hood tempa, dot dash wheels ($4-6)
19. white body, silver-gray base, blue hood tempa, dot dash wheels ($4-6)
20. white body, silver-gray base, blue hood tempa, 5 crown wheels ($4-6)
21. white body, pearly silver base, blue hood tempa, dot dash wheels, Macau casting ($4-6)
22. dark blue body, silver-gray base, no tempa, dot dash wheels, Manaus casting ($50-75)(BR)

NOTE: Available as a Bulgarian casting. Assorted colors available ($15-25)

MB16-D F.1 RACER, issued 1984 (USA)
MB 6-D F.1 RACER, issued 1984 (ROW)

NOTE: in 1985 an identical casting to MB 16-D was released in the USA only as MB65-D. Both models ran concurrently in the US range. Only certain variations appear on either model and are listed accordingly. English release models are listed here. See wheel type chart for wheel reference types. Chrome and unchromed wheels refers to the lettering on the wheel sides.

1. red body, black metal base, black driver, black "Pirelli" airfoil, (5) front wheels, (11) chromed rear wheels, chrome exhausts, "Fiat 3" tempa, Macau casting ($2-4)
2. red body, black metal base, black driver, black "Pirelli" airfoil, (11) front wheels, (12) unchromed rear wheels, chrome exhausts, "Fiat 3" tempa, Macau casting ($2-4)
3. white/ orange/ green body, black metal base, yellow driver, yellow "Watson's" airfoil, (11) front wheels, (12) chromed rear wheels, "Mr. Juicy/ Sunkist" tempa, Macau casting ($20-25)(HK)
4. yellow body, black metal base, dark red driver, dark red "Goodyear" airfoil, (11) front wheels, (12) chromed rear wheels, "Matchbox Racing Team" tempa, Macau casting ($2-4)
5. white body, blue metal base, blue driver, blue "Shell" airfoil, (11) front wheels, (12) chromed rear wheels, "Matchbox/ Goodyear" tempa, Macau casting ($5-8)(KS)(GS)
6. white body, blue metal base, blue driver, blue "Shell" airfoil, (11) front wheels, (12) unchromed rear wheels, "Matchbox/ Goodyear" tempa, Macau casting ($5-8)(KS)(GS)
7. red body, black plastic base, black driver, black "Pirelli" airfoil, (11) front wheels, (12) unchromed rear wheels, "Fiat 3" tempa, Macau casting ($2-4)(KS)
8. white body, blue plastic base, blue driver, blue "Shell" airfoil, (11) front wheels, (12) unchromed rear wheels, "Matchbox/ Goodyear" tempa, Macau casting ($2-4)(GS)
9. white body, blue plastic base, blue driver, blue "Shell" airfoil, (11) front wheels, (12) unchromed rear wheels, "Matchbox/ Goodyear" tempa, Thailand casting ($2-4)(GS)

MB16-E FORD LTD POLICE CAR, issued 1987 (USA)
MB51-H FORD LTD POLICE CAR, issued 1987 (ROW)

NOTE: All models with white interior, blue windows, red/ blue dome lights & 8 dot wheels unless otherwise noted.

1. white body, chrome base, "Police PD-21" tempa, Macau casting ($1-2)
2. dark purple body, chrome base, "Police PD-21" tempa, Macau casting ($3-4)(SC)
3. raspberry red body, chrome base, "Police PD-21" tempa, Macau casting ($3-4)(SC)
4. red body, chrome base, "Fire Dept. Fire Chief" tempa, Macau casting ($2-4)(MC)
5. red body, chrome base, "Fire Dept. Fire Chief" tempa, Thailand casting ($2-4)(MC)
6. white body, chrome base, "Police PD-21" tempa, Thailand casting ($1-2)
7. white body, chrome base, no tempa, Thailand casting ($10-15)(GF)
8. white body, blue base, Police face & cartoon figures tempa, 8 dot red wheels (yellow hubs), Thailand casting ($6-8)(LL)
9. dark blue body, chrome base, "Police R-25" tempa, Thailand casting ($3-5)(TH)
10. white body, chrome base, "Police PD-21" without silver tempa on door shield, Thailand casting ($1-2)
11. white body, black base with bar code, "Police PD-21" & "Intercom City" tempa, Thailand casting ($10-15)(IC)
12. white body, chrome base, "Police PD-21" & "Intercom City" tempa, Thailand casting ($10-15)
13. white body, chrome base, "17 Police" tempa, Thailand casting ($1-2)(MP)
14. white body, blue base, Police face & cartoon figures tempa, 8 dot yellow wheels, Thailand casting ($12-15)(LL)
15. blue body, chrome base, "Police 16" & white band tempa, Thailand casting ($2-4)(CC)
16. black body, chrome base, "Police Unit 3" & gold star tempa, Thailand casting ($1-2)(MP)
17. red body, chrome base, "Fire Chief" & "FD No. 1" in gold print, Thailand casting ($1-2)(MP)
18. white body, chrome base, "Police PD-21" with blue background tempa, Thailand casting ($4-6)
19. white body, chrome base, blue "Police" & star logo tempa, Thailand casting ($1-2)(MP)
20. metallic blue body, chrome base, "State Police SP16" tempa, Thailand casting ($1-2)
21. metallic gold body, chrome base, no tempa, Thailand casting ($10-15)(CH)

NOTE: Versions 22-24 with all blue dome lights and chrome disc with rubber tires.

22. black & tan body, white & black interior, chrome base, "Florida State Trooper" tempa, Thailand casting ($3-5)(PC8)
23. dark blue & gray body, white & black interior, chrome base, "State Police Virginia" tempa, Thailand casting ($3-5)(PC8)
24. white body, gray & black interior, chrome base, "State Police New Jersey" tempa, Thailand casting ($3-5)(PC8)
25. blue body, clear windows, chrome base, "Unit 22 Police" with white band tempa, Thailand casting ($1-2)(MP)
26. metallic brown-gold body, chrome base, "Sheriff S-27" tempa, Thailand

casting ($1-2)
27. white body, chrome base, "Sheriff S-27" tempa, Thailand base ($1-2)(MW24)
28. white body, chrome base, "Sheriff S-27" tempa, China casting ($1-2)(MW24)
29. white body, chrome base, "Sheriff S-27" tempa, 5 spoke concave star wheels, China casting ($15-20)(MW24)
30. blue body, clear windows, chrome base, "Unit 22 Police" & white band tempa, China casting ($1-2)(MP)
31. silver-gray body, silver-gray interior, chrome base, "Police" with shield & red design tempa, China casting ($1-2)(MP)

MB17-A HORSE BOX, issued 1970
1. red body, green box, gray door ($25-40)
2. red-orange body, green box, gray door ($25-40)
3. mustard body, green box, gray door ($20-35)
4. red-orange body, light gray box, light brown door ($20-35)
5. light orange body, light gray box, light brown door ($20-35)

MB17-B THE LONDONER, issued 1972
NOTE: Following models with 5 spoke wheels and white interior unless otherwise noted.
1. red body, black metal base, "Swinging London" (type 1) labels ($8-12)
2. red body, black metal base, "Swinging London" (type 2) labels ($8-12)
3. red body, charcoal metal base, "Swinging London" (type 2) labels ($8-12)
4. red body, unpainted metal base with screw mounts cast, "Swinging London" (type 1) labels ($18-25)(GW)
5. gold plated body, unpainted metal base with screw mounts cast, "Swinging London" (type 1) labels ($750-1000)(GW)
6. silver plated body, unpainted metal base with screw mounts cast, "Swinging London" (type 1) labels ($750-1000)(GW)
7. red body, black metal base, "Preston Guild Merchant 1972" labels ($150-200)(LE)
8. red body, black metal base, "London/ Kensington Hilton" labels ($150-200)(LE)
9. red body, unpainted metal base, "London/ Kensington Hilton" labels ($150-200)(LE)
10. red body, black metal base, "Typhoo Tea" labels ($250-350)(CN)
11. red body, black metal base, "Impel 73" labels ($50-75)(LE)
12. red body, unpainted metal base, "Impel 73" labels ($50-75)(LE)
13. red body, black metal base, "Berger Paints" labels ($8-12)
14. red body, unpainted metal base, "Berger Paints" labels ($8-12)
15. red body, black metal base "ICP Interchemicals & Plastics" labels ($750+)(LE)
16. red body, black metal base, "Borregaard Paper" labels ($750+)(LE)
17. red body, black metal base, "Sellotape Selbstklebebander" labels ($750+)(LE)
18. red body, black metal base, "Sellotape Packaging Systems" labels ($150-200)(LE)
19. red body, black metal base, "Sellotape Electrical Tapes" labels ($750+)(LE)
20. red body, black metal base, "Sellotape International Operations" labels ($750+)(LE)
21. red body, black metal base, "Chambourcy Yogurt" labels ($85-110)(OP)
22. red body, black metal base, "Esso Extra Petrol" labels ($35-50)
23. coffee & cream body, black metal base, "Berger Paints" labels ($175-250)
24. coffee & cream body, black metal base, "Impel 76" labels ($85-110)(LE)
25. red body, black metal base, "Selfridges" labels ($60-75)(UK)
26. red body, black metal base, "Aviemore Centre/ Santa Claus Land" labels ($65-80)(LE)
27. red body, black metal base, "C Amcel" labels ($175-225)(LE)
28. red body, black metal base, "Baron of Beef" labels ($175-225)(LE)
29. lemon & red body, black metal base, "Swinging London" (type 2) labels ($350-500)(BR)
30. red body, black metal base, "A.I.M. Building Fund 1976" labels ($40-60)(LE)
NOTE: the following models are with dot dash wheels.
31. red body, black metal base, "A.I.M. Building Fund 1976" labels ($40-60)(LE)
32. red body, charcoal metal base, "Berger Paints" labels ($6-8)
33. red body, black metal base, "Berger Paints" labels ($6-8)
34. red body, unpainted metal base, "Berger Paints" labels ($6-8)
35. red body, black metal base, no labels ($6-8)
36. white & red body, unpainted metal base, "Berger Paints" labels ($350-500)(BR)
37. yellow & red body, unpainted metal base, "Berger Paints" labels ($350-500)(BR)
38. white & blue body, unpainted metal base, "Berger Paints" labels ($500-750)(BR)
39. yellow & blue body, unpainted metal base, "Berger Paints" labels ($500-750)(BR)
40. metallic red body, unpainted metal base, "Lufthansa" labels ($500-750)(BR)
41. red body, black metal base, "Army & Navy" labels ($50-65)(UK)
42. red body, charcoal metal base, "Army & Navy" labels ($60-65)(UK)
43. red body, black metal base, "Eduscho Kaffee" labels ($500-750)(GR)
44. orange body, black metal base, "Jacob's- The Biscuit Makers" labels ($25-40)(IR)
45. orange body, charcoal metal base, "Jacob's- The Biscuit Makers" labels ($25-40)(IR)
46. red body, charcoal metal base, "Jacob's- The Biscuit Makers" labels ($65-80)(IR)
47. red body, black metal base, "Jacob's- The Biscuit Makers" labels ($65-80)(IR)
48. red body, black metal base, "Ilford Hp5 Film" labels ($350-500)(LE)
49. red body, black metal base, "Museum of London" labels ($50-65)(UK)
50. red body, unpainted metal base, "Museum of London" labels ($50-65)(UK)
51. red body, charcoal metal base, "Museum of London" labels ($50-65)(UK)
52. red body, black metal base, "Silver Jubilee" labels ($175-225)(UK)
NOTE: Versions 53-55 with red interiors.
53. silver-gray body, charcoal metal base, "Silver Jubilee" labels ($10-15)(UK)
54. silver-gray body, unpainted metal base, "Silver Jubilee" labels ($10-15)(UK)
55. silver-gray body, charcoal metal base, "Berger Paints" labels ($75-100)
56. blue body, charcoal metal base, "Deutschlands Autopartner" labels ($35-50)(GR)
57. blue body, black metal base, "Deutschlands Autopartner" labels ($35-50)(GR)
58. blue body, black metal base, "Matchbox 1953- 1978" labels ($35-50)
59. blue body, charcoal metal base, "Matchbox 1953- 1978" labels ($35-50)
60. orange body, charcoal metal base, "Matchbox 1953- 1978" labels ($75-100)
61. red body, black metal base, "Matchbox 1953- 1978" labels ($6-8)
62. red body, black metal base, "Busch Gardens" labels ($40-65)(US)
63. red body, brown metal base, "Berger Paints" labels ($7-10)
64. red body, charcoal metal base, "Berger Paints" labels ($6-8)
65. red body, gray metal base, "Berger Paints" labels ($6-8)
66. red body, black metal base, "The Bisto Bus" labels ($8-12)(UK)(OP)
67. red body, black plastic base, "The Bisto Bus" labels ($8-12)(UK)(OP)
68. red body, black plastic base, "Berger Paints" labels ($6-8)
69. red body, black metal base, "3rd A.I.M. Inc. Convention & Toy Show 1979" labels ($25-40)(C2)
70. red body, brown metal base, "The Bisto Bus" labels ($81-12)(UK)(OP)

MB17-C LONDON BUS, issued 1982
MB51-F LONDON BUS, reissued 1985 (USA)
MB28-F LONDON BUS, reissued 1990 (USA)
NOTE: All models listed with white interior & black base unless otherwise noted.
1. red upper & lower body, "Berger Paints" labels, England casting ($10-15)
2. red upper & lower body, "Laker Skytrain" labels, England casting ($7-10)
3. white upper body, powder blue lower body, "Matchbox No. 1/ Montepna" labels, England casting ($25-40)(GK)
4. dark green upper & lower body, "Chesterfield Centenary" labels, England casting ($10-15)(UK)
5. red upper & lower body, "Matchbox London Bus" labels, England casting ($3-5)
6. red upper & lower body, "Matchbox London Bus" labels, brown base, England casting ($10-15)
7. red upper & lower body, "Nice To Meet You! Japan 1984" labels, England casting ($15-20)(JP)
8. red upper & lower body,
labels, England casting ($15-20)(JP)
9. red upper & lower body, "York Festival & Mystery Plays" labels, England base ($10-15)(UK)
10. dark blue upper & lower body, "Nestles Milkybar" labels, England base ($10-15)(UK)
11. dark green upper & lower body, "Rowntrees Fruit Gums" labels, England casting ($10-15)(UK)
12. dark blue upper & lower body, "Keddies No. 1 in Essex" labels, England casting ($40-65)(UK)
13. maroon upper & lower body, "Rapport" labels, England casting ($8-12)(UK)
14. white upper body, black lower body, "Torvale Fisher Engineering Co." labels, England casting ($8-12)(UK)
15. white upper body, orange lower body, "WH Smith Travel" labels, England casting ($10-15)(UK)
16. red upper & lower body, "Matchbox London Bus" labels, Macau casting ($3-4)
17. red upper & lower body, "Nestles Milkybar" labels, Macau casting ($10-15)
18. red upper & lower body, "Rowntrees Fruit Gums" labels, Macau casting ($10-15)
19. red upper & lower body, "Matchbox No. 1/ Montepna" labels, England casting ($150-200)(GK)
20. red upper & lower body, You'll ♥ New York" labels, Macau casting ($2-4)
21. blue upper body, white lower body, "Space for Youth 1985/ Staffordshire Police" labels, Macau casting ($8-12)(UK)
22. blue upper & lower body, "Cityrama" labels, Macau casting ($8-12)
23. red upper & lower body, no labels, England casting ($3-5)
24. red upper & lower body, "You'll ♥ New York" labels, China casting ($2-4)
25. red upper & lower body, "Nuremberg 1986" labels, Macau casting ($100-150)(GR)
26. red upper & lower body, "1st M.I.C.A. Convention" labels, Macau casting ($250-300)(UK)
27. red upper & lower body, "1st M.I.C.A. Convention" labels, England casting ($250-300)(UK)
28. red upper & lower body, "1st M.I.C.A. Convention" labels, China casting ($250-300)(UK)
29. red upper & lower body, "Around London Tour Bus" labels, China casting ($2-3)
30. blue upper & lower body, "National Tramway Museum" labels, China casting ($8-12)(UK)
31. white upper body, dull red lower body, "Midland Bus Transport Museum" labels, China casting ($8-12)(UK)
32. dull red upper & lower body, "Band-Aid Plasters Playbus" labels, China casting ($8-12)(UK)(OP)
33. blue upper & lower body, "National Girobank" labels, China casting ($8-12)(UK)
34. red upper & lower body, "Matchbox- Niagara Falls" labels, China casting ($6-8)(CN)
35. red upper & lower body, "Feria Del Juguete Valencia, 12 Febrero 1987" labels, China casting ($175-225)(SP)
36. beige upper body, blue lower body, tan interior, "West Midlands Travel" labels, China casting ($8-12)(UK)
37. white upper & lower body, red interior, "M.I.C.A. Matchbox International Collectors Association" labels, China casting ($8-12)(UK)
38. white upper body, white & dark blue lower body, "Denny- Happy 1000th Birthday, Dublin" labels ($8-12)(IR)
39. red upper & lower body, orange-yellow interior, orange-yellow wheels with blue hubs, "123 abc" sides tempa & "My First Matchbox Nuremberg 1990" roof tempa, China casting ($10-15)(GR)
40. red upper & lower body, orange-yellow interior, orange-yellow wheels with blue hubs, "123 abc" sides tempa & teddy bear with "abc" roof tempa, China casting ($6-8)(LL)
41. red upper & lower body, no labels, China casting ($4-6)
42. yellow upper & lower body, "It's The Real Thing- Coke" labels, China casting ($12-18)(CN)
43. maroon upper & lower body, "Corning Glass Center" labels, China casting ($8-12)(US)
44. chrome plated upper & lower body, "Celebrating A Decade of Matchbox Conventions" labels, China casting ($25-40)(C2)
45. red upper & lower body, "Markfield Project Support Appeal 92" labels, China casting ($15-20)(UK)
46. red upper & lower body, "London Wide Tour Bus" labels, China casting ($1-2)
47. white upper & lower body, no labels, China casting ($10-15)(GF)
48. red upper & lower body, orange-yellow interior & wheels (plain hubs), "123 abc" sides tempa & teddy bear with "abc" roof tempa, China casting ($6-8)(LL)
49. red upper & lower body, white interior, "Takashimaya" labels, Macau casting ($100-125) (JP)
50. white upper & lower body, white interior, no labels, China casting ($20-25)(ASAP-blank)
51. white upper & lower body, white interior, "American International Recovery" (on roof) tempa, China casting ($100+)(ASAP)

MB17-D AMX PROSTOCKER, issued 1983 (USA)
MB 9-E AMX PROSTOCKER, issued 1983 (ROW)
1. pearly silver body, black metal base, 5 arch wheels, red interior, red & black stripes with "AMX" tempa, Macau casting ($2-4)
2. pearly silver body, black metal base, dot dash wheels, red interior, red & black stripes with "AMX" tempa, Macau casting ($2-4)
3. maroon body, black metal base, dot dash wheels, black interior, "Dr. Pepper" tempa, Macau casting ($5-8)
4. maroon body, black plastic base, dot dash wheels, black interior, "Dr. Pepper" tempa, Macau casting ($5-8)
5. silver-gray body, black plastic base, dot dash wheels, black interior, red & black stripes with "AMX" tempa, China casting ($8-10)(MP)
NOTE: Available as a Hungarian and Bulgarian casting. Assorted colors available ($15-25).

MB17-E FORD ESCORT CABRIOLET, issued 1985 (USA)
MB37-G FORD ESCORT CABRIOLET, issued 1985 (ROW)
NOTE: All models with clear windows, gray interior, black tonneau & bumpers
1. white body & base, 8 dot silver wheels, no tow hook, "XR3i" tempa, Macau casting ($2-4)
2. white body & base, 8 dot gold wheels, no tow hook, "XR3i" tempa, Macau casting ($4-6)
3. white body & base, starburst wheels, no tow hook, "3" with stripes tempa, Macau casting ($3-5)(SF)
4. white body & base, 5 arch wheels, no tow hook, "XR3i" tempa, Macau casting ($2-4)
5. red body & base, 8 dot silver wheels, no tow hook, "XR3i" & "Ford" tempa, Macau casting ($8-12)
6. white body & base, 8 dot silver wheels, with tow hook, "XR3i" tempa, Macau casting ($2-4)(TP)
7. white body & base, 8 dot white wheels, with tow hook, "XR3i" tempa, Macau casting ($3-5)
8. metallic blue body & base, laser wheels, with tow hook, "3" with stripes tempa, Macau casting ($3-5)(LW)
9. white body & base, starburst wheels, with tow hook, "3" with stripes tempa, Macau casting ($3-5)(SF)
10. dark blue body & base, 8 dot silver wheels, with tow hook, "XR3i" tempa, Macau casting ($2-3)(TP)
11. white body & base, 8 dot silver wheels, with tow hook, "XR3i" tempa, Thailand casting ($2-3)(TP)
12. dark blue body & base, 8 dot silver wheels, with tow hook, "XR3i" tempa, Thailand casting ($2-3)(TP)
13. metallic blue body & base, 8 dot silver wheels, with tow hook, white & orange spatter tempa, Thailand casting ($2-3)(TP)
14. white body & base, 8 dot silver wheels, with tow hook, "XR3i " tempa, China casting ($2-4)
15. white body & base, red interior, 8 dot silver wheels, with tow hook, "Ocean Explorer" tempa ($1-2)(MP)

MB17-F DODGE DAKOTA, issued 1987 (USA)
MB50-F DODGE DAKOTA, issued 1990 (ROW)
1. bright red body, chrome base, chrome rollbar, black interior, clear windows, black & white stripes (plain sides) tempa, Macau casting ($3-5)

2. bright red body, chrome base, chrome rollbar, black interior, clear windows, black & white stripes & "Dakota ST" tempa, Macau casting ($1-2)
3. dark red body, chrome base, black rollbar, black interior, clear windows, black & white stripes & "Dakota ST" tempa, China casting ($1-2)
4. metallic green body, chrome base, black rollbar, black interior, clear windows, "MB Construction" & stripes tempa, China casting ($3-5)(AP)
5. white body, chrome base, white rollbar, white interior, blue windows, no tempa, China casting ($10-15)(GF)
6. blue body, chrome base, black rollbar, black interior, clear windows, black & white stripes & "Dakota ST" tempa, China casting ($8-12)(GS)
7. florescent orange body, black base with bar code, white rollbar, white interior, clear windows, "Fire Chief 1- Intercom City" tempa, China casting ($10-15)(IC)
8. fluorescent orange body, chrome base, white rollbar, white interior, clear windows, "Fire Chief 1- Intercom City" tempa, China casting ($12-15)
9. purple body, chrome base, chrome rollbar, gray interior, clear windows, neon yellow & pink stripes tempa, China casting ($1-2)(MP)
10. olive body, black base, black rollbar, black interior, clear windows, white bands tempa, China casting ($25-35)(CHI)(MP)
11. olive body, chrome base, chrome rollbar, gray interior, clear windows, white bands, China casting ($35-50)(CHI)(MP)
12. lemon body, chrome base, black rollbar, black interior, clear windows, "Highway Crew- Crew Chief" tempa ($1-2)(MP)

MB17-G FERRARI 456GT, issued 1994 (USA)
MB41-J FERRARI 456GT, issued 1994 (ROW)
1. blue body, tan interior, clear windows, "456GT" tempa, gold 6-spoke spiral wheels, China casting ($1-2)
2. dark purple body, neon yellow interior, clear windows, white design on hood, roof, trunk & sides tempa, silver 6-spoke spiral wheels, China casting ($1-2)
3. dark purple body, neon yellow interior, clear windows, white design on sides only tempa, silver 6-spoke spiral wheels, China casting ($1-2)
4. metallic red body, brown interior, clear windows, no tempa, silver 6 spoke spiral wheels China casting ($2-4)
5. metallic gold body, black interior, clear windows, no tempa, silver 6 spoke spiral wheels, China casting ($10-15)(CH)
6. metallic red body, brown interior, clear windows, no tempa, 5 spoke concave star wheels, China casting ($1-2)
7. dark purple body, gray interior, clear windows, "Matchbox Racing Rush 11" tempa, 5 spoke concave star wheels, China casting ($1-2)
8. red body, black & brown interior, clear windows, "Ferrari" logo tempa, chrome disc with rubber tires, Thailand casting ($3-5)(JC)(PC)
9. dark metallic red body, black interior, clear windows, "Ferrari" logo tempa, 5 spoke concave star wheels, China casting ($1-2)
10. black body, black & tan interior, clear windows, detailed trim tempa, chrome disc with rubber tires, China casting ($3-5)(PC15)

MB18-A FIELD CAR, issued 1970
1. yellow body, red-brown roof, unpainted base, ivory interior, no labels, 5 spoke wheels ($20-30)
2. yellow body, red-brown roof, unpainted base, ivory interior, no labels, 4 spoke wheels ($20-30)
3. yellow body, red-brown roof, silver-gray base, ivory interior, no labels, 4 spoke wheels ($25-35)
NOTE: All olive body models have black hubs, all others with silver hubs unless noted.
4. olive body, tan roof, black base, black interior, "A" label, 4 spoke wheels ($5-7)(TP)
5. olive body, tan roof, black base, black interior, "RA391" labels, 4 spoke wheels ($5-7)(TP)
6. olive body, tan roof, black base, black interior, "A" label, 5 spoke wheels ($5-7)(TP)
7. olive body, tan roof, black base, black interior, "RA391" label, 5 spoke wheels ($5-7)(TP)
8. olive body, tan roof, black base, black interior, star label, 5 spoke wheels ($25-40)(TP)
9. olive drab body, tan roof, black base, black interior, "A" label, 4 spoke wheels ($65-80)(TP)
10. olive drab body, tan roof, black base, black interior, "A" label, 5 spoke wheels ($65-80)(TP)
11. white body, black roof, black base, black interior, checker label, 4 spoke (silver hubs) wheels ($300-450)(TP)
12. white body, black roof, black base, black interior, checker label, 4 spoke (black hubs) wheels ($300-450)(TP)
13. dull orange body, black roof, black base, black interior, checker label, 5 spoke wheels ($4-6)(TP)
14. dull orange body, black roof, black base, black interior, checker label, 4 spoke wheels ($4-6)(TP)
15. dull orange body, black roof, black base, black interior, checker label, 4 spoke (black hubs) wheels ($4-6)(TP)
16. dull orange body, black roof, silver-gray base, black interior, checker label, 4 spoke wheels ($4-6)(TP)
17. metallic red body, tan roof, black base, black interior, "44" label, 4 spoke wheels ($4-6)(TP)
18. metallic red body, tan roof, black base, black interior, "44" label, 4 spoke (black hubs) wheels ($4-6)(TP)
19. metallic red body, tan roof, silver-gray base, black interior, "44" label, 4 spoke wheels ($4-6)(TP)
20. metallic red body, tan roof, silver-gray base, black interior, checker label, 4 spoke (black hubs) wheels ($4-6)(TP)
21. metallic red body, tan roof, black base, black interior, checker label, 4 spoke wheels ($4-6)(TP)
22. dark orange body, black roof, black base, black interior, no label, 4 spoke wheels ($4-6)(TP)
23. dark orange body, black roof, black base, black interior, "179" tempa, 4 spoke wheels ($5-7)(LE)
24. dark orange body, black roof, silver-gray base, black interior, "179" tempa, 4 spoke wheels ($5-7)(TP)
25. dark orange body, tan roof, silver-gray base, black interior, "179" tempa, 4 spoke wheels ($5-7)(LE)
26. dark orange body, black roof, black base, black interior, "179" tempa, 5 spoke wheels ($5-7)(LE)
27. dark orange body, black roof, black base, white interior, "179" tempa, 4 spoke wheels ($8-10)(LE)
28. dark yellow body, tan roof, black base, black interior, checker label, 4 spoke wheels ($4-6)(TP)
29. dark yellow body, black roof, black base, black interior, checker label, 4 spoke wheels ($4-6)(TP)
30. dark yellow body, black roof, black base, black interior, checker label, 5 spoke wheels ($4-6)(TP)
31. orange body, black roof, black base, white interior, "179" tempa, 4 spoke wheels ($6-8)(TP)
32. orange body, tan roof, black base, black interior, "179" tempa, 4 spoke wheels ($6-8)(TP)
33. orange body, tan roof, black base, black interior, "179" tempa, 4 spoke wheels ($6-8)(TP)
34. orange body, black roof, black base, black interior, checker label, 4 spoke wheels ($4-6)(TP)
35. orange body, tan roof, black base, white interior, "44" label, 4 spoke wheels ($6-8)(TP)
NOTE: models listed as (LE) were issued as limited edition "Bushwacker".

MB18-B HONDARORA, issued 1975
1. red body, chrome handlebars, no driver, chrome engine, with label, black seat, wire wheels ($10-15)
2. red body, black handlebars, no driver, chrome engine, with label, black seat, wire wheels ($5-7)
3. red body, black handlebars, no driver, chrome engine, no label, black seat, wire wheels ($5-7)
4. red body, black handlebars, no driver, chrome engine, with label, white seat, wire wheels ($95-125)
5. orange body, black handlebars, no driver, chrome engine, with label, black seat, wire wheels ($8-12)(KS)
6. olive drab body, black handlebars, no driver, black engine, no label, black seat, wire wheels ($50-75)(TP)
7. olive body, black handlebars, no driver, black engine, no label, black seat, wire wheels ($7-10)(TP)
8. red body, black handlebars, no driver, black engine, no label, black seat, wire wheels ($5-7)
9. red body, black handlebars, no driver, chrome engine, no label, black seat, mag wheels ($5-7)
10. red body, black handlebars, no driver, black engine, no label, black seat, mag wheels ($5-7)
11. metallic red body, black handlebars, no driver, chrome engine, no label, black seat, wire wheels ($75-100)(BR)
12. green body, black handlebars, no driver, chrome engine, no label, black seat, mag wheels ($5-7)
13. green body, black handlebars, no driver, black engine, no label, black seat, mag wheels ($5-7)
14. yellow body, black handlebars, no driver, chrome engine, no label, black seat, mag wheels ($4-6)
15. yellow body, black handlebars, tan driver, chrome engine, no label, black seat, mag wheels ($4-6)
16. yellow body, black handlebars, brown driver, chrome engine, no label, black seat, mag wheels ($4-6)
17. yellow body, black handlebars, green driver, chrome engine, no label, black seat, mag wheels ($50-75)(GR)
NOTE: Above models all with England casting.
18. yellow body, black handlebars, tan driver, chrome engine, no label, black seat, mag wheels, Macau casting ($3-5)
19. pearly silver body, black handlebars, red driver, black engine, with tempa, black seat, mag wheels, Macau casting ($8-12)(JP)
20. pearly silver body, black handlebars, red driver, black engine, with tempa, charcoal seat, mag wheels, Macau casting ($8-12)(JP)
21. orange body, black handlebars, tan driver, chrome engine, no label, black seat, mag wheels, Macau casting ($3-5)

MB18-C FIRE ENGINE, issued 1984
NOTE: All models with blue windows
1. red body, chrome base, white ladder, black turret, 5 arch wheels, no tempa, Macau casting ($1-2)
2. red body, chrome base, white ladder, black turret, 8 dot wheels, no tempa, Macau casting ($1-2)
3. red body, chrome base, white ladder, black turret, 5 arch wheels, no tempa, China casting ($1-2)
4. red body, chrome base, white ladder, black turret, 5 arch wheels, "Fire Dept." & shield tempa, China casting ($1-2)
5. yellow body, chrome base, white ladder, black turret, 8 dot wheels, no tempa, Macau casting ($2-4)(MP)
6. red body, chrome base, white ladder, black turret, 8 dot wheels, Japanese lettered tempa, Macau casting ($8-12)(JP)(GS)
7. red body, chrome base, white ladder, black turret, "Fire Dept." & shield tempa, Macau casting ($1-2)
8. red body, chrome base, yellow ladder, black turret, 8 dot blue wheels (yellow hubs), fireman head tempa, Macau casting ($6-8)(LL)
9. red body, chrome base, white ladder, black turret, 8 dot wheels, "3" & crest tempa, Macau casting ($3-5)(GS)
10. red body, chrome base, white ladder, black turret, 8 dot wheels, "Fire Dept." & shield tempa, Thailand casting ($1-2)
11. red body, chrome base, white ladder, black turret, 5 arch wheels, "Fire Dept." & shield tempa, no origin cast ($8-12)(MP)
12. red body, chrome base, white ladder, black turret, 8 dot wheels, "3" & crest tempa, Thailand casting ($1-2)(GS)
13. yellow body, chrome base, white ladder, black turret, 8 dot wheels, no tempa, Thailand casting ($3-5)(MP)
14. red body, blue base, green & blue ladder, yellow turret, 8 dot blue wheels (yellow hubs), fireman head tempa, Macau casting ($6-8)(LL)
15. red body, blue base, green & blue ladder, yellow turret, 8 dot blue wheels (yellow hubs), fireman head tempa, Thailand casting ($6-8)(LL)
16. red body, blue base, green & blue ladder, yellow turret, 8 dot blue wheels (plain hubs), fireman head tempa, Thailand casting ($6-8)(LL)
17. florescent orange body, chrome base, white ladder, black turret, 8 dot wheels, "4" & checkers tempa, Thailand casting ($1-2)
18. white body, white base, white ladder, white turret, 8 dot wheels, no tempa, Thailand casting ($10-15)(GF)
19. florescent orange body, black base with bar code, white ladder, black turret, 8 dot wheels, "5" & "Intercom City" tempa, China casting ($10-15)(IC)
20. fluorescent orange body, chrome base, white ladder, black turret, 8 dot wheels, "5" & "Intercom City" tempa, China casting ($7-10)
21. fluorescent orange body, chrome base, white ladder, black turret, 8 dot wheels, "Metro Fire Dept." tempa, Thailand casting ($1-2)(MP)
22. red body, chrome base, white ladder, black turret, 8 dot wheels, "Metro Fire Dept." & detailed trim tempa, Thailand casting ($2-4)(CC)
23.white & red body, chrome base, silver-gray ladder, 8 dot wheels, gold crest & pinstriping tempa, Thailand casting ($1-2)(MP)
24. red body, black base, white ladder, black turret, 8 dot wheels, "4" & checkers tempa, Thailand casting ($7-10)
25. red body, black base, white ladder, black turret, 8 dot wheels, "FD No. 1" tempa, China casting ($1-2)(MP)
26. white body, chrome base, orange ladder, black turret,, 8 dot wheels, "Metro" tempa, China casting ($1-2)
27. yellow body, chrome base, gray ladder, black turret,, 8 dot wheels, "Matchbox Fire Dept." & red stripe tempa, China casting ($1-2)(MP)
28. yellow body, chrome base, gray ladder, black turret,, chrome disc with rubber tires, "Ladder 3 Bay District" tempa, China casting ($3-5)(PC7)
29. white & red body, chrome base, white ladder, black turret, chrome disc with rubber tires, "Springfield Fire Dept." tempa, China casting ($3-5)(PC7)
30. red body, chrome base, white ladder with lever, black turret, 8 dot wheels, "FD" tempa, China casting ($1-2)(AS)(AP)
31. metallic green-gold body, black base, white ladder, black turret, 8 dot wheels, no tempa, China casting ($5-10)(CH)
32. red body, chrome base, white ladder, black turret, 8 dot wheels, white stripe tempa, China casting ($1-2)
33. red body, chrome base, gray ladder, black turret, 8 dot wheels, gold stripe tempa, China casting ($1-2)(MP)
34. white body, chrome base, translucent red ladder, black turret, 8 dot wheels, red band tempa, China casting ($1-2)(MW23)
35. lemon & white body, chrome base, gray ladder, black turret, chrome disc with rubber wheels, "Park Ridge Fire Dept." tempa , China casting ($3-5)(PC21)
36. red & white body, chrome base, white ladder, black turret, chrome disc with rubber tires, "Laurel Springs Fire Rescue" tempa, China casting ($3-5)(PC21)

MB19-A LOTUS RACER, issued 1970
1. dark purple body, unpainted base, round "3" labels ($35-50)

MB19-B ROAD DRAGSTER, issued 1970
1. red body, unpainted base, ivory interior, "8" labels ($15-20)
2. red-orange body, unpainted base, ivory interior, "8" labels ($15-20)
3. red-orange body, silver-gray base, ivory interior, "8" labels ($15-20)
4. red-orange body, unpainted base, ivory interior, no labels ($15-20)
5. red-orange body, unpainted base, ivory interior, scorpion labels ($35-50)
6. red-orange body, silver-gray base, ivory interior, scorpion labels ($35-50)
7. red-orange body, unpainted base, white interior, "8" labels ($15-20)
8. pinkish red body, unpainted base, ivory interior, small "Wynn's" labels ($85-125)(LE)
9. pinkish red body, unpainted base, ivory interior, large "Wynn's" labels ($85-125)(LE)
10. purple body, unpainted base, ivory interior, "8" labels ($18-25)
11. purple body, unpainted base, ivory interior, scorpion labels ($35-50)
12. metallic red body, unpainted base, ivory interior, "8" labels ($18-25)

MB19-C CEMENT TRUCK, issued 1976
1. red body, orange yellow barrel, red stripes, green windows, unpainted base ($5-8)
2. red body, orange-yellow barrel, black stripes, green windows, unpainted base ($5-8)
3. red body, orange-yellow barrel, red stripes, blue-green windows, unpainted base ($5-8)
4. red body, orange-yellow barrel, no stripes, blue-green windows, unpainted base ($5-8)
5. red body, orange-yellow barrel, no stripes, green windows, unpainted base ($5-8)
6. red body, orange-yellow barrel, red stripes, no windows, unpainted base ($5-8)
7. red body, gray barrel, red stripes, no windows, unpainted base ($5-8)
8. red body, gray barrel, red stripes, green windows, unpainted base ($5-8)
9. red body, gray barrel, red stripes, purple windows, unpainted base ($5-8)
10. red body, orange barrel, red stripes, purple windows, unpainted base ($5-8)
11. red body, orange barrel, red stripes, green windows, unpainted base ($5-8)
12. red body, lemon barrel, red stripes, green windows, unpainted base

($5-8)
13. red body, lemon barrel, red stripes, purple windows, unpainted base ($5-8)
14. red body, orange-yellow barrel, red stripes, green windows, silver-gray base ($5-8)
15. red body, lemon barrel, no stripes, green windows, unpainted base ($5-8)

MB19-D PETERBILT CEMENT TRUCK, issued 1982
1. emerald green body, orange barrel, chrome exhausts, yellow "Big Pete" tempa, amber windows, black mounts, chrome base, England casting ($2-4)
2. emerald green body, orange barrel, chrome exhausts, white "Big Pete" tempa, amber windows, black mounts, chrome base, England casting ($2-4)
3. pale green body, orange barrel, chrome exhausts, yellow/ white "Big Pete" tempa, amber windows, black mounts, chrome base, Macau casting ($2-4)
4. dark green body, orange barrel, chrome exhausts, yellow/ white "Big Pete" tempa, amber windows, black mounts, chrome base, Macau casting ($2-4)
5. dark green body, orange barrel, chrome exhausts, yellow/white "Big Pete" tempa, amber windows, charcoal mounts, chrome base, Macau casting ($2-4)
6. dark green body, orange barrel, chrome exhausts, yellow/ white "Big Pete" tempa, clear windows, black mounts, chrome base, Macau casting ($2-4)
7. blue body, lemon barrel, chrome exhausts, "Kwik Set Cement" tempa, clear windows, black mounts, chrome base, Macau casting ($1-2)
8. blue body, orange barrel, chrome exhausts, "Kwik Set Cement" (roof only) tempa, clear windows, black mounts, chrome base, Macau casting ($8-12)
9. yellow body, orange barrel, chrome exhausts, "Dirty Dumper" tempa, clear windows, black mounts, chrome base, Macau casting ($60-80)
10. yellow body, gray barrel, chrome exhausts, "Pace Construction" tempa, clear windows, black mounts, chrome base, Macau casting ($2-3)(MP)
11. blue body, lemon barrel, gray exhausts, "Kwik Set Cement" tempa, clear windows, black mounts, chrome base, Macau casting ($1-2)
12. yellow body, gray barrel, gray exhausts, "Pace Construction" tempa, clear windows, black mounts, chrome base, Macau casting ($2-3)(MP)
13. red body, lime barrel, lime exhausts, face & stripe tempa, clear windows, yellow mounts, blue base, yellow wheels with blue hubs, Macau casting ($6-8)(LL)
14. light pink body, white barrel, gray exhausts, "Readymix" tempa, clear windows, light pink mounts, black base, Thailand casting ($8-12)(AU)
15. blue body, lemon barrel, gray exhausts, "Kwik Set Cement" tempa, clear windows, black mounts, chrome base, Thailand casting ($1-2)
16. yellow body, dark gray barrel, gray exhausts, "Pace Construction" tempa, clear windows, black mounts, Thailand casting ($3-4)(MC)
17. red body, lime barrel, lime exhausts, face & stripe tempa, clear windows, yellow mounts, blue base, yellow wheels with blue hubs, Thailand casting ($6-8)(LL)
18. red body, lime barrel, lime exhausts, face & stripes tempa, clear windows, yellow mounts, blue base, yellow wheels with plain hubs, Thailand casting ($6-8)(LL)
19. orange-yellow body, red barrel, gray exhausts, "Pace Construction" tempa, clear windows, black mounts, chrome base, Thailand casting ($1-2)
20. red body, orange barrel, gray exhausts, man tempa, clear windows, black mounts, gray base, Manaus casting ($35-50)(BR)
21. red body, orange barrel, gray exhausts, man tempa, clear windows, dark gray mounts, gray base, Manaus casting ($35-50)(BR)
22. white body, orange barrel, gray exhausts, "Cement Company" tempa, black mounts, gray base, Manaus casting ($30-45)(BR)
23. fluorescent orange body, black barrel, dark gray exhausts, no tempa, silver-gray mounts, Thailand casting ($1-2)(MP)
24. florescent orange body, gray barrel, gray exhausts, no tempa, black mounts, chrome base, Thailand casting ($1-2)(MP)
25. orange-yellow body, orange barrel, gray exhausts, "Pace Construction" tempa, black mounts, black base, Thailand casting ($4-5)
26. red body, black barrel, gray exhausts, white stripes tempa, gray mounts, black base, China casting ($1-2)
27. pumpkin body, gray barrel, gray exhausts, "Matchbox" tempa, black mounts, chrome base, China casting ($1-2)(MP)
28. metallic gold body, white barrel, black exhausts, no tempa, black mounts, chrome base, China casting ($5-10)(CH)
29. powder blue body, black barrel, chrome exhausts, white stripes tempa, gray mounts, chrome base, China casting ($2-3)
30. metallic red body, black barrel, chrome exhausts, white stripes tempa, gray mounts, chrome base, China casting ($1-2)(MW8)
31. lemon body, green barrel, chrome exhausts, "Highway Crew" tempa, black mounts, chrome base, China casting ($1-2)(MP)
32. red body, white barrel, chrome exhausts, white stripes tempa, black mounts, chrome base, China casting ($25-30)(MW10)
NOTE: Above model packaged as #10 Peterbilt Quarry Truck in 1998.

MB20-A LAMBORGHINI MARZAL, issued 1969
1. red body, unpainted base, no labels ($18-25)
2. red body, unpainted base, with labels ($18-25)(GS)
3. salmon body, unpainted base, no labels ($15-20)
4. salmon body, unpainted base, with labels ($18-25)(GS)
5. salmon body, silver-gray base, no labels ($15-20)
6. yellow body, unpainted base, no labels ($35-50)(BS)
7. hot pink body, unpainted base, no labels ($15-20)
8. hot pink body, unpainted base, with labels ($18-25)(GS)
9. orange-pink body, unpainted base, no labels ($15-20)

MB20-B POLICE PATROL, issued 1975
NOTE: All models with silver hubs and Lesney, England casting unless otherwise noted.
1. white body, unpainted base, frosted windows, orange dome/ spinner, 3/16" wide "Police" labels, maltese cross wheels ($8-12)
2. white body, unpainted base, blue frosted windows, orange dome/ spinner, 3/16" wide "Police" labels, maltese cross wheels ($8-12)
3. white body, unpainted base, frosted windows, orange dome/ spinner, 1/8" wide "Police" labels, maltese cross wheels ($8-12)
4. white body, unpainted base, frosted windows, orange dome/ spinner, 1/8" wide "Police" labels, 5 spoke wheels ($8-12)
5. white body, unpainted base, blue frosted windows, orange dome/ spinner, 1/8" wide "Police" labels, maltese cross wheels ($8-12)
6. white body, unpainted base, yellow frosted windows, orange dome/ spinner, 1/8" wide "Police" labels, maltese cross wheels ($8-12)
7. olive drab body, unpainted base, frosted windows, orange dome/ spinner, "Ambulance" labels, 5 spoke wheels, black hubs ($65-80)(TP)
8. olive drab body, unpainted base, frosted windows, orange dome/ spinner, "Ambulance" labels, maltese cross wheels, black hubs ($65-80)(TP)
9. olive drab body, unpainted base, frosted windows, orange dome/ spinner, red & yellow "Police" labels, maltese cross wheels, black hubs ($65-80)(TP)
10. olive body, unpainted base, frosted windows, orange dome/ spinner, red & yellow "Police" labels, maltese cross wheels, black hubs ($6-8)(TP)
11. olive body, unpainted base, frosted windows, orange dome/ spinner, red & yellow "Police" labels, maltese cross wheels, silver hubs ($7-10)(TP)
12. olive body, unpainted base, frosted windows, orange dome/ spinner, "Ambulance" labels, 5 spoke wheels, black hubs ($6-8)(TP)
13. olive body, unpainted base, frosted windows, orange dome/ spinner, 1/8" wide "Police" labels, 5 spoke wheels, black hubs ($15-20)(TP)
14. olive body, unpainted base, frosted windows, orange dome/ spinner, "Ambulance" labels, maltese cross wheels, black hubs ($6-8)(TP)
15. olive body, unpainted base, frosted windows, orange dome/ spinner, 1/8" wide "Police" labels, maltese cross wheels, black hubs ($6-8)(TP)
16. orange body, unpainted base, frosted windows, orange dome/ spinner, "Site Engineer" labels, maltese cross wheels ($15-20)(GS)
17. orange body, unpainted base, frosted windows, orange dome/ spinner, "Site Engineer" labels, 5 spoke wheels, black hubs ($15-20)(GS)
18. orange body, unpainted base, blue frosted windows, orange dome/ spinner, "Site Engineer" labels, maltese cross wheels ($15-20)(GS)
19. orange body, unpainted base, frosted windows, orange dome/ spinner, 1/8" wide "Police" labels ($18-25)(GS)
20. white body, unpainted base, frosted windows, orange dome/ spinner, "Site Engineer" labels, maltese cross wheels ($18-25)
21. white body, unpainted base, frosted windows, orange dome/ spinner, 1/8" wide "Police" labels, maltese cross wheels, black hubs ($8-12)
22. white body, unpainted base, amber frosted windows, orange dome/ spinner, 1/8" wide "Police" labels, maltese cross wheels ($8-12)
23. white body, unpainted base, frosted windows, blue dome, orange spinner, 1/8" wide "Police" labels, maltese cross wheels ($6-8)
24. white body, unpainted base, frosted windows, yellow dome, blue spinner, 1/8" wide "Police" labels, maltese cross wheels ($6-8)
25. white body, unpainted base, frosted windows, blue dome/ spinner, 1/8" wide "Police" labels, maltese cross wheels ($6-8)
26. white body, black base, frosted windows, blue dome/ spinner, 1/8" wide "Police" labels, maltese cross wheels ($8-12)
27. white body, unpainted base, frosted windows, blue dome, orange spinner, small "Police" labels, maltese cross wheels ($18-25)
28. white body, unpainted base, frosted windows, yellow dome, blue spinner, small "Police" labels, maltese cross wheels ($18-25)
29. white body, unpainted base, frosted windows, yellow dome, orange spinner, small "Police" labels, maltese cross wheels ($18-25)
30. white body, black base, frosted windows, blue dome, orange spinner, 1/8" wide "Police" labels, maltese cross wheels ($8-12)
31. white body, unpainted base, frosted windows, yellow dome, orange spinner, 1/8" wide "Police" labels, maltese cross wheels ($6-8)
32. blue body, unpainted base, frosted windows, orange dome/ spinner, "Paris Dakar 81" labels, maltese cross wheels ($35-50)(FR)
33. blue body, unpainted base, frosted windows, yellow dome/ spinner, "Paris Dakar 81" labels, maltese cross wheels ($35-50)(FR)
34. blue body, unpainted base, frosted windows, yellow dome, orange spinner, "Paris Dakar 81" labels, maltese cross wheels ($35-50)(FR)
35. white body, unpainted base, frosted windows, blue dome/ spinner, checkered "Police" labels, maltese cross wheels ($8-12)
36. white body, black base, frosted windows, blue dome/ spinner, checkered "Police:" labels, maltese cross wheels ($8-12)
37. white body, charcoal base, frosted windows, blue dome/ spinner, checkered "Police" labels, maltese cross wheels ($8-12)
38. white body, black base, frosted windows, blue dome/ spinner, "County Sheriff" labels, maltese cross wheels ($8-12)
39. white body, unpainted base, frosted windows, blue dome/ spinner, "County Sheriff" labels & blue roof tempa, maltese cross wheels ($8-12)
40. white body, black base, frosted windows, blue dome/ spinner, "County Sheriff" labels & blue roof tempa, maltese cross wheels($8-12)
41. metallic sand body, black base, frosted windows, red dome/ spinner, "Paris Dakar 83" labels, maltese cross wheels ($6-8)
42. beige body, black base, frosted windows, red dome/ spinner, "Paris Dakar 83" labels, maltese cross wheels ($6-8)
NOTE: Following models with "Matchbox International, England" bases
43. beige body, black base, frosted windows, red dome/ spinner, "Paris Dakar 83" tempa, maltese cross wheels ($4-6)
44. beige body, unpainted base, frosted windows, red dome/ spinner, "Paris Dakar 83" tempa, maltese cross wheels ($6-8)
45. white & black body, black base, frosted windows, red dome/ spinner, Japanese lettered tempa, maltese cross wheels ($8-12)(JP)
NOTE: Available as an Hungarian casting. Assorted colors available ($15-25)

MB20-C 4 X 4 JEEP, issued 1982 (USA)
MB14-F 4 X 4 JEEP, issued 1984 (ROW)
1. white body, black metal base, black interior, red canopy, "Desert Dawg" tempa, England casting ($3-5)
2. black body, black metal base, red interior, white canopy, "Laredo" tempa, Macau casting ($1-2)
3. black body, black metal base, red interior, white canopy, "Laredo" tempa, Hong Kong casting ($18-25)
4. dark tan body, black metal base, black interior, red canopy, "Golden Eagle" tempa, England casting ($18-25)
5. red body, black metal base, gray interior, white canopy, "Golden Eagle" tempa, Macau casting ($7-10)
6. olive body, black metal base, black interior, tan canopy, black & tan camouflage tempa, Macau casting ($4-6)(CM)
7. olive body, black plastic base, black interior, tan canopy, black & tan camouflage tempa, Macau casting ($4-6)(CM)
8. black body, black plastic base, red interior, white canopy, "Laredo" tempa, Macau casting ($1-2)
9. yellow body, black plastic base, blue interior, lime canopy, caricature tempa, red wheels with green hubs, Macau casting ($6-8)(LL)
10. black body, black plastic base, red interior, white canopy, "Laredo" tempa, Thailand casting ($1-2)
11. red body, greenish black metal base, gray interior, white canopy, "Golden Eagle" tempa, Macau casting ($7-10)
12. yellow body, black plastic base, blue interior, lime canopy, caricature tempa, red wheels with plain hubs, Thailand casting ($6-8)(LL)
13. black body, black plastic base, red interior, red canopy, "Laredo" tempa, Macau casting ($12-18)
14. yellow body, black plastic base, black interior, black roof, geometric hood design tempa, Thailand casting ($1-2)(MP)
NOTE: Above models with right hand drive. Below models with left hand drive unless otherwise noted.
15. yellow body, black plastic base, black interior, black roof, geometric hood design tempa, Thailand casting ($1-2)(MP)
16. beige body, black plastic base, black interior, beige roof, right hand drive, camouflage tempa, Thailand casting ($1-2)
17. beige body, black plastic base, black interior, beige roof, camouflage tempa, Thailand casting ($1-2)
18. pink-tan body, black plastic base, black interior, tan roof, green & brown camouflage tempa, Thailand casting ($1-2)(MP)
19. olive body, black plastic base, black interior, black roof, star & "V-9872-3" tempa, Thailand casting ($1-2)
20. beige body, black plastic base, black interior, black canopy, brown camouflage tempa, Thailand casting ($1-2)(MP)
21. dark sand body, black plastic base, black interior, dark sand canopy, star & "V-9873-3" tempa, Thailand casting ($1-2)(MP)
22. olive body, black plastic base, black interior, black canopy, red cross & "RB104" tempa, Thailand casting ($1-2)(PS)
23. pale olive body, black plastic base, black interior, pale olive canopy, white cross & "RB104" tempa, Thailand casting ($1-2)(PS)
24. light olive body, black plastic base, black interior, olive roof, red cross & "M*A*S*H" tempa, China casting ($4-6)(STR)
25. pale olive body, black plastic base, black interior, pale olive roof, white cross & "RB104" tempa, China casting ($1-2)(PS)

MB20-D VOLVO CONTAINER TRUCK, issued 1985 (ROW)
MB23-G VOLVO CONTAINER TRUCK, issued 1987 (USA)
MB62-I VOLVO CONTAINER TRUCK, reissued 1990 (ROW)
NOTE: all models with black base, amber windows, 5 arch wheels unless otherwise noted.
1. blue body, white container, "Coldfresh" labels, Macau casting ($3-5)
2. white body, white container, "Scotch Corner" labels, Macau casting ($8-12)(SC)
3. gray body, gray container, "Supersave Drugstores" labels, Macau casting ($8-12)(UK)
4. blue body, white container, "MB1-75 #1 in Volume Sales" labels, Macau casting ($35-50)(UK)
5. blue body, white container, "MB1-75 #1 in Volume Sales" labels, China casting ($35-50)(UK)
6. blue body, white container, "Coldfresh" labels, China casting ($3-5)
7. white body, white container, "Federal Express" labels, China casting ($3-5)
8. blue body, white container, "Unic" (towards front or rear) labels, China casting ($8-12)(BE)
9. blue body, blue container, "Crooke's Healthcare" labels, China casting ($6-8)(UK)
10. white body, white container, "Kellogg's/ Milch-Lait-Latte" labels, China casting ($35-50)(SW)(GR)
11. white body, white container, "TNT Ipec" labels, China casting ($4-6)(TC)
12. green body, gray container, "Hikkoshi Semmon Center" (in Japanese) labels, China casting ($10-15)(JP)
13. blue body, blue container, "Allders" labels, China casting ($6-8)(UK)
14. white body, white container, "XP Parcels" labels China casting ($4-6)(MP)
15. blue body, blue container, "Comma Performance Motor Oils" labels, China casting ($8-12)(UK)(OP)
16. blue body, white container, "Kellogg's/ Milch-Lait-Latte" labels, China casting ($35-50)(GR)(SW)
17. white body, white container, "Federal Express" (container) labels & "XP Parcels" doors tempa, China casting ($15-20)
18. red body, brown container, "Merkur Kaffee" labels, China casting ($8-12)(SW)
19. green body, white container, "M" & green stripe labels, China casting ($8-12)(SW)

20. red body, white container, "Denner" labels, China casting ($8-12)(SW)
21. white body, white container, "Family Trust" labels, China casting ($8-12)(CN)
22. blue body, red container, "Christiansaen" labels, China casting ($8-12)(BE)
23. white body, dark cream container, "Federal Express" labels, China casting ($2-3)
24. white body, white container, "Kit Kat" labels, China casting ($25-40)(UK)
25. white body, white container, "Yorkie" labels, China casting ($25-40)(UK)
26. red body, white container, "Big Top Circus" labels, China casting ($1-2)
27. white body, powder blue container, "Co Op- People Who Care" labels, China casting ($6-8)(UK)
28. blue body, white container, "Big Top Circus" labels, China casting ($8-12)(GS)
29. white body, powder blue container, "99 Tea" labels, China casting ($7-10)(UK)(OP)
30. black body, black container, "Cool Paint Co." labels, dark gray base, China casting ($1-2)
31. orange body, orange container, "Polar Power" labels, gray base, blue windows, China casting ($3-5)(WR)(GS)
32. white & red body, white container, "Auto Palace" labels, black base, China casting ($5-7)(US)
33. florescent orange body, yellow container, "Matchbox Get In The Fast Lane" labels with cab tempa, black windows, black base, China casting ($1-2)
34. florescent orange body, yellow container, "Matchbox Get In The Fast Lane" labels without cab tempa, black windows, black base, China casting ($1-2)
35. purple body, purple container, "Continental Aero" labels, gray base ($8-12)(US)
36. yellow body, yellow container, black windows, "Action System" labels, dark gray base, China casting ($8-12)(OP)
37. black body, yellow container, "Matchbox Auto Products" labels, China casting ($1-2)
38. turquoise body, black container, smoke windows, "Matchbox Auto Products" labels, China casting ($1-2)(MP)
39. dark turquoise body, white container, smoke windows, "Sagamore Insurance" tempa, China casting ($85-110)(US)
40. metallic gold body, black container, black windows, no labels, China casting ($5-10)(CH)
41. white body, white container, "Matchbox asi 33000" tempa, China casting ($75+)(ASAP)
42. white body, white container, "PC Van Go" (left side only) tempa, China casting ($50+)(ASAP)
43. white body, white container, "Dupont Answers" labels, China casting ($50+)(ASAP)
44. white body, white container, "Dupont Floor Covering" labels, China casting ($50+)(ASAP)
45. white body, white container, "CFU" in red (right side only) tempa, China casting ($25+)(ASAP)
46. white body, white container, "CFU" in blue (right side only) tempa, China casting ($50+)(ASAP)
47. red body, yellow container, black windows, "Matchbox Animals" labels, China casting ($1-2)(MW44)
48. red body, blue container, black windows, "Matchbox" with red arrow labels ($1-2)(MW1-ROW)
49. white body, white container, "Two Men and A Truck" tempa, China casting ($10-15)(ASAP)
50. white body, white container, "Harty Press" labels, China casting ($100+)(ASAP)
51. blue body, yellow container, "Airways Air Cargo" labels, China casting ($1-2)(MP)
52. white body, white container, "Bill Cairns- Let Bill Move you" tempa, China casting ($20+)(ASAP)
53. white body, blue container, blue windows, "The Matchbox Times" labels, China casting ($1-2)(MP)
54. white body, white container, no labels, China casting ($15-25)(ASAP blank)
55. white body, white container, "RCA" tempa, China casting ($75+)(ASAP)
56. white body, white container, "HiSpeed/Garvens" tempa, China casting ($25+)(ASAP)

MB20-E VOLKSWAGEN TRANSPORTER, issued 1988 (ROW)

NOTE: All models with blue windows & dome lights, gray interior.

1. white body, black base, 8 dot silver wheels, orange stripe & cross tempa, Macau casting ($2-4)
2. black body, black base, 8 dot black wheels, green cross & "LS2081" tempa, Macau casting ($4-6)(CM)
3. white body, black base, 8 dot silver wheels, red stripe & cross tempa, Macau casting ($2-4)
4. white body, black base, 8 dot silver wheels, red stripe & cross tempa, China casting ($2-4)
5. black body, black base, 8 dot black wheels, green cross & "LS2081" tempa, China casting ($4-6)(CM)
6. white body, white base, 8 dot silver wheels, no tempa, China casting ($10-15)(GF)
7. white body, black base, 8 dot silver wheels, red stripe/ cross & "Ambulance" tempa, China casting ($1-2)
8. white body, black base, 8 dot silver wheels, green "Ambulance" with orange dashes & "Paramedic" logo tempa, China casting ($2-3)

MB20-F PONTIAC FIREBIRD RAM AIR, issued 1997 (USA)
MB66-H PONTIAC FIREBIRD RAM AIR, issued 1997 (ROW)

NOTE: All models listed with clear windows & black base.

1. lemon body, black interior, 5 spoke concave star wheels, "Formula V-8/ Ram Air" tempa, Thailand casting ($1-2)
2. silver-gray body, black & maroon interior, chrome disc with rubber tires, detailed trim tempa, Thailand casting ($3-5)(PC14)
3. black body, tan interior, 5 spoke concave star wheels, "Formula V-8/ Ram Air" tempa, Thailand casting ($1-2)(MW72)
4. black body, tan interior, 5 spoke concave star wheels, "Formula V-8/ Ram Air" tempa, China casting ($1-2)(MW72)
5. metallic gold body, black interior, 5 spoke concave star wheels, no tempa, Thailand casting ($8-12)(CH)
6. metallic gold body, black interior, 5 spoke concave star wheels, no tempa, China casting ($5-10)(CH)

MB21-A FODEN CEMENT TRUCK, issued 1970

1. yellow body, yellow barrel, green base ($20-35)
2. bright yellow body, yellow barrel, green base ($20-35)
3. bright yellow body, yellow barrel, dark green base ($20-35)

MB21-B ROD ROLLER, issued 1973

1. yellow body, green base, hood label, metallic red rear wheels ($18-25)
2. yellow body, green base, hood label, red rear wheels ($15-18)
3. yellow body, green base, hood label, black rear wheels ($12-15)
4. yellow body, black base, hood label, black rear wheels ($15-18)
5. yellow body, green base, no label, black rear wheels ($12-15)
6. orange-yellow body, black base, hood label, black rear wheels ($15-18)
7. orange-yellow body, green base, hood label, black rear wheels ($12-15)

MB21-C RENAULT 5TL, issued 1978

NOTE: Following models with dot dash silver wheels and England casting unless otherwise noted. Tailgate color matches body color.

1. yellow body, tan interior, silver-gray base, clear windows, "Le Car" tempa ($4-6)
2. yellow body, tan interior, black base, clear windows, "Le Car" tempa ($4-6)
3. yellow body, tan interior, silver-gray base, amber windows, "Le Car" tempa ($4-6)
4. yellow body, tan interior, black base, amber windows, Le Car" tempa ($4-6)
5. yellow body, red interior, black base, clear windows, "Le Car" tempa ($8-12)
6. yellow body, red interior, silver-gray base, clear windows, "Le Car" tempa ($8-12)
7. yellow body, tan interior, charcoal base, clear windows, "Le Car" tempa ($4-6)
8. yellow body, tan interior, charcoal base, amber windows, "Le Car" tempa ($4-6)
9. yellow body, gray-yellow interior, charcoal base, clear windows, "Le Car" tempa ($4-6)
10. blue body, tan interior, silver-gray base, clear windows, no tempa, black hubs ($4-6)
11. blue body, tan interior, silver-gray base, clear windows, no tempa ($4-6)
12. blue body, tan interior, black base, clear windows, no tempa ($4-6)
13. blue body, tan interior, silver-gray base, amber windows, no tempa ($4-6)
14. blue body, tan interior, black base, amber windows, no tempa ($4-6)
15. blue body, tan interior, charcoal base, clear windows, no tempa, ($4-6)
16. blue body, red interior, silver-gray base, clear windows, no tempa ($8-12)
17. blue body, red interior, black base, clear windows, no tempa ($8-12)
18. silver-gray body, tan interior, silver-gray base, clear windows, no tempa ($18-25)
19. silver-gray body, tan interior, black base, clear windows, no tempa ($18-25)
20. silver-gray body, red interior, black base, clear windows, "A5" tempa ($15-20)
21. silver-gray body, red interior, silver-gray base, clear windows, "A5" tempa ($15-20)
22. silver-gray body, red interior, silver-gray base, clear windows, no tempa ($4-6)
23. silver-gray body, red interior, black base, clear windows, "Le Car" tempa ($4-6)
24. silver-gray body, red interior, charcoal base, clear windows, "Le Car" tempa ($4-6)
25. silver-gray body, red interior, black base, amber windows, "Le Car" tempa ($4-6)
26. silver-gray body, red interior, charcoal base, amber windows, "Le Car" tempa ($4-6)
27. silver-gray body, red interior, charcoal base, clear windows, "Le Car" tempa, black hubs ($4-6)
28. silver-gray body, red interior, blue-gray base, orange windows, "Le Car" tempa ($4-6)
29. silver-gray body, red interior, gray-brown base, clear windows, "Le Car" tempa ($4-6)
30. white body, tan interior, black base, clear windows, "Renault" tempa ($3-5)
31. white body, tan interior, charcoal base, clear windows, "Renault" tempa ($3-5)
32. white body, light yellow interior, black base, clear windows, "Renault" tempa($3-5)
33. white body, light yellow interior, charcoal base, clear windows, "Renault" tempa ($4-6)
34. white body, white interior, black base, clear windows, "Renault" tempa ($4-6)
35. white body, tan interior, black base, clear windows, "Renault" tempa (plain roof) ($4-6)
36. white body, tan interior, black base, clear windows, "Renault" tempa (plain sides) ($8-12)
37. white body, tan interior, black base, clear windows, "Roloil" tempa ($3-5)
38. white body, dark yellow interior, black base, clear windows, "Roloil" tempa ($3-5)
39. white body, white interior, black base, clear windows, "Roloil" tempa ($3-5)
40. white body, tan interior, orange base, clear windows, "Roloil" tempa ($15-20)
41. red body, orange interior, orange base, clear windows, "Turbo" tempa ($15-20)(JP)
42. red body, tan interior, black base, clear windows, "Turbo" tempa ($18-25)
43. white body, tan interior, black base, clear windows, "Roloil" tempa, Macau casting ($3-4)(TP)
44. pearly silver body, black interior, black base, clear windows, "Scrambler" tempa, Macau casting ($4-6)(TP)
45. powder blue body, tan interior, black base, clear windows, no tempa, Manaus casting ($75-100)(BR)
46. white body, tan interior, cream base, clear windows, "Roloil" tempa, Manaus casting ($35-50)(BR)
47. white body, tan interior, black base, clear windows, "Roloil" tempa, Manaus casting ($35-50)(BR)

NOTE: Available as a Bulgarian casting ($15-25)

MB21-D CORVETTE PACE CAR, issued 1983 (USA)

NOTE: all models with 5 arch front & 5 crown rear wheels but other wheel combinations exist.

1. pearly silver body, red interior & base, without "Pace" on trunk, Macau casting ($5-8)
2. pearly silver body, red interior & base, with "Pace" on trunk, Macau casting ($5-8)

MB21-E CHEVY BREAKDOWN VAN, issued 1985
MB53-F CHEVY BREAKDOWN VAN, reissued 1990 (USA)

NOTE: All models with blue windows, black tow hook, 8 spoke silver wheels unless otherwise noted.

1. red body, pearly silver base, silver-gray interior, white boom, "24 Hour Service" tempa, Macau casting ($1-2)
2. red body, pearly gray base, silver-gray interior, white boom, "24 Hour Service" tempa, China casting ($1-2)
3. red body, pearly gray base, silver-gray interior, white boom, "24 Hours" with white stripes tempa, China casting ($2-3)(MP)
4. yellow body, black base, black interior, black boom, "Auto Relay 24 Hr. Tow" tempa, China casting ($1-2)
5. black body, gray base, gray interior, gray boom, yellow stripes tempa, black hubs, China casting ($4-6)(CM)
6. black body, gray base, gray interior, gray boom, yellow stripes tempa, silver hubs, China casting ($5-7)(CM)
7. red body, yellow base, silver-gray interior, green boom, cartoon towed car tempa, blue wheels with yellow hubs, China casting ($6-8)(LL)
8. dark orange body, black base, orange-yellow interior, orange-yellow boom, "Auto Relay 24 Hr. Tow" tempa, China casting ($3-5)(AP)
9. white body, black base, black interior, black boom, "Auto Rescue" tempa, China casting ($2-4)(EM)
10. white body, white base, red interior, white boom, no tempa, red windows, China casting ($10-15)(GF)
11. orange-yellow body, greenish black base, black interior, black boom, "Auto Relay 24 Hr. Tow" tempa, China casting ($1-2)
12. red body, yellow base, silver-gray interior, green boom, cartoon towed car tempa, all blue wheels, China casting ($6-8)(LL)
13. florescent orange body, black base with bar code, black interior, black boom, "Intercom City Auto Service 7" tempa, China casting ($10-15)(IC)
14. black body, black base, black interior, red boom & hook, "24" with hand & car logo tempa, China casting ($1-2)(MP)
15. lemon body, black base, red windows, black interior, black boom, sling hook, "Rob's Towing 24 Hours" tempa, China casting ($1-2)(AS)
16. matt olive body, silver-gray base, smoke windows, pearly silver boom & sling hook, "Gen IV" & "The Lost World" tempa, China casting ($5-8)(JR)
17. silver-gray body, black base, red windows, black boom & sling hook, "Rob's Towing 24 Hours" tempa, China casting ($1-2)(AP)
18. black body, gray base, gray boom, 5 crown wheels with black hubs, yellow stripes & Commando logo tempa, China casting ($20-25)(CHI)(MP)

MB21-F GMC WRECKER, issued 1987 (USA)
MB71-F GMC WRECKER, issued 1987 (ROW)

NOTE: Following models with white rear bed, white boom, black hook, cloudy amber windows, 8 spoke wheels unless otherwise noted.

1. white body, unpainted metal base, "Frank's Getty" with phone no. tempa, Macau casting ($1-2)
2. white body, unpainted metal base, "Accessory Wholesalers Inc." tempa, Macau casting ($18-25)(US)
3. white body, chrome plastic base, "Frank's Getty" with phone no. tempa, Macau casting ($1-2)
4. white body, chrome plastic base, "Frank's Getty" with phone no. tempa, China casting ($1-2)
5. white body, chrome plastic base, "Frank's Getty" with phone no. tempa, Thailand casting ($1-2)
6. white body, chrome plastic base, "Frank's Getty" with phone no. tempa, no origin cast ($3-5)
7. white body, chrome plastic base, "Frank's Getty" tempa without phone no. tempa, China casting ($1-2)
8. white body, chrome plastic base, "Frank's Getty" tempa without phone no. (solid color tempa), Thailand casting ($1-2)
9. black body, chrome plastic base, "Official Wrecker Indy 500" tempa, Thailand casting ($5-8)(IN)

10. white body, chrome plastic base, "Police/Metro Emergency" tempa, Thailand casting ($1-2)(MP)
11. white body, chrome plastic base, "Polioe/Metro Emergency" tempa, Thailand casting ($1-2)(MP) *NOTE: misspelled Police (POLIOE).*
12. red body, chrome plastic base, black boom, "Ron's Towing" tempa, Thailand casting ($2-4)(CC)
13. white body, chrome plastic base, florescent orange boom, "3 Rescue", checkers & wrench design tempa, Thailand casting ($2-4)(Fl)
14. black body, chrome plastic base, white boom, "Police Emergency Unit 4" & gold star tempa, Thailand casting ($1-2)(MP)
15. dark purple body, chrome plastic base, neon yellow boom, "Park Hill Towing" with hood design tempa, Thailand casting ($1-2)
16. dark purple body, chrome plastic base, neon yellow boom, "Park Hill Towing" without hood design tempa, Thailand casting ($1-2)
17. red body, chrome plastic base, neon yellow boom, "Park Hill Towing" without hood design tempa, China casting ($1-2)
18. metallic gold body, chrome plastic base, black boom, no tempa, China casting ($5-10)(CH)
19. white body, chrome plastic base, florescent orange boom, "3 Rescue", checkers & wrench design tempa, China casting ($1-2)(Fl)
20. dark purple body, chrome plastic base, neon yellow boom, "Park Hill Towing" without hood design tempa, China casting ($2-4)
21. orange body, chrome plastic base, black boom, "Park Hill Towing" without hood design tempa, orange hook, China casting ($5-8)(ROW)
22. white body, chrome plastic base, black boom, "Matchbox 24 Hr. Towing" tempa, China casting ($2-4)(MP)
23. white body, chrome plastic base, red windows, blue boom, "CAA Member Service" tempa, China casting ($100-150)(CN)
24. white body, chrome plastic base, amber windows, blue boom, "CAA Member Service" tempa, China casting ($10-15)(CN)
25. white body, chrome plastic base, white boom, "Matchbox 33000" tempa, China casting ($50+)(ASAP)
26. white body, chrome plastic base, white boom, "Phil's Body Works" tempa, China casting ($100+)(ASAP)
27. black body, chrome plastic base, white boom, "Matchbox" with yellow & white design tempa, China casting ($1-2)(MW63)
28. white body, chrome plastic base, white boom, "PTROI" tempa, China casting ($20-35)(ASAP)
29. white body, chrome plastic base, white boom, no tempa, China casting ($20-25)(ASAP blank)
30. white body, chrome plastic base, white boom, "American International Recovery" tempa, China casting ($100+)(ASAP)

MB22-A PONTIAC GRAND PRIX, issued 1970
1. red body, gray interior, black base ($2000+)
2. dark purple body, gray interior, black base ($50-65)
3. light purple body, gray interior, black base ($50-65)

MB22-B FREEMAN INTERCITY COMMUTER, issued 1970
1. purple body, unpainted base, ivory interior, no labels ($15-18)
2. purple body, unpainted base, ivory interior, with labels ($15-18)
3. gold body, unpainted base, ivory interior, with labels ($15-18)
4. magenta body, unpainted base, ivory interior, no labels ($15-18)
5. magenta body, unpainted base, ivory interior, with labels ($15-18)
6. magenta body, silver-gray base, ivory interior, no labels ($15-18)
7. magenta body, silver-gray base, ivory interior, with labels ($15-18)
8. magenta body, unpainted base, white interior, no labels ($15-18)

MB22-C BLAZE BUSTER, issued 1975
1. red body, white ladder, unpainted base, chrome interior, 5 spoke wheels "Fire" labels ($250-400)
2. red body, black ladder, unpainted base, chrome interior, 5 spoke wheels, "Fire" labels ($20-35)
3. red body, yellow ladder, unpainted base, chrome interior, 5 spoke wheels, "Fire" labels ($5-8)
4. red body, yellow ladder, unpainted (label) base, chrome interior, 5 spoke wheels, "Fire" labels ($35-50)(BR)
5. red body, yellow ladder, gray (label) base, chrome interior, 5 spoke wheels, "Fire" label s ($65-85)(BR)
6. red body, yellow ladder, black base, chrome interior, 5 spoke wheels, "Fire" labels ($5-8)
7. red body, yellow ladder, black base, white interior, 5 spoke wheels, "Fire" labels ($5-8)
8. red body, yellow ladder, black base, white interior, 4 spoke wheels, "Fire" labels ($5-8)
9. red body, yellow ladder, charcoal base, white interior, 5 spoke wheels, "Fire" labels ($5-8)
10. red body, yellow ladder, charcoal base, white interior, 4 spoke wheels, "Fire" labels ($5-8)
11. dark red body, yellow ladder, black base, white interior, 4 spoke wheels, "Fire" labels ($5-8)
12. dark red body, yellow ladder, charcoal base, white interior, 5 spoke wheels, "Fire" labels ($5-8)
13. dark red body, yellow ladder, gray-brown base, white interior, 5 spoke wheels, "Fire" labels ($5-8)
14. dull red body, orange-yellow ladder, black base, white interior, 5 spoke wheels, "Fire" labels ($5-8)
15. dull red body, orange-yellow ladder, black base, white interior, 5 spoke wheels, "No. 32" labels ($8-12)
NOTE: Available as a Bulgarian casting. Assorted variations available ($8-15)

MB22-D 4 X 4 MINI PICKUP, issued 1982 (USA)
MB35-E 4 X 4 MINI PICKUP, issued 1986 (ROW)
1. silver-gray body, unpainted metal base, white stepped roof, "Big Foot" tempa, England casting ($4-6)
2. silver-gray body, unpainted metal base, white stepped roof, "Big Foot" tempa (plain sides), England casting ($5-8)
3. silver-gray body, unpainted metal base, white flat roof, "Big Foot" tempa, England casting ($4-6)
4. silver-gray body, silver-gray metal base, white flat roof, "Big Foot" tempa, England casting ($4-6)
5. silver-gray body, unpainted metal base, black roll bar, "Big Foot" tempa, England casting ($35-50)
6. pearly silver body, black metal base, white flat roof, "Big Foot" tempa, Hong Kong casting ($5-8)
7. pearly silver body, black metal base, white flat roof, "Big Foot" tempa, Macau casting ($4-6)
8. red body, black metal base, white flat roof, "Aspen Ski Holidays" tempa, Macau casting ($2-4)
9. white body, black metal base, white flat roof, "SLD Pump Service" tempa, Macau casting ($10-15)(UK)
10. red body, black plastic base, white flat roof, "Aspen Ski Holidays" tempa, Macau casting ($2-3)
11. red body, black plastic base, white flat roof, "Aspen Ski Holidays" tempa, Thailand casting ($2-3)

MB22-E JAGUAR XK120, issued 1984 (ROW)
NOTE: All models with 5 crown wheels unless otherwise noted.
1. dark green body, red interior, silver-gray base, clear windshield, no tempa, England casting ($2-4)
2. dark green body, red interior, unpainted base, clear windshield, no tempa, England casting ($2-4)
3. dark green body, red interior, pearly silver base, clear windshield, no tempa, Macau casting ($2-4)
4. dark green body, red interior, pearly silver base, amber windshield, no tempa, Macau casting ($2-4)
5. cream body, red interior, pearly silver base, clear windshield, "414" tempa, Macau casting ($1-2)
6. white body, dark maroon interior, pearly silver base, chrome windshield, detailed trim tempa, gray disc with rubber tires, Macau casting ($5-8)(WC)
7. dark cream body, dark red interior, pearly silver base, clear windshield, "414" tempa, Macau casting ($1-2)
8. cream body, red interior, pearly silver base, clear windshield, "414" tempa, Thailand casting ($1-2)
9. white body, purplish black interior, pearly silver base, chrome windshield, detailed trim tempa, gray disc with rubber tires, Thailand casting ($5-8)(WC)
10. white body, orange interior, pearly silver base, amber windshield, blue & orange flash tempa, Thailand casting ($3-5)(DM)
11. red body, white interior, pearly silver base, clear windshield, 5 crown wheels, no tempa, Thailand casting ($2-4)(SS)
12. black body, orange interior, pearly silver base, clear windshield, 5 crown wheels, detailed trim tempa, Thailand casting ($2-4)(CC)
13. dark green body, tan/brown interior, black base, clear windshield, chrome disc with rubber tires, detailed trim tempa, China casting ($3-5)(PC3)
14. red body, mustard/brown interior, black base, clear windshield, chrome disc with rubber tires, detailed trim tempa, China casting ($3-5)(PC6)
15. black body, mustard & brown interior, black base, clear windshield, chrome disc with rubber tires, detailed trim tempa, China casting ($3-5)(SC3)
16. pale olive body, maroon interior, black base, clear windshield, no tempa, China casting ($2-4)
17. dark green body, tan interior, black base, clear windshield, no tempa, gold 6 spoke spiral wheels, China casting ($75+)(CHI)
18. red body, tan interior, black base, clear windshield,, no tempa, gold 6 spoke spiral wheels, China casting ($75+)(CHI)

MB22-G VECTRA CAVALIER Gsi 2000, issued 1990 (USA)
MB41-G VECTRA CAVALIER Gsi 2000, issued 1990 (ROW)
NOTE: All models with black base, clear windows, gray interior, 8 dot wheels, no tempa.
1. metallic red body, Macau casting ($1-2)
2. metallic pink-red body, Macau casting ($1-2)
3. metallic pink-red body, China casting ($1-2)
4. green body, China casting ($8-12)(GR)(GS)

MB22-H LAMBORGHINI DIABLO, issued 1992 (USA)
MB49-F LAMBORGHINI DIABLO, issued 1992 (ROW)
1. yellow body, yellow base, black interior, clear windows, 8 dot wheels, "Diablo" tempa, China casting ($1-2)
2. red body, red base, black interior, chrome windows, gray disc with rubbers tires, detailed trim tempa, China casting ($5-8)(WC)
3. fluorescent yellow body, fluorescent yellow base, clear windows, black interior, 8 dot wheels, small "Lamborghini" logo tempa, China casting ($2-4)(SS)
4. red body, red base, black interior, clear windows, black interior, 8 dot wheels, "Diablo" tempa, Thailand casting ($50-75)(SP)(UK)
5. black body, black base, chrome windows, black interior, gray disc rubber tires, no tempa, Thailand casting ($2-4)(WC)
6. yellow body, yellow base, clear windows, black interior, 8 dot wheels, "Diablo" tempa, Thailand casting ($1-2)
7. yellow body, yellow base, clear windows, black interior, 6-spoke gold spiral wheels, "Diablo" tempa, Thailand casting ($2-3)
8. metallic blue & black body, black base, clear windows, orange interior, 6-spoke gold spiral wheels, orange & white flash tempa, Thailand casting ($1-2)
9. hot pink body, black base, clear windows, black interior, silver 6-spoke spiral wheels, black blotches tempa, Thailand casting ($1-2)(MP)
10. florescent yellow body, black base, clear windows, pink interior, silver 6-spoke spiral wheels, black blotches tempa, Thailand casting ($1-2)
11. silver body, black base, amber windows, white interior, silver 6-spoke spiral wheels, orange & yellow flames tempa, Thailand casting ($3-5)(MT)
12. dark purple body, black base, clear windows, orange interior, silver 6-spoke spiral wheels, white blotches tempa, Thailand casting ($1-2)(MP)
13. metallic mauve body, mauve base, clear windows, blue/black interior, chrome disc with rubber tires, detailed trim tempa, Thailand casting ($3-5)(PC3)
14. red body, black base, clear windows, yellow interior, silver 6-spoke spiral wheels, black blotches tempa, Thailand casting ($3-5)
15. silver-gray body, gray base, clear windows, blue/black interior, chrome disc with rubber tires, detailed trim tempa, Thailand casting ($3-5)(PC6)
16. yellow body, yellow base, clear windows, gray/black interior, chrome disc with rubber tires, detailed trim tempa, Thailand casting ($3-5)(PC1)(AU)
17. blue body, blue base, clear windows, blue/ gray interior, chrome disc with rubber tires, detailed trim tempa, Thailand casting ($3-5)(SC2)
18. blue body, black base, clear windows, brown interior, 5 spoke concave star wheels, white "Diablo" with white & black design tempa, Thailand casting ($1-2)
19. metallic gold body, black base, clear windows, black interior, silver 6 spoke spiral wheels, no tempa, Thailand casting ($5-10)(CH)
20. white body, black base, clear windows, blue & gray interior, chrome disc with rubber tires, detailed trim tempa, Thailand casting ($15-20)(GC)
21. metallic gold body, black base, clear windows, black interior, 5 spoke concave star wheels, no tempa, Thailand casting ($10-15)(CH)
22. blue body, black painted base, clear windows, brown interior, 5 spoke concave star wheels, white "Diablo" with black & white design tempa, Thailand casting ($2-4)(MP)
23. black body, black base, clear windows, red interior, 5 spoke concave star wheels, "Lamborghini" tempa, Thailand casting ($1-2)(ROW)
24. metallic turquoise body, black base, clear windows, black & gray interior, chrome disc with rubber tires, detailed trim tempa, Thailand casting ($3-5)(JP)(PC)
25. red body, black base, clear windows, black & red interior, chrome disc with rubber tires, detailed trim tempa, Thailand casting ($3-5)(SC4)
26. yellow chrome body, black base, black interior, 5 spoke concave star wheels, orange/white/dark pink tempa, Thailand casting ($1-2)(MP)
27. metallic purple body, purple base, black & gray interior, chrome disc with rubber tires, detailed trim tempa, Thailand casting ($3-5)(SC5)
28. gold body, gold base, gray & black interior, chrome disc with rubber tires, detailed trim tempa, Thailand casting ($3-5)(PC19)
29. yellow chrome body, black interior, 5 spoke concave star wheels, orange/white/dark pink tempa, China casting ($1-2)(MP)

MB23-A VOLKSWAGEN CAMPER/ DORMOBILE, issued 1970
1. blue body, unpainted base, orange interior, clear windows, no labels, 5 spoke wheels, orange roof cast ($15-18)
2. blue body, unpainted base, orange interior, clear windows, sailboat labels, 5 spoke wheels, orange roof cast ($15-18)
3. orange body, unpainted base, orange interior, clear windows, sailboat labels, 5 spoke wheels, orange roof cast ($125-175)
4. orange body, unpainted base, white interior, clear windows, sailboat labels, 5 spoke wheels, orange roof cast ($12-15)
5. orange body, unpainted base, white interior, clear windows, no labels, 5 spoke wheels, orange roof cast ($12-15)
6. olive body, black base, no interior, blue windows, cross labels, dot dash wheels with silver hubs ($6-8)(TP)
7. olive body, black base, no interior, blue windows, cross labels, dot dash wheels with black hubs ($6-8)(TP)
8. white body, black base, no interior, green windows, "Pizza Van" tempa, dot dash wheels with black hubs ($8-12)(LE)
9. white body, black base, no interior, green windows, "Pizza Van" tempa, dot dash wheels with silver hubs ($8-12)(LE)
10. white body, black base, no interior, green windows, "Pizza Van" tempa, 5 arch wheels ($8-12)(LE)
NOTE: Available as an Hungarian casting. Assorted colors available. Casting has the opening roof with various "Pizza Van" color variations ($15-35)

MB23-B ATLAS, issued 1975
NOTE: All models with England casting unless otherwise noted.
1. blue body, orange dump, unpainted base, amber windows, chrome interior, spiro wheels, with labels ($8-12)
2. blue body, orange dump, unpainted base, amber windows, chrome interior, spiro wheels, no labels ($8-12)
3. blue body, orange dump, unpainted base, amber windows, chrome interior, dot dash wheels, no labels ($8-12)
4. blue body, orange dump, unpainted base, amber windows, gray interior, dot dash wheels, no labels ($8-12)
5. blue body, orange dump, silver-gray base, amber windows, gray interior, dot dash wheels, no labels ($8-12)
6. blue body, orange dump, unpainted base, clear windows, gray interior, dot dash wheels ($8-12)
7. blue body, orange dump, silver-gray base, clear windows, gray interior, dot dash wheels ($8-12)
8. blue body, orange dump, silver-gray base, clear windows, orange interior, dot dash wheels ($8-12)
9. blue body, silver-gray dump, silver-gray base, clear windows, gray interior, dot dash wheels ($10-15)
10. red body, silver-gray dump, silver-gray base, clear windows, gray interior, dot dash wheels ($7-10)
11. red body, silver-gray dump, silver-gray base, clear windows, black interior, dot dash wheels ($7-10)
12. mid blue body, yellow dump, black plastic base, clear windows, gray interior, maltese cross wheels, China casting ($7-10)(MP)

MB23-C GT350 MUSTANG, issued 1981 (USA)
1. white body, blue interior, 5 arch wheels, black base, blue stripes tempa, Hong Kong casting ($8-12)

MB23-D AUDI QUATTRO, issued 1982 (USA)
MB25-F AUDI QUATTRO, issued 1982 (ROW)
NOTE: All models with black interior.
1. white body, charcoal base, clear windows, 5 arch wheels, "Audi 20" tempa, England casting ($2-4)
2. white body, black base, clear windows, 5 arch wheels, "Audi 20" tempa, England casting ($2-4)
3. white body, black base, clear windows, 5 arch wheels, "Audi 20" (plain sides) tempa, England casting ($2-4)
4. white body, black base, clear windows, 5 arch wheels, "Audi 20" tempa, Macau casting ($2-4)
5. white body, black base, light amber windows, 5 arch wheels, "Audi 20" tempa, Macau casting ($2-4)
6. white body, black base, clear windows, 5 arch wheels, "Duckhams/ Pirelli" tempa, Macau casting ($3-5)
7. white body, black base, clear windows, 5 arch wheels, "Duckhams/ Pirelli" (plain hood) tempa, Macau casting ($3-5)
8. white body, black base, clear windows, 5 arch wheels, "Duckhams" (without "Pirelli") tempa, Macau casting ($3-5)
9. white body, black base, amber windows, 5 arch wheels, "Duckhams/ Pirelli" tempa, Macau casting ($3-5)
10. plum body, black base, clear windows, 5 arch wheels, "Quattro 0000" tempa, Macau casting ($2-4)
11. plum body, black base, clear windows, 8 dot wheels, "Quattro 0000" tempa, Macau casting ($2-4)
12. dark blue body, black base, clear windows, 8 dot wheels, "Quattro 0000" & "Audi" tempa, Macau casting ($8-12)
13. dark blue body, black base, amber windows, 8 dot wheels, "Quattro 0000" & "Audi" tempa, Macau casting ($8-12)
14. dark plum body, black base, clear windows, 5 arch wheels, "Quattro 0000" tempa, China casting ($2-4)
15. dark gray body, black base, clear windows, 5 arch wheels, "0000 Quattro" & "Audi" tempa, China casting ($2-4)
16. dark blue body, black base, clear windows, 5 arch wheels, & "Audi 2584584" & "FT" tempa, China casting ($35-50)(CHI)
17. white body, black base, clear windows, 8 dot wheels, "Audi 20" tempa, Manaus casting ($35-50)(BR)
18. green body, black base, clear windows, 8 dot wheels, two-tone green band & silver "Audi" tempa, Manaus casting ($35-50)(BR)
19. dark cream body, black base, clear windows, 8 dot wheels, "Audi 20" tempa, Manaus casting ($35-50)(BR)

MB23-F HONDA ATC, issued 1985 (USA)
1. red body with blue painted seat, red handlebars, yellow wheels, Macau casting ($8-10)
2. red body with blue painted seat, red handlebars, yellow wheels, China casting ($8-10)
3. fluorescent green body with black painted seat, florescent orange handlebars, white wheels, China casting ($4-6)(KS)
4. fluorescent green body with black painted seat, fluorescent orange handlebars, white wheels, Macau casting ($3-5)(KS)

MB24-A ROLLS ROYCE SILVER SHADOW, issued 1970
NOTE: All models with ivory interior, clear windows
1. light metallic red body, black base ($12-15)
2. dark metallic red body, black base ($12-15)
3. dark metallic red body, gray base ($12-15)
4. dark metallic red body, charcoal base ($12-15)
5. dark metallic red body, silver-gray base ($12-15)
6. dark metallic red body, metallic green base ($15-18)
7. dark metallic red body, pink base ($15-18)
8. metallic gold body, black base ($15-18)(JP)
9. metallic gold body, unpainted base ($15-18)(JP)
NOTE: Available as a Bulgarian casting ($25-35)

MB24-B TEAM MATCHBOX, issued 1973
1. yellow body, white driver, "8" label, maltese cross rear wheels, no trailer ($225-275)
2. yellow body, white driver, "4" label, maltese cross rear wheels, no trailer ($300-375)(GS)
3. blue body, white driver, "1" label, maltese cross rear wheels, no trailer ($300-375)(GS)
4. blue body, white driver, "5" label, maltese cross rear wheels, no trailer ($300-375)(GS)
5. green body, white driver, "5" label, maltese cross rear wheels, no trailer ($45-60)(GS)
6. green body, white driver, "5" label, 5 arch rear wheels, no trailer ($45-60)(GS)
7. green body, white driver, "8" label, maltese cross rear wheels, no trailer ($45-60)(GS)
8. red body, white driver, "8" label, 5 arch rear wheels, no trailer ($6-8)
9. red body, white driver, "8" label, maltese cross rear wheels, no trailer ($6-8)
10. red body, white driver, "8" label, maltese cross rear wheels, no trailer, label on base ($50-65)(BR)
11. red body, white driver, "44" label, maltese cross rear wheels, no trailer ($5-7)(GS)
12. red body, white driver, "44" label, maltese cross rear wheels, with trailer ($5-7)(TP)
13. red body, lemon driver, "44" label, maltese cross rear wheels, no trailer ($18-25)(GS)
14. orange body, tan driver, "44" label, maltese cross rear wheels, no trailer ($50-75)(GS)
15. orange body, tan driver, "44" label, maltese cross rear wheels, with trailer ($50-75)(TP)
16. orange body, lemon driver, "44" label, maltese cross rear wheels, no trailer ($50-75)(GS)
17. orange body, lemon driver, "44" label, 5 spoke front wheels & maltese cross rear wheels, with trailer ($50-75)(TP)

MB24-C SHUNTER, issued 1979
1. dark green body, red metal undercarriage, red base, tan panel, "Rail Freight" labels, England casting ($7-10)
2. dark green body, red metal undercarriage, red base, tan panel, "D1496-RF" labels, England casting ($7-10)
3. light yellow body, red metal undercarriage, red base, tan panel, "D1496-RF" labels, England casting ($4-6)
4. light yellow body, red metal undercarriage, red base, brown panel, "D1496-RF" labels, England casting ($4-6)
5. light yellow body, red metal undercarriage, red base, no panel, "D1496-RF" labels, England casting ($4-6)
6. dark yellow body, red metal undercarriage, red base, tan panel, "D1496-RF" labels, England casting ($4-6)
7. dark yellow body, red metal undercarriage, red base, brown panel, "D1496-RF" labels, England casting ($4-6)
8. dark yellow body, red metal undercarriage, red base, no panel, "D1496-RF" labels, England casting ($4-6)
9. dark yellow body, metallic red undercarriage, red base, tan panel, "D1496-RF" labels, no origin casting ($75-100)(BR)
10. dark yellow body, red plastic undercarriage, red base, no panel, "D1496-RF" labels, England casting ($4-6)
11. dark yellow body, red plastic undercarriage, black base, no panel, "D1496-RF" labels, England casting ($5-8)
12. dark yellow body, yellow plastic undercarriage, black base, no panel, "D1496-RF" labels, England casting ($75-100)
13. dark yellow body, red plastic undercarriage, black base, no panel, "D1496-RF" tempa, Macau casting ($2-4)(MC)
14. dark yellow body, red plastic undercarriage, black base, no panel, "D1496-RF" tempa, China casting ($2-4)(MC)
15. orange-yellow body, red plastic undercarriage, black base, no panel, "D1496-RF" tempa, China casting ($2-4)(TP)

MB24-D DATSUN 280ZX, issued 1981 (USA)
NOTE: all models with clear windows, black base & Hong Kong casting.
1. black body, white interior, red hood tempa, maltese cross wheels ($2-4)
2. black body, white interior, red hood tempa, 5 spoke wheels ($2-4)
3. black body, dull red interior, red hood tempa, 5 spoke wheels ($3-5)
4. black body, dull red interior, no tempa, 5 spoke wheels ($3-5)

MB24-E DATSUN 280ZX, issued 1983
NOTE: All models with black base, tan interior & clear windows unless otherwise noted.
1. black body, 5 arch silver wheels, gold pin stripe tempa, Macau casting ($2-4)
2. black body, 5 arch silver wheels, "Turbo ZX" tempa, Macau casting ($2-4)
3. white body, 5 arch silver wheels, red & blue "Turbo 33" tempa, Macau casting ($8-12)(JP)
4. black body, small starburst wheels, orange/yellow/white "Turbo" tempa, Macau casting ($3-5)(SF)
5. black body, large starburst wheels, orange/yellow/white "Turbo" tempa, Macau casting ($3-5)(SF)
6. black body, 5 arch gold wheels, "Turbo ZX" tempa, Macau casting ($7-10)
7. black body, 8 dot gold wheels, "Turbo ZX" tempa, Macau casting ($10-15)
8. black body, laser wheels, orange/yellow/white tempa, Macau casting ($3-5)(LW)
9. charcoal gray body, laser wheels, orange/yellow/white tempa, Macau casting ($6-8)(LW)
10. red body, starburst wheels, black interior, black modified windows & doors, black & orange tempa, Macau casting, includes plastic armament ($6-8)(RB)
11. metallic red body, gray interior, dot dash wheels, black base, no tempa, China casting ($50-75)(CHI)

MB24-F NISSAN 300ZX, issued 1986
1. pearly silver body, light brown interior, 8 dot wheels, black base, gold stripe with "Turbo" tempa, Macau casting ($2-4)
2. pearly silver body, light brown interior, 5 arch wheels, black base, gold stripe with "Turbo" tempa, Macau casting ($2-4)
3. white body, red interior, 8 dot wheels, green base, "Fujicolor" tempa, Macau casting ($2-4)
4. red body, light brown interior, starburst wheels, black base, red & orange stripes tempa, Macau casting ($3-5)(SF)
5. metallic red body, light brown interior, laser wheels, black base, red & orange stripes tempa, Macau casting ($3-5)(LW)
6. white body, red interior, 8 dot wheels, black base "96 BP Racing Team" tempa, Macau casting ($8-12)(DU)
7. yellow body, red interior, 8 dot wheels, green base, "4 Monkey Racing Team" tempa, Macau casting ($8-12)(HK)

MB24-H FERRARI F40, issued 1989 (USA)
MB70-F FERRARI F40, issued 1989 (ROW)
NOTE: All models with black base unless otherwise noted.
1. red body, clear windows, black interior, 8 dot wheels, "Ferrari" logo tempa, Macau casting ($1-2)
2. red body, chrome windows, black interior, gray disc with rubber tires, "Ferrari" logo tempa, Macau casting ($5-8)(WC)
3. chrome plated body, clear windows, black interior, 8 dot wheels, no tempa, Macau casting ($12-18)(C2)
4. dull red body, clear windows, black interior, 8 dot wheels, "Ferrari" logo tempa, Macau casting ($1-2)
5. red body, clear windows, black interior, 8 dot wheels, "Ferrari" logo tempa, Thailand casting ($1-2)
6. dull red body, clear windows, black interior, 8 dot wheels, "Ferrari" logo tempa, China casting ($1-2)
7. red body, chrome/black windows, no interior, silver/yellow lightning wheels, lemon stripe & "40" tempa, China casting ($2-4)(LT)
8. lemon body, blue-chrome/black windows, no interior, pink/yellow lightning wheels, blue with "F40" tempa, China casting ($2-4)(LT)
9. lemon body, blue-chrome/black windows, no interior, peach/yellow lightning wheels, blue with "F40" tempa, China casting ($2-4)(LT)
10. lemon body, blue-chrome/black windows, no interior, silver/red lightning wheels, blue with "F40" tempa, China casting ($2-4)(LT)
11. white body, blue-chrome/black windows, no interior, peach/silver lightning wheels, "F40" tempa, China casting ($3-5)(LT)
12. black body, black/chrome windows, no interior, pink/silver lightning wheels, China casting ($3-5)(LT)
13. red body, black windows, black interior, 8 dot wheels, yellow & white "F40" tempa, Thailand casting ($3-5)(TH)
14. yellow body, chrome windows, black interior, gray disc with rubber tires, detailed trim tempa, China casting ($5-8)(WC)
15. red body, clear windows, black interior, 8 dot wheels, "Ferrari" (all yellow) logo tempa, Thailand casting ($1-2)
16. black body, clear windows, black interior, 8 dot wheels, "It's Matchbox '93- Tyco" tempa, Thailand casting ($30-45)(US)
17. red body, clear windows, black interior, 8 dot wheels, small "Ferrari" logo & painted tail lights tempa, Thailand casting ($2-3)(SS)
18. red body, clear windows, black interior, 8 dot wheels, yellow & black "Ferrari" logo tempa, Intercom City base, Thailand casting ($35-50)(IC)
19. red body, clear windows, black interior, gold 6-spoke spiral wheels, yellow & black "Ferrari" logo tempa, Thailand casting ($2-3)
20. orange body, opaque yellow windows, no interior, gold 6-spoke spiral wheels, black blotches tempa, Thailand casting ($1-2)
21. chrome plated body, pink windows, white interior & base, gold 6-spoke spiral wheels, no tempa, Thailand casting ($2-4)(GF)
22. iridescent white body, clear windows, blue interior, silver 6-spoke spiral wheels, small "Ferrari" logo & detailed trim tempa, Thailand casting ($2-4)(CC)
23. metallic red & black body, clear windows, black interior, silver 6-spoke spiral wheels, no tempa ($1-2)(MP)
24. orange body, opaque yellow windows, no interior, silver 6-spoke spiral wheels, black blotches tempa, Thailand casting ($1-2)
25. red body, clear windows, black interior, silver 6-spoke spiral wheels, "Ferrari" logo tempa, Thailand casting ($2-4)
26. silver body, pink windows, white interior, silver 6-spoke spiral wheels, yellow & pink stripes tempa, Thailand casting ($3-5)(MT)
27. metallic red & purple body, clear windows, black interior, silver 6-spoke spiral wheels, no tempa, Thailand casting ($1-2)
28. white & orange body, clear windows, black interior, silver 6-spoke spiral wheels, no tempa, Thailand casting ($1-2)(MP)
29. dark purple body, orange windows, white interior, 5 spoke concave star wheels, orange & white design tempa, Thailand casting ($1-2)(MP)
30. light blue chrome body, red windows, white interior, 5 spoke concave star wheels, purple & yellow tempa, Thailand casting ($1-2)(MP)
31. black body, clear windows, tan & black interior, chrome disc with rubber tires, small "Ferrari" logo & detailed trim tempa, Thailand casting ($3-5)(PC2-ROW)
32. lemon body, clear windows, black & red interior, chrome disc with rubber tires, detailed trim tempa, Thailand casting ($3-5)(PC10)
33. red body, clear windows, black interior, silver 6 spoke spiral wheels, "Old Eight" tempa, Thailand casting ($75-100)(BR)
34. metallic purple-red & dark purple body, clear windows, black interior, 5 spoke concave star wheels, Thailand casting ($1-2)
35. lemon body, clear windows, black interior, 5 spoke concave star wheels, red stripe & black horse on hood tempa, Thailand casting ($1-2)
36. metallic gold body, clear windows, black interior, no tempa, silver 6 spoke spiral wheels, Thailand casting ($5-10)(CH)
37. metallic gold body, clear windows, black interior, no tempa, 5 spoke concave star wheels, Thailand casting ($25-40)(CH)
38. red body, clear windows, black & red interior, detailed trim & small logo tempa, 5 spoke concave star wheels, Thailand casting ($15-20)(GC)
39. iridescent white body, clear windows, red interior, red stripe & black horse on hood tempa, 5 spoke concave star wheels, Thailand casting ($1-2)(MW57)
40. red chrome body, clear windows, white interior, light blue & yellow tempa, 5 spoke concave star wheels, Thailand casting ($1-2)(MP)
41. metallic burgundy body, clear windows, white interior, light blue & yellow tempa, 5 spoke concave star wheels, Thailand casting ($1-2)(MP)
42. silver-gray body, clear windows, red & black interior, detailed trim tempa, chrome mags with rubber tires, Thailand casting ($3-5)(PC19)
43. red chrome body, clear windows, white interior, light blue & yellow tempa, 5 spoke concave star wheels, China casting ($1-2)(MP)
44. iridescent white body, clear windows, red interior, red stripe & black horse on hood tempa, 5 spoke concave star wheels, China casting ($1-2)(MW57)

MB25-A FORD CORTINA, issued 1970
1. light brown body, unpainted base ($50-75)
2. light blue body, unpainted base ($18-25)
3. dark blue body, unpainted base ($18-25)
NOTE: Available as an Hungarian & Bulgarian casting. Assorted colors available. ($15-25)

MB25-B MOD TRACTOR, issued 1972
1. purple body, black base, yellow seat, maltese cross front wheels, headlights cast on fenders ($12-15)
NOTE: All below models with "V" cast on fenders.
2 purple body, black base, yellow seat, maltese cross front wheels ($10-15)
3. purple body, unpainted base, yellow seat, maltese cross front wheels ($10-15)
4. purple body, black base, red seat, maltese cross front wheels ($35-50)
5. purple body, black base, yellow seat, 4 spoke front wheels ($10-15)
6. purple body, black base, yellow seat, 5 crown front wheels ($10-15)
7. purple body, black base, yellow seat, 5 spoke front wheels ($10-15)
8. red body, black base, yellow seat, maltese cross front wheels ($7-10)(TP)
9. red body, black base, yellow seat, 5 crown front wheels ($7-10)(TP)
10. red body, black base, yellow seat, 5 spoke front wheels ($7-10)(TP)

MB25-C FLAT CAR & CONTAINER, issued 1979
1. black flatbed, dark tan container, opening doors, "NYK" labels, England casting ($6-8)
2. black flatbed, dark tan container, opening doors, "United States Lines" labels, England casting ($8-12)
3. black flatbed, dark tan container, opening doors, "Sealand" labels, England casting ($6-8)
4. black flatbed, dark tan container, opening doors, "OCL" labels, England casting ($10-15)
5. black flatbed, chocolate container, opening doors, "NYK" labels, England casting ($15-20)
6. black flatbed, light tan container, opening doors, "NYK' labels, England casting ($6-8)
7. charcoal flatbed, light tan container, opening doors, "NYK" labels, England casting ($6-8)
8. charcoal flatbed, dark tan container, opening doors, "NYK" labels, England casting ($6-8)
9. black flatbed, beige container, opening doors, "NYK" labels, England casting ($10-15)
10. black flatbed, coffee container, opening doors, "NYK" labels, England casting ($6-8)
11. charcoal flatbed, yellow-tan container, opening doors, "NYK" labels, England casting ($6-8)
12. black flatbed, blue container, cast doors, "United States Lines" labels, England casting ($40-60)(PS)
13. black flatbed, blue container, cast doors, "Sealand" labels, England casting ($40-60)(PS)
14. black flatbed, dark blue container, cast doors, "Sealand" labels, England casting ($40-60)(PS)
15. black flatbed, orange container, cast doors, "NYK" labels, England casting ($40-60)(PS)
16. black flatbed, orange container, cast doors, "OCL" labels, England casting ($40-60)(PS)
17. black flatbed, red container, cast doors, "NYK" labels, England casting ($40-60)(PS)
18. black flatbed, white container, cast doors, no labels, China casting ($10-15)(PS)
19. black flatbed, yellow container, cast doors, no labels, China casting ($10-15)(PS)
NOTE: for versions 18 & 19, the playset these come in has a separate label sheet for application to the containers.

MB25-D TOYOTA CELICA GT, issued 1981 (USA)
1. blue body, white interior, "78" tempa, maltese cross wheels, flat base ($4-6)
2. blue body, ivory interior, "78" tempa, maltese cross wheels, flat base ($4-6)
3. blue body, ivory interior, "78" tempa, 5 spoke star wheels, flat base ($4-6)
4. blue body, blue interior, "78" tempa, 5 spoke wheels, flat base ($4-6)
5. yellow body, blue interior, "Yellow Fever" tempa, 5 spoke wheels- all small size, raised rear base ($35-50)
6. yellow body, blue interior, "Yellow Fever" tempa, 5 spoke small front & 5 spoke large rear wheels, raised rear base ($4-6)

MB25-E AMBULANCE, issued 1983 (USA)
MB25-E AMBULANCE, issued 1990 (ROW)
NOTE: all models with cream interior, blue windows, white rear doors & dot dash wheels unless otherwise noted.
1. white body, pearly silver base, "Pacific Ambulance" tempa, Macau casting ($4-6)
2. white body, unpainted base, "Pacific Ambulance" tempa, Hong Kong casting ($4-6)
3. white body, pearly silver base, "Paramedics E11" with orange band tempa, Macau casting ($1-2)
4. white body, dark gray base, "Paramedics E11" with orange band tempa, Macau casting ($1-2)
5. white body, pearly silver base, "Paramedics E11" with orange band tempa, China casting ($1-2)
6. white body, pearly silver base, "EMT Ambulance" tempa, China casting ($3-4)(AP)
7. white body, white base, no tempa, China casting ($10-15)(GF)
8. yellow body, pearly silver base, "Paramedics E11" with orange band tempa, China casting ($8-12)(GS)
9. florescent orange body, black base with bar code, "Ambulance 7/ Intercom City" tempa, China casting ($10-15)(IC)
10. fluorescent orange body, black base (without barcode), "Ambulance 7/Intercom City" tempa, China casting ($8-12)
11. florescent yellow body & rear doors, silver-gray base, "Emergency Unit 3/ 3 EMT" tempa, China casting ($2-4)(CC)
12. white body, pearly silver base, "Paramedics/ Dial 911" with dark orange band without roof tempa, China casting ($2-3)
13. white body, pearly silver base, "Paramedics/ Dial 911" with neon orange band without roof tempa, China casting ($2-3)
14. red body & rear doors, black base, "Fire Rescue" tempa, China casting ($1-2)(MP)
15. white body, pearly silver base, "Ambulance" with red & blue design tempa, China casting ($1-2)
16. white body, pearly silver base, "Action System" tempa, China casting ($7-10)(OP)
17. white body, pearly gray base, "Matchbox Ambulance Dial 911" tempa, China casting ($1-2)(MP)
18. white body, pearly silver base, orange band on sides tempa, China casting ($25-40)(ASAP blank)
19. white body, pearly silver base, orange band on side with "Manhattan National Life" on hood tempa, China casting ($100+)(ASAP)

MB25-J BMW Z3 ROADSTER, issued 1997 (USA)
MB61-H BMW Z3 ROADSTER, issued 1997 (ROW)
NOTE: All models with clear windows & black base unless otherwise noted.
1. metallic blue body, tan & black interior, chrome disc with rubber tires, detailed trim tempa, Thailand casting ($4-6)(IG)
2. unpainted body, tan interior, chrome disc with rubber tires, no tempa, Thailand casting ($4-6)(IG)
3. red body, black interior, 5 spoke concave star wheels, white splash & "Z3" tempa, Thailand casting ($1-2)
4. red body, black interior, 5 spoke concave star wheels, white splash, "Z3" & "Fiery Driven" tempa, Thailand casting ($100+)
5. red body, black interior, 5 spoke concave star wheels, no interior, Thailand casting ($2-4)(ROW)
6. silver-gray body, maroon & red interior, chrome disc with rubber tires, Thailand casting ($3-5)(PC12)
7. red body, gray & black interior, chrome disc with rubber tires, detailed trim tempa, Thailand casting ($3-5)(PC16)
8. blue body, gray interior, 5 spoke concave star wheels, white splash & "Z3" tempa, Thailand casting ($1-2)(MW5)
9. blue body, gray interior, 5 spoke concave star wheels, white splash & "Z3" tempa, China casting ($1-2)(MW5)
10. metallic gold body, black interior, 5 spoke concave star wheels, no tempa, China casting ($5-10)(CH)
11. red body, black interior, 5 spoke concave star wheels, white splash, "Z3" & "Espe" tempa, Thailand casting ($100+)(ASAP)

MB26-A GMC TIPPER, issued 1970
1. red body, silver-gray dump, green chassis, 4 spoke wheels ($25-40)
2. red body, silver-gray dump, green chassis, spiro wheels ($25-40)

MB26-B BIG BANGER, issued 1972
1. red body, blue windows, unpainted base, "Big Banger" labels ($15-18)
2. red body, amber windows, unpainted base, "Big Banger" labels ($15-18)

MB26-C SITE DUMPER, issued 1976
NOTE: the front wheels are considered the large wheels on this model! All wheels are silver hubs unless noted otherwise.
1. yellow body & dump, black base, black interior, 5 spoke front & dot dash rear wheels ($4-6)
2. yellow body & dump, black base, black interior, 5 spoke front & 5 crown rear wheels ($4-6)
3. yellow body, red dump, black base, black interior, 5 spoke front & 5 arch rear wheels ($4-6)
4. yellow body, red dump, black base, black interior, 5 arch front & 5 crown rear wheels ($4-6)
5. yellow body, red dump, brown base, black interior, 5 arch front & 5 crown rear wheels ($7-10)
6. yellow body, red dump, brown base, black interior, 5 spoke front & 5 arch rear wheels ($4-6)
7. yellow body, red dump, charcoal base, black interior, 5 arch front & 5 crown rear wheels ($4-6)
8. yellow body, red dump, black base, black interior, 5 spoke front & 5 crown rear wheels ($4-6)
9. yellow body, red dump, black base, black interior, 5 spoke (black hubs) front & 5 crown rear wheels ($4-6)
10. orange-red body, red dump, black base, white interior, 5 arch front & 5 crown rear wheels ($150-250)
11. orange-red body, silver-gray dump, charcoal base, white interior, 5 arch front & 5 crown rear wheels ($4-6)
12. orange-red body, silver-gray dump, black base, white interior, 5 arch front & 5 crown rear wheels ($4-6)
13. orange-red body, silver-gray dump, black base, white interior, 5 arch front & 5 crown rear wheels, yellow hubs ($6-8)
14. orange-red body, silver-gray dump, charcoal base, white interior, 5 arch front & 5 crown rear wheels, yellow hubs ($6-8)
15. red body, silver-gray dump, silver-gray base, white interior, 5 arch front & 5 crown rear wheels, yellow hubs ($10-15)

MB26-D COSMIC BLUES, issued 1982 (USA)
MB41-H COSMIC BLUES, reissued 1991 (USA)
NOTE: Below models with blue windows & black base unless otherwise noted.
1. white body, clear windows, maltese cross front & maltese cross rear wheels, chrome exhausts, "Cosmic Blues" tempa, Hong Kong casting ($15-20)
2. white body, maltese cross front & maltese cross rear wheels, chrome exhausts, "Cosmic Blues" tempa, Hong Kong casting ($3-5)
3. white body, 5 crown front & maltese cross rear wheels, chrome exhausts, "Cosmic Blues" tempa, Macau casting ($1-2)
4. white body, 5 crown front & rear wheels, chrome exhausts, "Cosmic Blues" tempa, Macau casting ($1-2)
5. white body, 5 arch front & 5 crown rear wheels, chrome exhausts, "Cosmic Blues" tempa, China casting ($1-2)
6. blue body, 5 arch front & 5 crown rear wheels, chrome exhausts, "Cosmic Blues" tempa, China casting ($1-2)
7. blue body, 5 arch front & 5 crown rear wheels, black exhausts, "Cosmic Blues" tempa, China casting ($1-2)
8. orange body, 5 arch front & 5 crown rear wheels, black exhausts, "Hemi" & stripes tempa, China casting ($1-2)
9. orange body, 5 arch front & 5 crown rear wheels, black exhausts, "Hemi" & stripes tempa, Thailand casting ($1-2)
10. black body, pearly silver base, 5 arch front & 5 crown rear wheels, gray exhausts, white & orange flames tempa, pearly silver base, Thailand casting ($1-2)
11. orange-red body, 5 arch front & 5 crown rear wheels, gray exhausts, "Dandelion/ Dsylexicon" tempa, black base, Thailand casting ($7-10)(US)
12. black body, 5 arch front & 5 crown rear wheels, gray exhausts, orange & white flames tempa, Thailand casting ($1-2)
13. metallic green body, 5 arch front & 5 crown rear wheels, black exhausts, orange & white flames tempa, Thailand casting ($1-2)
14. metallic gold body, 5 arch front & 5 crown rear wheels, black exhausts, no tempa, Thailand casting ($5-10)(CH26)
15. red body, chrome base, 5 arch front & 5 crown rear wheels, chrome exhausts, "Big Banger" tempa ($3-5)(PC13)

MB26-E VOLVO CABLE TRUCK, issued 1982 (ROW)
1. orange body, red base, gray cable, green windows, 5 arch wheels ($18-25)
2. orange body, red base, gray cable, blue windows, 5 arch wheels ($18-25)
3. orange body, red base, gray cable, blue windows, maltese cross wheels ($18-25)
4. orange body, red base, gray cable, blue windows, 5 spoke wheels ($18-25)
5. orange body, red base, gray cable, blue windows, 5 crown wheels ($18-25)
6. orange body, black base, gray cable, blue windows, maltese cross wheels ($18-25)
7. orange body, black base, gray cable, blue windows, 5 spoke wheels ($18-25)
8. orange body, black base, gray cable, blue windows, 5 arch wheels ($18-25)
9. orange body, black base, gray cable, blue windows, 5 crown wheels ($18-25)
10. orange body, black base, dark gray cable, blue windows, 5 crown wheels ($18-25)
11. orange body, charcoal base, dark gray cable, blue windows, 5 arch wheels ($18-25)
12. yellow body, black base, dark gray cable, blue windows, 5 arch wheels ($20-30)
13. yellow body, black base, dark gray cable, blue windows, 5 crown wheels ($20-30)
14. red body, black base, dark gray cable, blue windows, 5 arch wheels ($25-40)

MB26-F VOLVO TILT TRUCK, issued 1984 (ROW)
MB49-G VOLVO TILT TRUCK, issued 1990 (USA)
NOTE: All models with blue windows, silver hubs, black base unless otherwise noted.
1. metallic blue body, yellow canopy, no tempa, England casting ($25-35)
2. metallic blue body, yellow canopy, "Fresh Fruit Co." tempa, England casting ($3-5)
3. metallic blue body, yellow canopy, "Fresh Fruit Co." tempa, Macau casting ($2-4)
4. yellow body, yellow canopy, "Ferrymasters Groupage" tempa, Macau casting ($2-4)
5. yellow body, yellow canopy, "Ferrymasters Groupage" tempa, China casting ($2-4)
6. white body, white canopy, "Federal Express" tempa, China casting ($2-4)
7. dark blue body, yellow canopy, "Michelin" tempa, dark gray base, China casting ($1-2)
8. olive body, tan canopy, "LS2020" tempa, black hubs, China casting ($15-20)(CM)
9. black body, dark gray canopy, "LS1509" tempa, black hubs, China casting ($15-20)(CM)
10.. blue body, blue canopy, "Henniez" tempa, China casting ($8-12)(SW)
11. red body, green canopy, cartoon face & forklift tempa, yellow wheels, red hubs, China casting ($6-8)(LL)
12. red body, no canopy, "123" on doors tempa, yellow wheels, blue hubs, China casting ($6-8)(LL)
13. red body, green canopy, cartoon face & forklift tempa, yellow wheels, blue hubs, China casting ($6-8)(LL)
14. white body, white container, "Pirelli Gripping Stuff" & gray tread pattern tempa, China casting ($1-2)
15. white body, white container, "Pirelli Gripping Stuff" & black tread pattern tempa, China casting ($1-2)
16. red body, green canopy, cartoon face & forklift tempa, yellow wheels, plain hubs, China casting ($6-8)(LL)
17. red body, white canopy, "Big Top Circus" tempa, China casting ($2-4)(AV)

MB26-G BMW 5 SERIES, issued 1989 (USA)
MB31-H BMW 5 SERIES, issued 1989 (ROW)
1. dark charcoal body, black base, no tempa, Macau casting ($2-4)
2. dark charcoal body, black base, no tempa, Thailand casting ($2-4)
3. white body, white base, "Fina 31/ BMW Team/ Sachs/ Bilstein" tempa, Thailand casting ($2-4)
4. white body, white base, "Fina 31/ BMW Team" without "Sachs/ Bilstein" tempa, Thailand casting ($2-4)
5. red body, red base, no tempa, Thailand casting ($3-5)(SS)
6. white body, white base, "31 BMW Team" without "Fina" & "Michelin"

tempa, Thailand casting ($2-3)

MB27-A MERCEDES 230SL, issued 1970
1. cream body, red interior, unpainted base ($25-40)
2. off white body, red interior, unpainted base ($25-40)
3. yellow body, red interior, unpainted base ($20-25)
4. yellow body, black interior, unpainted base ($15-20)
NOTE: Available as an Hungarian and Bulgarian casting. Assorted colors available ($15-25)

MB27-B LAMBORGHINI COUNTACH, issued 1973
1. yellow body, unpainted base, chrome interior, purple windows, "3" label ($10-15)
2. yellow body, black base, chrome interior, purple windows, "3" label ($10-15)
3. yellow body, unpainted base, chrome interior, red windows, "3" label ($10-15)
4. yellow body, black base, chrome interior, red windows, "3" label ($10-15)
5. yellow body, silver-gray base, chrome interior, purple windows, "3" label ($10-15)
6. yellow body, black base, chrome interior, amber windows, "3" label ($10-15)
7. red body, black base, chrome interior, amber windows, "3" label ($10-15)
8. red body, black base, chrome interior, red windows, "3" label ($10-15)
9. red body, unpainted base, chrome interior, amber windows, lime tempa ($7-10)
10. red body, black base, chrome interior, amber windows, lime tempa ($7-10)
11. red body, black base, chrome interior, red windows, lime tempa ($7-10)
12. red body, unpainted base, chrome interior, blue-green windows, lime tempa ($7-10)
13. red body, black base, chrome interior, blue-green windows, lime tempa ($7-10)
14. red body, black base, light gray interior, blue-green windows, lime tempa ($7-10)
15. red body, unpainted base, light gray interior, blue-green windows, lime tempa ($7-10)
16. red body, black base, light gray interior, blue-green windows, green tempa ($7-10)
17. red body, black base, light gray interior, green windows, lime tempa ($7-10)
18. red body, black base, light gray interior, green windows, green tempa ($7-10)
19. red body, brown base, light gray interior, blue-green windows, lime tempa ($7-10)
20. red body, brown base, dark gray interior, blue-green windows, lime tempa ($7-10)
21. red body, charcoal base, light gray interior, blue-green windows, lime tempa ($7-10)
22. red body, charcoal base, dark gray interior, blue-green windows, lime tempa ($7-10)
23. red body, charcoal base, yellow interior, blue-green windows, lime tempa ($7-10)
24. red body, charcoal base, yellow interior, smoke windows, lime tempa ($7-10)
25. red body, gray-brown base, yellow interior, smoke windows, lime tempa ($7-10)
26. red body, charcoal base, white interior, smoke windows, lime tempa ($7-10)
27. red body, charcoal base, white interior, blue-green windows, lime tempa ($7-10)
28. red body, black base, white interior, clear windows, lime tempa ($7-10)
29. red body, gray-brown base, white interior, clear windows, lime tempa ($7-10)
30. red body, charcoal base, tan interior, blue-green windows, lime tempa ($7-10)
31. red body, charcoal base, tan interior, clear windows, lime tempa ($7-10)
32. red body, black base, tan interior, clear windows, lime tempa ($7-10)
33. red body, black base, tan interior, blue-green windows, lime tempa ($7-10)
34. red body, unpainted base, tan interior, blue-green windows, lime tempa ($7-10)
35. red body, charcoal base, tan interior, purple windows, lime tempa ($7-10)
36. red body, gray-brown base, tan interior, purple windows, lime tempa ($7-10)
37. red body, unpainted base, light gray interior, green windows, lime tempa ($7-10)
38. red body, charcoal base, light gray interior, purple windows, lime tempa ($7-10)
39. red body, black base, dark gray interior, purple windows, lime tempa ($7-10)
40. red body, blue-gray base, dark gray interior, purple windows, lime tempa ($7-10)
41. red body, charcoal base, dark gray interior, smoke windows, lime tempa ($7-10)
42. red body, black base, yellow interior, blue-green windows, lime tempa ($7-10)
43. yellow body, pearly silver base, light gray interior, blue-green windows, no labels ($150-200)(BR)
44. dark green body, pearly silver base, light gray interior, blue-green windows, "Shell" labels ($500-750)(BR)

MB27-C SWEPT WING JET, issued 1981
1. dark red body, white wings & base, amber-red windows, no tempa, England casting ($2-4)
2. dark red body, white wings & base, red windows, no tempa, England casting ($2-4)
3. dark red body, white wings & base, pink windows, no tempa, England casting ($2-4)
4. dark red body, white wings & base, red windows, black & red tempa, England casting ($2-4)
5. dark red body, white wings & base, red windows, black & red tempa, Macau casting ($2-4)
6. rose red body, white wings & base, red windows, black & red tempa, Macau casting ($2-4)
7. dark red body, light gray wings, white base, red windows, black & red tempa, Macau casting ($4-6)
8. dark red body, white wings & base, red windows, black & red tempa, China casting ($2-4)
9. black body, dark gray wings, gray base, red windows, yellow & black camouflage tempa, Macau casting ($3-5)(CM)

MB27-D JEEP CHEROKEE, issued 1986
MB73-F JEEP CHEROKEE, reissued 1994 (USA)
MB51-J JEEP CHEROKEE, reissued 1996 (ROW)
NOTE: All models with clear windows & 8 spoke wheels. When interior is noted, this includes the color of the side molding.
1. white body, black interior, black metal base, "Quadtrak" tempa, Macau casting ($3-5)
2. beige body, black interior, black metal base, "Holiday Club" tempa, Macau casting ($2-4)(TP)
3. yellow body, dark gray interior, black metal base, "Forest Ranger County Park" tempa, Macau casting ($7-10)
4. yellow body, dark gray interior, black metal base, "Mr. Fixer" tempa, Macau casting ($1-2)
5. bright yellow body, dark gray interior, black metal base, "BP Chief" & green/ red stripes tempa, Macau casting ($8-12)(DU)
6. orange-yellow body, dark gray interior, black metal base, "Mr. Fixer" tempa, Macau casting ($1-2)
7. light pea green body, dark gray interior, black metal base, "Mr. Fixer" tempa, Macau casting ($3-4)(SC)
8. light brown body, dark gray interior, black metal base, "Mr. Fixer" tempa, Macau casting ($3-4)(SC)
9. dark brown body, dark gray interior, black metal base, "Mr. Fixer" tempa, Macau casting ($3-4)(SC)
10. beige body, dark gray interior, black metal base, "Holiday Club" tempa, Macau casting ($2-4)(TP)
11. yellow body, dark gray interior, black plastic base, "Mr. Fixer" tempa, Macau casting ($1-2)
12. reddish brown body, dark gray interior, black plastic base, "Mr. Fixer" tempa, Macau casting ($2-3)(SC)
13. dark brown body, dark gray interior, black plastic base, "Mr. Fixer" tempa, Macau casting ($2-3)(SC)
14. white body, dark gray interior, black plastic base, "National Ski Patrol" tempa, Macau casting ($8-12)(US)
15. beige body, dark gray interior, black plastic base, "Holiday Club" tempa, Thailand casting ($2-4)(MP)
16. orange-yellow body, dark gray interior, black plastic base, "Mr. Fixer" tempa, Thailand casting ($2-4)
17. silver-gray body, black interior, black plastic base, "Sport" & "Jeep" tempa, Thailand casting ($2-4)
18. dark purple body, dark orange interior, black plastic base, white & orange flames tempa, Thailand casting ($1-2)
19. dark purple body, dark orange interior, black plastic base, white & orange flames tempa, China casting ($1-2)
20. medium green body, black interior, black plastic base, no tempa, Thailand casting ($18-25)(BE)
21. blue body, dark gray interior, gray plastic base, "Hellmann's/ Best Foods" tempa, China casting ($75-100)(US)
22. red body, black interior, black plastic base, "Fire Chief/ FD No. 1" tempa, blue dome lights cast, China casting ($1-2)(MP)
23. red body, black & gray interior, black plastic base, "Fire Chief" tempa, blue dome lights cast, chrome disc with rubber tires, China casting ($3-5)(PC7)
24. dark green body, beige interior, black plastic base, no tempa, China casting ($1-2)(MP)
25. dark purple body, red-orange interior, black plastic base, white & orange flames tempa, China casting ($1-2)
26. black body, black interior, black plastic base, pink-red & white flames tempa, China casting ($1-2)
27. white body, dark blue interior, black plastic base, "Rescue EMT" tempa, China casting ($1-2)(MP)
28. white body, black interior, black plastic base, no tempa, China casting ($25-40)(ASAP blank)
29. black body, red interior, black plastic base, no tempa, China casting ($25-40)(ASAP blank)
30. black body, red interior, black plastic base, "American International Recovery" tempa, China casting ($100+)(ASAP)

MB27-F TAILGATOR, issued 1994
NOTE: All models with opaque black windows & painted eyes & teeth tempa.
1. lime body, lime base, gold 6-spoke spiral wheels, China casting ($1-2)
2. lime body, lime base, silver 6-spoke spiral wheels, China casting ($1-2)
3. dark green body, dark green base, silver 6-spoke spiral wheels, China casting ($2-3)
4. metallic gold body, silver 6-spoke spiral wheels, China casting ($10-15)(CH)
5. dark green body, dark green base, 5 spoke concave star wheels, China casting ($2-4)
6. dark purple body, dark purple base, 5 spoke concave star wheels, China casting ($1-2)
7. black body, black base, 5 spoke concave star wheels, China casting ($1-2)
8. metallic gold body, yellow base, gold 6 spoke spiral wheels, China casting ($100+)(CHI)

MB28-A MACK DUMP TRUCK, issued 1970
1. pea green body, unpainted base, spiro wheels, black axle covers ($20-35)
2. pea green body, unpainted base, spiro wheels, red axle covers ($20-35)
3. olive drab body, black base, dot dash wheels, no axle covers ($65-80)(TP)
4. olive body, black base, dot dash wheels,. no axle covers ($6-8)(TP)

MB28-B STOAT, issued 1974
1. gold body, unpainted base, silver hubs ($8-12)
2. gold body, black base, silver hubs ($8-12)
3. olive drab body, black base, black hubs ($65-80)(TP)
4. olive body, black base, silver hubs ($7-10)(TP)
5. olive body, black base, black hubs ($6-8)(TP)

MB28-C LINCOLN CONTINENTAL MK V, issued 1979
1. pinkish-red body, unpainted base, tan interior, white roof ($3-5)
2. dark red body, unpainted base, tan interior, white roof ($3-5)
3. dark red body, unpainted base, gray interior, white roof ($4-6)
4. dark red body, unpainted base, brown interior, white roof ($4-6)
5. dark red body, unpainted base, chocolate interior, white roof ($5-7)
NOTE: Available as a Bulgarian casting. Assorted colors available ($15-25)

MB28-D FORMULA 5000, issued 1982
1. tan body, unpainted metal base, white driver, chrome engine, 5 arch front & maltese cross rear wheels, England casting ($3-5)
2. tan body, black metal base, white driver, chrome engine, 5 arch front & maltese cross rear wheels, England casting ($3-5)
3. tan body, black metal base, white driver, chrome engine, 5 arch front & 5 spoke rear wheels, England casting ($3-5)
4. tan body, black metal base, white driver, chrome engine, dot dash front & dot dash rear wheels, England casting ($3-5)
5. tan body, black metal base, white driver, chrome engine, 5 arch front & dot dash rear wheels, Macau casting ($3-5)
6. tan body, black plastic base, white driver, chrome engine, 4 spoke front & maltese cross rear wheels, Manaus casting ($35-50)(BR)
7. rust red body, black plastic base, cream driver, gray engine, dot dash front & 8 spoke rear wheels, Manaus casting ($35-50)(BR)
8. dark green body, charcoal plastic base, white driver, 8 dot front & 8 spoke rear wheels, gray engine, Manaus casting ($30-45)(BR)
9. powder blue body, black plastic base, white driver, 8 dot front & 8 spoke rear wheels, gray engine, Manaus casting ($35-50)(BR)

MB28-E DODGE DAYTONA, issued 1984
NOTE: All models with clear windows & black interior. "Las Vegas" model is a different casting and is listed separately at the end of this section.
1. maroon body, silver-gray base with black insert, 8 dot silver wheels, no tempa, England casting ($3-5)
2. maroon body, silver-gray base with dark gray insert, 5 arch wheels, no tempa, England casting ($3-5)
3. maroon body, silver-gray base with dark gray insert, 8 dot silver wheels, no tempa, England casting ($3-5)
4. maroon body, silver-gray base with no insert, 8 dot silver wheels, no tempa, Macau casting ($50-75)
5. pearly silver body, black base, 8 dot silver wheels, red & black stripes tempa, Macau casting ($2-4)
6. pearly silver body, black base, large 5 crown wheels, red & black stripes tempa, Macau casting ($5-8)
7. pearly silver body, black base, dot dash wheels, red & black stripes tempa, Macau casting ($5-8)
8. pearly silver body, black base, 8 dot gold wheels, red & black stripes tempa, Macau casting ($4-6)
9. white body, blue base, starburst wheels, red & blue stripes with "8" tempa, Macau casting ($3-5)(SF)
10. white body, blue base, laser wheels, red & blue stripes with "8" tempa, Macau casting ($3-5)(LW)
11. plum body, gold base, starburst wheels, red/yellow/dark blue tempa, gray redesigned windows, Macau casting, includes plastic armament ($6-8)(RB)
12. dark blue body, black base, 8 dot silver wheels, "5 Goat Racing Team" tempa, Macau casting ($8-12)(HK)
13. red body, red base, 8 dot silver wheels, yellow & blue "Turbo Z" tempa, Macau casting ($2-3)
14. red body, red base, 8 dot silver wheels, yellow & blue "Turbo Z" tempa, hood cast shut, Macau casting ($2-3)
15. red body, red base, starburst wheels, yellow & blue "Turbo Z" tempa, hood cast shut, China casting ($5-7)(GS)

MB28-H FORKLIFT TRUCK, issued 1991 (USA)
MB61-F FORKLIFT TRUCK, issued 1991 (ROW)
NOTE: All models with black forks & arms, black base & 4 spoke wheels.
1. lime green body, red & white stripes tempa, Thailand casting ($1-2)
2. white body, red stripes tempa, Thailand casting ($2-4)(TC)
3. florescent green body, red & white stripes tempa, Thailand casting ($1-2)
4. orange-yellow body, red stripes tempa, Thailand casting ($2-4)(GS)
5. bright lime body, red & white stripes tempa, Thailand casting ($1-2)

MB28-L MITSUBISHI SPYDER, issued 1995 (USA)
MB22-J MITSUBISHI SPYDER, issued 1995 (ROW)
NOTE: All models with clear windshield & black base.
1. metallic blue body, green interior, white & green hood & side splash tempa, 6-spoke spiral wheels, Thailand casting ($1-2)
2. metallic blue body, green interior, no tempa, 6-spoke spiral wheels, Thailand casting ($2-4)
3. metallic blue body, white interior, no tempa, 6-spoke spiral wheels, Thailand casting ($1-2)
4. red body, dark gray interior, 6-spoke spiral wheels, no tempa, Thailand casting ($1-2)(MP)
5. red body, dark gray & black interior, chrome disc with rubber tires, detailed trim tempa, Thailand casting ($3-5)(PC1)
6. black body, dark gray & black interior, chrome disc with rubber tires, detailed trim tempa, Thailand casting ($3-5)(SC1)
7. silver-gray body, red & black interior, chrome disc with rubber tires, detailed trim tempa, Thailand casting ($3-5)(PC-JC)
8. metallic green body, gray & black interior, chrome disc with rubber tires, detailed trim tempa, Thailand casting ($3-5)(PC4)
9. metallic gold body, black interior, 6 spoke spiral wheels, no tempa., Thailand casting ($5-10)(CH)
10. lemon body, gray interior, 5 spoke concave star wheels, "Spyder" tempa, Thailand casting ($1-2)
11. black body, red interior, 5 spoke concave star wheels, "Spyder" tempa, Thailand casting ($1-2)(MP)
12. metallic blue body, gray & black interior, chrome disc with rubber wheels, detailed tempa, Thailand casting ($15-20)(GC)
13. black body, red interior, 5 spoke concave star wheels, "The Red Back" with spider & web tempa, Thailand casting ($3-5)(AU)
14. metallic gold body, black interior, 5 spoke concave star wheels, no tempa, Thailand casting ($10-15)(CH)
15. lemon body, gray & black interior, chrome disc with detailed trim tempa, Thailand casting ($3-5)(PC12)
16. red body, gray interior, 5 spoke concave star wheels, skeleton & "Raptor" tempa, Thailand casting ($1-2)(MP)
17. iridescent white body, maroon & black interior, chrome disc with rubber tires, detailed trim tempa, Thailand casting ($3-5)(PC16)
18. dark green body, tan interior, 5 spoke concave star wheels, "Spyder" tempa , Thailand casting ($1-2)(MW69)
19. dark green body, tan interior, 5 spoke concave star wheels, "Spyder" tempa, China casting ($1-2)(MW69)
20. red body, gray interior, 5 spoke concave star wheels, skeleton & "Raptor" tempa, China casting ($1-2)(MP)
21. black body, red interior, 5 spoke concave star wheels, "Spyder" tempa, China casting ($1-2)(MP)
22. metallic gold body, black interior, 6 spoke spiral wheels, no tempa, China casting ($5-10)(CH)

MB29-A FIRE PUMPER, issued 1970
1. red body, no water gun cast, no labels, 5 spoke wheels ($50-75)
2. red body, water gun cast, "P1" tempa, dot dash wheels ($7-10)(CR)
3. red body, water gun cast, "P1" tempa, 5 spoke wheels ($7-10)(CR)

MB29-B RACING MINI, issued 1970
1. bronze body, unpainted base, ivory interior, "29" orange outline labels, 5 spoke wheels ($15-20)
2. orange body, unpainted base, ivory interior, "29" orange outline labels, 5 spoke wheels ($10-15)
3. orange body, unpainted base, cream interior, "29" orange outline labels, 5 spoke wheels ($10-15)
4. orange body, silver-gray base, cream interior, "29" orange outline labels, 5 spoke wheels ($10-15)
5. orange body, unpainted base, ivory interior, "29" green outline labels, 5 spoke wheels ($10-15)
6. orange body, unpainted base, cream interior, "29" green outline labels, 5 spoke wheels ($10-15)
7. orange body, silver-gray base, cream interior, "29" green outline labels, 5 spoke wheels ($10-15)
8. orange body, silver-gray base, ivory interior, "29" green outline labels, 5 spoke wheels ($10-15)
9. red-orange body, unpainted base, ivory interior, "29" green outline labels, 5 spoke wheels ($10-15)
10. red body, unpainted base, ivory interior, "29" green outline labels, 5 spoke wheels ($10-15)
11. red body, unpainted base, cream interior, "29" green outline labels, 5 spoke wheels ($10-15)
12. red body, unpainted base, ivory interior, "29" green outline labels, 5 spoke center cut wheels ($5-7)(TP)
13. red body, unpainted base, ivory interior, "3" labels, 5 spoke center cut wheels ($15-18)(TP)
14. red body, unpainted base, ivory interior, no labels, 5 spoke center cut wheels ($5-7)(TP)
15. red body, unpainted base, ivory interior, "29" green outline labels, dot dash wheels ($5-7)(TP)

MB29-C TRACTOR SHOVEL, issued 1976
NOTE: All models listed with silver hubs unless otherwise noted.
1. light yellow body, red shovel, yellow base, chrome motor, no tempa, England casting ($8-12)
2. light yellow body, red shovel, yellow base, chrome motor, no tempa, black hubs, England casting ($10-15)
3. lime body, lemon shovel, lemon base, chrome motor, no tempa, England casting ($100-175)(GR)
4. dark yellow body, red shovel, yellow base, chrome motor, no tempa, England casting ($4-6)
5. dark yellow body, red shovel, yellow base, black motor, no tempa, England casting ($4-6)
6. dark yellow body, red shovel, pale tan base, black motor, no tempa, England casting ($4-6)
7. dark yellow body, red shovel, pale tan base, black motor, no tempa, yellow hubs, England casting ($6-8)
8. dark yellow body, maroon shovel, pale tan base, black motor, no tempa, yellow hubs, England casting ($6-8)
9. dark yellow body, maroon shovel, yellow base, black motor, no tempa, yellow hubs, England casting ($6-8)
10. dark yellow body, maroon shovel, lemon base, black motor, no tempa, England casting ($4-6)
11. dark yellow body, red shovel, lemon base, black motor, no tempa, England casting ($4-6)
12. dark yellow body, red shovel, black base, black motor, no tempa, England casting ($4-6)
13. dark yellow body, black shovel, yellow base, black motor, no tempa, England casting ($4-6)
14. dark yellow body, black shovel, lemon base, black motor, no tempa, England casting ($4-6)
15. dark yellow body, black shovel, pale tan base, black motor, no tempa, England casting ($4-6)
16. dark orange body, red shovel, black base, gray motor, no tempa, England casting ($50-75)
17. dark orange body, black shovel, black base, gray motor, no tempa, England casting ($8-10)
18. light orange body, black shovel, black base, gray motor, no tempa, England casting ($8-10)
19. dark yellow body, black shovel, black base, black motor, black stripes with "C" tempa, England casting ($2-4)
20. dark yellow body, black shovel, black base, black stripes tempa,, England casting ($2-4)
21. dark yellow body, black shovel, black base, gray motor, black stripes tempa, England casting ($2-4)
22. dark yellow body, black shovel, black base, gray motor, no tempa, England casting ($2-4)
23. purple body, black shovel, black base, black motor, lime & orange tempa, Macau casting, includes plastic armament ($6-8)(RB)
24. dark yellow body, red shovel, black base, black motor, black stripes tempa, Macau casting ($2-3)(TC)
25. dark yellow body, black shovel, black base, black motor, "Thomae Mucosolvan" tempa, Macau casting ($15-25)(GR)
26. light orange body, black shovel, black base, black motor, "Thomae Mucosolvan" tempa, Macau casting ($20-30)(GR)
27. blue body, red shovel, black base, red motor, yellow wheels with orange hubs, green stripes tempa, Macau casting ($6-8)(LL)
28. light yellow body, black shovel, black base, black motor, "Thomae Mucosolvan" tempa, Macau casting ($18-25)(GR)
29. light yellow body, black shovel, black base, black motor, "Thomae Mucosolvan" tempa, Thailand casting ($18-25)(GR)
30. dark yellow body, black shovel, black base, black motor, black stripes tempa, Thailand casting ($1-2)
31. dark yellow body, red shovel, black base, black motor, red stripes tempa, Thailand casting ($1-2)
32. light yellow body, black shovel, black base, black motor, "Thomae MucosolvanS" tempa, Thailand casting ($20-25)(GR)
33. blue body, black shovel, black base, black motor, "Spasmo Mucosolvan" tempa, Thailand casting ($10-15)(GR)
NOTE: below models with tow hook cast unless otherwise noted.
34. light yellow body, black shovel, black base, black motor, "Thomae Mucosolvan" on roof tempa, Thailand casting ($18-25)(GR)
35. blue body, black shovel, black base, black motor, "Spasmo Mucosolvan" on roof tempa, Thailand casting ($12-15)(GR)
36. dark yellow body, red shovel, black base, black motor, red stripes tempa, Thailand casting ($1-2)
37. fluorescent orange body, black shovel, black base, black motor, no tempa, Thailand casting ($1-2)(MP)
38. orange body, silver—gray shovel, black base, black motor, black stripes tempa, Thailand casting ($1-2)
39. orange body, silver—gray shovel, black base, black motor, black stripes tempa, China casting ($1-2)
40. orange body, silver-gray shovel, black base, black motor, black stripes tempa, Thailand casting ($1-2)
41. florescent orange body, silver—gray shovel, black base, black motor, no tempa, China casting ($1-2)(MP)
42. orange body, silver-gray shovel, black base, black motor, no tempa, Thailand casting ($1-2)(MP) 43. pumpkin body, gray shovel, black base, black motor, no tempa, China casting ($1-2)(MP)
44. light orange body, red shovel with lever, black base, black motor, red stripes tempa, China casting ($1-2)(AS)(AP)
45. metallic gold body, black shovel, black base, black motor, no tempa, China casting ($5-10)(CH)
46. light red body, silver-gray shovel, black base, black motor, no tempa, China casting ($1-2)
47. pink-red body, silver-gray shovel, black base, black motor, "Thomae MucosolvanS" tempa, China casting ($25-40)(GR)
48. blue body, black shovel, black base, black motor, "Thomae Mucosolvan" tempa, China casting ($25-40)(GR)
49. red body, black shovel, black base, black motor, no tempa, China casting ($1-2)
50. white body, silver-gray shovel,, black base, silver-gray motor, tow hook cast, China casting ($1-2)(MW13)

MB30-A EIGHT WHEEL CRANE, issued 1970
1. red body, orange crane boom, unpainted base, yellow hook ($350-500)
2. red body, gold crane boom, unpainted base, yellow hook ($35-50)

MB30-B BEACH BUGGY, issued 1970
1. pink body, yellow spatter, white interior, unpainted base ($20-25)
2. pink body, yellow spatter, yellow interior, unpainted base ($12-15)
3. lavender body, yellow spatter, yellow interior, unpainted base ($15-20)

MB30-C SWAMP RAT, issued 1976
1. olive deck, light tan hull, tan man, "Swamp Rats" labels, England casting ($5-8)
2. olive deck, dark tan hull, tan man, "Swamp Rats" labels, England casting ($5-8)
3. olive deck, pinkish-tan hull, tan man, "Swamp Rats" labels, England casting ($5-8)
4. olive deck, dark tan hull, tan man, no labels, England casting ($5-8)
5. olive deck, tan hull, tan man, tan & black camouflage tempa, Macau casting ($4-6)(CM)
6. olive deck, tan hull, black man, tan & black camouflage tempa, China casting ($12-15)(CM)

MB30-D LEYLAND ARTICULATED TRUCK, issued 1982 (ROW)
NOTE: All models with red windows, England casting unless otherwise noted.
1. blue cab, white cab base, silver-gray dump, no panel cast, no tempa ($2-4)
2. blue cab, yellow cab base, silver-gray dump, no panel cast, no tempa ($2-4)
3. bright blue cab, yellow cab base, silver-gray dump, no panel cast, no tempa ($2-4)
4. bright blue cab, yellow cab base, yellow dump, cast panel, "International" tempa ($3-5)
5. red cab, yellow cab base, silver-gray dump, no panel cast, no tempa ($7-10)
6. red cab, yellow cab base, yellow dump, cast panel, "International" tempa ($6-8)
7. blue cab, yellow cab base, yellow dump, cast panel, "International" tempa ($6-8)
8. bright blue cab, lemon cab base, yellow dump, cast panel, "International" tempa ($3-5)
9. bright blue cab, white cab base, yellow dump, cast panel, "International" tempa ($3-5)
10. bright blue cab, yellow cab base, bright blue dump, cast panel, "Pauls" tempa ($25-40)(UK)
11. bright blue cab, lemon cab base, bright blue dump, cast panel, "Pauls" tempa ($25-40)(UK)
12. bright blue cab, white cab base, bright blue dump, cast panel, "Pauls" tempa ($25-40)(UK)
13. bright blue cab, lemon cab base, yellow dump, cast panel, amber windows, "International" tempa, Macau casting ($3-5)

MB30-E PETERBILT QUARRY TRUCK, issued 1982 (USA)
MB23-E PETERBILT QUARRY TRUCK, issued 1982 (ROW)
1. yellow body, light gray dump, amber windows, chrome exhausts & base, "Dirty Dumper" tempa, England casting ($2-4)
2. yellow body, dark gray dump, amber windows, chrome exhausts & base, "Dirty Dumper" tempa, England casting ($2-4)
3. yellow body, silver-gray dump, amber windows, chrome exhausts & base, "Dirty Dumper" tempa, England casting ($2-4)
4. yellow body, silver-gray dump, clear windows, chrome exhausts & base, "Dirty Dumper" tempa, England casting ($2-4)
5. yellow body, dark gray dump, amber windows, chrome exhausts & base, "Dirty Dumper" tempa, Macau casting ($1-2)
6. yellow-orange body, dark gray dump, amber windows, chrome exhausts & base, "Dirty Dumper" tempa, Macau casting ($1-2)
7. yellow-orange body, dark gray dump, clear windows, chrome exhausts & base, "Dirty Dumper" tempa, Macau casting ($1-2)
8. light yellow body, dark gray dump, clear windows, chrome exhausts & base, "Pace" tempa, Macau casting ($1-2)
9. dark yellow body, dark gray dump, clear windows, chrome exhausts & base, "Pace" tempa, Macau casting ($1-2)
10. dark yellow body, dark gray dump, clear windows, gray exhausts, chrome base, "Pace" tempa, Macau casting ($1-2)
11. orange body, dark gray dump, clear windows, chrome exhausts & base, "Losinger" tempa, Macau casting ($8-12)(SW)
12. dark yellow body, dark gray dump, clear windows, gray exhausts, chrome base, "Pace" tempa, Thailand casting ($1-2)
13. dark yellow body, red dump, clear windows, gray exhausts, chrome base, "Pace" tempa, Thailand casting ($1-2)
14. white body, silver-gray dump, clear windows, gray exhausts & base, "Cement Company" tempa, Manaus casting ($35-50)(BR)
15. orange-yellow body, red dump, clear windows, gray exhausts, black base with bar code, "Pace" & "Intercom City" tempa, China casting ($10-15)(IC)
16. red body, gray dump, gray base, gray exhausts, "530SP" & stripes tempa, Manaus casting ($30-45)(BR)
17. white body, silver-gray dump, gray base, gray exhausts, "Construction" tempa, Manaus casting ($35-50)(BR)
18. fluorescent orange body, black dump, chrome base, black exhausts, no tempa, Thailand casting ($1-2)(MP)
19. red body, red dump, gray base, gray exhausts, "530SP" tempa, Manaus casting ($30-45)(BR)
20. orange-yellow body, red dump, chrome base, gray exhausts, "Pace" tempa, China casting ($2-4)
21. pumpkin body, gray dump, chrome base, dark gray exhausts, "Matchbox" tempa, China casting ($1-2)(MP)
22. orange-yellow body, red dump, chrome base, gray exhausts, no tempa, China casting ($1-2)
23. white body, dark turquoise dump, chrome base, gray exhausts,

"Sagamore Insurance" tempa, China casting ($85-110)(US)
24. dark yellow body, yellow dump, chrome base, chrome exhausts, "CAT" tempa, China casting ($2-3)(CT)
25. red body, dark gray dump, chrome base, chrome exhausts, white stripes tempa, China casting ($1-2)(MW10)

MB30-F MERCEDES 'G' WAGON, issued 1985 (ROW)
NOTE: All models with silver-gray interior except Lasertronic models which have no interior fitted. All models with 8 spoke wheels.
1. red body, white roof, black base, blue windows & dome lights, white "Rescue Unit" & checkers tempa, Macau casting ($2-3)
2. orange body, white roof, black base, blue windows & dome lights, "Lufthansa" tempa, Macau casting ($3-5)(GS)
3. white body, white roof, black base, blue windows & dome lights, "Polizei" & checkers tempa, Macau casting ($2-4)(TP)
4. white body, white roof, black base, blue windows & dome lights, "Polizei" with green doors & hood tempa, Macau casting ($2-4)
5. red body, white roof, black base, blue windows & dome lights, yellow "Rescue Unit" & checkers tempa, Macau casting ($2-3)(MC)
6. olive body, tan roof, black base, blue windows & dome lights, red cross in circle & "LS 2014" tempa, black hubs, Macau casting ($4-6)(CM)
7. white body, orange roof, orange base, blue windows & dome lights, "Ambulance" & checkers tempa, Macau casting ($3-5)(MC)
8. white body, white roof, black base, black windows, green dome lights, "Auto Rescue 24 Hrs. Towing" tempa, Macau casting ($8-12)(SR)
9. red body, red roof, black base, black windows, red dome lights, "Fire Metro Airport" tempa, Macau casting ($8-12)(SR)
10. navy blue body, navy blue roof, black base, black windows, red dome lights, "Swat Unit Team Support" tempa, Macau casting ($8-12)(SR)
11. red body, white roof, black base, blue windows & dome lights, yellow "Rescue Unit" & checkers, Thailand casting ($2-3)(MC)
12. white body, white roof, black base, blue windows & dome lights, "Polizei" with green hood & doors tempa, Thailand casting ($1-2)
13. white body, dark orange roof, orange base, blue windows & dome lights, "Ambulance" & checkers tempa, Thailand casting ($2-3)(MC)
14. white body, white roof, black base, blue windows & dome lights, "Lufthansa" tempa, Thailand casting ($1-2)(MP)
15. florescent orange body, white roof, black base, blue windows & dome lights, "Auto Rescue 24 Hrs. Towing", Thailand casting ($1-2)
16. white body, florescent orange roof & base, blue windows & dome lights, "Marine Rescue" & checkers tempa, Thailand casting ($2-3)(EM)
17. florescent orange body, white roof, black base with bar code, blue windows & dome lights, "Police 8" & "Intercom City" tempa, Thailand casting ($10-15)(IC)
18. florescent orange body, white roof, black base, blue windows & dome lights, white hood with "Rescue" & checker design on sides tempa, Thailand casting ($1-2)(EM)
19. red body, white roof, black base, black windows, red dome lights, "Matchbox Rescue Unit/ Fire Dept." tempa, China casting ($3-5)(LS)
20. lemon body, white roof, black base, black windows, greenish yellow dome lights, "Beach Patrol Unit 2" tempa, China casting ($3-5)(LS)
21. yellow body, black roof, black base, black windows, greenish-yellow dome lights, "Tough Construction- Construction Foreman" tempa, China casting ($3-5)(LS)
22. red body, gray roof, black base, black windows, red dome lights, "Matchbox Rescue Unit" tempa, China casting ($3-5)(LS)
23. beige body, dark green roof, black base, black windows, greenish yellow dome lights, green stripes tempa, China casting ($4-6)(LS)(Avon)
24. dark red body, white roof, black base, black windows, red dome lights, "Matchbox Fires Rescue Dept." tempa, China casting ($4-6)(LS)(Avon)

MB30-G TOYOTA SUPRA, issued 1995 (USA)
MB60-I TOYOTA SUPRA, issued 1995 (ROW)
NOTE: below models with gloss black base & Thailand casting unless otherwise noted.
1. white body, gray interior, smoke windows, red & yellow hood & sides design tempa, 6-spoke spiral wheels ($1-2)
2. white body, red interior, smoke windows, red & yellow side tempa, 6-spoke spiral wheels ($1-2)
3. florescent orange body, black interior, clear windows, "Matchbox Get In The Fast Lane/ Toy Fair 1996" tempa, chrome disc with rubber tires ($18-25)(US)
4. florescent yellow body, black interior, clear windows, "Matchbox Get In The Fast Lane/ Toy Fair 1996" tempa, chrome disc with rubber tires ($18-25)(UK)
5. iridescent white body, red interior, clear windows, detailed trim tempa, chrome disc with rubber tires ($3-5)(PC1)
6. copper body, red/black interior, clear windows, detailed trim tempa, chrome disc with rubber tires ($3-5)(SC1)
7. yellow body, gray/black interior, clear windows, detailed trim tempa, chrome disc with rubber tires ($3-5)(PC)(JC)
8. charcoal body, red/black interior, clear windows, detailed trim tempa, chrome disc with rubber tires ($3-5)(PC4)
9. red body, yellow interior, smoke windows, orange & white side tempa, 6-spoke spiral wheels ($2-4)
10. red body, silver-gray interior, smoke windows, white & black design tempa,, 5 spoke concave star wheels ($1-2)(MP
11. chrome body, purple interior, clear windows, purple & pink design tempa, 5 spoke concave star wheels ($1-2)
12. red body, yellow interior, smoke windows, orange and white side tempa, 5 spoke concave star wheels ($2-4)
13. black body, tan & black interior, clear windows, detailed trim tempa, chrome disc with rubber tires ($15-20)(GC)
14. metallic gold body, black interior, clear windows, no tempa, 5 spoke concave star wheels ($5-10)(CH)
15. greenish gold body, black interior, clear windows, no tempa, 5 spoke concave star wheels ($5-10)(CH)
16. blue chrome body, white interior, clear windows, pink/orange/white, 5 spoke concave star wheels ($1-2)(MP)
17. non chrome blue, white interior, clear windows, pink/orange/white, 5 spoke concave star wheels ($1-2)(MP)
18. black body, tan interior, clear windows, gold "Supra" tempa, 5 spoke concave star wheels ($1-2)(MW44-ROW)
19. pale blue chrome body, clear windows, pink/orange/white tempa, 5 spoke concave star wheels ($1-2)(MP)
20. pale blue chrome body, clear windows, pink/orange/white tempa, 5 spoke concave star wheels, China casting ($1-2)(MP)
21. black body, tan interior, clear windows, gold "Supra" tempa, 5 spoke concave star wheels, China casting ($1-2)(MW44-ROW)
NOTE: versions 16, 17 & 19 can be found in multiple shades of blue.

MB30-I CHEVY TAHOE POLICE, issued 1998
NOTE: All models with clear windows, red dome lights, chrome base & China casting unless otherwise noted.
1. white body, gray interior, "Police Unit 4" tempa, 5 spoke concave star wheels ($1-2)
2. black body, red interior, "Matchbox Official Collectors Club" tempa , 5 spoke concave star wheels ($5-8)
NOTE: Above model was available only to collectors joining a club.
3. green & yellow body, tan interior, "York Fair Police 1998" tempa , 5 spoke concave star wheels ($7-10)(US)
4. white body, gray interior, "Salt Lake Police" tempa , chrome disc with rubber tires (for price see note below)(PC22)
NOTE: The above model was scheduled in 1998 to be released with 5 other models for Premiere set #22. At the time of this book going to print, the series was prematurely cancelled and only 4 of the 6 were produced and in less than scheduled quantities. This piece ended up being a 1400 piece run. If production resumes in 1998 on PC22 this model will be valued at $3-5 like all other Premiere editions. If the production does not resume this model will value at ($15-25).

MB31-A LINCOLN CONTINENTAL, issued 1970
1. mint green body, unpainted base ($2000+)
2. green-gold body, unpainted base ($45-60)

MB31-B VOLKSDRAGON, issued 1971
1. red body, unpainted base, purple windows, cream interior, eyes label ($12-15)
2. red body, unpainted base, purple windows, yellow interior, eyes label ($12-15)
3. red body, unpainted base, clear windows, yellow interior, eyes label ($12-15)
4. red body, silver-gray base, clear windows, yellow interior, eyes label ($12-15)
5. red body, silver-gray base, purple windows, yellow interior, eyes label ($12-15)
6. red body, unpainted base, purple windows, yellow interior, flower label ($15-20)
7. red body, silver-gray base, purple windows, yellow interior, flower label ($15-20)
8. red body, unpainted base, purple windows, yellow interior, no label ($12-15)
9. red body, silver-gray base, purple windows, yellow interior, no label ($12-15)
10. red body, unpainted base, purple windows, white interior, eyes label ($12-15)

MB31-C CARAVAN, issued 1977
NOTE: Following models with clear windows unless otherwise noted.
1. white body, unpainted base, orange door, ivory interior, orange labels, England casting ($3-5)
2. white body, unpainted base, orange door, light yellow interior, orange labels, England casting ($3-5)
3. white body, unpainted base, yellow door, light yellow interior, orange labels, England casting ($3-5)
4. white body, unpainted base, yellow door, ivory interior, orange labels, England casting ($3-5)
5. white body, unpainted base, orange door, tan interior, orange labels, England casting ($3-5)
6. white body, unpainted base, light blue door, tan interior, orange labels, England casting ($3-5)
7. white body, unpainted base, light blue door, light yellow interior, orange labels, England casting ($3-5)
8. white body, unpainted base, light blue door, light brown interior, orange labels, England casting ($3-5)
9. white body, unpainted base, light blue door, light yellow interior, blue labels, England casting ($3-5)
10. white body, unpainted base, dark blue door, light yellow interior, blue labels, England casting ($3-5)
11. white body, unpainted base, light blue door, light yellow interior, no labels, England casting ($3-5)
12. white body, unpainted base, dark blue door, light yellow interior, no labels, England casting ($3-5)
13. white body, silver-gray base, dark blue door, light yellow interior, blue labels, England casting ($3-5)
14. white body, unpainted base, dark blue door, orange-yellow interior, blue labels, England casting ($3-5)
15. white body, black base, chocolate door, yellow interior, "Mobile 500" tempa, England casting ($2-4)(TP)
16. white body, black base, chocolate door, orange-yellow interior, "Mobile 500" tempa, England casting ($2-4)(TP)
17. white body, pearly silver base, chocolate door, lemon interior, amber windows, "Mobile 500" tempa, Macau casting ($2-4)(TP)
18. white body, black base, chocolate door, cream interior, amber windows, "Mobile 500" tempa, no origin cast ($2-4)(TP)
19. beige body, black base, chocolate door, cream interior, amber windows, "Mobile 500" tempa, no origin cast ($2-4)(TP)
20. gray body, black base, gray door, cream interior, amber windows, blue & red stripes tempa, no origin cast ($1-2)(TP)
21. white body, black base, red door, cream interior, yellow/orange/red stripes tempa, no origin cast ($2-3)(MC)
22. white body, black base, white door, cream interior, blue windows, blue/maroon/orange design tempa, no origin cast ($1-2)(TP)
23. white body, black base, white door, silver-gray interior, amber windows, "Caravan 2000" tempa, no origin cast ($1-2)(MP)
24. white body, black base, white door, silver-gray interior, amber windows, "Caravan 2000" tempa, China casting ($1-2)(MP)
NOTE: Available as a Bulgarian casting. Bases are cast blank. Assorted colors available ($15-25)

MB31-D MAZDA RX7, issued 1982 (USA)
1. white body, ivory interior, wide side stripe tempa, maltese cross wheels ($3-5)
2. white body, ivory interior, wide side tempa, 5 spoke wheels ($3-5)
3. white body, ivory interior, thin side stripe tempa, maltese cross wheels ($3-5)
4. white body, tan interior, wide side stripe tempa, 5 spoke wheels ($3-5)
5. white body, tan interior, thin side stripe tempa, 5 spoke wheels ($3-5)
6. black body, tan interior, gold side stripe tempa, 5 spoke wheels ($3-5)

MB31-E MAZDA RX7, issued 1983
1. black body, red interior, 5 arch wheels, gold side stripe tempa , Macau casting ($2-4)
2. white body, red interior, 5 arch wheels, "7" with stripes tempa, Macau casting ($2-4)
3. black body, red interior, 5 arch wheels, "RX7" & "Mazda" tempa, Manaus casting ($35-50)(BR)
4. black body, red interior, dot dash wheels, "RX7" & "Mazda" tempa, Manaus casting ($35-50)(BR)
NOTE: Available as a Bulgarian casting. Assorted colors available ($15-25)

MB31-G STERLING, issued 1988 (USA)
MB 2-F STERLING, issued 1988 (ROW)
NOTE: All models with smoke gray windows, tan interior and 8 dot wheels unless otherwise noted.
1. metallic red body, charcoal base, no tempa, Macau casting ($1-2)
2. pearly silver body, metallic blue base, laser wheels, blue/white/red stripes tempa, Macau casting ($4-6)(LW)
3. metallic red body, charcoal base, no tempa, China casting ($1-2)
4. blue body, yellow base, blue wheels with yellow hubs, exposed engine & tools design tempa, China casting ($6-8)(LL)
5. blue body, orange-yellow base, blue wheels with yellow hubs, exposed engine & tools design tempa, China casting ($6-8)(LL)
6. silver-gray body, metallic blue base, black door posts tempa, China casting ($1-2)
7. yellow body, yellow base, no tempa, China casting ($8-12)(GR)(GS)
8. silver-gray body, metallic blue base, black doors posts & "Rover Sterling" tempa, China casting ($1-2)
9. silver-gray body, metallic blue base, "Rover Sterling" tempa, China casting ($1-2)
10. white body, white base, white interior, no tempa, China casting ($10-15)(GF)
11. blue body, orange-yellow base, red interior, all blue wheels, exposed engine design & tools tempa, China casting ($6-8)(LL)

MB31-I NISSAN PRAIRIE, issued 1991 (USA)
MB21-G NISSAN PRAIRIE, issued 1991 (ROW)
1. metallic blue body, black base, clear windows, blue interior, silver sides tempa, China casting ($5-7)
2. silver-gray body, black base, clear windows, blue interior, "Nissan" tempa, China casting ($2-3)
3. white body, white base, green windows, white interior, no tempa, China casting ($10-15)(GF)
4. red body, black base, clear windows, blue interior, "Nissan" tempa, China casting ($8-12)(GS)
5. white body, black base, clear windows, blue interior, "Paramedic PS" tempa, China casting ($2-3)
6. dark green body, black base, clear windows, tan interior, gold "Nissan" tempa, China casting ($1-2)(MW45-ROW)
7. yellow body, black base, clear windows, black interior, "Citywide Taxi Service" tempa, China casting ($1-2)(MP)

MB31-J JAGUAR XJ220, issued 1993 (USA)
MB26-I JAGUAR XJ220, issued 1993 (ROW)
1. silver-gray body, red interior, clear windows, 8 dot wheels, no tempa, Thailand casting ($2-3)(SS)
2. dark blue body, ivory interior, clear windows, 8 dot wheels, no tempa, Thailand casting ($1-2)
3. purple body, ivory interior, chrome windows, gray disc with rubber tires, detailed tempa, Thailand casting ($2-4)(WC)
4. fluorescent yellow (left side) & fluorescent orange (right side) body, blue interior, smoke windows, 6-spoke gold spiral wheels, geometric design tempa, Thailand casting ($1-2)
5. dark blue body, ivory interior, clear windows, gold 6-spoke spiral wheels, "Jaguar" logo tempa, Thailand casting ($2-3)
6. dark blue body, white interior, smoke windows, gold 6-spoke spiral wheels, "50" & "XJ220" tempa, Thailand casting ($2-3)(GS)
7. chrome plated body, white interior & base, amber windows, gold 6-

spoke spiral wheels, no tempa, Thailand casting ($2-4)(GF)
8. silver-gray body, blue interior, smoke windows, silver 6-spoke spiral wheels, blue & yellow design tempa, Thailand casting ($1-2)(MP)
9. florescent yellow (left side) & florescent orange (right side) body, blue interior, smoke windows, silver 6-spoke spiral wheels, geometric design tempa, Thailand casting ($1-2)
10. florescent orange body, blue interior, smoke windows, silver 6-spoke spiral wheels, geometric design tempa, Thailand casting ($1-2)
11. metallic red & black body, yellow interior, clear windows, silver 6-spoke spiral wheels, no tempa, Thailand casting ($1-2)(MP)
12. dark blue body, ivory interior, clear windows, silver 6-spoke spiral wheels, gold "Jaguar" logo tempa, Thailand casting ($3-5)
13. dark blue body, ivory interior, smoke windows, silver 6-spoke spiral wheels, "50" & "XJ220" tempa, Thailand casting ($3-5)(GS)
14. dark green body, ivory interior, smoke windows, silver 6 spoke spiral wheels, white & lime flames tempa, Thailand casting ($1-2)(MP)
15. metallic turquoise body, yellow interior, smoke windows, 5 spoke concave star wheels, yellow & white flames, Thailand casting ($1-2)
16. metallic gold body, black interior, clear windows, silver 6 spoke spiral wheels, no tempa, Thailand casting ($5-10)(CH)
17. metallic blue body, gray & black interior, chrome disc with rubber tires, detailed trim tempa, Thailand casting ($3-5)(PC2-ROW)
18. metallic maroon, gray & black interior, chrome disc with rubber tires, detailed trim tempa, Thailand casting ($3-5)(PC10)
19. dark blue body, white interior, silver 6 spoke spiral wheels, "Old Eight" tempa, Thailand casting ($75-100)(BR)
20. dark green body, tan interior, 5 spoke concave star wheels, "Jaguar" tempa, Thailand casting ($1-2)(MW75-ROW)
21. dark green body, gray & black interior, chrome disc with rubber tires, detailed trim tempa, Thailand casting ($3-5)(PC19)
22. dark green body, tan interior, 5 spoke concave star wheels, "Jaguar" tempa, China casting ($1-2)(MW75-ROW)

MB31-L 1957 CHEVY BEL AIR, issued 1998

NOTE: All models with clear windows, chrome base and China casting.
1. bright blue body & roof, blue & white interior, silver flash & detailed trim tempa, chrome disc with rubber tires ($4-6)(FE)
2. unpainted body, gray roof, white interior, no tempa, chrome disc with rubber tires ($4-6)(FE)
3. black body & roof, white interior, green & white design tempa, 5 spoke concave star wheels ($1-2)(MW31)
4. maroonish purple body, beige roof, beige & maroon interior, silver flash & "Matchbox Premiere Collectors Club" tempa, chrome mags with rubber tires ($10-15)(PC Club)

MB32-A LEYLAND TANKER, issued 1970

1. blue cab, white tank, chrome base, "Aral" labels ($50-75)
2. green cab, white tank, chrome base, "BP" labels ($15-20)
3. green cab, white tank, gray base, "BP" labels ($18-25)
4. red cab, white tank, chrome base, "N.A.M.C./ The Miniature Vehicle" labels ($400-600)(LE)
5. purple cab, silver-gray tank, chrome base, "National Association of Matchbox Collectors" labels ($173-223)(C2)
6. purple cab, silver/gray tank, chrome base, no labels ($125-175)

NOTE: Although issued back in 1972 with "National Association of Matchbox" labels, unlabelled versions were not offered for sale until 1994. Less than 300 probably exist this way.

MB32-B MASERATI BORA, issued 1972

1. burgundy body, unpainted base, "8" label, no tow hook, 5 spoke wheels ($25-40)
2. burgundy body, light green base, "8" label, no tow hook, 5 spoke wheels ($8-12)
3. burgundy body, dark green base, "8" label, no tow hook, 5 spoke wheels ($8-12)
4. burgundy body, dark green base, no label, no tow hook, 5 spoke wheels ($8-12)
5. burgundy body, dark green base, "8" label, no tow hook, 5 arch wheels ($8-12)
6. burgundy body, dark green base, "3" label, no tow hook, 5 arch wheels ($10-15)
7. burgundy body, metallic green base, "8" label, no tow hook, 5 arch wheels ($8-12)
8. gold body, silver-gray base, no label, with tow hook, 5 arch wheels ($15-20)(TP)

MB32-C FIELD GUN, issued 1978

1. olive body, olive guard, no plastic base, 5 arch black wheels ($5-7)(TP)
2. olive body, olive guard, tan plastic base, 5 arch black wheels ($5-7)
3. olive body, olive guard, tan plastic base, dot dash silver wheels ($25-40)
4. olive body, black guard, tan plastic base (with tab), 5 arch black wheels ($65-80)(BR)
5. green body, green guard, tan plastic base (with tab), 5 arch black wheels ($75-100)(BR)

MB32-D ATLAS EXCAVATOR, issued 1981
MB 6-F ATLAS EXCAVATOR, reissued 1990 (USA)

1. dark orange body, black scoop, black platform, gray base, no tempa, England casting ($6-8)
2. dark orange body, black scoop, charcoal platform, gray base, no tempa, England casting ($6-8)
3. light orange body, black scoop, black platform, gray base, no tempa, England casting ($6-8)
4. light orange body, black scoop, charcoal platform, gray base, no tempa, England casting ($6-8)
5. yellow body, black scoop, black platform, gray base, black stripes with "C" tempa, England casting ($2-4)
6. yellow body, black scoop, black platform, black base, black stripes with "C" tempa, England casting ($2-4)
7. yellow body, black scoop, black platform, black base, black stripes tempa, England casting ($2-4)
8. yellow body, black scoop, black platform, black base, black stripes tempa, Macau casting ($1-2)
9. yellow-orange body, black scoop, black platform, black base, black stripes tempa, Macau casting ($1-2)
10. light yellow body, yellow scoop, light yellow platform & base, "JCB" labels, Macau casting ($7-10)(GS)
11. yellow body, black scoop, black platform, black base, black stripes tempa, Thailand casting ($1-2)
12. yellow body, red scoop, black platform, black base, red stripes tempa, Thailand casting ($1-2)
13. fluorescent orange body, black scoop, black platform, black base, no tempa, Thailand casting ($1-2)(MP)
14. red body, red scoop, black platform, black base, black & white stripes tempa, Thailand casting ($1-2)
15. red body, red scoop, black platform, black base, white stripes tempa, Thailand casting ($1-2)
16. metallic gold body, black scoop, black platform, black base, no tempa, Thailand casting ($5-10)(CH6)
17. dull orange body, orange scoop, black platform, black base, black & white stripes tempa, Thailand casting ($1-2)
18. bright orange body, orange scoop, black platform, black base, black & white stripes tempa, Thailand casting ($1-2)
19. bright lime body, lime scoop, black platform, black base, black & white stripes tempa, Thailand casting ($1-2)
20. bright lime body, lime scoop, black platform, black base, black & white stripes tempa, China casting ($1-2)

MB32-E MODIFIED RACER, issued 1988 (USA)
MB12-G MODIFIED RACER, issued 1988 (ROW)

NOTE: All models with chrome base & racing special slicks
1. orange body, black interior, chrome exhausts, "12" tempa, Macau casting ($1-2)
2. rose red body, black interior, chrome exhausts, "12" tempa, Macau casting ($3-4)(SC)
3. pale orange body, black interior, chrome exhausts, "12" tempa, Macau casting ($3-4)(SC)
4. orange body, black interior, black exhausts, "12" tempa, Macau casting ($1-2)
5. red body, black interior, black exhausts, "12" tempa, Macau casting ($3-4)(SC)
6. pale orange body, black interior, black exhausts, "12" tempa, Macau casting ($3-4)(SC)
7. orange body, black interior, black exhausts, "12" tempa, China casting ($1-2)
8. red body, black interior, chrome exhausts, "Mike 15" tempa, China casting ($4-6)(NM)
9. yellow body, green interior, chrome exhausts, "44 Reggie/ Magnum Oils" tempa, China casting ($4-6)(NM)
10. white body, red interior, chrome exhausts, "U2 Jamie" tempa, China casting ($4-6)(NM)
11. white body, black interior, chrome exhausts, "1 Tony/ Universal Joint Sales" tempa, China casting ($4-6)(NM)
12. dark purple body, black interior, black exhausts, "12" tempa, China casting ($3-4)(AP)
13. chrome plated body, black interior, black exhausts, no tempa, China casting ($12-18)(C2)
14. red body, red interior, black exhausts, "36" & Stripes tempa, China casting ($4-6)(NM)
15. red body, orange-yellow interior, black exhausts, "12" & stripes tempa, China casting ($4-6)(NM)
16. white & blue body, blue interior, black exhausts, "ADAP 15" tempa, China casting ($4-6)(NM)
17. white body, translucent blue interior, black exhausts, "41" & stripes tempa, China casting ($4-6)(NM)
18. white body, lavender interior, black exhausts, no tempa, China casting ($10-15)(GF)
19. red body, red interior, chrome exhausts, "38 Jerry Cook" tempa, China casting ($4-6)(NM)
20. white body, orange interior, chrome exhausts, "Maynard Troyer" tempa, China casting ($4-6)(NM)
21. dark blue body, black interior, chrome exhausts, "3 Ron Bouchard" tempa, China casting ($4-6)(NM)
22. orange-yellow body, red interior, chrome exhausts, "4 Bugs" tempa, China casting ($4-6)(NM)
23. red body, red interior, chrome exhausts, "42 Jamie Tomaino" tempa, China casting ($4-6)(NM)
24. orange-yellow body, red interior, chrome exhausts, "4 Satch Wirley" tempa, China casting ($4-6)(NM)
25. dark blue body, blue interior, chrome interior, "3 Doug Heveron" tempa, China casting ($4-6)(NM)
26. black body, black interior, chrome exhausts, "21 George Kent" tempa, China casting ($4-6)(NM)
27. dark blue body, black interior, chrome exhausts, "12" tempa, China casting ($8-12)(GS)
28. blue body, black interior, chrome exhausts, "3 Mike McLaughlin" tempa, China casting ($4-6)(NM)
29. black body, red interior, chrome exhausts, "44 Rick Fuller" tempa, China casting ($4-6)(NM)
30. black body, red interior, chrome exhausts, "7 NY" tempa, China casting ($4-6)(NM)
31. red body, red interior, chrome exhausts, "25 Jan Leaty" tempa, China casting ($4-6) (NM)
32. red body, red interior, chrome exhausts, "69 Parts Peddler" tempa, China casting ($4-6)(NM)
33. red body, white interior, chrome exhausts, "12 Sherri Cup" tempa, China casting ($4-6)(NM)
34. orange body, orange interior, chrome exhausts, "61 BR DeWitt" tempa, China casting ($4-6)(NM)
35. blue body, yellow interior, chrome exhausts, "24 Jimmy Spencer" tempa, China casting ($4-6)(NM)
36. white body, red interior, chrome exhausts, "99 Phil's Chevrolet" tempa, China casting ($4-6)(NM)
37. white body, green interior, chrome exhausts, "Polar 77" tempa, China casting ($4-6) (NM)
38. red body, red interior, chrome exhausts, "2X" tempa, China casting ($4-6)(NM)
39. dark blue body, white interior, chrome exhausts, "11 Hummels", China casting ($4-6) (NM)
40. powder blue body, powder blue interior, chrome exhausts, "5" tempa, China casting ($4-6)(NM)
41. red body, red interior, chrome exhausts, "15 Wayne Anderson" tempa, China casting ($4-6)(NM)
42. yellow body, dark blue interior, chrome exhausts, "56 Miller Brick Co." tempa, China casting ($4-6)(NM)
43. white & powder blue body, powder blue interior, chrome exhausts, "31 Tony Ferrante" tempa, China casting ($4-6)(NM)
44. metallic blue body, black interior, chrome exhausts, "JVB27- Jan Leaty" tempa, China casting ($4-6)(NM)
45. orange body, black interior, chrome exhausts, "73" tempa, China casting ($4-6)(NM)
46. white body, red interior, chrome exhausts, "1" tempa, China casting ($4-6)(NM)
47. red body, red interior, chrome exhausts, "37" tempa, China casting ($4-6)(NM)
48. red body, red interior, chrome exhausts, "Craz 8" tempa, China casting ($4-6)(NM)
49. red body, red interior, chrome exhausts, "21 Spearpoint Auto" tempa, China casting ($4-6)(NM)
50. white & orange body, orange interior, chrome exhausts, "17 Perth Amboy Spring" tempa, China casting ($4-6)(NM)
51. black body, pale orange interior, chrome exhausts, "39 Fyne Lyne" tempa, China casting ($4-6)(NM)
52. black & gold body, red interior, chrome exhausts, "0" tempa, China casting ($4-6)(NM)
53. black body, white interior, chrome exhausts, "1" with pink & white stripes tempa, Thailand casting ($1-2)(MP)
54. blue & silver/ gray body, silver/ gray interior, chrome exhausts, "Collector's Toys 95/ Gary's" tempa, Thailand casting ($5-8)(TC)(PL)

MB32-G 1970 EL CAMINO, issued 1998

NOTE: All models with clear windows & China casting unless otherwise noted.
1. red body, black & white interior, 2 white hood stripes tempa, chrome base, chrome disc with rubber tires ($4-6)(FE)
2. unpainted body, black interior, no tempa, chrome base, chrome disc with rubber tires ($4-6)(FE)
3. metallic gold body, black interior, 2 black hood stripes tempa, chrome base, 5 spoke concave star wheels ($1-2)(MW32)

NOTE: Above model found in various shades of gold from light to dark.
4. metallic gold body, black interior, 2 black hood stripes tempa, translucent white base, 5 spoke concave star wheels ($50-75)(MW32)
5. red & white body, black interior, "Coca Cola" tempa, chrome base, chrome disc with rubber tires ($4-6)(PC)

MB33-A LAMBORGHINI MIURA, issued 1969

NOTE: all models with 5 spoke wheel unless noted.
1. yellow body, red interior, unpainted base ($75-90)
2. dark bronze body, red interior, unpainted base ($25-40)
3. light bronze body, red interior, unpainted base ($18-25)
4. dark gold body, red interior, unpainted base ($18-25)
5. dark gold body, ivory interior, unpainted base ($15-20)
6. light gold body, ivory interior, unpainted base ($15-20)
7. light gold body, ivory interior, dark red base ($15-20)
8. light gold body, ivory interior, florescent red base ($15-20)
9. light gold body, ivory interior, bright florescent red base ($15-20)
10. light gold body, ivory interior, black base ($15-20)
11. light gold body, ivory interior, black base, dot dash wheels ($15-20)

NOTE: Available as a Bulgarian casting. Assorted colors available ($65-90)

MB33-B DATSUN 126X, issued 1973

1. yellow body, orange base, no tempa ($10-15)
2. yellow body, unpainted base, no tempa ($25-40)
3. yellow body, orange base, orange & red flames tempa ($15-18)
4. yellow body, orange base, black & red flames tempa ($15-18)

MB33-C POLICE MOTORCYCLE, issued 1977

NOTE: Following models with England casting unless otherwise noted.
1. white body, "Police" label, white seat, dark blue rider, chrome motor, wire wheels ($5-7)
2. white body, "Police" label, white seat, dark blue- painted rider, chrome motor, wire wheels ($5-7)(KS)
3. white body, "Police" label, white seat, navy blue rider, chrome motor, wire wheels ($5-7)
4. white body, "Police" label, white seat, light blue rider, chrome motor, wire wheels ($5-7)
5. white body, "Police" label, white seat, gray-blue rider, chrome motor,

wire wheels ($5-7)
6. cream body, "Polizei" label, green seat, green rider, chrome motor, wire wheels ($25-40)(GR)
7. cream body, "Polizei" label, green seat, green rider, black motor, wire wheels ($25-40)(GR)
8. white body, "Polizei" label, green seat, green rider, chrome motor, wire wheels ($20-35)(KS)
9. white body, "Polizei" label, green seat, green rider, black motor, wire wheels ($20-35)(KS)
10. white body, "Polizei" label, green seat, green rider- painted, black motor, wire wheels ($20-35)(GR)
11. white body, "Police" label, white seat, navy blue rider, black motor, wire wheels ($5-7)
12. white body, "Police" label, white seat, navy blue- painted rider, black motor, wire wheels ($5-7)
13. white body, "Police" label, white seat, blue rider, black motor, wire wheels ($5-7)
14. white body, "Police" label, white seat, navy blue- painted rider, black motor, mag wheels ($5-7)
15. white body, "Police" label, white seat, light blue- painted rider, black motor, mag wheels ($5-7)
16. white body, "Polizei" label, green seat, green- painted rider, black motor, mag wheels ($20-35)(GR)
17. white body, "Police" label, green seat, dark blue rider, black motor, mag wheels ($15-20)
18. black body, "L.A.P.D." label, white seat, light blue rider, chrome motor, mag wheels ($6-8)(CR)
19. white body, "Police" label, black seat, dark blue rider, chrome motor, mag wheels ($5-7)
20. white body, "4" label, red seat & airdam, no rider, chrome motor, mag wheels ($12-15)(KS)
21. white body, "Police" label, black seat, shiny blue rider, chrome motor, mag wheels, Macau casting ($2-4)
22. white body, "Honda" & "Police" labels, white seat, bright blue rider, chrome motor, mag wheels, Macau casting ($2-4)
23. black body, "Police" tempa, white seat, dark blue- painted rider, chrome motor, mag wheels, Macau casting ($2-4)
24. white body, Japanese lettered tempa, white seat, dark blue rider, chrome motor, mag wheels, Macau casting ($8-12)(JP)

MB33-D VOLKSWAGEN GOLF GTi, issued 1985 (USA)
MB56-E VOLKSWAGEN GOLF GTi, issued 1985 (ROW)
MB63-G VOLKSWAGEN GOLF GTi, reissued 1991 (ROW)
NOTE: All models with black interior, grille & bumpers, clear windows.
1. red body & base, 8 dot silver wheels, black & silver "Golf GTi" tempa, Macau casting ($2-4)
2. red body & base, 8 dot silver wheels, white "GTi" tempa, Macau casting ($2-4)
3. red body & base, 8 dot gold wheels, white "GTi" tempa, Macau casting ($3-5)
4. red body & base, dot dash wheels, white "GTi" tempa, Macau casting ($3-5)
5. white body & base, 8 dot silver wheels, "Federal Express" tempa, Macau casting ($3-5)(GS)
6. white body & base, 8 dot silver wheels, "Quantum" tempa, Macau casting ($6-8)(UK)
7. dark gray body & base, 8 dot silver wheels, silver sides tempa, Macau casting ($2-4)(TP)
8. yellow body & base, 8 dot silver wheels, "PTT" tempa, Macau casting ($8-12)(SW)
9. dark gray body & base, 8 dot silver wheels, silver sides tempa, Thailand casting ($2-4)(TP)
10. white body & base, 8 dot silver wheels, "Abstract" tempa, Thailand casting ($3-5)(UK)
11. white body & base, 8 dot silver wheels, "Lippische Landes-Zeitung" tempa, Thailand casting ($15-20)(GR)

MB33-F RENAULT 11, issued 1986 (ROW)
MB43-F RENAULT 11, issued 1986 (USA)
NOTE: All models with gray plastic base and clear windows.
1. metallic blue body, gray interior, 8 dot wheels, gray side tempa, "Taxi Parisien" roof sign, England casting ($10-15)(JB)
2. black body, gray interior, dot dash wheels, "Turbo" & silver stripes tempa, England casting ($2-4)
3. black body, gray interior, 8 dot wheels, no tempa, England casting ($2-4)
4. black body, gray interior, 8 dot wheels, "Turbo" & silver stripes tempa, England casting ($2-4)
5. black body, tan interior, dot dash wheels, "Turbo" & silver stripes tempa, England casting ($2-4)
6. black body, tan interior, dot dash wheels, "Turbo" & silver stripes tempa, Macau casting ($2-4)
7. black body, tan interior, 8 dot dash wheels, "Turbo" & silver stripes tempa, Macau casting ($2-4)
8. black body, tan interior, dot dash wheels, "Turbo" & silver stripes tempa, China casting ($2-4)
9. black body, tan interior, 8 dot wheels, "Turbo" & silver stripes tempa, China casting ($2-4)
NOTE: Available as a Bulgarian casting. Assorted colors available ($15-25)

MB33-G UTILITY TRUCK, issued 1989 (USA)
MB74-I UTILITY TRUCK, issued 1989 (ROW)
NOTE: All models with blue windows & 8 spoke wheels.
1. gray body, black base, white boom, turret & bucket, "Energy Inc." tempa, Macau casting ($1-2)
2. red body, yellow base, blue turret, no boom or bucket, "53"/ circle/bolt tempa, yellow wheels with blue hubs, China casting ($6-8)(LL)
3. red body, yellow base, yellow turret, no boom or bucket, "53"/circle/bolt tempa, yellow wheels with blue hubs, China casting ($6-8)(LL)
4. red body, yellow base, blue & yellow boom, blue turret, lime bucket, "53"/circle/bolt tempa, yellow wheels with blue hubs, China casting ($6-8)(LL)
5. red body, yellow base, blue & lime boom, yellow turret, blue bucket, "53"/circle/bolt tempa, yellow wheels with blue hubs, China casting ($6-8)(LL)
6. gray body, black base, white boom, turret & bucket, "Energy Inc." tempa, China casting ($1-2)
7. orange-yellow body, black base, white boom, turret & bucket, "Energy Inc." with red cab front tempa, China casting ($3-4)(AP)
8. dark yellow body, black base, white boom, turret & bucket, "Telephone Co. Unit 4" & checkers tempa, Thailand casting ($1-2)
9. green body, black base, white boom, turret & bucket, "Intercom City"/"Service" & checkers tempa, Thailand casting ($7-10)(IC)
10. cream body, green base, green boom, turret & bucket, "Tree Care 14" (light green) tempa, China casting ($1-2)
11. cream body, green base, green boom, turret & bucket, "Tree Care 14" (dark green) tempa, China casting ($1-2)
12. dark yellow body, black base, white boom, turret & bucket, "Telephone Co. Unit 4" & black checkers tempa, China casting ($1-2)
13. metallic green body, gray base, white boom, turret & bucket, "Tree Care 14" tempa, China casting ($1-2)
14. metallic gold body, black base, black boom, turret & bucket, no tempa, China casting ($10-15)(CH)
15. silver-gray body, black base, red boom, turret & bucket, "Global Electric" tempa, China casting ($1-2)(MP)
16. silver-gray body, black base, dark red boom, turret & bucket, "Global Electric" tempa, China casting ($1-2)(MP)
17. silver-gray body, black base, maroon boom, turret & bucket, "Global Electric" tempa, China casting ($1-2)(MP)
18. blue body, chrome base, yellow boom, turret & bucket, "P & L Co. Response Unit 20" tempa, China casting ($1-2)
19. red body, chrome base, white boom, turret & bucket, "Matchbox Fire Dept." tempa, China casting ($1-2)(MP)
20. orange body, chrome base, white boom, turret & bucket, "P & L Response Unit 20" tempa, China casting ($1-2)(MW9)
21. black body, gray base, green boom, turret & bucket, "Highway Crew-Caution High Voltage Unit #45" tempa, China casting ($1-2)(MP)
22. white body, chrome base, white boom, turret & bucket, no tempa, China casting ($25-40)(ASAP blank)
23. white body, chrome base, white boom, turret & bucket, "American International Recovery" tempa, China casting ($100+)(ASAP)
24. white body, chrome base, yellow boom, turret & bucket, "GI" temps, China casting ($20+)(ASAP)

MB34-A FORMULA 1, issued 1971
NOTE: All models with clear windshields and unpainted base unless otherwise noted.
1. metallic pink body, "16" yellow label, 4 spoke front & rear wheels ($15-20)
2. metallic pink body, "16" yellow label, spiro front & rear wheels ($15-20)
3. metallic pink body, "16" yellow & "Wynn's" label, 4 spoke front & rear wheels ($75-125)(UK)
4. metallic blue body, "15" label, 4 spoke front & rear wheels ($12-15)(GS)
5. blue body, "15" label, 4 spoke front & 5 spoke rear wheels ($12-15)(GS)
6. blue body, "16" blue label, 4 spoke front & 5 spoke rear wheels, amber windshield ($12-15)(GS)
7. blue body, "15" label, maltese cross front & 5 spoke rear wheels ($12-15)(GS)
8. orange body, "16" blue label, 4 spoke front & rear wheels ($12-15)
9. orange body, "16" blue label, maltese cross front & 5 spoke rear wheels ($12-15)
10. orange body, "16" blue label, maltese cross front & 5 spoke rear wheels, amber windshield ($12-15)
11. orange body, "16" yellow label, 4 spoke front & rear wheels ($12-15)
12. orange body, "16" yellow label, maltese cross front & 5 spoke rear wheels ($12-15)
13. orange-yellow body, "16" blue label, 4 spoke front & 5 spoke rear wheels ($12-15)
14. yellow body, "16" blue label, 4 spoke front & rear wheels ($12-15)
15. yellow body, "16" blue label, maltese cross front & 5 spoke rear wheels ($12-15)
16. yellow body, "16" blue label, maltese cross front & 5 spoke rear wheels, amber windshield ($12-15)
17. yellow body, "16" yellow label, maltese cross front & 5 spoke rear wheels ($12-15)
18. yellow body, "16" blue label, maltese cross front & 5 spoke rear wheels, silver-gray base ($12-15)
19. yellow body, "16" blue label, 4 spoke front & 5 spoke rear wheels ($12-15)
20. yellow body, "16" blue label, 4 spoke front & maltese cross rear wheels ($12-15)
21. yellow body, "15" label, maltese cross front & 5 spoke rear wheels ($12-15)
22. yellow body, "16" yellow label, maltese cross front & 5 spoke rear wheels, amber windshield ($12-15)

MB34-B VANTASTIC, issued 1975
NOTE: All models with 5 arch front and dot dash rear wheels unless otherwise noted.
1. orange body, unpainted base, blue-green windows, with motor, fish-like side label ($10-15)
2. orange body, white base, blue-green windows, with motor, fish-like side labels ($10-15)
3. orange body, white base, blue-green windows, with motor, stripes side label ($10-15)
4. orange body, white base, blue-green windows, no motor, "34" hood & stripes side labels ($8-12)
5. orange body, white base, blue-green windows, no motor, "34" hood & no side labels ($8-12)
6. orange body, white base, clear windows, no motor, "34" hood & no side labels ($8-12)
7. orange body, white base, blue-green windows, no motor, "34" hood & no side labels, 5 arch rear wheels ($8-12)
8. orange body, white base, blue-green windows, no motor, "34" hood & no side labels, dot dash front wheels ($8-12)
9. orange body, white base, blue-green windows, no motor, sunburst hood & no side labels ($15-20)
10. orange body, white base, blue-green windows, no motor, "Jaffa Mobile" hood & no side labels ($375-450)
11. orange body, white base (with tab), blue-green windows, no motor, "34" hood & no side labels ($65-80)(BR)
12. orange body, white base (with tab), blue-green windows, no motor, "3" hood & no side labels ($75-100)(BR)
13. orange body, white base, blue-green windows, no motor, "34" hood & no side labels, 5 crown rear wheels ($8-12)

MB34-C CHEVY PROSTOCKER, issued 1981
NOTE: Versions 12 onwards have a revised headlight grille casting that incorporates an airfoil below the headlights.
1. white body, red interior, clear windows, unpainted base, no tempa, 5 arch front & 5 crown rear wheels, England casting ($15-20)
2. white body, red interior, clear windows, unpainted base, "34" (plain sides) tempa, 5 arch front & 5 crown rear wheels, England casting ($5-8)
3. white body, red interior, clear windows, unpainted base, "34" tempa, 5 arch front & rear wheels, England casting ($5-8)
4. white body, red interior, clear windows, unpainted base, "34" tempa, 5 arch front & 5 crown rear wheels, England casting ($5-8)
5. white body, red interior, clear windows, unpainted base, "34" tempa, 5 crown front & rear wheels, England casting ($5-8)
6. white body, red interior, clear windows, unpainted base, "34" tempa, 5 crown front & 5 arch rear wheels, England casting ($5-8)
7. white body, red interior, clear windows, silver-gray base, "34" tempa, dot dash front & 5 crown rear wheels, England casting ($5-8)
8. white body, red interior, clear windows, silver-gray base, "34" tempa, 5 arch front & 5 crown rear wheels, England casting ($5-8)
9. white body, red interior, clear windows, silver-gray base, "34" tempa, 5 arch front & rear wheels, England casting ($5-8)
10. white body, red interior, clear windows, silver-gray base, "34" tempa, 5 crown front & rear wheels, England casting ($5-8)
11. white body, red interior, clear windows, silver-gray base, "34" tempa, 5 crown front & 5 arch rear wheels, England casting ($5-8)
12. white body, red interior, clear windows, red base, "34" tempa, 5 arch front & 5 crown rear wheels, England casting ($15-20)
13. yellow-orange body, black interior, clear windows, black base, "4" & stripes tempa, 5 arch front & 5 crown rear wheels, Macau casting ($2-4)
14. yellow-orange body, black interior, clear windows, black base, "4" & stripes tempa, 5 spoke front & 5 crown rear wheels, Macau casting ($2-4)
15. yellow-orange body, black interior, clear windows, black base, "4" & stripes tempa, 5 spoke front & rear wheels, Macau casting ($2-4)
16. white body, red interior, amber windows, black base, "Pepsi 14" tempa, 5 spoke front & 5 crown rear wheels, Macau casting ($2-4)
17. white body, red interior, amber windows, black base, "Pepsi 14" tempa, 5 arch front & 5 crown rear wheels, Macau casting ($2-4)
18. white body, black interior, clear windows, black base, "Pepsi 14" tempa, 5 arch front & 5 crown rear wheels, Macau casting ($65-90)(TM)
19. white body, black interior, clear windows, black base, "Pepsi 14" tempa, 5 spoke front & 5 crown rear wheels, Macau casting ($65-90)(TM)
20. white body, red interior, clear windows, black base, "Superstar 217" tempa, 5 arch front & 5 crown rear wheels, Macau casting ($3-5)(TM)
21. black body, red interior, clear windows, black base, "Haley's Comet" tempa, starburst wheels, Macau casting ($8-12)(MP)
22. white & orange body, red interior, clear windows, black base, "21 355CID" tempa, starburst wheels, Macau casting ($4-6)(SF)
23. white & orange body, red interior, clear windows, black base, "21 355CID" tempa, laser wheels, Macau casting ($4-6)(LW)
24. white body, red interior, clear windows, black base, "7 Up" tempa, 5 arch front & 5 crown rear wheels, Macau casting ($3-5)(TM)
25. white body, black interior, clear windows, black base, "7 Up" tempa, 5 arch front & 5 crown rear wheels, Macau casting ($75-100)(TM)
26. white body, red interior, clear windows, black base, "Pepsi 14" tempa, 5 arch front & 5 crown rear wheels, Macau casting ($3-5)
27. white body, red interior, clear windows, black base, "Pepsi 14" tempa, 5 arch front & 5 crown rear wheels, Thailand casting ($3-5)(GS)
28. blue & white body, black interior, clear windows, silver-gray base, "70 Bailey Excavating" tempa, Goodyear slicks, Thailand casting ($4-6)(WR)(TC)

MB34-D FORD RS200, issued 1987
1. white body, black base, clear windows, silver-gray interior, blue with "7" tempa, Macau casting ($1-2)
2. blue body, black base, clear windows, silver-gray interior, white with "2" tempa, China casting ($1-2)
3. mid blue body, black base, clear windows, silver-gray interior, white with "2" tempa, China casting ($1-2)
4. white body, black base, clear windows, silver-gray interior, red with "7" tempa, China casting ($1-2)
5. white body, white base, purple windows, white interior, no tempa, China casting ($10-15)(GF)
6. dark blue body, dark blue base, clear windows, silver-gray interior, no tempa, China casting ($8-12)(GR)(GS)

7. white body, black base, clear windows, silver-gray interior, red & blue with "7" tempa, China casting ($1-2)
8. white body, greenish black base, clear windows, silver-gray interior, red & blue with "7" tempa, China casting ($1-2)

MB34-E SPRINT RACER, issued 1990 (USA)
MB72-J SPRINT RACER, issued 1990 (ROW)
NOTE: All models with black base, chrome airfoils, Goodyear front slicks, racing special rear slicks.
1. red body, white driver, "2 Rollin Thunder" tempa, China casting ($1-2)
2. red body, white driver, "Williams 5M" (blue letters) tempa, China casting ($4-6)(NM)
3. red body, white driver, "Williams 5M" (white letters) tempa, China casting ($75-100)(NM)
4. black body, white driver, "TMC 1" tempa, China casting ($4-6)(NM)
5. white body, red driver, "Maxim 11" tempa, China casting ($4-6)(NM)
6. white body, red driver, "Schnee 8D" tempa, China casting ($4-6)(NM)
7. yellow body, white driver, "Ben Cook & Sons 33x" tempa, China casting ($4-6)(NM)
8. blue body, white driver, "Ben Allen 1a" tempa, China casting ($4-6)(NM)
9. metallic blue body, white driver, "Lucky 7" tempa, China casting ($3-5)(AP)
10. red body, white driver, "7 Joe Gaerte" tempa, China casting ($4-6)(NM)
11. red body, white driver, "4 Gambler" tempa, China casting ($4-6)(NM)
12. yellow body, white driver, "17 F&G Classics Eash" tempa, China casting ($4-6)(NM)
13. yellow body, white driver, "7c Vivarin- D. Blaney" (purple background) tempa, China casting ($4-6)(NM)
14. powder blue body, white driver, "69 Schnee- D. Krietz" tempa, China casting ($4-6)(NM)
15. black body, white driver, "49 Doug Wolfgang" labels, China casting ($4-6)(NM)
16. metallic blue body, white driver, "2 Rollin Thunder" tempa, China casting ($8-12)(GS)
17. black body, white driver, "TMC 1" tempa, China casting ($4-6)(NM)
18. black body, white driver, "JW Hunt 69" tempa, China casting ($4-6)(NM)
19. orange body, white driver, "Williams Payless 5m" tempa, China casting ($4-6)(NM)
20. white body, red driver, "Alvis O Rock 69" tempa, China casting ($4-6)(NM)
21. yellow body, white driver, "Vivarin" (blue background) tempa, China casting ($7-10) (NM)
22. red body, white driver, "Rollin' Thunder 2" (all red "2") tempa, China casting ($1-2)
23. red body, white driver, "Allweld 14" tempa, China casting ($4-6)(NM)
24. red body, white driver, "lW Lew" tempa, China casting ($4-6)(NM)
25. white & dark blue body, white driver, "Valvoline 11" tempa, China casting ($4-6)(NM)
26. white/red & dark blue body, white driver, "Casey Luna 10" tempa, China casting ($4-6) (NM)
27. white body, blue driver, "Weitkerk's Livestock 29" tempa, China casting ($4-6)(NM)
28. gold body, red driver, "Vandermark & Wahlie lm" tempa, China casting ($4-6)(NM)
29. red body, white driver, "Shoff 23s" tempa, China casting ($4-6)(NM)
30. black body, black driver, "Gebhart's 4j" tempa, China casting ($4-6)(NM)
31. purple body, yellow driver, "Hot Shot 34" tempa, Thailand casting ($1-2)(MP)

MB34-G PLYMOUTH PROWLER, issued 1995 (USA)
MB 6-H PLYMOUTH PROWLER, issued 1995 (ROW)
1. plum body, gray base, clear windshield, gray interior, 6 spoke spiral wheels, silver grille, Thailand casting ($1-2)
NOTE: Version 1 appears in multiple shade variations from light to dark
2. yellow body, gray base, smoke windshield, gray interior, chrome disc with rubber tires, "Matchbox 1996 Line Preview" tempa, Thailand casting ($275-350)(US)
3. plum body, gray base, clear windshield, gray interior, 6-spoke spiral wheels, plain grille, Thailand casting ($1-2)
4. plum body, gray base with painted detail, clear windshield, gray/ purple interior, chrome disc with rubber tires, detailed trim tempa, Thailand casting ($100-150)(PC1)
5. plum body, gray base, clear windshield, gray/purple interior, chrome disc with rubber tires, detailed trim tempa, Thailand casting ($7-10)(PC1)
6. red body, black base, smoke windshield, black interior, 6-spoke spiral wheels, "Prowler" tempa, Thailand casting ($1-2)(MP)
7. black body, gray base, smoke windshield, purple interior, 6-spoke spiral wheels, "Prowler" tempa, Thailand casting ($1-2)(MP)
8. white body, blue base, clear windshield, blue interior, 6-spoke spiral wheels, "Tyco Playtime Toy Fair 96" tempa, Thailand casting ($35-50)(US)
9. white body, blue base, clear windshield, blue interior, 6-spoke spiral wheels, "Tyco Playtime Dallas 96" tempa, Thailand casting ($35-50)(US)
10. white body, blue base, clear windshield, blue interior, 6-spoke spiral wheels, "Tyco Playtime Hong Kong 96" tempa, Thailand casting ($35-50)(US)(HK)
11. charcoal body, gray base, clear windshield, gray/purple interior, chrome disc with rubber tires, detailed trim tempa, Thailand casting ($7-10)(SC1)
12. red body, gray base, clear windshield, gray/red interior, chrome disc with rubber tires, detailed trim tempa, Thailand casting ($3-5)(PC)(JC)
13. silver-gray body, gray base, clear windshield, gray/purple interior, chrome disc with rubber tires, detailed trim tempa, Thailand casting ($3-5)(PC4)
14. dark metallic blue body, gray base, clear windshield, black interior, chrome disc with rubber tires, detailed trim tempa, Thailand casting ($7-10)(PC1-ROW)
15. metallic gold body, black base, clear windshield, black interior, 6 spoke spiral wheels, no tempa, Thailand casting ($5-10)(CH)
16. blue body, black base, clear windshield, green interior, 5 spoke concave star wheels, green & white design tempa, Thailand casting ($1-2)(MP)
17. black body, black base, clear windshield, orange interior, chrome disc with rubber tires, "Toy Fair 97- Matchbox" tempa, Thailand casting ($75-100)(US)
18. black body, black base, clear windshield, yellow interior, chrome disc with rubber tires, "Toy Fair- 97- Matchbox" tempa, Thailand casting ($15-25)(UK)
19. iridescent white body, silver-gray base, clear windshield, purple interior, 5 spoke concave star wheels, "Prowler" tempa, Thailand casting ($1-2)(MP)
20. plum body, gray base, smoke windshield, gray interior, 5 spoke concave star wheels, no tempa, Thailand casting ($2-4)
21. black body, gray base, clear windshield, red interior, chrome disc with rubber tires, detailed trim tempa, Thailand casting ($15-20)(GC)
22. plum body, gray base, smoke windshield, gray interior, 6 spoke spiral wheels, "16th Annual Matchbox USA Convention 1997" decals, Thailand base ($10-15)(C2)
23. metallic gold body, black base, clear windshield, black interior, 5 spoke concave star wheels, no tempa, Thailand casting ($15-25)(CH)
24. plum body, gray base, smoke windshield, gray interior, silver 6 spoke spiral wheels, "Mattel Wheels- Driving To Win" tempa, Thailand casting ($250-400)(C2)
25. plum body, gray base, smoke windshield, gray interior, 5 spoke concave star wheels, "Mattel Wheels- Driving To Win" tempa, Thailand casting ($250-400)(C2)
26. metallic purple body, gray base, clear windshield, gray interior, chrome disc with rubber tires, detailed trim tempa, Thailand casting ($3-5)(PC14)
27. metallic red body, gray base, smoke windshield, gray interior, 5 spoke concave star wheels, no tempa, Thailand casting ($2-3)
28. metallic red body, gray base, clear windshield, black interior, chrome disc with rubber tires, detailed trim tempa, Thailand casting ($3-5)(SC4)
29. dark orange body, gray base, clear windshield, gray interior, chrome disc with rubber tires, detailed trim tempa, Thailand casting ($3-5)(PC16)
30. yellow body, gray base, clear windshield, gray & black interior, chrome disc with rubber tires, detailed trim tempa, Thailand casting ($3-5)(SC5)
31. maroon body, gray base, clear windshield, gray interior, chrome disc with rubber tires, detailed trim tempa, Thailand casting ($3-5)(GS)
32. metallic tan body, black base, clear windshield, black interior, 5 spoke concave star wheels, no tempa, Thailand casting ($1-2)(MW18)
33. metallic tan body, black base, clear windshield, black interior, 5 spoke concave star wheels, no tempa, China casting ($1-2)(MW18)
34. blue body, black base, clear windshield, green interior, 5 spoke concave star wheels, green & white flames tempa, China casting ($1-2)(MP)
35. metallic gold body, black base, clear windshield, black interior, 6 spoke spiral wheels, no tempa, China casting ($8-12)(CH)
36. plum body, gray base, clear windshield, white interior, chrome disc with rubber tires, detailed trim tempa, China casting ($3-5)(GS-Chrysler)

MB34-I '33 FORD COUPE, issued 1998
NOTE: All models with clear windows, black interior, chrome engine, black base, China casting unless otherwise noted
1. unpainted body, Goodyear rubber tires, no tempa ($4-6)(FE)
2. black body, Goodyear rubber tires, red stripe tempa ($4-6)(FE)
3. maroon body, Goodyear slicks wheels, black & yellow design tempa ($1-2)(MW34)

MB35-A MERRYWEATHER FIRE ENGINE, issued 1970
1. metallic red body, light gray base, 2 clips on base, 5 spoke wheels ($15-18)
2. bright red body, light gray base, 2 clips on base, 5 spoke wheels ($12-15)
3. bright red body, tan base, 2 clips on base, 5 spoke wheels ($18-25)
4. bright red body, light gray base, 4 rivets on base, 5 spoke wheels ($12-15)
5. bright red body, black base, 4 rivets on base, 5 spoke wheels ($18-25)
6. bright red body, light gray base, 4 rivets on base, 5 arch wheels ($12-15)
7. bright red body, light gray base, 4 rivets on base, dot dash wheels ($5-8)(TP)

MB35-B FANDANGO, issued 1975
1. white body, red base, clear windows, red interior, silver prop, "6" label ($15-20)
2. white body, red base, clear windows, red interior, red prop, "35" label ($8-12)
3. white body, red base, clear windows, red interior, silver prop, "35" label ($8-12)
4. white body, unpainted base, clear windows, red interior, silver prop, "35" label ($8-12)
5. red body, red base, clear windows, ivory interior, silver prop, "35" label ($10-15)
6. red body, unpainted base, clear windows, ivory interior, silver prop, "35" label ($8-12)
7. red body, white base, clear windows, ivory interior, silver prop, "35" label ($8-12)
8. red body, white base, clear windows, ivory interior, red prop, "35" label ($8-12)
9. red body, white base, clear windows, ivory interior, light blue prop, "35" label ($8-12)
10. red body, unpainted base, clear windows, ivory interior, light blue prop, "35" label ($8-12)
11. red body, unpainted base, clear windows, cream interior, mid blue prop, "35" label ($8-12)
12. red body, unpainted base, clear windows, white interior, dark blue prop, "35" label ($8-12)
13. red body, unpainted base, purple windows, cream interior, dark blue prop, "35" label ($8-12)
14. red body, unpainted base, clear windows, white interior, light blue prop, "35" label ($8-12)
15. purple body, charcoal base, clear windows, white interior, light blue prop, "35" label ($500-750)(BR)
16. red body, black base, clear windows, white interior, light blue prop, "35" label ($60-85)(BR)
17. red body, red base, clear windows, red interior, silver prop, "35" label ($50-75)
18. red body, unpainted base, clear windows, white interior, dark blue prop, sunburst label ($15-20)
19. red body, unpainted base, purple windows, ivory interior, dark blue prop, "35" label ($8-12)

MB35-C PONTIAC T-ROOF, issued 1982 (USA)
MB16-C PONTIAC T-ROOF, issued 1983 (ROW)
1. black body, unpainted base, red interior, green eagle & "Turbo" tempa, England casting ($2-4)
2. black body, silver-gray base, red interior, green eagle & "Turbo" tempa, England casting ($2-4)
3. black body, pearly silver base, red interior, white eagle & "Trans Am" tempa, Macau casting ($2-4)
4. black body, pearly silver base, red interior, yellow eagle & "Trans Am" tempa, Macau casting ($2-4)
5. black body, pearly silver base, red interior, orange tiger stripes tempa, Macau casting ($12-15)(UK)(OP)
6. pearly silver body, black base, red interior, red/orange/yellow eagle & red/orange stripes tempa, Macau casting ($2-3)
7. red body, black base, red interior, "3 Rooster Racing Tram" tempa, Macau casting ($8-12)(HK)
NOTE: Available as a Bulgarian casting. Assorted colors available ($15-25)

MB35-D ZOO TRUCK, issued 1982 (ROW)
NOTE: all models with England casting unless otherwise noted.
1. red body, red base, blue cage, orange-yellow lions, 5 arch wheels ($18-25)
2. red body, black base, blue cage, orange-yellow lions, 5 arch wheels ($18-25)
3. red body, black base, blue cage, lemon lions, 5 arch wheels ($18-25)
4. red body, black base, blue cage, orange-yellow lions, 5 spoke wheels ($18-25)
5. red body, charcoal base, blue cage, orange-yellow lions, 5 arch wheels ($18-25)
6. red body, black base, blue cage, orange-yellow lions, maltese cross wheels ($18-25)
7. red body, black base, gray cage, brown lions, 5 arch wheels ($18-25)
8. red body, black base, gray cage, tan lions, 5 arch wheels ($18-25)
9. red body, black base, gray cage, light tan lions, 5 arch wheels ($18-25)
10. red body, black base, gray cage, white lions, 5 arch wheels ($25-40)
11. red body, black base, gray cage, orange-yellow lions, 5 arch wheels ($18-25)
12. orange body, black base, blue cage, orange-yellow lions, maltese cross wheels ($18-25)
13. orange body, black base, gray cage, dark tan lions, 5 arch wheels ($18-25)
14. red body, black base, gray cage, tan lions, 5 arch wheels, Macau casting ($18-25)

MB35-F LAND ROVER, issued 1987 (USA)
MB16-F LAND ROVER, issued 1987 (ROW)
NOTE: All models with clear windows, black interior/ grille and silver dot dash wheels unless otherwise noted.
1. blue body, pearly gray base, white roof, yellow & orange stripes tempa, Macau casting ($2-3)
2. green body, pearly gray base, white roof, yellow & orange stripes tempa, Macau casting ($1-2)(MC)
3. dark blue body, pearly gray base, white roof, "RN Royal Navy" tempa, Macau casting ($2-3)(GS)
4. red body, pearly gray base, white roof, blue & gray stripes with "County" tempa, Macau casting ($1-2)
5. black body, dark gray base, dark gray roof & interior, gray & yellow camouflage tempa, black hubs, Macau casting ($4-5)(CM)
6. white body, pearly gray base, white roof, black & red stripes with "County" tempa, Macau casting ($1-2)(TP)
7. white body, pearly gray base, white roof, black & red stripes with "County" tempa, Thailand casting ($1-2)(TP)
8. green body, pearly gray base, white roof, yellow & orange stripes tempa, Thailand casting ($1-2)(MC)(TP)
9. red body, pearly gray base, white roof, blue & gray stripes with "County" tempa, Thailand casting ($1-2)
10. dark blue body, pearly gray base, white roof, "RN Royal Navy" tempa, Thailand casting ($2-3)(GS)
11. light gray & dark navy body, dark navy base, light gray roof, red stripe tempa, Thailand casting ($3-4)(MC)
12. yellow body, pearly silver base, white roof, large "Park Ranger" tempa, Thailand casting ($1-2)
13. white body, white base, blue roof, "KLM" tempa, Thailand casting ($3-5)(MP)
14. white body, white base, blue roof, "SAS" tempa, Thailand casting ($3-5)(MP)
15. white body, white base, green roof, "Alitalia" tempa, Thailand casting ($3-5)(MP)
16. white body, pearly silver base, white roof, "Bacardi Rum" tempa, Thailand casting ($25-40)(TP)(OP)
17. yellow body, yellow base, white roof, small "Park Ranger" tempa, Thailand casting ($1-2)
18. red body, black base, white roof, "Red Arrows/ Royal Air Force"

tempa, Thailand casting ($3-5)(MC)
19. white body, white base, white roof, pink windows, neon red interior, no tempa, Thailand casting ($10-15)(GF)
20. white body, pearly silver base, white roof, "Rescue Police" & checkers tempa, Thailand casting ($1-2)(EM)
21. white body, red base, white roof, red interior, "Circus Circus" tempa, Thailand casting ($2-4)(MC)
22. white body, pearly silver base, green roof, "Garden Festival Wales" tempa, Thailand casting ($6-8)(WL)(GS)
23. yellow body, pearly silver base, white roof, small "Park Ranger" tempa, Thailand casting ($1-2)
24. orange body, pearly silver base, black roof, "Safari Park" & black stripes tempa, Thailand casting ($1-2)(MP)
25. white body, pearly silver base, white roof, "55 Rijkspolitie" tempa, Thailand casting ($3-5)(CY)(DU)
26. white body, dark blue base, white roof, pink interior, smoke windows, neon pink/ neon yellow & blue side splash tempa, Thailand casting ($2-5)
27. red body, black base, white roof, yellow interior, clear windows, "Red Valley Camp" tempa, Thailand casting ($1-2)(MP)
28. lemon body, black base, black roof, black interior, clear windows, "Mountain Trails" tempa, Thailand casting ($1-2)(MP)
29. dark green body, pearly silver base, white roof, black interior, clear windows, small "Land Rover" tempa, Thailand casting ($1-2)
30. white body, black base, black roof, red interior, clear windows, black design & "Land Rover" tempa, China casting ($1-2)(MW53-ROW)
31. lemon body, black base, black roof, black interior, clear windows, "Mountain Trails" tempa, China casting ($1-2)(MP)
32. red body, black base, white roof, yellow interior, clear windows, "Red Valley Camp" tempa, China casting ($1-2)(MP)

MB35-H PONTIAC GRAND PRIX, issued 1992 (USA)
MB22-I PONTIAC GRAND PRIX, issued 1993 (ROW)
NOTE: All models with clear windows & black base unless otherwise noted.
1. bright yellow body, black interior, Goodyear slicks, "Pennzoil 30" tempa, China casting ($3-5)(WR)
2. bright yellow body, black interior, gray disc with rubber tires, "Pennzoil 30" tempa, China casting ($4-6)(WR)(TC)
3. blue body, black interior, Goodyear slicks, "STP 43" tempa, China casting ($3-5)(WR)
4. blue body, black interior, blue disc with rubber tires, "STP 43" tempa, China casting ($4-6)(WR)(TC)
5. blue body, black interior, black disc with rubber tires, "Rumple 70/ Son's" tempa, China casting ($4-6)(WR)(TC)
6. yellow body, gray interior, Goodyear slicks, "White House Apple Juice 4" tempa, China casting ($4-6)(WR)(OP)
7. yellow body, gray interior, 9 spoke Goodyear slicks, "White House Apple Juice 4" tempa, China casting ($4-6)(WR)(OP)
8. black body, black interior, Goodyear slicks, "Pontiac Excitement 2" tempa, China casting ($3-5)(WR)
9. black body, black interior, black disc with rubber tires, "Pontiac Excitement 2" tempa, China casting ($4-6)(WR)(TC)
10. black & green body, black interior, Goodyear slicks, "Mello Yello 42" tempa, China casting ($3-4)(WR)
11. black & green body, black interior, black disc with rubber tires, "Mello Yello 42" tempa, China casting ($4-6)(WR)(TC)
12. blue & white body, gray interior, Goodyear slicks, "Evinrude 89" tempa, China casting ($4-6)(WR)
13. matt yellow body, black interior, Goodyear slicks, "Country Time 68" tempa, China casting ($3-5)(WR)
14. white & yellow body, red interior, Goodyear slicks, "Medford Speed Shop/ Valtrol 48" tempa, China casting ($4-6)(WR)
NOTE: All below with Goodyear slicks unless noted.
15. white & red body, blue interior, "Nastrak 1" tempa, China casting ($3-5)(GS)(WR)
16. red body, gray interior, "Nastrak 2" tempa, China casting ($3-5)(GS)(WR)
17. red & yellow body, gray interior, "Nastrak 3" tempa, China casting ($3-5)(GS)(WR)
18. red-brown body, gray interior, "Nastrak 4" tempa, China casting ($3-5)(GS)(WR)
19. red & yellow body, red interior, "Nastrak 5" tempa, China casting ($3-5)(GS)(WR)
20. blue & white body, blue interior, "Nastrak 6" tempa, China casting ($3-5)(GS)(WR)
21. white & black body, black interior, "White Rose Collectibles 93" tempa, China casting ($25-30)(WR)
22. fluorescent yellow body, black interior, gold 6-spoke spiral wheels, "Pro Auto 10" tempa, Thailand casting ($1-2)
23. black body, blue interior, silver 6-spoke spiral wheels, "Outlaw Auto 7" tempa, Thailand casting ($2-3)
24. orange-yellow body, black interior, Goodyear slicks wheels, "Pennzoil 30" tempa, China casting ($12-18)(WR)

MB35-I PONTIAC STOCK CAR, issued 1993 (USA)
1. yellow body, black interior, Goodyear slicks, "Pro Auto 10" tempa, Thailand casting ($1-2)(MP)
2. fluorescent yellow body, black interior, Goodyear slicks, "Seaside 15" tempa, Thailand casting ($3-5)
3. black body, silver-gray interior, Goodyear slicks, "Dirt Devil" (white print), Thailand casting ($3-5)(WR)
4. black body, silver-gray interior, Goodyear slicks, "Dirt Devil" (orange print), Thailand casting ($3-5)(WR)(TC)
5. black body, silver-gray interior, black disc with rubber tires, "Dirt Devil" (white print) tempa, Thailand casting ($3-5)(WR)(TC)
6. black body, silver-gray interior, Goodyear slicks, "Duron 66" tempa, Thailand casting ($7-10)(WR)
7. orange body, red interior, Goodyear slicks, "Burn Foundation/ Motorsports 94" tempa, Thailand casting ($15-18)(US)
8. purple body, translucent red interior, Goodyear slicks, "JP Graphics" tempa, Thailand casting ($1-2)(MP)

MB35-J AMG MERCEDES C CLASS, issued 1996 (USA)
MB75-F AMG MERCEDES C CLASS, issued 1996 (ROW)
1. metallic blue body, gray interior, clear windows, silver 6-spoke spiral wheels, "25 Camsport" tempa, China casting ($1-2)
2. silver-gray body, gray interior, clear windows, 5 spoke concave star wheels, "25 Camsport" tempa, China casting ($1-2)(MP)
3. metallic gold body, black interior, clear windows, 6 spoke spiral wheels, no tempa, China casting ($5-10)(CH)
4. metallic blue body, gray interior, clear windows, 5 spoke concave star wheels, "25 Camsport" tempa, China casting ($3-5)
5. lemon body, red interior, clear windows, 5 spoke concave star wheels, "25 Camsport" tempa, China casting ($1-2)
6. silver-gray & florescent orange body, black/gray/white interior, clear windows, chrome disc with rubber tires, "Team Matchbox 1" tempa, China casting ($3-5)(PC15)

MB36-A OPEL DIPLOMAT, issued 1970
1. green-gold body, black base, plain grille ($25-40)
2. dark gold body, black base, plain grille ($25-40)
3. dark gold body, black base, silver grille ($25-40)
4. light gold body, black base, silver grille ($25-40)

MB36-B HOT ROD DRAGUAR, issued 1970
1. red body, unpainted base, orange interior, clear windows, with label ($15-20)
2. red body, unpainted base, orange interior, clear windows, no label ($15-20)
3. red body, unpainted base, ivory interior, clear windows, with label ($15-20)
4. red body, unpainted base, light yellow interior, clear windows, with label ($15-20)
5. red body, unpainted base, light yellow interior, clear windows, no label ($15-20)
6. pink body, unpainted base, light yellow interior, clear windows, with label ($15-20)
7. pink body, unpainted base, light yellow interior, amber windows, with label ($15-20)
8. pink body, unpainted base, white interior, clear windows, with label ($15-20)
9. pink body, unpainted base, light yellow interior, yellow windows, with label ($15-20)
10. pink body, unpainted base, dark yellow interior, amber windows, with label ($15-20)
11. pink body, unpainted base, dark yellow interior, yellow windows, with label ($15-20)
12. pink body, unpainted base, white interior, amber windows, with label ($15-20)
13. pink body, unpainted base, light yellow interior, amber windows, with label ($15-20)
14. pink body, unpainted base, light yellow interior, clear windows, no label ($15-20)

MB36-C FORMULA 5000, issued 1975
NOTE: All models with unpainted base & 5 spoke front wheels.
1. orange body, blue driver, "5000" hood & spoiler label, 5 arch rear wheels ($8-12)
2. orange body, blue driver, "5000" hood & spoiler label, maltese cross rear wheels ($8-12)
3. orange body, yellow-orange driver, "5000" hood & spoiler label, maltese cross rear wheels ($8-12)
4. red body, yellow-orange driver, "5000" hood & spoiler label, maltese cross rear wheels ($7-10)
5. red body, yellow-orange driver, "Texaco" hood label, "Marlboro" spoiler label, maltese cross rear wheels ($7-10)
6. red body, yellow-orange driver, "Texaco" hood label, no spoiler label , maltese cross rear wheels ($7-10)
7. red body, yellow-orange driver, "Texaco" hood label, "Champion" spoiler label, maltese cross rear wheels ($7-10)
8. red body, lemon driver, "Texaco" hood label, "Champion" spoiler label, maltese cross rear wheels ($7-10)
9. red body, yellow-orange driver, "Texaco" hood label, "Champion" spoiler label, maltese cross rear wheels, tab on base ($45-60)(BR)
10. white body, yellow-orange driver, "Texaco" hood label, "Champion" spoiler label, maltese cross rear wheels, tab on base ($300-450)(BR)
11. red body, yellow-orange driver, "Texaco" hood label, "Champion" spoiler label, dot dash rear wheels ($7-10)

MB36-D REFUSE TRUCK, issued 1980
All models with red windows & 5 arch wheels unless otherwise noted. Version 2 with red or orange windows.
1. red body, orange-yellow dump & hatch, silver-gray base, no label, red trigger, without "Colectomatic" cast on front of dump, England casting ($18-25)
2. red body, orange-yellow dump & hatch, silver-gray base, no label, red trigger, England casting ($2-4)
3. red body, orange-yellow dump & hatch, unpainted base, no label, red trigger, England casting ($2-4)
4. magenta body, orange-yellow dump & hatch, silver-gray base, no label, red trigger, England casting ($2-4)
5. blue body, yellow dump & hatch, silver-gray base, "Metro" label, red trigger, England casting ($3-5)
6. blue body, yellow dump & hatch, silver-gray base, "Metro" label, black trigger, England casting ($3-5)
7. blue body, orange dump & hatch, silver-gray base, "Metro" label, red trigger , England casting ($2-4)
8. blue body, orange dump & hatch, silver-gray base, "Metro" label, black trigger, England casting ($2-4)
9. blue body, orange dump, yellow hatch, silver-gray base, no label, red trigger, England casting ($5-7)
10. blue body, dull orange dump, yellow hatch, silver-gray base, no label, red trigger, England casting ($5-7)
11. blue body, orange dump & hatch, pearly silver base, "Metro" label, red trigger, Macau casting ($2-4)
12. white body, blue dump & hatch, light metallic gray base, "Metro" label, blue trigger, Macau casting ($2-3)
13. white body, blue dump & hatch, pearly silver base, Japanese lettered tempa, blue trigger, Macau casting ($8-12)(JP)
14. white body, blue dump & hatch, light metallic gray base, no label, blue trigger, Macau casting ($2-3)
15. white body, blue dump & hatch, pearly silver base, "Metro" label, red trigger, purple windows, China casting ($2-3)
16. green body, yellow dump & hatch, pearly gray base, "State City" tempa, red trigger, China casting ($1-2)
17. green body, lemon dump & hatch, pearly gray base, "State City" tempa, red trigger, China casting ($1-2)
18. orange body, gray dump & hatch, black base, "Refuse Disposal" tempa, red trigger, China casting ($1-2)
19. green body, light yellow dump & hatch, black base, "Refuse Disposal" tempa, red trigger, China casting ($1-2)
20. red body, light yellow dump & hatch, black base, "Refuse Disposal" tempa, red trigger, China casting ($8-12)(GS)
21. orange body, white dump & hatch, black base, orange trigger, "Refuse Disposal" tempa, China casting ($1-2)
22. pale orange body, white dump & hatch, black base, orange trigger, "Refusal Disposal" without dump tempa, China casting ($1-2)
23. red body, silver-gray dump & hatch, black base, red trigger, smoke windows, caricature tempa, China casting ($1-2)
24. white body, blue dump & hatch, black base, red trigger, red arrows & caricature tempa, China casting ($3-5)(MP)
25. metallic gold body, white dump & hatch, black base, black trigger, no tempa, China casting ($5-10)(CH)
26. orange-yellow body, dark blue dump & hatch, black base, orange-yellow trigger, "Metro DPW Unit 17" tempa ($1-2)
27. white body, white dump & hatch, black base, white trigger, no tempa, China casting ($25-40)(ASAP blank)
28. white body, white dump & hatch, black base, white trigger, "Bulldog Castor Co." tempa, China casting ($75+)(ASAP)
29. white body, white dump & hatch, black base, white trigger, maroon design tempa, China casting ($75+)(ASAP)
30. white body, white dump & hatch, black base, white trigger, "Waste Industries" tempa, China casting ($75+)(ASAP)
31. orange body, orange dump & hatch, black base, black trigger, "Metro DPW Unit 17" tempa, China casting ($1-2)(MW7)
32. dark green body, clear windows, silver-gray dump & hatch, black base, red trigger, "Recycle" tempa, China casting ($1-2)(MP)
33. dark green body, clear windows, silver-gray dump & hatch, black base, black trigger, "Recycle" tempa, China casting ($1-2)(MP)
34. white body, white dump & hatch, black base, black trigger, "Metro DPW" tempa, China casting ($2-4)(MP)

MB36-E 1957 CHEVY BEL AIR CONVERTIBLE, issued 1998
NOTE: All models with clear windshield, chrome base & China casting unless otherwise noted.
1. black body, white interior, chrome disc with rubber tires, "Toy Fair 98-Matchbox" ($85-110)(US)
2. red body, red & white interior, chrome disc with rubber tires, silver flash & detailed trim tempa ($4-6)(FE)
3. unpainted body, white interior, chrome disc with rubber tires, no tempa ($4-6)(FE)
4. turquoise body, white interior, 5 spoke concave star wheels, silver flash with purple & white design tempa ($1-2)(MW36)
5. turquoise body, white interior, chrome disc with rubber tires, silver flash with purple & white design tempa ($100+)
NOTE: The above model was found packaged as a First Edition but is probably done so as a manufacturing error.

MB37-A CATTLE TRUCK, issued 1970
1. light yellow body, gray box ($25-40)
2. orange-yellow body, gray box ($25-40)
3. orange body, gray box ($25-40)
4. orange body, silver-gray box ($25-40)

MB37-B SOOPA COOPA, issued 1972
1. light blue body, unpainted base, no labels, maltese cross wheels ($15-20)
2. mid blue body, unpainted base, no labels, maltese cross wheels ($15-20)
3. mid blue body, silver-gray base, no labels, maltese cross wheels ($15-20)
4. dark blue body, unpainted base, no labels, maltese cross wheels ($15-20)
5. dark blue body, unpainted base, no labels, 5 spoke wheels ($15-20)
6. pink body, unpainted base, flower label, maltese cross wheels ($18-25)
7. pink body, red base, flower label, maltese cross wheels ($50-75)
8. orange body, unpainted base, "Jaffa Mobile" labels, maltese cross wheels ($100-150)(OP)

MB37-C SKIP TRUCK, issued 1976
1. red body, yellow skip, black base, amber windows, chrome interior ($5-7)
2. red body, yellow skip, black base, amber windows, gray interior ($4-6)
3. red body, yellow skip, black base, clear windows, gray interior ($4-6)
4. red body, yellow skip, unpainted base, clear windows, gray interior

($4-6)
5. red body, yellow skip, black base, light blue windows, gray interior ($4-6)
6. red body, yellow skip, black base, smoke windows, gray interior ($4-6)
7. red body, yellow skip, brown base, clear windows, gray interior ($7-10)
8. red body, yellow skip, brown base, smoke windows, gray interior ($7-10)
9. red body, yellow skip, charcoal base, clear windows, gray interior ($4-6)
10. red body, blue skip, black base, clear windows, gray interior ($90-125)
11. red body, yellow skip, black base, clear windows, orange interior ($4-6)
12. orange-red body, yellow skip, black base, clear windows, gray interior ($4-6)
13. orange-red body, yellow skip, black base, smoke windows, gray interior ($4-6)
14. orange body, red skip, black base, clear windows, gray interior ($85-110)(GR)
15. orange body, yellow skip, black base, clear windows, gray interior ($85-110)(GR)
16. blue body, yellow skip, charcoal base, clear windows, gray interior ($3-5)
17. blue body, yellow skip, silver-gray base, clear windows, gray interior ($3-5)
18. blue body, yellow skip, black base, clear windows, gray interior ($3-5)
19. blue body, yellow skip, black base, clear windows, black interior ($5-8)
20. dark blue body, yellow skip, charcoal base, clear windows, gray interior ($200-300)(BR)

MB37-D SUNBURNER, issued 1981 (USA)
1. black body, black base, red interior, yellow & red flames tempa, England casting ($3-5)
2. black body, black base, red interior, green & red flames tempa, England casting ($3-5)
3. black body, black base, red interior, yellow & red flames tempa, Macau casting ($3-5)
4. black body, black base, red interior, yellow & red flames tempa, Hong Kong casting ($3-5)

MB37-E MATRA RANCHO, issued 1982 (ROW)
1. turquoise body & base, no tempa, blue tailgate, 5 arch silver wheels, England casting ($8-12)
2. light blue body & base, no tempa, blue tailgate, 5 arch silver wheels, England casting ($8-12)
3. light blue body & base, no tempa, blue tailgate, dot dash wheels, England casting ($8-12)
4. yellow body & base, red stripe tempa, yellow tailgate, 5 arch silver wheels, England casting ($7-10)
5. navy blue body, white base, "Surf Rescue" tempa, blue tailgate, 5 arch silver wheels, England casting ($4-6)(TP)
6. dark blue body, black base, no tempa, blue tailgate, 5 arch silver wheels, England casting ($7-10)
7. dark blue body, black base, no tempa, blue tailgate, 5 arch gold wheels, England casting ($15-18)
8. dark blue body, yellow base, no tempa, yellow tailgate, 5 arch gold wheels, England casting ($18-25)(TP)
9. dark blue body, yellow base, no tempa, yellow tailgate, 5 arch silver wheels, England casting ($15-18)(TP)
10. dark blue body & base, no tempa, blue tailgate, 5 arch gold wheels, England casting ($15-18)
11. yellow body & base, no tempa, yellow tailgate, 5 arch silver wheels, England casting ($6-8)
12. yellow body & base, red stripe tempa, yellow tailgate, 5 arch gold wheels, England casting ($15-18)
13. navy blue body, white base, "Surf Rescue" tempa, blue tailgate, 5 arch silver wheels, England casting ($3-5)(TP)
14. navy blue body, white base, "Surf Rescue" tempa, black tailgate, 5 arch silver wheels, England casting ($4-6)
15. navy blue body, yellow base, "Surf Rescue" tempa, black tailgate, 5 arch silver wheels, England casting ($12-15)(TP)
16. black body, white base, "Surf Rescue" tempa, black tailgate, 5 arch silver wheels, Macau casting ($3-5)(TP)
17. orange body, black base, "Surf 2" tempa, orange tailgate, 5 arch silver wheels, Macau casting ($2-4)(TP)
18. florescent yellow body, yellow base, "Marine Rescue" tempa, florescent yellow tailgate, 5 arch silver wheels, China casting ($1-2)(EM)
19. white body, white base, white interior & tailgate, amber windows, no tempa, 5 arch silver wheels, China casting ($10-15)(GF)
20. blue body, yellow base, "Marine Rescue" (gold) tempa, blue tailgate, clear windows, 5 arch silver wheels, China casting ($3-5)(MP)
NOTE: Available as Bulgarian casting. Assorted colors available ($15-25)

MB37-F JEEP 4 X 4, issued 1984 (USA)
MB25-I JEEP 4 X 4, issued 1994 (ROW)
1. black body, pearly silver metal base, black interior, red/orange/yellow tempa, Macau casting ($2-3)
2. black body, pearly silver metal base, black interior, red/orange/yellow tempa, China casting ($2-3)
3. white body, pearly silver metal base, black interior, orange/red/blue tempa, Macau casting ($1-2)
4. white body, pearly silver metal base, black interior, orange/red/blue tempa, China casting ($1-2)
5. white body, gray plastic base, black interior, orange/red/blue tempa, Macau casting ($1-2)
6. white body, gray plastic base, black interior, orange/red/blue tempa, Thailand casting ($1-2)
7. white body, gray plastic base, black interior, orange/red/blue tempa, China casting ($1-2)
8. dark florescent orange body, gray plastic base, black interior, "Cool Mud" with hood tempa, China casting ($1-2)
9. dark florescent orange body, gray plastic base, black interior, "Cool Mud" without hood tempa, China casting ($1-2)
10. metallic red body, gray plastic base, black interior, none tempa, China casting ($1-2)(MP)
11. pink body, gray plastic base, black interior, "Cool Mud" without hood tempa, China casting ($2-4)
12. metallic gold body, black plastic base, black interior, no tempa, China casting ($10-15)(CH)
13. beige body, dark gray plastic base, black interior, green stripes tempa, China casting ($1-2)(AS)(AP)
14. metallic blue body, dark gray plastic base, black interior, orange flames tempa, China casting ($1-2)(MP)
15. silver-gray body, black plastic base, black interior, purple & pink flames tempa, China casting ($1-2)(AS)
16. powder blue body, dark gray plastic base, black interior, "Cool Mud" & black design tempa, China casting ($2-4)
17. yellow body, dark gray plastic base, black interior, red flames tempa, China casting ($1-2)(MP)
18. bright blue body, dark gray plastic base, black interior, white splash tempa, China casting ($1-2)(MW52)

MB37-I 1970 BOSS MUSTANG, issued 1998
1. lemon body, white interior, chrome disc with rubber tires, black stripe tempa, lemon base, China casting ($4-6)(FE)
2. unpainted body, white interior, chrome disc with rubber tires, no tempa, chrome base, China casting ($4-6)(FE)
3. purple body, yellow interior, 5 spoke concave star wheels, "Boss" with stripes tempa, chrome base, China casting ($1-2)(MW37)
4. purple body, yellow interior, 5 spoke concave star wheels, "Boss" with stripes tempa, translucent white base, China casting ($50-75)(MW37)
5. black body, white interior, 5 spoke concave star wheels, silver design tempa, chrome base, China casting ($2-4)(RT)
6. black body, white interior, 5 spoke concave star wheels, silver design tempa, translucent white base, China casting ($50-75)

MB38-A HONDA MOTORCYCLE & TRAILER, issued 1970
1. blue cycle, light yellow trailer, "Honda" labels, 5 spoke wheels ($15-18)
2. purple cycle, light yellow trailer, "Honda" labels, 5 spoke wheels ($20-30)
3. pink cycle, light yellow trailer, "Honda" labels, 5 spoke wheels ($20-30)
4. blue-green cycle, orange trailer, no labels, 5 spoke center cut wheels ($5-7)(TP)
5. blue-green cycle, orange trailer, "Honda" labels, 5 spoke center cut wheels ($5-7)(TP)
6. blue-green cycle, dark yellow trailer, no labels, 5 spoke center cut wheels ($5-7)(TP)
7. blue-green cycle, dark yellow trailer, "Honda" labels, 5 spoke center cut wheels ($5-7)(TP)

MB38-B STINGEROO, issued 1973
1. purple body, chrome handlebars ($350-400)
2. purple body, purple handlebars ($15-18)
3. purple body, blue-gray handlebars ($18-25)

MB38-C JEEP, issued 1976
1. olive body, black base, star label, no gun or roof cast, black hubs ($18-25)(TP)
2. olive drab body, black base, "21 * 11" label, no gun or roof cast, black hubs ($65-80)(TP)
3. olive body, black base, "21 * 11" label, no gun or roof cast, black hubs ($8-12)(TP)
4. olive body, black base, star label gun cast, black hubs ($8-12)
5. olive body, black base, "21 * 11" label, gun cast, silver hubs ($8-12)
6. olive body, black base, "21 * 11" label, gun cast, black hubs ($5-7)
7. green body, black base, no label, gun cast, silver hubs ($150-225)(BR)
8. green body, charcoal base, "21 * 11" label, gun cast, silver hubs ($150-225)(BR)
9. yellow body, black base, "Gliding Club" label, no gun or roof cast, silver hubs ($8-12)(TP)
10. yellow body, black base, "Gliding Club" label, no gun or roof cast, black hubs ($8-12)(TP)
11. red body, black base, "Gliding Club" label, no gun or roof cast, silver hubs ($350-450)(TP)
12. blue body, white base, "U.S. Mail" tempa, white roof, silver hubs ($6-8)
13. powder blue body, white base, "U.S. Mail" tempa, white roof, silver hubs ($8-12)
NOTE: All models have "No. 38 Jeep" cast on base.

MB38-D FORD CAMPER, issued 1980
1. orange-red body, green cab windows, beige camper, amber camper windows, No. 35 cast on base ($50-75)
2. orange-red body, green cab windows, beige camper, no camper windows ($4-6)
3. orange-red body, blue-green windows, beige camper, no camper windows ($4-6)
4. red body, blue-green cab windows, beige camper, no camper windows ($4-6)
5. red body, green cab windows, beige camper, no camper windows ($4-6)

MB38-E MODEL A FORD VAN, issued 1982
NOTE: Following models with clear windows, black sub base,, chrome grille & 5 crown front & dot dash rear wheels unless otherwise noted.
1. blue body, black chassis, white roof, amber windows, "Champion" labels, England casting ($5-7)
2. blue body, black chassis, white roof, "Champion" labels, England casting ($5-7)
NOTE: All models below with Macau base unless otherwise noted.
3. blue body, black chassis, white roof, "Champion" labels ($4-6)
4. blue body, black chassis, white roof, "Kellogg's" labels ($7-10)(UK)(OP)
5. blue body, black chassis, white roof, "Matchbox On The Move in 84" labels ($20-40)(US)
6. blue body, black chassis, white roof, "Matchbox On The Move in 84" labels with "Toy Fair 84" roof label ($20-40)(US)
7. white body, blue chassis, red roof, "Pepsi" with "Come Alive" tempa ($7-10)
8. white body, blue chassis, red roof, "Pepsi" without "Come Alive" tempa ($4-6)
9. white body, blue chassis, red roof, "Matchbox USA" labels ($20-35)(US)
10. white body, blue chassis, red roof, "Ben Franklin" labels ($500-700)(US)
11. red body, black chassis, black roof, "Arnotts Biscuits" tempa ($7-10)(AU)
12. gray body, red chassis, red roof, "Tittensor First School" tempa ($5-8)(UK)
13. beige body, brown chassis, brown roof, "Larklane Motor Museum" tempa ($5-8)(UK)
14. dark blue body, black chassis, red roof, "Bass Museum" tempa ($5-8)(UK)
15. yellow body, green chassis, green roof, "Toy Collectors Pocket Guide" tempa ($6-8)(UK)
16. white body, black chassis, black roof, "The Australian" tempa ($6-8)(AU)
17. olive body, black chassis, black roof, "BBC 1925" tempa ($6-8)(UK)
18. dark blue body, black chassis, black roof, "Matchbox Speedshop" with yellow pinstriping tempa, 5 arch front & chromed racing special rear wheels ($75-100)
19. dark blue body, black chassis, black roof, "Matchbox Speedshop" with yellow pinstriping tempa, 5 arch front & unchromed racing special rear wheels ($1-2)
20. dark blue body, black chassis, black roof, "Matchbox Speedshop" with orange pinstriping tempa, 5 arch front & unchromed racing special rear wheels ($1-2)
21. cream body, green chassis, green roof, "H.H. Brain" tempa ($18-25)(UK)(OP)
22. powder blue body, dark blue chassis, red roof, "Isle of Man TT86" tempa ($5-7)(UK)
23. dark green body, black chassis, dark green roof, "Weetabix/ Sanitarium Food" tempa ($7-10)(AU)(OP)
24. dark blue body, red chassis, white roof, "Smiths Potato Crisps" tempa ($7-10)(AU)(OP)
25. black body, red chassis, red roof, "Isle of Man TT87" tempa ($5-7)(UK)
26. dark yellow body, blue chassis, blue roof, "Junior Matchbox Club" tempa ($6-8)(CN)
27. black body, black chassis, black roof, "2nd M.I.C.A. Convention" decals ($375-450)(UK)
28. white body, black chassis, black roof, "Chesty Bonds" tempa ($5-7)(AU)
29. red body, black chassis, black roof, "I.O.M. Post Office" tempa ($6-8)(UK)
30. blue body, black chassis, black roof, "Silvo" tempa ($7-10)(UK)
31. red body, black chassis, black roof, "W.H. Smith & Sons" tempa ($18-25)(UK)(OP)
32. red body, black chassis, black roof, "Dewhurst Master Butcher" tempa ($8-12)(UK)
33. dark olive body, red chassis, red roof, "John West Salmon" tempa ($8-12)(AU)(OP)
34. light blue body, black chassis, white roof, "Kellogg's Rice Krispies" labels ($8-12)(UK)(OP)
35. dark blue body, black chassis, red roof, "Matchbox- This Van Delivers" with phone # on doors tempa ($12-18)(HK)
36. dark blue body, black chassis, red roof, "Matchbox- This Van Delivers" without phone # on doors ($60-75)(UK)
37. red body, black chassis, black roof, gold grille, "Royal Mail" tempa ($6-8)(UK)(MP)
38. orange body, black chassis, black roof, "North America M.I.C.A. Convention 1988" tempa ($6-8)(US)
39. yellow body, black chassis, red roof, "Isle of Man TT88" tempa ($5-7)(UK)
40. yellow body, yellow chassis, red roof, "3rd M.I.C.A. Convention" tempa ($8-12)(UK)
41. yellow body, dark blue chassis, white roof, "James Neale & Sons" tempa ($8-12)(UK)
42. red body, black chassis, black roof, "I.O.M. Post Office" with phone # on rear doors tempa ($6-8)(UK)
43. red body, black chassis, black roof, "Manx Cattery" labels ($12-15)(UK)
44. red body, black chassis, black roof, "Mervyn Wynne" labels ($12-15)(UK)
45. dark orange body, black chassis, black roof, "P.M.G." tempa ($7-10)(AU)
46. red body, black chassis, black roof, "Alex Munro Master Butcher" tempa ($8-12)(UK)
47. red body, black chassis, black roof, "Rayner's Crusha" tempa ($8-12)(UK)(OP)
48. red body, greenish black chassis, black roof, "Rayner's Crusha" tempa ($8-12)(UK)(OP)
49. powder blue body, dark gray chassis, dark gray roof, "Chester Heraldry Centre" tempa ($6-8)(UK)
50. yellow body, black chassis, red roof, "Barratt's Sherbet" tempa ($10-15)(UK)(OP)
51. blue body, black chassis, blue roof, "Guernsey Post" tempa ($5-7)(UK)
52. dark green body, black chassis, black roof, "Historical Collection/ Powerhouse" tempa ($6-8)(AU)
53. dark green body, greenish black chassis, black roof, "Historical

Collection/ Powerhouse" tempa ($6-8)(AU)
54. brown body, black chassis, black roof, "Cobb of Knightsbridge" tempa ($7-10)(UK)
55. red body, black chassis, black roof, "Big Sister" tempa ($6-8)(AU)(OP)
56. powder blue body & roof, dark gray chassis, "Chester Toy Museum" labels ($6-8)(UK)
57. green body, black chassis, yellow roof, "Rowntree's Table Jelly" tempa ($8-12)(UK)(OP)
58. blue body, silver-gray chassis, gray roof, "Nat West Action Bank" tempa ($6-8)(UK)
59. black body, light maroon chassis, red roof, "Uniroyal Royal Care" tempa ($18-25)(CN)
60. yellow body, black chassis, black roof, "Matchbox Series Model A Ford Van" tempa ($2-3)
61. yellow body, black chassis, black roof, 5 arch front wheels, "Matchbox Series Model A Ford Van" tempa ($2-3)
62. light yellow body, black chassis, black roof, "W.H. Smith & Sons" tempa ($12-15)(UK)
63. dark green body, dark green chassis & roof, "Green's Sponge Mixture" tempa ($8-12)(UK)(OP)
64. olive green body, red-brown chassis & roof, black grille & hubs, "Aldershot- 4th M.I.C.A. Convention" tempa ($8-10)(UK)
65. black body, orange chassis, orange roof, "2nd M.I.C.A. NA Convention 1989" tempa ($6-8)(US)
66. yellow body, blue chassis, blue roof, "Welcome Ye To Chester" labels ($15-20)(UK)(C2)
67. dark blue body, black chassis, black roof, "Cheeses of England & Wales" tempa ($10-15)(UK)(OP)
68. cream body, red chassis, red roof, "Isle of Man TT89" tempa ($5-7)(UK)
69. cream body, black chassis, black roof, "Jordan's" tempa ($10-15)(UK)(OP)
70. dark blue body, black chassis, black roof, "Ribena" tempa ($8-12)(UK)
71. yellow body, red chassis, red roof, "Barratt's Sherbet" tempa ($8-12)(UK)
72. yellow body, black chassis, black roof, "Barratt's Sherbet" tempa ($8-12)(UK)
73. light blue body, blue chassis, blue roof, "Junior Matchbox Club- The Gang" tempa ($6-8)(CN)
74. dark blue body, cream chassis & roof, "Lightwater Theme Park Valley" tempa ($6-8)(UK)
75. red body, blue chassis, blue roof, "Tandy Electronics" tempa ($12-15)(AU)
76. light gray body, dark gray chassis, dark gray roof, "Moorland Centre" tempa ($6-8)(UK)
77. black body, orange chassis, orange roof, "Baltimore Orioles 1989" tempa ($6-8)(WR)
78. yellow body, dark green chassis & roof, "York Fair 1989" tempa ($6-8)(WR)
79. silver body, silver chassis, black roof, "Matchbox Collectors Club 1989" labels ($125-150)(C2)
80. white body, red chassis, blue roof, "Ten Years Lion" tempa ($7-10)(UK)
81. white body, black chassis, black roof, "Jacky Maeder" tempa ($8-12)(SW)
82. cream body, brown chassis, brown roof, "Johnson's Seeds" tempa ($8-12)(UK)(OP)
83. red body, red chassis, red roof, "Asda Baked Beans" tempa ($7-10)(UK)(OP)
84. dark blue body, dark blue chassis & roof, "Matchbox 40th Anniversary 1990" ($7-10)(US)
85. white body, blue chassis, white roof, "New York Yankees 1990" tempa ($3-5)(WR)
86. white body, blue chassis, white roof, "Los Angeles Dodgers 1990" tempa ($3-5)(WR)
87. white body, blue chassis, white roof, "Texas Rangers 1990" tempa ($3-5)(WR)
88. white body, blue chassis, white roof, "Chicago White Sox 1990" tempa ($3-5)(WR)
89. white body, blue chassis, white roof, "Houston Astros 1990" tempa ($3-5)(WR)
90. white body, blue chassis, white roof, "Atlanta Braves 1990" tempa ($3-5)(WR)
91. white body, blue chassis, white roof, "Cleveland Indians 1990" tempa ($3-5)(WR)
92. white body, blue chassis, white roof, "New York Mets 1990" tempa ($3-5)(WR)
93. white body, blue chassis, white roof, "Minnesota Twins 1990" tempa ($3-5)(WR)
94. white body, blue chassis, white roof, "Toronto Blue Jays 1990" tempa ($3-5)(WR)
95. white body, mid blue base, white roof, "Milwaukee Brewers 1990" tempa ($3-5)(WR)
96. white body, mid blue base, red roof, "Chicago Cubs 1990" tempa ($3-5)(WR)
97. white body, blue chassis, orange roof, "Detroit Tigers 1990" tempa ($3-5)(WR)
98. white body, blue chassis, yellow roof, "Mariners 1990" tempa ($3-5)(WR)
99. white body, red chassis, white roof, "Boston Red Sox 1990" tempa ($3-5)(WR)
100. white body, red chassis, white roof, "Cincinnati Reds 1990" tempa ($3-5)(WR)
101. white body, red chassis, white roof, "St. Louis Cardinals 1990" tempa ($3-5)(WR)
102. white body, red chassis, white roof, "Montreal Expos 1990" tempa ($3-5)(WR)
103. white body, red chassis, yellow roof, "California Angels 1990" tempa ($3-5)(WR)
104. white body, maroon chassis, white roof, "Philadelphia Phillies 1990" tempa ($3-5)(WR)
105. white body, black chassis, white roof, "San Francisco Giants 1990" tempa ($3-5)(WR)
106. white body, black chassis & roof, "Pittsburgh Pirates 1990" tempa ($3-5)(WR)
107. white body, brown chassis, orange roof, "San Diego Padres 1990" tempa ($3-5)(WR)
108. powder blue body, blue chassis, white roof, "Kansas City Royals 1990" tempa ($3-5)(WR)
109. black body, orange chassis, black roof, "Baltimore Orioles 1990" tempa ($3-5)(WR)
110. yellow body, green chassis, white roof, "Oakland A's 1990" tempa ($3-5)(WR)
111. yellow body, red chassis, red roof, "Pava" tempa ($8-12)(DK)
112. dark blue body, black chassis, black roof, "Swarfega" tempa ($18-25)(UK)(OP)
113. dark blue body, black chassis, black roof, "Kellogg's Rice Krispies" tempa ($4-6)(US)(OP)
114. dark green body, dark green chassis & roof, "Carmelle" tempa ($15-20)(SU)
115. dark blue body, black chassis, black roof, "Lyceum Theatre" tempa ($6-8)(UK)
116. light blue body, black chassis, white roof, "Fresh Dairy Cream" tempa ($8-12)(UK)(OP)
117. yellow body, red chassis, red roof, "Drink Coca Cola" with brown bottles tempa ($7-10)(CN)
118. yellow body, red chassis, red roof, "Drink Coca Cola" with red bottles tempa ($8-12)(SW)
119. yellow body, dark green chassis & roof, "Drink Coca Cola" tempa ($7-10)(CN)
120. white body, maroon chassis, white roof, "Matchbox USA 9th Annual Convention 1990" tempa ($8-10)
121. blue body, red chassis, yellow roof, "Isle of Man TT90" tempa ($5-7)(UK)
122. florescent green body, florescent orange chassis, black roof, "Matchbox Collectors Club 1990" labels ($85-110)(C2)
123. dark blue body, white chassis, white roof, "Penn State 1990" tempa ($6-8)(WR)
124. white body, dark blue chassis, dark blue roof, "Penn State 1990" tempa ($6-8)(WR)
125. cream body, red chassis, red roof, "York Fair 1990- 225 Years" tempa ($5-7)(WR)
126. white body, navy blue chassis, orange roof, "Bears 1990" tempa ($3-5)(WR)
127. white body, blue chassis, blue roof, "Colts 1990" tempa ($3-5)(WR)
128. white body, green chassis, green roof, "Jets 1990" tempa ($3-5)(WR)
129. white body, red-brown chassis, maroon roof, "Cardinals 1990" tempa ($3-5)(WR)
130. white body, red chassis, lemon roof, "KC Chiefs 1990" tempa ($3-5)(WR)
131. navy blue body, yellow chassis, white roof, "Chargers 1990" tempa ($3-5)(WR)
132. blue body, white chassis, white roof, "Giants 1990" tempa ($3-5)(WR)
133. blue body, red chassis, white roof, "Bills 1990" tempa ($3-5)(WR)
134. bright blue body, red chassis, bright blue roof, "Oilers 1990" tempa ($3-5)(WR)
135. silver-gray body, blue chassis, white roof, "Seahawks 1990" tempa ($3-5)(WR)
136. silver-gray body, light blue chassis, white roof, "Lions 1990" tempa ($3-5)(WR)
137. silver-gray body, navy blue chassis, & roof, "Cowboys 1990" tempa ($3-5)(WR)
138. silver-gray body, black chassis, black roof, "Raiders 1990" tempa ($3-5)(WR)
139. silver-gray body, green chassis, white roof, "Eagles 1990" tempa ($3-5)(WR)
140. green-gold body, black chassis, white roof, "Saints 1990" tempa ($3-5)(WR)
141. gold body, red chassis, white roof, "49ers 1990" tempa ($3-5)(WR)
142. red body, black chassis, light gray roof, "Falcons 1990" tempa ($3-5)(WR)
143. red body, white chassis, blue roof, "Patriots 1990" tempa ($3-5)(WR)
144. red-brown body, lemon chassis, white roof, "Redskins 1990" tempa ($3 5)(WR)
145. dark orange body, brown chassis, white roof, "Browns 1990" tempa ($3-5)(WR)
146. dark orange body, blue chassis, orange roof, "Broncos 1990" tempa ($3-5)(WR)
147. light orange body, black chassis, black roof, "Buccaneers 1990" tempa ($3-5)(WR)
148. blue-green body, orange chassis, white roof, "Dolphins 1990" tempa ($3-5)(WR)
149. olive body, lemon chassis, white roof, "Packers 1990" tempa ($3-5)(WR)
150. yellow body, blue chassis, yellow roof, "Rams 1990" tempa ($3-5)(WR)
151. yellow body, black chassis, yellow roof, "Steelers 1990" tempa ($3-5)(WR)
152. black body, dark orange chassis, white roof, "Bengals 1990" tempa ($3-5)(WR)
153. purple body, purple chassis, yellow roof, "Vikings 1990" tempa, ($3-5)(WR)
154. metallic green body & chassis, green roof, "Canada Dry" tempa ($8-12)(CN)
155. dark blue body, black chassis, black roof, "Kellogg's Rice Krispies" tempa, Thailand casting ($4-6)(US)(OP)
156. cream body, green chassis, green roof, "William Lusty" tempa ($6-8)(UK)
157. dark plum body, black chassis, black roof, "Johnnie Walker" tempa ($18-25)(UK)(OP)
158. blue body, black chassis, blue roof, "Mitre 10" tempa ($7-10)(AU)
159. orange-red body, black chassis, black roof, "Tyne Brand" tempa ($12-15)(UK)(OP)
160. dark blue body, black chassis, black roof, "Tyne Brand" tempa ($12-15)(UK)(OP)
161. cream body, green chassis, red roof, "PG Tips" tempa ($12-15)(UK)(OP)
162. powder blue body, dark gray chassis & roof, "Open Every Day" tempa on doors, plain main panel ($12-15)(MP)
163. dark blue body, black chassis, black roof, "Kellogg's Rice Krispies" tempa, China casting ($4-6)(US)(OP)
164. white body, black chassis, black roof, "Rutter Bros. Dairy" tempa ($6-8)(WR)
165. dark blue body, black chassis, white roof, "Lyons Tea" tempa ($6-8)(UK)

NOTE: following models with China casting unless otherwise noted.

166. yellow body, black chassis, black roof, black grille, "Matchbox Dinky Toy Convention 1991" ($8-12)(UK)
167. white body, red chassis, dark blue roof, "Indians 1991" tempa ($3-5)(WR)
168. white body, red chassis, dark blue roof, "Yankees 1991" tempa ($3-5)(WR)
169. white body, red chassis, white roof, "Cardinals 1991" tempa ($3-5)(WR)
170. white body, yellow chassis, white roof, "Brewers 1991" tempa ($3-5)(WR)
171. white body, black chassis, dark gray roof, "White Sox 1991" tempa ($3-5)(WR)
172. lemon body, blue chassis, mid blue roof, "Mariners 1991" tempa ($3-5)(WR)
173. orange-yellow body, red chassis, dark blue roof, "Angels 1991" tempa ($3-5)(WR)
174. orange body, black chassis, white roof, "Orioles 1991" tempa ($3-5)(WR)
175. orange body, blue chassis, white roof, "Mets 1991" tempa ($3-5)(WR)
176. orange body, dark blue chassis, orange-yellow roof, "Astros 1991" tempa ($3-5)(WR)
177. red body, blue chassis, white roof, "Rangers 1991" tempa ($3-5)(WR)
178. red body, white chassis, white roof, "Cubs 1991" tempa ($3-5)(WR)
179. red body, red chassis, white roof, "Reds 1991" tempa ($3-5)(WR)
180. dark maroon body & chassis, white roof, "Phillies 1991" tempa ($3-5)(WR)
181. dark blue body, red chassis, white roof, "Red Sox 1991" tempa ($3-5)(WR)
182. dark blue body, red chassis, white roof, "Twins 1991" tempa ($3-5)(WR)
183. blue body, red chassis, white roof, "Braves 1991" tempa ($3-5)(WR)
184. blue body, baby blue chassis, white roof, "Royals 1991" tempa ($3-5)(WR)
185. medium blue body, blue chassis, white roof, "Blue Jays 1991" tempa ($3-5)(WR)
186. baby blue body, red chassis, white roof, "Expos 1991" tempa ($3-5)(WR)
187. pearly silver body, blue chassis, orange roof, "Dodgers 1991" tempa ($3-5)(WR)
188. pearly silver body, dark blue chassis, orange roof, "Padres 1991" tempa ($3-5)(WR)
189. silver-gray body, dark blue chassis, orange roof, "Tigers 1991" tempa ($3-5)(WR)
190. lavender gray body, black chassis, orange roof, "Giants 1991" tempa ($3-5)(WR)
191. black body, yellow chassis, white roof, "Pirates 1991" tempa ($3-5)(WR)
192. green body, yellow chassis, white roof, "Athletics 1991" tempa ($3-5)(WR)
193. powder blue body, blue chassis, red roof, gold grille, "Isle of Man TT91" tempa ($5-7)(UK)
194. orange-yellow body, black chassis, black roof, "Celebrating A Decade of Matchbox Conventions 1991" tempa ($8-10)(US)
195. white body, dark pink chassis, black roof, "Matchbox Collectors Club 1991" labels, Macau casting ($60-75)(C2)
196. chrome plated body, red chassis, red roof, "15th Anniversary Matchbox USA 1991" tempa, Macau casting ($35-50)(C2)
197. light yellow body, light blue chassis & roof, "Dairylea" tempa ($15-20)(UK)(OP)
198. white body, white chassis & sub-base, white roof & grille, no tempa ($10-15)(GF)
199. yellow body, green chassis, white roof, "Notre Dame 1991" tempa ($5-7)(WR)
200. silver-gray body, red chassis, white roof, "UNLV 1991" tempa ($5-7)(WR)
201. white body, blue chassis, blue roof, "Rugby Child Development Centre" tempa ($7-10)(UK)
202. dark plum body, black chassis, black roof, "Johnnie Walker" tempa, Thailand casting ($18-25)(UK)
203. red body, black chassis, black roof, "Mervyn Wynne" with black island on doors tempa, Macau casting ($18-25)(UK)
204. silver-gray body, turquoise chassis & roof, "York Fair 1991" tempa ($6-8)(WR)

NOTE: football set models for 1991 have roof blades cast with labels applied.
205. lemon body, maroon chassis, maroon roof, "Redskins 1991" tempa ($3-5)(WR)
206. lemon body, red chassis, white roof, "Chiefs 1991" tempa ($3-5)(WR)
207. yellow body, navy blue chassis, navy blue roof, "Chargers 1991" tempa ($3-5)(WR)
208. yellow body, black chassis, black roof, "Steelers 1991" ($3-5)(WR)
209. yellow body, dark blue chassis, dark blue roof, "Rams 1991" tempa ($3-5)(WR)
210. lemon body, purple chassis, purple roof, "Vikings 1991" tempa ($3-5)(WR)
211. orange body, blue-green chassis & roof, "Dolphins 1991" tempa ($3-5)(WR)
212. dark orange body, dark blue chassis & roof, "Broncos 1991" tempa ($3-5)(WR)
213. dark orange body, black chassis, black roof, "Bengals 1991" tempa ($3-5)(WR)
214. light orange body, red chassis, white roof, "Buccaneers 1991" tempa ($3-5)(WR)
215. white body, dark orange chassis, navy blue roof, "Bears 1991" tempa ($3-5)(WR)
216. white body, dull green chassis & roof, "Jets 1991" tempa ($3-5)(WR)
217. white body, dark blue chassis, red roof, "Bills 1991" tempa ($3-5)(WR)
218. white body, dark blue chassis & roof, "Giants 1991" tempa ($3-5)(WR)
219. white body, green-gold chassis, black roof, "Saints 1991" tempa ($3-5)(WR)
220. blue body, silver-gray chassis, white roof, "Lions 1991" tempa ($3-5)(WR)
221. bright blue body, red chassis, white roof, "Oilers 1991" tempa ($3-5)(WR)
222. red body, black chassis, black roof, "Falcons 1991" tempa ($3-5)(WR)
223. red body, gold chassis, gold roof, "49ers 1991" tempa ($3-5)(WR)
224. maroon body, white chassis, white roof, "Cardinals 1991" tempa ($3-5)(WR)
225. brown body, brown chassis, orange roof, "Browns 1991" tempa ($3-5)(WR)
226. black body, silver-gray chassis, white roof, "Raiders 1991" tempa ($3-5)(WR)
227. dark blue body, green chassis, white roof, "Seahawks 1991" tempa ($3-5)(WR)
228. dark blue body, white chassis, white roof, "Colts 1991" tempa ($3-5)(WR)
229. dark blue body, red chassis, red roof, "Patriots 1991" tempa ($3-5)(WR)
230. navy blue body, silver-gray chassis, purple-blue roof, "Cowboys 1991" tempa ($3-5)(WR)
231. olive body, yellow chassis, yellow roof, "Packers 1991" tempa ($3-5)(WR)
232. silver-gray body, green chassis, green roof, "Eagles 1991" tempa ($3-5)(WR)
233. orange-yellow body, purple chassis, white roof, "University of Washington 1992" tempa ($4-6)(WR)
234. dark yellow body, black chassis, white roof, "University of Colorado 1992" tempa ($4-6)(WR)
235. yellow body, navy blue chassis, yellow roof, "University of Michigan 1992" tempa ($4-6)(WR)
236. dark orange body, blue chassis, white roof, "Clemson University 1992" tempa ($4-6)(WR)
237. dark orange body, blue chassis, white roof, "Syracuse University 1992" tempa ($4-6)(WR)
238. white body, dark blue chassis, dark blue roof, "Penn State 1991" tempa ($6-8)(WR)
NOTE: following models with Thailand casting unless otherwise noted. The 1992 hockey set models are only available as paired editions. ($10-15) per pair (WR)
239. red body, blue chassis, white roof, "Canadiennes (logo) 1917" tempa
240. white body, red chassis, white roof, "Canadiennes (logo) 1992" tempa
241. black body, red chassis, white roof, "Chicago Black Hawks 1917" tempa
242. white body, black chassis, white roof, Indian's head (Black Hawk logo) "1992" tempa
243. tan body, brown chassis, white roof, "Boston Bruins 1917" tempa
244. black body, yellow chassis, white roof, Bruin's logo & "1992" tempa
245. red body, white chassis, white roof, Redwings logo & "1917" tempa
246. white body, red chassis, white roof, Redwings logo & "1992" tempa
247. bright red body, red chassis, white roof, "Rangers 1917" tempa
248. white body, bright blue chassis, white roof, "New York Rangers 1992" tempa
249. navy blue body, white chassis, white roof, "Toronto Maple Leafs 1917" tempa
250. white body, blue chassis, white roof, "Toronto Maple Leafs 1992" tempa
NOTE: Following models with China casting unless otherwise noted. #251-256 sold only as a set ($30-40)(AU)
251. lime body, black chassis, black roof, "Milo" tempa
252. red body, black chassis, black roof, "Uncle Toby's" tempa
253. dark blue body, black chassis, black roof, "IXL" tempa
254. orange body, black chassis, black roof, "Billy Tea" tempa
255. beige body, black chassis, black roof, "Aeroplane Jelly" tempa
256. dark purple body, black chassis, black roof, "Violet Crumble" tempa
257. powder blue body & chassis, white roof, "North Carolina 1992" tempa ($4-6)(WR)
258. white body, orange chassis, white roof, "Tennessee Vol. 1992" tempa ($4-6)(WR)
259. white body, blue chassis, blue roof, "Camperdown Cumberland" tempa ($10-15)(AU)
260. white body, white chassis, white roof, amber windows, no tempa, Thailand casting ($10-15)(GF)
261. brown body, black chassis, black roof, "Cobb of Knightsbridge" tempa, Thailand casting ($8-12)(UK)
262. white body, black chassis, red roof, "Big Ben" tempa ($6-8)(AU)
263. white body, white chassis, white roof, "Matthew Walker" tempa ($8-12)(UK)
264. red body, black chassis, black roof, "McVities Digestive" tempa ($12-15)(UK)(OP)
265. orange-yellow body, green chassis, green roof, "1st M.I.C.A. Australia Convention 1992" tempa ($8-12)(AU)
266. red body, black chassis, black roof, "Pritt Stick" tempa ($7-10)(UK)(OP)
267. black body, black chassis, black roof, "City Ford" tempa, China casting ($7-10)(AU)
268. orange body, black chassis, black roof, "P.M.G." tempa ($8-12)(AU)
269. brass plated body, black chassis, black roof, "Matchbox Collectors Club 1992" tempa ($40-65)(C2)
270. pale gray body, brown chassis, brown roof, "Yardley" tempa ($8-12)(UK)
271. white body, white chassis, white roof, no tempa ($10-15)(GF)
NOTE: Following models with Thailand casting unless otherwise noted.
272. orange body, black chassis, black roof, "Philadelphia Flyers 1993" tempa ($6-8)(WR)
273. black body, silver-gray chassis & roof, "LA Kings 1993" tempa ($6-8)(WR)
274. white body, red chassis, blue roof, "Washington Capitals 1993" tempa ($6-8)(WR)
275. white body, metallic turquoise chassis, black roof, "San Jose Sharks 1993" tempa ($6-8)(WR)
NOTE: Versions #276-281 sold only as a set ($35-40)(AU)
276. purple body, black chassis, black roof, "Tyrrells Dry Red" tempa
277. red body, black chassis, black roof, "McWilliams Cream Sherry" tempa
278. brown body, black chassis, black roof, "Yalumba Port" tempa
279. blue body, black chassis, black roof, "Houghton White Burgundy" tempa
280. green body, black chassis, black roof, "Penfold's" tempa
281. black body, black chassis, black roof, "Hardy's Black Bottle" tempa
282. dark green body, dark green chassis, black roof, "Selfridge & Co." tempa, China casting ($5-7)(UK)
283. green body, green chassis, green roof, "William Lusty" tempa, China casting ($6-8)(UK)
284. yellow body, greenish black chassis, black roof, "Matchbox Series Model A Ford Van" tempa ($2-3)
285. yellow body, black chassis, black roof, "Matchbox Series Model A Ford Van" tempa ($2-3)
286. red body, white chassis, white roof, "Vileda" tempa, China casting ($8-12)(UK)(OP)
287. dark blue body, white chassis, red roof, "Dale Farms" tempa, China casting ($6-8)(UK)
288. cream body, red chassis, red roof, "Indiana Hoosiers 1993" tempa, China casting ($4-6)(WR)
289. red body, yellow chassis, dark blue roof, "8th MICA Event" tempa, China casting ($10-15)(UK)
290. red body, yellow chassis, black roof, "1st MICA European Convention", China casting ($12-18)(GR)
291. black body, black chassis, black roof, "Gowings" tempa, China casting ($8-12)(AU)
292. white body, red chassis, black roof, "Georgia" tempa, China casting ($4-6)(WR)
293. black body, green chassis, green roof, "Matchbox Collectors Club 1993" labels, China casting ($15-25)(C2)
294. green body, red chassis, red roof, "Merry Christmas 1993" labels, China casting ($25-45)(C2)
295. cream body, blue chassis, green roof with blade, "York Fair 1993" tempa, China casting ($4-6)(WR)
296. dark cream body, blue chassis, cream roof, "Pure Cod Liver Oil" tempa, Thailand casting ($4-6)(GS)
297. green body, blue chassis, green roof, "Vicks" tempa, Thailand casting ($4-6)(GS)
298. blue body, dark blue chassis, blue roof, "Milk of Magnesia" tempa, Thailand casting ($4-6)(GS)
299. red body, dark blue chassis, red roof, "Tiger Balm" tempa, Thailand casting ($4-6)(GS)
300. dark blue body, dark blue chassis, dark blue roof, "Alka-Seltzer" tempa, Thailand casting ($4-6)(GS)
301. tan body, brown chassis, tan roof, "Bayer Aspirin" tempa, Thailand casting ($4-6)(GS)
302. yellow body, red chassis, yellow roof, "Vegemite" tempa, Thailand casting ($7-10) (AU)
303. lime body, orange chassis, orange roof, "True Value Hardware" tempa, Thailand casting ($7-10)(AU)
304. maroon body, beige chassis, beige roof, "Automodel Exchange" tempa, Thailand casting ($7-10)(AU)
305. maroon body, maroon chassis, white roof, "Matchbox 1991" labels, China casting ($50-75)(CHI)
306. blue body, red chassis, white roof, "Matchbox 1991" labels, China casting ($50-75)(CHI)
307. orange body, black chassis, white roof, "Matchbox 1991" labels, China casting ($50-75)(CHI)
308. white body, red chassis, blue roof, "Matchbox 1991" labels, China casting ($50-75)(CHI)
309. green body, yellow chassis, white roof, "Matchbox 1991" labels, China casting ($50-75)(CHI)
310. silver-gray body, black chassis, orange roof, "Matchbox 1991" labels, China casting ($50-75)(CHI)
NOTE: 305-310 are relabeled at the Chinese factory over baseball vans and issued on the Chinese market. These 6 are confirmed with 22 more possible versions!
311. white body, red chassis, powder blue roof, "Ironbridge Telford 1994-MICA 9" tempa, Thailand casting ($12-15)(UK)
312. white body, red chassis, lime roof, "Dusseldorf Deutschland 94" tempa, Thailand casting ($12-15)(GR)
313. fluorescent orange & yellow body, yellow chassis, orange roof, "Get In The Fast Lane Matchbox" tempa, Thailand casting ($7-10)(US)
314. black body, maroon chassis, maroon roof, "Hershey, Penn.-MICA 7" labels, Macau casting ($12-15)(C2)
315. green body, green chassis, green roof, "Young's Sheep Dips" tempa, Thailand casting ($7-10)(AU)
316. beige body, blue chassis, blue roof, kangaroo & MICA logo tempa, Macau casting (base secured by screws) ($90-125)(AU)(C2)
317. tan body, blue chassis, blue roof, kangaroo & MICA logo tempa, Thailand casting ($7-10)(AU)
NOTE: versions 318-323 only available as a set ($25-35)
318. cream body, red chassis, red roof, "Gerry Cottle's Circus" tempa, Thailand casting
319. white body, red chassis, blue roof, "Circus Barum" tempa, Thailand casting
320. yellow body, red chassis, red roof, "Circus Oz" tempa, Thailand casting
321. red body, black chassis, red roof, "Circus Krone" tempa, Thailand casting
322. red body, black chassis, black roof, "Chipperfield's Circus" tempa, Thailand casting
323. blue body, blue chassis, blue roof, "Big Apple Circus" tempa, Thailand casting
324. metallic gold body, green chassis, green roof, "Matchbox Collectors Club Christmas 1994", Thailand casting ($5-7)(US)
325. white body, red chassis, white roof, "Hansell's" tempa, Thailand casting($7-10)(AU)(OP)
326. white body, black chassis, red roof, "Matchbox" tempa , Thailand casting ($20-30)(AU)
327. gold body, black chassis, black roof, "Memories 1993" tempa, Macau casting ($400-600)(C2)
NOTE: All models below with Thailand casting unless noted.
328. brown body, cocoa brown chassis, white roof, "Matchbox & Lesney Toy Museum" tempa, 5 crown rear wheels ($8-12)(US)
329. cocoa brown body, black chassis, cocoa brown roof, "Beechworth Bakery" tempa, ($5-7)(AU)
330. cocoa brown body, black chassis, yellow roof, "Beechworth Bakery" ($15-25)(AU)
331. silver-gray body, black chassis, black roof, "10th MICA Convention" tempa ($8-12)(UK)
332. brown body, cocoa brown chassis, white roof, "Matchbox & Lesney Toy Museum" tempa ($5-7)(US)
333. red body, black chassis, black roof, "Postes Canada Post" tempa ($5-7)(GS)
334. red body, black chassis, black roof, "De Post" tempa ($5-7)(GS)
335. orange-red body, black chassis, black roof, "Australia Post" tempa ($5-7)(GS)
336. yellow body, black chassis, white roof, "Reichspost" tempa ($5-7)(GS)
337. blue body, blue chassis, white roof, "Guernsey Post Office" tempa ($5-7)(GS)
338. white body, white chassis, white roof, "U.S. Mail" tempa ($5-7)(GS)
339. white body, red chassis, red roof, "Sydney Swans" tempa ($7-10)(AU)
340. white body, white chassis, red roof, "St. Kilda Saints" tempa ($7-10)(AU)
341. white body, blue chassis, white roof, "No. Melbourne Kangaroos" tempa ($7-10)(AU)
342. blue body, yellow chassis, blue roof, "West Coast Eagles" tempa ($7-10)(AU)
343. blue body, red chassis, blue roof, "Fitzroy Lions" tempa ($7-10)(AU)
344. blue body, red chassis, red roof, "Footscray Bulldogs" tempa ($7-10)(AU)
345. dark blue body, chassis & roof, "Carlton Blues" tempa ($7-10)(AU)
346. dark blue body, white chassis, dark blue roof, "Geelong Cats" tempa ($7-10)(AU)
347. dark blue body, red chassis, dark blue roof, "Melbourne Demons" tempa ($7-10)(AU)
348. dark blue body, red chassis, yellow roof, "Adelaide Crows" tempa ($7-10)((AU)
349. purple body, red chassis, purple roof, "Fremantle Dockers" tempa ($7-10)(AU)
350. black body, yellow chassis, black roof, "Richmond Tigers" tempa ($7-10)(AU)
351. black body, white chassis, black roof, "Collingwood Magpies" tempa ($7-10)(AU)
352. black body, red chassis, black roof, "Essendon Bombers" tempa ($7-10)(AU)
353. brown body, yellow chassis, brown roof, "Hawthorn Hawks" tempa ($7-10)(AU)
354. rose body, yellow chassis, rose roof, "Brisbane Bears" tempa ($7-10)(AU)
355. blue body, red chassis & roof, "Eastern Suburbs" tempa ($7-10)(AU)
356. blue body, red chassis & roof, "Newcastle Knights" tempa ($7-10)(AU)
357. blue body, yellow chassis, blue roof, "Parramatta Eels" tempa ($7-10)(AU)
358. dark blue body, red chassis & roof, So. Queensland Crushers" tempa ($7-10)(AU)
359. dark blue body, gray chassis & roof, "No. Queensland Cowboys"

tempa ($7-10)(AU)
360. light blue body, black chassis, bright blue roof, "Cronulla Sharks" tempa ($7-10)(AU)
361. black body, red chassis, black roof, "Penrith Panthers" tempa ($7-10)(AU)
362. black body, white chassis, black roof, "Western Suburbs" tempa ($7-10(AU)
363. black body, white chassis, red roof, "No. Sydney Bears" tempa ($7-10)(AU)
364. orange body, white chassis, black roof, "Balmain Tigers" tempa ($7-10)(AU)
365. red body, white chassis & roof, "Western Reds" tempa ($7-10)(AU)
366. red body, white chassis, red roof, "Illawarra Steelers" tempa ($7-10)(AU)
367. dark red body, white chassis, dark red roof, "Sea Eagles" tempa ($7-10)(AU)
368. light plum body, white chassis, yellow roof, "Brisbane Broncos" tempa ($7-10)(AU)
369. white body, blue chassis, white roof, "C-B Bulldogs" tempa ($7-10)(AU)
370. white body, black chassis, white roof, "Gold Coast Seagulls" tempa ($7-10)(AU)
371. white body, red chassis, white roof, "St. George" tempa ($7-10)(AU)
372. green body, blue chassis & roof, "Auckland Warriors" tempa ($7-10)(AU)
373. bright green body, red chassis, bright green roof, "So. Sydney Rabbitohs" tempa ($7-10)(AU)
374. bright lime body, white chassis, blue roof, "Canberra Raiders" tempa ($7-10)(AU)
375. white body, green chassis, turquoise roof, "Gold Coast Rollers" tempa ($7-10)(AU)
376. white body, yellow chassis, white roof, "Perth Wildcats" tempa ($7-10)(AU)
377. purple body, orange-yellow chassis, white roof, "Sydney Kings" tempa ($7-10)(AU)
378. turquoise body, purple chassis, white roof, "No. Melbourne Giants" tempa ($7-10)(AU)
379. dark blue body, red chassis & roof, "Adelaide Super Sixers" tempa ($7-10)(AU)
380. dark blue & white body, red chassis & roof, "Geelong Supercats" tempa ($7-10)(AU)
381. dark blue body, red chassis & roof, "Newcastle Falcons" tempa ($7-10)(AU)
382. black body, red chassis, blue roof, "Magic" tempa ($7-10)(AU)
383. red body, yellow chassis, red roof, "Melbourne Tigers" tempa ($7-10)(AU)
384. red body, blue chassis, red roof, "Canberra Cannons" tempa ($7-10)(AU)
385. red & white body, red chassis & roof, "Illawarra Hawks" tempa ($7-10)(AU)
386. yellow body, salmon chassis, red roof, "Townsville Suns" tempa ($7-10)(AU)
387. orange-yellow body, red chassis & roof, "Tassie Devils" tempa ($7-10)(AU)
388. orange-yellow body, blue chassis, orange-yellow roof, "Brisbane Bullets" tempa ($7-10)(AU)
389. yellow body & chassis, black roof, "Matchbox For Serious Collectors" tempa ($8-12)(GR)
390. yellow body, bright blue chassis, blue roof, "RACQ 90" tempa ($10-15)(AU)
391. dark blue body, black chassis, white roof, "Kellogg's" tempa ($40-55)(SD)(OP)
392. bright orchid body, black roof & chassis, "Kellogg's Raisin Bran" tempa ($8-12)(US)(OP)
393. dark orchid body, black roof & chassis, "Kellogg's Raisin Bran" tempa ($8-12)(US)(OP)
394. orange body, black chassis & roof, "Kellogg's Frosted Mini Wheats" tempa ($8-12)(US)(OP)
NOTE: Following models with China casting, unless noted
395. red-brown body, dark cream chassis, cream roof, "XITH MICA Convention" tempa ($10-15)(UK)
396. fawn body, red chassis & roof, "Street's Ice Cream" tempa ($15-20)(AU)
397. dark blue body, red chassis, yellow roof, "Smith's Crisps" tempa ($15-20)(AU)
398. yellow body, red chassis, yellow roof, "Shell Motor Oil" tempa ($15-20)(AU)
399. cream body & chassis, red roof, "Coca Cola" tempa ($15-20)(AU)
400. violet body, dark gold chassis, violet roof, "Cadbury's Chocolate" tempa ($15-20)(AU)
401. dark orchid body, black roof & chassis, "Kellogg's Raisin Bran" tempa ($8-12)(US)(OP)
402. pale orange body, black roof & chassis, "Kellogg's Frosted Mini Wheats" tempa ($8-12)(US)(OP)
403. brown body, cocoa brown chassis, white roof, "Greater Pennsylvania Toy Show" decals, Thailand casting ($8-12)(C2)
404. brown body, cocoa brown chassis, white roof, "LaRue Bros. Auto Inc." decals, Thailand casting ($8-12)(C2)
405. white body, blue chassis & roof, "Shipyard Brewing Co." tempa, rubber tires ($8-12)(MB1)(CL)
406. cream body, green chassis, dark green roof, "Kentucky Pride- Dixie Lexington Brewery" tempa , rubber tires($8-12)(MB2)(CL)
407. blue body, black chassis & roof, "Left Hand Brewing Co." tempa, rubber tires ($8-12)(MB3)(CL)
408. yellow body, black chassis & red roof, "Kellogg's Eggo" tempa ($10-15)(US)(OP)
409. purple body, black chassis & roof, "Continental Aero" tempa ($8-12)(US)
410. florescent orange body, blue chassis & roof, "3rd MICA Australia Convention 1996" labels, base screws ($85-110)(C2)
411. dark blue body, black chassis, yellow roof, "Sammler Treffen 1988" tempa, 5 arch front & racing special rear wheels, Macau casting ($150-250)(C2)
NOTE: this model was only just documented as a German code 2 in early 1997.
412. green body, metallic gold chassis & roof, "Fish Tales Ales" tempa, rubber tires ($8-12)(MB4)(CL)
413. blue body, blue chassis & roof, "Big Apple Circus" tempa ($5-8)(US)
414. white body, blue chassis, red roof, "Auto 1" tempa ($5-8)(AU)
415. white body, black chassis & roof, "TMLP" tempa ($30-40)(ASAP)
416. white body, black chassis & roof, "Brew Works" tempa ($100+)(ASAP)
417. red body, black chassis & roof, "Canadian Tire" tempa ($4-6)(CN)(GS)
418. red body, black chassis & roof, "Canadian Tire Corp'n" tempa ($4-6)(CN)(GS)
419. red body, black chassis & roof, "Canadian Tire Associate Store" tempa ($4-6)(CN)(GS)
420. black body, red chassis & roof, "Moto Master" tempa ($4-6)(CN)(GS)
421. white body, blue chassis, red roof, "Bendigo National Swapmeet" tempa ($10-15)(AU)(C2)
422. white body, black chassis & roof, "Dutchway Farm Market" tempa ($10-15)(ASAP)
423. white body, black chassis & roof, "Matchbox 33000" tempa ($75+)(ASAP)
424. white body, black chassis & roof, "Smith Kline Beecham" tempa ($100+)(ASAP)
425. white body, black chassis & roof, "Farmers Auto Loans/ Farmers Insurance Group" tempa ($100+)(ASAP)
426. bright blue body, yellow chassis & roof, "Hudson Lager" tempa, rubber tires ($8-12)(MB)(CL)
427. red body, blue chassis, white roof, "Big Apple Circus" tempa ($50-75)(US)
428. red body, black chassis & roof, "Beechworth Bakery" tempa ($3-5)(AU)
429. white body, black chassis & roof, "Melcer Tile 30 Years" tempa ($100+)(ASAP)
430. white body, black chassis & roof, "Carroll County Fair" tempa ($50+)(ASAP)
431. white body, black chassis & roof, "Two Men and A Truck" tempa ($10-15)(ASAP)
432. white body, black chassis & roof, "Corning Building Co." tempa ($75+)(ASAP)
433. white body, black chassis & roof, no tempa ($25-40)(ASAP blank)
434. light neon orange body, black chassis & roof, "Cave Creek Chili Beer" tempa, rubber tires ($8-12)(MB)(CL)
435. green body, yellow chassis & roof, "River-Horse Lager" tempa, rubber tires ($8-12)(MB)(CL)
436. red body, black chassis & roof, "Coca Cola Quality Assurance" tempa, rubber tires ($4-6)(PC)
437. white body, blue chassis & roof, "Special Edition 76" labels ($1-2)(MW76)
438. white body, black chassis & roof, "Avant Garde Drum & Bugle Corps" tempa ($10-15)(ASAP)

MB38-F FORD COURIER, issued 1992 (ROW)
1. white body, white metal base, gray interior, "Courier" tempa, China casting ($12-15)(UK)(LE)
2. lilac body, lilac plastic base, gray interior, "Milka" tempa, China casting ($2-3)
3. dark blue body, black plastic base, gray interior, "Matchbox- The Ideal Premium" tempa , China casting ($20-25)(GR)
4. dark lilac body, dark lilac plastic base, "Milka" tempa, Thailand casting ($1-3)
5. red body, red base, "Axa Insurance?" tempa, Thailand casting ($75-100)(LD)(UK)
6. red body, red base, "Ford County Emergency Services" tempa, Thailand casting ($12-18)(LD)(US)
7. red body, red base, "Australian Matchbox News" with "Club Member" on roof tempa, Thailand casting ($75-100)(LD)(AU)
8. red body, red base, "Australian Matchbox News" tempa, Thailand casting ($15-20)(LD)(AU)
9. dark blue body, dark blue base, "Australian Matchbox News" tempa, Thailand casting ($15 20)(LD)(AU)
10. white body, white base, "Dent Magician" tempa, Thailand casting ($45-60)(LD)(UK)
11. dark blue body, dark blue base, "Axa" tempa, Thailand casting ($18-25)(LD)(UK)
12. dark blue body, dark blue base, "Benedick's Coffee Service", Thailand casting ($12-18)(LD)(US)

MB38-G FORD COURIER, issued 1992 (UK)
1. red body, red metal base, gray interior, no tempa, China casting ($12-15)(LE)
NOTE: MB38-G features side cast windows, whereas MB38-F features no side windows.

MB38-H MERCEDES 600SEL, issued 1992 (USA)
MB39-G MERCEDES 600SEL, issued 1992 (ROW)
1. silver—gray body, gray base, clear windows, light gray interior, 8 dot wheels, gray sides tempa, China casting ($1-2)
2. silver—gray body, gray base, clear windows, light gray interior, 8 dot wheels, gray sides tempa, Thailand casting ($1-2)
3. metallic brown body, brown base, clear windows, light gray interior, 8 dot wheels, brown sides tempa, Thailand casting ($2-3)(SS)
4. black body, charcoal base, clear windows, lt./dk. gray interior, chrome disc with rubber tires, detailed trim tempa, Thailand casting ($3-5)(PC2)
5. blue body, charcoal base, clear windows, lt./dk. gray interior, chrome disc with rubber tires, detailed trim & charcoal sides tempa, Thailand casting ($3-5)(PC5)
6. dark green body, charcoal base, clear windows, lt./dk gray interior, chrome disc with rubber tires, detailed trim & charcoal sides tempa, Thailand casting ($3-5)(PC1)(AU)
7. white body, charcoal base, clear windows, lt./dk. gray interior, chrome disc with rubber tires, detailed trim & charcoal sides tempa, Thailand casting ($3-5)(SC2)
8. metallic red body, charcoal base, clear windows, gray & black interior, chrome disc with rubber tires, charcoal sides tempa, Thailand casting ($8-12)(UC)
9. silver blue body, silver-gray base, clear windows, lt./dk/. gray interior, chrome disc with rubber tires, silver-gray sides tempa, Thailand casting ($3-5)(JC)(PC)

MB38-I CORVETTE STINGRAY III, issued 1994
NOTE: All models with black base unless otherwise noted.
1. dark purple body, clear windshield, dark gray interior, gold 6-spoke spiral wheels, pink & white tempa, Thailand casting ($1-2)
2. dark purple body, purple base, chrome windshield, dark gray interior, gray disc with rubber tires, detailed trim tempa, Thailand casting ($2-4)(WC)
3. red body, clear windshield, black interior, gold 6-spoke spiral wheels, "7-Eleven" tempa, Thailand casting ($4-6)(US)
4. florescent yellow body, smoke windshield, gray interior, silver 6-spoke spiral wheels, "Ice Breaker" tempa, Thailand casting ($7-10)(PS)
5. florescent orange body, smoke windshield, gray interior, silver 6-spoke spiral wheels, "Ice Breaker" tempa, Thailand casting ($7-10)(PS)
6. florescent orange & yellow body, smoke windshield, black interior, silver 6-spoke spiral wheels, "Matchbox Get In The Fast Lane/ Toy Fair 1995" tempa, Thailand casting ($18-25)(US)
7. yellow & florescent orange body, smoke windshield, black interior, silver 6-spoke spiral wheels, "Matchbox Get In The Fast Lane/ Toy Fair 1995" tempa, Thailand casting ($85-100)(UK)(GR)
8. dark purple body, smoke windshield, gray interior, silver 6-spoke spiral wheels, pink & white hood & side design tempa, Thailand casting ($1-2)
9. dark purple body, smoke windshield, light gray interior, silver 6-spoke spiral wheels, pink & white side design tempa, Thailand casting ($1-2)
10. red body, chrome windshield, black interior, chrome disc with rubber tires, detailed trim tempa, Thailand casting ($20-35)(US)(OP)
11. silver body, amber windshield, white interior, silver 6-spoke spiral wheels, peach & white design tempa, Thailand casting ($3-5)(MT)
12. dark purple & metallic blue body, smoke windshield, white interior, silver 6-spoke spiral wheels, no tempa, Thailand casting ($1-2)(MP)
13. black & florescent orange body, smoke windshield, white interior, silver 6-spoke spiral wheels, no tempa, Thailand casting ($2-4)(MP)
14. white body, smoke windshield, blue interior, silver 6-spoke spiral wheels, blue & black spray design tempa, Thailand casting ($1-2)(MP)
15. metallic blue body, clear windshield, lt./dk. gray interior, chrome disc with rubber tires, detailed trim tempa, Thailand casting ($3-5)(PC2)
16. white body, smoke windshield, red interior, silver 6-spoke spiral wheels, red & yellow design tempa, Thailand casting ($2-4)
17. lemon body, clear windshield, lt./dk. gray interior, chrome disc with rubber tires, detailed trim tempa, Thailand casting ($3-5)(PC5)
18. metallic gold body, clear windshield, black interior, silver 6-spoke spiral wheels, no tempa, Thailand casting ($10-15)(CH)
19. silver-gray body, clear windshield, black & 2 tone gray interior, chrome disc with rubber tires, detailed trim tempa, Thailand casting ($3-5)(SC2)
20. red body, chrome windshield, black interior, chrome disc with rubber tires, "Matchbox USA 97" tempa, Thailand casting ($100-150)(C2)
21. black body, clear windshield, red & gray interior, chrome disc with rubber tires, detailed trim tempa, Thailand casting ($15-20)(GC)
22. blue chrome body, clear windshield, gray interior, 5 spoke concave star wheels, pink & orange tempa, Thailand casting ($1-2)(MP)
23. white body, smoke windshield, red interior, 5 spoke concave star wheels, red & yellow side design tempa, Thailand casting ($2-4)
24. blue body, clear windshield, gray interior, 5 spoke concave star wheels, orange & white stripes with "Corvette" tempa, Thailand casting ($1-2)
25. red body, clear windshield, brown & black interior, chrome disc with rubber tires, detailed trim tempa, Thailand casting ($3-5)(PC12)
26. iridescent white body, clear windshield, brown & black interior, chrome disc with rubber tires, detailed trim tempa, Thailand casting ($3-5)(SC4)
27. crimson body, clear windshield, dark & light gray interior, chrome disc with rubber tires, detailed trim, Thailand casting ($3-5)(PC16)
28. crimson body, clear windshield, dark & light gray interior, 5 spoke concave star wheels, detailed trim tempa, Thailand casting ($50+)(found as PC16)
29. red body, clear windshield, gray interior, 5 spoke concave star wheels, blue & white stripes with "Corvette" tempa, Thailand casting ($1-2)(MW2)
30. red body, clear windshield, gray interior, 5 spoke concave star wheels, blue & white stripes with "Corvette" tempa, China casting ($1-2)(MW2)

MB39-A CLIPPER, issued 1973
1. magenta body, unpainted base, yellow interior, amber windows, chrome tailpipes ($10-15)
2. magenta body, green base, yellow interior, amber windows, chrome tailpipes ($10-15)
3. magenta body, green base, yellow interior, clear windows, chrome tailpipes ($10-15)
4. magenta body, unpainted base, yellow interior, amber windows, white tailpipes ($10-15)

5. magenta body, green base, yellow interior, amber windows, white tailpipes ($10-15)
6. magenta body, green base, yellow interior, clear windows, white tailpipes ($10-15)
7. hot pink body, green base, yellow interior, amber windows, chrome tailpipes ($150-250)
NOTE: Available as a Bulgarian casting. Assorted colors available ($60-85)

MB39-B ROLLS ROYCE SILVER SHADOW, issued 1979
NOTE: Following models with England casting unless otherwise noted.
1. silver—gray body, unpainted base, red interior, clear windows, dot dash wheels ($4-6)
2. matt gray body, unpainted base, red interior, clear windows, dot dash wheels ($4-6)
3. red body, unpainted base, ivory interior, clear windows, dot dash wheels ($4-6)
4. red body, unpainted base, light yellow interior, clear windows, dot dash wheels ($3-5)
5. red body, unpainted base, brown interior, clear windows, dot dash wheels ($4-6)
6. dark tan body, unpainted base, white interior, clear windows, dot dash wheels ($2-4)
7. light tan body, unpainted base, white interior, clear windows, dot dash wheels ($2-4)
8. light tan body, silver-gray base, white interior, clear windows, dot dash wheels ($2-4)
9. light tan body, silver-gray base, white interior, clear windows, 5 arch wheels ($2-4)
10. light tan body, unpainted base, white interior, smoke windows, dot dash wheels ($2-4)
11. light tan body, unpainted base, white interior, amber windows, dot dash wheels ($3-5)
12. light tan body, silver-gray base, white interior, amber windows, dot dash wheels ($3-5)
13. plum body, unpainted base, white interior, clear windows, dot dash wheels ($4-6)
14. plum body, silver-gray base, white interior, clear windows, dot dash wheels ($4-6)
15. plum body, black base, white interior, clear windows, dot dash wheels ($4-6)
16. black body, black base, gray interior, clear windows, dot dash wheels, China casting ($50-75)(CHI)
17. maroon body, pearly silver base, white interior, clear windows, dot dash wheels, Macau casting ($4-6)
NOTE: Available as an Hungarian casting. Assorted colors available ($15-25)

MB39-C TOYOTA SUPRA, issued 1983 (USA)
MB60-E TOYOTA SUPRA, issued 1983 (ROW)
NOTE: All models feature red interior & black hatch unless otherwise noted.
1. white body, black base, clear windows, 5 arch wheels, "41" tempa, Macau casting ($2-4)
2. white body, black base, light amber windows, 5 arch wheels, "41" tempa, Macau casting ($2-4)
3. white body, charcoal base, light amber windows, 5 arch wheels, "41" tempa, Macau casting ($2-4)
4. red body, black base, clear windows, 5 arch wheels, "Twin Cam 24" tempa, Macau casting ($7-10) (JP)
5. dark red body, black base, clear windows, 8 dot wheels, "Twin Cam 24" tempa, Macau casting ($7-10)(JP)
6. white body, black base, clear windows, 5 arch wheels, "Supra" & pinstripes tempa, Macau casting ($2-4)
7. white body, black base, clear windows, 8 dot wheels, "Supra" & pinstripes tempa, Macau casting ($2-4)
8. white body, black base, clear windows, 8 dot wheels, red/blue/yellow design tempa, Macau casting ($8-12)(DY)
NOTE: Available as a Bulgarian casting. Assorted colors available ($15-25)

MB39-D BMW CABRIOLET, issued 1985
MB28-I BMW CABRIOLET, reissued 1991 (ROW)
1. metallic silver blue body & base, red-brown interior, 8 dot silver wheels, no tow hook, "323i" tempa, Macau casting ($2-3)
2. metallic silver blue body & base, red-brown interior, dot dash wheels, no tow hook, "323i " tempa, Macau casting ($2-3)
3. red body & base, red-brown interior, 8 dot gold wheels, no tow hook, "323i" tempa, Macau casting ($1-2)
4. red body & base, red-brown interior, 8 dot silver wheels, no tow hook, "323i" tempa, Macau casting ($1-2)
5. red body & base, red-brown interior, 5 arch wheels, no tow hook, "323i" tempa, Macau casting ($2-3)
6. white body & base, red-brown interior, starburst wheels, no tow hook, "Alpina" tempa, Macau casting ($3-5)(SF)
7. white body & base, red-brown interior, 8 dot silver wheels, no tow hook, "BMW" & "323i" tempa, Macau casting ($8-12)
8. white body & base, red-brown interior, 8 dot silver wheels, with tow hook, "BMW" & "323i" tempa, Macau casting ($8-12)
9. red body & base, red-brown interior, 8 dot silver wheels, with tow hook, "Gliding Club" tempa, Macau casting ($3-4)(TP)
10. white body & base, red-brown interior, starburst wheels, with tow hook, "Alpina" tempa, Macau casting ($3-5)(SF)
11. white body & base, red-brown interior, laser wheels, with tow hook, "Alpina" tempa, Macau casting ($3-5)(LW)
12. dark blue body, black base, black interior, 8 dot silver wheels, with tow hook, "323i" & "BP" tempa, Macau casting ($8-12)(DU)
13. silver-blue body & base, gray interior, 8 dot silver wheels, with tow hook, dark blue stripe tempa, Macau casting ($2-4)(TP)
14. light silver-blue body & base, gray interior, 8 dot silver wheels, with tow hook, dark blue stripe tempa, Thailand casting ($2-4)(TP)
15. red body & base, red-brown interior, 8 dot silver wheels, with tow hook, "323i" tempa, Thailand casting ($1-2)
16. white body & base, gray interior, 8 dot silver wheels, with tow hook, blue & red with "323i" tempa, Thailand casting ($2-3)(TP)
17. white body & base, maroon interior, 8 dot silver wheels, with tow hook, purple/orange/blue tempa, Thailand casting ($1-2)(TP)
18. metallic silver blue body & base, red-brown interior, 8 dot silver wheels, with tow hook, "323i" tempa, Thailand casting ($1-2)(SP)

MB39-E FORD BRONCO II, issued 1987 (USA)
MB35-G FORD BRONCO II, issued 1988 (ROW)
NOTE: All models with clear windows, black tire carrier, maltese cross wheels unless otherwise noted.
1. white body, chrome base, red interior, "Bronco" & stripes tempa, Macau casting ($1-2)
2. dark brown body, chrome base, red interior, "Bronco" & stripes tempa, Macau casting ($3-4)(SC)
3. orange body, chrome base, red interior, "Bronco" & stripes tempa, Macau casting ($3-4)(SC)
4. white body, chrome base, red interior, "Coast Guard Beach Patrol" tempa, Macau casting ($1-2)
5. white body, chrome base, red interior, "Coast Guard Beach Patrol" tempa, Thailand casting ($1-2)
6. bright yellow body, chrome base, red interior, flames & "4X4" tempa, Thailand casting ($6-8)(US)(OP)
7. red body, blue base, orange-yellow interior, map & compass tempa, all yellow wheels, no spare tire carrier, Thailand casting ($6-8)(LL)
8. metallic blue body, chrome base, silver-gray interior, white splash marks & orange "4X4 Bronco" tempa, with window tempa, Thailand casting ($1-2)
9. metallic blue body, chrome base, silver-gray interior, white splash marks & orange "4X4 Bronco" tempa, with plain window, Thailand casting ($1-2)
10. white body, chrome base, red interior, "Police PD-22" tempa, Thailand casting ($1-3)(EM)
11. red body, chrome base, silver— g-ray interior, "4X4 Bronco" & splash marks tempa, Thailand casting ($1-2)(MP)
12. metallic green body, chrome base, tan interior, tan fenders tempa, Thailand casting ($2-4)(CC)
13. fluorescent orange body, chrome base, black interior, black zebra stripes tempa, Thailand casting ($1-2)(MP)
14. black body, chrome base, red interior, "Piranha" & fish design tempa, Thailand casting ($1-2)
15. black body, chrome base, red interior, fish design only tempa, Thailand casting ($1-2)
16. yellow body, chrome base, blue interior, "World 4 Kids" tempa, Thailand casting ($18-25)(AU)
17. white body, chrome base, black interior, black zebra stripes tempa, Thailand casting ($1-2)(MP)
18. black body, chrome base, red interior, fish design only tempa, China casting ($1-2)
19. silver-gray body, chrome base, blue interior, fish design only tempa, China casting ($2-3)
20. white body, chrome base, red interior, "Luigi's Pizza" tempa, China casting ($1-2)
21. metallic gold body, chrome base, black interior, no tempa, China casting ($5-10)(CH)
22. purple body, chrome base, gray interior, white stripes tempa, China casting ($1-2)(MP)
23. black body, chrome base, black interior, "Kidz 1.75FM" with pink & yellow stripes tempa, China casting ($4-6)(AU)
24. red body, chrome base, black interior, "Luigi's Pizza" tempa, China casting ($1-2)(MW51)

MB39-I 1971 CAMARO Z-28, issued 1998
1. green body, clear windows, black interior, dual white stripes tempa, 5 spoke concave star wheels black base, China casting ($1-2)
NOTE: Above model in various shades from light to dark.

MB40-A VAUXHALL GUILDSMAN, issued 1971
NOTE: version 1 label has star in black or blue background)
1. pink body, unpainted base, green windows, flames label, 5 spoke wheels ($12-15)
2. pink body, silver-gray base, green windows, flames label, 5 spoke wheels ($12-15)
3. pink body, unpainted base, green windows, "40" tempa, 5 spoke wheels ($15-20)
4. red body, unpainted base, green windows, flames label, 5 spoke wheels ($10-15)
5. red body, unpainted base, amber windows, flames label, 5 spoke wheels ($10-15)
6. red body, unpainted base, amber windows, flames label, dot dash wheels ($10-15)
7. red body, unpainted base, green windows, "40" tempa, 5 spoke wheels ($10-15)
8. red body, unpainted base, amber windows, "40" tempa, 5 spoke wheels ($10-15)
9. red body, unpainted base, amber windows, "40" tempa, dot dash wheels ($10-15)
10. red body, silver-gray base, amber windows, "40" tempa, dot dash wheels ($10-15)
11. cherry red body, unpainted base, amber windows, "40" tempa, 5 spoke wheels ($10-15)
NOTE: Available as a Bulgarian casting. Assorted colors available ($15-25)

MB40-B HORSE BOX, issued 1977
NOTE: All models with dot dash wheels & England casting unless noted otherwise.
1. red body, beige box, light brown door, black base, green windows ($45-60)
2. orange body, beige box, light brown door, black base, green windows ($4-6)
3. orange body, bone white box, light brown door, black base, green windows (4-6)
4. orange body, beige box, light brown door, silver-gray base, green windows ($4-6)
5. orange body, beige box, dark brown door, black base, green windows ($4-6)
6. orange body, beige box, dark brown door, charcoal base, green windows ($4-6)
7. orange body, beige box, dark brown door, charcoal base, clear windows ($8-10)
8. orange body, beige box, dark brown door, charcoal base, purple windows ($5-8)
9. orange body, beige box, dark brown door, unpainted base, green windows ($4-6)
10. light green body, beige box, dark brown door, unpainted base, green windows ($5-8)
11. light green body, beige box, white door, unpainted base, green windows ($5-8)
12. dark green body, beige box, dark brown door, black base, green windows ($5-8)
13. dark green body, beige box, dark brown door, unpainted base, green windows ($5-8)
14. dark green body, beige box, gray-brown door, unpainted base, green windows ($5-8)
15. dark green body, beige box, dark brown door, charcoal base, green windows ($5-8)
16. dark green body, beige box, dark brown door, silver-gray base, green windows ($5-8)
17. dark green body, beige box, lime door, black base, green windows ($7-10)
18. dark green body, beige box, lime door, silver-gray base, green windows ($7-10)
19. dark green body, translucent bone box, dark brown door, unpainted base, green windows ($7-10)
20. dark green body, chocolate box, white door, unpainted base, green windows ($10-15)
21. red body, chocolate box, white door, silver-gray base, green windows ($10-15)
22. red body, chocolate box, white door, black base, green windows ($10-15)
23. orange body, cream box, lime door, black base, green windows ($10-15)
24. orange body, chocolate box, white door, black base, green windows ($6-8)
25. orange body, chocolate box, white door, unpainted base, green windows ($6-8)
26. orange body, chocolate box, white door, silver-gray base, green windows ($6-8)
27. orange body, chocolate box, lime door, black base, green windows ($6-8)
28. yellow body, chocolate box, white door, black base, green windows ($6-8)
29. yellow body, chocolate box, lime door, black base, green windows ($6-8)
30. dark orange body, beige box, gray-brown door, charcoal base, green windows ($6-8)
31. dark orange body, chocolate box, lime door, black base, green windows ($4-6)
32. dark orange body, chocolate box, lime door, unpainted base, green windows ($4-6)
33. dark orange body, chocolate box, lime door, unpainted base, green windows, black hubs ($5-8)
34. dark orange body, chocolate box, lime door, black base, green windows, black hubs ($5-8)
35. dark orange body, chocolate box, white door, black base, green windows ($4-6)
36. orange body, chocolate box, white door, black base, green windows, Macau casting ($4-6)
37. blue body, yellow box, lime door, red base, green windows, caricature tempa, lime wheels with red hubs, Macau casting ($6-8)(LL)
38. blue body, yellow box, lime door, red base, green windows, caricature tempa, lime wheels with blue hubs, Thailand casting ($15-20)(LL)
NOTE: Versions 39 to 41 with 8 dot wheels.
39. red body, dark tan box, dark brown door, black base, green windows, Manaus casting ($35-50)(BR)
40. red body, dark tan box, light brown door, black base, green windows, Manaus casting ($35-50)(BR)
41. red body, dark tan box, chocolate door, black base, green windows, Manaus casting ($35-50)(BR)
42. white body, white box, white door, red base, blue windows, "Circus Circus" tempa, Thailand casting ($3-5)(MC)
43. yellow body, chocolate box, white door, black base, amber windows, Thailand casting ($2-4)(FM)(GS)
44. blue body, yellow box, lime door, red base, green windows, caricature tempa, all lime wheels, Thailand casting ($15-20)(LL)

MB40-C CORVETTE T-ROOF, issued 1982 (USA)
MB62-E CORVETTE T-ROOF, issued 1982 (ROW)
MB58-F CORVETTE T-ROOF, reissued 1991 (USA)
NOTE: All models with clear windows unless otherwise noted.
1. white body, gray interior, unpainted metal base, stripes tempa, 5 arch front & 5 crown rear wheels, England casting ($4-6)
2. white body, gray interior, unpainted metal base, stripes tempa, 5 arch front & rear wheels, England casting ($4-6)
3. white body, gray interior, unpainted metal base, stripes tempa, 5 crown front & rear wheels, England casting ($4-6)
4. white body, gray interior, unpainted metal base, stripes tempa, 5 crown front & 5 arch rear wheels, England casting ($4-6)
5. white body, gray interior, silver-gray metal base, stripes tempa, 5 arch front & 5 crown rear wheels, England casting ($4-6)
6. white body, red interior, red metal base, stripes tempa, 5 arch front & 5 crown rear wheels, Macau casting ($2-3)
7. white body, red interior, red metal base, stripes tempa, 5 crown front & 5 arch rear wheels, Macau casting ($2-3)
8. white body, red interior, red metal base, stripes tempa, 5 crown front & rear wheels, Macau casting ($2-3)
9. dark blue body, red interior, pearly silver metal base, flames tempa, 5 arch front & 5 crown rear wheels Macau casting ($2-3)
10. dark blue body, red interior, pearly silver metal base, flames tempa, 5 arch front & 5 crown rear wheels, Macau casting ($3-5)
11. dark blue body, red interior, pearly silver metal base, flames tempa, starburst wheels, Macau casting ($75-100)
12. yellow body, silver-gray interior, black metal base, "Corvette" tempa, 5 arch front & 5 crown rear wheels, Macau casting ($1-2)
13. yellow body, silver-gray interior, black plastic base, "Corvette" tempa, 5 arch front & 5 crown rear wheels, Macau casting ($1-2)
14. yellow body, silver-gray interior, black plastic base, "Corvette" tempa, 5 arch front & 5 crown rear wheels, China casting ($1-2)
15. dark blue body, red interior, black plastic base, yellow & red stripes tempa, 4 arch wheels, Manaus casting ($35-50)(BR)
16. dark blue body, red interior, black plastic base, yellow & red stripes tempa, 8 spoke wheels, Manaus casting ($35-50)(BR)
17. dark orange body, black interior, gray plastic base, detailed trim tempa, gray disc with rubber tires, chrome windshield, China casting ($5-8)(WC)
18. red body, white interior, gray plastic base, "Vette" & Chevy logo tempa, 5 arch front & 5 crown rear wheels, China casting ($1-2)
19. metallic blue body, dark gray interior, silver-gray plastic base, detailed trim tempa, gray disc w/rubber tires, chrome windshield, China casting ($5-8)(WC)
20. black body, black interior, silver-gray plastic base, "22" & stripes tempa, black disc with rubber tires, China casting ($5-7)(WP)
21. dark cream body, red interior, silver/gray plastic base, red & gray stripes tempa, 8 dot wheels, Manaus casting ($30-45)(BR)
22. dark gray body, white interior, gray plastic base, white stripes & "Corvette" tempa, 5 arch front & 5 crown rear wheels, Thailand casting ($2-4)(GS)
23. red body, white interior, gray plastic base, "Vette" & white design tempa, 5 arch front & 5 crown rear wheels, Thailand casting ($1-2)
24. dark teal blue body, pink interior, gray plastic base, white & pink grid tempa, gold 6 spoke spiral wheels, Thailand casting ($1-2)
25. dark green body, orange interior, chrome base, detailed trim tempa, silver 6 spoke spiral wheels, Thailand casting ($2-4)(CC)
26. red body, white interior, gray plastic base, "Vette" & white design tempa, silver 6 spoke spiral wheels, Thailand casting ($1-2)
27. white & black body, pink interior, gray plastic base, pink design tempa, silver 6 spoke spiral wheels, Thailand casting ($1-2)
28. white & black body, pink interior, gray plastic base, pink design tempa, silver 6 spoke spiral wheels, China casting ($1-2)
29. white body, black interior, gray plastic base, pink design tempa, silver 6 spoke spiral wheels, China casting ($1-2)
30. silver/gray body, purple interior, gray plastic base, white & purple design tempa, silver 6 spoke spiral wheels, China casting ($1-2)
31. silver-gray body, purple interior, gray plastic base, white & purple design tempa, 5 spoke concave star wheels, China casting ($2-4)
32. candy apple red body, black & white interior, chrome plastic base, black & white design tempa, chrome disc with rubber tires, China casting ($3-5)(PC9)
33. yellow body, black & white interior, chrome plastic base, detailed trim tempa, chrome disc with rubber tires, China casting ($3-5)(CP)
34. red body, black & red interior, chrome plastic base, detailed trim tempa, chrome disc with rubber tires, China casting ($3-5)(CP)
35. green body, black interior, gray plastic base, white & purple design tempa, 5 spoke concave star wheels, China casting ($1-2)
36. dark green body, chrome plastic base, white & black interior, detailed trim tempa, chrome disc with rubber tires, China casting ($3-5)(CP)
37. black body, chrome plastic base, red & black interior, detailed trim tempa, chrome disc with rubber tires, China casting ($3-5)(CP)
38. bright blue body, chrome plastic base, black & white interior, detailed trim tempa, chrome disc with rubber tires, China casting ($3-5)(CP)
39. white body, chrome plastic base, red & black interior, detailed trim tempa, chrome disc with rubber tires, China casting ($3-5)(CP)
40. salmon pink body, chrome plastic base, black & white interior, detailed trim tempa, chrome disc with rubber tires, China casting ($15-20)(GC)
41. metallic red body, gray plastic base, black interior, white & purple design tempa, 5 spoke concave star wheels, China casting ($1-2)(MW74)
42. metallic gold body, chrome plastic base, black interior, no tempa, 5 spoke concave star wheels, China casting ($5-10)(CH58)

MB40-D ROCKET TRANSPORTER, issued 1985 (ROW)
MB60-H ROCKET TRANSPORTER, issued 1990 (USA)
1. white body, blue windows, white rockets, "NASA" with US flag tempa, silver hubs, Macau casting ($1-2)
2. white body, blue windows, white rockets, "NASA" with US flag tempa, silver hubs, China casting ($1-2)
3. black body, blue windows, dark gray rockets, yellow & gray camouflage tempa, black hubs, China casting ($25-35)(CM)
4. white body, blue windows, white rockets, "NASA" with checkers tempa, silver hubs, China casting ($1-2)
5. pink-tan body, smoke windows, pink-tan rockets, green & brown camouflage tempa, black hubs, Thailand casting ($1-2)(MP)
6. white body, blue windows, white rockets, "NASA" with checkers tempa, silver hubs, Thailand casting ($1-2)
7. white body, blue windows, white rockets (rocket has print on 1 side only), "NASA" with checkers tempa, silver hubs, Thailand casting ($1-2)
8. green body, smoke green windows, green rockets, black hubs, black & brown camouflage tempa, Thailand casting ($1-2)(MP)
9. olive body, smoke green windows, olive rockets, black hubs, "T-7871-6" tempa, Thailand casting ($1-2)
10. beige body, smoke windows, black rockets, black hubs, brown camouflage tempa, Thailand casting ($1-2)(MP)
11. white body, smoke green windows, gray rockets, black hubs, gray & olive camouflage tempa, Thailand casting ($1-2)(MP)
12. dark sand body, smoke windows, dark sand rockets, black hubs, "T-7871-6" & star tempa, Thailand casting ($1-2)(MP)
13. black body, blue windows, red rockets, black hubs, skull & crossbones tempa, Thailand casting ($3-5)(AU)
14. white body, smoke windows, olive rockets, black hubs, gray & olive camouflage tempa, Thailand casting ($1-2)(PS)
15. black body, smoke green windows, black rockets, black hubs, green & brown camouflage tempa, Thailand casting ($1-2)(MP)
16. black body, smoke green windows, black rockets, black hubs, green & brown camouflage tempa, China casting ($1-2)(MP)

MB40-F ROAD ROLLER, issued 1991 (USA)
MB68-H ROAD ROLLER, issued 1991 (ROW)
1. dark orange body, & base, dark gray interior, 5 crown rear wheels, blue stripes tempa, Thailand casting ($1-2)
2. orange-yellow body & base, dark gray interior, 5 crown rear wheels, red stripes & design tempa, Thailand casting ($1-2)
3. orange body & base, dark gray interior, 5 crown rear wheels, black stripes & design tempa, Thailand casting ($1-2)(MP)

MB40-G FORD MONDEO, issued 1995 (USA)
MB33-I FORD MONDEO, issued 1995 (ROW)
1. blue body, tan interior, 6-spoke spiral wheels, "15ICS" with blue "Mondeo" tempa, Thailand casting ($1-2)
2. blue body, tan interior, 6-spoke spiral wheels, "15ICS" with red "Mondeo" tempa, Thailand casting ($1-2)
3. blue body, tan interior, 5 spoke concave star wheels, "Ford" logo tempa, Thailand casting ($1-2)
4. white body, red interior, 5 spoke concave star wheels, "Airport Security" tempa, China casting ($10-15)(PS)

MB40-H 1969 CAMARO SS-396, issued 1997
NOTE: All models with clear windows, black base & China casting unless otherwise noted
1. metallic blue body, black interior, 5 spoke concave star wheels, "Camaro SS" & dual white stripes tempa ($1-2)
2. red body, black interior, 5 spoke concave star wheels, dual white stripes tempa ($1-2)(AP)
3. dark green body, white & black interior, dual white stripes tempa ($3-5)(PC17)
4. metallic blue body, black interior, 5 spoke concave star wheels, dual white stripes & "Great Camaro Gathering 1997" tempa ($35-50)(C2)
5. white body, bright red interior, 5 spoke concave star wheels, dual black stripes tempa ($1-2)(MW33)
6. white body, dark red interior, 5 spoke concave star wheels, dual black stripes tempa ($1-2)(MW33)
7. orange body, white & black interior, chrome disc with rubber wheels, white & black stripes tempa ($3-5)(PC20)
8. metallic gold body, black interior, 5 spoke concave star wheels, no tempa ($5-10)(CH)

MB40-I FJ HOLDEN VAN , issued 1998 (ROW)
MB282 FJ HOLDEN VAN, issued 1995 (AU)
NOTE: All models listed with clear windows, black interior, black base, solid disc wheels & China casting unless otherwise note. This model was never given a series number until 1998 when it was introduced in the ROW line in 1998
1. white body, "Kids World" & blue oblong tempa ($4-6)(AU)
2. orange-red body, "Royal Mail" tempa ($4-6)(AU)
3. white body, "Auto One" tempa ($4-6)(AU)
4. black body, no tempa ($4-6)(AU)
5. black body, "Sunday Age/ View" tempa ($25-35)(LD)(AU)
6. black body, "Automodels for Model Cars 1995" tempa ($25-35)(LD)(AU)
7. baby blue body, "Your Own Promotional Van/ Matchbox- Your Logo Here" tempa ($20-25)(AU)
8. black body, "Automodels For Model Cars 1996" tempa ($25-35)(LD)(AU)
9. white & dark blue body, "Premiers 1995" tempa ($3-5)(AU)
10. white & black body, "Magpies" tempa ($3-5)(AU)
11. white & dark blue body, "Cats" tempa ($3-5)(AU)
12. white & dark blue body, "Blues" tempa ($3-5)(AU)
13. white & blue body, "Kangaroos" tempa ($3-5)(AU)
14. red & white body, "Sydney" tempa ($3-5)(AU)
15. red & green body, "Dockers" tempa ($3-5)(AU)
16. red & blue body, "Bulldogs" tempa ($3-5)(AU)
17. red & dark blue body, "Demons" tempa ($3-5)(AU)
18. red & black body "Bombers" tempa ($3-5)(AU)
19. light red & black body, "Saints" tempa ($3-5)(AU)
20. burgundy & yellow body, "Bears" tempa ($3-5)(AU)
21. brown & yellow body, "Hawks" tempa ($3-5)(AU)
22. yellow & blue body, "West Coast" tempa ($3-5)(AU)
23. yellow & dark blue body, "Crows" tempa ($3-5)(AU)
24. yellow & black body, "Tigers" tempa ($3-5)(AU)
25. red & blue body, "lions" tempa ($3-5)(AU)
26. baby blue body, "Bevic" tempa ($18-25)(AU)
27. blue body, "True Blue" tempa ($3-5)(AU)
28. red body, "Matchbox" tempa, China casting ($1-2)(MW40-ROW)
29. white body, "Laverne & Shirley/ Shotz" tempa, China casting ($4-6)(STR)

MB41-A FORD GT, issued 1970
1. white body, black base, "6" label, 5 spoke wheels ($12-15)
2. white body, light green base, "6" label, 5 spoke wheels ($12-15)
3. white body, dark green base, "6" label, 5 spoke wheels ($12-15)
4. bronze body, black base, "6" label, 5 spoke wheels ($12-15)
5. bronze body, light yellow base, "6" label, 5 spoke wheels ($12-15)
6. bronze body, dark yellow base, "6" label, 5 spoke wheels ($12-15)
7. bronze body, green base, "6" label, 5 spoke wheels ($12-15)
8. bronze body, charcoal base, "6" label, 5 spoke wheels ($12-15)
9. bronze body, light gray base, "6" label, 5 spoke wheels ($12-15)
10. bronze body, dark gray base, "6" label, 5 spoke wheels ($12-15)
11. white body, black base, cat head label, 5 spoke wheels ($15-20)
12. white body, black base, "6" label (from MB62-C Renault), 5 spoke wheels ($18-25)
13. white body, black base, "6" label (from MB62-C Renault), dot dash wheels ($18-25)
14. yellow body, black base, no label, dot dash wheels ($650-800)(MP)(IT)
NOTE: Available as an Hungarian and Bulgarian casting. Assorted colors available. ($15-25)

MB41-B SIVA SPYDER, issued 1972
NOTE: All models with clear windows unless otherwise noted.
1. red body, no tempa, cream interior, chrome body strap, 5 spoke wheels ($15-20)
2. red body, no tempa, cream interior, black body strap, 5 spoke wheels ($12-15)
3. red body, no tempa, white interior, black body strap, 5 spoke wheels ($12-15)
4. red body, no tempa, ivory interior, black body strap, 5 spoke wheels ($12-15)
5. red body, no tempa, ivory interior, black body strap, 4 spoke wheels ($12-15)
6. dark blue body, stripes tempa, ivory interior, black body strap, 5 spoke wheels ($15-18)
7. dark blue body, stripes tempa, white interior, black body strap, 5 spoke wheels ($15-18)
8. dark blue body, stripes tempa, cream interior, black body strap, 5 spoke wheels ($15-18)
9. powder blue body, spider & web tempa, ivory interior, black body strap, 5 spoke wheels ($15-18)(LE)
10. powder blue body, spider & web tempa, ivory interior, black body strap, 5 spoke wheels, black windows ($15-18)(LE)

MB41-C AMBULANCE, issued 1977
1. white body, unpainted base, gray interior, "Ambulance" & cross labels ($5-8)
2. white body, unpainted base, light yellow interior, "Ambulance" & cross labels ($5-8)
3. white body, unpainted base, orange interior, "Ambulance" & cross labels ($7-10)
4. white body, unpainted (tab) base, gray interior, "Ambulance" & cross labels ($25-50)(BR)
5. white body, unpainted base, gray interior, "Emergency Medical Service" labels ($5-8)
6. white body, unpainted base, light yellow interior, "Emergency Medical Service" labels ($5-8)
7. white body, unpainted base, orange interior, "Emergency Medical Service" labels ($7-10)
8. white body, unpainted base, dark tan interior, "Emergency Medical Service" labels ($5-8)
9. white body, silver-gray base, light yellow interior, "Emergency Medical Service" labels ($5-8)
10. white body, unpainted base, gray interior, "Ambulance" & EMS logo labels ($5-8)
11. white body, silver-gray base, gray interior, "Ambulance" & EMS logo labels ($5-8)
12. white body, unpainted base, gray interior, small "Ambulance" labels ($15-18)
13. silver-gray body, unpainted base, gray interior, "Paris Dakar 81" labels ($25-30)(FR)
14. red body, unpainted base, gray interior, "Notarzt" tempa ($25-40)(GR)
15. white body, unpainted base, gray interior, maroon "Pacific Ambulance" tempa ($6-8)(CR)
16. white body, unpainted base, gray interior, red "Pacific Ambulance" tempa ($6-8)(CR)
17. white body, silver-gray base, gray interior, red "Pacific Ambulance" tempa ($6-8)(CR)

MB41-D KENWORTH AERODYNE, issued 1982 (USA)
NOTE: Other variations on this model exist as cabs to Convoy models but these are not listed as singles. England base models 1-3 have "Lesney"

cast. Version 4 onwards with England base have "Matchbox International" cast.
1. red body, amber windows, black & white flared stripes tempa, England base ($3-5)
2. red body, clear windows, black & white flared stripes tempa, England casting ($3-5)
3. red body, clear windows, black & white straight stripes tempa, England casting ($3-5)
4. red body, clear windows, black & white straight stripes tempa, England casting ($3-5)
5. red body, clear windows, black & white curved stripes tempa, England casting ($3-5)
6. black body, clear windows, orange/yellow/white stripes tempa, Macau casting ($4-6)
7. pearly silver body, clear windows, red & blue stripes tempa, Macau casting ($3-5)
8. blue body, clear windows, no tempa, Macau casting ($4-6)(MP)
NOTE: Above model normally associated with CY-9A Mitre 10 Convoy but found as a release in multipacks

MB41-F JAGUAR XJ6, issued 1987 (USA)
MB 1-E JAGUAR XJ6, issued 1987 (ROW)
NOTE: Following models with black base, clear windows and 8 dot wheels.
1. metallic red body, tan interior, no tempa, doors open, metal base, Macau casting ($1-2)
2. black body, maroon interior, "W&M" & crest tempa, doors open, metal base, Macau casting ($25-40)(UK)(OP)
3. green body, maroon interior, "Redoxon/ Jaguar" tempa, doors open, metal base, Macau casting ($18-25)(HK)
4. white body, black interior, no tempa, doors open, metal base, Macau casting($7-10)(KS)
5. metallic red body, tan interior, no tempa, doors open, metal base, Thailand casting ($1-2)
NOTE: Versions 1-5 with doors cast open & metal bases. Below versions doors cast shut & plastic bases.
6. blue body, black base, tan interior, clear windows, 8 dot wheels, no tempa, Thailand casting ($2-3)(SS)
7. white body, black base, tan interior, clear windows, 8 dot wheels, "Police" with shield & checkers tempa, Thailand casting ($2-4)
8. metallic blue body, blue base, tan interior, chrome windows, gray disc with rubber tires, detailed trim tempa, Thailand casting ($2-4)(WC)
9. met. silver blue body, black base, white interior, blue windows, 8 dot wheels, no tempa, Thailand casting ($2-4)(GS)
10. dark green body, black base, black & tan interior, clear windows, chrome disc with rubber tires, detailed trim tempa, Thailand casting ($8-12)(UC)
11. charcoal body, charcoal base, black & red interior, clear windows, chrome disc with rubber tires, detailed trim tempa, Thailand casting ($3-5)(JC)(PC)
12. white body, gray base, blue interior, clear windows, 8 dot wheels, "Police" with shield & checkers tempa , Thailand casting($1-2)(MW27-ROW)
13. white body, gray base, blue interior, clear windows, 8 dot wheels, "Police" with shield & checkers tempa , China casting($1-2)(MW27-ROW)

MB42-A IRON FAIRY CRANE, issued 1970
NOTE: all models with yellow base, yellow interior, 4 spoke wheels & yellow hook.
1. red body, yellow boom ($65-80)
2. red body, lime boom ($250-350)
3. dark orange-red body, yellow boom ($40-55)
4. dark orange-red body, lime boom ($40-55)
5. light orange-red body, lime boom ($40-55)

MB42-B TYRE FRYER, issued 1972
1. light blue body, black base, yellow interior, no labels, 5 spoke front wheels ($12-15)
2. mid blue body, unpainted base, yellow interior, no labels, 5 spoke front wheels ($12-15)
3. mid blue body, black base, yellow interior, no labels, 5 spoke front wheels ($12-15)
4. mid blue body, black base, yellow interior, no labels, maltese cross front wheels ($12-15)
5. mid blue body, black base, orange-yellow interior, no labels, 5 spoke front wheels ($12-15)
6. dark blue body, black base, yellow interior, no labels, 5 spoke front wheels ($12-15)
7. orange body, black base, yellow interior, "Jaffa Mobile" labels, 5 spoke front wheels ($85-110)(UK)(OP)

MB42-C MERCEDES CONTAINER TRUCK, issued 1977
1. red body, beige container, red roof & doors, black base, blue windows, "Sealand" labels ($5-7)
2. red body, beige container, red roof & doors, unpainted base, blue windows, "Sealand" labels ($5-7)
3. red body, beige container, red roof & doors, unpainted base, blue windows, "N.Y.K." labels ($5-7)
4. red body, beige container, red roof & doors, black base, blue windows, "N.Y.K." labels ($5-7)
5. red body, beige container, red roof & doors, unpainted base, blue windows, "N.Y.K." labels, black hubs ($5-7)
6. red body, beige container, red roof & doors, unpainted base, blue windows, "Sealand" labels, black hubs ($5-7)
7. red body, beige container, red roof & doors, unpainted base, blue windows, "O.C.L." labels ($10-15)
8. yellow body, yellow container, roof & doors, black base, blue windows, "Deutsche Bundespost" labels ($25-40)(GR)
9. red body, beige container, red roof & doors, unpainted base, blue windows, "Confern" labels ($35-45)(GR)
10. red body, yellow-tan container, red roof & doors, unpainted base, blue windows, "Sealand" labels ($5-7)
11. red body, white container, red roof & doors, blue windows, "Matchbox" labels ($8-12)
12. red body, white container, red roof & doors, purple windows, "Matchbox" labels ($8-12)
13. red body, white container, red roof & doors, unpainted base, purple windows, "Mayflower" labels ($8-12)
14. red body, white container, red roof & doors, unpainted base, blue windows, "Mayflower" labels ($8-12)
15. red body, white container, red roof & doors, unpainted base, blue windows, "Confern" applied over "Mayflower" labels ($45-60)
16. green body, green container, yellow roof & doors, unpainted base, blue windows, "Confern" applied over "Mayflower" labels ($100-150)
17. green body, green container, yellow roof & doors, unpainted base, purple windows, "Confern" applied over "Mayflower" labels ($100-150)
18. green body, green container, yellow roof & doors, unpainted base, purple windows, "Mayflower" labels ($6-8)
19. green body, green container, yellow roof & doors, unpainted base, red windows, "Mayflower" labels ($6-8)
20. green body, green container, orange roof & doors, unpainted base, red windows, "Mayflower" labels ($6-8)
21. green body, green container, orange roof & doors, unpainted base, purple windows, "Mayflower" labels ($6-8)
22. green body, green container, orange roof & doors, unpainted base, blue windows, "Mayflower" labels ($6-8)
23. blue body, blue container, roof & doors, unpainted base, blue windows, "Karstadt" labels ($35-50)(GR)
24. red body, gray plastic dump, unpainted base, blue windows , white label with stripes ($50-75)(PS)

MB42-D 1957 FORD THUNDERBIRD, issued 1982
1. red body, unpainted metal base, white interior, clear windows, no tempa, dot dash wheels, England casting ($3-5)
2. red body, unpainted metal base, white interior, clear windows, no tempa, 5 arch wheels, England casting ($3-5)
3. red body, silver-gray base, white interior, clear windows, 5 arch wheels, no tempa, England casting ($3-5)
4. cream & red body, pearly silver metal base, clear windows, red interior, with tempa, Macau casting ($3-5)
5. cream & red body, pearly silver metal base, light amber windows, with tempa, 5 arch wheels, Macau casting ($3-5)
6. cream & red body, pearly silver metal base, clear windows, with tempa, 5 arch wheels, China casting ($3-5)
7. black body, pearly silver metal base, red interior, clear windows, no tempa, 5 arch wheels, China casting ($3-5)
8. black body, pearly silver metal base, red interior, clear windows, dot dash front & 5 arch rear wheels, China casting ($3-5)
9. turquoise body, pearly silver metal base, white interior, clear windows, 5 arch wheels, , "Chubby's" tempa, China casting ($8-12)(US)
10. black body, chrome plastic base, red & white interior, clear windows, chrome disc with rubber tires, detailed trim tempa, China casting ($3-5)(PC3)
11. red body, chrome plastic base, white interior, clear windows, 5 arch wheels, "Celebrating Patsy" tempa, China casting ($12-15)(US)
12. met. candy red body, chrome plastic base, white & red interior, clear windows, chrome disc with rubber tires, detailed trim tempa, China casting ($3-5)(PC6)
13. turquoise body, chrome plastic base, white & turquoise interior, clear windows, chrome disc with rubber tires, detailed trim tempa, China casting ($10-15)(YST)
14. iridescent white body, chrome plastic base, red interior, clear windows, 5 arch wheels, no tempa, China casting ($1-2)(MP)
15. red body, chrome plastic base, white & red interior, clear windshield, chrome disc with rubber tires, detailed trim tempa, China casting ($3-5)(SC3)
16. blue body, chrome plastic base, white & red interior, clear windshield, chrome disc with rubber tires, yellow & orange flames tempa, China casting ($3-5)(PC11)
15. white body, chrome plastic base, red & pink interior, clear windshield, chrome disc with rubber tires, detailed trim tempa, China casting ($15-20)(GC)
16. blue body, chrome plastic base, white interior, clear windshield, 5 arch wheels, yellow & orange flames tempa, China casting ($50+)(CHI)
17. lemon body, chrome plastic base, black & white interior, clear windshield, chrome disc with rubber tires, detailed trim tempa, China casting ($3-5)(PC17)
18. metallic silver body, chrome plastic base, blue & white tempa, clear windshield, chrome disc with rubber tires, T-Bird design tempa, China casting ($3-5)(PC20)

MB42-E FAUN CRANE TRUCK, issued 1984 (ROW)
MB42-E FAUN CRANE TRUCK, issued 1987 (USA)
1. yellow body, yellow metal crane cab, black boom, red hook, "Reynolds Crane Hire" tempa, England casting ($2-3)
2. yellow body, yellow metal crane cab, black boom, red hook, "Reynolds Crane Hire" tempa, Macau casting ($1-2)
3. yellow body, yellow metal crane cab, black boom, red hook, "Reynolds Crane Hire" tempa, China casting ($1-2)
4. yellow body, yellow metal crane cab, black boom, red hook, no tempa, Macau casting ($2-3)(MC)
5. yellow body, yellow plastic crane cab, black boom, red hook, "Reynolds Crane Hire" tempa, Thailand casting ($1-2)
6. yellow body, yellow plastic crane cab, black boom, red hook, no tempa, Thailand casting ($2-3)(MC)
7. yellow body, red plastic cane cab, black boom, red hook, bridge & road design tempa, Thailand casting ($1-2)
8. yellow body, florescent orange plastic crane cab, black boom, red hook, checkers & "IC" logo tempa, bar code on base, China casting ($10-15)(IC)
9. yellow body, fluorescent orange plastic crane cab, black boom, red hook, checkers & "IC" logo tempa, (base without bar code), China casting ($12-15)
10. orange body, gray plastic crane cab, black boom, gray hook, bridge & road design tempa, Thailand casting ($1-2)(MP)
11. florescent orange body, black plastic crane cab, silver-gray boom, black hook, no tempa, Thailand casting ($1-2)
12. florescent orange body, gray plastic crane cab, black boom, gray hook, no tempa, China casting ($1-2)(MP)
13. pale florescent orange body, black plastic crane cab, silver-gray boom, black hook, no tempa, China casting ($1-2)
14. dark orange body, black plastic crane cab, black boom, black hook, no tempa, China casting ($1-2)
15. light orange body, black plastic crane cab, yellow & lemon boom with lever, black hook, road design tempa, China casting ($1-2)(AS)
16. metallic gold body, black plastic crane cab, black boom, black hook, no tempa, China casting ($5-10)(CH)
17. powder blue body, black plastic crane cab, silver-gray boom, black hook, no tempa, China casting ($1-2)
18. red body, black plastic crane cab, silver-gray boom, black hook, no tempa, China casting ($1-2)(MW15)
19. blue-green body, black plastic cab, silver-gray boom, black hook, dolphin & waves tempa, China casting ($2-4)(AV)

MB43-A PONY TRAILER, issued 1970
NOTE: versions 1 to 14 with two white plastic horses. Versions 15 to 18 with two black plastic horses.
1. yellow body, light green base, no label, gray tailgate, 5 spoke wheels, England casting ($18-25)
2. yellow body, dark green base, no label, gray tailgate, 5 spoke wheels, England casting ($18-25)
3. orange body, black base, horse head label, brown tailgate, 5 spoke center cut wheels, England casting ($4-6)(TP)
4. orange body, charcoal base, horse head label, brown tailgate, 5 spoke center cut wheels, England casting ($4-6)(TP)
5. orange body, black base, no label, brown tailgate, 5 spoke center cut wheels, England casting ($4-6)(TP)
6. beige body, black base, horse head label, brown tailgate, 5 spoke center cut wheels, England casting ($4-6)(TP)
7. beige body, charcoal base, horse head label, brown tailgate, 5 spoke center cut wheels, England casting ($4-6)(TP)
8. beige body, black base, no label, brown tailgate, 5 spoke center cut wheels, England casting ($4-6)(TP)
9. beige body, silver-gray base, no label, lime tailgate, dot dash wheels, England casting ($7-10)(TP)
10. beige body, unpainted base, no label, lime tailgate, dot dash wheels, England casting ($7-10)(TP)
11. beige body, black base, horse head label, brown tailgate, dot dash wheels, England casting ($3-5)(TP)
12. beige body, black base, "Silver Shoes" tempa, brown tailgate, dot dash wheels, England casting ($4-6)
13. beige body, black base, "Silver Shoes" tempa, white tailgate, dot dash wheels, Macau casting ($2-3)(TP)
14. beige body, black base, "Silver Shoes" tempa, white tailgate, dot dash wheels, no origin cast ($2-3)(TP)
15. white body, black base, "Polizei" & checkers tempa, blue-gray tailgate, dot dash wheels, no origin cast ($2-3)(TP)
16. white body, black base, horse silhouette tempa, lime tailgate, dot dash wheels, no origin cast ($1-2)(TP)
17. green body with white roof, black base, "Polizei" tempa, green tailgate, dot dash wheels, no origin cast ($1-2)(TP)
18. white body with red roof, black base, black & red dashed stripes tempa, white tailgate, dot dash wheels, no origin cast ($1-2)(TP)

MB43-B DRAGON WHEELS, issued 1972
NOTE: all models with chrome interior, amber windows & maltese cross rear wheels unless otherwise noted.
1. light green body, black base, 5 spoke front wheels ($15-18)
2. dark green body, black base, 5 spoke front wheels ($15-18)
3. dark green body, unpainted base, 5 spoke front wheels ($15-18)
4. dark green body, blue-gray base, 5 spoke front wheels ($15-18)
5. dark green body, gray base, 5 spoke front wheels ($15-18)
6. dark green body, black base, dot dash front wheels ($15-18)
7. dark green body, black base, dot dash front & rear wheels ($15-18)

MB43-C 0-4-0 STEAM LOCO, issued 1978
NOTE: all models with black train wheels unless otherwise noted.
1. red body, black boiler, black base, "4345" labels, England casting ($4-6)
2. red body, black boiler, black base, "NP" labels, England casting ($8-12)
3. red body, charcoal boiler, black base, "4345" labels, England casting ($4-6)
4. cherry red body, black boiler, black base, "4345" labels, England casting ($4-6)
5. metallic red body, black boiler, black base, "4345" labels, no origin cast ($150-200)(BR)
6. green body, black boiler, black base, "4345" labels, England casting ($8-12)
7. green body, black boiler, black base, "NP" labels, England casting ($5-8)(TP)
8. black body, black boiler, black base, "British Railways" tempa, Macau

casting ($6-8)(UK)
9. red body, black boiler, black base, "4345" tempa, Macau casting ($2-4)(MC)
10. green body, black boiler, black base, "4345" tempa, Macau casting ($2-4)(MC)
11. green body, black boiler, black base, "West Somerset Railway" tempa, Macau casting ($6-8)(UK)
12. red body, black boiler, black base, "North Yorkshire Moors" (all white) tempa, Macau casting ($6-8)(UK)
13. red body, black boiler, black base, "North Yorkshire Moors Railway" (white & black) tempa, Macau casting ($15-20)(SW)
14. yellow body, red boiler, blue base & wheels, "123/efg" tempa, Macau casting ($6-8)(LL)
15. blue body, black boiler, black base, "Hutchinson" tempa, Macau casting ($6-8)(UK)
16. green body, black boiler, black base, white emblem tempa, Macau casting ($15-20)(UK)(OP)
17. matt olive body, black boiler, black base, "GWR" tempa, Macau casting ($6-8)(UK)
18. matt black body, black spoiler, black base, "British Railways" tempa, Macau casting ($6-8)(UK)
19. yellow body, lime boiler, blue base & wheels, "123/ 456" tempa, Macau casting ($6-8)(LL)
20. blue body, black boiler, black base, red coachline tempa, Macau casting ($6-8)(UK)
21. yellow body, lime boiler, blue base & wheels, "123/ 456" tempa, China casting ($6-8)(LL)
22. green body, black boiler, black base, "British Railways" (red, black & white) tempa, China casting ($1-2)
23. red body, black boiler, black base, "4345" tempa, China casting ($2-3)(MP)
24. green body, black boiler, black base, white Kellogg's rooster head tempa, China casting ($75-100)(FR)(DU)(OP)
25. white body, white boiler, white base, no tempa, China casting ($10-15)(GF)
26. green body, black boiler, black base, "British Railways" (red & white) tempa, China casting ($1-2)
25. red-brown body, black boiler, black base, "Gold Rush Australia" tempa, China casting ($4-6)(AU)

MB43-D PETERBILT CONVENTIONAL, issued 1982 (USA)

NOTE: Other variations exist as components to Convoy models. Only single releases are listed here. England bases are either (L) Lesney or (M) Matchbox International. All models with chrome exhausts unless otherwise noted.

1. black body, amber windows, white & red design tempa, England (L) casting ($4-6)
2. black body, clear windows, white & red design tempa, England (L) casting ($4-6)
3. black body, amber windows, white & red "Ace" tempa, England (L) casting ($4-6)
4. black body, clear windows, white & red "Ace" tempa, England (L) tempa ($4-6)
5. black body, clear windows, white & brown "Ace" tempa, England (L) tempa ($4-6)
6. black body, amber windows, white & black design tempa, England (L) casting ($4-6)
7. black body, amber windows, white & red "Ace" tempa, England (M) casting ($2-4)
8. black body, clear windows, white & red "Ace" tempa, England (M) casting ($2-4)
9. black body, clear windows, white & red "Z" pattern tempa, England (M) casting ($3-5)
10. black body, amber windows, white & red "Z" pattern tempa, Macau casting ($2-4)
11. white body, clear windows, gray exhausts, "NASA" & rocket tempa, Macau casting ($3-5)(MP)

MB43-E MERCEDES 500 SEC, issued 1984

1. white body, black metal base, clear windows, blue interior, 8 dot silver wheels, "AMG" tempa, Macau casting ($2-4)
2. red body, black metal base, clear windows, black interior, 8 dot silver wheels, "AMG" tempa, Macau casting ($2-3)
3. red body, black metal base, clear windows, black interior, starburst wheels, "AMG" with stripes tempa, Macau casting ($3-5)(SF)
4. white body, black metal base, clear windows, black interior, 8 dot gold wheels, red & blue with "7" tempa, Macau casting ($2-4)
5. white body, black metal base, clear windows, black interior, 8 dot silver wheels, red & blue with "7" tempa, Macau casting ($2-4)
6. white body, black metal base, clear windows, black interior, starburst wheels, red & blue with "7" tempa, Macau casting ($75-100)
7. white body, black metal base, clear windows, black interior, 8 dot silver wheels, "AMG" on hood & sides tempa, Macau casting ($6-8)
8. black body, black metal base, clear windows, brown interior, 8 dot silver wheels, "500SEC" tempa, Macau casting ($2-3)
9. metallic red body, black metal base, clear windows, black interior, laser wheels, "AMG" & stripes tempa, Macau casting ($3-5)(LW)
10. red body, pearly silver metal base, clear windows, brown interior, 8 dot silver wheels, green & yellow stripes tempa, Macau casting ($8-12)(DU)
11. white body, pearly silver metal base, clear windows, brown interior, 8 dot silver wheels, "1 Pig Racing Team" tempa, Macau casting ($8-12)(HK)
12. black body, pearly silver metal base, clear windows, brown interior, 8 dot silver wheels, "500SEC" & stripe tempa, Macau casting ($2-3)
13. metallic red body, pearly silver metal base, clear windows, black interior, laser wheels, "AMG" & stripes tempa, Macau casting ($3-5)(LW)
14. white body, pearly silver metal base, clear windows, brown interior, 8 dot silver wheels, "500SEC" & silver stripe tempa, Macau casting ($18-25)(SU)
15. black body, black metal base, clear windows, brown interior, 8 dot silver wheels, "Redoxon/ 500SEC AMG" tempa, Macau casting ($18-25)(HK)
16. white body, black metal base, chrome windows, no interior, gray disc with rubber tires, detailed trim tempa, Macau casting ($5-8)(WC)
17. black body, black metal base, navy blue windows, no interior, 8 dot silver wheels, "Pace Car Heuer" tempa, amber dome lights, Macau casting ($7-10)(SR)
18. black body, black plastic base, navy blue windows, no interior, 8 dot silver wheels, "Pace Heuer" tempa, amber dome lights, Macau casting ($7-10)(SR)
19. white body, black metal base, black windows, no interior, 8 dot silver wheels, "Police" tempa, red dome lights, Macau casting ($7-10)(SR)
20. white body, black plastic base, black windows, no interior, 8 dot silver wheels, "Police" tempa, red dome lights, Macau casting ($7-10)(SR)
21. cream body, black metal base, black windows, no interior, 8 dot silver wheels, "Emergency Doctor" tempa, green dome lights, Macau casting ($7-10)(SR)
22. cream body, black plastic base, black windows, no interior, 8 dot silver wheels, "Emergency Doctor" tempa, green dome lights, Macau casting ($7-10)(SR)
23. cream body, black metal base, black windows, no interior, 8 dot silver wheels, "Emergency Doctor/ Rescue 911" tempa, green dome lights, China casting ($7-10)(SR)
24. white body, black metal base, black windows, no interior, 8 dot silver wheels, "Police/ Rescue 911" tempa, red dome lights, China casting ($7-10)(SR)
25. black body, black metal base, black windows, no interior, 8 dot silver wheels, "Pace Car Heuer/ Rescue 911" tempa, green dome lights, China casting ($7-10)(SR)
26. red body, silver-gray metal base, clear windows, brown interior, starburst wheels, "AMG" with stripes tempa, Macau casting ($3-5)(SF)
27. white body, black plastic base, black windows, no interior, 8 dot silver wheels, "Police 17" & blue stripe tempa, red dome lights, China casting ($3-5)(LS)
28. olive body, black plastic base, black windows, no interior, 8 dot silver wheels, "Matchbox Military Police MP-090196" tempa, green—yellow dome lights, China casting ($3-5)(LS)
29. dull olive body, black plastic base, black windows, no interior, 8 dot silver wheels, "Matchbox Military Police MP-090196" tempa, amber dome lights, China casting ($3-5)(LS)
30. silver-gray body, black plastic base, black windows, no interior, 8 dot silver wheels, "Police 17" & blue stripe tempa, red dome lights, China casting ($3-5)(LS)

MB43-G LINCOLN TOWN CAR, issued 1989 (USA)
MB24-G LINCOLN TOWN CAR, issued 1989 (ROW)

NOTE: All models with red interior, smoke windows & black base unless otherwise noted.

1. white body, metal base, dot dash wheels, no tempa, Macau casting ($1-2)
2. black body, plastic base, gray disc with rubber tires, no tempa, chrome windows, Macau casting ($5-8)(WC)
3. white body, plastic base, dot dash wheels, no tempa, Thailand casting ($1-2)
4. silver-gray body, plastic base, dot dash wheels, pink & yellow design tempa, Thailand casting ($2-3)(DM)
5. orange-yellow body, plastic base, dot dash (blue) wheels, face on hood tempa, Thailand casting ($10-15)(LL)
6. metallic maroon body, plastic base, dot dash wheels, brown rear half of roof tempa, Thailand casting ($2-4)
7. metallic maroon body, plastic base, dot dash wheels, no tempa, Thailand casting ($1-2)
8. charcoal body, plastic base, chrome disc with rubber tires, purple rear half of roof tempa, China casting ($8-12)(UC)

MB43-I CAMARO Z28, issued 1994 (USA)
MB56H CAMARO Z28, issued 1994 (ROW)

NOTE: All models with black base.

1. black body, gray interior, clear windows, gold 6-spoke spiral wheels, purple/blue/white tempa, Thailand casting ($1-2)
2. white body, no interior, chrome windows, gray disc with rubber tires, black roof tempa, Thailand casting ($2-4)(WC)
3. metallic light gold body, black interior, clear windows, chrome disc with rubber tires, "Matchbox Collectors Club" tempa, Thailand casting ($10-15)(US)
4. florescent orange body, black interior, smoke windows, silver 6-spoke spiral wheels, "Matchbox Get In The Fast Lane- 95 Premium Show" tempa, Thailand casting ($25-45)(US)
5. silver body, white interior, amber windows, silver 6-spoke spiral wheels, lavender/ purple & blue tempa, Thailand casting ($3-5)(MT)
6. black body, gray interior, smoke windows, silver 6-spoke spiral wheels, purple/ blue & white hood & side design tempa, Thailand casting ($1-2)
7. black body, white interior, clear windows, silver 6-spoke spiral wheels, purple/ blue & white side design only tempa, Thailand casting ($1-2)
8. florescent orange body, black interior, smoke windows, silver 6-spoke spiral wheels, "Matchbox Get In The Fast Lane- Melbourne Motor Show 96" tempa, Thailand casting ($25-45)(AU)
9. dark green body, dk. tan/ black interior, clear windows, chrome disc with rubber tires, black roof & detailed trim tempa, Thailand casting ($3-5)(PC2)
10. metallic blue body, gray/ black interior, clear windows, chrome disc with rubber tires, black roof & detailed trim tempa, Thailand casting ($3-5)(PC)(JC)
11. metallic charcoal body, blue interior, clear windows, silver 6-spoke spiral wheels, purple/ blue & white side design only tempa, Thailand casting ($1-2)
12. red body, black/ brown interior, clear windows, chrome disc with rubber tires, black roof & detailed trim tempa, Thailand casting ($3-5)(PC5)
13. dark purple body, black/ gray interior, clear windows, chrome disc with rubber tires, black roof & detailed trim tempa, Thailand casting ($3-5)(SC2)
14. purple chrome body, white interior, yellow windows, 5 spoke concave star wheels, orange & yellow tempa, Thailand casting ($1-2)(MP)
15. metallic charcoal body, blue interior, clear windows, 5 spoke concave star wheels, purple/blue & white design tempa, Thailand casting ($1-2)
16. candy apple red body, black & gray interior, clear windows, chrome disc with rubber tires, black roof tempa, Thailand casting ($15-20)(GC)
17. orange body, dark gray & white interior, clear windows, chrome disc with rubber tires, dual white stripes tempa, Thailand casting ($3-5)(PC14)
18. metallic gold body, black interior, clear windows, 5 spoke concave star wheels, no tempa, Thailand casting ($5-10)(CH)
19. silver-gray body, blue interior, smoke windows, 5 spoke concave star wheels, blue/ red & white design tempa, Thailand casting ($1-2)
20. fluorescent orange body, black interior, smoke windows, silver 6 spoke spiral wheels, "Matchbox Get in The Fast Lane/ Sydney Motor Show" tempa, Thailand casting ($15-25)(C2)
21. lemon body, gray & black interior, clear windows, chrome disc with rubber tires, black roof tempa, Thailand casting ($3-5)(SC4)
22. metallic turquoise body, black & gray interior, clear windows, chrome disc with rubber tires, black roof tempa, Thailand casting ($3-5)(SC5)
23. metallic purple body, silver-gray interior, clear windows, 5 spoke concave star wheels, checkers & salmon flash tempa, Thailand casting ($1-2)(MW75)
24. metallic light gold body, black interior, clear windows, chrome disc with rubber tires, "Great Camaro Gathering II 1998" tempa, Thailand casting ($35-50)(C2)
25. dark gold chrome body, white interior, yellow windows, 5 spoke concave star wheels, blue & yellow tempa, China casting ($1-2)(MP)
26. metallic purple body, silver-gray interior, clear windows, 5 spoke concave star wheels, checkers & salmon flash tempa, China casting ($1-2)(MW75)

MB44-A GMC REFRIGERATOR TRUCK, issued 1970

1. red body, turquoise container, black axle covers ($45-60)
2. yellow body, red container, black axle covers ($20-30)
3. yellow body, red container, red axle covers ($20-30)
4. yellow body, turquoise container, black axle covers ($2000+)

MB44-B BOSS MUSTANG, issued 1972

1. yellow body, black hood, unpainted base, no tempa, maltese cross wheels ($6-8)
2. yellow body, black hood, silver-gray base, no tempa, maltese cross wheels ($6-8)
3. yellow body, black hood, unpainted base, no tempa, 5 spoke front & maltese cross rear wheels ($6-8)
4. lemon body, black hood, unpainted base, no tempa, maltese cross wheels ($6-8)
5. dark green body & hood, unpainted base, with tempa, maltese cross wheels ($8-12)(LE)

NOTE: Above model issued as Limited Edition "Cobra Mustang"

MB44-C PASSENGER COACH, issued 1978

NOTE: all models with black base & black train wheels unless otherwise noted.

1. red body, flat beige roof, light green windows, train wheels, red "431 432" labels, England casting ($4-6)
2. red body, flat bone roof, light green windows, train wheels, red "431 432" labels, England casting ($4-6)
3. red body, flat beige roof, dark green windows, train wheels, red "431 432" labels, England casting ($4-6)
4. red body, flat beige roof, dark green windows, dot dash wheels,, red "431 432" labels, England casting ($6-8)\
5. red body, flat beige roof, green windows, train wheels, "NYK" labels, no origin cast ($100-150)(BR)
6. red body, flat beige roof, clear windows, train wheels, red "431 432" labels, England casting ($4-6)
7. red body, flat bone roof, clear windows, train wheels, red "431 432" labels, England casting ($4-6)
8. red body, flat beige roof, no windows, train wheels, red "431 432" labels, England casting ($4-6)
9. red body, flat bone roof, no windows, train wheels, red "431 432" labels, England casting ($4-6)
10. red body, flat cream roof, no windows, train wheels, "GWR" labels, England casting ($8-12)
11 red body, flat beige roof, no windows, train wheels, "GWR" labels, England casting ($8-12)
12. red body, flat beige roof, no windows, train wheels, "5810-6102" labels, England casting ($8-12)
13. red body, flat cream roof, no windows, train wheels, "5810-6102" labels, England casting ($8-12)
14. red body, flat beige roof, no windows, dot dash wheels, "5810-6102" labels, England casting ($8-12)
15. red body, flat tan roof, no windows, dot dash wheels, "5810-6102" labels, England casting ($8-12)
16. red body, flat beige roof, no windows, dot dash wheels, red "431 432" labels, England casting ($4-6)
17. red body, flat tan roof, no windows, dot dash wheels, red "431 432" labels, England casting ($4-6)

18. red body, flat tan roof, no windows, dot dash wheels, green "431 432" labels, England casting ($4-6)
19. red body, flat beige roof, no windows, dot dash wheels, green "431 432" labels, England casting ($4-6)
20. green body, flat beige roof, no windows, train wheels, red "431 432" labels, England casting ($8-12)
21. green body, raised beige roof, no windows, train wheels, "5810-6102" labels, England casting ($6-8)(TP)
22. red body, raised beige roof, no windows, dot dash wheels, "5810-6102" labels, England casting ($8-12)
23. red body, raised beige roof, no windows, train wheels, red "431 432" labels, England casting ($7-10)
24. red body, flat cream roof, no windows, train wheels, "431 432" tempa, Macau casting ($2-3)
25. lime & yellow body, flat red roof, blue base, no windows, blue train wheels, 2 figures with clock tempa, Macau casting ($6-8)(LL)
26. lime & yellow body, flat red roof, blue base, no windows, blue train wheels, 2 figures with clock tempa, China casting ($6-8)(LL)
27. green body, flat beige roof, no windows, train wheels, "British Railways" tempa, China casting ($2-3)(TP)
28. red body, flat cream roof, no windows, train wheels, "431 432" tempa, China casting ($1-2)(MP)
29. red body, flat cream roof, no windows, train wheels, "431 432" tempa, very small "Kellogg's" label on base, China casting ($18-25)(DU)(OP)
30. white body, flat white roof, white base, no windows, no tempa, China casting ($10-15)(GF)

MB44-D 4 X 4 CHEVY VAN, issued 1982 (USA)
MB68-D 4 X 4 CHEVY VAN, issued 1983 (ROW)
MB26-H 4 X 4 CHEVY VAN, reissued 1991 (USA)
MB10-E 4 X 4 CHEVY VAN, reissued 1993 (ROW)

1. light green body, black metal base, "Ridin High" tempa with plain hood, England casting ($3-5)
2. light green body, black metal base, "Ridin High" tempa with black horseshoes on hood, England casting ($3-5)
3. dark green body, black metal base, "Ridin High" tempa with black horseshoes on hood, England casting ($3-5)
4. dark green body, black metal base, "Ridin High" tempa with white horseshoes on hood, England casting ($7-10)
5. dark emerald green body, black metal base, "Ridin High" tempa with black horseshoes on hood, England casting ($15-18)
6. white body, black metal base, "Matchbox Racing" tempa, Macau casting ($2-3)
7. white body, black metal base, "Tokyo Giants/ Matsumoto 2" labels, Macau casting ($8-12)(JP)
8. white body, black metal base, "Tokyo Giants/ Shinozuka 6" labels, Macau casting ($8-12)(JP)
9. white body, black metal base, "Tokyo Giants/ Hara 8" labels, Macau casting ($8-12)(JP)
10. white body, black metal base, "Tokyo Giants/ Yamakura 15" labels, Macau casting ($8-12)(JP)
11. white body, black metal base, "Tokyo Giants/ Sadaoka 20" labels, Macau casting ($8-12)(JP)
12. white body, black metal base, "Tokyo Giants/ Nakahata 24" labels, Macau casting ($8-12)(JP)
13. white body, black metal base, "Tokyo Giants/ Nishimoto 26" labels, Macau casting ($8-12)(JP)
14. white body, black metal base, "Tokyo Giants/ Egawa 30" labels, Macau casting ($8-12)(JP)
15. white body, black metal base, "Castrol Racing Team" tempa, Macau casting ($7-10)(AU)
16. white body, silver-gray metal base, "Matchbox Motorsports" tempa, Macau casting ($1-2)
17. white body, gray plastic base, "Matchbox Motorsports" tempa, Macau casting ($1-2)
18. white body, gray plastic base, "Matchbox Motorsports" tempa, Thailand casting ($1-2)
19. white body, black plastic base, no tempa, Thailand casting ($10-15)(GF)
20. fluorescent yellow body, gray plastic base, blue & pink design tempa, Thailand casting ($1-2)
21. black body, gray plastic base, pink & green design tempa, Thailand casting ($1-2)(MP)
22. white body, gray plastic base, "Surf's Up" with wave design tempa, Thailand casting ($1-2)(MP)
23. black body, gray plastic base, "S.W.A.T. Unit 5" & gold star tempa, Thailand casting ($1-2)(MP)
24. green & purple body, gray plastic base, "23rd National Truck-In" tempa, Thailand casting ($8-12)(US)
25. white body, gray plastic base, purple & green design tempa, Thailand casting ($1-2)
26. red body, gray plastic base, "Claws" tempa, Thailand casting ($1-2)
27. metallic gold body, black plastic base, no tempa, Thailand casting ($5-10)(CH26)
28. black body, gray plastic base, skeleton & "Stegosaurus" tempa, Thailand casting ($1-2)(MP)
29. black body, gray plastic base, skeleton & "Stegosaurus" tempa, China casting ($1-2)(MP)
30. white body, gray plastic base, "Matchbox Motorsports/ PA Matchbox Collectors Club 20th Anniversary" tempa, Thailand casting ($10-15)(ASAP)

MB44-E CITROEN 15CV, issued 1983 (ROW)
NOTE: All models with 5 crown wheels unless otherwise noted.
1. black body, chrome base, light gray interior, England casting ($2-3)
2. black body, chrome base, silver-gray interior, England casting ($2-3)
3. black body, chrome base, beige interior, England casting ($2-3)
4. black body, chrome base, white interior, England casting ($2-3)
5. black body, chrome base, silver-gray interior, Macau casting ($2-3)
6. dark blue body, chrome base, silver-gray interior, Macau casting ($2-3)
7. dark blue body, chrome base, red interior, Macau casting ($2-3)
8. dark green body, chrome base, red interior, Macau casting ($8-12)(DY)
9. black body, gray base, cream interior, 5 arch wheels, China casting ($4-6)(MP)

MB44-F DATSUN 280ZX POLICE CAR, issued 1987 (JP)
1. white & black body, clear windows, opaque red dome lights, tan interior, black base, Japanese lettered tempa, 5 arch wheels, Macau casting ($8-12)(JP)

MB44-G SKODA 130LR, issued 1987 (ROW)
NOTE: All models with powder blue base, red trunk, black interior, clear windows and 8 dot wheels.
1. white body, "Skoda 44" with "Duckhams" on sides tempa, Macau casting ($2-4)
2. white body, "Skoda 44" without "Duckhams" on sides tempa, Macau casting ($2-4)
3. white body, "Skoda 44" with "Duckhams" on sides tempa, China casting ($2-4)

MB44-H 1921 MODEL T FORD VAN, issued 1990
NOTE: All models with clear windshield, plastic chassis & black plastic spoked wheels unless otherwise noted.
1. yellow body, red roof, blue chassis, "Bird's Custard Powder" tempa, Macau casting ($1-2)
2. cream body, dark blue roof, dark blue chassis, "5th MICA Convention 1990" tempa, Macau casting ($8-10)(UK)
3. cream body, dark blue roof, dark blue chassis, "3rd MICA NA Convention 1990" tempa, Macau casting ($8-10)(US)
4. red body with black hood, black roof, black chassis, "Royal Mail GR" tempa, Macau casting ($7-10)(UK)
5. white body, powder blue roof & chassis, "Para 90" tempa, Macau casting ($8-10)(UK)
6. white body, powder blue roof & chassis, "Chester Doll Hospital/ World's Largest Matchbox Display" tempa, Macau casting ($8-10)(UK)
7. dark green body, black roof, dark charcoal chassis, "Swarfega" tempa, Macau casting ($35-50)(UK)(OP)
8. black body, black roof & chassis, "Mars" tempa, Macau casting ($10-15)(UK)
9. cream body, red roof, green chassis, "PG Tips" tempa, Macau casting ($15-20)(UK)(OP)
10. cream body, red roof, green chassis, "PG Tips" tempa, China casting ($15-20)(UK)(OP)
11. yellow body, red roof, blue chassis, "Bird's Custard Powder" tempa, China casting ($2-3)
12. black body, black roof & chassis, "4th M.I.C.A. NA Convention/ Detroit Motor City" tempa, China casting ($8-12)(US)
13. red body, red roof, black chassis, "Mars" tempa, China casting ($15-20)(UK)
14. white body, powder blue roof & chassis, "M.I.C.A. 7- I Could Have Danced All Night" labels, Macau casting ($10-15)(UK)(C2)
15. cream body, dark blue roof & chassis, "Greetings From Philadelphia 1992/ MICA NA" labels, Macau casting ($10-15)(US)(C2)
16. white body, red roof, dark blue chassis, "Lloyds" tempa, China casting ($10-15)(UK)
17. black body, black roof & chassis, "William Lusty" tempa, China casting ($6-8)(UK)
18. white body, red roof, dark blue chassis, "Dale Farm" tempa, China casting ($7-10)(UK)
19. powder blue body, black roof, dark blue chassis, "Goodyear Tyres" tempa, China casting ($1-2)
20. dark blue body, black roof & chassis, "Kellogg's Corn Flakes" tempa, China casting ($15-20)(AU)(OP)
21. black body, black roof & chassis, "Philadelphia MICA NA" labels, China casting ($10-15)(C2)
22. white body, black roof & chassis, "Financial Times" tempa, China casting ($8-12)(UK)
23. red body, black roof & chassis, "Matchbox Toy Delivery" tempa, China casting ($2-4) (CC)
24. yellow body, red roof & chassis, "Vegemite" tempa, China casting ($7-10)(AU)(OP)
25. yellow body, blue roof & chassis, "Chesdale" tempa, China casting ($7-10)(AU)(OP)
26. blue body, yellow roof & chassis, "Kraft" tempa, China casting ($7-10)(AU)(OP)
27. blue body, red roof & chassis, "Craig's" tempa, China casting ($7-10)(AU)(OP)
28. orange-red body, black roof & chassis, "P.M.G." tempa, China casting ($7-10)(AU)
NOTE: All models below with China casting unless otherwise noted.
29. dark blue body & roof, black plastic chassis, "Matchbox USA 95" tempa ($15-25)(LD)(US)
30. white body, blue roof, black plastic chassis, "Lowestoft Town Football Club/ Blues of Crown Meadow" tempa ($25-40)(LD)(UK)
31. white body, white roof, black plastic chassis, "Lowestoft Town Football Club/ John Grose Ford" tempa ($25-40)(LD)(UK)
32. white body, white roof, black plastic chassis, "Lowestoft Town Football Club/ Blues of Crown Meadow" with "John Grose Ford" on roof tempa ($175-250)(LD)(UK)
33. white body, white roof, black plastic chassis, "Freihofer's" tempa ($12-15)(LD)(US)
34. white body, white roof, black plastic chassis, "Matchbox Drive Your Name Home" tempa ($18-25)(LD)(UK)
35. dark blue body & roof, black plastic chassis, "Matchbox Drive Your Name Home" tempa ($18-25)(LD)(UK)
36. red body, red roof, black plastic chassis, "Matchbox Drive Your Name Home" tempa ($18-25)(LD)(UK)
37. red body, red roof, black plastic chassis, "Matchbox Official Visitor" tempa ($50-75)(LD)(UK)
38. white body & roof, black plastic chassis, "50 Years Liberation/ War & Occupation Museum" tempa ($18-25)(LD)(DU)
39. white body & roof, black plastic chassis, "1939 1945/ War & Occupation Museum" tempa ($18-25)(LD)(DU)
40. orange body & roof, black plastic chassis, "Jacob's" tempa ($18-25)(IR)(OP)
41. white body & roof, black plastic chassis, "The Royal Tournament" labels ($18-25)(LD)(UK)
42. white body & roof, black plastic chassis, "The Royal Tournament" with "Earl's Court" rear labels ($125-175)(LD)(UK)
43. dark blue body & roof, black plastic chassis, "BASC/ Beccles Amateur Sailing Club" tempa ($35-50)(LD)(UK)
44. dark blue body & roof, black plastic chassis, "TTK" tempa ($35-50)(LD)(UK)
45. green body, red roof, green metal chassis, "Matchbox Collectibles" tempa ($35-50)(CL)
46. red body, green roof, red metal chassis, "Klaus Toys" tempa ($35-50)(CL)
NOTE: Above two models issued only with Holiday Express Train.
47. white body & roof, black plastic chassis, "7th Jan 1996- Farnham Maltings 1" tempa ($15-25)(LD)(UK)
48. white body & roof, black plastic chassis, "Matchbox USA 96" tempa (base secured with screws) ($18-25)(LD)(US)
49. red body & roof, black plastic chassis, "Matchbox USA 96" tempa ($18-25)(LD)(US)
50. red body & roof, black plastic chassis, "Bradford AFC" tempa ($18-25)(LD)(UK)
51. yellow body, red roof, blue plastic chassis, "Kellogg's Corn Pops" tempa ($8-12)(US)(OP)
52. florescent lime body, black roof & plastic chassis, "Kellogg's Apple Jacks" tempa ($8-12)(US)(OP)
53. yellow body, red roof, black plastic chassis, "Kellogg's Eggo" tempa ($18-25)(US)(OP)
54. white body & roof, black plastic chassis, "10th March 1996- Farnham Maltings 2" tempa ($15-25)(LD)(UK)
55. purple body & roof, black plastic chassis, "Continental Aero" tempa ($12-15)(US)
56. dark blue body & roof, black plastic chassis, "Ford On Show" tempa ($75-100)(LD)(UK)
57. black body & roof, black metal chassis, "Your Own Promotional Vehicle/ Matchbox- Put Your Logo Here" tempa ($18-25)(AU) Special edition in gift box ($75-125)(AU)
58. dark blue body & roof, black plastic chassis, "Matchbox USA 15th Annual Toy Show" tempa ($18-25)(LD)(US)
59. red body & roof, black plastic chassis, "Matchbox USA 15th Annual Toy Show" tempa ($18-25)(LD)(US)
60. yellow body & roof, black plastic chassis, "Matchbox USA 15th Annual Toy Show" tempa (base secured by screws) ($75-125)(LD)(US)
61. cream body , white roof, blue plastic chassis, Macau casting, "26th May 1996- Farnham Maltings 3" tempa (base secured by screws) ($18-25)(LD)(UK)
62. white body & roof, black metal chassis, "26th May 1996- Farnham Maltings 3" tempa ($18-25)(LD)(UK)
63. black body & roof, black metal chassis, "SAE International" tempa ($35-50)(US)
64. red body & roof, black plastic chassis, "1896 1996" tempa ($15-20)(LD)(UK)
65. dark blue body & roof, black plastic chassis, "Stirling Old Town Jail" tempa ($50-75)(LD)(UK)
66. white body & roof, black metal chassis, "North Walsham Carnival 1996" tempa ($18-25)(LD)(UK)
NOTE: Models listed below with same team names are packaged only as two packs with a special pewter medallion. *Each set of two is ($40-60) each pair*
67. white body, tan-beige roof & metal chassis, "St. Kilda Saints 1897" tempa(AU)
68. white body, red roof & metal chassis, "St. Kilda Saints 1996" tempa(AU)
69. black body, tan-beige roof & metal chassis, "Essendon Bombers 1897" tempa(AU)
70. black body, black roof & metal chassis, "Essendon Bombers 1996" tempa(AU)
71. dark blue body, tan-beige roof & metal chassis, "Fitzroy Lions 1897" tempa(AU)
72. pink-red body, dark blue roof & metal chassis, "Fitzroy Lions 1996" tempa(AU)
73. dark blue body, tan-beige roof & metal chassis, "Carlton Blues 1897" tempa(AU)
74. dark blue body & roof, black metal chassis, "Carlton Blues 1996" tempa(AU)
75. dark blue body, tan-beige roof & metal chassis, "Melbourne Demons 1897" tempa(AU)
76. dark blue body & roof, pink-red metal chassis, "Melbourne Demons 1996" tempa(AU)
77. white body, tan-beige roof & metal chassis, "Collingwood Magpies 1897" tempa(AU)
78. white body, black roof & metal chassis, "Collingwood Magpies 1996" tempa(AU)
79. white body, tan-beige roof & metal chassis, "South Melbourne 1897" tempa(AU)
80. white body, red roof & metal chassis, "South Melbourne 1996"

tempa(AU)
81. dark blue body, tan-beige roof & metal chassis, "Geelong Cats 1897" tempa(AU)
82. dark blue body & roof, dark blue metal chassis, "Geelong Cats 1996" tempa(AU)
NOTE: Following three models with rubber tires
83. blue body, red roof & metal chassis, "North Coast Brewing Company-Scrimshaw" tempa ($8-12)(MB1)(CL)
84. black body, red roof & metal chassis, "Firehouse Brewing Co." tempa ($8-12)(MB2)(CL)
85. green body, black roof, red metal chassis, "Holy Cow/ Ambler Gambler" tempa ($8-12)(MB3)(CL)
86. dark blue body & roof, black plastic chassis, "DM David Meek" tempa ($50-75)(LD)(UK)
87. white body & roof, black metal chassis, "8th Sep 1996- Farnham Maltings 4" tempa ($18-25)(LD)(UK)
88. white body & roof, black metal chassis, "Cromer Carnival 1996" ($18-25)(LD)(UK)
89. white body & roof, black metal chassis, "Springfest Extravaganza 1996" tempa ($18-25)(LD)AU)
90. red body & roof, black plastic chassis, "Springfest Extravaganza 1996" tempa ($18-25)(LD)(AU)
91. red body & roof, black plastic chassis, "Bendigo National Swapmeet 1996" tempa ($18-25)(LD)(AU)
92. white body & roof, black metal chassis, "Bendigo National Swapmeet 1996" tempa ($18-25)(LD)(AU)
93. red body & roof, black plastic chassis, "Merry Christmas/Best Wishes from Carr Collectaables" ($35-50)(LD)(UK)
94. red body & roof, black plastic base, "8th Super Southern Swapmeet" tempa ($8-12)(LD)(AU)
95. yellow & roof , black plastic base, "8th Super Southern Swapmeet" tempa ($8-12)(LD)(AU)
96. white body & roof, black plastic base, "Runnymeade Meccano Guild" tempa ($10-15)(LD)(UK)
97.red body, green roof, black plastic base, "Runnymeade Meccano Guild" tempa ($10-15)(LD)(UK)
98. gold body, green roof & metal base, "Anderson Valley" tempa, rubber tires ($8-12)(MB5)(CL)
99. red body, blue roof, gold metal base, "Red Tail Ale" tempa, rubber tires ($8-12)(MB6)(CL)
100. white body & roof, black metal base, "Farnham 6 16th March 1997" tempa ($10-15)(LD)(UK)
101. yellow body & roof, black plastic base, "Adtrucks" tempa ($10-15)(LD)(UK)
102. light beige body & roof, dark rose metal base, "Haig's Chocolates" tempa, dark rose spoked wheels ($10-15)(AU)
103. white body & roof, black plastic base, "Farnham 6 16th March 1997" tempa ($10-15)(LD)(UK)
104. yellow body & roof, blue metal base, "Weidman's Brewery" tempa, rubber tires ($81-12)(MB4)(CL)
105. yellow body & roof, black plastic base, "Great Yarmouth/ Wellesley Main Grandstand" tempa ($10-15)(LD)(UK)
106. yellow body & roof, black plastic base, "Great Yarmouth/ The Bloaters" tempa ($10-15)(LD)(UK)
107. yellow body & roof, black plastic base, "15 Jaar Model Auto 97" tempa ($10-15)(LD)(DU)
108. yellow body & roof, black plastic base, "Bishop's Move" tempa ($10-15)(LD)(UK)
109. yellow body & roof, black plastic base, "16th Matchbox USA Toy Show" tempa ($10-15)(LD)(US)
110. white body & roof, black plastic base, "16th Matchbox USA Toy Show" tempa ($10-15)(LD)(US)
111. white body & roof, black metal base, "16th Matchbox USA Toy Show" tempa ($10-15)(LD)(US)
112. white body & roof, black metal base, "Farnham 7 - May 1997" tempa ($10-15)(LD)(UK)
113. white body & roof, black plastic base., "Farnham 7- May 1997" tempa ($10-15)(LD)(UK)
114. white body & roof, black plastic base, "Dyspraxia Foundation" tempa ($10-15)(LD)(UK)
115. white body & roof, black plastic base, "NGK- The Heartbeat of The Engine" tempa ($50-75)(LD)(UK)
116. white body & roof, black plastic base, "Starlec" tempa ($10-15)(LD)(UK)
117. yellow body & roof, black plastic base, "Kia-Ora" tempa ($10-15)(LD)(UK)
118. yellow body & roof, black plastic base, "Bala Lake Railway" tempa ($10-15)(LD)(UK)
119. red body & roof, black plastic base, "Cromer Carnival 1997" tempa ($10-15)(LD)(UK)
120. red body & roof, black plastic base, "Encyclopedia of Matchbox Toys" tempa ($10-15)(LD)(UK)
121. yellow body & roof, black plastic base, "Encyclopedia of Matchbox Toys" (blue letters) tempa ($15-25)(LD)(US)
122. yellow body & roof, black plastic base, "Encyclopedia of Matchbox Toys" (black letters) tempa ($15-25)(LD)(US)
123. white body & roof, black plastic base, "40th Anniversary Spar" tempa ($100-150)(LD)(UK)
124. white body & roof, black plastic base, "Finlaystone" tempa ($10-15)(LD)(UK)
125. yellow body & roof, black plastic base, "Finlaystone" tempa ($10-15)(LD)(UK)
126. yellow body & roof, black plastic base, "St. Marien Sandersleben" tempa ($15-20)(LD)(GR)
127. red body & roof, black plastic base, "St. Marien Sandersleben" tempa ($20-40)(LD)(GR)
128. white body & roof, black plastic base, "St. Marien Sandersleben" tempa ($35-50)(LD)(GR)
129. white body & roof, black plastic base, "Farnham 8- 11th Sept 1997" tempa ($10-15)(LD)(UK)
130. blue body, red roof & base, "Mastercraft" tempa, rubber tires ($4-6)(CN)(GS)
131. pink-red body, dark blue roof & base, "Crazy Clown" tempa, ($8-12)(AU)
132. red body & roof, black plastic base, "Merry Christmas Australian Matchbox" tempa ($15-20)(C2)
133. white body & roof, black plastic base, "5th Anniversary Australian Matchbox News" tempa ($15-20)(C2)
134. white body & roof, black plastic base, "Mundesley Inshore Lifeboat" tempa ($10-15)(LD)(UK)
135. yellow body & roof, black plastic base, "Evening Gazette Car Awards 1997" tempa ($10-15)(LD)(UK)
136. dark cream body & roof, black plastic base, "Encyclopedia of Matchbox Toys" tempa ($35-50)(LD)(US)
137. dark cream body & roof, black plastic base, "Catalogue of Matchbox Toys" tempa ($15-18)(LD)(US)
138. yellow body & roof, black plastic base, "Catalogue of Matchbox Toys" tempa ($50-75)(LD)(US)
139. white body & roof, black plastic base, "Ferne Animal Sanctuary" tempa ($10-15)(LD)(UK)
140. white body & roof, black plastic base, "MD" tempa ($10-15)(LD)(UK)
141. yellow body & roof, black plastic base, "QATC & EMC Projects/ QA Testing Centre" tempa ($20-30)(LD)(UK)
142. dark cream body & roof, black plastic base, "Bostik" tempa ($10-15)(LD)(UK)
143. dark cream body & roof, black plastic base, "The Story of Mann" tempa ($10-15)(LD)(UK)
144. yellow body & roof, black plastic base, "Ford Motor Co." tempa ($20-30)(LD)(UK)
145. blue body, red roof & metal base, "Sea Dog Brewing Co." tempa ($8-12)(MB)(CL)
146. yellow body & roof, black plastic base, "MCCD 1998" tempa ($50-75)(LD)(GR)
147. white body & roof, black plastic base, "MCCD 1998" tempa ($15-20)(LD)(GR)
148. red body & roof, black plastic base, "MCCD 1998" tempa ($15-20)(LD)(GR)
149. dark cream body & roof, black plastic base, "MCCD 1998" tempa ($40-60)(LD)(GR)
150. dark cream body & roof, black plastic base, "Norwich Citadel-Salvation Army" tempa ($10-15)(LD)(UK)
151. yellow body & roof, black plastic base, "Norwich Citadel- Salvation Army" tempa ($10-15)(LD)(UK)
152. white body & roof, black plastic base, "NGK- The UK's No. 1 Professional Plug" tempa ($65-80)(LD)(UK)
153. pink-beige body, dark green roof & metal base, "Mt. Wilson Wheat Beer" tempa, rubber tires ($8-12)(MB)(CL)
154. pale orange body, orange-red roof & metal base, "Zonker Stout" tempa, rubber tires ($8-12)(MB)(CL)
155. dark cream body 7 roof, blue plastic base, "Barrettine The Independent Choice" tempa ($12-15)(LD)(UK)

MB44-I FORD PROBE, issued 1994

NOTE: All models with clear windows & black base.
1. black body, blue interior, gold 6-spoke spiral wheels, blue & red tempa, Thailand casting ($1-2)
2. black body, blue interior, gold 6-spoke spiral wheels, blue & red tempa, China casting ($1-2)
3. metallic red body, black interior, silver 6-spoke spiral wheels, orange & yellow design tempa , China casting ($1-2)
4. metallic red body, black interior, silver 6-spoke spiral wheels, peach & white design tempa, China casting ($1-2)
5. dark purple body, black interior, silver 6-spoke spiral wheels, green & white design tempa, China casting ($2-3)
6. metallic red body, black interior, silver 6-spoke spiral wheels, yellow & peach design with "Princeton Nassau-Conover" on hood tempa, China casting ($15-20)(C2)
7. metallic gold body, black interior, silver 6-spoke spiral wheels, no tempa, China casting ($10-15)(CH)
8. dark purple body, black interior, 5 spoke concave star wheels, green & white design tempa , China casting ($2-4)
9. metallic blue body, gray & black interior, chrome disc with rubber tires, gray flames tempa, engine cast , China casting ($3-5)(PC9)
10. metallic bronze body, black interior, 5 spoke concave star wheels, blue & white design tempa, China casting ($1-2)

MB45-A FORD GROUP 6, issued 1970

1. non-metallic green body, unpainted base, clear windows, chrome motor, round "7" label ($175-225)
2. green body, unpainted base, clear windows, chrome motor, round "7" label ($12-15)
3. green body, black base, clear windows, chrome motor, round "7" label ($12-15)
4. green body, black base, clear windows, chrome motor, round "7" & "Burmah" label ($12-15)(GS)
5. green body, black base, clear windows, chrome motor, square "7" label ($12-15)
6. green body, unpainted base, clear windows, chrome motor, square "7" & "Burmah" label ($12-15)(GS)
7. green body, black base, clear windows, chrome motor, square "7" & "Burmah" label ($12-15)(GS)
8. green body, pink base, clear windows, chrome motor, "45" & "Burmah" label ($12-15)(GS)
9. green body, black base, clear windows, chrome motor, "45" & "Burmah" label ($12-15)(GS)
10. green body, yellow base, clear windows, chrome motor, "45" & "Burmah" label ($12-15)(GS)
11. green body, charcoal base, clear windows, chrome motor, "45" & "Burmah" label ($12-15)(GS)
12. green body, black base, clear windows, chrome motor, "45" label ($12-15)
13. green body, gray base, clear windows, chrome motor, "45" label ($12-15)
14. green body, yellow base, clear windows, chrome motor, "45" label ($12-15)
15. green body, pink base, clear windows, chrome motor, "45" label ($12-15)
16. green body, pink base, amber windows, chrome motor, "45" label ($12-15)
17. lime body, black base, amber windows, chrome motor, "45" label ($12-15)
18. lime body, charcoal base, amber windows, chrome motor, "45" label ($12-15)
19. lime body, gray base, amber windows, chrome motor, "45" label ($12-15)
20. lime body, light gray base, amber windows, chrome motor, "45" label ($12-15)
21. lime body, pink base, amber windows, chrome motor, "45" label ($12-15)
22. lime body, yellow base, amber windows, chrome motor, "45" label ($12-15)
23. lime body, gray base, amber windows, chrome motor, "45" & "Burmah" label ($12-15)(GS)
24. lime body, black base, amber windows, gray motor, "45" label ($12-15)
25. lime body, charcoal base, amber windows, gray motor, "45" label ($12-15)
26. lime body, gray base, amber windows, gray motor, "45" label ($12-15)
27. purple body, gray base, amber windows, chrome motor, "45" label ($12-15)
28. purple body, black base, amber windows, gray motor, "45" label ($12-15)
29. purple body, black base, amber windows, chrome motor, "45" label ($12-15)
30. purple body, green base, amber windows, chrome motor, "45" label ($12-15)
31. purple body, black base, amber windows, chrome motor, eyes label ($12-15)
32. purple body, green base, amber windows, chrome motor, eyes label ($12-15)
NOTE: All above models with ivory interior.
33. purple body, black base, amber windows, chrome motor, eyes label, white interior ($12-15)
34. purple body, green base, amber windows, chrome motor, eyes label, white interior ($12-15)
35. purple body, green base, amber windows, chrome motor, no label, white interior ($12-15)

MB45-B BMW 3.0 CSL, issued 1976

NOTE: All models with 5 arch wheels unless otherwise noted.
1. orange body, light yellow interior, green windows, "BMW" hood label ($6-8)
2. orange body, light yellow interior, green windows, no hood label ($6-8)
3. white body, light yellow interior, green windows, green hood & trunk with "Polizei" labels, amber dome light ($35-45)(GR)(JP)
4. white body, light yellow interior, green windows, green hood & trunk with "Polizei" labels, blue dome light ($35-45)(GR)(JP)
5. white body, light yellow interior, green windows, green hood & trunk tempa ($85-110)(GR)
6. white body, light yellow interior, green windows, "BMW" & "Manhalter" label ($50-65)(AS)
7. orange body, ivory interior, green windows, "BMW" hood label ($6-8)
8. orange body, light yellow interior, clear windows, "BMW" hood label ($7-10)
9. orange body, ivory interior, clear windows, "BMW" hood label ($7-10)
10. orange body, light yellow interior, dark green windows, "BMW" hood label ($7-10)
11. orange body, ivory interior, dark green windows, "BMW" hood label ($7-10)
12. orange body, light yellow interior, green windows, "BMW" hood label, dot dash wheels ($8-12)
13. red body, light yellow interior, green windows, no hood label ($65-80)(GS)
NOTE: Available as an Hungarian & Bulgarian casting. Assorted colors available ($15-35)

MB45-C KENWORTH AERODYNE, issued 1982

NOTE: Other versions exist as components to Convoy models. Only models issued as single releases are listed here.
1. white body, amber windows, chrome exhausts, brown & blue stripes tempa, England casting ($3-5)
2. white body, amber windows, chrome exhausts, brown & blue stripes tempa, Macau casting ($2-4)
3. pearly silver body, amber windows, chrome exhausts, purple & orange tempa, Macau casting ($2-4)
4. white body, amber windows, chrome exhausts, "Chef Boyardee" label, Macau casting ($35-50)(US)(OP)
5. red body, amber windows, chrome exhausts, yellow/orange/white stripes

tempa, Macau casting ($1-2)
6. red body, amber windows, chrome exhausts, orange/yellow/white stripes tempa, Macau casting ($1-2)
7. red body, amber windows, gray exhausts, yellow/orange/white stripes tempa, Macau casting ($1-2)
8. red body, amber windows, gray exhausts, yellow/orange/white stripes tempa, Thailand casting ($1-2)(MP)

MB45-E HIGHWAY MAINTENANCE VEHICLE, issued 1990 (USA)
MB69-G HIGHWAY MAINTENANCE VEHICLE, issued 1990 (ROW)
NOTE. All models with black base, amber windows & 8 spoke wheels.
1. pale lemon body, pale lemon dump & plow, "Int'l Airport Authority 45" tempa, China casting ($1-2)
2. red body, gray dump & plow, "Aspen Snow Removal" tempa, China casting ($2-4)(AP)
3. pale lemon body, red dump & plow, "Int'l Airport Authority 45" tempa, China casting ($1-2)
4. dark orange body, red dump & plow, "Int'l Airport Authority 45" tempa, China casting ($8-12)(GS)
5. green body, yellow dump & plow, "Intercom City" tempa, Thailand casting ($7-10)(IC)
6. pale lemon body, red dump & plow, "Int'l Airport Authority 45" tempa, Thailand casting ($1-2)
7. orange body, gray dump & plow, "Highway Maintenance 45" tempa, Thailand casting ($2-4)(CC)
8. white body, blue dump & plow, ""Highway Dept." with hood design tempa, China casting ($1-2)
9. white body, blue dump & plow, "Highway Dept." without hood design tempa, China casting ($1-2)
10. pumpkin body, gray dump & plow, "Matchbox" tempa, China casting ($1-2)(MP)
11. orange body, black dump & plow, "Road Crew" tempa, China casting ($1-2)
12. metallic gold body, black dump & plow, none tempa, China casting ($5-10)(CH)
13. red body, black dump & plow, "Matchbox Road Crew" tempa, China casting ($1-2)(MW11)
14. florescent green body, black dump, yellow plow, "Highway Crew" tempa, China casting ($1-2)(MP)

MB46-A MERCEDES 300 SE, issued 1970
NOTE: All models with silver hubs unless otherwise noted.
1. blue body, unpainted base, opening doors & trunk, no labels, 5 spoke wheels ($75-90)
2. dark gold body, unpainted base, opening doors & trunk, no labels, 5 spoke wheels ($20-25)
3. light gold body, unpainted base, opening doors & trunk, no labels, 5 spoke wheels ($20-25)
4. light gold body, unpainted base, cast doors, opening trunk, no labels, 5 spoke wheels ($20-25)
5. olive body, unpainted base, cast doors & trunk, "Staff" labels, 5 arch wheels with black hubs ($7-10)(TP)
6. olive body, unpainted base, cast doors & trunk, "Staff" labels, dot dash wheels with black hubs ($7-10)(TP)
7. silver—gray body, unpainted base, cast doors & trunk, no labels, dot dash wheels ($85-110)(MP)
8. silver—gray body, unpainted base, cast doors & trunk, no labels, dot dash wheels with black hubs ($85-110)(MP)
NOTE: Available as a Bulgarian casting. Assorted colors available. ($20-30)

MB46-B STRETCHA FETCHA, issued 1972
1. white body, unpainted base, blue windows, "Ambulance" labels, light yellow interior, maltese cross wheels ($12-15)
2. white body, red base, blue windows, "Ambulance" labels, light yellow interior, maltese cross wheels ($12-15)
3. white body, red base, blue windows, "Ambulance" labels, cream interior, maltese cross wheels ($12-15)
4. white body, red base, blue windows, cross labels light yellow interior, maltese cross wheels ($12-15)
5. white body, red base, blue windows, "Ambulance" labels, light yellow interior, 5 spoke wheels ($12-15)
6. white body, red base, blue windows, "Ambulance" labels, light yellow interior, 4 spoke wheels ($12-15)
7. red body, red base, blue windows, "Unfall Rettung" labels, light yellow interior, maltese cross wheels ($35-45)(GR)
8. white body, red base, blue windows, no labels, light yellow interior, maltese cross wheels ($12-15)
9. white body, red base, amber windows, "Ambulance" labels, light yellow interior, maltese cross wheels ($15-18)
10. white body, red base, amber windows, cross labels, light yellow interior, maltese cross wheels ($15-18)
11. lime body, black base, amber windows, "Viper Van" tempa, light yellow interior, maltese cross wheels ($12-15)(LE)
12. lime body, white base, amber windows, "Viper Van" tempa, light yellow interior, maltese cross wheels ($12-15)(LE)
13. lime body, white base, amber windows, "Viper Van" tempa, cream interior, maltese cross wheels ($12-15)(LE)
14. lime body, unpainted base, amber windows, "Viper Van" tempa, light yellow interior, maltese cross wheels ($12-15)(LE)
NOTE: Versions 11-14 issued as a limited edition in US as "Viper Van".

MB46-C FORD TRACTOR, issued 1978
NOTE: All models without tempa unless otherwise noted.
1. blue body, unpainted base, light yellow interior, yellow harrow, black front & rear hubs, England casting ($3-5)
2. blue body, unpainted base, light yellow interior, orange harrow, black front & rear hubs, England casting ($3-5)
3. blue body, unpainted base, light yellow interior, no harrow, black front & rear hubs, England casting ($3-5)(TP)
4. blue body, unpainted base, light yellow interior, yellow harrow, yellow front & rear hubs, England casting ($3-5)
5. blue body, unpainted base, dark yellow interior, yellow harrow, black front & rear hubs, England casting ($3-5)
6. blue body, unpainted base, white interior, yellow harrow, yellow rear hubs only, England casting ($3-5)
7. blue body, unpainted base, white interior, yellow harrow, yellow front & rear hubs, England casting ($3-5)
8. lime body, unpainted base, light yellow interior, yellow harrow, yellow front & rear hubs, England casting ($5-7)
9. green body, unpainted base, light yellow interior, yellow harrow, yellow front & rear hubs, England casting ($5-7)
10. mid blue body, unpainted base (tab), light yellow interior, yellow harrow, yellow front & rear hubs, no origin cast ($65-80)(BR)
11. blue body, pearly silver base, white interior, no harrow, gold front & rear hubs, Macau casting ($2-3)(TP)
12. yellow body, pearly silver base, black interior, no harrow, orange front & rear hubs, orange stripe tempa, Macau casting ($1-2)(TP)
13. yellow body, pearly silver base, black interior, red harrow, orange front & rear hubs, orange stripe tempa, Macau casting ($1-2)(GS)
14. green body, pearly silver base, white interior, red harrow, orange front & rear hubs, no tempa, Macau casting ($1-2)(MC)
15. green body, pearly silver base, black interior, no harrow, orange front & rear hubs, Macau casting ($1-2)(MP)
16. green body, pearly silver base, black interior, no harrow, orange front & rear hubs, Thailand casting ($1-2)(TP)
17. green body, pearly silver base, black interior, yellow harrow, orange front & rear hubs, Thailand casting ($1-2)(MC)

MB46-D HOT CHOCOLATE/ BEETLE STREAKER, issued 1981 (USA)
NOTE: versions 1 & 2 cast with "Hot Chocolate" as base name. Versions 3 onward cast with "Beetle Streaker" as base name. All models with 5 arch front wheels unless otherwise noted.
1. black body, black base, white roof stripes with brown sides tempa, Hong Kong casting ($4-6)
2. black body, black base, no roof stripes with brown sides tempa, Hong Kong casting ($8-12)
3. silver blue body, pearly silver base, "Big Blue" tempa, Macau casting ($3-5)
4. silver blue body, pearly silver base, "Big Blue" tempa, Hong Kong casting ($3-5)
5. blue body, pearly silver base, "Big Blue" tempa, Hong Kong casting ($3-5)
6. blue body, light gray base, "Big Blue" tempa, Hong Kong casting ($3-5)
7. silver blue body, light gray base, "Big Blue" tempa, Hong Kong casting ($3-5)
8. dark blue body, pearly silver base, "Big Blue" tempa, Macau casting ($3-5)
9. blue body, light gray base, "Big Blue" tempa, 5 spoke front wheels, Hong Kong casting ($3-5)

MB46-F MISSION HELICOPTER, issued 1985 (USA)
MB57-F MISSION HELICOPTER, issued 1985 (ROW)
NOTE: All versions with blue windows except 18 & 24 with smoke windows.
1. dark blue body, silver-gray base & skis, white tail & blades, orange tempa, Macau casting ($1-2)
2. red body, white base & skis, white tail & blades, "Sheriff Air 1" tempa, Macau casting ($1-2)
3. olive green body, tan base & skis, tan tail & blades, star & emblem tempa, Macau casting ($2-3)(SB)
4. red body, white base & skis, white tail & blades, "Rebels/ Rescue/ Air 1" tempa, Macau casting ($1-2)(MC)
5. dark blue body, silver-gray base & skis, white tail & blades, bullseye tempa, Macau casting ($2-3)(GS)
6. olive green body, black base & skis, black tail & blades, "AC15" & logo tempa, Macau casting ($4-5)(CM)
7. black body, dark gray base & skis, dark gray tail, yellow blades, "AC99" & logo tempa, Macau casting ($4-5)(CM)
8. red body, white base & skis, white tail & blades, "Sheriff Air 1" tempa, Thailand casting ($1-2)
9. dark blue body, silver-gray base & skis, white tail & blades, bullseye tempa, Thailand casting ($2-3)
10. red body, white base & skis, white tail & blades, "Rebels/ Rescue/ Air 1" tempa, Thailand casting ($1-2)(MC)
11. olive green body, bright tan base & skis, bright tan tail & blades, star & emblem tempa, Thailand casting ($2-3)(SB)
12. olive green body, pink-tan base & skis, pink-tan tail & blades, star & emblem tempa, Thailand casting ($2-3)(SB)
13. white body, dark blue base & skis, white tail & blades, "Police" & crest tempa, Thailand casting ($1-2)
14. green body, white base & skis, white tail & blades, "Polizei" tempa, Thailand casting ($2-3)(CY)
15. black body, white base & skis, white tail & blades, "Police" tempa, Thailand casting ($2-3)(CY)
16. white body, fluorescent orange base/skis, white tail & blades, "Metro Swat 7" tempa, Thailand casting ($1-2)(MP)
17. beige body, yellow-tan base/skis, yellow-tan tail & blades, camouflage tempa, Thailand casting ($1-2)
18. white body, fluorescent orange base/skis, white tail & blades, "Politie 06-11" tempa, Thailand casting ($3-4)(DU)(CY)
19. white body, blue base/skis, white tail & blades, "Intercom City/Police" tempa, Thailand casting ($7-10)(IC)
20. white body, red base/skis, white tail & blades, "Sky" tempa, Thailand casting ($2-3) (NM)
21. yellow body, blue base/skis, white tail & blades, "Canon" tempa, Thailand casting ($2-3)(NM)
22. white body, blue base/skis, white tail & blades, green crest & "Rescue" tempa, Thailand casting ($3-4)(MP)
23. black body, white base & skis, white tail & blades, "Police Unit 2" & gold star tempa, Thailand casting ($1-2)(MP)
24. pink-tan body, tan base & skis, tan tail & blades, green & brown camouflage tempa, Thailand casting ($1-2)(MP)
NOTE: Following models with blue windows unless noted.
25. white body, tan base & skis, tan tail & blades, "Rescue" & green logo tempa, Thailand casting ($2-4)(MP)
26. white body, red base & skis, red tail, white blades, "Aces" & ace logo tempa, Thailand casting ($2-3)(CY)
27. olive body, black base & skis, olive tail, black blades, star & "T-7521-6" tempa, Thailand casting ($1-2)
28. green body, green base & skis, green tail, black blades, green smoke windows, black & brown camouflage tempa, Thailand casting ($1-2)(MP)
29. white body, black base & skis, black tail & blades, "Police Unit 3" tempa, Thailand casting ($1-2)(MP)
30. florescent lime body, black base & skis, neon blue tail, black blades, "12 Air Patrol" tempa, Thailand casting ($1-2)(MP)
31. blue body, white base & skis, blue tail, silver-gray blades, "Police Air Rescue" tempa, Thailand casting ($1-2)
32. beige body, smoke windows, black base & skis, beige tail, black blades, brown camouflage tempa ($1-2)(MP)
33. white body, black base & skis, white tail & blades, "Police"" tempa, Thailand casting ($1-2)
34. white body, smoke windows, gray base & skis, white tail & blades, gray & olive camouflage tempa, Thailand casting ($1-2)(MP)
35. black body, amber windows, black base & skis, black tail & blades, "INGEN" & "Lost World" tempa, gray armament attached, Thailand casting ($5-8)(JR)
36. white body, red windows, black base & skis, black & tail blades, black camouflage tempa, Thailand casting ($1-2)(PS)
37. pale gray body, red windows, black base & skis, black tail & blades, black camouflage tempa, Thailand casting ($1-2)(PS)
38. metallic gold body, smoke windows, black base & skis, black tail & blades, no tempa, Thailand casting ($5-10)(CH)
39. khaki tan body, dark smoke windows, black base & skis, black tail & blades, "AT-7521" & star tempa, Thailand casting ($1-2)(MW49)
40. black body, smoke green windows, brown base & skis, brown tail & blades, green & brown camouflage tempa, Thailand casting ($1-2)(MP)
41. black base, smoke green windows, brown base & skis, brown tail & blades, green & brown camouflage tempa, China casting ($1-2)(MP)
42. blue body, white base & skis, blue tail, silver-gray blades, "Police Air Rescue" tempa, China casting ($1-2)(MP)
43. florescent lime body, blue base & skis, neon blue tail, black blades, "12 Air Patrol" tempa, China casting ($1-2)(MP)
44. pale gray body, smoke windows, black base & skis, black tail & blades, black camouflage tempa, China casting ($1-2)(MP)
45. khaki tan body, dark smoke windows, black base & skis, black tail & blades, "AT-7521" & star tempa, China casting ($1-2)(MW49)
46. black body, blue base & skis, blue tail & blades, "SWAT Stand Clear 000256" tempa, China casting ($1-2)(MP)

MB46-H CHEVY TAHOE, issued 1998
NOTE: All models with clear windows, chrome base & China casting
1. dark green body, tan & black interior, chrome disc with rubber tires, silver band & detailed trim tempa ($4-6)(FE)
2. unpainted base, tan interior, chrome disc with rubber tires, no tempa ($4-6)(FE)
3. metallic red body, tan interior, 5 spoke concave star wheels, "454" & white & yellow design tempa ($1-2)(MW46)
4. dark metallic red body, tan interior, 5 spoke concave star wheels, "454" & white & yellow design tempa ($1-2)(MW46)

MB47-A DAF TIPPER TRUCK, issued 1970casting ($
1. silver—gray body, yellow container, gray roof, red base ($25-35)
2. silver—gray body, dark yellow container, gray roof, red base ($25-35)

MB47-B BEACH HOPPER, issued 1974
1. dark blue body, windshield cast, silver-gray base, orange interior, tan driver ($20-25)
2. dark blue body, windshield cast, pink base, orange interior, tan driver ($12-15)
3. dark blue body, windscreen cast, pink base, orange interior, tan driver ($12-15)
4. dark blue body, windscreen cast, pink base, orange interior, pink-tan driver ($12-15)
5. dark blue body, windscreen cast, pink base, yellow interior, pink-tan driver ($15-18)
6. dark blue body, windscreen cast, pink base, yellow interior, tan driver ($15-18)
7. dark blue body, windscreen cast, salmon base, orange interior, tan driver ($12-15)
8. dark blue body, windscreen cast, lavender base, orange interior, tan driver ($12-15)
9. dark blue body, windscreen cast, unpainted base, orange interior, tan driver ($12-15)
10. dark blue body, windscreen cast, unpainted base, light orange interior,

tan driver ($12-15)

MB47-C PANNIER LOCO, issued 1979
1. dark green body, black frame, black base ($4-6)
2. light green body, black frame, black base ($4-6)
3. light green body, black frame, brown base ($7-10)
4. light green body, black frame, unpainted base ($4-6)
5. light green body, black frame, charcoal base ($4-6)
6. light green body, black frame, blue-gray base ($4-6)
7. light green body, black frame, charcoal brown base ($4-6)
8. light green body, charcoal frame, black base ($4-6)

MB47-D JAGUAR SS 100, issued 1982
1. red body, partially painted hood, gray base, tan interior, England casting ($7-10)
2. red body, red hood, gray base, tan interior, England casting ($2-4)
3. red body, red hood, black base, tan interior, England casting ($2-4)
4. red body, red hood, gray base, tan interior, Macau casting ($2-3)
5. red body, red hood, black base, tan interior, Macau casting ($2-3)
6. dark blue body, pearly silver hood, black base, white interior, Macau casting ($4-6)
7. dark green body, red hood, black base, black interior, Thailand casting ($12-15)(UK)(OP) & (US)(GS)
8. silver-gray body with dark gray hood, blue interior, Thailand casting ($3-5)(GS)

MB47-E SCHOOL BUS, issued 1985 (USA)
MB47-E SCHOOL BUS, issued 1987 (ROW)
NOTE: All models with black interior, black base, clear windows & dot dash wheels unless otherwise noted. Early models cast with small window in two sizes in lower section of rear door. Later models cast solid with black painted tempa.
1. yellow body, "School District 2" tempa, Macau casting ($1-2)
2. yellow body, "School District 2" tempa, China casting ($1-2)
3. olive body, "Govt. Property" tempa, China casting ($8-12)(US)
4. yellow body, "School District 2" tempa with "Chef Boyardee" hood label, China casting ($8-12)(US)(OP)
5. orange-yellow body, "School District 2" tempa with "Chef Boyardee" hood label, China casting ($8-12)(US)(OP)
6. orange-yellow body, "School District 2" tempa, China casting ($1-2)
7. orange-yellow body, "1 + 2 = 3 abc" tempa, red base, green wheels with red hubs, China casting ($6-8)(LL)
8. orange-yellow body, "1 + 2 = 3 abc" tempa, red base, green wheels with blue hubs, China casting ($6-8)(LL)
9. orange-yellow body, "School District 2" tempa, Thailand casting ($10-15)
10. orange-yellow body, "St. Paul Public Schools" tempa, China casting ($25-45)(US)
11. blue body, "Police 88" tempa, China casting ($2-4)(AP)
12. dark blue body, "Hofstra University" tempa, China casting ($7-10)(US)
13. yellow body, "Harvey World Travel" tempa, China casting ($7-10)(AU)
14. dark orange body, "School District 2" tempa, China casting ($8-12)(GS)
15. white & dark blue body, "Penn State- The Loop" tempa, China casting ($6-8)(WR)
16. orange-yellow body, red base, "1 + 2 = 3 abc" tempa, all green wheels, China casting ($4-6)(LL)
17. dark pink body, black base, "Mt. Laurel Preschool" tempa, China casting ($2-4)(CC)
18. orange-yellow body, black base, "School District 2" without rear tempa, China casting ($1-2)
19. orange-yellow body, black base, "Carpenter High School" tempa, China casting ($1-2)
20. metallic gold body, black base, no tempa, China casting ($10-15)(CH)
21. orange-yellow body, red interior, black base, "Matchbox Elementary School" tempa, China casting ($1-2)(MP)
22. olive body, black base, "Gov't Property" with Commando hood logo tempa, China casting ($25-40)(CHI)(MP)
23. orange-yellow body, black base, "Cap'n Crunch- Quaker Oats" tempa, China casting ($100+)(ASAP)
24. orange-yellow body, black base, "Go Team Go- Oaklyn Middle School PS33" tempa, China casting ($1-2)
25. orange-yellow body, black base, "Montgomery High School" tempa, China casting ($15-20)(C2)
26. orange-yellow body, black base, no tempa, China casting ($20-35)(ASAP blank)
27. orange yellow body, black base, "Vancom" tempa, China casting ($75-100)(US)
28. orange-yellow body, black base, "Van Lear" tempa, China casting ($75+)(ASAP)
29. lemon body, dark green interior, "Go Team Go- Oaklyn Middle School PS33" tempa, China casting ($1-2)(MW12)
30. orange-yellow body, black base, "RCA" tempa, China casting ($75+)(ASAP)

MB47-G M2 BRADLEY TANK, issued 1998
1. beige body & turret, black gun, black base, star & "T-0927" tempa, China casting ($1-2)(MW47)

MB48-A DODGE DUMP TRUCK, issued 1970
1. blue body, yellow dump, 5 spoke front & rear wheels ($25-40)
2. metallic blue body, yellow dump, 5 spoke front & rear wheels ($25-40)
3. metallic blue body, yellow dump, 4 spoke front & spiro rear wheels ($25-40)
4. metallic blue body, yellow dump, 4 spoke front & rear wheels ($25-40)

MB48-B PI-EYED PIPER, issued 1972
1. blue body, amber windows, 8 stacks engine, "8" roof label ($15-18)
2. blue body, blue windows, 8 stacks engine, "8" roof label ($15-18)
3. red body, blue windows, single engine (as MB26-B), "Big Banger" labels ($85-110)

MB48-C SAMBRON JACKLIFT, issued 1977
NOTE: most versions can be found with combinations of yellow & yellow-orange forks & arms. The yellow-orange is only slightly darker on this particular model.
1. yellow body, yellow forks & arm, black base, 4 spoke wheels, silver hubs ($5-7)
2. yellow body, yellow forks & arm, black base, 5 arch wheels, silver hubs ($5-7)
3. yellow body, yellow forks & arm, brown base, 5 arch wheels, silver hubs ($7-10)
4. yellow body, yellow forks & arm, charcoal base, 5 arch wheels, silver hubs ($5-7)
5. yellow body, yellow forks & arm, black base, 5 arch wheels, silver hubs, "Sambron" tempa ($350-500)
6. yellow body, yellow forks & arm, charcoal base, 5 arch wheels, yellow hubs ($7-10)
7. yellow body, black forks, yellow arm, charcoal base, 5 arch wheels, silver hubs ($5-7)
8. yellow body, black forks & arm, black base, 5 arch wheels, silver hubs ($5-7)
9. yellow-orange body, yellow forks & arm, black base, 5 arch wheels, silver hubs ($5-7)

MB48-D RED RIDER, issued 1982 (USA)
NOTE: Versions 1-7 with white flames tempa.
1. red body, maltese cross front & rear wheels, Hong Kong casting ($4-6)
2. red body, maltese cross front & rear wheels, England casting ($4-6)
3. red body, maltese cross front & rear wheels, Macau casting ($1-2)
4. red body, maltese cross front & 5 crown rear wheels, Macau casting ($1-2)
5. red body, 5 spoke front & 5 crown rear wheels, Macau casting ($1-2)
6. red body, 5 arch front & 5 crown rear wheels, China casting ($1-2)
7. dark red body, 5 arch front & 5 crown rear wheels, China casting ($1-2)
8. dark blue body, 5 arch front & 5 crown rear wheels, "8" tempa, China casting ($3-5)(PC13)

MB48-E UNIMOG WITH PLOW, issued 1983 (ROW)
1. yellow body, white base & plow, black plow stripes, amber windows, white canopy, "Rescue" tempa, England casting ($8-10)
2. yellow body, yellow-orange base & plow, black plow stripes, amber windows, white canopy, "Rescue" tempa, England casting ($3-5)
3. yellow body, black base & plow, no plow stripes, amber windows, white canopy, "Rescue" tempa, England casting ($8-10)
4. yellow body, yellow-orange base & plow, black plow stripes, amber windows, no canopy, "Rescue" tempa, England casting ($3-5)
5. yellow body, lemon base & plow, black plow stripes, amber windows, white canopy, "Rescue" tempa, Macau casting ($2-4)
6. red body, red base & plow, white plow stripes, amber windows, white canopy, "UR83" tempa, Macau casting ($2-4)(TP)
7. white body, yellow base & plow, black plow stripes, red windows, no canopy, red & dark blue stripes tempa, Macau casting, includes plastic armament ($6-8)(RB)
8. white body, orange base & plow, black plow stripes, amber windows, orange canopy, "C&S" tempa, Macau casting ($2-4)(TP)
9. white body, orange base & plow, black plow stripes, amber windows, orange canopy, "C&S" tempa, Thailand casting ($2-4)(TP)
10. white body, yellow base & plow, black plow stripes, red windows, no canopy, red & dark blue stripes tempa, Thailand casting, includes plastic armament ($8-12)(JP) (Tomy box)
11. white body, light olive base & plow, no plow stripes, amber windows, light olive canopy, gray & olive camouflage tempa, black hubs, Thailand casting ($2-4)(PS)

MB48-F VAUXHALL ASTRA/ OPEL KADETT, issued 1986 (ROW)
NOTE: early model bases cast "Vauxhall Astra" only. Later models cast "Vauxhall Astra/ Opel Kadett". All models with clear windows.
1. red body, black base, black interior, 8 dot silver wheels, "GTE" & stripe tempa, Macau casting ($2-4)
2. red body, black base, black interior, 5 arch wheels, "GTE" & stripe tempa, Macau casting ($2-4)
3. white body, black base, black interior, 8 dot silver wheels, "AC Delco 48" tempa, Macau casting ($1-2)
4. white body, black base, black interior, 8 dot white wheels, "AC Delco 48" tempa, Macau casting ($2-4)
5. yellow body, blue base, black interior, 8 dot silver wheels, "Mobile Phone/ Telecom" tempa, Macau casting ($3-5)(GS)
6. black body, black base, black interior, 8 dot silver wheels, "BP 52" & yellow band tempa, Macau casting ($8-12)(DU)
7. white body, black base, black interior, 8 dot silver wheels, "AC Delco 48" tempa, China casting ($1-2)
8. white body, black base, blue interior, 8 dot silver wheels, "STP 7/ Sphere Drake" tempa, China casting ($1-2)
9. yellow body, yellow base, blue interior, 8 dot silver wheels, no tempa, China casting ($8-12)(GR)(GS)
10. white body, black base, blue interior, 8 dot silver wheels, "STP/ Sphere" without "7" tempa, China casting ($1-2)

MB48-H 1956 FORD PICKUP, issued 1997
NOTE: All models with clear windows ,chrome base & China casting unless otherwise noted.
1. black body, red & white interior, chrome disc with rubber tires, white roof tempa ($4-6)(IG)
2. unpainted body, red interior, chrome disc with rubber tires, no tempa ($4-6)(IG)
3. dark purple body, gray interior, 5 spoke concave star wheels, white & peach flames tempa ($2-3)
4. metallic red body, tan interior, 5 spoke concave star wheels, "Happy Days" tempa ($4-6)(STR)
5. red body, white & red interior, chrome disc with rubber tires, detailed trim tempa ($3-5)(PC17)
6. red body, white interior, 5 spoke concave star wheels, no tempa ($1-2)(MW35)
7. metallic blue body, blue & gray interior, chrome disc with rubber tires, white roof & "Matchbox Toy Show Hershey 98" tempa ($10-15)(US)
8. turquoise body, black & white interior, chrome disc with rubber tires, pink & purple pinstriping tempa ($3-5)(PC20)
9. light pumpkin body, maroon & white interior, chrome disc with rubber tires, maroon roof & "MBRR Service" tempa ($25-40)(CL)
10. metallic gold body, black interior, 5 spoke concave star wheels, no tempa ($5-10)(CH)
11. red body, white interior, 5 spoke concave star wheels, "Matchbox USA" logo & "www.matchbox-usa.com" decals ($10-15)(C2)
12. red body, black interior, chrome disc with rubber tires, white roof & "Coca Cola in Bottles" tempa ($4-6)(PC)

MB49-A UNIMOG, issued 1970
1. blue body, plain grille, red base, spiro wheels, no label, no shellbox ($18-25)
2. blue body, silver grille, red base, spiro wheels, no label, no shellbox ($18-25)
3. blue-green body, plain grille, red base, spiro wheels, no label, no shellbox ($18-25)
4. bright blue body, plain grille, red base, spiro wheels, no label, no shellbox ($18-25)
5. metallic blue body, plain grille, red base, spiro wheels, no label, no shellbox ($18-25)
6. metallic blue body, silver grille, red base, spiro wheels, no label, no shellbox ($18-25)
7. olive body, plain grille, olive base, dot dash wheels, star label, no shellbox ($75-100)(TP)
8. olive body, plain grille, olive base, dot dash wheels, star label, with shellbox ($75-100)(TP)
9. olive body, plain grille, olive base, dot dash wheels, "A" label, with shellbox ($7-10)(TP)

MB49-B CHOP SUEY, issued 1973
1. magenta body, chrome handlebars ($350-425)
2. magenta body, orange handlebars ($15-20)
3. magenta body, red handlebars ($12-15)
4. magenta body, black handlebars ($20-25)(MP)
5. magenta body, dark red handlebars ($12-15)

MB49-C CRANE TRUCK, issued 1976
1. yellow body, yellow boom, dark green windows, no labels, dot dash wheels ($4-6)
2. yellow body, yellow boom, dark green windows, no labels, 5 arch wheels ($4-6)
3. yellow body, yellow boom, light green windows, no labels, 5 arch wheels ($4-6)
4. dark red body, yellow boom, dark green windows, no labels, 5 arch wheels ($60-75)(GR)
5. bright red body, yellow boom, clear windows, no labels, 5 arch wheels ($60-75)(GR)
6. yellow body, black boom, dark green windows, no labels, 5 arch wheels ($4-6)
7. yellow body, black boom, red windows, no labels, 5 arch wheels ($4-6)
8. yellow body, black boom, purple windows, no labels, 5 arch wheels ($4-6)
9. yellow body, black boom, dark green windows, "A-1 Crane" labels with stripes & "C" tempa, 5 arch wheels ($3-5)
10. yellow body, black boom, dark green windows, "A-1 Crane" labels with stripes tempa, 5 arch wheels ($3-5)
11. yellow body, black boom, blue windows, stripes only tempa, 5 arch wheels ($8-12)

MB49-D SAND DIGGER, issued 1983
1. emerald green body, black base, ivory interior, "Sand Digger" tempa, Macau casting ($2-3)
2. very dark green body, black base, ivory interior, "Sand Digger" tempa, Macau casting ($2-3)
3. red body, black base, white interior, "Dune Man" tempa, Macau casting ($2-3)
4. red body, black base, rust red interior, "Dune Man" tempa, Macau casting ($2-3)
5. red body, black base, rust red interior, "Dune Man" tempa, China casting ($2-3)
NOTE: Available as a Bulgarian casting. Assorted colors available ($15-25)

MB49-E PEUGEOT QUASAR, issued 1986
MB72-M PEUGEOT QUASAR, reissued 1995 (USA)
1. white body & base, chrome interior, smoke gray windows, 8 dot silver wheels, "Quasar" tempa, Macau casting ($2-3)
2. dark blue body, black base, chrome interior, smoke gray windows, starburst wheels, "9" & pink stripes tempa, Macau casting ($3-5)(SF)
3. metallic blue body, black base, chrome interior, smoke gray windows, laser wheels, "9" & pink stripes tempa, Macau casting ($3-5)(LW)
4. white body & base, chrome interior, smoke gray windows, 8 dot white

wheels, "Quasar" tempa, Macau casting ($2-4)
5. black body & base, no interior, red modified windows, starburst wheels, lime & orange stripes tempa, Macau casting, includes plastic armament ($5-8)(RB)
6. plum body & base, chrome interior, smoke gray windows with purple tempa, 8 dot silver wheels, "Quasar" tempa, Macau casting ($1-2)
7. plum body & base, chrome interior, smoke gray windows, 8 dot silver wheels, "Quasar" tempa, Macau casting ($1-2)
8. yellow body, lime base, red interior, smoke gray windows, 8 dot blue wheels with yellow hubs, "3" with stripes & flames tempa, Macau casting ($6-8)(LL)
9. yellow body, lime base, red interior, smoke gray windows, 8 dot blue wheels with yellow hubs, "3" with stripes & flames tempa, China casting ($6-8)(LL)
10. orange-yellow body, lime base, red interior, smoke gray windows, 8 dot blue wheels with yellow hubs, "3" with stripes & flames tempa, China casting ($6-8)(LL)
11. plum body & base, chrome interior, smoke gray windows, 8 dot silver wheels, "Quasar" tempa, China casting ($1-2)
NOTE: Version 11 was briefly reintroduced in the US as MB72 in 1995 ($1-2)
12. orange-yellow body, lime base, red interior, smoke gray windows, 8 dot all blue wheels, "3" with stripes & flames tempa, China casting ($6-8)(LL)

MB49-H BMW 850i, issued 1993 (USA)
MB 2-H BMW 850i, issued 1993 (ROW)
NOTE: all models with clear windows unless otherwise noted.
1. silver/gray body, silver/gray base, blue interior, 8 dot wheels, no tempa, Thailand casting ($2-3)
2. silver body, silver base, blue interior, 8 dot wheels, no tempa , Thailand casting ($2-4)
3. white body, white base, red interior, 8 dot wheels, no tempa, Thailand casting ($3-5)(SS)
4. metallic charcoal body, met. charcoal base, chrome windows, red interior, gray disc with rubber tires, detailed trim tempa, Thailand casting ($2-4)(WC)
5. black body, black base, neon yellow interior, 6-spoke gold spiral wheels, yellow flash & "850i" tempa, Thailand casting ($1-2)
6. black body, black base, neon yellow interior, 6-spoke gold spiral wheels, yellow flash & "850i" tempa, China casting ($1-2)
7. silver-gray body, silver/gray base, blue interior, 6-spoke gold spiral wheels, no tempa, Thailand casting ($2-3)
8. black body, black base, florescent yellow interior, silver 6-spoke spiral wheels, yellow flash & "850i" tempa, China casting ($2-4)
9. red body, red base, white interior, silver 6-spoke spiral wheels, "Ripper" on sides with skull on hood tempa, China casting ($1-2)
10. red body, red base, white interior, silver 6-spoke spiral wheels, "Ripper" on sides only tempa, China casting ($1-2)
11. red body, red base, white interior, silver 6-spoke spiral wheels, no tempa, China casting ($25-50)(US) *(issued with Kentucky Fried Chicken Kids Meal)*
12. dark plum body, black base, tan & black interior, chrome disc with rubber tires, detailed trim tempa , China casting ($8-12)(UC)
13. red body, red base, white interior, 5 spoke concave star wheels, "Ripper" on sides only tempa, China casting ($2-4)
14. black body, black base, black interior, 5 spoke concave star wheels, "Go Tigers! 1997" tempa, China casting ($3-5)(AU)
15. black body, black base, neon yellow interior, 5 spoke concave star wheels, yellow flash & "850i " tempa, China casting ($2-4)
16. dark blue body, black base, tan interior, 8 dot wheels, no tempa, China casting ($1-2)
17. candy red body, black base, black & tan interior, chrome disc with rubber tires, detailed trim tempa, Thailand casting ($3-5)(JC)(PC)
18. red body, black base, black & red interior, chrome disc with rubber tires, detailed trim tempa, Thailand casting ($3-5)(PC15)
19. metallic red body, metallic red base, tan interior, 5 spoke concave star wheels, no tempa, China casting ($1-2)(MW73-ROW)

MB49-I VOLKSWAGEN CONCEPT 1, issued 1996 (USA)
MB58-G VOLKSWAGEN CONCEPT 1, issued 1996 (ROW)
All models with clear windows.
1. red body, red base, black interior, black roof tempa, 6-spoke spiral wheels, Thailand casting ($1-2)
2. red body, red base, black interior, black roof & "Mark I V.W.S." tempa, chrome disc with rubber tires, Thailand casting ($8-12)(US)
3. metallic gold body, black base, black interior, no tempa, 6 spoke spiral wheels, Thailand casting ($5-10)(CH)
4. metallic purple body, black base, gray interior, black roof tempa, 5 spoke concave star wheels, Thailand casting ($1-2)(MP)
Version 4 can also come with inverted hood logo.
5. red body, red base, black interior, black roof tempa, 5 spoke concave star wheels, Thailand casting ($3-5)
6. green body, red base, black interior, black roof tempa, 5 spoke concave star wheels, Thailand casting ($100+)
7. green body, green base, black interior, black roof tempa, 5 spoke concave star wheels, Thailand casting ($1-3)
NOTE: version 7 can come with inverted front & rear logos or with only one inverted or both correctly positioned.
8. orange body, orange base, black interior, black roof tempa, 5 spoke concave star wheels, Thailand casting ($1-2)(MW17)
NOTE: version 8 can come with inverted or correctly positioned logos.
9. red body, red base, black interior, black roof tempa & "17th Annual Matchbox USA Convention 1998" decals, 6 spoke spiral wheels, Thailand casting ($12-18)(C2)
10. green body, green base, black interior, black roof tempa & "17th Annual Matchbox USA Convention 1998" decals, 5 spoke concave star wheels, Thailand casting ($12-18)(C2)
11. orange body, orange base, black interior, black roof tempa, 5 spoke concave star wheels, China casting ($1-2)(MW17)
12. red body, black base, black interior, white roof , "Coca Cola" & "Always Coca Cola" logo tempa, chrome disc with rubber tires, China casting ($4-6)(PC)
13. orange body, orange base, black interior, black roof, "Hope Spring Cancer Support Centre 1998" tempa, 5 spoke concave star wheels, China casting ($15-25)(C2)
14. light brown body, orange base, black interior, black roof, "Hope Spring Cancer Support Centre 1998" tempa, 5 spoke concave star wheels, China casting ($100+)(C2)
15. brown body, orange base, black interior, black roof, "Hope Spring Cancer Support Centre 1998" tempa, 5 spoke concave star wheels, China casting ($100+)(C2)
16. dark brown body, orange base, black interior, black roof, "Hope Spring Cancer Support Centre 1998" tempa, 5 spoke concave star wheels, China casting ($100+)(C2)
NOTE: Versions 14-16 are limited to only 25 pieces of each and were given out to persons directly involved with Hope Spring charities.

MB50-A KENNEL TRUCK, issued 1970
1. metallic green body, black base, chrome grille ($25-40)
2. metallic green body, light yellow base, chrome grille ($25-40)
3. metallic green body, dark yellow base, chrome grille ($25-40)
4. metallic green body, gray base, chrome grille ($25-40)
5. metallic green body, charcoal base, chrome grille ($25-40)
6. apple green body, black base, chrome grille ($25-40)
7. apple green body, charcoal base, chrome grille ($25-40)
8. apple green body, gray base, chrome grille ($25-40)
9. apple green body, black base, white grille ($25-40)
10. apple green body, charcoal base, white grille ($25-40)
11. apple green body, gray base, white grille ($25-40)
12. apple green body, unpainted base, white grille ($25-40)

MB50-B ARTICULATED DUMP TRUCK, issued 1973
NOTE: all models with black cab base, maltese cross front & 5 spoke rear wheels although other combinations exist.
1. orange-yellow cab, purple windows, blue dump, orange-yellow trailer base, with label s ($6-8)
2. orange-yellow cab, purple windows, blue dump, orange-yellow trailer base ($3-5)
3. yellow cab, purple windows, blue dump, orange-yellow trailer base, with labels ($6-8)
4. orange-yellow cab, purple windows, blue dump, orange trailer base ($3-5)
5. orange-yellow cab, red windows, blue dump, orange-yellow trailer base ($3-5)
6. yellow cab, purple windows, blue dump, lemon trailer base ($3-5)
7. orange-yellow cab, purple windows, blue dump, lemon trailer base, with tow hook ($4-6)(TP)
8. yellow cab, purple windows, blue dump, lemon trailer base, with tow hook ($4-6)(TP)
9. yellow cab, red windows, blue dump, orange trailer base ($3-5)
10. yellow cab, red windows, blue dump, lemon trailer base ($3-5)
11. yellow cab, purple windows, dark blue dump, lemon trailer base, with tow hook ($85-110)(BR)
12. yellow cab, purple windows, very dark blue dump, orange-yellow trailer base ($175-200)(BR)
13. red cab, purple windows, blue dump, red trailer base ($35-45)
14. red cab, red windows, blue dump, red trailer base ($35-45)
15. red cab, red windows, silver-gray dump, red trailer base, with tow hook ($8-12)(TP)
16. red body, purple windows, silver-gray dump, red trailer base, with tow hook ($8-12)(TP)

MB50-C ARTICULATED TRAILER, issued 1980 (TP)
1. blue dump, yellow trailer base ($4-6)(TP)
2. silver-gray dump, red trailer base ($6-8)(TP)

MB50-D HARLEY-DAVIDSON MOTORCYCLE, issued 1980
1. light tan body, black handlebars, no driver, England casting ($3-5)
2. dark tan body, black handlebars, no driver, England casting ($3-5)
3. light copper body, black handlebars, tan driver, England casting ($3-5)
4. mid tan body, black handlebars, tan driver, England casting ($3-5)
5. dark tan body, black handlebars, tan driver, England casting ($3-5)
6. dark tan body, black handlebars, brown driver, England casting ($3-5)
7. brown body, black handlebars, tan driver, Macau casting ($2-3)
8. dark metallic tan body, black handlebars, brown driver, Macau casting ($2-3)
9. light blue body, chrome handlebars, no driver, Thailand casting ($2-3)(HD)
10. orange body, chrome handlebars, no driver, Thailand casting ($2-3)(HD)
11. silver-gray body, chrome handlebars, Thailand casting ($2-3)(HD)
12. metallic red body, chrome handlebars, Thailand casting ($2-3)(HD)
13. metallic blue body, chrome handlebars, Thailand casting ($2-3)(HD)
14. white body, chrome handlebars, Thailand casting ($2-3)(HD)(PS)
15. orange-red body, chrome handlebars, Thailand casting ($2-3)(HD)(PS)
16. metallic charcoal body, chrome handlebars, Thailand casting ($2-3)(HD)
17. dark purple body, chrome handlebars, Thailand casting ($2-3)(HD)
18. fluorescent yellow body, chrome handlebars, Thailand casting ($2-3)(HD)(GS)
19. dark orange body, chrome handlebars, Thailand casting ($2-3)(HD)(GS)
20. metallic turquoise body, chrome handlebars, Thailand casting ($2-3)(HD)(GS)
21. yellow body, chrome handlebars, Thailand casting ($2-3)(HD)
22. gold plated body, chrome handlebars, Thailand casting ($2-3)(HD)
23. dark orange body, chrome handlebars, Thailand casting ($2-3)(HD)
24. turquoise body, chrome handlebars, Thailand casting ($2-3)(HD)
25. florescent orange body, chrome handlebars, China casting ($7-10)(HD)
26. red body, chrome handlebars, China casting ($2-3)(HD)

MB50-E CHEVY BLAZER, issued 1984
NOTE: All models with white interior & antenna, blue windows & dome lights, maltese cross wheels unless otherwise noted.
1. white body, chrome base, "Sheriff 7" tempa, Macau casting ($1-2)
2. white body, black base, "Sheriff 7" tempa, Macau casting ($1-2)
3. grape body, black base, orange/red/black tempa, Macau casting, includes plastic armament ($5-8)(RB)
4. white body, black base, "Sheriff 7" tempa, Thailand casting ($1-2)
5. white body, black base, "Sheriff 7" (without red hood print) tempa, Manaus casting ($45-60)(BR)
NOTE: Version 1-5 dome lights cast with metal strip in center. Versions 6 onward cast with one piece plastic unit.
6. white body, black base, blue windows, "Metro EMS" tempa, Thailand casting ($1-2)(MP)
7. white body, chrome base, chrome windows, blue/peach/magenta tempa, Thailand casting ($2-4)(ST)
8. black body, chrome base, chrome windows, pink & yellow tempa, Thailand casting ($2-4)(ST)
9. white body, black base, blue windows, "Sheriff 7" tempa, Thailand casting ($1-2)
10. white body, black base, blue windows, "7 Eleven" tempa, Thailand casting ($4-6)(US)
11. metallic red body, black base, blue windows, no tempa, Thailand casting ($1-2)(MP)
12. black body, chrome base, blue windows, "Police Unit 3" & gold star tempa, Thailand casting ($1-2)(MP)
13. blue body, chrome base, blue windows, "Police 50/ Police Dial 911" & star tempa, Thailand casting ($1-2)
14. blue body, chrome base, red windows, "Police 50/ Police Dial 911" & star tempa, Thailand casting ($1-2)
16. white body, chrome base, blue windows, "Police Unit 3" tempa, Thailand casting ($1-2)(MP)
17. black & white body, chrome base, blue windows, "Emergency Unit 50/ Off Road Patrol" tempa, Thailand casting ($1-2)
18. blue & white body, chrome base, blue windows, "Police Unit 14" tempa, Thailand casting ($1-2)(MP)
19. metallic gold body, chrome base, blue windows, no tempa, Thailand casting ($5-10)(CH)
20. white & black body, chrome base, blue windows, "Emergency Unit 50/ Off Road Patrol" tempa, Thailand casting ($1-2)(MW22)
21. white & black body, chrome base, blue windows, "Emergency Unit 50/ Off Road Patrol" tempa, China casting ($1-2)(MW22)
22. blue & white body, chrome base, blue windows, "Police 50/ Police Dial 911" tempa, China casting ($1-2)(MP)
23. beige & green body, chrome base, blue windows, "Park Police" tempa,, tan interior & antenna, China casting ($1-2)(MP)

MB50-H HARLEY-DAVIDSON CHOPPER, issued 1993 (HD)
1. metallic maroon body, chrome handlebars, white tempa, Thailand casting ($2-3)
2. yellow body, chrome handlebars, white tempa, Thailand casting ($2-3)
3. dk. fluorescent orange body, chrome handlebars, black flames tempa, Thailand casting ($2-3)(GS)
4. silver-gray body, chrome handlebars, white tempa, Thailand casting ($2-3)(GS)
5. red body, chrome handlebars, Thailand casting ($2-3)
6. gold plated body, chrome handlebars, Thailand casting ($2-3)
7. metallic blue body, chrome handlebars, Thailand casting ($2-3)
8. dark purple body, chrome handlebars, China casting ($7-10)
9. turquoise body, chrome handlebars, Thailand casting ($12-15)
10. pale florescent orange body, chrome handlebars, black flames tempa, China casting ($2-3)
11. black body, chrome handlebars, China casting ($2-3)
12. blue body, chrome handlebars, China casting ($2-3)

MB50-I HARLEY-DAVIDSON ELECTRAGLIDE, issued 1993 (HD)
1. white body, chrome handlebars, blue saddlebags, "Police" tempa, Thailand casting ($2-3)
2. black body, chrome handlebars, black saddlebags, "MBPD" tempa, Thailand casting ($2-3)
3. metallic blue body, chrome handlebars, black saddlebags, "MBPD" tempa, Thailand casting ($2-3)(GS)
4. pale gray body, chrome handlebars, black saddlebags, "MBPD" tempa, Thailand casting ($2-3)
5. gold plated body, chrome handlebars, black saddlebags, "Harley-Davidson" tempa, Thailand casting ($2-3)
6. orange-red body, chrome handlebars, orange saddlebags, "PMG" tempa, China casting ($10-15)(AU)
7. metallic red body, chrome handlebars, black saddlebags, no tempa, "Harley Davidson" tempa, China casting ($7-10)
8. dark blue body, chrome handlebars, black saddlebags, "Harley-Davidson" tempa, China casting ($2-3)
9. red body, chrome handlebars, black saddlebags, "Harley-Davidson" tempa, China casting ($2-3)
10. white body, chrome handlebars, white saddlebags, "MBPD" tempa, China casting ($2-3)
11. black body, chrome handlebars, black saddlebags, "Harley Davidson" tempa, China casting ($2-3)

MB50-J 1997 FORD F150 PICKUP, issued 1998

NOTE: All models listed with clear windows, chrome base, China base.

1. unpainted body, tan interior, Goodyear rubber tires, no tempa ($4-6)(FE)
2. black body, black & tan interior, Goodyear rubber slicks beige band tempa ($4-6)(FE)
3. black body, black & tan interior, Goodyear rubber slicks, pink-tan band tempa ($4-6)(FE)
4. red body, black interior, Goodyear rubber slicks, "4X4 Off Road" tempa ($1-2)(MW50)
5. black body, black & tan interior, Goodyear rubber tires, pink-tan band with "Matchbox/MDM/630-681-2101" tempa ($35-50)(C2)
6. black body, black & tan interior, Goodyear rubber tires, beige band with "Matchbox/MDM/630-681-2101" tempa ($35-50)(C2)
7. unpainted body, tan interior, Goodyear rubber tires, "Matchbox/MDM/630-681-2101" tempa ($35-50)(C2)

MB51-A EIGHT WHEEL TIPPER, issued 1970

1. yellow cab, silver-gray dump, chrome base, "Pointer" labels ($25-40)
2. yellow cab, silver-gray dump, chrome base, no labels ($25-40)
3. yellow cab, silver-gray dump, gray base, "Pointer" labels ($25-40)
4. yellow cab, silver-gray dump, gray base, no labels ($25-40)

MB51-B CITROEN S.M., issued 1972

1. bronze body, orange interior, unpainted base, no labels, 5 spoke wheels ($20-30)
2. bronze body, cream interior, unpainted base, no labels, 5 spoke wheels ($8-12)
3. bronze body, cream interior, silver-gray base, no labels, 5 spoke wheels ($8-12)
4. bronze body, light yellow interior, unpainted base, no labels, 5 spoke wheels ($8-12)
5. bronze body, dark yellow interior, unpainted base, no labels, 5 spoke wheels ($8-12)
6. bronze body, tan interior, unpainted base, no labels, 5 spoke wheels ($8-12)
7. metallic blue body, tan interior, unpainted base, no labels, 5 spoke wheels ($15-18)
8. metallic blue body, tan interior, unpainted base, "8" tempa, 5 spoke wheels ($8-12)
9. metallic blue body, dark yellow interior, unpainted base, "8" tempa, 5 spoke wheels ($8-12)
10. metallic blue body, ivory interior, unpainted base, "8" tempa, 5 spoke wheels ($8-12)
11. metallic blue body, lemon interior, unpainted base, "8" tempa, 5 spoke wheels ($8-12)
12. metallic blue body, lemon interior, unpainted base, "8" tempa, dot dash wheels ($8-12)
13. metallic blue body, yellow-orange interior, unpainted base, "8" tempa, dot dash wheels ($8-12)
14. metallic blue body, tan interior, unpainted base, "8" tempa, dot dash wheels ($8-12)
15. metallic blue body, yellow-orange interior, unpainted base, with label, dot dash wheels, roof rack ($5-8)(TP)
16. metallic blue body, red interior, unpainted base, with label, dot dash wheels, roof rack ($50-75)(TP)

NOTE: Available as an Hungarian & Bulgarian casting. Assorted colors available ($15-35)

MB51-C COMBINE HARVESTER, issued 1978

1. red body, black base, solid black wheels, no hubs, yellow rotor & chute, no tempa, England casting ($4-6)
2. red body, black base, black Superfast wheels, black hubs, yellow rotor & chute, no tempa, England casting ($4-6)
3. red body, black base, black Superfast wheels, yellow hubs, yellow rotor & chute, no tempa, England casting ($4-6)
4. red body, no base, black Superfast wheels, black hubs, yellow rotor & chute, no tempa, England casting ($4-6)
5. red body, no base, black Superfast wheels, yellow hubs, yellow rotor & chute, no tempa, England casting ($4-6)
6. orange body, black base, solid black wheels, yellow rotor & chute, no tempa, no origin cast (tab) ($350-500)(BR)
7. dark green body, black base, solid black wheels, yellow rotor & chute, no tempa, no origin cast (tab) ($350-500)(BR)
8. yellow body, no base, solid black wheels, red rotor & chute, "2" with stripes tempa, Macau casting ($1-2)(MC)
9. orange-yellow body, no base, solid black wheels, red rotor & chute, "2" with stripes tempa, Macau casting ($1-2)(MC)
10. lime & blue body, no base, solid red wheels, yellow rotor, lime chute, faces/gears/ haystack tempa, Macau casting ($6-8)(LL)
11. lime & blue body, no base, solid red wheels, yellow rotor, lime chute, faces/gears/ haystack tempa, Thailand casting ($6-8)(LL)
12. orange-yellow body, no base, solid black wheels, maroon rotor & chute, "2" with stripes tempa, Thailand casting ($1-2)(MC)

MB51-D MIDNIGHT MAGIC, issued 1981 (USA)

1. black body, silver sides, pearly silver base, 5 spoke front & maltese cross rear wheels, Hong Kong casting ($3-5)
2. black body, silver sides, pearly silver base, maltese cross front & 5 spoke rear wheels, Hong Kong casting ($3-5)
3. black body, silver sides, pearly silver base, 5 spoke front & rear wheels, Hong Kong casting ($3-5)
4. black body, silver sides, pearly white base, 5 spoke front & maltese cross rear wheels, Macau casting ($2-3)
5. black body, silver sides, pearly silver base, 5 spoke front & maltese cross rear wheels, Macau casting ($2-3)
6. black body, silver sides, unpainted base, 5 spoke front & maltese cross rear wheels, Hong Kong casting ($2-3)

NOTE: Available as a Bulgarian casting. Assorted colors available ($15-25)

MB51-G CAMARO IROC Z28, issued 1986 (USA)
MB68-F CAMARO IROC Z28, issued 1986 (ROW)

NOTE: All models with black base, silver-gray interior & clear windows unless otherwise noted.

1. apple green body, metal base, 8 dot wheels, "IROC Z" tempa, Macau casting ($4-6)
2. apple green body, metal base, 5 arch wheels, "IROC Z" tempa, Macau casting ($4-6)
3. blue body, metal base, 5 arch wheels, "IROC Z" on sides only tempa, Macau casting ($2-4)
4. blue body, metal base, 8 dot wheels, "IROC Z" on sides only tempa, Macau casting ($2-4)
5. red body, metal base, starburst wheels, "Carter/ Goodyear" tempa, Macau casting ($3-5)(SF)
6. metallic red body, metal base, laser wheels, "Carter/ Goodyear" tempa, Macau casting ($3-5)(LW)
7. blue body, metal base, 8 dot wheels, "IROC Z" hood & sides tempa without extra black line, Macau casting ($2-4)
8. blue body, metal base, 8 dot wheels, "IROC Z" hood & sides tempa with extra black line, Macau casting ($2-4)
9. lemon body, metal base, 8 dot wheels, "IROC Z" with stripes tempa, Macau casting ($1-2)
10. metallic copper body, metal base, laser wheels, "Carter/ Goodyear" tempa, Macau casting ($4-6)(LW)
11. blue-green body, metal base, 8 dot wheels, "BP Stunt Team" & stripes tempa, Macau casting ($8-12)(DU)
12. lemon body, plastic base, 8 dot wheels, "IROC Z" with stripes tempa, Macau casting ($1-2)
13. lemon body, plastic base, 8 dot wheels, "IROC Z" with stripes tempa, Thailand casting ($1-2)
14. metallic blue body, plastic base, 8 dot wheels, black windows, "350Z" with pink/ purple/ lime stripes tempa, Thailand casting ($3-5)(TH)
15. black body, plastic base, 8 dot wheels, "Z28" with orange bands & white stripes tempa, Thailand casting ($1-2)
16. red body, plastic base, 8 dot wheels, white stripes tempa, Thailand casting ($2-3)(SS)
17. dark purple body, plastic base, 8 dot wheels, silver band & "Z28" tempa, Thailand casting ($2-4)(CC)

MB51-K FORD AMBULANCE, issued 1997
MB17-H FORD AMBULANCE, issued 1997

NOTE: All models listed with smoke windows, red dome lights & China casting

1. white body, chrome base, chrome disc with rubber tires, "Ambulance Dial 911" ($4-6)(IG)
2. unpainted body, chrome base, chrome disc with rubber tires, no tempa ($4-6)(IG)
3. white body, chrome base, 8 dot wheels, "27 Matchbox Ambulance" with blue & silver tempa ($1-2)
4. yellow body, chrome base, 8 dot wheels, "York Fair Emergency 1997" tempa ($5-8)(WR)
5. yellow body, chrome base, 8 dot wheels, "27 Matchbox Ambulance" with blue & silver tempa ($1-2) (MW25)
6. yellow body, translucent white base, 8 dot wheels, "27 Matchbox Ambulance" with blue & silver tempa ($50-75)(MW25)
7. red body, chrome base, chrome disc with rubber tires, "Fire Rescue" with white band tempa ($3-5)(PC21)
8. metallic gold body, chrome base, 8 dot wheels, no tempa ($5-10)(CH)
9. white body, chrome base, 8 dot wheels, maroon cab & "County EMS" tempa ($1-2)(MP)
10. white body, chrome base, 8 dot wheels, no tempa ($25-40)(ASAP blank)
11. white body, chrome base, 8 dot wheels, "American International Recovery" tempa ($100+)(ASAP)

MB52-A DODGE CHARGER, issued 1970

1. pinkish red body, green base, no labels ($10-15)
2. pale red body, green base, no labels ($10-15)
3. pale red body, green base, "5" on roof with side labels ($10-15)(GS)
4. dark red body, green base, "5" on roof with side labels ($10-15)(GS)
5. dark red body, green base, no labels ($10-15)
6. dark red body, green base, yellow & black hood label ($10-15)
7. magenta body, green base, no labels ($10-15)
8. purple body, green base, no labels ($15-20)
9. lime body, bright red base, no labels ($10-15)
10. lime body, red base, no labels ($10-15)
11. lime body, red base, "5" on roof with sides labels ($15-20)(GS)
12. lime body, red base, "Castrol" hood label ($500-750)
13. lime body, unpainted base, no labels ($10-15)

MB52-B POLICE LAUNCH, issued 1976

1. white deck, blue hull, light blue figures, dark blue windows, "Police" labels, horns cast, England casting ($5-7)
2. white deck, blue hull (tab), light blue figures, dark blue windows, "Police" labels, horns cast, no origin cast ($50-65)(BR)
3. white deck, blue hull, light blue figures, dark blue windows, "Police" labels, hatch cast, England casting ($4-6)
4. white deck, blue hull, light blue figures, opaque blue windows, "Police" labels, hatch cast, England casting ($4-6)
5. white deck,, dark blue hull, light blue figures, light blue windows, "Police" labels, hatch cast, England casting ($4-6)
6. white deck, dark blue hull, light blue figures, opaque blue windows, "Police" labels, hatch cast, England casting ($4-6)
7. white deck, red hull, orange-yellow figures, light blue windows, "LA Fire" labels, hatch cast, England casting ($6-8)(CR)
8. white deck, red hull, light blue figures, light blue windows, "LA Fire" labels, hatch cast, England casting ($10-15)(CR)
9. black deck, dark gray hull, dark gray figures, light blue windows, tan & gray camouflage tempa, hatch cast, Macau casting ($4-5)(CM)
10. white deck, blue hull, red figures & wheels, light blue windows, "123" & rope pattern tempa, hatch cast, Macau casting ($6-8)(LL)
11. white deck, blue hull, red figures & wheels, light blue windows, "123" & rope pattern tempa, hatch cast, Thailand casting ($6-8)(LL)
12. white deck white hull, white figures, light blue windows, no tempa, hatch cast, China casting ($10-15)(GF)
13. white deck, blue hull with brown painted base, blue figures, clear windows, "Amity Police/ Jaws" tempa, horns cast, China casting ($4-6)(STR)
14. yellow deck, black hull, red figures, clear windows, "Rescue B-1" with red & white stripe tempa, horns cast, China casting ($2-4)(RT)
15. white deck, dark blue hull, dark blue figures, blue windows, "Police" & orange stripes tempa, horns cast, China casting ($2-4)(AV)

MB52-C BMW M1, issued 1981

1. silver-gray body, black base, clear windows, red interior, "52" tempa ($2-4)
2. silver-gray body, blue-gray base, clear windows, red interior, "52" tempa ($2-4)
3. silver-gray body, blue-gray base, smoke windows, red interior, "52" tempa ($2-4)
4. silver-gray body, black base, amber windows, red interior, "52" tempa ($12-15)
5. silver-gray body, black base, green windows, red interior, "52" tempa ($60-75)
6. silver-gray body, black base, clear windows, pink-red interior, "52" tempa ($2-4)
7. silver-gray body, black base, amber windows, pink-red interior, "52" tempa ($12-15)

MB52-D BMW M1, issued 1983

NOTE; this is a highly modified version to MB52-C in which the hood has been cast closed with a spoiler added to the front & rear of the body. All models with black plastic base, clear windows, 5 arch wheels unless otherwise noted.

1. white body, black interior, "BMW M1" tempa, Macau casting ($2-3)
2. black body, red interior, "Pirelli 59" tempa, Macau casting ($3-5)
3. yellow body, black interior, "11" with stripes tempa, Macau casting ($1-2)
4. yellow body, black interior, "11" with stripes tempa, China casting ($1-2)
5. yellow body, black interior, "11" with stripes tempa (all black "Bell" logo & all red "Champion" logo), China casting ($1-2)
6. bright red body, black interior, "1" with stripes tempa, Macau casting ($1-2)
7. red body, black interior, "1" with stripes tempa, Macau casting ($1-2)
8. dark yellow body, black interior, chrome windows, gray disc with rubber tires, detailed trim tempa, China casting ($5-8)(WC)
9. chrome plated body, black interior, no tempa, Macau casting ($12-18)(C2)
10. chrome plated body, black interior, no tempa, China casting ($12-18)(C2)
11. bright red body, black interior, "1" with stripes tempa, Thailand casting ($1-2)
12. black body, red interior, "Pirelli 59" tempa, Manaus casting ($35-50)(BR)
13. metallic blue body, black & gray interior, detailed trim tempa, chrome disc with rubber tires, Thailand casting ($15-20)(GC)

MB52-E ISUZU AMIGO, issued 1991

NOTE: All models with chrome base, & dot dash wheels

1. metallic blue body, gray interior, "Isuzu Amigo" tempa, Thailand casting ($5-7)
2. lemon body, gray interior, pink stripes & design tempa, Thailand casting ($2-3)(DM)
3. red body, gray interior, "Amigo" with silver & orange stripes tempa, Thailand casting ($2-3)
4. white body, neon orange interior, blue splash tempa, Thailand casting ($1-2)(MP)
5. purple body, black interior, skeleton & "Hadrosaur" tempa, Thailand casting ($1-2)(MP)
6. purple body, black interior, skeleton & "Hadrosaur" tempa, China casting ($1-2)(MP)
7. white body, neon orange interior, blue splash tempa, China casting ($1-2)(MP)
8. navy blue body, gray interior, green splash tempa, China casting ($1-2)(MP)

MB52-F FORD ESCORT COSWORTH, issued 1994

NOTE: All models listed with clear windows.

1. white body, white spoiler & base, blue interior, gold 6-spoke spiral wheels, "Mobil l/Michelin 5" tempa, Thailand casting ($1-2)
2. white body, white spoiler & base, blue interior, gold 6-spoke spiral wheels, "Mobil l/Michelin 5" tempa, China casting ($1-2)
3. white body, white spoiler & base, blue interior, silver 6-spoke spiral wheels, "Mobil 1/ Michelin 5" tempa, China casting ($1-2)
4. white body, white spoiler, blue base, white interior, silver 6-spoke spiral wheels, "Mobil 1/ Michelin 5" tempa, China casting ($2-4)

5. metallic red body, red spoiler & base, white interior, silver 6-spoke spiral wheels, lime & white design tempa, China casting ($1-2)
6. white body, white spoiler & base, blue interior, silver 6 spoke spiral wheels, "Ford 23" & black design tempa, China casting ($1-2)(MP)
7. red body, black spoiler, red base, light gray interior, silver 6 spoke spiral wheels, "5" with yellow splash tempa, China casting ($3-5)(MP)
8. white body, white spoiler & base, white interior, silver 6 spoke spiral wheels, "MOL" with orange & 2 tone green stripes tempa, China casting ($25-40)(HU)
9. metallic gold body, black spoiler & base, black interior, silver 6 spoko spiral wheels, no tempa , China casting ($5-10)(CH)
10. white body, dark blue spoiler, white base, dark blue interior, 5 spoke concave star wheels, "Matchbox 3" tempa, China casting ($1-2)(MP)
11. metallic red body, black spoiler, red base, white interior, 5 spoke concave star wheels, lime & white design tempa, China casting ($2-3)
12. red body, black spoiler, red base, light gray interior, 5 spoke concave star wheels, "5" on yellow splash tempa, China casting ($1-2)(MP)
13. black body, black spoiler & base, light gray interior, 5 spoke concave star wheels, "1" with yellow & white design tempa, China casting ($1-2)

MB53-A FORD ZODIAC MK IV, issued 1970
1. light blue body, unpainted base ($350-425)
2. light green body, unpainted base ($15-20)
3. mid green body, unpainted base ($15-20)
4. dark green body, unpainted base, ($15-20)
5. emerald green body, unpainted base ($15-20)
6. apple green body, unpainted base ($25-30)

MB53-B TANZARA, issued 1972
1. orange body, unpainted base, chrome interior, blue-green windows, no tempa ($12-15)
2. orange body, unpainted base, chrome interior, amber windows, no tempa ($15-18)
3. white body, unpainted base, chrome interior, amber windows, no tempa ($18-25)
4. white body, unpainted base, chrome interior, amber windows, orange stripes tempa ($12-15)
5. white body, unpainted base, chrome interior, amber windows, red stripes tempa ($12-15)
6. white body, silver-gray base, chrome interior, amber windows, red stripes tempa ($12-15)
7. white body, unpainted base, chrome interior, blue-green windows, red stripes tempa ($15-20)
8. white body, unpainted base, red interior, amber windows, red stripes tempa ($25-40)

MB53-C JEEP CJ6, issued 1977
1. red body, tan roof, orange-yellow interior, unpainted base, no tempa ($4-6)
2. red body, tan roof, orange-yellow interior, silver-gray base, no tempa ($4-6)
3. red body, tan roof, orange-yellow interior, unpainted base, no tempa, black hubs ($5-7)
4. red body, light tan roof, orange-yellow interior, unpainted base, no tempa ($4-6)
5. red body, tan roof, light orange interior, unpainted base, no tempa ($4-6)
6. red body, tan roof, black interior, unpainted base, no tempa ($5-8)
7. green body, tan roof, orange-yellow interior, unpainted base, no tempa ($5-8)
8. green body, tan roof, orange-yellow interior, silver-gray base, no tempa ($5-8)
9. green body, tan roof, black interior, unpainted base, no tempa ($4-6)
10. light green body, pink-tan roof, black interior, unpainted base, no tempa ($4-6)
11. light yellow body, brown roof, black interior, black base, stripes tempa ($5-7)
12. yellow body, brown roof, black interior, black base, stripes tempa ($5-7)
13. yellow body, brown roof, black interior, charcoal base, stripes tempa ($4-6)
NOTE: Available as an Hungarian casting. Assorted colors available. ($15-25)

MB53-D FLARESIDE PICKUP, issued 1982
MB55-J FLARESIDE PICKUP, reissued 1994
1. blue body, charcoal base, white interior, clear windows, 8 spoke wheels, "326 Baja Bouncer" tempa, England casting ($2-4)
2. blue body, black base, white interior, clear windows, 8 spoke wheels, "326 Baja Bouncer" tempa, England casting ($2-4)
3. blue body, black base, white interior, clear windows, 8 spoke wheels, "326 Baja Bouncer" (plain sides) tempa, England casting ($4-6)
4. blue body, black base, white interior, clear windows, 8 spoke wheels, "326 Baja Bouncer" (plain hood) tempa, England casting ($4-6)
5. blue body, black base, white interior, blue windows, 8 spoke wheels, "326 Baja Bouncer" tempa, England casting ($45-60)
6. orange body, black base, white interior, clear windows, 8 spoke wheels, "326 Baja Bouncer" tempa, Macau casting ($2-4)
7. yellow body, black base, white interior, clear windows, 8 spoke wheels, "Ford 460" tempa, Macau casting ($175-225)
8. yellow body, black base, black interior, clear windows, 8 spoke wheels, "Ford 460" tempa, Macau casting ($35-50)
9. yellow body, black base, black interior, clear windows, racing slicks (chromed letters) wheels, "Ford 460" tempa, Macau casting ($2-3)
10. yellow body, black base, black interior, clear windows, racing slicks (unchromed letters) wheels, "Ford 460" tempa, Macau casting ($1-2)
11. khaki green body, black base, black interior, opaque green windows, dark purple & blue design tempa, racing slicks wheels, Macau casting, includes plastic armament ($5-8)(RB)
12. white body, black base, black interior, clear windows, "Deb" tempa, racing slicks wheels, Macau casting ($35-50)(UK)(OP)
13. red body, black base, white interior, clear windows, "326 Baja Bouncer" tempa, 8 spoke wheels, Manaus casting ($75-100)(BR)
14. lime body, yellow base, red interior, clear windows, jack & wheel design tempa, red racing slicks, Thailand casting ($6-8)(LL)
15. red body, black base, black interior, clear windows, "Bill Elliot 11" tempa, racing slicks wheels ($5-7)(WR)(TC)
16. fluorescent yellow body, chrome base, no interior, chrome windows, racing slicks (unchromed letters), pink/red/blue flash tempa, Thailand casting ($2-4)(ST)
17. metallic blue body, chrome base, no interior, chrome windows, racing slicks (unchromed letters), yellow with orange flames tempa, Thailand casting ($2-4)(ST)
18. red body, chrome base, black interior, clear windows, racing slicks (unchromed letters), orange & yellow flames tempa, Thailand casting ($1-2)
19. dark yellow body, black base, black interior, clear windows, racing slicks (unchromed letters), "Ford 460" tempa, Thailand casting ($2-4)(MP)
20. white body, chrome base, chrome interior, clear windows, racing slicks (gray insert), silver band & red stripe tempa, Thailand casting ($2-4)(CC)
21. dark blue body, black base, chrome interior, clear windows, racing slicks (unchromed letters), "QC Quality Care 15" tempa, Thailand casting ($3-5)(WR)(TC)
22. florescent orange body, chrome base, black interior, clear windows, racing slicks, black front design tempa, China casting ($1-2)
23. red body, chrome base, black interior, clear windows, racing slicks, orange & yellow flames tempa, China casting ($1-2)
24. silver-gray body, chrome base, purple interior, clear windows, racing slicks, purple & lavender flames tempa, China casting ($1-2)(MP)
25. blue body, chrome base, pale orange interior, clear windows, racing slicks, white splash tempa, China casting ($1-2)
26. blue body, chrome base, dark orange interior, clear windows, racing slicks, white splash tempa, China casting ($1-2)
27. silver-gray body, black interior, clear windows, racing slicks, "Jay's Flight Team" tempa, China casting, includes black launcher & white glider ($2-4)(AS)
28. met. green-gold body, black interior, chrome base, clear windows, racing slicks, no tempa, China casting ($5-10)(CH55)
29. black body, yellow interior, chrome base, clear windows, racing slicks, orange & yellow flames tempa, China casting ($1-2)(MP)
30. dark purple body, gray interior, chrome base, clear windows, racing slicks, white splash tempa, China casting ($1-2)(MW55)
31. silver-gray body, black interior, clear windows, racing slicks, "Jay's Flight Team" tempa, China casting ($1-2)(LS)(Avon)

MB53-G FORD LTD TAXI, issued 1992 (USA)
MB56-G FORD LTD TAXI, issued 1992 (ROW)
1. yellow body, chrome base, blue interior, clear windows, 8 dot wheels, "Radio XYZ Cab" & checkers tempa, Thailand casting ($3-5)
2. yellow body, chrome base, white interior, clear windows, 8 dot wheels, checkers & "Taxi" tempa, Thailand casting ($4-6)(STR)

MB53-H RHINO ROD, issued 1994 (USA)
MB24-J RHINO ROD, issued 1994 (ROW)
NOTE" All models listed with white horns, chrome engine & rear bumper.
1. dark gray body, gray base, red painted eyes tempa, gold 6-spoke spiral wheels, China casting ($1-2)
2. dark gray body, gray base, orange painted eyes tempa, silver 6-spoke spiral wheels, China casting ($1-2)
3. dark gray body, gray base, black painted eyes tempa, silver 6-spoke spiral wheels, China casting ($1-2)
4. black body, black base, white painted eyes tempa, silver 6-spoke spiral wheels, China casting ($1-2)
5. black body, black base, white painted eyes tempa, 5 spoke concave star wheels, China casting ($2-4)
6. pale gray body, light gray base , red painted eyes tempa, 5 spoke concave star wheels, China casting ($1-2)
7. metallic gold body, black base, black painted eyes tempa, 5 spoke concave star wheels, China casting ($5-10)(CH)
8. metallic dark gray body, dark charcoal base, yellow painted eyes, 5 spoke concave star wheels, China casting ($1-2)(MW43)

MB54-A S&S CADILLAC AMBULANCE, issued 1970
1. white body, black base, plain grille ($35-50)
2. white body, black base, silver grille ($35-50)
3. off white body, black base, plain grille ($35-50)

MB54-B FORD CAPRI, issued 1971
1. light peach body, black hood, ivory interior, unpainted base, 5 spoke wheels ($12-15)
2. dark peach body, black hood, ivory interior, unpainted base, 5 spoke wheels ($12-15)
3. purple body & hood, ivory interior, unpainted base, 5 spoke wheels ($10-15)
4. purple body & hood, white interior, unpainted base, 5 spoke wheels ($10-15)
5. purple body & hood, ivory interior, silver-gray base, 5 spoke wheels ($10-15)
6. purple body & hood, ivory interior, unpainted base, maltese cross wheels ($10-15)
7. orange body & hood, ivory interior, unpainted base, 5 spoke wheels ($7-10)(TP)

MB54-C PERSONNEL CARRIER, issued 1976
1. olive body, green windows, no rear seats, dot dash silver wheels ($4-6)
2. olive body, green windows, tan rear seats, dot dash silver wheels ($4-6)
3. olive body, green windows, tan rear seats, dot dash black wheels ($4-6)
4. olive body, blue-green windows, tan rear seats, dot dash black wheels ($4-6)

MB54-D MOBILE HOME, issued 1980
1. ivory body, black base, dark brown door, no tempa ($3-5)
2. ivory body, charcoal base, dark brown door, no tempa ($3-5)
3. cream body, black base, dark brown door, no tempa ($3-5)
4. cream body, charcoal base, dark brown door, no tempa ($3-5)
5. cream body, black base, chocolate door, no tempa ($3-5)
6. cream body, charcoal base, chocolate door, no tempa ($3-5)
7. white body, charcoal base, light brown door, no tempa ($3-5)
8. white body, gray-brown base, light brown door, no tempa ($3-5)
9. white body, gray-brown base, dark brown door, no tempa ($3-5)
10. white body, black base, light brown door, no tempa ($3-5)
11. white body, black base, dark brown door, no tempa ($3-5)
12. white body, charcoal base, light brown door, stripes tempa ($4-6)
13. white body, charcoal base, dark brown door, stripes tempa ($4-6)

MB54-E NASA TRACKING VEHICLE, issued 1982
1. white body, black base, red door, clear windows, no side tempa, dot dash wheels, England casting ($4-6)
2. white body, black base, red door, clear windows, with side tempa, dot dash wheels, England casting ($3-5)
3. white body, charcoal base, red door, clear windows, with side tempa, dot dash wheels, England casting ($3-5)
4. white body, black base, red door, clear windows, with side tempa, dot dash wheels, Macau casting ($2-3)
5. white body, black base, maroon door, clear windows, with side tempa, dot dash wheels, Macau casting ($2-3)
6. white body, black base, red door, blue windows, with side tempa, dot dash wheels, Macau casting ($3-5)
7. white body, black base, red door, blue windows, with side tempa, 8 dot wheels, Macau casting ($3-5)
8. white body, black base, maroon door, blue windows, with side tempa, dot dash wheels, Macau casting ($3-5)

MB54-F COMMAND VEHICLE, issued 1984
NOTE: All models with black base & blue windows.
1. red body with white painted roof, metal base, 8 dot silver wheels, chrome beacons, red pumper, "Foam Unit" & checkerboard tempa, Macau casting ($35-50)
2. yellow body, metal base, 8 dot silver wheels, chrome beacons, red pumper, "Foam Unit 3 Metro Airport" tempa, Macau casting ($2-4)
3. red body, metal base, 8 dot silver wheels, chrome beacons, red pumper, "Foam Unit 3 Metro Airport" tempa, Macau casting ($2-3)
4. red body, metal base, dot dash wheels, chrome beacons, red pumper, "Foam Unit 3 Metro Airport" tempa, Macau casting ($2-3)
5. red body, plastic base, dot dash wheels, chrome beacons, red pumper, "Foam Unit 3 Metro Airport" tempa, Macau casting ($2-3)
6. red body, plastic base, 8 dot silver wheels, chrome beacons, red pumper, "Foam Unit 3 Metro Airport" tempa, Macau casting ($2-3)
7. red body, plastic base, 8 dot gold wheels, chrome beacons, red pumper, "Foam Unit 3 Metro Airport" tempa, Macau casting ($18-25)
8. white body, plastic base, 8 dot silver wheels, chrome beacons & radar, "NASA Space Shuttle Command Center" tempa, Macau casting ($3-4)(TC)
9. yellow body, plastic base, 8 dot silver wheels, chrome beacons, red pumper, "Foam Unit 3 Metro Airport" tempa, Macau casting ($2-3)(MP)
10. red body, plastic base, 8 dot silver wheels, chrome beacons, red pumper, "3" & Japanese lettered tempa, Macau casting ($8-12)(JP)(GS)
11. olive body, plastic base, 8 dot black wheels, black beacons & radar, "9" & red/ white stripes tempa, Macau casting ($4-5)(CM)
12. olive body, plastic base, 8 dot silver wheels, black beacons & radar, "9" & red/ white stripes tempa, Macau casting ($18-25)(CM)
13. black body, plastic base, 8 dot black wheels, dark gray beacons & radar, "LS150" & yellow stripes tempa, Macau casting ($4-5)(CM)
14. yellow body, plastic base, 8 dot silver wheels, black beacons, red pumper, "Foam Unit 3 Metro Airport" tempa, Macau casting ($2-4)
15. red body, plastic base, 8 dot silver wheels, black beacons, red pumper, "Foam Unit 3 Metro Airport" tempa, Macau casting ($2-4)
16. white body, plastic base, 8 dot silver wheels, black beacons, chrome radar, "NASA Space Shuttle Command Center" tempa, Macau casting ($2-4)
17. red body, plastic base, 8 dot silver wheels, black beacons, red pumper, "Foam Unit 3 Metro Airport" tempa, Thailand casting ($1-2)
18. yellow body, plastic base, 8 dot silver wheels, black beacons, red pumper, "Foam Unit 3 Metro Airport" tempa, Thailand casting ($1-2)
19. white body, plastic base, 8 dot silver wheels, black beacons, chrome radar, "NASA Space Shuttle Command Center" tempa, Thailand casting ($1-2)
20. florescent orange body, plastic base, 8 dot silver wheels, chrome beacons & pumper, "Foam Unit/ City Airport/ Emergency Rescue" tempa, Thailand casting ($1-2)(EM)
21. red body, plastic base, 8 dot silver wheels, silver beacons, silver pumper, "Fire Rescue" with gold crest, white band & black & gold stripes tempa, Thailand casting ($1-2)(MP)
22. black body, brown plastic base, 8 dot black wheels, brown beacons, brown pumper, brown & green camouflage tempa, Thailand casting ($1-2)(MP)
23. blue body, plastic base, 8 dot silver wheels, silver beacons, silver pumper, "Command Center" tempa, Thailand casting ($1-2)(MP)

24. blue body, plastic base, 8 dot silver wheels, silver beacons, silver pumper, "Command Center" tempa, China casting ($1-2)(MP)
25. black body, brown plastic base, 8 dot black wheels, brown beacons, brown pumper, brown & green camouflage tempa, China casting ($1-2)(MP)

MB54-G CHEVY LUMINA, issued 1989
NOTE: the body casting for MB54-G is based on a redesigned casting of the MB10-D Buick LeSabre with different size window and redesigned grille. All models with clear windows & Goodyear slicks.
1. matt pink & white body, white base, black interior, "Superflo 46" tempa, Macau casting ($6-8)(DT)
2. dark pink & white body, white base, black interior, "Superflo 46" tempa, Macau casting ($6-8)(DT)
3. matt green & lime body, green base, black interior, "City Chevrolet 46" tempa, Macau casting ($4-6)(DT)
4. bright green & lime body, green base, black interior, "City Chevrolet 46" tempa, Macau casting ($4-6)(DT)
5. bright orange & blue body, orange base, black interior, "Hardees 18" tempa, Macau casting ($6-8)(DT)
6. black body, black base, red interior, "Exxon 51" without roof signature tempa, Macau casting ($6-8)(DT)
7. black body, black base, red interior, "Exxon 51" with roof signature tempa, Macau casting ($6-8)(DT)
8. black body, green base, gray interior, "Mello Yello 51" tempa, Macau casting ($6-8)(DT)
9. white body, white base, white interior, no tempa, Thailand casting ($10-15)(GF)
NOTE: Due to the demand of "Days of Thunder" at the time, Matchbox couldn't keep up supply. They asked the company that makes Racing Champions to supply their castings and place them in Matchbox blistercards. These are quickly identified as the base of the model faces down against the blistercard. ($8-12) each.

MB54-H CHEVY LUMINA, issued 1990
NOTE: All models wit h black base unless otherwise noted.
1. dark pink & white body, clear windows, black interior, Goodyear slicks, "Superflo 46" tempa, Macau casting ($6-8)(DT)
2. green & lime body, clear windows, black interior, Goodyear slicks, "City Chevrolet 46" tempa, Macau casting ($6-8)(DT)
3. bright orange & blue body, clear windows, black interior, Goodyear slicks, "Hardees 18" tempa, Macau casting ($6-8)(DT)
4. black body, clear windows, red interior, Goodyear slicks, large "Exxon 51" (with signature) tempa, Macau casting ($6-8)(DT)
5. black body, clear windows, red interior, Goodyear slicks, small "Exxon 51" (without signature) tempa, Macau casting ($25-40)(DT)
6. black body, clear windows, gray interior, Goodyear slicks, "Mello Yello 51" tempa, Macau casting ($4-6)(DT)
7. black body, clear windows, red interior, Goodyear slicks, "Goodwrench 3/ GM" without "Western Steer" & plain trunk tempa, Macau casting ($12-15)(WR)
8. dark blue body, clear windows, gray interior, Goodyear slicks, "Matchbox Motorsports 35" tempa, Macau casting ($2-3)
9. dark blue body, clear windows, gray interior, Goodyear slicks, "Matchbox Motorsports 35" tempa, China casting ($2-3)
10. black body, clear windows, red interior, Goodyear slicks, "Goodwrench 3/ GM" without "Western Steer" with trunk tempa, China casting ($7-10)(WR)
11. white body, clear windows, black interior, Goodyear slicks, "PG Tags" tempa, Macau casting ($85-110)(UK)(OP)
12. chrome plated body, clear windows, gray interior, Goodyear slicks, no tempa, Macau casting ($15-18)(C2)
13. white & florescent yellow body, blue-chrome & black windows, no interior, lightning wheels, blue spatter & lightning bolts tempa, China casting ($7-10)(LT)(PS)
14. white & black body, chrome & black windows, no interior, lightning wheels, pink spatter & lightning bolts tempa, China casting ($7-10)(LT)(PS)
15. black body, clear windows, red interior, black disc with rubber tires, "Goodwrench 3/GM" with "Western Steer" tempa, China casting ($5-7)(WR)(TC)
16. orange-yellow body, clear windows, black interior, black disc with rubber tires, "Kodak Film 4 Racing" tempa, China casting ($5-7)(WR)(TC)
17. yellow body, clear windows, black interior, Goodyear slicks, "MAC Tool Distributors 10" tempa, China casting ($15-20)(WR)
18. red & yellow body, clear windows, black interior, Goodyear slicks, "Matchbox Racing 7" tempa, China casting ($2-3)(HS)
19. white & metallic blue body, clear windows, red interior, Goodyear slicks, "Matchbox Racing 1" tempa, China casting ($2-3)(HS)
20. white body, clear windows, gray interior, Goodyear slicks, "Team Goodyear 11" tempa, China casting ($2-3)(HS)
21. orange body, clear windows, black interior, Goodyear slicks, "Team Goodyear 22" tempa, China casting ($2-3)(HS)
22. black body, clear windows, red interior, Goodyear slicks, "Champion 4" tempa, China casting ($2-3)(HS)
23. yellow body, clear windows, gray interior, Goodyear slicks, "Champion 3" tempa, China casting ($2-3)(HS)
24. orange-yellow body, clear windows, black interior, Goodyear slicks, "Kodak Film 4 Racing" tempa, China casting ($3-4)(WR)
25. florescent orange & white body, clear windows, black interior, gray disc with rubber tires, "Purolator 10" tempa, China casting ($4-5)(WR)(TC)
26. dark pink & white body, clear windows, black interior, Goodyear slicks, "Superflo 46" tempa, China casting ($3-5)(DT)
27. green & lime body, clear windows, black interior, Goodyear slicks, "City Chevrolet 46" tempa, China casting ($3-5)(DT)
28. bright orange & blue body, clear windows, black interior, Goodyear slicks, "Hardees 18" tempa, China casting ($3-5)(DT)
29. black body, clear windows, red interior, Goodyear slicks, "Exxon 51" tempa, China casting ($3-5)(DT)
30. black body, clear windows, gray interior, Goodyear slicks, "Mello Yello 51" tempa, China casting ($3-5)(DT)
31. black body, clear windows, red interior, gray disc with rubber tires, "Goodwrench 3/ GM" with "Western Steer" tempa, China casting ($6-8)(WR)(TC)
32. black body, clear windows, red interior, gray disc with rubber tires, "Goodwrench 3/ GM" without "Western Steer" tempa, China casting ($15-25)(WR)(Winross promo)
33. matt black body, clear windows, red interior, gray disc with rubber tires, "3" & "GM Parts" tempa, China casting ($15-25)(WR)(Winross promo)
34. white & green body, clear windows, silver-gray interior, gold disc with rubber tires, "Hendricks 25" tempa, China casting ($6-8)(WR)(TC)
35. florescent green body, clear windows, silver-gray interior, Goodyear slicks, "Matchbox Motorsports 35" tempa, China casting ($2-3)
36. black body, clear windows, red interior, Goodyear slicks, "Goodwrench/ GM/ Mom N Pops" with "Western Steer" tempa, China casting ($6-8)(WR)(OP)
37. white & orange body, clear windows, orange interior, Goodyear slicks, "Ferree Chevrolet 49" tempa, China casting ($3-5)(WR)
38. yellow & orange body, black & chrome windows, no interior, lightning wheels, red spatter & lightning bolts tempa, China casting ($3-4)(LT)(PS)
39. green & white body, black & chrome windows, no interior, lightning wheels, purple spatter & lightning bolts tempa, China casting ($3-4)(LT)(PS)
40. dark purple & white body, clear windows, silver-gray interior, Goodyear slicks, "Phil Parsons Racing 29/ Matchbox" tempa, China casting ($12-15)(WR)
41. dark purple & white body, clear windows, silver-gray interior, Goodyear slicks, "White Rose Collectibles 29/ Matchbox" tempa, China casting ($3-5)(WR)
42. maroon body, clear windows, silver-gray interior, Goodyear slicks, "Penrose 44/ Fire Cracker Sausage/ Big Mama" tempa, China casting ($6-8)(WR)
43. lime & black body, clear windows, silver-gray interior, Goodyear slicks, "Interstate Batteries 18" tempa, China casting ($3-5)(WR)
44. metallic blue & white body, clear windows, red interior, Goodyear slicks, "Raybestos 12" tempa, China casting ($3-5)(WR)
45. metallic blue & white body, clear windows, red interior, Goodyear slicks, "Raybestos 12" without "Tic Tac" logo tempa, China casting ($75-100)(WR)
46. florescent orange & white body, clear windows, black interior, 9 spoke Goodyear slicks, "Purolator 10" tempa, China casting ($3-5)(WR)
47. florescent orange & white body, clear windows, black interior, Goodyear slicks wheels, "Purolator 10" tempa, China casting ($3-5)(WR)
48. black body, clear windows, gray interior, Goodyear slicks, "Stanley Tools 92" tempa, China casting ($3-5)(WR)
49. black body, clear windows, gray interior, 9 spoke Goodyear slicks, "Stanley Tools 92" tempa, China casting ($3-5)(WR)
50. maroon body, clear windows, silver-gray interior, Goodyear slicks, "Slim Jim 44" tempa, China casting ($6-8)(WR)
51. florescent green body, clear windows, silver-gray interior, Goodyear slicks, "Matchbox Motorsports 35" (without black grille) tempa, China casting ($1-2)
52. yellow body, clear windows, silver-gray interior, Goodyear slicks, "MAC Tools 7" tempa, China casting ($7-10)(WR)
53. lemon & white body, clear windows, gray interior, yellow disc with rubber tires, "Texas Pete/ Lozito's 87" tempa, Thailand casting ($4-6)(WR)
54. black body, clear windows, red interior, 9 spoke Goodyear slicks, "Goodwrench 3/ GM" with "Western Steer" tempa, China casting ($3-5)(WR)
55. black body, gray interior, Goodyear slicks, "TIC Financial 8" tempa, Thailand casting ($3-5)(WR)
56. black body, gray interior, Goodyear slicks, "Moly Black Gold 98" tempa, Thailand casting ($3-5)(WR)
57. black body, red interior, Goodyear slicks, "Ireland 31" tempa, Thailand casting ($3-5)(WR)
58. dark blue body, gray interior, Goodyear slicks, "Sunoco Ultra 94" tempa, Thailand casting ($3-5)(WR)
59. white body, red interior, Goodyear slicks, "Freedom Village/ Jasper 55" tempa, Thailand casting ($3-5)(WR)
60. white body, red interior, Goodyear slicks, "Matchbox/White Rose 29" tempa, Thailand casting ($3-5)(WR)
61. red body, gray interior, Goodyear slicks, "Performance Parts 12" tempa, Thailand casting ($1-2)
62. white body, red interior, Goodyear slicks, "Matchbox/White Rose 29-Brad's Toys" tempa, Thailand casting ($6-8)(WR)
63. white body, red interior, Goodyear slicks, "Matchbox/White Rose 29-Matchbox Road Museum" tempa, Thailand casting ($6-8)(WR)
64. white body, red interior, Goodyear slicks, "Matchbox/White Rose 29-Diecast Toy Exchange" tempa, Thailand casting ($6-8)(WR)
65. white body, red interior, Goodyear slicks, "Matchbox/White Rose 29-Craig Hill" tempa, Thailand casting ($6-8)(WR)
66. white body, red interior, Goodyear slicks, "Matchbox/White Rose 29-Cars Plus" tempa, Thailand casting ($6-8)(WR)
67. white body, red interior, Goodyear slicks, "Matchbox/White Rose 29—Kiddie Kar Kollectibles" tempa, Thailand casting ($6-8)(WR)
68. baby blue body, gray interior, Goodyear slicks, "Performance Parts 12" tempa, Thailand casting ($1-2)(MP)
69. light blue body, gray interior, Goodyear slicks, "Performance Parts 12" tempa, Thailand casting ($1-2)(MP)
70. yellow & red body, red interior, Goodyear slicks, "Matchbox USA 12" tempa, Thailand casting ($6-8)(US)
NOTE: Above models with white-lettered slicks, below with yellow-lettered slicks unless otherwise noted
71. red & white body, silver-gray interior, Goodyear slicks, "Dentyne 87" tempa, Thailand casting ($3-5)(WR)
72. metallic blue & neon orange body, red interior, Goodyear slicks, "Dupont 24" tempa, Thailand casting ($3-5)(WR)
73. red body, gray interior, Goodyear slicks, "Active 32" tempa, Thailand casting ($3-5)(WR)
74. black body, orange interior, Goodyear slicks, "WFE 69" tempa, Thailand casting ($15-18)(WR)
75. white body, red interior, Goodyear slicks, "MW Windows/Freedom 14" tempa, China casting ($3-5)(WR)
76. fluorescent yellow & lime body, silver/gray interior, Goodyear slicks, "Manheim 41" tempa, China casting ($3-5)(WR)
77. black body, red interior, gray disc with rubber tires, "Goodwrench 3" with large "Goodwrench" on sides & revised small logos tempa, China casting ($4-7)(WR)(TC)
78. flat black body, red interior, Goodyear slicks, "GM" & "Goodwrench" tempa, China casting ($4-7)(WR)(TC)
79. black body, red interior, Goodyear slicks, "Virginia is for Lovers 25" tempa, China casting ($3-5)(WR)
80. white & blue body, red interior, Goodyear slicks, "American Zoom 93" tempa, China casting ($10-15)(WR)
81. yellow body, gray interior, Goodyear slicks, "Pic N Pay Shoes/Shoe City 32" tempa, China casting ($3-5)(WR)
82. metallic blue body, silver—gray interior, Goodyear slicks, "Dupont 99" tempa, China casting ($3-5)(WR)
83. blue body, black interior, Goodyear slicks, "Enck's Custom Catering 71" tempa, China casting ($3-5)(WR)
84. metallic blue & neon orange body, silver-gray interior, black disc with rubber tires, "Dupont 24" tempa, China casting ($4-6)(WR)(TC)
85. gold plated body, red interior, black disc with rubber tires, "Rookie of The Year 1993" tempa, China casting ($7-10)(WR)(TC)
86. yellow body, gray interior, Goodyear slicks, "Dewalt 08" (gray print) tempa, China casting ($3-5)(WR)
87. yellow body, gray interior, Goodyear slicks, "Dewalt 08" (lavender print) tempa, China casting ($3-5)(WR)
88. metallic turquoise & pink body, gray interior, Goodyear slicks, "FDP Brakes 9" tempa, China casting ($3-5)(WR)
89. white body, gray interior, Goodyear slicks, "Cintas 87" tempa, China casting ($7-10) (WR)
90. yellow & red body, black interior, Goodyear slicks, "Matchbox USA 13" tempa, Thailand casting ($6-8)(US)
91. dark purple body, gray interior, Goodyear slicks, "Performance Parts 12" tempa, Thailand casting ($2-4)(CC)
92. yellow body, gray interior, Goodyear slicks, "Nationwise Auto Parts" tempa, Thailand casting ($20-35)(US)
93. red body, gray interior, Goodyear slicks, white lettered "Performance Parts 12" tempa, Thailand casting ($4-6)(Aquafresh)
94. white body, red interior, Goodyear slicks, white base, no tempa, Thailand casting ($5-8)(GF)
95. silver- gray body, red interior, Goodyear slicks, "Matchbox USA 14" tempa, Thailand casting ($6-10)(US)(PR)
96. black body, red interior, black disc with rubber tires, "Goodwrench 3/ Sydney Motorshow 1997", China casting ($20-30)(C2)
97. black body, red interior, black disc with rubber tires, "Goodwrench 3/ Melbourne Motor Show" tempa, China casting ($20-30)(C2)
98. white body, white base, red interior, Goodyear slicks, "Avis" tempa, China casting ($50+)(ASAP)
99. white body, white base, red interior, Goodyear slicks, "Drive/ A-Pix Entertainment" tempa, China casting ($100+)(ASAP)
100. white body, white base, red interior, Goodyear slicks, no tempa, China casting ($15-25)(ASAP blank)

MB54-J ABRAMS TANK, issued 1995 (USA)
MB61-G ABRAMS TANK, issued 1995 (ROW)
1. beige body, turret & gun, beige base, brown & white camouflage tempa, Thailand casting ($1-2)
2. olive body, turret & gun, olive base, star & "T-7521-6" tempa, Thailand casting ($1-2)
3. green body, turret & gun, green base, black & brown camouflage tempa, Thailand casting ($1-2)(MP)
4. beige body & turret, black gun, black base, brown camouflage tempa, Thailand casting ($1-2)(MP)
5. white body & turret, gray gun, gray base, ray & olive camouflage tempa, Thailand casting ($1-2)(MP)
6. dark sand body & turret, black gun, dark sand base, "T-7521-6" & star tempa, Thailand casting ($2-4)(MP)
7. olive body & turret, gray gun, black base, gray & brown camouflage tempa, Thailand casting ($1-2)(PS)
8. black body, turret & gun, black base, rose & white design tempa, Thailand casting ($3-5)(AU)
9. black body & turret , brown gun, green & brown camouflage tempa, Thailand casting ($1-2)(MP)
10. black body & turret, brown gun, green & brown camouflage tempa, China casting ($1-2)(MP)

MB54-K FORD CROWN VICTORIA POLICE CAR, issued 1997 (USA)
MB38-J FORD CROWN VICTORIA POLICE CAR, issued 1997 (ROW)
NOTE: All models listed with clear windows & black base.
1. blue body, red dome lights, gray interior, 8 dot wheels, "D-22 Police" tempa, Thailand casting ($2-4)
2. black body, red dome lights, gray interior, 5 spoke concave star wheels, "D-22 Police" tempa, Thailand casting ($1-2)(MW28)
3. dark burgundy body, red dome lights, black & gray interior, chrome

disc with rubber tires, "State Police "(Minnesota) tempa, Thailand casting ($3-5)(PC18)
4. white body, blue & red dome lights, black & gray interior, chrome disc with rubber tires, "SD Highway Patrol" tempa, Thailand casting ($3-5)(PC18)
5. black body, blue dome lights, black & gray interior, chrome disc with rubber tires, "Montana Highway Patrol" tempa, Thailand casting ($3-5)(PC18)
6. black body, red dome lights, gray interior, 5 spoke concave star wheels, "D-22 Police" tempa, China casting ($1-2)(MW28)
7. white body, red dome lights, gray interior, 5 spoke concave star wheels, "Drive/ A-Pix Entertainment" tempa, China casting ($100+)(ASAP)
8. metallic gold body, red dome lights, black interior, 5 spoke concave star wheels, no tempa, China casting ($5-10)(CH)
9. white body, red dome lights, gray interior, 5 spoke concave star wheels, no tempa, China casting ($25-40)(ASAP blank)
10. blue body, red dome lights, gray interior, 5 spoke concave star wheels, "Police K-9 Canine Unit" tempa, China casting ($1-2)(MP)
11. white body, red dome lights, gray interior, 5 spoke concave star wheels, "IAC Police" tempa, China casting ($75+)(ASAP)
12. white body, red dome lights, gray interior, 5 spoke concave star wheels, "Aegis NT" tempa, China casting ($50+)(ASAP)
13. white body, red & blue dome lights, black & tan interior, chrome disc with rubber tires, "Dallas Police" tempa, China casting ($75+)(PC22)
NOTE: See notes on 30I Chevy on Tahoe.

MB54-L HOLDEN COMMODORE, issued 1997 (AU)
MB64-H HOLDEN COMMODORE, issued 1998 (ROW)
NOTE: All models listed with clear windows, black base & China casting unless otherwise noted.
1. white body, white interior, chrome disc with rubber tires, Thailand casting, "Castrol 11" ($15-20)(AU) 2. metallic silver body, black interior, chrome disc with rubber tires, "Australia's First" tempa ($10-15)(IG)(AU)
3. unpainted body, black interior, chrome disc with rubber tires, 5 spoke concave star wheels, no tempa ($10-15)(IG)(AU)
4. white body, white interior & base, 5 spoke concave star wheels, "Commodore Race Team 25" tempa ($3-5)(AU)
5. red & dark blue body, white interior, 5 spoke concave star wheels, "Bulldogs 1998" tempa ($3-5)(AU) 6. red & dark blue body, white interior, 5 spoke concave star wheels "Demons 1998" tempa ($3-5)(AU)
7. red & black body, white interior, 5 spoke concave star wheels, "Bombers 1998" tempa ($3-5)(AU)
8. red & green body, white interior, 5 spoke concave star wheels, "Fremantle 1998" tempa ($3-5)(AU)
9. white & red body, white interior, 5 spoke concave star wheels, "Saints 1998" tempa ($3-5)(AU)
10. white & black body, white interior, 5 spoke concave star wheels, "Magpies 1998" tempa ($3-5)(AU)
11. turquoise & black body, white interior, 5 spoke concave star wheels, "Power 1998" tempa ($3-5)(AU)
12. yellow & brown body, white interior, 5 spoke concave star wheels, "Hawks 1998" tempa ($3-5)(AU)
13. pumpkin body, blue interior, 5 spoke concave star wheels, white design with "99 Holden Commodore" tempa (MW64-ROW)

MB55-A MERCURY POLICE CAR, issued 1970
1. white body, unpainted base, blue dome light ($15-20)
2. white body, unpainted base, red dome light ($15-20)

MB55-B MERCURY POLICE COMMUTER, issued 1971
1. white body, unpainted base, shield hood & side labels, red dome lights ($15-18)
2. white body, unpainted base, red & yellow "Police" hood & side labels, red dome lights ($15-18)
3. white body, silver-gray base, red & yellow "Police" hood & side labels, red dome lights ($15-18)
4. white body, unpainted base, red & yellow "Police" hood label only, red dome lights ($15-18)
5. white body, silver-gray base, red & yellow "Police" hood label only, red dome lights ($15-18)
6. white body, unpainted base, red & yellow "Police" hood & side labels, amber dome lights ($85-110)

MB55-C HELLRAISER, issued 1975
NOTE: all models with 5 crown front & dot dash rear wheels unless otherwise noted.
1. white body, unpainted base, red interior, clear windshield, stars & stripes label ($15-18)
2. white body, unpainted base, red interior, clear windshield, stars & stripes label, dot dash front wheels ($15-18)
3. blue body, unpainted base, ivory interior, clear windshield, stars & stripes label ($12-15)
4. blue body, silver-gray base, ivory interior, clear windshield, stars & stripes label ($12-15)
5. blue body, silver-gray base, ivory interior, clear windshield, no label ($12-15)
6. blue body, silver-gray base, red interior, clear windshield, stars & stripes label ($12-15)
7. blue body, silver-gray base, red interior, amber windshield, stars & stripes label ($12-15)
8. blue body, silver-gray base, red interior, clear windshield, "3" label ($12-15)
9. blue body, silver-gray base, ivory interior, clear windshield, "3" label ($12-15)

MB55-D FORD CORTINA, issued 1979
1. green body, unpainted base, red interior, clear windows, no tempa, dot dash wheels, doors open, England casting ($4-6)
2. metallic green body, unpainted base, red interior, clear windows, no tempa, dot dash wheels, doors open, England casting ($4-6)
3. bright metallic green body, unpainted base, light yellow interior, clear windows, no tempa, dot dash wheels, doors open, England casting ($4-6)
4. metallic red body, unpainted base, light yellow interior, clear windows, no tempa, dot dash wheels, doors open, England casting ($4-6)
5. light tan body, unpainted base, light yellow interior, clear windows, black stripe tempa, dot dash wheels, doors open, England casting ($3-5)
6. light tan body, unpainted base, white interior, clear windows, black stripe tempa, dot dash wheels, doors open, England casting ($3-5)
7. light tan body, unpainted base, white interior, clear windows, black stripe tempa, 5 arch wheels, doors open, England casting ($3-5)
8. light tan body, silver-gray base, white interior, clear windows, black stripe tempa, dot dash wheels, doors open, England casting ($3-5)
9. light tan body, unpainted base, white interior, clear windows,. no tempa, dot dash wheels, doors open, England casting ($3-5)
10. red body, silver-gray base, white interior, opaque white windows, no tempa, dot dash wheels, doors cast, England casting ($12-15)(PS)
11. red body, unpainted base, white interior, opaque white windows, no tempa, dot dash wheels, doors cast, England casting ($12-15)(PS)
12. red body, silver-gray base, white interior, clear windows, no tempa, dot dash wheels, doors cast, England casting ($3-5)
13. red body, unpainted base, white interior, clear windows, no tempa, dot dash wheels, doors cast, England casting ($3-5)
14. red body, black base, white interior, clear windows, no tempa, dot dash wheels, doors cast, England casting ($3-5)
15. red body, silver-gray base, white interior, clear windows, black stripe tempa, dot dash wheels, doors cast, England casting ($3-5)(TP)
16. red body, unpainted base, white interior, clear windows, black stripe tempa, dot dash wheels, doors cast, England casting ($3-5)(TP)
17. red body, unpainted base, brown interior, clear windows, black stripe tempa, dot dash wheels, doors cast, England casting ($3-5)(TP)
18. red body, silver-gray base, white interior, clear windows, white & orange flames tempa, dot dash wheels, doors cast, China casting ($150-200)(CHI)
19. orange-red body, black base, yellow interior, clear windows, "Nigel Cooper for Matchbox Toys/ Christmas 96" tempa, dot dash wheels, doors cast, Bulgaria casting ($35-50)(UK)
20. red body, silver-gray base, white interior, clear windows, no tempa, dot dash wheels, doors cast, China casting ($7-10)(MP)
NOTE: Available as a Bulgarian casting. Assorted colors available. ($15-25)

MB55-F RACING PORSCHE, issued 1983 (USA)
MB41-E RACING PORSCHE, issued 1983 (ROW)
NOTE: All models with black base & clear windows unless otherwise noted.
1. powder blue body, black interior, 8 dot silver wheels, "Elf 71 Sachs" tempa, Macau casting ($2-4)
2. baby blue body, black interior, 8 dot silver wheels, "Elf 71 Sachs" tempa, Macau casting ($2-4)
3. white body, black interior, 8 dot silver wheels, "Cadbury Buttons" tempa, Macau casting ($8-12)(UK)
4. red body, black interior, starburst wheels, "Autotech 35" tempa, Macau casting ($3-5)(SF)
5. metallic red body, black interior, laser wheels, "Autotech 35" tempa, Macau casting ($3-5)(LW)
6. white body, black interior, 8 dot gold wheels, "Porsche 10" tempa, Macau casting ($4-6)
7. white body, black interior, 8 dot silver wheels, "Porsche 10" tempa, Macau casting ($2-4)
8. baby blue body, black interior, 8 dot gold wheels, "Elf 71 Sachs" tempa, Macau casting ($40-65)
9. black body, black interior, 8 dot silver wheels, "11 Ox Racing Team" tempa, Macau casting ($8-12)(HK)
10. red body, tan interior, 8 dot silver wheels, "41 Porsche" tempa, Macau casting ($1-2)
11. red body, tan interior, 8 dot silver wheels, "Porsche" logo tempa, Thailand casting ($2-4)(MC)
12. yellow body, tan interior, 8 dot silver wheels, "Porsche 10" tempa, Macau casting ($2-4)(MP)
13. lemon body, no interior, gray disc with rubber tires, chrome windows, detailed trim tempa, China casting ($5-8)(WC)
14. white body, no interior, lightning wheels, blue-chrome & black windows, orange stripes with "935" tempa, China casting ($2-4)(LT)
15. black body, no interior, lightning wheels, black & chrome windows, lime stripes with "935" tempa, China casting ($2-4)(LT)
16. iridescent cream body, gray interior, gray disc with rubber tires, chrome windows, detailed trim tempa, China casting ($5-8)(WC)
17. yellow body, black interior, 8 dot silver wheels, "Porsche 10" tempa, Thailand casting ($2-4)(MP)
18. powder blue body, black interior, dot dash wheels, "FAR Porsche 71 Sachs" tempa, silver-gray base, Manaus casting ($35-50)(BR)
19. powder blue body, black interior, 8 dot silver wheels, "FAR Porsche 71 Sachs" tempa, silver-gray base, Manaus casting ($35-50)(BR)
20. white body, black interior, 8 dot wheels, "Elf/ Porsche/71 Sachs" with green wavy line & lavender stripes tempa, silver-gray base, Manaus casting ($35-50)(BR)

MB55-G MERCURY SABLE WAGON, issued 1987 (USA)
MB33-F MERCURY SABLE WAGON, issued 1989 (ROW)
1. white body, gray base, silver-gray interior, clear windows, 8 dot wheels, gray side stripe tempa, white painted hatch, Macau casting ($2-4)
2. white body, gray base, silver-gray interior, clear windows, 8 dot wheels, gray side stripe tempa, white painted hatch, China casting ($2-4)
3. white body, gray base, silver-gray interior, clear windows, 8 dot wheels, light gray side stripe tempa, clear hatch, China casting ($25-40)(CHI)
4. pea green body, silver-gray interior, clear windows, 8 dot wheels, woodgrain sides & "The Brady Bunch" tempa, lime painted hatch, China casting ($4-6)(STR)

MB55-K FLARESIDE PICKUP with LOAD, issued 1994 (WR)
NOTE: All models below with chrome base, black interior, white rear load, slicks with gray inserts wheels.
1. gold body, "Royals 94" tempa ($3-5)(WR)
2. gold body, "Astros 94" tempa ($3-5)(WR)
3. silver—gray body, "White Sox 94" tempa ($3-5)(WR)
4. black body, "Pirates 94" tempa ($3-5)(WR)
5. black body, "Orioles 94" tempa ($3-5)(WR)
6. black body, "Reds 94" tempa ($3-5)(WR)
7. red body, "Phillies 94" tempa ($3-5)(WR)
8. red body, "Yankees 94" tempa ($3-5)(WR)
9. red body, "Indians 94" tempa ($3-5)(WR)
10. red body, "Cubs 94" tempa ($3-5)(WR)
11. dark green body, "Athletics 94" tempa ($3-5)(WR)
12. dark green body, "Brewers 94-25th Anniversary" tempa ($3-5)(WR)
13. blue-green body, "Marlins 94" tempa ($3-5)(WR)
14. dark blue-green body, "Mariners 94" tempa ($3-5)(WR)
15. purple body, "Rockies 94" tempa ($3-5)(WR)
16. dark blue body, "Angels 94" tempa ($3-5)(WR)
17. blue body, "Mets 94" tempa ($3-5)(WR)
18. blue body, "Dodgers 94" tempa ($3-5)(WR)
19. blue body, "St. Louis Cardinals 94" tempa ($3-5)(WR)
20. blue body, "Expos 94" tempa ($3-5)(WR)
21. dull blue body, "Twins 94" tempa ($3-5)(WR)
22. metallic blue body, "Braves 94" tempa ($3-5)(WR)
23. light blue body, "Blue Jays 94" tempa ($3-5)(WR)
24. dark gray body, "Red Sox 94" tempa ($3-5)(WR)
25. khaki gray body, "Rangers 94" tempa ($3-5)(WR)
26. orange body, "Tigers 94" tempa ($3-5)(WR)
27. orange body, "Giants 94" tempa ($3-5)(WR)
28. orange body, "Padres 94" tempa ($3-5)(WR)
29. dark blue body, "Penn State Nittany Lions 94" tempa ($4-6)(WR)
30. white body, "Baltimore Football 1994" tempa ($4-6)(WR)

MB56-A BMC PININFARINA, issued 1969
1. gold body, unpainted base, no hood or side labels ($15-20)
2. gold body, unpainted base, hood label only ($15-20)(GS)
3. gold body, unpainted base, with hood & side labels ($15-20)(GS)
4. peach body, unpainted base, no labels ($20-25)
5. orange body, unpainted base, no labels ($15-20)
6. orange body, unpainted base, with hood & side labels ($15-20)(GS)
7. orange body, silver-gray base, no labels ($15-20)

MB56-B HI-TAILER, issued 1974
1. white body, unpainted base, blue driver, "MB5" labels, 5 spoke front wheels ($7-10)
2. white body, unpainted base, blue driver, "MB5" labels, maltese cross front wheels ($7-10)
3. white body, unpainted base, yellow-orange driver, "MB5" labels, 5 spoke front wheels ($7-10)
4. white body, red base, yellow-orange driver, "MB5" labels, 5 spoke front wheels ($8-12)
5. white body, red base, yellow-orange driver, "Martini" labels, 5 spoke front wheels ($8-12)
6. white body, red base, lemon driver, "Martini" labels, 5 spoke front wheels ($8-12)

MB56-C MERCEDES 450SEL, issued 1979
1. blue body, unpainted base, tan interior, clear windows, no tempa, England casting ($2-4)
2. blue body, unpainted base, red interior, clear windows, no tempa, England casting ($6-8)
3. beige body, unpainted base, tan interior, clear windows, no tempa, red "Taxi" sign, England casting ($2-4)
4. beige body, unpainted base, dark tan interior, clear windows, no tempa, red "Taxi" sign, England casting ($2-4)
5. beige body, silver-gray base, dark tan interior, clear windows, no tempa, red "Taxi" sign, England casting ($2-4)
6. beige body, silver-gray base, chocolate interior, clear windows, no tempa, red "Taxi" sign, England casting ($3-5)
7. white body, silver-gray base, tan interior, blue windows & dome light, chrome beacon, no tempa, England casting ($7-10)
8. white & green body, silver-gray base, tan interior, blue windows & dome light, chrome beacon, "Polizei" tempa, England casting ($2-4)
9. white & dark green body, unpainted base, tan interior, blue windows & dome light, chrome beacon, "Polizei" tempa, England casting ($2-4)
10. white & dark green body, unpainted base, tan interior, blue windows & dome light, black beacon, "Polizei" tempa, England casting ($2-4)
11. white & dark green body, silver-gray base, tan interior, blue windows & dome light, black beacon, "Polizei" tempa, England casting ($2-4)
12. white & dark green body, unpainted base, tan interior, blue windows & dome light, black beacon, "Polizei" (plain sides) tempa, England casting ($2-4)
13. white & light green body, pearly silver base, tan interior, blue windows & dome light, black beacon, Macau casting ($2-4)
NOTE: Available as a Bulgarian casting. Assorted colors available ($15-25)

MB56-D PETERBILT TANKER, issued 1982 (USA)

MB 5-E PETERBILT TANKER, issued 1982 (ROW)
1. blue body, white tank, amber windows, chrome base & exhausts, "Milk" with red "Milk" door tempa, England casting ($4-6)
2. blue body, white tank, amber windows, chrome base & exhausts, "Milk" with white "Milk" door tempa, England casting ($3-5)
3. blue body, white tank, amber windows, chrome base & exhausts, "Milk" with no door tempa, England casting ($3-5)
4. blue body, white tank, clear windows, chrome base & exhausts, "Milk" with no door tempa, England casting ($3-5)
5. blue body, white tank, clear windows, chrome base & exhausts, "Milk" with white "Milk" door tempa, England casting ($3-5)
6. black body, yellow tank, amber windows, chrome base & exhausts, "Supergas" tempa, Macau casting ($2-4)
7. black body, orange-yellow tank, amber windows, chrome base & exhausts, "Supergas" tempa, Macau casting ($2-4)
8. white body, gray tank, amber windows, chrome base & exhausts, "Shell" tempa, Macau casting ($2-4)
9. red body, chrome tank, clear windows, chrome base & exhausts, "Getty" tempa, Macau casting ($2-4)
10. white body, yellow tank, amber windows, chrome base & exhausts, "Supergas" tempa, Macau casting ($25-40)
11. white body, gray tank, amber windows, chrome base & exhausts, "Ampol" tempa, Macau casting ($7-10)(AU)
12. white body, gray tank, clear windows, chrome base & exhausts, "Shell" tempa, Macau casting ($2-4)
13. black body, black tank, clear windows, chrome base & exhausts, "Amoco" tempa, Macau casting ($3-5)
14. black body, chrome tank, clear windows, chrome base & exhausts, "Amoco" tempa, Macau casting ($60-75)
15. black body, white tank, clear windows, chrome base & exhausts, "Amoco" tempa, Macau casting ($35-50)
16. white body, white tank, clear windows, chrome base & exhausts, "Amoco' tempa, Macau casting ($2-4)
17. red body, chrome tank, clear windows, chrome base & exhausts, "Amoco" on tank & "Getty" on doors tempa, Macau casting ($40-65)
18. white body, white tank, clear windows, chrome base & exhausts, no tempa, Macau casting ($40-55)
19. blue body, white tank, clear windows, chrome base & exhausts, no tempa, England casting ($5-8)
20. olive body, olive tank, clear windows, black base & exhausts, "Gas" tempa, Macau casting ($4-5)(CM)
21. white body, chrome tank, clear windows, chrome base, gray exhausts, "Shell" tempa, Macau casting ($1-2)
22. lime body, yellow tank, clear windows, blue base, red exhausts, gas pump & stripes tempa, red wheels with yellow hubs, Macau casting ($6-8)(LL)
23. lime body, yellow tank, clear windows, blue base, red exhausts, gas pump & stripes tempa, red wheels with yellow hubs, Thailand casting ($6-8)(LL)
24. lime body, yellow tank, clear windows, blue base, red exhausts, gas pump & stripes tempa, red wheels (plain hubs), Thailand casting ($6-8)(LL)
25. white body, chrome tank, clear windows, chrome base, gray exhausts, "Shell" tempa, Thailand casting ($1-2)
26. white body, white tank, blue windows, chrome base, gray exhausts, no tempa, Thailand casting ($10-15)(GF)
27. black body, black tank, clear windows, chrome base & exhausts, "Indy Racing Fuel" tempa, Thailand casting ($12-15)(IN)
28. black body, black tank, clear windows, gray base & exhausts, "Matchbox" & "Getty" tempa, gold hubs, Manaus casting ($35-50)(BR)
29. black body, black tank, clear windows, gray base & exhausts, "Matchbox" & "Getty" tempa, silver hubs, Manaus casting ($35-50)(BR)
30. white body, chrome tank, clear windows, chrome base & gray exhausts, "Shell" (without yellow on cab) tempa, Thailand casting ($1-2)
31. white body, chrome tank, clear windows, black base with bar code, gray exhausts, "Shell" with "IC" door logo tempa, China casting ($10-15)(IC)
32. white body, cream tank, clear windows, gray base, gray exhausts, "Esso" tempa, Manaus casting ($30-45)(BR)
33. black & white body, black tank, clear windows, chrome exhausts, chrome base, "Official Indy Fuel Truck" tempa, Thailand casting ($7-10)(IN)
34. white body, chrome tank, clear windows, gray exhausts, chrome base, "Shell" with "IC" logo on doors tempa, China casting ($12-15)
35. blue body, white tank, clear windows, gray exhausts, chrome base, "Fresh Milk" tempa, Thailand casting ($20-25) (FM)(GS)
36. white & red body, white tank, clear windows, gray exhausts, chrome base, "Avia" tempa, Thailand casting ($12-18)(BE)
37. white body, chrome tank, clear windows, gray exhausts, chrome base, "Shell" tank tempa, red line on cab tempa, China casting ($1-2)
38. white body, green tank, clear windows, gray exhausts, chrome base, "BP" tempa, China casting ($8-12)(AU)
39. neon yellow body, chrome tank, clear windows, chrome exhausts, chrome base, "Airways Caution Jet Fuel" tempa, China casting ($1-2)(MP)
40. white body, chrome tank, clear windows, chrome exhausts, chrome base, no tempa, China casting ($25-40)(ASAP blank)
41. white body, chrome tank, clear windows, chrome exhausts, chrome base, "American International Recovery" tempa, China casting ($100+)(ASAP)

MB56-I ISUZU RODEO, issued 1995 (USA)
MB59-I VAUXHALL FRONTERA, issued 1995 (ROW)
NOTE: Model has different names printed on the baseplate on U.S. vs. ROW issues. All models with 8 spoke wheels & black roof luggage.
1. black body, white interior, blue windows, silver- gray "Rodeo" base, pink spatter on hood & sides tempa, Thailand casting ($1-2)
2. white body, white interior, blue windows, black "Frontera" base, brown spatter on hood & sides tempa, Thailand casting ($3-5)
3. white body, white interior, blue windows, black "Frontera" base, no tempa, Thailand casting ($12-15)
4. black body, white interior, blue windows, silver-gray ""Rodeo" base, pink spatter on sides only tempa, Thailand casting ($1-2)
5. white body, white interior, blue windows, silver—gray "Rodeo" base, pink spatter on sides only tempa, Thailand casting ($2-4)
6. metallic gold body, white interior, blue windows, black "Rodeo" base, no tempa, Thailand casting ($5-10)(CH)
7. red body, white interior, blue windows, silver-gray "Rodeo" base, "Power Parts 21" tempa, Thailand casting ($2-3)
8. metallic red body, black interior, blue windows, black "Frontera" base, no tempa, Thailand casting ($2-3)
9. green body, white interior, blue windows, gray (no name) base, skeleton & "Brontosaurus" tempa , Thailand casting ($1-2)(MP)
10. silver-gray body, maroon interior, clear windows, silver-gray "Frontera" base, no tempa, Thailand casting ($1-2)
11. black body, light gray interior, clear windows, silver-gray "Rodeo" base, red & white design tempa, Thailand casting ($1-2)(MP)
12. black body, light gray interior, clear windows, silver-gray "Rodeo" base, red & white design tempa, China casting ($1-2)(MP)
13. green body, white interior, blue windows, gray (no name) base, skeleton & " Brontosaurus" tempa, China casting ($1-2)(MP)

MB57-A LAND ROVER FIRE ENGINE, issued 1970
1. red body, blue windows & dome light,, gray base, "Kent Fire Brigade" labels, white ladder, 5 spoke wheels ($45-60)

MB57-B ECCLES CARAVAN, issued 1970
1. cream body, orange roof, green interior, stripe label, black axle cover, 5 spoke wheels ($10-15)
2. cream body, orange roof, green interior, brown stripe & flower label, black axle cover, 5 spoke wheels ($10-15)
3. cream body, orange roof, green interior, brown stripe & flower label, red axle cover, 5 spoke wheels ($10-15)
4. light yellow body, orange roof, green interior, brown stripe & flower label, black axle cover, 5 spoke wheels ($10-15)
5. dark yellow body, dark orange roof, white interior, black stripe & flower label, black axle cover, 5 spoke center cut wheels ($5-7)(TP)
6. dark yellow body, dark orange roof, white interior, dots label, black axle cover, 5 spoke center cut wheels ($7-10)(TP)
7. beige body, dark orange roof, white interior, black stripe & flower label, black axle cover, 5 spoke center cut wheels ($5-7)(TP)
8. beige body, dark orange roof, white interior, stripe with seagull label, black axle cover, 5 spoke center cut wheels ($7-10)(TP)
9. white body, dark orange roof, white interior, "Sun Set" tempa, black axle cover, 5 spoke center cut wheels ($8-12)(TP)

MB57-C WILDLIFE TRUCK, issued 1973
1. yellow body, unpainted base, red windows, amber canopy, orange lion, hood label ($5-7)
2. yellow body, unpainted base, red windows, light blue canopy, orange lion, hood label ($5-7)
3. yellow body, unpainted base, red windows, clear canopy, orange lion, hood label ($5-7)
4. yellow body, silver-gray base, red windows, amber canopy, orange lion, hood label ($5-7)
5. yellow body, unpainted base, red windows, amber canopy, orange lion, hood label ($5-7)
6. yellow body, unpainted base, red windows, smoke canopy, brown lion, hood label, ($5-7)
7. yellow body, unpainted base, red windows, light blue canopy, brown lion, hood label ($5-7)
8. yellow body, unpainted base, red windows, clear canopy, brown lion, hood label ($5-7)
9. yellow body, unpainted base, red windows, amber canopy, brown lion, hood label ($5-7)
10. yellow body, unpainted base, no windows, clear canopy, brown lion, hood label ($5-7)
11. yellow body, unpainted base, orange windows, smoke canopy, brown lion, hood label ($5-7)
12. white body, unpainted base, red windows, light blue canopy, brown lion, stripes tempa ($5-7)
13. white body, unpainted base, red windows, light blue canopy, red-brown lion, stripes tempa ($5-7)
14. white body, unpainted base, red windows, clear canopy, brown lion, stripes tempa ($5-7)
15. white body, unpainted base, red windows, clear canopy, red-brown lion, stripes tempa ($5-7)
16. white body, unpainted base, red windows, smoke canopy, brown lion, stripes tempa ($5-7)
17. white body, unpainted base, red windows, smoke canopy, red-brown lion, stripes tempa ($5-7)
18. white body, unpainted base, purple windows, clear canopy, brown lion, stripes tempa ($5-7)
19. white body, unpainted base, purple windows, clear canopy, red-brown lion, stripes tempa ($5-7)
20. white body, unpainted base, purple windows, smoke canopy, brown lion, stripes tempa ($5-7)
21. white body, unpainted base, purple windows, smoke canopy, red-brown lion, stripes tempa ($5-7)
22. white body, unpainted base, purple windows, light blue canopy, brown lion, stripes tempa ($5-7)
23. white body, unpainted base, purple windows, light blue canopy, red-brown lion, stripes tempa ($5-7)
24. white body, unpainted base, orange windows, clear canopy, brown lion, stripes tempa ($5-7)
25. white body, unpainted base, orange windows, clear canopy, red-brown lion, stripes tempa ($5-7)
26. white body, unpainted base, orange windows, smoke canopy, brown lion, stripes tempa ($5-7)
27. white body, unpainted base, orange windows, smoke canopy, red-brown lion, stripes tempa ($5-7)
28. white body, unpainted base, orange windows, light blue canopy, brown lion, stripes tempa ($5-7)
29. white body, unpainted base, orange windows, light blue canopy, red-brown lion, stripes tempa ($5-7)

MB57-D 4 X 4 MINI PICKUP, issued 1982 (USA)
1. orange-red body, unpainted metal base, blue windows, white/silver/black stripes tempa, England casting ($3-5)
2. dark red body, unpainted metal base, blue windows, white/silver/black stripes tempa, England casting ($3-5)
3. dark red body, silver-gray metal base, blue windows, white/silver/black stripes tempa, England casting ($3-5)
4. dark powder blue body, black metal base, blue windows, "Mountain Man" tempa, Hong Kong casting ($2-3)
5. light powder blue body, black metal base, blue windows, "Mountain Man" tempa, Macau casting ($2-3)
6. baby blue body, black metal base, blue windows, "Mountain Man" tempa, Macau casting ($2-3)
7. baby blue body, black plastic base, blue windows, "Mountain Man" tempa, Macau casting ($1-2)
8. baby blue body, black plastic base, blue windows, "Mountain Man" tempa, Thailand casting ($1-2)

MB57-E CARMICHAEL COMMANDO, issued 1982 (ROW)
1. white body, black base, gray interior, "Police Rescue" tempa, England casting ($18-25)
2. white body, charcoal base, gray interior, "Police Rescue" tempa England casting ($18-25)
3. red body, black base, gray interior, "Fire" tempa, England casting ($15-18)
4. red body, charcoal base, gray interior, "Fire" tempa, England casting ($15-18)
5. red body, black base, gray interior, "Fire" tempa, Macau casting ($15-18)
NOTE: Available as a Bulgarian casting. Assorted colors available. ($15-25)

MB57-H MACK AUXILIARY POWER TRUCK, issued 1991 (USA)
MB50-G MACK AUXILIARY POWER TRUCK, issued 1991 (ROW)
NOTE: All models with chrome base, white roof, red windows & 8 spoke wheels unless otherwise noted.
1. yellow body, chrome & yellow roof fixtures, "Floodlight Heavy Rescue" & door shield tempa, China casting ($2-3)
2. florescent orange body, chrome & yellow roof fixtures, "Fire Rescue Unit 2" & checkers with "Floodlight Heavy Rescue" tempa, China casting ($1-2)
3. white body, chrome & white roof fixtures, no roof or body tempa, China casting ($10-15)(GF)
4. red body, chrome & yellow roof fixtures, "Fire Rescue Unit 2" & "Floodlight Heavy Rescue" tempa, China casting ($8-12)(GS)
5. orange body, chrome & yellow roof fixtures, "Reithoffer's" tempa, China casting ($4-6)(WR)(GS)
6. florescent orange body, black & yellow roof fixtures, black base, "Fire Rescue Unit 2" with blue & white checkers tempa, China casting ($4-6)
7. red body, chrome & yellow roof fixtures, chrome base, "Shrewsbury Fire Co." with white painted roof tempa, China casting ($10-15)(WR)
8. red body, chrome & black roof fixtures, chrome base, "Floodlight Rescue Unit/ Fire Rescue" tempa, China casting ($5-7)
9. white body, chrome & black roof fixtures, chrome base, "Bridge & Highway Dept. 57" tempa, China casting ($1-2)
10. orange-red body, chrome & yellow roof fixtures, chrome base, "Fire Rescue Unit 2/ Action System" tempa ($7-10)(OP)
11. metallic gold body, blue windows, chrome & yellow roof fixtures, chrome base, "Floodlight Rescue Unit" tempa, China casting ($10-15)(CH)
12. red body, blue windows, chrome & black roof fixtures, chrome base, "Matchbox Fire Rescue/ Fire Dept." tempa, China casting ($1-2)(MP)
13. red & white body, chrome & black roof fixtures, chrome base, chrome disc with rubber tires, "Acorn Hill Fire Dept." , China casting ($3-5)(PC7)
14. yellow body, chrome & black roof fixtures, chrome base, "Bridge & Highway Dept. 57" tempa, China casting ($2-3)
15. red body, chrome & black roof fixtures, chrome base, "Clearbrook Fire & Rescue" tempa, China casting ($8-12)(US)
16. white body, blue windows, chrome & black roof fixtures, chrome base, "Matchbox Fire Rescue/ Fire Dept." tempa, China casting ($1-2)(MP)
17. red body, chrome & black roof fixtures, chrome base, "Bridge & Highway Rescue Dept. 57" tempa, China casting ($1-2)(MW21)
18. metallic red & white body, chrome & black roof fixtures, chrome base, chrome disc with rubber tires, "Eagle Point Fire Rescue", China casting ($3-5)(PC21)
19. red body, chrome & black roof fixtures, chrome base, no tempa, China casting ($25-40)(ASAP blank)
20. red body, chrome & black roof fixtures, chrome base, "American International Recovery" tempa, China casting ($100+)(ASAP)

MB58-A DAF GIRDER TRUCK, issued 1970
1. cream body, red base, red girders ($65-80)
2. green-gold body, red base, red girders ($20-30)

MB58-B WOOSH-N-PUSH, issued 1972
1. yellow body, red interior, flower label, maltese cross front wheels ($15-18)
2. yellow body, red interior, flower label, 5 spoke front wheels ($15-18)
3. yellow body, red interior, "2" label, maltese cross front wheels ($15-18)
4. yellow body, red interior, "2" label, 5 spoke front wheels ($15-18)
5. yellow body, light yellow interior, "2" label, maltese cross front wheels ($15-18)
6. metallic red body, light yellow interior, "2" label, maltese cross front wheels ($15-18)
7. magenta body, light yellow interior, "2" label, maltese cross front wheels ($15-18)
8. magenta body, light yellow interior, "8" label, maltese cross front wheels ($15-18)

MB58-C FAUN DUMP TRUCK, issued 1976
1. orange-yellow body & dump, no tempa ($3-5)
2. yellow body & dump, no tempa ($3-5)
3. yellow body, red dump, no tempa ($20-35)
4. yellow body & dump, "CAT" tempa ($4-6)

MB58-D RUFF TREK, issued 1983
NOTE: All models with black base, & 8 spoke wheels unless otherwise noted.
1. tan body, red interior, amber windows, "Ruff Trek" tempa, black load, Macau casting ($2-4)
2. white body, red interior, amber windows, "Ruff Trek" tempa, black load, Macau casting ($7-10)(JP)
3. white body, red interior, amber windows, "217" tempa, black load, Macau casting ($3-4)(TM)
4. white body, red interior, clear windows, "217" tempa, black load, Macau casting ($3-4)(TM)
5. white body, black interior, clear windows, "Brut/ Faberge" tempa, black load, Macau casting ($3-4)(TM)
6. white body, red interior, clear windows, "Brut/ Faberge" tempa, black load, Macau casting ($40-60)(TM)
7. dark blue body, red interior, clear windows, "STP/ Goodyear" tempa, black load, Macau casting ($45-60)(TM)
8. white body, red interior, clear windows, "7 Up" tempa, black load, Macau casting ($3-4)(TM)
9. brown body, red interior, olive green windows, red/yellow/blue tempa, green rear load, Macau casting, includes plastic armament ($5-8)(RB)
10. white body, black interior, clear windows, flames tempa, black load, Macau casting ($8-12)(GS)(JB)
11. yellow body, black interior, clear windows, "Matchbox Rescue Team Support" tempa, black load, Macau casting ($3-5)(MC)
12. yellow body, black interior, clear windows, black load, "Matchbox Rescue Team Support" tempa, Thailand casting ($3-5)(MC)
13. brown body, red interior, dark olive windows, red/yellow/blue tempa, dark green load, Thailand casting, includes plastic armament ($10-15)(JP) (Tomy box)

MB58-E MERCEDES BENZ 300E, issued 1986
NOTE: All models with black base, clear windows & 8 dot wheels.
1. silver blue body, dark blue interior, no tempa, Macau casting ($1-2)
2. silver blue body, dark blue interior, no tempa, Thailand casting ($1-2)
3. white body, tan interior, green stripe & silver star with "Polizei 5075" tempa, Thailand casting ($1-2)
4. white body, tan interior, green stripe (without star) & "Polizei 5075" tempa, Thailand casting ($1-2)
5. white body, dark blue interior, "61 Rijkspolitie" tempa, Thailand casting ($4-6)(DU) (CY)
6. white body, tan interior, green stripes & "Polizei 5075" tempa, China casting ($2-4)
7. blue-gray body, gray interior, "Go Blues! 1997" tempa, China casting ($3-5)(AU)

MB58-H 1939 CHEVY SEDAN DELIVERY, issued 1997 (AU)
MB245 1939 CHEVY SEDAN DELIVERY, issued 1992 (WR)
NOTE: This is a larger casting than the MB215 and has the rear bumper omitted. All models below with clear windows, silver 5 crown wheels, silver-gray base & China casting unless otherwise noted.
1. white body, brown chassis, "Browns 1992" tempa ($3-5)(WR)
2. white body, red-brown chassis, "Redskins 1992" tempa ($3-5)(WR)
3. white body, orange chassis, "Buccaneers 1992" tempa ($3-5)(WR)
4. white body, red chassis, "Falcons 1992" tempa ($3-5)(WR)
5. white body, turquoise chassis, "Dolphins 1992" tempa ($3-5)(WR)
6. white body, dark blue chassis, "Patriots 1992" tempa ($3-5)(WR)
7. white body, dark blue chassis, "Bills 1992" tempa ($3-5)(WR)
8. white body, dark blue chassis, "Colts 1992" tempa ($3-5)(WR)
9. white body, bright blue chassis, "Oilers 1992" tempa ($3-5)(WR)
10. white body, green chassis, "Jets 1992" tempa ($3-5)(WR)
11. white body, green chassis, "Eagles 1992" tempa ($3-5)(WR)
12. yellow body, purple chassis, "Vikings 1992" tempa ($3-5)(WR)
13. yellow body, black chassis, "Steelers 1992" tempa ($3-5)(WR)
14. yellow body, dark blue chassis, "Chargers 1992" tempa ($3-5)(WR)
15. yellow body, mid blue chassis, "LA Rams 1992" tempa ($3-5)(WR)
16. bright yellow body, green chassis, "Packers 1992" tempa ($3-5)(WR)
17. bright yellow body, red chassis, "Chiefs 1992" tempa ($3-5)(WR)
18. bright yellow body, red-brown chassis, "Cardinals 1992" tempa($3-5)(WR)
19. orange body, black chassis, "Bengals 1992" tempa ($3-5)(WR)
20. orange body, dark blue chassis, "Bears 1992" tempa ($3-5)(WR)
21. orange body, mid blue chassis, "Broncos 1992" tempa ($3-5)(WR)
22. gold body, red chassis, "49ers 1992" tempa ($3-5)(WR)
23. green-gold body, black chassis, "Saints 1992" tempa ($3-5)(WR)
24. silver-gray body, black chassis, "Raiders 1992" tempa ($3-5)(WR)
25. silver-gray body, dark blue chassis, "Cowboys 1992" tempa ($3-5)(WR)
26. silver-gray body, mid blue chassis, "Seahawks 1992" tempa ($3-5)(WR)
27. silver-gray body, bright blue chassis, "Lions 1992" tempa ($3-5)(WR)
28. red body, dark blue chassis, "Giants 1992" tempa ($3-5)(WR)
29. florescent orange body, lavender chassis, "York Fair 1992" tempa ($6-8)(WR)
30. bright blue body, yellow chassis, "Brewers 1993" tempa ($5-7)(WR)
31. dark blue body, orange chassis, "Astros 1993" tempa ($5-7)(WR)
32. dark blue body, red chassis, "Red Sox 1993" tempa ($5-7)(WR)
33. dark blue body, red chassis, "Twins 1993" tempa ($5-7)(WR)
34. blue body, red chassis, "Expos 1993" tempa ($5-7)(WR)
35. blue body, bright blue chassis, "Toronto Blue Jays 1993" tempa ($5-7)(WR)
36. blue body, orange chassis, "NY Mets 1993" tempa ($5-7)(WR)
37. blue body, white chassis, "Dodgers 1993" tempa ($5-7)(WR)
38. gray body, black chassis, "Giants 1993" tempa ($5-7)(WR)
39. gray body, dark blue chassis, "Indians 1993" tempa ($5-7)(WR)
40. gray body, red chassis, "Chicago Cubs 1993" tempa ($5-7)(WR)
41. silver-gray body, black chassis, "White Sox 1993" tempa ($5-7)(WR)
42. silver-gray body, blue-green chassis, "Mariners 1993" tempa ($5-7)(WR)
43. orange-yellow body, green chassis, "Oakland A's 1993" tempa ($5-7)(WR)
44. black body, lemon chassis, "Pirates 1993" tempa ($5-7)(WR)
45. black body, purple chassis, "Rockies 1993" tempa ($5-7)(WR)
46. red body, black chassis, "Reds 1993" tempa ($5-7)(WR)
47. red body, dark blue chassis, "Cardinals 1993" tempa ($5-7)(WR)
48. red body, white chassis, "Phillies 1993" tempa ($5-7)(WR)
49. white body, orange chassis, "Padres 1993" tempa ($5-7)(WR)
50. white body, dark blue chassis, "Angels 1993" tempa ($5-7)(WR)
51. white body, light blue chassis, "Marlins 1993" tempa ($5-7)(WR)
52. white body, blue chassis, "Yankees 1993" tempa ($5-7)(WR)
53. white body, blue chassis, "Tigers 1993" tempa ($5-7)(WR)
54. white body, metallic blue chassis, "Braves 1993" tempa ($5-7)(WR)
55. white body, red chassis, "Rangers 1993" tempa ($5-7)(WR)
56. powder blue body, dark blue chassis, "Royals 1993" tempa ($5-7)(WR)
57. orange body, black chassis, "Orioles 1993" tempa ($5-7)(WR)
58. red-brown body, yellow chassis, "Redskins 1993" tempa ($5-7)(WR)
59. white body, orange chassis, "Reithoffer's-Tickets for All Attractions" tempa ($4-6) (WR)(GS)
60. white & blue body, blue chassis, gold grille & wheels, "Penn State 1993" tempa ($5-7)(WR)
61 white body, dark blue chassis, "Florida Panthers 1993" tempa ($5-7)(WR)
62. white body, grape chassis, "Mighty Ducks 1993" tempa ($5-7)(WR)
63 white body, blue chassis, "Washington Capitals 20th Anniversary 1974-1994" tempa ($5-7)(WR)
64. black body, gold chassis, "Dallas Stars 1993" tempa ($5-7)(WR)
65. light blue body, lavender chassis, gold grille & wheels, "York Fair 1994" tempa ($5-7)(WR)
66. red body, white chassis, "1995 Temecula Rod Run" tempa, China casting ($10-15)(WR)
67. yellow body, black chassis, "Pioneer Distributors-Gowings" tempa, China casting ($10-15)(AU)
68. florescent orange body & chassis, "Matchbox Get In The Fast Lane-Hershey 1995" tempa, China casting ($8-12)(US)
69. red body, purple chassis, "Raptors 1995" tempa ($8-12)(AU)
70. red body, blue chassis, "Detroit Pistons 1995" tempa ($8-12)(AU)
71. dark red body, dark blue chassis, "Denver Nuggets 1995" tempa ($8-12)(AU)
72. orange body, purple chassis, "Phoenix Suns 1995" tempa ($8-12)(AU)
73. orange-yellow body, dark blue chassis, "Pacers 1995" tempa ($8-12)(AU)
74. lavender body, orange-yellow chassis, "Los Angeles Lakers 1995" tempa ($8-12)(AU)
75. blue-green body, orange chassis, "Knicks 1995" tempa ($8-12)(AU)
76. blue body, white chassis, "Orlando Magic 1995" tempa ($8-12)(AU)
77. dark blue body, orange-yellow chassis, "Golden State Warriors 1995" tempa ($15-20)(AU)
78. dark blue body, orange chassis, "San Antonio Spurs 1995" tempa ($8-12)(AU)
79. dark blue body, red chassis, "Chicago Bulls 1995" tempa ($8-12)(AU)
80. dark blue body, red chassis, "Houston Rockets 1995" tempa ($8-12)(AU)
81. dark green body, orange-yellow chassis, "Seattle Sonics 1995" tempa ($8-12)(AU)
82. green body, orange-yellow chassis, "Utah Jazz 1995" tempa ($8-12)(AU)
83. green body, white chassis, "Boston Celtics 1995" tempa ($8-12)(AU)
84. green body, blue chassis, "Dallas Mavericks 1995" tempa ($8-12)(AU)
85. black body, turquoise chassis, "Vancouver Grizzlies 1995" tempa ($8-12)(AU)
86. turquoise body, blue chassis, "Charlotte Hornets 1995" tempa ($8-12)(AU)
87. dark purple & black body, blue-green chassis, chrome disc with rubber tires, "San Andreas Brewing Co." ($8-12)(MB)(CL)
88. silver blue & black body, cream chassis, chrome disc with rubber tires, "Blue Ridge Brewing Co./ Hawksbill Lager" tempa ($8-12)(MB)(CL)
89. red & black body, black chassis, chrome disc with rubber tires, "Dubuque Red" tempa ($8-12)(MB)(CL)
90. white & black body, lavender chassis & base, chrome disc with rubber tires, "Samuel Adams" tempa ($8-12)(MB)(CL)
91. yellow & black body, red chassis & base, chrome disc with rubber tires, "Red Ale" tempa ($8-12)(MB)(CL)
92. yellow & black body, green chassis & base, chrome disc with rubber tires, "Gator Lager Beer" tempa ($8-12)(MB)(CL)
93. black body & chassis, money bags & bullet marks tempa ($4-6)(AU)

MB59-A FORD GALAXIE FIRE CHIEF, issued 1970
1. red body, blue dome light, decal on hood, label on sides ($25-40)
2. red body, blue dome light, label on hood & sides ($25-40)
3. red body, blue dome light, label on sides only ($25-40)

MB59-B MERCURY FIRE CHIEF, issued 1971
NOTE: Following models cast with driver & passenger in interior
1. red body, unpainted base, clear windows, dome light, ivory interior, 5 spoke wheels, "Fire Chief" in square hood label, shield side label, England casting ($12-15)
2. red body, unpainted base, clear windows, dome light, ivory interior, 5 spoke wheels, helmet & axes hood label, shield side label, England casting ($12-15)
3. red body, unpainted base, clear windows, dome light, ivory interior, 5 spoke wheels, helmet & axes hood & side labels, England casting ($8-12)
4. red body, unpainted base, clear windows, dome light, ivory interior, 5 spoke wheels, helmet & axes hood label only, England casting ($8-12)
5. red body, silver-gray base, clear windows, dome light, ivory interior, 5 spoke wheels, helmet & axes hood label only, England casting ($8-12)
6. red body, unpainted base, clear windows, dome light, ivory interior, 5 spoke wheels, "Fire Chief" in square hood label, helmet & axes side labels, England casting ($12-15)
7. red body, unpainted base, clear windows, dome light, ivory interior, 5 spoke wheels, red & yellow "Fire Chief" hood label, helmet & axes side labels, England casting ($12-15)
8. red body, unpainted base, clear windows, dome light, ivory interior, dot dash wheels, helmet & axes hood & side labels, England casting ($8-12)
NOTE: Following models cast without driver & passenger in interior.
9. red body, unpainted base, clear windows, dome light, ivory interior, dot dash wheels, helmet & axes hood & side labels, England casting ($8-12)
10. red body, unpainted base, clear windows, bar light, ivory interior, dot dash wheels, no hood labels, "Fire" with shield side labels, England casting ($5-7)(TP)
11. red body, unpainted base, clear windows, bar light, ivory interior, dot dash wheels, red & yellow "Fire Chief" hood label, "Fire" with shield side labels, England casting ($5-7)(TP)
12. white body, unpainted base, purple windows, bar light, ivory interior, dot dash wheels, no hood label, "Police" with shield side labels, England casting ($30-45)(TP)
13. white body, unpainted base, blue windows, bar light, ivory interior, dot dash wheels, "Los Angeles Police" tempa, England casting ($6-8)(CR)
14. white body, unpainted base, clear windows, bar light, ivory interior, dot dash wheels, "Los Angeles Police" tempa, England casting ($6-8)(CR)
15. red body, unpainted base, clear windows, bar light, ivory interior, dot dash wheels, "Los Angeles Fire Dept." tempa, England casting ($6-8)(CR)
16. white body, unpainted base, clear windows, bar light, ivory interior, dot dash wheels, "Police" with shield & black fenders tempa, England casting ($8-12)
17. white body, unpainted base, clear windows, bar light, white interior, dot dash wheels, "Police" with shield & black fenders tempa, England casting ($8-12)
18. white body, unpainted base, blue windows, bar light, white interior, dot dash wheels, "Police" with shield & black fenders tempa, England casting ($8-12)
19. white body, unpainted base, purple windows, bar light, ivory interior, dot dash wheels, "Police" with shield & black fenders tempa, England casting ($35-50)
20. white body, unpainted base, purple windows, bar light, white interior, dot dash wheels, "Police" with shield & black fenders tempa, England casting ($35-50)
21. white body, unpainted base, blue windows, bar light, white interior, dot dash wheels, "Metro Police" tempa, England casting ($8-12)
22. white body, silver-gray base, blue windows, bar light, white interior, dot dash wheels, "Metro Police" tempa, England casting ($8-12)
23. white body, silver-gray base, blue windows, bar light, white interior, dot dash wheels, "Los Angeles Police" tempa, England casting ($6-8)(CR)
24. white body, silver-gray base, blue windows, bar light, white interior, dot dash wheels, "Los Angeles Police" on hood, "Metro Police" on sides tempa, England casting ($25-40)
25. white body, silver-gray base, blue windows, bar light, white interior, dot dash wheels, "Metro" on hood tempa, shield on sides tempa, England casting ($8-12)
26. white body, silver-gray base, blue windows, bar light, white interior, dot dash wheels, "Metro Police" without black fenders tempa, England casting ($8-12)
27. red body, unpainted base, purple windows, bar light, ivory interior, dot dash wheels, no hood label, "Fire' with shield side labels, England casting ($35-50)
28. white body, unpainted base, clear windows, bar light, white interior, dot dash wheels, "Metro Police" tempa, England casting ($8-12)
29. white body, silver-gray base, smoke windows, bar light, white interior, dot dash wheels, "Metro Police" tempa, England casting ($8-12)
30. white body, unpainted base, blue windows, bar light, white interior, dot dash wheels, no labels, England casting ($8-12)
31. white body, silver-gray base, blue windows, bar light, white interior, dot dash wheels, "201" hood tempa, "Metro" side tempa, England casting ($8-12)
32. white body, unpainted base, clear windows, bar light, white interior, dot dash wheels, no labels, England casting ($8-12)
33. white body, silver-gray base, clear windows, bar light, white interior, dot dash wheels, no labels, England casting ($8-12)
34. white body, unpainted base, clear windows, bar light, ivory interior, dot dash wheels, "Police" with shield tempa, England casting ($8-12)

35. white body, unpainted base, blue windows, bar light, ivory interior, dot dash wheels, "Metro" on hood, shield on sides tempa, England casting ($8-12)
36. white body, unpainted base, clear windows, bar light, ivory interior, dot dash wheels, "Metro" on hood, shield on sides tempa, England casting ($8-12)
37. white body, unpainted base, smoke windows, bar light, ivory interior, dot dash wheels, "Metro" on hood, shield on sides tempa, England casting ($8-12)
38. white body, silver-gray base, clear windows, bar light, white interior, dot dash wheels, "Metro" with black fenders tempa, England casting ($8-12)
39. white body, pearly silver base, blue windows, bar light, gray interior, starburst wheels, "State Police" tempa, Macau casting ($3-5)(SF)
40. white body, black base, blue windows, bar light, gray interior, starburst wheels, "State Police" tempa, Macau casting ($7-10)(SF)
41. white body, pearly silver base, blue windows, bar light, gray interior, laser wheels, "State Police" tempa, Macau casting ($3-5)(LW)
42. black body, black base, blue windows, bar light, gray interior, "Haley's Comet" tempa, Macau casting ($7-10)(MP)
43. metallic blue body, pearly silver base, blue windows, bar light, gray interior, starburst wheels, yellow/blue/red tempa, Macau casting, includes plastic armament ($5-8)(RB)

MB59-C PLANET SCOUT, issued 1975

NOTE: All models with 5 crown front & dot dash rear wheels but other combinations do exist.

1. metallic green upper body, lime chassis, amber windows ($12-15)
2. metallic green upper body, apple green chassis, amber windows ($12-15)
3. red upper body, beige chassis, amber windows ($12-15)
4. avocado upper body, black chassis, amber windows ($25-35)(AV)
5. avocado upper body, black chassis, purple windows ($25-35)(AV)
6. metallic blue body, black chassis, purple windows ($40-55)(AV)

NOTE: Available as a Bulgarian casting. Assorted colors available ($10-25)

MB59-D PORSCHE 928, issued 1980

NOTE: Following models with 5 arch wheels unless otherwise noted.

1. light tan body, black base, ivory interior, clear windows, no tempa, England casting ($4-6)
2. light tan body, black base, cream interior, clear windows, no tempa, England casting ($4-6)
3. light tan body, black base, brown interior, clear windows, no tempa, England casting ($4-6)
4. gray-brown body, black base, brown interior, clear windows, no tempa, England casting ($4-6)
5. light tan body, black base, milky tan interior, clear windows, no tempa, England casting ($4-6)
6. mid tan body, black base, brown interior, clear windows, no tempa, England casting ($4-6)
7. mid tan body, black base, brown interior, amber windows, no tempa, England casting ($4-6)
8. mid tan body, black base, tan interior, amber windows, no tempa, England casting ($4-6)
9. mid tan body, black base, brown interior, orange windows, no tempa, England casting ($4-6)
10. dark tan body, black base, brown interior, clear windows, no tempa, England casting ($4-6)
11. dark tan body, black base, brown interior, amber windows, no tempa, England casting ($4-6)
12. light tan body, charcoal base, brown interior, orange windows, no tempa, England casting ($4-6)
13. mid tan body, charcoal base, brown interior, clear windows, no tempa, England casting ($4-6)
14. dark tan body, charcoal base, brown interior, clear windows, no tempa, England casting ($4-6)
15. dark tan body, black base, brown interior, orange windows, no tempa, England casting ($4-6)
16. dark tan body, charcoal base, tan interior, amber windows, no tempa, England casting ($4-6)
17. dark tan body, brown base, brown interior, amber windows, no tempa, England casting ($7-10)
18. dark tan body, brown base, tan interior, amber windows, no tempa, England casting ($7-10)
19. blue body, black base, tan interior, clear windows, no tempa, England casting ($4-6)
20. blue body, black base, brown interior, clear windows, no tempa, England casting ($4-6)
21. blue body, charcoal base, brown interior, clear windows, no tempa, England casting ($4-6)
22. blue body, silver-gray base, brown interior, clear windows, no tempa, England casting ($4-6)
23. blue body, silver-gray base, tan interior, clear windows, no tempa, England casting ($4-6)
24. black body, silver-gray base, brown interior, clear windows, "Porsche" & stripes tempa, England casting ($8 12)
25. black body, silver-gray base, red interior, clear windows, "Porsche" & stripes tempa, England casting ($3-5)
26. black body, unpainted base red interior, clear windows, "Porsche" & stripes tempa, England casting ($3-5)
27. black body, pearly silver base, red interior, clear windows, "Porsche" & stripes tempa, Macau casting ($2-4)
28. black body, pearly silver base, red interior, light amber windows, "Porsche" & stripes tempa, Macau casting ($2-4)
29. light metallic gray body & base, red interior, clear windows, purple & blue tempa, Macau casting ($3-5)
30. pearly silver body, & base, red interior, clear windows, "Martini Racing Porsche" tempa, Macau casting ($7-10)(JP)
31. white & metallic blue body, white base, red interior, clear windows, "28" with "Cale Jenkins" tempa, starburst wheels, Macau casting ($3-5)(SF)
32. white & metallic blue body, white base, red interior, clear windows, "28" without "Cale Jenkins" tempa, starburst wheels, Macau casting ($3-5)(SF)
33. white & metallic blue body, white base, red interior, clear windows, "28" with "Cale Jenkins" tempa, laser wheels, Macau casting ($3-5)(LW)
34. white & metallic blue body, white base, red interior, clear windows, "28" without "Cale Jenkins" tempa, laser wheels, Macau casting ($3-5)(LW)
35. orange body, pearly silver base, red interior, clear windows, "Lufthansa" tempa, Macau casting ($4-6)(GS)
36. charcoal gray body & base, no interior, chrome windows, detailed trim tempa, gray disc with rubber tires, doors cast shut, Macau casting ($5-8)(WC)
37. charcoal gray body & base, no interior, chrome windows, detailed trim tempa, gray disc with rubber tires, doors cast shut, Thailand casting ($5-8)(WC)
38. white body, white base, red interior, clear windows, "56 Porsche" with red stripes tempa, starburst wheels, doors cast shut, China casting ($12-15)(PS)
39. yellow body, pearly silver base, red interior, clear windows, "Porsche 928" & logo tempa, starburst wheels, doors cast shut, China casting ($12-15)(PS)
40. silver-gray body, silver-gray base, purple & gray interior, clear windows, "928S" & detailed trim tempa, chrome disc with rubber tires, Thailand casting ($3-5)(JC)(PC)

MB59-F T-BIRD TURBO COUPE, issued 1987 (USA)
MB61-D T-BIRD TURBO COUPE, issued 1987 (ROW)
MB28-J T-BIRD TURBO COUPE, reissued 1992 (ROW)

1. plum body & base, clear windows, silver-gray interior, 8 dot wheels, "Turbo Coupe" tempa, Macau casting ($1-2)
2. metallic gold body & base, clear windows, silver-gray interior, laser wheels, "56 Motorcraft" tempa, Macau casting ($3-5)(LW)
3. light pea green body & base, clear windows, silver-gray interior, 8 dot wheels, "Turbo Coupe" tempa, Macau casting ($3-4)(SC)
4. dark brown body & base, clear windows, silver-gray interior, 8 dot wheels, "Turbo Coupe" tempa, Macau casting ($3-4)(SC)
5. pink body & base, clear windows, silver-gray interior, 8 dot wheels, "Turbo Coupe" tempa, Macau casting ($3-4)(SC)
6. dark purple body & base, clear windows, silver-gray interior, 8 dot wheels, "Turbo Coupe" tempa, Macau casting ($3-4)(SC)
7. silver-gray body & base, chrome windows, red interior, gray disc with rubber tires, detailed trim tempa, Macau casting ($5-8)(WC)
8. silver-gray body & base, chrome windows, black interior, gray disc with rubber tires, detailed trim tempa, Macau casting ($55-70)(WC)
9. plum body & base, clear windows, silver—gray interior, 8 dot wheels, "Turbo Coupe" tempa, Thailand casting ($1-2)
10. bright plum body & base, clear windows, silver—gray interior, 8 dot wheels, "Turbo Coupe" tempa, Thailand casting ($1-2)
11. metallic blue body, florescent pink base, clear windows, silver-gray interior, 8 dot wheels, stripes tempa, Thailand casting ($1-2)
12. metallic red body & base, clear windows, silver-gray interior, 8 dot wheels, small wing logos tempa, Thailand casting ($3-4)(SS)
13. gold body & base, clear windows, ivory/ black interior, chrome disc with rubber tires, detailed trim tempa, Thailand casting ($3-5)(PC1)
14. charcoal body & base, clear windows, red/ black interior, chrome disc with rubber tires, detailed trim tempa, Thailand casting ($3-5)(PC)(JC)
15. dark green body & base, clear windows, black/ ivory interior, chrome disc with rubber tires, detailed trim tempa, Thailand casting ($3-5)(PC4)
16. red body & base, clear windows, black/ ivory interior, chrome disc with rubber tires, detailed trim tempa, Thailand casting ($3-5)(SC2)
17. white body & base, clear windows, red & black interior, chrome disc with rubber tires, detailed trim tempa, Thailand casting ($15-20)(GC)
18. black body, charcoal base, clear windows, black & gray interior, chrome disc with rubber tires, detailed trim & blue side stripe tempa, Thailand casting ($3-5)(SC5)

MB59-G ASTON MARTIN DB-7, issued 1994 (USA)
MB63-I ASTON MARTIN DB-7, issued 1994 (ROW)

1. metallic green body, tan interior, clear windows, gold 6-spoke spiral wheels, "DB-7" & stripe tempa, Thailand casting ($1-2)
2. metallic green body, tan interior, clear windows, gold 6-spoke spiral wheels, no tempa, Thailand casting ($1-2)
3. charcoal gray body, tan interior, chrome windows, gray disc with rubber tires, detailed trim tempa, Thailand casting ($2-4)(WC)
4. blue body, tan interior, clear windows, silver 6-spoke spiral wheels, no tempa, Thailand casting ($3-5)
5. silver—gray body, gray/ black interior, clear windows, chrome disc with rubber tires, detailed trim tempa, Thailand casting ($6-10)(PC1-ROW)
6. silver blue body, black interior, clear windows, chrome disc with rubber tires, detailed trim tempa, Thailand casting ($8-12)(UC)
7. pearl white body, black & brown interior, clear windows, chrome disc with rubber tires, detailed trim tempa, Thailand casting ($3-5)(PC10)
8. blue body, tan interior, clear windows, 5 spoke concave star wheels, no tempa, Thailand casting ($2-3)
9. candy red body, black & brown interior, clear windows, chrome disc with rubber tires, detailed trim tempa, Thailand casting ($3-5)(JC)(PC)

MB59-H CAMARO Z-28 POLICE CAR, issued 1995 (USA)
MB56-J CAMARO Z-28 POLICE CAR, issued 1995 (ROW)

1. black body, white interior, smoke windows, 6 spoke spiral wheels, red dome lights, "Police" with gold on white star on doors tempa, Thailand casting ($1-2)
2. black body, white interior, smoke windows, 6 spoke spiral wheels, red dome lights, "Police" with black on white star on doors tempa, Thailand casting ($1-2)
3. white body, white interior, smoke windows, 6 spoke spiral wheels, red dome lights, blue "Police" with star logo tempa, Thailand casting ($1-2)(MP)
4. black & white body, black & gray interior, clear windows, chrome disc with rubber tires, red dome lights, "Highway Patrol" tempa, Thailand casting ($3-5)(PC8)
5. white & black body, black & gray interior, clear windows, chrome disc with rubber tires, blue dome lights, "Texas Dept. Public Safety Trooper" tempa, Thailand casting ($3-5)(PC8)
6. bright blue body, black & blue interior, clear windows, chrome disc with rubber tires, red dome lights, "NY State Police" tempa, Thailand casting ($3-5)(PC8)
7. blue body, white interior, blue windows, 5 spoke concave star wheels, red dome lights, "Police Unit 4" tempa, Thailand casting ($1-2)(MP)
8. white body, blue interior, clear windows, 5 spoke concave star wheels, blue dome lights, "Matchbox Police" tempa, Thailand casting ($1-2)
9. metallic gold body, black interior, clear windows, 6 spoke spiral wheels, red dome lights, no tempa, Thailand casting ($5-10)(CH)
10. black body, white interior, blue windows, 5 spoke concave star wheels, red dome lights, "Matchbox Police 911" tempa, Thailand casting ($1-2)(MW27)
11. black body, black & gray interior, clear windows, chrome disc with rubber tires, red dome lights, "Kansas Highway Patrol", Thailand casting ($3-5)(PC18)
12. metallic blue & silver-gray body, black & gray interior, clear windows, chrome disc with rubber tires, red & blue dome lights, "Nevada Highway Patrol" tempa, Thailand casting ($3-5)(PC18)
13. white body, black & gray interior, clear windows, red & blue dome lights, chrome disc with rubber tires, "Utah Highway Patrol" tempa, Thailand casting ($3-5)(PC18)
14. black body, white interior, blue windows, red dome lights, 5 spoke concave star wheels, "Matchbox Police 911" tempa, China casting ($1-2)(MW27)
15. blue body, white interior, blue windows, red dome lights, 5 spoke concave star wheels, "Matchbox Police" tempa, China casting ($1-2)(MP)
16. white body, black interior, clear windows, red dome lights, 5 spoke concave star wheels, "Highway Patrol/ DWI Enforcement" tempa, China casting ($1-2)(MP)
17. white body, black & blue interior, clear windows, red & blue dome lights, chrome disc with rubber tires, "City of Miami Police 7630" tempa, China casting ($75+)(PC22)

NOTE: See notes for MB30I Chevy Tahoe.

MB60-A SITE HUT TRUCK, issued 1970

1. blue body, blue windows, yellow plastic building with green roof , chrome base, 5 spoke wheels, ($25-40)

MB60-B LOTUS SUPER SEVEN, issued 1971

NOTE: All models with unpainted base, black interior, clear windshield & 4 spoke wheels.

1. orange body, flames labels ($15-18)
2. yellow body, flames labels ($50-75)
3. yellow body, checkers & "60" tempa ($18-25)

MB60-C HOLDEN PICK-UP, issued 1977

1. maroon body, orange interior, amber windows, yellow cycles, "500" label ($12-15)
2. maroon body, light yellow interior, amber windows, yellow cycles, "500" label ($12-15)
3. red body, light yellow interior, amber windows, yellow cycles, "500" label ($7-10)
4. red body, light yellow interior, orange windows, yellow cycles, "500" label ($7-10)
5. red body, light yellow interior, amber windows, lemon cycles, "500" label ($7-10)
6. red body, light yellow interior, clear windows, yellow cycles, "500" label ($7-10)
7. red body, light yellow interior, amber windows, yellow cycles, star label ($20-25)
8. red body, red interior, amber windows, yellow cycles, "500" label ($8-12)
9. red body, red interior, amber windows, olive cycles, "500" label ($10-15)
10. red body, red interior, orange windows, olive cycles, "500" label ($10-15)
11. red body, red interior, amber windows, olive cycles, sunburst label ($10-15)
12. red body, red interior, orange windows, olive cycles, sunburst label ($10-15)
13. cream body, red interior, amber windows, yellow cycles, "Superbike" labels ($8-12)
14. cream body, red interior, amber windows, red cycles, "Superbike" labels ($6-8)
15. cream body, red interior, orange windows, red cycles, "Superbike" labels ($6-8)
16. cream body, tan interior, amber windows, red cycles, "Superbike" labels ($6-8)
17. cream body, tan interior, amber windows, yellow cycles, "Superbike" labels ($6-8)
18. white body, red interior, amber windows, red cycles, "Superbike" labels ($12-15)
19. cream body, red interior, amber windows, red cycles, "Honda" labels ($15-20)

20. metallic blue body, light yellow interior, orange windows, yellow cycles, "Paris Dakar 81" label ($35-50)(FR)

MB60-D PISTON POPPER, issued 1982 (USA)

NOTE: All models with unpainted base, amber windows & maltese cross rear wheels unless otherwise noted.

1. yellow body, red interior, maltese cross front wheels, no tempa, England casting ($7-10)
2. yellow body, red interior, 5 spoke front wheels, "60" towards front side tempa, no trunk tempa, England casting ($5-7)
3. yellow body, red interior, 5 spoke front wheels, "60" towards rear side tempa, no trunk tempa, England casting ($5-7)
4. yellow body, red interior, 5 spoke front wheels, "60" towards rear side tempa, with trunk tempa, England casting ($5-7)
5. yellow body, white interior, 5 spoke front wheels, "60" towards rear side tempa, with trunk tempa, England casting ($10-15)
6. yellow body, red interior, 5 spoke front wheels, no side tempa, with trunk tempa, England casting ($7-10)
7. orange body, red interior, 5 spoke front wheels, unpainted base, "Sunkist" tempa, Hong Kong casting ($4-6)
8. orange body, red interior, 5 spoke front wheels, black base, "Sunkist" tempa, Macau casting ($4-6)

MB60-F PONTIAC FIREBIRD RACER, issued 1985 (USA)
MB12-F PONTIAC FIREBIRD RACER, issued 1985 (ROW)
MB48-G PONTIAC FIREBIRD RACER, reissued 1993 (USA)
MB48-G PONTIAC FIREBIRD RACER, reissued 1994 (ROW)

NOTE: All models with clear windows unless otherwise noted.

1. yellow body, blue metal base, red interior, 8 dot silver wheels, "Son of A Gun 55" tempa, Macau casting ($4-6)
2. yellow body, blue metal base, red interior, 8 dot silver wheels, "Pirelli 56" tempa, Macau casting ($4-6)
3. yellow body, blue metal base, red interior, 8 dot gold wheels, "Son of A Gun 55" tempa, Macau casting ($4-6)
4. yellow body, blue metal base, red interior, 8 dot gold wheels, "Pirelli 56" tempa, Macau casting ($4-6)
5. yellow body, blue metal base, red interior, dot dash wheels, "Son of A Gun 55" tempa, Macau casting ($4-6)
6. yellow body, blue metal base, red interior, dot dash wheels, "Pirelli 56" tempa, Macau casting ($4-6)
7. yellow body, blue metal base, red interior, 8 dot silver wheels, "Pirelli 56" (plain sides) tempa, Macau casting ($4-6)
8. powder blue body, blue metal base, gray interior, starburst wheels, "10" with blue & yellow tempa, Macau casting ($3-5)(SF)
9. metallic blue body, blue metal base, gray interior, laser wheels, "10" with blue & yellow tempa, Macau casting ($3-5)(LW)
10. white body, blue metal base, red interior, 5 arch wheels, "Fast Eddies 15" tempa, Macau casting ($2-4)
11. white body, blue metal base, red interior, 8 dot silver wheels, "Fast Eddies 15" tempa, Macau casting ($2-4)
12. white body, blue metal base, red interior, 8 dot silver wheels, "6 Horse Racing Team" tempa, Macau casting ($8-12)(HK)
13. dark brown body, blue metal base, red interior, 8 dot silver wheels, "Fast Eddies 15" tempa, Macau casting ($7-10)(SC)
14. light pea green body, blue metal base, red interior, 8 dot silver wheels, "Fast Eddies 15" tempa, Macau casting ($7-10)(SC)
15. white body, blue plastic base, red interior, 8 dot silver wheels, "Fast Eddies 15" tempa, Macau casting ($3-5)
16. powder blue body, blue plastic base, gray interior, starburst wheels, "10" with blue & yellow tempa, Macau casting ($7-10)(SF)
17. yellow body, red plastic base, red interior, starburst wheels, "10" with red & white stripes tempa, Macau casting ($15-20)(SF)
18. metallic blue body, blue plastic base, gray interior, laser wheels, "10" with yellow & blue stripes tempa, Macau casting ($7-10)(LW)
19. white body, blue plastic base, red interior, starburst wheels, "Fast Eddies 15" tempa, China casting ($6-8)(GS)
20. black body, pink plastic base, silver-gray interior, 8 dot wheels, blue & pink tempa, Thailand casting ($2-3)
21. fluorescent pink body, bright yellow plastic base, gold 6-spoke spiral wheels, yellow & white design tempa, Thailand casting ($1-2)
22. purple body, bright yellow plastic base, gold 6-spoke spiral wheels, yellow & white design tempa, Thailand casting ($6-8)(PS)
23. florescent pink body, bright yellow plastic base, silver 6-spoke spiral wheels, yellow & white hood & side design tempa, Thailand casting ($1-2)
24. dark florescent pink body, bright yellow plastic base, silver 6-spoke spiral wheels, yellow & white side design only tempa, China casting ($1-2)
25. metallic turquoise body, bright yellow plastic base, silver 6-spoke spiral wheels, yellow & white hood & sides design tempa, China casting ($2-4)
26. silver-gray body, dark gray plastic base, chrome disc with rubber tires, two tone blue design tempa, China casting ($3-5)(PC9)
27. black body, black plastic base, 5 spoke concave star wheels, "Go Pies! 1997" tempa, China casting ($3-5)(AU)

MB60-G FORD TRANSIT VAN, issued 1986 (USA)
MB57-G FORD TRANSIT VAN, issued 1990 (USA)

NOTE: All models with clear windows, dark gray base, gray interior & 8 dot wheels unless otherwise noted.

1. red body, left hand drive, "Motorsport" tempa, Macau casting ($2-4)
2. red body, right hand drive, no tempa, Macau casting ($30-45)(UK)
3. red body, left hand drive, no tempa, Macau casting ($2-4)
4. red body, left hand drive, "Motorsport" tempa, dot dash wheels, Macau casting ($3-5)
5. white body, left hand drive, red cross & stripe with gray rectangle tempa, Macau casting ($2-3)
6. white body, left hand drive, "Federal Express" tempa, Macau casting ($2-3)
7. yellow body, left hand drive, "British Telecom" tempa, Macau casting ($4-6)(GS)
8. red body, left hand drive, "Australia Post" tempa, Macau casting ($6-8)(AU)
9. white body, left hand drive, red cross & stripe with gray rectangle tempa, China casting ($2-4)
10. white body, right hand drive, "Unichem" tempa, Macau casting ($7-10)(UK)
11. white body, right hand drive, "JCB Site Shop" tempa, Macau casting ($6-8)(GS)
12. white body, left hand drive, "Federal Express" tempa, China casting ($1-2)
13. white body, right hand drive, "XP Express Parcels" tempa, China casting ($6-8)(UK)
14. red body & base, right hand drive- black interior, "Royal Mail" tempa, Macau casting ($5-8)(UK)(MP)
15. orange-red body, left hand drive, "Australia Post- We Deliver" tempa, Chinas casting ($6-8)(AU)
16. white body, left hand drive, "Wigwam" tempa, China casting ($7-10)(DU)
17. lime green body, left hand drive, no tempa, China casting ($12-15)(DU)
18. white body, right hand drive, "Wishing Well Appeal", China casting ($6-8)(UK)
19. white body, left hand drive, "Wella" tempa, China casting ($6-8)(GR)
20. white body, right hand drive, "Australia Telecom" tempa, China casting ($6-8)(AU)
21. white body, left hand drive, "XP Express Parcels" tempa, China casting ($4-6)(UK)
22. white body, right hand drive, "Federal Express" tempa, China casting ($3-5)
23. white body, right hand drive, "Peter Cox Preservation" tempa, China casting ($7-10)(UK)
24. white body, left hand drive, "Kiosk" tempa, China casting ($8-12)(SW)
25. red body, left hand drive, "Blick" tempa, China casting ($8-12)(SW)
26. orange body, left hand drive, "Ovomaltine" tempa, China casting ($8-12)(SW)
27. silver-gray body, left hand drive, "Isostar/ Perform/ Powerplay" tempa, China casting ($8-12)(SW)
28. white body, left hand drive, "Kellogg's" tempa, China casting ($60-75)(SW)(AS)(OP)
29. white body, right hand drive, "Kellogg's" tempa, China casting ($60-75)(SW)(AS)(OP)
30. yellow body, left hand drive, "Ryder" tempa, China casting ($2-3)
31. white body, left hand drive, "DCS" tempa, China casting ($85-110)(SC)
32. white body, left hand drive, white interior & base, amber windows, no tempa, China casting ($10-15)(GF)
33. white body, left hand drive, "Supertoys" tempa, China casting ($20-25)(IR)
34. metallic green body, left hand drive, "Taronga Zoomobile" tempa ($6-8)(AU)
35. white body, left hand drive, "McKesson" tempa, China casting ($50-75)(US)
36. yellow body, left hand drive, "Cadbury's Flake" tempa, China casting ($1-2)
37. white body, left hand drive, "Garden Festival Wales" tempa, China casting ($5-8)(WL)(GS)
38. powder blue & white body, left hand drive, "OCS" tempa, China casting ($15-18)(AU)
39. white body, left hand drive, "Matchbox" tempa, China casting ($2-3)
40. orange-red body with all white roof, left hand drive, "Australia Post- We Deliver" tempa, China casting ($3-5)(AU)(GS)
41. yellow body, left hand drive, "Express Post" tempa, China casting ($3-5)(AU)(GS)
42. red body, left hand drive, "14th Annual Toy Show- Ft. Washington, PA" tempa, China casting ($18-25)(US)(LD)
43. white body, left hand drive, "Hankook Tyres" tempa, China casting ($25-40)(US)(LD)
44. red body, left hand drive, "Brantho-Korrux" tempa, China casting ($25-40)(GR)(LD)
45. red body, left hand drive, "Viewmaster" tempa, China casting ($85-90)(US)(LD)

NOTE: Above model only available in wooden box display with viewer & special reel

46. white body, left hand drive, "Viewmaster" tempa, China casting ($18-25)(US)(LD)
47. white body, left hand drive, "Pickfords Record Management", China casting ($25-50)(UK)(LD)
48. red body, left hand drive, "Kit Kat" tempa, China casting ($20-30)(UK)(LD)
49. white & teal body, left hand drive, "Hilton" with red letters tempa, China casting ($18-25)(US)(LD)
50. white & teal body, left hand drive, "Hilton" with black letters tempa, China casting ($15-18)(US)(LD)
51. white body, left hand drive, "97.5 PST" tempa, China casting ($15-18)(US)(LD)
52. dark blue body, left hand drive, "97.5 PST" tempa, China casting ($18-25)(US)(LD)
53. dark blue body, left hand drive, "Midwest Diecast Miniatures" tempa, China casting ($12-15)(US)(LD)
54. white body, left hand drive, "24th National Truck In 1996" tempa, China casting ($12-15)(US)(LD)
55. red body, left hand drive, "24th National Truck In 1996" tempa, China casting ($18-25)(US)(LD)
56. red body, left hand drive, "Smoke Detectors Saves Lives" tempa, China casting ($15-18)(US)(LD)
57. dark blue body, left hand drive, "Scooter's Snowboard Shoppe" tempa, China casting ($18-25)(US)(LD)
58. red body, left hand drive, "Hankook" tempa, China casting ($12-15)(Malta)(LD)
59. red body, left hand drive, "Waterway Recovery Group" tempa, China casting ($12-15)(UK)(LD)
60. red body, left hand drive, "Manrose Extractor Fans" tempa, China casting ($12-15)(UK)(LD)
61. red body, left hand drive, "Magna" tempa, China casting ($100-150)(UK)(LD)
62. red body, left hand drive, "Belfast Evening Telegraph" tempa, China casting ($100-150)(IR)(LD)
63. dark blue body, left hand drive, "NSVA- 25th Anniversary Members Van" ($25-40)(UK)(LD)
64. dark blue body, left hand drive, "NSVA- 25th Anniversary Committee Van" ($100-150)(UK)(LD)

MB61-A BLUE SHARK, issued 1971

1. dark blue body, clear windshield, unpainted base, "86" label ($15-18)
2. dark blue body, clear windshield, silver-gray base, "86" label ($15-18)
3. dark blue body, amber windshield, unpainted base, "86" label ($15-18)
4. dark blue body, amber windshield, silver-gray base, "86" label ($15-18)
5. dark blue body, clear windshield, unpainted base, "69" label ($15-18)
6. dark blue body, amber windshield, unpainted base, "69" label ($15-18)
7. dark blue body, clear windshield, silver-gray base, "69" label ($15-18)
8. dark blue body, amber windshield, silver-gray base, "69" label ($15-18)
9. dark blue body, clear windshield, unpainted base, scorpion label ($25-40)
10. dark blue body, amber windshield, unpainted base, scorpion label ($25-40)

MB61-B WRECK TRUCK, issued 1978

1. red body, black base, amber windows, white booms, red hooks, no tempa ($4-6)
2. red body, black base, blue windows, white booms, red hooks, no tempa ($8-12)
3. red body, charcoal base, amber windows, white booms, red hooks, no tempa ($4-6)
4. red body, black base, amber windows, white booms, black hooks, no tempa ($4-6)
5. red body, black base, amber windows, red booms, red hooks, no tempa ($6-8)
6. red body, charcoal base, amber windows, red booms, red hooks, no tempa ($6-8)
7. red body, black base, amber windows, red booms, black hooks, no tempa ($6-8)
8. bright yellow body, black base, amber windows, white booms, red hooks, no tempa ($4-6)
9. dull yellow body, black base, amber windows, white booms, red hooks, no tempa ($4-6)
10. bright yellow body, charcoal base, amber windows, green booms, red hooks, no tempa, ($5-7)
11. dull yellow body, charcoal base, amber windows, green booms, red hooks, no tempa ($5-7)
12. bright yellow body, black base, amber windows, green booms, black hooks, no tempa ($5-7)
13. dull yellow body, black base, amber windows, green booms, black hooks, no tempa ($5-7)
14. bright yellow body, charcoal base, amber windows, green booms, black hooks, no tempa ($5-7)
15. dull yellow body, charcoal base, amber windows, green booms, black hooks, no tempa ($5-7)
16. bright yellow body, black base, amber windows, red booms, red hooks, no tempa ($4-6)
17. dull yellow body, black base, amber windows, red booms, red hooks, no tempa ($4-6)
18. bright yellow body, charcoal base, amber windows, red booms, red hooks, no tempa ($4-6)
19. dull yellow body, charcoal base, amber windows, red booms, red hooks, no tempa ($4-6)
20. bright yellow body, blue-gray base, amber windows, red booms, red hooks, no tempa ($4-6)
21. dull yellow body, blue-gray base, amber windows, red booms, red hooks, no tempa ($4-6)
22. bright yellow body, unpainted base, amber windows, red booms, black hooks, no tempa ($4-6)
23. dull yellow body, unpainted base, amber windows, red booms, black hooks, no tempa ($4-6)
24. red body, black base, amber windows, white booms, red hooks, "24 Hour" tempa ($5-7)(TP)
25. white body, charcoal base (tab), amber windows, white booms, red hooks, red stripe label ($450-600)(BR)
26. orange-red body, black base (tab), amber windows, white booms, red hooks, no tempa ($225-300)(BR)
27. bright yellow body, blue-gray base, amber windows, red booms, black hooks, no tempa ($4-6)
28. bright yellow body, blue-gray base, amber windows, white booms, red hooks, no tempa ($5-8)
29. bright yellow body, brown base, amber windows, red booms, black hooks, no tempa ($7-10)
30. dull yellow body, brown base, amber windows, red booms, black hooks, no tempa ($7-10)
31. lemon body, blue-gray base, amber windows, white booms, red hooks, no tempa ($10-15)

MB61-C PETERBILT WRECKER, issued 1982

1. blue body, black booms, amber windows, chrome exhausts & base, no tempa, England casting ($150-200)(GS)
2. orange body, black booms, amber windows, chrome exhausts & base,

black "Eddie's Wrecker" tempa, England casting ($4-6)
3. orange body, black booms, clear windows, chrome exhausts & base, black "Eddie's Wrecker" tempa, England casting ($4-6)
4. orange body, black booms, amber windows, chrome exhausts & base, white "Eddie's Wrecker" tempa, England casting ($4-6)
5. white body, black booms, amber windows, chrome exhausts & base, black "9" tempa, Macau casting ($2-3)
6. white body, black booms, clear windows, chrome exhausts & base, black "9" tempa, Macau casting ($2-3)
7. white body, black booms, amber windows, chrome exhausts & base, blue "9" tempa, Macau casting ($1-2)
8. white body, blue booms, amber windows, chrome exhausts & base, blue "9" tempa, Macau casting ($1-2)
9. white body, blue booms, clear windows, chrome exhausts & base, blue "911" tempa, Macau casting ($1-2)
10. white body, orange booms, clear windows, chrome exhausts & base, "SFPD" & star tempa, Macau casting ($1-2)
11. white body, dull orange booms, clear windows, chrome exhausts & base, "SFPD" & star tempa, Macau casting ($1-2)
12. orange body, dark green booms, dark green windows, gray exhausts & base, black stripes tempa, Macau casting includes plastic armament ($5-8)(RB)
13. olive body, black booms, clear windows, black exhausts & base, "8" with red/white stripes tempa, Macau casting ($4-5)(CM)
14. white body, orange booms, clear windows, gray exhausts, chrome base, "SFPD" & star tempa , Macau casting ($1-2)
15. white body, orange booms, clear windows, gray exhausts, chrome base, "SFPD" & star tempa, Thailand casting ($1-2)(MC)
16. orange body, dark green booms, dark green windows, gray exhausts & base, black stripes tempa, Thailand casting ($8-12)(JP) (Tomy box)
17. red body, black booms, clear windows, gray exhausts & base, "Police" tempa, Manaus casting ($35-50)(BR)
18. white body, black booms, clear windows, gray exhausts, chrome base, black "9" tempa, Manaus casting ($35-50)(BR)
19. blue body, black booms, clear windows, gray exhausts & base, "C.P. City Police" tempa, Manaus casting ($30-45)(BR)
20. white body, dull orange booms, clear windows, gray exhausts, black base, "Police M9" & "Intercom City" tempa, Thailand casting ($7-10)(IC)
21. white body, orange booms, clear windows, chrome exhausts & base, "Police PD-22" & checkers tempa, Thailand casting ($2-4)(TP)

MB61-E NISSAN 300ZX, issued 1990 (USA)
MB37-H NISSAN 300ZX, issued 1990 (ROW)

1. yellow body, smoke gray windows, white interior, 8 dot wheels, outlined "300ZX" tempa, Macau casting ($1-2)
2. chrome plated body, smoke gray windows, white interior, 8 dot wheels, no tempa, Macau casting ($12-18)(C2)
3. chrome plated body, smoke gray windows, white interior, 8 dot wheels, no tempa, Thailand casting ($12-18)(C2)
4. yellow body, smoke gray windows, white interior, 8 dot wheels, outlined "300ZX" tempa, Thailand casting ($1-2)
5. iridescent cream body, chrome windows, pink interior, gray disc with rubber tires, detailed trim tempa, China casting ($5-8)(WC)
6. iridescent cream body, chrome windows, dark gray interior, gray disc with rubber tires, detailed trim tempa, China casting ($5-8)(WC)
7. iridescent cream body, chrome windows, white interior, gray disc with rubber tires, detailed trim tempa, China casting ($5-8)(WC)
8. iridescent pink-cream body, blue-chrome & black windows, no interior, peach & silver lightning wheels, "Turbo Z" tempa, China casting ($2-3)(LT)
9. iridescent pink-cream body, blue-chrome & black windows, no interior, pink & silver lightning wheels, "Turbo Z" tempa, China casting ($2-3)(LT)
10. metallic blue body, chrome & black windows, no interior, lightning wheels, "300ZX" tempa, China casting ($2-3)(LT)
11. bright orange body, blue-chrome & black windows, no interior, lightning wheels, "300ZX" tempa, China casting ($2-3)(LT)
12. lemon body, black & chrome windows, no interior, lightning wheels, "Turbo Z" tempa, China casting ($2-3)(LT)
13. yellow body, clear windows, white interior, 8 dot wheels, outlined "300ZX" tempa, China casting ($1-2)
14. yellow body, clear windows, white interior, 8 dot wheels, solid "300ZX" tempa, China casting ($1-2)
15. metallic red body, chrome windows, dark gray interior, gray disc with rubber tires, detailed trim tempa, China casting ($5-8)(WC)
16. metallic red body, black & chrome windows, no interior, silver & yellow lightning wheels, "Turbo Z" tempa, China casting ($5-8)(LT)(US)(OP)
17. metallic red body, black & chrome windows, no interior, pink & red lightning wheels, "Turbo Z" tempa, China casting ($5-8)(LT)(US)(OP)
18. white, lime & pink body, black & chrome windows, no interior, lightning wheels, "Z" & "Turbo" tempa, China casting ($2-3)(LT)
19. white, orange & black body, black & chrome windows, no interior, lightning wheels, "Z" & "Turbo" tempa, China casting ($2-3)(LT)
20. dark teal blue body, clear windows, pink interior, gold 6-spoke spiral wheels, yellow & pink streaks tempa, Thailand casting ($1-2)
21. yellow body, clear windows, gray interior, 8 dot wheels, "300ZX" tempa & "Nationwise Auto Parts" labels, Thailand casting ($20-35)(US)
22. silver-gray & metallic blue body, clear windows, florescent orange interior, silver 6-spoke spiral wheels, steel grid pattern tempa, China casting ($1-2)
23. flat black body, clear windows, florescent orange interior, silver 6-spoke spiral wheels, white lines on side with orange & white lines on hood tempa, China casting ($3-5)
24. black body, clear windows, pink interior, silver 6-spoke spiral wheels, white swirls tempa, China casting ($1-2)
25. metallic gold body, clear windows, black interior, silver 6-spoke spiral wheels, no tempa, China casting ($10-15)(CH)
26. yellow body, clear windows, white interior, 8 dot wheels, solid "300ZX" tempa, Thailand casting ($1-2)
27. silver-gray & metallic blue body, clear windows, florescent orange interior, silver 6 spoke spiral wheels, Thailand casting ($1-2)
28. black body, clear windows, pink interior, 5 spoke concave star wheels, white swirls tempa, China casting ($1-2)
29. silver body, clear windows, orange interior, 5 spoke concave star wheels, yellow & orange design with "ZX" tempa, China casting ($1-2)
30. lemon body, clear windows, black & gray interior, chrome disc with rubber tires, detailed trim tempa, China casting ($3-5)(PC15)
31. white body, clear windows, silver-gray interior, 5 spoke concave star wheels, orange & yellow design with "ZX" tempa, China casting ($1-2)(MW43-ROW)

MB62-A MERCURY COUGAR, issued 1970

1. green body, unpainted base, red interior ($25-40)
2. yellow-green body, unpainted base, red interior ($25-40)

MB62-B MERCURY COUGAR DRAGSTER, issued 1970

1. yellow-green body, unpainted base, 5 spoke rear wheels "Rat Rod" labels ($15-20)
2. yellow-green body, unpainted base, 4 spoke rear wheels, "Rat Rod" labels ($15-20)
3. dark lime body, unpainted base, 4 spoke rear wheels, "Rat Rod" labels ($15-20)
4. dark lime body, silver-gray base, 4 spoke rear wheels, "Rat Rod" labels ($15-20)
5. dark lime body, unpainted base, 4 spoke rear wheels, "Wildcat" labels ($20-25)

MB62-C RENAULT 17TL, issued 1974

1. dark red body, "9" hood label, 5 spoke wheels ($7-10)
2. orange-red body, "9" hood label, 5 spoke wheels ($7-10)
3. orange-red body, "6" hood label, 5 spoke wheels ($7-10)
4. orange-red body, "Fire" side labels, 5 spoke wheels ($12-15)
5. orange-red body, "6" hood label, maltese cross wheels ($7-10)
6. orange body, "6" hood label, 5 spoke wheels ($7-10)

MB62-D CHEVROLET CORVETTE, issued 1979

NOTE: Most versions exist with combinations of all 5 arch wheels, all 5 crown wheels, 5 arch front & 5 crown rear wheels and vice versa, unless otherwise noted.

1. red body, unpainted base, gray interior, clear windows, white hood & side tempa, no "Corvette" cast at rear or front, England casting ($35-50)
2. red body, unpainted base, gray interior, clear windows, white hood & sides tempa, England casting ($4-6)
3. red body, unpainted base, gray interior, clear windows, white hood tempa only, England casting ($4-6)
4. red body, unpainted base, black interior, clear windows, white hood & sides tempa, England casting ($4-6)
5. red body, unpainted base, black interior, clear windows, white hood tempa only, England casting ($4-6)
6. red body, unpainted base, white interior, clear windows, white hood tempa only, England casting ($4-6)
7. black body, unpainted base, gray interior, clear windows, green & orange stripes hood tempa, England casting ($3-5)
8. black body, silver-gray base, gray interior, clear windows, green & orange stripes hood tempa, England casting ($3-5)
9. black body, unpainted base, gray interior, opaque windows, green & orange stripes hood tempa, England casting ($10-15)(PS)
10. black body, red base, gray interior, clear windows, yellow & orange stripes hood tempa, Macau casting ($2-4)
11. black body, silver-gray base, gray interior, clear windows, "The Force" tempa, Macau casting ($2-4)
12. black body, pearly silver base, gray interior, clear windows, "The Force" tempa, Macau casting ($2-4)
13. green body, pearly silver base, gray interior, clear windows, "Brut/ Faberge" tempa, Macau casting ($6-8)(TM)
14. black body, pearly silver base, red interior, clear windows, "Turbo Vette" tempa, starburst wheels, Macau casting ($3-5)(SF)
15. black body, pearly silver base, red interior, clear windows, "Turbo Vette" tempa, laser wheels, Macau casting ($3-5)(LW)
16. metallic red body, pearly silver base, red interior, clear windows, "Turbo Vette" tempa, laser wheels, Macau casting ($10-15)(LW)
17. black body, red plastic base, red interior, clear windows, "The Force" tempa, 8 spoke wheels, Manaus casting ($35-50)(BR)

NOTE: Following models with plastic base, clear windows, gray disc with rubber tires & China casting unless otherwise noted.

18. blue body, white base, dark blue interior, "Dodgers 1992" tempa ($3-5)(WR)
19. blue body, pumpkin orange base, dark blue interior, "Royals 1992" tempa ($3-5)(WR)
20. blue body, dark blue base, black interior, "Mariners 1992" tempa ($3-5)(WR)
21. blue body, dark silver-gray base, gray interior, "Rockies 1992" tempa ($3-5)(WR)
22. blue body, bright orange base, black interior, "Mets 1992" tempa ($3-5)(WR)
23. dark blue body, white base, red interior, "Red Sox 1992" tempa ($3-5)(WR)
24. dark blue body, gray base, black interior, "Twins 1992" tempa ($3-5)(WR)
25. metallic blue body, red base, black interior, "Braves 1992" tempa ($3-5)(WR)
26. bright blue body, dark blue base, black interior, "Blue Jays 1992" tempa ($3-5)(WR)
27. powder blue body, white base, dark blue interior, "Expos 1992" tempa ($3-5)(WR)
28. green body, dark yellow base, dark yellow interior, "Athletics 1992" tempa ($3-5)(WR)
29. yellow body, red base, red interior, "Angels 1992" tempa ($3-5)(WR)
30. orange body, silver-gray base, dark blue interior, "Tigers 1992" tempa ($3-5)(WR)
31. gray body, black base, red interior, "Giants 1992" tempa ($3-5)(WR)
32. white body, yellow base, dark blue interior, "Brewers 1992" tempa ($3-5)(WR)
33. white body, dark blue base, dark blue interior, "Indians 1992" tempa ($3-5)(WR)
34. white body, dark blue base, dark blue interior, "Padres 1992" tempa ($3-5)(WR)
35. white body, blue base, orange interior, "Astros 1992" tempa ($3-5)(WR)
36. white body, turquoise base, orange interior, "Marlins 1992" tempa ($3-5)(WR)
37. white body, red base, red interior, "Yankees 1992" tempa ($3-5)(WR)
38. red body, white base, black interior, "Reds 1992" tempa ($3-5)(WR)
39. red body, white base, dark blue interior, "Phillies 1992" tempa ($3-5)(WR)
40. red body, white base, dark blue interior, "Cubs 1992" tempa ($3-5)(WR)
41. red body, white base, red interior, "Cardinals 1992" tempa ($3-5)(WR)
42. red body, blue base, dark blue interior, "Rangers 1992" tempa ($3-5)(WR)
43. black body, white base, black interior, "Pirates 1992" tempa ($3-5)(WR)
44. black body, white base, orange interior, "Orioles 1992" tempa ($3-5)(WR)
45. black body, silver-gray base, red interior, "White Sox 1992" tempa ($3-5)(WR)
46. white body, red base, red interior, "Cooperstown 1993" tempa ($3-5)(WR)
47. white body, gray base, maroon interior, red stripes tempa, 5 arch front & 5 crown rear wheels, Thailand casting ($2-4)(GS)
48. black body, silver-gray base, gray interior, opaque windows, "The Force" tempa, Macau casting ($8-12)(PS)
49. silver-gray body, gray base, purple interior, clear windows, white & purple design tempa, China casting ($8-12)(PS)

MB62-F ROLLS ROYCE SILVER CLOUD, issued 1986 (USA)
MB31-F ROLLS ROYCE SILVER CLOUD, issued 1986 (ROW)

1. silver-gray body, chrome base, dark gray interior, clear windows, dot dash wheels, England casting ($8-10)(JB)
2. cream body, chrome base, dark gray interior, clear windows, dot dash wheels, England casting ($1-2)
3. cream body, chrome base, dark gray interior, clear windows, dot dash wheels, Macau casting ($1-2)
4. green-gold body, chrome base, black interior, chrome windows, gray disc with rubber tires, Macau casting ($5-8)(WC)
5. green-gold body, chrome base, black interior, chrome windows, gray disc with rubber tires, Thailand casting ($5-8)(WC)
6. cream body, chrome base, dark gray interior, clear windows, dot dash wheels, Thailand casting ($1-2)
7. plum body, chrome base, purple & gray interior, clear windows, chrome disc with rubber tires, Thailand casting ($18-25)(GC)

MB62-G VOLVO 760, issued 1986 (ROW)

NOTE: All models with black base & 8 dot wheels unless otherwise noted.

1. pearly silver body, black interior, clear windows, Macau casting ($2-3)
2. dark silver-gray body, black interior, clear windows, China casting ($2-3)
3. plum body, black interior, clear windows, China casting ($2-3)
4. dark plum body, black interior, clear windows, China casting ($2-3)
5. white body & base, white interior, amber windows, China casting ($10-15)(GF)
6. silver-gray body, black base, gray & blue interior, clear windows, chrome disc with rubber tires, detailed trim tempa, China casting ($8-12)(UC)

MB62-H OLDSMOBILE AEROTECH, issued 1989 (USA)
MB64-F OLDSMOBILE AEROTECH, issued 1989 (ROW)

NOTE: all models with gray plastic base & smoke windows unless otherwise noted.

1. silver-gray body, "Quad 4/ Aerotech/ Oldsmobile" tempa, 8 dot wheels, Macau casting ($1-2)
2. silver-gray body, "Quad 4/ Aerotech/ Oldsmobile" tempa, 8 dot wheels, Thailand casting ($1-2)
3. florescent orange body, "Aerotech" tempa, 8 dot wheels, Thailand casting ($1-2)
4. dark purple & white body, purple flash & "Aerotech" tempa, gold 6 spoke spiral wheels, Thailand casting ($1-2)
5. dark purple & white body, purple flash & "Aerotech" tempa, silver 6-spoke spiral wheels, China casting ($1-2)
6. dark purple & white body, purple flash without "Aerotech" tempa, silver 6-spoke spiral wheels, China casting ($1-2)

MB62-J STREET STREAK, issued 1996 (USA)
MB72-N STREET STREAK, issued 1996 (ROW)

1. purple & white body, smoke windows, 6-spoke spiral wheels, Thailand casting ($3-5)
2. florescent orange & black body, black windows, 6-spoke spiral wheels, Thailand casting ($1-2)(MP)
3. dark red & silver-gray body, chrome windows, 5 spoke concave star wheels, Thailand casting ($1-2)
4. red & black body, chrome windows, 5 spoke concave star wheels, Thailand casting ($1-2)(MP)
5. metallic gold body, smoke windows, 5 spoke concave star wheels,

Thailand casting ($5-10)(CH)
6. blue & silver-gray body , chrome windows, 5 spoke concave star wheels, Thailand casting ($1-2)(MW16)
7. blue & silver-gray body, chrome windows, 5 spoke concave star wheels, China casting ($1-2)(MW16)

MB63-A DODGE CRANE TRUCK, issued 1970
1. yellow body, green windows, yellow hook, black axle covers ($25-40)
2. yellow body, green windows, yellow hook, red axle covers ($25-40)

MB63-B FREEWAY GAS TANKER, issued 1973
NOTE: All models with white tank and maltese cross front & 5 spoke rear wheels unless otherwise noted. Other wheel combinations can exist.
1. "Castrol" labels, red cab with black base, red trailer base, purple windows ($90-120)
2. "Burmah" labels, red cab with black base, red trailer base, purple windows ($6-8)
3. "Burmah" labels, red cab with black base, red trailer base, purple windows, with tow hook ($6-8)(TP)
4. "Octane" labels, olive cab with black base, black trailer base with olive tank, purple windows ($7-10)(TP)
5. French flag labels, olive drab cab with black base, black trailer base with olive tank, purple windows ($65-80)(TP)
6. Canadian flag labels, olive drab cab with black base, black trailer base with olive tank, purple windows ($125-175)(TP)
7. "Aral" labels, blue cab with black base, blue trailer base, purple windows ($25-40)
8. "Chevron" labels, red cab with black base, red trailer base, purple windows ($6-8)
9. "Chevron" labels, red cab with black base, red trailer base, purple windows, with tow hook ($6-8)(TP)
10. "Shell" labels, white cab with yellow base, yellow trailer base, purple windows ($6-8)
11. "Shell" labels, white cab with yellow base, dark yellow trailer base, purple windows ($6-8)
12. "Shell" labels, white cab with yellow base, yellow trailer base, purple windows, with tow hook ($6-8)(TP)
13. "Shell" labels, white cab with yellow base, yellow trailer base, red windows ($6-8)
14. "Shell" labels, white cab with yellow base, dark yellow trailer base, red windows ($6-8)
15. "Shell" labels, white cab with yellow base, yellow trailer base, amber windows ($6-8)
16. "Shell" labels, yellow cab with black base, yellow trailer base, purple windows ($8-12)
17. "Shell" labels, yellow cab with black base, dark yellow trailer base, purple windows ($8-12)
18. "Exxon" labels, white cab with black base, white trailer base, purple windows ($7-10)
19. "Exxon" labels, white cab with yellow base, yellow trailer base, purple windows ($20-25)
20. "Exxon" labels, white cab with yellow base, white trailer base, purple windows, with tow hook ($6-8)(TP)
21. "Exxon" labels, red cab with black base, white trailer base, purple windows, with tow hook ($50-75)(TP)
22. "BP" labels, white cab with black base, green trailer base, purple windows ($8-12)
23. "BP" labels, white cab with yellow base, yellow trailer base, purple windows, with tow hook ($50-75)(TP)

MB63-C FREEWAY GAS TRAILER, issued 1978 (TP)
NOTE: All models with white tank.
1. red coupling, red base, "Burmah" labels ($6-8)
2. red coupling, red base, "Chevron" labels ($6-8)
3. yellow coupling, yellow base, "Shell" labels ($6-8)
4. yellow coupling, dark yellow base, "Shell" labels ($6-8)
5. yellow coupling, white base, "Exxon" labels ($7-10)
6. red coupling, white base, "Exxon" labels ($55-65)
7. yellow coupling, yellow base, "BP" labels ($30-45)
8. white coupling, yellow base, "BP" labels ($6-8)

MB63-D DODGE CHALLENGER, issued 1982 (USA)
1. green body, dark green & white "2" tempa, white interior, 5 spoke star wheels ($10-15)
2. green body, dark green & white "2" tempa, white interior, 5 spoke wheels ($10-15)
3. green body, dark green & white "2" tempa, white interior, maltese cross wheels ($10-15)
4. green body, black "2" tempa, green interior, 5 spoke wheels ($10-15)

MB63-E SNORKEL, issued 1982 (USA)
MB13-E SNORKEL, issued 1983 (ROW)
NOTE: Following models with black interior, white boom & 5 arch wheels unless otherwise noted.
1. red body, gray base, unpainted base insert, "Los Angeles" tempa, England casting ($6-8)(CR)
2. red body, gray base, silver-gray base insert, "Los Angeles" tempa, England casting ($6-8)(CR)
3. red body, black base, black metal base insert, "Metro Fire" tempa, Macau casting ($1-2)
4. red body, black base, black plastic base insert, "Metro Fire" tempa, Macau casting ($1-2)
5. red body, black base, black plastic base insert, "Metro Fire" tempa, China casting ($1-2)
6. dull red body, black base, black plastic base insert, "Fire Dept." & shield tempa, China casting ($1-2)
7. red body, black base, black plastic base insert, Japanese lettered tempa, China casting ($8-12)(JP)
8. greenish yellow body, black base, black plastic base insert, "Fire Dept." & shield tempa, China casting ($3-4)(AP)
9. florescent orange body, black base, black plastic base insert, "Rescue Unit 1 Fire" & checkers tempa, China casting ($1-2)
10. white body, white base, white plastic base insert, no tempa, China casting ($10-15)(GF)
11. red body, black base, black plastic base insert, "Rescue Unit 1 Fire" & checkers tempa, China casting ($8-12)(GS)
12. florescent orange body, black base, black plastic insert with bar code, "Rescue Unit 1 Fire", checkers & "IC" logo tempa, China casting ($10-15)(IC)
NOTE: below versions with silver-gray boom unless otherwise noted.
13. red body, blue interior, black plastic base insert, "12th Rescue Squad" with gold outline tempa, China casting ($1-2)
14. red body, blue interior, black plastic base insert, "12th Rescue Squad" with white outline tempa, China casting ($1-2)
15. white & red body, blue interior, black plastic base insert, "FD No. 1 Fire Dept." tempa, China casting ($1-2)(MP)
16. white body, black interior, black plastic base insert, "Matchbox Fire Dept." & red stripes tempa, China casting ($1-2)(MP)
17. dark purple body, black interior, black plastic base insert, "Matchbox Fire Dept." tempa, China casting ($1-2)
18. metallic gold body, black interior, black boom, black plastic base insert, no tempa, China casting ($5-10)(CH)
19. red body, gray & black interior, black boom, black plastic base insert, "Richfield Co." tempa, chrome disc with rubber tires, China casting ($3-5)(PC7)
20. red body, black interior, black plastic base insert, "Matchbox Fire Dept." tempa, China casting ($1-2)(MW26)
21. metallic red body, gray & black interior, white boom, black plastic base insert, "Seaside Fire Co./ Snorkel Unit 2" tempa, chrome disc with rubber tires, China casting ($3-5)(PC21)
22. white body, black interior, gray boom, black plastic base insert, no tempa, China casting ($25-40)(ASAP blank)

MB63-J FORD FALCON, issued 1997 (AU)
MB68-K FORD FALCON, issued 1998 (ROW)
NOTE: All models listed with clear windows. China casting
1. white body, white interior, white base, chrome disc with rubber tires, "Australian Open 1997" tempa ($7-10)(AU)
2. white body, white interior, black base, chrome disc with rubber tires, "Castrol 25" tempa ($15-20)(AU)
3. white body, gray interior, black base, 5 spoke concave star wheels, "Go Cats! 1997" tempa ($3-5)(AU)
4. gold body, black interior, black base, chrome disc with rubber tires, "Australia's First" tempa ($10-15)(IG)(AU)
5. unpainted body, black interior, black base, chrome disc with rubber tires, no tempa ($10-15)(IG)(AU)
6. white & dark blue body, gray interior, gray base, 5 spoke concave star wheels, "Ford 75" tempa ($2-4)(AU)
7. blue body, gray interior, gray base, yellow disc with rubber tires, "Mitre 10 Accent Paint Racing" tempa ($7-10)(AU)
8. white & mid blue body, white interior, black base, 5 spoke concave star wheels, "Kangaroos 1998" tempa ($3-5)(AU)
9. white & dark blue body, white interior, black base, 5 spoke concave star wheels, "Blues 1998" tempa ($3-5)(AU)
10. white & black body, white interior, black base, 5 spoke concave star wheels, "Cats 1998" tempa ($3-5)(AU)
11. white & red body, white interior, black base, 5 spoke concave star wheels, "Swans 1998" tempa ($3-5)(AU)
12. yellow & plum body, white interior, black base, 5 spoke concave star wheels, "Brisbane 1998" tempa ($3-5)(AU)
13. yellow & dark blue body, white interior, black base, 5 spoke concave star wheels, "Eagles 1998" tempa ($3-5)(AU)
14. yellow & black body, white interior, black base, 5 spoke concave star wheels, "Tigers 1998" tempa ($3-5)(AU)
15. red & dark blue body, white interior, black base, 5 spoke concave star wheels, "Crows 1998" tempa ($3-5)(AU)
16. metallic grape body, white interior, black base, 5 spoke concave star wheels, "Ford Falcon 4" tempa ($1-2)(MW68-ROW)

MB64-A MG 1100, issued 1970
1. green body, unpainted base ($175-250)
2. light blue body, unpainted base ($30-45)
3. dark blue body, unpainted base ($30-45)

MB64-B SLINGSHOT DRAGSTER, issued 1971
1. pink body, black base, black pipes, "9" with flames label ($15-20)
2. orange body, black base, black pipes, "9" with flames label ($125-150)
3. orange body, unpainted base, red pipes, "9" with flames label ($125-150)
4. steel blue body, black base, black pipes, "9" with flames label ($15-18)
5. steel blue body, unpainted base, red pipes, "9" with flames label ($15-18)
6. steel blue body, black base, red pipes, "9" with flames label ($15-18)
7. steel blue body, black base, red pipes, star with flames label ($50-75)
8. steel blue body, black base, red pipes, "3" with stripe label ($18-25)

MB64-C FIRE CHIEF CAR, issued 1976
1. red body, plain shield labels, 5 arch front & 5 crown rear wheels ($8-12)
2. red body, outline shield labels, 5 arch front & 5 crown rear wheels ($8-12)
3. red body, outline shield labels, 5 arch front & rear wheels ($8-12)
4. red body, outline shield labels, 5 crown front & rear wheels ($8-12)

MB64-D CATERPILLAR BULLDOZER, issued 1979
MB 9-G CATERPILLAR BULLDOZER, reissued 1986 (ROW)
NOTE: All models with black treads unless otherwise noted.
1. yellow body, yellow blade, unpainted metal base, orange rollers, tan canopy, no tempa, England casting ($4-6)
2. yellow body, yellow blade, unpainted metal base, yellow-orange rollers, tan canopy, no tempa, England casting ($4-6)
3. yellow body, yellow blade, unpainted metal base, dark yellow rollers, tan canopy, no tempa, England casting ($4-6)
4. yellow body, yellow blade, unpainted metal base, lemon rollers, tan canopy, no tempa, England casting ($4-6)
5. yellow body, yellow blade, unpainted metal base, lemon rollers, black canopy, "C" tempa, England casting ($4-6)
6. yellow body, yellow blade, unpainted metal base, yellow-orange rollers, black canopy, "C" tempa, England casting ($4-6)
7. yellow body, yellow blade, unpainted metal base, dark yellow rollers, black canopy, "C" tempa, England casting ($4-6)
8. yellow body, black blade, unpainted metal base, lemon rollers, black canopy, "C" tempa, England casting ($4-6)
9. yellow body, black blade, unpainted metal base, lemon rollers, black canopy, "C Cat" tempa, England casting ($4-6)
10. yellow body, black blade, silver-gray metal base, lemon rollers, black canopy, "C" tempa, England casting ($4-6)
11. yellow body, yellow blade, silver-gray metal base, lemon rollers, black canopy, "C" tempa, England casting ($4-6)
12. yellow body, black blade, unpainted metal base, lemon rollers, tan canopy, "C Cat" tempa, England casting ($4-6)
13. yellow body, yellow blade, unpainted metal base, lemon rollers, tan canopy, "C Cat" tempa, England casting ($4-6)
14. yellow body, no blade, silver-gray base, lemon rollers, black canopy, "C Cat" tempa, England casting ($12-15)
15. yellow body, yellow blade, pearly silver metal base, lemon rollers, black canopy, "C Cat" tempa, Macau casting ($1-2)
16. yellow body, yellow blade, pearly silver metal base, lemon rollers, black canopy, "C Cat" tempa, China casting ($1-2)
17. yellow body, yellow blade, pearly silver metal base, lemon rollers, black canopy, no tempa, Macau casting ($1-2)
18. yellow body, gray blade, pearly silver metal base, lemon rollers, black canopy, no tempa, Macau casting ($2-3)(MP)
19. red body, yellow blade, blue metal base, blue rollers, yellow treads, blue canopy, yellow stripes tempa, Macau casting ($6-8)(LL)
20. orange body, orange blade, pearly silver metal base, orange rollers, black canopy, "Losinger" tempa, Macau casting ($8-12)(SW)
21. yellow body, yellow blade, light gray plastic base, yellow rollers, black canopy, no tempa, Thailand casting ($1-2)
22. yellow body, yellow blade, dark gray plastic base, yellow rollers, black canopy, no tempa, Thailand casting ($1-2)
23. yellow body, dark gray blade, light gray plastic base, yellow rollers, black canopy, no tempa, Thailand casting ($1-2)
24. red body, lime blade, yellow plastic base, lemon rollers, yellow treads, blue canopy, gravel design tempa, Thailand casting ($6-8)(LL)
25. orange-yellow body, yellow blade, light gray plastic base, yellow rollers, black canopy, no tempa, Thailand casting ($1-2)
26. orange-yellow body, yellow blade, light gray plastic base, yellow rollers, red canopy, red stripes (blade) tempa, Thailand casting ($1-2)
27. orange-yellow body, yellow blade, silver-gray plastic base, yellow rollers, red canopy, red stripes (blade) tempa, Thailand casting ($1-2)
28. orange body, orange blade, silver-gray plastic base, orange rollers, black canopy, black stripes (blade) tempa, Thailand casting ($1-2)(MP)
29. dark orange body, silver-gray blade, silver-gray plastic base, dark orange rollers, black canopy, detailed trim tempa, Thailand casting ($2-4)(CC)
30. fluorescent orange body, black blade, silver-gray plastic base, orange rollers, black canopy, no tempa, Thailand casting ($1-2)(MP)
31. orange-yellow body, yellow blade, silver-gray plastic base, yellow rollers, red canopy, no tempa (plain blade), Thailand casting ($1-2)
32. florescent orange body, gray blade, black plastic base, orange rollers, black canopy, no tempa, China casting ($1-2)(MP)
33. red body, silver-gray blade, silver-gray plastic base, red rollers, black canopy, no tempa, China casting ($1-2)
34. pumpkin body, gray blade, black plastic base, yellow rollers, black canopy, no tempa, China casting ($1-2)(MP)
35. neon yellow body, gray blade, gray plastic base, black rollers, black canopy, no tempa, China casting ($1-2)
36. orange-yellow body, black blade, gray plastic base, black rollers, yellow canopy, "Matchbox" & detailed trim tempa, China casting ($2-4)(PC-CY)
37. orange body, orange blade, silver-gray plastic base, orange rollers, orange canopy, "Metro DPW" (blade) tempa, China casting ($1-2)(MW14)
38. yellow body, black blade, silver-gray plastic base, yellow rollers, yellow canopy, small "C" & detailed trim tempa, China casting ($2-4)(PC-CY)

MB65-A SAAB SONNET, issued 1973
1. blue body, unpainted base, yellow interior ($10-15)
2. white body, unpainted base, yellow interior ($250-350)(MP)

MB65-B AIRPORT COACH, issued 1977
NOTE: All models with dot dash wheels unless otherwise noted.
1. blue body, "American Airlines" labels, amber windows, light yellow interior, unpainted base, England casting ($4-6)
2. blue body, "American Airlines" labels, clear windows, light yellow interior, unpainted base, England casting ($4-6)
3. blue body, "American Airlines" labels, amber windows, light yellow interior, unpainted (tab) base, no origin cast ($35-50)(BR)
4. blue body, "American Airlines" labels, clear windows, ivory interior, unpainted base, England casting ($4-6)
5. blue body, "American Airlines" labels, amber windows, ivory interior, unpainted base, England casting ($4-6)
6. blue body, "American Airlines" labels, clear windows, cream interior, unpainted base, England casting ($4-6)

7. blue body, "British Airways" labels, amber windows, light yellow interior, unpainted base, England casting ($4-6)
8. blue body, "British Airways" labels, clear windows, light yellow interior, unpainted base, England casting ($4-6)
9. blue body, "British Airways" labels, amber windows, light yellow interior, unpainted base (tab), no origin cast ($35-50)(BR)
10. blue body, "British Airways" labels, clear windows, ivory interior, unpainted base, England casting ($4-6)
11. blue body, "British Airways" labels, amber windows, ivory interior, unpainted base, England casting ($4-6)
12. blue body, "Lufthansa" labels, amber windows, light yellow interior, unpainted base, England casting ($4-6)
13. blue body, "Lufthansa" labels, clear windows, light yellow interior, unpainted base, England casting ($4-6)
14. blue body, "Lufthansa" labels, amber windows, light yellow interior, unpainted base (tab), no origin cast ($35-50)(BR)
15. blue body, "Lufthansa" labels, clear windows, ivory interior, unpainted base, England casting ($4-6)
16. blue body, "Lufthansa" labels, amber windows, ivory interior, unpainted base, England casting ($4-6)
17. red body, "Qantas" labels, amber windows, light yellow interior, unpainted base, England casting ($8-12)
18. red body, "Qantas" labels, amber windows, light yellow interior, silver-gray base, England casting ($8-12)
19. red body, "TWA" labels, amber windows, light yellow interior, unpainted base, England casting ($7-10)
20. red body, "TWA" labels, amber windows, light yellow interior, silver-gray base, England casting ($7-10)
21. orange body, "Schulbus" labels, amber windows, light yellow interior, unpainted base, England casting ($35-45)(GR)
22. blue body, "British" labels, amber windows, light yellow interior, unpainted base, England casting ($7-10)
23. blue body, "British" labels, amber windows, light yellow interior, silver-gray base, England casting ($7-10)
24. white body, "Alitalia" labels, amber windows, light yellow interior, unpainted base, England casting ($7-10)
25. white body, "Alitalia" labels, amber windows, light yellow interior, silver-gray base, England casting ($7-10)
26. white body, "Lufthansa" labels, amber windows, light yellow interior, silver-gray base, England casting ($25-40)
27. white body, "Alitalia" tempa, amber windows, light yellow interior, pearly silver base, Macau casting ($3-5)
28. orange body, "Lufthansa" tempa, amber windows, light yellow interior, pearly silver base, Macau casting ($3-5)(GS)
29. orange body, "Pan Am" tempa, amber windows, light yellow interior, pearly silver base, Macau casting ($3-5)(GS)
30. white body, "Stork SB" tempa, amber windows, light yellow interior, pearly silver base, Macau casting ($8-12)(AU)(OP)
31. red body, "Virgin Atlantic" tempa, amber windows, light yellow interior, pearly silver base, Macau casting ($3-5)(GS)
32. blue body, "Australian" tempa, amber windows, light yellow interior, pearly silver base, Macau casting ($7-10)(AU)
33. blue body, "Girobank" labels, blue windows, light yellow interior, pearly silver base, Macau casting ($7-10)(UK)
NOTE: Above models all with white plastic roof.
34. white body, green roof, "Alitalia" tempa, amber windows, white interior, white base, Thailand casting ($5-7)(MP)
35. white body, blue roof, "KLM" tempa, amber windows, white interior, white base, Thailand casting ($5-7)(MP)
36. white body, blue roof, "SAS" tempa, amber windows, white interior, white base, Thailand casting ($5-7)(MP)
37. white body & roof, "Lufthansa" tempa, amber windows, white interior, pearly silver base, Thailand casting ($5-7)(MP)
38. red body, white roof, "Virgin Atlantic" tempa, amber windows, white interior, pearly silver base, Thailand casting ($3-5)
39. red body, white roof, "TWA" tempa, amber windows, white interior, white plastic base, Manaus casting ($35-50)(BR)
40. green body, white roof, "TWA" tempa, amber windows, white interior, white plastic base, 8 dot wheels, Manaus casting ($45-60)(BR)

MB65-C BANDAG BANDIT, issued 1982 (USA)
1. black body, green & white stripes tempa, "Tyrone" & 4 stripes on airfoil, 5 crown front & dot dash rear wheels, England casting ($3-5)
2. black body, green & white stripes tempa, "Tyrone" & 4 stripes on airfoil, dot dash front & rear wheels, England casting ($3-5)
3. black body, green & white stripes tempa, "Tyrone" & 2 stripes on airfoil, 5 crown front & dot dash wheels, England casting ($3-5)
4. black body, green & white stripes tempa, "Tyrone" & 2 stripes on airfoil, dot dash front & rear wheels, England casting ($3-5)
5. black body, green & white stripes tempa, plain airfoil, 5 crown front & dot dash rear wheels, England casting ($3-5)
6. black body, green & white stripes tempa, "Tyrone" & 4 stripes on airfoil, 5 crown front & rear wheels, England casting ($3-5)
7. black body, yellow & white stripes tempa, "Tyrone" & no stripes on airfoil, 5 crown front & dot dash rear wheels, Macau casting ($1-2)
8. black body, yellow & white stripes tempa, "Tyrone" & 4 stripes on airfoil, 5 crown front & dot dash rear wheels, Macau casting ($1-2)
9. black body, yellow & white stripes tempa, plain airfoil, maltese cross front wheels & dot dash rear wheels, China casting ($4-6)

MB65-D F.1 RACER, issued 1985 (USA)
NOTE: All models with 8 dot front & racing special rear wheels unless otherwise noted.
1. dark blue body, black metal base, red driver, red "Goodyear" airfoil, 5 arch front wheels, chrome lettered rear wheels, chrome exhausts, "20 Bosch STP" tempa, Macau casting ($4-6)
2. dark blue body, black metal base, red driver, red "Goodyear" airfoil, 5 arch front wheels, unchromed rear wheels, chrome exhausts, "20 Bosch STP" tempa, Macau casting ($4-6)
3. yellow body, black metal base, red driver, red "Goodyear" airfoil, chrome exhausts, "Matchbox Racing Team" tempa, Macau casting ($2-3)
4. yellow body, black metal base, dark red driver, dark red "Goodyear" airfoil, chrome exhausts, "Matchbox Racing Team" tempa, Macau casting ($2—3)
5. pink body, black metal base, red driver, red "Goodyear" airfoil, chrome exhausts, "Matchbox Racing Team" tempa, Macau casting ($3-4)(SC)
6. light pea green body, black metal base, red driver, red "Goodyear" airfoil, chrome exhausts, "Matchbox Racing Team" tempa, Macau casting ($3-4)(SC)
7. light peach body, black metal base, red driver, red "Goodyear" airfoil, chrome exhausts, "Matchbox Racing Team" tempa, Macau casting ($3-4)(SC)
8. red body, black plastic base, red driver, red "Goodyear" airfoil, black exhausts, "Matchbox Racing Team" tempa, Macau casting ($3-4)(SC)
9. orange body, black plastic base, red driver, red "Goodyear" airfoil, black exhausts, "Matchbox Racing Team" tempa, Macau casting ($3-4)(SC)
10. yellow body, black plastic base, red driver, red "Goodyear" airfoil, black exhausts, "Matchbox Racing Team" tempa, Macau casting ($1-2)
11. white body, red plastic base, red driver, red plain airfoil, blue wheels with yellow hubs, lime exhausts, "123456" & flames tempa, Macau casting ($6-8)(LL)
12. white body, red plastic base, red driver, red plain airfoil, blue wheels with yellow hubs, lime exhausts, "123456" & flames" tempa, Thailand casting ($6-8)(LL)
13. yellow body, black plastic base, red driver, red "Goodyear" airfoil, black exhausts, "Matchbox Racing Team" tempa, Thailand casting ($1-2)
14. white/hot pink/blue body, black plastic base, pink driver, pink "Rain-X" airfoil, black exhausts, "Amway/Speedway 22" tempa, China casting ($3-5)(IN)
15. dark blue & white body, black plastic base, dark blue driver, dark blue "Valvoline" airfoil, black exhausts, "Valvoline 5" tempa, China casting ($3-5)(IN)
16. orange-yellow & blue body, black plastic base, yellow driver, yellow "Kraco" airfoil, black exhausts, "Kraco/Otter Pops 18" tempa, China casting ($3-5)(IN)
17. lemon & black body, black plastic base, lemon driver, lemon "Goodyear" airfoil, black exhausts, "Indy 11" tempa, China casting ($3-5)(IN)
18. lemon & black body, black plastic base, lemon driver, lemon "Indy" airfoil, black exhausts, "Indy 11" tempa, China casting ($4-6)(IN)
19. black body, black plastic base, black driver, black "Havoline" airfoil, black exhausts, "Havoline 86" tempa, China casting ($3-5)(IN)
20. chrome plated body, black plastic base, red driver, red "Goodyear" airfoil, black exhausts, no tempa, Thailand casting ($12-18)(C2)
21. yellow body, black plastic base, red driver, red "Goodyear" airfoil, black exhausts, "Matchbox Racing Team" tempa, China casting ($1-2)
22. orange-yellow & blue body, black plastic base, orange-yellow driver, orange-yellow "Kraco" airfoil, black exhausts, "Kraco 18" tempa, Thailand casting ($3-5)(IN)
23. yellow body, black plastic base, maroon driver, maroon "Goodyear" airfoil, black exhausts, "Matchbox Racing Team" tempa, Thailand casting ($1-2)
24. white/hot pink/blue body, black plastic base, pink driver, pink "Rain-X" airfoil, black exhausts, "Amway/Speedway 22" tempa, Thailand casting ($3-5)(IN)
25. blue & white body, black plastic base, blue driver, blue "Mitre 10" airfoil, black exhausts, "Mitre 10/Larkham/Taubmans 3" tempa, Thailand casting ($6-8)(AU)(TC)
26. white body, black plastic base, plum driver, plum "Hyflo" airfoil, black exhausts, "Hyflo Exhausts 5" tempa, Thailand casting ($1-2)(MP)
27. black body, black plastic base, black driver, black "Rad" airfoil, black exhausts, "Rad 5" with green & white stripes tempa, Thailand casting ($1-2)
28. blue body, black plastic base, blue driver, blue "Mitre 10" airfoil, black exhausts, "Mitre 10/2/M10" tempa, Thailand casting ($5-7)(AU)(CY)
29. white & dark orange body, black plastic base, orange driver, orange "AGFA" airfoil, black exhausts, "AGFA Film 29" tempa, Thailand casting ($7-10)(US)
30. white & red body, black plastic base, red driver, red "AGFA" airfoil, black exhausts, "AGFA Film 29" tempa, Thailand casting ($7-10)(US)
31. black body, black plastic base, black driver, black "Rad" airfoil, black exhausts, "Rad 5" with white stripes only tempa, Thailand casting ($4-6) (Aquafresh)
32. red body, black plastic base, black driver, black airfoil, black exhausts, "3 Tech Racing" tempa, Thailand casting ($1-2)(MP)

MB65-G FORD F150 PICKUP, issued 1995
NOTE: All models with clear windows & chrome base unless otherwise noted.
1. red body, black interior, chrome rollbar, white band tempa, Thailand casting ($1-2)
2. red body, black interior, black rollbar, white band tempa, Thailand casting ($1-2)
3. purple body, black interior, chrome rollbar, greenish yellow design tempa, China casting ($1-2)(MP)
4. red body, black interior, black rollbar, white band tempa, China casting ($1-2)
5. dark metallic blue, black interior, black rollbar, silver band tempa, China casting ($1-2)
6. red body, black interior, chrome rollbar, "Ford" with white & blue tempa, China casting ($1-2)(MP)
7. black body, gray interior, chrome rollbar, red band tempa, China casting ($1-2)
8. metallic tan body, black interior, chrome rollbar, white & blue splash tempa, China casting ($1-2)(MP)
9. metallic gold body, black interior, chrome rollbar, no tempa, China casting ($5-10)(CH)
10. iridescent white body, dark blue interior, dark blue rollbar, pink & blue with "Ford" tempa, China casting ($1-2)(MW53)

MB66-A GREYHOUND BUS, issued 1970
1. silver-gray body, black base, red rear axle cover ($25-40)
2. silver-gray body, black base, black rear axle cover ($25-40)
3. silver-gray body, pink base, black rear axle cover ($25-40)
4. silver-gray body, light yellow base, black rear axle cover ($25-40)
5. silver-gray body, dark yellow base, black rear axle cover ($25-40)

MB66-B MAZDA RX500, issued 1971
NOTE: Versions 1 to 11 with England casting. Version 12 with Hong Kong casting.
1. orange body, unpainted base, amber windows, chrome interior, no tempa, 5 spoke wheels ($50-75)
2. orange body, unpainted base, purple windows, chrome interior, no tempa, 5 spoke wheels ($10-15)
3. orange body, white base, purple windows, chrome interior, no tempa, 5 spoke wheels ($10-15)
4. red body, white base, purple windows, chrome interior, no tempa, 5 spoke wheels ($18-25)
5. red body, white base, purple windows, tan interior, no tempa, 5 spoke wheels ($18-25)
6. red body, white base, purple windows, chrome interior, "Castrol" labels, 5 spoke wheels ($650-800)
7. red body, white base, purple windows, chrome interior, "77" tempa, 5 spoke wheels ($12-15)
8. red body, white base, amber windows, chrome interior, "77" tempa, 5 spoke wheels ($8-12)
9. red body, white base, amber windows, chrome interior, "77" tempa, 5 arch wheels ($8-12)
10. red body, unpainted base, amber windows, chrome interior, "77" tempa, 5 arch wheels ($8-12)
11. red body, white base, amber windows, tan interior, "77" tempa, 5 arch wheels ($8-12)
12. green body, pearly silver base, amber windows, chrome interior, "66" tempa, 5 arch wheels ($10-15)(US)
NOTE: Available as a Bulgarian casting. Assorted colors available. ($15-25)

MB66-C FORD TRANSIT, issued 1977
1. dark orange body, unpainted base, light yellow interior, blue-green windows, brown cargo ($6-8)
2. dark orange body, unpainted base, tan interior, blue-green windows, brown cargo ($6-8)
3. dark orange body, unpainted base, light yellow interior, blue-green windows, dark tan cargo ($6-8)
4. dark orange body, unpainted base, light yellow interior, dark green windows, dark tan cargo ($6-8)
5. dark orange body, unpainted base, tan interior, amber windows, light tan cargo ($6-8)
6. dark orange body, unpainted base, olive interior, amber windows, light tan cargo ($6-8)
7. dark orange body, unpainted base, light yellow interior, amber windows, light tan cargo ($6-8)
8. dark orange body, unpainted base, white interior, amber windows, light tan cargo ($6-8)
9. dark orange body, unpainted base, olive interior, amber windows, brown cargo ($6-8)
10. dark orange body, unpainted base, olive interior, dark green windows, light tan cargo ($6-8)
11. dark orange body, unpainted base, olive interior, blue-green windows, dark tan cargo ($6-8)
12. dark orange body, unpainted base, olive interior, amber windows, dark tan cargo ($6-8)
13. dark orange body, unpainted (tab) base, cream interior, blue-green windows, light tan cargo ($35-50)(BR)
14. light orange body, unpainted base, cream interior, blue-green windows, light tan cargo ($6-8)
15. light orange body, black base, cream interior, blue-green windows, light tan cargo ($6-8)
16. light orange body, unpainted base, olive interior, blue-green windows, light tan cargo ($6-8)
17. light orange body, unpainted base, cream interior, blue-green windows, dark tan cargo ($6-8)
18. light orange body, black base, cream interior, blue-green windows, dark tan cargo ($6-8)
19. light orange body, charcoal base, lemon interior, green windows, dark tan cargo ($6-8)
20. light orange body, charcoal base, cream interior, blue-green windows, light tan cargo ($6-8)

MB66-D SUPER BOSS, issued 1982
NOTE: all models with chrome base & 5 crown front wheels unless otherwise noted.
1. white body, no "Detroit Diesel" on roof, green windows, dot dash rear wheels, tempa & 4 stripes on spoiler, England casting ($2-4)
2. white body, no "Detroit Diesel" on roof, green windows, dot dash rear wheels, no tempa on spoiler, England casting ($2-4)
3. white body, no "Detroit Diesel" on roof, green windows, dot dash rear wheels, tempa & 2 stripes on spoiler, England casting ($2-4)
4. white body, with "Detroit Diesel" on roof, green windows, dot dash rear wheels, no tempa on spoiler, England casting ($2-4)

5. white body, with "Detroit Diesel" on roof, green windows, 5 arch rear wheels, no tempa on spoiler, England casting ($2-4)
6. white body, with "Detroit Diesel" on roof, red windows, 5 arch rear wheels, no tempa on spoiler, England casting ($7-10)(CY)
7. white body, no "Detroit Diesel" on roof, dot dash rear wheels, tempa & 4 stripes on spoiler, Macau casting ($1-2)
8. white body, with "Detroit Diesel" on roof, dot dash rear wheels, decal & 4 stripes on spoiler, Macau casting ($1-2)
9. white body, with "Detroit Diesel" on roof, dot dash rear wheels, decal & no stripes on spoiler, Macau casting ($1-2)
10. white body no "Detroit Diesel" on roof, dot dash rear wheels, decal & 4 stripes on rear spoiler, Macau casting ($1-2)
11. white body no "Detroit Di[illegible] dash rear wheels, tempa & 4 stripes on spoiler, China casting ($1-2)
12. white body, with "Detroit Diesel" on roof, maltese cross front & dot dash rear wheels, plain spoiler, China casting ($1-2)
13. tan body, orange/yellow/black stripes tempa, dot dash rear wheels, silver-gray armament replaces spoiler, Macau casting, includes plastic armament ($5-8)(RB)
14. white body, no "Detroit Diesel" on roof, dot dash rear wheels, plain spoiler, China casting ($2-3)
15. white body, no tempa, dot dash rear wheels, China casting ($10-15)(GF)

MB66-E SAUBER GROUP C RACER, issued 1984 (USA)
MB46-E SAUBER GROUP C RACER, issued 1984 (ROW)
1. red body, clear windows, ivory interior, black airfoil, 8 dot silver wheels, "BASF Cassettes" tempa, Macau casting ($3-5)
2. red body, clear windows, ivory interior, black airfoil, 8 dot gold wheels, "BASF Cassettes" tempa, Macau casting ($3-5)
3. white body, clear windows, ivory interior, black airfoil, 8 dot silver wheels, "Jr. Matchbox Collector's Club" tempa, Macau casting ($8-12)(AU)
4. white body, clear windows, ivory interior, black airfoil, 8 dot gold wheels, "61 Sauber Castrol" tempa, Macau casting ($2-3)
5. white body, clear windows, ivory interior, black airfoil, 8 dot silver wheels, "61 Sauber Castrol" tempa, Macau casting ($1-2)
6. yellow body, clear windows, ivory interior, blue airfoil, starburst wheels, orange & blue tempa, Macau casting ($3-5)(SF)
7. yellow body, clear windows, ivory interior, blue airfoil, laser wheels, orange & blue tempa, Macau casting ($3-5)(LW)
8. black body, black windows, ivory interior, black airfoil, starburst wheels, "Cargantua" tempa, Macau casting ($15-18)(PS)
9. pink-red body, dark blue windows, no interior or airfoil, starburst wheels, black/white/yellow tempa, Macau casting, includes plastic armament ($5-8)(RB)
10. white & orange body, clear windows, ivory interior, orange airfoil, 8 dot silver wheels, "Bisotherm/Baustein" tempa, Macau casting ($8-12)(SW)
11. red body, clear windows, black interior, red airfoil, 8 dot silver wheels, "Royal Mail Swiftair" tempa, Macau casting ($5-7)(UK)(MP)
12. robin egg blue body, clear windows, dark blue interior, black airfoil, 8 dot silver wheels, "Grand Prix 46" tempa, Macau casting ($4-6)(MP)
13. white body, clear windows, ivory interior, black airfoil, 8 dot silver wheels, "Grand Prix 46" tempa, Thailand casting ($1-2)
14. chrome plated body, clear windows, ivory interior, black airfoil, 8 dot silver wheels, no tempa, Macau casting ($12-18)(C2)
15. florescent pink & blue body, chrome & black windows, black interior, blue airfoil, lightning wheels, "Matchbox" & flames tempa, China casting ($3-4)(LT)
16. florescent orange & yellow body, blue-chrome & black windows, black interior, florescent yellow airfoil, lightning wheels, lightning bolts tempa, China casting ($3-4)(LT)
17. florescent yellow & orange body, blue-chrome & black windows, black interior, florescent yellow airfoil, lightning wheels, "Lightning" & flames tempa, China casting ($3-4)(LT)
18. blue & florescent pink body, chrome & black windows, black interior, blue airfoil, lightning wheels, "Lightning" & flames tempa, China casting ($3-4)(LT)
19. white body, clear windows, ivory interior, 8 dot silver wheels, black airfoil, "Grand Prix 46" tempa, China casting ($1-2)
20. yellow & red body, clear windows, red interior, 8 dot silver wheels, red airfoil, "Matchbox USA 11th Annual Convention & Toy Show 1992" tempa, China casting ($10-12)(US)
21. red & white body, clear windows, ivory interior, red airfoil, 8 dot silver wheels, "Champion 51" tempa, China casting ($1-2)
22. red & white body, clear windows, ivory interior, maroon airfoil, 8 dot silver wheels, "Champion 51" tempa, China casting ($1-2)
23. red & white body, clear windows, ivory interior, maroon airfoil, 8 dot silver wheels, "Champion 51" tempa, Thailand casting ($1-2)
24. white body, clear windows, pink interior, pink airfoil, gold 6 spoke spiral wheels, "50" & blue/pink design tempa, Thailand casting ($1-2)
25. white body, clear windows, ivory interior, black airfoil, gold 6 spoke spiral wheels, "Grand Prix 46" tempa, Thailand casting ($2-3)
26. white body & base, blue windows, white interior, white airfoil, gold 6 spoke spiral wheels, no tempa, Thailand casting ($7-10)(GF)
27. white body, clear windows, pink interior, pink airfoil, silver 6 spoke spiral wheels, "50" & blue/pink design tempa, Thailand casting ($1-2)
28. white body, blue windows, white interior, pink airfoil, silver 6 spoke spiral wheels, "50" & blue (sides only) & pink (hood only) tempa, Thailand casting ($1-2)
29. white body, blue windows, white interior, pink airfoil, silver 6 spoke spiral wheels, "50" & blue (sides only) & pink (hood only) tempa, China casting ($1-2)
30. white body, clear windows, ivory interior, black airfoil, silver 6 spoke spiral wheels, "Grand Prix 46" tempa, Thailand casting ($3-5)
31. white body, clear windows, red interior, blue airfoil, silver 6 spoke spiral wheels, "50" & red stripes tempa, China casting ($1-2)(MP)
32. white body, clear windows, ivory interior, black airfoil, 8 dot silver wheels, "Grand Prix 46" tempa, Macau casting ($1-2)
33. white body, clear windows, ivory interior, black airfoil, silver 6 spoke spiral wheels, "Grand Prix 46" tempa, China casting ($1-2)

MB66-F ROLLS ROYCE SILVER SPIRIT, issued 1987 (ROW)
MB55-H ROLLS ROYCE SILVER SPIRIT, issued 1990 (USA)
MB73-G ROLLS ROYCE SILVER SPIRIT, reissued 1995 (USA)
NOTE: All models with black base, clear windows & 8 dot wheels.
1. tan body, tan interior, no tempa, Macau casting ($2-4)
2. green-gold body, tan interior, no tempa, Macau casting ($3-5)
3. metallic red body, tan interior, no tempa, Macau casting ($1-2)
4. metallic red body, tan interior, no tempa, Thailand casting ($1-2)
5. metallic red body, cream interior, crest tempa, Thailand casting ($1-2)
6. metallic red body, tan interior, no tempa, China casting ($1-2)

MB66-G OPEL CALIBRA, issued 1997 (USA)
MB46-G OPEL CALIBRA, issued 1997 (ROW)
NOTE: below models with 5 spoke concave star wheels, black base and China casting unless otherwise noted.
1. orange body, gray interior, smoke windows, "33 Opel Racing" & "Calibra" tempa ($1-2)
2. white body, red interior, clear windows, "World Cup/ France 98" tempa ($1-2)(MP)
3. white body, yellow interior, clear windows, "World Cup/ France 98" tempa ($1-2)(MW65)
4. white body, blue interior, clear windows, "World Cup/ France 98" tempa ($1-2)(AP)
5. metallic gold, black interior, clear windows, no tempa ($5-10)(CH)

MB66-H MGF, issued 1998
1. yellow body, clear windshield, black interior, 5 spoke concave star wheels, orange band & "MG" logo tempa, China casting ($1-2)

MB67-A VOLKSWAGEN 1600TL, issued 1970
1. red body, unpainted base ($85-110)
2. pale grape body, unpainted base ($20-30)
3. light purple body, unpainted base ($20-30)
4. dark purple body, unpainted base ($20-30)
5. metallic purple body, unpainted base, ($20-30)
6. pink body, unpainted base ($18-25)

MB67-B HOT ROCKER, issued 1973
1. yellow-green body, unpainted base, 5 spoke wheels ($12-15)
2. lime green body, unpainted base, 5 spoke wheels ($12-15)
3. apple green body, unpainted base, 5 spoke wheels ($12-15)
4. apple green body, silver-gray base, 5 spoke wheels ($12-15)
5. apple green body, unpainted base, maltese cross wheels ($12-15)
6. orange-red body, unpainted base, 5 spoke wheels ($10-15)

MB67-C DATSUN 260Z, issued 1978
1. burgundy body, doors open, black base, light yellow interior, clear windows, no tempa, England casting ($3-5)
2. burgundy body, doors open, black base, dark yellow interior, clear windows, no tempa, England casting ($3-5)
3. burgundy body, doors open, charcoal base, light yellow interior, clear windows, no tempa, England casting ($3-5)
4. purple body, doors open, charcoal base, light yellow interior, clear windows, no tempa, England casting ($8-12)
5. magenta body, doors open, black base, light yellow interior, clear windows, no tempa, England casting ($5-8)
6. magenta body, doors open, black base, light yellow interior, smoke windows, no tempa, England casting ($5-8)
7. blue body, doors open, black base, light yellow interior, clear windows, no tempa, England casting ($6-8)(TP)
8. blue body, doors open, black base, red interior, clear windows, no tempa, England casting ($6-8)(TP)
9. blue body, doors open, gray-brown base, red interior, clear windows, no tempa, England casting ($6-8)(TP)
10. silver-gray body, doors open, blue-gray base, red interior, clear windows, no tempa, England casting ($2-4)
11. silver-gray body, doors open, charcoal base, red interior, clear windows, no tempa, England casting ($2-4)
12. silver-gray body, doors open, charcoal base, red interior, smoke windows, no tempa, England casting ($2-4)
13. silver-gray body, doors open, gray-brown base, red interior, clear windows, no tempa, England casting ($2-4)
14. silver-gray body, doors open, gray-brown base, red interior, smoke windows, no tempa, England casting ($2-4)
15. silver-gray body, doors open, black base, red interior, clear windows, no tempa, England casting ($2-4)
16. silver-gray body, doors open, black base, red interior, smoke windows, no tempa, England casting ($2-4)
17. silver-gray body, doors open, blue-gray base, light yellow interior, clear windows, no tempa, England casting ($6-8)
18. silver-gray body, doors open, black base, white interior, clear windows, red & black tempa, England casting ($2-4)
19. silver-gray body, doors open, black base, white interior, smoke windows, red & black tempa, England casting ($2-4)
20. silver-gray body, doors open, charcoal base, white interior, clear windows, red & black tempa, England casting ($2-4)
NOTE: Above England base models with "Lesney" cast. Below England base models with "Matchbox International" cast.
21. black body, black base, white interior, clear windows, no tempa, England casting ($3-5)
22. black body, black base, black interior, opaque windows, no tempa, England casting ($8-12)
23. silver-gray body, black base, black interior, clear windows, 2 tone blue tempa, England casting ($2-4)
24. black body, black base, black interior, milky opaque windows, no tempa, England casting ($8-12)
25. silver-gray body, black base, black interior, clear windows, no tempa, England casting ($5-8)
26. silver-gray body, black base, black interior, opaque windows, no tempa, England casting ($8-12)
27. silver-gray body, black base, black interior, clear windows, green & blue tempa, China casting ($125-175)(CHI)
28. silver-gray body, silver-gray base, black interior, clear windows, two-tone blue tempa, England casting ($4-6)
29. silver-gray body, silver-gray base, black interior, clear windows, no tempa, England casting ($3-5)
30. silver-gray body, black base, red interior, clear windows, no tempa, China casting ($8-12)
31. black body, black base, black interior, clear windows, no tempa, England casting ($4-6)
32. black body, black base, white interior, opaque windows, no tempa, England casting ($8-12)
NOTE: Available as a Bulgarian casting. Assorted colors available ($15-25)

MB67-D FLAME OUT, issued 1983 (USA)
1. white body, red windows, maltese cross rear wheels, Macau casting ($4-6)
2. white body, red windows, 5 crown rear wheels, Macau casting ($4-6)

MB67-F LAMBORGHINI COUNTACH, issued 1985 (USA)
MB11-F LAMBORGHINI COUNTACH, issued 1985 (ROW)
1. red body & metal base, tan interior, clear windows, 5 arch silver wheels, "Lamborghini" logo tempa, Macau casting ($2-3)
2. red body & metal base, tan interior, clear windows, 8 dot silver wheels, "Lamborghini" logo tempa, Macau casting ($2-3)
3. red body & metal base, tan interior, clear windows, 8 dot gold wheels, "Lamborghini" logo tempa, Macau casting ($8-12)
4. black body & metal base, tan interior, clear windows, 5 arch silver wheels, "5" with stripes tempa, Macau casting ($2-3)
5. black body & metal base, tan interior, clear windows, 8 dot gold wheels, "5" with stripes tempa, Macau casting ($3-5)
6. white body & metal base, dark blue interior, clear windows, starburst wheels, "LP500S" & stripes tempa, Macau casting ($3-5)(SF)
7. metallic pearly silver body & metal base, dark blue interior, clear windows, laser wheels, "LP500S" & stripes tempa, Macau casting ($3-5)(LW)
8. red body & metal base, tan interior, clear windows, 5 arch silver wheels, green "15" & "BP" tempa, Macau casting ($8-12)(DU)
9. yellow body & metal base, clear windows, 5 arch silver wheels, "10 Tiger Racing Team" tempa, Macau casting ($8-12)(HK)
10. yellow body & metal base, white interior, clear windows, 5 arch silver wheels, "Countach" & "Lamborghini" logo tempa, Macau casting ($2-3)
11. canary yellow body & metal base, white interior, chrome windows, gray disc w/rubber tires, "LP500" tempa, Macau casting ($5-8)(WC)
13. black body & metal base, white interior, clear windows, starburst wheels, "LP500" with stripes tempa, Macau casting ($12-15)(SF)
14. chrome plated body & metal base, white interior, clear windows, 5 arch wheels, no tempa, Macau casting ($12-18)(C2)
15. red body & metal base, white interior, clear windows, 5 arch wheels, "Countach" tempa, Thailand casting ($1-2)
16. red body & metal base, white interior, chrome windows, gray disc w/ rubber tires, "Countach" & detailed trim tempa, China casting ($5-8)(WC)
17. red body & metal base, white interior, clear windows, 5 arch wheels, "Countach" tempa, China casting ($1-2)
18. white body & metal base, white interior, clear windows, 5 arch wheels, no tempa, China casting ($10-15)(GF)
19. iridescent cream & metal base, white interior, black windows, 5 arch wheels, "Countach" & logo tempa, Thailand casting ($3-5)(TH)
20. fluorescent green body, black plastic base, white interior, clear windows, 5 arch silver wheels, small logo tempa, Thailand casting ($2-3)(SS)
21. red body, black plastic (barcode) base, white interior, clear windows, 5 arch silver wheels, "Countach" & "Lamborghini" logos tempa, Thailand casting ($35-50)(IC)
22. fluorescent yellow & blue body, blue plastic base, pink interior, clear windows, gold 6 spoke spiral wheels, blue design on sides & hood tempa, Thailand casting ($1-2)
23. red body, red plastic base, white interior, clear windows, gold 6 spoke spiral wheels, "Countach" & "Lamborghini" logos tempa, Thailand casting ($2-3)
24. white body, white plastic base, white interior, pink windows, gold 6 spoke spiral wheels, no tempa, Thailand casting ($2-4)(GF)
25. silver-gray body, silver-gray plastic base, maroon interior, clear windows, silver 6 spoke spiral wheels, "Countach" & detailed trim tempa, Thailand casting ($2-4)(CC)
26. fluorescent yellow & blue body, blue plastic base, pink interior, clear windows, gold 6 spoke spiral wheels, blue design on sides only tempa, Thailand casting ($4-6)(Aquafresh)
27. metallic blue body, blue plastic base, white interior, pink windows, silver 6 spoke spiral wheels, no tempa, Thailand casting ($4-6)(MP)
28. florescent yellow & blue body, blue plastic base, pink interior, clear windows, silver 6 spoke spiral wheels, blue design on sides & hood tempa, Thailand casting ($1-2)
29. silver body, black plastic base, white interior, red windows, silver 6 spoke spiral wheels, lavender/blue & white design tempa, Thailand casting ($3-5)(MT)
30. metallic red body, black plastic base, gray interior, clear windows, silver 6 spoke spiral wheels, "Lamborghini" tempa, Thailand casting ($1-2)

31. red body, black plastic base, black interior, clear windows, silver 6 spoke spiral wheels, "Lamborghini" tempa, Thailand casting ($1-2)(MP)
32. red body, red plastic base, white interior, clear windows, silver 6 spoke spiral wheels, "Countach" tempa, Thailand casting ($3-5)
33. metallic gold body, black plastic base, black interior, clear windows, silver 6 spoke spiral wheels, no tempa, Thailand casting ($10-15)(CH)
34. red chrome body, black plastic base, white interior, yellow windows, 5 spoke concave star wheels, purple/ white/ yellow design tempa, Thailand casting ($1-2)(MP)
35. red body, black plastic base, black interior, clear windows, chrome disc with rubber tires, detailed trim tempa, Thailand casting ($8-12)(UC)
36. metallic red body, black plastic base, gray interior, clear windows, 5 spoke concave star wheels, "Lamborghini" tempa, Thailand casting ($1-2)
37. white body, white plastic base, black & brown interior, clear windows, chrome disc with rubber tires, detailed trim tempa, Thailand casting ($3-5)(PC2-ROW)
38. metallic purple body, purple plastic base, gray & black interior, clear windows, chrome disc with rubber tires, detailed trim tempa, Thailand casting ($3-5)(PC10)
39. red body, red plastic base, white interior, clear windows, 5 spoke concave star wheels, "Countach" tempa, Thailand casting ($1-2)
40.black body, black plastic base, red interior, clear windows, 5 spoke concave star wheels, "Lamborghini" tempa, Thailand casting ($1-2)
41. dark green body, black plastic base, tan interior, clear windows, 5 spoke concave star wheels, "Lamborghini" tempa, Thailand casting ($1-2)(MW60)
42. dark orange body, orange base, black & tan interior, clear windows, chrome disc with rubber tires, detailed trim tempa, Thailand casting ($15-20)(GC)
43. dark green body, black plastic base, tan interior, clear windows, 5 spoke concave star wheels, "Lamborghini" tempa, China casting ($1-2)(MW60)

MB67-G IKARUS COACH, issued 1986 (ROW)
NOTE: All models with black base & dot dash wheels. The interior is part of the body casting.
1. white body, orange roof, smoke windows, "Voyager" tempa, Macau casting ($2-4)
2. white body, orange roof, clear windows, "Voyager" tempa, Macau casting ($2-4)
3. white body, orange roof, amber windows, "Voyager" tempa, Macau casting ($2-4)
4. cream body, cream roof, smoke windows, "Ikarus" tempa, Macau casting ($2-4)
5. white body, red roof, clear windows, "Gibraltar" tempa, Macau casting ($5-7)(SP)
6. 6. white body, green roof, smoke windows, "City Line Tourist" tempa, China casting ($2-4)
7. white & orange body, white roof, smoke windows, "Airport Limousine 237" tempa, China casting ($8-12)(JP)(GS)
8. white body, orange roof, smoke windows, "Voyager" tempa, China casting ($2-3)
9. white body, white roof, smoke windows, "Canary Island" tempa, China casting ($7-10)(UK)
10. beige body, brown roof, smoke windows, "Marti" tempa, China casting ($8-12)(SW)
11. white body, red roof, smoke windows, "Gibraltar" tempa, China casting ($5-7)(SP)
12. white body,, green roof, smoke windows, /2384584" & "FT" tempa, China casting ($30-50)(CHI)
13. white body, white roof, smoke windows, "Espana" tempa, China casting ($1-2)
14. white body, red roof, smoke windows, smiling face tempa, China casting ($3-5)(MP)
15. white body, red roof, blue windows, "World Cup Tour Bus" tempa, China casting ($1-2)(MP)
16. yellow body, white roof, smoke windows, sunset scene tempa, China casting ($1-2)(MW2-ROW)
17. white body, white roof, smoke windows, no tempa, China casting ($25-40)(ASAP blank)

MB67-H FORD EXPEDITION, issued 1999
1. bright blue body, clear windows, tan interior, no tempa, chrome disc with rubber tires, China casting ($4-5)(FE)
2. unpainted bdy, clear windows, tan interior, no tempa, chrome disc with rubber tires, China casting ($4-5)(FE)

MB68-A PORSCHE 910, issued 1970
1. red body, amber windows, "68" hood label ($12-15)
2. red body, amber windows, "68" hood & side labels ($12-15)(GS)
3. red body, clear windows, "68" hood label ($12-15)
4. red body, amber windows, "45" hood label ($15-18)
5. red body, clear windows, "45" hood label ($15-18)
6. white body, amber windows, no labels ($35-50)(BM)

MB68-B COSMOBILE, issued 1975
NOTE: Most variations appear with small wheels front & rear, both large wheels front & rear or with front wheels on back and back wheels on front.
1. blue body, yellow base, chrome interior, amber windows ($12-15)
2. blue body, yellow base, white interior, amber windows ($12-15)
3. red body, beige base, chrome interior, amber windows ($15-18)
4. red body, beige base, white interior, amber windows ($15-18)
5. avocado body, black base, white interior, purple windows ($25-35)(AV)
6. avocado body, black base, chrome interior, purple windows ($25-35)(AV)
7. avocado body, black base, chrome interior, amber windows ($30-40)(AV)
8. metallic blue body, black base, chrome interior, purple windows ($40-55)(AV)

MB68-C CHEVY VAN, issued 1979
NOTE: Most variations appear with both small front & rear wheels, both large front & rear wheels or with front wheels on back and back wheels on front.
1. orange body, unpainted base, clear windows, wide blue & narrow red stripes tempa, England casting ($30-40)
2. orange body, unpainted base, blue windows, wide blue & narrow red stripes tempa, England casting ($3-5)
3. orange body, unpainted base, blue windows, wide blue & white narrow stripes tempa, England casting ($4-6)
4. orange body, unpainted base, blue windows, wide red & black narrow stripes tempa, England casting ($4-6)
5. orange body, unpainted base, orange windows, wide red & narrow black stripes tempa, England casting ($4-6)
6. orange body, unpainted base, red windows, wide red & narrow black stripes tempa, England casting ($4-6)
7. orange body, unpainted base, green windows, wide red & black narrow stripes tempa, England casting ($6-8)
8. dark orange body, unpainted base, blue windows, wide red & black narrow stripes tempa, England casting ($15-20)
9. orange body, unpainted base, blue windows, no tempa, England casting ($8-12)
10. orange body, unpainted base, blue windows, "Matchbox Collectors Club" labels, England casting ($20-25)(LE)
11. white body, unpainted base, blue windows, "USA 1" tempa, England casting ($8-12)
12. white body, unpainted base, blue windows, "Adidas" tempa, England casting ($35-45)(GR)
13. green body, unpainted base, blue windows, "Chevy" with brown stripes tempa, England casting ($8-12)
14. green body, unpainted base, blue windows, "Chevy" with yellow stripes tempa, England casting ($8-12)
15. silver-gray body, unpainted base, blue windows, "Vanpire" tempa, England casting ($3-5)
16. silver-gray body, silver-gray base, blue windows, "Vanpire" tempa, England casting ($3-5)
17. yellow body, unpainted base, blue windows, "Matchbox Collecting" with kangaroo tempa, England casting ($10-15)(AU)
18. pearly silver body, black base, blue windows, "Vanpire" tempa, Macau casting ($3-5)
19. yellow body, pearly silver base, blue windows, "Pepsi Challenge" tempa, Macau casting($4-6)(TM)
20. white & maroon tempa, pearly silver base, blue windows, "Dr. Pepper" tempa, Macau casting ($7-10)(TM)
21. bright yellow body, pearly silver base, blue windows, "STP Son of A Gun" tempa, Macau casting ($50-65)(TM)
22. black body, pearly silver base, blue windows, "Goodwrench Racing Team Pit Crew" tempa, Macau casting ($4-6)(WR)(TC)
23. black body, silver-gray base, blue windows, "Goodwrench Racing Team Pit Crew" tempa, Thailand casting ($4-6)(WR)(TC)
24. orange-yellow body, silver-gray base, blue windows, "Kodak Film 4 Racing" tempa, Thailand casting ($4-6)(WR)(TC)
25. white body, silver-gray base, blue windows, gold hubs, "25" & green design tempa, Thailand casting ($4-6)(WR)(TC)
26. black body, silver-gray base, blue windows, "Goodwrench 5 Time National Champion Dale Earnhardt" tempa, Thailand casting ($4-6)(WR)(TC)
27. bright yellow body, silver-gray base, blue windows, "Pennzoil 30" tempa, Thailand casting ($4-6)(WR)(TC)
28. blue & florescent orange body, silver-gray base, blue windows, "43 STP Oil Treatment" tempa, Thailand casting ($4-6)(WR)(TC)
29. black body, silver-gray base, blue windows, "Pontiac Excitement 2" tempa, Thailand casting ($4-6)(WR)(TC)
30. black & green body, silver-gray base, blue windows, "Mello Yello 42" tempa, Thailand casting ($4-6)(WR)(TC)
31. florescent orange & white body, silver-gray base, blue windows, "Purolator 10" tempa, Thailand casting ($4-6)(WR)(TC)
32. blue & dark orange body, silver-gray base, blue windows, "21st National Truckin' VAM" tempa, Thailand casting ($8-12)(US)
33. white & yellow body, yellow base, blue windows, "Renault Canon Williams" tempa, Thailand casting ($4-6)(MN)
34. orange-yellow body, silver-gray base, clear windows, "DeWalt 08" tempa, Thailand casting ($4-6)(WR)(TC)
35. powder blue body, silver-gray base, blue windows, "Boston Gas" & white band tempa, Thailand casting ($75-100)(US)
36. orange body, silver-gray base, blue windows, blue & red stripes tempa, Thailand casting ($3-5)(PC13)
37. black body, silver-gray base, blue windows, "Automodels 98912244" & "Sydney Motorshow" tempa, Thailand casting ($15-20)(AU)(C2)
38. black body, silver-gray base, blue windows, "Automodels 98912244" & "Melbourne Motorshow" tempa, Thailand casting ($15-20)(AU)(C2)
39. white body, white base, blue windows, "Sears Home Central" tempa, Thailand casting ($100+)(ASAP)
40. white body, white base, blue windows, "MCI Scholar Award" tempa, Thailand casting ($100+)(ASAP)
41. white body, white base, blue windows, "Consolidated Engineering" tempa, Thailand casting ($100+)(ASAP)
42. white body, white base, blue windows, "American International Recovery" (black lettering) tempa, Thailand casting ($100+)(ASAP)
43. white body, white base, blue windows, "American International Recovery" (blue lettering) tempa, Thailand casting ($100+)(ASAP)
44. white body, white base, blue windows, no tempa, Thailand casting ($25-40)(ASAP blank)
45. white body, white base, blue windows, "Sears Home Central Max I Rewards", Thailand casting ($75+)(ASAP)

MB68-E DODGE CARAVAN, issued 1984 (USA)
MB64-E DODGE CARAVAN, issued 1984 (ROW)
NOTE: Model with cast door and "Las Vegas" base listed at end of this section. Early models cast "1983," later ones cast "1984." All models with clear windows & chrome base unless otherwise noted.
1. burgundy body, maroon door & interior, black stripe tempa, England casting ($15-20)(US)
2. silver-gray body, gray door, maroon interior, black stripe tempa, England casting ($6-8)
3. silver-gray body, gray door, brown-red interior, black stripe tempa, England casting ($6-8)
4. black body, black door, maroon interior, no tempa, England casting ($5-8)
5. black body black door, maroon interior, silver side stripe tempa, England casting ($3-5)
6. black body, black door, maroon interior, silver stripe tempa, Macau casting ($2-4)
7. black body, black door, maroon interior, silver & gold stripes tempa, Macau casting ($2-4)
8. white body, white door, maroon interior, "Pan Am" tempa, Macau casting ($3-5)(GS)
9. white body, white door, maroon interior, "Caravan" with stripes tempa, Macau casting ($2-4)
10. white body, white door, maroon interior, "Fly Virgin Atlantic" tempa, Macau casting ($3-5)(GS)
11. black body, black door, maroon interior, silver stripe tempa with "Adidas" hood label, England casting ($250-300)(US)
12. black body, black door, maroon interior, green & yellow stripes tempa, Macau casting ($8-12)(DU)
13. white body, white door, maroon interior, "NASA Shuttle Personnel" tempa, Macau casting ($3-5)(MP)
14. light gray & dark navy body, light gray door, red interior, "British Airways" tempa, Thailand casting ($3-5)(MC)
15. red body, red door, black interior & base, "Red Arrows/Royal Air Force" tempa, Thailand casting ($3-5)(MC)
16. black body, black door, red interior, gray base, silver & gold stripes tempa, Manaus casting ($35-50)(BR)
17. light gray & dark navy body, gray door, red interior, "British Airways" tempa, black (barcode) base, Thailand casting ($35-50)(IC)
18. black body, black door, maroon interior, silver & gold stripes tempa, China casting ($3-5)

MB68-G TV NEWS TRUCK, issued 1989 (USA)
MB73-D TV NEWS TRUCK, issued 1989 (ROW)
NOTE: All models with frosted windows & dot dash wheels. Later issues with non-frosted windows.
1. dark blue body, silver-gray roof, orange roof units, amber windows, black base, "75 News/MB TV Mobile One" tempa, Macau casting ($1-2)
2. dark blue body, silver-gray roof, orange roof units, amber windows, black base, "75 News/MB TV Mobile One" tempa, Thailand casting ($1-2)
3. dark blue body, silver-gray roof, pale orange roof units, amber windows, black base, "75 News/MB TV Mobile One" tempa, Thailand casting ($1-2)
4. white body, white roof, orange roof units, amber windows, white base, no tempa, Thailand casting ($10-15)(GF)
5. white body, white roof, brown roof units, amber windows, white base, no tempa, Thailand casting ($10-15)(GF)
6. white body, dark blue roof, white roof units, blue windows, black base, "Sky Satellite Television" tempa, Thailand casting ($1-2)
7. white body, blue roof, white roof units, blue windows, black base, "Rock TV" tempa, Thailand casting ($1-2)
8. white body, blue roof, white roof units, blue windows, black base, "Intercom City TV" tempa, Thailand casting ($7-10)(IC)
9. white body, blue roof, white roof units, blue windows, black base, "Sky Satellite TV" tempa, China casting ($2-3)
10. yellow body, red roof, black roof units, blue windows, red base, "Matchbox Cable TV" tempa, China casting ($1-2)(MP)
11.white body, blue roof, dark red roof units, clear windows, red base, "World Cup Mobile Unit Television" tempa, China casting ($1-2)(MP)
12. black body, dark gray roof, dark gray roof units, clear windows, dark gray base, "Mission Impossible" tempa, China casting ($4-6)(STR)
13. blue body, yellow roof, lime roof units, smoke windows, dark gray base, "TV 6" tempa, China casting ($1-2)(MW3-ROW)
14. white body, yellow roof, lime roof units, clear windows, silver-gray base, no tempa, China casting ($25-40)(ASAP blank)
15. white body, yellow roof, lime roof units, clear windows, silver-gray base, "American International Recovery" tempa, China casting ($100+)(ASAP)
16. white body, blue roof, white roof units, blue windows, blue base, "World Cup Mobile Unit Television" tempa, China casting ($1-2)(AP)
17. black body, red roof, yellow roof units, clear windows, red base, "Matchbox Channel 4" tempa, China casting ($1-2)(MP)

MB68-I STINGER, issued 1995
1. black & yellow upper & lower body, clear propeller wings, yellow mid & rear fins, black stand, Thailand casting ($1-2)
2. gold & black upper lower body, clear propeller wings, gold mid & rear fins, black stand, Thailand casting ($5-10)(CH)
3. orange & black upper lower body, clear propeller wings, orange mid & rear fins, black stand, Thailand casting ($1-2)
4. green & black upper & lower body, clear propeller wings, green mid & rear fins, black stand, Thailand casting ($1-2)(MW41)
5. green & black upper & lower body, clear propeller wings, green mid & rear fins, black stand, China casting ($1-2)(MW41)

MB68-J PORSCHE 911 GT1, issued 1998 (USA)
MB58-I PORSCHE 911 GT1, issued 1998 (ROW)
1. white body, black interior, clear windows, white spoiler, 5 spoke concave star wheels, black base, "911 GT1" tempa, China casting ($1-2)

MB69-A ROLLS ROYCE SILVER SHADOW COUPE, issued 1969
1. blue body, orange-brown interior, tan tonneau, black base ($20-25)
2. blue body, orange-brown interior, tan tonneau, light yellow base ($20-25)
3. blue body, orange-brown interior, tan tonneau, dark yellow base ($20-25)
4. metallic gold body, orange-brown interior, tan tonneau, tan base ($20-25)
5. metallic gold body, orange-brown interior, tan tonneau, light yellow base ($20-25)
6. metallic gold body, orange-brown interior, tan tonneau, dark yellow base ($20-25)
7. metallic gold body, orange-brown interior, tan tonneau, black base ($20-25)
8. metallic gold body, orange-brown interior, tan tonneau, silver base ($20-25)
9. metallic gold body, orange-brown interior, black tonneau, black base ($20-25)
10. metallic gold body, orange-brown interior, black tonneau, silver base ($20-25)
11. metallic gold body, orange-brown interior, black tonneau, charcoal base ($20-25)
12. metallic gold body, orange-brown interior, black tonneau, light yellow base ($20-25)
13. metallic gold body, ivory interior, black tonneau, black base ($20-25)
14. metallic gold body, ivory interior, black tonneau, gray base ($20-25)
15. dark gold body, orange-brown interior, black tonneau, black base ($20-25)
16. dark gold body, orange-brown interior, black tonneau, silver base ($20-25)
17. dark gold body, orange-brown interior, black tonneau, charcoal base ($20-25)
18. dark gold body, ivory interior, black tonneau, silver base($20-25)
19. lime gold body, orange-brown interior, black tonneau, charcoal base ($20-25)
20. lime gold body, ivory interior, black tonneau, charcoal base ($20-25)
21. lime gold body, ivory interior, black tonneau, black base ($20-25)
22. lime gold body, ivory interior, black tonneau, silver base ($20-25)

MB69-B TURBO FURY, issued 1973
1. red body, black base, clear windshield, "69" label, 5 spoke wheels ($15-18)
2. red body, black base, amber windshield, "69" label, 5 spoke wheels ($15-18)
3. red body, black base, clear windshield, "86" label, 5 spoke wheels ($15-18)
4. red body, black base, clear windshield, "86" label, 4 spoke wheels ($15-18)
5. red body, black base, clear windshield, scorpion label, 4 spoke wheels ($25-40)
6. red body, black base, clear windshield, scorpion label, 5 spoke wheels ($25-40)

MB69-C ARMORED TRUCK, issued 1978
1. red body, silver-gray base, clear windows, 5 crown wheels, "Wells Fargo/ 732-2031" tempa, England casting ($25-40)
2. red body, silver-gray base, blue windows, 5 crown wheels, no tempa, England casting ($20-35)
3. red body, silver-gray base, blue windows, 5 crown wheels, "Wells Fargo/ 732-2031" tempa, England casting ($4-6)
4. red body, silver-gray base, blue windows, 5 arch wheels, "Wells Fargo/ 732-2031" tempa, England casting ($4-6)
5. red body, unpainted base, blue windows, 5 crown wheels, "Wells Fargo/ 732-2031" tempa, England casting ($4-6)
6. red body, silver-gray base, blue windows, 5 crown wheels, "Wells Fargo/ QZ-2031" tempa, England casting ($4-6)
7. green body, silver-gray base, blue windows, 5 crown wheels, "Dresdner Bank" tempa, England base ($35-45)(GR)
8. dark olive body, pearly silver base, blue windows, 5 crown wheels, "Dresdner Bank" tempa, Macau casting ($60-75)(GR)

MB69-D '33 WILLYS STREET ROD, issued 1982 (USA)
1. white body, unpainted metal base, orange flames tempa, dot dash rear wheels, England casting ($3-5)
2. white body, unpainted metal base, red flames tempa, dot dash rear wheels, England casting ($3-5)
3. white body, silver-gray metal base, orange flames tempa, dot dash rear wheels, England casting ($3-5)
4. white body, silver-gray metal base, red flames tempa, dot dash rear wheels, England casting ($3-5)
5. dark blue body, pearly silver metal base, orange flames tempa, dot dash rear wheels, Macau casting ($1-2)
6. dark blue body, pearly silver metal base, red flames tempa, dot dash rear wheels, Macau casting ($1-2)
7. dark blue body, light gray metal base, red flames tempa, dot dash rear wheels, Hong Kong casting ($1-2)
8. dark blue body, light gray metal base, red flames tempa, 5 spoke rear wheels, Hong Kong casting ($1-2)
9. dark blue body, black plastic base, red flames tempa, dot dash rear wheels, Macau casting ($1-2)
10. dark blue body, black plastic base, red flames tempa, dot dash rear wheels, China casting ($1-2)
11. black body, black plastic base, red flames tempa, dot dash rear wheels, China casting ($7-10)(US)(OP)
12. iridescent cream body, black plastic base, pink & yellow flames & "Pro Street" tempa, dot dash rear wheels, China casting ($1-2)
13. iridescent cream body, black plastic base, pink & yellow flames without "Pro Street" tempa, dot dash rear wheels, China casting ($2-4)
14. metallic turquoise body, black plastic base, pink & white design tempa, dot dash rear wheels, China casting ($1-2)(MP)
15. black body, black plastic base, pink & white tempa, dot dash rear wheels, China casting ($5-7)
16. turquoise body, black plastic base, pink/ purple/ white tempa, dot dash rear wheels, China casting ($1-2)(MP)
17. grape body, black plastic base, "Bad To The Bone" & crossbones tempa, dot dash rear wheels, China casting ($3-5)(AU)
18. iridescent white body, black plastic base, "Grease" & silver flash tempa, dot dash rear wheels, China casting ($4-6)(STR)

MB69-F VOLVO 480ES, issued 1988 (ROW)
NOTE: All models with gray interior & smoke windows.
1. pearly silver body, gray metal base, laser wheels, "Volvo 480" with dual green stripes tempa, Macau casting ($3-5)(LW)
2. white body, gray metal base, 8 dot wheels, "Volvo" & "480ES" tempa, Macau casting ($2-3)
3. white body, gray metal base, 8 dot wheels, "480ES" tempa, Macau casting ($2-3)
4. white body, gray plastic base, 8 dot wheels, "480ES" tempa, Macau casting ($2-3)
5. white body, gray plastic base, 8 dot wheels, "Volvo" & "480ES" tempa, China casting ($5-7)
6. white body, gray metal base, 8 dot wheels, "Toys City" roof label, Macau casting ($75-100)(Malaysian)

MB69-G 1968 FORD MUSTANG COBRA JET, issued 1997 (USA)
MB20-F 1968 FORD MUSTANG COBRA JET, issued 1997 (ROW)
NOTE: All models with clear windows and China casting unless otherwise noted.
1. black body, red & black interior, chrome disc with rubber tires, black base, red pinstripe tempa ($4-6)(IG)
2. unpainted body, chrome interior, chrome disc with rubber tires, black base, no tempa ($4-6)(IG)
3. yellow body, chrome interior, 5 spoke concave star wheels, yellow base, purple & white tempa ($1-2)
4. silver blue body, black & blue interior, chrome disc with rubber tires, black painted base, black stripes tempa ($12-18)(CL)
5. white body, black & red interior, chrome disc with rubber tires, black base, black on hood & red pinstripes tempa ($3-5)(PC17)
6. bright blue body, chrome interior, 5 spoke concave star wheels, black base, orange & white tempa ($1-2)(MW40)
7. red body, tan & black interior, chrome disc with rubber tires, white & black stripes tempa ($3-5)(PC20)
8. bright blue body, translucent white interior, 5 spoke concave star wheels with black hubs, orange & white tempa ($50-75)(MW40)
9. medium blue body, chrome interior, 5 spoke concave star wheels, orange & white tempa ($1-2)(MW40)
10. dark blue body, chrome interior, 5 spoke concave star wheels, orange & white tempa ($1-2)(MW40)

MB70-A FORD GRIT SPREADER, issued 1970
1. red cab & chassis, yellow dump, 5 spoke wheels ($25-40)
2. red cab & chassis, yellow dump, 4 spoke wheels ($25-40)

MB70-B DODGE DRAGSTER, issued 1971
1. hot pink body, black base, light green snake label, 4 spoke rear wheels ($15-20)
2. dark pink body, black base, light green snake label, 4 spoke rear wheels ($15-20)
3. dark pink body, unpainted base, light green snake label, 4 spoke rear wheels ($15-20)
4. dark pink body, light green base, light green snake label, 4 spoke rear wheels ($15-20)
5. dark pink body, light yellow base, light green snake label, 4 spoke rear wheels ($15-20)
6. dark pink body, dark yellow base, light green snake label, 4 spoke rear wheels ($15-20)
7. dark pink body, tan base, light green snake label, 4 spoke rear wheels ($15-20)
8. dark pink body, lavender base, light green snake label, 4 spoke rear wheels ($15-20)
9. dark pink body, charcoal base, light green snake label, 4 spoke rear wheels ($15-20)
10. dark pink body, black base, light green snake label, 5 spoke rear wheels ($15-20)
11. dark pink body, black base, dark green snake label, 4 spoke rear wheels ($15-20)
12. dark pink body, black base, "Rat Rod" label, 4 spoke rear wheels ($25-35)
13. dark pink body, black base, "Wildcat" label, 4 spoke rear wheels ($25-35)
14. dark pink body, black base, star with flame label, 4 spoke rear wheels ($100-150)
15. dark pink body, black base, "Castrol" label, 4 spoke rear wheels ($750-1000)

MB70-C SELF PROPELLED GUN, issued 1976
1. olive green body & base, black treads, no tempa, England casting ($2-4)
2. olive green body & base, tan treads, no tempa, England casting ($2-4)
3. matt olive green body & base, tan treads, no tempa, England casting ($2-4)
4. black body, dark gray base, tan treads, gray & yellow camouflage, tempa, Macau casting ($4-5)(CM)
5. olive green body & base, tan treads, tan & black camouflage tempa, Macau casting ($4-5)(CM)
6. olive green body & base, tan treads, tan & black camouflage tempa, China casting ($6-8)(CM)

MB70-D FERRARI 308 GTB, issued 1981
1. red body & base, no tempa, 5 arch wheels, black interior, clear windows, England casting ($2-4)
2. red body, orange-red base, no tempa, 5 arch wheels, black interior, clear windows, England casting ($2-4)
3. orange-red body & base, no tempa, 5 arch wheels, black interior, clear windows, England casting ($2-4)
4. orange-red body & base, "Ferrari" tempa, 5 arch wheels, black interior, clear windows, England casting ($2-4)
5. orange-red body & base, "Ferrari" tempa, 5 arch wheels, black interior, amber windows, England casting ($2-4)
6. orange-red body, silver-gray base, "Ferrari" tempa, 5 arch wheels, black interior, clear windows, England casting ($8-12)
7. orange-red body, pearly silver base, "Ferrari" & logo tempa, 5 arch wheels, black interior, clear windows, Macau casting ($2-3)
8. orange-red body, pearly silver base, "Ferrari" & logo tempa, 5 spoke wheels, black interior, clear windows, Macau casting ($2-3)
9. dark red body, pearly silver base, "Ferrari" & logo tempa, 5 spoke wheels, black interior, clear windows, Macau casting ($2-3)
10. red body, blue base, "Pioneer 39" tempa, 5 arch wheels, white interior, clear windows, Macau casting ($2-3)
11. yellow body, red base, "Ferrari 308GTB" tempa, starburst wheels, black interior, clear windows, Macau casting ($3-5)(SF)
12. yellow body, red base, "Ferrari 308GTB" tempa, laser wheels, black interior, clear windows, Macau casting ($3-5)(LW)
13. orange body, blue base, "12 Rat Racing Team" tempa, 5 arch wheels, white interior, clear windows, Macau casting ($8-12)(HK)
14. red body & base, "Data East/Secret Service" tempa, 5 arch wheels, black interior, clear windows, Macau casting ($65-80)(CN)
15. red body & base, detailed trim tempa, gray disc w/rubber tires, black interior, chrome windows, Macau casting ($5-8)(WC)
16. red body & base, rectangular "Ferrari" logo on hood tempa, 5 arch wheels, black interior, clear windows, Macau casting ($2-3)(MP)
17. red body & base, rectangular "Ferrari" logo on hood tempa, 5 arch wheels, black interior, clear windows, Thailand casting ($2-3)(MC)
18. white body & base, no tempa, 5 arch wheels, black interior, green windows, Thailand casting ($10-15)(GF)
19. lemon body & base, geometric designs tempa, 5 arch wheels, black interior, clear windows, Thailand casting ($2-4)(DM)
20. red body, gray plastic base, 8 dot wheels, black interior, clear windows, "Ferrari" on sides tempa, Manaus casting ($8-25)(BR)
21. red body, gray plastic base, 4 arch wheels, black interior, clear windows, "Ferrari" on sides tempa, Manaus casting ($18-25)(BR)
22. red body, red plastic base, 5 spoke concave star wheels, yellow-orange & black interior, clear windows, "Magnum P.I." & black roof tempa, China casting ($4-6)(STR)

MB70-E FORD CARGO SKIP TRUCK, issued 1989 (USA)
MB45-D FORD CARGO SKIP TRUCK, issued 1987 (ROW)
NOTE: All models with blue windows & 8 spoke wheels.
1. yellow body, pearly gray metal dump, black base & arms, orange stripe tempa, Macau casting ($1-2)
2. blue body, red metal dump, yellow base & arms, white stripe tempa, yellow wheels with orange hubs, Macau casting ($6-8)(LL)
3. yellow body, pearly gray metal dump, black base & arms, orange stripe tempa, Thailand casting ($1-2)
4. yellow body, gray plastic dump, black base & arms, orange stripe tempa, Macau casting ($1-2)
5. yellow body, gray plastic dump, black base & arms, orange stripe tempa, Thailand casting ($1-2)
6. yellow body, red plastic dump, black base & arms, no tempa, Thailand casting ($1-2)
7. orange-yellow body, red plastic dump, black base, yellow arms, no tempa, China casting ($2-4)

MB70-H 1970 PONTIAC GTO, issued 1996 (USA)
MB64-G 1970 PONTIAC GTO, issued 1996 (ROW)
NOTE: All models with clear windows, black base & China casting unless otherwise noted.
1. orange body & spoiler, black interior, blue & yellow tempa, 6 spoke spiral wheels ($1-2)
2. silver-gray body, gray spoiler, blue/black interior, blue & yellow tempa, chrome disc w/rubber tires ($5-8)(PC3)
3. white body & spoiler, blue/black interior, blue & yellow tempa, chrome disc w/rubber tires ($5-8)(PC6)
4. dark purple body, white/purple interior, detailed trim tempa, chrome disc w/rubber tires ($12-18)(CL)
5. black body, black interior, yellow & red tempa, 5 spoke concave star wheels ($1-2)(MP)
6. dark green body, tan & black interior, orange & yellow tempa, chrome disc with rubber tires ($3-5)(SC3)
7. yellow body, black & gray interior, green & blue flames tempa, chrome disc with rubber tires ($3-5)(PC9)
8. orange body, black interior, blue & yellow tempa, 5 spoke concave star wheels ($100+)
9. red body, black interior, blue & yellow tempa, 6 spoke spiral wheels ($100+)
10. red body, black interior, blue & yellow tempa, 5 spoke concave star wheels ($2-3)
11. metallic blue body, black & gray interior, red & white tempa, chrome disc with rubber tires ($15-20)(GC)
12. metallic gold body, black interior, no tempa, 5 spoke concave star wheels ($5-10)(CH)
13. lemon body, black interior, red & blue tempa, 5 spoke concave star wheels ($1-2)(MW38)
14. dark green body, tan & black interior, orange & yellow tempa, 6 spoke

spiral wheels ($75+)(CHI)
15. silver-gray body, dark blue & black interior, black & yellow tempa, 6 spoke spiral wheels ($75+)(CHI)
16. dark charcoal body, purplish & black interior, red & white tempa, chrome disc with rubber tires ($3-5)(PC17)
17. dark blue body, gray & black interior, white/yellow/orange/red tempa, chrome disc with rubber tires ($3-5)(PC20)

MB70-I MERCEDES E CLASS, issued 1998
1. charcoal body, dark red interior, clear windows, 5 spoke concave star wheels, black base, red pinstripe & " E Class" tempa, China casting ($1-2)

MB71-A FORD HEAVY WRECK TRUCK, issued 1970
1. red cab, white body, red clip axle covers, silver hubs, red hook, "Esso" labels ($25-40)
2. red cab, white body, black clip axle covers, silver hubs, red hook, "Esso" labels ($25-40)
3. red cab, white body, black clip axle covers, silver hubs, yellow hook, "Esso" labels ($25-40)
4. olive green cab & body, riveted axle covers, black hubs, black hook, "3LGS64" labels ($8-12)(TP)
5. olive green cab & body, riveted axle covers, silver hubs, black hook, "3LGS64" labels ($8-12)(TP)
6. blue cab & body, riveted axle covers, silver hubs, black hook, no labels ($175-225)(MP)
7. blue cab & body, riveted axle covers, black hubs, black hook, no labels ($175-225)(MP)

MB71-B JUMBO JET, issued 1973
1. dark blue body, light blue handlebars ($15-20)
2. dark blue body, dark blue handlebars ($15-20)

MB71-C CATTLE TRUCK, issued 1976
MB12-I CATTLE TRUCK, reissued 1992 (ROW)
NOTE: All models with 5 crown front & rear wheels & England casting unless otherwise noted. First 14 variations listed with two black cows.
1. bronze body, orange-yellow stakes, dark green windows, unpainted base, no tow hook ($3-5)
2. bronze body, orange-yellow stakes, dark green windows, silver-gray base, no tow hook ($3-5)
3. bronze body, orange-yellow stakes, blue windows, unpainted base, no tow hook ($3-5)
4. bronze body, orange-yellow stakes, blue windows, silver-gray base, no tow hook ($3-5)
5. bronze body, light yellow stakes, blue windows, silver-gray base, no tow hook ($3-5)
6. bronze body, yellow stakes, blue windows, silver-gray base, no tow hook ($3-5)
7. bronze body, orange-yellow stakes, light green windows, silver-gray base, no tow hook ($3-5)
8. bronze body, orange-yellow stakes, purple windows, silver-gray base, no tow hook ($3-5)
9. bronze body, orange-yellow stakes, orange windows, silver-gray base, no tow hook ($3-5)
10. bronze body, orange-yellow stakes, blue windows, silver-gray base, black tow hook ($3-5)(TP)
11. dull red body, beige stakes, blue windows, silver-gray base, black tow hook ($3-5)(TP)
12. dull red body, cream stakes, blue windows, silver-gray base, black tow hook ($3-5)(TP)
13. dull red body, beige stakes, red windows, silver-gray base, black tow hook ($3-5)(TP)
14. dull red body, beige stakes, purple windows, silver-gray base, black tow hook ($3-5)(TP)
15. dull red body, beige stakes, blue windows, silver-gray base, black tow hook, brown cows ($3-5)(TP)
NOTE: Due to permutations of the cows, green bodied models can be found with brown, coffee, or white cows with earliest green versions having brown cows only.
16. light green body, beige stakes, orange windows, silver-gray base, no tow hook ($6-8)
17. dark green body, beige stakes, orange windows, silver-gray base, no tow hook ($6-8)
18. light green body, orange-yellow stakes, orange windows, silver gray base, no tow hook ($3-5)
19. light green body, orange-yellow stakes, red windows, silver-gray base, no tow hook ($3-5)
20. dark green body, orange-yellow stakes, orange windows, silver-gray base, no tow hook ($3-5)
21. dark green body, orange-yellow stakes, red windows, silver-gray base, no tow hook ($3-5)
22. dark green body, chocolate stakes, red windows, silver-gray base, no tow hook ($6-8)
23. dark green body, chocolate stakes, amber windows, black base, no tow hook ($6-8)
24. dark green body, chocolate stakes, amber windows, silver-gray base, no tow hook ($6-8)
25. dark green body, chocolate stakes, amber windows, black base, no tow hook ($6-8)
26. dark green body, chocolate stakes, clear windows, silver-gray base, no tow hook ($6-8)
27. dark green body, chocolate stakes, clear windows, black base, no tow hook ($6-8)
28. metallic green body, chocolate stakes, red windows, silver-gray base, no tow hook ($6-8)
29. metallic green body, chocolate stakes, red windows, black base, no tow hook ($6-8)
30. metallic green body, chocolate stakes, amber windows, silver-gray base, no tow hook ($6-8)
31. metallic green body, chocolate stakes, amber windows, black base, no tow hook ($6-8)
32. metallic green body, chocolate stakes, clear windows, silver-gray base, no tow hook ($6-8)
33. metallic green body, chocolate stakes, clear windows, black base, no tow hook ($6-8)
34. dark green body, brown stakes, red windows, silver-gray base, no tow hook ($6-8)
35. dark green body, brown stakes, red windows, black base, no tow hook ($6-8)
36. dark green body, brown stakes, amber windows, silver-gray base, no tow hook ($6-8)
37. dark green body, brown stakes, amber windows, black base, no tow hook ($6-8)
38. dark green body, brown stakes, clear windows, silver-gray base, no tow hook ($6-8)
39. dark green body, brown stakes, clear windows, black base, no tow hook ($6-8)
40. metallic green body, brown stakes, red windows, silver-gray base, no tow hook ($6-8)
41. metallic green body, brown stakes, red windows, black base, no tow hook ($6-8)
42. metallic green body, brown stakes, amber windows, silver-gray base, no tow hook ($6-8)
43. metallic green body, brown stakes, amber windows, black base, no tow hook ($6-8)
44. metallic green body, brown stakes, clear windows, silver-gray base, no tow hook ($6-8)
45. metallic green body, brown stakes, clear windows, black base, no tow hook ($6-8)
NOTE: Due to permutations, yellow bodied models can be found with coffee or red-brown cows.
46. yellow body, chocolate stakes, red windows, silver-gray base, no tow hook ($3-5)
47. yellow body, chocolate stakes, red windows, silver-gray base, black tow hook ($3-5)(TP)
48. yellow body, chocolate stakes, amber windows, silver-gray base, no tow hook ($3-5)
49. yellow body, chocolate stakes, amber windows, silver-gray base, black tow hook ($3-5)(TP)
50. yellow body, chocolate stakes, clear windows, silver-gray base, no tow hook ($3-5)
51. yellow body, chocolate stakes, clear windows, silver-gray base, black tow hook ($3-5)(TP)
52. yellow body, chocolate stakes, red windows, black base, no tow hook ($3-5)
53. yellow body, chocolate stakes, red windows, black base, black tow hook ($3-5)(TP)
54. yellow body, chocolate stakes, red windows, unpainted base, no tow hook ($3-5)
55. yellow body, chocolate stakes, red windows, unpainted base, black tow hook ($3-5)(TP)
56. yellow body, chocolate stakes, red windows, silver-gray base, black tow hook ($3-5)(TP)
57. yellow body, chocolate stakes, red windows, black base, black tow hook ($3-5)(TP)
58. yellow body, chocolate stakes, red windows, black base, no tow hook, dot dash rear wheels ($7-10)
59. yellow body, chocolate stakes, amber windows, black base, no tow hook, dot dash rear wheels ($7-10)
60. yellow body, chocolate stakes, red windows, black base, no tow hook, 5 arch rear wheels ($7-10)
61. yellow body, chocolate stakes, red windows, black base, no tow hook, 5 arch front & rear wheels ($7-10)
62. yellow body, tan stakes, red windows, unpainted base, no tow hook ($4-6)
63. yellow body, tan stakes, red windows, black base, no tow hook ($4-6)
64. yellow body, tan stakes, amber windows, black base, no tow hook ($4-6)
65. dull red body, beige stakes, blue windows, silver-gray base, no tow hook, 5 arch front & rear wheels ($7-10)
66. powder blue body, chocolate stakes, red windows, black base, black cows, black tow hook, 5 crown wheels, Macau casting ($2-4)(TP)
67. red body, yellow stakes, red windows, yellow base, no cows, red tow hook, 5 crown blue wheels with yellow hubs, cow head tempa, Macau casting ($6-8)(LL)
68. green body, yellow stakes, red windows, black base, black cows, black tow hook, 5 crown wheels, Macau casting ($1-2)(TP)
69. green body, yellow stakes, red windows, black base, black cows, black tow hook, 5 crown wheels, Thailand casting ($1-2)(TP)
70. green body, yellow stakes, red windows, black base, black cows, no tow hook, 5 crown wheels, Thailand casting ($1-2)
71. yellow body, chocolate stakes, red windows, black base, no tow hook, 5 crown wheels, Macau casting ($1-2)

MB71-D 1962 CORVETTE, issued 1982 (USA)
MB32-F 1962 CORVETTE, reissued 1994 (USA)
MB72-L 1962 CORVETTE, reissued 1994 (ROW)
1. dark blue body & base, blue interior, white tempa, 5 arch silver wheels, England casting ($3-5)
2. dark blue body & base, blue interior, white tempa, maltese cross wheels, England casting ($3-5)
3. dark blue body & base, chrome interior, white tempa, 5 arch silver wheels, England casting ($3-5)
4. dark blue body & base, chrome interior, white tempa, maltese cross wheels, England casting ($3-5)
5. white body & base, blue interior, red tempa, 5 arch silver wheels, England casting ($7-10)
6. white body & base, chrome interior, red tempa, 5 arch silver wheels, England casting ($7-10)
7. white body, dark blue base, chrome interior, red tempa, 5 arch silver wheels, England casting ($7-10)
NOTE: All models with chrome interior & clear windows unless otherwise noted.
8. white body & base, red flames tempa, 5 arch silver wheels, Macau casting ($2-4)
9. white body & base, orange flames tempa, 5 arch silver wheels, Macau casting ($2-4)
10. white body & base, red flames tempa, 5 arch silver wheels, Hong Kong casting ($2-4)
11. white body & base, orange flames tempa, 5 arch silver wheels, Hong Kong casting ($2-4)
12. bright blue body & base, "Firestone" tempa, 5 arch silver wheels, Macau casting ($7-10)(JP)
13. orange body & base, "11" & white stripe tempa, small starburst wheels, Macau casting ($3-5)(SF)
14. orange body & base, "11" & white stripe tempa, large starburst wheels, Macau casting ($3-5)(SF)
15. red body & base, "454 Rat" tempa, 5 arch gold wheels, Macau casting ($2-3)
16. red body & base, "454 Rat" tempa, 5 arch silver wheels, Macau casting ($2-3)
17. metallic copper body & base, "11" & white stripe tempa, laser wheels, Macau casting ($3-5)(LW)
18. metallic green body & base, "11" & white stripe tempa, laser wheels, Macau casting ($3-5)(LW)
19. rose red body & base, "Heinz 57" tempa, 5 arch silver wheels, Macau casting ($25-35)(US)
20. turquoise body & base, white roof tempa, gray disc w/rubber tires, China casting ($3-4)(WC)
21. white body & base, no tempa, 5 arch silver wheels, China casting ($6-8)(GF)
22. red body & base, "454 Rat" tempa, 5 arch silver wheels, China casting ($1-2)
23. metallic copper body & base, "4" & black roof tempa, black disc w/ rubber tires, China casting ($5-8)(WP)
24. red body & base, white roof & side flash tempa, 5 arch silver wheels, Thailand casting ($2-4)(GS)
25. metallic blue body & base, blue & red design tempa, gold 6 spoke spiral wheels, Thailand casting ($1-2)
26. black body & base, white roof & side flash tempa, silver 6 spoke spiral wheels, China casting ($2-4)(CC)
27. metallic red body & base, white roof with "Matchbox/DMB & B" tempa, chrome disc w/rubber tires, Thailand casting ($275-350)(US)
28. metallic red body & base, white roof with "Matchbox/DMB & B" tempa, gray disc w/rubber tires, Thailand casting ($275-350)(US)
29. metallic blue body & base, white & red design tempa, silver 6 spoke spiral wheels, Thailand casting ($1-2)
30. blue body & base, white & red design (sides only) tempa, silver 6 spoke spiral wheels, China casting ($1-2)
31. metallic red body & base, "Corvette 62" tempa, silver 6 spoke spiral wheels, China casting ($1-2)(MP)
32. candy red body & base, red chrome & white interior, white roof tempa, chrome disc w/rubber tires, China casting ($3-5)(PC3)
33. gold body & base, gold & white interior, white roof tempa, chrome disc w/rubber tires, China casting ($3-5)(PC6)
34. metallic blue body & base, white & red design tempa, silver 6 spoke spiral wheels, China casting ($1-2)
35. white body & base, orange flames tempa, silver 6 spoke spiral wheels, China casting ($2-4)
36. white body & base, orange flames tempa, 5 spoke concave star wheels, China casting ($1-2)
37. dark purple body & base, yellow tiger stripes tempa, 5 spoke concave star wheels, China casting ($1-2)(MP)
38. red body & base, "Chubby's/ Pepsi Cola" tempa, 5 spoke concave star wheels, China casting ($5-10)(US)
39. lemon body & base, yellow & black interior, white roof tempa, chrome disc with rubber tires, China casting ($3-5)(SC3)
40. black body & base, white & black interior, silver/ blue/ purple tempa, chrome disc with rubber tires, engine cast on hood, China casting ($3-5)(PC9)
41. silver-gray body & base, silver & black interior, white roof & side flash tempa, chrome disc with rubber tires, China casting ($3-5)(CP)
42. blue body & base, blue & white interior, white roof & side flash tempa, chrome disc with rubber tires, China casting ($3-5)(CP)
43. purple body & base, purple & white interior, orange & yellow flames tempa, chrome disc with rubber tires, China casting ($3-5)(PC11)
44. white body & base, red & black interior, white roof & side flash tempa, chrome disc with rubber tires, China casting ($3-5)(CP)
45. red body & base, red & white interior, white roof & side flash tempa, chrome disc with rubber tires, China casting ($3-5)(CP)
46. red body & base, white stripes & "62" on roof tempa, 5 spoke concave star wheels, China casting ($4-6)(AU)
47. lemon body & base, yellow & black interior, white roof & side flash tempa, gold 6 spoke spiral wheels, China casting ($75+)(CH)
48. metallic gold body & base, no tempa, 5 spoke concave star wheels, China casting ($5-10)(CH)
49. black body & base, black & white interior, white roof & side flash

tempa, chrome disc with rubber tires, China casting ($3-5)(CP)
50. metallic blue body & base, met. blue & white interior, white roof & side flash tempa, chrome disc with rubber tires, China casting ($3-5)(CP)
51. purple body, red base, red & white interior, orange & yellow flames tempa, blue windows, 5 spoke concave star wheels, engine cast on hood, China casting ($75+)(CHI)
52. purple body, red base, purple & white interior, orange & yellow flames tempa, blue windows, 5 spoke concave star wheels, engine cast on hood, China casting ($75+)(CHI)
53. red body & base, white stripes only tempa, 5 spoke concave star wheels, China casting ($4-6)(AU)
54. black body & base, pink roof & "Matchbox/ Hot August Nights 1998" tempa, chrome disc with rubber tires, China casting ($12-18)(US)
55. red body & base, white roof & side flash with "Animal House" tempa, 5 spoke concave star wheels, China casting ($4-6)(STR)
56. silver-gray body, red base, blue & white interior, white roof & side flash tempa, gold 6 spoke spiral wheels, China casting ($75+)(CHI)
57. metallic blue body, blue base, blue & white interior, white roof & side flash tempa, 5 spoke concave star wheels, China casting ($75+)(CHI)
58. blue body, red base, red & black interior, white roof & side flash tempa, gold 6 spoke spiral wheels, China casting ($75+)(CHI)
59. pale red body, white base, white & black interior, white stripes & "62" on roof tempa, gold 6 spoke spiral wheels, China casting ($75+)(CHI)

MB71-G PORSCHE 944 TURBO, issued 1989 (USA)
MB59-E PORSCHE 944 TURBO, issued 1989 (ROW)
1. red body, black base, tan interior, clear windows, 8 dot wheels, doors open, "944 Turbo" & logo tempa, Macau casting ($1-2)
2. black body, black base, no interior, chrome windows, gray disc w/rubber tires, doors cast, "944 Turbo" & detailed trim tempa, Macau casting ($5-8)(WC)
3. red body, black base, tan interior, clear windows, 8 dot wheels, doors open, "944 Turbo/Credit Charge" tempa, Macau casting ($7-10)(UK)
4. black body, black base, tan interior, clear windows, 8 dot wheels, doors open, "944 Turbo" & logo tempa, Macau casting ($2-3)(KS)
5. white body, black base, tan interior, clear windows, 8 dot wheels, doors open, "Duckhams" tempa, Macau casting ($15-20)(UK)(OP)
6. white body, black base, tan interior, clear windows, 8 dot wheels, doors open, "Duckhams" tempa, Thailand casting ($15-20)(UK)(OP)
7. black body, black base, no interior, chrome windows, gray disc w/rubber tires, doors cast, "944 Turbo" & detailed trim tempa, Thailand casting ($5-8)(WC)
8. metallic green body, black base, tan interior, clear windows, 8 dot wheels, doors open, "944 Turbo" & logo tempa, Thailand casting ($1-2)
9. yellow body, black base, black interior, clear windows, doors open, "944 Turbo" tempa, 8 dot wheels, Thailand casting ($2-4)(CC)
10. red body, black base, black & red interior, clear windows, doors open, "944 Turbo" & detailed trim tempa, Thailand casting ($3-5)(PC2-ROW)
11. candy red body, black base, tan & black interior, clear windows, doors open, detailed trim tempa, Thailand casting ($15-20)(GC)
12. iridescent white body, black base, brown & black interior, clear windows, doors open, "944 Turbo" & detailed trim tempa, Thailand casting ($3-5)(PC19)
13. metallic green body, black base, clear windows, door open, "944 Turbo" & "American International Recovery" tempa, 8 dot wheels, Thailand casting ($100+)(ASAP promo)

MB71-H MUSTANG COBRA, issued 1995 (USA)
MB43-J MUSTANG COBRA, issued 1995 (ROW)
1. red body, smoke windows, gray interior, cobra on black hood tempa, 6 spoke spiral wheels, Thailand casting ($1-2)
2. white body, smoke windows, green interior, cobra on black hood tempa, 6 spoke spiral wheels, Thailand casting ($1-2)(MP)
3. red body, clear windows, red/ivory interior, detailed trim tempa, chrome disc w/rubber tires, Thailand casting ($3-5)(PC2)
4. dark purple body, clear windows, white/black interior, detailed trim tempa, chrome disc w/rubber tires, Thailand casting ($3-5)(PC)(JC)
5. black body, smoke windows, orange-brown interior, cobra on gray hood tempa, 6 spoke spiral wheels, Thailand casting ($2-4)
6. white body, clear windows, ivory/red interior, detailed trim tempa, chrome disc w/rubber tires, Thailand casting ($3-5)(PC5)
7. black body, clear windows, black/tan interior, detailed trim tempa, chrome disc w/rubber tires, Thailand casting ($3-5)(SC2)
8. white body, clear windows, light blue interior, "Ford Pace Car" & black design tempa, 5 spoke concave star wheels, Thailand casting ($1-2)(MP)
9. pumpkin body, clear windows, white & gray interior, detailed trim tempa, chrome disc with rubber tires, Thailand casting ($15-20)(GC)
10.metallic blue body, clear windows, translucent yellow interior, lime horse design tempa, 5 spoke concave star wheels, Thailand casting ($1-2)
11. metallic gold body, clear windows, gray interior, no tempa, 6 spoke spiral wheels, Thailand casting ($5-10)(CH)
12. metallic blue body, clear windows, white & gray interior, detailed trim tempa, chrome disc with rubber tires, Thailand casting ($3-5)(SC4)
13. gold body, clear windows, white & gray interior, detailed trim tempa, chrome disc with rubber tires, Thailand casting ($3-5)(PC14)
14. slate blue body, clear windows, brown & tan interior, detailed trim tempa, chrome disc with rubber tires, Thailand casting ($3-5)(PC16)
15. dark green body, clear windows, white & gray interior, detailed trim tempa, chrome disc with rubber tires, Thailand casting ($3-5)(SC5)
16. metallic red body, clear windows, gray interior, lime horse design tempa, 5 spoke concave star wheels, Thailand casting ($1-2)(MW73)
17. pink body, smoke windows, white interior, "71st Shenandoah Apple Blossom Festival 1998" tempa, 5 spoke concave star wheels, Thailand casting ($8-12)(US)
18. metallic red body, clear windows, mid gray interior, lime horse design tempa, 5 spoke concave star wheels with black hubs, Thailand casting ($15-20)(MW73)
19. metallic red body, clear windows, mid gray interior, lime horse design tempa, 5 spoke concave star wheels with black hubs, China casting ($15-20)(MW73)
20. metallic red body, clear windows, mid gray interior, lime horse design tempa, 5 spoke concave star wheels, China casting ($1-2)(MW73)
21. metallic rose body, clear windows, white interior, lime horse design tempa, 5 spoke concave star wheels, China casting ($1-2)(MW73)
22. light rose red body, clear windows, white interior, lime horse design tempa, 5 spoke concave star wheels, China casting ($1-2)(MW73)
NOTE: There are numerous intermediate shades of body & tempa color on versions 16 & 18-22.
23. white body, clear windows, light blue interior, "Ford Pace Car" & black design tempa, 5 spoke concave star wheels, China casting ($1-2)(MP)
24. red body, smoke windows, tan interior, no tempa, 5 spoke concave star wheels, China casting ($1-2)(MP)

MB71-I JAGUAR XK8, issued 1998
NOTE: All models with clear windows, black base & China casting unless otherwise noted.
1. metallic red body, pale tan & black interior, chrome disc with rubber tires, detailed trim tempa ($4-6)(FE)
2. unpainted body, pale tan interior, chrome disc with rubber tires, no tempa ($4-6)(FE)
3. metallic blue body, silver-gray interior, 5 spoke concave star wheels, silver band & "Jaguar XK8" tempa ($1-2)(MW71)

MB72-A JEEP, issued 1970
1. yellow body, red interior, red axle covers ($25-40)
2. yellow body, red interior, black axle covers ($25-40)
3. yellow-orange body, red interior, black axle covers ($25-40)
4. bright yellow body, red interior, black axle covers ($25-40)

MB72-B HOVERCRAFT SRN6, issued 1972
1. white body, black base, blue windows, with labels ($5-7)
2. white body, black base, no windows, with labels ($5-7)
3. white body, black base, no windows, without labels ($5-7)

MB72-C BOMAG ROAD ROLLER, issued 1979
1. yellow body & base, red interior, yellow hubs ($4-6)
2. yellow body & base, red interior, silver hubs ($3-5)

MB72-D MAXI TAXI, issued 1981 (USA)
1. yellow body, black base, "M" towards upper left on roof, Hong Kong casting ($7-10)
2. yellow body, black base, "I" towards upper right on roof, Hong Kong casting ($2-4)
3. yellow body, black base, no roof tempa, Hong Kong casting ($3-5)
4. yellow body, black base, "M" towards upper left on roof, Macau casting ($3-5)

MB72-E DODGE DELIVERY TRUCK, issued 1982 (ROW)
NOTE: All models with 5 arch wheels unless otherwise noted.
1. red body, white container, silver wheels, "Pepsi" labels, England casting ($4-6)
2. red body, white container, gold wheels, "Pepsi" labels, England casting ($4-6)
3. red body, white container, silver wheels, "Smith's" labels, England casting ($4-6)(UK)(OP)
4. red body, white container, gold wheels, "Smith's" labels, England casting ($4-6)(UK)(OP)
5. red body, white container, silver wheels, "Kellogg's" labels, England casting ($4-6)
6. red body, white container, gold wheels, "Kellogg's" labels, England casting ($4-6)
NOTE: All models below with blue windows, black base & silver wheels unless otherwise noted.
7. red body, white container, "Kellogg's" tempa, Macau casting ($4-6)
8. white body, white container, "Street's Ice Cream" tempa, Macau casting ($6-8)(AU)
9. yellow body, yellow container, "Hertz" tempa, Macau casting ($2-4)
10. orange-yellow body & container, "Hertz" tempa, Macau casting ($2-4)
11. red body, red container, "Royal Mail Parcels" tempa , Macau casting ($5-7)(UK)
12. red body, white container, "Kellogg's/Milch-Lait-Latte" tempa, Macau casting ($35-50)(GR)(SW)
13. white body, white container, "Jetspress Road Express" tempa, Macau casting ($6-8)(AU)
14. green body, white container, "Minties" tempa, Macau casting ($6-8)(AU)
15. orange-yellow body, yellow container, "Risi" tempa, Macau casting ($15-25)(SP)
16. blue body, blue container, "Mitre 10" tempa, Macau casting ($6-8)(AU)
17. red body, dark yellow container, "Nestle Chokito" tempa, Macau casting ($6-8)(AU)
18. red body, container & base, red windows, "Kit Kat" tempa, Macau casting ($7-10)(UK)(OP)
19. blue body & base, blue container, "Yorkie" tempa, Macau casting ($7-10)(UK)(OP)
20. white body, white container, "Pirelli Gripping Stuff" tempa, Macau casting ($3-5)(TC)
21. red body, white container, "Matchbox U.S.A. Sheraton Inc. 1989" tempa, Macau casting ($8-12)(US)
22. white body, white container, "XP Express Parcels Systems" tempa, Macau casting ($3-5)(TC)
23. dark green body, orange container, "C Plus Orange" tempa, Macau casting ($10-15)(CN)
24. light gray & dark navy body, light gray container, "British Airways Cargo" tempa, Thailand casting ($3-5)(MC)
25. white body, white container, "Wigwam" tempa, Thailand casting ($7-10)(CY)(DU)
26. white body, white container, "XP Express Parcels Systems" tempa, Thailand casting ($3-5)(TC)
27. red body, white container, "Big Top Circus" tempa, 5 crown wheels, Thailand casting ($3-5)(TP)
28. blue body & container, "St. Ivel Gold" tempa, Thailand casting ($10-15)(UK)(OP)
29. blue body & container, "Stena Line Freight" tempa, Thailand casting ($12-15)(UK)(LD)
30. white body & container, "MD" tempa, Thailand casting ($12-15)(UK)(LD)

MB72-F SAND RACER, issued 1984 (USA)
1. white body, pearly silver base, black interior & roll bar, "Goodyear 211" tempa, 5 crown front & racing special rear wheels, Macau casting ($18-25)

MB72-G AIRPLANE TRANSPORTER, issued 1985 (USA)
MB65-E AIRPLANE TRANSPORTER, issued 1985 (ROW)
1. yellow body, blue windows, "Rescue" & checkers tempa, plastic plane with red wings & white undercarriage, Macau casting ($6-8)
2. yellow body, blue windows, "Rescue" & checkers tempa, plastic plane with white wings & red undercarriage, Macau casting ($6-8)
3. yellow body, blue windows, "Rescue" & checkers tempa, plastic plane with white wings & red undercarriage, China casting ($6-8)
4. white body, blue windows, "NASA" tempa, plastic plane with white wings & undercarriage, Macau casting ($3-5)(MP)
5. olive body, blue windows, black & tan camouflage tempa, black hubs, plastic plane with olive wings & undercarriage, China casting ($35-50)(CM)
6. yellow body, blue windows, "Rescue" & checkers tempa, plastic plane with red wings & white undercarriage, China casting ($6-8)
7. white body, smoke windows, gray & olive camouflage tempa, black hubs, plastic plane with white wings & gray undercarriage, Thailand casting ($3-5)(MP)
8. white body, smoke windows, "Rescue" with red checkers tempa, plastic plane with black wings & red undercarriage, Thailand casting ($2-4)(MP)

MB72-I CADILLAC ALLANTE, issued 1987 (USA)
MB65-F CADILLAC ALLANTE, issued 1987 (ROW)
1. silver-gray body, red interior, clear windshield, 8 dot wheels, no tempa, Macau casting ($1-2)
2. black body, red interior, clear windshield, laser wheels, red & silver stripes tempa, Macau casting ($3-5)(LW)
3. pink body, gray interior, clear windshield, 8 dot wheels, "Cadillac" tempa, Macau casting ($1-2)
4. light pink body, gray interior, clear windshield, 8 dot wheels, "Cadillac" tempa, China casting ($1-2)
5. silver-gray body, red interior, clear windshield, 8 dot wheels, no tempa, China casting ($1-2)
6. charcoal body, red interior, chrome windshield, gray disc w/rubber tires, no tempa, Macau casting ($5-8)(WC)
7. white body, red interior, clear windshield, gray disc w/rubber tires, no tempa, China casting ($100-150)(US)
8. bright pink body, gray interior, clear windshield, 8 dot wheels, "Cadillac" tempa, Thailand casting ($1-2)
9. pink body, white interior, clear windshield, 8 dot wheels, green zig zags & blue stripes tempa, Thailand casting ($1-2)
10. metallic red body, gray interior, clear windshield, 8 dot wheels, "Official Pace Car 76th Indy" tempa, Thailand casting ($7-10)(N)
11. metallic red body, dark gray interior, chrome windows, gray disc w/ rubber tires, no tempa, Thailand casting ($3-4)(WC)
12. pink body, white interior, clear windshield, 8 dot wheels, green zig zags & blue stripes tempa, China casting ($1-2)
13. white body, red & black interior, clear windshield, chrome disc with rubber tires, detailed trim tempa, Thailand casting ($8-12)(UC)
14. cream body, black & tan interior, clear windshield, chrome disc with rubber tires, detailed trim tempa, Thailand casting ($3-5)(JC)(PC)

MB72-K DODGE ZOO TRUCK, issued 1992 (ROW)
1. white body, blue windows, silver-gray cage with brown lions red/orange/ yellow stripes tempa, 5 arch wheels, black base, Thailand casting ($3-5)(MC)

MB72-O CHEVY K-1500 PICKUP, issued 1996 (USA)
NOTE: All models with clear windows, chrome rollbar & base, maltese cross wheels & China casting unless otherwise noted.
1. black body, gray interior, yellow & pink tempa ($1-2)
2. florescent orange body, black interior, blue mountain design tempa ($1-2)(MP)
3. metallic gold body, black interior, no tempa ($10-15)(CH)
4. florescent lime body, black interior, neon orange/black/white & "454" tempa ($1-2)(MP)
5. yellow body, black interior, red & white tempa ($1-2)(MP)
6. red body, gray interior, yellow/black/white "454" tempa ($1-2)(MP)
7. white body, blue interior, "World Cup Field Maintenance/ France 98" tempa ($1-2)(MP)
8. metallic blue body, gray interior, green & white tempa ($1-2)(MW54)
9. metallic blue body, gray interior, red & white tempa ($1-2)(MP)

MB73-A MERCURY COMMUTER, issued 1970
1. lime body, unpainted base, no labels ($20-25)
2. red body, unpainted base, cow head label ($20-25)

3. red body, unpainted base, cat head label ($20-25)
4. red body, silver-gray base, cat head label ($20-25)

MB73-B WEASEL, issued 1974
MB70-G WEASEL, reissued 1993 (USA)
NOTE: Versions 1 to 9 with black turret.
1. metallic green body & base, green base insert, silver hubs, no tempa, England casting ($4-6)
2. olive drab body, metallic green base, green base insert, black hubs, no tempa, England casting ($65-80)(TP)
3. olive green body, metallic green base, green base insert, black hubs, no tempa, England casting ($6-8)(TP)
4. olive green body & base, green base insert, black hubs, no tempa, England casting ($6-8)(TP)
5. olive green body & base, green base insert, silver hubs, no tempa, England casting ($6-8)(TP)
6. bright olive body & base, black base insert, silver hubs, no tempa, England casting ($6-8)(TP)
7. bright olive body & base, black base insert, black hubs, no tempa, England casting ($6-8)(TP)
8. olive green body & base, black base insert, black hubs, tan & black camouflage tempa, Macau casting ($4-5)(CM)
9. black body & base, black base insert, black hubs, yellow & gray camouflage tempa, Macau casting ($4-5)(CM)
10.beige body, black base, black base insert, black hubs, brown/black/white camouflage tempa, beige turret, China casting ($1-2)
11.beige body, black base, black base insert, black hubs, brown/black/white camouflage tempa, beige turret, Thailand casting ($1-2)
12. pink-tan body, black base, black base insert, black hubs, green & brown camouflage tempa, light tan turret, Thailand casting ($1-2)(MP)
13. olive body, black base, black base insert, black hubs, star & "M-3173" tempa, olive turret, Thailand casting ($2-3)
NOTE: Some of this version model was packaged in blisterpacks as #77 in error ($2-3)
14. green body & turret, black base, black base insert, black hubs, black & brown camouflage tempa, Thailand casting ($1-2)(MP)

MB73-C MODEL A FORD, issued 1979
NOTE: Some variations may be found with 5 crown (front wheels) used on the rear axles
1. cream body, dark green fenders with spare tire cast, green windows, no tempa, 5 crown front & dot dash rear wheels, England casting ($6-8)
2. cream body, dark green fenders, green windows, no tempa, 5 crown front & dot dash rear wheels, England casting ($4-6)
3. cream body, dark green fenders, no windows, no tempa, 5 crown front & dot dash rear wheels, England casting ($4-6)
4. green body, dark green fenders, green windows, no tempa, 5 crown front & dot dash rear wheels, England casting ($4-6)
5. green body, dark green fenders, no windows, no tempa, 5 crown front & dot dash rear wheels, England casting ($4-6)
6. beige body, brown fenders, amber windows, no tempa, 5 crown front & dot dash rear wheels, England casting ($4-6)
7. beige body, brown fenders, clear windows, no tempa, 5 crown front & dot dash rear wheels, England casting ($4-6)
8. beige body, brown fenders, clear windows, no tempa, 5 crown front & dot dash rear wheels, Macau casting ($2-4)
9. red body, black fenders, clear windows, no tempa, 5 crown front & dot dash rear wheels, Macau casting ($2-4)
10. black body & fenders, clear windows, flames tempa, 5 arch front & racing special rear wheels, Macau casting ($2-4)
11. purple body, yellow fenders, clear windows, stripes tempa, 5 arch front & racing special rear wheels, Macau casting ($3-5)
12. yellow body, red fenders, clear windows, "Pava" tempa, 5 arch front & racing special rear wheels, Macau casting ($8-12)(DK)
13. red body, dark green fenders, clear windows, no tempa, 5 crown front & dot dash wheels, Macau casting ($15-20)(UK)(OP)
14. red body, dark green fenders, clear windows, no tempa, 5 crown front & dot dash rear wheels, Thailand casting ($15-20)(UK)(OP)
15. red body, dark green fenders, clear windows, no tempa, 5 crown front & dot dash rear wheels, China casting ($15-20)(UK)(OP)
16. purple body, yellow chassis, clear windows, stripes tempa, 5 arch front & racing special rear wheels, Thailand casting ($2-4)
17. orange-yellow body, white fenders, clear windows, "GT" & yellow jacket tempa, 5 crown front & dot dash rear wheels, Thailand casting ($6-8)(WR)
18. powder blue body, red chassis, clear windows, clown tempa, yellow 5 arch front & racing special rear wheels, Thailand casting ($7-10)(MC)
19. white body, pink chassis, clear windows, zigzag design tempa, 5 arch front & racing special rear wheels, Thailand casting ($2-3)
20. dark blue body & chassis, clear windows, green & pink grid tempa, 5 arch front & racing special rear wheels, Thailand casting ($1-2)(MP)
21. metallic red body & chassis, clear windows, black roof & detailed trim tempa, 5 arch front & gray disc insert racing special rear wheels, Thailand casting ($2-4)(CC)
22. red body & chassis, clear windows, blue & yellow tempa, 5 arch front & racing special rear wheels, Thailand casting ($1-2)(MP)
23. metallic gold body, black chassis, clear windows, "Matchbox Collectors Club" tempa, 5 crown front & dot dash rear wheels, Thailand casting ($10-15)(US)
24. white body, dark purple chassis, clear windows, "Temecula Rod Run 1996" tempa, 5 arch front & racing special rear wheels, Thailand casting ($8-12)(WR)
25. metallic gold body, black chassis, clear windows, "American Iron Cruise 96/Memory Lane" tempa, 5 crown front & dot dash rear wheels, Thailand casting ($15-25)(C2)
26. dark gray body, black chassis, clear windows, "The Untouchables" & bullet marks tempa, 5 crown front & 5 crown rear wheels, China casting ($4-6)(STR)

MB73-E MERCEDES TRACTOR, issued 1990 (USA)
MB27-E MERCEDES TRACTOR, issued 1990 (ROW)
1. pea green upper body, olive chassis & interior, pea green wheels, no tempa, Macau casting ($1-2)
2. pea green upper body, olive chassis & interior, pea green wheels, no tempa, Thailand casting ($1-2)
3. green upper body, pale yellow chassis & interior, green wheels, no tempa, Thailand casting ($2-4)(TP)(TC)
4. pea green upper body, olive chassis & interior, pea green wheels, "MB Trac" tempa, Thailand casting ($1-2)
5. dark green upper body, black plastic chassis, olive interior, pea green wheels, no tempa, Thailand casting ($2-4)(FM)

MB73-H ROTWHEELER, issued 1995 (USA)
MB47-F ROTWHEELER, issued 1995 (ROW)
NOTE: All models with chrome eyes & engine and Goodyear slicks.
1. brown body, brown base, red upper & lower gums with black collar tempa, Thailand casting ($1-2)
2. brown body, brown base, brown upper & red lower gums with black collar tempa, Thailand casting ($1-2)
3. black body, black base, red upper & lower gums with red collar tempa, Thailand casting ($1-2)
4. metallic gold, black base, red upper & lower gums with plain collar tempa, Thailand casting ($5-10)(CH)
5. red body, red base, red upper & lower gums with black collar tempa, Thailand casting ($1-2)(MW42)
6. red body, dark red base, red upper & lower gums with black collar tempa, Thailand casting ($1-2)(MW42)
7. red body, dark red base, red upper & lower gums with black collar tempa, China casting ($1-2)(MW42)

MB74-A DAIMLER BUS, issued 1970
NOTE: All versions can be found with red or black axle covers.
1. red body & base, "Esso Extra Petrol" labels ($18-25)
2. red body, pink-red base, "Esso Extra Petrol" labels ($18-25)
3. pink-red body, red base, "Esso Extra Petrol" labels ($18-25)
4. pink-red body & base, "Esso Extra Petrol" labels ($18-25)
5. red body & base, "The Baron of Beef" labels ($175-225)(LE)
6. red body & base, "Inn On The Park" labels ($200-275)(LE)
7. red body & base, "The Miniature Vehicle/N.A.M.C." labels ($200-275)(US)
8. red body & base, "Beefeater Gin" labels ($300-450)(LE)
9. red body & base, "Fly Cyprus Airways/ London Frankfurt Athens Nicosia" labels ($250-400)(LE)
NOTE: Superfast models in green can not be verified to exist!

MB74-B TOE JOE, issued 1972
1. lime body, unpainted base, green booms, red hooks, 5 spoke wheels ($4-6)
2. lime body, silver-gray base, green booms, red hooks, 5 spoke wheels ($4-6)
3. lime body, unpainted base, green booms, red hooks, maltese cross wheels ($4-6)
4. lime body, black base, green booms, red hooks, 5 arch wheels ($4-6)
5. lime body, unpainted base, green booms, black hooks, 5 arch wheels ($4-6)
6. dark lime body, black base, green booms, red hooks, 5 arch wheels ($4-6)
7. dark lime body, black base, red booms, black hooks, 5 arch wheels ($15-18)(TP)
8. dark lime body, unpainted base, red booms, black hooks, dot dash wheels ($15-18)(TP)
9. dark lime body, black base, white booms, black hooks, 5 arch wheels ($125-175)(TP)
10. yellow body, unpainted base, green booms, black hooks, 5 arch wheels ($15-18)(TP)
11. yellow body, unpainted base, red booms, black hooks, 5 arch wheels ($3-5)(TP)
12. yellow body, black base, red booms, black hooks, 5 arch wheels ($3-5)(TP)
13. yellow body, black base, red booms, black hooks, 5 spoke wheels ($3-5)(TP)
14. yellow body, black base, red booms, black hooks, dot dash wheels ($4-6)(TP)
15. yellow-orange body, unpainted base, red booms, black hooks, 5 arch wheels ($3-5)(TP)
16. yellow-orange body, unpainted base, red booms, black hooks, 5 arch wheels, "Hitchhiker" labels ($125-175)(TP)
17. red body, black base, green booms, black hooks, 5 arch wheels ($150-200)(TP)
18. red body, black base, red booms, black hooks, 5 arch wheels ($150-200)(TP)
19. red body, black base, red booms, red hooks, 5 arch wheels ($150-200)(TP)

MB74-C COUGAR VILLAGER, issued 1978
1. light green body, green tailgate, yellow interior, unpainted base ($2-4)
2. light green body, green tailgate, yellow-orange interior, unpainted base ($2-4)
3. dark green body, green tailgate, yellow interior, unpainted base ($2-4)
4. dark green body, green tailgate, yellow-orange interior, unpainted base ($2-4)
5. very dark green body, green tailgate, yellow interior, unpainted base ($2-4)
6. very dark green body, green tailgate, yellow-orange interior, unpainted base ($2-4)
7. dark blue body, blue tailgate, yellow interior, unpainted base ($2-4)
8. dark blue body, blue tailgate, yellow-orange interior, unpainted base ($2-4)
9. olive green body, green tailgate, yellow interior, unpainted (tab) base ($375-450)(BR)
NOTE: Available as a Bulgarian casting. Assorted colors available ($15-25)

MB74-D ORANGE PEEL, issued 1981 (USA)
1. white body, black base, dark orange "Orange Peel" tempa, 5 arch front wheels, Hong Kong casting ($3-5)
2. white body, black base, light orange "Orange Peel" tempa, 5 arch front wheels, Macau casting ($3-5)
3. white body, black base, light orange "Orange Peel" tempa, 5 arch front wheels, Hong Kong casting ($3-5)
4. white body, black base, light orange "Orange Peel" tempa, maltese cross front wheels, Macau casting ($3-5)
5. purple body, black base, white/yellow/green flames tempa, 5 arch front wheels, China casting ($1-2)(AV)
6. pink body, black base, dark green with snake tempa, 5 arch front wheels, China casting ($3-5)(PC13)

MB74-F MUSTANG GT, issued 1984 (USA)
NOTE: All models with black base, clear windows & 5 arch front wheels
1. light orange body, racing special rear wheels, yellow & blue stripes tempa, Macau casting ($2-4)
2. dark orange body, racing special rear wheels, yellow & blue stripes tempa, Macau casting ($2-4)
3. dark orange body, racing special rear wheels, orange & blue stripes tempa, Macau casting ($2-4)
4. dark orange body, dot dash rear wheels, yellow & blue stripes tempa, China casting ($2-4)
5. dull orange body, dot dash rear wheels, yellow & blue stripes tempa, China casting ($2-4)
6. pearly silver body, racing special rear wheels, purple & yellow stripes tempa, China casting ($2-4)
7. white body, racing special rear wheels, red squiggly lines tempa, Thailand casting ($1-2)(MP)
8. red body, racing special rear wheels, black stripes tempa, China casting ($1-2)(MP)

MB74-H GRAND PRIX RACING CAR, issued 1987 (USA)
MB14-H GRAND PRIX RACING CAR, issued 1987 (ROW)
1. white & powder blue body, dark blue base, red driver, black airfoil, "15/Goodyear/Shell" tempa,, Macau casting ($3-4)
2. red body, black base, white driver, black airfoil, "27 Fiat" tempa, Macau casting ($1-2)
3. red body, black base, white driver, black airfoil, "27 Fiat" tempa, Thailand casting ($1-2)
4. yellow body & base, red driver, dark yellow airfoil, "Pennzoil 2" tempa, China casting ($3-4)(IN)
5. dark orange & white body, white base, red driver, orange airfoil, "Indy 4" tempa, China casting ($3-4)(IN)
6. dark yellow body & base, red driver, orange-yellow airfoil, "Squirt" tempa, Thailand casting ($18-25)(US)(OP)
7. chrome plated body, black base, white driver, black airfoil, no tempa, Thailand casting ($12-18)(C2)
8. red body, black base, white driver, black airfoil, "27 Fiat" tempa, China casting ($1-2)
9. red body, black (plastic) base, white driver, black airfoil, "27 Fiat" tempa, China casting ($15-20)
10. red body, black base, white driver, black airfoil, "Scotch/Target" tempa, Thailand casting ($3-4)(IN)
11. blue body & base, yellow driver, blue airfoil, "Panasonic 7" tempa, Thailand casting ($3-4)(IN)
12. white & blue body, blue base, red driver, blue airfoil, "Indy 76" tempa, Thailand casting ($3-4)(IN)
13. white & black body, black metal base, red driver, black airfoil, "Havoline/K-Mart 6" tempa, Thailand casting ($3-4)(IN)
14. yellow body & base, red driver, yellow airfoil, "Pennzoil 4" tempa, Thailand casting ($3-4)(IN)
15. orange/lavender/white body, lavender base, white driver, white airfoil, "Indy 1" tempa, Thailand casting ($4-6)(IN)
16. white & black body, black metal base, red driver, black airfoils, "Texaco/K-Mart 1" tempa, Thailand casting ($3-4)(IN)
17. black body, black metal base, pink driver, black airfoils, "Indy 5" & green/pink spatter tempa, Thailand casting ($3-4)(IN)
18. yellow body, yellow metal base, red driver, yellow airfoils, "Pennzoil 8" tempa, Thailand casting ($3-4)(IN)
19. red body, red metal base, white driver, black airfoils, "Scotch 9" tempa, Thailand casting ($3-4)(IN)
20. blue body, blue metal base, silver-gray driver, blue airfoils, "Mackenzie 15" tempa, Thailand casting ($3-4)(IN)
21. blue & yellow body, blue metal base, yellow driver, blue airfoils, "Panasonic 11" tempa, Thailand casting ($3-4)(IN)
22. blue & white body, blue metal base, red driver, blue airfoils, "Valvoline/Kraco 3" tempa, Thailand casting ($3-4)(IN)
23. white body, blue metal base, red driver, white airfoils, "Indy 500" & "77" tempa, Thailand casting ($3-4)(IN)(KS)
24. white body, white metal base, green driver, white airfoils, "XP 6" tempa, all black slicks, Thailand casting ($8-12)(DU)
25. white body, pink metal base, blue driver, white airfoils, "7" & blue dots tempa, Thailand casting ($1-2)
26. fluorescent orange & yellow body, yellow metal base, white driver, yellow airfoils, "Matchbox Get in the Fast Lane 7" tempa, Thailand casting

($2-4)(CC)
27. green & white body, green metal base, black driver, white airfoils, "4" & black lines tempa, Thailand casting ($1-2)(MP)
28. white body, pink metal base, blue driver, white airfoils, "7" & blue dots tempa, Thailand casting ($1-2)
29. white & orange body, black metal base, black driver, white airfoils, "4" & black lines tempa, Thailand casting ($1-2)(MP)
30. dark purple body, black metal base, white driver, neon yellow airfoils, "Matchbox 20" tempa, China casting ($1-2)(MP)
31. metallic tan body, metallic tan metal base, white driver, tan airfoils, "Peugeot/ Special 11" tempa, China casting ($2-3)(ROW)
32. red body, black metal base, white driver, black airfoils, "Kids World/ Fiat" tempa, China casting ($35-50)(AU)
33. red body, black metal base, white driver, black airfoils, "Fiat 27" tempa, China casting ($2-4)

MB74-J FORMULA ONE RACER, issued 1996 (USA)
MB246 FORMULA ONE, issued 1994 (MN/F1)
NOTE: All models with yellow wheel lettering unless otherwise noted.
1. blue & white body, blue driver, white airfoil, black base (cast "Williams Renault"), white wheel lettering, "Canon Williams 5" tempa, Thailand casting ($4-6)(MN)
2. blue & white body, blue driver, white airfoil, black base, "Canon Williams 0" tempa, Thailand casting ($3-5)(Fl)
3. white body, white driver, white airfoil, black base, "Footwork 9" tempa, Thailand casting ($3-5)(Fl)
4. red body, white driver, red airfoil, black base, "Fiat 27" tempa, Thailand casting ($3-5)(Fl)
5. black body, white driver, black airfoil, black base, "Liqui Moly 30" tempa, Thailand casting ($3-5)(Fl)
6. red body, white driver, black airfoil, black base, "Fiat 27" without white band around top tempa, Thailand casting ($3-5)(F1)
7. blue & white body, blue driver, black airfoil, black base, "Elf/Renault 0" with red, white & gold trim tempa, Thailand casting ($3-5)(F1)
8. white body, white driver, white airfoil, black base, "Uliveto/Lee Cooper, Ford 9" tempa, Thailand casting ($3-5)(F1)
9. white body, white driver, white airfoil, black base, "Mobil 1/Loctite/ Hitachi 72" tempa, Thailand casting ($3-5)(F1)
10. blue body, white driver, blue airfoil, black base, "Sasol 14" tempa, Thailand casting ($3-5)(F1)
11. white body, dark blue driver, orange airfoil, black base, "MB Racing 1" tempa, Thailand casting ($1-2)
12. white body, white driver, white airfoil, black base, "BP/ Footwork 9" tempa, Thailand casting ($3-5)(F1)
13. red body, black driver, black airfoil, black base, "Ferrari 27 Pioneer" without white band tempa, China casting ($3-5)(F1)
14. blue & white body, white driver, white airfoil, black base, "Renault Elf 0" tempa, China casting ($3-5)(F1)
15. white body, white driver, white airfoil, black base, "Uliveto/Lee Cooper 9" tempa, China casting ($3-5)(F1)
16. blue body, white driver, black airfoil, black base, "Sasol 14" tempa, China casting ($3-5)(F1)
NOTE: Below models with white lettered wheels unless otherwise noted.
17. metallic gold body, white driver, black airfoil, metallic gold base, no tempa, China casting ($5-10)(CH)
18. orange body, dark blue driver, dark blue airfoil, black base, "MB Racing 1" tempa, China casting ($1-2)
19. white body, dark blue driver, dark blue airfoil, black base, "MB Racing 1" tempa, China casting ($1-2)
20. lemon body, black driver, red airfoil, red base, "MB Racing 1" tempa, China casting ($1-2)(MW61)
21. white body, black driver, black airfoil, black base, no tempa, China casting ($25-40)(ASAP blank)
22. white body, black driver, black airfoil, black base, "STB" tempa, China casting ($100+)(ASAP)
23. white body, black driver, black airfoil, black base, "IFS" tempa, China casting ($100+)(ASAP)

MB75-A FERRARI BERLINETTA, issued 1970
NOTE: All models with unpainted base, ivory interior, clear windows & 5 spoke wheels.
1. light green body, plain grille ($75-90)
2. dark green body, plain grille ($75-90)
3. red body, plain grille ($25-35)
4. red body, silver grille ($25-35)

MB75-B ALFA CARABO, issued 1971
1. light purple body, unpainted base, no tempa, 5 spoke wheels ($15-18)
2. light purple body, yellow base, no tempa, 5 spoke wheels ($15-18)
3. pink body, yellow base, no tempa, 5 spoke wheels ($75-100)
4. pink body, yellow base, with tempa, 5 spoke wheels ($18-25)
5. red body, yellow base, with tempa, 5 spoke wheels ($8-12)
6. red body, yellow base, with tempa, 5 arch wheels ($8-12)(JP)

MB75-C SEASPRITE HELICOPTER, issued 1977
1. white body, red base, blue windows, "Rescue" labels ($4-6)
2. white body, red base, green windows, "Rescue" labels ($4-6)
3. white body, red base, purple windows, "Rescue" labels ($4-6)
4. white body, red base, red windows, "Rescue" labels ($4-6)
5. dark cream body, red (etched) base, blue windows, "Rescue" labels ($250-350)(BR)
6. dark green body, red (etched) base, blue windows, "Rescue" labels ($350-500)(BR)
NOTE: Available as a Bulgarian casting. Assorted colors available ($10-25)

MB75-D HELICOPTER, issued 1982
NOTE: All models with black blades unless otherwise noted.
1. white body, orange base, black interior & skis, amber windows, "MB TV News" tempa, England casting ($3-5)
2. white body, black base, black interior & skis, clear windows, "MB TV News" tempa, England casting ($8-12)
3. white body, black base, gray interior & skis, clear windows, "MB TV News" tempa, England casting ($8-12)
4. white body, black base, gray interior & skis, clear windows, "36 Police" tempa, England casting ($4-6)
5. white body, black base, gray interior & skis, amber windows, "36 Police" tempa, England casting ($4-6)
6. white body, black base, black interior & skis, clear windows, "36 Police" tempa, England casting ($4-6)
7. white body, black base, black interior & skis, amber windows, "36 Police" tempa, England casting ($4-6)
8. silver-gray body, orange base, gray interior & skis, amber windows, "-600-" tempa, England casting ($2-4)(CY)
9. silver-gray body, orange base, gray interior & skis, clear windows, "-600-" tempa, England casting ($2-4)(CY)
10. silver-gray body, orange base, black interior & skis, amber windows, "-600-" tempa, England casting ($2-4)(CY)
11. silver-gray body, orange base, black interior & skis, clear windows, "-600-" tempa, England casting ($2-4)(CY)
12. silver-gray body, black base, gray interior & skis, amber windows, "-600-" tempa, England casting ($2-4)(CY)
13. silver-gray body, black base, black interior & skis, amber windows, "-600-" tempa, England casting ($2-4)(CY)
14. white body, orange base, gray interior & skis, amber windows, "Police 36" tempa, England casting ($15-20)
15. white body, black base, gray interior & skis, amber windows, "Rescue" tempa ($2-4)
16. white body, black base, black interior & skis, amber windows, "Rescue" tempa, England casting ($2-4)
17. pearly gray body, orange base, gray interior & skis, amber windows, "-600-" tempa, Macau casting ($2-4)(CY)
18. white body, orange base, black interior & skis, amber windows, blue "Rescue" tempa, Macau casting ($2-4)
19. white body, black base, gray interior & skis, amber windows, blue "Rescue" tempa, Macau casting ($2-4)
20. black body, black base, gray interior & skis, amber windows, "Air Car" tempa, Macau casting ($2-4)(CY)
21. white body, red base, gray interior & skis, amber windows, "Fire Dept." tempa, Macau casting ($2-4)(MP)
22. white body, red base, gray interior & skis, amber windows, "NASA" tempa, Macau casting ($2-4)(MP)
23. white body, red base, black interior & skis, amber windows, "Virgin Atlantic" tempa, Macau casting ($2-4)(GS)
24. white body, yellow base, red interior & skis, amber windows, "JCB" tempa, white blades, Macau casting ($4-6)(GS)
25. white body, lemon base, gray interior & skis, amber windows, "Fire Dept." tempa, Macau casting ($2-4)(MP)
26. white body, dull orange base, gray interior & skis, amber windows, black "Rescue" tempa, Macau casting ($2-4)
27. red body, white base, gray interior & skis, amber windows, "Red Rebels" tempa, white blades, Macau casting ($2-4)(MC)
28. white body, black base, gray interior & skis, amber windows, Japanese lettered tempa, Macau casting ($8-12)(JP)(GS)
29. red body, white base, gray interior & skis, amber windows, "Fire Dept." tempa, white blades, Macau casting ($2-4)(TC)
30. white body, lemon base, gray interior & skis, amber windows, "Fire Dept." tempa, Thailand casting ($2-3)(MP)
31. black body, black base, gray interior & skis, amber windows, "Air Car" tempa, Thailand casting ($2-3)(CY)
32. white body, black base, gray interior & skis, amber windows, "Rescue" tempa, Thailand casting ($2-3)(MC)
33. white body, yellow base, lime interior & skis, amber windows, "123456" tempa, blue & yellow blades, Macau casting ($6-8)(LL)
34. white body, yellow base, lime interior & skis, amber windows, "123456" tempa, blue & yellow blades, Thailand casting ($6-8)(LL)
35. red body, white base, gray interior & skis, amber windows, "Red Rebels" tempa, white blades, Thailand casting ($1-2)(MC)
36. red body, white base, gray interior & skis, clear windows, "Royal Air Force" tempa, Thailand casting ($2-3)(MC)
37. red body, white base, gray interior & skis, amber windows, "Fire Dept." tempa, white blades, Thailand casting ($1-2)(MP)
38. white body, florescent orange base, gray interior & skis, amber windows, "Air Rescue 10" & "IC" logo tempa, Thailand casting ($10-15)(IC)
39. red body, white base, white interior & skis, blue windows, "Fire Dept." tempa, white blades, Thailand casting ($1-2)(MP)
40. white body, fluorescent orange base, silver-gray interior & skis, blue windows, blue checkers tempa, Thailand casting ($1-2)(EM)
41. white body, red base, silver-gray interior & skis, blue windows, "Aerobatic Team" tempa, Thailand casting ($2-4)(MP)
42. white body, red base, silver-gray interior & skis, blue windows, "Fire Rescue" tempa, China casting ($1-2)(AV)(AP)
43. red body, white base, white interior & skis, blue windows, gray blades, "Fire Dept." tempa, China casting ($1-2)
44. white body, red base, black interior & skis, amber windows, "Fire Dept." tempa, China casting ($1-2)(MW29)
45. red body, white base, white interior & skis, blue windows, gray blades, "Airways Tours" tempa, China casting ($1-2)(MP)
46. metallic gold body, white base, white interior & skis, blue windows, no tempa, China casting ($5-10)(CH)
47. white body, black base, black interior & skis, amber windows, "Newscam/ News 8" tempa, China casting ($2-4)(RT)
48. red body, red base, black interior & skis, amber windows, "Fire Dept." tempa, China casting ($1-2)(MP)
49. white body, orange base, silver-gray interior & skis, blue windows, "Police" tempa, white blades, China casting ($2-4)(AV)

MB75-E FERRARI TESTAROSSA, issued 1986
1. red body & base, black interior, clear windows, 8 dot wheels, "Ferrari" logo tempa, Macau casting ($1-2)
2. black body & base, black interior, clear windows, starburst wheels, silver with logo tempa, Macau casting ($3-5)(SF)
3. metallic pearly silver body & base, black interior, clear windows, laser wheels, gold with logos tempa, Macau casting ($3-5)(LW)
4. yellow body, black base, no interior, dark blue modified windows, starburst wheels, red/blue/yellow tempa, Macau casting, includes plastic armament ($5-8)(RB)
5. yellow body & base, black interior, clear windows, 8 dot wheels, "9 Rabbit Racing Team" tempa, Macau casting ($8-12)(HK)
6. metallic red body & base, black interior, clear windows, laser wheels, silver with logos tempa, Macau casting ($3-5)(LW)
7. orange-red body, black base, black interior, clear windows, 8 dot wheels, "Ferrari" logo tempa, Macau casting ($3-4)(SCC)
8. dark red body, black base, black interior, clear windows, 8 dot wheels, "Ferrari" logo tempa, Macau casting ($3-4)(SC)
9. orange body, black base, black interior, clear windows, 8 dot wheels, "Ferrari" logo tempa, Macau casting ($3-4)(SC)
10. rose red body, black base, black interior, clear windows, 8 dot wheels, "Ferrari" logo tempa, Macau casting ($3-4)(SC)
11. red body & base, black interior, clear windows, 8 dot wheels, "Redoxon" tempa, Macau casting ($20-35)(HK)
12. red body & base, black interior, chrome windows, gray disc w/rubber tires, detailed trim tempa, Macau casting ($5-8)(WC)
13. red body, lime base, lime interior, clear windows, 8 dot yellow wheels with blue hubs, "1" with face & checkered flag tempa, Macau casting ($6-8)(LL)
14. red body & base, black interior, clear windows, 8 dot wheels, "Ferrari" logo tempa, Thailand casting ($1-2)
15. red body & base, black interior, chrome windows, gray disc w/rubber tires, detailed trim tempa, Thailand casting ($5-8)(WC)
16. white body & base, black interior, chrome windows, gray disc w/rubber tires, detailed trim tempa, Thailand casting ($5-8)(WC)
17. red body & base, black interior, clear windows, starburst wheels, silver with logos tempa, Macau casting ($8-12)(SF)
18. red body & base, black interior, clear windows, 8 dot wheels, "Ferrari" logo tempa, China casting ($1-2)
19. white body & base, black interior, clear windows, 8 dot wheels, no tempa, China casting ($10-15)(GF)
20. red body & base, black interior, clear windows, 8 dot wheels, "Lloyds/ Ferrari" tempa, China casting ($7-10)(UK)
21. red body & base, black interior, clear windows, 8 dot wheels, "Ferrari" logo (all yellow background) tempa, China casting ($1-2)
22. red body & base, black interior, clear windows, 8 dot wheels, small "Ferrari" logo & painted tail lights tempa, Thailand casting ($2-3)(SS)
23. fluorescent yellow body & base, black interior, clear windows, gold 6 spoke spiral wheels, black stripes & pink flash tempa, Thailand casting ($1-2)
24. red body & base, black interior, clear windows, gold 6 spoke spiral wheels, all yellow background "Ferrari" logo tempa, Thailand casting ($2-3)
25. metallic blue body & base, black interior, clear windows, silver 6 spoke spiral wheels, small "Ferrari" logo tempa, Thailand casting ($2-4)(CC)
26. metallic red body & base, black interior, clear windows, silver 6 spoke spiral wheels, no tempa, Thailand casting ($1-2)(MP)
27. florescent yellow body & base, black interior, clear windows, silver 6 spoke spiral wheels, black stripes & pink flash tempa, Thailand casting ($1-2)
NOTE: Some versions of this model are packaged in blisterpacks as #78 in error ($1-2)
28. red body & base, black interior, clear windows, silver 6 spoke spiral wheels, "Ferrari" logo tempa, Thailand casting ($3-5)
29. silver-gray body & base, black & red interior, clear windows, chrome disc w/rubber tires, detailed trim tempa, Thailand casting ($18-25)(GC)
30. black body & base, black & red interior, clear windows, chrome disc with rubber tires, detailed trim tempa, Thailand casting ($3-5)(PC10)
31. yellow body & base, black & red interior, clear windows, chrome disc with rubber tires, detailed trim tempa, Thailand casting ($3-5)(PC2-ROW)
32. red body & base, black & red interior, clear windows, chrome disc with rubber tires, detailed trim tempa, Thailand casting ($3-5)(PC19)
33. white body, white plastic base, brown & black interior, clear windows, 5 spoke concave star wheels, "Miami Vice" tempa, China casting ($4-6)(STR)

MB75-G FERRARI F50, issued 1996 (USA)
MB21-H FERRARI F50, issued 1996 (ROW)
NOTE: All models with clear windows, black base & China casting unless otherwise noted.
1. red body, black interior, 6 spoke spiral wheels, "Ferrari" logo tempa ($1-2)
2. metallic gold body, black interior, 6 spoke spiral wheels, no tempa ($10-15)(CH)
3. red body, black interior, 5 spoke concave star wheels, "Ferrari F50" & yellow/ white stripes tempa ($1-2)(MP)
4. red body, black interior, 5 spoke concave star wheels, "Ferrari" logo tempa ($2-3)
5. red body, black interior, chrome disc with rubber tires, detailed trim tempa ($8-12)(UC)
6. rose red body, black interior, 5 spoke concave star wheels, "Go Swans!

1997" tempa ($3-5)(AU)
7. lemon body, black interior, 5 spoke concave star wheels, small "Ferrari" logo tempa ($1-2)
8. black body, dark red interior, 5 spoke concave star wheels, small "Ferrari" logo tempa ($1-2)(MW59)
9. silver-gray body, black & red interior, chrome disc with rubber tires, detailed trim tempa ($3-5)(PC15)
10. yellow body, black & red interior, chrome disc with rubber tires, detailed trim tempa ($3-5)(TRU)

MB76-A MAZDA RX7, issued 1981 (USA)(AU)
1. light green body, no tempa ($15-20)(AU)
2. blue body, no tempa ($2-4)(US-Speedsticks)
3. blue body, black stripe "RX7" tempa ($20-30)(US)
4. blue body, red & white stripes tempa ($4-8)(US)(LE) (issued as "Boulevard Blaster")

MB77-A TOYOTA CELICA XX, issued 1981 (USA)(AU)
1. red body, no tempa ($3-5)(AU) & (US-Speedsticks)
2. red body, "Sunburner" tempa ($4-8)(US)(LE) (issued as "Sunburner Celica")

MB78-A FAIRLADY Z, issued 1981 (USA)(AU)
1. black body, no tempa ($2-4)(AU)(US-Speedsticks)
2. black body, "Z" tempa ($4-8)(US)(LE) (issued as "Phantom Z")
3. pearly white body, no tempa ($15-20)(AU)

MB79-A GALANT ETERNA, issued 1981 (USA)(AU)
1. light green body, no tempa ($2-4) (AU)(US-Speedsticks)
2. dark green body, no tempa ($2-4) (AU)(US-Speedsticks)
3. light green body, cream & red "Hot Points" tempa ($4-8)(US)(LE) (issued as "Hot Points Challenger")
4. light green body, white & red "Hot Points" tempa ($4-8)(US)(LE) (issued as "Hot Points Challenger")

MB-2 SAVANNA RX-7, issued 1979 (JP)
1. green body, stripe & "RX7" tempa, Japan casting ($15-20)(JP)
2. yellow body, stripe & "RX7" tempa, Japan casting ($15-20)(JP)

MB-5 FAIRLADY Z, issued 1979 (JP)
1. red body, dot dash wheels, Japan casting ($15-20)(JP)
2. pearly silver body, dot dash wheels, Japan casting ($15-20)(JP)

MB J-21 TOYOTA CELICA XX, issued 1979 (JP)
1. cream body, Japan casting, "J-21" cast on base ($15-20)(JP)
2. red body, Japan casting, "J-21" cast on base ($15-20)(JP)

MB J-22 GALANT ETERNA, issued 1979 (JP)
1. red body, Japan casting, "J-22" cast on base ($15-20)(JP)
2. yellow body, Japan casting, "J-22" cast on base ($15-20)(JP)

NOTE: As of the end of 1996, the following models were not included in the normal 1-75 range. Some of these were promotional castings offered through White Rose Collectibles. These are identified with MB or WR frame numbers, while others were offered through the Farming series and Two Packs.

MB215 CHEVY PANEL VAN, issued 1995 (USA)
NOTE: This is a smaller size than the MB245 Chevy Panel Van, notably marked by a rear bumper that is omitted on the larger casting. All models with clear windows, 8 dot wheels, black base & Thailand casting unless otherwise noted.
1. metallic red body & chassis, "American Iron Cruise 95" tempa ($12-18)(US)
2. metallic green body, black chassis, "Seasons Greetings-Matchbox Collectors Club 1995" tempa ($8-12)(US)
3. florescent orange body & chassis, "Matchbox Get In The Fast Lane-Hershey Convention 1996" tempa ($8-12)(US)
4. purple body, black chassis, "Continental Aero" tempa ($10-15)(US)
5. metallic green body, black chassis, "American Iron Cruise 1998" tempa ($15-20)(C2)

MB217 D.I.R.T. MODIFIED, issued 1992 (WR)
1. powder blue body, red interior, chrome base, "White Rose Collectibles 1" tempa, Thailand casting ($60-75)(WR)
2. orange-yellow body, red interior, chrome base, "7X Turbo Blue" tempa, Thailand casting ($5-7)(WR)
3. orange-yellow body, blue interior, blue base, "91 Wheels" tempa, Thailand casting ($5-7)(WR)
4. orange & white body, red interior, chrome base, "9 Kinney" tempa, Thailand casting ($5-7)(WR)
5. red body, red interior, chrome base, "72 Auto Palace" tempa, Thailand casting ($5-7)(WR)
6. brown body, black interior, chrome base, "1 Phil's Chevrolet" tempa, Thailand casting ($5-7)(WR)
7. white body, red interior, chrome base, "6 Freightliner" tempa, Thailand casting ($5-7)(WR)
8. white body, red interior, chrome base, "1 Steak Out Restaurants" tempa, Thailand casting ($6-8)(WR)
9. blue body, red interior, chrome base, "35" tempa, Thailand casting ($6-8)(WR)
10. orange & yellow body, orange interior, chrome base, "12 BR Dewitt" tempa, Thailand casting ($6-8)(WR)
11. dark blue & white body, red interior, chrome base, "74 Smith Brothers" tempa, Thailand casting ($6-8)(WR)
12. white body, black interior, chrome base, "14 R.P. LeFrois" tempa, Thailand casting ($6-8)(WR)
13. white & black body, red interior, chrome base, "115 Doherty Bros." tempa, Thailand casting ($6-8)(WR)
14. red, white & black body, black interior, chrome base, "21 Alfair Studio" tempa, Thailand casting ($6-8)(WR)
15. white & orange body, blue interior, chrome base, "44 Pontiac/Kneisel Race Cars" tempa, Thailand casting ($6-8)(WR)

MB236 FORD TRACTOR, issued 1993 (FM)
1. blue body, red scoop, light yellow interior, pearly silver base, gray hubs with black tires, Thailand casting ($3-5)(FM)

MB237 TRACTOR SHOVEL, issued 1993 (FM)
NOTE: Although cast No.29 on the base, the frame number "MB237" is cast on the forks which makes this into a new model.
1. red body, red scoop, gray arms, black base, black interior/motor, no tempa, Thailand casting ($3-5)(FM)

MB262 CHRYSLER VOYAGER, issued 1994 (BE)
NOTE: This is a modified casting of the MB68E/64E Dodge Caravan.
1. blue body & side door, chrome base, 8 spoke wheels, detailed trim tempa, Thailand casting ($15-18)(BE)
NOTE: Roof label lettering can read in either direction
2. blue body & side door, chrome base, detailed trim tempa & "Kipling" roof label, 8 spoke wheels, Thailand casting ($15-18)(BE)

NOTE: MB267, MB268 & MB269 are new castings and are much larger than their previous counterparts at MB54H, MB7G and MB35I respectively
.

MB267 CHEVY LUMINA, issued 1994 (WR)
NOTE: All models below with clear windows, black disc rubber tires (Goodyear unless noted) & China casting.
1. white & dark blue body, black interior, "White Rose Series II in '94" tempa ($4-6)(WR)
2. white/powder blue/dark blue body, black interior, "White Rose Collectibles 94" tempa ($25-35)(WR)
3. metallic blue & orange body, silver-gray interior, "Dupont 24/1993 Rookie of the Year" tempa ($3-5)(WR)
4. orange & white body, gray interior, "Kodak Funsaver 4" tempa ($3-5)(WR)
5. dark blue & yellow body, black interior, Hoosier tires, "Matchbox-White Rose Collectibles 29" tempa ($3-5)(WR)
6. fluorescent lime body, black interior, white lettered "Manheim Auctions 7" tempa ($3-5)(WR)
7. red & yellow body, black interior, "Kellogg's Corn Flakes 5" tempa ($3-5)(WR)
8. white body, black interior, Hoosier tires, "Baltimore Colts 29" tempa ($18-25)(WR)
9. yellow body, gray interior, "Pic N Pay/Shoe World 32" tempa ($8-12)(WR)
10. yellow-orange body, black interior, "Kodak 4" tempa ($3-5)(WR)
11. red body, gray interior, "Fiddle Faddle 34" tempa ($3-5)(WR)
12. white/gray/black body, gray interior, Hoosier tires, "Western Auto 17" tempa ($3-5)(WR)
13. gold plated body, red interior, "Six Time Champion 3 Dale Earnhardt" tempa ($18-25)(WR)
14. red & yellow body, black interior, yellow disc wheels, "Kellogg's Corn Flakes 5" tempa ($4-6)(WR)(TC)
15. gray body, red interior, "Kellogg's 5" tempa ($4-6)(WR)(TC)
16. fluorescent lime body, black interior, Hoosier tires, "Manheim Auctions 7" (black letters) tempa ($4-6)(WR)(TC)
17. fluorescent lime body, black interior, lime disc wheels, "Manheim Auctions 7" (white letters) tempa ($4-6)(WR)(TC)
18. orange body, gray interior, "Polaroid 46" tempa ($18-25)(WR)
19. white & blue body, gray interior, "AC-Delco 52" tempa ($3-5)(WR)
20. black & yellow body, red interior, "Meineke 41" tempa ($4-5)(WR)
21. black body, gray interior, "Stanley 92" tempa ($4-5)(WR)
22. gold plated body, gray interior, "Lifetime Achievement Award-Harry Gant" tempa ($20-25)(WR)
23. yellow body, gray interior, "DeWalt 08" tempa ($4-5)(WR)(TM)
24. metallic blue body, gray interior, "Dupont Automotive Finishes 2" tempa ($3-5)(WR)
25. red body, gray interior, "Detroit Gasket/MGM Brake 70" tempa ($3-5)(WR)
26. black & orange-yellow body, red interior, "Caterpillar 95" tempa ($3-5)(WR)
27. pink red & yellow body, gray interior, "Lipton Tea 74" tempa ($3-5)(WR)
28. blue-green & purple body, gray interior, "Vermont Teddy Bear" tempa ($3-5)(WR)
29. orange-red & white body, gray interior, "Tracey Lawrence/Yamaha 1" tempa ($8-12)(WR)
30. white body, gray interior, "Luxaire 99" tempa ($3-5)(WR)
31. gold plated body, red interior, "7 Time Champion 3" tempa ($20-25)(WR)
32. purple body, black interior, "Kandi & Steve/ October 1, 1994" tempa ($250-500)(WR)
33. white body, black interior, "Diecast Digest 01" tempa ($3-5)(WR)
34. cream body, gray interior, "December 10, 1994/ Steph & Mike/ The Desenberg's" ($250-500)(WR)

MB268 FORD THUNDERBIRD, issued 1994 (WR)
NOTE: Below models with clear windows, black disc rubber tires Goodyear, China casting unless noted otherwise
1. blue body, gray interior, "Factory Stores of America 75" tempa ($3-5)(WR)
2. black body, gray interior, "Winn Dixie 60" tempa ($3-5)(WR)
3. white/red/dark blue body, gray interior, "Valvoline 6/Reese's" tempa ($3-5)(WR)
4. black body, gray interior, "Ford Motorsports 2" tempa ($3-5)(WR)
5. metallic blue & white body, gray interior, "Family Channel 16" tempa ($3-5)(WR)
6. green body, gray interior, "Quaker State 26" tempa ($3-5)(WR)
7. black body, gray interior, "Petron Plus 55" tempa ($15-20)(WR)
8. black body, gray interior, "Exide Batteries 7" tempa ($3-5)(WR)
9. metallic blue & powder blue body, gray interior, "Quality Care 15" tempa ($3-5)(WR)
10. black body, gray interior, "Fingerhut 98" tempa ($3-5)(WR)
11. white body, gray interior, Hoosier tires, "Hooters 19" tempa ($3-5)(WR)
12. metallic blue body, gray interior, Hoosier tires, "Raybestos 8" tempa ($3-5)(WR)
13. yellow & purple body, gray interior, "Smokin' Joe 23" tempa, sealed in plexibox with yellow base stand ($20-25)(WR)
14. yellow & purple body, black interior, "Smokin' Joe 23" tempa, sealed in plexibox with purple base stand ($20-25)(WR)
15. red body, red interior, "McDonald's 94" tempa ($3-5)(WR)
16. green body, gray interior, "Quaker State 26" tempa ($3-5)(WR)
17. black & pink body, gray interior, "Fingerhut 98" tempa ($3-5)(WR)
18. black body, black interior, "McDonald's/Batman Forever 94" tempa ($10-15)(WR)
19. gold plated body, red interior, "1994 Rookie of The Year-8 Jeff Burton" tempa ($20-25)(WR)
20. bright blue & yellow body, gray interior, "Lowe's 11" tempa ($3-5)(WR)
21. turquoise & black body, gray interior, "Heilig-Meyers 90" tempa ($3-5)(WR)
22. black body, gray interior, "Exide Batteries 7" tempa ($3-5)(WR)
23. gold plated body, red interior, "1994 Most Popular Driver-Bill Elliot" tempa ($20-25)(WR)
24. blue & white body, gray interior, "Raybestos 8" tempa ($3-5)(WR)
25. white & dark blue body, gray interior, "Valvoline/Cummins 6" tempa ($3-5)(WR)
26. multi-color body, black interior, "Mane N Tail/Straight Arrow 12" tempa ($3-5)(WR)
27. black body, red interior, "Havoline 28" tempa ($3-5)(WR)
28. blue & orange body, gray interior, "Purex Dial 40" tempa ($3-5)(WR)
29. black body, black interior, "Burn Foundation/Motorsports 96" tempa ($7-10)(US)
30. blue body, black interior, "Kleenex 40" tempa ($3-5)(WR)
31. blue body, gray interior, slicks, "Kleenex 40" tempa ($10-15)(WR)
32. red & orange body, gray interior, "Citgo 21" tempa ($3-5)(WR)
33. purple body, red interior, "K-Mart/Little Caesars 37" tempa ($3-5)(WR)
34. orange body, black interior, Hoosier tires, "White Rose Collectibles 00" tempa ($10-15)(WR)
35. blue body, gray interior, "New Holland 94" tempa ($3-5)(WR)
36. black body, gray interior, "Exide 99" tempa ($3-5)(WR)

MB269 GRAND PRIX PONTIAC, issued 1994 (WR)
NOTE: Following models with clear windows, black disc rubber tires Goodyear, China casting unless noted otherwise
1. yellow/black & red/blue body, black interior, "Black Flag 43/French's 43" tempa ($35-40)(WR)
2. black body, black interior, "Black Flag 43" tempa ($3-5)(WR)
3. black body, gray interior, "Kendall 40" tempa ($3-5)(WR)
4. yellow body, black interior, "French's 43" tempa ($3-5)(WR)
5. yellow body, yellow interior & wheels, "Pennzoil 30" tempa ($3-5)(WR)
6. blue body, black interior, "Richard Petty Pit Tour 43" tempa ($10-15)(WR)
7. dark blue & white body, black interior, "Cobra 24" tempa ($10-15)(WR)
8. metallic blue & pink body, black interior, "Coors Light 42" tempa, sealed in plexibox with silver-gray stand ($20-25)(WR)
9. light blue body, gray interior, "USA Bobsled Team 43" tempa ($10-15)(WR)
10. silver-gray, metallic blue & pink body, black interior, "Coors Light 42" tempa, sealed in plexibox with white stand ($20-25)(WR)
11. red body, gray interior, "Hulkster 43" tempa ($6-8)(WR)(TC)

MB283 CHEVY MONTE CARLO, issued 1995 (WR)
NOTE: Below models with black base, clear windows, Goodyear rubber tires & China casting unless noted.
1. florescent pink body, black interior, "Matchbox 1995/1" tempa ($85-125)(US)
2. florescent yellow body, black interior, "Matchbox 1995/1" tempa ($85-125)(US)
NOTE: Above two models used as raffle prizes at the 1995 Hershey, PA convention
3. yellow & red body, black interior, "Kellogg's 5" tempa ($3-5)(WR)
4. red body, gray interior, "Lipton Tea 74" tempa ($3-5)(WR)
5. orange-yellow body, black interior, "Dewalt 1" tempa ($3-5)(WR)
6. black body, black interior, "Goodwrench 3" tempa ($3-5)(WR)
7. blue & white body, black interior, "Hyde Tools 08" tempa ($3-5)(WR)
8. purplish & yellow body, black interior, "Burger King 87" tempa ($3-5)(WR)
9. blue & white body, black interior, "Bell South Mobility 87" tempa ($10-15)(WR)
10. white body, black interior, "The Budget Gourmet" tempa ($3-5)(WR)
11. red body, black interior, "Budweiser 25" tempa, sealed in plexibox ($20-25)(WR)
12. green & black body, gray interior, "Interstate Batteries" tempa ($3-5)(WR)
13. metallic blue & florescent orange body, gray interior, "Dupont 24" tempa ($3-5)(WR)
14. black body, red interior, yellow wheel hubs, "Caterpillar/Cat 95" tempa

($6-8)(WR)(TC)
15. blue body, red interior, "Lance Snacks 43" tempa ($3-5)(WR)
16. gold plated body, black interior, "1995 Rookie of The Year-Ricky Craven 41" tempa ($20-25)(WR)
17. gold plated body, gray interior, "1995 Champion-Lipton Tea 74" tempa ($20-25)(WR)
18. orange-yellow body, black interior, "Kodak Film 4" tempa ($3-5)(WR)
19. red & yellow body, gray interior, "Royal Oak Charcoal 34" tempa ($3-5)(WR)
20. mid blue body, black interior, "Channellock 10" tempa ($3-5)(WR)
21. gold plated body, gray interior, "Dupont 95 Points Champion" tempa ($20-25)(WR)
22. orange-yellow body, black interior, "Caterpillar/Cat 95" tempa ($3-5)(WR)
23. white & green body, gray interior, "Kodiak 41" tempa, sealed in plexibox ($20-25)(WR)
24. black & orange-yellow body, black interior, "Burger King 87" tempa ($7-10)(WR)
25. blue/white/red body, gray interior, "Lance Snacks 43" tempa ($3-5)(WR)
26. black body, red interior, "Hype 88" tempa ($3-5)(WR)
27. red body, black interior, "Budweiser 25" tempa, sealed in glass bottle ($25-35)(WR)
28. blue/ white/ dark rose, black interior, "White Rose Collectibles 96" tempa ($8-12)(WR)
29. lemon & red body, black interior, "Kellogg's Corn Flakes 5" tempa ($3-5)(WR)
30. gold plated body, black interior, "Kellogg's Corn Flakes 5/ 1996 Champion" tempa ($20-25)(WR)
31. dark blue/ silver-gray/ pale yellow body, gray interior, "Coors Light 40" tempa, sealed in glass bottle ($25-35)(WR)
32. black & orange-yellow body, red interior, "Caterpillar 96" tempa ($3-5)(WR)
33. blue body, gray interior, "Fina 74" tempa ($3-5)(WR)
34. gold plated body, gray interior, "Fina 74- 1996 Champion" ($20-25)(WR)
35. green & white body, gray interior, "Skoal 33" tempa, sealed in plexibox with Convoy ($25-35)(WR)

MB284 CHEVROLET SUPER TRUCK, issued 1995 (WR)
NOTE: Below models with clear windows, Goodyear rubber tires, black base & China casting unless noted otherwise.
1. black body, black interior, "Goodwrench 3" tempa ($3-5)(WR)
2. black body, black interior, "Sears Diehard 1" tempa ($3-5)(WR)
3. white, blue & red body, red interior, "Total 6" tempa ($3-5)(WR)
4. gold plated body, red interior, "3-1995 Super Truck Champion" tempa ($20-25)(WR)
5. black body, blue-green interior, "The Magic Mile 96" tempa ($7-10)(WR)
6. grape body, gray interior, "Westview Capital 33" tempa ($3-5)(WR)
7. grape body, gray interior, "Manheim Auctions 33" tempa ($3-5)(WR)
8. blue/ white/ red body, red interior, "Lance Snacks 43" tempa ($3-5)(WR)
9. metallic blue & orange body, red interior, "Dupont 24" tempa ($3-5)(WR)

MB285 ICE MAKER, issued 1995 (WR)
1. red lower body, white upper body, chrome wheels, black groomer, blue driver, "White Rose collectibles-No. 1 In Sports 1995" tempa ($75-100)(WR)
NOTE: The 1995 Hockey series models had bases altered from "Matchbox" to "White Rose Collectibles," however a small quantity (1-5) of each were found with "Matchbox" still cast on the base. Because of this rarity there is no firm $ value on these as most belong in private collections and none have been offered on the market. Those teams reported include Hartford Whalers, Chicago Blackhawks, New York Rangers, Philadelphia Flyers, Toronto Mapleleafs, Ottawa Senators, Detroit Redwings, San Jose Sharks, Washington Capitals & Tampa Bay Lightning. Others may exist but have not been reported.

MB315 VOLVO TRUCK, issued 1997 (AP/AV)
1. blue body, black stakes, tan load, amber windows, 5 arch wheels, black base, "MB Builders" tempa, China casting ($3-4)(AP)
2. blue-green body, clear aquarium load, smoke windows, 5 arch wheels, silver-gray base, dolphin & waves tempa, China casting ($3-4)(AV)

MB318 FORD CARGO SKIP TRUCK, issued 1997
1. light beige body, black cage, black base & arms (with lever), green stripes tempa, China casting ($2-4)(AV)(AP)
2. bright green body, black cage, black base & arms (with lever), dark green camouflage & "The Lost World" tempa, China casting ($5-8)(JR)
3. red body, silver-gray cage, silver-gray base & arms (with lever), "Big Top Circus" tempa, China casting ($2-4)(AV)

MB319 MERCEDES AAV, issued 1997 (JR)
1. light green body, light gray base (without base name), black painted windows, turret with arms on roof, "The Lost World" & green camouflage tempa ($5-8)(JR)

MB331 UNIMOG, issued 1997
1. bright green body, silver-gray base & plow, no plow stripes, amber windows, black stake bed, "The Lost World" tempa, black hubs, Thailand casting includes metal dinosaur ($5-8)(JR)

MB337 MERCEDES AAV, issued 1997 (JR)
1. light green body, light gray base (with base name), black painted windows, luggage rack on roof, "The Lost World" & green camouflage tempa ($5-8)(JR)

MB338 1938 DODGE AIRFLOW VAN, issued 1998 (CL)
1. mustard body, black roof, chassis & base, gold wheels & grille, "Catamount Porter" tempa ($8-12)(MB)
2. red body & roof, green-gold chassis, black base, gold wheels & grille, "Penn Brewery St. Nikolaus Bock Bier" tempa ($8-12)(MB)
3. lemon body & roof, pale green chassis, black base, gold wheels & grille, "Zephyr Golden Ale" tempa ($8-12)(MB)

MB339 1937 MACK JUNIOR VAN, issued 1998 (CL)
1. dark green body, light lime chassis, black base, silver wheels & grille, "Arapahoe Amber Ale" tempa ($8-12)(MB)
2. black body, salmon pink chassis, black base, silver wheels & grille, "Dixie Jazz Beer" tempa ($8-12)(MB)
3. lemon body, red chassis, black base, gold wheels & grille, "Pony Express" tempa ($8-12)(MB)

NOTE: Models MB343 through MB350 were originally Hot Wheel castings and were retooled into Matchbox castings. MB349 was to have been the retooled Hot Wheel Peterbilt Dump Truck but this was changed to include the MB30-E Peterbilt Quarry Truck in the Caterpillar series instead.

MB343 EXCAVATOR, issued 1998
1. orange-yellow body & plastic arm, black treads, yellow base, "CAT" tempa ($3-4)(CT)

MB344 DUMP TRUCK, issued 1998
1. orange yellow cab, dump & base, "Caterpillar" tempa, yellow hubs ($3-4)(CT)

MB345 BULLDOZER, issued 1998
1. orange-yellow body, blade & arms, yellow plastic base, black treads, "CAT" tempa ($3-4)(CT)

MB346 WHEEL LOADER, issued 1998
1. orange-yellow body & base, yellow plastic bucket, yellow hubs, "CAT" tempa ($3-4)(CT)

MB347 ROAD ROLLER, issued 1998
1. orange-yellow body, black rollers & base, "Caterpillar" tempa ($3-4)(CT)

MB348 SCRAPER, issued 1998
1. orange-yellow plastic cab & rear, orange-yellow metal mid section, yellow hubs, "CAT" tempa ($3-4)(CT)

MB350 MOTOR GRADER, issued 1998
1. orange-yellow plastic body, orange-yellow metal base, 8 spoke wheels, "Caterpillar" tempa ($3-4)(CT)

MB351 CHALLENGER AG TRACTOR, issued 1998
1. orange-yellow body, yellow plastic roof, smoke green windows, black base, wheels & treads, "CAT" tempa ($3-4)(CT)

MB352 TRAILER, issued 1998
1. orange-yellow plastic body, orange-yellow metal chassis, yellow wheels, black treads ($3-4)(CT)

MB353 BACKHOE/ LOADER, issued 1998
1. orange-yellow body, yellow-orange plastic shovel, arms, backhoe & wheels, "CAT" tempa ($3-4)(CT)

MB354 SOIL COMPACTOR, issued 1998
1. orange-yellow body, orange-yellow plastic grader & base, smoke green windows, yellow studded wheels, "CAT" tempa ($3-4)(CT)

MB388 PETERBILT DUMP TRUCK W/PLOW, issued 1998
1. orange-yellow body, orange-yellow dump, chrome plated base & plow, "CAT" tempa, clear windows, 8 spoke wheels, China casting ($3-5)(PS)

MB710 TIPPING TRAILER, issued 1993 (FM)
1. red plastic bed, silver-gray chassis, black tailgate, gray wheels with black plastic tires ($2-4)(FM)

MB711 FARM TRAILER, issued 1993 (FM)
1. yellow stake body, silver-gray base, gray wheels with black plastic tires ($2-4)(FM)

MB712 SEEDER, issued 1993 (FM)
1. green body, yellow wheels, silver-gray spreader, black tires ($2-4)(FM)

MB713 ROTOVATOR, issued 1993 (FM)
1. blue body, gray rotors ($2-4)(FM)

MB720 SIDE TIPPER, issued 1977 (TP)
1. yellow body, black base, red tipper, black wheels, no tempa, England casting ($2-4)(TP)
2. yellow body, black base, black tipper, black wheels, no tempa, England casting ($3-5)(TP)
3. yellow body, black base, red tipper, black wheels, no tempa, Macau casting ($2-4)(TP)
4. blue body, red base, yellow tipper, blue wheels, "4567/ABCD" tempa, Macau casting ($6-8)(LL)
5. yellow body, black base, red tipper, black wheels, no tempa, China casting ($2-4)(TP)

MB791 MOTORCYCLE TRAILER, issued 1979
1. blue body, lemon cycles, 5 spoke center cut wheels, England casting ($2-4)(TP)
2. blue body, yellow cycles, 5 spoke center cut wheels, England casting ($2-4)(TP)
3. red body, yellow cycles, 5 spoke center cut wheels, England casting ($2-4)(TP)
4. yellow body, black cycles, 5 spoke center cut wheels, England casting ($2-4)(TP)
5. yellow body, dark green cycles, 5 spoke center cut wheels, England casting ($15-20)(TP)
6. yellow body, yellow cycles, dot dash wheels, England casting ($7-10)
NOTE: versions 5 & 6 found as single boxed releases in the US.
7. yellow body, red cycles, dot dash wheels, England casting ($2-4)(TP)
8. yellow body, red cycles, dot dash wheels, Macau casting ($2-4)(TP)
9. yellow body, red cycles, dot dash wheels, no origin cast ($2-4)(TP)
10. beige body, black cycles, dot dash wheels, no origin cast ($2-4)(TP)
11. pearly silver body, black cycles, dot dash wheels, no origin cast ($2-4)(TP)
12. black body, dark red cycles, dot dash wheels, no origin cast ($1-2)(MP)
13. black body, dark red cycles, dot dash wheels, China casting ($1-2)(MP)

MB792 CATTLE TRAILER, issued 1979 (TP)
NOTE: All models with black wheels and silver hubs unless otherwise noted.
1. red body, light beige stakes, black cows, England casting ($2-4)(TP)
2. red body, dark beige stakes, black cows, England casting ($2-4)(TP)
3. red body, dark beige stakes, brown cows, England casting ($2-4)(TP)
4. yellow body, chocolate stakes, coffee cows, England casting ($2-4)(TP)
5. red body, orange-yellow stakes, black cows, England casting ($2-4)(TP)
6. yellow body, chocolate stakes, red-brown cows, England casting ($2-4)(TP)
7. yellow body, chocolate stakes, coffee cows, Macau casting ($2-4)(TP)
8. powder blue body, chocolate stakes, black cows, no origin cast ($2-4)(TP)
9. yellow body, chocolate stakes, coffee cows, no origin cast ($2-4)(TP)
10. green body, yellow stakes, black cows, no origin cast ($2-4)(TP)
11. red body, yellow stakes, blue wheels with yellow hubs, no cows, no origin cast ($6-8)(LL)

MB793 INFLATABLE, issued 1984 (TP)
1. orange deck, white hull & seats, black motor, no tempa, England casting; black trailer with no tempa, England casting ($2-4)(TP)
2. orange deck, white hull & seats, black motor, blue "SR" tempa, England casting; black trailer with no tempa, England casting ($2-4)(TP)
3. orange body, white hull & seats, black motor, red "SR" tempa, England casting; black trailer with no tempa, England casting ($2-4)(TP)
4. lemon deck, white hull & seats, black motor, blue "SR" tempa, England casting; black trailer with no tempa, England casting ($5-8)(TP)
5. red deck, white hull & seats, black motor, blue "SR" tempa, England casting; black trailer with no tempa, England casting ($5-8)(TP)
6. orange deck, white hull & seats, black motor, blue "SR" tempa, Macau casting; black trailer with no tempa, Macau casting ($2-4)(TP)
7. black deck, orange hull & seats, white motor, no tempa, no origin cast; black trailer with "2" tempa, no origin cast ($2-4)(TP)
8. orange deck, black hull & seats, black motor, blue "SR" tempa, no origin cast; black trailer with no tempa, no origin cast ($2-4)(TP)
9. orange deck, black hull & seats, white motor, no tempa, no origin cast; white trailer with dark blue & red stripes tempa, no origin cast ($2-4)(TP)
10. dark blue deck, gray hull & seats, white motor, no tempa, no origin cast; white trailer with blue & red stripes tempa, no origin cast ($2-4)(TP)
11. orange deck, silver-gray hull & seats, white motor, "Rescue" tempa, no origin cast; white trailer with blue anchor tempa, no origin cast ($2-4)(TP)
12. orange deck, black hull & seats, white motor, "R1" tempa, no origin cast; white trailer with "Rescue" & stripes tempa, no origin cast ($2-4)(TP)
13. orange deck, black hull & seats, white motor, anchor emblem tempa, no origin cast; white trailer with black & orange stripe tempa, no origin cast ($2-4)(TP)
14. red deck, yellow hull & seats, black motor, "Red Valley Camp" tempa, no origin cast; black trailer with no tempa, no origin cast ($1-2)(MP)
15. red deck, yellow hull & seats, black motor, "Red Valley Camp" tempa, no origin cast; black trailer with no tempa, China casting ($1-2)(MP)

MB794 GLIDING TRANSPORTER, issued 1976
NOTE: All models with white glider & wings, dot dash wheels.
1. yellow body, light amber canopy, "Gliding Club" labels, England casting ($2-4)(TP)
2. yellow body, dark amber canopy, "Gliding Club" labels, England casting ($2-4)(TP)
3. green body, clear canopy, no labels, England casting ($2-4)(TP)
4. green body, clear canopy, "Seagull Gliding Club" labels, England casting ($2-4)(TP)
5. red body, dark amber canopy, "Gliding Club" labels, England casting ($350-450)(TP)
6. dark green body, dark amber canopy, "Seagull Gliding Club" labels, England casting ($2-4)(TP)
7. red body, clear canopy, "Auto Glide" tempa, no origin cast ($2-4)(TP)
8. dark blue body, clear canopy, yellow stripes tempa, no origin cast ($2-4)(TP)
9. lemon body, clear canopy, purple & pink spatter tempa, no origin cast ($2-4)(TP)

NOTE: In 1996, most of the White Rose castings were no longer issued with

"MB" frame numbers. Each had its own type of identification number.

FS001/WR002 FORD F800 DELIVERY VAN, issued 1995 (WR)
NOTE: Below models with clear windows, chrome disc with rubber tires unless otherwise noted.
1. green body & base, orange-yellow container, "York Fair 1995" tempa ($7-10)(WR)
2. red body, black base, orange-yellow container, "Hulkster/Hogan 43" tempa ($7-10)(WR)(TC)
3. dark blue body, silver-gray base, white container with blue roof, "We Are Penn State 95" tempa ($7-10)(WR)
4. white body, base & container, "UGI Gas Service" tempa ($8-12)(WR)
5. red body & base, white container, "World Series 1995-Atlanta Braves Champs" tempa ($8-12)(WR)
6. blue body & base, white container, "World Series 1995-Atlanta Braves Champs" tempa ($8-12)(WR)
7. red body, gold base & wheels, white container, "All Star Game 1996" tempa ($8-12)(WR)
8. blue body & base, white container, "KC Royals 1996" tempa ($6-8)(WR)
9. blue body & base, white container, "Chicago Cubs 1996" tempa ($6-8)(WR)
10. blue body & base, red container, "Philadelphia Phillies 1996" tempa ($6-8)(WR)
11. dark blue body & base, red container, "Boston Red Sox 1996" tempa ($6-8)(WR)
12. dark blue body & base, red container, "St. Louis Cardinals 1996" tempa ($6-8)(WR)
13. dark blue body & base, orange container, "Detroit Tigers 1996" tempa ($6-8)(WR)
14. dark blue body & base, orange container, "San Diego Padres 1996" tempa ($6-8)(WR)
15. dark blue body & base, gold container, "Milwaukee Brewers 1996" tempa ($6-8)(WR)
16. mid blue body & base, dark blue container, "Toronto Blue Jays 1996" tempa ($6-8)(WR)
17. purple body & base, silver-gray container, "Colorado Rockies 1996" tempa ($6-8)(WR)
18. blue-green body & base, dark blue container, "Seattle Mariners 1996" tempa ($6-8)(WR)
19. black body & base, turquoise container, "Florida Marlins 1996" tempa ($6-8)(WR)
20. black body & base, orange container, "San Francisco Giants 1996" tempa ($6-8)(WR)
21. black body & base, white container, "Chicago White Sox 1996" tempa ($6-8)(WR)
22. orange body & base, blue container, "New York Mets 1996" tempa ($6-8)(WR)
23. orange body & base, black container, "Baltimore Orioles 1996" tempa ($6-8)(WR)
24. red body & base, blue container, "Montreal Expos 1996" tempa ($6-8)(WR)
25. red body & base, blue container, "Atlanta Braves 1996" tempa ($6-8)(WR)
26. red body & base, dark blue container, "Minnesota Twins 1996" tempa ($6-8)(WR)
27. pink-red body & base, dark blue container, "Cleveland Indians 1996" tempa ($6-8)(WR)
28. yellow body & base, black container, "Pittsburgh Pirates 1996" tempa ($6-8)(WR)
29. yellow body & base, green container, "Oakland Athletics 1996" tempa ($6-8)(WR)
30. gold body & base, dark blue container, "Houston Astros 1996" tempa ($6-8)(WR)
31. silver-gray body & base, dark blue container, "California Angels 1996" tempa ($6-8)(WR)
32. light gray body & base, red container, "Texas Rangers 1996" tempa ($6-8)(WR)
33. white body & base, pink-red container, "Cincinnati Reds 1996" tempa ($6-8)(WR)
34. white body & base, blue container, "New York Yankees 1996" tempa ($6-8)(WR)
35. white body & base, blue container, "Los Angeles Dodgers 1996" tempa ($6-8)(WR)
36. green body & base, white container, "Rutters Dairy Celebrates 75 Years" tempa ($15-20)(WR)
37. orange body, black base, white container, "Preston-The 151 Line" tempa ($15-20)(WR)
38. white body, black base, white container, "Cat Racing" tempa ($6-8)(WR)(TC)
39. red body & base, white container, "Bill Elliot/M/10" tempa ($6-8)(WR)(TC)
40. white body, dark gray base, white container, "ABC Sports" tempa ($10-15)(WR)
41. white body, white base, white container, "Quality You Can See-Maple Donuts" tempa ($7-10)(WR)
42. white body, dark blue base, white container, "NY Yankees World Series 1996" tempa ($7-10)(WR)
43. white body, base & container, "All Star Game 1997- Indians" tempa ($6-8)(WR)
44. white body, base & container, "York Daily Record" tempa ($6-8)(WR)
45. blue body, white base & container, "Dutch Valley" tempa ($6-8)(WR)
46. white body, blue base, white container, "American Lung Association" tempa ($7-10)(WR)

FS002 FORD F800 DELIVERY VAN, issued 1996 (WR)
NOTE: This model differs from the FS001/WR002 in that the container overhangs the cab. Below models with clear windows, chrome wheels with rubber tires & China casting unless noted otherwise.
1. beige body, dark brown base, beige container, "York Fair 1996" tempa ($7-10)(WR)
2. metallic silver body, dark blue base, metallic silver container, "Nittany Lions/PSU 1996" tempa ($7-10)(WR)
3. white body, dark blue base, white container with dark blue roof, "Penn State 1996" tempa, blue wheels ($7-10)(WR)
4. blue body, dark blue base, white container, "All Star Game 1997" tempa ($6-8)(WR)

FST FORD SUPER TRUCK, issued 1996 (WR)
NOTE: Below models with clear windows, Goodyear rubber tires, black base & China casting unless otherwise noted.
1. black body, black interior, "Exide 7" tempa ($3-5)(WR)
2. yellow body, yellow interior, "Ortho 21" tempa ($3-5)(WR)
3. white & green body, white interior, "Quaker State 24" tempa ($3-5)(WR)
4. blue & white body, red interior, "Team ASE 2" tempa ($3-5)(WR)
5. white body, white interior, "Larry's Heavenly/Petron Plus 78" tempa ($5-7)(WR)
6. white & red body, red interior, "Remax 6" tempa ($5-7)(WR)

MLB97 PLYMOUTH PROWLER, issued 1997 (WR)
NOTE: Although this model looks exactly like the MB34-G Plymouth Prowler, this is a new casting produced by White Rose Collectibles and the notable difference between the two castings is that the MB34-G has a PLASTIC base whereas this casting has a METAL base. There is no notation cast inside this model to identify this casting with any frame number like standard models. The only discernable catalog reference number is an "MLB97" cast inside box flaps so this will be used to identify this particular model.
NOTE: All models with dark gray interiors with painted dashboards on some versions, clear windshield, 5 spoke concave star wheels & silver-gray metal base.
1. iridescent white body, "Houston Astros 1997" tempa ($4-6)(WR)
2. iridescent white body, "Anaheim Angels 1998" tempa ($4-6)(WR)
3. iridescent white body, "Montreal Expos 1997" tempa ($4-6)(WR)
4. silver-gray body, "Florida Marlins 1997" tempa ($4-6)(WR)
5. silver-gray body, "Seattle Mariners 1997" tempa ($4-6)(WR)
6. silver-gray body, "San Diego Padres 1997" tempa ($4-6)(WR)
7. silver-gray body, New York Yankees 1997" tempa ($4-6)(WR)
8. silver-gray body, "Cleveland Indians 1997" tempa ($4-6)(WR)
9. metallic tan body, "St. Louis Cardinals 1997" tempa ($4-6)(WR)
10. metallic tan body, "Atlanta Braves 1997" tempa ($4-6)(WR)
11. metallic tan body, "Kansas City Royals 1997" tempa ($4-6)(WR)
12. metallic orange body, "Detroit Tigers 1997" tempa ($4-6)(WR)
13. metallic orange body, "New York Mets 1997" tempa ($4-6)(WR)
14. black body, "Baltimore Orioles 1997" tempa ($4-6)(WR)
15. black body, "Chicago White Sox 1997" tempa ($4-6)(WR)
16. black body, "Pittsburgh Pirates 1997" tempa ($4-6)(WR)
17. black body, "San Francisco Giants 1997" tempa ($4-6)(WR)
18. metallic green body, "Oakland A's 1997" tempa ($4-6)(WR)
19. metallic green body, "Milwaukee Brewers 1997" tempa ($4-6)(WR)
20. metallic blue body, "Minnesota Twins 1997" tempa ($4-6)(WR)
21. metallic blue body, "Chicago Cubs 1997" tempa ($4-6)(WR)
22. metallic blue body, "Los Angeles Dodgers 1997" tempa ($4-6)(WR)
23. metallic blue body, "Toronto Blue Jays 1997" tempa ($4-6)(WR)
24. metallic red body, "Boston Red Sox 1997" tempa ($4-6)(WR)
25. metallic red body, "Texas Rangers 1997" tempa ($4-6)(WR)
26. metallic red body, "Philadelphia Phillies 1997" tempa ($4-6)(WR)
27. metallic red body, "Cincinnati Reds 1997" tempa ($4-6)(WR)
28. dark met. purple body, "Colorado Rockies 1997" tempa ($4-6)(WR)
29. metallic purple body, "Tampa Bay Devil Rays Inaugural Season 1998" tempa ($4-6)(WR)
30. metallic purple body, "Arizona Diamondbacks Inaugural Season 1998" tempa ($4-6)(WR)
31. turquoise body, "World Series 1997 Champions Marlins" tempa ($4-6)(WR)
32. turquoise body, "World Series 1997 Champions Marlins" tempa, sealed in bat-shaped glass bottle ($30-45)(WR)

WRP01 1996 PONTIAC GRAND PRIX, issued 1996 (WR)
1. dark green body, clear windows, gray interior, "White Rose Collectibles/ December 25" tempa, China casting ($50-75)(WR)
2. black body, clear windows, gray interior, "MBNA America 72" tempa, China casting ($4-6)(WR)
3. red & blue body, clear windows, gray interior, "Skittles 36/ Starburst" tempa ($4-6)(WR)
4. red body, clear windows, gray interior, "White Rose Collectibles/ Merry Christmas 1997" tempa ($35-50)(WR)

WRP02 1996 FORD THUNDERBIRD, issued 1996 (WR)
NOTE: This model is modified from the MB268, notably the grille & new base casting. Below models with clear windows, black base, Goodyear rubber tires & China casting unless noted otherwise.
1. white & blue body, red interior, "Valvoline 6" tempa ($3-5)(WR)
2. red & white body, red interior, "McDonald's 94" tempa ($3-5)(WR)
3. metallic blue & white body, gray interior, "Family Channel/Primestar 16" tempa ($3-5)(WR)
4. black body, gray interior, "Miller Racing 2" tempa, encased in glass bottle on wooden stand ($50-75)(WR)
5. white body, gray interior, "Jasper/Federal Mogul 77" tempa ($3-5)(WR)
6. blue body, black interior, "Spam 9" tempa ($3-5)(WR)
7. blue body, red interior, "QC Quality Care/Red Carpet Lease 88" tempa ($3-5)(WR)
8. red & white body, red interior & wheels, "McDonald's 94" tempa ($6-8)(WR)(TC)
9. red body, red interior, "McDonald's/Monopoly 94" tempa ($8-12)(WR)
10. orange & blue body, black interior, "Badcock 12" tempa ($8-12)(WR)
11. purple & turquoise body, gray interior, "Hayes Modems 15" tempa ($8-12)(WR)
12. red body, red interior, "McDonald's 94" tempa ($3-5)(WR)
13. blue body, gray interior, "New Holland 94" tempa ($3-5)(WR)
14. orange-yellow body, red interior, "Caterpillar 97" tempa ($3-5)(WR)
15. metallic green body, gray interior, "Remington 75" tempa, sealed in glass bottle ($25-35)(WR)
16. blue body, black interior, "Mac Tonight" tempa ($18-25)(WR)
17. dark blue & white body, black interior, "Miller Lite" tempa, sealed in plexibox with Convoy ($20-30)(WR)
18. brown-gold body, gray interior, "QVC 7" tempa ($3-5)(WR)
19. dark red body, gray interior, "Circuit City 8" tempa ($3-5)(WR)
20. grape body, black interior, "Remington Stren 75" tempa, sealed in glass bottle ($25-35)(WR)
21. olive, tan & black camouflage body, gray interior, "Remington 75" tempa, sealed in glass bottle ($25-35)(WR)

TACO BELL MATCHBOX MADNESS VEHICLES, issued 1998
NOTE: These four vehicles have been retooled by an independent company Strottman International Inc. through a license agreement with Mattel Toys using Matchbox's pattern molds. Strottman International Inc.(S.I.I.) is a manufacturing company that supplies Taco Bell with their toy give-aways. This is why they are not listed under the original casting number. The baseplates are cast "Made in China by S.I.I." They have no frame numbers so are grouped here together.
VW CONCEPT- red with black fenders & base, silver painted windows, swirl & lines design, 6 spoke spiral wheels ($3-5)
'62 CORVETTE- black body, windows & base, dual white stripes, Taco Bell logo & red side band tempa, 5 spoke concave star wheels ($3-5)
HUMVEE- black & base, silver painted windows, white & red swirls tempa, 8 spoke wheels with black hubs ($3-5)
FIREBIRD FORMULA- black body with silver painted windows, black base, "Taco Bell" with red & white flames tempa, 6 spoke spiral wheels ($3-5)

DODGE DAYTONA, issued 1983 (VEGAS)
1. burgundy body, black interior, clear windows, silver-gray base, casting closed, base cast "Expressly For Dodge Las Vegas", England casting ($75-100)(VG)

DODGE CARAVAN, issued 1983 (VEGAS)
1. burgundy body, maroon interior, clear windows, chrome base, casting closed, base cast "Expressly for Dodge Las Vegas", 8 spoke wheels, England casting ($75-100)(VG)

DODGE PLAQUE, issued 1983
1. above two models mounted by Velcro to a wooden plinth with gold plate denoting models made for Las Vegas with Lee Iacocca signature ($500-750)(VG)

Roman Numeral Editions

The following models have Roman numeral designations on their bases. Although some look like their original counterparts, these are listed here because of the base number!

MB I SILVER STREAK, issued 1978 (USA)
1. yellow body, amber windows, cat head label, chrome motor ($35-50)
2. yellow body, amber windows, cat head label, black motor ($75-100)
3. chrome plated body, black windows, stripes tempa, black motor ($10-15)

MB II SLEET-N-SNOW, issued 1978 (USA)
1. blue body, white base, white canopy, silver hubs, "U.S. Mail" tempa ($8-12)
2. dull blue body, white base, white canopy, silver hubs, "U.S. Mail" tempa ($8-12)
3. powder blue body, white base, white canopy, silver hubs, "U.S. Mail" tempa ($8-12)
4. olive body, black base, gun cast, black hubs, "21 * 11" labels ($15-20)
5. yellow body, black base, no canopy or gun, black hubs, "Gliding Club" labels ($15-20)(TP)
6. yellow body, black base, no canopy or gun, silver hubs, "Gliding Club" labels ($15-20)(TP)

MB III WHITE LIGHTNING, issued 1978 (USA)
1. cream body, black engine stacks ($10-15)
2. white body, black engine stacks ($10-15)
3. white body, dark gray engine stacks ($10-15)

MB IV FLYING BEETLE, issued 1978 (USA)
1. orange body, black windows, flesh colored driver ($10-15)

MB V HOT SMOKER, issued 1978 (USA)
1. yellow body, black base, 5 spoke front & 4 spoke rear wheels ($10-15)
2. yellow body, black base, 5 spoke front & rear wheels ($10-15)
3. yellow body, black base, 5 spoke front & maltese cross rear wheels

($10-15)
4. yellow body, charcoal base, 5 spoke front & 4 spoke rear wheels ($10-15)
5. yellow body, black base, dot dash front & rear wheels ($10-15)
6. yellow body, black base, dot dash front & 5 crown rear wheels ($10-15)
7. yellow body, black base, 5 spoke front & 5 crown rear wheels ($10-15)

MB VI LADY BUG, issued 1978 (USA)
1. red body, purple windows, yellow interior, eyes labels ($15-20)
2. black body, purple windows, yellow interior, flames & beetle tempa ($10-15)

MB VII BROWN SUGAR, issued 1978 (USA)
1. brown body, white base, black windows, brown background & outlined cherries labels ($10-15)
2. brown body, white base, black windows, brown background & solid cherries labels ($10-15)
3. dark brown body, white base, blue windows, brown background & outlined cherries labels ($10-15)
4. brown body, white base, blue windows, brown background & outlined cherries labels ($10-15)
5. brown body, white base, blue windows, brown background & solid cherries labels ($10-15)
6. brown body, white base, blue windows, tan background & solid cherries labels ($10-15)
7. brown body, white base, amber windows, brown background & solid cherries labels ($10-15)
8. brown body, white base, amber windows, tan background & solid cherries labels ($10-15)
9. red-brown body, white base, amber windows, tan background & solid cherries labels ($10-15)
10. dark brown body, white base, amber windows, brown background & solid cherries labels ($10-15)

MB VIII BLACK WIDOW, issued 1978 (USA)
1. powder blue body, clear windows ($15-20)
2. powder blue body, black windows ($10-15)

MB IX FLAMIN MANTA, issued 1978 (USA)
1. light yellow body, chrome interior, amber windows, flames tempa ($10-15)
2. dark yellow body, chrome interior, amber windows, flames tempa ($10-15)
Available as a Bulgarian casting. Assorted colors available ($35-50)

MB X GOLDEN X, issued 1978 (USA)
1. yellow body, black base, amber windows, red & black flames tempa ($35-50)
2. gold plated body, black base, black windows, light green tempa ($10-15)
3. gold plated body, black base, black windows, dark green tempa ($10-15)

Super GT's

Super GT's are a type of miniature. These models are based on older 1970s castings in which interiors are no longer fitted, the windows are solid in color (opaque) and opening features are cast shut. The original name for the line was to be the "Budget Range" and models were designated with "BR" numbers. All models are in paired numbers i.e. BR1/2, BR3/4, etc. The line was introduced in 1985 and ran through 1988. This line consists of varied tempa and wheel variations. Model names do not appear on the castings. Model names are taken from the original name in the 1970s. The first Chinese made Super GT range in 1987 contained all the basic color variations previously made in England. The only exceptions being the gold Monteverdi and the green Hairy Hustler. For 1988, they were all recolored. In 1990, some models were reissued in neon colors called "Neon Racers" and these are denoted with "NR"

BR1/2 Iso Grifo	BR21/22 Alfa Carabo
BR3/4 Gruesome Twosome	BR23/24 Vantastic
BR5/6 Datsun 126X	BR25/26 Ford Escort
BR7/8 Siva Spyder	BR27/28 Lamborghini Marzal
BR9/10 Lotus Europa	BR29/30 Maserati Bora
BR11/12 Saab Sonnet	BR31/32 Fandango
BR13/14 Hairy Hustler	BR33/34 Hi-Tailer
BR15/16 Monteverdi Hai	BR35/36 Porsche 910
BR17/18 Fire Chief	BR37/38 Ford Capri
BR19/20 Ford Group 6	BR39/40 DeTomasso Pantera

BR 1/2 ISO GRIFO, issued 1985
1. cream body, 8 dot wheels, black windows, red & black tempa, England casting ($3-5)
2. cream body, 8 dot wheels, white glow windows, red & black tempa, England casting ($12-15)
3. pale yellow body, 8 dot wheels, black windows, red & black tempa, England casting ($7-10)
4. pale yellow body, dot dash wheels, black windows, red & black tempa, England casting ($7-10)
5. yellow body, 8 dot wheels, black windows, red & black tempa, England casting ($7-10)
6. yellow body, dot dash wheels, black windows, red & black tempa, England casting ($7-10)
7. light blue body, 8 dot wheels, black windows, black & purple tempa, England casting ($4-6)
8. metallic blue body, 8 dot wheels, black windows, lime & maroon with "57" tempa, England casting ($3-5)
9. metallic blue body, 8 dot wheels, white glow windows, lime & red with "57" tempa, England casting ($12-15)
10. metallic blue body, 8 dot wheels, black windows, lemon & brown with "57" tempa, England casting ($4-6)
11. metallic blue body, 8 dot wheels, black windows, yellow & red with "57" tempa, England casting ($4-6)
12. metallic blue body, 8 dot wheels, black windows, red & black tempa, England casting ($7-10)
13. metallic blue body, 8 dot wheels, black windows, purple & back tempa, England casting ($7-10)
14. metallic blue body, dot dash wheels, black windows, purple & black tempa, England casting ($7-10)
15. metallic blue body, 8 dot wheels, black windows, maroon & black tempa, England casting ($7-10)
16. metallic blue body, 8 dot wheels, black windows, lime & red with "57" tempa, China casting ($7-10)
17. bright green body, 8 dot wheels, black windows, white & black with "57" tempa, China base ($3-5)
18. cream body, 8 dot wheels, black windows, red & black tempa, China casting ($6-8)
19. yellow body, 8 dot wheels, black windows, red & black tempa, China casting ($3-5)

BR3/4 GRUESOME TWOSOME, issued 1985
NOTE: All models below with black windows & 8 dot wheels unless otherwise noted.
1. yellow body, blue & orange with "Gruesome" tempa, England casting ($4-6)
2. yellow body, green & orange with "Gruesome" tempa, England casting ($4-6)
3. powder blue body, white arrow design tempa, England casting ($4-6)
4. powder blue body, white arrow design with no tempa on tail, England casting ($4-6)
5. dark blue body, white arrow design tempa, England casting ($5-8)
6. yellow body, blue & orange with "Gruesome" tempa, China casting ($7-10)
7. white body, red & black with "Gruesome" tempa, China casting ($3-5)
8. white body, red & black with "Gruesome" tempa, white glow windows, China casting ($20-25)
9. gray body, dark blue arrow design tempa, China casting ($3-5)
10. florescent orange body, yellow & black tempa, China casting ($4-6)(NR)
11. powder blue body, white arrow design with no tempa on tail, China casting ($4-6)

BR5/6 DATSUN 126X, issued 1985
1. dark blue body, 5 arch wheels, black windows, gold & white tempa, England casting ($4-6)
2. dark blue body, 8 dot wheels, black windows, gold & white tempa, England casting ($4-6)
3. silver body, 5 arch wheels, black windows, green & red stripes tempa, England casting ($4-6)
4. silver body, 8 dot wheels, black windows, green & red stripes tempa, England casting ($4-6)
5. silver-gray body, 5 arch wheels, black windows, green & red stripes tempa, England casting ($4-6)
6. pearly silver body, 5 arch wheels, black windows, green & red stripes tempa, China casting ($7-10)
7. powder blue body, 5 arch wheels, black windows, white & blue stripes tempa, China casting ($3-5)
8. beige body, 5 arch wheels, black windows, 2 tone blue tempa, China casting ($3-5)
9. beige body, 5 arch wheels, white glow windows, 2 tone blue tempa, China casting ($20-25)
10. dark blue body, 5 arch wheels, black windows, gold & white tempa, China casting ($4-6)

BR7/8 SIVA SPYDER, issued 1985
NOTE: All models fitted with black windows.
1. orange-yellow body, 8 dot wheels, black & white "Turbo" tempa, England casting ($4-6)
2. orange-yellow body, dot dash wheels, black & white "Turbo" tempa, England casting ($7-10)
3. yellow body, 8 dot wheels, black & red "Turbo" tempa, England casting ($7-10)
4. yellow body, 8 dot wheels, black & white "Turbo" tempa, England casting ($7-10)
5. white body, 8 dot wheels, blue & lemon tempa, England casting ($4-6)
6. white body, 8 dot wheels, blue & yellow tempa, England casting ($4-6)
7. white body, dot dash wheels, blue & yellow tempa, England casting ($4-6)
8. blue body, 8 dot wheels, white & black tempa, England casting ($7-10)
9. gray body, 8 dot wheels, white & black tempa, England casting ($7-10)
10. gray body, 8 dot wheels, gray & black tempa, England casting ($7-10)
11. white body, 8 dot wheels, blue & yellow tempa, China casting ($7-10)
12. dark red body, 8 dot wheels, white & gold tempa, China casting ($3-5)
13. orange-yellow body, 8 dot wheels, black & white "Turbo" tempa, China casting ($7-10)
14. yellow body, 8 dot wheels, black & red "Turbo" tempa, China casting ($3-5)

BR9/10 LOTUS EUROPA, issued 1985
NOTE: All models with black windows & 8 dot wheels.
1. white body, red & black with "1" tempa, England casting ($4-6)
2. metallic blue body, lemon leaf pattern tempa, England casting ($4-6)
3. metallic blue body, cream leaf pattern tempa, England casting ($4-6)
4. metallic blue body, yellow leaf pattern tempa, England casting ($4-6)
5. purple body, gold leaf pattern tempa, China casting ($3-5)
6. white body, red & black with "1" tempa, China casting ($7-10)
7. blue body, yellow & black with "1" tempa, China casting ($3-5)
8. metallic blue body, lemon leaf pattern tempa, China casting ($3-5)

BR11/12 SAAB SONNET, issued 1985
NOTE: All models fitted with black windows.
1. orange body, 8 dot wheels, white & red with "5" tempa, England casting ($4-6)
2. light tan body, 8 dot wheels, white & red triangle tempa, England casting ($4-6)
3. dark tan body, 8 dot wheels, white & red triangle tempa, England casting ($4-6)
4. light tan body, dot dash wheels, white & red triangle tempa, England casting ($4-6)
5. light tan body, 8 dot wheels, white & red with "5" tempa, England casting ($7-10)
6. blue body, 8 dot wheels, white & red triangle tempa, England casting ($7-10)
7. light tan body, dot dash wheels, white & red triangle tempa, England casting ($3-5)
8. light tan body, 8 dot wheels, yellow & black triangle tempa, China casting ($7-10)
9. powder blue body, 8 dot wheels, yellow & black triangle tempa, China casting ($3-5)
10. orange body, 8 dot wheels, white & red with "5" tempa, China casting ($7-10)
11. green body, 8 dot wheels, white & gold with "5" tempa, China casting ($3-5)

BR13/14 HAIRY HUSTLER, issued 1985
NOTE: All models fitted with black windows
1. lemon body, 5 crown wheels, black & red "L" & reverse "F" with "7" on roof with tail stripes tempa, England casting ($4-6)
2. yellow body, 5 crown wheels, black & red "L" & reverse "F" with "7" on roof with tail stripes tempa, England casting ($4-6)
3. yellow body, 5 crown wheels, black & red "L" & reverse "F" tempa only, England casting ($7-10)
4. yellow body, 5 arch front & 5 crown rear wheels, black & red "L" & reverse "F" with "7" on roof with tail stripes tempa, England casting ($4-6)
5. yellow body, 5 arch wheels, black & red "L" & reverse "F" with "7" on roof with tail stripes tempa, England casting ($4-6)
6. yellow body, 5 crown front & 5 arch rear wheels, black & red "L" & reverse "F" tempa with "7" on roof with tail stripes tempa, England casting ($4-6)
7. yellow body, 8 dot wheels, black & red "L" & reverse "F" with "7" on roof with tail stripes tempa, England casting ($4-6)
8. green body, 5 crown wheels, yellow & black with "2" tempa, England casting ($4-6)
9. green body, 5 arch front & 5 crown rear wheels, yellow & black with "2" tempa, England casting ($4-6)
10. dark green body, 5 crown wheels, yellow & black with "2" tempa, England casting ($7-10)
11. gray body, 5 crown wheels, red & black with "2" tempa, China casting ($3-5)
12. yellow body, 5 crown wheels, black & red "L" & reverse "F" with "7" on roof with tail stripes tempa, China casting ($7-10)
13. red body, 5 crown wheels, white & yellow "L" & reverse "F" with "7" on roof with tail stripes tempa, China casting ($3-5)

BR15/16 MONTEVERDI HAI, issued 1985
1. green body, 8 dot wheels, black windows, no tempa, England casting ($12-15)
2. green body, 8 dot wheels, black windows, black windows, white & gold tempa, England casting ($4-6)
3. green body, dot dash wheels, black windows, white & gold tempa, England casting ($6-8)
4. green body, 8 dot wheels, white glow windows, white & gold tempa, England casting ($12-15)
5. black body, 8 dot wheels, white glow windows, white & gold tempa, England casting ($15-20)
6. yellow body, 8 dot wheels, black windows, white & gold tempa, England casting ($50-65)
7. light tan body, 8 dot wheels, black windows, blue & white with "28" tempa, England casting ($4-6)
8. light tan body, 8 dot wheels, black windows, green & white with "28" tempa, England casting ($6-8)
9. mid tan body, 8 dot wheels, black windows, black & white with "28" tempa, England casting ($6-8)
10. dark tan body, 8 dot wheels, black windows, green & white with "28" tempa, England casting ($6-8)
11. gold body, 8 dot wheels, black windows, blue & white with "28" tempa, England casting ($7-10)
12. white body, 8 dot wheels, black windows, orange & black with "28" tempa, China casting ($30-45)
13. orange body, 8 dot wheels, black windows, red & blue with "28" tempa, China casting ($3-5)
14. green body, 8 dot wheels, black windows, white & gold tempa, China casting ($7-10)
15. blue body, 8 dot wheels, black windows, red & lime tempa, China casting ($3-5)

16. florescent pink body, 8 dot wheels, black windows, black & yellow tempa, China casting ($4-6)(NR)
17. tan body, dot dash wheels, black windows, blue & white with "28" tempa, China casting ($8-12)

BR17/18 FIRE CHIEF
NOTE: All models fitted with black windows. There can be other combinations of front & rear wheels to make other permutations.
1. white body, 5 crown wheels, "Police" tempa, England casting ($4-6)
2. white body, 5 arch front & 5 crown rear wheels, "Police" tempa, England casting (4-6)
3. white body, 5 arch wheels, "Police" tempa, England casting ($4-6)
4. red body, 5 crown wheels, white "Rescue" tempa, England casting ($4-6)
5. red body, 5 arch front & 5 crown rear wheels, white "Rescue" tempa, England casting ($4-6)
6. red body, 5 crown wheels, white "Rescue" tempa, England casting ($4-6)
7. orange body, 5 crown wheels, black "Rescue" tempa, China casting ($3-5)
8. white body, 5 crown wheels, "Police" tempa, China casting ($7-10)
9. blue body, 5 crown wheels, "Police" tempa, China casting ($3-5)
10. white body, 8 dot wheels, "Police" tempa, England casting ($7-10)
11. red body, 5 crown wheels, "Rescue" tempa, China casting ($3-5)

BR19/20 FORD GROUP 6, issued 1985
NOTE: All models with black windows.
1. white body, 8 dot wheels, red & black "18" tempa, England casting ($4-6)
2. white body, dot dash wheels, pink & black "18" tempa, England casting ($4-6)
3. yellow body, 8 dot wheels, red & black "18" tempa, England casting ($7-10)
4. red body, 8 dot wheels, white & yellow "2" tempa, England casting ($4-6)
5. red body, dot dash wheels, white & yellow "2" tempa, England casting ($4-6)
6. red body, 8 dot wheels, white & yellow "2" tempa, China casting ($7-10)
7. gray body, 8 dot wheels, purple & white "2" tempa, China casting ($3-5)
8. white body, 8 dot wheels, red & black "18" tempa, China casting ($7-10)
9. dark red body, 8 dot wheels, blue & black "18" tempa, China casting ($3-5)
10. florescent lime body, 8 dot wheels, yellow & black "18" tempa, China casting ($4-6)(NR)

BR21/22 ALFA CARABO, issued 1985
NOTE: All models fitted with black windows & 8 dot wheels. Various shades of the panel tempa exist on the silver model.
1. silver body., light & dark blue panels tempa, England casting ($4-6)
2. silver body, light blue & dark green panels tempa, England casting ($4-6)
3. silver body, no tempa, England casting ($12-15)
4. green body, dark blue & white panels tempa, England casting ($12-15)
5. beige body, light & dark blue panels tempa, England casting ($35-50)
6. yellow body, blue & green panels tempa, England casting ($35-50)
7. yellow body, light & dark blue panels tempa, England casting ($35-50)
8. silver body, white & blue panels tempa, England casting ($7-10)
9. orange body, blue & white with "6" tempa, England casting ($4-6)
10. orange body, blue & white with "6" tempa, 5 crown wheels, England casting ($7-10)
11. orange body, no tempa, England casting ($12-15)
12. orange body, dark & light blue panels tempa, England casting ($12-15)
13. orange body, green & light blue panels tempa, England casting ($12-15)
14. silver body, black & blue panels tempa, 5 arch wheels, England casting ($7-10)
15. green body, black & blue panels tempa, England casting ($7-10)
16. orange body, blue & white with "6" tempa, 5 arch wheels, England casting ($4-6)
17. pearly silver body, black & dark blue panels tempa, China casting ($7-10)
18. powder blue body, yellow & white panels tempa, China casting ($3-5)
19. green body, gold & white with "6" tempa, China casting ($3-5)
20. orange body, blue & white with "6" tempa, China casting ($3-5)

BR23/24 VANTASTIC, issued 1986
1. beige body, blue & red "Starfire" tempa, black windows, China casting ($3-5)
2. blue body, red & yellow with "51" tempa, black windows, China casting ($3-5)

BR25/26 FORD ESCORT, issued 1985
NOTE: All models with black windows and 8 dot wheels.
1. red body, gold & white with "10" tempa, England casting ($4-6)
2. red body, blue & white with "10" tempa, England casting ($4-6)
3. blue body, blue & white with "10" tempa, England casting ($5-8)
4. beige body, light & mid blue with "9" tempa, England casting ($4-6)
5. beige body, light blue & green with "9" tempa, England casting ($4-6)
6. yellow body, light & dark blue with "9" tempa, England casting ($15-18)
7. blue body, yellow & dark blue with "9" tempa, China casting ($3-5)
8. purple body, white & black with "10" tempa, China casting ($3-5)
9. red body, gold & white with "10" tempa, China casting ($3-5)
10. beige body, light & dark blue with "9" tempa, China casting ($3-5)

BR27/28 LAMBORGHINI MARZAL, issued 1985
NOTE: All models with black windows & 8 dot wheels unless otherwise noted.
1. green body, white & yellow with "8" tempa, dot dash wheels, England casting ($7-10)
2. green body, white & yellow with "8" tempa, England casting ($4-6)
3. green body, black & gray with "16" tempa, England casting ($12-15)
4. blue body, white & yellow with "8" tempa, England casting ($7-10)
5. cream body, black & gray with "16" tempa, England casting ($4-6)
6. white body, black & gray with "16" tempa, England casting ($12-15)
7. green body, white & yellow with "8" tempa, 5 arch wheels, England casting ($5-8)
8. cream body, black & gray with "16" tempa, 5 arch wheels, England casting ($5-8)
9. cream body, black & gray with "16" tempa, China casting ($7-10)
10. yellow body, blue & gold with "16" tempa, China casting ($3-5)
11. green body, white & yellow with "8" tempa, China casting ($7-10)
12. red body, black & red with "8" tempa, China casting ($3-5)

BR29/30 MASERATI BORA, issued 1985
NOTE: All models with black windows & 8 dot wheels unless otherwise noted. The tempa on the yellow model exists in varying shades.
1. yellow body, blue & orange tempa, England casting ($4-6)
2. yellow body, green & orange tempa, England casting ($4-6)
3. yellow body, green & orange tempa, dot dash wheels, England casting ($7-10)
4. yellow body, purple & orange tempa, England casting ($4-6)
5. yellow body, blue & brown tempa, England casting ($4-6)
6. light blue body, dark blue & white with "70" tempa, England casting ($4-6)
7. light blue body, black & white with "70" tempa, England casting ($4-6)
8. light blue body, black & white with "70" tempa, dot dash wheels, England casting ($7-10)
9. dark blue body, black & white with "70" tempa, England casting ($6-8)
10. dark blue body, black & white with "70" tempa, dot dash wheels, England casting ($7-10)
11. light blue body, black & white with "70" tempa, China casting ($7-10)
12. beige body, 2 tone blue with "70" tempa, China casting ($3-5)
13. yellow body, blue & orange tempa, China casting ($7-10)
14. powder blue body, purple & black tempa, China casting ($3-5)
15. florescent lime body, black & white with "70" tempa, China casting ($4-6)(NR)

BR31/32 FANDANGO, issued 1985
NOTE: All models fitted with black windows.
1. yellow body, 5 crown wheels, blue & red with "19" tempa, England casting ($4-6)
2. yellow body, 5 arch front & 5 crown rear wheels, blue & red with "19" tempa, England casting ($4-6)
3. maroon body, 5 crown wheels, white & yellow with "217" & white prop tempa, England casting ($4-6)
4. maroon body, 5 crown wheels, white & yellow with "217" & unpainted prop tempa, England casting ($4-6)
5. maroon body, 5 arch front & 5 crown rear wheels, white & yellow with "217" & white prop tempa, England casting ($4-6)
6. maroon body, 5 arch front & 5 crown rear wheels, white & yellow with "217" & white prop tempa, China casting ($7-10)
7. yellow body, 5 arch front & 5 crown rear wheels, red & black with "217" & red prop tempa, China casting ($3-5)
8. lemon body, 5 arch front & 5 crown rear wheels, blue & red with "19" tempa, China casting ($7-10)
9. gray body, 5 arch front & 5 crown rear wheels, gray & red with "19" tempa, China casting ($3-5)

BR33/34 HI-TAILER, issued 1986
1. lemon body, black & red with "Super 61" tempa, China casting ($3-5)
2. yellow body, black & red with "Super 61" tempa, China casting ($3-5)
3. white body, black & red with "45" tempa, China casting ($3-5)

BR35/36 PORSCHE 910, issued 1985
NOTE: All models fitted with black windows.
1. dark blue body, 8 dot wheels, blue & white with "49" tempa, England casting ($4-6)
2. light blue body, 8 dot wheels, blue & white with "49" tempa, England casting ($4-6)
3. light blue body, dot dash wheels, blue & white with "49" tempa, England casting ($4-6)
4. light blue body, dot dash wheels, black "3" & "Drive" tempa, England casting ($7-10)
5. light blue body, 8 dot wheels, black "3" & "Drive" tempa, England casting ($7-10)
6. silver body, 8 dot wheels, black "3" & "Drive" tempa, England casting ($4-6)
7. silver-gray body, 8 dot wheels, black "3" & "Drive" tempa, England casting ($4-6)
8. silver body, 8 dot wheels, black & white with "49" tempa, England casting ($7-10)
9. silver body, dot dash wheels, black & white with "49" tempa, England casting ($7-10)
10. pearly silver body, dot dash wheels, black "3" & "Drive" tempa, China casting ($7-10)
11. white body, 5 arch wheels, red "3" & "Drive" tempa, China casting ($3-5)
12. light blue body, 5 arch wheels, black with "49" tempa, China casting ($7-10)
13. lime body, 5 arch wheels, gold & white with "49" tempa, China casting ($3-5)
14. florescent orange body, 5 arch wheels, dark blue & yellow with "49" tempa, China casting ($4-6)(NR)

BR37/38 FORD CAPRI, issued 1986
1. cream body, red-brown & green with "48" tempa, China casting ($3-5)
2. blue body, red & white with "8" tempa, China casting ($3-5)

BR39/40 DE TOMASO PANTERA, issued 1986
1. maroon body, orange & white with "4X4" tempa, China casting ($3-5)
2. orange body, blue & brown with "Ace" tempa, China casting ($3-5)
3. florescent yellow body, blue-green & orange with "4X4" tempa, China casting ($4-6)(NR)

Originals

In 1988, Matchbox Toys decided to celebrate the fortieth anniversary of Matchbox Toys by recreating five miniatures that were made back in the early 1950s. The recreated toys were based on the 1A Road Roller, 4A Tractor, 5A London Bus, 7A Milk Float, and 9A Dennis Fire Engine. All were produced as closely as possible to original colors. These were then packaged in a limited-edition gift set in English or German text. A French version was also supposed to have been issued in gold plate but this idea was canceled. In 1991, these same five models were reissued as singles under the name "Originals" and packaged with recreated boxes but in new colors. These were numbered as MX101 through MX105. The series continued with ten new editions as Series 2 and 3 with series 4 being a repeat of Series 1 in new colors.

MX101-A ROAD ROLLER, issued 1988
1. green body, red rollers, double post roof pillars ($3-5)(GS)
2. dark blue body, red rollers, double post roof pillars ($2-4)
3. dark blue body, red rollers, single post roof pillars ($2-4)
4. orange body, red rollers, single post roof pillars ($3-5)

MX102-A TRACTOR, issued 1988
1. red body, silver metal wheels ($3-5)(GS)
2. green body, silver metal wheels ($2-4)
3. powder blue body, silver metal wheels ($3-5)

MX103-A LONDON BUS, issued 1988
1. red body, "Buy Matchbox Series" tempa, silver metal wheels ($3-5)
2. red body, yellow background "Matchbox Originals" tempa, silver metal wheels ($2-4)
NOTE: Above model with box art reading "Players Please" on box ($12-15)
3. red body, "Matchbox Originals" (white background) tempa, silver metal wheels ($3-5)

MX104-A MILK FLOAT, issued 1988
1. orange body, brown horse, silver metal wheels ($3-5)(GS)
2. powder blue body, brown horse, silver metal wheels ($2-4)
3. green body, brown horse, silver metal wheels ($3-5)

MX105-A DENNIS FIRE ENGINES, issued 1988
1. red body, red flywheel, silver metal wheels ($3-5)(GS)
2. red body, yellow flywheel, silver metal wheels ($2-4)
3. red body, white flywheel, silver metal wheels ($3-5)

MX106-A QUARRY TRUCK, issued 1992
1. blue body, gray dump, silver metal wheels ($2-4)

MX107-A WRECK TRUCK, issued 1992
1. red body, yellow boom & hook, silver metal wheels ($2-4)

MX108-A MGA, issued 1992
1. dark green body & base, cream driver, silver metal wheels ($2-4)

MX109-A CONCRETE TRUCK, issued 1992
1. orange body, gray barrel, silver metal wheels ($2-4)

MX110-A JAGUAR XK140, issued 1992
1. black body, black base, silver metal wheels ($2-4)

MX111-A ROAD TANKER, issued 1994
1. powder blue body, silver metal wheels, China casting ($2-4)

MX112-A LAND ROVER, issued 1994
1. green body, light tan driver, silver metal wheels, China casting ($2-4)

MX113-A REMOVALS VAN, issued 1994
1. dark blue body, "Matchbox Removals Service" tempa, silver metal wheels, China casting ($2-4)
2. dark blue body, "BAMCA- Bay Area Matchbox Collectors Association" decals, silver metal wheels, China casting ($20-25)(C2)
3. dark blue body, "Mitre 10" tempa, silver metal wheels, China casting ($15-20)(AU)

MX114-A CATERPILLAR BULLDOZER, issued 1994
1. yellow body, red blade, black treads, silver metal rollers, China casting ($2-4)

MX115-A MASERATI RACER, issued 1994
1. red body, cream driver, "52" in circle tempa, black plastic wheels, China casting ($2-4)

Twin Packs

Originally introduced as "Two Packs" in 1976, this diecast line features paired models. Over the years, the line's name has been called

"900 Series" and "Hitch 'N Haul," and in 1984 it became known as "Twin Packs." Along with the standard Twin Packs range, several other combinations of two vehicles were issued including Matchmates and other individualized pairs.

NOTE: values quoted for Twin Packs are for sealed blisterpacks. Models removed from the blisterpacks can be quoted by their single issue price only. Some models may be "rare" as a twin-pack combination, but worth substantially less individually!

TP 1-A MERCEDES TRUCK & TRAILER, issued 1976
1. red MB1-A & red MB2-A, yellow canopies, "Transcontinental" labels ($12-15)
2. red MB1-A & red MB2-A, orange-yellow canopies, "Transcontinental" labels ($12-15)
3. powder blue MB1-A & MB2-A, orange-yellow canopies, "I.M.S." labels ($25-30)

TP 2-A MOD TRACTOR & TRAILER, issued 1976
1. red MB25-B Mod Tractor & yellow 40C Hay Trailer ($15-20)

TP 2-B POLICE CAR & FIRE ENGINE, issued 1979
1. white MB59-B Mercury & red MB35-A Merryweather Fire Engine ($10-15)
2. white MB59-B Mercury & red MB22-C Blaze Buster ($15-20)

TP 2-C ARTICULATED PETROL TANKER, issued 1981
1. red cab & trailer, white tank, green windows, "Exxon" labels ($10-15)
2. red cab & trailer, white tank, amber windows, "Exxon" labels ($10-15)

TP 3-A PONY TRAILER SET, issued 1976
1. lime MB 9-B AMX Javelin & orange MB43-A Pony Trailer ($10-15)
2. metallic blue MB9-B Javelin & orange MB43-A Pony Trailer ($10-15)
3. red MB53-C Jeep CJ6 & orange MB43-A Pony Trailer ($20-25)
4. red MB53-C Jeep CJ6 & beige MB43-A Pony Trailer ($20-25)
5. blue MB9-B Javelin (doors cast) & beige MB43-A Pony Trailer ($10-15)
6. green MB9-B Javelin (doors cast) & beige MB43-A Pony Trailer ($10-15)
7. red MB18-A Field Car with "44" label & beige MB43-A Pony Trailer ($25-40)
8. blue MB9-B Javelin (doors cast) with white tempa & beige MB43-A Pony Trailer ($15-18)
9. red MB9-B Javelin (doors cast) & beige MB43-A Pony Trailer ($65-80)
10. green MB9-B Javelin (doors cast) & orange MB43-A Pony Trailer ($10-15)

TP 4-A HOLIDAY SET, issued 1976
1. orange MB54-B Ford Capri & cream MB57-B Eccles with flower & stripe label ($20-25)
2. red MB40-A Guildsman with label & yellow MB57-B Eccles with flower & stripe label ($20-25)
3. red MB40-A Guildsman with label & yellow MB57-B Eccles with dots label ($20-25)
4. red MB40-A Guildsman with label & yellow MB57-B Eccles with no label ($20-25)
5. red MB40-A Guildsman with tempa & yellow MB57-B Eccles with flower & stripe label ($20-25)
6. pink MB40-A Guildsman with label & pale yellow MB57-B Eccles with flower & stripe label ($25-35)
7. red MB40-A Guildsman with no label & white MB31-C Caravan with seagull label ($25-35)
8. lime MB9-B Javelin & yellow MB57-B Eccles with flower & stripe label ($10-15)
9. metallic blue MB9-B Javelin (doors cast) & yellow MB57-B Eccles with flower & stripe label ($10-15)
10. dark green MB9-B Javelin (doors cast) & yellow MB57-B Eccles with flower & stripe label ($10-15)
11. green MB7-C VW Golf & yellow MB57-B Eccles with flower & stripe label ($15-20)
12. green MB7-C VW Golf & beige MB57-B Eccles with flower & stripe label ($15-20)
13. green MB7-C VW Golf & beige MB57-B Eccles with seagull label ($18-25)
14. red MB7-C VW Golf & yellow MB57-B Eccles with flower & stripe label ($18-25)
15. yellow MB7-C VW Golf & yellow MB57-B Eccles with flower & stripe label ($18-25)
16. blue MB67-C Datsun 260Z & yellow MB57-B Eccles with flower & stripe label ($35-50)
17. blue MB21-C Renault 5TL & yellow MB57-B Eccles with flower & stripe label ($35-50)
18. gold MB32-B Maserati Bora & beige MB57-B Eccles with flower & stripe label ($25-40)
19. gold MB32-B Maserati Bora & beige MB57-B Eccles with dots label ($25-40)
20. gold MB32-B Maserati Bora & beige MB57-B Eccles with seagull label ($25-40)

TP 5-A WEEKENDER, issued 1976
1. orange MB54-B Ford Capri & blue/white MB9-A Boat & Trailer ($15-20)
2. red-orange MB67-B Hot Rocker & blue/white MB9-A Boat & Trailer ($15-20)
3. white MB9-C Ford Escort with "Dunlop" labels & blue/white MB9-A Boat & Trailer ($35-50)
4. black MB5-A Lotus Europa with "JPS" tempa & blue/white MB9-A Boat & Trailer ($35-50)
5. brown MB3-C Porsche Turbo & blue/white MB9-A Boat & Trailer ($35-50)
6. red MB7-C VW Golf & blue/white MB9-A Boat & Trailer ($10-15)
7. white MB9-C Ford Escort with "Phantom" labels & blue/white MB9-A Boat & Trailer ($35-50)
8. blue MB9-C Ford Escort with "Phantom" labels & blue/white MB9-A Boat & Trailer ($35-50)

TP 6-A BREAKDOWN SET, issued 1976
1. green MB74-B Toe Joe with green booms & orange MB29-B Racing Mini with "29" labels ($12-15)
2. red MB74-B Toe Joe with green booms & orange MB29-B Racing Mini with "29" labels ($250-275)
3. red MB74-B Toe Joe with red booms & orange MB29-B Racing Mini with "29" labels ($250-275)
4. green MB74-B Toe Joe with green booms & orange MB20-B Police Patrol with "Site Engineer" labels ($25-40)
5. yellow MB74-B Toe Joe with red booms & orange MB29-B Racing Mini with "29" labels ($12-15)
6. yellow MB74-B Toe Joe with red booms & white MB15-A VW 1500 with "137" labels ($35-45)
7. yellow MB74-B Toe Joe with red booms & blue MB65-A Saab Sonnet ($35-50)
8. yellow MB74-B Toe Joe with green booms & orange MB29-B Racing Mini with "29" labels ($12-15)
9. green MB74-B Toe Joe with green booms & orange MB29-B Racing Mini with "3" labels ($15-18)
10. green MB74-B Toe Joe with white booms & orange MB29-B Racing Mini with "29" labels ($200-250)
11. red MB74-B Toe Joe with green booms & orange MB20-B Police Patrol with "Site Engineer" labels ($250-275)
12. yellow MB74-B Toe Joe with red booms & orange MB20-B Police Patrol with "Site Engineer" labels ($25-40)
13. red MB74-B Toe Joe with red booms & white MB15-A VW 1500 with "137" labels ($250-275)
14. red MB61-B Wrecker with white booms & orange MB29-B Racing Mini with "29" labels ($10-15)
15. yellow MB61-B Wrecker with red booms & MB29-B Racing Mini with "29" labels ($10-15)
16. red MB61-B Wrecker with white booms & "24 Hour" tempa & orange MB29-B Racing Mini with no labels ($10-15)
17. red MB61-B Wrecker with red booms & MB29-B Racing Mini with "3" labels ($15-20)

TP 7-A EMERGENCY SET, issued 1976
1. white MB46B Stretcha Fetcha & MB59-B Mercury Fire Chief ($10-15)
2. white MB46-B Stretcha Fetcha & red MB64-C Fire Chief ($10-15)

TP 7-B GLIDER SET, issued 1977
1. yellow MB38-C Jeep with black base & yellow trailer with "Gliding Club" labels ($10-15)
2. yellow MB38-C Jeep with white base & yellow trailer with "Gliding Club" labels ($10-15)
3. yellow MB38-C Jeep with white base & yellow trailer with no labels ($10-15)
4. red MB38-C Jeep with black base & red trailer with "Gliding Club" labels ($750-1000)
5. yellow MB18-A Field Car with checker label & yellow trailer with "Gliding Club" labels ($35-50)
6. green MB9-C Ford Escort with "Seagull" labels & green trailer with "Seagull" labels ($8-12)

TP 8-A TRANSPORTER SET, issued 1976
1. red MB17-B The Londoner with "Swinging London" labels & white/black MB72-B Hovercraft ($15-20)

TP 8-B FIELD CAR & HONDA WITH TRAILER, issued 1977
1. orange MB18-A Field Car with checker label & orange trailer with "Honda" labels ($12-15)
2. orange MB18-A Field Car with checker label & orange trailer with no labels ($12-15)
3. white MB18-A Field Car with checker label & orange trailer with "Honda" labels ($500-650)
4. yellow MB18-A Field Car with checker label & orange trailer with no labels ($12-15)
5. yellow MB18-A Field Car with checker label & yellow trailer with no labels ($12-15)
6. dark orange MB18-A Field Car with no labels & orange trailer with "Honda" labels ($15-20)
7. dark orange MB18-A Field Car with "179" tempa & orange trailer with no labels ($18-25)
8. yellow MB18-A Field Car with checker label & yellow trailer with "Honda" labels ($12-15)

TP 9-A FIELD CAR & TEAM MATCHBOX, issued 1978
1. red MB18-A Field Car with "44" label & red MB24-B Team with "44" label ($12-15)
2. orange MB18-A Field Car with "44" label & orange MB24-B Team with "44" label ($75-100)
3. orange MB18-A Field Car with checker label & orange MB24-B Team with "44" label ($75-100)

TP10-A FIRE CHIEF & AMBULANCE, issued 1978
1. red MB59-B Mercury Fire Chief & white MB3-A Mercedes Ambulance ($12-15)
2. red MB64-C Fire Chief & white MB3-A Mercedes Ambulance ($12-15)

TP11-A MILITARY JEEP & MILITARY CYCLE, issued 1977
NOTE: The MB2-B Jeep can also exist in any of the below combinations.
1. olive drab MB38-C Jeep with no gun & star label & olive drab MB18-B Hondarora ($130-165)
2. olive MB38-C Jeep with no gun & star label & olive MB18-B Hondarora ($15-18)
3. olive MB38-C Jeep with no gun & "21 * 11" label & olive MB18-B Hondarora ($15-18)
4. olive MB38-C Jeep with gun & "21 * 11" label & olive MB18-B Hondarora ($15-18)
5. olive MB18-A Field Car with star label & olive MB18-B Hondarora ($25-40)

TP11-B TRACTOR & HAY TRAILER, issued 1979
1. blue MB46-C Tractor & yellow 40-C Hay Trailer with no stakes ($15-20)
2. blue MB46-C Tractor & blue 40-C Hay Trailer with black stakes ($15-20)
3. blue MB46-C Tractor & beige 40-C Hay Trailer with black stakes ($125-175)
4. lime MB46-C Tractor & beige 40-C Hay Trailer with black stakes ($125-175)
5. lime MB46-C Tractor & red 40-C Hay Trailer with black stakes ($15-20)

TP12-A POLICE PATROL & FIELD CAR, issued 1977
1. olive drab MB20-B Police Patrol with "Ambulance" labels & olive drab MB18-A Field Car with "A" labels ($130-165)
2. olive drab MB20-B Police Patrol with "Police" labels & olive drab MB18-A Field Car with "A" labels ($130-165)
3. olive MB20-B Police Patrol with "Police" labels & olive MB18-A Field Car with "A" labels ($15-20)
4. olive MB20-B Police Patrol with "Ambulance" labels & olive MB18-A Field Car with "3RA391" label ($15-20)

TP12-B DORMOBILE & FIELD CAR, issued 1977
1. olive MB23-A Dormobile with "Ambulance" labels & olive MB18-A Field Car with "3RA391" label ($15-20)

TP13-A MILITARY SCOUT & ARMORED CAR, issued 1977
1. olive drab MB28-B Stoat & olive drab MB73-B Weasel ($130-165)
2. olive MB28-B Stoat & olive MB73-B Weasel ($12-15)

TP13-B UNIMOG & ARMORED CAR, issued 1978
1. olive MB49-A Unimog with "A" label & olive MB73-B Weasel ($12-15)

TP13-C UNIMOG & FIELD GUN, issued 1978
1. olive MB49-A Unimog with star label (no ammo box) & olive MB32-C Field Gun ($75-100)
2. olive MB49-A Unimog with "A" label (with ammo box) & olive MB32-C Field Gun ($12-15)

TP14-A MILITARY GAS TANKER & RADAR TRUCK, issued 1977
1. olive drab MB63-B Tanker with Canadian flag label & olive drab MB16-A Badger ($150-175)
2. olive drab MB63-B Tanker with French flag label & olive drab MB16-A Badger ($130-165)
3. olive MB63-B Tanker with "High Octane" labels & olive MB16-A Badger ($15-18)

TP14-B MILITARY AMBULANCE & STAFF CAR, issued 1977
1. olive MB3-A Mercedes Ambulance & olive MB46-A Mercedes 300SE ($15-18)

TP15-A MILITARY TRUCK & TRAILER, issued 1977
1. olive drab MB1-A Mercedes Truck & olive drab MB2-A Mercedes Trailer with "48350USA" labels ($130-165)
2. olive drab MB1-A Mercedes Truck with "48350USA" labels & olive drab MB2-A Mercedes Trailer with "4TS702K" labels ($130-165)
3. olive drab MB1-A Mercedes Truck & olive drab MB2-A Mercedes Trailer with "4TS702K" labels ($130-165)
4. olive MB1-A Mercedes Truck & MB2-A Mercedes Trailer with "48350USA" labels ($15-18)
5. olive MB1-A Mercedes Truck & olive MB2-A Mercedes Trailer with "4TS702K" labels ($15-18)

TP16-A MILITARY DUMP TRUCK & BULLDOZER, issued 1977
1. olive drab MB28-A Mack Dump & olive drab 16D Case Bulldozer ($130-165)
2. olive MB28-A Mack Dump & olive 16D Case Bulldozer ($15-18)

TP16-B MILITARY WRECK TRUCK & ALVIS STALWART, issued 1979
1. olive MB71-A Wreck Truck & olive 61B Alvis Stalwart with "3LGS64" labels ($15-20)

TP16-C ARTICULATED TRUCK & TRAILER, issued 1980
1. MB50-B Articulated Truck with yellow cab/blue dump & MB50-C Trailer with blue dump ($10-15)
2. MB50-B Articulated Truck with lemon cab/blue dump & MB50-C Trailer with blue dump ($10-15)
3. MB50-B Articulated Truck with red cab/silver-gray dump & MB50-C Trailer with silver-gray dump ($20-30)

TP17-A DOUBLE TANKER SET, issued 1979
1. red cab/trailer MB63-B Tanker & red/white MB63-C Trailer with "Burmah" labels ($12-15)
2. red cab/trailer MB63-B Tanker with "Chevron" labels & red/white

MB63-C Trailer with "Burmah" labels ($15-20)
3. red cab/trailer MB63-B Tanker & red/white MB63-C Trailer with "Chevron" labels ($12-15)
4. white cab/yellow trailer MB63-B Tanker & yellow/white MB63-C Trailer with "Shell" labels ($12-15)
5. white cab/. trailer MB63-B Tanker & white MB63-C Trailer with "Exxon" labels ($12-15)
6. white cab/yellow trailer MB63-B Tanker & yellow/white MB63-C Trailer with "Exxon" labels ($25-35)
7. red cab/white trailer MB63-B Tanker & white MB63-C Trailer with "Exxon" labels ($100-150)
8. white cab/green trailer MB63-B Tanker & green/white MB63-C Trailer with "BP" labels ($20-35)

TP18-A WATER SPORTER, issued 1979
1. red MB7-C VW Golf & MB5-B Seafire with red deck & white hull ($10-15)
2. red MB7-C VW Golf & MB5-B Seafire with white deck & brown hull ($100-150)
3. red MB7-C VW Golf & MB5-B Seafire with white deck & blue hull ($15-20)
4. red MB9-B AMX Javelin & MB5-B Seafire with dark red deck & white hull ($50-75)

TP19-A CATTLE TRUCK & TRAILER, issued 1979
1. red MB71-C Cattle Truck & Cattle Trailer with beige stakes & black cows ($10-15)
2. red MB71-C Cattle Truck & Cattle Trailer with beige stakes & brown cows ($10-15)
3. red MB71-C Cattle Truck & Cattle Trailer with orange stakes & dark brown cows ($15-20)

TP20-A SHUNTER & SIDE TIPPER, issued 1979
1. yellow MB24-C Shunter & yellow Side Tipper with red dump ($12-15)
2. yellow MB24-C Shunter & yellow Side Tipper with black dump ($15-18)

TP21-A MOTORCYCLE SET, issued 1979
1. blue MB21-C Renault 5TL & blue trailer with yellow cycles ($15-18)
2. blue MB67-C Datsun 260Z & blue trailer with yellow cycles ($15-18)
3. blue MB51-B Citroen & blue trailer with yellow cycles ($8-12)
4. blue MB51-B Citroen & blue trailer with red cycles ($25-40)
5. blue MB67-C Datsun 260Z & blue trailer with lemon cycles ($15-18)

TP22-A DOUBLE CONTAINER TRUCK, issued 1979
1. bronze cab, beige containers, amber windows, "OCL" labels ($10-15)
2. bronze cab, cream containers, amber windows, "OCL" labels ($10-15)
3. bronze cab, milky white containers, amber windows, "OCL" labels ($12-15)
4. bronze cab, beige containers, no windows, "OCL" labels ($10-15)
5. red cab, beige containers, amber windows, "OCL" labels ($12-15)
6. red cab, light yellow containers, amber windows, "OCL" labels ($12-15)
7. red cab, milky white containers, amber windows, "OCL" labels ($12-15)
9. red cab, light blue containers, amber windows, "Sealand" labels ($100-150)
10. red cab, red containers, amber windows, "NYK" labels ($100-150)
11. dark green cab, beige containers, amber windows, "OCL" labels ($100-150)
12. dark green cab, orange containers, amber windows, "OCL" labels ($150-200)

TP23-A COVERED CONTAINER TRUCK, issued 1979
1. red cab, amber windows, solid lettered "Firestone" labels ($10-15)
2. red cab, amber windows, outlined lettered "Firestone" labels ($10-15)
3. red cab, no windows, outlined lettered "Firestone" labels ($10-15)

TP24-A CONTAINER TRUCK, issued 1979
1. red cab, solid lettered "Firestone" labels ($25-35)
2. red cab, outlined lettered "Firestone" labels ($35-50)
3. red cab, "Matchbox" (towards rear) labels ($12-15)
4. red cab, "Matchbox" (towards front) labels ($12-15)
5. yellow cab, "Matchbox" (towards front) labels ($35-50)

TP25-A PIPE TRUCK, issued 1979
1. yellow cab, amber windows, silver-gray flatbed, orange pipes ($35-50)
2. yellow cab, amber windows, black flatbed, orange pipes ($35-50)
3. dark green cab, amber windows, silver-gray flatbed, orange pipes ($12-15)
4. dark green cab, amber windows, black flatbed, orange pipes ($12-15)
5. dark green cab, no windows, black flatbed, orange pipes ($12-15)
6. bronze cab, amber windows, black flatbed, orange pipes ($75-100)

TP26-A BOAT TRANSPORTER, issued 1981
1. blue cab, green windows, silver-gray trailer, beige & red boat ($35-50)
2. blue cab, amber windows, silver-gray trailer, beige & red boat ($10-15)

TP27-A STEAM LOCO & CABOOSE, issued 1981
1. green MB43-C 0-4-0 Loco with "NP" labels & green MB44-C Coach with "5810-6102" labels ($12-15)

TP28-A FORD CORTINA & CARAVAN, issued 1982
1. tan MB55-D Ford Cortina & white MB57-B Eccles with "Sunset" tempa ($12-15)

TP29-A TRUCK & BOAT, issued 1982
1. blue MB53-D Flareside Pickup & blue/white MB9-A Boat & Trailer ($10-15)
2. blue MB53-D Flareside Pickup & black/white MB9-A Boat & Trailer ($60-80)
3. orange MB18-A Field Car with "44" label & black/white MB9-A Boat & Trailer ($100-125)

TP30-A SEAFIRE BOAT SET, issued 1982
1. dark orange MB18-A Field Car with "179" tempa & MB5-B Seafire with white deck & blue hull ($50-75)
2. dark orange MB18-A Field Car with "44" label & MB5-B Seafire with black deck & yellow hull ($50-75)
3. silver-gray MB67-C Datsun 260Z & MB5-B Seafire with black deck & yellow hull ($10-15)
4. silver-gray MB67-C Datsun 260Z & MB5-B Seafire with red deck & yellow hull ($50-75)

TP31-A CITROEN & MOTORCYCLE TRAILER, issued 1982
1. yellow MB12-D Citroen with "Team Matchbox" tempa & red trailer with yellow cycles ($10-15)

TP32-A WRECK TRUCK & DODGE CHALLENGER, issued 1982
1. yellow MB74-B Toe Joe with red booms & Hitchhiker" labels & orange MB1-D Dodge ($150-200)
2. red MB61-B Wrecker with white booms & "24 Hour" tempa & orange MB1-D Dodge ($8-12)
3. yellow MB61-B Wrecker with red booms & orange MB1-D Dodge ($18-25)

TP101-A MATRA RANCHO & PONY TRAILER, issued 1984
1. MB37-E Matra Rancho in blue with blue base & beige MB43-A Pony Trailer ($8-12)
2. MB37-E Matra Rancho in blue with black base & beige MB43-A Pony Trailer ($8-12)
3. MB37-E Matra Rancho in blue with yellow base & beige MB43-A Pony Trailer ($15-25)
4. MB37-E Matra Rancho in yellow with yellow base & beige MB43-A Pony Trailer ($8-12)
5. MB37-E Matra Rancho in blue with white base & beige MB43-A Pony Trailer ($8-12)

TP102-A FORD ESCORT & GLIDER TRANSPORTER, issued 1984
1. light green MB9-C Ford Escort & dark green Glider Transporter with "Seagull" labels ($15-18)
2. dark green MB9-C Ford Escort & dark green Glider Transporter with "Seagull" labels ($7-10)

TP103-A CATTLE TRUCK & TRAILER, issued 1984
1. red MB71-C Cattle Truck & Cattle Trailer with beige stakes & brown cows, England casting ($8-10)
2. red MB71-C Cattle Truck & Cattle Trailer with beige stakes & coffee cows, England casting ($8-10)
3. yellow MB71-C Cattle Truck & Cattle Trailer with chocolate stakes & red-brown cows, England casting ($8-10)
4. powder blue MB71-C Cattle Truck & Cattle Trailer with chocolate stakes & black cows, Macau casting ($8-12)
5. green MB71-C Cattle Truck & Cattle Trailer with yellow stakes & black cows, Thailand casting ($7-10)
6. yellow MB71-C Cattle Truck & Cattle Trailer with chocolate stakes & red-brown cows, Macau casting ($7-10)
7. green MB71-C Cattle Truck & Cattle Trailer with yellow stakes & black cows, Macau casting ($7-10)

TP104-A STEAM LOCOMOTIVE & PASSENGER COACH, issued 1984
1. red MB43-C 0-4-0 Loco with "4345" labels & red MB44-C Coach with flat tan roof & "431 432" labels ($10-15)
2. red MB43-C 0-4-0 Loco with "4345" labels & red MB44-C Coach with flat beige roof & "431 432" labels ($10-15)
3. red MB43-C 0-4-0 Loco with "4345" labels & red MB44-C Coach with flat beige roof & "5810 6102" labels ($15-18)
4. red MB43-C 0-4-0 Loco with "4345" labels & red MB44-C Coach with flat tan roof & "5810 6102" labels ($15-18)
5. red MB43-C 0-4-0 Loco with "4345" labels & MB44-C Coach with raised beige roof & "5810 6102" labels ($15-18)
6. red MB43-C 0-4-0 Loco with "4345" labels & red MB44-C Coach with raised beige roof & "431 432" labels ($15-18)

TP105-A DATSUN & BOAT, issued 1984
1. MB67-C Datsun 260Z in black with no tempa & MB9-A Boat with blue deck, white hull & blue trailer ($10-15)
NOTE: Datsun with clear or opaque windows, England casting with either Lesney or Matchbox International cast.

TP106-A RENAULT & MOTORCYCLE TRAILER, issued 1984
1. white MB21-C Renault with green tempa & yellow trailer with red cycles, England casting ($10-15)
2. white MB21-C Renault with pink/yellow tempa & yellow trailer with red cycles, England casting ($10-15)
3. white MB21-C Renault with pink/yellow tempa & yellow trailer with olive cycles, England casting ($15-18)
4. white MB21-C Renault with pink/yellow tempa & yellow trailer with black cycles, England casting ($15-18)
5. white MB21-C Renault with pink/yellow tempa & yellow trailer with black cycles, Macau casting ($15-18)
6. pearly silver MB21-C Renault with "Scrambler" tempa & pearly silver trailer with black cycles, Macau casting ($15-18)

TP107-A DATSUN & CARAVAN, issued 1984
1. silver-gray MB67-C Datsun 260Z with 2 tone blue stripes & white MB31-C Caravan with "Mobile 500" tempa ($10-15)

TP108-A TRACTOR & TRAILER, issued 1984
1. blue MB46-C Tractor & red 40C Hay Trailer, England or Macau casting ($8-12)
2. yellow MB46-C Tractor & yellow 40C Hay Trailer, Macau casting ($8-12)
3. green MB46-C Tractor & yellow 40C Hay Trailer, Macau or Thailand casting ($8-12)

TP109-A CITROEN & BOAT, issued 1984
NOTE: Versions 1 to 8 with England castings.
1. white MB12-D Citroen with "Marine" tempa; MB9-A Boat with blue deck, white hull, blue trailer & no labels ($15-20)
2. white MB12-D Citroen with "Marine" tempa; MB9-A Boat with blue deck, white hull, blue trailer & "8" label ($15-20)
3. white MB12-D Citroen with "Marine" tempa; MB9-A Boat with white deck, blue hull, blue trailer & "8" label ($15-20)
4. white MB12-D Citroen with "Marine" tempa; MB9-A Boat with white deck, blue hull, orange trailer & "8" label ($15-20)
5. white MB12-D Citroen with "Ambulance" tempa; MB9-A Boat with blue deck, white hull, orange trailer & no label ($25-40)
6. white MB12-D Citroen with "Ambulance" tempa; MB9-A Boat with white deck, blue hull, orange trailer & "8" label ($15-20)
7. white MB12-D Citroen with "Ambulance" tempa; MB9-A Boat with white deck, white hull, orange trailer & "8" label ($15-20)
8. dark green MB9-C Ford Escort with "Seagull" labels; MB9-A Boat with white deck, blue hull, orange trailer & "8" label ($50-75)
9. white MB12-D Citroen with "Marine" tempa; MB9-A Boat with white deck, white hull, orange trailer & "8" tempa, Macau casting ($15-20)

TP110-A MATRA RANCHO & INFLATABLE, issued 1984
1. MB37-E Matra Rancho in navy blue with white base & tempa; Inflatable with orange deck, white hull & no tempa, black trailer ($10-15)
2. MB37-E Matra Rancho in navy blue with white base & tempa; Inflatable with orange deck, white hull & "SR" tempa, black trailer ($10-15)
3. MB37-E Matra Rancho in black with white base & tempa; Inflatable with orange deck, white hull & "SR" tempa, black trailer ($10-15)
4. MB37-E Matra Rancho in navy blue with white base & tempa; Inflatable with yellow deck, white hull & "SR" tempa, black trailer ($12-18)
5. MB37-E Matra Rancho in orange with black base & tempa; Inflatable with black deck, orange hull & "2" tempa, white trailer ($10-15)

TP111-A FORD CORTINA & PONY TRAILER, issued 1984
1. tan MB55-D Ford Cortina with black stripe & beige MB43-A Pony Trailer with horse head label ($8-12)
2. red MB55-D Ford Cortina with black stripe & beige MB43-A Pony Trailer with "Silver Shoes" tempa ($8-12)

TP112-A UNIMOG & TRAILER, issued 1984
1. MB48-E Unimog & MB2-A Trailer in yellow with white canopies and "Alpine Rescue" labels, England casting ($10-15)
2. MB48-E Unimog & MB2-A Trailer in yellow with white canopies and "Alpine Rescue" tempa, Macau casting ($10-15)
3. MB48-E Unimog & MB2-A Trailer in red with white canopies and "Unfall Rettung" tempa, Macau casting ($10-15)
4. MB48-E Unimog & MB2-A Trailer in white with orange canopies with "GES" tempa, Macau or Thailand casting ($10-15)

TP113-A PORSCHE & CARAVAN, issued 1985
1. black MB3-C Porsche with gold tempa & white MB31-C Caravan with "Mobile 500" tempa ($15-18)

TP114-A VOLKSWAGEN & PONY TRAILER, issued 1985
1. black MB7-C VW Golf with red tempa & beige MB43-A Pony Trailer with "Silver Shoes" tempa ($15-18)

TP115-A FORD ESCORT & BOAT, issued 1987
1. MB17D/MB37-F Ford Escort in white with "XR3i" tempa; MB9-A Boat with white deck, white hull, black trailer & "Seaspray" tempa, Macau or Thailand casting ($8-12)
2. MB17-D/MB37-F Ford Escort in metallic blue with spatter tempa; MB9-A Boat with blue deck, blue hull, black trailer & spatter tempa, Thailand casting ($8-12)

TP116-A JEEP CHEROKEE & CARAVAN, issued 1987
1. MB27-D Jeep Cherokee in beige with "Holiday Club:" tempa & MB31-C Caravan in beige with "500" tempa ($8-12)

TP117-A MERCEDES G WAGON & PONY TRAILER, issued 1987
1. MB30-F Mercedes in white with "Polizei" checkered tempa & MB43-A Pony Trailer in white with "Polizei" checkered tempa, Macau casting ($8-12)
2. MB30-F Mercedes in white with green "Polizei" tempa & MB43-A Pony Trailer in green with "Polizei" tempa, Macau or Thailand casting ($8-12)

TP118-A BMW CABRIOLET & GLIDER TRANSPORTER, issued 1987
1. MB39-D BMW in red with "Gliding Club" tempa & Glider Transporter in red with "Auto Glide" tempa ($12-15)

TP119-A FLARESIDE PICKUP & SEAFIRE, issued 1987
1. MB53-D Flareside in yellow with "Ford" tempa & MB5-B Seafire in yellow with blue hull & "460" tempa ($8-12)

TP120-A VOLKSWAGEN & INFLATABLE, issued 1989
1. MB33-D/MB56-E Volkswagen in dark gray & Inflatable with orange deck, black hull, white trailer with red & blue tempa, Macau or Thailand casting ($8-12)

TP121-A LAND ROVER & SEAFIRE, issued 1989
1. MB35-F/MB16-F Land Rover in white with "County" tempa' MB5-B Seafire with white deck, red hull, red tempa, white plastic trailer with blue & red tempa, Macau or Thailand casting ($8-12)
2. MB35-F/MB16-F Land Rover in white with "Bacardi" tempa; MB5-B Seafire with white deck,, white hull, "Bacardi" tempa with white metal trailer, Thailand casting (from MB9-A) ($50-75)(UK)(OP)

TP122-A PORSCHE & GLIDER TRANSPORTER, issued 1989
1. MB3-C Porsche in dark blue with yellow tempa; Transporter in dark blue with white glider & yellow tempa , Macau or Thailand casting ($7-10)
2. MB3-C Porsche in yellow with spatter tempa; Transporter in yellow with hot pink glider & spatter tempa, Thailand casting ($8-12)

TP123-A BMW CABRIOLET & CARAVAN, issued 1989
1. MB39-D BMW in silver blue with dark blue stripe; MB31-C Caravan in gray with orange tempa ($8-12)
2. MB39-D BMW in white with geometric tempa; MB31-C Caravan in white with geometric design tempa ($8-12)

TP124-A LOCOMOTIVE & PASSENGER COACH, issued 1991
1. green MB43-C 0-4-0 Loco with "British Railways" tempa & green MB44-C Coach with "British Railways" tempa, ($8-12)

TP125-A SHUNTER & TIPPER, issued 1991
1. MB24-C Shunter in yellow, ex-TP20 Side Tipper in yellow with red dump, China casting ($8-10)

TP126-A MERCEDES TRACTOR & TRAILER, issued 1991
1. MB73-E/MB27-E Mercedes Tractor in yellow & green; 40-C Hay Trailer in yellow ($8-10)

TP127-A BMW CABRIOLET & INFLATABLE, issued 1991
1. MB39-D BMW in white with red & blue tempa; Inflatable in dark blue with gray hull. white trailer with red & blue tempa ($8-10)

TP128-A CIRCUS SET, issued 1992
1. MB72-E Dodge Truck in red with white container & "Big Top Circus" tempa; MB2-A Mercedes Trailer in red with white canopy & "Big Top Circus" tempa ($8-12)

TP129-A ISUZU AMIGO & SEAFIRE, issued 1992
1. MB52-E Isuzu in red; MB5-B Seafire in red with white hull with "Surf Rider" tempa, white plastic trailer ($7-10)

TP130-A LAND ROVER & PONY TRAILER, issued 1992
1. MB35-F/MB16-F Land Rover in white; MB43-A Pony Trailer in white with red roof & red/black stripes tempa ($7-10)

TP131-A MERCEDES G WAGON & INFLATABLE, issued 1992
1. MB30-F Mercedes in white with orange roof & "Marine Rescue" tempa; Inflatable in florescent orange with gray hull with "Rescue" tempa & white trailer ($7-10)

CS-81 BULLDOZER & TRACTOR SHOVEL, issued 1992
1. MB64-D Bulldozer in yellow with red roof; MB29-C Tractor Shovel in yellow with red shovel, with plastic accessories ($6-8)

CS-82 PETERBILT QUARRY TRUCK & EXCAVATOR, issued 1992
1. MB30-E/MB23-E Peterbilt in yellow with red dump; MB32-D/MB6-F Excavator in yellow with red scoop, with plastic accessories ($6-8)

CS-83 ROAD ROLLER & FAUN CRANE, issued 1992
1. MB40-E/MB68-H Road Roller in yellow; MB42-E Crane in yellow with red cab, includes plastic accessories ($6-8)

EM-81 SNORKEL & FOAM PUMPER, issued 1992
1. MB63-E/MB13-C Snorkel in florescent orange & MB54 Foam Pumper in florescent orange, with plastic accessories ($6-8)

EM-83 AUXILIARY POWER TRUCK & AMBULANCE, issued 1992
1. MB57-H/MB50-G Power Truck in florescent orange & MB25-E Ambulance in white, with plastic accessories ($6-8)

010120 LIMITED EDITION CHRISTMAS OFFER, issued 1984
1. 2 assorted vehicles esp. U.K. versions using a Christmas stocking sleeve ($12-15)

010301 DODGE INSTANT WINNER GAME, issued 1984
1. MB28-E Dodge Daytona in maroon; MB68-E/MB64-E Dodge Caravan in black ($20-25)

32350 DAYS OF THUNDER RACE CAR CHALLENGE, issued 1990
1. 2X MB54-F Chevy Lumina in "Superflo" & "City Chevrolet" liveries ($10-15)
2. 2X MB54-G Chevy Lumina in "Hardees" & "Mello Yello" liveries ($10-15)

FM-100 FARMING TWIN PACK, issued 1993
1. includes MB73-E Mercedes Tractor & MB712 Seeder ($4-6)

2. includes MB73-E Mercedes Tractor & MB711 Hay Trailer ($4-6)
3. includes MB237 Tractor Shovel & MB710 Tipping Trailer ($4-6)
4. includes MB246 Ford Tractor & MB711 Hay Trailer ($4-6)
5. includes MB246 Ford Tractor & MB713 Rotovator ($4-6)

NM-810 NIGEL MANSELL TWINPACKS, issued 1994
1. includes MB246 Formula 1 & MB74-H Grand Prix Racer ($4-6)
2 includes MB246 Formula 1 & MB46-F Mission Helicopter ($4-6)
3 includes MB246 Formula 1 & MB68-C Chevy Van ($4-6)

GRAFFIC TRAFFIC HOT METALS, issued 1994
1. includes MB2-G Corvette & MB31-J Jaguar XJ220 ($5-7)
2. includes MB7-F Porsche 959 & MB24-H Ferrari F40 ($5-7)

GRAFFIC TRAFFIC METAL FLAKES, issued 1994
1. includes MB7-G Ford Thunderbird & MB67-F Lamborghini Countach ($5-7)
2. includes MB54-H Chevy Lumina & MB66-E Sauber Group C Racer ($5-7)

32660 INDY 500 CLOSEST FINISH EVER, issued 1993
1. includes MB74-H (2x) in Valvoline & Mackenzie liveries ($6-10)(IN)

Matchmates

M-01-A CITROEN MATCHMATES, issued 1984
1. MB12-D Citroen in white with "Marine" tempa & MB44-E Citroen 15CV in black ($10-15)

M-02-A FORD MATCHMATES, issued 1984
1. MB38-E Model A Ford Van in white/red/blue with "Pepsi" tempa & MB73-C Model A Ford in tan/brown ($10-15)

M-03-A JAGUAR MATCHMATES, issued 1984
1. MB22-E Jaguar XK120 in green & MB47-D Jaguar SS in red ($10-15)

M-04-A JEEP MATCHMATES, issued 1984
1. MB5-D Jeep in brown & MB20-C Jeep in black ($10-15)

M-05-A CORVETTE MATCHMATES, issued 1984
1. MB14-D 1984 Corvette in red & MB21-D Corvette in pearly silver ($10-15)

M-06-A KENWORTH MATCHMATES, issued 1984
1. MB41-D Kenworth in black & MB45-C Kenworth in pearly silver ($10-15)

Theme and Gift Packs

This section covers three-pack, five-pack, and other multiple-pack sets issued in themes or for other purposes. Like the gift sets, different prefixes are used as well as serial numbers to identify sets. A few sets have no identification. Prefixes used include MP (Multi Pack), MB (Matchbox), EM (Emergency), CS (Construction), SB (Skybuster), and GF (Graffic Traffic). For values, add up price of each individual item and add 10-20 percent for sealed items.

MP-1 FIVE PACK, issued 1979 (UK)
1. assorted vehicles
NOTE: This set included such vehicles as the white Piston Popper, white Saab Sonnet, blue Ford Heavy Wrecker, silver Mercedes 300SE, etc.

MP-101 EMERGENCY SET, issued 1988 (ROW)
1. contains MB8-G, MB21-E, MB60-F

MP-102 CONSTRUCTION SET, issued 1988 (ROW)
1. contains MB19-D, MB64-D, MB70-E

MP-103 AIRPORT FIRE SET, issued 1988 (ROW)
1. contains MB18-C, MB54-F, MB75-D

MP-104 4 X 4 SET, issued 1988 (ROW)
1. contains MB5-D, MB20-C, MB37-F
2. includes MB13-D, MB22-D, MB53-D ($5-8)

MP-105 DRAGSTER SET, issued 1988(ROW)
1. contains MB26-D, MB48-D, MB69-D

MP-106 PORSCHE SET, issued 1988 (ROW)
1. contains MB3-C, MB7-F, MB55-F

MP-107 FARM SET, issued 1989 (ROW)
1. contains MB46-C, MB51-C, MB71-C
2. contains MB46-C, MB51-C, MB71-C ("Boot's" package-UK)

MP-108 NASA SET, issued 1989 (ROW)
1. contains MB54-F, MB68-E, MB72-F in NASA liveries

MP-109 FERRARI SET, issued 1990 (ROW)
1. contains MB24-F, MB70-D, MB75-E

MP-803 FERRARI SET, issued 1989 (ROW)
1. MB24-F MB70-D, MB75-E (red package)
2. MB24-F, MB70-D, MB75-E (gray package-Italy)

MP-804 PORSCHE SET, issued 1989 (ROW)
1. MB3-C, MB7-F, MB71-F in black (red package)

MP-805 HOBBY SET, issued 1991 (DU/AS/GR)
1. contains MB27-D, MB31-C, TP21 Trailer
2. contains MB31-C, MB39-D, TP110 Inflatable Raft
3. contains MB35-F, MB5-B, MB43-A
4. contains MB3-C, MB9-A, TP7 Glider

MB-170 BUY 2/GET 1 FREE AT WOOLWORTH'S (UK)
1. contains three assorted miniatures (contents vary)

MB-803 MOTORPLAY, issued 1989 (Early Learning Center)
NOTE: In 1993 these were reissued numbered "2358".
1. contains MB19-D, MB64-D, MB70-E
2. contains MB8-G, MB21-F, MB60-G
3. contains MB4-E, MB17-C, MB66-G

MB-831 SUPER VALUE PACK-FREE SKYBUSTER, issued 1991 (UK)
1. contains 4 miniatures & 1 Skybuster (contents vary)

MB837 SUPER VALUE PACK, issued 1992 (ROW)
1. contains six assorted miniatures (contents vary)

MB-838 TRAINPLAY, issued 1991 (Early Learning Center)
NOTE: In 1993 these were reissued numbered "2140"
1. contains MB43-C and 2X MB44-C

MB844 CHRISTMAS FOUR PACK, issued 1992 (ROW)
1. contains four assorted miniatures in an outer sleeve (contents vary)

MB-858 SUPER VALUE PACK, issued 1990 (ROW)
1. contains three assorted miniatures (contents vary)

MB-860 BUY 2/GET 1 FREE, issued 1987 (UK)
1. contains three assorted miniatures (contents vary)

MB-861 SONDERPREIS, issued 1987 (GR)
1. contains three assorted miniatures (contents vary)

MB-862 THREE PIECE SET, issued 1987 (ROW)
1. contains three assorted miniatures (contents vary)

MB-868 TRE AL PREZZO DI DUE, issued 1987 (IT)
1. contains three assorted miniatures (contents vary)

SB-150 SKYBUSTERS GIFT SET, issued 1990 (ROW)
1. contains 2 miniatures and 1 Skybuster (contents vary)

1100 THREE PACK ASSORTMENTS, issued 1993 (USA)
1. "Construction" includes MB40-H, MB42-E, MB64-D ($3-5)
2. "Racing" includes MB7-G, MB35-I, MB54-H ($3-5)
3. "Hot Rods" includes MB2-G, MB4-D, MB73-C ($3-5)

1101 METRO POLICE SET, issued 1987 (USA)
1. contains MB10-C, MB46-F, MB50-E
2. contains MB16-E, MB46-F, MB50-E

1102 METRO FIRE DEPT., issued 1987 (USA)
1. contains MB18-C, MB25-E, MB63-E

1103 SPORTS RACERS, issued 1987 (USA)
1. contains MB2-E, MB55-F, MB67-F
2. contains MB10-D, MB32-E, MB51-G

1104 4 X 4 MOUNTAIN ADVENTURE, issued 1989 (USA)
1. contains MB5-D, MB13-D, MB39-E
2. contains MB5-D, MB20-C, MB37-F

1105 HOT ROD DRIVE-IN, issued 1989 (USA)
1. contains MB4-D, MB40-C, MB73-C
2. contains MB2-G, MB4-D, MB69-D
3. contains MB2-G, MB66-F, MB73-C

1106 TRUCK STOP, issued 1989 (USA)
1. contains MB8-F, MB30-E, MB45-C
2. contains MB8-H, MB30-E, MB45-C

0312 PUFFY STICKERS, issued 1983 (USA)
1. Track Burners contain MB11-E, MB34-C, MB55-F
2. Off Road 4X4 contains MB7-D, MB13-D, MB22-D
3. Street Racers contains MB4-D, MB40-C, MB71-D

2420 AIRPLAY issued 1993 (Early Learning Center)

1. includes one Skybuster, one MB75-C & accessories (contents vary)($4-6)(ELC)

2501 ROADBLASTERS, issued 1987
1. contains 3 miniatures with armament (contents vary)

010779 FREE RIDE, BUY 2 GET 1 FREE, issued 1985 (USA)
1. contains three assorted miniatures (contents vary)

010787 HALLEY'S COMET BUY 2 GET 1 FREE , issued 1985 (USA)
1. contains two assorted miniatures with "Haley's Comet" version of either MB12-E, MB34-C or MB59-B

25823 SUPER VALUE PACK WITH FREE POSTER, issued 1990 (USA)
1. contains five assorted miniatures with poster (contents vary)
NOTE: A European version of this set was numbered MB-823)

32900 DREAM MACHINES, issued 1992 (USA)
1. contains MB14-G, MB43-F, MB53-F
2. contains MB5-D, MB22-E, MB70-D

38320 GRAFFIC TRAFFIC BODY SWOPPERS, issued 1993
1. set includes three plastic bodies (van, car & jeep) with one metal interchangeable chassis ($7-10)

SB-807 BUY 2 SKYBUSTERS, GET 2 CARS FREE, issued 1990 (ROW)
1. contains 2 assorted miniatures & 2 assorted Skybusters (contents vary)

GF-180 GRAFFIC TRAFFIC THREE PACK, issued 1991
1. contains 3 assorted miniatures (contents vary)

1000 PS SET, issued 1977 (GR)
1. contains MB29-C3, MB37-C14 & MB49-C4 or C5 in an outer sleeve

LONDON LIFE, issued 1987 (UK)
1. contains MB4-E, MB17-C, MB66-G

LE MANS, issued 1987 (UK)
1. contains MB55-F, MB66-E, MB67-G

CONSTRUCTION, issued 1987 (UK)
1. contains MB30-E, MB32-D, MB64-D

ROYAL MAIL BY PROMOD, issued 1987 (UK)
1. contains MB38-E, MB60-G, MB66-E in Royal Mail liveries

GERMAN FIVE PACK CHRISTMAS STOCKING, issued 1986 (GR)
1. contains five assorted miniatures (contents vary)

GERMAN FOUR PACK EASTER EGG, issued 1988 (GR)
1. contains four assorted miniatures shaped like an Easter egg (contents vary)

SUPER GT CHRISTMAS STOCKING, issued 1991 (UK)
1. contains five assorted Super GT's (contents vary)

SUPER GT THREE & FOUR PACKS, issued 1987
1. contains three assorted Super GT's (contents vary)
2. contains four assorted Super GT's (contents vary)

COLECAO MATCHBOX FOUR PACK, issued 1993 (BR)
1. "Racing" includes MB9-D, MB15-E, MB28-D, MB55-F ($120-160)(BR)
2. "Drivers" includes MB6-B, MB25-E, MB40-C, MB70-D ($120-160)(BR)
3. "Truck" includes MB19-D, MB30-E, MB56-D, MB61-C ($120-160)(BR)

PRICE BUSTERS, issued 1993 & 1994
1. includes two Convoys (contents vary)($8-10)(UK)
2. includes one Skybuster & one miniature (contents vary)($4-6)(UK)
3. includes one Special (contents vary)($3-5)(UK)
4. includes three miniatures (contents vary)($3-5)(ROW)
NOTE: Price Buster 3 packs come in two different shapes. The models are arranged in one vertical row or in a triangular arrangement.

060032 FIVE PACK ASSORTMENTS, issued 1993/94
1. "Racing" includes MB7-G, MB10-D, MB35-H, MB54-H, MB65-D ($5-8)
2. "Emergency" includes MB16-E, MB18-C, MB21-F, MB46-F, MB50-E ($5-8)
3. "Off Road" includes MB5-D, MB20-C, MB35-F, MB39-E, MB44-D ($5-8)

FM-110 FARMING GIFT SET, issued 1993
1. includes MB35-F, MB73-E, MB237, Tipping Trailer & Rotovator ($7-10)

FM-120 FARMING GIFT SET, issued 1993
1. includes MB40-C, MB51-C, MB73-E, MB237, Hay Trailer, Rotovator & Seeder ($10-12)

FM-130 FARMING GIFT SET, issued 1993
1. includes MB35-F, MB40-A, MB43-A, MB51-C, MB56-D, MB71-C, MB236, MB237, Hay Trailer, Tipping Trailer, Rotovator, Seeder & plastic accessories ($35-50)

NM-830 NIGEL MANSELL COLLECTION- FORMULA 1 GIFT SET, issued 1994
1. contains MB46-F, MB68-C, MB68-G, MB246 & CY-24-A ($18-25)

NM-832 NIGEL MANSELL COLLECTION- INDY GIFT SET, issued 1994
1. contains MB21-F, (2X)MB74-H, CY-104-A & Team Transporter ($18-25)

11920 40TH ANNIVERSARY CORVETTE GIFT SET, issued 1994
1. contains MB2-G, MB14-G, MB40-C, MB62-D, MB71-D ($12-18)(US)

50021 JAGUAR GIFT SET, issued 1994
1. includes MB22-E, MB31-J, MB41-F, MB47-D, CY-24-A ($12-15)

50022 SUPER CARS GIFT SET, issued 1994
1. includes MB7-F, MB22-H, MB24-H, MB31-J, MB67-H, MB75-E ($10-13)

15 PIECE SUPER COLLECTION GIFT SET, issued 1993
1. includes 15 miniatures (contents vary)($15-18)

REITHOFFER'S CIRCUS GIFT SET, issued 1994
1. includes MB20-D, MB50-H, MB215, CY-104-A, CY-109-A ($25-40)(WR)

DISNEY HOLIDAY STOCKING, issued 1979
1. consists of three Disney vehicles each individually blisterpacked and enclosed with outer sleeve (contents vary)

Convoy

This series includes mostly trailer trucks. First introduced in 1982, the series branched off as White Rose Collectibles to include castings exclusive to that promotional concern. In 1993, the Convoy name was replaced by the name "Super Rigs," although 'CY' numbers are still used to identify these.

CY-1-A KENWORTH CAR TRANSPORTER, issued 1982
1. red cab with white/yellow/blue stripes, chrome exhausts, red trailer with beige ramp & white stripes, England casting ($8-12)
2. red cab with black/blue/white stripes, chrome exhausts, red trailer with beige ramp & white stripes, England casting ($8-12)
3. red cab with black/blue/white stripes, chrome exhausts, red trailer with beige ramp & white stripes, England casting ($8-12)
4. red cab with black/blue/white stripes & "4" roof label, chrome exhausts, red trailer with beige ramp & no stripes, England casting ($150-175)
5. red cab with white/yellow/black stripes, chrome exhausts, red trailer with beige ramp & no stripes, Macau casting ($6-8)
6. red cab with white/yellow/black stripes, chrome exhausts, red trailer with beige ramp with stripes Macau casting ($6-8)
7. yellow cab with blue & purple tempa, chrome exhaust, dark blue trailer with yellow ramp, Macau casting ($6-8)
8. yellow cab with blue & purple tempa, gray exhausts, dark blue trailer with yellow ramp, Macau casting ($6-8)
9. yellow cab with blue & purple tempa, gray exhausts, dark blue trailer with yellow ramp, Thailand casting ($6-8)
10. blue cab with yellow & orange tempa, chrome exhausts, blue trailer with yellow ramp, Thailand casting ($4-6)
11. blue cab with yellow & orange tempa, chrome exhausts, blue trailer with yellow ramp, China casting ($4-6)

CY-2-A KENWORTH ROCKET TRANSPORTER, issued 1982
1. silver-gray cab with tempa on front, chrome exhausts, white SB-3B Space Shuttle, England casting ($12-15)(GS)
2. silver-gray cab with tempa on front, chrome exhausts, white plastic rocket, England casting ($8-12)
3. silver-gray cab without tempa on front, chrome exhausts, white plastic rocket, England casting ($8-12)
4. pearly silver cab, chrome exhausts, white plastic rocket, Macau casting ($6-8)
5. white cab, chrome exhausts, white plastic rocket, Macau casting ($5-7)
6. white cab, gray exhausts, white plastic rocket, Macau casting ($5-7)
7. white cab, gray exhausts, white plastic rocket, Thailand casting ($5-7)
8. white cab, gray exhausts, chrome plastic rocket, Thailand casting ($4-5)
9. white cab, gray exhausts, chrome plastic rocket, China casting ($4-5)

CY-3-A DOUBLE CONTAINER TRUCK, issued 1982
1. MB41-D cab in red, chrome exhausts, clear windows, beige containers, black trailer, "Uniroyal" labels, England casting ($15-18)
2. MB43-D cab in red, chrome exhausts, amber windows, beige containers, black trailer, "Uniroyal" labels, England casting ($12-15)
3. MB43-D cab in red, chrome exhausts, clear windows, beige containers, black trailer, "Uniroyal" labels, England casting ($12-15)
4. MB43-D cab in red, chrome exhausts, clear windows, light tan containers, black trailer, "Uniroyal" labels, England casting ($12-15)
5. MB43-D cab in red, chrome exhausts, clear windows, beige containers, white trailer, "Uniroyal" labels, England casting ($20-25)
6. MB43-D cab in red, chrome exhausts, clear windows, cream containers, white trailer, "Uniroyal" labels, England casting ($20-25)
7. MB41-D cab in red, chrome exhausts, clear windows, beige containers, white trailer, "Uniroyal" labels, England casting ($20-25)
8. MB43-D cab in red, chrome exhausts, clear windows, brown containers, black trailer, "Uniroyal" labels, England casting ($10-15)
9. MB45-C cab in white, chrome exhausts, amber windows, beige containers, "Pepsi" labels, Macau casting ($350-500)
10. MB43-D cab in black, chrome exhausts, clear windows, cream containers, "Pepsi" labels, England casting ($350-500)
11. MB43-D cab in black, chrome exhausts, clear windows, cream containers, black trailer, "Federal Express" labels, Macau casting ($15-18)
12. MB43-D cab in white, chrome exhausts, clear windows, beige containers, black trailer, "Federal Express" labels, England casting ($15-18)
13. MB43-D cab in white, chrome exhausts, clear windows, white containers, black trailer, "Federal Express" tempa, Macau casting ($6-8)
14. MB41-D cab in red, chrome exhausts, clear windows, light tan containers, white trailer, "Mayflower" labels, England casting ($1000+)
15. MB43-D cab in white, gray exhausts, clear windows, white containers, black trailer, "Federal Express" tempa, Macau casting ($6-8)
16. MB43-D cab in white, gray exhausts, clear windows, white containers, black trailer, "Federal Express" tempa, Thailand casting ($4-5)
17. MB45-C cab in white, chrome exhausts, amber windows, beige containers, black trailer, "Smith's Crisps" labels, Macau casting ($350-500)
18. MB41-D cab in red, chrome exhausts & antennas, clear windows, black containers, yellow trailer, "Matchbox" tempa, China casting, rubber tires ($8-10)(PC)

CY-3-B KENWORTH BOX TRUCK, issued 1985 (AU)
1. red cab, red container, yellow trailer, "Linfox" tempa, Macau casting ($12-15)(AU)

CY-4-A KENWORTH BOAT TRANSPORTER, issued 1982
1. light orange cab, boat with light orange hull & green windows, silver-gray trailer, England casting ($8-12)
2. light orange cab, boat with dark orange hull & green windows, silver-gray trailer, England casting ($8-12)
3. dark orange cab, boat with dark orange hull & green windows, silver-gray trailer, England casting ($8-12)
4. dark orange cab, boat with light orange hull & green windows, silver-gray trailer, England casting ($8-12)
5. dark orange cab, boat with dark orange hull & red windows, silver-gray trailer, England casting ($10-15)
6. dark orange cab, boat with dark orange hull & clear windows, silver-gray trailer, England casting ($10-15)
7. dark orange cab, boat with dark orange hull & green windows, pearly silver trailer, Macau casting ($6-8)
8. very light orange cab, boat with dark orange hull & green windows, pearly silver trailer, Macau casting ($6-8)

CY-4-B SCANIA BOX TRUCK, issued 1985 (AU)
1. white cab, white container, black trailer, "Ansett" (towards front) labels ($12-15)(AU)
2. white cab, white container, black trailer, "Ansett" (towards rear) labels ($12-15)(AU)

CY-5-A PETERBILT COVERED TRUCK, issued 1982
1. MB43-D cab in white, chrome exhausts, amber windows, green cover, white trailer, "Interstate Trucking" labels, England casting ($8-12)
2. MB43-D cab in white, chrome exhausts, clear windows, green cover, white trailer, "Interstate Trucking" labels, England casting ($8-12)
3. MB41-D cab in green, chrome exhausts, clear windows, green cover, white trailer, "Interstate Trucking" labels, England casting ($18-25)
4. MB43-D cab in green, chrome exhausts, clear windows, green cover, white trailer, "Interstate Trucking" tempa, Macau casting ($12-15)
5. MB43-D cab in yellow, chrome exhausts, clear windows, yellow cover, pearly silver trailer, "Michelin" tempa, Macau casting ($8-12)
6. MB43-D cab in orange, chrome exhausts, clear windows, light gray cover, pearly silver trailer, "Walt's Fresh Farm Produce" tempa, Macau casting ($6-8)
7. MB43-D cab in orange, gray exhausts, clear windows, light gray cover, pearly silver trailer, "Walt's Fresh Farm Produce" tempa, Macau casting ($6-8)
8. MB43-D cab in orange, gray exhausts, clear windows, light gray cover, pearly silver trailer, "Walt's Fresh Farm Produce" tempa, Thailand casting ($4-6)

CY-6-A KENWORTH HORSE BOX, issued 1982
1. green cab with yellow & black stripes, beige trailer, green doors, silver-gray base, "Blue Grass Farms" tempa, England casting ($8-12)
2. green cab with white & black stripes, beige trailer, green doors, silver-gray base, "Blue Grass Farms" tempa, England casting ($8-12)
3. green cab with white & black stripes, beige trailer, green doors, silver-gray base, "Blue Grass" tempa, England casting ($8-12)
4. green cab with white & black stripes, tan trailer, green doors, silver-gray base, no tempa, England casting ($8-12)
5. green cab with white & black stripes, beige trailer, green doors, pearly silver base, "Blue Grass Farms" tempa, Macau casting ($8-12)
6. green cab with white & black stripes, beige trailer, white doors, pearly silver base, "Blue Grass Farms" tempa, Macau casting ($8-12)
7. green cab with orange & yellow stripes, beige trailer, green door, pearly silver trailer base, Thailand casting, green & orange stripes with horse silhouette tempa ($6-8)(FM)

CY-7-A PETERBILT GAS TANKER, issued 1982
NOTE: All models with 8 spoke wheels & no antennas cast unless otherwise noted.
1. MB43-D cab in black with yellow & orange "Supergas" tempa, amber windows, yellow tank, black trailer base, "Supergas" labels, England casting ($8-12)

2. MB43-D cab in black with white & red "Super" tempa, amber windows, yellow tank, black trailer base, "Supergas" labels, England casting ($8-12)
3. MB43-D cab in black with white & red "Super" tempa, clear windows, yellow tank, black trailer base, "Supergas" labels, England casting ($8-12)
4. MB41-D cab in black with red & gray stripes tempa, amber windows, yellow tank, black trailer base, "Supergas" labels, England casting ($10-15)
5. MB41-D cab in black with red & gray stripes tempa, clear windows, yellow tank, black trailer base, "Supergas" labels, England casting ($10-15)
6. MB45-C cab in white with red & yellow stripes tempa, amber windows, yellow tank, black trailer base, "Supergas" labels, England casting ($10-15)
7. MB43-D cab in white with no tempa, light amber windows, white tank, black trailer base, "Supergas" labels, England casting ($1000+)
8. MB43-D cab in black with yellow & red "Z" tempa, clear windows, orange-yellow tank, black trailer base, "Supergas" tempa, Macau casting ($8-12)
9. MB43-D cab in red with "Getty" tempa, clear windows, chrome tank, pearly silver trailer base, "Getty" tempa, Macau casting ($6-8)
10. MB43-D cab in silver-gray with "Arco" tempa, clear windows, chrome tank, silver-gray trailer base, "Arco" tempa, China casting, rubber tires, antennas cast ($8-10)(PC)

CY-7-B FORD AEROMAX GAS TANKER, issued 1998
1. bright blue cab with black chassis, chrome tank with blue chassis, "Exxon" tempa, antennas cast, rubber tires ($8-10)(PC)
2. white cab with white chassis, white tank with white chassis, no tempa, no antennas cast, 8 spoke wheels ($35-50)(ASAP blank)

CY-8-A KENWORTH BOX TRUCK, issued 1982
1. MB45-C cab in white with red & yellow tempa, red container with white roof & doors, "Matchbox" labels, England casting ($85-110)
2. MB45-C cab in white with red & yellow tempa, red container with white roof & doors, "Redcap" labels, England casting ($45-60)
3. MB45-C cab in white with brown & blue tempa, red container with white roof & doors, "Redcap" labels, England casting ($45-60)
4. MB41-D cab in red with black & white tempa, red container with white roof & doors, "Redcap" labels, England casting ($45-60)
5. MB41-D cab in red with black & white tempa, red container with white roof & black doors, "Redcap" labels, England casting ($45-60)
6. MB41-D cab in red with black & white tempa, red container with black roof & doors, "Redcap" labels, England casting ($150-200)
7. MB41-D cab in red with black & white tempa, red container with black roof & white doors, "Redcap" labels, England casting ($150-200)
8. MB45-C cab in white with brown & blue tempa, red container with white roof & doors, "Ski Fruit Yogurt" labels, England casting ($100-150)(AU)(C2)
9. MB45-C cab in white with orange & yellow tempa, red container with white roof & doors, "Ski Fruit Yogurt" labels, England casting ($100-150)(AU)(C2)
10. MB45-C cab in white with orange & yellow tempa, red container with white roof & doors, "Redcap" labels, England casting ($45-60)
11. MB45-C cab in silver-gray/blue with yellow & red tempa, silver-gray container with blue roof & doors, "Matchbox Showliner" labels, Macau casting ($300-375)(UK)
12. MB45-C cab in white with red band tempa, white container with white roof & doors, "K-Line" tempa, Macau casting ($300-450)(US)
13. MB45-C cab in white with yellow/red/blue tempa, white container with white roof & doors, "Matchbox" tempa, Macau casting ($12-15)
14. MB45-C cab in white with yellow/red/blue tempa, white container with white roof & doors, "Matchbox" tempa with "This Truck Delivers 1988" roof label, Macau casting ($40-60)(UK)
15. MB45-C cab in white with yellow/red/blue tempa, white container with white roof & doors, "Matchbox" tempa with "This Truck Delivers 1989" roof label, Macau casting ($350-500)(HK)
16. MB45-C cab in white with red band tempa, red container with red roof & doors, "K-Line" tempa, Macau casting ($125-175)(US)
17. MB45-C cab in black with "Harley-Davidson" tempa, black container with black roof & doors, "Harley-Davidson" labels, Macau casting ($5-8)(HD)
18. MB45-C cab in red with white band tempa, red container with red roof & doors, Thailand casting, "Nintendo" tempa ($4-5)
NOTE: above model was originally a preproduction in 1990 but with Macau casting!
19. MB45-C cab in white with "KFC" tempa, white container, roof & doors, Thailand casting, "KFC" labels ($3-5)
20. MB45-C cab in red with "Pizza Hut" tempa, white container, roof & doors, Thailand casting, "Pizza Hut" labels ($3-5)
21. MB45-C cab in white with "Matchbox" tempa, white container with white roof & doors, Thailand casting, "Matchbox/Universal Group" tempa ($450-600)(HK)
22. MB45-C cab in white with "K" tempa, red container, roof & doors with black base, Thailand casting, "K-Line" tempa ($150-200)(US)
23. MB45-C cab in black with "Pizza Hut" tempa, white container, roof & doors with black base, Thailand casting, "Pizza Hut" labels ($3-5)
24. MB45-C cab in black with "Pizza Hut" tempa, white container, roof & doors with black base, China casting, "Pizza Hut" labels ($3-5)
25. MB45-C cab in blue with "Matchbox" tempa, blue container, roof, doors & base, China casting, "Matchbox Action System" labels ($3-5)
26. MB45-C cab in white with "B & L" tempa, white container, roof, doors & base, China casting, "Baldwin & Lyons Inc." labels ($250-500)(US)
27. MB45-C cab in yellow with "Nintendo" tempa, yellow container, roof, doors & base, China casting, "Super Mario 64- Nintendo" labels ($3-5)

CY-9-A KENWORTH BOX TRUCK, issued 1982
NOTE: All models with amber windows, 8 spoke wheels, no antennas & chrome exhausts unless otherwise noted.
1. MB41-D cab in black, black container, "Midnight X-Press" labels, England casting ($8-12)
2. MB41-D cab in black, clear windows, black container, "Midnight X-Press" labels, England casting ($8-12)
3. MB45-C cab in black, amber windows, black container, "Midnight X-Press" tempa, England casting ($40-60)
4. MB41-D cab in black, black container, "Midnight X-Press" tempa, Macau casting ($6-8)
5. MB41-D cab in black, black container, "Moving In New Directions" tempa, Macau casting ($125-175)(AU)
6. MB41-D cab in black, black container, "Moving In New Directions" tempa with "Personal Contact Is Barry Oxford" roof label, Macau casting ($250-300)(AU)
7. MB41-D cab in black, black container, "Moving In New Directions" tempa with "Personal Contact Is Anita Jones" roof label, Macau casting ($250-300)(AU)
8. MB41-D cab in black, black container, "Moving In New Directions" tempa with "Personal Contact Is Keith Mottram" roof label, Macau casting ($250-300)(AU)
9. MB41-D cab in black, black container, "Moving In New Directions" tempa with "Personal Contact Is Terry Blyton" roof label ($250-300)(AU)
10. MB41-D cab in black, black container, "Moving In New Directions" tempa with "Personal Contact Is Jenny Brindley" roof label ($250-300)(AU)
11. MB41-D cab in black, yellow container, "Stanley" tempa, Macau casting ($12-15)(US)(OP)
12. DAF cab in yellow, yellow container, "IPEC" tempa, Macau casting ($12-15)(AU)
13. MB41-D cab in white, white container, "Paul Arpin Van Lines" tempa, Macau casting ($10-15)(US)
14. MB41-D cab in white, white container, "Matchbox/Compliments Macau Diecast Co. Ltd.," Macau casting ($1000+)
15. MB41-D cab in white, white container, "Matchbox-In Celebration of Universal Group's 20th Anniversary" tempa, Macau casting ($1000+)
16. MB41-D cab in white, white container, "Canadian Tire" tempa, Macau casting ($10-15)(CN)
17. MB41-D cab in white, white container, "Merry Christmas 1988 MICA Members" with calendar roof label ($25-40)(C2)
18. MB41-D cab in blue, blue container, "Mitre 10" tempa, Macau casting ($10-15)(AU)
19. MB41-D cab in blue, white container, "Spaulding" tempa, Macau casting ($25-40)(US)
20. MB41-D cab in white, white container, "Merry Christmas MICA Members 1990" labels with calendar roof label ($25-40)(C2)
21. MB41-D cab in black, black container, "Midnight X-Press" tempa, Thailand casting ($4-6)
22. MB41-D cab in black, black container, "Cool Paint Co." labels, Thailand casting ($4-6)
23. MB41-D cab in black, black container, Thailand casting, "Cool Paint Co." labels applied over "Midnight X-Press" ($4-5)
24. MB41-D cab in white, white container, Thailand casting, "Truckin' USA" labels ($4-5)
25. MB41-D cab in white, white container, Thailand casting, "Hershey's" labels ($4-5)
26. MB41-D cab in white, white container, Thailand casting, "Paul Arpin Van Lines" with "NFL" logo ($12-18)
27. MB41-D cab in white, white container & base, Thailand casting, "Hershey's" (with small candy bar) labels ($8-12)
28. MB41-D cab in orange, orange container & base, Thailand casting, "Reese's" labels ($3-5)
29. MB41-D cab in red, red container & base, Thailand casting, "Skittles" labels ($3-5)
30. MB41-D cab in silver/gray, orange container, silver/gray base, Thailand casting, "Skittles" labels ($3-5)
31. MB41-D cab in white, red container, white base, Thailand casting, "Skittles" labels ($3-5)
32. MB41-D cab in yellow, yellow container & base, Thailand casting, "M & M's" labels ($3-5)
33. MB41-D cab in black, black container & base, Thailand casting, "Roller Blade" labels ($3-5)
34. MB41-D cab in black, black container & base, China casting, "Roller Blade" labels ($3-5)
35. MB41-D cab in yellow, yellow container & base, China casting, "M & M's" labels ($3-5)
36. MB41-D cab in bright blue, red container & base, China casting, "Kellogg's Froot Loops" labels ($3-5)
NOTE: Version 36 with either "Matchbox International" or "Mattel Inc." cab casting.
37. MB41-D cab in lemon, lemon container, black base, China casting, "Stop. Go. Pennzoil" tempa, rubber tires, antennas cast ($8-10)(PC)
38. MB41-D cab in red, red container, black base, China casting, "Coca-Cola" with sideways bottle tempa, rubber tires, antennas cast ($8-10)(PC)

CY-10-A RACING TRANSPORTER, issued 1983
1. white body, "Tyrone Malone" tempa, MB66-D Super Boss with green windows (20-25)
2. white body, "Tyrone Malone" tempa, MB66-D Super Boss with red windows ($25-35)

CY-11-A KENWORTH HELICOPTER TRANSPORTER, issued 1983
NOTE: helicopter comes in combinations of clear or amber windows, orange or black base and gray or black interior to make additional permutations to this list.
1. silver-gray cab with "Ace Hire" tempa, chrome exhausts; MB75-D Helicopter in silver-gray with "-600-" tempa, silver-gray trailer, England casting ($8-12)
2. pearly silver cab with "Ace Hire" tempa, chrome exhausts; MB75-D Helicopter in pearly silver with "-600-" tempa, pearly silver trailer, Macau casting ($7-10)
3. black cab with "Air Car" tempa, chrome exhausts; MB75-D Helicopter in black with "Air Car" tempa, pearly silver trailer, Macau casting ($7-10)
4. black cab with "Air Car" tempa, gray exhausts; MB75-D Helicopter in black with "Air Car" tempa, pearly silver trailer, Macau casting ($6-8)
5. dark blue cab with white & gold stripes tempa, chrome exhausts; MB75-D Helicopter in white with "Rescue" tempa, pearly silver trailer, Macau casting ($8-12)(MC)
6. dark blue cab with white & gold stripes tempa, gray exhausts; MB75-D Helicopter in white with "Rescue" tempa, pearly silver trailer, Macau casting ($8-12)(MC)
7. black cab with "Air Car" tempa, gray exhausts; MB75-D Helicopter in black with "Air Car" tempa, pearly silver trailer, Thailand casting ($5-7)
8. dark blue cab with white & gold stripes tempa, gray exhausts: MB75-D Helicopter in white with "Rescue" tempa, pearly silver trailer, Thailand casting ($8-12)(MC)

CY-12-A KENWORTH PLANE TRANSPORTER, issued 1984
1. white cab with blue & dark green tempa, silver-gray trailer, blue plane with "Darts" tempa, England casting ($12-15)
2. white cab with blue & brown tempa, silver-gray trailer, blue plane with "Darts" tempa, England casting ($12-15)
3. white cab with 2 tone blue tempa, pearly silver trailer, blue plane with "Darts" tempa, Macau casting ($8-12)

CY-13-A PETERBILT FIRE ENGINE, issued 1984
1. MB43-D cab in red, red trailer with white lettered "8" & "Fire Dept." tempa, white ladder, England casting ($15-18)
2. MB45-C cab in red with "Denver" label, red trailer with white lettered "8" & "Fire Dept." tempa, white ladder, England casting ($1000+)
3. Peterbilt with dome lights in red, red trailer with white lettered "8" & "Fire Dept." tempa, white ladder, Macau casting ($7-10)
4. Peterbilt with dome lights in red, red trailer with yellow lettered "8" & "Fire Dept." tempa, white ladder, Macau casting ($7-10)
5. Peterbilt with dome lights in red, red trailer with white lettered "8" & yellow lettered "Fire Dept." tempa, white ladder, Macau casting ($8-12)
6. Peterbilt with dome lights in red, red trailer with white lettered "8" & "Fire Dept." tempa, white ladder, Thailand casting ($4-6)
7. Peterbilt with dome lights in florescent orange, florescent orange trailer with "City Fire Dept. 15" & checkers tempa, white ladder, Thailand casting ($4-6)(EM)
8. Peterbilt with dome lights in red, red trailer with white lettered "8" & "Fire Dept." tempa, white ladder, China casting ($4-6)

CY-14-A KENWORTH BOAT TRANSPORTER, issued 1985
1. white cab, white boat, pearly silver trailer with brown cradle ($8-12)

CY-15-A PETERBILT TRACKING VEHICLE, issued 1985
1. white cab with "NASA" tempa, chrome exhausts, white container with pearly silver base, "NASA" tempa, Macau casting ($6-8)
2. yellow cab with no tempa, chrome exhausts, yellow container with pearly silver base, "British Telecom" tempa, Macau casting ($8-12)(GS)
3. powder blue cab with "Satellite TV" & bolt tempa, chrome exhausts, powder blue container with pearly silver base, "MB TV News" tempa, Macau casting ($12-15)
4. powder blue cab with "Peterbilt" & bolt tempa, chrome exhausts, powder blue container with pearly silver base, "MB TV News" tempa, Macau casting ($6-8)
5. powder blue cab with "Peterbilt" & bolt tempa, gray exhausts, powder blue container with pearly silver base, "MB TV News" tempa, Macau casting ($6-8)
6. olive cab with "Strike Team" tempa, black base & exhausts, olive container with olive base, "LS2009" tempa, Macau casting ($20-25)(CM)
7. dark blue cab with "Peterbilt" & bolt tempa, gray exhausts, dark blue container with pearly silver base, "MB TV News" tempa, Macau casting ($6-8)
8. dark blue cab with "Peterbilt" & bolt tempa, gray exhausts, dark blue container with pearly silver base, "MB TV News" tempa, Thailand casting ($6-8)
9. powder blue cab with "Peterbilt" & bolt tempa, gray exhausts, powder blue container with pearly silver base, "MB TV News" tempa, Thailand casting ($6-8)
10. white cab with "Sky TV" tempa, gray exhausts, white container with pearly silver base, "Sky Satellite TV" tempa, Thailand casting ($4-5)
11. white cab with "Sky TV" tempa, chrome exhausts, white container with pearly silver base, "Sky Satellite TV" tempa, Thailand casting ($4-5

CY-16-A SCANIA BOX TRUCK, issued 1985
NOTE: All cabs with chrome base unless otherwise noted.
1. white cab, green chassis, white container with black base, "7 Up" (towards rear) labels, Macau casting ($12-15)(US)
2. white cab, green chassis, white container with black base, "7 Up" (towards front) labels, Macau casting ($12-15)(US)
3. white cab, green chassis, white container with black base, "7 Up" (upside down) labels, Macau casting ($20-35)(US)
4. white cab, dark blue chassis, dark blue container with white base "Duckham's Oils" tempa, Macau casting ($10-15)
5. purple cab & chassis, white container with purple base, "Edwin Shirley" tempa, Macau casting ($12-15)(UK)
6. white cab, black chassis, white container with black base, "Wimpey" tempa, Macau casting ($12-15)(UK)
7. red cab, white chassis, red container with white base, "Kentucky Fried Chicken" tempa, Macau casting ($12-15)(UK)
8. white cab, blue chassis, white container with blue base, "Signa

Toothpaste" tempa, Macau casting ($12-15)(UK)
9. white cab, red chassis, red container with red base, "Heinz Tomato Ketchup Squeezable" labels, Macau casting ($12-15)(UK)
10. yellow cab, white chassis, white container with red base, "Weetabix" labels, Macau casting ($12-15)(UK)
11. blue cab, white chassis, blue container with blue base, "Matey Bubble Bath" tempa, Macau casting ($12-15)(UK)
12. white cab, black chassis, white container with black base, "Golden Wonder Potato Crisps" tempa, Macau casting ($12-15)(UK)
13. white cab, red chassis, white container with red base, "Merchant Tire Auto & Auto Centers" tempa, Macau casting ($10-15)(US)
14. white cab, red chassis, white container with red base, "Merry Christmas 1988 MICA Members" with calendar roof label, Macau casting ($25-40)(C2)
15. yellow cab, white chassis, black base, yellow container & yellow base, "Weetabix" tempa, Macau casting ($12-15)(UK)
16. purple cab, red chassis, black base, purple container with red base, "Ribena" tempa, Macau casting ($12-15)(UK)
17. red cab, white chassis, black base, red container with white base, "Kentucky Fried Chicken" tempa, Macau casting ($12-15)(UK)
18. white cab, green chassis, white container with black base, "Merry Christmas 1989 MICA Members" with calendar roof label ($25-40)(C2)
19. white cab, blue chassis, white container with blue base, "Goodyear Vector" tempa, Thailand casting ($6-8)
20. white cab/dark gray chassis & chrome base, white container with black trailer, Thailand casting, "Saudia" labels ($50-75)(SU)

CY-17-A SCANIA PETROL TANKER, issued 1985
1. white cab, blue chassis with chrome base, white tank with blue base, "Amoco" tempa, Macau casting ($6-8)
2. red cab & chassis with chrome base, red tank with red base, "Tizer" tempa, Macau casting ($12-15)(UK)
3. white cab, green chassis with chrome base, white tank with green base, "Diet 7 Up" tempa, Macau casting ($12-15)(UK)
4. orange cab & chassis with chrome base, orange tank with white base, "Cadbury's Fudge" tempa, Macau casting ($12-15)(UK)
5. white cab, dark gray chassis with chrome base, chrome tank with dark gray base, "Shell" tempa, Macau casting ($6-8)
6. white cab, dark gray chassis with black base, chrome tank with dark gray base, "Shell" tempa, Macau casting ($6-8)
7. white cab, dark gray chassis with black base, chrome tank with dark gray base, "Shell" tempa, Thailand casting ($6-8)
8. white cab, dark gray chassis with black base, white tank with dark gray base, "Feoso" tempa, Thailand casting ($35-45)(CHI)

CY-18-A SCANIA DOUBLE CONTAINER TRUCK, issued 1986
1. blue cab with black interior, yellow chassis, dark blue containers, yellow trailer base, "Varta Batteries" tempa ($30-45)
2. blue cab with gray interior, yellow chassis, dark blue containers, yellow trailer base, "Varta Batteries" tempa ($10-15)
3. white cab, dark blue chassis, white containers, dark blue trailer base, "Wall's Ice Cream" tempa ($12-15)(UK)
4. red cab & chassis, red containers, red trailer base, "Kit Kat" tempa ($12-15)(UK)
5. orange cab, brown chassis, orange containers, brown trailer base, "Breakaway" tempa ($12-15)(UK)
6. white cab, green chassis, white containers, green trailer base, "7 Up" tempa ($12-15)(UK)
7. red cab, black chassis, red containers, black trailer base, "Beefeater Steak Houses" tempa ($12-15)(UK)

CY-18-B FORD AEROMAX DOUBLE CONTAINER TRUCK, issued 1993
1. black cab & chassis, black flatbed with black containers, "Charitoys 1993" tempa, no antennas cast, 8 spoke wheels, Thailand casting ($30-40)(WR)
2. white cab with black chassis, blue flatbed with white containers, "American Airlines" tempa, antennas cast, rubber tires, China casting ($8-10)(PC)
3. orange cab with black chassis, black flatbed with white containers, "U-Haul" labels, antennas cast, rubber tires, China casting ($8-10)(PC)

CY-19-A PETERBILT BOX TRUCK, issued 1987
1. white cab, white container with pearly silver base, "Ansett Wridgways" tempa ($15-20)

CY-20-A ARTICULATED DUMP TRUCK, issued 1987
1. MB45-C cab in yellow, chrome exhausts, yellow trailer with black base, "Taylor Woodrow" tempa, Macau casting ($6-8)
2. MB8-F cab in pink with chrome base, pink trailer with black base, "Readymix" tempa, Macau casting ($15-18)(AU)
3. MB45-C cab in yellow, chrome exhausts, yellow trailer with black base, "Eurobran" tempa, Macau casting ($6-8)
4. MB45-C cab in yellow, chrome exhausts, yellow trailer with black base, black & white road design tempa, Macau casting ($6-8)
5. MB45-C cab in green, chrome exhausts, yellow trailer with black base, "Eurobran" tempa, Macau casting ($6-8)
6. MB45-C cab in green, gray exhausts, yellow trailer with black base, "Eurobran" tempa, Macau casting ($6-8)(MC)
7. MB45-C cab in yellow, gray exhausts, yellow trailer with black base, "Taylor Woodrow" tempa, Macau casting ($6-8)
8. MB8-F cab in pink with black base, pink trailer with black base, "Readymix" tempa, Macau casting ($18-25)(AU)
9. MB45-C cab in green, gray exhausts, yellow trailer with black base, "Eurobran" tempa, Thailand casting ($5-7)
10. MB45-C cab in red, gray exhausts, yellow trailer with black base, red design tempa, Thailand casting ($4-5)(CS)

CY-21-A DAF AIRCRAFT TRANSPORTER, issued 1987
1. white cab, blue chassis with "Space Cab" tempa, dark blue trailer, orange plane with "Airtrainer" tempa, Macau casting ($7-10)
2. white cab, dark blue chassis with "Red Rebels" tempa, white trailer, red plane with "Red Rebels" tempa, Macau casting ($6-8)(MC)
3. black cab, gray chassis with "AC102" tempa, black trailer, black plane with "AC102" tempa, Macau casting ($25-40)(CM)
4. white cab & chassis with no tempa, white trailer, white plane with no tempa, Thailand casting ($15-25)(GF)(GS)
5. white cab, red chassis with "Aerobatic Team" & "Flying Aces" tempa, red trailer, blue plane with "Flying Aces" tempa, Thailand casting ($6-9)
6. white cab, dark blue chassis with "Red Rebels" tempa, white trailer, red plane with "Red Rebels" tempa, Thailand casting ($4-6)
7. white cab, red chassis with "Aerobatic Team" & "Flying Aces" tempa, red trailer, blue plane with "Flying Aces" tempa, China casting ($4-6)

CY-22-A DAF BOAT TRANSPORTER, issued 1987
1. white cab, blue chassis with "Lakeside" tempa, dark blue trailer, boat with white deck, red hull & "Shark" tempa, Macau casting ($7-10)
2. white cab, blue chassis with "P & G" tempa, dark blue trailer, boat with white deck, orange-brown hull & "CG22" tempa, Macau casting ($7-10)
3. white cab, black chassis with "Coast Guard" tempa, black trailer, boat with gray deck, white hull & "Coast Guard" tempa, Macau casting ($6-8)
4. white cab, black chassis with "Coast Guard" tempa, black trailer, boat with gray deck, white hull & "Coast Guard" tempa, Thailand casting ($5-7)
5. white cab, florescent orange chassis with "Rescue 3" & checkers tempa, florescent orange trailer, boat with florescent orange deck, white hull & "Marine Rescue" tempa, Thailand casting ($4-5)(EM)

CY-23-A SCANIA COVERED TRUCK, issued 1988
1. yellow cab, blue chassis with chrome base, yellow canopy with blue trailer sides on pearly silver base, "Michelin" tempa ($7-10)
2. yellow cab, blue chassis with black base, yellow canopy with blue sides on pearly silver trailer, "Michelin" tempa ($7-10)

CY-24-A DAF BOX TRUCK, issued 1988
1. red cab with black chassis, red container with pearly silver base, "Ferrari" tempa, Macau casting ($6-8)
2. blue cab with black chassis, blue container with black base, "Pickfords" tempa, Macau casting ($6-8)
3. white cab with black chassis, white container with pearly silver base, "Porsche" labels, Macau casting ($5-7)
4. white cab with black chassis, white container with pearly silver base, "Porsche" tempa, Thailand casting ($5-7)
5. red cab with black chassis, dark red container with pearly silver base, "Ferrari" tempa, Thailand casting ($5-7)
6. white cab with red chassis, white container with red base, "Circus Circus" labels, Thailand casting ($5-7)(MC)
7. white cab with black chassis, white container with black base, Thailand casting, "Saudia" labels ($50-75)(SU)
8. blue body with black chassis, blue container with black base, Thailand casting, "Mitre 10 Racing" labels ($10-15)(AU)(TC)
9. white body with black chassis, black container with black base, Thailand casting, "Bassett's Liquorice Allsorts" labels ($8-12)(UK)
10. white body with black chassis, yellow container with black base, Thailand casting, "Bassett's Jelly Babies" labels ($8-12)(UK)
11. dark green body with green chassis, dark green container with black base, Thailand casting, "Jaguar" tempa ($5-7)(GS)
12. orange/red cab with white roof with black chassis, orange/red container with black base, Thailand casting, "Parcel Post" labels ($8-12)(AU)(GS)
13. white cab with dark blue chassis, white container with dark blue base, Thailand casting, "Renault Elf/ Canon Williams" labels ($7-10)(MN)

CY-25-A DAF CONTAINER TRUCK, issued 1989
1. yellow cab & chassis, yellow container with yellow base, "IPEC" tempa, Macau casting ($12-15)(AU issued as CY-9)
2. blue cab & chassis, blue container with blue base, "Crooke's Healthcare" tempa, Macau casting ($12-15)(UK)
3. white & orange cab, black chassis, white container with black base, "Unigate" tempa, Macau casting ($12-15)(UK)
4. red cab, black chassis, red container with black base, "Royal Mail Parcels" tempa, Macau casting ($12-15)(UK)
5. blue cab & chassis, blue container with blue base, "Comma Performance Oil" tempa, Macau casting ($12-15)(UK)
6. white cab, bright blue chassis, white container with bright blue base, "Leisure World" tempa, Macau casting ($12-15)(UK)
7. white cab, blue chassis, white container with black chassis, "Pepsi Team Suzuki" tempa, Macau casting ($12-15)
8. white & orange cab, orange chassis, white container with orange base, "TNT IPEC" tempa, Macau casting ($8-12)(TC)
9. white cab, blue chassis, white container with blue base, "Pioneer" labels, Macau casting ($12-15)(UK)
10. metallic gold cab & chassis, black container with black base, "Duracell" tempa ($12-15)(UK)
11. yellow container, black chassis, yellow container with black base, "Zweifel Pomy Chips" tempa, Macau casting ($12-15)(SW)
12. green cab & chassis, white container with black base, "M" & orange stripe tempa, Macau casting ($12-15)(SW)
13. white cab, red chassis, white container with red base, "Toblerone" tempa, Macau casting ($7-10)
14. white cab, black chassis, white container with black base, "Pirelli Gripping Stuff" tempa, Macau casting ($7-10)(TC)
15. white cab, black chassis, white container with black base, "XP" tempa, Macau casting ($7-10)(TC)
16. white cab, red chassis, white container with red base, "Toblerone" tempa, Thailand casting ($6-8)
17. white cab, yellow chassis, white container with yellow base, "HB Racing" tempa, Thailand casting ($25-40)(AS)
18. white cab, green chassis, white container with green base, "Garden Festival Wales" tempa, Thailand casting ($12-15)(WL)(GS)
19. brown cab, black chassis, light gray container with black chassis, "United Parcel Service" tempa, Thailand casting ($20-25)(UK)
20. blue cab, black chassis, red container with white chassis, "World Cup" labels, China casting ($3-5)
NOTE: Version 20 with either "Matchbox International" or "Mattel Inc." cast cab.

CY-26-A DAF DOUBLE CONTAINER TRUCK, issued 1989
1. powder blue cab, black chassis, dark blue containers with black trailer, "P & O" tempa, Macau casting ($10-12)
2. powder blue cab, black chassis, dark blue containers with black trailer, "P & O" tempa, Thailand casting ($10-12)

CY-27-A MACK CONTAINER TRUCK, issued 1990
NOTE: All models with 8 spoke wheels & no antennas cast unless otherwise noted.
1. white cab, black chassis, white container with black base, "The Greatest Name In Trucks-Mack" labels, Macau casting ($12-15)
2. chrome plated cab, black chassis, black container with black base, "Celebrating A Decade of Matchbox Conventions 1991" labels, Macau casting ($30-45)(C2)
3. black cab & chassis, black container with black base, "Body Glove" labels, Thailand casting ($4-6)
4. black cab, blue chassis, blue container with black base, "Oreo" labels, Thailand casting ($8-12)
5. white cab, black chassis, white container with white base, "Nothing Else Is A Pepsi" labels, Thailand casting ($3-5)
6. white cab, black chassis, white container with white base, "Fed Ex" labels, Thailand casting ($3-5)
7. blue cab & chassis, blue container with blue base, "Planters" labels, China casting ($3-5)
NOTE: Version 7 comes with or without "TM" next to Mr. Peanut on cab & container.
8. blue cab, black chassis, blue container with blue base, "Planters" labels, China casting ($3-5)
9. white cab & chassis, white container with white base, "Haagen-Dazs It's Just Perfect" labels, China casting, rubber tires, antennas cast ($15-25)(GC)
10. black cab & chassis, black container with black base, "Matchbox" labels, China casting ($8-12)
11. red cab, black chassis, white container with gray base, "Ringling Bros., Barnum & Bailey" labels, China casting ($3-5)
12. powder blue cab, black chassis, powder blue container with gray base, "Ben & Jerry's" labels, China casting ($3-5)
13. white cab, black chassis, blue container with blue base, "Kroger Quality Guaranteed" labels, China casting ($6-8)(US)
14. white cab, black chassis, white container with white base, "Safeway Food & Drug" labels, China casting ($6-8)(US)
15. white cab, black chassis, white container with white base, "Lucky" labels, China casting ($6-8)(US)

CY-28-A MACK DOUBLE CONTAINER TRUCK, issued 1990
1. white cab, black chassis, white containers with black trailer, "Big Top Circus" tempa ($10-15)
2. white cab, blue chassis, white container with blue trailer, "Big Top Circus" tempa ($6-8)
3. white cab, black chassis, white containers with black trailer, "DHL Worldwide Express" tempa ($5-7)(TC)
4. red cab, black chassis, white containers with red trailer, "Big Top Circus" tempa ($4-5)

CY-29-A MACK AIRCRAFT TRANSPORTER, issued 1991
1. red cab, black chassis, white carriage with black trailer, red plane with "Red Rebels" tempa ($4-6)

CY-30-A GROVE CRANE, issued 1992
1. orange-yellow body, red crane cab, yellow boom, red hook, "AT1100" tempa ($10-15)(CS)
2. orange-yellow body, red crane cab, yellow boom, maroon hook, "AT1100" tempa ($10-15)(CS)

CY-31-A MACK PIPE TRUCK, issued 1992
1. red cab, black chassis, red trailer with silver-gray sides, black trailer base, yellow plastic pipes ($8-12)(CS)

CY-32-A MACK SHOVEL TRANSPORTER, issued 1992
1. orange-yellow cab, red chassis, red trailer, MB29-C Tractor Shovel in yellow with red shovel ($8-12)(CS)

CY-32-A PETERBILT LOWLOADER WITH BULLDOZER, issued 1998
1. orange-yellow cab with "Matchbox" tempa, orange-yellow trailer, antennas cast, rubber tires, includes MB64-D36 Caterpillar Bulldozer ($8-10)(PC)
2. yellow cab with "CAT" tempa, yellow trailer, antennas cast, rubber tires, includes MB64-D38 Caterpillar Bulldozer ($8-10)(PC)

CY-33-A MACK HELICOPTER TRANSPORTER, issued 1992
1. white cab, blue chassis, white carriage with blue base, "Police" tempa; MB46-F Mission Helicopter in white & dark blue ($7-10)(EM)

2. white cab, green chassis, green carriage with silver-gray base, "Polizei" tempa; MB46-F Mission Helicopter in green & white ($7-10)(EM)
3. white cab, black chassis, white carriage with black base, "Police" tempa; MB46-F Mission Helicopter in black & white ($7-10)(EM)
4. white cab, black chassis, white carriage with black base, "Rijkspolitie" tempa; MB46-F Mission Helicopter in white & neon orange ($18-25)(DU)(EM)

CY-34-A PETERBILT EMERGENCY CENTER, issued 1992
1. florescent orange cab, florescent orange trailer with gray roof & white boom, "Rescue" with checkers tempa ($8-12)(EM)

CY-35-A MACK TANKER, issued 1992
1. white & florescent green cab, florescent green chassis, chrome base, chrome tank with florescent green base, "Orange Juice" tempa, no antennas cast, 8 spoke wheels, Thailand casting ($7-10)
2. white & florescent green cab, florescent green chassis, gray base, chrome tank with florescent green base, "Orange Juice" tempa, no antennas cast, 8 spoke wheels, Thailand casting ($6-8)
3. yellow cab with black chassis, chrome base, chrome tank with dark green base, "Shell" tempa, antennas cast, rubber tires, China casting ($8-10)(PC)

CY-36-A KENWORTH TRANSPORTER, issued 1992
NOTE: All models with 8 spoke wheels & no antennas cast unless otherwise noted.
1. white cab, white container with black base, "Charitoys" labels, Thailand casting ($25-35)(US)
2. orange cab, black container with black base, "Trick Truckin" labels, Thailand casting ($4-6)
3. fluorescent orange cab, yellow container with black base, "Matchbox-Get in the Fast Lane" labels, Thailand casting ($4-5)
4. fluorescent orange cab, yellow container with black base, "Matchbox-Get in the Fast Lane" labels, China casting ($4-5)
5. powder blue cab, powder blue container with black base, "RTF-Safety Information" labels, Thailand casting ($50-75)(AU)
6. dark blue cab, dark blue container with black base, "Heritage Design" labels, China casting, rubber tires, antennas cast ($8-10)(GS)

CY-37-A FORD AEROMAX TRANSPORTER, issued 1993 (continued)
1. yellow cab, black chassis, yellow container, "Radical Cams" labels, 8 spoke wheels ($4-5)
2. red cab, black chassis, yellow container, "RTF-Safety Information" labels, 8 spoke wheels ($35-50)(AU)(C2)
3. white cab, black chassis, white container, "North American" tempa, rubber tires, antennas cast ($8-10)(PC)

CY-38-A KENWORTH CONTAINER TRUCK, issued 1993
1. MB45-C cab in black, black container, "Matchbox Racing 5" labels ($4-5)

CY-39-A FORD AEROMAX BOX TRUCK, issued 1994
NOTE: All models with 8 spoke wheels, no antennas cast unless otherwise noted
1. white cab with black chassis, white container with white base, "Pepsi/ Diet Pepsi" labels ($4-5)
2. yellow cab with black chassis, yellow container with yellow base, "Cheerios" labels ($4-5)
3. red cab with red chassis, red container with red base, "Heinz Tomato Ketchup Squeezable!" labels ($6-8)(UK)
4. blue cab with blue chassis, blue container with blue base, "Oreo" labels, Thailand casting ($3-5)
5. dark blue cab with dark blue chassis, dark blue container & base, "Hawaiian Punch" labels, Thailand casting ($3-5)
6. orange cab with black chassis, orange container & base, "Honey Nut Cheerios" labels, Thailand casting ($3-5)
7. silver/gray cab with black chassis, white container & base, "Pepsi/Diet Pepsi" labels, Thailand casting ($3-5)
8. white cab with black chassis, orange container with white chassis, "Honey Nut Cheerios" labels, Thailand casting ($5-7)
9. white cab with blue chassis, blue container with white chassis, "Hawaiian Punch" labels, Thailand casting ($3-5)
10. black cab with blue chassis, blue container with black base, "Oreo" labels, Thailand casting ($3-5)
11. white cab with black chassis, white container & base, "Fed Ex" labels, Thailand casting ($3-5)
12. white cab with black chassis, white container with black base, "Fed Ex" labels, China casting ($3-5)
13. white cab & chassis, white container & base, "Nothing Else Is A Pepsi" labels, China casting ($3-5)
14. black cab with blue chassis, blue container with black base, "Oreo" labels, China casting ($3-5)
15. black cab & chassis, black container & base, "Body Glove" labels, China casting ($3-5)
16. green cab, black chassis, green container & base, "Collector's Choice Upper Deck" labels, China casting ($3-5)
17. white cab & chassis, white container & base, "Barnes Van Lines" tempa, China casting ($100+)(ASAP)
18. white cab & chassis, white container & base, "Oh What Those Oats Can Do!" labels, China casting ($100+)(ASAP)
19. white cab & chassis, white container & base, "Ryder Transportation Services" tempa, China casting ($100+)(ASAP)
20. white cab & chassis, white container & base, "Pocahontas PFG" tempa, China casting ($100+)(ASAP)
21. white cab & chassis, white container & base, no labels, China casting ($50-75)(ASAP blank)
22. white cab & chassis, white container & base, "Atlas Van Lines- Thomas of California" tempa, China casting ($100+)(ASAP)
23. white cab & chassis, white container & base, "International Airport Center 1-888-Lease-Us" tempa, China casting ($50+)(ASAP)
24. white cab & chassis, white container & base, "McLane Distribution Services" tempa, China casting ($100+)(ASAP)
25. white cab & chassis, white container & base, "Castleberry's" tempa, China casting ($20-30)(ASAP)(OP)
26. white cab & chassis, white container & base, "Austex" tempa, China casting ($20-30)(ASAP)(OP)
27. pale red cab, black chassis, red container, black base, "Coca-Cola" with Santa Claus labels, China casting, rubber tires ($25-40)(US)
28. white cab & chassis, white container & base, "Klockner Optima Waste-free Films" labels, China casting ($100+)(ASAP)
29. white cab, black chassis, white container & base, "K-B Toys" tempa, China casting , rubber tires, antennas cast ($15-25)(GC)
30. white cab & chassis, white container & base, "Super Pretzel" labels, China casting ($8-12)(US)(OP)
31. white cab, black chassis, white container & base, "Midas Auto Systems Experts" tempa, China casting, rubber tires, antennas cast ($8-10)(PC)
32. blue cab, black chassis, blue container & base, "Goodyear #1 in Tires" tempa, China casting, rubber tires, antennas cast ($8-10)(PC)
33. white cab & chassis, white container & base, "Mobile Process Technology" tempa, China casting ($100+)(ASAP)
34. white cab & chassis, white container & base, "Metal Industries/ Capitol" tempa, China casting ($45-60)(ASAP)
35. white cab, black chassis, powder blue container, white base, "Coca-Cola" with polar bear labels, China casting ($3-5)
36. white cab & chassis, white container & base, "PYA/ Monarch Foodservice Distributors" tempa, China casting ($100+)(ASAP)
37. white cab & chassis, white container & base, "Monarch Foodservice Distributors" tempa, China casting ($100+)(ASAP)
38. white cab & chassis, white container & base, "EFI- Set your ideas on Fiery" labels, China casting ($100+)(ASAP)
39. white cab & chassis, white container & base, "Albertsons" labels, China casting ($6-8)(US)
40. white cab & chassis, white container & base, "Rite Screen" tempa, China casting ($25-40)(ASAP)
41. white cab & chassis, white container & base, "MI Metals" tempa, China casting ($25-40)(ASAP)
42. white cab & chassis, white container & base, "MI Plastics" tempa, China casting ($25-40)(ASAP)
43. white cab & chassis, white container & base, "MI Home Products" tempa, China casting ($25-40)(ASAP)
44. bright blue cab & chassis, bright blue container & base, "Toys R Us 50 Years Forever Fun" labels, China casting, rubber tires, antennas cast ($8-10)(TRU-PC)
45. red cab, black chassis, red container & base, "Coca Cola" with Santa Claus labels, China casting ($15-25)(US)
46. white cab & chassis, white container & base, "Simplot" tempa, China casting ($100+)(ASAP)
47. white cab, black chassis, white container & base, "Vons Seafood" labels, China casting ($6-8)(US)
48. white cab, black chassis, white container & base, "At a Glance Millennium Tour" tempa, China casting ($100+)(ASAP)
NOTE: Due to the fluctuating Nascar market and the "dumping" of product into close out stores, please consult Nascar related magazines for any changes in prices that may occur.

CY-104-A KENWORTH SUPERSTAR TRANSPORTER, issued 1989
1. white cab with "STP" logo, white container with black base, "Richard Petty/STP" labels ($175-250)(WR)
2. white cab, white container with black base, "Neil Bonnett/Citgo" labels ($100-125)(WR)
3. white cab, white container with black base, "Hardee's Racing" labels ($100-125)(WR)
4. black cab, black container with silver-gray base, "Goodwrench Racing Team" labels ($200-275)(WR)
NOTE: All models listed below with black trailer base.
5. white cab, dark blue container, "Goodyear Racing" labels ($75-100)
6. black cab, black container, "Exxon 51" labels ($25-40)(DT)
7. black & green cab, black container, "Mello Yello 51" labels ($25-40)(DT)
8. orange cab, orange container, "Hardees 18" labels ($25-40)(DT)
9. pink cab, white container, "Superflo 46" labels ($35-40)(DT)
10. white cab, white container, "City Chevrolet" labels ($25-40)(DT)
11. white cab with red & blue tempa, white container, "Richard Petty/ STP" labels ($90-125)(WR)
NOTE: Above models with Macau casting, below models with Thailand casting.
12. black cab, black container, "Goodwrench Racing Team" labels ($60-85)(WR)
13. gold cab without "6" on doors, gold container, "Folgers" labels ($50-75)(WR)
14. white cab, white container, "Trop Artic" with "Dick Trickle" labels ($35-50)(WR)
15. white & blue cab, white container, "Valvoline" labels ($7-10)(IN)
16. yellow cab, yellow container, "Pennzoil 4" labels ($7-10)(IN)
17. gold cab with "6" on doors, gold container, "Folgers" labels ($25-35)(WR)
18. black cab, black container, "Goodwrench Racing Team" with team car depicted on sides labels ($20-35)(WR)
19. dark blue cab, dark blue container, "94 Sunoco" without "Sterling Marlin" on labels ($250-300)(WR)
20. dark blue cab, dark blue container, "94 Sunoco" with "Sterling Marlin" on labels ($250-300)(WR)
21. white cab, white container, "Crown Moroso" labels ($35-50)(WR)
22. black cab, black container, "Texaco Havoline/Davey Allison" labels ($35-50)(WR)
23. white cab, white container, "Richard Petty" with portrait labels ($25-40)(WR)
24. dark blue cab, white container, "Penn State 1855-1991" labels ($12-15)(WR)
25. white cab, white container, "Trop Artic" with "Lake Speed" labels ($18-25)(WR)
26. blue cab, blue container, "Maxwell House Racing" labels ($7-10)(WR)
27. white cab, white container, "Ken Schraeder 25" labels ($10-15)(WR)
28. orange-yellow cab, orange-yellow container, "Kodak Racing" labels ($7-10)(WR)
29. white cab, white container, "Purolator" with red car labels ($60-75)(WR)
30. white cab, white container, "Purolator" with orange car labels ($18-20)(WR)
31. white cab, white container, "Western Auto 17" labels ($10-15)(WR)
32. white cab, white container, "Country Time" labels ($10-15)(WR)
33. black cab, black container, "MAC Tools" labels ($20-35)(WR)
34. black cab, black container, "Mello Yello 42" labels ($10-15)(WR)
35. black cab, black container, "Alliance" labels ($15-20)(WR)
36. yellow cab, yellow container, "Pennzoil 2" labels ($7-10)(IN)
37. white cab, white container, "Panasonic" labels ($7-10)(IN)
38. white cab, white container, "K-Mart/Havoline" labels ($10-15)(IN)
39. yellow cab, yellow container, "Pennzoil" (Waltrip) labels ($7-10)(WR)
41. white cab, white container, "STP-Richard Petty Fan Appreciation Tour 1992" labels ($18-25)(WR)
42. white cab, white container, "Baby Ruth Racing" labels ($7-10)
43. black cab, black container, "Goodwrench Racing Team" with checkered flags labels ($15-20)(WR)
44. metallic blue body, blue container, "Raybestos" labels ($7-10)(WR)
45. black cab, red container, "Slim Jim Racing Team" labels ($10-15)(WR)
46. white & green cab, white container, "Quaker State" labels ($7-10)(WR)
47. blue & white cab, blue container, "Evinrude 89" labels ($7-10)(WR)
48. white cab, white container, "Jasper Engines 55" labels ($7-10)(WR)
49. black cab, black container, "MAC Tools Racing" (Harry Gant) labels ($15-18)(WR)
50. black cab, black container, "Martin Birrane-Team Ireland" labels ($7-10)
51. white cab, white container, "Penn State Nittany Lions-Happy Valley Express" labels ($10-15)(WR)
52. black cab, black container, "Chevrolet Racing" (bowtie) labels ($12-15)(WR)
53. black cab, black container, "Moly Black Gold 98 Racing" labels ($12-15)(WR)
54. blue cab, blue container, "Sunoco Ultra 98" (LaBonte) labels ($12-15)(WR)
55. white cab, white container, "Baby Ruth Racing" (Burton) labels ($12-15)(WR)
56. white cab, white container, "Mackenzie Indy Racing" labels ($8-12)(IN)
57. white & blue cab, white container, "Valvoline Racing" with "Goodyear" labels ($8-12) (IN)
58. black cab, black container, "Alliance 59" (2nd issue)labels ($12-15)(WR)
59. black cab, black container, "Dirt Devil" labels ($12-15)(WR)
60. metallic blue cab, blue container, "Dupont Racing Team 24" labels ($12-15)(WR)
61. red cab, red container, "Dentyne Racing" labels ($12-15)(WR)
62. black cab, black container, "Meineke Racing Team 12" labels ($12-15)(WR)
63. orange cab, orange container, "Reithoffer's Antique Carousel" labels ($7-10)(WR)(GS)
64. blue cab, blue container, "Maxwell House" (B. LaBonte) labels ($12-15)
65. black cab, black container, "Mac Tools/Davey Allison" labels ($20-35)(WR)
66. red cab, red container, "King of Speed-Mac Tools" labels ($18-20)(WR)
67. red cab, white container, "Indiana University-Go Big Red" labels ($12-15)(WR)
68. white cab, blue container, "Raybestos 8" labels ($12-15)(WR)
69. orange-red cab, black container, "Staff America Racing" labels ($12-15)(WR)
70. black cab, black container, "Bojangles Racing Team" labels ($12-15)(WR)
71. gold & blue cab, dark blue container, "Penn State 1993" labels ($12-15)(WR)
72. white cab, white container, "Dupont 99" labels ($12-15)(WR)
73. red cab, red container, "Nastrak" labels ($12-15)(WR)(GS)
74. blue cab, yellow container, "Mannheim" labels ($12-15)(WR)

CY-104-B SCANIA BOX TRUCK, issued 1997 (AU)
NOTE: All models with black interior, clear windows, black cab & trailer chassis.
1. dark blue & white cab, dark blue container, "Carlton Blue Go Blues!" labels ($12-15)(AU)
2. dark blue & white cab, dark blue container, "Geelong Cats Go Cats!" labels ($12-15)(AU)
3. black & white cab, black container, "Collingwood Magpies Go Pies!" labels ($12-15)(AU)
4. black & yellow cab, black container, "Richmond Tigers Go Tigers!" labels ($12-15)(AU)
5. turquoise & white cab, turquoise container, "Port Power Go Power!" labels ($12-15)(AU)
6. red & black cab, red container, "Essendon Bombers Go Bombers!" labels ($12-15)(AU)
7. red & white cab, red container, "Sydney Swans Go Swans!" labels ($12-15)(AU)

8. dark blue & white cab, dark blue container, "Blues 1998" labels ($12-15)(AU)
9. dark blue & white cab, dark blue container, "Cats 1998" labels ($12-15)(AU)
10. dark blue & white cab, dark blue container, Crows 1998" labels ($12-15)(AU)
11. dark blue & white cab, blue container, "Eagles 1998" labels ($12-15)(AU)
12. blue & white cab, blue container, "Demons 1998" labels ($12-15)(AU)
13. blue & white cab, blue container, "Kangaroos 1998" labels ($12-15)(AU)
14. blue & white cab, blue container, "Bulldogs 1998" labels ($12-15)(AU)
15. turquoise & white cab, turquoise container, "Power 1998" labels ($12-15)(AU)
16. black & white cab, black container, "Tigers 1998" labels ($12-15)(AU)
17. black & white cab, black container, "Magpies 1998" labels ($12-15)(AU)
18. brown & white cab, brown container, "Hawks 1998" labels ($12-15)(AU)
19. green & white cab, green container, "Fremantle 1998" labels ($12-15)(AU)
20. red & white cab, red container, "Saints 1998" labels ($12-15)(AU)
21. red & white cab, red container, "Swans 1998" labels ($12-15)(AU)
22. red & white cab, red container, "Brisbane 1998" labels ($12-15)(AU)
23. red & white cab, red container, "Bombers 1998" labels ($12-15)(AU)

CY-105-A KENWORTH GAS TRUCK, issued 1989
1. MB41-D cab in white, white tank with black base, gold & black stripes tempa, Macau casting ($15-20)(JB)(GS)
2. MB41-D cab in white, white tank with matt gray base, "Shell" tempa, China casting ($12-15)(GS)
3. MB45-C cab in white, white tank with matt gray base, "Shell" tempa, China casting ($35-50)(GS)

CY-106-A PETERBILT ARTICULATED TIPPER, issued 1990 (AU)
1. pink cab, gray tipper with black base, "Readymix" tempa ($12-15)(AU)

CY-106-B PETERBILT CONTAINER TRUCK, issued 1997
1. white cab, chrome base, white container & base, "Quad Graphics" labels, 8 spoke wheels ($15-25)(US)
2. grape cab, chrome base, yellow container with grape base, "Nickelodeon" labels, 8 spoke wheels ($3-5)
NOTE: Version 2 cab base can be cast "Matchbox International" or "Mattel Inc."
3. orange cab, chrome base, orange container with black base, "Matchbox Premiere Collection" labels, rubber tires, antennas cast ($8-10)(PC)

CY-107-A MACK SUPERSTAR TRANSPORTER, issued 1990
NOTE: All models with 8 spoke wheels & no antennas cast unless otherwise noted.
1. orange cab, black container, "Baltimore Orioles" labels ($15-20)(WR)
2. red cab, white container, "Melling Racing 9" labels ($50-75)(WR)
3. red & white cab, maroon container, "Nascar-America's Ultimate Motorsport" labels ($75-90)(WR)
4. blue cab, white container, "Bill Elliot 9" labels ($18-25)(WR)
5. white & blue cab, white container, "ADAP/Auto Palace" labels ($18-25)(WR)
6. white cab, white container, "Ferree Chevrolet 49" labels ($7-10)(WR)
7. black cab, black container, "Interstate Batteries" labels ($7-10)(WR)
8. black cab, black container, "Active Racing 32" labels ($12-15)(WR)
9. white cab, white container, "MW Windows Racing" labels ($12-15)(WR)
10. red cab, red container, "Fiddle Faddle" labels ($12-15)(WR)
11. black cab, black container, "Armor All" tempa, rubber tires, antennas cast ($8-10)(PC)

CY-108-A DAF AIRCRAFT TRANSPORTER, issued 1992
1. red cab, red carriage with red trailer base; SB37-A Hawk with roundels & white stripe livery ($8-12)

CY-109-A FORD AEROMAX SUPERSTAR TRANSPORTER, issued 1991
NOTE: All models with 8 spoke wheels & no antennas cast unless otherwise noted.
1. gold cab, gold container, "Folgers" labels ($15-20)(WR)
2. blue cab, white container, "Bill Elliot 9" labels ($15-20)(WR)
3. white cab, white container, "Hooters Racing" labels ($25-40)(WR)
4. black cab, black container, "Texaco Havoline/Davey Allison" labels ($25-40)(WR)
5. white cab, dark blue container, "Goodyear Racing" labels ($10-15)(WR)
6. red cab, red container, "Melling Performance 9" labels ($10-15)(WR)
7. red cab, red container, "Motorcraft" labels ($10-15)(WR)
8. white cab, dark blue container, "Penn State Nittany Lions" labels ($10-15)(WR)
9. red-brown cab, red-brown container, "Washington Redskins Super Bowl Champions" labels ($50-75)(WR)
10. white cab, white container, "Snickers Racing Team" labels ($10-15)(WR)
11. black cab, black container, "Stanley Mechanic Tools 92" labels ($7-10)(WR)
12. green cab, red container, "Merry Christmas White Rose Collectibles 1992" labels ($250-300)(WR)
13. blue cab, blue container, "Matchbox 29 Racing" labels ($12-15)(WR)
14. white cab, white container, "Purex" labels, ($12-15)(WR)
15. red cab, white container, "Wood Brothers—Citgo" labels ($12-15)(WR)
16. yellow cab, yellow container, "Matchbox Hong Kong Men of the Years 1982-1992" tempa ($250-350)(HK)
17. black cab, black container, "54th All Star Game" labels ($12-15)(WR)
18. black cab, turquoise container, "1993 Florida Marlins" labels ($12-15)(WR)
19. black cab, purple container, "1993 Colorado Rockies" labels ($12-15)(WR)
20. silver-gray cab, dark blue container, "Cowboys Super Bowl Champions" labels ($15-18)(WR)
21. orange cab, orange container "Reithoffer's Thunderbolt" labels ($7-10)(WR)(GS)
22. black cab, black container, "Virginia is for Lovers 25" labels ($12-15)(WR)
23. black cab, red container, "Falcons 1993" labels ($9-12)(WR)
24. black cab, black container, "Steelers 1993" labels ($9-12)(WR)
25. white cab, blue container, "Patriots 1993" labels ($9-12)(WR)
26. white cab, purple container, "Vikings 1993" labels ($9-12)(WR)
27. white cab, red container, "Oilers 1993" labels ($9-12)(WR)
28. white cab, red container, "Buccaneers 1993" labels ($9-12)(WR)
29. white cab, orange container, "Broncos 1993" labels ($9-12)(WR)
30. white cab, blue container, "Rams 1993" labels ($9-12)(WR)
31. orange cab, black container, "Bengals 1993" labels ($9-12)(WR)
32. orange cab, brown container, "Browns 1993" labels ($9-12)(WR)
33. red cab, blue container, "Bills 1993" labels ($9-12)(WR)
34. red cab, yellow container, "KC Chiefs 1993" labels ($9-12)(WR)
35. red-brown cab, yellow container, "Redskins 1993" labels ($9-12)(WR)
36. red-brown cab, white container, "Cardinals 1993" labels ($9-12)(WR)
37. green-gold cab, black container, "Saints 1993" labels ($9-12)(WR)
38. gold cab, gold container, "49ers 1993" labels ($9-12)(WR)
39. blue-green cab, orange container, "Dolphins 1993" labels ($9-12)(WR)
40. green cab, black container, "Jets 1993" labels ($9-12)(WR)
41. green cab, white container, "Eagles 1993" labels ($9-12)(WR)
42. dull green cab, yellow container, "Packers 1993" labels ($9-12)(WR)
43. blue cab, red container, "Giants 1993" labels ($9-12)(WR)
44. blue cab, white container, "Colts 1993" labels ($9-12)(WR)
45. dark blue cab, orange container, "Bears 1993" labels ($9-12)(WR)
46. dark blue cab, yellow container, "Chargers 1993" labels ($9-12)(WR)
47. silver-gray cab, green container, "Seahawks 1993" labels ($9-12)(WR)
48. silver-gray cab, blue container, "Lions 1993" labels ($9-12)(WR)
49. silver-gray cab, dark blue container, "Cowboys 1993" labels ($9-12)(WR)
50. silver-gray cab, black container, "Raiders 1993" labels ($9-12)(WR)
51. black & red cab, black container, "Cappio" labels ($12-15)(WR)
52. yellow cab, yellow container, "Dewalt 08-B. Dotter" labels ($12-15)(WR)
53. white & blue cab, white container, "Valvoline" labels ($12-15)(WR)
54. sea green cab, white container, "Matchbox Road Museum" labels ($12-15)(WR)
55. orange-red cab, orange-red container, "Parcel Post Australia" labels ($18-25)(AU)
56. white cab, white container, "Proball Paintball" labels ($12-15)(US)
57. white cab, white container, "Fastway Couriers" labels ($12-15)(AU)
58. white cab, white container, "Gold Coast Rollers" labels ($18-25)(AU)
59. white cab, white container, "Newcastle Falcons" labels ($18-25)(AU)
60. white cab, white container, "Wildcats" labels ($18-25)(AU)
61. white cab, white container, "Illawarra Hawks" labels ($18-25)(AU)
62. white cab, white container, "Brisbane Bullets" labels ($18-25)(AU)
63. white & purple cab, white container, "Sydney Kings" labels ($18-25)(AU)
64. orange cab, white container, "Townsville Suns" labels ($18-25)(AU)
65. orange-red cab, orange-red container, "Canberra Cannons" labels ($18-25)(AU)
66. red cab, dark blue container, "Geelong Supercats" labels ($18-25)(AU)
67. green cab, green container, "Devils" labels ($18-25)(AU)
68. blue-green cab, blue-green container, "North Melbourne Giants" labels ($18-25)(AU)
69. blue cab, blue container, "Adelaide 36ers" labels ($18-25)(AU)
70. black cab, black container, "Magic" labels ($18-25)(AU)
71. black cab, black container, "Melbourne Tigers" labels ($18-25)(AU)

CY-110-A KENWORTH SUPERSTAR TRANSPORTER, issued 1992
NOTE: All models with 8 spoke wheels & no antennas cast unless otherwise noted.
1. black cab, black container, "Rusty Wallace-Pontiac" labels ($10-15)(WR)
2. black cab, black container, "TIC Racing 8" labels ($12-15)(WR)
3. orange cab, black container, "Pic N Pay Shoes" labels ($12-15)(WR)
NOTE: Versions 4-6 with rubber tires & antennas cast
4. green cab, green container, "Mayflower" tempa ($8-10)(PC)
5. black cab, black container, "Jiffy Lube- Drive In Drive Out Drive On" tempa ($8-10)(PC)
6. gray cab, white container, "Snap-On" tempa ($8-10)(PC)

CY-111-A TEAM TRANSPORTER, issued 1989
1. white transporter, gray exhausts, "[illegible] Racing Team" tempa; includes MB16-D F.1 in white with "Matchbox" tempa ($12-15)(MC)
2. orange transporter, chrome exhausts; includes MB54-G Chevy Lumina in orange-both with "Hardees 18" tempa ($15-20)(DT)
3. orange transporter, chrome exhausts; includes MB54-H Chevy Lumina in orange-both with "Hardees 18" tempa ($15-20)(DT)
4. black & green transporter, chrome exhausts; includes MB54-G Chevy Lumina in black & green-both with "Mello Yello 51" tempa ($15-20)(DT)
5. black & green transporter, chrome exhausts; includes MB54-H Chevy Lumina in black & green-both with "Mello Yello 51" tempa ($15-20)(DT)
6. blue & white transporter, chrome exhausts; includes MB65-D F.1 Racer in blue & white-both with "Valvoline" tempa ($10-15)(IN)
7. yellow transporter, chrome exhausts; includes MB74-H G.P. Racer in yellow-both with "Pennzoil 4" livery ($10-15)(IN)
8. pink/white/blue transporter, chrome exhausts; includes MB65-D F.1 Racer in pink/white/blue-both with "Amway" tempa ($25-30)(IN)
9. white & black transporter, chrome exhausts; includes MB74-H G.P. Racer in white & black both with "Havoline 5" tempa ($10-15)(IN)
10. lemon transporter, chrome exhausts,; includes MB74-H G.P. Racer in lemon-both with "Pennzoil 2" tempa ($10-15)(IN)
11. lavender/orange/white transporter, chrome exhausts; includes MB74-H G.P. Racer in lavender/orange/white-both with "Indy 1" tempa ($20-25)(IN)
12. white transporter, chrome exhausts; includes MB54-G Chevy Lumina-both with no tempa ($15-20)(GF)
13. blue & white transporter, chrome exhausts; includes MB65-D F.1 Racer in blue & white-both with "Mitre 10" tempa ($15-20)(AU)
14. white/black transporter with chrome exhausts; includes MB74-H G.P. Racer in white/black with "Havoline 6" livery $8-12)(MN)
15. white & dark blue transporter with chrome exhausts, "Valvoline Kraco 3" tempa; includes MB74-H G.P. Racer in dark blue/white, "Valvoline 3" tempa, Thailand castings ($6-8)(IN)
16. red transporter with chrome exhausts, "Target/Scotch 9" tempa; includes MB74-H G.P. Racer in red with "Scotch 9" tempa, Thailand castings ($20-25)(IN)
17. blue transporter with chrome exhausts, "Panasonic 11" tempa; includes MB74-H G.P. Racer in blue with "Panasonic 11" tempa, Thailand castings ($6-8)(IN)
18. blue transporter with chrome exhausts, "Mackenzie 15" tempa; includes MB74-H G.P. Racer in blue with "Mackenzie 15" tempa, Thailand castings ($6-8)(IN)
19. red transporter with chrome exhausts, "Ferrari" tempa; MB246 Formula 1 in red with "Fiat 27" tempa, Thailand castings ($6-8)(Fl)
20. white & dark blue transporter with chrome exhausts, "Canon Williams 0/Renault Elf" tempa; MB246 Formula 1 in dark blue & white, "Canon Williams 0" tempa, Thailand castings ($6-8)(Fl)
21. red transporter with chrome exhausts & black ramp, "Ferrari 27" tempa, MB74-J in red with "Ferrari 27" tempa, Thailand castings ($6-8)(F1)
22. white & blue transporter with chrome exhausts, "Renault Elf 0" tempa, MB74-J in white & blue with "Elf Renault 0" tempa, Thailand castings ($6-8)(F1)
23. blue & white transporter with chrome exhausts & blue ramp, "Arrows" tempa, MB74-J in white with "Uliveto 9" tempa, Thailand castings ($6-8)(F1)
24. red transporter with chrome exhausts & black ramp, "Ferrari 27" tempa, MB74-J in red with "Ferrari 27" tempa, China castings ($6-8)(F1)
25. blue & white transporter with chrome exhausts & blue ramp, "Arrows" tempa, MB74-J in white with "Uliveto 9" tempa, China castings ($4-6)(F1)
26. white & blue transporter with chrome exhausts, "Renault Elf 0" tempa, MB74-J in white & blue with "Elf Renault 0" tempa, China castings ($4-6)(F1)

CY-112-A KENWORTH T600 SUPERSTAR TRANSPORTER, issued 1994
1. red cab with chrome chassis, green container, "Merry Christmas 1993" labels ($150-225)(WR)
2. black cab with chrome chassis, yellow container, "White Rose Series II in '94" labels ($12-15)(WR)
3. yellow cab with chrome chassis, yellow container, "White House Apple Juice Racing" (pink lettering) labels ($12-15)(WR)
4. dark blue cab with chrome chassis, yellow container, "Matchbox/White Rose 29" labels ($12-15)(WR)
5. black cab with chrome chassis, red container, "Phillies-National League Champions 1993" labels ($12-15)(WR)
6. white cab with chrome chassis, white container, "Factory Stores of America" labels ($12-15)(WR)
7. yellow cab with red chassis, red container, "Kellogg's Racing 5" labels ($12-15)(WR)
8. white cab with chrome chassis, white container, "Manheim Auctions 7" labels ($12-15)(WR)
9. black cab with chrome chassis, black container, "Shoe World 32" labels ($12-15)(WR)
10. black cab with chrome chassis, black container, "Baltimore Orioles 94" labels ($12-15)(WR)
11. black cab with chrome chassis, red container, "65th All Star Game-Pittsburgh Pirates 1994" labels ($12-15)(WR)
12. purple cab with chrome chassis, black container, "Colorado Rockies" labels ($12-15)(WR)
13. black cab with chrome chassis, black container, "Carolina Panthers-Inaugural Season 1995" labels ($12-15)(WR)
14. blue-green cab with chrome chassis, blue-green container, "Jacksonville Jaguars Inaugural Season 1995" labels ($12-15)(WR)
15. yellow cab with chrome chassis, yellow container, "White House Apple Juice Racing" (red lettering) labels ($20-25)(WR)(OP)
16. black cab with chrome chassis, black container, "Goodwrench Racing" labels ($12-15)(WR)
17. powder blue cab with dark blue chassis, dark blue container, "Penn State 94" labels ($12-15)(WR)
18. white body with dark gray chassis, white container, "AC-Delco" labels ($12-15)(WR)
19. metallic blue cab with chrome chassis, dark blue container, "Dupont Racing" labels ($12-15)(WR)
20. orange/yellow cab with black chassis, white container, "Kodak Funsaver Racing" labels ($12-15)(WR)
21. white cab with chrome chassis, black container, "Western Auto 17" labels ($12-15)(WR)
22. silver-gray cab with chrome chassis, gray container, "Cowboys Super Bowl" labels ($12-15)(WR)
23. white cab with chrome chassis, white container, "Black Flag/French's" labels ($12-15)(WR)

24. black cab with black chassis, black container, "Kendall Motor Oil Racing" labels ($12-15)(WR)
25. black cab with chrome chassis, black container, "Orioles 40 Years" labels ($12-15)(WR)
26. white cab with white chassis, white container, "Polaroid" labels ($12-15)
27. black cab with black chassis, black container, "Goodwrench Racing Team" with "Snap-On Tools" roof label ($18-25)
28. green cab with chrome chassis, white container, "Merry Christmas 1994 from White Rose Collectibles" labels ($100-150)
29. powder blue cab with chrome chassis, dark blue container, "Penn State 94" labels ($50-75)(WR)
30. metallic blue cab with chrome chassis, blue container, "Dupont Automotive Refinishes" labels ($12-15)(WR)
31. blue & yellow cab with yellow chassis, blue container, "Straight Arrow Motorsports 12" labels ($12-15)(WR)
32. red cab with chrome chassis, red container, "Detroit Gasket Racing 72" labels ($12-15)
33. red cab with black chassis, red container, "Bosal Exhaust Systems" labels ($12-15)(US)
34. black cab & chassis, black container, "Florida State University" labels ($12-15)(WR)
35. white cab with chrome chassis, white container, "Luxaire 99" labels ($12-15)(WR)
36. red cab & chassis, red container, "Lipton Tea 74" labels ($12-15)
37. white cab with chrome chassis, turquoise container, "Vermont Teddy Bear Co. 71" labels ($12-15)
NOTE: Following versions with chrome chassis & white container
38. dark blue cab, "Minnesota Twins 95" labels ($8-12)(WR)
39. dark blue cab, "New York Yankees 95" labels ($8-12)(WR)
40. dark blue cab, "Cleveland Indians 95" labels ($8-12)(WR)
41. dark blue cab, "San Diego Padres 95" labels ($8-12)(WR)
42. blue cab, "Atlanta Braves 95" labels ($8-12)(WR)
43. blue cab, "Philadelphia Phillies 95" labels ($8-12)(WR)
44. blue cab, "Los Angeles Dodgers 95" labels ($8-12)(WR)
45. light blue cab, "Toronto Blue Jays 95" labels ($8-12)(WR)
46. purple cab, "Colorado Rockies 95" labels ($8-12)(WR)
47. blue-green cab, "Seattle Mariners 95" labels ($8-12)(WR)
48. green cab, "Milwaukee Brewers 95" labels ($8-12)(WR)
49. black cab, "Chicago White Sox 95" labels ($8-12)(WR)
50. black cab, "San Francisco Giants 95" labels ($8-12)(WR)
51. black cab, "Florida Marlins 95" labels ($8-12)(WR)
52. silver-gray cab, "California Angels 95" labels ($8-12)(WR)
53. gold cab, "Houston Astros 95" labels ($8-12)(WR)
54. gold cab, "Kansas City Royals 95" labels ($8-12)(WR)
55. yellow cab, "Pittsburgh Pirates 95" labels ($8-12)(WR)
56. yellow cab, "Oakland Athletics 95" labels ($8-12)(WR)
57. orange cab, "Baltimore Orioles 95" labels ($8-12)(WR)
58. orange cab, "Detroit Tigers 95" labels ($8-12)(WR)
59. orange cab, "New York Mets 95" labels ($8-12)(WR)
60. red cab, "Chicago Cubs 95" labels ($8-12)(WR)
61. red cab, "Montreal Expos 95" labels ($8-12)(WR)
62. red cab, "St. Louis Cardinals 95" labels ($8-12)(WR)
63. red cab, "Boston Red Sox 95" labels ($8-12)(WR)
64. red cab, "Texas Rangers 95" labels ($8-12)(WR)
65. pink-red cab, "Cincinnati Reds 95" labels ($8-12)(WR)
66. dark blue cab with chrome chassis, dark blue container, "66th All Star Game" labels ($10-15)(WR)
67. black cab with chrome chassis, black container, "DeWalt Racing 1/ Peebles" labels ($12-15)(WR)
68. orange-yellow cab with chrome chassis, orange-yellow container, "Kodak Film Racing 4" labels ($12-15)(WR)
69. white cab with chrome chassis, gold container, "49ers Super Bowl XXIX" labels ($12-15)(WR)
70. silver-gray cab with chrome chassis, gray container, "Coors Light-Silver Bullet" labels, sealed in plexi box ($25-30)(WR)
71. white cab with chrome chassis, white container, "Hyde Tools Racing Team" labels ($12-15)(WR)
72. black cab & chassis, black container, "Goodwrench Service" (Monte Carlo) labels ($12-15)(WR)
73. black cab & chassis, black container, "Goodwrench Service" (Super Truck) labels ($12-15)(WR)
74. red cab & chassis, red container, "Total Racing" (Super Truck) ($12-15)(WR)
75. purple cab with chrome chassis, purple container, "Burger King" labels ($12-15)(WR)
76. red cab & chassis, white container, "The Budget Gourmet Racing" labels ($12-15)(WR)
77. navy blue cab with chrome chassis, navy blue container, "University of Michigan 95" labels ($12-15)(WR)
78. white cab with chrome chassis, light blue container, "University of North Carolina Tar Heels 95" labels ($12-15)(WR)
79. white cab with orange chassis, orange container, "University of Tennessee Vols 95" labels ($12-15)(WR)
80. red cab with chrome chassis, red container, "University of Georgia Bulldogs 95" labels ($12-15)(WR)
81. white cab with chrome chassis, dark blue container, "Penn State 95" labels ($12-15)(WR)
82. black cab with chrome chassis, black container, "Sears Die Hard" (Super Truck) labels ($12-15)(WR)
83. dark blue & orange cab with orange chassis, dark blue container, "Purex Dial 40" labels ($12-15)(WR)
NOTE: Below models with chrome chassis
84. red & blue cab, blue container, "New England Patriots 1995" labels ($8-12)(WR)
85. red & blue cab, blue container, "New York Giants 1995" labels ($8-12)(WR)
86. red & blue cab, blue container, "Buffalo Bills 1995" labels ($8-12)(WR)
87. red & blue cab, black container, "Atlanta Falcons 1995" labels ($8-12)(WR)
88. orange & turquoise cab, blue-green container, "Miami Dolphins 1995" labels ($8-12)(WR)
89. orange & blue cab, blue container, "Denver Broncos 1995" labels ($8-12)(WR)
90. orange & navy blue cab, blue container, "Chicago Bears 1995" labels ($8-12)(WR)
91. orange & black cab, black container, "Cincinnati Bengals 1995" labels ($8-12)(WR)
92. orange & brown cab, brown container, "Cleveland Browns 1995" labels ($8-12)(WR)
93. orange & red cab, red container, "Tampa Bay Buccaneers 1995" labels ($8-12)(WR)
94. yellow & olive cab, olive green container, "Green Bay Packers 1995" labels ($8-12)(WR)
95. yellow & blue cab, blue container, "St. Louis Rams 1995" labels ($8-12)(WR)
96. yellow & dark blue cab, dark blue container, "San Diego Chargers 1995" labels ($8-12)(WR)
97. yellow & dark blue cab, dark blue container, "Minnesota Vikings 1995" labels ($8-12)(WR)
98. yellow & black cab, black container, "Pittsburgh Steelers 95" labels ($8-12)(WR)
99. yellow & maroon cab, dark red container, "Washington Redskins 1995" labels ($8-12)(WR)
100. yellow & maroon cab, dark red container, "Arizona Cardinals 1995" labels ($8-12)(WR)
101. yellow & red cab, red container, "Kansas City Chiefs 1995" labels ($8-12)(WR)
102. gold & red cab, red container, "San Francisco 49ers 1995" labels ($8-12)(WR)
103. gold & black cab, black container, "New Orleans Saints 1995" labels ($8-12)(WR)
104. silver & blue cab, blue container, "Detroit Lions 1995" labels ($8-12)(WR)
105. silver & dark blue cab, dark blue container, "Dallas Cowboys 1995" labels ($8-12)(WR)
106. silver & black cab, black container, "Oakland Raiders 1995" labels ($8-12)(WR)
107. silver & green cab, green container, "Philadelphia Eagles 1995" labels ($8-12)(WR)
108. blue & black cab, black container, "Carolina Panthers 1995" labels ($8-12)(WR)
109. light blue & red cab, red container, "Houston Oilers 1995" labels ($8-12)(WR)
110. dark green & black cab, black container, "New York Jets 1995 labels ($8-12)(WR)
111. green & blue cab, blue container, "Seattle Seahawks 1995" labels ($8-12)(WR)
112. white & blue cab, blue container, "Indianapolis Colts 1995" labels ($8-12)(WR)
113. mustard & turquoise cab, turquoise container, "Jacksonville Jaguars 1995" labels ($8-12)(WR)
114. red cab & chassis, red container, "Budweiser King of Beers" labels, sealed in plexi box ($35-50)(WR)
115. yellow cab & chassis, yellow container, "Caterpillar Racing" labels ($12-15)(WR)
116. white cab with chrome chassis, white container. "Lance Snacks Racing" labels ($12-15)(WR)
117. black & orange cab with chrome chassis, black container, "Baltimore Orioles 96" labels ($12-15)(WR)
118. dark blue & red cab with chrome chassis, , dark blue container, "Cleveland Indians 96" labels ($12-15)(WR)
119. red cab & chassis, red container, "Royal Oak Charcoal Briquets" labels ($12-15)(WR)
120. white cab & chassis, white container, "Channellock Racing" labels ($12-15)(WR)
121. black cab & chassis, black container, "MBNA Racing" labels ($12-15)(WR)
122. white cab & chassis, white container, "Q Quaker State Racing" labels ($12-15)(WR)
123. white cab & chassis, dark green container, "Kodiak Racing" labels ($20-30)(WR)
124. red cab, chrome chassis, green container, "Merry Christmas 96" labels ($125-175)(WR)
125. black cab, black chassis, black container, "88 Hype Racing Team" labels ($12-15)(WR)
126. red & white cab, blue chassis, blue container, "New York Yankees World Series Champions" labels ($12-15)(WR)
127. red & white cab, blue chassis, blue container, "Cleveland Welcomes the 1997 All-Star Game" labels ($12-15)(WR)
128. blue cab, chrome base, blue container, "Fina" labels ($12-15)(WR)
129. red cab & chassis, red container, "Team Remax Racing" labels ($12-15)(WR)
130. red cab & chassis, red container, "Skittles Racing Team" labels ($12-15)(WR)
131. lemon cab, red chassis, red container, "Kellogg's 5 Racing Team" labels ($12-15)(WR)
132. orange & green cab, chrome chassis, orange container, "Baltimore Orioles 1997" labels ($12-15)(WR)
133. orange cab, chrome chassis, gray container, "Go Tennessee Vols" labels ($12-15)(WR)
134. blue cab, chrome chassis, gray container, "Jay Hawks" labels ($12-15)(WR)
135. red cab, chrome chassis, gray container, "Nebraska Huskers" labels ($12-15)(WR)
136. silver-gray cab, chrome base, gray container, "Penn State 1997" labels ($12-15)(WR)
137. silver-gray cab, purple chassis, gray container, "Kansas State" labels ($12-15)(WR)
138. silver-gray cab, blue chassis, gray container, "Kentucky Wildcats" labels ($12-15)(WR)
139. silver-gray cab, red chassis, red container, "Go Big Red" labels ($12-15)(WR)
140. dark blue cab, chrome chassis, dark blue container, "Wolverines" labels ($12-15)(WR)
141. dark blue cab, chrome chassis, gray container, "Seminoles" labels ($12-15)(WR)
142. black cab & chassis, black container, "Timber Wolf Racing" labels ($12-15)(WR)
143. green & silver cab, chrome base, gray container, "Associated Truck Parts" & numerous logos labels ($12-15)(WR)

CY-113-A FORD AEROMAX SUPERSTAR TRANSPORTER, issued 1994

1. metallic blue cab with blue chassis, blue container, "Family Channel" labels ($12-15)(WR)
2. blue cab with red chassis, blue container, "Quality Care Racing" labels ($12-15)(WR)
3. white cab with white chassis, white container, "7 Exide Batteries" labels ($12-15)(WR)
4. white cab with white chassis, white container, "Hooters Racing" labels ($12-15)(WR)
5. black cab with chrome chassis, black container, "Fingerhut Racing" labels ($12-15)(WR)
6. white cab with chrome chassis, blue container, "Colts 94" labels ($10-12)(WR)
7. white cab with chrome chassis, light blue container, "Oilers 94" labels ($10-12)(WR)
8. white cab with chrome chassis, dark blue container, "Chargers 94" labels ($10-12)(WR)
9. white cab with chrome chassis, black container, "Raiders 94" labels ($10-12)(WR)
10. white cab with chrome chassis, red container, "Bills 94" labels ($10-12)(WR)
11. yellow cab with chrome chassis, red container, "Cardinals 94" labels ($10-12)(WR)
12. yellow cab with chrome chassis, red container, "KC Chiefs 94" labels ($10-12)(WR)
13. yellow cab with chrome chassis, green container, "Packers 94" labels ($10-12)(WR)
14. yellow cab with chrome chassis, black container, "Steelers 94" labels ($10-12)(WR)
15. orange cab with chrome chassis, red container, "Buccaneers 94" labels ($10-12)(WR)
16. orange cab with chrome chassis, white container, "Browns 94" labels ($10-12)(WR)
17. orange cab with chrome chassis, white container, "Bengals 94" labels ($10-12)(WR)
18. orange cab with chrome chassis, turquoise container, "Dolphins 94" labels ($10-12)(WR)
19. red-brown cab with chrome chassis, yellow container, "Redskins 94" labels ($10-12)(WR)
20. red cab with chrome chassis, dark blue container, "Patriots 94" labels ($10-12)(WR)
21. red cab with chrome chassis, black container, "Falcons 94" labels ($10-12)(WR)
22. silver-gray cab with chrome chassis, dark blue container, "Cowboys 94" labels ($10-12)(WR)
23. gold cab with chrome chassis, red container, "SF 49ers" labels ($10-12)(WR)
24. green-gold cab with chrome chassis, black container, "Saints 94" labels ($10-12)(WR)
25. purple cab with chrome chassis, yellow container, "Vikings" labels ($10-12)(WR)
26. dark blue cab with chrome chassis, white container, "Giants 94" labels ($10-12)(WR)
27. dark blue cab with chrome chassis, orange container, "Bears 94" labels ($10-12)(WR)
28. bright blue cab with chrome chassis, orange container, "Broncos 94" labels ($10-12)(WR)
29. blue cab with chrome chassis, yellow container, "Rams 94" labels ($10-12)(WR)
30. blue cab with chrome chassis, gray container, "Lions 94" labels ($10-12)(WR)
31. green cab with chrome chassis, gray container, "Eagles 94" labels ($10-12)(WR)
32. green cab with chrome chassis, white container, "Jets 94" labels ($10-12)(WR)
33. bright green cab with chrome chassis, gray container, "Seahawks 94" labels ($10-12)(WR)
34. red cab & chassis, red container, "McDonald's Racing Team" labels ($12-15)(WR)
35. green cab with yellow chassis, green container, "Quaker State Racing Team" labels ($12-15)(WR)
36. blue & yellow cab with yellow chassis, blue container, "Team Lowe's Racing" labels ($12-15)(WR)
37. black cab & chassis, black container, "Helig-Myers" labels ($12-15)(WR)
38. white & blue cab with blue chassis, blue container, "Valvoline Rousch

Racing" labels ($12-15)(WR)
39. metallic blue cab with blue chassis, blue container, "Raybestos Racing" labels ($12-15)(WR)
40. black cab with chrome chassis, black container, "Havoline" labels ($12-15)(WR)
41. black cab & chassis, black container, "Winn Dixie Racing" labels ($12-15)(WR)
42. red cab & chassis, red container, "Happy Holidays" labels ($175-250)(WR)
43. blue cab with lemon chassis, blue container, "Kleenex Racing 40" labels ($12-15)(WR)
44. red cab with gold chassis & wheels, red container, All-Star Game 1996" labels ($12-15)(WR)
45. white cab & chassis, white container, "K-Mart/Little Caesars" labels ($12-15)(WR)
46. white cab with red chassis, white container, "Jasper Engines & Transmissions" labels ($12-15)(WR)
47. red & black cab with red chassis, red container, "McDonald's Racing" with two-line "McDonald's" roof label ($12-15)(WR)
48. blue cab with orange chassis, blue container, "Team ASE" labels ($12-15)(WR)
49. orange cab with blue chassis, orange container, "Florida Gators 96" labels ($12-15)(WR)
50. dark blue & yellow cab with yellow chassis, dark blue container, "Michigan 96" labels ($12-15)(WR)
51. white & red cab with black chassis, red container, "Nebraska Huskers 96" labels ($12-15)(WR)
52. white & orange cab with orange chassis, orange container, "Syracuse University Orangemen 96" labels ($12-15)(WR)
53. black cab with red chassis, red container, "Maryland Terrapins 96" labels ($12-15)(WR)
54. dark blue & white cab with white chassis, dark blue container, "Penn State Nittany Lions 96" labels ($12-15)(WR)
55. pale orange cab with chrome chassis, black container, "Super Bowl XXX" labels ($12-15)(WR)
56. dark blue cab with red chassis, dark blue container, "Quality Care Ford Credit Racing" labels ($12-15)(WR)
57. dark blue cab & chassis, dark blue container, "Spam Racing" labels ($12-15)(WR)
58. white & dark blue cab with dark blue chassis, dark blue container, "Penn State 96" labels ($12-15)(WR)
NOTE: All below models with chrome chassis
59. dark blue & silver cab, gray container, "Patriots 96" labels ($8-12)(WR)
60. dark blue & silver cab, gray container, "Cowboys 1996" labels ($8-12)(WR)
61. dark blue & red cab, red container, "Giants 1996" labels ($8-12)(WR)
62. dark blue & green cab, green container, "Seahawks 96" labels ($8-12)(WR)
63. dark blue & yellow cab, yellow container, "Chargers 1996" labels ($8-12)(WR)
64. dark blue & yellow cab, yellow container, "Rams 96" labels ($8-12)(WR)
65. dark blue & orange cab, orange container, "Bears 96" labels ($8-12)(WR)
66. blue & silver cab, gray container, "Lions 96" labels ($8-12)(WR)
67. bright blue & orange cab, orange container, "Broncos 96" labels ($8-12)(WR)
68. bright blue & red cab, red container, "Bills 96" labels ($8-12)(WR)
69. blue-green & orange cab, orange container, "Dolphins 96" labels ($8-12)(WR)
70. turquoise & mustard cab, mustard container, "Jacksonville Jaguars 96" labels ($8-12)(WR)
71. black & orange cab, orange container, "Bengals 96" labels ($8-12)(WR)
72. black & red cab, red container, "Falcons 96" labels ($8-12)(WR)
73. black & silver cab, gray container, "Raiders 96" labels ($8-12)(WR)
74. black & gold cab, gold container, "Saints 96" labels ($8-12)(WR)
75. black & yellow cab, yellow container, "Steelers 96" labels ($8-12)(WR)
76. black & green cab, green container, "Jets 96" labels ($8-12)(WR)
77. black & purple cab, purple container, "Ravens Inaugural Season 1996" labels ($8-12)(WR)
78. black & blue cab, blue container, "Panthers 96" labels ($8-12)(WR)
79. black & dark blue-green cab, dark blue-green container, "Eagles 96" labels ($8-12)(WR)
80. purple & yellow cab, yellow container, "Vikings 96" labels ($8-12)(WR)
81. green & yellow cab, yellow container, "Packers 96" labels ($8-12)(WR)
82. rose & gold cab, gold container, "49ers 96" labels ($8-12)(WR)
83. rose & yellow cab, yellow container, "Cardinals 96" labels ($8-12)(WR)
84. rose & yellow cab, yellow container, "Redskins 96" labels ($8-12)(WR)
85. red & yellow cab, yellow container, "Chiefs 96" labels ($8-12)(WR)
86. red & orange cab, orange container, "Buccaneers 96" labels ($8-12)(WR)
87. red & light blue cab, light blue container, "Oilers 96" labels ($8-12)(WR)
88. white & dark blue cab, blue container, "Colts 96" labels ($8-12)(WR)
89. black cab with chrome chassis, black container, "Associated Truck & Brake Supply" labels ($15-25)(WR)
90. black cab & chassis, black container, "Exide 99 Racing Team" ($10-15)(WR)
91. black cab, chrome chassis, black container, "Miller Lite Racing" labels ($25-35)(WR)
92. silver-gray cab, chrome chassis, gray container, "68th All-Star Game 1997" labels ($12-15)(WR)
93. white cab, chrome chassis, white container, "New Holland" labels ($12-15)(WR)
NOTE: Versions 94-123 all with chrome chassis.
94. blue & red cab, blue container, "1997 New England Patriots" labels ($10-15)(WR)
95. blue & red cab, blue container, "1997 New York Giants" labels ($10-15)(WR)
96. blue & red cab, blue container, "1997 Buffalo Bills" labels ($10-15)(WR)
97. blue & red cab, blue container, "1997 Atlanta Falcons" labels ($10-15)(WR)
98. blue & orange cab, blue container, "1997 Denver Broncos" labels ($10-15)(WR)
99. blue & yellow cab, blue container, "1997 San Diego Chargers" labels ($10-15)(WR)
100. dark blue & orange cab, dark blue container, "1997 Cincinnati Bengals" labels ($10-15)(WR)
101. dark blue & yellow cab, dark blue container, "1997 St. Louis Rams" labels ($10-15)(WR)
102. dark blue & orange cab, blue container, "1997 Chicago Bears" labels ($10-15)(WR)
103. dark blue & mustard cab, blue container, "1997 Baltimore Ravens" labels ($10-15)(WR)
104. blue & black cab, dark blue container, "1997 Indianapolis Colts" labels ($10-15)(WR)
105. blue & green cab, blue container, "1997 Seattle Seahawks" labels ($10-15)(WR)
106. blue-green & mustard cab, blue-green container, "1997 Jacksonville Jaguars" labels ($10-15)(WR)
107. blue-green & orange cab, blue-green container, "1997 Miami Dolphins" tempa ($10-15)(WR)
108. purple & yellow cab, purple container, "1997 Minnesota Vikings" labels ($10-15)(WR)
109. black & silver-gray cab, black containers, "1997 Oakland Raiders" labels ($10-15)(WR)
110. black & blue cab, black container, "1997 Carolina Panthers" labels ($10-15)(WR)
111. black & dark green cab, black container, "1997 New York Jets" labels ($10-15)(WR)
112. black & mustard cab, black container, "1997 New Orleans Saints" labels ($10-15)(WR)
113. black & yellow cab, black container, "1997 Pittsburgh Steelers" labels ($10-15)(WR)
114. black & dark green cab, black container, "1997 Philadelphia Eagles" labels ($10-15)(WR)
115. dark green & yellow cab, dark green container, "1997 Green Bay Packers" labels ($10-15)(WR)
116. silver-gray & dark blue cab, blue container, "1997 Dallas Cowboys" labels ($10-15)(WR)
117. silver-gray & blue cab, gray container, "1997 Detroit Lions" labels ($10-15)(WR)
118. red & yellow cab, red container, "1997 Kansas City Chiefs" labels ($10-15)(WR)
119. red & blue cab, red container, "1997 Tennessee Oilers" labels ($10-15)(WR)
120. orange & red cab, red container, "1997 Tampa Bay Buccaneers" labels ($10-15)(WR)
121. rose & yellow cab, rose container, "1997 Washington Redskins" labels ($10-15)(WR)
122. rose & yellow cab, rose container, "1997 Arizona Cardinals" labels ($10-15)(WR)
123. rose & gold cab, red container, "1997 San Francisco 49ers" labels ($10-15)(WR)
124. green & yellow cab, green container, "Packers Super Bowl XXXI" labels ($12-15)(WR)
125. blue cab, chrome chassis, white container, "Miller Lite" labels, sealed in plexibox ($25-30)(WR)
126. dark red cab, chrome chassis, dark red container, "Circuit City 8" labels ($12-15)(WR)
127. white cab & chassis, white container, "QVC Racing Team 7" labels ($12-15)(WR)
128. green cab, chrome chassis, red container, "Merry Christmas Happy New Year- White Rose Collectibles 1997" labels ($150-250(WR)

CY-203-A CONSTRUCTION LOW LOADER, issued 1989
1. yellow cab, pearly silver trailer, MB32 Excavator, Macau castings ($8-12)(MC)
2. yellow cab, pearly silver trailer, MB32 Excavator, Thailand castings ($8-12)(MC)

CY-803-A SCANIA LOW LOADER WITH DODGE TRUCK, issued 1992 (DU)
1. red cab with silver-gray trailer; MB72-E Dodge Truck with "Wigwam" tempa ($20-25)(DU)

ADT01 KENWORTH RACING TRANSPORTER, issued 1998 (WR)
NOTE: All models with metal chassis & container with black metal base, chrome wheels with rubber tires.
1. orange-yellow cab & chassis, orange-yellow container, "Caterpillar" tempa ($12-18)(WR)
2. white cab, silver-gray chassis, green container, "Skoal Bandit Racing" tempa, sealed in plexibox with matching car ($25-35)(WR)
3. red cab, silver-gray chassis, red container, "Budweiser King of Beers Racing" tempa, sealed in plexibox with matching car ($25-35)(WR)
4. lemon cab, red chassis & container, "Kellogg's Racing" tempa, sealed in plexibox with matching car ($25-35)(WR)

ADT02 FORD AEROMAX RACING TRANSPORTER, issued 1998 (WR)
NOTE: All models with metal chassis & container with black metal base, chrome wheels with rubber tires.
1. blue cab & chassis, blue container, "McDonald's Racing Team- Mac Tonight" tempa, sealed in plexibox with matching car ($25-35)(WR)
2. red & black cab, red chassis & container, "McDonald's Racing Team" tempa, sealed in plexibox with matching car ($25-25)(WR)
3. dark blue cab, white chassis & container, "Miller Lite" tempa, sealed in plexibox with matching car ($25-35)(WR)

MLBPA97 FORD AEROMAX TEAM MATES DOUBLE TANDEMS, issued 1998 (WR)
NOTE: All models with silver-gray cab chassis and tandem coupling hitch, chrome interior, clear windows, chrome disc with rubber tires
1. black & orange cab, black front container with orange roof & "Orioles" tempa; white rear container with orange roof & "Cal Ripken, Jr. 8" tempa ($60-75)(WR)
2. black & orange cab, black front container with black roof & "Giants" tempa; white rear container with orange roof & "Barry Bonds 25" tempa ($35-50)(WR)
3. black & silver-gray cab, black front container with black roof & "White Sox" tempa; white rear container with silver-gray roof & "Frank Thomas 35" tempa ($35-50)(WR)
4. white & red container, white front container with white roof & "Reds" tempa; white rear container with red roof & "Barry Larkin 11" tempa ($35-50)(WR)
5. silver-gray & blue cab, silver-gray front container with silver-gray roof & "Yankees" tempa; white rear container with dark blue roof & "Derek Jeter 2" tempa ($35-50)(WR)
6. blue & white cab, blue front container with blue roof & "Dodgers" tempa; white rear container with white roof & "Hideo Nomo 16" tempa ($35-50)(WR)
7. blue & red cab, blue front container with blue roof & "Braves" tempa; white rear container with red roof & "Greg Maddux 31" tempa ($35-50)(WR)
8. dark blue & silver-gray cab, dark blue front container with dark blue roof & "Mariners" tempa; white rear container with silver-gray roof & "Ken Griffey, Jr. 24" tempa ($35-50)(WR)

35236 POLICE K-9 UNIT, issued 1998 (RT)
1. blue MB41-D Kenworth cab, blue container with silver-gray base, red dome lights, "Police K-9 Search Unit" labels ($7-10)(RT)

35237 LAUNCH CONTROL, issued 1998 (RT)
1. red MB45-C Kenworth cab, gray container with black base, red dome lights, "Launch Control" labels ($7-10)(RT)
NOTE: Above two models from Real Talkin' series issued only with a serial number.

Collectibles Convoys

In 1997, Matchbox Collectibles started offering a new line of Convoys which were cast "Matchbox Ultra" on the baseplates but used a "CCY" rather than "CY" designation. The containers on the box trucks were newly tooled to a longer length and now made out of metal. The tanker series also featured newly tooled trailers but the top halves were still cast in plastic. All models in the series have rubber tires and antennas cast to the cab.

CCY-01 PETERBILT CONTAINER TRUCK, issued 1997
1. black cab with chrome airfoil cast, black container with silver-gray base, "Miller Genuine Draft" tempa ($25-30)

CCY-02 FORD AEROMAX CONTAINER TRUCK, issued 1997
1. red cab with black chassis, white container with silver-gray base, "Red Dog- you are your own dog" tempa ($25-30)
2. black cab with black chassis, black container with silver-gray base, "Dos Equis XX" tempa ($25-30)
3. black & green cab, black chassis, black container with silver-gray base, "Tomorrow's Thrills Today! Action Sportster" ($25-30)

CCY-03 KENWORTH CONTAINER TRUCK, issued 1997
1. dark green cab, dark green cab with silver-gray base, "The Moose Is Loose" tempa ($25-30)
2. dark beige & gray cab, green container, "The Harley Davidson Motorcycle 1909" tempa ($25-30)

CCY-04 KENWORTH CONTAINER TRUCK, issued 1997
1. white & blue cab, white container with blue roof & silver-gray base, "Longnecks Corona Extra" tempa ($25-35)
2. light pea green & gray cab, light orange container with silver-gray base, "1929 WL 45" Twin Harley-Davidson" tempa ($25-35)

CCY-05 MACK CONTAINER TRUCK, issued 1997
1. orange & red cab with black chassis, orange container with silver-gray base, "Honey Brown Lager" tempa ($25-35)
2. black cab & chassis, black container, black container with silver-gray base, "Built Like A Mack Truck" tempa ($25-30)
3. dark blue cab with black chassis, dark blue container with silver-gray base, "Labatt Blue" tempa ($25-30)

CCY-06 PETERBILT CONTAINER TRUCK, issued 1997
1. white & red cab, red container with silver-gray base, "PBRme ASAP! Pabst Blue Ribbon" tempa ($25-35)
2. black cab, black container with dark gray base, "Jim Beam" tempa ($30-35)

3. red cab, red container with silver-gray base, "Budweiser King of Beers" tempa ($25-35)

CCY-07 SCANIA CONTAINER TRUCK, issued 1998
1. white cab with black chassis, white container with black base, "Skol Skol" tempa ($25-35)
2. white cab with black chassis, white container with black base, "XXXX Castlemaine" tempa ($25-35)

CCY-08 DAF CONTAINER TRUCK, issued 1998
1. dark green with black chassis, orange-yellow container with green roof & silver-gray base, "Holsten Pils" tempa ($25-35)

CCY-09 PETERBILT TANKER, issued 1998
1. black cab, silver-gray tank & base, "Take It To The Star Texaco" tempa ($25-30)

CCY-10 FORD AEROMAX TANKER, issued 1998
1. dark blue cab with silver-gray chassis, silver-gray tank & base, "Sunoco Ultra 94 Octane" tempa ($25-30)

CCY-11 MACK TANKER, issued 1998
1. white cab with gray chassis, white tank with gray base, "Citgo the Sign of Quality" tempa ($25-35)
2. yellow cab with light gray chassis, chrome tank with light gray base, "Formula Shell" tempa ($25-35)

CCY-12 KENWORTH TANKER, issued 1998
1. gray cab, silver-gray tank & base, "Mobil" tempa ($25-35)

CCY-13 DAF TANKER, issued 1998
1. white & green cab with gray chassis, green & white tank with gray base, "BP" tempa ($25-35)

Team Matchbox and Team Convoy

Team Matchbox was first introduced in 1985 as a secondary Convoy line which included team transporters and two vehicles. By 1988, the line was renamed Team Convoy. Team Convoy included some of the Team Matchbox, but also included a combination of one Convoy plus one miniature. Several models were never numbered, however in late 1992, a CY-111 was issued for Australia which includes a Team Matchbox type issue. As this has a CY rather than a TM or TC number, these are listed in the Convoy section. White Rose Collectibles introduced Team Convoy sets in 1990 with numbers starting at TC-54.

TM 1-A PEPSI TEAM, issued 1985
TC-7-A PEPSI TEAM, reissued 1988
1. yellow transporter with ramp clips toward rear; includes MB34-C Prostocker & MB68-C Chevy Van in "Pepsi" liveries ($18-25)
2. yellow transporter with ramp clips toward front; includes MB34-C Prostocker & MB68-C Chevy Van in "Pepsi" liveries ($18-25)

TM-2-A SUPERSTAR TEAM, issued 1985
1. white transporter with ramp clips toward rear; includes MB34-C Prostocker & MB58-D Ruff Trek in "Superstar" liveries ($18-25)
2. white transporter with ramp clips toward front; includes MB34-C Prostocker & MB58-D Ruff Trek in "Superstar" liveries ($18-25)

TM-3-A DR. PEPPER TEAM, issued 1985
1. white transporter with ramp clips toward rear; includes MB17-D Prostocker & MB68-C Chevy Van in "Dr. Pepper" liveries ($30-50)
2. white transporter with ramp clips toward front; includes MB17-D Prostocker & MB68-C Chevy Van in "Dr. Pepper" liveries ($30-50)

TM-4-A BRUT TEAM, issued 1985
1. white transporter with ramp clips toward rear; includes MB62-D Corvette & MB58-D Ruff Trek in "Brut" liveries ($20-25)
2. white transporter with ramp clips toward front; includes MB62-D Corvette & MB58-D Ruff Trek in "Brut" liveries ($20-25)

TM-5-A 7 UP TEAM, issued 1985
TC-8-A 7 UP TEAM, reissued 1988
1. green transporter with ramp clips toward rear; includes MB34-C Prostocker & MB58-D Ruff Trek in "7 Up" liveries ($25-40)
2. green transporter with ramp clips toward front; includes MB34-C Prostocker & MB58-D Ruff Trek in "7 Up" liveries ($25-40)

TM-6-A DUCKHAMS TEAM, issued 1985
TC-9-A DUCKHAMS TEAM, reissued 1988
1. dark blue transporter; includes MB15-D Ford Sierra & MB6-H Ford Supervan II in "Duckhams QXR" liveries ($18-25)

TM-X-A STP TEAMS, issued 1985 (no identification #)
1. dark blue transporter; includes MB65-D F.1 Racer & MB58-D Ruff Trek in "STP 20" liveries ($175-225)(US)
2. yellow transporter; includes MB60-F Firebird Racer & MB68-C Chevy Van in "STP Son of A Gun" liveries ($175-225)(US)

TC-01-A FIRE SET, issued 1988
1. includes CY-13-A in red with MB54-E Command Vehicle in red ($10-15)

TC-02-A TANKER SET, issued 1988
1. includes CY-17-A in "Shell" livery with MB56-D Tanker in "Shell" livery ($10-15)

TC-03-A CONSTRUCTION SET, issued 1988
1. includes CY-20-A in yellow with MB29-C Tractor Shovel in yellow ($8-12)

TC-04-A CARGO SET, issued 1988
1. includes CY-25-A DAF Box Truck & MB20-D Volvo Container Truck in "TNT Ipec" liveries ($15-20)
2. includes CY-25-A DAF Box Truck & MB72-E Dodge Delivery Truck in "XP Parcels" liveries ($15-20)

TC-05-A NASA SET, issued 1988
1. includes CY-2-A Rocket Transporter & MB54-E Command Vehicle in "NASA" liveries ($8-12)

TC-05-B TEAM KELLOGGS, issued 1994
1. dark blue transporter, Thailand casting; MB267 Lumina in yellow & red, China casting; MB267 Lumina in gray, China casting-all with "Kellogg's Racing 5" tempa ($15-18)(WR)

TC-06-A RESCUE SET, issued 1988
1. includes CY-22-A Boat Transporter & MB75-D Helicopter in "Rescue" liveries ($8-12)

TC-07-A PEPSI TEAM (see TM-1-A)

TC-07-B TEAM MANHEIM AUCTIONS, issued 1994
1. fluorescent green transporter, Thailand casting; MB267 Luminas in fluorescent green-one with black lettering, other with white lettering, China castings-all with "Manheim Auctions 7" tempa ($15-18)(WR)

TC-08-A 7 UP TEAM (see TM-5-A)

TC-08-B TEAM DEWALT, issued 1994
1. orange-yellow transporter, Thailand casting; MB267 in orange-yellow, China casting; MB68-C Chevy Van in orange-yellow, Thailand casting-all with "DeWalt 08" tempa ($15-18)(WR)

TC-09-A DUCKHAMS TEAM (see TM-6-A)

TC-10-A FUJI TEAM, issued 1988
1. white & green transporter, chrome exhausts; includes MB24-E Nissan 300ZX & MB6-H Ford Supervan II in "Fuji Racing Team" liveries ($20-25)
2. white & green transporter, gray exhausts; includes MB24-E Nissan 300ZX & MB6-H Ford Supervan II in "Fuji Racing Team" liveries ($20-25)

TC-11-A PIRELLI TEAM, issued 1989
1. white transporter, chrome exhausts, includes MB7-F Porsche 959 & MB72-E Dodge Truck in "Pirelli Gripping Stuff" liveries ($18-25)
2. white transporter, gray exhausts, includes MB7-F Porsche 959 & MB72-E Dodge Truck in "Pirelli Gripping Stuff" liveries ($18-25)

TC-12-A TIZER TEAM, issued 1989
1. red transporter, chrome exhausts, includes MB15-D Ford Sierra & MB6-H Ford Supervan II in "Tizer" liveries ($18-25)
2. red transporter, gray exhausts, includes MB15-D Ford Sierra & MB6-H Ford Supervan II in "Tizer" liveries ($18-25)

TC-13-A TV NEWS SET, issued 1990
1. includes CY-15-A Tracking Vehicle & MB68-G TV Van in dark blue with "MB TV News" liveries ($8-12)
2. includes CY-15-A Tracking Vehicle & MB68-G TV Van in white with "Sky Satellite TV" liveries ($8-12)

TC-14-A FERRARI SET, issued 1990
1. includes CY-24-A in red & MB74-H G.P. Racer in red with "Ferrari" liveries ($7-10)
2. includes CY-24-A in red & MB70-D Ferrari in red with "Ferrari" liveries ($7-10)

TC-15-A PIRELLI SET, issued 1990
1. includes CY-25-A DAF Container & MB7-F Porsche 959 in white with "Pirelli Gripping Stuff" liveries ($12-15)

TC-15-B TEAM QUALITY CARE, issued 1994
1. bright blue transporter, Thailand casting; MB267 Lumina in bright blue, China casting; MB53-D Flareside in bright blue, Thailand casting-all in "Quality Care 15" tempa ($15-18)(WR)

TC-16-A COAST GUARD SET, issued 1990
1. includes CY-22-A DAF Boat Transporter & MB39-E Ford Bronco II in "Coast Guard" liveries ($7-10)

TC-17-A FARM SET, issued 1991
1. includes CY-20-A Tipper Truck with green cab & yellow dump with "Eurobran" livery with MB73-E Mercedes Tractor in yellow & green ($7-10)

TC-18-A TRANSPORT SET, issued 1991
1. includes CY-28-A Mack Double Container in white with "DHL" livery with MB28-H Fork Lift Truck in white with red stripes ($10-15)

TC-24-A TEAM DUPONT, issued 1993
1. metallic blue transporter, Thailand casting; MB54-H Lumina in metallic blue & orange, China casting, MB54-H Lumina in gold plate, China casting-all with "Dupont 24" tempa ($15-18)(WR)

TC-40-A DIRT DEVIL TEAM, issued 1993
1. black transporter, Thailand casting; MB35-I Pontiacs in black, one with white "40" & other with orange "40," Thailand castings-all in "Dirt Devil 40" tempa ($15-18)(WR)

TC-43-A HULKSTER TEAM, issued 1995
1. red transporter, Thailand casting; MB269 Pontiac in red, China casting; WR002 F800 Ford in red with orange/yellow container, China casting; all with "Hulkster 43/Hogan" liveries ($15-20)(WR)

TC-54-A GOODWRENCH RACING TEAM, issued 1990
1. black transporter with "GM" roof tempa & no door tempa; MB54-H Chevy Lumina in black with Goodyear slicks, plain trunk & no "Western Steer" emblem; MB68-C Chevy Van in black-all with "Goodwrench Racing," Macau castings ($125-150)(WR)
2. black transporter with "GM" roof tempa & "1990 Champion" on door, Thailand casting; MB54-H Chevy Lumina in black with Goodyear slicks, with trunk design & no "Western Steer" tempa, China casting; MB68-C Chevy Van in black, Thailand casting-all with "Goodwrench Racing" ($25-40)(WR)
3. black transporter with "GM" on roof tempa & "1990 Champion" on doors, Thailand casting; MB54-H Chevy Lumina in black with black disc & rubber tires, with trunk design & with "Western Steer" tempa, China casting; MB68-C Chevy Van in black, Thailand casting-all with "Goodwrench Racing" ($20-35)(WR)
4. black transporter with "GM" on roof tempa & "1990 Champion" on door, Thailand casting; MB54-H Chevy Lumina in black with gray disc & rubber tires, with trunk design & with "Western Steer" tempa, China casting; MB68-C Chevy Van in black, Thailand casting-all with "Goodwrench Racing" ($20-35)(WR)
5. black transporter with "Dale Earnhardt" roof tempa & "1990 Champion" on doors, Thailand casting; MB54-H Chevy Lumina in black with black disc & rubber tires, with trunk design & with "Western Steer" tempa, China casting; MB68-C Chevy Van in black, Thailand casting-all with "Goodwrench Racing" ($15-20)(WR)
6. black transporter with "Dale Earnhardt" on roof tempa & "1991 Champion" on doors, Thailand casting; MB54-H Chevy Lumina in black with black disc & rubber tires, with trunk design & with "Western Steer" tempa, China casting; MB68-C Chevy Van in black with "5 Time Champion" tempa, Thailand casting-all with "Goodwrench Racing" ($15-20)(WR)
7. black transporter with "Dale Earnhardt" roof signature & "1991 Champion" on door, Thailand casting; MB54-H Chevy Lumina in black with gray disc & rubber tires, with trunk design & with "Western Steer," China casting: MB54-H Chevy Lumina in matt black with "GM" on hood & "Goodwrench" on sides, slicks, Thailand casting-all with "Goodwrench Racing" tempa ($15-18)(WR)

TC-56-A PUROLATOR RACING TEAM, issued 1991
1. white & florescent orange transporter, Thailand casting; MB54-H Chevy Lumina in white & florescent orange, China casting; MB68-C Chevy Van in white & florescent orange, Thailand casting-all with "Purolator 10 Racing Team" liveries ($18-25)(WR)

TC-57-A KODAK RACING TEAM, issued 1991
1. orange-yellow transporter, Thailand casting; MB54-H Chevy Lumina in orange-yellow, China casting; MB68-C Chevy Van in orange-yellow, Thailand casting-all with "Kodak 4 Racing" liveries ($15-20)(WR)

TC-59-A SCHRAEDER RACING TEAM, issued 1991
1. white & green transporter, gold hubs, Thailand casting; MB54-H Chevy Lumina in white & green with gold disc wheels, China casting; MB68-C Chevy Van in white & green with gold hubs, Thailand casting-all with "Schraeder 25" liveries ($15-20)

TC-60-A PENNZOIL RACING TEAM, issued 1992
1. yellow transporter, Thailand casting; MB35-H Pontiac in yellow, China casting; MB68-C Chevy Van in yellow, Thailand casting-all with "Pennzoil" liveries ($15-20)(WR)

TC-61-A STP (PETTY) TEAM, issued 1992
1. blue transporter, Thailand casting; MB35-H Pontiac in blue with blue wheels, China casting; MB68-C Chevy Van in blue, Thailand casting-all with "STP Oil Treatment" liveries ($15-20)(WR)

TC-62-A MELLO YELLO RACING TEAM, issued 1992
1. black & green transporter, Thailand casting; MB35-H Pontiac in green & black, China casting; MB68-C Chevy Van in black & green, Thailand casting-all with "Mello Yello 42" liveries ($15-20)(WR)

TC-63-A J.D. McDUFFIE RACING TEAM, issued 1992
1. blue transporter, Thailand casting; MB35-H Pontiac in blue, China casting; MB34-C Chevy Prostocker in blue & white, Thailand casting-all with "Rumple 70," "Son's" or "J.D. McDuffie" liveries ($25-40)(WR)

TC-64-A PONTIAC EXCITEMENT TEAM, issued 1992
1. black transporter, Thailand casting; MB35-H Pontiac in black, China casting; MB68-C Chevy Van in black, Thailand casting-all with "Pontiac Excitement" & "Rusty Wallace" liveries ($15-20)(WR)

TC-65-A BILL ELLIOT RACING TEAM, issued 1992
1. red transporter, Thailand casting; MB7-G Ford Thunderbird in red, China casting; MB53-D Flareside Pickup in red, Thailand casting-all with "Bill Elliot 11 Racing" liveries ($15-20)(WR)

TC-66-A TEXACO/HAVOLINE TEAM, issued 1993
1. black transporter, Thailand casting; MB54-H Lumina in black, Thailand casting; MB7-G Ford Thunderbird in matt black, Thailand casting-all in "Texaco/Havoline 28" tempa ($25-40) (WR)

TC-67-A HOOTERS TEAM, issued 1993
1. white transporter, Thailand casting; MB54-H Lumina in white & orange, Thailand casting; MB7-G Ford Thunderbird in gray, Thailand casting-all with "Hooters 7" tempa ($25-40)(WR)

TC-68-A COUNTRY TIME TEAM, issued 1993
1. yellow transporter, Thailand casting; MB7-G Thunderbird in yellow, Thailand casting; MB7-G Thunderbird in pink, Thailand casting-all with "Country Time 68" tempa ($15-18)(WR)

TC-95-A AUTO PALACE RACING TEAM, issued 1995
1. blue & silver transporter, Thailand casting; MB32-E Modified Racer in blue & silver, China casting. Both in "Auto Palace 95" liveries ($12-18)(PR)

TC-95-B TEAM CATERPILLAR, issued 1996
1. yellow & black transporter, China casting; MB283 Chevy Monte Carlo in black & yellow, China casting; WR002 Ford Delivery in white, China casting-all with "95 Cat Racing" liveries ($12-18)(WR)

TC-96-A TEAM McDONALD'S, issued 1996
1. red transporter with red wheels, China casting; WRP02 Ford Thunderbird in red & white with red wheels, China casting; WR002 Ford Delivery with red cab & white container, silver wheels, China casting-all with "94 "McDonald's" or "Bill Elliot" liveries ($12-18)(WR)

TC-98-A TEAM BOJANGLES, issued 1994
1. yellow transporter, Thailand casting; MB7-G Thunderbird in yellow, Thailand casting; MB7-G Thunderbird in black, Thailand casting-all in "Bojangles 98" tempa ($15-18) (WR)

TC-98-B TEAM FINGERHUT, issued 1995
1. black transporter, Thailand casting; MB268 Ford Thunderbird in black, China casting; MB68-C Chevy Van in black, Thailand casting. All with "Fingerhut 98" liveries ($15-20)(WR)

TC-111-A TEAM MITRE 10, issued 1993 (AU)
1. CY-10-A transporter in blue with MB65-D F.1 Racer-"Mitre 10" tempa ($12-15)(AU)

Models of Yesteryear

The Models of Yesteryear were introduced in 1956 when the Y-1-A Allchin Traction Engine was introduced. The first fourteen models have been classified as the "first series." The line never extended past Y-16 until 1973 when numbers started to be added to the line as opposed to always replacing lower numbers with the new models like in the miniatures range. The numbers continued up to Y-48 and skipped up to Y-61 and continued through to Y-66. Most standard "Y" prefix ceased to be used in 1993 when Tyco started a three-letter prefix to identify the Yesteryear series such as YTF for Taste of France, YGB for Great Beers and so forth. Yesteryears were produced in England up until 1985 and although Lesney ceased to exist in 1982, the Lesney name carried on for several years afterwards in the Yesteryear range. The year 1993 also marked the "Matchbox Collectibles" division of Tyco. Although mainly dealing with Yesteryears or the Dinky range, Matchbox Collectibles entered into other ranges and these are discussed in a separate section of this book. Many Code 2s were issued by both Lesney, Tyco Toys and Mattel in the Yesteryear range and these are denoted with (C2).

Y-1-A 1925 ALLCHIN TRACTION ENGINE, issued 1956
1. green body, straight unpainted treads, copper boiler door ($125-150)
2. green body, diagonal unpainted treads, copper boiler door ($85-100)
3. green body, diagonal red painted treads, copper boiler door ($75-90)
4. green body, diagonal unpainted treads, gold boiler door ($85-100)
5. green body, diagonal red painted treads, gold boiler door ($75-90)
6. green body, smooth unpainted treads, gold boiler door ($450-600)
7. green body, diagonal unpainted treads, silver boiler door ($125-150)

Y-1-B 1911 FORD MODEL T, issued 1964
1. red body & chassis, black roof, black seats, red metal steering wheel ($18-25)
2. red body & chassis, black roof, black seats, black plastic steering wheel ($18-25)
3. silver plated body & chassis, red roof & seats, black plastic steering wheel ($45-60)
4. gold plated body & chassis, red roof & seats, black plastic steering wheel ($45-60)
5. silver plated body & chassis, black roof & seats, black plastic steering wheel ($50-65)
6. cream body, red chassis, maroon roof, red seats, black plastic steering wheel ($18-25)
7. white body, red chassis, red roof & seats, black plastic steering wheel ($25-40)
8. cream body, red chassis, black roof, red seats, black plastic steering wheel ($175-250)
9. black body & chassis, black roof, black seats, black plastic steering wheel ($300-450)(LE)(US)
10. black body & chassis, black roof, tan seats, black plastic steering wheel ($15-25) (LE)(Connoisseur set)

Y-1-C 1936 JAGUAR SS100, issued 1977
1. cream body & chassis, black seats, black wall tires, England casting ($10-15)
2. silver-blue body & chassis, black seats, black wall tires, England casting ($10-15)
3. silver-blue body & chassis, black seats, whitewall tires, England casting ($10-15)
4. dark green body & chassis, black seats, whitewall tires, England casting ($10-15)
5. light yellow body & chassis, black seats, whitewall tires, England casting ($75-100)
6. dark yellow body & chassis, black seats, whitewall tires, Macau casting, includes 2 piece diorama ($12-15)
7. red body & chassis, black seats, black wall tires, China casting ($15-18)

Y-2-A 1911 'B' TYPE LONDON BUS, issued 1956
1. red body, unpainted wheels, black driver, 4 over 4 side windows ($250-275)
2. red body, unpainted wheels, blue driver, 4 over 4 side windows ($250-275)
3. red body, unpainted wheels, black driver, 8 over 4 side windows ($60-75)
4. red body, unpainted wheels, blue driver, 8 over 4 side windows ($60-75)
5. red body, black wheels, black driver, 8 over 4 side windows ($60-75)
6. red body, black wheels, blue driver, 8 over 4 side windows ($60-75)

Y-2-B 1911 RENAULT TWO SEATER, issued 1963
1. green body, unplated dashboard & wheels, green metal steering wheel ($30-35)
2. green body, brass dashboard & wheels, green metal steering wheel ($20-25)
3. green body, brass dashboard & wheels, black plastic steering wheel ($20-25)
4. silver plated body, silver plated dashboard, wheels & steering wheel ($45-60)

Y-2-C 1914 PRINCE HENRY VAUXHALL, issued 1970
1. dark red body & chassis, silver hood, white seats, red radiator, brass 24 spoke wheels ($18-25)
2. red body & chassis, silver hood, white seats, red radiator, brass 24 spoke wheels ($18-25)
3. red body & chassis, silver hood, white seats, black radiator, brass 24 spoke wheels ($18-25)
4. blue body & chassis, silver hood, red seats, black radiator, silver 24 spoke wheels ($1000+)
5. blue body & chassis, silver hood, white seats, black radiator, silver 24 spoke wheels ($18-25)
6. blue body & chassis, silver hood, white seats, black radiator, brass 24 spoke wheels ($25-40)
7. blue body & chassis, silver hood, white seats, black radiator, silver 12-spoke wheels ($18-25)
8. red body, black chassis, silver hood, white seats, black radiator, red 12-spoke wheels ($15-20)
9. red body, black chassis, silver hood, white seats, black radiator, red 12-spoke wheels, whitewall tires ($15-20)
10. red body, black chassis, silver hood, white seats, black radiator, silver 24 spoke wheels, ($25-40)
11. silver plated body, chassis & hood, maroon seats & radiator, silver 24 spoke wheels ($45-60)
12. gold plated body, chassis & hood, maroon seats & radiator, gold 24 spoke wheels ($45-60)

Y-2-D 1930 BENTLEY 4-1/2 LITRE, issued 1985
1. dark green body & base, green fenders, reddish brown interior, green wheels, door flag tempa, England casting ($12-15)
2. dark green body & base, dark green fenders, reddish brown interior, green wheels, door flag tempa, Macau casting ($12-15)
3. dark blue body & base, dark blue fenders, black interior, blue wheels, door flag tempa, Macau casting ($10-15)
4. dark blue body & base, dark blue fenders, black interior, blue wheels, door flag tempa, China casting ($25-35)
5. purple body & base, black fenders, brown interior, chrome wheels, no tempa, China casting ($15-18)

Y-3-A 1907 LONDON 'E' CLASS TRAMCAR, issued 1956
1. red body, cream roof, gray metal wheels, "Dewars" decals ($500-650)
2. red body, cream roof, gray metal wheels, "News of The World" decals ($60-75)
3. red body, white roof, gray plastic wheels, "News of The World" decals ($60-75)
4. red body, white roof, black plastic wheels, "News of The World" decals ($60-75)

Y-3-B 1910 BENZ LIMOUSINE, issued 1966
1. cream body, green roof, seats & grille, metal steering wheel, high cast headlights ($40-50)
2. cream body, green roof, red seats & grille, metal steering wheel, high cast headlights ($40-50)
NOTE: Below models with lower cast headlights
3. cream body, green roof, seats & grille, metal steering wheel ($25-40)
4. cream body, chartreuse roof, green seats & grille, metal steering wheel ($150-175)
5. cream body, chartreuse roof, red seats & grille, metal steering wheel ($150-175)
6. cream body, green roof, red seats & grille, metal steering wheel ($35-50)
7. light green body, green roof, seats & grille, metal steering wheel ($60-75)
8. light green body, green roof, red seats & grille, metal steering wheel ($60-75)
9. light green body, chartreuse roof, red seats & grille, metal steering wheel ($25-40)
10. light green body, chartreuse roof, red seats, green grille, metal steering wheel ($25-40)
11. light green body, chartreuse roof, red seats, black grille, metal steering wheel ($35-50)
12. light green body, chartreuse roof, red seats & grille, plastic steering wheel ($25-40)
13. light green body, chartreuse roof, red seats, green grille, plastic steering wheel ($25-40)
14. light green body, chartreuse roof, red seats, black grille, plastic steering wheel ($25-40)
15. light green body, black roof, red seats & grille, metal steering wheel ($18-25)
16. light green body, black roof, red seats & grille, metal steering wheel ($18-25)
17. light green body, black roof, red seats & grille, plastic steering wheels ($18-25)
18. light green body, black roof, red seats, green grille, plastic steering wheel ($18-25)
19. dark green body, chartreuse roof, red seats & grille, plastic steering wheel ($45-60)
20. dark green body, chartreuse roof, red seats, green grille, plastic steering wheel ($45-60)
21. dark green body, black roof, red seats & grille, plastic steering wheel ($15-20)
22. dark green body, black roof, red seats, green grille, plastic steering wheel ($18-25)
23. black body with blue sides tempa, black roof, brown grille, plastic steering wheel ($15-25)(Connoisseur set)

Y-3-C 1934 RILEY MPH, issued 1974
1. purple body & chassis, white seats & radiator, silver 24 spoke wheels, no labels ($25-40)
2. purple-red body & chassis, white seats & radiator, silver 24 spoke wheels, no labels ($20-30)
3. dark red body & chassis, white seats & radiator, silver 24 spoke wheels, no labels ($18-25)
4. dark red body & chassis, white seats & radiator, silver 12-spoke wheels, no labels ($18-25)
5. light red body & chassis, white seats & radiator, silver 24 spoke wheels, no labels ($18-25)
6. light red body & chassis, white seats & radiator, silver 12-spoke wheels, no labels ($18-25)
7. light red body & chassis, white seats & radiator, red 12-spoke wheels, no labels ($25-40)
8. red body & silver plated chassis, black seats & radiator, silver 12-spoke wheels, no labels ($45-60)
9. blue body & chassis, white seats & radiator, silver 24 spoke wheels, "6" label ($15-20)
10. blue body & chassis, white seats & radiator, silver 24 spoke wheels, "9" label ($15-20)
11. blue body & chassis, white seats & radiator, silver 24 spoke wheels, "3" label ($25-40)
12. blue body & chassis, white seats & radiator, silver 12-spoke wheels, "5" label ($15-20)
13. blue body & chassis, white seats & radiator, silver 12-spoke wheels, "9" label ($15-20)
14. blue body & chassis, white seats & radiator, silver 24 spoke wheels, whitewalls, "6" label ($15-20)

Y-3-D MODEL T FORD TANKER, issued 1981
1. dark green body, black chassis, red tank, white roof, red 12-spoke wheels, "BP" tempa, England casting ($12-18)
2. dark green body, black chassis, red tank, white roof, gold 12-spoke wheels, "BP" tempa, England casting ($35-50)
3. green body, black chassis, green tank, white roof, gold 12-spoke wheels, "Zerolene" tempa, England casting ($50-100)
4. blue body, black chassis, blue tank, white roof, gold 12-spoke wheels, "Express Dairy" tempa, England casting ($12-15)
5. blue body, black chassis, blue tank, white roof, red 12-spoke wheels, "Express Dairy" tempa, England casting ($25-40)
6. cream body, maroon chassis, maroon tank, white roof, red 12-spoke wheels, whitewalls, "Carnation Farm Products" tempa, England casting ($12-15)
NOTE: Above models with black seats, models below with tan seats unless otherwise noted.
7. blue & red body, black chassis, blue tank, blue roof, red 12-spoke wheels, "Mobiloil" tempa, England casting ($15-18)
8. blue & red body, black chassis, blue tank, blue roof, red 24 spoke wheels, "Mobiloil" tempa, England casting ($25-40)
9. dark green body, black chassis, dark green tank, white roof, red 12-spoke wheels, "Castrol" tempa, England casting ($25-35)
NOTE: Above models cast "Lesney," below models cast "Matchbox International"
10. dark green body, black chassis, dark green tank, white roof, gold 12-spoke wheels, "Castrol" tempa, England casting ($12-15)
11. dark green body, brown chassis, dark green tank, white roof, red 12-spoke wheels, "Castrol" tempa, England casting ($150-250)
12. yellow body, black chassis, yellow tank, white roof, black seat, red 12-spoke wheels, "Shell" tempa, Macau casting ($12-15)

13. white body, black chassis, white tank, white roof, tan seat, red 12 spoke wheels, "Haines Gas Services" tempa, England casting ($85-125)(C2)
14. white body, black chassis, white tank, blue roof, tan seat, red 12 spoke wheels, "Haines Gas Services" tempa, England casting ($150-200)(C2)

Y-3-E 1912 MODEL T TANKER, issued 1985
1. red body, black chassis, red tank & roof, gold 12-spoke wheels, "Red Crown Gasoline" tempa ($18-25)(LE)

Y-4-A SENTINEL STEAM WAGON, issued 1956
1. blue body, unpainted metal wheels ($60-75)
2. blue body, black plastic wheels ($175-250)

Y-4-B SHAND MASON HORSE DRAWN FIRE ENGINE, issued 1960
1. red body, gray horses, "Kent" decals, gold boiler ($1000+)
2. red body, white horses, "Kent" decals, gold boiler ($150-175)
3. red body, white horses, blue bordered "London" decals, gold boiler ($150-175)
4. red body, white horses, black bordered "London" decals, gold boiler ($150-175)
5. red body, white horses, black bordered "London" decals, silver boiler ($150-175)
6. red body, black horses, black bordered "London" decals, silver boiler ($150-175)
7. red body, black horses, black bordered "London" decals, gold boiler ($135-150)
8. red body, black horses, gold bordered "London" decals, gold boiler ($135-150)
9. red body, black horses, gold bordered "London" decals, silver boiler ($150-175)

Y-4-C 1909 OPEL COUPE, issued 1967
NOTE: Below models with brass 12-spoke wheels unless otherwise noted.
1. white body & chassis, maroon seats & grille, smooth tan roof ($25-40)
2. white body & chassis, maroon seats, red grille, smooth tan roof ($25-40)
3. white body & chassis, red seats & grille, smooth tan roof ($18-25)
4. white body & chassis, red seats & grille, textured tan roof ($35-50)
5. gold plated body & chassis, red seats & grille, smooth red roof ($45-60)
6. silver plated body & chassis, red seats & grille, smooth red roof ($45-60)
7. orange body & black chassis, maroon seats, white grille, 24 spoke silver wheels, textured black roof ($18-20)
8. orange body, black chassis, maroon seats, white grille, 12-spoke silver wheels, textured black roof ($20-25)
9. red body, dark red chassis, red seats, black grille, textured tan roof ($15-25)(LE) (Connoisseur set)

Y-4-D 1930 MODEL "J" DUESENBERG, issued 1976
1. white body, orange-red chassis, yellow roof & seats, 24 spoke wheels, England casting ($1500+)
2. red body & chassis, black roof & seats, 24 spoke wheels, England casting ($18-25)
3. red body & chassis, black roof & seats, 12-spoke wheels, England casting ($18-25)
4. red body & chassis, black roof & seats, solid disc wheels, England casting ($25-40)
5. two-tone green body, dark green chassis, black roof & seats, solid disc wheels, England casting ($18-25)
6. two-tone green body, dark green chassis, black roof & seats, 24 spoke wheels, England casting ($18-25)
7. two-tone green body, dark green chassis, green roof & seats, 24 spoke wheels, England casting ($18-25)
8. two-tone green body, dark green chassis, green roof & seats, 12-spoke wheels , England casting ($18-25)
9. brown & beige body, brown chassis, light tan roof & seats, solid disc wheels, England casting ($15-18)
10. brown & beige body, brown chassis, light tan roof & seats, 24 spoke disc wheels, England casting ($15-18)
11. brown & beige body, brown chassis, dark tan roof & seats, 24 spoke wheels, England casting ($15-18)
NOTE: Above models with "Lesney" cast, below models with "Matchbox International" base.
12. brown & beige body, brown chassis, rust brown roof & seats, 24 spoke wheels, England casting ($15-18)
13. silver-blue body, blue chassis, black roof & seats, 24 spoke blue wheels, England casting ($15-18)
14. silver-blue body, blue chassis, black roof & seats, 24 spoke light blue wheels, England casting ($15-18)
15. powder blue body, blue chassis, creamy tan roof & seats, 24 spoke chrome wheels,. England casting ($15-18)
16. silver-blue body, blue chassis, black roof & seats, 24 spoke blue wheels, China casting ($25-40)
17. purplish maroon body, dark beige chassis, black roof, dark beige/purple interior, 24 spoke chrome wheels with white wall tires, China casting ($25-30)

Y-5-A 1929 LEMANS BENTLEY, issued 1958
1. green body, silver radiator & grille, gray tonneau, silver steering wheel ($150-175)
2. green body, silver radiator, green grille, gray tonneau, silver steering wheel ($150-175)
3. green body, gold radiator, green grille, gray tonneau, silver steering wheel ($150-175)
4. green body, gold radiator, green grille, green tonneau, silver steering wheel ($60-75)
5. green body, green radiator & grille, green tonneau, silver steering wheel ($60-75)
6. green body, gold radiator, green grille, green tonneau, green steering wheel ($60-75)

Y-5-B 1929 4 1/2 LITRE BENTLEY, issued 1962
1. metallic apple green body & radiator shell, green seats & tonneau, "5" decal ($350-400)
2. metallic apple green body & radiator shell, red seats & tonneau, "5" decal ($350-400)
3. metallic green body & radiator shell, green seats & tonneau, "5" decal ($350-400)
4. green body & radiator shell, green seats & tonneau, "5" decal ($25-35)
5. green body & radiator shell, red seats & tonneau, "5" decal ($25-35)
6. green body, unpainted radiator shell, green seats & tonneau, "5" decal ($18-25)
7. green body, unpainted radiator shell, red seats & tonneau, "3" decal ($35-50)
8. green body, unpainted radiator shell, red seats & tonneau, "6" decal ($50-60)
9. silver plated body & radiator shell, green seats & tonneau, "5" decal ($50-65)
10. silver plated body & radiator shell, red seats & tonneau, "5" decal ($50-65)

Y-5-C 1907 PEUGEOT, issued 1969
1. yellow body & chassis, black roof, red seats & grille, amber windows, brass 12-spoke wheels ($15-20)
2. yellow body & chassis, black roof, red seats & grille, clear windows, brass 12-spoke wheels ($50-75)
3. bronze body, chassis & roof, black seats & grille, amber windows, brass 12-spoke wheels ($18-25)
4. orange-gold body, chassis & roof, black seats & grille, amber windows, brass 12-spoke wheels ($18-25)
5. bronze body, chassis & roof, black seats & grille, clear windows, silver 12-spoke wheels ($18-25)
6. orange-gold body, chassis & roof, black seats & grille, clear windows, silver 12-spoke wheels ($18-25)
7. bronze body, black chassis & roof, black seats & grille, amber windows, silver 12-spoke wheels ($125-150)
8. orange-gold body, black chassis & roof, black seats & grille, amber windows, silver 12-spoke wheels ($125-150)
9. orange-gold body, chassis & roof, black seats, red grille, amber windows, silver 12-spoke wheels ($18-25)
10. orange-gold body, chassis & roof, black seats & grille, amber windows, silver 24 spoke wheels ($20-25)

Y-5-D 1927 TALBOT VAN, issued 1978
NOTE: All models with black seat & England casting unless otherwise noted.
1. green body, black chassis & roof, green 12-spoke wheels, "Lipton's Tea" with crest tempa ($15-20)
2. green body, black chassis & roof, silver 12-spoke wheels, "Lipton's Tea" with crest tempa ($25-40)
3. green body, black chassis & roof, green 12-spoke wheels, "Lipton's City Road" tempa ($12-15)
4. green body, black chassis & roof, silver 12-spoke wheels, "Lipton's City Road" tempa ($25-40)
5. green body, black chassis & roof, silver 24 spoke wheels, "Lipton's City Road" tempa ($25-40)
6. green body, black roof & chassis, green 12-spoke wheels, "2nd AIM Convention 1978" labels ($125-150)(C2)
7. blue body, black chassis & roof, silver 12-spoke wheels, "Chocolat Menier" tempa ($15-20)
8. blue body, black chassis & roof, red 12-spoke wheels, "Chocolat Menier" tempa ($25-40)
9. blue body, black chassis & roof, silver 12-spoke wheels, "Crawley Swapmeet" labels ($150-225)(C2)
10. yellow body & chassis, black roof, red 12-spoke wheels, "Taystee" tempa ($12-15)
11. yellow body & chassis, black roof, red 12-spoke wheels, whitewalls, "Taystee" tempa ($12-15)
12. yellow body & chassis, black roof, red 12-spoke wheels, "Taystee" (square) labels ($75-90)(C2)
13. yellow body & chassis, black roof, red 12-spoke wheels, "Merita" labels ($35-50)(C2)
14. yellow body & chassis, black roof, red 12-spoke wheels, "Langendorf" labels ($35-50)(C2)
15. yellow body & chassis, black roof, red 12-spoke wheels, "Greenwich Appeal" labels ($150-200)(C2)
16. yellow body & chassis, black roof, red 12-spoke wheels, "Ironbridge Museum" labels ($150-200)(C2)
17. yellow body & chassis, black roof, red 12-spoke wheels, "Bee's Art" labels ($125-150)(C2)
18. yellow body, black chassis & roof, red 12-spoke wheels, "Taystee" tempa ($12-15)
19. yellow body, black chassis & roof, red 12-spoke wheels, whitewalls, "Taystee" tempa ($12-15)
20. yellow body, black chassis & roof, red disc wheels, "Taystee" tempa ($25-40)
21. powder blue body, black chassis, light gray roof, red 12-spoke wheels, whitewalls, "Nestles Milk" tempa ($25-40)
22. powder blue body, black chassis, dark gray roof, red 12-spoke wheels, whitewalls, "Nestles Milk" tempa ($15-20)
23. cream body & chassis, green roof, red 12-spoke wheels, "Chivers" tempa ($12-15)
24. cream body & chassis, green roof, red 12-spoke wheels, whitewalls, "Chivers" tempa ($12-15)
25. brown body, beige chassis & roof, silver 12-spoke wheels, "Wright's Coal Tar" tempa ($12-15)
26. brown body, beige chassis & roof, gold 12-spoke wheels, "Wright's Coal Tar" tempa ($12-15)
27. blue & gray body, blue chassis, black roof with white roof sign, silver 12-spoke wheels, "1st Dutch Swapmeet" labels ($300-400)(C2)
28. blue body & chassis, black roof, silver 12-spoke wheels, "Frasers" labels ($350-500)(C2)
29. powder blue body, black chassis & roof, red 12-spoke wheels, "Nestles Milk" tempa ($85-110)
30. blue body, black chassis, white roof, 12 spoke silver wheels, "EverReady" tempa ($12-15)
31. blue body, black chassis, white roof, 12-spoke silver wheels, tan seat, "EverReady" tempa ($12-15)
32. black body & chassis, yellow roof, 12-spoke yellow wheels, tan seat, "Dunlop" labels ($15-18)
33. black body & chassis, yellow roof, 12-spoke yellow wheels, "Dunlop" labels ($12-15)
34. cream body, green chassis & roof, 12-spoke olive wheels, tan seat, "Rose's Lime Juice" tempa ($15-18)
35. cream body, green chassis & roof, 12-spoke olive wheels, black seat, "Rose's Lime Juice," Macau casting ($15-18)
36. green body, black chassis, white roof, 12-spoke gold wheels, tan seat, "Lyle's Golden" tempa, Macau casting ($12-15)
37. black body & chassis, yellow roof, 12-spoke yellow wheels, tan seat, "AIM 25th Anniversary" labels ($60-85)(C2)

Y-5-E 1929 LEYLAND TITAN, issued 1989
1. lime green body, dark green fenders & base, cream roof, tan seats, "Robin The New Starch" tempa, Macau casting ($15-18)
2. blue body, black fenders & base, cream roof, tan seats, "Swan Fountpens." This model is issued in a framed cabinet with one model assembled & the other disassembled, Macau casting ($75-100)
3. maroon body, black fenders & base, cream roof, tan seats, "Newcastle Brown Ale" tempa, China casting ($15-18)
4. maroon body, black fenders & base, cream roof, tan seats, "MICA for collectors of Matchbox" labels, China casting ($35-50)(C2)
5. blue body, black fenders & base, cream roof, tan seats, "Swan Fountpens" tempa, Macau casting (packaged in limited issue box) ($25-40)(UK)

Y-6-A 1916 AEC "Y" TYPE LORRY, issued 1957
1. light gray body, metal wheels ($125-150)
2. dark gray body, metal wheels ($150-175)
3. dark gray body, black plastic wheels ($1200+)

Y-6-B 1926 TYPE 35 BUGATTI, issued 1961
1. blue body, red dash & floor, gray plastic tires, "6" decal ($150-225)
2. blue body, red dash & floor, black plastic tires, "6" decal ($25-40)
3. blue body, red dash & floor, black plastic tires, "6" decal, blue grille ($70-80)
4. blue body, red dash & floor, black plastic tires, "9" decal ($35-50)
5. blue body, white dash & floor, black plastic tires, "6" decal ($150-200)
6. red body, white dash & floor, black plastic tires, "6" decal ($20-30)
7. red body, white dash & floor, black plastic tires, "5" decal ($50-65)
8. red body, black dash & floor, black plastic tires, "6" decal ($150-200)
9. red body, white dash & floor, black plastic tires, "9" decal ($40-50)
10. silver plated body, dash & floor, black plastic tires, no decal ($350-500)

Y-6-C 1913 CADILLAC, issued 1967
1. yellow-gold body, & chassis, maroon roof, grille & seat ($20-25)
2. dark gold body & chassis, maroon roof, grille & seat ($20-25)
3. dark gold body & chassis, maroon roof, grille & seat, "913" base date ($45-60)
4. brown gold body & chassis, maroon roof, grille & seat ($20-25)
5. silver plated body & chassis, maroon roof, grille & seat ($250-325)
6. gold plated body & chassis, maroon roof, grille & seat ($250-325)
NOTE: Above models with 12-spoke brass wheels.
7. green body & chassis, black roof, yellow grille & seat, brass 12-spoke wheels ($25-40)
8. green body & chassis, black roof, yellow grille & seat, silver 12-spoke wheels ($15-20)
9. green body & chassis, black roof, yellow grille & seat, red 12-spoke wheels ($35-50)

Y-6-D ROLLS ROYCE FIRE ENGINE, issued 1977
1. red body & chassis, dark brown ladder, black seat, 24 spoke gold wheels ($20-25)
2. red body & chassis, dark brown ladder, black seat, 12-spoke gold wheels ($10-15)
3. red body & chassis, red-brown ladder, black seat, 12-spoke gold wheels ($10-15)
4. red body & chassis, red-brown ladder, black seat, 12-spoke silver wheels (20-25)
5. red body & chassis, orange-brown ladder, black seat, 12-spoke gold wheels ($10-15)
6. red body & chassis, orange-brown ladder, red seat, 12-spoke gold wheels ($150-200)
7. red body & chassis, white ladder, black seat, 12-spoke gold wheels ($10-15)
8. red body, black chassis, white ladder, black seat, 12-spoke gold wheels ($10-15)

Y-6-E 1932 MERCEDES BENZ LORRY, issued 1988
1. cream body, black fenders, dark gray base, cream canopy, red wheels, "Stuttgarter Hofbrau" tempa, Macau casting ($12-15)

Y-7-A 1914 7 TON LEYLAND VAN, issued 1957
1. dark red-brown body, cream roof, metal wheels, without central line on decal ($1000+)
2. dark red-brown body, white roof, metal wheels, full text decal ($75-100)
3. dark red-brown body, cream roof, metal wheels, full text decal ($75-100)
4. light red-brown body, cream roof, metal wheels, full text decal ($75-100)
5. light red-brown body, cream roof, black plastic wheels, full text decal ($1200+)

Y-7-B 1913 MERCER RACEABOUT, issued 1961
1. lilac body & grille, gray plastic tires ($250-350)
2. lilac body & grille, black plastic tires ($35-50)
3. yellow body & grille, black plastic tires ($20-35)
4. yellow body, gold grille, black plastic tires ($20-25)
5. silver plated body & grille, black plastic tires ($250-300)
6. gold plated body & grille, black plastic tires ($450-600)

Y-7-C 1912 ROLLS ROYCE, issued 1968
NOTE: Below models with brass 12-spoke wheels.
1. silver-gray body, red base, smooth gray roof, red seats & grille ($20-35)
2. silver-gray body, red base, smooth red roof, red seats & grille ($150-200)
3. silver-gray body, red base, ribbed gray roof, red seats & grille ($175-200)
4. silver-gray body, red base, ribbed red roof, red seats & grille ($25-40)
5. silver plated body & base, smooth gray roof, red seats & grille ($50-60)
6. silver plated body & base, ribbed gray roof, red seats & grille ($50-60)
7. silver plated body & base, ribbed red roof, red seats & grille ($50-60)
8. gold plated body & base, ribbed red roof, red seats & grille ($50-60)
9. gold body with silver hood, red base, ribbed red roof, red seats & grille ($25-40)
10. gold body with silver hood, red base, ribbed red roof, black seats, red grille ($25-40)
11. gold body, red base, ribbed red roof, red seats & grille ($20-30)
12. gold body, red base, ribbed red roof, black seats & grille ($20-30)
NOTE: Below models with silver 12-spoke wheels.
13. gold body, red base, ribbed red roof, red seats & grille ($15-18)
14. gold body, red base, ribbed red roof, black seats & grille ($15-18)
NOTE: Below models with red 12-spoke wheels.
15. gold body, red base, ribbed red roof, black seats & grille ($25-40)
16. yellow body, black base, ribbed black roof, black seats & grille ($10-15)
17. yellow body, black base, ribbed black roof, black seats & grille, whitewalls ($10-15)
18. yellow body, black base, ribbed black roof, black seats & grille, "Duchy of Cornwall" labels ($150-200)(C2)

Y-7-D 1930 MODEL A FORD WRECK TRUCK, issued 1985
1. orange body, black chassis, brown interior, dark green boom, orange wheels, "Barlow Motor Sales" tempa, England casting ($10-15)
2. orange body, black chassis, brown interior, dark green boom, orange wheels, "Barlow Motor Sales" tempa, Macau casting ($20-25)
3. yellow body, black chassis, brown interior, gray boom, red wheels, "Shell" tempa, Macau casting ($10-15)

Y-8-A 1926 MORRIS COWLEY "BULLNOSE," issued 1958
1. light tan body, brown base, copper wheels ($75-90)
2. light tan body, brown base, unplated wheels ($75-90)
3. dark tan body, brown base, unplated wheels ($75-90)

Y-8-B 1914 SUNBEAM MOTORCYCLE & SIDECAR, issued 1962
1. silver plated body, black sidecar seat ($1200+)
2. silver plated body, bright green sidecar seat ($350-500)
3. silver plated body, dark green sidecar seat ($50-75)

Y-8-C 1914 STUTZ ROADSTER, issued 1969
1. metallic red body & chassis, smooth tan roof, 12-spoke brass wheels, gold gas tank ($50-75)
2. metallic red body & chassis, smooth tan roof, 12-spoke brass wheels, copper gas tank ($15-20)
3. metallic red body & chassis, smooth tan roof, 12-spoke brass wheels, copper gas tank ($15-20)
4. blue body & chassis, textured black roof, 12-spoke silver wheels, copper gas tank ($12-15)
5. blue body & chassis, textured black roof, 24 spoke silver wheels, copper gas tank ($15-20)

Y-8-D 1945 M.G. TD, issued 1978
1. green body & chassis, tan roof, red interior, "3" label, red 12-spoke wheels ($35-50)
2. green body & chassis, tan roof, red interior, "3" label, silver 12-spoke wheels ($15-18)
3. green body & chassis, tan roof, tan interior, "3" label, silver 24 spoke wheels ($75-100)
4. green body & chassis, tan roof, black interior, "3" label, silver 24 spoke wheels ($50-75)
5. red body & chassis, tan roof, red interior, no labels, silver 24 spoke wheels ($50-75)
6. red body & chassis, tan roof, black interior, no labels, silver 24 spoke wheels ($12-15)
7. red body & chassis, brown roof, black interior, no labels, silver 24 spoke wheels ($12-15)
8. red body & chassis, rust roof, black interior, no labels, silver 24 spoke wheels ($15-18)
9. blue body & chassis, tan roof, black interior, no labels, silver 24 spoke wheels ($12-15)
10. blue body & chassis, tan roof & interior, silver 24 spoke wheels ($12-15)
11. blue body & chassis, rust roof, tan interior, silver 24 spoke wheels ($12-15)
12. cream body, brown chassis, tan roof & interior, silver 24 spoke wheels ($12-15)
13. cream body, brown chassis, rust roof, tan interior, silver 24 spoke wheels ($12-15)
14. cream body, brown chassis, rust roof, light tan interior, silver 24 spoke wheels ($12-15)

Y-8-E 1917 YORKSHIRE STEAM WAGON, issued 1987
1. plum body, black chassis, gray cab roof, tan canopy, red wheels, "Johnnie Walker Whisky" tempa, Macau casting ($15-18)
2. green body, black chassis, white cab roof & canopy, "Samuel Smith" tempa. This model is in a framed cabinet unit. The disassembled model has parts in chrome plate and the canopy has no tempa, Macau casting ($125-150)
3. dark blue body, black chassis, gray cab roof, white sack load, cream wheels, "William Prichard Millennium Flour" tempa, Macau casting ($15-18)
4. yellow body, black chassis, beige cab roof & canopy, yellow wheels, "Fyffes" tempa, China casting ($15-18)

Y-9-A FOWLER SHOWMAN'S ENGINE, issued 1958
1. dark maroon body, cream roof, copper boiler, gold roof supports, cream roof spreaders, black base insert ($100-135)
2. dark maroon body, cream roof, copper boiler, gold roof supports, cream roof spreaders, dark maroon base insert ($90-110)
3. light maroon body, cream roof, gold boiler, gold roof supports, cream roof spreaders, light maroon base insert ($90-110)
4. light maroon body, cream roof, gold boiler, white roof supports & roof spreaders, light maroon base insert ($90-110)
5. light maroon body, cream roof, gold boiler, gold roof supports & roof spreaders, light maroon base insert ($90-110)
6. light maroon body, white roof, gold boiler, gold roof supports & roof spreaders, light maroon base insert ($90-110)
7. light maroon body, cream roof, silver boiler, silver roof supports & roof spreaders, light maroon base insert ($90-110)
8. light maroon body, white roof, copper boiler, gold roof supports, cream roof spreaders, black base insert ($100-135)
9. red body, cream roof, gold boiler, gold roof supports & roof spreaders, red base insert ($90-110)
10. red body, white roof, gold boiler, gold roof supports & roof spreaders, red base insert ($90-110)
11. red body, cream roof, gold boiler, cream roof supports & roof spreaders, red base insert ($90-110)
12. red body, white roof, gold boiler, silver roof supports & roof spreaders, red base insert ($90-110)
13. red body, white roof, silver boiler, silver roof supports & roof spreaders, red base insert ($90-110)
14. red body, white roof, silver boiler, gold roof supports & roof spreaders, red base insert ($90-110)
15. red body, white roof, gold boiler, gold roof supports & roof spreaders, black base insert ($100-135)

Y-9-B 1912 SIMPLEX, issued 1968
1. yellow-green body & chassis, smooth tan roof, red seats & grille ($25-35)
2. dark green body & chassis, smooth tan roof, red seats & grille ($25-35)
3. dark green body & chassis, textured tan roof, red seats & grille ($40-50)
4. bronze-gold body, red-brown chassis, textured black roof, red seats & grille ($65-80)
5. bronze-gold body, red-brown chassis, textured black roof, dark red seats & grille ($65-80)
6. pale gold body, orange-red chassis, black textured roof, dark red seats, yellow grille ($50-75)
7. pale gold body, orange-red chassis, black textured roof, yellow seats & grille ($50-75)
NOTE: Above models with brass 12-spoke wheels, below models as noted.
8. orange-red body & chassis, black textured roof, yellow seats & grille, silver 12-spoke wheels ($12-15)
9. dark red body & chassis, textured black roof,. yellow seats & grille, silver 12-spoke wheels ($12-15)
10. dark red body & chassis, yellow roof & seats, black grille, red 12-spoke wheels ($12-15)
11. dark red body & chassis, orange-yellow roof, yellow seats & grille, 12-spoke red wheels ($12-15)
12. yellow body, black chassis, black roof, tan seats, black grille, gold 12-spoke wheels ($12-15)
13. yellow body, black chassis, yellow roof, tan seats, black grille, gold 12-spoke wheels, includes 2 piece diorama ($25-40)
14. yellow body, black chassis, black roof, tan seats, black grille, gold 12-spoke wheels, includes 2 piece diorama ($12-15)

Y-9-C 1920 LEYLAND 3 TON LORRY, issued 1985
1. dark green body, red chassis, black base, tan seats, green wheels, "A. Luff & Sons" tempa, Macau casting ($25-40)(LE)
2. dark green body, red chassis, charcoal base, tan seats, green wheels, "A. Luff & Sons" tempa, Macau casting ($25-40)(LE)

Y-9-D 1936 LEYLAND CUB FIRE ENGINE, issued 1989
1. red body & fenders, black roof, brown ladder, red flywheel & wheels, "Works Fire Service" tempa, Macau casting ($200-275)(LE)

Y-10-A 1908 GRAND PRIX MERCEDES, issued 1958
1. white body, light green seats, silver trim ($125-150)
2. cream body, light green seats, silver trim ($75-90)
3. cream body, light green seats, gold trim ($75-90)
4. cream body, dark green seats, gold trim ($75-90)
5. cream body, dark green seats, silver trim ($75-90)
6. cream body, dark green seats, no trim ($75-90)

Y-10-B 1928 MERCEDES-BENZ 36/220, issued 1963
1. white body, beige dashboard, double spare tires ($45-60)
2. white body, beige dashboard, single spare tire ($18-25)
3. gold plated body & dashboard, single spare tire ($45-60)
4. silver plated body & dashboard, single spare tire ($45-60)
5. silver plated body & dashboard, double spare tires ($45-60)

Y-10-C 1906 ROLLS ROYCE SILVER GHOST, issued 1969
1. lime body, gray-brown chassis, maroon seats & grille, brass wheels ($15-20)
2. lime body, gray-brown chassis, brown-red seats, maroon grille, brass wheels ($15-20)
3. white body, purple-red chassis, maroon seats & grille, silver wheels ($15-20)
4. white body, purple-red chassis, maroon seats, black grille, silver wheels ($15-20)
5. white body, purple-red chassis, black seats & grille, silver wheels ($15-20)
6. white body, red chassis, black seats & grille, silver wheels ($15-20)
7. white body, red chassis, black seats & grille, red wheels ($25-40)
8. silver-gray body & chassis, maroon seats, black grille, red wheels ($15-18)
9. silver-gray body & chassis, yellow seats, black grille, red wheels ($20-30)
10. silver-gray body & chassis, yellow seats, black grille, silver wheels ($25-40)
11. silver plated body & chassis maroon seats & grille, silver wheels ($45-60)
12. gold plated body & chassis, maroon seats & grille, gold wheels ($45-60)

Y-10-D 1957 MASERATI 250F, issued 1986
1. red body & base, black seat, chrome wheels, Macau casting ($15-18)
2. red body & base, black seat, silver painted wheels, Macau casting ($15-18)

Y-10-E 1931 "DIDDLER" TROLLEY BUS, issued 1988
1. red body, brown interior, gray roof, "Ronuk" & "Jeyes' Kills" labels, Macau casting ($25-35)(LE)

Y-11-A 1920 AVELING PORTER STEAM ROLLER, issued 1958
1. green body, black roof supports, dark brown flywheel ($75-90)
2. green body, black roof supports, matt black flywheel ($75-90)
3. green body, black roof supports, gloss black flywheel ($75-90)
4. green body, green roof supports, dark brown flywheel ($75-90)
5. green body, green roof supports, matt black flywheel ($75-90)
6. green body, green roof supports, gloss black flywheel ($75-90)

Y-11-B 1912 PACKARD LANDAULET, issued 1964
1. red body, black interior, metal steering wheel, unplated grille & wheels ($18-25)
2. red body, black interior, metal steering wheel, brass grille & wheels ($18-25)
3. red body, black interior, plastic steering wheel, unplated grille & wheels ($18-25)
4. red body, black interior, plastic steering wheel, brass grille & wheels ($18-25)
5. dark red body, black interior, plastic steering wheel, brass grille & wheels ($18-25)
6. beige & brown body, brown interior, plastic steering wheel, brass grille & wheels ($15-25) (Connoisseur set)

Y-11-C 1938 LAGONDA DROPHEAD COUPE, issued 1972
1. gold body, purple chassis, black interior & grille, brass 24 spoke wheels ($850-1000)
2. gold body, dark red chassis, black interior & grille, brass 24 spoke wheels ($250-400)
3. gold body, bright red ("strawberry") chassis, black interior & grille, brass 24 spoke wheels ($250-400)
4. gold body, purplish maroon chassis, black interior & grille, black interior & grille, brass 24 spoke wheels ($45-60)
5. copper body, gold chassis, black interior & grille, brass 24 spoke wheels ($15-20)
6. copper body, gold chassis, black interior & grille, silver 24 spoke wheels ($15-20)
7. copper body, gold chassis, black interior & grille, silver 12-spoke wheels ($15-20)
8. copper body, gold chassis, dark red interior & grille, silver 12-spoke wheels ($18-25)
9. beige body, black chassis, maroon interior, black grille, silver disc wheels ($15-20)
10. beige body, black chassis, dark red interior, black grille, silver disc wheels ($15-20)
11. beige body, black chassis, dark red interior & grille, silver disc wheels ($15-20)
12. beige body, black chassis, black interior & grille, silver disc wheels ($15-20)
13. plum body & chassis, black interior & grille, silver 24 spoke wheels ($20-25)(GS)
14. plum body & chassis, maroon interior & grille, silver 24 spoke wheels ($35-50)(GS)

Y-11-D 1932 BUGATTI TYPE 51, issued 1986
1. blue body & base, brown interior with gray dashboard, silver painted wheels, "4" tempa, England casting ($10-15)
2. blue body & base, black interior with cream dashboard, chrome wheels, "6" tempa, Macau casting ($10-15)

Y-12-A 1899 LONDON HORSE DRAWN BUS, issued 1959
1. red body, beige driver & seats, light brown horses ($75-100)
2. red body, beige driver & seats, dark brown horses ($75-100)
3. red body, pink-cream driver & seats, dark brown horses ($85-110)

Y-12-B 1909 THOMAS FLYABOUT, issued 1967
NOTE: All models with 12 spoke wheels unless otherwise noted.
1. blue body & chassis, smooth tan roof, yellow seats & grille ($1000+)
2. blue body & chassis, smooth tan roof, dark red seats & grille ($15-18)
3. blue body & chassis, textured tan roof, dark red seats & grille ($15-18)
4. silver plated body & chassis, textured tan roof, dark red seats & grille ($45-60)
5. gold plated body & chassis, textured tan roof, dark red seats & grille ($45-60)
6. purple-red body & chassis, textured black roof, white seats, black grille ($15-18)
7. purple-red body & chassis, textured black roof, white seats, black grille, 24 spoke wheels ($25 35)
8. red body & chassis, textured black roof, white seats, black grille ($60-75)

Y-12-C MODEL T FORD VAN, issued 1978
1. cream body, black chassis & roof, black seat, red 12-spoke wheels, "Coca Cola" tempa ($35-50)
2. cream body, black chassis & roof, black seat, silver 12-spoke wheels, "Coca Cola" tempa ($60-75)
3. yellow body, black chassis & roof, black seat, red 12-spoke wheels, "Colman's Mustard" tempa ($12-15)
4. yellow body, black chassis & roof, dark black seat, silver 24 spoke wheels, "Colman's Mustard" tempa ($50-75)
5. yellow body, black chassis & roof, black seat, silver 12-spoke wheels, "Colman's Mustard" tempa ($50-75)
6. yellow body, black chassis & roof, black seat, red 12-spoke wheels, "Suze" tempa ($12-15)
7. yellow body, black chassis & roof, black seat, silver 24 spoke wheels, "Suze" tempa ($50-75)
8. yellow body, black chassis & roof, black seat, silver 12-spoke wheels, "Suze" tempa ($50-75)
9. yellow body, black chassis & roof, black seat, red 12-spoke wheels, "Deans For Toys" labels ($175-250)(C2)
10. yellow body, black chassis & roof, black seat, red 12-spoke wheels, "Camberley News" tempa ($225-275)(C2)
11. yellow body, black chassis & roof, black seat, red 12-spoke wheels, "Cada Toys" labels ($175-250)(C2)
12. yellow body, black chassis & roof, black seat, red 12-spoke wheels, "Model Collectors Extravaganza" labels ($175-250)C2)
13. white & maroon body, black chassis & roof, black seat, red 12-spoke wheels, "Bang & Olufsen" tempa ($300-450)(C2)
14. blue body, black chassis, white roof, black seat, red 12-spoke wheels, "Smith's Crisps" tempa ($12-15)
15. blue body, black chassis, white roof, tan seat, red 12-spoke wheels, "Smith's Crisps" tempa ($12-15)
16. green body, dark green chassis, gray roof, black seat, yellow 12-spoke wheels, "25th Anniversary of Yesteryear" tempa ($12-15)
17. blue body, black chassis, yellow roof, black seat, red 12-spoke wheels, "Bird's Custard" tempa ($12-15)
18. blue body, black chassis, yellow roof, tan seat, red 12-spoke wheels, "Bird's Custard" tempa ($12-15)
19. blue body, black chassis, white roof, black seat, gold 12-spoke wheels, "Cerebos Salt" tempa ($12-15)
20. red body, black chassis & roof, black seat, gold 12-spoke wheels, "Arnott's Biscuits" labels ($250-350)(AU)
21. dark green body, black chassis, beige roof, black seat, gold 12-spoke wheels, "Harrods" tempa ($15-18)
22. dark green body, black chassis, beige roof, tan seat, gold 12-spoke wheels, "Harrods" tempa ($15-18)
23. yellow body, black chassis & roof, black seat, red 12-spoke wheels, "Sunlight Seife" labels ($150-200)(GR)
24. red body, black chassis & roof, black seat, red 12-spoke wheels, "Royal Mail" tempa ($12-15)
25. black body & chassis, white roof, tan seat, gold 12-spoke wheels, "Captain Morgan" decals ($12-15)
26. black body & chassis, white roof, tan seat, gold 12-spoke wheels, "Captain Morgan" labels ($12-15)
27. blue body, black chassis, white roof, black seat, gold 12-spoke wheels, "Hoover" tempa ($1000+)(LE)
28. orange body, black chassis & roof, black seat, silver disc wheels, "Hoover" tempa ($25-40)
29. orange body, black chassis & roof, black seat, black 12-spoke wheels, "Hoover" tempa ($12-15)
30. tan-brown body, brown chassis & roof, black seat, gold 12-spoke wheels, "Motor 100" tempa ($25-40)
31. tan-brown body, brown chassis & roof, black seat, red 12-spoke wheels, "Motor 100" tempa ($12-15)
32. white body, blue chassis, red roof, black seat, red 12-spoke wheels, "Pepsi Cola" tempa ($25-40)
33. white body, blue chassis, red roof, black seat, silver 12-spoke wheels, "Pepsi Cola" tempa ($12-15)
34. white body, blue chassis, red roof, tan seat, silver 12-spoke wheels, "Pepsi Cola" tempa ($12-15)
35 light gray body, green chassis, gray roof with pickle cast, black seat, red 12-spoke wheels, "Heinz 57" tempa ($15-25)
36 blue body, black chassis, yellow roof, black seat, gold 12-spoke wheels, "Rosella" tempa ($15-20)
37. orange-yellow body, green chassis & roof, green seat, gold wheels, "Junior Matchbox Collectors Club" tempa, China casting ($25-35)
38. orange-yellow body, blue roof, green chassis, green seat, gold wheels, "Junior Matchbox Collectors Club" tempa, China casting ($500-750)
39. olive body, olive roof, olive chassis, pale yellow seat, olive wheels, "Field Ambulance" & red crosses in white circles tempa, China casting ($25-35)(CL)
40. red-brown body & roof, black chassis, black seat, red wheels, "MICA Members Weekend 1997" decals, England casting ($50-75)(C2)
41. red-brown body & roof, black chassis, black seat, gold wheels, "MICA Members Weekend 1997" decals, England casting ($50-75)(C2)

Y-12-D 1912 MODEL T FORD PICKUP, issued 1986
1. blue body, base & roof, tan seats, gold wheels, "Imbach" tempa ($18-25)(LE)
2. blue body, base & roof, tan seats, red wheels, "Imbach" tempa ($25-40)(LE)

Y-12-E STEPHENSON'S ROCKET, issued 1987
1. yellow engine with yellow wheels & white stack; tender in yellow with yellow barrel, Macau casting ($20-35)(LE)

Y-12-F 1937 GMC VAN, issued 1988
1. black body with gray painted roof, black chassis, tan interior, chrome wheels, "Goblin" tempa, Macau casting ($50-65)
2. black body, black chassis, tan interior, chrome wheels, "Goblin" tempa, Macau casting ($12-15)
3. cream body, green chassis, black interior, chrome wheels, "Baxter's" tempa, Macau casting ($12-15)
4. dark blue body, black chassis, tan interior, red wheels, "Goanna" tempa, China casting ($15-18)
5. white body, black chassis, tan interior, chrome wheels, "MSS" tempa, China casting ($25-50)(C2)
6. white body, black chassis, tan interior, silver painted wheels, "MSS" tempa, Macau casting ($45-60)(C2)
7. yellow body, blue chassis, tan interior, silver painted wheels, "2nd Dusseldorf Spielzeugmarkte" tempa, China casting ($60-85)(C2)

Y-13-A 1868 SANTA FE LOCOMOTIVE, issued 1959
1. light green body, maroon engine ($500-750)
2. dark green body, maroon engine ($75-90)

Y-13-B 1911 DAIMLER, issued 1966
1. yellow body, black chassis, black seats & grille ($25-40)
2. yellow body, black chassis, maroon seats, black grille ($18-25)
3. yellow body, black chassis, maroon seats & grille ($18-25)
4. silver plated body & chassis, maroon seats, black grille ($45-60)
5. gold plated body & chassis, maroon seats, black grille ($45-60)
6. dark gold plated body & chassis, maroon seats, black grille ($45-60)
7. blue body, powder blue chassis, brown chassis, black grille ($15-25)(LE) (Connoisseur set)

Y-13-C 1918 CROSSLEY, issued 1974
Note:All models with England casting unless otherwise noted.
1. blue-gray body & chassis, cream seat, tan roof & grille, tan canopy, "RAF" & cross labels, silver 12-spoke wheels ($35-45)
2. blue-gray body & chassis, cream seat, tan roof & grille, tan canopy, "RAF" & cross labels, silver 24 spoke wheels ($35-45)
3. blue-gray body & chassis, cream seat, olive roof & grille, olive canopy,. "RAF" & cross labels, silver 24 spoke wheels ($40-60)
4. blue-gray body & chassis, cream seat, black roof & grille, black canopy, "RAF" & cross labels, silver 24 spoke wheels ($250-400)
5. gold plated body & chassis, maroon seat, black roof & grille, black canopy, "RAF" & cross labels, gold 24 spoke wheels ($250-400)
6. gold plated body & chassis, maroon seat, black roof, tan grille, black canopy, "RAF" & cross labels, gold 24 spoke wheels ($250-400)
7. gold plated body & chassis, maroon seat, black roof, tan grille, black coal load, "Coal & Coke" labels, gold 24 spoke wheels ($45-60)
8. gold plated body & chassis, maroon seat, black roof & grille, black coal load, "Coal & Coke" labels, gold 24 spoke wheels ($45-60)
9. red body, black chassis, black seat, roof & grille, black coal load, "Coal & Coke" labels red 12-spoke wheels ($12-15)
10. red body, black chassis, black seat, yellow roof, black grille, yellow canopy, "UK Matchbox 800 Members" labels, red 12-spoke wheels ($275-400)(C2)
11. red body, black chassis, black seat, black grille, gray canopy, "Surrey Model Fair & Swapmeet" labels, red 12-spoke wheels ($225-300)(C2)
12. red body, black chassis, black seat, black grille, gray canopy, "Aspects & Images" labels, red 12-spoke wheels ($225-300)(C2)
13. cream body, black chassis, maroon seat, green roof & grille, green canopy, "Carlsberg" labels, silver 12-spoke wheels ($12-15)
14. cream body, black chassis, maroon seat, green roof & grille, green canopy, "Carlsberg" labels, gold 12-spoke wheels ($12-15)
12. dark green body, black chassis, maroon seat, cream roof, black grille, cream canopy, "Warings" labels with cream background, gold 12-spoke wheels ($15-20)
13. dark green body, black chassis, maroon seat, white roof, black grille, white canopy, "Warings" labels with cream background, gold 12-spoke wheels ($18-25)
14. dark green body, black chassis, maroon seat, white roof, black grille, white canopy, "Warings" labels with white background, gold 12-spoke wheels ($15-20)
15. yellow body, black chassis, black seat, black roof & grille, black coal load, "Kohle & Koks" tempa, black 12-spoke wheels, Macau casting ($15-18)
16. maroon body, cream chassis, maroon seat, cream roof, cream canopies, "XIth MICA Convention" tempa, gold 12 spoke wheels, Macau casting ($45-60)(C2)
17. dark blue body, black chassis, tan roof & seat, black grille, porcelain flower load, "Sherwood Florist" tempa, gold 12-spoke wheels, no origin cast ($35-40)(CL)

Y-14-A 1903 DUKE OF CONNAUGHT, issued 1959
1. green body, brown frame, gold boiler door ($75-90)
2. green body, brown frame, silver boiler door ($75-90)

Y-14-B 1911 MAXWELL ROADSTER, issued 1965
1. turquoise body & chassis, black roof, maroon seats, black grille, gold gas tank ($35-50)
2. turquoise body & chassis, black roof, maroon seats, black grille, copper gas tank ($15-20)
3. turquoise body & chassis, black roof, maroon seats, red grille, copper gas tank ($15-20)
4. silver plated body & chassis, red roof, red seats & grille, plated gas tank ($45-60)
5. gold plated body & chassis, red roof, red seats & grille, plated gas tank ($45-60)
6. gold plated body & chassis, maroon roof, maroon seats & grille, plated gas tank ($45-60)
7. beige body, green chassis, black roof, black seats & grille, copper gas tank ($15-18)(LE) (Connoisseur set)

Y-14-C 1931 STUTZ BEARCAT, issued 1974
1. lime body, dark green chassis, red seats & grille, silver 24 spoke wheels, England casting ($15-18)
2. cream & red body, red chassis, black seats & grille, silver 24 spoke wheels, England casting ($15-18)
3. cream & red body, red chassis, black seats, maroon grille, silver 24 spoke wheels, England casting ($15-18)
4. cream & red body, red chassis, black seats, maroon grille, red 12-spoke wheels, England casting ($25-40)
5. cream & red body, red chassis, black seats, maroon grille, red disc wheels, England casting ($25-40)
6. cream body, green chassis, red seats, maroon grille, silver 24 spoke wheels, England casting ($12-15)
7. cream body, green chassis, black seats, maroon grille, silver 24 spoke wheels, England casting ($12-15)
8. cream body, green chassis, black seats & grille, silver 24 spoke wheels, England casting ($12-15)
9. blue body, dark gray chassis, tan seats, black grille, silver 12-spoke wheels, England casting ($15-18)
10. dark blue & cream body, blue chassis, red seats, black grille, silver 12-spoke wheels, Macau casting ($18-25)

Y-14-D 1935 E.R.A., issued 1986
1. black body & base, silver-gray exhausts, grille & steering wheel, brown interior, chrome plated wheels, "7" tempa, England casting ($10-15)
2. blue body, yellow base, dark silver-gray exhaust, grille & steering wheel, black interior, yellow wheels, "4" tempa, England casting ($10-15)
3. blue body, yellow base, dark silver-gray exhaust, grille & steering wheel, black interior, yellow wheels, "4" tempa, China casting ($10-15)

Y-15-A 1907 ROLLS ROYCE SILVER GHOST, issued 1960
1. silver-green body, black seats, gray plastic tires, unplated wheels ($45-60)
2. silver-green body, black seats, gray plastic tires, brass wheels ($45-60)
3. silver-green body, black seats, black plastic tires, brass wheels ($18-25)
4. silver-green body, black seats, black plastic tires, unplated wheels ($18-25)
5. gold plated body, black seats, black plastic tires, plated wheels ($45-60)
6. gold plated body, green seats, black plastic tires, plated wheels ($45-60)
7. silver plated body, black seats, black plastic tires, plated wheels ($45-60)
8. silver plated body, green seat, black plastic tires, plated wheels ($45-60)

Y-15-B PACKARD VICTORIA, issued 1969
1. tan body, brown chassis, maroon roof, grille, seats & trunk, brass 24 spoke wheels ($15-20)
2. tan body, brown chassis, maroon roof, red grille, maroon seats & trunk, brass 24 spoke wheels ($15-20)
3. green-gold body, brown chassis, maroon roof, grille, seats & trunk, silver 24 spoke wheels ($15-18)
4. green-gold body, brown chassis, maroon roof, grille, seats & trunk, silver 12-spoke wheels ($15-18)
5. green-gold body, brown chassis, black roof, maroon grille, seats & trunk, silver 24 spoke wheels ($15-18)
6. gold plated body & chassis, maroon roof, seats & trunk, red grille, gold 24 spoke wheels ($45-60)
7. gold plated body & chassis, red roof & grille, maroon seats & trunk, gold 24 spoke wheels ($45-60)
8. gold plated body & chassis, red roof, grille & trunk, maroon seats, gold 24 spoke wheels ($45-60)
9. black & red body, black chassis, black roof, grille & trunk, maroon seats, silver disc wheels ($15-20)
10. black & red body, black chassis, white roof, black grille & trunk, maroon seats, silver disc wheels ($12-15)
11. black & red body, black chassis, white roof, black grille & trunk, maroon seats, 24 spoke silver wheels ($12-15)
12. beige body, brown chassis, white roof, maroon grille & seats, black trunk, red 12-spoke wheels ($50-65)
13. beige body, brown chassis, tan roof & seats, black grille & trunk, red 12-spoke wheels ($15-18)
14. beige body, brown chassis, tan roof & seats, black grille & trunk, red 24 spoke wheels ($25-40)
15. beige body, brown chassis, rust roof, tan seats, black grille & trunk, red 12-spoke wheels ($25-40)

Y-15-C PRESTON TYPE TRAMCAR, issued 1987
1. red body, white window area, dark gray roof, dark gray base, brown interior, "Swan Vestas" tempa, Macau casting ($12-15)
2. red body, white window area, dark gray roof, dark gray base, brown interior, "Swan Vestas" tempa. This model comes in a framed cabinet

with a disassembled version in chrome plate with no tempa, Macau casting ($75-100)
3. blue body, cream window area, blue roof, dark gray base, brown interior, "Swan Soap" tempa, Macau casting ($12-15)
4. orange-red body, cream window area, light gray roof, black base, brown interior, "Golden Shred" tempa, Macau casting ($12-15)
5. brown body, cream window area, light gray roof, black base, black interior, "Zebra Grate" tempa, China casting ($12-15)

Y-16-A 1904 SPYKER, issued 1961
1. light green body, dark green fenders, black plastic tires ($1500+)
2. maroon body & fenders, black plastic tires ($1000+)
3. light yellow body & fenders, gray plastic tires ($90-110)
4. light yellow body & fenders, black plastic tires ($18-25)
5. dark yellow body & fenders, black plastic tires ($15-20)
6. silver plated body & fenders, black plastic tires ($45-60)

Y-16-B 1928 MERCEDES BENZ SS, issued 1972
NOTE: All models with England casting unless otherwise noted.
1. silver-gray body, red chassis, black roof, grille, seats & trunk, brass 24 spoke wheels ($50-75)
2. light green body, dark emerald green chassis, black roof, grille, seats & trunk, silver 24 spoke wheels ($175-250)
3. light green body & chassis, black roof, grille, seats & trunk, silver 24 spoke wheels ($15-20)
4. light green body & chassis, black roof, grille, seats & trunk, silver 12-spoke wheels ($15-20)
5. light green body & chassis, green roof, grille, seats & trunk, silver 24 spoke wheels ($125-150)
6. dark green body & chassis, black roof, seats & trunk, green grille, silver 24 spoke wheels ($15-20)
7. dark green body & chassis, black roof & seats, green grille & trunk, silver 24 spoke wheels ($18-25)
8. dark green body & chassis, black, roof, grille, seats & trunk, silver 24 spoke wheels ($15-20)
9. white body & chassis, black roof, grille, seats & trunk, silver 24 spoke wheels ($15-20)
10. white body & chassis, black roof, seats, grille & trunk, silver 24 spoke wheels, whitewalls ($15-20)
11. white body & chassis, black roof, grille, seats & trunk, silver 12-spoke wheels ($15-20)
12. white body & chassis, black roof, seats, grille & trunk, silver 12-spoke wheels, whitewalls ($15-20)
13. blue & gray body, blue chassis, black roof, grille seats & trunk, silver 12-spoke wheels, whitewalls ($18-25)
14. blue & light blue body, blue chassis, black roof, grille, seats & trunk, silver 12-spoke wheels, whitewalls ($18-25)
15. blue & beige body, blue chassis, black roof, grille, seats & trunk, silver 12-spoke wheels, white walls ($18-25)
16. blue & beige body, blue chassis, black roof, grille, seats & trunk, silver 12-spoke wheels ($18-25)
17. red body, silver-gray chassis, no roof, black grille, seats & trunk, red 24 spoke wheels ($18-25)
18. lavender-gray body, black chassis, black roof, grille, seats & trunk, silver 24 spoke wheels, whitewalls, Macau casting ($20-25)

Y-16-C 1960 FERRARI DINO 246/V12, issued 1986
1. red body & base, black interior, gray exhaust, chrome wheels, "17" tempa, Macau casting ($15-18)
2. red body & base, black interior, gray exhaust, silver painted wheels, "17" tempa, Macau casting ($15-18)

Y-16-D 1922 SCANIA VABIS POSTBUS, issued 1988
1. yellow body, black chassis, gray roof, reddish brown interior, gold wheels, yellow skis, Macau casting ($25-40)(LE)

Y-16-E SCAMMELL 100 TON TRANSPORTER & CLASS 2-4-0 LOCO, issued 1989
1. dark blue cab with red chassis, blue trailer, red wheels, "Pickfords" livery; Locomotive in black, Macau casting ($85-110)(LE)

Y-17-A 1938 HISPANO SUIZA, issued 1975
1. red body, black chassis, black roof & grille, silver 24 spoke wheels, England casting ($15-18)
2. light blue & powder blue body, light blue chassis, black roof & grille, silver disc wheels, England casting ($15 18)
3. light blue & powder blue body, black chassis, black roof & grille, silver disc wheels, England casting ($15-18)
4. light blue & powder blue body, black chassis, black roof & grille, silver 24 spoke wheels, England casting ($18-25)
5. green body, dark green chassis, black roof & interior, green grille, gold 24 spoke wheels, includes 2 piece plastic diorama, England casting ($15-20)
6. green body, dark green chassis, black roof, interior & grille, gold 24 spoke wheels, includes 2 piece plastic diorama, England casting ($15-20)
7. green body, dark green chassis, black roof, interior & grille, gold 24 spoke wheels, includes 2 piece plastic diorama, Macau casting ($15-20)
8. green & lime body, green chassis, white roof, cream interior, black grille, silver 24 spoke wheels, whitewalls, Macau casting ($18-25)
9. dark blue body & chassis, tan interior, black roof & grille, gold 24 spoke wheels & headlights, whitewalls, China casting ($20-25)
10. dark pea green body & chassis, dark tan sides tempa, tan roof & interior, black grille, gold 24 spoke wheels & headlights, whitewalls, no origin cast ($30-35)(CL)

Y-18-A 1937 CORD 812, issued 1979
1. red body & chassis, red base, white roof & interior, silver disc wheels, England casting ($12-15)
2. red body & chassis, red base, white roof & interior, silver 12-spoke wheels, England casting ($20-35)
3. red body & chassis, red base, white roof & interior, silver 24 spoke wheels, England casting ($20-35)
4. plum body & chassis, black base, white roof & interior, silver 24 spoke wheels, England casting ($25-40)
5. plum body & chassis, black base, white roof & interior, silver disc wheels, England casting ($25-40)
6. pale yellow body & chassis, black base, tan roof & interior, silver 24 spoke wheels, Macau casting ($20-25)
7. pale yellow body & chassis, black base, tan roof & interior, silver 24 spoke wheels, "Matchbox Collectibles 1998 Dealer Conference", Macau casting ($1000+)

Y-18-B 1918 ATKINSON STEAM LORRY, issued 1985
1. green body, red base, green wheels, "Sand & Gravel" tempa, England casting ($18-25)(LE)

Y-18-C 1918 ATKINSON STEAM LORRY, issued 1986
1. yellow body, black base, yellow wheels, no load, "Blue Circle Portland Cement" tempa, England casting ($15-18)
2. red body, black base, red wheels, beige sack load, "Burghfield Mills Reading" tempa, Macau casting ($15-18)

Y-18-D 1918 ATKINSON D-TYPE STEAM LORRY, issued 1987
1. blue body, black base, red wheels, brown barrels with gold chain, "Bass & Co." tempa, Macau casting ($18-25)(LE)
2. cream body, red base, gold wheels, porcelain landscapers load, "F.C. Conybeare Gardeners Chilham, Kent" tempa ($35-40)(CL)

Y-19-A 1935 AUBURN 851 SUPERCHARGED ROADSTER, issued 1980
1. khaki & beige body, brown chassis, orange seat, silver disc wheels, whitewalls, England casting ($25-40)
2. khaki & beige body, brown chassis, orange seat, red disc wheels, whitewalls, England casting ($15-18)
3. khaki & beige body, brown chassis, red seat, red disc wheels, whitewalls, England casting ($15-18)
4. khaki & beige body, dark brown chassis, red seat, red disc wheels, whitewalls, England casting ($15-18)
5. khaki & beige body, dark brown chassis, red seat, red disc wheels, black walls, England casting ($15-18)
6. cream body, black chassis, red seat, red disc wheels, England casting ($12-15)
7. white & blue body, white chassis, blue seat, blue 24 spoke wheels, England casting ($18-25)
8. beige & cream body, beige chassis, tan seat, silver 24 spoke wheels, whitewalls, Macau casting ($18-25)

Y-19-B FOWLER B6 SHOWMAN'S ENGINE, issued 1986
1. blue body, cream roof, black boiler, red wheels, gray tires, "Hey-Ho Come To The Fair" tempa, Macau casting ($20-35)(LE)
2. blue body, white roof, black boiler, red wheels, gray tires, "Hey-Ho Come To The Fair" tempa, Macau casting ($20-25)(LE)
3. yellow body, white roof, black boiler, red wheels, gray tires, "Lesney Products & Co. Amusements" tempa, China casting ($25-35)(LE)
4. red body, dark cream roof, black boiler, dark cream wheels, black tires, "Billy Smart's Coronation Amusements" tempa, China casting ($35-50)(LE)
5. red body, dark cream roof, black boiler, red wheels, black tires, "L.J. Searle & Sons Contractors Horsham" tempa, China casting ($30-35)(CL)

Y-19-C 1929 MORRIS LIGHT VAN, issued 1988
NOTE: This model differs from Y-47-A in that it has a small window cast on the body sides.
1. blue body, white roof, black chassis, brown interior, red 12 spoke wheels, "Brasso" tempa, Macau casting ($15-18)
2. blue body, yellow roof, black chassis, brown interior, silver 12 spoke wheels, "Michelin" tempa, Macau casting ($15-18)
3. brown body, white roof, black chassis, brown interior, silver 12 spoke wheels, "Sainsbury" tempa, Macau casting ($15-18)
4. blue body, white roof, black chassis, brown interior, red 12 spoke wheels, "Brasso" tempa, China casting ($25-35)
5. blue body, white roof, black chassis, brown interior, red 12 spoke wheels, "Vitakraft" tempa, Macau casting ($85-110)(C2)
6. blue body, yellow roof, black chassis, brown interior, silver 12 spoke wheels, "Vitakraft" tempa, Macau casting ($60-85)(C2)
7. white body, maroonish purple roof, black chassis, silver 12 spoke wheels, "The Black Light Display" tempa, Macau casting ($50-75)(C2)

Y-20-A 1937 MERCEDES BENZ 540K, issued 1981
1. silver-gray body, black chassis, red seats, silver 24 spoke wheels, England casting ($12-15)
2. silver-gray body, black chassis, orange-red seats, silver 24 spoke wheels, England casting ($12-15)
3. silver-gray body, black chassis, orange-red seats, silver disc wheels, England casting ($20-35)
4. silver-gray body, black chassis, orange-red seats, red disc wheels, England casting ($25-40)
5. silver-gray body, black chassis, orange-red seats, red 12-spoke wheels, England casting ($25-40)
6. white body & chassis, red seats, red 24 spoke wheels, whitewalls, England casting ($12-15)
7. white body & chassis, red seats, red 24 spoke wheels, black walls, England casting ($12-15)
8. red body & chassis, red seats, red 24 spoke wheels, includes 2 piece plastic diorama, Macau casting ($15-20)
9. black body & chassis, red seats, silver 24 spoke wheels, Macau casting ($15-18)
10. black body & chassis, red seats, silver 24 spoke wheels, China casting ($15-18)
11. dark red body & chassis, black seats, silver 24 spoke wheels, China casting ($18-25)(CL)

Y-21-A 1930 MODEL A FORD "WOODY WAGON," issued 1981
1. yellow hood, brown rear body, black chassis, orange interior, open cast windows, England casting ($25-40)
2. yellow hood, brown rear body, black chassis, red interior, open cast windows, England casting ($25-40)
3. yellow hood, brown rear body, brown chassis, red interior, open cast windows, England casting ($12-15)
4. metallic bronze hood, brown rear body, brown chassis, cream interior, "A&J Box" tempa, England casting ($10-15)
5. orange-brown hood, brown rear body, brown chassis, cream interior, "A&J Box" tempa, England casting (with Lesney or International base)($10-15)
NOTE: Following models with "Matchbox International" cast.
6. blue hood, dark cream rear body, black chassis, cream interior, "Carter's Seeds" tempa, England casting ($25-40)
7. blue hood, dark cream rear body, black chassis, brown interior, "Carter's Seeds" tempa, England casting ($10-15)
8. blue hood, pale cream rear body, black chassis, brown interior, "Carter's Seeds" tempa, England casting ($10-15)
9. blue hood, pale cream rear body, blue chassis, white interior, "Pepsi Cola" tempa, China casting ($20-25)

Y-21-B 1920 AVELING PORTER STEAM ROLLER, issued 1987
1. green body, green wheels with gray tires, red front wheel frame, gold roof supports, black stack, gray roof (without inscription underneath), "James Young & Sons Edinburgh" tempa, Macau casting ($250-350)(LE)
2. green body, green wheels with gray tires, red front wheel frame, gold roof supports, black stack, gray roof (with inscription underneath), "James Young & Sons Edinburgh" tempa, Macau casting ($20-30)(LE)
3. green body, green wheels with gray tires, green front wheel frame, red roof supports, black stack, black roof, "F. Dibnah & Sons Steeplejacks Bolton 531303", China casting ($35-50)(LE)

Y-21-C 1957 BMW 507. issued 1988
1. blue body & hood, black roof, red interior, clear windshield, chrome wheels, black base, Macau casting ($15-20)(LE)

Y-21-D FORD MODEL TT VAN, issued 1989
1. green body, black chassis, red roof, gray interior, red wheels, silver grille, "O for an Osram Lamp" tempa, Macau casting ($15-18)
2. green body, black chassis, red roof, gray interior, red wheels, black grille, "O for an Osram Lamp" tempa, Macau casting ($15-18)
3. beige body, black chassis, beige roof, gray-brown interior, red wheels, "My Bread" tempa, Macau casting ($12-15)
4. black body, black chassis, black roof, gray interior, gold wheels, "Drambuie" tempa, China casting ($12-15)
5. black body, black chassis, black roof, gray interior, gold wheels, "Antiques Road Show-Next Generation 1992" decals, China casting ($1500+)(LE)
NOTE: Following two models are only issued as a pair in a boxed set and not individually available ($1500+)(AU)
6. dark blue body, dark blue chassis & roof, gray interior, gold wheels, "Jenny Kee" & 'Waratah" painting tempa, China casting
7. dark green body, dark green chassis & roof, gray interior, gold wheels, "Pro Hart" & 'Lunchtime' painting tempa, China casting
8. blue-green body, black chassis, white roof, gray interior, gold wheels, "Classic Toys" decals, China casting ($60-75)(C2)
9. white body, black chassis, turquoise roof, gray interior, gold wheels, "bph Barclays Property Holding Limited" tempa, China casting ($500-750)(C2)

Y-22-A MODEL A FORD VAN, issued 1982
1. red body, black chassis, black roof, silver 12-spoke wheels, "OXO" tempa, England casting ($10-15)
2. yellow body, black chassis, red roof, silver 12-spoke wheels, "Maggi's" tempa, England casting ($10-15)
3. beige body, brown chassis, red roof, silver 24 spoke wheels, "Toblerone" tempa, England casting ($10-15)
4. red body, black chassis, black roof, black 24 spoke wheels, "Canada Poste" tempa, England casting ($12-15)
5. cream body, red chassis, red roof, gold 24 spoke wheels, "Walter's Palm Toffee" tempa, England casting ($12-15)
6. reddish brown body, brown chassis, white roof, silver 24 spoke wheels, "Spratt's," England casting ($12-15)
7. blue body, black chassis, white roof, silver 12-spoke wheels, "Lyon's Tea" tempa, England casting ($12-15)
8. white body, black chassis, black roof, red 12-spoke wheels, "Cherry Blossom" tempa, Macau casting ($15-18)
9. white body, black chassis, black roof, red 12-spoke wheels, "Cherry Blossom" tempa, China casting ($25-35)
10. blue body, black chassis, white roof, silver 12-spoke wheels, "Lyon's Tea" tempa, China casting ($25-35)
11. white body, black chassis, black roof, orange disc wheels, "Pratt's" tempa, China casting ($15-18)
12. orange body, blue chassis, black roof, orange wheels, "Bravo Colonel" tempa, China casting ($60-75)(C2)
13. orange body, blue chassis, black roof, orange wheels, "Bravo Colonel" tempa, Macau casting ($60-75)(C2)

14. orange body, blue chassis, black roof, orange wheels, "Bravo Colonel" tempa, England casting ($60-75)(C2)
15. reddish brown body, brown chassis, white roof, chrome wheels, "Matchbox & Lesney Toy Museum" tempa, England casting ($60-75)(C2)

Y-23-A 1922 AEC 'S' TYPE BUS, issued 1982
1. red body & upper deck, chocolate interior, red wheels, "Schweppes Tonic Water" labels, England casting ($18-25)
2. red body & upper deck, light tan interior, red wheels, "Schweppes Tonic Water" labels, England casting ($15-18)
3. red body & upper deck, tan interior, red wheels, "Schweppes" labels, England casting ($12-15)
4. red body & upper deck, tan interior, red wheels, "Maples Furniture" labels, England casting ($15-20)(GS)
5. red body & upper deck, tan interior, red wheels, "The RAC" labels, England casting ($12-15)
6. brown body, cream upper deck, chocolate interior, dark red wheels, "Haig" labels, England casting ($12-15)
7. red body & upper deck, tan interior, red wheels, "Kellogg's Rice Krispies" labels, Macau casting ($12-15)
8. blue body, cream upper deck, chocolate interior, cream wheels, "Lifebuoy Soap" labels, Macau casting ($12-15)

Y-23-B 1923 MACK PETROL TANKER, issued 1989
1. red body, fenders & roof, red tank, "Texaco" tempa, Macau casting ($12-15)
2. red body, fenders & roof, white tank, "Conoco" tempa, Macau casting ($10-15)
3. orange body, fenders & roof, orange tank, white lettered "Supertest Petroleum Corporation" tempa, Macau casting ($50-75)(C2)
4. orange body, fenders & roof, orange tank, black lettered "Supertest Petroleum Corporation" tempa, Macau casting ($50-75)(C2)
5. desert sand body, fenders & roof, desert sand tank, "Military Refueller" tempa, Macau casting ($60-75)(C2)
6. dark gray body, fenders & roof, dark gray tank, "Military Refueller" tempa, Macau casting ($100-150)(C2)

Y-24-A 1928 BUGATTI TYPE 44. issued 1983
1. black body & chassis, tan interior, silver 12-spoke wheels, full yellow tempa, England casting ($12-15)
black body & chassis, tan interior, silver 12-spoke wheels, pinstriped lemon tempa, England casting ($12-15)
black body & chassis, black interior, silver 24 spoke wheels, pinstriped lemon tempa, England casting ($18-25)
4. gray body, plum chassis, tan interior, silver disc wheels, pinstriped plum tempa, includes 2 piece plastic diorama, Macau casting ($15-18)
5. black body & chassis, tan interior, silver 12-spoke wheels, pinstriped red tempa, Macau casting ($15-18)
6. black body & chassis, tan interior, silver 24 spoke wheels, pale yellow basket weave design tempa, China casting ($20-25)

Y-25-A 1910 RENAULT TYPE AG VAN, issued 1983
1. green body, dark green chassis, white roof & interior, gold 12 spoke wheels, "Perrier" tempa, England casting ($12-15)
2. green body, dark green chassis, white roof & interior, red 12-spoke wheels, "Perrier" tempa, England casting ($25-40)
3. yellow body, blue chassis, white roof, black interior, yellow 12-spoke wheels, "James Neale & Sons" tempa, England casting ($15-20)
4. yellow body, dark blue chassis, white roof, black interior, yellow 12-spoke wheels, "James Neale & Sons" tempa, England casting ($35-50)
5. yellow body, dark blue chassis, white roof, black interior, red 12-spoke wheels, "James Neale & Sons" tempa, England casting ($45-60)
6. silver-gray body & chassis, white roof, maroon interior, red 12-spoke wheels, "Duckhams Oils" tempa, England casting ($15-18)
7. powder blue body, dark blue chassis, white roof, maroon interior, gold 12-spoke wheels, "Eagle Pencils" tempa, England casting ($15-18)
8. red body, black chassis, white roof & interior, black 12-spoke wheels, "Tunnock's" tempa, England casting ($15-18)
9. green body, black chassis, white roof, maroon interior, gold 12-spoke wheels, "Delhaize" tempa, Macau casting ($15-18)
10. lavender body, black chassis, white roof, brown interior, gold 12-spoke wheels, "Suchard Chocolat" tempa, Macau casting ($15-18)

Y-25-B 1910 RENAULT TYPE AG AMBULANCE, issued 1986
1. olive body & roof, black chassis, brown interior, 12-spoke olive wheels, red cross & "British Red Cross Society-St. John Ambulance Assn." tempa, England casting ($18-25)(LE)

Y-26-A 1913 CROSSLEY BEER LORRY, issued 1983
1. light blue body, black chassis, tan canopy, brown barrels, maroon seat, black grille, "Lowenbrau" tempa, England casting ($12-15)
2. light blue body, black chassis, light tan canopy, brown barrels, maroon seat, black grille, "Lowenbrau" tempa, England casting ($12-15)
3. light blue body, black chassis, light tan canopy, gray-brown barrels, maroon seat, black grille, "Lowenbrau" tempa, England casting ($12-15)
4. black body, reddish brown chassis, black canopy, dark brown barrels, brown seat, black grille, "Romford Brewery" tempa, England casting ($12-15)
5. white body, red chassis, maroon canopy, dark brown barrels, maroon seat & grille, "Gonzales Byass" tempa, England casting ($12-15)
6. white body, red chassis, maroon canopy, brown barrel load, maroon seat & grille, "De Bortoli" tempa, England casting ($60-75)(C2)

Y-27-A 1922 FODEN STEAM WAGON, issued 1985
1. blue body, red chassis, gray roof & rear canopy, red wheels, without tow hook, "Pickfords" tempa, England casting ($15-18)
2. blue body, red chassis, gray roof & rear canopy, red wheels, with tow hook, "Pickfords" tempa, England casting ($25-40)
3. brown body, black chassis, tan roof & rear canopy, tan wheels, "Hovis" tempa, England casting ($12-15)
4. light brown body, black chassis, black roof & rear canopy, "Tate & Lyle" tempa, England casting ($12-15)
5. cream body, dark green chassis, greenish black roof, beige sack load, red wheels, "Spillers" tempa, England casting ($12-15)
6. dark blue body, black chassis, black roof, brown barrel load, red wheels, "Guinness" tempa, Macau casting ($15-18)
7. dark green body, brown chassis, brown roof, cream sack load, dark green wheels, "Joseph Rank" tempa, Macau casting ($15-18)
8. black body, red chassis, cream roof, brown barrel load, red wheels, "McMullen" tempa, China casting ($15-18)
9. black body, red chassis, red roof, brown barrel load, red wheels, "Fullers" tempa, China casting ($25-35)(UK)
10. maroon body, yellow chassis, yellow roof, yellow rear canopy, red wheels, "MICA 1996 Club Member" tempa, China casting ($25-35)(UK)
11. gray body, red chassis, red roof, tan bed with no load, red wheels, "MICA Chester 1998" tempa, China casting ($50-75)(C2)
12. gray body, black chassis, black roof, dark tan bed with no load, red wheels, "MICA Chester 1998" tempa, China casting ($50-75)(C2)
13. red-brown body, black chassis, black roof, porcelain lumber load, gold wheels, "F. Parker & Co." tempa, China casting ($75-100)(CL)

Y-27-B 1922 FODEN STEAM WAGON & TRAILER, issued 1986
1. dark green body with white roof, red chassis, white canopies on both wagon & trailer, "Frasers" tempa, England casting ($25-40)(LE)

Y-28-A 1907 UNIC TAXI, issued 1984
1. maroon body, black chassis & roof, with window frame tempa, red wheels, plastic meter, England casting ($10-15)
2. maroon body, black chassis & roof, without window frame tempa, red wheels, plastic meter, England casting ($10-15)
3. maroon body, black chassis & roof, without window frame tempa, red wheels, metal meter, England casting ($10-15)
4. maroon body, black chassis & roof, with window frame tempa, red wheels, metal meter, England casting ($10-15)
5. maroon body, black chassis & roof, with window frame tempa, maroon wheels, metal meter, England casting ($10-15)
6. maroon body, black chassis & roof, without window frame tempa, maroon wheels, metal meter, England casting ($10-15)
7. blue body, black chassis & roof, without window frame tempa, maroon wheels, metal meter, England casting ($10-15)
8. blue body, black chassis & roof, without window frame tempa, red wheels, metal meter, England casting ($10-15)
9. white body, black chassis & roof, without window frame tempa, gold wheels, metal meter, Macau casting ($10-15)

Y-29-A WALKER ELECTRIC VAN, issued 1985
1. olive body, beige canopy, olive wheels, tan interior, "Harrods Ltd." tempa, England casting ($15-18)(UK)
2. green body, green canopy, red wheels, tan interior, "Joseph Lucas" tempa, England casting ($12-15)
3. dark blue body, gray canopy, dark blue wheels, tan interior, "His Master's Voice" tempa, Macau casting ($10-15)
4. olive body, dark olive canopy, olive wheels, red-brown interior, "Harrods Special Bread" tempa, England casting ($12-15)

Y-30-A 1920 MODEL AC MACK TRUCK, issued 1985
1. light blue body, dark blue chassis, dark gray cab roof, dark blue fenders, brown wheels, light blue container with dark gray roof, "Acorn Storage" tempa, England casting ($15-18)
2. light blue body, dark blue chassis, dark gray cab roof & fenders, brown wheels, light blue container with dark gray roof, "Acorn Storage" tempa, England casting ($15-18)
3. cream body & cab roof, dark green chassis & fenders, cream wheels, cream container with tan roof, "Artic Ice Cream" tempa, Macau casting ($12-15)
4. red body, cab roof & fenders, black chassis, tan wheels, red container with tan roof, "Kiwi Boot Polish" labels, Macau casting ($12-15)
5. dark red body & cab roof, black fenders, gray chassis, red wheels, dark red container with black roof, "Mack Allentown, Penna." tempa, no origin cast ($25-30)(CL)

Y-30-B 1920 MACK CANVASBACK TRUCK, issued 1985
1. yellow body & cab roof, dark brown fenders, black chassis, red wheels, tan canopy on yellow bed, "Consolidated Transport" tempa, England casting ($15-18)(LE)
2. dark blue body & cab roof, dark blue fenders, black chassis, silver wheels, porcelain load on pea green bed, "Fisherman's Wharf Pier 39" tempa, China casting ($30-40)(CL)

Y-31-A 1931 MORRIS PANTECHNICON, issued 1990
1. red cab & container, white container roof, red wheels, black base, "Kemp's Biscuits" tempa, Macau casting ($15-18)
2. orange-yellow cab, container & container roof, red wheels, black base, "Weetabix" tempa, China casting ($15-18)

Y-32-A 1917 YORKSHIRE STEAM WAGON, issued 1990
1. plum body, black chassis, cream cab roof & wheels, "Samuel Smith" tempa, Macau casting ($15-18)
NOTE: Base can be cast "Y-8" or "Y-32"

Y-32-B 1932 MERCEDES BENZ LORRY, issued 1998
NOTE: This model is a reissue of Y-6-E & Y-42-A
1. dark green cab & body, gray roof, black fenders, gray chassis, gray interior & wheels, porcelain load of vegetables in bed, "O'Neill Family Produce" tempa, no origin cast ($30-40)(CL)

Y-33-A 1920 MACK TRUCK, issued 1990
NOTE: Reissue of Y-30 but base is cast Y-23!
1. blue body, gray cab roof, blue container with gray roof, blue wheels, dark blue chassis, "Goodyear" tempa, Macau casting ($15-18)

Y-33-B 1957 BMW507, issued 1998
NOTE: This model is a reissue of Y-21-C.
1. dark cream body, hood & base, black roof & interior, silver wheels, China casting ($30-40)(CL)

Y-34-A 1933 CADILLAC V-16, issued 1990
1. dark blue body & chassis, brown interior, cream roof, Macau casting ($15-18)
2. white body, dark blue chassis, black interior, black roof, China casting ($15-18)

Y-34-B 1937 GMC VAN, issued 1996
NOTE: This model is a reissue of Y-12F.
1. powder blue body, dark blue chassis, tan interior, solid chrome wheels, "Chester Toy Museum" tempa, China casting ($25-35)(UK)
2. powder blue body, dark blue chassis, tan interior, small gold spoked wheels, "Chester Toy Museum" tempa, China casting ($250-450)(UK)
3. dark olive body & chassis, light tan interior, solid olive wheels, red crosses on white squares & "Ambulance" tempa, no origin cast ($25-30)(CL)

Y-35-A 1930 MODEL A FORD PICKUP, issued 1990
1. cream body, black roof & chassis, brown interior, yellow wheels, cream front bumper, "W. Clifford & Sons" & "Fresh Farm Milk" tempa, Macau casting ($15-18)
2. blue body, cream roof & chassis, brown interior, cream wheels, blue front bumper, "From Our Devon Creamery-Ambrosia" tempa, China casting ($15-18)

Y-35-B 1922 SCANIA VABIS BUS, issued 1997
NOTE: This model is a reissue of Y-16-D.
1. dark green body & roof, black fenders & base, brown interior & skis, gold wheels, porcelain roof load, "Snow Mountain Inn" tempa, no origin cast ($30-40)(CL)

Y-36-A 1926 ROLLS ROYCE PHANTOM I, issued 1990
1. plum body, black roof & chassis, brown interior, China casting ($15-18)
2. blue body, black roof & chassis, brown interior, China casting ($15-18)

Y-37-A 1931 GARRETT STEAM WAGON, issued 1990
1. powder blue body with white roof, powder blue container with white roof, dark blue chassis, blue wheels, "Chubb's Safe Deposits" tempa, Macau casting ($15-18)
2. dark blue cab & cab roof, dark cream container with white roof, dark blue chassis, red wheels, "Milkmaid Brand Milk" tempa, China casting ($15-18)
3. gray body & roof, yellow container with gray roof, gray chassis, red wheels, "Year Ten 1984 1994 MICA" decals, China casting ($35-50)(C2)
4. dark blue body & roof, yellow container with dark blue roof, dark blue chassis, red wheels, "Year Ten 1984 1994 MICA" decals, China casting ($500-750)(C2)
5. lime green body & gray roof, lime green container with gray roof, black chassis, yellow wheels, "All Roads To the Garrett are Smooth Roads" tempa, China casting ($85-12)(C2)
6. lime green body & dark green roof, lime green container & dark green roof, black chassis, yellow wheels, "All Roads To the Garrett are Smooth Roads" tempa, China casting ($$60-75)(C2)

Y-38-A ROLLS ROYCE ARMORED CAR, issued 1990
1. khaki tan body, chassis & turret, khaki tan wheels, small red/white/blue roundels tempa, Macau casting ($25-30)(LE)

Y-39-A 1820 ENGLISH STAGE COACH, issued 1990
1. black body with maroon door, red chassis, hitch & wheels, 4 horses with one each in brown, white, red-brown & dark brown, five painted figures, China casting ($45-60)(LE)

Y-39-B FORD MODEL TT VAN, issued 1996
NOTE: This model is a reissue of Y-21-D.
1. white body, red roof & chassis, silver wheels, "Starting Our 20th Year in 1996-Matchbox USA" tempa, China casting ($25-35)(US)
2. black body, dark gray roof & chassis, silver wheels, "Jack Daniel's Old No. 7 Brand" tempa, China casting ($35-45)(CL)

Y-40-A 1931 MERCEDES BENZ TYPE 770, issued 1991
1. dark gray body & chassis, dark blue roof, maroon interior, chrome wheels, China casting ($15-20)

Y-41-A 1932 MERCEDES BENZ TRUCK, issued 1991
1. dark green body with dark gray roof, black fenders, gray base, red wheels, light gray casting load with brown bed, "Howaldtswerke A.G. Kiel" tempa, China casting ($15-20)
NOTE: Base still cast "Y-6"

Y-42-A ALBION CX27, issued 1991
1. white cab, powder blue bed, dark blue chassis, black interior, blue wheels,

chrome milk churn load, "Libby's" tempa, China casting ($15-20)

Y-43-A 1905 BUSCH STEAM FIRE ENGINE, issued 1991
1. dark green body & chassis, bluish boiler, red wheels with black tire rims, 4 dark blue painted figures, small lettered tempa, China casting ($50-65)(LE)

Y-44-A 1910 RENAULT BUS, issued 1991
1. orange-yellow body, black chassis, light red roof, brown seats, red wheels, "Wesserling-Bussang" tempa, China casting ($150-200)
2. orange-yellow body, black chassis, dark red roof, brown seats, red wheels, "Wesserling-Bussang" tempa, China casting ($150-200)
3. orange-yellow body, black chassis, black roof, brown seats, red wheels, "Wesserling-Bussang" tempa, China casting ($15-20)

Y-45-A 1930 BUGATTI ROYALE, issued 1991
1. black body with blue flash tempa, black chassis, dark blue interior, chrome wheels, China casting ($15-20)
2. black body with blue flash tempa, black chassis, dark purplish blue interior, chrome wheels, China casting ($15-20)

Y-46-A 1868 MERRYWEATHER FIRE ENGINE, issued 1991
1. red body & chassis, red wheels & tow bar, black rear base section, two white horses, four dark blue firemen, "Tehidy House" tempa, China casting ($45-60)(LE)

Y-47-A 1929 MORRIS VAN, issued 1991
1. black body & chassis, yellow roof, silver wheels, brown interior, "Chocolat Lindt" labels, China casting ($15-20)
2. black body & chassis, yellow roof, silver wheels, brown interior, "Antiques Road Show 1991" labels, China casting ($1500+)
3. black body & chassis, yellow roof, chrome wheels, brown interior, "Churton's Fine Scotch Whisky/The Chairman's Choice" tempa, China casting ($45-60)(C2)
NOTE: Versions 1-3 & 5 with "Y-19" cast, below model with "Y-47." Reissue of Y-19-C but without side window cast.
4. green body, red roof & chassis, brown interior, "Fuller's Brewery" tempa, China casting ($25-35)(UK)
5. white body, maroonish purple roof, black chassis, "The Black Light display" tempa, Macau casting ($50-75)(C2)

Y-48-A 1931 GARRETT STEAM WAGON, issued 1996
NOTE: This model is a reissue of Y-37-A.
1. dark blue cab body with white roof, dark blue container with white roof, red chassis, red wheels, "Removals & Warehousing-Pickfords" tempa ($45-55)(LE)
2. red cab body with yellow roof, red container with yellow roof, black chassis, red wheels, "Chester Mystery Plays" tempa ($45-55)(LE)

NOTE: No Yesteryear models were issued with the numbers Y-49 through Y-60 except for Y-52 & 53.

Y-52-A MACK TRUCK, issued 1998
NOTE: This model is a reissue of Y-30-A
1. bright blue cab & container, purple container roof, black interior & base, gold wheels, "Matchbox Collectibles Inaugural Collectors Edition 1998" tempa ($30-35)(CL)

Y-53-A 1931 MERCEDES BENZ TYPE 770, issued 1998
NOTE: This model is a reissue of Y-40-A.
1. red-brown body, black roof & base, gray interior, chrome wheels, no origin cast ($30-40)(CL)

Y-61-A 1933 CADILLAC FIRE ENGINE, issued 1992
1. red body & chassis, brown ladder with red roof rack, red dome lights, black interior, silver wheels, "Feuerwehr Aarau" tempa, China casting ($18-25)

Y-62-A 1932 FORD AA PICKUP, issued 1992
1. lime body, gray roof, black chassis, red wheels, brown sack load, "G.W. Peacock Haulage" tempa, China casting ($20-30)
2. dark green body, black roof, maroonish purple chassis, gold wheels, porcelain snowmen load, "Happy Holidays from Clayton Feed & Grain" tempa, no origin cast ($40-45)(CL)

Y-63-A 1939 BEDFORD TRUCK, issued 1992
1. red cab, brown bed, black chassis, black interior, silver wheels, real stone load, "George Farrar Yorkshire Stone" tempa, China casting ($20-30)

Y-64-A 1938 LINCOLN ZEPHYR, issued 1992
1. cream body & chassis, brown interior, yellowish cream tonneau, no windshield, China casting ($35-50)
2. plum body & chassis, tan interior, white tonneau, clear windshield, China casting ($20-25)

Y-65-A AUSTIN 7—BMW—ROSENGART SET, issued 1992
1. three model set includes Austin 7 in red with black chassis, brown interior, silver wire wheels, "Castrol" tempa; BMW in white with black chassis, brown interior, silver wire wheels; Rosengart in blue with black chassis & roof, brown interior, silver disc wheels, China castings ($45-50)(LE)

Y-65-B AUSTIN 7 VAN, issued 1992
1 light & dark green body with black chassis, white interior, "The Yesteryear Book" tempa, China casting ($45-60)(C2)
2. light & dark green body with black chassis, blue interior, "The Yesteryear Book" tempa, China casting ($60-75)(C2)
3. yellow body with salmon chassis, brown interior, "Sun Valley Gold" tempa, China casting ($8-12)(MB1)
4. red body with blue chassis, brown interior, "Wild Goose Brewery" tempa, China casting ($8-12)(MB2)
5. green body with black chassis, dark gray interior, "Ozark Brewing Co." tempa, China casting ($8-12)(MB3)
6. white body with red chassis, dark blue interior, "Dinky-MICA European Convention 1996" tempa, China casting ($30-40)(DU)
7. powder blue body with dark blue roof & chassis, red interior, "Aldershot-Royal Army Reserve Corps" tempa, China casting ($18-25)
8. dark blue body & chassis, tan interior, "5th Euro-MICA 1997" tempa, China casting ($18-25)

Y-66-A GOLD STATE COACH, issued 1992
1. gold plated body & horsebar, opaque blue windows, white horses with painted features, China casting ($15-25)(LE)

Y-901 JAGUAR SS100, issued 1991
1. pewter casting with free standing wooden plinth ($75-100)(LE)

YTF01 1947 CITROEN H-TYPE VAN, issued 1993
1. pink body, gray interior, clear windows, cream hubs, "Evian" tempa, China casting ($15-20)

YTF02 1947 CITROEN H-TYPE VAN, issued 1993
1. cream & dark blue body, gray interior, clear windows, cream hubs, "Martell Cordon Bleu" tempa, China casting ($15-20)

YTF03 1947 CITROEN H-TYPE VAN, issued 1993
1. white & lime body, gray interior, clear windows, lime hubs, "Yoplait" tempa, China casting ($15-20)

YTF04 1947 CITROEN H-TYPE VAN, issued 1993
1. cream body, gray interior, clear windows, red hubs, "Brie Marcillat" tempa, China casting ($15-20)

YTF05 1947 CITROEN H-TYPE VAN, issued 1993
1. silver/gray body with maroon roof, gray interior, clear windows, maroon hubs, "Champagne Taittinger" tempa, China casting ($15-20)
2. silver-gray body with maroon roof, gray interior, clear windows, maroon hubs, "Brisbane International Motor Show" tempa (tempa does not extend onto right side door), China casting($50-70)(AU)(C2)
3. silver-gray body with maroon roof, gray interior, clear windows, maroon wheels, "Brisbane International Motor Show" tempa (tempa extends onto right side door), China casting ($65-85)(AU)(C2)
4. silver-gray body with maroon roof, gray interior, clear windows, maroon wheels, "15th Annual Matchbox USA Convention & Toy Show" with rear door print, China casting ($200-250)(US)(C2)

YTF06 1947 CITROEN H-TYPE VAN, issued 1993
1. cream body with red roof, gray interior, clear windows, red hubs, "Moutarde de Meaux Pommery" tempa, China casting ($15-20)
2. cream body with red roof, gray interior, clear windows, red hubs, "15th Annual Matchbox USA Convention & Toy Show" (blue lettering) tempa, China casting ($60-85)(C2)
3. cream body with red roof, gray interior, clear windows, red hubs, "15th Annual Matchbox USA Convention & Toy Show" (red lettering) tempa, China casting ($100-150)(C2)

YGB01 1930 MODEL A FORD VAN, issued 1993
NOTE: Model is a reissue of Y-22-A
1. dark yellow body, black chassis, red roof, red 24 spoke wheels, "Castlemaine XXXX" tempa, China casting ($15-20)

YGB02 FORD MODEL TT VAN, issued 1993
NOTE: Model is a reissue of Y-21-D.
1. beige body, green chassis, red roof, gray interior, red wheels, silver grille, "Beck & Co. " tempa, with side window cast, China casting ($15-20)
2. beige body, green chassis, red roof, gray interior, red wheels, silver grille, "Beck & Co." tempa, without side window cast, China casting ($15-20)

YGB03 1931 GARRETT STEAM WAGON, issued 1993
1. dark green cab, dark green container with red roof, black chassis, red wheels, "The Swan Brewery Co LTD " tempa, China casting ($15-20)

YGB04 1929 MORRIS LIGHT VAN, issued 1993
NOTE: Model is a reissue of Y-47-A.
1. dark green body, red roof & chassis, gold wheels & grille, brown interior, "Fuller's" tempa, China casting ($15-20)

YGB05 1932 FORD AA PICKUP, issued 1993
NOTE: Model is a reissue of Y-62-A.
1. dark green body with cream roof, black chassis, red wheels, cream canopy, "Carlsberg Pilsner" tempa, China casting ($15-20)

YGB06 1932 MERCEDES BENZ LORRY, issued 1993
NOTE: Model is a reissue of Y-6-E.
1. cream body, black fenders & base, orange canopy, red wheels, "Holsten Brauerei" tempa on canopy, "Holsten-Bier" tempa on bed sides, China casting ($15-20)

YGB07 1910 RENAULT TYPE AG VAN, issued 1994
NOTE: Model is a reissue of Y-25-B.
1. white body, dark blue hood & chassis, red plastic roof, gold 12 spoke wheels, windscreen & grille, maroon interior, "Kronenbourg" tempa, China casting ($15-20)

YGB08 1937 GMC VAN, issued 1994
NOTE: Model is a reissue of Y-12-F.
1. dark metallic blue-green body, black chassis, tan interior, red wheels, "Steinlager" tempa, China casting ($15-20)
2. lemon body, dark blue chassis, tan interior, silver painted wheels, "2nd Dusseldorf Spielzeugmarkte" tempa, China casting ($60-75)(C2)

YGB09 1920 MODEL AC MACK, issued 1994
NOTE: Model is a reissue of Y-30-A/Y-33-A.
1. dark green cab, roof & fenders, red chassis, dark green container with black roof, red wheels, "Moosehead Beer" tempa, China casting ($15-20)

YGB10 1927 TALBOT VAN, issued 1994
NOTE: Model is a reissue of Y-5-D
1. rich brown body, cream roof, black chassis, tan seat, red 12 spoke wheels, gold grille & windscreen, "South Pacific Export Lager" tempa, China casting ($15-20)

YGB11 1927 FODEN STEAM WAGON, issued 1994
NOTE: Model is a reissue of Y-27-A.
1. dark brown body, black chassis, cream roof, cream rear canopy, red wheels, "Whitbread's Ale & Stout" tempa ($15-18)

YGB12 1917 YORKSHIRE STEAM WAGON, issued 1994
NOTE: Model is a reissue of Y-8-E.
1. blue body, black chassis, white cab roof & canopy, red wheels, "Lowenbrau" tempa, China casting ($15-20)

YGB13 FORD MODEL TT VAN, issued 1995
NOTE: Model is a reissue of Y-21D.
1. dark blue body, black chassis, cream roof, gray interior, gold wheels & grille, "Anchor Steam Beer" (very detailed design) tempa, China casting ($15-20)
2. dark blue body, black chassis, cream roof, gray interior, gold wheels & grille, "Anchor Steam Beer" (less detailed design) tempa, China casting ($15-20)
3. dark blue body, black chassis, cream roof, gray interior, gold wheels & grille, "3rd MICA Convention Sydney" tempa, China casting ($65-95)(AU)(C2)
4. dark blue body, black chassis, cream roof, gray interior, gold wheels & grille, "RAC Vic.- RACV" tempa, China casting ($150-250)(C2)

YGB14 1912 MODEL T FORD VAN, issued 1995
NOTE: Model is a reissue of Y-12-D.
1. maroon body, cream roof, black chassis, black seat, gold wheels, "Kirin Lager" tempa, China casting ($15-20)
2. maroon body, cream roof, black chassis, black seat, gold wheels, "DMM" & "Matchbox Collectors Club" tempa, China casting ($65-80)(C2)

YGB15 GARRETT STEAM WAGON, issued 1995
NOTE: Model is a reissue of Y-37-A.
1. pale yellow cab & body, red chassis & wheels, "Flower's Fine Ale" tempa, China casting ($15-20)

YGB16 MODEL AA FORD TRUCK, issued 1995
1. dark blue body, white rear canopy, black chassis, gold wheels, "Corona Extra" tempa, China casting ($15-20)

YGB17 MERCEDES-BENZ LORRY, issued 1995
NOTE: Model is a reissue of Y-6-E.
1. white body, black fenders, red canopy & chassis, chrome wheels, "Henninger- Brau" tempa, China casting ($15-20)

YGB18 MORRIS PANTECHNICON, issued 1995
NOTE: Model is a reissue of Y-31-A.
1. green body, beige roof & fenders, black base, beige wheels, "Cascade" tempa, China casting ($15-20)

YGB19 1912 MODEL T FORD, issued 1996
NOTE: Model is a reissue of Y-12-D.
1. orange-red body, blue roof & seat, black chassis, gold wheels, "Yuengling's" tempa, China casting ($15-20)
2. orange-red body, blue roof & seat, black chassis, gold wheels, "DMM" & "Matchbox Collectors Club" tempa, China casting ($125-175)(C2)

YGB20 MODEL AA FORD TRUCK, issued 1996
1. orange-red body & canopy, black cab roof & chassis, "Stroh's Beer" tempa, gold wheels, China casting ($15-20)

YGB21 MERCEDES BENZ LORRY, issued 1996
1. white body, green roof & chassis, chrome wheels, "DAB Pils- Das Bier von Weltruf" tempa, China casting ($15-20)

YGB22 ATKINSON STEAM WAGON, issued 1996
1. black body, cream roof, gray chassis, gold wheels, "Beamish Special Stout Cork" tempa, China casting ($15-20)

YGB23 MACK AC TRUCK, issued 1996
1. green body, brown canopy, black chassis, red wheels, "Tsingtao Beer" tempa, China casting ($15-20)

YGB24 BEDFORD PICKUP, issued 1996
NOTE: Model is a reissue of Y-63-A.
1. blue body, black chassis, chrome wheels, brown barrel load, "Toohey's" tempa, China casting ($15-20)

YHS01 GYPSY CARAVAN, issued 1993
1. red body, white roof, beige chassis & wheels, white metal horse, painted figures, green & gold tempa, China casting ($50-65)

YHS02 LONDON OMNIBUS, issued 1993
1. cream body, brown plastic upper deck, brown seats, yellow chassis & wheels, white & brown horses (2), clear windows, painted figures, "Oakey's Knife Polish" upper deck labels, "Baker St. & Waterloo" body tempa, China casting ($50-65)

YHS03 WELLS FARGO STAGE COACH, issued 1993
1. red-brown body, black roof, light brown undercarriage, pale yellow wheels, brown & bright brown horses (4), painted figures, brown luggage, "Wells Fargo & Co." tempa, China casting ($50-65)

YFE01 MACK FIRE ENGINE, issued 1994
1. red body and chassis, white bed, dark brown ladders, chrome wheels, gold coachlines tempa, China casting ($30-40)

YFE02 LAND ROVER FIRE ENGINE, issued 1994
1. red body with black chassis, clear windows, brown ladder, red wheels; support trailer in red with red wheels, China casting ($25-30)
2. red body with black chassis, clear windows, brown ladder, chrome wheels; support trailer in red with chrome wheels, China casting ($30-40)
3. yellow body with black chassis, clear windows, brown ladder, yellow wheels; support trailer in yellow with yellow wheels, China casting ($85-110)(AU)

YFE03 CADILLAC FIRE ENGINE, issued 1994
1. red body with red chassis, brown ladder & hoses, China casting ($30-40)

YFE04 BEDFORD FIRE TANKER, issued 1995
1. red body & tank, white hoses, chrome wheels, no tempa, China casting ($30-40)
2. red body & tank, black hoses, chrome wheels, "Belrose Volunteer Bush Fire Brigade" tempa, China casting ($85-110)(AU)

YFE05 MERCEDES BENZ LADDER TRUCK, issued 1995
1. red body & chassis, chrome wheels, no tempa, China casting ($30-40)

YFE06 MODEL AA FORD FIRE ENGINE, issued 1995
1. red body & chassis, chrome wheels, no tempa, China casting ($30-40)

YFE07 MERCEDES KS15 FIRE TRUCK, issued 1995
1. red body, white chassis, chrome wheels, China casting ($30-40)
2. dark green body, black chassis, black wheels, China casting ($45-55)(LE)(GR)

YFE08 LEYLAND CUB FIRE ENGINE, issued 1995
1. red body, black roof, brown ladder, "Leyland" & pinstripes tempa, China casting ($30-40)

YFE09 FORD AA OPEN BACK FIRE ENGINE, issued 1996
1. red body & chassis, chrome wheels, China casting ($30-40)

YFE10 GMC RESCUE VEHICLE, issued 1996
1. red body, white chassis, brown ladder, "FDNY Rescue Squad" tempa, chrome wheels, China casting ($30-40)
2. white body with yellow roof, brown ladder, "Cessnock Rescue Squad" tempa, chrome wheels, China casting ($45-55)(LE)(AU)

YFE11 MACK AC TANKER, issued 1996
NOTE: Model is a reissue of Y-23-B.
1. red body & chassis, chrome tank, "Tanker No. 1/ Fire Dept. No. 1" tempa, chrome wheels, China casting ($30-40)

YFE12 MODEL A FORD FIRE CHIEF'S CAR, issued 1996
1. red body, black roof, brown seat, "FDNY" tempa, chrome wheels, China casting ($30-40)

YFE13 CITROEN H-TYPE INTEGRAL VAN FIRE ENGINE, issued 1997
NOTE: Model is a reissue from the YTF series body castings.
1. red body, brown ladder, red wheels, chrome roof rack, black base, "Longueville" tempa, no origin cast ($30-40)

YFE14 1953 FORD FIRE TRUCK, issued 1997
1. red body, brown interior, red wheels, black chassis, yellow & white hoses, "Garden City F.D. No. 1" tempa, no origin cast ($30-40)

YFE15 1935 MACK PUMPER, issued 1997
1. red body & chassis, black seats, dark brown ladder, white hoses, red seats, no origin cast ($30-40)

YFE16 DODGE ROUTE VAN CANTEEN, issued 1997
1. red body with white painted fenders, white opening panel on right side, silver wheels, black base, "Springfield Fire Brigade Auxiliary" tempa, no origin cast ($30-40)

YFE17 1939 BEDFORD FIRE TRUCK, issued 1997
1. red body & fenders, black base, tan interior, black hoses, dark brown ladder, red wheels, "City of Manchester Fire Brigade" tempa, China casting ($30-40)

YFE18 1950 FORD E.83.W VAN & SUPPORT TRAILER, issued 1997
1. red body, black fenders & base, brown ladder & white hoses, "Emergency Fire Services" tempa; red trailer with white & tannish hoses, China castings ($30-40)

YFE19 1904 MERRYWEATHER FIRE ENGINE, issued 1998
1. red body & removable engine cover, red wheels with black tires, black hoses, China casting ($30-40)

YFE20 1912 BENZ MOTORSPRITZE FIRE ENGINE, issued 1998
1. red body, black chassis, black seats, brown ladder, red ladder holder & wheels, white hoses, China casting ($30-40)

YFE21 1907 SEAGRAVE AC53, issued 1998
1. white body & chassis, white wheels with black tires, maroon seats, copper water tanks, "V.F.D." tempa, China casting ($30-40)

YFE22 1916 MODEL T FIRE ENGINE, issued 1998
1. red body & chassis, brown ladder, black seats, red painted & chrome wheels, black hoses, China casting ($30-40)

YFE23 1906 WATEROUS S/P PUMPER, issued 1998
1. red body & chassis, black seats, gunmetal gray drive-train, white hoses & tires, red wheels, China casting ($30-40)

YFE24 1911 MACK PUMPER, issued 1998
1. red body & chassis, black base, brown seats, white tires & hoses, red wheels, "U.F.A.L.M." tempa, China casting ($30-40)

YSFE01 1930 AHRENS-FOX QUAD FIRE ENGINE, issued 1994
1. red body with black chassis, red wheels, gold coachlines tempa, China casting, available with wooden plinth ($90-100)

YSFE02 LEYLAND CUB FIRE ENGINE, issued 1996
1. red body, black roof, brown ladder, "Leyland" & pinstriping tempa (identical to YFE08 except base number & looser chains) ($45-60)

YSFE03 BUSCH FIRE ENGINE, issued 1996
NOTE: Model is a reissue of Y-43-A but without firemen cast.
1. dark green body, red boiler, dark green wheels ($60-75)

YSFE04 1927 AHRENS-FOX N-S-4, issued 1998
1. Red body & chassis, red wheels, black seats & hoses, brown ladders, "Lockland F.D." tempa, China casting ($65-75)

YSFE05 1868 MERRYWEATHER FIRE ENGINE, issued 1997
NOTE: Model is a reissue of Y-46 but without firemen cast.
1. red body & wheels, gold plated boiler, porcelain hose rack, two brown horses, China casting ($60-75)

YCC01 CHRISTMAS TREASURES, issued 1994
1. metallic green with black chassis, "Season Greetings 1994" tempa, China casting
2. powder blue with black chassis, "Peace On Earth 1994" tempa, China casting
3. red body with black chassis, "Merry Christmas 1994" tempa, China casting
4. white body with black chassis, "Happy Holiday 1994" tempa, China casting
NOTE: Versions 1-4 issued as set of 4 only ($25-35). The code 2 models listed below are made up from broken sets and are cast "YCC01" on the base.
5. red body with black chassis, black roof sign reads "Erlangen 23.03.1997", "Erste Matchbox Borse Erlangen" tempa, China casting ($45-60)(C2)
6. dull gray body with black chassis, black roof sign reads "Stuttgart 06.09.1997", "Models of Yesteryear" tempa, China casting ($45-60)(C2)
7. light red body with black chassis, blue interior, pale tan roof, pale tan roof sign reads "6th MICA Europe Convention", tulips design tempa, China casting ($35-50)(C2)
8. light red body with black chassis, white interior, pale tan roof, pale tan roof sign reads "6th MICA European Convention", tulips design tempa, China casting ($50-75)(C2)

YCC02 CHRISTMAS TREASURES, issued 1995
1. metallic green body with black chassis, "Seasons Greetings 1995" tempa, China casting
2. metallic gold body with black chassis, "Peace On Earth 1995" tempa, China casting
3. red body with black chassis, "Merry Christmas 1995" tempa, China casting
4. iridescent white body with black chassis, "Happy Holiday 1995" tempa, China casting
NOTE: Above models issued as a set of 4 only ($25-35) The code 2 models listed below are made up from broken sets and are cast "YCC02" on the base.
5. light yellow body & chassis with dark yellow roof, dark yellow roof sign reads "Magazine Delivery Van" tempa, "City of Chester MICA 14th March 1998" tempa, China casting ($30-45)(C2)

YCC03 CHRISTMAS TREASURES, issued 1996
1. dark blue Road Roller
2. green tractor
3. red fire engine
4. yellow Maserati Racer

NOTE: Above models issued as a set of 4 only ($20-25)

GS95-01 FAO SCHWARZ GIFT SET, issued 1995
1. red body with black chassis, rocking horse logo tempa, China casting
2. purple body with black chassis, rocking horse logo tempa, China casting
3. turquoise body with black chassis, rocking horse logo tempa, China casting
4. yellow body with black chassis, rocking horse logo tempa, China casting
NOTE: Above models issued as a set of 4 only ($25-35)

YPP01 1910 RENAULT TYPE AG VAN, issued 1995
1. blue hood & chassis, yellow body, red roof, gold wheels, "Le Figaro" tempa, China casting ($20-25)
(based on Y-25-A)

YPP02 1931 MORRIS PANTECHNICON, issued 1995
1. cream cab & container, gray container roof, cream wheels, black base, "The Times" tempa, China casting ($20-25)
2. black cab, yellow container, white container roof, silver wheels, red base, "Classic Toys For A Jolly Colorful Read" tempa, China casting ($50-75)(UK)
3. cream cab & container, green roof & fenders, silver wheels, gray base, "Lesney Products & Company Limited 1947-1997" tempa, China casting ($45-55)(LE)

YPP03 MERCEDES BENZ LORRY, issued 1996
1. green body, cream roof, dark gray chassis, black base, "Morgenpost" tempa, China casting ($20-25)
2. gray body, black roof & chassis, black base, "100 Jahre Dieselmotor 1 Jahr MCCD" tempa, China casting ($75-100)(C2)

YPP04 DODGE ROUTEMASTER, issued 1995
1. blue body, chrome wheels, "New York Times" tempa, China casting ($20-25)
2. cream body with maroon fenders, chrome wheels, "Express Delivery" tempa, China casting ($45-60)(AU)
3. red body, chrome wheels, "The Hershey Herald" labels, China casting ($125-150)(C2)
4. black body, chrome wheels, "The Hershey Herald" labels, China casting ($100-175)(C2)

YPP05 MODEL AA FORD TRUCK, issued 1995
1. dark blue body, white container with tan tarp, chrome wheels, "Los Angeles Times" tempa, China casting ($20-25)

YPP06 MACK AC TRUCK, issued 1995
1. red body, gray chassis, white roof, brown-gold wheels, "PRAVDA" (Cyrillic) tempa, China casting ($20-25)
(based on Y-30-B)

YPP07 1937 GMC VAN, issued 1996
1. white body, white chassis, red interior, chrome wheels, "The Australian" tempa, China casting ($15-20) (based on Y-12-F)

YPP08 1930 MODEL A FORD VAN, issued 1995
1. blue body, chassis & roof, chrome wheels, "The Washington Post" tempa, China casting ($15-20) (based on Y-22-A)
2. blue body, chassis & roof, chrome wheels, "16th Annual Matchbox USA Toy Show 1997", China casting ($85-110)(C2)

YAS01 STEPHENSON'S ROCKET, issued 1996
NOTE: Model is a reissue of Y-12-E.
1. yellow engine body with yellow wheels & white stack; tender in yellow with yellow barrel, China casting ($20-25)

YAS02 1922 FODEN STEAM LORRY, issued 1996
NOTE: Model is a reissue of Y-27-A.
1. cream body, red chassis, red roof, dark charcoal porcelain coal load, red wheels, China casting ($20-25)
2. cream body, red chassis, red roof, black porcelain coal load, red wheels, China casting ($20-25)

YAS03 1920 AVELING PORTER STEAM ROLLER, issued 1996
NOTE: Model is a reissue of Y-21-B.
1. blue body, gray wheels, black stack, white roof, small black worm gear, "PB Coulson & Sons" tempa, China casting ($20-25)
2. blue body, gray wheels, black stack, white roof, small gold plated worm gear, "PB Coulson & Son" tempa, China casting ($20-25)

YAS04 YORKSHIRE STEAM WAGON, issued 1996
1. black body, red roof & chassis, porcelain stone load, "De Selby Quarries Ltd." tempa, China casting ($20-25)

YAS05 FOWLER B6 SHOWMAN'S ENGINE, issued 1996
NOTE: Model is a reissue of Y-19-B.
1. maroon body, white roof, black boiler, maroon wheels, "John Hoadley's Mammoth Fair" tempa, China casting ($20-25)

YAS06 ATKINSON LOGGER, issued 1996
1. green body, red chassis, green wheels, porcelain log load, China casting ($20-25)
NOTE: Log casting can be found in several widths & lengths.

YAS07 FOWLER B6 SHOWMAN'S ENGINE WITH CRANE, issued 1997
1. black body, roof, stack & crane jib, gold roof supports, black wheels

with gray tires, "Marstons Road Services Ltd./ E. Box Ltd." tempa, China casting ($25-30)

YAS08 1912 BURREL TRACTION ENGINE, issued 1997
1. dark green body, white roof with gold supports, black boiler stack, red wheels with gray tires, "Woods, Sadd, Moore & Co. Ltd. Loddon" tempa, China casting ($25-30)

YAS09 1929 GARRETT STEAM WAGON, issued 1997
1. dark green cab & flatbed body, gray roof, black interior, red wheels, black chassis, porcelain drain pipe load with gold chains, "Rainford Potteries Ltd. Rainford Nr. St. Helens" tempa, China casting ($25-30)

YAS10 1918 ATKINSON STEAM WAGON, issued 1997
NOTE: Model is a reissue of Y-18-D.
1. yellow cab & flatbed body, yellow wheels, black chassis, porcelain load, "City of Westminster Works, Sewers & Highways" tempa, China casting ($25-30)

YAS11 1917 YORKSHIRE STEAM WAGON, issued 1997
1. brown cab & flatbed body, cream roof & wheels, porcelain railroad ties & tracks load, "1087 Great Western Railway Co." tempa, China casting ($25-30)

YAS12 1922 FODEN STEAM WAGON, issued 1997
NOTE: Model is reissue of Y-27-A.
1. gray cab & flatbed body, black roof & chassis, yellow wheels, porcelain barrel load, "R. Brett & Sons" tempa, China casting ($25-30)

YET01 PRESTON TYPE TRAMCAR, issued 1996
NOTE: Model is a reissue of Y-15-C.
1. blue body, cream window area, red roof, brown base, cream interior, "Yorkshire Relish" tempa, China casting ($20-25)

YET02 1929 LEYLAND TITAN, issued 1996
NOTE: Model is a reissue of Y-5-E.
1. orange & green body, maroon fenders & base, dark gray roof, cream interior, "Van Houten's Cocoa" tempa, China casting ($20-25)

YET03 1931 "DIDDLER" TROLLEY BUS, issued 1996
NOTE: Model is a reissue of Y-10-E.
1. red body & base, gray roof, "Lion Black Lead" tempa, China casting ($20-25)

YET04 1922 SCANIA VABIS BUS, issued 1996
1. dark blue body, black chassis, gray roof with header "Kaffe DG Rich," gold wheels, "Stockholm Automobil Trafik Aktiebolag" tempa, China casting ($20-25)

YET05 1922 AEC 'S' TYPE BUS, issued 1996
NOTE: Model is a reissue of Y-23-A.
1. green body & chassis, tan interior, cream window area & wheels, "Kennedys" tempa, China casting ($20-25)

YET06 1910 RENAULT TYPE AG BUS, issued 1996
NOTE: Model is a reissue of Y-44-A.
1. pea green body & chassis, beige roof & rear body, gold wheels, "St. Symphorien Coise Paris" tempa, China casting ($20-25)

YSC01 1922 SCANIA VABIS POSTBUS, issued 1995
1. iridescent white body & chassis, gold coachlines tempa, gold wheels, porcelain tree attached to roof, China casting ($100-150)
NOTE: Tree on roof comes in different lengths. Based on Y-16-D casting.

YSC02 1955 CHEVY PICKUP, issued 1996
1. red body, red interior, porcelain tree & accessories in bed ($45-60)

YSC03 FORD AA FIRE ENGINE WITH SANTA, issued 1996
1. red body, white chassis, gold trim, porcelain Santa in rear ($50-75)

YSC04 1932 FORD AA FIRE ENGINE, issued 1997
1. red body & chassis, chrome trim, brown ladder & hoses, "Clayton Fire Brigade" tempa, porcelain Santa & Mrs. Claus with presents in rear ($40-45)

YCH01 MODEL T FORD VAN, issued 1995
NOTE: Model is a reissue of Y-12-D
1. yellow body, red roof & chassis, gold wheels, "Ronald McDonald House" tempa, China casting ($125-175)(AU)

YCH02/1 MODEL FORD TT VAN, issued 1996
YCH02/2 MODEL A FORD VAN, issued 1996
NOTE: Models are reissues of Y-21-D & Y-22-A respectively and only issued as a boxed pair except for version #3.
1. Model TT Van: red body, yellow roof & chassis, gold wheels, "Ronald McDonald Charities of Australia" tempa, China casting with Model A Van: light blue body, dark blue roof & chassis, silver wheels, "Camp Quality" tempa, China casting ($100-150)(AU)
2. Model TT Van: red body, roof & chassis, chrome wheels, "Ronald McDonald Charities of Australia" tempa, China casting with Model A Ford Van: light blue body, roof & chassis, silver wheels, "Camp Quality" tempa, China casting ($350-500)(AU)
3. Model TT Van: red body, yellow roof & chassis, gold wheels, "Magical Million 11th Annual Ball 1997" tempa, China casting, mounted in thin black plexiglass plinth ($250-350)(C2)
NOTE: The above model was made as a code 2 from existing stocks. The

Model A Van version was sent to Camp Quality in loose form mounted to wooden plinths with no decoration change.
4. Model TT Van: red body, yellow roof & chassis, silver wheels, "Tyco" tempa, China casting with Model A Ford Van: light blue body, dark blue roof & chassis, silver wheels, "Matchbox" tempa, China casting ($1500+)
NOTE: The above model pair was available in a similar but plain box as version 1 & 2 and given out at a charity fund raiser in Hong Kong at Christmas 1997. Only 50 sets were produced.

YCH03 & YCH05 *NOTE: No models issued at these numbers!*

YCH04 1929 MORRIS LIGHT VAN, issued 1997
NOTE: Model is a reissue of Y-47-A.
1. pale yellow body, dark blue roof, black chassis, brown interior, chrome wheels, "RSPCA" tempa, China casting ($45-55)

YCH06 1920 MACK AC, issued 1998
NOTE: Model is a reissue of Y-30-A & Y-33-A.
1. red cab, roof & fenders, red container with red roof, red wheels, Hamburglar with "Ronald McDonald House" tempa, China casting ($45-50)(AU)

YCH07 1930 FORD MODEL A FORD VAN, issued 1998
NOTE: Model is a reissue of Y-22-A.
1. white body, red roof, chassis & wheels, blue interior, "Ronald McDonald House" with McDonald characters tempa, China casting ($45-50)(AU)

YCH08 1932 MERCEDES BENZ L5, issued 1998
NOTE: Model is a reissue of YPP03.
1. dark yellow body, red roofs & chassis, red interior, chrome wheels, "Ronald McDonald House" & Grimace tempa, China casting ($45-50)(AU)

YCH09 1931 MORRIS VAN, issued 1998
NOTE: Model is a reissue of YPP02.
1. blue body, dark blue roof & fenders, red base, chrome wheels, "Ronald McDonald House" & Ronald McDonald tempa, China casting ($45-50)(AU)

YCH10 1955 FJ/2104 PANEL VAN, issued 1998
NOTE: Model is a reissue of YHN01.
1. powder blue body, powder blue interior & wheels, "Ronald McDonald House- Sydney Newcastle" tempa, black base, China casting ($45-50)(AU)

YMS01 1911 MODEL T FORD, issued 1996
NOTE: Model is a reissue of Y-1-B.
1. black body with gold coachlines, brown interior, black roof, gold wheels ($20-25)

YMS02 1910 BENZ LIMOUSINE, issued 1996
NOTE: Model is a reissue of Y-3-B.
1. dark blue body & chassis, gold coachlines, black roof & interior, gold wheels ($20-25)

YMS03 1909 OPEL COUPE, issued 1996
NOTE: Model is a reissue of Y-4-C.
1. yellow body & chassis, black coachlines, black roof & interior, gold wheels ($20-25)

YMS04 1912 PACKARD LANDALET, issued 1996
NOTE: Model is a reissue of Y-11-B.
1. iridescent white body & chassis, black interior, gold wheels ($20-25)

YMS05 1911 DAIMLER, issued 1996
NOTE: Model is a reissue of Y-13-B.
1. maroon body & chassis, light brown seats, gold coachlines, gold wheels ($20-25)

YMS06 1911 MAXWELL ROADSTER, issued 1996
NOTE: Model is a reissue of Y-14-B.
1. red body & chassis, black roof & interior, gold coachlines, gold wheels ($20-25)

YMC01 1970 CHEVELLE SS 454, issued 1996
1. red body, black interior, chrome wheels, black base, dual black stripes on hood & trunk tempa ($30-35)
2. red body, black interior, chrome wheels, black base, "Mattel" logo on roof, dual black stripes hood & trunk with "Annual Operations Meeting 1998" on sides tempa ($750+)

YMC02 1971 CUDA 440 6-PACK, issued 1997
1. yellow body, black side tempa, black interior, black base, chrome wheels ($30-35)

YMC03 1967 PONTIAC GTO, issued 1996
1. silver blue body with dark blue roof, blue interior, black base, chrome wheels ($30-35)

YMC04 1970 ROAD RUNNER HEMI, issued 1996
1. metallic lime green body, black hood stripes, black interior, black base, chrome wheels ($30-35)

YMC05 1970 MUSTANG BOSS 429, issued 1997

1. orange body, black hood air scoop & rear fin, black interior, black base, chrome wheels ($30-35)
2. yellow body, "It's The Real Thing- Coca Cola" tempa, red interior, black base ("Dinky" imprinted), chrome wheels ($30-35)

YMC06 1968 CAMARO SS 396, issued 1997
1. black body, red interior, red pinstriping across hood & sides tempa, black base, chrome wheels ($30-35)
2. black body with yellow roof, red interior, yellow hood & trunk bands with "Coca Cola It's Twice Time" tempa, black base ("Dinky" imprinted), chrome wheels ($30-35)

YMC07 1970 PLYMOUTH GTX, issued 1998
NOTE: Model is a reissue of YMC04.
1. apple green body, black interior, white side stripes tempa, black base, chrome wheels ($30-35)

YMC08 1966 CHEVELLE SS396, issued 1998
1. metallic cranberry body, dark cranberry interior, detailed trim tempa, black base, chrome wheels ($30-35)

YMC09 1966 FORD FAIRLANE 500XL, issued 1998
1. dark blue body, white interior with black dashboard, detailed trim tempa, black base, chrome wheels ($30-35)

YMC10 1969 DODGE CHARGER, issued 1998
1. orange-red body, brown interior, black painted roof, rear black band on trunk tempa, black base, chrome wheels ($30-35)

YMC11 1970 OLDSMOBILE 442, issued 1998
1. white body, black interior, black hood design &side pinstripes tempa, black base, chrome wheels ($30-35)

YMC12 1971 DODGE CHALLENGER R/T, issued 1998
1. purple body, white interior with black dashboard, white side stripes tempa, black base, chrome wheels ($30-35)

YRS01 1955 CHEVROLET PICKUP TRUCK, issued 1996
1. red body, charcoal boom, red interior & wheels, detailed bed accessories, "Fred's Service/Emergency AAA" tempa ($30-35)

YRS02 1953 FORD F100, issued 1996
1. black body with white roof, white interior, chrome wheels, detailed bed accessories, "Flying A Tires" tempa ($30-35)

YRS03 1956 CHEVROLET 3100, issued 1996
1. dark blue body, dark blue interior, blue wheels, detailed bed accessories, "Harris Bros. Mobilgas" tempa ($30-35)

YRS04 1954 FORD F100, issued 1996
1. green body with yellow plow, beige interior, green wheels, detailed bed accessories, "Sinclair" tempa ($30-35)

YRS05 1957 CHEVROLET 3100, issued 1997
1. pale yellow body, black painted roof, brown interior, pale yellow wheels, brown stakes with dark brown bed, "Ray's Dixie Gasoline Service" tempa ($30-35)
2. turquoise body, cream painted roof, turquoise interior & wheels, light brown bed, small cab logo tempa ($30-35)

YRS06 1955 FORD F-150 PICKUP, issued 1998
1. white body, black painted roof, red interior, chrome wheels with white wall tires, "Santa Fe Red Crown Gasoline" tempa, black rear canopy with "Route US 66" tempa ($45-50)
2. white body, black painted roof, red interior, chrome wheels with white wall tires, "Santa Fe Red Crown Gasoline" tempa, black rear canopy with "Route US 84" tempa ($30-35)
3. red body, white interior, red dome light cast, chrome wheels with white wall tires, "County Fire Marshall" tempa, porcelain rear load of fire equipment & Dalmatian dogs ($35-45)

YIS01 1955 CHEVROLET 3100 PICKUP, issued 1998
NOTE: Model is a reissue of YRS05.
1. black body, black interior, chrome wheels, brown stakes, porcelain crates load, "Harley Davidson Motorcycles" tempa ($30-35)

YIS02 1955 FORD F150 PICKUP, issued 1998
1. dark yellow body, black painted roof, brown interior, yellow wheels, "Peoria Tractor & Equipment Co./ Caterpillar" tempa, porcelain tool box & two tires rear load ($30-35)

YIS03 1956 CHEVROLET 3100 PICKUP, issued 1998
1. baby blue body, baby blue interior & wheels, "Chevrolet Motors", "Chevrolet" logo & "Genuine Parts" tempa, porcelain load of two engine blocks ($30-35)

YIS04 1957 CHEVROLET 3100 PICKUP, issued 1998
1. white body, blue painted roof, blue interior & wheels, "AA American Ground Service" tempa, porcelain luggage load tempa ($30-35)

YIS05 1954 FORD F-100 PICKUP, issued 1998
1. pale rose red body, gray interior, rose red wheels, gold dome light, "PRR" tempa, porcelain railroad track & accessories load ($30-35)

YIS06 1953 FORD F150, issued 1998
1. red body, yellow-tan interior, chrome wheels, "Genuine Ford Parts/ Factory Service" tempa, two porcelain engine blocks for rear load ($30-35)

YHN01 1955 FJ/2104 PANEL VAN, issued 1997
1. dark gray body, red interior, dark gray wheels, black base, no tempa, China casting ($45-55)(AU)
2. white body, red interior, white wheels, black base, "Auto One 1" tempa, China casting ($45-55)(AU)
3. white body, red interior, white wheels, black base, "Australian Model Collectors Club" tempa, China casting ($85-110)(C2)
4. dark yellow body, red interior, yellow wheels, black base, "Automodels [illegible] Galligan" tempa, China casting ($45-55)(AU)
5. dark beige body, red interior, beige wheels, black base, dome lights & horns cast on roof, "Temora District Ambulance" tempa, China casting ($45-55)(AU)
6. dark yellow body, red interior, yellow wheels, black base, "An Evening Aboard the Love Boat" tempa, China casting, mounted on blue wooden plinth ($175-250)(C2)

YHN02 1954 FJ/2106 UTILITY, issued 1997
1. dark navy blue body, light blue interior, black wheels, removable black rear canopy, China casting ($45-55)(AU)

YHN03 1951 50/2106 UTILITY, issued 1997
1. khaki tan body, brown interior, khaki tan wheels, removable brown plastic canopy, China casting ($45-55)(AU)

YWG01 1930 FORD MODEL A VAN, issued 1997
NOTE: Model is a reissue of Y-22-A.
1. dark blue body & roof sign, white roof, brown interior, black chassis, gold wheels, "Ballantine's" tempa, China casting ($20-25)

YWG02 1921 MODEL TT FORD VAN, issued 1997
NOTE: Model is a reissue of Y-21-D.
1. black, fenders & roof, beige container & roof sign, red wheels, "Long John" tempa, China casting ($20-25)

YWG03 1929 MORRIS LIGHT VAN, issued 1997
NOTE: Model is a reissue of Y-47-A.
1. dark yellow body. Black roof, chassis & roof sign, brown interior, gold wheels, "Cutty Sark Scots Whisky" tempa, China casting ($20-25)

YWG04 1937 GMC VAN, issued 1997
NOTE: Model is a reissue of Y-12-F.
1. white body & roof sign, dark green roof & chassis, brown interior, white wheels, "Laphroaig Islay Malt Whisky" tempa, China casting ($20-25)

YWG05 1912 MODEL T FORD VAN, issued 1997
NOTE: Model is a reissue of Y-12-C.
1. olive green body with beige painted side panels, beige roof sign, black roof, seats & chassis, gold wheels, "Sheep Dip The Original Oldbury" tempa, China casting ($20-25)

YWG06 1932 FORD AA TRUCK, issued 1997
NOTE: Model is a reissue of YGB16.
1. cocoa brown body, beige roof & roof sign, black interior & chassis, gold wheels, "Teacher's" tempa, China casting ($20-25)

YPC01 1957 CHEVROLET PICKUP, issued 1998
NOTE: Model is a reissue of YRS05.
1. red & yellow body, black interior, red wheels, yellow stakes, two metal vending machines as rear load, "The Coca Cola Company… It's The Real Thing/ Atlanta Bottling Co." tempa, China casting ($30-35)

YPC02 1937 GMC VAN, issued 1998
NOTE: Model is a reissue of Y-12-F.
1. red body & roof blade with "Nine Million Drinks A Day" tempa, black roof & chassis, light tan interior, chrome wheels, "Drink Coca Cola Special Delivery" tempa, China casting ($30-35)

YPC03 1920 MACK AC TRUCK, issued 1998
NOTE: Model is a reissue of Y-30-B with new load.
1. black cab & roof, red fenders & bed, gray base, gold wheels, "Coca Cola" tempa, red & yellow sign load with "Stoneliegh Pharmacy Drink Coca Cola" tempa, China casting ($30-35)

YPC04 1912 MODEL T FORD VAN, issued 1998
NOTE: Model is a reissue of Y-12-C.
1. red body with yellow painted cab area, yellow roof with red roof blade, black chassis, blue seats, "Ice Cold Coca Cola Sold Here" tempa, China casting ($30-35)

YPC05 1930 MODEL A FORD PICKUP, issued 1998
NOTE: Model is a reissue of Y-35-A with new load.
1. black body, red rear bed & chassis, yellow roof, brown seats, gold wheels, "Atlanta Bottling Company Atlanta, Georgia" & "Coca Cola" logo tempa, red Coca Cola ice chest as rear load, China casting ($30-35)

YPC06 1932 FORD AA TRUCK, issued 1998
1. yellow cab with red painted engine covers, red roof & rear bed, black chassis, gold wheels, "Delicious Coca Cola Refreshing" tempa, yellow & red rear load with cases of soda, China casting ($30-35)

YSL001 CRESCENT LIMITED, issued 1994
1. dark green locomotive & coal tender, "Crescent Limited" tempa, issued with wooden plinth which features two pieces of railroad track (actual casting made by Mantua for Matchbox Collectibles)($195-225)

YYM36791 HORSE DRAWN WAGON, issued 1998
1. white body & wheels, gray horse, "Anheruser Busch Brew'g Ass'n" tempa ($50-60)

YYM36793 #1, issued 1998
Note: This model is a reissue of Y-35-B
1. red body, white roof, green fenders & base, brown interior, red skis, gold wheels, porcelain roof load, "North Pole Mail Delivery" tempa, China casting ($35-40)(CL)

Dinky

The Dinky name has been around since the 1930s. Meccano owned the trademark until their bankruptcy in 1979. Nearly a decade later, Matchbox obtained the Dinky trademark from Kenner Toys to market a new line of 1/43-scale vehicles. This was in 1988. At that time, no new molds were available, so in order not to lose the trademark rights, Matchbox scrambled to release six miniatures in Dinky blisterpacks. The original idea was to take the new Commando line and issue that as Dinky. In fact, preproductions of the miniature Commando series carry this trademark. It is also of note that the MB6-B Mercedes made in Bulgaria also features the Dinky name, but for reasons unknown. By 1993, the Dinky name, although still in use, was not used as a marketing tool by Tyco Toys. In 1997 Dinkys were resurrected as a brand in the Collectibles range. Also in 1997, other than a "DY" prefix were used to designate Dinky models i.e. "VEM" amongst others. At the end of 1998 there were some Dinky model bases printed with Yesteryear and Ultra model numbers. See those respective numbers (YMC05, YMC06 & CCV06) for those particular Dinky issues.

DY-1-A 1967 SERIES 1-1/2 E TYPE JAGUAR, issued 1989
1. dark green body & base, black roof, tan interior, Macau casting ($10-15)
2. yellow body & base, black roof, black interior, China casting ($17-20)
3. black body, black roof, tan interior, black China base, ($17-20)

DY-2-A 1957 CHEVROLET BELAIR SPORTS COUPE, issued 1989
1. red body, white roof, red interior, pearly silver base, detailed trim tempa, Macau casting ($17-20)
2. black body & roof, red & black interior, black base, red/orange/yellow flames tempa, no origin cast ($35-40)(CL)

DY-3-A 1965 MGB-GT, issued 1989
1. blue body, black painted roof, red interior, black base, Macau casting ($10-15)
2. orange body, black interior, black base, China casting ($10-15)

DY-4-A 1950 FORD E.83.W VAN, issued 1989
1. yellow-orange body, red interior, yellow-orange hubcaps, black base, "Heinz 57 Varieties" tempa, China casting ($10-15)
2. olive body, red interior, silver hubcaps, olive base, "Radio Times" tempa, China casting ($10-15)
3. lime body, red interior, silver hubcaps, black base, "I'm A Dinky" tempa, China casting ($350-500)(C2)
4. dark gray body, red interior, silver hubcaps, black base, "5th MICA European Convention" tempa, China casting ($60-85)(C2)
5. dark gray body, red interior, orange-yellow hubcaps, black base, "5th MICA European Convention" tempa, China casting ($60-85)(C2)

DY-5-A 1949 FORD V-8 PILOT, issued 1989
1. black body & base, tan interior, Macau casting ($10-15)
2. silver-gray body with black painted roof, maroon interior, silver-gray base, China casting ($10-15)
3. tan body with black painted roof, maroon interior, tan base, China casting ($10-15)

DY-6-A 1951 VOLKSWAGEN DELUXE SEDAN, issued 1989
1. powder blue body with gray painted roof, light gray interior, powder blue wheels, black base, Macau casting ($18-25)
2. black body with gray painted roof, light gray interior, black wheels, black base, China casting ($17-20)
3. red body with gray painted roof, light gray interior, red wheels, black base, China casting ($17-20)

DY-7-A 1959 CADILLAC COUPE DE VILLE, issued 1989
1. metallic red body, cream roof, tan interior with orange steering wheel, black base, China casting ($17-20)
2. pink body, cream roof, cream interior with red steering wheel, black base, China casting ($17-20)
3. pink body, cream roof, cream interior with red steering wheel, black China base, "Dinky Toy Club of America 1st Toy Show" decal ($125-150)(C2)

DY-8-A 1948 COMMER 8 CWT VAN, issued 1989
1. red body, red-brown interior, black base, "Sharp's Toffee" tempa, Macau casting ($10-15)
2. dark blue body, gray interior, black base, "His Master's Voice" tempa, China casting ($10-15)
3. dark blue body, gray interior, black base, "Motorfair 91" labels, China casting ($50-65)(C2)
4. dark blue body, gray interior, black China casting, "Classic Toys" labels ($25-40)(C2)

DY-9-A 1949 LAND ROVER SERIES 1.80, issued 1989
1. green body & windscreen, green wheels, black interior, tan canopy, black base, Macau casting ($10-15)
2. yellow body & windscreen, black wheels, black interior, tan canopy, black base, "AA Road Service" tempa, China casting ($17-20)

DY-10-A 1950 MERCEDES BENZ KONFERENZ TYPE OMNIBUS O-3500, issued 1989
1. cream body with blue hood & fenders, red interior, clear windows, "Reiseburo Ruoff Stuttgart" tempa, China casting ($50-75)(LE)

DY-11-A 1948 TUCKER TORPEDO, issued 1990
1. metallic red body, brown interior, black base, Macau casting ($17-20)
2. metallic blue body, white interior, black base, China casting ($17-20)
3. yellow body, tan interior, black base, no origin cast ($35-40)(CL)

DY-12-A 1955 MERCEDES 300SL, issued 1990
1. cream body & base, red interior, China casting ($10-15)
2. silver-gray body & base, red interior, China casting (see DY-902)
3. black body & base, cream interior, China casting ($10-15)

DY-13-A 1955 BENTLEY 'R' TYPE CONTINENTAL, issued 1990
1. silver blue body, black interior, black base, China casting ($10-15)
2. dark blue body, tan interior, black base, China casting ($17-20)

DY-14-A 1946 DELAHAYE 145 CHAPRON, issued 1990
1. dark metallic blue body, red interior, black base, China casting ($10-15)
2. metallic red body, tan interior, black base, China casting ($10-15)

DY-15-A 1952 AUSTIN A40 GV4 10-CWT. VAN, issued 1990
1. red body, tan interior, black base, "Brooke Bond Tea" tempa, China casting ($10-15)
2. yellow body, black interior, black base, "Dinky Toys" tempa, China casting ($10-15)
3. white body, tan interior, black base, red wheels, "Major Print & Design Limited" tempa, China casting ($50-75)(C2)
4. dark gray body, tan interior, black base, red wheels, "Dinky For Matchbox Collectors/4th MICA European Convention" tempa, China casting ($50-75)(C2)
5. light gray body, black interior, black base, red wheels, "Dinky For Matchbox Collectors-4th MICA European Convention" tempa, China casting ($65-85)(C2)
6. dark gray body, brown interior, black base, black wheels, "Dinky For Matchbox Collectors- 4th MICA European Convention" tempa, China casting ($65-85)(C2)
6. yellow body, black interior, black base, "Matchbox at Rugby" labels, China casting ($500+)
NOTE: Approximately 50 of these models were made and given out to Matchbox staff at the closure of the Rugby offices.

DY-16-A 1967 FORD MUSTANG FASTBACK 2+2, issued 1990
1. dark green body, black interior, black base, no tempa, China casting ($10-15)
2. white body, red interior, black base, no tempa, China casting ($17-20)
3. light metallic green body, black interior, black base, no tempa, China casting ($17-20)
4. red body, tan & black interior, black base, white stripes tempa, no origin cast ($20-25)(CL)
5. red body, tan & black interior, black base, white stripes tempa with "Dinky Club of America 4th Show 9/27/98" trunk decal, no origin cast ($60-85)(C2)

DY-17-A 1939 TRIUMPH DOLOMITE, issued 1990
1. red body, black roof & interior, maroon wheels, red base, China casting ($15-25)(LE)

DY-18-A 1967 SERIES 1-1/2 E TYPE JAGUAR CONVERTIBLE, issued 1990
1. red body & base, brown interior, clear windshield, Macau casting ($10-15)
2. cream body & base, red interior, clear windshield, China casting (see DY-903)
3. black body & base, red interior, clear windshield, China casting ($17-20)

DY-19-A 1973 MGB-GT V8, issued 1990
1. brownish body, black interior, black base, Macau casting ($10-15)
2. red body, black interior, black base, China casting ($17-20)

DY-20-A 1965 TRIUMPH TR4-IRS, issued 1991
1. white body & base, black interior & tonneau, China casting ($10-15)
2. red body & base, black interior & tonneau, China casting (see DY-903)

DY-21-A 1964 AUSTIN MINI COOPER 'S', issued 1991
1. cream body with black roof, red interior, cream base, no labels, China casting ($10-15)
2. cream body with black roof, red interior, cream base, small side labels depicting steering wheel & flags, China casting ($60-85)(C2)
3. cream body with dome light added, black interior, cream China base ($85-100)(C2)
4. dark green body with white roof, black interior, dark green China base, rally design tempa ($60-85)(C2)

5. dark green body with cream roof, black interior, dark green China base, rally design tempa ($60-85)(C2)

DY-22-A 1952 CITROEN 15CV 6 CYL, issued 1991
1. black body & base, tan interior, cream wheels, China casting ($10-15)
2. cream body & base, brown interior, cream wheels, China casting ($10-15)

DY-23-A 1956 CHEVROLET CORVETTE, issued 1991
1. red body & base, cream side flash, red roof & interior, China casting ($10-15)
2. metallic copper body & base, cream side flash, metallic copper roof, cream interior, China casting ($17-20)

DY-24-A 1973 FERRARI DINO 246, issued 1991
1. red body & base, black roof & interior, China casting ($17-20)
2. metallic blue body & base, black roof, cream interior (see DY-902)

DY-25-A 1958 PORSCHE 356A COUPE, issued 1991
1. silver-gray body, red interior, cream wheels, black base, China casting ($10-15)
2. red body, cream interior, cream wheels, black base, China casting (see DY-902)

DY-26-A 1958 STUDEBAKER GOLDEN HAWK, issued 1991
1. metallic brown body, cream side flash, red interior, black base, China casting ($17-20)

DY-27-A 1957 CHEVROLET BEL AIR COUPE CONVERTIBLE, issued 1991
1. powder blue body, brown & blue interior, silver-gray base, China casting ($90-125)
2. powder blue body, cream & blue interior, silver-gray base, China casting ($17-20)
3. red body, red & white interior, black base, no origin cast ($25-30)(CL)

DY-28-A 1969 TRIUMPH STAG, issued 1992
1. white body & base, red interior, China casting ($10-15)
2. white body & base, red interior, small label depicting steering wheel & flags & "1992" hood & trunk labels, China casting ($50-75)(C2)
3. dark green body, red interior, green China base ($17-20)

DY-29-A 1953 BUICK SKYLARK, issued 1992
1. powder blue body, white & blue interior, white tonneau, black base, China casting ($17-20)

DY-30-A 1956 AUSTIN HEALEY, issued 1992
1. dark green body, black seats & tonneau, black base, no tempa, China casting ($17-20)
2. silver blue body, cream seats & tonneau, black base, no tempa, China casting (see DY-903)
3. dark green body, black seats & tonneau, black base, "Dinky Club of America 3rd Show 9/27/97" decal, China casting ($75-100)(C2)
4. red body, white seats, black tonneau, black base, "UK Austin Healey Club" tempa, China casting ($65-90)(C2)
5. white body, black seats & tonneau, black base, "UK Austin Healey Club" tempa, China casting ($250+)(C2)

DY-31-A 1955 FORD THUNDERBIRD, issued 1992
1. red body, red & white interior, black base, China casting ($17-20)

DY-32-A 1957 CITROEN 2CV, issued 1992
1. gray body & base, dark gray painted roof, gray & white interior, cream wheels, China casting ($17-20)

DY-33-A 1962 MERCEDES BENZ 300SL CONVERTIBLE, issued 1995
1. dark blue body & base, red interior, no tempa, China casting ($17-20)
2. dark blue body & base, red interior, "Dinky Toy Club of America 2nd Toy Show" decal, China casting ($75-100)(C2)
3. silver-gray body & base, red interior, "The Dinky Book" tempa, China casting ($65-80)(C2)

DY-34-A no model issued at this number.
NOTE: This was intended to be the Citroen Van but this was placed into the Yesteryear series instead.

DY35-A 1968 VW KARMANN GHIA, issued 1995
1. red body & base, black & tan interior, cream tonneau, China casting ($17-20)

DY-36-A 1960 JAGUAR XK150, issued 1995
1. cream body, red interior, black tonneau, black base, China casting ($17-20)

DY-902-A THREE PIECE DINKY SET, issued 1991
1. wooden plinth with DY-12-A3, DY-24-A2 & DY-25-A2 ($35-50)

DY-903-A THREE PIECE DINKY SET, issued 1992
1. wooden plinth with DY-18-A2, DY-20-A2 & DY-30-A2 ($50-75)

DY-921 1967 SERIES 1-1/2 E TYPE JAGUAR, issued 1992
1. pewter casting mounted to wooden plinth ($35-50)

DYG01 1967 FORD MUSTANG FASTBACK 2 + 2, issued 1996
NOTE: Model is a reissue of DY-16-A.
1. dark blue, red interior, black China base ($17-20)

DYG02 1957 CHEVROLET BELAIR SPORTS COUPE, issued 1996
NOTE: Model is a reissue of DY-2-A.
1. red body, white roof, black & red interior, black base ($17-20)
2. metallic light lavender body, white roof, black & silver interior, black base ($30-35)

DYG03 1958 STUDEBAKER GOLDEN HAWK, issued 1996
NOTE: Model is a reissue of DY-26-A.
1. blue-green body with white flash, black & white interior, black base ($17-20)

DYG04 1953 BUICK SKYLARK, issued 1996
NOTE: Model is a reissue of DY-29-A.
1. light yellow body, tan & yellow interior, tan tonneau, black base ($17-20)

DYG05 1959 CADILLAC CONVERTIBLE, issued 1996
1. black body, red interior, black tonneau, black base ($17-20)

DYG06 1956 CHEVROLET CORVETTE, issued 1996
NOTE: Model is a reissue of DY-23-A.
1. black body with white side flash, black (removable) roof, red interior, black base ($17-20)

DYG07 1948 TUCKER TORPEDO, issued 1996
NOTE: Model is a reissue of DY-11-A.
1. dark green body, tan interior, black base ($17-20)

DYG08 1955 FORD THUNDERBIRD, issued 1996
1. turquoise body & base, white removable roof, white & turquoise interior, no tempa ($17-20)
2. turquoise body & base, turquoise roof (secured), white & turquoise interior, "Maple Leaf Thunderbird Club 1996-1997" tempa ($85-110)(C2)
3. white body & base, white roof (secured), red interior, "Maple Leaf Thunderbird Club 1996-1997" tempa ($250+)(C2)
4. black body & base, red roof (secured), red interior, "Americans Prefer Taste Coca Cola" tempa ($30-35)

DYG09 1959 CHEVROLET IMPALA, issued 1998
1. white body, dark red interior, black tonneau, white wall tires, black base ($20-25)

DYG10 1947 CHRYSLER TOWN & COUNTRY, issued 1998
1. khaki tan body, khaki tan interior with printed seats, khaki tan wheels, tan panels with wood effect panels, black base ($20-25)

DYG11 1958 BUICK SPECIAL, issued 1998
1. metallic blue-green body, white interior & tonneau, white wall tires, black base ($20-25)

DYG12 1956 FORD FAIRLANE, issued 1998
1. white body, blue roof & side panels, white & blue interior, white wall tires, black base ($20-25)

DYG13 1953 CADILLAC ELDORADO, issued 1998
1. black body, white plastic roof, white & black interior, white wall tires, black base ($20-25)

DYG14 1948 DESOTO, issued 1998
1. purplish maroon body, tan interior, maroon wheels, black base ($20-25)

DYG15 1958 NASH METROPOLITAN, issued 1998
1. turquoise upper body, white lower body, white interior with turquoise tempa, turquoise wheels with white wall tires, black base ($20-25)

DYG16 1955 CHEVROLET BEL AIR, issued 1998
1. red body, cream roof & trunk, red & white interior, white wall tires, black base ($20-30)

DYB01 TRIUMPH TR8, issued 1998
1. dark green body, brown roof & interior, chrome wheels, black plastic base ($20-30)

DYB02 1967 SERIES 1-1/2 "E" TYPE JAGUAR, issued 1998
NOTE: Model is a reissue of DY-18-A
1. red body, brown & black interior, chrome wheels with white wall tires, black painted base ($20-30)

DYB03 1955 MORGAN, issued 1998
1. black body, brown seat, tonneau & hood strap, chrome wheels, black base ($20-30)

DYB04 1956 AUSTIN HEALEY, issued 1998
NOTE: Model is a reissue of DY-30-A.
1. dark cream body, black interior & tonneau, chrome wheels, black base ($20-30)

DYB05 MGB, issued 1998
1. light yellow body, black roof & interior, chrome wheels, black plastic base ($20-30)

DYB06 1960 ASTON MARTIN DB4, issued 1998
1. silver-gray body, red interior, light green tinted windows, chrome wheels, black plastic base ($20-30)

DYB07 1961 LOTUS SUPER SEVEN, issued 1998
1. red body, brown interior, black doors & tonneau, chrome wheels, black plastic base ($20-30)

VEM01 1949 VOLKSWAGEN CABRIO, issued 1997
1. black body with red painted sides, khaki tan interior, black tonneau, red wheels, black base ($20-30)

VEM02 1959 AUSTIN SEVEN, issued 1997
1. red body, white & black interior, cream wheels, black base ($20-30)

VEM03 1949 CITROEN 2CV, issued 1997
1. light gunmetal body & base, dark gray interior & wheels ($20-30)

VEM04 1955 MESSERSCHMIDT KR 200, issued 1997
1. yellow body, black fenders & base, yellow interior with black tempa, chrome wheels, clear windshield with light blue tinted roof ($20-30)

VEM05 1962 WOLSELEY HORNET, issued 1997
1. purplish maroon body, cream roof, light brown interior, chrome wheels, black base ($20-30)

VEM06 1966 FIAT 500, issued 1997
1. light green body, cream interior & roof roll, chrome wheels, black base ($20-30)

VEM07 1962 RENAULT 4L, issued 1997
1. slate blue body, tan interior, khaki tan wheels with chrome hubcaps, black roof openings, black base ($20-30)

VCV01 1957 CHEVROLET NOMAD, issued 1998
1. black body, cream roof, black & white interior, white wall tires, black base ($20-25)

Accessory Packs

Accessory Packs was a short-lived series introduced in 1957. The series included mostly non-vehicles but did include one wheeled model.

A-1-A ESSO PETROL PUMPS & SIGN, issued 1957
1. red metal pumps & sign with "Esso" decals ($75-100)

A-1-B BP PETROL PUMPS & SIGN, issued 1963
1. white metal pumps & sign with "BP" decals ($50-75)

A-1-C SERVICE RAMP, issued 1970
1. gold ramp with red handle, "Castrol" label ($25-45)

A-2-A BEDFORD CAR TRANSPORTER, issued 1957
1. blue cab & trailer, black lettered decals, metal wheels ($150-175)
2. blue cab & trailer, orange lettered decals, gray plastic wheels ($150-175)
3. blue cab & trailer, orange lettered decals, black plastic wheels ($200-250)
4. red cab, gray trailer, orange lettered decals, black plastic wheels ($250-300)

A-3-A GARAGE, issued 1957
1. yellow building, maroon roof, green doors, with unpainted connecting clip ($65-90)

A-3-B BRROOMSTICK, issued 1971
1. contains assorted Superfast vehicles with an orange handle with a label and elastic string. Most notable models are MB20-A Lamborghini Marzal in yellow & MB68-A Porsche 910 in white. Also released under the name Zing-O-Matic in the USA. For price add 25% to value of model included in a sealed blisterpack.

A-4-A ROAD SIGNS, issued 1960
1. eight metal road signs with different decals on each ($50-75)
NOTE: Two sets of six plastic signs on a cardboard display were not issued by Lesney. These are pirate issues (see elsewhere)

A-5-A HOME STORE, issued 1961
1. cream building with light green roof ($75-90)

Major Packs

Major Packs were introduced in 1957 as a companion to the 1-75 series in a larger scale. As the King-Size series was introduced three years later, the Major Packs were slowly phased out and some were merged into the King-Size range. By 1967, the series had ended. Major Packs are the "up and coming" Matchbox collectible as prices have soared on this range since 1992. In 1996, the Matchbox International Collectors Club started a series of code two models in which they paired a Yesteryear/Dinky model with either an MB38 Model A Van or Y-65 Austin 7 Van. These were packaged as "Major Packs" and numbered M-1 through M-6. These are listed separately after the Lesney models.

M-1-A CATERPILLAR EARTH SCRAPER, issued 1957
1. yellow body, silver metal wheels, black plastic tires ($100-150)

M-1-B BP AUTOTANKER, issued 1961
1. yellow and green body, "BP" decals, black plastic wheels ($45-60)

M-2-A BEDFORD ICE CREAM TRUCK, issued 1957
1. light blue cab, cream trailer, metal wheels ($150-175)
2. light blue cab, cream trailer, gray plastic wheels ($150-175)

M-2-B BEDFORD TRACTOR & YORK TRAILER, issued 1961
1. orange cab, silver-gray trailer, orange base & doors, "Davies Tyres" decals, gray plastic wheels ($350-500)
2. orange cab, silver-gray trailer, orange base & doors, "Davies Tyres" decals, black plastic wheels ($150-175)
3. [illegible] trailer, maroon base & doors, "LEP" decals, black plastic wheels ($350-500)
4. silver-gray cab, maroon trailer, black base & orange doors, "LEP" decals, black plastic wheels ($150-175)
5. silver-gray cab, maroon trailer, black base & doors, "LEP" decals, black plastic wheels ($150-175)

M-3-A THORNYCROFT ANTAR & CENTURION TANK, issued 1959
1. olive green body, black plastic wheels; metal wheels on tank ($150-175)
2. olive green body, black plastic wheels, gray plastic wheels on tank ($150-175)
3. olive green body, black plastic wheels; black plastic wheels on tank ($150-175)

M-4-A RUSTON BUCYRUS POWER SHOVEL, issued 1959
1. maroon body, yellow shovel assembly, green treads, red lettered decals ($150-175)
2. maroon body, yellow shovel assembly, green treads, yellow lettered decals ($150-175)
3. maroon body, yellow shovel assembly, gray treads, yellow lettered decals ($150-175)

M-4-B GMC TRACTOR & FRUEHAUF HOPPER TRAIN, issued 1964
1. dark red cab, silver-gray hoppers, red plastic wheels with gray plastic tires ($150-200)
2. dark red cab, silver-gray hoppers, red plastic wheels with black plastic tires ($100-125)

M-5-A MASSEY FERGUSON COMBINE HARVESTER, issued 1960
1. red body, silver metal front wheels, black plastic rear wheels ($90-125)
2. red body, orange plastic front wheels, black plastic rear wheels ($90-125)
3. red body, yellow plastic front wheels, black plastic rear wheels ($750+)
4. red body, orange plastic front & rear wheels ($90-125)
5. red body, yellow plastic front & rear wheels ($90-125)

M-6-A PICKFORDS 200 TON TRANSPORTER, issued 1960
1. blue cab, maroon trailer, black plastic wheels ($150-200)
2. blue cab, dark red trailer, black plastic wheels ($150-200)

M-6-B RACING CAR TRANSPORTER, issued 1965
1. green body, black plastic tires ($50-65)

M-7-A JENNINGS CATTLE TRUCK, issued 1960
1. red cab, tan trailer & rear door, gray plastic wheels ($125-175)
2. red cab, tan trailer & rear door, black plastic wheels ($125-175)
3. red cab, dark tan trailer, red rear door, black plastic wheels ($125-175)

M-8-A MOBILGAS PETROL TANKER, issued 1960
1. red cab & trailer, gray plastic wheels ($150-200)
2. red cab & trailer, black plastic wheels ($350-500)

M-8-B GUY WARRIOR CAR TRANSPORTER, issued 1964
1. blue-green cab, orange trailer, orange wheels with gray plastic tires ($75-100)

M-9-A INTERSTATE DOUBLE FREIGHTER, issued 1962
1. blue cab, pearly gray containers, unpainted connector, yellow background decals ($150-200)
2. blue cab, pearly gray containers, blue connector, yellow background decals ($150-200)
3. blue cab, silver-gray containers, unpainted connector, yellow background decals ($150-200)
4. blue cab, silver-gray containers, blue connector, yellow background decals ($150-200)
5. blue cab, silver-gray containers, unpainted connector, orange background decals ($150-200)
NOTE: The rear doors can be silver-gray or blue on most variations as well as two different black plastic wheels being used for further permutations.

M-10-A DINKUM DUMPER, issued 1962
1. yellow body & dump, silver metal wheels, black plastic tires ($75-95)
2. yellow body & dump, red plastic wheels, black plastic tires ($75-95)

CODE 2 "MAJOR PACKS" ($150-250)

M-1 MAJOR PACK- includes Y-13-C & MB38-E for "11th MICA UK Convention"
M-2 MAJOR PACK- includes DY-15-A & Y-65-A for "4th MICA European Convention"
M-3 MAJOR PACK- includes Y-47-A & Y-65-A for "12th MICA UK Convention"
M-4 MAJOR PACK- includes DY-4-A & Y-65-A for "5th European MICA Convention"
M-5 MAJOR PACK- includes Y-27-A & Y-65-A for "13th MICA UK Convention"
M-6 MAJOR PACK- includes Y-37-A & Y-65-A for "6th MICA European Convention"

King-Size, Superkings, and Speedkings

The King-Size range was introduced in 1960 as a larger scale version to the earlier released Major Pack series. The most popular of the series are the pre-1969 models without the Superfast wheels attached. Like the Major Packs, the values on this vintage series have increased dramatically since 1992. The series continues today, but most Superkings are now sold only in Europe. The range has not been imported into the United States since the early 1990s.

K-1-A WEATHERILL HYDRAULIC EXCAVATOR, issued 1960
1. yellow body & shovel, black wheels with gray plastic tires ($85-100)

K-1-B HOVERINGHAM TIPPER TRUCK, issued 1964
1. red cab & chassis, orange dumper, "Hoveringham" decals ($50-75)
2. red cab & chassis, orange dumper, "Hoveringham" labels ($50-75)

K-1-C O & K EXCAVATOR, issued 1970
1. red body, silver-gray arm & shovel, amber windows, red wheels with black plastic tires, red & white "O&K" labels ($35-50)
2. red body, silver-gray arm & shovel, amber windows, 4 spoke Superfast wheels, red & white "O&K" labels ($18-25)
3. red body, silver-gray arm & shovel, amber windows, 4 spoke Superfast wheels, yellow & black "O&K" labels ($18-25)
4. red body, silver-gray arm & shovel, clear windows, treaded Superfast wheels, yellow & black "O&K" labels ($18-25)

K-2-A MUIR HILL DUMPER, issued 1960
1. red body & dump, green metal wheels, gray plastic tires ($65-80)
3. red body & dump, green metal wheels, black plastic tires ($65-80)

K-2-B K.W. DUMP TRUCK, issued 1964
1. yellow body & dump, red plastic wheels with black plastic tires ($60-85)

K-2-C SCAMMELL HEAVY WRECK TRUCK, issued 1969
1. white body, green windows, red grille, unpainted base, red wheels with black plastic tires, silver hooks ($85-100)
2. white body, amber windows, red grille, unpainted base, red wheels with black plastic tires, silver hooks ($40-55)
3. gold body, amber windows, red grille, unpainted base, red wheels with black plastic tires, silver hooks ($70-85)
4. gold body, amber windows, red grille, unpainted base, Superfast wheels, silver hooks ($20-30)
5. gold body, amber windows, red grille, red base, Superfast wheels, silver hooks ($20-30)
6. gold body, amber windows, red grille, red base, Superfast wheels, gold hooks ($20-30)
7. gold body, amber windows, black grille, red base, Superfast wheels, gold hooks ($20-30)
8. gold body, clear windows, red grille, red base, Superfast wheels, gold hooks ($20-30)

K-2-D CAR RECOVERY VEHICLE, issued 1977
1. green body, "Car Recovery" labels, red ramps; K-37-A in red with green base, black interior, gray roof, "3" label ($20-25)
2. green body, "Car Recovery" labels, red ramps; K-37-A in red with green base, gray interior & roof, "3" label ($20-25)
3. green body, "Car Recovery" labels, red ramps; K-37-A in red with green base, gray interior, black roof, "3" label ($20-25)
4. green body, "Car Recovery" labels, red ramps; K-37-A in red with orange base, black interior, gray roof, "3" label ($20-25)
5. green body, "Car Recovery" labels, black ramps; K-37-A in red with green base, gray interior, gray roof, "3" label ($20-25)
6. green body, "24 Hour" labels, red ramps; K-37-A in red with green base, gray interior, gray roof, "3" label ($20-25)
7. metallic blue body, "24 Hour" labels, black ramps; K-59-A in beige ($20-25)
8. metallic blue body, "24 Hour" labels, red ramps; K-59-A in beige ($20-25)
NOTE: 1-8 & 10 transporters with amber, 9 & 10 fitted with clear windows, gray interior
9. metallic blue body, "24 Hour" labels, red ramps; K-59-A in beige ($20-25)
10. tan & white body with white bed, "Race Haulage" labels, red ramps; K-60-B in red with "207 Cobra" tempa & green windows ($35-45)
11. tan & white body , "Race Haulage" labels, red ramps; K-60-B in metallic red with "207 Cobra" tempa & amber windows ($35-45)
12. yellow body, "im Auftrag des-ADAC" labels, red ramps; K-48-A in silver-gray with black roof ($40-50)(GR)

K-3-A CATERPILLAR BULLDOZER, issued 1960
1. yellow body, gray metal rollers ($60-85)
2. yellow body, red plastic rollers ($60-85)
3. yellow body, yellow plastic rollers ($60-85)

K-3-B HATRA TRACTOR SHOVEL, issued 1965
1. orange body & shovel, red plastic wheels, black plastic tires ($55-75)

K-3-C MASSEY FERGUSON TRACTOR & TRAILER, issued 1970
1. red tractor, red trailer with yellow chassis, yellow wheels with black tires ($35-50)

K-3-D MOD TRACTOR & TRAILER, issued 1974
1. metallic blue body, red seat & grille, stars & stripes labels, metallic blue trailer ($15-20)
2. metallic blue body, yellow seat, red grille, stars & stripes labels, metallic blue trailer ($15-20)
3. metallic blue body, red seat, yellow grille, stars & stripes labels, metallic blue trailer ($15-20)
4. metallic blue body, yellow seat & grille, stars & stripes labels, metallic blue trailer ($15-20)
5. blue-green body, yellow seat & grille, no labels, blue-green trailer ($65-80)

K-3-E GRAIN TRANSPORTER, issued 1981
1. red cab with white chassis, red trailer chassis, white tank, small "Kellogg's" labels ($25-35)
2. red cab with white chassis, red trailer chassis, white tank, large "Kellogg's" labels ($25-35)
3. green cab with white chassis, green trailer chassis, white tank, "Heidelberger Zement" labels ($45-60)(GR)

K-4-A INTERNATIONAL TRACTOR, issued 1960
1. red body, green metal wheels, black plastic tires ($65-80)
2. red body, red metal wheels, black plastic tires ($65-80)
3. red body, red plastic wheels, black plastic tires ($65-80)
4. red body, orange plastic wheels, black plastic tires ($65-80)

K-4-B G.M.C. TRACTOR & FRUEHAUF HOPPER TRAIN, issued 1967
1. dark red cab, silver-gray hoppers, red plastic wheels, gray plastic tires ($175-250)
2. dark red cab, silver-gray hoppers, red plastic wheels, black plastic tires ($100-150)

K-4-C LEYLAND TIPPER, issued 1969
1. dark red cab, silver-gray dump, chrome base, "LE Transport" labels, black plastic tires ($35-45)
2. dark red cab, silver-gray dump, chrome base, "W. Wates" labels, black plastic tires ($35-45)
3. pea green cab & dump, chrome base, "W. Wates" labels, black plastic tires ($500+)
4. orange-red cab, pea green dump, chrome base, "W. Wates" labels, black plastic tires ($35-45)
5. orange-red cab, metallic lime dump, chrome base, "W. Wates" labels, black plastic tires ($50-60)
6. orange-red cab, metallic lime dump, green base, "W. Wates" labels, Superfast wheels ($20-30)
7. orange-red cab, metallic lime dump, dark green base, no labels, Superfast wheels ($20-30)
8. powder blue cab, silver-gray dump & base, miner & cave labels, Superfast wheels ($50-75)(MX)

K-4-D BIG TIPPER, issued 1974
1. metallic red body, yellow dump, 3 stripes labels, with press-a-matic ($15-18)
2. metallic red body, yellow dump, "Laing" labels, with press-a-matic ($15-18)
3. red body, yellow dump, 3 stripes labels, with press-a-matic ($15-18)
5. metallic red body, yellow dump, 3 stripes labels, without press-a-matic ($15-18)
6. metallic red body, yellow dump, "Laing" labels, without press-a-matic ($15-18)
7. red body, yellow dump, 3 stripes labels, without press-a-matic ($15-18)
8. red body, yellow dump, "Laing" labels, without press-a-matic ($15-18)
9. red body, dark yellow dump, "Laing" labels, without press-a-matic ($15-18)

K-5-A FODEN TIPPER TRUCK, issued 1961
1. yellow cab & dump, silver metal wheels, black plastic tires ($65-80)
2. yellow cab & dump, red plastic wheels, black plastic tires ($60-75)

K-5-B RACING CAR TRANSPORTER, issued 1967
1. green body, red plastic wheels, black plastic tires ($40-50)

K-5-C MUIR HILL TRACTOR & TRAILER, issued 1972
1. yellow body, red chassis, blue driver, amber windows, "Muir Hill" labels ($25-35)
2. yellow body, red chassis, white driver, amber windows, "Muir Hill" labels ($25-35)
3. yellow body, red chassis, white driver, clear windows, "Muir Hill" labels ($25-35)
4. dark & light blue body, red chassis, white driver, amber windows, "Hoch & Tief" labels ($45-60)(GR)

K-6-A ALLIS-CHALMERS EARTH SCRAPER, issued 1961
1. orange body, silver metal wheels, black plastic tires ($90-125)
2. orange body, red plastic wheels, black plastic tires ($90-125)

K-6-B MERCEDES BENZ "BINZ" AMBULANCE, issued 1967

1. cream body, decals, silver wheels with black plastic tires ($30-40)
2. cream body, labels, silver wheels with black plastic tires ($30-40)
3. off white body, labels, silver wheels with black plastic wheels ($30-40)
NOTE: combinations of decal & labels on hood & sides exist on all versions.

K-6-C CEMENT MIXER, issued 1971
1. blue body, red chassis, yellow barrel, tan box on top of cab, amber windows ($18-25)
2. blue body, red chassis, yellow barrel, black box on top of cab, amber windows ($18-25)
3. blue body, red chassis, yellow barrel, black box on top of cab, clear windows ($18-25)

K-6-D MOTORCYCLE TRANSPORTER, issued 1976
1. dark blue body, "Team Honda" labels, exposed engine, MB18-B red Hondarora ($15-20)
2. dark blue body, "Team Honda" labels, exposed engine, MB18-B orange Hondarora ($15-20)
3. dark blue body, "Team Honda" labels, no engine-hood label, MB18-B red Hondarora ($15-20)
4. dark blue body, "Team Honda" labels, no engine-hood label, MB18-B orange Hondarora ($15-20)

K-7-A CURTISS WRIGHT REAR DUMPER, issued 1961
1. yellow body, silver metal wheels, black plastic tires ($90-125)

K-7-B REFUSE TRUCK, issued 1967
1. red cab, all silver-gray rear tipper, "Cleansing Service" decals, black plastic tires ($35-50)
2. red cab, all silver-gray rear tipper, "Cleansing Service" labels, black plastic tires ($35-50)
3. red cab, all silver-gray rear tipper, "Cleansing Service" labels, Superfast wheels ($20-25)
4. red cab, red front & silver-gray rear tipper, "Cleansing Service" labels, Superfast wheels ($20-25)
5. dark blue cab, all orange rear tipper, yellow/black/white labels, Superfast wheels ($50-75)(MX)

K-7-C RACING CAR TRANSPORTER, issued 1973
1. yellow body, red tailgate, black interior, amber windows & canopy, "Team Matchbox" labels; MB34-A in pink ($25-40)
2. yellow body, red tailgate, black interior, amber windows & canopy, "Team Matchbox" labels; MB24-B in green ($60-75)
3. yellow body, red tailgate, black interior, amber windows & canopy, "Team Matchbox" labels; MB24-B in red ($20-35)
4. yellow body, red tailgate, black interior, amber windows & canopy, "Team Matchbox" labels; MB34-A in yellow ($25-40)
5. yellow body, red tailgate, blue interior, amber windows & canopy, "Team Matchbox" labels; MB34-A in yellow ($25-40)
6. yellow body, red tailgate, blue interior, clear windows, amber canopy, "Team Matchbox" labels; MB34-A in yellow ($25-40)
7. yellow body, red tailgate, blue interior, clear windows & amber canopy, "Team Matchbox" labels; MB36-C in red ($25-40)
8. yellow body, red tailgate, black interior, clear windows & canopy, "Team Matchbox" labels; MB34-A in yellow ($25-40)
9. white body & tailgate, black interior, clear windows & canopy, "Martini Racing" labels; MB56-B in white ($35-45)
10. white body & tailgate, black interior, clear windows, orange canopy, "Martini Racing" labels; MB56-B in white ($35-45)

K-8-A PRIME MOVER & CATERPILLAR TRACTOR, issued 1962
1. orange mover & trailer with silver metal wheels, tractor with metal rollers ($175-250)
2. orange mover & trailer with silver metal wheels, tractor with orange plastic rollers ($175-250)
3. orange mover & trailer with red plastic wheels, tractor with metal rollers ($175-250)
4. orange mover & trailer with red plastic wheels, tractor with red plastic rollers ($175-250)
5. orange mover & trailer with red plastic wheels, tractor with orange plastic rollers ($175-250)
6. orange mover & trailer with red plastic wheels, tractor with yellow plastic rollers ($175-250)

K-8-B GUY WARRIOR CAR TRANSPORTER, issued 1967
1. blue-green cab, orange trailer, orange wheels, gray plastic tires ($60-75)
1. blue-green cab, orange trailer, orange wheels, black plastic tires ($60-75)
3. blue-green cab, orange trailer, red wheels, black plastic tires ($60-75)
4. blue-green cab, yellow trailer, red wheels, black plastic tires ($500+)
5. yellow cab, yellow trailer, red wheels, black plastic tires ($50-65)

K-8-C CATERPILLAR TRAXCAVATOR, issued 1970
1. yellow body & bucket, yellow rollers, green treads ($25-30)
2. light yellow body, orange bucket, yellow rollers, green treads ($25-30)
3. light yellow body, orange bucket, black rollers, green treads ($25-30)
4. yellow-orange body, orange bucket, black rollers, green treads ($25-30)
5. yellow-orange body, orange bucket, black rollers, black treads ($25-30)
6. silver-gray body, orange bucket, black rollers, black treads ($50-75)(MX)

K-8-D ANIMAL TRANSPORTER, issued 1980
1. orange cab, brown chassis, beige container, "Anitran" labels ($25-35)
2. orange cab, brown chassis, light tan container, "Anitran" labels ($25-35)
3. orange cab, brown chassis, dark tan container, "Anitran" labels ($25-35)

K-8-E FERRARI F40, issued 1989
1. red body, clear windows, small logo tempa, China casting ($6-8)
2. white body, amber windows, no tempa, China casting ($10-15)(GF)
3. white body, black windows, "Ferrari" tempa, China casting ($6-8)(Alarm Car)
4. red body, black windows, "Ferrari" tempa, China casting ($6-8)(Alarm Car)
5. lime body, clear windows, red interior, yellow base & wheels, caricature tempa, China casting ($6-8)(LL)

K-9-A DIESEL ROAD ROLLER, issued 1962
1. green body, red metal rollers, gray driver ($75-100)
2. green body, red metal rollers, red driver ($50-75)

K-9-B CLAAS COMBINE HARVESTER, issued 1967
1. green body, red rotor, green & white "Claas" decal, white driver ($35-50)
2. green body, red rotor, green & white "Claas" label no driver ($35-50)
3. green body, red rotor, green & white "Claas" label, white driver ($35-50)
4. red body, yellow rotor, green & white "Claas" label, tan driver ($50-75)
5. red body, yellow rotor, red & white "Claas" label, tan driver ($35-50)
6. red body, yellow rotor, red & white "Claas" label, no driver ($35-50)

K-9-C FIRE TENDER, issued 1973
1. red body, amber windows, gray extension ladder ($15-20)
2. red body, clear windows, gray extension ladder ($15-20)
3. red body, amber windows, black extension ladder ($15-20)
4. red body, amber windows, white extension ladder ($15-20)

K-10-A AVELING-BARFORD TRACTOR SHOVEL, issued 1963
1. blue-green body, silver metal wheels, air cleaner cast ($75-100)
2. blue-green body, red plastic wheels, air cleaner cast ($75-100)
3. blue-green body, red plastic wheels, no air cleaner cast ($75-100)
4. mint green body, red plastic wheels, no air cleaner cast ($75-100)

K-10-B PIPE TRUCK, issued 1967
1. yellow body & trailer, decals, gray plastic pipes, black plastic tires ($50-75)
2. yellow body & trailer, labels, gray plastic pipes, black plastic tires ($50-65)
3. pinkish purple body & trailer, labels, gray plastic pipes, Superfast wheels ($20-30)
4. pinkish purple body & trailer, labels, yellow plastic pipes, Superfast wheels ($20-30)
5. metallic purple body & trailer, labels, yellow pipes, Superfast wheels ($20-30)
6. metallic purple body & trailer, labels, orange pipes, Superfast wheels ($20-30)

K-10-C CAR TRANSPORTER, issued 1976
1. red body & trailer, amber windows, "Auto Transport" labels ($20-25)
2. red body & trailer, clear windows, "Auto Transport" labels ($20-25)
3. red body & trailer, amber windows, mustang horse labels (from K-60-A) ($25-35)
4. red body & trailer, amber windows, "4" labels ($25-35)

K-10-D BEDFORD CAR TRANSPORTER, issued 1981
1. metallic blue body & trailer, white metal ramp, "Bedford" & "Courier" labels ($18-25)

K-11-A FORDSON TRACTOR & FARM TRAILER, issued 1963
1. blue tractor, silver steering wheel, orange metal wheels ($60-75)
2. blue tractor, silver steering wheel, orange plastic wheels ($60-75)
3. blue tractor, blue steering wheel, orange plastic wheels ($60-75)
4. blue tractor, blue steering wheel, red plastic wheels ($60-75)

K-11-B DAF CAR TRANSPORTER, issued 1969
1. metallic blue cab, clear windows, unpainted base, gold trailer, black wheel blocks, "DAF" labels, black plastic tires ($85-110)
2. yellow cab, clear windows, unpainted base, yellow & orange trailer, black wheel blocks, "DAF" labels, black plastic tires ($50-65)
3. yellow cab, clear windows, unpainted base, yellow & orange trailer, red wheel blocks, "DAF" labels, black plastic tires ($50-65)
4. yellow cab, blue windows, unpainted base, yellow & red trailer, red wheel blocks, "DAF" labels, Superfast wheels ($25-40)
5. yellow cab, clear windows, unpainted base, yellow & red trailer, red wheel blocks, "DAF" labels, Superfast wheels ($25-40)
6. yellow cab, clear windows, metallic red base, yellow & red trailer, red wheel blocks, "DAF" labels, Superfast wheels ($25-40)
7. yellow cab, clear windows, metallic red base, yellow & orange trailer, red wheel blocks, "DAF" labels, Superfast wheels ($25-40)
8. yellow cab, clear windows, metallic red base, yellow & orange trailer, red wheel blocks, stripes labels, Superfast wheels ($25-40)

K-11-C BREAKDOWN TRUCK, issued 1976
1. yellow body, silver-gray base, white booms, red hooks, "AA" labels ($12-15)
2. yellow body, black base, white booms, red hooks, "AA" labels ($12-15)
3. yellow body, black base, white booms, red hooks, "Shell Recovery" labels ($12-15)
4. red body, black base, white booms, red hooks, "Falck-Zonen" labels ($75-100)(SW)

K-11-D DODGE DELIVERY VAN, issued 1981
1. yellow body, "Michelin" labels ($12-15)
2. blue body, "Frankfurter Allgemeine" labels ($35-50)(GR)
3. blue body, "Suchard Express" labels ($35-50)(FR)
4. yellow body, "Suchard Express" labels ($50-75)(FR)

K-12-A HEAVY BREAKDOWN WRECK TRUCK, issued 1963
1. green body, silver metal wheels, no roof lights cast ($60-80)
2. green body, red plastic wheels, no roof lights cast ($60-80)
3. green body, red plastic wheels, with roof lights cast ($60-80)

K-12-B SCAMMELL CRANE TRUCK, issued 1969
1. yellow body & crane, unpainted base, red plastic wheels, black plastic tires ($40-55)
2. orange body & crane, silver-gray base, Superfast wheels ($20-25)
3. orange body & crane, gray base, Superfast wheels ($20-25)
4. silver-gray body, red crane, red base, Superfast wheels ($50-75)(MX)

K-12-C HERCULES MOBILE CRANE, issued 1975
1. yellow body & crane, yellow hook, "Laing" labels ($18-25)
2. yellow body & crane, red hook, "Laing" labels ($18-25)
3. dark & light blue body, red crane, red hook, "Hoch & Tief" labels ($45-60)(GR)

K-13-A READYMIX CONCRETE TRUCK, issued 1963
1. orange body, silver metal wheels, "Readymix" decals ($60-80)
2. orange body, red plastic wheels, "Readymix" decals ($60-80)
3. orange body, red plastic wheels, "RMC" decals ($60-80)

K-13-B BUILDING TRANSPORTER, issued 1971
1. light green body, unpainted base, blue windows ($20-25)
2. light green body, red base, blue windows ($20-25)
3. light green body, red base, clear windows, ($20-25)
4. light green body, yellow base, clear windows ($20-25)
5. light green body, olive green base, clear windows ($20-25)
6. lime green body, red base, clear windows ($20-25)
7. lime green body, yellow base, clear windows ($20-25)
8. lime green body, black base, clear windows ($20-25)

K-13-C AIRCRAFT TRANSPORTER, issued 1976
1. red body, yellow base, amber windows, white interior, "X4" label, white plane ($15-20)
2. red body, yellow base, amber windows, brown interior, "X4" label, white plane ($15-20)
3. red body, yellow base, amber windows, gray interior, "X4" label, white plane ($15-20)
4. red body, yellow base, clear windows, white interior, "X4" label, white plane ($15-20)
5. red body, yellow base, clear windows, white interior, "12" label, brown plane with white wings ($18-25)
6. silver-gray body, red base, amber windows, white interior, no labels, white plane ($15-20)
7. silver-gray body, red base, amber windows, white interior, stripes label, white plane ($15-20)
8. silver-gray body, red base, clear windows, white interior, stripes label, white plane ($15-20)

K-14-A TAYLOR JUMBO CRANE, issued 1964
1. yellow body & crane, yellow weight box, red plastic wheels ($50-65)
2. yellow body & crane, red weight box, red plastic wheels ($50-65)

K-14-B SCAMMELL FREIGHT TRUCK, issued 1971
1. metallic blue cab, bronze-red container with white roof, "LEP" labels, silver-gray base ($15-20)
2. metallic blue cab, bronze-red container with white roof, "LEP" labels, gray base ($15-20)

K-14-C HEAVY BREAKDOWN TRUCK, issued 1977
1. white cab & chassis, red rear section, amber windows, "Shell Recovery" labels ($15-18)
2. white cab & chassis, red rear section, clear windows, "Shell Recovery" labels ($15-18)

K-15-A MERRYWEATHER FIRE ENGINE, issued 1964
1. red body, gray ladder, red plastic wheels, black plastic tires ($60-75)
2. red body, gray ladder, Superfast wheels ($35-45)
3. red body, silver-gray ladder, Superfast wheels ($35-45)
4. metallic red body, silver-gray ladder, Superfast wheels ($35-45)
5. metallic red body, silver-gray ladder, Superfast wheels ($50-75)(MX)
6. red body, silver-gray ladder, Superfast wheels ($50-75)(MX)

K-15-B THE LONDONER, issued 1973
1. red upper & lower body, yellow interior, "Swinging London Carnaby Street" labels, with bell cast, England casting ($25-40)
2. red upper & lower body, yellow interior, "Swinging London Carnaby Street" labels, without bell cast, England casting ($12-15)
3. red upper & lower body, white interior, "Swinging London Carnaby Street" labels, England casting ($12-15)
4. silver-gray upper & lower body, red interior, "Silver Jubilee 1952-1977" labels, England casting ($20-25)(UK)
5. red upper & lower body, yellow interior, "Enter A Different World-Harrods" labels, England casting ($20-25)(UK)
6. red upper & lower body, yellow interior, "Hamley's" labels, England casting ($20-25)
7. red upper & lower body, yellow interior, "Tourist London-By Bus" labels, mounted on plastic stand, England casting ($20-25)(UK)
8. red upper & lower body, yellow interior, "Harrods for more than money can buy" labels, England casting ($20-25)
9. red upper & lower body, yellow interior, "London Dungeon" labels, England casting ($15-18)
10. red upper & lower body, brown interior, "London Dungeon" labels, England casting ($15-18)

11. metallic silver upper & lower body, blue interior, "London Dungeon" labels, England casting ($20-25)
12. metallic silver upper & lower body, blue interior, "The Royal Wedding" labels, England casting ($20-25)
13. red upper & lower body, yellow interior, "Firestone" labels, England casting ($20-25)
14. powder blue upper & white/dark blue lower body, black interior, "1234-1984 Parish Church 750th Anniversary" labels, England casting ($20-25)(UK)
15. powder blue upper & white lower body, orange-yellow interior, "Macleans Toothpaste" labels, England casting ($20-25)(UK)
16. blue upper & lower body, gray interior, "Alton Towers" labels, England casting ($20-25)(UK)
17. dark cream upper & blue lower body, blue interior, "Telegraph & Argus" labels, England casting ($20-25)(UK)
18. red upper & lower body, orange-yellow interior, "Nestles Milkybar" labels, England casting ($15-18)
19. white upper & red lower body, orange-yellow interior, "Nestles Milkybar" labels, England casting ($15-18)
20. red upper & lower body, orange-yellow interior, "Petticoat Lane" labels, England casting ($10-15)
21. yellow upper & brown lower body, yellow interior, "Butterkist Butter Toffee Popcorn" labels, England casting ($25-40)(UK)(OP)
22. red upper & lower body, orange-yellow interior, "London Wide Tour Bus" labels, England casting ($10-15)
23. red upper & lower body, yellow interior, "The Planetarium" labels, Macau casting ($10-15)
24. red upper & lower body, yellow interior, "Besuchen Sie Berlin Hauptstadt Der DDR" labels, Macau casting ($25-40)(GR)
25. red upper & lower body, yellow interior, Chinese lettered side labels with "Matchbox" roof label, China casting ($250-400)(CHI)
26. red upper & lower body, yellow interior, "Around London Tour Bus" labels, China casting ($10-12)
27. yellow upper & lower deck, blue interior, red wheels, "1 2 3 4" & blue/red stripe sides and "Save the Children" roof tempa, China casting ($7-10)(LL)
28. silver-gray upper & lower deck, blue interior, "Cada Toys" labels, England casting ($150-250)(C2)

K-15-C THE LONDONER, issued 1982
1. beige body, black interior, "Berlin ist eine Reise Wert!" labels ($12-15)
NOTE: This model is cast different than the K-15B in that the doors are cast on the opposite side to all other versions.

K-16-A DODGE TRACTOR WITH TWIN TIPPERS, issued 1966
1. green cab & base, yellow tippers, red plastic wheels, black plastic tires ($125-175)
2. yellow cab, black base, powder blue tippers, black axle covers, Superfast wheels ($85-110)
3. yellow cab, blue base, powder blue tippers, brown axle covers, Superfast wheels ($85-110)

K-16-B PETROL TANKER, issued 1974
NOTE: Model permutations exist on hose colors (yellow, black or white), cab connectors (black, gray, blue, white or yellow), axle covers (gold, gray, brown, black & green) and grilles (yellow, red or white). All models with white tank & maltese cross wheels unless otherwise noted.
1. "Texaco" labels, red cab & tank bottom, chrome tank strip, green windows, chrome interior, with hood labels ($20-25)
2. "Texaco" labels, metallic red cab, red tank bottom, chrome tank strip, green windows, chrome interior, hood labels ($20-25)
3. "Texaco" labels, metallic red cab, red tank bottom, chrome tank strip, green windows, chrome interior, with hood labels, triangle in circle door labels ($20-25)
4. "Texaco" labels, metallic red cab, red tank bottom, chrome tank strip, green windows, chrome interior, without hood labels ($20-25)
5. "Texaco" labels, red cab & tank bottom, chrome tank strip, green windows, chrome interior, without hood labels ($20-25)
6. "Texaco" labels, red cab & tank bottom, chrome tank strip, clear windows, chrome interior, without hood labels ($20-25)
7. "Texaco" labels, red cab & tank bottom, black tank strip, green windows, chrome interior, without hood labels ($20-25)
8. "Texaco" labels, red cab & tank bottom, black tank strip, clear windows, chrome interior, without hood labels ($20-25)
9. "Texaco" labels, green cab & tank bottom, chrome tank strip, green windows, chrome interior ($85-110)(US)
10. "Quaker State" labels, green cab & tank bottom, chrome tank strip, green windows, chrome interior ($85-110)(CN)
11. "Shell" labels, white cab, yellow tank bottom, chrome tank strip, green windows, chrome interior ($20-25)
12. "Shell" labels, white cab, yellow tank bottom, black tank strip, green windows, chrome interior ($20-25)
13. "Shell" labels, white cab, yellow tank bottom, black tank strip, clear windows, chrome interior ($20-25)
14. "Exxon" labels, white cab & tank bottom, chrome tank strip, green windows, chrome interior ($20-25)
15. "Exxon" labels, white cab & tank bottom, black tank strip, green windows, chrome interior ($20-25)
16. "Exxon" labels, white cab & tank bottom, black tank strip, green windows, black interior ($20-25)
17. "Exxon" labels, white cab & tank bottom, black tank strip, clear windows, chrome interior ($20-25)
18. "Aral" (blue on white) labels, dark blue cab, dark blue tank bottom, chrome tank strip, green windows, chrome interior ($40-60)
19. "Aral' (white on blue) labels, dark blue cab, dark blue tank bottom, chrome tank strip, green windows, chrome interior ($40-60)
20. "Aral" (white on blue) labels, light blue cab & tank bottom, chrome tank strip, green windows, chrome interior ($40-60)
21. "Aral" (clouds) labels, light blue tank bottom, chrome tank strip, green windows, chrome interior ($40-60)
22. "Aral" (clouds) labels, light blue cab & tank bottom, black tank strip, clear windows, chrome interior ($40-60)
23. "Total" labels, white cab & tank bottom, chrome tank strip, green windows, chrome interior ($40-60)
24. "Total" labels, white cab, red tank bottom, chrome tank strip, green windows, chrome interior ($40-60)
25. "Total" labels, white cab, red tank bottom, black tank strip, clear windows, chrome interior ($40-60)
26. "BP" labels, white tank, yellow tank bottom, chrome tank strip, green windows, chrome interior ($500+)
27. "LEP International Transport" labels, metallic red cab, red tank bottom, chrome tank strip, green windows, chrome interior ($500)
28. "Chemco" labels, black cab, yellow tank top & bottom, green windows, chrome interior, mag wheels ($20-25)

K-17-A LOW LOADER WITH BULLDOZER, issued 1967
1. green cab & trailer, "Laing" decals, black plastic tires; red & dark yellow bulldozer, red rollers, green treads, "Laing" decals ($90-125)
2. green cab & trailer, "Taylor Woodrow' decals, black plastic tires; red & dark yellow bulldozer, yellow rollers, green treads, "Taylor Woodrow" decals ($90-125)
3. lime green cab & trailer, "Taylor Woodrow" decals, Superfast wheels; orange & yellow bulldozer, yellow rollers, green treads, "Taylor Woodrow" decals ($75-100)
4. florescent red cab, lime green trailer, "Taylor Woodrow" decals, Superfast wheels; orange & yellow bulldozer, yellow rollers, green treads, "Taylor Woodrow" decals ($50-75)
5. florescent red cab, lime green trailer, "Taylor Woodrow" decals, Superfast wheels; orange & yellow bulldozer, yellow rollers, black treads, "Taylor Woodrow" decals ($50-75)

K-17-B SCAMMELL ARTICULATED CONTAINER TRUCK, issued 1974
NOTE: Some models are available with either yellow or black grilles.
1. metallic red cab, red trailer chassis, yellow containers with blue roofs, "Gentransco" labels ($18-25)
2. metallic red cab, red trailer chassis, orange containers with blue roofs, "Gentransco" labels ($18-25)
3. metallic red cab, red trailer chassis, orange containers with orange roofs, "Gentransco" labels ($18-25)
4. metallic red cab, red trailer chassis, white containers with blue roofs, "Gentransco" labels ($18-25)
5. metallic red cab, red trailer chassis, white containers with orange roofs, "Gentransco" labels ($18-25)
6. metallic red cab, red trailer chassis, white containers with black roofs, "Gentransco" labels, ($18-25)
7. metallic red cab, red trailer chassis, white containers with red roofs, "Gentransco" labels ($18-25)
8. metallic red cab, blue trailer chassis, white containers with blue roofs, "Gentransco" labels($18-25)
9. blue cab, blue trailer chassis, white containers with blue roofs, "Gentransco" labels ($20-25)
10. metallic red cab, red trailer chassis, white containers with blue roofs, "Ginny Vogue Dolls" labels ($250-400)(US)
11. metallic red cab, black trailer chassis, white containers with blue roofs, "Gentransco" labels ($18-25)
12. metallic red cab, white trailer chassis, white containers with blue roofs, "Gentransco" labels ($18-25)
13. yellow cab, black trailer chassis, yellow containers with dark yellow roofs, "Gentransco" labels ($20-25)
14. yellow cab, black trailer chassis, yellow containers with yellow roofs, "DBP" labels ($30-45)(GR)
15. yellow cab, black trailer chassis, yellow containers with yellow roofs, "Deutsche Bundespost" labels ($30-45)(GR)
16. blue cab, white trailer chassis, white containers with blue roofs, "Pppick-up a Penguin" labels ($18-25)(UK)
17. white cab, black trailer chassis, white containers with green roofs, "7 Up" labels ($18-25)

K-18-A ARTICULATED HORSE BOX, issued 1967
NOTE: All models with unpainted cab base unless otherwise noted.
1. red cab, tan box, black plastic tires, gray rear trailer interior ($50-75)
2. red cab, tan box, black plastic tires, green rear trailer interior ($50-75)
3. red cab, tan box, black plastic tires, red rear trailer interior ($50-75)
4. red cab, tan box, black plastic tires, brown rear trailer interior ($50-75)
5. red cab, tan box, black plastic tires, mottled color trailer interior ($50-75)
6. red cab, silver-gray base, tan box, Superfast wheels, green rear trailer interior ($25-40)
7. red cab, silver-gray base, orange box, Superfast wheels, green rear trailer interior ($25-40)
8. red cab, gray base, orange box, Superfast wheels, green rear trailer interior ($25-40)

K-18-B ARTICULATED TIPPER TRUCK, issued 1974
1. red cab, silver-gray chassis, black trailer chassis, yellow tipper, stripes labels on cab & tipper, without cast panel ($18-25)
2. metallic red cab, silver-gray chassis, black trailer chassis, yellow tipper, stripes labels on cab & tipper, without cast panel ($18-25)
3. metallic red cab, silver-gray chassis, black trailer chassis, yellow tipper, stripes label on tipper, without cast panel ($18-25)
4. silver-gray cab, red chassis, red trailer chassis, silver-gray tipper, stripes label on tipper, without cast panel ($18-25)
5. silver-gray cab, red chassis, red trailer chassis, silver-gray tipper, "Tarmac" labels on tipper, without cast panel ($18-25)
6. silver-gray cab, red chassis, red trailer chassis, yellow tipper, "Tarmac" labels on tipper with door labels, without cast panel ($18-25)
7. yellow cab, black chassis, black trailer chassis, yellow tipper, "US Steel" labels on tipper & cab, without cast panel ($18-25)
8. silver-gray cab, red chassis, red trailer chassis, silver-gray tipper, "Tarmac" label on tipper with door labels, with cast panel ($18-25)
9. dark blue cab, red chassis, red trailer chassis, powder blue tipper, "Hoch & Tief" labels on tipper, without cast panel ($45-60)(GR)
10. white cab, black chassis, black trailer chassis, silver-gray tipper, "Condor" labels on tipper, with cast panel ($45-60)

K-19-A SCAMMEL TIPPER TRUCK, issued 1967
1. red cab, yellow tipper, black grille, decals, black plastic tires ($40-60)
2. red cab, yellow tipper, black grille, labels, black plastic tires ($40-60)
3. red cab, orange-yellow tipper, black grille, labels, black plastic tires ($40-60)
4. metallic red cab, orange-yellow tipper, red grille, Superfast wheels ($25-40)
5. metallic red cab, orange-yellow tipper, black grille, Superfast wheels ($25-40)

K-19-B SECURITY TRUCK, issued 1979
1. white cab & chassis, yellow roof, "Group 4" labels ($12-15)
2. white cab & chassis, orange roof, "Group 4" labels ($12-15)
3. white cab & chassis, orange roof, "Fort Knox" labels ($12-15)
4. white cab & chassis, red roof, "Fort Knox" labels ($12-15)

K-20-A TRACTOR TRANSPORTER, issued 1968
1. red cab with yellow tanks, red trailer, 3 all blue tractors, black plastic tires ($125-175)
2. red cab with red tanks, red trailer, 3 all blue tractors, black plastic tires ($125-175)
3. florescent red cab, yellow trailer, 3 all blue tractors, Superfast wheels ($125-175)
4. blue cab, yellow trailer, 3 orange tractors, Superfast wheels ($250-300)(MX)
5. blue cab, silver-gray trailer, 3 orange tractors, Superfast wheels ($250-300)(MX)
6. blue cab, gold trailer, 3 orange tractors, Superfast wheels ($250-300)(MX)
7. red cab, silver-gray trailer, 3 orange tractors, Superfast wheels ($250-300)(MX)

K-20-B CARGO HAULER & PALLET LOADER, issued 1973
NOTE: Includes K-15-B Fork Lift. These can be various versions for any given variation. The mounts for the barrels, spare tire & motor can be red or orange on some versions.
1. metallic green body, red base, yellow barrels ($20-25)
2. metallic green body, yellow base, yellow barrels ($20-25)
3. metallic green body, black base, yellow barrels ($20-25)
4. metallic green body, olive green base, yellow barrels ($20-25)
5. lime green body, yellow base, yellow barrels ($20-25)
6. lime green body, yellow base, blue barrels ($20-25)
7. lime green body, black base, yellow barrels ($20-25)
8. lime green body, red base, yellow barrels ($20-25)

K-20-C PETERBILT WRECKER, issued 1979
1. dark green body, unpainted roof mount, red dome lights, unpainted base ($15-20)
2. dark green body, white roof mount, red dome lights, unpainted base ($15-20)
3. dark green body, unpainted roof mount, orange dome lights, unpainted base ($15-20)
4. white body, unpainted roof mount, orange dome lights, unpainted base ($50-75)
5. dark green body, white roof mount, red dome lights, silver-gray base ($15-20)
6. dark green body, unpainted roof mount, blue dome lights, silver-gray base ($15-20)
7. light green body, unpainted roof mount, red dome lights, silver-gray base ($15-20)

K-21-A MERCURY COUGAR, issued 1968
1. gold body, white interior, black plastic tires ($75-100)
2. gold body, red interior, black plastic tires ($60-75)

K-21-B COUGAR DRAGSTER, issued 1971
1. light pink body, "Dinamite" labels ($15-20)
2. dark pink body, "Dinamite" labels ($15-20)
3. purple body, "Dinamite" labels ($15-20)
4. burgundy body, "Dinamite" labels ($15-20)
5. purple body, "Bender" labels ($18-25)

K-21-C TRACTOR TRANSPORTER, issued 1974
1. blue body, yellow interior, amber windows, silver-gray base, yellow ramp, (2) MB25-B Mod Tractors ($20-25)

K-21-D FORD TRANSCONTINENTAL, issued 1979
1. blue cab, white chassis, white tarp, clear dome lights, maltese cross wheels, "Santa Fe" livery ($25-35)
2. blue cab, white chassis, white tarp, amber dome lights, maltese cross wheels, "Santa Fe" livery ($25-35)
3. blue cab, white chassis, white tarp, blue dome lights, maltese cross wheels, "Santa Fe" livery ($25-35)

4. yellow cab, yellow chassis, green tarp, amber dome lights, maltese cross wheels, "Continental" livery ($25-35)
5. yellow cab, yellow chassis, green tarp, amber dome lights, mag wheels, "Continental" livery ($25-35)
6. yellow cab, yellow chassis, green tarp, blue dome lights, mag wheels, "Continental" livery ($25-35)
7. yellow cab, white chassis, blue bed, green tarp, blue dome lights, mag wheels, "Continental" livery ($35-50)
8. green cab, white chassis, white tarp, blue dome lights, mag wheels, "Nichts geht uber Barenmarke" livery ($45-60)(GR)
9. yellow cab, blue chassis, blue tarp, amber dome lights, mag wheels, "Danzas" livery ($45-60)(FR)
10. green cab, white chassis, white tarp, amber dome lights, mag wheels, "Polara" livery ($45-60)(GR)
11. yellow cab, white chassis, yellow tarp, blue dome lights, mag wheels, "Weetabix" livery ($45-60)(UK)
12. blue cab, white chassis, solid orange canopy, white roof mount, mag wheels, "Sunkist" livery ($35-50)

K-22-A DODGE CHARGER, issued 1969
1. dark blue body, pale blue interior, black plastic tires ($60-75)

K-22-B DODGE DRAGSTER, issued 1971
1. pinkish-orange body, "Bender" labels ($15-20)
2. orange body, "Bender" labels ($15-20)
3. light orange body, "Bender" labels ($15-20)
4. orange body, "Dinamite" labels ($18-25)

K-22-C SRN6 HOVERCRAFT, issued 1974
1. blue deck, white hull, white window section, "SRN6" & "Seaspeed" labels ($12-15)
2. white deck, black hull, red window section, "Calais-Ramsgate" & Hoverlloyd" labels ($12-15)
3. white deck, black hull, red window section, "SRN6" & "Seaspeed" labels ($12-15)
4. white deck, white hull, white window section, "SRN6" & "Seaspeed" labels ($50-75)

K-23-A MERCURY POLICE COMMUTER, issued 1969
1. white body, black plastic tires ($40-60)
2. white body, Superfast wheels ($20-30)

K-23-B LOWLOADER & BULLDOZER, issued 1974
1. metallic blue cab, silver-gray base, yellow interior, gold trailer, red bulldozer with yellow base & blade ($18-25)
2. dark blue cab, red base, black interior, pale blue trailer, dark blue bulldozer with red base & blade, "Hoch & Tief" labels ($45-60)(GR)
3. yellow cab, silver-gray base, black interior, orange trailer, yellow bulldozer with silver-gray base & blade ($18-25)
4. red cab, silver-gray base, yellow interior, gold trailer, red bulldozer with yellow base & blade ($18-25)
5. orange cab, silver-gray base, black interior, orange trailer, yellow bulldozer with silver-gray base & blade ($18-25)

K-24-A LAMBORGHINI MIURA, issued 1969
1. red body & trunk, clear windows, unpainted base, no hood label, silver plastic wheels , black plastic tires, no tow hook ($40-55)
2. red body & trunk, clear windows, unpainted base, no hood label, silver plastic mag wheels, black plastic tires, no tow hook ($40-55)
3. bronze body & trunk, clear windows, unpainted base, no hood label, spiro wheels, no tow hook ($12-15)
4. bronze body & trunk, clear windows, unpainted base, no hood label, spiro wheels, with tow hook ($12-15)
5. bronze body & trunk, amber windows, unpainted base, no hood label, 5 spoke wheels, with tow hook ($12-15)
6. burgundy body & trunk, clear windows, unpainted base, with hood label, spiro wheels, with tow hook ($12-15)
7. burgundy body & trunk, amber windows, unpainted base, with hood label, spiro wheels, with tow hook ($12-15)
8. burgundy body & trunk, clear windows, yellow base, with hood label, spiro wheels, with tow hook ($12-15)
9. burgundy body & trunk, clear windows, yellow base, no hood label, spiro wheels, with tow hook ($12-15)
10. blue body, yellow trunk, amber windows, unpainted base, with hood label, spiro wheels, with tow hook ($12-15)
11. blue body, yellow trunk, clear windows, yellow base, with hood label, spiro wheels, with tow hook ($12-15)
12. blue body, yellow trunk, amber windows, yellow base, with hood label, spiro wheels, with tow hook ($12-15)
13. blue body, yellow trunk, clear windows, yellow base, with hood label, 5 spoke wheels, with tow hook ($12-15)
14. blue body, yellow trunk, amber windows, yellow base, with hood label, 5 spoke wheels, with tow hook ($12-15)
15. blue body, yellow trunk, amber windows, unpainted base, with hood label, 5 spoke wheels, with tow hook ($12-15)
16. blue body, yellow trunk, clear windows, silver-gray base, with hood label, 5 spoke wheels, with tow hook ($12-15)

K-24-B SCAMMELL CONTAINER TRUCK, issued 1976
1. red body, white container, red roof, "Crowe" labels ($12-15)
2. red body, white container, orange roof, "Crowe" labels ($12-15)
3. red body, orange container, red roof, "Michelin" labels ($15-18)
4. red body, white container, red roof, "Bauknecht Komplettkuchen" labels ($25-40)(GR)
5. red body, white container, red roof, "Gentransco" labels ($15-18)
6. red body, white container, blue roof, "Gentransco" labels ($15-18)

K-25-A POWERBOAT & TRAILER, issued 1971
NOTE: All models with white hull and yellow trailer.
1. orange deck, white prop, "Seaburst" boat labels, "Super 70" outboard labels ($12-15)
2. orange deck, red prop, "Seaburst" boat labels, "Super 70" outboard labels ($12-15)
3. red deck, red prop, "Chrysler" boat labels, "Super 70" outboard labels ($12-15)
4. orange deck, red prop, "Chrysler" boat & outboard labels ($12-15)
5. orange deck, red prop, "Seaburst" boat labels, "Chrysler" outboard labels ($12-15)
6. orange deck, blue prop, "Chrysler" boat & outboard labels ($12-15)

K-25-B DIGGER AND PLOW, issued 1977
1. red body, base & plow, amber windows, silver-gray backhoe & scoop, red wheels, England casting ($25-30)
2. orange body, base & plow, amber windows, silver-gray backhoe & scoop, red wheels, England casting ($18-25)
3. yellow body & base, red plow, amber windows, yellow backhoe, red scoop, red wheels, England casting ($15-20)
4. yellow body, base & plow, amber windows, yellow backhoe & scoop, yellow wheels, no origin cast ($15-20)
5. yellow body & base, red plow, amber windows, yellow backhoe, red scoop, red wheels, China casting ($15-20)
6. green body, yellow base, no plow, amber windows, silver-gray backhoe, green scoop, yellow wheels, China casting ($15-20)(FM)

K-26-A MERCEDES BENZ "BINZ" AMBULANCE, issued 1971
1. white body, white interior, blue windows ($12-15)

K-26-B CEMENT TRUCK, issued 1978
1. yellow body, black base, gray barrel with red stripes, clear windows, "McAlpine" labels ($12-15)
2. yellow body, black base, gray barrel with black stripes, clear windows, "McAlpine" labels ($12-15)
3. blue body, red base, light blue barrel with red stripes, clear windows, "Hoch & Tief" labels ($30-45)(GR)
4. yellow body, red base, gray barrel with red stripes, clear windows, "McAlpine" labels ($15-20)
5. yellow body, black base, gray barrel with black stripes, amber windows, "McAlpine" labels ($12-15)
6. red body, red base, gray barrel with red stripes, clear windows, "McAlpine" labels ($18-25)

K-27-A CAMPING CRUISER, issued 1971
1. yellow body, amber front & rear windows, orange roof, dots labels ($12-15)
2. yellow body, clear front & amber rear windows, orange roof, dots labels ($12-15)
3. yellow body, clear front & rear windows, orange roof, dots labels ($12-15)

K-27-B BOAT TRANSPORTER, issued 1978
NOTE: All versions with white cab chassis & maltese cross wheels except "Miss Solo" versions with red cab chassis & mag wheels. All boats with white deck & hull.
1. white cab, amber windows, red trailer ramp, amber boat windshield, "Miss Embassy" labels ($15-20)
2. red cab, amber windows, red trailer ramp, amber boat windshield, "Miss Embassy" labels ($15-20)
3. red cab, clear windows, red trailer ramp, blue boat windshield, "Miss Embassy" labels ($15-20)
4. white cab, amber windows, orange trailer ramp, amber boat windshield, "Benihana" labels ($15-20)
5. red cab, amber windows, orange trailer ramp, amber boat windshield, "Benihana" labels ($15-18)
6. orange & white cab, amber windows, orange trailer ramp, amber boat windshield, "Benihana" labels ($15-20)
7. white cab, clear windows, orange trailer ramp, amber boat windshield, "Benihana" labels ($15-20)
8. orange cab, amber windows, orange trailer ramp, blue boat windshield, "Benihana" labels ($15-20)
9. orange cab, amber windows, orange trailer ramp, amber boat windshield, "Benihana" labels ($15-20)
10. red cab, amber windows, red trailer ramp, amber boat windshield, "Matchbox" labels ($15-20)
11. orange cab, amber windows, red trailer ramp, amber boat windshield, "Matchbox" labels ($15-20)
12. white cab, amber windows, black trailer ramp, amber boat windshield, "Miss Solo" labels ($15-20)
13. white cab with red roof, amber windows, black trailer ramp, amber boat windshield, "Miss Solo" labels ($15-20)

K-27-C FORD BOAT TRANSPORTER, issued 1983
1. white cab, clear windows, black trailer ramp, amber boat windshield, red & blue stripes with "506" labels ($25-35)

K-28-A DRAG PACK, issued 1971
1. lime green Mercury, light pink Dragster, yellow trailer with yellow platform ($20-30)
2. metallic green Mercury, light pink Dragster, yellow trailer with yellow platform ($20-30)
3. lime green Mercury, purple Dragster, yellow trailer with yellow platform ($20-30)
4. metallic green Mercury, purple Dragster, yellow trailer with orange-yellow platform ($20-30)
5. metallic green Mercury, purple Dragster, yellow trailer with yellow platform ($20-30)
6. dark lime Mercury, dark pink Dragster, yellow trailer with orange-yellow platform ($20-30)

K-28-B SKIP TRUCK, issued 1978
1. orange cab, orange-yellow containers, black base, "Hales" labels ($12-15)
2. red cab, yellow containers, black base, "Hales" labels ($12-15)
3. blue & red cab, light blue containers, "Hoch & Tief" labels ($30-45)(GR)

K-29-A MIURA SEABURST SET, issued 1971
NOTE: Different versions of the K-24-A Miuras & K-25-A Powerboat can make up endless permutations.
1. K-24-A Miura in bronze & K-25-A Powerboat with orange deck ($25-35)
2. K-24-A Miura in burgundy & K-25-A Powerboat with orange deck ($25-35)
3. K-24-A Miura in blue & yellow & K-25-A Powerboat with red deck ($25-35)

K-29-B FORD DELIVERY VAN, issued 1978
1. orange & white cab, white chassis, gray container, "U-Haul" labels ($15-18)
2. orange cab, white chassis, gray container, "U-Haul" labels ($20-25)
3. red cab, white chassis, red container, "Avis" labels ($15-18)
4. white cab, white chassis, red container, "Avis" labels ($35-50)
5. white cab, dark green chassis, lime container, "Mr. Softy" labels ($30-45)(GR)
6. white cab, white chassis, lime container, "Mr. Softy" labels ($25-35)
7. turquoise cab & chassis, turquoise container, "75 Express" labels ($30-45)(FR)
8. blue cab, white chassis, white container with blue roof, "Elefanten Junge Mode" labels ($30-45)(GR)
9. blue cab, white chassis, white container with blue roof, "Jelly Babies" labels ($25-40)(UK)
10. blue cab, white chassis, white container with blue roof, "TAA" labels ($25-40)(UK)

K-30-A MERCEDES C.111, issued 1972
1. gold body, red base, purple windows, black headlight covers, no label, battery compartment ($100-150)(GR)
2. gold body, red base, purple windows, black headlight covers, no label ($12-15)
3. lime body, gold base, amber windows, gold headlight covers, no label ($10-15)
4. lime body, gold base, amber windows, black headlight covers, no label ($10-15)
5. lime body, gold base, purple windows, gold headlight covers, no label ($10-15)
6. lime body, gold base, clear windows, black headlight covers, no label ($10-15)
7. lime body, orange base, amber windows, black headlight covers, no label ($10-15)
8. dark lime body, gold base, amber windows, black headlight covers, no label ($10-15)
9. blue body, white base, amber windows, black headlight covers, "3" label ($10-15)
NOTE: Available as a Bulgarian casting. Assorted colors available ($30-50)

K-30-B UNIMOG & COMPRESSOR, issued 1978
1. beige body, with brown base, brown compressor ($15-18)
2. gray body with brown base, brown compressor ($25-40)

K-31-A BERTONE RUNABOUT, issued 1971
1. orange body, lime base, green windows, serpent labels ($12-15)
2. orange body, lime base, clear windows, serpent labels ($15-18)

K-31-B PETERBILT REFRIGERATOR TRUCK, issued 1978
1. white cab, blue chassis, white container with white roof, "Iglo Langnese" labels ($50-75)
2. white cab, black chassis, white container with white roof, "Iglo Langnese" labels ($50-75)
3. white cab, blue chassis, white container with white roof, "Christian Salvesen" labels ($50-75)
4. red cab & chassis with white hood, roof & sleeper, red container with white roof, "Coca Cola" labels ($45-60)
5. red cab & chassis with white roof & sleeper, red container with white roof, "Coca Cola" labels ($45-60)
6. red cab & chassis with white sleeper, red container with white roof, "Coca Cola" labels ($45-60)
7. red cab & chassis, red container with white roof, "Coca Cola" labels ($45-60)
8. white cab, black chassis, white container with white roof, "Glaces Gervais" labels ($85-110)(FR)
9. white cab, blue chassis, white container with blue roof, "Pepsi Cola" labels ($45-60)
10. white cab, black chassis, white container with white roof, "Burger King" labels ($50-75)
11. white cab, blue chassis, white container with white roof, "Trink 10" labels ($50-75)(GR)
12. white cab, red chassis, white container with white roof, "Trink 10" labels ($50-75)(GR)
13. white cab, blue chassis, white container with white roof, "Acorn Duro-Penta" labels ($500-750)(SA)
14. powder blue cab, blue chassis, powder blue container & roof, "Euro-

Express" labels ($35-50)
15. white cab, blue chassis, white container with blue roof, "Pepsi Cola" labels, mag wheels ($45-60)

K-32-A SHOVEL NOSE, issued 1972
1. yellow body, black base, black interior, clear windows, "2" labels ($12-15)
2. yellow body, black base, black interior, clear windows, "4" label ($12-15)
3. yellow body, black base, black interior, amber windows, "2" label ($12-15)
4. yellow body, black base, black interior, amber windows, "4" label ($12-15)
5. yellow body, yellow base, yellow interior, clear windows, "4" label ($18-25)

K-32-B FARM UNIMOG & TRAILER, issued 1978
1. gray body with brown base, brown plastic insert in cab bed, gray trailer ($15-18)
2. gray body with brown base, yellow plastic insert in cab bed, gray trailer ($15-18)

K-33-A CITROEN S.M., issued 1972
1. magenta body, silver-gray base, green windows, with tow hook ($12-15)
2. magenta body, silver-gray base, green windows, no tow hook ($12-15)

K-33-B CARGO HAULER, issued 1979
1. blue cab, white chassis, white trailer, white center post with black crane, "US Steel" livery ($18-25)
2. yellow cab, silver-gray chassis, yellow trailer, red center post with beige crane, "K" livery ($18-25)
3. yellow cab, silver-gray chassis, yellow trailer, red center post with beige crane, "MW" livery ($18-25)
4. yellow cab, silver-gray chassis, yellow trailer, red center post with black crane, "MW" livery ($18-25)
5. yellow cab, silver-gray chassis, yellow trailer, white center post with beige crane, "MW" livery ($18-25)
6. yellow cab, white chassis, orange trailer, white center post with yellow crane, "Gauntlet" livery ($25-40)
7. blue cab, white chassis, orange trailer, white center post with black crane, "Gauntlet" livery ($18-25)

K-34-A THUNDERCLAP, issued 1972
1. yellow body, "Matchbox 34" labels with yellow background ($12-15)
2. yellow body, "Matchbox 34" labels with white background ($12-15)
3. black body, "Matchbox 1" labels ($12-15)

K-34-B PALLET LOADER & FORKLIFT, issued 1979
1. white cab, dark blue chassis, blue tarp, "K" livery; MB15-B Forklift with long red forks ($35-50)
2. white body, dark blue chassis, blue tarp, "MW" livery; MB15-B Forklift with long red forks ($35-50)
3. white body, red chassis, white tarp, "KM International" livery; MB15-B Forklift with long red forks ($35-50)

K-35-A LIGHTNING, issued 1972
1. red body, "Flame Out" labels ($175-225)(UK)
2. red body, "35 Team Matchbox" hood label, "Firestone" spoiler label, irregular "35" side labels ($12-15)
3. white body, "35 Team Matchbox" hood label, "Firestone" spoiler label, irregular "35" side labels ($12-15)
4. white body, "35 Team Matchbox" hood label, "Texaco" spoiler label, irregular "35" side labels ($12-15)
5. white body, "35 STP Champion" hood label, "Texaco" spoiler label, rectangular "35" side labels ($12-15)

K-35-B MASSEY FERGUSON TRACTOR & TRAILER, issued 1979
1. red tractor with silver-gray base, white canopy; red trailer with silver-gray base, England casting ($15-20)
2. red tractor with silver-gray base, white canopy; red trailer with silver-gray base, Macau casting ($12-15)(Early Learning Centre)
3. red tractor with silver-gray base, white canopy; red trailer with silver-gray base, China casting ($12-15)(FM)

K-36-A BANDALERO, issued 1972
1. blue body, red base, white interior, amber windows ($12-15)
2. blue body, red base, white interior, clear windows ($12-15)
3. blue body, red base, yellow interior, clear windows ($12-15)
4. blue body, red base, yellow interior, amber windows ($12-15)
5. blue body, black base, yellow interior, amber windows ($12-15)
6. blue body, black base, white interior, amber windows ($12-15)

K-36-B CONSTRUCTION TRANSPORTER, issued 1978
1. dark yellow body, black plastic ramp & supports; MB26-C Site Dumper & MB29-C Tractor Shovel ($18-25)
2. dark yellow body, yellow plastic ramp & supports; MB26-C Site Dumper & MB29-C Tractor Shovel ($18-25)
3. dark yellow body, black plastic ramp & supports; MB26-C Site Dumper & MB48-C Sambron ($18-25)
4. dark yellow body, black plastic ramp & supports; Superking Lime Mercury ($25-30)

K-37-A SAND CAT, issued 1973
1. orange body with green spatter, orange base, black roof & interior, hood ornament with label ($12-15)
2. red body, green base, black roof, gray interior, "3" label ($12-15)(K-2-D)
3. red body, green base, gray roof & interior, "3" label ($12-15)(K-2-D)
4. red body, green base, gray roof, black interior, "3" label ($12-15)(K-2-D)
5. red body, orange base, gray roof & interior, "3" label ($12-15)(K-2-D)
6. gold plated body, orange base, black roof & interior, stripes label, mounted to ashtray ($50-75)(GW)

K-37-B LEYLAND TIPPER, issued 1979
1. yellow cab & chassis, red tipper, silver-gray base, "Laing" labels ($12-15)

K-38-A GUS'S GULPER, issued 1973
1. pink body, yellow interior, yellow rollbar ($12-15)
2. pink body, orange interior, orange rollbar ($12-15)
3. dark pink body, light yellow interior, light yellow rollbar ($12-15)
4. white body, yellow interior, yellow rollbar ($150-200)

K-38-B DODGE AMBULANCE, issued 1980
1. white body, orange painted hood & side stripe, reversed "Ambulance" hood label, blue & white medical cross on sides ($15-18)
2. white body, orange side stripe, reversed "Ambulance" hood label, "Ambulance" side labels ($15-18)
3. white body, "Notarzt" hood & side labels ($35-45)(GR)

K-39-A MILLIGAN'S MILL, issued 1973
1. light green body, orange interior & rollbar, clear windows, flames roof label, red "Firestone" rear label ($12-15)
2. dark green body, orange interior & rollbar, clear windows, flames roof label, red "Firestone" rear label ($12-15)
3. dark green body, yellow interior, orange rollbar, clear windows, flames roof label, red "Firestone" rear label ($12-15)
4. dark green body, yellow interior & rollbar, clear windows, flames roof label, red "Firestone" rear label ($12-15)
5. dark green body, orange interior & rollbar, clear windows, stars & stripes roof label, blue "Firestone" rear label ($15-18)
6. dark green body, orange interior & rollbar, blue windows, flames roof label, red "Firestone" rear label ($12-15)

K-39-B SNORKEL FIRE ENGINE, issued 1980
1. red body & base, silver painted roof & rear, black interior, amber windows & dome lights, red background "County Fire Department" labels, England casting ($18-25)
2. red body & base, plain roof & rear, black interior, blue windows & dome lights, clear background "County Fire Department" labels, Macau casting ($18-25)

K-40-A BLAZE TRAILER, issued 1973
1. red body, yellow base, orange interior, amber windows, orange antennae, blue dome lights ($12-15)
2. red body, yellow base, yellow interior, clear windows, yellow antennae, blue dome lights ($12-15)
3. red body, yellow base, orange interior, clear windows, orange antennae, blue dome lights ($12-15)
4. red body, black base, yellow interior, clear windows, yellow antennae, blue dome lights ($12-15)
5. red body, yellow base, yellow interior, clear windows, black antennae, blue dome lights ($12-15)
6. red body, yellow base, yellow interior, amber windows, black antennae, blue dome lights ($12-15)
7. red body, yellow base, yellow interior, clear windows, black antennae, amber dome lights ($12-15)

K-40-B DELIVERY TRUCK, issued 1980
1. white body with red roof, red chassis, blue container roof, "Pepsi Cola" livery ($15-20)
2. white body with blue roof, blue chassis, blue container roof, "Pepsi Cola" livery ($15-20)
3. white body, blue chassis, white container roof, "Frohliches Durstloschen" livery ($35-50)(GR)

K-41-A FUZZ BUGGY, issued 1973
1. white body, black base, amber windows, yellow interior, blue dome lights, black steering wheel ($12-15)
2. white body, black base, amber windows, yellow interior, amber dome lights, yellow steering wheel ($12-15)
3. white body, black base, amber windows, yellow-orange interior, amber dome lights, white steering wheel ($12-15)
4. white body, black base, clear windows, white interior, amber dome lights, white steering wheel ($12-15)
5. white body, black base, clear windows, yellow interior, blue dome lights, white steering wheel ($12-15)
6. white body, black base, clear windows, white interior, blue dome lights, white steering wheel ($12-15)
7. white body, black base, amber windows, yellow interior, amber dome lights, white steering wheel ($12-15)
8. white body, black base, clear windows, yellow interior, amber dome lights, white steering wheel ($12-15)
9. white body, red base, amber windows, yellow interior, amber dome lights, white steering wheel ($15-20)
10. white body, red base, clear windows, yellow interior, amber dome lights, white steering wheel ($15-20)

K-41-B BRABHAM BT 44B, issued 1977
1. red body, base & spoiler, "Martini-Brabham 7" tempa with "Goodyear" on front airfoils ($12-15)
2. red body, base & airfoil, "Martini-Brabham 7" tempa without "Goodyear" on front airfoils ($12-15)

K-41-C JCB EXCAVATOR, issued 1981
1. yellow body, base & excavator arm, red scoop, "808" & "JCB" labels ($25-40)

K-42-A NISSAN 270ZX, issued 1973
1. orange body, green base, yellow interior, green windows, "8" labels ($12-15)
2. orange body, green base, yellow interior, clear windows, "8" labels ($12-15)

K-42-B TRAXCAVATOR ROAD RIPPER, issued 1979
1. yellow body, base & shovel, red metal ripper, black plastic roof, England casting ($15-20)
2. yellow body & base, yellow plastic shovel & rear ripper, black plastic roof, England casting ($12-15)(K-117-A)
3. yellow body & base, red plastic shovel & ripper, red plastic roof, China casting ($12-15)(CS)

K-43-A CAMBUSTER, issued 1973
1. yellow body, black base, green windows ($12-15)
2. yellow body, black base, clear windows ($12-15)
3. yellow body, black base, amber windows ($12-15)
4. yellow body, yellow base, green windows ($12-15)
5. yellow body, yellow base, amber windows ($12-15)

K-43-B LOG TRANSPORTER, issued 1981
1. yellow body, red chassis, orange boom, three brown plastic logs, England casting ($18-25)
2. yellow body, red chassis, red boom, three gray plastic pipes, China casting ($15-18)(CS)

K-44-A BAZOOKA, issued 1973
1. red body, yellow base, amber windows, "Bazooka" side labels ($12-15)
2. red body, yellow base, amber windows, "Firestone" side labels ($15-18)
3. red body, black base, amber windows, "Bazooka" side labels ($12-15)
4. red body, black base, green windows, "Bazooka" side labels ($12-15)
5. red body, yellow base, green windows, "Bazooka" side labels ($12-15)
6. red body, black base, amber windows, "Firestone" side labels ($15-18)

K-44-B SURTEES FORMULA 1, issued 1977
1. white body & base, red airfoil, "Chesterfield 18" labels ($12-15)

K-44-C BRIDGE LAYER, issued 1981
1. beige cab with brown chassis, beige trailer with brown arm, red plastic bridge ($90-125)
2. beige cab with brown chassis, beige trailer with brown arm, orange plastic bridge ($90-125)
3. beige cab with brown chassis, beige trailer with brown arm, yellow plastic bridge ($90125)

K-45-A MARAUDER, issued 1973
1. burgundy body, green base, clear windshield, orange interior & airfoil, white driver, "7" labels ($12-15)
2. burgundy body, green base, clear windshield, yellow interior & airfoil, white driver, "7" labels ($12-15)
3. burgundy body, green base, clear windshield, yellow interior, orange airfoil, white driver, "7" labels ($12-15)
4. burgundy body, green base, clear windshield, orange interior, yellow airfoil, white driver, "7" labels ($12-15)
5. burgundy body, green base, clear windshield, yellow interior & airfoil, tan driver, "7" labels ($12-15)
6. burgundy body, green base, amber windshield, yellow interior & airfoil, white driver, "7" labels ($12-15)
7. red body, black base, clear windshield, yellow interior & airfoil, white driver, "Cibie" labels ($12-15)

K-46-A RACING CAR PACK, issued 1973
1. yellow Mercury with red roof rack; K-34-A1 in yellow; yellow trailer with blue platform ($25-40)
2. yellow Mercury with red roof rack; K-34-A2 in yellow; yellow trailer with blue platform ($25-40)
3. yellow Mercury with red roof rack; K-34-A3 in black; yellow trailer with blue platform ($25-40)
4. yellow Mercury with red roof rack; K-35-A5 in white; yellow trailer with blue platform ($25-40)
5. yellow Mercury with red roof rack; K-35-A4 in white, yellow trailer with blue platform ($25-40)
6. yellow Mercury with red roof rack; K-35-A2 in red; yellow trailer with blue platform ($25-40)
7. yellow Mercury with red roof rack; K-35-A4 in white; yellow trailer with black platform ($25-40)
8. yellow Mercury with maroon roof rack; K-35-A5 in white; yellow trailer with blue platform ($25-40)
9. lime Mercury with red roof rack; K-34-A1 in yellow; yellow trailer with blue platform ($25-40)

K-47-A EASY RIDER, issued 1973
1. blue body & seat, tannish brown rider, flames label ($12-15)
2. blue body & seat, orange rider, flames label ($12-15)
3. blue body & seat, white rider, flames label ($50-75)

K-48-A MERCEDES 350 SLC, issued 1973
1. bronze body, silver-gray base, yellow interior, clear windows ($12-15)
2. bronze body, silver-gray base, yellow interior, amber windows ($12-15)
3. silver-gray body with black roof, silver-gray base, yellow interior, clear windows ($12-15)(K-2-D)

K-49-A AMBULANCE, issued 1973

1. white body, red roof, red interior, black base, clear windows, blue dome light, "Ambulance" labels ($12-15)
2. white body, red roof, red interior, black base, amber windows, blue dome light, "Ambulance" labels ($12-15)
3. white body, red roof, white interior, black base, clear windows, blue dome light, "Ambulance" labels ($12-15)
4. red body, cream roof, white interior, cream base, pale blue windows, blue dome light, "Malteser" labels ($25-40)(GR)
5. red body, cream roof, white interior, cream base, dark blue windows, clear dome light, "Malteser" labels ($25-40)(GR)

K-50-A STREET ROD, issued 1973
1. lime body, light green fenders, "Hot T" labels ($12-15)
2. lime body, dark green fenders, "Hot T" labels ($12-15)
3. dark green body & fenders, "Hot T" labels ($12-15)
4. orange body, gold plated fenders, no labels, mounted to pen stand ($50-75)(GW)

K-51-A BARRACUDA, issued 1973
1. blue body, yellow interior, orange airfoil, clear windshield, white driver, "5" labels ($12-15)
2. blue body, yellow interior & airfoil, clear windshield, white driver, "5" labels ($12-15)
3. blue body, orange interior, yellow airfoil, clear windshield, white driver, "5" labels ($12-15)
4. blue body, yellow interior, lemon airfoil, clear windshield, white driver, "5" labels ($12-15)
5. dark blue body, yellow interior & airfoil, clear windshield, white driver, "5" labels ($12-15)
6. dark blue body, yellow interior & airfoil, amber windshield, white driver, "5" labels ($12-15)
7. dark blue driver, yellow interior & airfoil, amber windshield, white driver with red helmet, "5" labels ($12-15)
8. white body, white interior, yellow airfoil, amber windshield, white driver with red helmet, "14" labels ($15-18)
9. white body, yellow interior & airfoil, amber windshield, white driver, "14" labels ($15-18)
10. white body, yellow interior, white airfoil, amber windshield, white driver with red helmet, "14" labels ($15-18)(KP)

K-52-A DATSUN 260Z, issued 1974
1. yellow body, red hood, "52" labels with red background ($12-15)
2. silver-gray body, red hood, "52" labels with red background ($12-15)
3. silver-gray body, red hood, "52" labels with black background ($12-15)
4. silver-gray body, black hood, "52" labels with red background ($12-15)
5. silver-gray body, black hood, "52" labels with black background ($12-15)
6. green body, white hood, "Cibie" labels ($12-15)(from K-76-A)
NOTE: Available as a Bulgarian casting. Assorted colors available ($30-50)

K-53-A HOT FIRE ENGINE, issued 1976
1. red body & chassis, black riders with gold helmets ($12-15)
2. red body & chassis, black riders with white helmets ($12-15)
3. red body & chassis, blue riders with white helmets ($12-15)
4. red body & chassis, blue riders with unpainted helmets ($12-15)

K-54-A AMX JAVELIN, issued 1976
1. burgundy body, green windows, "7" labels on roof, hood & sides ($12-15)
2. red body, dark green windows, "24" labels on sides only ($12-15)
3. red body, clear windows, "24" labels on roof & sides with stripes hood label ($12-15)
4. black body, clear windows, no labels ($15-20)(KP)

K-55-A CORVETTE CAPER CART, issued 1976
1. dark blue body, yellow interior, "55" labels ($12-15)
2. dark blue body, orange-yellow interior, "55" labels ($12-15)
3. bronze body with black roof, yellow interior, no labels ($12-15)
4. bronze body with black roof, orange-yellow interior, no labels ($12-15)
5. light blue body, white interior, no labels ($15-20)(KP)

K-56-A MASERATI BORA, issued 1976
1. silver-gray body, red base, yellow interior, clear windows, with labels on sides ($12-15)
2. silver-gray body, red base, orange interior, clear windows, with labels on sides ($12-15)
3. silver-gray body, red base, orange interior, amber windows, with labels on sides ($12-15)
4. silver-gray body, red base, yellow interior, amber windows, with labels on sides ($12-15)
5. gold body, gold base, orange interior, clear windows, no labels ($60-85)
6. red body, silver-gray base, yellow interior, clear windows, no labels ($15-20)(KP)
7. red body, silver-gray base, yellow interior, clear windows, "7" hood decal ($15-20)
NOTE: Available as a Bulgarian casting. Assorted colors available ($30-50)

K-57-A JAVELIN DRAG RACE PACK, issued 1976
1. K-54-A1 Javelin in burgundy; K-39-A2 Milligan's Mill with yellow trailer ($25-35)
2. K-54-A2 Javelin in red; K-39-A3 Milligan's Mill with yellow trailer ($25-35)
3. K-54-A2 Javelin in red; K-39-A4 Milligan's Mill with yellow trailer ($25-35)
4. K-54-A3 Javelin in red; K-39-A3 Milligan's Mill with yellow trailer ($25-35)
5. K-54-A1 Javelin in burgundy; K-38-A1 Gus's Gulper with yellow trailer ($25-35)

K-58-A CORVETTE POWERBOAT SET, issued 1976
1. K-55-A1 Corvette in dark blue; K-25-A3 Powerboat with red deck ($25-35)
2. K-55-A2 Corvette in dark blue; K-25-A3 Powerboat with red deck ($25-35)
3. K-55-A1 Corvette in dark blue; K-25-A4 Powerboat with orange deck ($25-35)
4. K-55-A1 Corvette in dark blue; K-25-A5 Powerboat with orange deck ($25-35)
5. K-55-A3 Corvette in bronze; K-25-A4 Powerboat with orange deck ($25-35)

K-59-A FORD CAPRI II, issued 1976
1. white body, red interior, "Capri II" labels ($15-18)
2. white body with black roof, red interior, "Capri II" labels ($12-15)
3. beige body with black roof, red interior, "Capri II" labels ($12-15)
4. beige body with brown roof, red interior, "Capri II" labels ($12-15)
5. beige body, red interior, no labels ($12-15)
6. metallic silver body, red interior, no labels ($15-20)(KP)
NOTE: Available as a Bulgarian casting. Assorted colors available ($30-50)

K-60-A FORD MUSTANG II, issued 1976
1. blue body, white interior, green windows, "20" labels ($12-15)

K-60-B COBRA MUSTANG, issued 1978
1. white body, white interior, green windows, "Cobra" tempa ($12-15)
2. red body, white interior, green windows, "207 Cobra" tempa ($20-25)(K-2-D)
3. metallic red body, white interior, clear windows, "207 Cobra" tempa ($20-25)(K-2-D)

K-61-A MERCEDES POLICE CAR, issued 1976
1. white body, hood & doors, yellow interior, amber windows, "Police" labels, 5 spoke wheels ($12-15)
2. white body, hood & doors, yellow interior, amber windows, "Polizei" labels, 5 spoke wheels ($12-15)
3. white body, green hood & doors, yellow interior, amber windows, "Polizei" labels, 5 spoke wheels ($35-45)(GR)
4. white body, hood & doors, yellow interior, amber windows, "Police" labels, 5 arch wheels ($12-15)
5. white body, green hood & doors, yellow interior, amber windows, "Polizei" labels, 5 arch wheels ($35-45)(GR)

K-62-A DOCTOR'S EMERGENCY CAR, issued 1977
1. white body, silver-gray base, amber windows & dome light, "Doctor" labels ($12-15)
2. white body, red base, amber windows & dome light, "Doctor" labels ($12-15)
NOTE: Available as a Bulgarian casting. Assorted colors available ($30-50)

K-63-A MERCEDES BENZ "BINZ" AMBULANCE, issued 1977
NOTE: This is essentially the same model as K-26-A, but "K-63" is cast on the base.
1. white body & interior, dark blue windows ($12-15)
2. white body & interior, light blue windows ($12-15)

K-64-A RANGE ROVER FIRE ENGINE, issued 1978
1. red body, amber dome light, yellow ladder, black firemen with gold helmets, "Fire Control" labels ($12-15)
2. red body, amber dome light, yellow ladder, black firemen with white helmets, "Fire Control" labels ($12-15)
3. red body, amber dome light, yellow ladder, black firemen with gold helmets, "Falck-Zonen" labels ($45-60)(SW)
4. red body, amber dome light, yellow ladder, blue firemen, "Fire Control" labels ($12-15)

K-65-A PLYMOUTH TRAIL DUSTER, issued 1979
1. red body, white base, amber windows, "Emergency Rescue" labels ($12-15)
2. green body, white base, amber windows, "Bergrettungswacht" labels ($40-50)(GR)

K-66-A JAGUAR XJ12 POLICE PATROL, issued 1979
1. white body, brown interior, light blue dome lights, maltese cross wheels, single blue stripe tempa, amber windows ($15-20)
2. white body, brown interior, light blue dome lights, maltese cross wheels, two blue stripes with central orange stripe tempa, amber windows ($15-20)
3. white body, brown interior, clear dome lights, maltese cross wheels, two blue stripes with central orange stripe tempa, amber windows ($15-20)
4. white body, brown interior, dark blue dome lights, maltese cross wheels, two blue stripes with central orange stripe tempa, amber windows ($15-20)
5. white body, black interior, dark blue dome lights, maltese cross wheels, two blue stripes with central orange stripe tempa, amber windows ($15-20)
6. white body, brown interior, dark blue dome lights, maltese cross wheels, two blue stripes without central orange stripe tempa, amber windows ($15-20)
7. white body, brown interior, dark blue dome lights, maltese cross wheels, solid blue stripe tempa, amber windows ($15-20)
8. white body, brown interior, dark blue dome lights, maltese cross wheels, "County Police" with checkered design tempa, amber windows ($15-20)
9. white body, brown interior, dark blue dome lights, mag wheels, "County Police" with checkered design tempa, amber windows ($15-20)
10. white body, ivory interior, dark blue dome lights, mag wheels, "County Police" with checkered design tempa, amber windows ($15-20)
11. white body, ivory interior, dark blue dome lights, mag wheels, "County Police" with checkered design tempa, clear windows ($15-20)
NOTE: Model issued with two MB33-C Police Motorcycles which include permutations to this list of variations. Available as a Bulgarian casting in a sedan version in assorted colors ($30-50).

K-67-A DODGE MONACO FIRE CHIEF CAR, issued 1978
1. yellow body, black base, white roof, red interior, amber windows, red dome lights, "Hackensack" tempa ($15-20)(US)
2. red body & base, white roof, yellow interior, amber windows, blue dome lights, "Fire Chief" tempa ($15-18)
3. red body & base, red roof, yellow interior, amber windows, blue dome lights, "Fire Chief" tempa ($15-18)

K-68-A DODGE MONACO & TRAILER, issued 1979
1. beige body & base, dark brown roof, red interior; beige canopy on beige trailer ($15-18)
2. beige body & base, dark brown roof red interior; black canopy on beige trailer ($15-18)

K-69-A SEDAN & EUROPA CARAVAN, issued 1980
1. Jaguar with blue body & base, brown interior, clear windows, maltese cross wheels; Caravan with white body, beige base, beige gas cover, 5 arch wheels ($25-35)
2. Jaguar with blue body & base, brown interior, clear windows, maltese cross wheels; Caravan with beige body, white base, white gas cover, 5 arch wheels ($25-35)
3. Jaguar with red body & base, ivory interior, clear windows, maltese cross wheels; Caravan with white body, beige base, white gas cover, 5 arch wheels ($25-35)
4. Jaguar with red body & base, ivory interior, clear windows, mag wheels; Caravan with white body, beige base, white gas cover, mag wheels ($25-35)
5. Jaguar with red body & base, ivory interior, clear windows, mag wheels; Caravan with white body, beige base, beige gas cover, mag wheels ($25-35)
6. Jaguar with red body & base, ivory interior, clear windows, mag wheels; Caravan with white body, beige base, unpainted gas cover, mag wheels ($25-35)
7. Jaguar with red body & base, ivory interior, clear windows, mag wheels; Caravan with white body, beige base, unpainted gas cover, 5 arch wheels ($25-35)
8. Jaguar with light brown body, brown base, white interior, amber windows, mag wheels; Caravan with white body, brown base, unpainted gas cover, 5 arch wheels ($25-35)
9. Volvo with red body, orange-yellow interior, clear windows, mag wheels; Caravan with white body, red base, unpainted gas cover, 5 arch wheels ($25-35)
10. Volvo with light brown body, orange-yellow interior, clear windows, mag wheels; Caravan with pale yellow body, light brown base, unpainted gas cover, 4 spoke wheels ($25-35)
NOTE: The K-66 Jaguar from this set is available as a Bulgarian casting. Assorted colors available ($30-50)

K-70-A PORSCHE TURBO, issued 1979
1. dark green body, lime base, black interior, clear windows, "Turbo" labels, England casting ($12-15)
2. lime body & base, black interior, clear windows, "Turbo" labels, England casting ($12-15)
3. black body & base, red interior, clear windows, black roof label & "Turbo" on sides tempa, England casting ($8-12)
4. black body & base, red interior, clear windows, "Turbo" on sides tempa, Macau casting ($8-12)
5. red body, black base, black interior, clear windows, no tempa, Macau casting ($8-12)
6. metallic red body, black base, cream interior, clear windows, "Turbo" tempa, Macau casting ($8-12)
7. red body, black base, red interior, clear windows, "Dragon Racing Team" tempa, Macau casting ($15-18)(HK)

K-71-A PORSCHE POLIZEI PATROL, issued 1980
1. white body, dark green doors, hood & trunk, white base cast 'K-70', blue dome light, clear windows, "Polizei" & "1705" labels, issued with two MB33-C Motorcycles ($60-75)(GR)

K-72-A BRABHAM BT44B, issued 1980
1. red body, base & spoiler, white driver, "Martini-Brabham 7" tempa, base cast 'K-72' ($12-15)
2. blue-green body, white base & spoiler, brown driver, no tempa, base cast 'K-72' ($15-20)(KP)
NOTE: Available as a Bulgarian casting. Assorted colors available ($30-50)

K-73-A SURTEES FORMULA 1, issued 1980
1. white body & base, red spoiler, white driver, "Chesterfield 18" labels, base cast 'K-73' ($15-20)
2. light tan body, black base & spoiler, brown driver, no labels, base cast 'K-73' ($15-20)(KP)

K-74-A VOLVO ESTATE, issued 1980
1. dark red body, black base, white interior, black roof label ($12-15)
2. dark red body, black base, white interior, no labels ($12-15)
3. blue body, black base, tan interior, no labels ($12-15)
4. metallic green body, black base, ivory interior, no labels ($12-15)
5. red body, black base, orange-yellow interior, no labels ($15-20)(K-69-A set)
6. light brown body, black base, orange-yellow interior, no labels ($15-20)(K-69-A set)

K-75-A AIRPORT FIRE TENDER, issued 1980
1. yellow body, red base, amber windows, "Airport Fire Tender" labels ($12-15)
2. yellow body, red base, amber windows, "Securite Aeroport" label ($50-75)(FR)
3. yellow body, red base, amber windows, "Flughafen-Feuerwehr" labels ($40-50)(GR)

K-76-A VOLVO RALLY SET, issued 1980
1. Volvo in white with tan roof rack; Datsun in green with "Cibie" labels ($25-35)
2. Volvo in white with brown roof rack; Datsun in green with "Cibie" labels ($25-35)

K-77-A HIGHWAY RESCUE VEHICLE, issued 1980
1. white body, orange base, amber windows, "Highway Rescue System" labels ($12-15)
2. white body, orange base, amber windows, "Secours Routier" labels ($50-75)(FR)
3. white body, orange base, amber windows, "Strassen Service" labels ($40-50)(GR)

K-78-A GRAN FURY POLICE CAR, issued 1980
1. blue & white body, blue interior, red dome lights on unpainted frame, "Polizei" decals, England casting ($12-15)
2. blue & white body, blue interior, red dome lights on unpainted frame, "Police" decals, England casting ($12-15)
3. black body, blue interior, red dome lights on unpainted frame, "Police" decals, England casting ($20-30)
4. black body, white interior, red dome lights on unpainted frame, "Police" decals, England casting ($15-20)
5. black body, white interior, red dome lights on white frame, "Police" decals, England casting ($15-20)
6. blue & white body, blue interior, red dome lights on white frame, "Police" decals, England casting ($12-15)
7. blue body, blue interior, red dome lights on white frame, "Police" decals, England casting ($12-15)
8. blue body, black interior, red dome lights on white frame, "Police" decals, England casting ($12-15)
9. blue body, black interior, blue dome lights on white frame, "Police" decals, England casting ($12-15)
10. blue body, blue interior, blue dome lights on white frame, "Police" decals, England casting ($12-15)
11. white body, blue interior, red dome lights on white frame, "City Police" tempa, England casting ($8-12)
12. white body, blue interior, blue dome lights on white frame, "City Police" tempa, Macau casting ($8-12)
13. white body, blue interior, blue dome lights on white frame, "City Police" tempa, China casting ($8-12)
14. maroon body, blue interior, blue dome lights on white frame, "Fire Dept./Fire Chief" tempa, Macau casting ($8-12)
15. maroon body, blue interior, blue dome lights on white frame, "Fire Dept./Fire Chief" tempa, China casting ($8-12)
16. red body, black interior, red dome lights on white frame, "IAAFC" decals, China casting ($12-15)(WR)
17. orange body, black interior, blue dome lights on white frame, "Lindberg City Police" tempa, China casting ($8-12)(EM)

K-79-A GRAN FURY TAXI, issued 1980
1. yellow body, red interior, black roof mount, assorted tempa & decals ($12-15)

K-80-A DODGE CUSTOM VAN, issued 1980
1. light blue body, clear windows, white interior with flowered pattern ($15-18)
2. light blue body, clear windows, white interior ($12-15)
3. dark blue body, clear windows, white interior ($12-15)

K-81-A SUZUKI MOTORCYCLE, issued 1981
1. white body, red shield, red driver with painted features, assorted decals ($12-15)
2. dark blue body, blue shield, blue driver with painted features, "Suzuki 30" labels ($12-15)

K-82-A BMW MOTORCYCLE, issued 1981
1. silver-gray body, black shield, blue driver with painted features, "BMW" label ($12-15)
2. silver-gray body, black shield, red driver with painted features, "BMW" labels ($12-15)
3. silver-gray body, gray shield, brown & yellow driver with painted features, "BMW" labels ($12-15)
4. black body, white shield, white driver with painted features, "Polizei" labels ($20-25)(GR)

K-83-AHARLEY-DAVIDSO MOTORCYCLE (ELECTRAGLIDE), issued 1981
1. white body & frame, tan gas tank, blue & black driver with painted features, "Police" labels, England casting ($12-15)
2. white body & frame, tan gas tank, blue & black driver with painted features, "Police" labels, Macau casting ($8-12)
NOTE: Below models have no driver fitted.
3. red body & frame, red gas tank, "Harley-Davidson" & silver pinstriping tempa, Thailand casting ($6-8)(HD)
4. dark blue body & frame, blue gas tank, "Harley-Davidson" & silver pinstriping tempa, Thailand casting ($6-8)(HD)
5. black body & frame, black gas tank, "Harley-Davidson" & silver pinstriping tempa, Thailand casting ($6-8)(HD)
6. red body & frame, red gas tank, "Harley-Davidson" & gold pinstriping tempa, Thailand casting ($6-8)(HD)
7. dark blue body & frame, dark blue gas tank, "Harley-Davidson" & gold pinstriping tempa, Thailand casting ($6-8)(HD)
8. black body & frame, black gas tank, "Harley-Davidson" & gold pinstriping tempa, Thailand casting ($6-8)(HD)
9. dark purple body & frame, dark purple gas tank, "Harley-Davidson" & gold pinstriping tempa, Thailand casting ($6-8)(HD)(GS)
10. white body & frame, blue gas tank, "MBPD 17" tempa, Thailand casting ($5-7)(HD)
11. black body & frame, black gas tank, "MBPD 17" tempa, Thailand casting ($5-7)(HD)
12. dark blue body & frame, dark blue gas tank, "Virginia State Police" tempa, Thailand casting ($5-7)(HD)
13. black/white body & frame, black gas tank, "California Highway Patrol" tempa, Thailand casting ($5-7)(HD)
14. black/white body & frame, black gas tank, "Kansas Highway Patrol" tempa, Thailand casting ($5-7)(HD)
15. cream body & frame, black gas tank, "Florida State Trooper" tempa, Thailand casting ($5-7)(HD)
16. gold plated body & frame, gold plated gas tank, "Harley-Davidson" tempa, Thailand casting ($6-8)(HD)
17. black & white body & frame, black gas tank, "M.B.P.D. 17/Dial 911" tempa, Thailand casting ($6-8)(HD)
18. cream body & frame, cream gas tank, "M.B.P.D./Police" tempa, Thailand casting ($6-8)(HD)
19. white body & frame, white gas tank, "M.B.P.D./Dial 911" tempa, Thailand casting ($6-8)(HD)
20. red body & frame, red gas tank, "Harley-Davidson" tempa, China casting ($6-8)(HD)

K-83-B HARLEY-DAVIDSON CHOPPER, issued 1994
1. red body, Thailand casting ($5-7)(HD)
2. blue body, Thailand casting ($5-7)(HD)
3. purple body, Thailand casting ($5-7)(HD)(GS)
4. gold plated body, Thailand casting (6-8)(HD)
5. black body Thailand casting ($6-8)(HD)
6. black & florescent orange body, Thailand casting ($6-8)(HD)
7. metallic red body, China casting ($6-8)(HD)
8. red body, China casting ($6-8)(HD)

K-83-C HARLEY-DAVIDSON SPORTSTER, issued 1994
1. turquoise body, Thailand casting ($5-7)(HD)
2. blue body, Thailand casting ($5-7)(HD)
3. red body, Thailand casting ($5-7)(HD)(GS)
4. black body, Thailand casting ($5-7)(HD) (Available with Tyco radio control)
5. gold plated body, Thailand casting ($6-8)(HD)
6. yellow body, China casting ($6-8)(HD)
7. florescent yellow body, China casting ($6-8)(HD)
8. purple body, China casting ($6-8)(HD)

K-84-A PEUGEOT 305, issued 1981
1. blue body, ivory interior, no tempa ($10-15)
2. white body, ivory interior, "14" & assorted logos tempa ($10-15)
3. white body, black interior, "10" & assorted logos tempa ($10-15)
4. metallic blue body, ivory interior, "5" & assorted logos tempa ($10-15)

K-85-A (NO MODEL ISSUED AT THIS NUMBER!)

K-86-A V.W. GOLF, issued 1981
1. black body, ivory interior, stripes tempa, white "Shell" gas pump accessory ($8-12)
2. white body, ivory interior, stripes tempa, white "Shell" gas pump accessory ($8-12)
3. yellow body, ivory interior, "ADAC StraBenwacht" tempa, white "Shell" gas tank accessory ($25-35)(GR)

K-87-A MASSEY FERGUSON TRACTOR & ROTARY RAKE, issued 1981
1. red tractor with silver-gray base, orange frame with yellow rakes, England casting ($15-20)
2. green tractor with silver-gray base, green frame with yellow rakes, China casting ($12-15)(FM)

K-88-A MONEY BOX, issued 1981
1. white cab, black base, white container with red roof, "Fort Knox" labels, England casting ($10-15)
2. white cab, black base, white container with red roof, "Matchbox" labels, England casting ($15-18)
3. white cab, black base, white container with red roof, "Volksbank Raiffeisenbank" labels, England casting ($35-45)(GR)
4. red cab, black base, ivory container with red roof, "Caisse D'Epargne" labels, England casting ($35-45)(FR)
5. orange cab, black base, light beige container with orange roof, "Caisse D'Epargne" labels, England casting ($35-45)(FR)
6. lime cab, black base, white container with lime roof, "De Speelboom Spaaravto" labels, China casting ($25-35)(DU)
NOTE: All models cast with 'K-19' on base but with slot cast on roof to deposit coins.

K-89-A FORESTRY RANGE ROVER & TRAILER, issued 1982
1. Rover in yellow with brown interior, gray grille, "Keilder Forest" on sides & stripes label on hood; trailer in yellow with two direction parallel stripes design labels ($15-20)
2. Rover in yellow with brown interior, black grille, "Keilder Forest" on sides & stripes label on hood; trailer in yellow with partial length label with one direction stripes labels ($15-20)
3. Rover in yellow with brown interior, gray grille, "Keilder Forest" on sides and "12" label on hood; trailer in yellow with full length label with one direction stripes labels ($15-20)

K-90-A MATRA RANCHO, issued 1982
1. red body & base, black interior & side molding, "Trans Globe Couriers" tempa, England casting ($12-15)
2. yellow body & base, black interior & side molding, "Pursuit Vehicle Interceptor 3000" labels, England casting ($12-15)
3. white body & base, black interior & side molding, "Coast Guard Patrol 70" tempa, England casting ($8-12)(K-104)
4. red body & base, black interior & side molding, "2 Fire Control Unit" tempa, Macau casting ($8-12)
5. red body & base, black interior & side molding, "2 Fire Control Unit" tempa, China casting ($7-10)

K-91-A MOTORCYCLE RACING SET, issued 1982
1. metallic silver Gran Fury with assorted decals & tempa; red trailer with two MB33-C Motorcycles with red windscreens ($35-50)

K-92-A HELICOPTER TRANSPORTER, issued 1982
1. yellow cab with green chassis, green trailer, white helicopter with green base & "Heli-Hire" tempa ($18-25)

K-93-A LAMP MAINTENANCE SET, issued 1982
1. yellow body, black chassis, orange boom, yellow bucket, stripes tempa. White lamp & green stand accessory ($15-18)

K-94 (NO MODEL ISSUED AT THIS NUMBER!)
NOTE: This was supposed to be a large Fire Tender with working water jets & hoses but due to cost problems and keeping the water tank leak-free, the project was abandoned.

K-95-A AUDI QUATTRO, issued 1982
1. white body, "Audi Sport 10" & assorted logos tempa, England casting ($10-15)
2. white body, "17" & assorted logos tempa, England casting ($10-15)
3. silver-gray body, "1" with black striping & assorted logos tempa, England casting ($8-12)
4. silver-gray body, "1" without striping & assorted logos tempa, England casting ($8-12)
5. white body, "Pirelli/Duckhams 10" & assorted logos tempa, England casting ($7-10)
6. metallic blue body, "0000" tempa, Macau casting ($7-10)
7. white body, "Pirelli/Duckhams 10" & assorted logos tempa, China casting ($7-10)

K-96-A VOLVO AMBULANCE, issued 1982
1. white body, red interior, orange roof mount, red stripes & cross tempa ($12-15)

K-97-A RANGE ROVER POLICE CAR, issued 1982
1. white body, brown interior, white roof mount, "Police" with orange stripe tempa ($12-15)

K-98-A FORESTRY UNIMOG & TRAILER, issued 1979
1. dark green body with red chassis, stripes labels, green trailer ($35-50)(GR)

K-98-B PORSCHE 944, issued 1983
1. silver-gray body, red interior, 2 tone blue with "Porsche 944" tempa, Macau casting ($7-10)
2. brown body, red interior, orange/brown with "Porsche 944" tempa, Macau casting ($7-10)
3. red body, black interior, "Porsche 944" tempa, Macau casting ($7-10)
4. silver-gray body, black interior, small logo tempa, Macau casting ($7-10)
5. black body, tan interior, small logo tempa, Macau casting ($8-12)(GS)
6. pearly white body, black interior, small logo tempa, China casting ($6-8)
7. yellow body, black interior, small logo tempa, China casting ($6-8)

K-99-A RANGE ROVER POLIZEI SET, issued 1979
1. cream body, green interior, green roof mount, "Polizei" tempa; issued with two MB33-C Motorcycles ($75-100)(GR)

K-99-B DODGE POLIZEI VAN, issued 1983
1. white body, green plastic roof, "Polizei" labels, England casting ($12-15)

K-100-A FORD SIERRA XR4i, issued 1983
1. white body, gray base, gray interior, no tempa, England casting ($8-12)
2. silver-gray body, gray base, gray interior, no tempa, England casting ($7-10)
3. powder blue body, gray base, gray interior, no tempa, England casting ($12-15)
4. red body, gray base, gray interior, small "XR4i" tempa, England casting ($12-15)
5. plum body, gray base, gray interior, no tempa, England casting ($12-15)
6. black body, gray base, gray interior, red stripe tempa, Macau casting ($7-10)
7. black body, gray base, gray interior, red stripe with "XR4i" tempa, Macau casting ($7-10)

NOTE: For models K-101-A through K-118-A see the next section entitled "Battlekings/Matchbox Military"

K-101-B RACING PORSCHE, issued 1983
1. metallic beige body, red dashboard, black interior, "TC Racing" & "Sunoco 16" tempa ($20-25)
2. red body, red dashboard & interior, "TC Racing" & "Sunoco 16" tempa ($7-10)
3. red body, red dashboard, black interior, "TC Racing" & "Sunoco 16" tempa ($7-10)
4. white body, red dashboard, black interior, "Team Porsche" & "9 Esso" with dark blue sides tempa ($7-10)
5. white body, red dashboard, black interior, "Team Porsche" & "9 Esso" with plain sides tempa ($7-10) (K-102)

K-102-B RACE SUPPORT SET, issued 1983
1. Dodge Van in yellow with red interior, "Team Porsche" labels; K-101-A5 Porsche in white ($18-25)

K-103-B PETERBILT TANKER, issued 1983
1. silver-gray cab with solid blue label, blue chassis, white plastic tank with blue chassis, "Comet" labels ($45-60)
2. white cab with solid blue stripe label, blue chassis, white plastic tank with blue chassis, "Comet" labels ($20-25)
3. white cab with two blue stripe tempa, blue chassis, white plastic tank with blue chassis, "Comet" labels ($20-25)

K-104-B RANCHO RESCUE SET, issued 1983
1. K-90-A Matra Rancho in white with "Coast Guard Patrol 70" tempa; K-25-A boat with white deck, blue hull, tan seats, "370" on sides only; white plastic cradle on orange trailer ($18-25)
2. K-90-A Matra Rancho in white with "Coast Guard Patrol 70" tempa; K-25-A boat with white deck, blue hull, tan seats, "370" on sides & deck; white plastic cradle on orange trailer ($18-25)
3. K-90-A Matra Rancho in white with "Coast Guard Patrol 70" tempa; K-25-A boat with white deck, blue hull, tan seats, "370" on sides & deck; black plastic cradle on orange trailer ($18-25)

K-105-B PETERBILT TIPPER, issued 1984
1. white body, black chassis, red plastic dump with red stripes, England casting ($12-15)
2. yellow body, black chassis, yellow plastic dump with "Taylor Woodrow" tempa, England casting ($12-15)

K-106-B SCAMMELL AIRCRAFT TRANSPORTER, issued 1984
1. red cab with silver-gray chassis, silver-gray trailer, red plastic airplane with "Aces" on wings, England casting ($15-20)

K-107-B POWERBOAT TRANSPORTER, issued 1984
1. white cab, blue chassis, no dome lights cast; white trailer with blue base; boat with white deck & hull, "Spearhead" labels, England casting ($20-25)

K-108-B PETERBILT DIGGER TRANSPORTER, issued 1984
1. yellow cab with black chassis, "Avro" tempa, black trailer; K-25-B in yellow with yellow base, amber windows, yellow backhoe with red scoop, red wheels, England castings ($25-30)
2. yellow cab with black chassis, "Avro" tempa, black trailer; K-25-B in yellow with yellow base, green windows, yellow backhoe with red scoop, red wheels, England castings ($25-30)

K-109-B IVECO TANKER, issued 1984
1. yellow cab with white front fenders, no dome lights, white tank, "Shell" labels, England casting ($8-12)
2. yellow cab with black front fenders, no dome lights, white tank, "Shell" labels, England casting ($8-12)

K-110-B FIRE ENGINE, issued 1985
1. red body, gray ladder, "008" tempa, England casting ($8-12)

K-111-B PETERBILT REFUSE TRUCK, issued 1985
1. orange body, gray chassis, orange dump, "Waste Beater" tempa, England casting ($12-15)

K-112-B FIRE SPOTTER TRANSPORTER, issued 1985
1. red cab & chassis with "Fire 23" tempa, red trailer, red plastic plane with chrome plated wings with "Fire," black cradle, cab features non-steerable wheels, England casting ($20-25)

K-113-B GARAGE TRANSPORTER, issued 1985
1. yellow cab with red chassis, no dome lights cast, red plastic trailer with black base, gray plastic garage, orange-yellow tarp with "Shell," England casting ($20-25)
2. yellow cab with red chassis, no dome lights cast, red plastic trailer with black base, gray plastic garage, white tarp with "Shell," England casting ($20-25)

K-114-B CRANE TRUCK, issued 1985
1. yellow body & crane cab, yellow boom, black extending boom, no roof tempa, "Taylor Woodrow" tempa on crane cab, black base, Macau casting ($15-20)
2. yellow body & crane cab, yellow boom, black extending boom, "113" roof tempa, "Cotras" tempa on crane cab, black base, Macau casting ($15-20)
3. yellow body, red crane cab, yellow boom, red extending boom, "113" roof tempa, red & white stripes tempa on crane cab, red base, China casting ($15-20)(CS)

K-115-B MERCEDES BENZ 190E, issued 1985
1. white body, black interior, chrome wheels, England casting ($7-10)
2. silver blue body, black interior, chrome wheels, Macau casting ($6-8)
3. black body, tan interior, chrome wheels, Macau casting ($6-8)
4. gunmetal gray body, red interior, chrome wheels, Macau casting ($6-8)
5. white body, black interior, red wheels, "Fuji" tempa, Macau casting ($6-8)
6. white body, black interior, red wheels, "Fuji" tempa, China casting ($6-8)
7. light silver green body, black interior, chrome wheels, China casting ($6-8)

K-116-B RACING CAR TRANSPORTER, issued 1985
1. red cab, black interior & front hubs, white chassis, no dome lights cast; trailer with red body, red base, "Ferrari" labels; includes 2X MB16-D in red ($20-25)
2. red cab, white interior & front hubs, white chassis, no dome lights cast; trailer with red body, red base, "Ferrari" labels; includes 2X MB16-D in red ($20-25)

K-117-B SCANIA BULLDOZER TRANSPORTER, issued 1985
1. yellow cab, brown chassis, "Taylor Woodrow" roof tempa; brown trailer with K-42-B3 Traxcavator Road Ripper, England castings ($25-30)

K-118-B ROAD CONSTRUCTION SET, issued 1985
1. Ford Truck with yellow cab & body with black chassis & white roof, small design tempa, England casting; support trailer in yellow, small design tempa, Macau casting; Unimog in yellow with black chassis, "115" & small design labels, Macau casting; compressor trailer in yellow with yellow cap & small design tempa, Macau casting ($35-45)

K-119-A FIRE RESCUE SET, issued 1985
1. Unimog in red, red interior with small "Fire" label on hood, "8 Fire Dept." labels on white canopy, "Fire Dept." labels on sides, England casting; K-110-B1 version Fire Truck; Compressor trailer in red, England casting ($25-35)

K-120-A CAR TRANSPORTER, issued 1986
1. white cab with black chassis, white trailer with pearly silver ramp, "Carrier" labels, Macau casting ($15-20)
2. white cab with black chassis, white trailer with white ramp, "Carrier" labels, Macau casting ($15-20)
3. yellow cab with red chassis, yellow trailer with red ramp, "Express Courier" labels, China casting ($15-18)

K-121-A PETERBILT WRECKER, issued 1986
NOTE: This is a reissue of K-20-C, but with steerable front wheels.
1. dark blue cab, white chassis & rear bed, red dome lights, black booms, "Highway Patrol City Police" tempa, Macau casting ($15-18)
2. dark blue cab, white chassis & rear bed, red dome lights, black booms, "Highway Patrol City Police" tempa, China casting ($15-18)

K-122-A DAF ROAD TRAIN, issued 1986
1. white cab, black chassis, white bed & canopies, amber dome lights, "Eurotrans" tempa, Macau casting ($18-25)
2. white cab, black chassis, red bed, white canopies, amber dome lights, "Toblerone" tempa, Macau casting ($25-35)(SW)
3. cream cab, dark gray chassis, cream bed, gray canopies, amber dome lights, "Marti" tempa, Macau casting ($25-35)(SW)
4. blue cab, black chassis, blue bed & canopies, amber dome lights, "Henniez" tempa, Macau casting ($25-35)(SW)
5. yellow cab, black chassis, yellow bed & canopies, amber dome lights, "Zweifel Pomy Chips" tempa, Macau casting ($25-35)(SW)

K-123-A LEYLAND CEMENT TRUCK, issued 1986
1. yellow-orange cab & body, red chassis, gray barrel with black stripes, road design tempa, red hubs, Macau casting ($7-10)
2. yellow-orange cab & body, red chassis, gray barrel with red on white stripes, red & white stripes tempa, China casting ($7-10)(CS)

K-124-A MERCEDES CONTAINER TRUCK, issued 1986
1. white cab, red interior & front wheel fenders, dark gray chassis, white container with dark gray chassis, red wheels, "7 Up" labels, England casting ($15-20)
2. pearly silver cab, black interior & front wheel fenders, black chassis, silver-gray container with black chassis, chrome wheels, gray background "Taglich Frisch" labels, China casting ($30-45)(GR)
3. pearly silver cab, black interior & front wheel fenders, black chassis, silver-gray container with black chassis, chrome wheels, clear background "Taglich Frisch" labels, China casting ($30-45)(GR)

K-125-A (NO MODEL ISSUED AT THIS NUMBER!)

K-126-A DAF HELICOPTER TRANSPORTER, issued 1986
1. blue cab with blue chassis, "Royal Navy" tempa, blue trailer; helicopter with dark blue body, bright orange pontoons, white interior, "RN Royal Navy" & "Rescue" tempa, Macau castings ($15-20)
2. white cab with powder blue chassis, "Coast Guard" tempa, powder blue trailer; helicopter with white body, orange pontoons, white interior, "Coast Guard" tempa, China castings ($15-20)
3. blue cab with blue chassis, "Royal Navy" tempa, blue trailer; helicopter with dark blue body, bright orange pontoons, white interior, "RN Royal Navy" & "Rescue" tempa, China castings ($15-18)

K-127-A PETERBILT TANKER, issued 1986
1. white cab with red chassis, white plastic tank with red chassis, red wheels, "Total" labels, Macau casting ($15-20)
2. red cab with red chassis, white plastic tank with light gray chassis, red wheels, "Getty" labels, Macau casting ($15-20)
NOTE: This is a reissue of K-103-B with the addition of steerable front axle.

K-127-B IVECO TANKER, issued 1989
1. blue cab with white chassis, blue plastic tank with white chassis, white wheels, "British Farm Produce-Milk" tempa, China casting ($25-40) (Early Learning Centre)

K-128-A DAF AIRCRAFT TRANSPORTER, issued 1986
1. red cab & chassis, red trailer with gray cradle; light brown plastic jet plane with olive/white/red tempa, Macau casting ($15-18)
2. red cab & chassis, red trailer with white cradle; silver-gray plastic spotter plane with red pontoons & wings, no tempa, China casting ($35-50)(UK) (released in Woolworth's)

K-129-A POWERBOAT TRANSPORTER, issued 1986
NOTE: This is a reissue of K-107-B in which dome lights have been added as well as steerable front axles.
1. white cab with blue chassis, blue stripes tempa, amber dome lights, cream plastic trailer with blue base, chrome wheels; boat with white deck & hull, "Spearhead" in blue letters with blue side stripes labels, England casting ($15-20)
2. blue cab with powder blue chassis, "Kruger" tempa, amber dome lights, gray plastic trailer with powder blue base, chrome wheels; boat with white deck & hull, "Spearhead" in blue letters with brown side stripes labels, England casting ($15-20)
3. blue cab with powder blue chassis, "Kruger" tempa, amber dome lights, gray plastic trailer with powder blue base, chrome wheels; boat with white deck & tan hull, "Spearhead" in brown letters with brown side stripes labels, England casting ($15-20)
4. blue cab with powder blue chassis, "Kruger" tempa, amber dome lights, gray plastic trailer with dark blue base, red wheels; boat with white deck & tan hull, "Spearhead" in brown letters with brown side stripes labels, England casting ($15-20)
5. white cab with black chassis, "Coast Guard" tempa, amber dome lights, gray plastic trailer with black base, chrome wheels; boat with light gray deck & white/black hull, "4439 Coast Guard" labels, Macau casting ($15-20)
6. white cab with powder blue chassis, "Coast Guard" tempa, amber dome lights, gray plastic trailer with powder blue base, white wheels; boat with light gray & florescent orange deck & white & black hull, "4439 Coast Guard" labels, China casting ($15-20)(EM)

K-130-A SCANIA DIGGER TRANSPORTER, issued 1986
1. yellow cab with brown chassis, "Plant Hire" & "B1" tempa, brown trailer; K-25-B in yellow with yellow base, amber windows, yellow backhoe with yellow scoop, yellow wheels, Macau casting ($20-25)

K-131-A IVECO PETROL TANKER, issued 1986
NOTE: This is a reissue of K-109-B with the addition of dome lights & steerable front axle.
1. yellow cab, amber dome lights, chrome wheels, white tank, "Shell" labels, England casting ($7-10)
2. red cab, amber dome lights, white wheels, red tank, "Texaco" labels, Macau casting ($12-15)
3. white cab, amber dome lights, white wheels, white tank, "Texaco" labels, Macau casting ($15-20)

K-132-A FIRE ENGINE, issued 1986
NOTE: This is a reissue of K-110-B with the addition of steerable front axle
1. red body, gray ladder, white interior, chrome wheels, "008" tempa, England casting ($8-12)
2. red body, white ladder, white interior, chrome wheels, "Fire 201" tempa, England casting ($8-12)
3. red body, white ladder, black interior, red wheels, "Fire 201" tempa, Macau casting ($8-12)

K-133-A IVECO REFUSE TRUCK, issued 1986
1. maroon cab & dump, maroon wheels, "Refuse City Corp." tempa, England casting ($10-15)
2. maroon cab & dump, red wheels, "Refuse City Corp." tempa, Macau casting ($10-15)
3. white cab & dump, white wheels, "Recycle" tempa, Macau casting ($10-15)
4. white cab & dump, red wheels, caricature tempa, Macau casting ($10-12)
5. white cab & dump, red wheels, caricature tempa, China casting ($10-12)
6. blue cab & dump, white wheels, "BFI 664" tempa, China casting ($50-75)(US)
7. blue cab, white dump, white wheels, "BFI 664" tempa, China casting ($75-125)(US)

K-134-A FIRE SPOTTER TRANSPORTER, issued 1986
NOTE: This is a reissue of K-112-B with the addition of a steerable front axle.
1. red cab with white chassis, "Patrol Unit 12 Fire" tempa, red trailer with brown cradle; plane in red with red pontoons & chrome wings, "12" on plane tail & "C-802 Fire" with red stripe on wings, Macau casting ($15-20)
2. red cab with white chassis, "Patrol Unit 12 Fire" tempa, red trailer with brown cradle; plane in red with red pontoons & chrome wings, "12" on plane tail & "C-802 Fire" with red stripe on wings, China casting ($15-20)
3. red cab with white chassis, "Patrol Unit 12 Fire" tempa, red trailer with white cradle; plane in silver-gray with red pontoon & wings, "12" on plane tail & "Fire" on wings, China casting ($15-20)(EM)

K-135-A GARAGE TRANSPORTER, issued 1986

NOTE: This is a reissue of K-113-B with the addition of dome lights & steerable front axle.
1. yellow cab with red chassis, red interior; dull red plastic trailer with black base; gray plastic garage, orange-yellow tarp with "Shell," England casting ($18-25)
2. yellow cab with red chassis, black interior; red plastic trailer with black base; gray plastic garage, yellow tarp with "Shell," Macau casting ($18-25)
3. red cab & chassis, black interior; gray plastic trailer with red base; gray plastic garage, red tarp with "Texaco," Macau casting ($18-25)

K-136-A RACING CAR TRANSPORTER, issued 1986
NOTE: This is a reissue of K-116-B with the addition of dome lights & steerable front axle.
1. red cab with white chassis, black interior, red container with dark gray base, white wheels, "Ferrari" labels; includes 2X MB16-D in red, England casting ($18-25)

K-137-A ROAD CONSTRUCTION SET, issued 1986
1. DAF Truck with orange-yellow body, black chassis, red stripe & small "1104" tempa, Macau casting; support trailer in yellow with black chassis, red stripe with "4172" tempa, England casting; Unimog in yellow with black chassis, red stripe with "126" tempa, England casting; compressor trailer in yellow with yellow canopy, red stripe with "1127" tempa, England casting ($30-45)

K-138-A FIRE RESCUE SET, issued 1986
1. Unimog with red body, black interior, "Fire" hood tempa, "9 Foam Pump" tempa on white canopy, "Fire Dept." on sides tempa, Macau casting; K-132-A1 Fire Engine; compressor trailer in red with red canopy, Macau casting ($25-30)

K-139-A IVECO TIPPER TRUCK, issued 1987
1. orange-yellow body & dump, black chassis, "Wimpey" tempa, Macau casting ($10-15)
2. orange-yellow body & dump, black chassis, "Department of Highways" tempa, Macau casting ($10-15)
3. red body & dump, black chassis, silver side stripe tempa, Macau casting ($10-15)
4. orange-yellow body, red dump & chassis, red & white stripes tempa, China casting ($8-12)(CS)

K-140-A CAR RECOVERY VEHICLE, issued 1987
1. white cab, blue chassis, white bed with white drop ramp, blue & red tempa, Macau casting ($8-12)
2. white cab, blue chassis, white bed with white drop ramp, blue/red tempa, China casting ($8-12)

K-141-A IVECO SKIP TRUCK, issued 1987
1. red cab, black chassis, gray dump, "ECD" tempa, Macau casting ($10-15)
2. red cab, red chassis, orange-yellow dump, no tempa, Macau casting ($10-15)

K-142-A BMW POLICE CAR, issued 1987
1. white body, black interior, "Polizei" with green hood & doors tempa, Macau casting ($8-12)
2. white body, black interior, "Police" with checkers tempa, Macau casting ($8-12)
3. white body, black interior, "Fina Pace Car" tempa, Macau casting ($8-12)

K-143-A BEDFORD EMERGENCY VAN, issued 1987
1. white body, blue windows, pink cross & stripe tempa, Macau casting ($8-12)

K-144-A LAND ROVER, issued 1987
1. yellow body & roof, blue dome lights, chrome wheels, "Frankfurt Flughafen" tempa, Macau casting ($8-12)
2. orange-yellow body & roof, amber dome lights, red wheels, "Heathrow Airport" tempa, Macau casting ($8-12)(UK)
3. orange-yellow body & roof, amber dome lights, red wheels, "Road Maintenance" tempa, Macau casting ($8-12)
4. green body, cream roof, amber dome lights, "Veterinary Surgeon" tempa, China casting ($15-18)(UK) (Early Learning Centre)

K-145-A IVECO TWIN TIPPER, issued 1988
1. orange cab, black chassis, "S&G" tempa, pearly silver twin tippers with black chassis, orange stripes tempa, Macau casting ($20-25)

K-146-A JAGUAR XJ6, issued 1988
1. white body, black interior, Macau casting ($10-15)(GS)
2. metallic red body, gray interior, Macau casting ($6-8)
3. metallic red body, gray interior, China casting ($6-8)
4. dark green body, brown interior, China casting, display stand ($15-18)(UC)
5. white body, maroon interior, China casting ($6-8)

K-147-A BMW 750iL, issued 1988
1. silver blue body, gray interior, Macau casting ($6-8)
2. silver blue body, gray interior, China casting ($6-8)
3. red body, gray interior, China casting ($25-40)(AU)
4. silver-gray body, white & black interior, China casting, display stand ($15-18)(UC)
5. black body, gray interior, blue-gray base, China casting ($6-8)
6. silver-gray body, black interior, gray base, China casting ($6-8)

K-148-A CRANE TRUCK, issued 1988
1. white cab, bed & crane post, red chassis, black plastic boom, blue stripe, "PEX" tempa, Macau casting ($15-18)

K-149-A FERRARI TESTAROSSA, issued 1988
1. red body, black & cream interior, red base, Macau casting ($6-8)
2, red body, black & cream interior, red base, detailed trim, China casting, display stand ($15-18)(UC)
3. red body, black & cream interior, red base, China casting ($6-8)

K-150-A LEYLAND TRUCK, issued 1988
1. blue cab & chassis, black base. Includes three interchangeable rear components-plastic container with "SMF" tempa, white tipper bed with "SMF" tempa & powder blue flatbed with "SMF" tempa, China casting ($15-20)
2. yellow cab, yellow chassis with red base; includes only tipper bed casting in yellow with white stripes tempa, China casting ($8-12)(CS12)

K-151-A SKIP TRUCK, issued 1988
1. orange-yellow cab & bed, black chassis, orange-yellow dump, orange skip arms, road design tempa, Macau casting ($6-8)
2. orange-yellow cab & bed, black chassis, orange-yellow dump, orange skip arms, road design tempa, China casting ($6-8)
3. orange-yellow cab, yellow bed, black chassis, yellow dump, orange skip arms, road design tempa, China casting ($6-8)
4. orange-yellow cab, yellow bed, red chassis, red dump & skip arms, white & red stripes tempa, China casting ($6-8)(CS)

K-152-A *NOTE: no model issued at this number.*

K-153-A JAGUAR XJ6 POLICE CAR, issued 1988
1. white body, black interior, blue dome lights, "Police" with checkers tempa, Macau casting ($7-10)
2. white body, black interior, "Police" with light peach band & blue striping tempa, China casting ($7-10)(EM)

K-154-A BMW 750iL POLICE CAR, issued 1988
1. white body, black interior, blue dome lights, "Polizei" with green doors, hood & trunk tempa, Macau casting ($7-10)
2. white body, black interior, blue dome lights, "Police" with orange & black stripes tempa, China casting ($7-10)

K-155-A FERRARI TESTAROSSA RALLYE, issued 1988
1. yellow body & base, black & cream interior, gold & black stripes with "61" tempa, Macau casting ($6-8)

K-156-A PORSCHE TURBO RALLYE, issued 1988
1. red body, white interior, black base, white with "18 Elf" & "Pioneer" tempa, Macau casting ($6-8)

K-157-A PORSCHE 944 RALLYE, issued 1988
1. orange-yellow body, black interior, "Turbo Porsche 944" with red & blue stripes tempa, Macau casting ($6-8)

K-158-A FORD SIERRA XR4i RALLYE, issued 1988
1. white body, gray interior, white base & wheels, "Total" tempa, China casting ($6-8)

K-159-A RACING CAR TRANSPORTER, issued 1988
1. white cab & chassis, black interior, white container with black chassis, "Porsche" tempa; includes 2X MB7-F Porsche 959 in white, Macau casting ($20-25)

K-160-A RACING CAR TRANSPORTER, issued 1988
1. white cab, blue chassis, black interior, white container with blue chassis, "Matchbox Formula Racing Team" labels; includes 2X MB16-D in white, Macau casting ($20-25)

K-161-A ROLLS ROYCE SILVER SPIRIT, issued 1989
1. silver-gray body, gray interior, black base, Macau casting ($6-8)
2. metallic red body, gray interior, black base, Macau casting ($10-12)(GS)

K-162-A SIERRA RS500 COSWORTH, issued 1989
1. white upper & lower body, dark gray interior with white steering wheel, white spoiler, white wheels, small "Cosworth" tempa, Macau casting ($6-8)
2. white upper body, dark gray lower body, dark gray interior with black steering wheel, dark blue spoiler, white wheels, "Gemini" & "British Open Rally Championship" tempa, Macau casting ($6-8)
3. black upper body, dark gray lower body, light gray interior with black steering wheel, black spoiler, chrome wheels, "Texaco 6" tempa, Macau casting ($6-8)
4. white upper & lower body, black interior with white steering wheel, black spoiler, white wheels, "Caltex Bond" tempa, Macau casting ($20-35)(AU)

K-163-A UNIMOG SNOW PLOW, issued 1989
1. orange body, black chassis, blue canopy on bed, orange plow with "Schmidt" tempa, Macau casting ($10-15)
2. orange body, black chassis, blue canopy on bed, orange plow with "Schmidt" tempa, China casting ($8-12)

K-164-A RANGE ROVER, issued 1989
1. dark blue body, gray interior, "Range Rover" on hood tempa, Macau casting ($6-8)
2. white body, gray interior, "Africa Safari Tours" & black zebra stripes tempa, China casting ($6-8)
3. beige body, gray interior, brown stripes tempa, China casting ($10-15)(UK) (Early Learning Center)
4. green body, gray interior, yellow & white stripes tempa, China casting ($6-8)(FM)

K-165-A RANGE ROVER POLICE, issued 1989
1. white body, black interior, blue stripe with yellow "Police" tempa, Macau casting ($6-8)
2. white body, black interior, orange band with blue "Police" tempa, China casting ($6-8)

K-166-A MERCEDES BENZ 190E TAXI, issued 1989
1. dark cream body, black interior, yellow "Taxi" roof sign, Macau casting ($6-8)

K-167-A FORD TRANSIT, issued 1990
1. lavender body with white roof, black interior, clear windows, chrome wheels, "Milka" labels, Macau casting ($12-15)
2. powder blue body with white roof, black interior, blue windows, chrome wheels, "Surf N Sun" labels, China casting ($7-10)
3. orange-yellow body with red roof, black interior, clear windows, red wheels, "Miller Construction Company" labels, China casting ($7-10)(CS)

K-168-A PORSCHE 911 CARRERA, issued 1990
1. red body, black interior, black base, "Carrera 4 Porsche" tempa, Macau casting ($6-8)
2. pearly white body, black interior, black base, "Carrera" tempa, with display stand, China casting ($15-18)(UC)
3. yellow body, black interior, black base, "Carrera 4 Porsche" tempa, China casting ($6-8)
4. red body, black interior, black base, "Carrera 4 Porsche" tempa, China casting ($6-8)

K-169-A FORD TRANSIT AMBULANCE, issued 1990
1. white body with cream roof, "Air Ambulance" with yellow band & orange stripe tempa, Macau casting ($7-10)
2. white body with cream roof, "Air Ambulance" with light orange & blue stripe tempa, China casting ($7-10)

K-170-A JCB EXCAVATOR, issued 1991
NOTE: This is a reissue of K-41-C.
1. orange-yellow body, chassis & crane booms, red cab & shovel, "JCB," "808" & red/white stripes tempa, China casting ($18-25)(CS)

K-171-A TOYOTA HI-LUX, issued 1990
1. white body, black interior, white bed, "Runnin Brave" & peacock feather design tempa; includes MB23-F Honda ATC in florescent green & orange, Macau castings ($15-20)
2. red body, gray interior, white bed, yellow stripes tempa; includes hay bale, 2 milk cans & plastic cow ($8-12)(FM)
3. white body, black interior, white bed, "Runnin' Brave" & peacock feather design tempa; includes MB23-F Honda ATC in fluorescent green/orange, China casting ($15-18)
4. black body, black interior, chrome windows, black bed, "Harley-Davidson Motorcycles" with blue & orange flames tempa, China casting ($7-10)(HD)(GS)

K-172-A MERCEDES BENZ 500SL, issued 1991
1. silver-gray body, blue interior, gray base, China casting ($6-8)
2. red body, dark gray interior, red base, display stand, China casting ($15-18)(UC)
3. metallic red body, gray interior, maroon base, China casting ($6-8)

K-173-A LAMBORGHINI DIABLO, issued 1992
1. yellow body, black interior, yellow base, "Diablo" tempa, China casting ($6-8)
2. black body, gray interior, black base, "Diablo" tempa, China casting ($6-8)

NOTE: no numbers issued for K-174 through K-178 & K-180 through K-185 or K-195 through K-198.

K-179-A SUZUKI SAMURAI, issued 1993
1. red body, black interior, white spare tire carrier, gold/white with "Suzuki" tempa, China casting ($7-10)

K-186-A PETERBILT CONTAINER TRUCK, issued 1995
1. black cab with chrome chassis, black container, "Jim Beam 200 Years" tempa ($50-65)(CL)
2. white cab with chrome chassis, white container with blue roof, "Tyco International" tempa ($750+)(US)
3. blue cab with chrome chassis, blue container, "Matchbox" tempa ($125-175)(CL)

K-187-A FREIGHTLINER CONTAINER TRUCK, issued 1997
1. red cab with red plastic airdam & plastic chassis, light purple windows, white container with red roof & chassis, chrome wheels, "Beefeater-The Spirit of London" tempa ($60-70)(CL)

K-188-A KENWORTH CABOVER, issued 1997
1. red body & airdam, black chassis, gold wheels & grille, "KW" logo tempa, free standing wood plinth included ($75-90)(CL)

K-188-B PETERBILT CONTAINER TRUCK, issued 1998
1. black cab with chrome chassis, black container, "Harley Davidson" & large flying eagle tempa ($75-100)(CL)

K-189-A PETERBILT CONTAINER TRUCK, issued 1997

1. black cab with chrome chassis, gray container with black roof & chassis, "Jack Daniel's Tennessee" tempa ($75-100)(CL)

K-190-A FREIGHTLINER CONTAINER TRUCK, issued 1996
1. dark green cab with black chassis, dark green container with dark green roof, "ingle ells ingle ells Don't Forget the J&B" tempa ($65-75)(CL)

K-191-B FREIGHTLINER CONTAINER TRUCK, issued 1998
1. blue cab & chassis, blue container, gold wheels, "The Stars and Stripes Forever 1897-1997" tempa ($75-100)(CL)

K-192-A PETERBILT LOWLOADER, issued 1998
1. powder blue cab, black chassis, "Pac Lease" tempa, brown flatbed trailer, two black Peterbilt cabs as load mounted atop porcelain crates ($75-100)(CL)

K-193-A PETERBILT 359 CABOVER CAB, issued 1998
1. dark green body, black chassis, "Peterbilt" logo tempa, chrome wheels ($40-60)(CL)

K-194-A KENWORTH W900 CAB, issued 1998
1. metallic blue body, black chassis, red stripes tempa, chrome wheels ($40-60)(CL)

K-199-A KENWORTH CONTAINER TRUCK, issued 1998
NOTE: This model is a reissue of K-188.
1. red body, black chassis, red container with silver-gray base, "Coca Cola" with Santa Claus tempa ($75-90)(CL)

K-200-A PETERBILT TANKER, issued 1998
1. yellow cab with gray chassis, chrome tank with gray chassis, "Formula Shell" tempa ($75-90)(CL)

K-201-A FREIGHTLINER CONTAINER TRUCK, issued 1998
NOTE: This model is a reissue of K-187.
1. Light red cab & chassis, light red container with dark gray base, "Budweiser" tempa ($75-90)(CL)

CS-5-A UNIMOG TAR SPRAYER, issued 1991
1. orange-yellow body, red chassis, black interior, red tank with white stripes tempa, red plastic tar sprayer units, China casting ($10-15)(CS)

FM-3-A SHOVEL TRACTOR, issued 1992
1. red body, silver-gray base, white shovel arms with red shovel, white plastic roof, red wheels, base cast 'K-35', China casting ($8-12)(FM)

FM-5-A MUIR HILL TRACTOR & TRAILER, issued 1992
1. K-25-C Muir Hill Tractor with green body, yellow chassis & wheels; trailer with green body & yellow chassis, 3 plastic logs ($12-15)(FM)

EM-13-A HELICOPTER, issued 1992
1. red body, white base, yellow pontoons with red stripes tempa, "Patrol Unit" & "4 Fire" tempa, no origin cast ($10-12)(EM)

EM-14-A SUZUKI SAMURAI, issued 1993
1. white body, black interior, white rear canopy & spare tire carrier, "Police" with crest, orange dashes & checkers tempa, China casting ($6-8)

EM-15-A MERCEDES BENZ 190E POLICE CAR, issued 1993
1. white body, brown interior, blue dome lights, "Rijkspolitie 61" tempa, China casting ($12-15)(DU)

FORD ESCORT COSWORTH, issued 1995 (no identification #)
1. yellow body, black base, black interior, "Michelin/Pilot" tempa, white wheels, China casting ($7-10)

MAZDA RX7, issued 1995 (no identification #)
1. metallic red body, tan interior, black base, chrome wheels, China casting ($7-10)

HARLEY-DAVIDSON SPRINGER SOFT TAIL, issued 1996 (no identification #)
1. purple body, China casting ($8-12)
2. metallic turquoise body, China casting ($8-12)
3. black body, China casting ($8-12)
4. metallic red body, China casting ($8-12)
5. white body, China casting ($8-12)
6. dark blue body, China casting ($8-12)
7. red body, China casting ($8-12)

1939 HARLEY-DAVIDSON KNUCKLEHEAD, issued 1996 (no identification #)
1. powder blue casting & gas tank, China casting ($8-12)
2. black body & red gas tank, China casting ($8-12)
3. white body & black gas tank, China casting ($8-12)
NOTE: Although these are two different castings, they were never issued under separate assortment numbers.

50713-A RAGE RIG WITH WRECKING TYRANNOSAURUS, issued 1997
1. olive body, black chassis, silver-gray sides, Tyrannosaurus in bed ($8-12)(JR)
NOTE: Tyrannosaurus can come in various shades.

50713-B RAGE RIG WITH RAGING STEGOSAURUS, issued 1997
1. blue-gray body, silver-gray sides, black base, brown stegosaurus in bed ($8-12)(JR)

RB-2521 A.L.T.R.A.C., issued 1988
1. pea green cab with dark blue chassis, dark blue trailer with pea green ramp; helicopter in pea green with brown base, "89" with red design tempa, plastic battle armament attachments, Macau casting ($45-60)(RB)

RB-2522 V.A.R.M.I.T., issued 1988
1. plum body & crane cab, yellow wheels, blue & yellow tempa, plastic battle armament attachments, Macau casting ($35-50)(RB)

RB-2531 T.R.A.P.P.E.R., issued 1988
1. brown body with black chassis, black trailer with large gray & dark blue plastic container attachment, green/blue/yellow tempa, plastic battle armament attachments, Macau casting ($45-60)(RB)

RB-2532 M.O.R.G., issued 1988
1. purple cab & chassis, yellow tempa, black plastic trailer with purple chassis, large plastic accessories as load, plastic battle armament attachments, Macau casting ($45-60)(RB)

32630 SPEEDWAY TEAM TRANSPORTER, issued 1991
1. black cab & chassis, black container, pink lettered "Indy" with "75th Indianapolis 500" labels, black chassis; includes MB65-D in black/yellow & MB74-H in orange/white ($18-25)(IN)
2. black cab & chassis, black container, yellow lettered "Indy" with "Indianapolis 500-the Seventy Sixth" labels; includes 2X MB74-H Racer-one in orange/lavender/white & one in white/blue ($18-25)(IN)
3. white & blue cab with black chassis, white container, "Indy 500" labels, dark gray trailer chassis; includes two MB74-H in white/blue with "Indy 77" tempa, China casting ($18-25)(IN)
4. white/yellow cab with blue chassis, white container, "Renault Elf/Canon Williams" labels, dark gray trailer chassis; includes two MB246 Formula 1 racers in white/blue, China casting ($18-25)(Fl)

Battlekings/Matchbox Military

In 1974, the Battlekings were released. Early versions were produced in bright metallic colors with later issues being done in more realistic military colors. The series was discontinued by 1980. There are numerous unrecorded variations on those below which include on the tanks in particular different color drive wheels which have a smooth or gear appearance. Some figures in the tanks can include tan, pink-tan and green combinations on most versions.

K-101-A SHERMAN TANK, issued 1974
1. gold body, silver-gray base, French flag labels, green rollers, gray treads ($20-25)
2. gold body, silver-gray base, "USA 48350" labels, green rollers, gray treads ($20-25)
3. gold body, silver-gray base, "USA 48350" labels, tan rollers, gray treads ($20-25)
4. tan & green camouflage body, black base, "USA 48350" labels, gray treads ($20-25)

K-102-A M48-A2 TANK, issued 1974
1. metallic green body, green rollers, white star in circle label ($20-25)
2. beige & brown camouflage body, green rollers, "Armored Div." label ($20-25)
3. tan & green camouflaged body, green rollers, "Armored Div." label ($20-25)
4. yellowish-green camouflage body, green rollers, "Armored Div." label ($20-25)
5. mottled green & dark brown body, green rollers, "Armored Div." label ($20-25)

K-103-A CHIEFTAIN TANK, issued 1974
1. metallic green body, "8" label, green rollers ($20-25)
2. metallic green body, "8" label, tan rollers ($20-25)
3. tan & green camouflage body, "8" label, green rollers ($20-25)
4. tan & green camouflage body, "8" label, tan rollers ($20-25)

K-104-A KING TIGER TANK, issued 1974
1. silver-gray body, cross & "23" labels, green rollers ($20-25)
2. silver-gray body, cross & "23" labels, tan rollers ($20-25)
3. silver-gray body with black camouflage, cross & "23" labels, green rollers ($20-25)

K-105-A HOVER RAIDER, issued 1974
1. metallic green body, tan base, chrome attachments, three black wheels & one white drive wheels ($20-25)
2. metallic green body, tan base, chrome attachments, four black wheels ($20-25)
3. olive green body, tan base, black attachments, four black wheels ($20-25)

K-106-A TANK TRANSPORTER, issued 1974
1. metallic green cab, amber windows, chrome interior, metallic green trailer, silver hubs; with K-102-A4 ($45-60)
2. olive green cab, clear windows, black interior, olive green trailer, silver hubs; with K-102-A4 ($45-60)
3. olive green cab, clear windows, chrome interior, olive green trailer, silver hubs; with K-102-A4 ($46-60)
4. olive green cab, clear windows, chrome interior, olive green trailer, black hubs; with K-102-A4 ($45-60)
5. olive green cab, clear windows, gray interior, olive green trailer, black hubs; with K-102-A4 ($45-60)
6. olive green body, clear windows, gray interior, olive green trailer, black hubs; with K-102-A3 ($45-60)
7. olive green body, clear windows, black interior, olive green trailer, black hubs; with K-102-A5 ($45-60)

K-107-A 155 MM. SELF PROPELLED GUN, issued 1974
1. olive green body, gold base & gun mount, "A" label ($20-25)
2. olive green body & base, gold gun mount, "A" label ($20-25)
3. olive green body & base, green gun mount, "A" label ($20-25)

K-108-A M3A1 HALF TRACK, issued 1974
1. metallic green body, charcoal brown base, greenish white interior, silver hubs, orange canopy, black treads ($20-25)
2. metallic green body, charcoal brown base, tan interior, silver hubs, orange canopy , black treads($20-25)
3. metallic green body, charcoal gray base, tan interior, silver hubs, tan canopy, black treads ($20-25)
4. olive green body, charcoal gray base, tan interior, black hubs, tan canopy, black treads ($20-25)
5. metallic green body, black base with tab, tan interior, silver hubs, orange canopy, tan treads ($60-85)(BR)

K-109-A M551 SHERIDAN, issued 1976
1. dark green body, black base, "7" label, gray treads ($20-25)
2. dark green body, black base, "7" label, black treads ($20-25)
3. dark olive & tan body, dark olive base, "7" label, gray treads ($25-30)

K-110-A RECOVERY VEHICLE, issued 1977
1. metallic green body, yellow interior, amber windows, silver hubs, "Repair 66" labels ($20-25)
2. olive green body, gray interior, clear windows, black hubs, "Repair 66" labels ($20-25)
3. olive green body, black interior, clear windows, black hubs, "Repair 66" labels ($20-25)

K-111-A MISSILE LAUNCHER, issued 1977
1. metallic green body, orange plastic launch pad & storage racks, silver hubs ($20-25)
2. olive green body, orange plastic launch pad & storage racks, black hubs ($20-25)
3. olive green body, yellow plastic launch pad & storage racks, black hubs ($20-25)
4. olive green body, red plastic launch pad & storage racks, black hubs ($30-40)

K-112-A DAF AMBULANCE, issued 1977
1. olive green body, tan cab roof & canopy ($18-25)
2. olive green body, orange cab roof & canopy ($18-25)

K-113-A MILITARY CRANE TRUCK, issued 1977
1. olive green body & crane, tan interior, clear windows ($25-35)
2. olive green body & crane, gray interior, clear windows ($25-35)

K-114-A ARMY AIRCRAFT TRANSPORTER, issued 1977
1. olive green body, brown plastic airplane with amber window ($25-35)
2. olive green body, brown plastic airplane with clear window ($25-35)
NOTE: Axle covers on either version can come in orange, gold or black amongst others.

K-115-A ARMY PETROL TANKER, issued 1977
1. olive green cab & trailer chassis, dark olive tank, "Army Flammable CD 34-96 M" labels ($25-40)
2. olive green cab, olive drab trailer chassis, dark olive tank, "Army Flammable CD 34-96 M" labels ($25-40)

K-116-A TROOP CARRIER & HOWITZER, issued 1977
1. olive green cab, tan canopy, olive green howitzer ($25-40)

K-117-A SELF PROPELLED "HAWK" ROCKET LAUNCHER, issued 1977
1. tan & green camouflage body, green base, red plastic rockets ($25-40)

K-118-A KAMAN SEASPRITE ARMY HELICOPTER, issued 1978
1. olive green body & base ($20-25)

MM-1-A MILITARY ARTICULATED TANKER, issued 1977
1. olive drab cab, dark olive trailer chassis, dark green tank, "8" labels ($65-80)
2. olive drab cab, dark olive trailer chassis, dark green tank, "Armored Div." labels ($100-150)
3. olive drab cab, olive drab trailer chassis, dark green tank, "Army Flammable CD 34-96 M" labels ($100-150)

MM-2-A ARMORED CAR TRANSPORTER, issued 1977
NOTE: various variations of the MB73-B Weasel can be included for further permutations.
1. olive drab body & base, "7" label; with MB73-B Weasel ($75-100)
2. olive drab body, black base, "8" label, with MB73-B Weasel ($75-100)

Seakings

K-301-A FRIGATE, issued 1976
1. red deck, silver-gray hull, "F109" labels ($15-20)

K-302-A CORVETTE, issued 1976
1. black deck, silver-gray hull, "C70" labels ($15-20)

K-303-A BATTLESHIP, issued 1976
1. brown deck, silver-gray hull, "110" labels ($15-20)

K-304-A AIRCRAFT CARRIER, issued 1976
1. blue deck, gray hull, red & white deck label ($15-20)
2. blue deck, gray hull, blue & yellow deck label ($15-20)

K-305-A SUBMARINE CHASER, issued 1976
1. light gray deck, blue-gray hull, "F101" labels ($15-20)

K-306-A CONVOY ESCORT, issued 1976
1. red deck, silver-gray hull, "C17" labels ($15-20)

K-307-A HELICOPTER CARRIER, issued 1976
1. brown deck, blue-gray hull, "114" labels ($15-20)

K-308-A GUIDED MISSILE DESTROYER, issued 1976
1. blue deck, silver-gray hull, "D02" labels ($15-20)

K-309-A SUBMARINE, issued 1978
1. black deck, dark blue hull, "117" labels ($15-20)

K-310-A ANTI-AIRCRAFT CRUISER, issued 1978
1. brown deck, silver-gray hull, "C115" labels ($15-20)

Adventure 2000

K-2001-A RAIDER COMMAND, issued 1977
1. two piece vehicle in avocado with black base, chrome interior, amber windows, "2000" labels ($25-40)

K-2002-A FLIGHT HUNTER, issued 1977
1. avocado body, black base, red wings, amber windows ($20-30)

K-2003-A CRUSADER TANK, issued 1977
1. avocado body, black chassis, amber windows ($20-30)

K-2004-A ROCKET STRIKER, issued 1977
1. avocado body, black chassis, red radar & rocket launch pad ($20-30)
2. avocado body, black chassis, yellow radar & rocket launch pad ($20-30)

K-2005-A COMMAND FORCE SET, issued 1977
1. set includes K-2004-A with avocado colored MB2-C, MB59-C & MB68-C (for value add individual items together)

K-2006-A SHUTTLE LAUNCHER, issued 1982
1. metallic blue body, black chassis, red launcher with cream saucers ($75-100)

Gold Collection King-size Rigs

This King-Size–type vehicle range includes six styles of Kenworth Transporters. Not part of the regular Superking range, these models sport serial numbers. Issued 1996 ($20-30) each.

42727	Nothing Else is a Pepsi
42728	Body Glove
42729	Roller Blade
42729(B)	Toys R Us Children's Benefit ($150-250)
42731	Matchbox Action System
42732	M & Ms
42733	Fed Ex
42734	Pizza Hut
42736	Oreo

Specials, Turbo Specials, and Alarm Cars

First making their mark in 1984, Specials were a series of race cars in approximately 1/43 scale. Although still available today, this series has yet to find a real niche in the Matchbox series. Although all models are cast "Specials," the model series underwent many different category names including LA Wheels, Super GT Sport, Superkings, Muscle Cars, and Alarm Cars. Some were introduced into the Graffic Traffic series. A secondary series called "Turbo Specials" feature pullback action with two-speed motor. Specials designated as Muscle Cars (MU), Alarm Cars (AL), LA Wheels (LA), Turbo Specials (TS), or King-Size (KS) only are denoted in the variation text.(GF) designates that the model was used as a Graffic Traffic issue.

SP-1/2-A KREMER PORSCHE, issued 1984
1. white body, brown interior, clear windows, "22 Grand Prix" tempa, chromed wheels, Macau casting ($6-8)(SP1)
2. white body, brown interior, clear windows, "35 Porsche" tempa, chromed wheels, Macau casting ($6-8)(SP1)
3. white body, brown interior, clear windows, "35 Porsche" tempa, chromed wheels, Macau casting ($6-8)(TS3)
4. white body, brown interior, clear windows, "35 Porsche" tempa, unchromed wheels, China casting ($6-8)(SP1)
5. pearly silver body, brown interior, clear windows, stripes & "19" tempa, chromed wheels, Macau casting ($6-8)(SP2)
6. maroon body, brown interior, clear windows, "Michelin 15" tempa, chromed wheels, Macau casting ($6-8)(TS3)
7. white body, brown interior, clear windows, green & yellow with "2" tempa, chromed wheels, Macau casting ($6-8)(SP2)
8. white body, brown interior, clear windows, green & yellow with "2" tempa, unchromed wheels, China casting ($6-8)(SP2)
9. white body, brown interior, clear windows, red & yellow with "2" tempa, unchromed wheels, China casting ($6-8)(SP2)
10. black body, brown interior, clear windows, "35 Porsche" tempa, unchromed wheels, China casting ($10-15)(LA)
11. white body & base, white interior, pink windows, no tempa, unchromed wheels, China casting ($10-15)(GF)
12. white body, brown interior, clear windows, "Lloyd's 1" tempa, unchromed wheels, China casting ($20-30)(UK)

SP-3/4-A FERRARI 512BB, issued 1984
1. blue body, black interior, clear windows, "Pioneer 11" tempa, chromed wheels, Macau casting ($6-8)(SP3)
2. red body, black interior, clear windows, "European University 11" tempa, chromed wheels, Macau casting ($6-8)(SP4)
3. black body, gray interior, clear windows, "Michelin 88" tempa, chromed wheels, Macau casting ($6-8)(SP4)
4. white body, black interior, clear windows, "Pioneer 11" tempa, chromed wheels, Macau casting ($8-10)(TS6)
5. orange body, gray interior, clear windows, "147" tempa, chromed wheels, Macau casting ($6-8)(SP3)
6. white body, gray interior, clear windows, "147" tempa, unchromed wheels, China casting ($6-8)(LA)
7. lime body, gray interior, clear windows, "Michelin 88" tempa, unchromed wheels, China casting ($6-8)(LA)
8. white body & base, white interior, amber windows, no tempa, unchromed wheels, China casting ($10-15)(GF)
9. white & black body, white interior, amber windows, pink flames & "512" tempa, white China base, unchromed wheels ($5-8)

SP-5/6-A LANCIA RALLYE, issued 1984
1. yellow body, dark gray interior, clear windows, "102" tempa, chromed wheels, Macau casting ($6-8)(SP5)
2. white body, dark gray interior, clear windows, "Martini Racing 1" tempa, chromed wheels, Macau casting ($6-8)(SP6)
3. green body, light gray interior, clear windows, "Pirelli 116" tempa, chromed wheels, Macau casting ($6-8)(SP5)
4. white body, dark gray interior, clear windows, "102" tempa, unchromed wheels, Macau casting ($6-8)(TS5)
5. dark blue body, light gray interior, clear windows, "Pirelli 16" tempa, unchromed wheels, China casting ($6-8)(LA)
6. white body & base, white interior, blue windows, no tempa, unchromed wheels, China casting ($10-15)(GF)

SP-7/8-A ZAKSPEED MUSTANG, issued 1984
1. white body, black interior, clear windows, "Ford 16" tempa, chromed wheels, Macau casting ($6-8)(SP7)
2. pearly silver body, black interior, clear windows, "Motul 28" tempa, chromed wheels, Macau casting ($6-8)(SP8)
3. yellow body, gray interior, clear windows, blue & red with "20" tempa, unchromed wheels, Macau casting ($6-8)(TS2)
4. black body, maroon interior, clear windows, "83" tempa, chromed wheels, Macau casting ($6-8)(SP8)
5. blue body, black interior, clear windows, "QXR Duckhams" tempa, chromed wheels, Macau casting ($6-8)(SP7)
6. black body, black interior, clear windows, "83" tempa, unchromed wheels, Macau casting ($6-8)(TS2)
7. orange body, maroon interior, clear windows, blue & red with "20" tempa, unchromed wheels, China casting ($6-8)(KS1)
8. blue body, black interior, clear windows, "QXR Duckhams" tempa, unchromed wheels, China casting ($6-8)(KS6)
9. white body, black interior, clear windows, blue stripes tempa, chromed wheels, China casting ($6-8)(MU)
10. orange body, black interior, clear windows, black stripes tempa, chromed wheels, China casting ($6-8)(MU)

SP- 9/10-A CHEVY PROSTOCKER, issued 1984
1. lemon body, brown interior, clear windows, "NGK 12" tempa, chromed wheels, black base, Macau casting ($6-8)(SP9)
2. metallic blue body, brown interior, clear windows, "Heuer 111" tempa, chromed wheels, black base, Macau casting ($6-8)(SP10)
3. green body, brown interior, clear windows, "Heuer 9" tempa, chromed wheels, black base, Macau casting ($6-8)(SP10)
4. green body, gray interior, clear windows, "Heuer 9" tempa, unchromed wheels, gray base, Macau casting ($6-8)(TS4)
5. white body, gray interior, clear windows, "Momo 5" tempa, unchromed wheels, gray base, Macau casting ($8-12)(TS4)
6. yellow body, brown interior, clear windows, "Heuer 9" tempa, unchromed wheels, black base, China casting ($6-8)(LA)
7. orange-yellow body, brown interior, clear windows, "Heuer 9" tempa, unchromed wheels, black base, China casting ($6-8)(KS)
8. dark blue body, gray interior, clear windows, white stripes & "SS454" tempa, chromed wheels, black base, China casting ($6-8)(MU)
9. red body, gray interior, clear windows, black stripes tempa, chromed wheels, black base, China casting ($6-8)(MU)

SP-9/10-B JAGUAR XJ220, issued 1993
1. red body, white interior, smoke windows, black base, chrome wheels, no tempa, China casting ($6-8)
2. blue body, white interior, smoke windows, black base, chrome wheels, no tempa, China casting ($6-8)

SP-11/12-A CHEVROLET CAMARO, issued 1984
1. white body, black interior, clear windows, "Goodyear 18" tempa, chromed wheels, Macau casting ($6-8)(SP11)
2. red body, black interior, clear windows, "56" tempa, chromed wheels, Macau casting ($6-8)(SP12)
3. white body, black interior, clear windows, "7 Total" tempa, chromed wheels, Macau casting ($6-8)(SP12)
4. white body, brown interior, clear windows, "Firestone 4" tempa, unchromed wheels, Macau casting ($6-8)(TS1)
5. white body, brown interior, clear windows, "7 Total" tempa, unchromed wheels, Macau casting ($6-8)(TS1)
6. white body, black interior, clear windows, "Michelin 3" tempa, chromed wheels, Macau casting ($6-8)(SP11)
7. white body, black interior, clear windows, "Michelin 3" tempa, unchromed wheels, China casting ($6-8)(LA)(KS)
8. yellow body, black interior, clear windows, "7 Total" tempa, unchromed wheels, China casting ($6-8)(LA)(KS)
9. white body, black interior, clear windows, orange & black stripes tempa, chromed wheels, China casting ($6-8)(MU)
10. black body, black interior, clear windows, orange & black stripes tempa, chromed wheels, China casting ($6-8)(MU)

SP-11-B FORD THUNDERBIRD, issued 1994
1. black body, black interior, black base, clear windows, "Texaco/Havoline 28" tempa, China casting ($10-15)
2. white body, gray interior, black base, clear windows, "US AIR/ US Air 77/ Jasper" tempa, China casting ($12-15)(US)

SP-12-B CHEVROLET LUMINA, issued 1994
1. orange/yellow body, black interior, black base, clear windows, "Kodak Film 4" tempa, China casting ($7-10)
2. blue body, black interior, black base, clear windows, "Mr. Salt 71" tempa, China casting ($8-12)(US)
3. red body, gray interior, black base, clear windows, "Bryant/Cafeteria 14" tempa, China casting ($8-12)(US)
4. blue body, black interior, black base, clear windows, "Mr. Salt 74" with rear print reading "Started 34th Finished 21st" tempa, China casting ($8-12)(US)
5. white body, black interior, black base, clear windows, "Wintech 1" with assorted colors & stripes tempa, no markings cast on base ($750+)(HK)

SP-13/14-A PORSCHE 959, issued 1986
1. red body, gray interior, clear windows, "Michelin 44" tempa, chromed wheels, Macau base ($6-8)(SP13)
2. white body, gray interior, clear windows, "53" with stripes tempa, chromed wheels, Macau casting ($6-8)(SP14)
3. black body, gray interior, clear windows, "Michelin 44" tempa, unchromed wheels, Macau casting ($6-8)(LA)
4. yellow body, gray interior, clear windows, "53" with stripes tempa, unchromed wheels, China casting ($6-8)(LA)
5. silver-gray body, tan interior, clear windows, "27" with stripes tempa, unchromed wheels, China casting ($8-12)(TS8)
6. silver-gray body, gray interior, clear windows, "3" with stripes tempa, unchromed wheels, China casting ($8-12)(KS)
7. white body, gray interior, blue windows, "Porsche 959" tempa, chromed wheels, China casting ($8-12)(KS)
8. white body, white interior, blue windows, no tempa, unchromed wheels, China casting ($10-15)(GF)
9. dark blue body, no interior, black windows, "Turbo" tempa, chromed wheels, China casting ($15-18)(AL)
10. black body, no interior, black windows, "Turbo" tempa, chromed wheels, China casting ($15-18)(AL)
11. red body, white interior & base, amber windows, caricature tempa, white wheels, China casting ($6-8)(LL)
12. white body, white interior, black base, clear windows, "959" with red, green & black lines tempa, China casting ($6-8)

Skybusters

Skybusters were first introduced in 1973. Early versions are cast with "SP" rather than "SB" numbers as the line was originally was to be called Super Planes. The Shanghai Universal Toy Co. (SUTC) was under contract from Tyco and now under contract with Mattel, Inc. to produce Skybusters. The same Matchbox Skybusters are also produced with a

"SUTC" casting with "Matchbox" & model number removed. These appear to be only offered for sale in China. No attempt has been made in this book to catalog these "SUTC" version castings.

SB-1-A LEAR JET, issued 1973
1. yellow fuselage, white undercarriage, "D-ILDE" labels, blue window, thin axles, England casting ($10-15)
NOTE: Below models with thick axles.
2. yellow body, white undercarriage, "D-ILDE" labels, blue window, England casting ($10-15)
3. yellow body, white undercarriage, "D-ILDE" tempa, blue window, England casting ($10-15)
4. yellow body, white undercarriage, "D-ILDE" tempa, clear window, England casting ($10-15)
5. lemon body, white undercarriage, "D-ILDE" tempa, clear window, Macau casting ($6-8)
6. red body, red undercarriage, "Datapost" tempa, clear window, Macau casting ($6-8)
7. purple body, white undercarriage, "Federal Express" tempa, clear window, Macau casting ($6-8)(GS)
8. white body, white undercarriage, "G-JCB" tempa, clear window, Macau casting ($8-12)(GS)
9. white body, white undercarriage, "U.S. Air Force" tempa, clear window, Macau casting ($-6)(US)
10. purple body, purple undercarriage, "U.S. Air Force" tempa, clear window, Macau casting ($6-8)(SC)
11. white body, white & orange undercarriage, "QX-Press Freight Delivery Service" tempa, clear window, Macau casting ($4-6)
12. white body, white undercarriage, "DHL" tempa, clear window, Thailand casting ($3-4)
13. white body, white undercarriage, "U.S. Air Force" tempa, clear window, Thailand casting ($3-4)(US)
14. white body, white undercarriage, "DHL" tempa, clear window, China casting ($3-4)

SB-2-A CORSAIR A7D, issued 1973
1. dark green body, white base, clear window, with tail label, thin axles, England casting ($10-15)
2. dark green body, white base, clear window, with tail label, thick axles, England casting ($10-15)
3. dark blue body, white base, clear window, with tail label, thick axles, England casting ($8-12)
4. dark blue body, white base, clear window, no tail label, thick axles, England casting ($8-12)
5. silver-blue body, white base, clear window, with tail label, thick axles, England casting ($8-12)
6. khaki tan body, white base, clear window, brown & green camouflage tempa, thick axles, Macau casting ($6-8)(US)
7. orange body, white base, clear window, olive & brown camouflage tempa, thick axles, Macau casting ($6-8)(SC)

SB-3-A A300 AIRBUS, issued 1973
1. white fuselage, silver-gray undercarriage, "Air France" labels, no tail label, thin axles, England casting ($10-15)
2. white fuselage, silver-gray undercarriage, "Air France" labels, 4 sided tail label, thin axles, England casting ($10-15)
3. white fuselage, silver-gray undercarriage, "Air France" labels, 5 sided tail label, thin axles, England casting ($10-15)
4. white fuselage, silver-gray undercarriage, no labels, 5 sided tail label, thin axles, England casting ($10-15)
5. white fuselage, silver-gray undercarriage, "Air France" labels, 5 sided tail label, thick axles, England casting ($10-15)
6. white fuselage, silver-gray undercarriage, "Air France" tempa, tempa on tail, thick axles, England casting ($8-12)
7. white fuselage, silver-gray undercarriage, "Lufthansa" tempa, tempa on tail, thick axles, England casting ($8-12)

SB-3-B NASA SPACE SHUTTLE, issued 1980
1. white body, gray base, "United States NASA" labels, England casting ($7-10)
2. white body, pearly silver base, "United States NASA" labels, Macau casting ($3-5)
3. white body, pearly silver base, "United States NASA" labels, Thailand casting ($3-5)
4. white body, white base, no labels, Thailand casting ($6-8)(GF)
5. white body, black base, "United States NASA" labels, China casting ($3-4)
6. white body, black base, upside-down "United States NASA" labels, China casting ($3-4)

SB-4-A MIRAGE F1, issued 1973
1. red body & base, clear window, thin axles, bulleyes on wings, England casting ($10-15)
2. red body & base, smoke window, thin axles, bulleyes on wings, England casting ($10-15)
NOTE: Below models with thick axles.
3. red body & base, clear window, bulleyes on wings, England casting ($10-15)
4. red body & base, smoke window, bulleyes on wings, England casting ($10-15)
5. light orange body, brown base, clear window, "122-18" tempa, Macau casting ($4-6)
6. dark orange body, brown base, clear window, "122-18" tempa, Macau casting ($4-6)
7. yellow body & base, clear window, blue stripes on red painted wings tempa, Macau casting ($3-5)(US)
8. white body & base, clear window, "ZE-164" with blue wings tempa, Macau casting ($3-5)(UK)
9. pink body & base, clear window, blue stripes on red painted wings tempa, Macau casting ($6-8)(SC)
10. blue body & base, clear window, white & red stripes tempa, Thailand casting ($3-5)
11. yellow body & base, clear window, blue stripes on red painted wings tempa, China casting ($3-4)
12. brown body, gray base, clear window, dark cream camouflage & bulleyes tempa, China casting ($3-4)

SB-5-A STARFIGHTER F104, issued 1973
1. white body, silver-gray base, blue window, thin axles, maple leaf labels, England casting ($10-15)
2. white body, silver-gray base, blue window, thick axles, maple leaf labels, England casting ($10-15)
3. red body, silver-gray base, blue window, thick axles, maple leaf labels, England casting ($10-15)

SB-6-A MIG 21, issued 1973
1. blue body, white base, clear window, thin axles, cut star labels, no tail label, England casting ($10-15)
2. blue body, white base, clear window, thin axles, cut star labels, with tail label, England casting ($10-15)
NOTE: All models below with thick axles
3. blue body, white base, clear window, cut star labels, with tail label, England casting ($10-15)
4. blue body, white base, clear window, round star labels, with tail label, England casting ($10-15)
5. silver-blue body, white base, clear window, round star labels, with tail label, England casting ($10-15)
6. silver-gray flecked body & base, clear window, star wing & tail tempa, Macau casting ($4-6)(US)
7. black body & base, clear window, lightning bolts on wings & scorpion & "3" on tail tempa, Macau casting ($4-6)(US)
8. light purple body & base, clear window, lightning bolts on wings & scorpion & "3" on tail tempa, Macau casting ($6-8)(SC)
9. black body & base, clear window, lightning bolt on wings & scorpion & "3" on tail tempa, Thailand casting ($3-5)(US)
10. pearly silver body & base, clear window, star wing & tail tempa, Thailand casting ($3-5)(US)
11. black body & base, clear window, lightning bolts on wings & scorpion & "3" on tail tempa, China casting ($3-4)
12. dark green body, gray base, clear window, red stars & "16" with pale green & olive camouflage tempa, China casting ($3-4)

SB-7-A JUNKERS 87B, issued 1973
1. green body, base & wings, thin axles, cross wing labels, swastika tail label, England casting ($10-15)
2. green body, base & wings, thick axles, cross wing labels, swastika tail label, England casting ($10-15)
3. black body, silver-gray base & wings, thin axles, cross wing labels, swastika tail label, England casting ($350-500)
4. black body, beige & brown base & wings, cross labels on wings & tail, Macau casting ($7-10)
5. green body, base & wings, thick axles, cross labels on wings & tail, Macau casting ($7-10)

SB-8-A SPITFIRE, issued 1973
1. dark brown body, gold base & wings, thin axles, light blue window, with tail label, England casting ($15-20)
2. dark brown body, gold base & wings, thin axles, clear window, with tail label, England casting ($15-20)
3. metallic green body, gold base & wings, thin axles, light blue window, with tail label, England casting ($10-15)
4. metallic green body, gold base & wings, thin axles, light blue window, no tail label, England casting ($10-15)
5. metallic green body, gold base & wings, thin axles, clear window,. with tail label, England casting ($10-15)
6. metallic green body, gold base & wings, thick axles, light blue window, with tail label, England casting ($10-15)
7. metallic green body, gold base & wings, thick axles, light blue window, no tail label, England casting ($10-15)
8. gold plated body, base & wings, no axles, clear windshield, no tail label, mounted on pen stand ($45-60)(GW)
9. light brown body, khaki base & wings, clear window, light brown camouflage tempa & bullseye labels, Macau casting ($7-10)
10. khaki body, base & wings, clear window, green camouflage tempa, Thailand casting ($20-25)(UK)(OP)

SB-9-A CESSNA 402, issued 1973
1. light green body, white base & wings, thin axles, light blue window, with labels, England casting ($10-15)
2. light green body, white base & wings, thin axles, clear window, with labels, England casting ($10-15)
3. dark green body, white base & wings, thin axles, clear window, with labels, England casting ($10-15)
NOTE: Below models all with thick axles
4. light green body, white base & wings, light blue window, with labels, England casting ($10-15)
5. light green body, white base & wings, clear window, with labels, England casting ($10-15)
6. pea green body, white base & wings, clear window, with tempa, England casting ($10-15)
7. light green body, white base & wings, light blue window, with tempa, England casting ($10-15)
8. light green body, white base & wings, clear window, with tempa, England casting ($10-15)
9. dark green body, white base & wings, light blue window, with tempa, England casting ($10-15)
10. dark green body, white base & wings, clear window, with tempa, England casting ($10-15)
11. dark green body, white base & wings, clear window, "N7873Q" tempa, Macau casting ($7-10)
12. brown body, beige base & wings, clear window, "N402CW" tempa, Macau casting ($6-8)
13. white body, red base & wings, clear window, "DHL World-Wide Express" tempa, Macau casting ($4-6)
14. blue body, yellow base & wings, clear window, "S7-402" etc. tempa, Macau casting ($4-6)
15. white body, red base & wings, clear window, "DHL World-Wide Express" tempa, Thailand casting ($3-5)
16. white body, base & wings, clear window, "Delivery Service DS" tempa, China casting ($10-15)

SB-10-A BOEING 747, issued 1973
1. white fuselage, dark blue undercarriage, thin axles, "BOAC" labels, England casting ($10-15)
2. white fuselage, dark blue undercarriage, thin axles, "British Airways" labels, England casting ($10-15)
NOTE: All models below with thick axles
3. white fuselage, dark blue undercarriage, "British Airways" labels, England casting ($10-15)
4. white fuselage, dark blue undercarriage, "British Airways" tempa, England casting ($10-15)
5. white fuselage, dark blue undercarriage, "Qantas" tempa, England casting ($10-15)
6. white fuselage, silver-gray undercarriage, "United States of America" tempa, England casting ($15-20)
7. white fuselage, silver-gray undercarriage, "MEA" tempa, England casting ($15-20)
8. white fuselage, silver plated undercarriage, no axles, "BOAC" labels, mounted on ashtray, England casting ($45-60)
9. white fuselage, gold plated undercarriage, no axles, "British Airways" labels, mounted on ashtray, England casting ($45-60)
10. white fuselage, dark blue undercarriage, "British" tempa, Macau casting ($15-20)
11. white fuselage, pearly silver undercarriage, "Cathay Pacific" tempa, Macau casting ($6-8)
12. white fuselage, pearly silver undercarriage, "British Caledonia" tempa, Macau casting ($8-12)
13. white fuselage, pearly silver undercarriage, "Lufthansa" tempa, Macau casting ($6-8)
14. white fuselage, pearly silver undercarriage, "Pan Am" tempa, Macau casting ($12-15)
15. white fuselage & undercarriage, "Virgin" tempa, Macau casting ($6-8)
16. powder blue fuselage, pearly silver undercarriage, "KLM" tempa, Macau casting ($6-8)
17. white body, pearly silver undercarriage, "Air Nippon" tempa, Macau casting ($12-15)(JP)(GS)
18. lime body, white undercarriage with pearly silver wings, "Aer Lingus" tempa, Macau casting ($6-8)
19. powder blue fuselage, pearly silver undercarriage, "KLM" tempa, Thailand casting ($3-5)
20. white fuselage, pearly silver undercarriage, "Pan Am" tempa, Thailand casting ($7-10)
21. white fuselage, pearly silver undercarriage, "Lufthansa" tempa, Thailand casting ($3-5)
22. white fuselage & undercarriage, "South African Airways" tempa, Thailand casting ($10-15)(GR)
23. white fuselage & undercarriage, "Virgin" tempa, Thailand casting ($3-5)
24. white fuselage, pearly silver undercarriage, "Saudi" tempa, Thailand casting ($3-5)
25. white fuselage, pearly silver undercarriage, "Olympic" tempa, Thailand casting ($3-5)
26. white fuselage, white undercarriage with pearly silver wings, "El Al" labels/tempa, Thailand casting ($7-10)(IS)
27. light gray fuselage, dark blue undercarriage, "British Airways" tempa, China casting ($3-4)

SB-11-A ALPHA JET, issued 1973
1. metallic red body, white base, thin axles, clear window, with labels, England casting ($10-15)
2. metallic red body, white base, thick axles, clear window, with labels, England casting ($10-15)
3. blue body, red base, thick axles, clear window, no tempa on wings, England casting ($15-20)
4. blue body & base, thick axles, clear window, "162" on wings tempa, Macau casting ($7-10)
5. white body, red base, thick axles, clear window, "AT39" on wings tempa, Macau casting ($7-10)
6. black body & base, thick axles, blue window, "AT39" & bullseyes on wings tempa, Macau casting ($20-30)(MP)(CHI)

SB-12-A SKYHAWK A-4F, issued 1973
1. dark blue body, white base, thin axles, clear window, "Navy" labels, England casting ($10-15)
2. dark blue body, white base, thick axles, clear window, "Navy" labels, England casting ($10-15)
3. dark blue body, white base, thick axles, clear window, "Marines" tempa, England casting ($10-15)

SB-12-B PITTS SPECIAL, issued 1980
1. metallic red body, white upper wings, red checkers tempa, cream driver, England casting ($8-12)
2. dark green body, white upper wings, red flares tempa, cream driver, Macau casting ($7-10)
3. blue body, white upper wings, "Matchbox" tempa, cream driver, Macau casting ($7-10)
4. red body, red upper wings, "Fly Virgin Atlantic" tempa, cream driver, Macau casting ($6-8)
5. red body, red upper wings, "Fly Virgin Atlantic" tempa, cream driver, Thailand casting ($3-5)
6. white body, white upper wings, no tempa, red driver, Thailand casting ($10-15)(GF)
7. white body, white upper wings, "Circus Circus" tempa, no driver, Thailand casting ($6-8)(GS)

SB-13-A DC.10, issued 1973
1. white fuselage, red undercarriage, thin axles, "Swissair" labels, England casting ($10-15)
2. white fuselage, red undercarriage, thin axles, "Swissair" tempa, England casting ($10-15)
3. white fuselage, silver-gray undercarriage, thin axles, "Swissair" tempa, England casting ($10-15)
NOTE: Models listed below with thick axles
4. white fuselage, red undercarriage, "Swissair" tempa, England casting ($10-15)
5. white fuselage, silver-gray undercarriage, "Swissair" tempa, England casting ($10-15)
6. white fuselage, silver-gray undercarriage, "United" tempa, England casting ($10-15)
7. white fuselage, pearly silver undercarriage, "Lufthansa" tempa, Macau casting ($6-8)
8. white fuselage, pearly silver undercarriage, "Alitalia" tempa, Macau casting ($6-8)
9. white fuselage & undercarriage, "Thai" tempa, Macau casting ($6-8)
10. white fuselage, pearly silver undercarriage, "Swissair" tempa, Macau casting ($6-8)
11. silver & red fuselage, pearly silver undercarriage, "Aeromexico" tempa, Macau casting ($6-8)
12. silver-gray fuselage, silver-gray undercarriage, "American" tempa, Macau casting ($6-8)
13. white fuselage & undercarriage, "UTA" tempa, Macau casting ($250-300)
14. white fuselage & undercarriage, "Thai" tempa, Thailand casting ($3-5)
15. silver & red fuselage, pearly silver undercarriage, "Aeromexico" tempa, Thailand casting ($3-5)
16. white fuselage & undercarriage, "Scandinavian" tempa, Thailand casting ($3-5)
17. silver-gray fuselage & undercarriage, "United" tempa, Thailand casting ($3-5)
18. white fuselage, silver-gray undercarriage, "Sabena" tempa, Thailand casting ($3-5)
19. powder blue fuselage, silver gray undercarriage, "KLM" tempa, China casting ($3-4)

SB-14-A CESSNA 210, issued 1973
1. orange-yellow body, white base & wings, thin axles, clear window, with labels, England casting ($10-15)
2. orange body, white base & wings, thin axles, clear window, with labels, England casting ($10-15)
3. orange body, white base & wings, thick axles, clear window, with labels, England casting ($10-15)
4. orange body, white base & wings, thick axles, clear window, with tempa, England casting ($10-15)

SB-15-A PHANTOM F4E, issued 1975
1. metallic red body, white base & wings, light blue window, red/white/blue wing labels, England casting ($10-15)
2. metallic red body, white base & wings, light blue window, red & blue wing labels, England casting ($10-15)
3. cherry red body, white base & wings, light blue window, red/white/blue wing labels, England casting ($10-15)
4. metallic red body, white base & wings, clear window, red/white/blue wing labels, Macau casting ($7-10)
5. gray body, base & wings, clear window, "Marines" with orange & yellow stripes tempa, Macau casting ($4-6)
6. pink body, base & wings, clear window, "Marines" with orange & yellow stripes tempa, Macau casting ($6-8)(SC)
7. gray body, base & wings, clear window, "Marines" with orange & yellow stripes tempa, Thailand casting ($3-5)
8. gray body, base & wings, clear window, "Marines" with orange & yellow stripes tempa, China casting ($3-4)
9. white body, base & wings, clear window, "5888 Navy" & emblems tempa, China casting ($3-4)

SB-16-A CORSAIR F4U, issued 1975
1. metallic blue body, clear window, star label on right wing, star label on left wing, England casting ($10-15)
2. metallic blue body, clear window, star label on right wing, "Navy" label on left wing, England casting ($10-15)
3. metallic blue body, clear window, "Navy" label on right wing, star label on left wing, England casting ($10-15)
4. orange body, clear window, star label on right wing, "Navy" label on left wing, England casting ($8-12)
5. orange body, clear window, "Navy" label on right wing, star label on left wing, England casting ($8-12)
6. light orange body, clear window, "Navy" label on right wing, star label on left wing, Macau casting ($7-10)

SB-17-A RAM ROD, issued 1976
1. red body, white base & wings, clear windows, 1-3/8" long wing labels, England casting ($10-15)
2. red body, white base & wings, clear windows, 1-1/8" long wing labels, England casting ($10-15)

SB-18-A WILD WIND, issued 1976
1. lime green body & wings, white base, "Wild" & "Wind" wing labels, "7" in circle tail label, England casting ($10-15)
2. lime green body & wings, white base, "Wild" & "Wind" wing labels, star tail label, England casting ($10-15)

SB-19-A PIPER COMANCHE, issued 1977
1. red body, yellow base & wings, chrome interior, "N246P" labels, England casting ($10-15)
2. white body, base & wings, silver-gray interior, "XP" tempa, Macau casting ($6-8)
3. beige body, dark blue base & wings, silver-gray interior, "Comanche" tempa, Macau casting ($4-6)
4. beige body, dark blue base & wings, silver-gray interior, "Comanche" tempa, Thailand casting ($3-5)
5. beige body, dark blue base & wings, silver/gray interior, "Comanche" tempa, China casting ($3-4)

SB-20-A HELICOPTER, issued 1977
1. olive upper & lower body, "Army" labels, England casting ($10-15)
2. white upper body, powder blue lower body, "Coast Guard" labels, England casting ($8-12)
3. white upper body, red lower body, "Police" labels, England casting ($8-12)
4. dark blue upper body, white lower body, "Air-Aid" tempa, Macau casting ($6-8)
5. dark blue upper & lower body, "Gendarmarie JAB" tempa, Macau casting ($250-300)(FR)

SB-21-A LIGHTNING, issued 1977
1. olive body & wings, gray base, smoke gray window, red side missiles, England casting ($8-12)
2. silver-gray body & wings, gray base, smoke gray window, red side missiles, England casting ($10-15)
3. silver-gray body, wings & base, smoke gray window, red side missiles, England casting ($8-12)

SB-22-A TORNADO, issued 1978
1. light gray body & wings, white base, pale gray camouflage, stripe only tail label, England casting ($7-10)
2. light gray body & wings, white base, pale gray camouflage, stripe with "01" tail label, England casting ($7-10)
3. dark gray body & wings, white base, light gray camouflage, stripe only tail label, England casting ($7-10)
4. dark gray body & wings, white base, light gray camouflage, stripe with "01" tail label, England casting ($7-10)
5. dark gray body & wings, white base, cream camouflage, stripe with "01" tail label, England casting ($7-10)
6. light gray body & wings, white base, "F132" & ornate design tempa, Macau casting ($6-8)
7. red body & wings, white base, white wings with "06" tempa, Macau casting ($6-8)(UK)
8. light purple body & wings, white base, "F132" & ornate design tempa, Macau casting ($6-8)(SC)
9. light gray body & wings, white base, "F132" & ornate design tempa, Thailand casting ($3-5)
10. blue-gray body & wings, blue-gray base, green camouflage & bullseye tempa, China casting ($3-4)

SB-23-A SUPERSONIC TRANSPORT, issued 1979
1. white body & base, "Air France" tempa, tempa tail print, with wing label, England casting ($7-10)
2. white body & base, "Singapore" tempa, tempa tail print, with wing label, England casting ($175-250)
3. white body & base, "Air France" tempa, Macau casting ($4-6)
4. white body & base, "Supersonic Airlines" tempa, Macau casting ($4-6)
5. white body & base, "Singapore Airlines" tempa, Macau casting ($175-250)
6. white body & base, "British Airways" tempa, Thailand casting ($3-5)
7. white body & base, "Air France" tempa, Thailand casting ($3-5)
8. white body & base, "Heinz 57" tempa, Thailand casting ($35-50)(US)
9. white body & base, no tempa, Thailand casting ($6-8)(GF)
10. white body & base, "British Airways" tempa, China casting ($3-4)

SB-24-A F.16 FIGHTER JET, issued 1979
1. white body, red base & wings, "USAF" label on right wing, star label on left wing, "U.S. Air Force" labels on sides, England casting ($7-10)
2. white body, red base & wings, "USAF" label on right wing, star label on left wing, no side labels, England casting ($7-10)
3. white body, red base & wings, star label on right & left wings, no side labels, England casting ($7-10)
4. white body, red base & wings, "USAF" label on right wing, star label on left wing, no side labels, Macau casting ($6-8)
5. red body, white base & wings, "USAF" tempa on right wing, star tempa on left wing, "United States Air Force" side tempa, Macau casting ($4-6)
6. light gray body, base & wings, "USAF" tempa on right wing, star tempa on left wing, "U.S. Air Force" side tempa with blue & dark gray camouflage, Macau casting ($4-6)(US)
7. white body, base & wings, black tempa on both wings, "USAF XXX" side tempa, Macau casting ($4-6)(UK)
8. light gray body, base & wings, "USAF" tempa on right wing, star tempa on left wing, "U.S. Air Force" side tempa with blue & dark gray camouflage, Thailand casting ($3-5)
9. light purple body, base & wings, "USAF" tempa on right wing, star tempa on left wing, "U.S. Air Force" side tempa with blue & dark gray camouflage, Macau casting ($6-8)(SC)
10. red body, white base & wings, "USAF" tempa on right wing, star tempa on left wing, "United States Air Force" side tempa, Thailand casting ($3-5)(UK)
11. white body, base & wings, no tempa, red windows, Thailand casting ($10-15)(GF)
12. light khaki tan body & wings, gray base, blue star in white circle & "106" tempa, China casting ($3-4)

SB-25-A RESCUE HELICOPTER, issued 1979
1. yellow upper & lower body, black interior, black exhausts, "Rescue" labels, England casting ($7-10)
2. yellow upper & lower body, white interior, chrome exhausts, "Rescue" labels, England casting ($7-10)
3. white & red upper body, white lower body, white interior, chrome exhausts, "Los Angeles City Fire Dept." labels ($10-15)(CR)
4. white upper body, blue lower body, white interior, chrome exhausts, no labels, England casting ($8-12)
5. dark blue upper & lower body, black interior, black exhausts, "Royal Air Force Rescue" tempa, Macau casting ($5-8)
6. white upper & lower body, orange interior, chrome exhausts, "Shell" tempa, Macau casting ($5-8)
7. white upper body, red lower body, tan interior, chrome exhausts, "007" tempa, Macau casting ($10-15)(JB)(GS)
8. dark blue upper & lower body, blue interior, black exhausts, "Royal Air Force Rescue" tempa, China casting ($3-4)
9. gray upper & lower body, gray interior, gray exhausts, "Royal Air Force Rescue" tempa, China casting ($3-4)

SB-26-A CESSNA FLOAT PLANE, issued 1981
1. red body, white base & wings, black skis, smoke gray window, "N264H" tempa, 'SB14' cast on base, England casting ($10-15)
2. red body, white base & wings, black skis, clear window, "N264H" tempa, Macau casting ($6-8)
3. black body, white base & wings, black skis, clear window, "C210F" tempa, Macau casting ($6-8)
4. red body, base & wings, black skis, clear window, "Fire" tempa, Macau casting ($3-5)
5. white body, base & wings, black skis, clear window, "007 James Bond" tempa, Macau casting ($10-15)(JB)(GS)
6. white body, base & wings, green skis & propeller, clear window, "National Park Service" tempa, China casting ($3-4)
7. white body, base & wings, green skis & propeller, clear window, "Forestry Service" tempa, China casting ($8-12)

SB-27-A HARRIER JET, issued 1981
1. white body & wings, red base, "Marines" tempa, clear window, England casting ($10-15)
2. white body & wings, red base, "Marines" tempa, clear window, Macau casting ($6-8)
3. light gray body & wings, white base, dark gray camouflage tempa, clear window, Macau casting ($4-6)
4. gray body & wings, white base, "Marines" & dark gray camouflage tempa, clear window, Macau casting ($4-6)(US)
5. metallic blue body & wings, white base, "Royal Navy" tempa, clear window, Macau casting ($4-6)(UK)
6. pea green body & wings, white base, "Marines" & olive camouflage tempa clear window, Macau casting ($6-8)(SC)
7. dark blue body & wings, white base, "Royal Navy" tempa, clear window, Thailand casting ($3-5)
8. light gray body & wings, white base, bullseye tempa, clear window, Thailand casting ($3-5)
9. gray body & wings,. white base, dark gray camouflage tempa, clear window, China casting ($3-4)
10. gray body, wings & base, bulleyes, 4 red "x" tempa, clear window, China casting ($3-4)

SB-28-A A300 AIRBUS, issued 1983
1. white fuselage, pearly silver undercarriage, "Lufthansa" tempa, Macau casting ($6-8)
2. white fuselage & undercarriage, "Alitalia" tempa, Macau casting ($6-8)
3. white fuselage & undercarriage, "Air France" tempa, Macau casting ($6-8)
4. powder blue fuselage, pearly silver undercarriage, "Korean Air" tempa, Macau casting ($5-8)
5. white fuselage & undercarriage, "Iberia" tempa, Macau casting ($5-8)
6. white fuselage & undercarriage, "Air Inter" tempa, Macau casting ($125-175)
7. white fuselage, pearly silver undercarriage, "Swissair" tempa, Macau casting ($5-8)
8. white fuselage & undercarriage, "Air France" tempa, Thailand casting ($3-5)
9. powder blue fuselage, white undercarriage, "Korean Air" tempa, Thailand casting ($3-5)
10. white fuselage & undercarriage, "Alitalia" tempa, Thailand casting ($3-5)
11. white fuselage & undercarriage, "Air Malta" tempa, Thailand casting ($20-30) (Malta)
12. white fuselage & undercarriage, "Swissair" tempa, Thailand casting

(\$3-5)
13. white fuselage & undercarriage, "Iberia" tempa, China casting (\$3-4)

SB-29-A SR-71 BLACKBIRD, issued 1990
1. black body, "U.S. Air Force" tempa, Macau casting (\$3-5)
2. black body, "U.S. Air Force" tempa, Thailand casting (\$3-5)
3. black body, "U.S. Air Force" tempa, China casting (\$3-4)
4. silver-gray body, "U.S. Air Force" tempa, China casting (\$60-85)(CHI)
5. silver-gray body with black painted front, black base, "U.S. Air Force" tempa, China casting (\$3-4)

SB-30-A GRUMMAN F-14 TOMCAT, issued 1990
1. gray fuselage, white undercarriage, "Navy" tempa, Macau casting (\$3-5)
2. gray fuselage, white undercarriage, "Navy" tempa, Thailand casting (\$3-5)
3. light gray fuselage & undercarriage, "115", "15" & emblem tempa, China casting (\$3-4)

SB-31-A BOEING 747-400, issued 1990
1. light gray fuselage, dark blue undercarriage, "British Airways" tempa, Thailand casting (\$4-6)(GS)
2. white fuselage, pearly silver undercarriage, "Cathay Pacific" tempa, Thailand casting (\$3-5)
3. white fuselage, pearly silver undercarriage, "Lufthansa" tempa, Thailand casting (\$3-5)
4. white fuselage, pearly silver undercarriage, "Singapore Airlines" tempa, Thailand casting (\$3-5)
5. white fuselage, silver-gray undercarriage, "Cathay Pacific" tempa, Thailand casting (\$3-5)(IC)

SB-32-A FAIRCHILD A-10 THUNDERBOLT, issued 1990
1. dark green body, green camouflage tempa, Macau casting (\$3-5)
2. dark green body, green camouflage tempa, Thailand casting (\$3-5)
3. tan body, brown camouflage & "USAF" tempa, China casting (\$3-4)
4. khaki tan body, green & orange fuzzy polka dots & emblem tempa, China casting (\$3-4)

SB-33-A BELL JET RANGER, issued 1990
1. white/blue body, white base, "Sky-Ranger" tempa, Macau casting (\$3-5)
2. white/blue body, white base, "Sky-Ranger" tempa, Thailand casting (\$3-5)
3. white/blue body, white base, "Sky-Ranger" tempa, China casting (\$3-4)

SB-34-A C-130 HERCULES, issued 1990
1. white body & undercarriage, "USCG" tempa, Macau casting (\$3-5)
2. white body & undercarriage, "USCG" tempa, Thailand casting (\$3-5)

SB-35-A MiL M-24 HIND-D, issued 1990
1. brown body, gray base, dark brown camouflage tempa, Thailand casting (\$3-5)
2. brown body, gray base, dark brown camouflage tempa, China casting (\$3-5)
3. khaki gray body, gray base, dark gray camouflage & "0709" tempa, China casting (\$3-4)

SB-36-A LOCKHEED F-117A (STEALTH), issued 1990
1. dark gray body & base, "USAF" tempa, Thailand casting (\$3-5)
2. white body & base, no tempa, Thailand casting (\$10-15)(GF)(GS)
3. dark gray body & base, "USAF" tempa, China casting (\$3-5)
4. black body & base, white emblems tempa, China casting (\$3-4)

SB-37-A HAWK, issued 1992
1. red body & base, "Royal Air Force" tempa, white under wings, Thailand casting (\$6-8)(UK)(OP)
2. red body & base, "Royal Air Force" tempa, plain underside, Thailand casting (\$3-5)

SB38-A BaE 146, issued 1992
1. white body gray base, "Dan-Air" tempa, Thailand casting (\$3-5)
2. white body & base, "Thai" tempa, Thailand casting (\$3-5)
3. white body, white base, "Continental" tempa, China casting (\$3-4)

SB-39-A BOEING STEARMAN, issued 1992
1. orange-yellow body & wings, "Crunchie" with printing on underside of wings tempa, Thailand casting (\$20-30)(UK)(OP)
2. orange-yellow body & wings, "Crunchie" without printing on underside of wings, Thailand casting (\$3-5)
3. white body & wings, "Circus Circus" tempa, Thailand casting (\$3-5)(MC)
4. silver-gray body & wings, "Australian National Airways" tempa, China casting (\$7-10)(AU)
5. dark blue body & wings, "Ditec" tempa, China casting (\$75-100)(GR)
6. dark blue body & yellow wings, "Ditec" tempa, China casting (\$75-100)(GR)
7. yellow body & dark blue wings, "Ditec" tempa, China casting (\$75-100)(GR)
8. yellow body & wings, "Ditec" tempa, China casting (\$75-100)(GR)

SB-40-A BOEING 737-300, issued 1992
1. white fuselage, dark blue undercarriage, "Britannia" tempa, Thailand casting (\$3-5)
2. powder blue body, silver-gray undercarriage, "KLM" tempa, Thailand casting (\$3-5)

SB41-A BOEING 777-200, issued 1997
1. white fuselage with blue base, silver-gray wings, "Boeing 777-200"

tempa, China casting (\$5-7)(IG)
2. unpainted fuselage, base & wings, no tempa, China casting (\$5-7)(IG)

HS212 CONCORDE JET, issued 1977
1. gold plated body, no casting marks, mounted on pen stand (\$45-60)(GW)

Character Toys:
Disney, Popeye, Looney Tunes & Sesame Street

In 1979, Lesney Products commissioned Universal Toys—the eventual buyer of Lesney in 1982—to produce a set of twelve Disney vehicles. This was extended in 1981 to include three King Features' characters from the Popeye cartoon series. In 1994, Matchbox Toys received the license for Looney Tunes. The license was taken over from Ertl. Only six diecast vehicles were issued. In 1997, Tyco Toys decided to move its Sesame Street diecast vehicles under the "Matchbox" brand. At the very end of 1998, six new castings were issued under the Fisher Price brand.

WD-1-A MICKEY MOUSE FIRE ENGINE, issued 1979
1. red body, silver-gray base, without casting to secure ladder, Hong Kong casting (\$50-75)
2. red body, silver-gray base, with casting to secure ladder, Hong Kong casting (\$25-30)
3. red body, pearly silver base, with casting to secure ladder, Macao casting (\$50-75)

WD-2-A DONALD DUCK BEACH BUGGY, issued 1979
1. orange body, black base, Hong Kong casting (\$20-25)
2. orange body, black base, Macao casting (\$50-75)

WD-3-A GOOFY'S BEETLE, issued 1979
1. yellow body, black base, ears not attached to shoulders, Hong Kong casting (\$75-100)
2. yellow body, black base, ears attached to shoulders, Hong Kong casting (\$20-25)
3. yellow body, black base, ears attached to shoulders, Macao casting (\$50-75)

WD-4-A MINNIE MOUSE LINCOLN, issued 1979
1. blue body, silver-gray base, Hong Kong casting (\$20-25)
2. blue body, pearly silver base, Macao casting (\$50-75)

WD-5-A MICKEY MOUSE JEEP, issued 1979
1. dark blue body, white base, "MM" on hood, Hong Kong casting (\$25-40)
2. dark blue body, white base, "Mickey's Mail Jeep" on hood, Hong Kong casting (\$20-25)
3. dark blue body, black base, "Mickey's Mail Jeep" on hood, Macao casting (\$50-75)

WD-6-A DONALD DUCK JEEP, issued 1979
1. white body, black base, Hong Kong casting (\$20-25)
2. white body, white base, Macao casting (\$50-75)

WD-7-A PINOCCHIO'S TRAVELING THEATER, issued 1979
1. lime green body, yellow theater, red grille, black base, Hong Kong casting (\$25-40)
2. lime green body, yellow theater, red grille, black base, Macao casting (\$50-75)

WD-8-A JIMINY CRICKET'S OLD TIMER, issued 1979
1. yellow body, red chassis, silver-gray base, Hong Kong casting (\$25-40)
2. yellow body, red chassis, pearly silver base, Macao casting (\$50-75)

WD-9-A GOOFY'S SPORTS CAR, issued 1980
1. blue body, silver-gray base, Hong Kong casting (\$25-40)
2. blue body, pearly silver base, Macao casting (\$50-75)

WD-10-A GOOFY'S TRAIN, issued 1980
1. red body, yellow chassis, black base, Hong Kong casting (\$50-75)
2. red body, yellow chassis, black base, Macao casting (\$60-80)

WD-11-A DONALD DUCK'S ICE CREAM VAN, issued 1980
1. white body, pink rear canopy, blue fenders, black base, Hong Kong casting (\$25-40)
2. white body, pink rear canopy, blue fenders, black base, Macao casting (\$50-75)

WD-12-A MICKEY MOUSE CORVETTE, issued 1980
1. red body, silver-gray base, Hong Kong casting (\$25-40)
2. red body, pearly silver base, Macao casting (\$50-75)

CS-13-A POPEYE'S SPINACH WAGON, issued 1981
1. yellow body, red fenders, green spinach can, black base, Hong Kong casting (\$25-40)

CS-14-A BLUTO'S ROAD ROLLER, issued 1981
1. blue body, yellow roller & wheels, black base, Hong Kong casting (\$25-40)

CS-15-A OLIVE OYL'S SPORTS CAR, issued 1981

1. white body, hood label applied right side up, black base, Hong Kong casting (\$25-40)
2. white body, hood label applied upside down, black base, Hong Kong casting (\$35-50)

BUGS BUNNY GROUP C RACER, issued 1994
1. white & orange body, "Bugs Bunny 1/ Looney Tunes Racing" & "What's Up Doc?" tempa, dark smoke windows, green airfoil, silver 6 spoke spiral wheels, Thailand casting (\$3-4)

BUGS BUNNY LUMINA, issued 1994
1. White & orange body, "Carrot Plugs 7" tempa, smoke windows, all black Goodyear slicks, Thailand casting (\$3-4)

WILE E. COYOTE LUMINA, issued 1994
1. White body, "Acme Anvils" & "Coyote Cams 99" tempa, smoke windows, all black Goodyear slicks, Thailand casting (\$3-4)

ROAD RUNNER DRAGSTER, issued 1994
1. Orange body, blue windows, chrome engine, "Acme" & "Beep! Beep! 2" tempa, 5 arch front & 5 crown rear wheels, Thailand casting (\$3-4)

DAFFY DUCK 4X4 PICKUP, issued 1994
1. Green body, purple roll bar, black plastic base, "Daffy's Diner" & "13 You're Despicable!!!" tempa, maltese cross wheels, Thailand casting (\$3-4)

TASMANIAN DEVIL'S SPRINT RACER, issued 1994
1. Yellow body, chrome airfoils, all black wheels, "Taz Oil 99" tempa, Thailand casting (\$3-4)

ERNIE'S DUMP TRUCK, issued 1997
1. blue body, red dump, yellow base, red wheels (\$3-4)

BERT'S TOW TRUCK, issued 1997
1. lime green body, blue boom, orange base, yellow wheels (\$3-4)

ELMO'S TAXI, issued 1997
1. dark yellow body, blue painted windows, red base, blue wheels, "Taxi" tempa (\$3-4)
2. light yellow body, blue painted windows, red base, blue wheels, "Taxi" tempa (\$3-4)
3. blue body, white painted windows, red base, yellow wheels, "30" tempa (\$3-4)(MP)

BIG BIRD'S FIRE ENGINE, issued 1997
1. red body & base, white rear section, yellow wheels (\$3-4)

COOKIE MONSTER'S SCHOOL BUS, issued 1997
1. dark yellow body, blue base, red wheels, "School Bus" tempa (\$3-4)
2. light yellow body, blue base, red wheels, "School Bus" tempa (\$3-4)

ZOE'S SPORTS CAR, issued 1997
1. orange-red body, blue painted windows, yellow base, blue wheels (\$3-4)

ERNIE'S POLICE CAR, issued 1998
1. white body, red base, blue wheels, black doors tempa (\$3-4)

OSCAR'S GARBAGE TRUCK, issued 1998
silver-gray cab, orange dump, yellow base, lime wheels (\$3-4)

BIG BIRD'S DUNE BUGGY, issued 1998
1. lime green body, blue rollbar, orange base, yellow wheels (\$3-4)

ELMO'S CEMENT TRUCK, issued 1998
1. blue cab, gray barrel on red mount, yellow base, red wheels (\$3-4)

COOKIE MONSTER'S AIRPLANE, issued 1998
1. white body with yellow cockpit area, red base, blue wheels, yellow propeller (\$3-4)

GROVER'S HELICOPTER, issued 1998
1. yellow body, red base, blue skis, gray propeller & rear fin (\$3-4)

BIG BIRD'S DELIVERY VAN, issued 1998
1. metallic red cab, yellow container, blue base, lime green wheels, "30 Years and Counting- 30- Sesame Street" tempa (\$3-4)(MP)

ERNIE'S DUNE BUGGY, issued 1998
1. light yellow body, blue rollbar, red base, blue wheels, "30" tempa (\$3-4)(MP)

ELMO'S DUMP TRUCK, issued 1998
1. lemon body, blue dump & wheels, yellow base (\$3-4)

BIG BIRD'S MAILUAN, issued 1998
1. rose red cab, white container, blue base & wheels, "S.S. Mail" tempa (\$3-4)

ERNIE'S CEMENT TRUCK, issued 1998
1. lemon body, red barrel, yellow rear & base, red wheels (\$3-4)

BABY BEAR'S BUGGY, issued 1998
1. lime body, orange roll bar & base, blue wheels, tree design tempa ($3-4)

TELLY'S FRONT LOADER, issued 1998
1. lemon body, lime shovel & wheels, yellow base ($3-4)

ERNIE'S CAR CARRIER, issued 1998
1. three piece set includes large car carrier with Ernie: blue cab, red ramp, white carrier, yellow base, red wheels. Elmo's Sports Car: light yellow body, blue airfoils, blue base, red wheels & Cookie Monster's Van: red cab, white container, yellow base, blue wheels, "Racing Elmo" tempa ($10-15)

Superchargers and Monster Wars

In 1984, Matchbox Toys entered the "Monster Truck" market with an item called "High Riders." Using two different clip-on chassis, a street car could become a 4X4 or a truck could become a street-type vehicle. Several different cars and trucks were used. High Riders are valued at $10-15 each. In 1986, Matchbox Toys improved upon the clip-on method by introducing "Superchargers." These monster trucks included permanent cast bases affixed to miniature-style body castings. Later on, monster cars were issued and called Mud Racers. A series of Monster tractors were introduced in 1988. By 1993, the entire Supercharger range was discontinued except for four Graffic Traffic entries. The line was resurrected in 1994, but now called "Monster Wars." The series included only six miniatures plus four large plastic vehicles in 1/43 scale. The series was discontinued in 1995.

SC-01-A BIG FOOT, issued 1986
1. metallic blue body, with or without tow slot, Macau casting ($10-15)
2. metallic blue body, with tow slot & rocker steering, Macau casting ($10-15)

SC-02-A USA 1, issued 1986
1. white body, without rocker steering, Macau casting ($10-15)
2. white body, with rocker steering, Macau casting ($10-15)

SC-03-A TAURUS, issued 1986
1. light red body, Macau casting ($12-15)
2. dark red body, Macau casting ($12-15)

SC-04-A ROLLIN THUNDER, issued 1986
1. orange body, without rocker steering, Macau casting ($10-15)
2. orange body, with rocker steering, Macau casting ($10-15)

SC-05-A FLYIN HI, issued 1986
1. white body, with spare tire, no rocker steering, Macau casting ($12-15)
2. white body, without spare tire, no rocker steering, Macau casting ($10-15)
3. white body, without spare tire, with rocker steering, Macau casting ($10-15)

SC-06-A AWESOME KONG II, issued 1986
1. red body, with or without tow slot, no rocker steering, Macau casting ($10-15)
2. red body, with tow slot, with rocker steering, Macau casting ($10-15)

SC-07-A MAD DOG II, issued 1986
1. yellow body, with or without tow slot, no rocker steering, Macau casting ($10-15)
2. yellow body, with tow slot, rocker steering, Macau casting ($10-15)

SC-08-A HAWK, issued 1986
1. black body, light gray interior, Macau casting ($15-20)
2. black body, dark gray interior, Macau casting ($15-20)

SC-09-A SO HIGH, issued 1987
1. yellow body, with or without tow slot, Macau casting ($15-20)

SC-10-A TOAD, issued 1987
1. red body, chrome exhausts, no rocker steering, Macau casting ($15-20)
2. red body, chrome exhausts, with rocker steering, Macau casting ($15-20)
3. red body, gray exhausts, with rocker steering, Macau casting ($15-20)

SC-11-A MUD RULER, issued 1989
1. 1984 Corvette casting, no rocker steering, black tires, Macau casting ($10-15)
2. 1984 Corvette casting, with rocker steering, black tires, Macau casting ($10-15)
3. 1987 Corvette casting, with rocker steering, black tires, Macau casting ($10-15)
4. 1987 Corvette casting, with rocker steering, neon yellow tires, Macau casting ($8-12)

SC-12-A BOG BUSTER, issued 1989
1. black body, no rocker steering, black tires, Macau casting ($10-15)
2. black body, with rocker steering, black tires, Macau casting ($10-15)
3. black body, with rocker steering, black tires, Thailand casting ($8-12)
4. black body, with rocker steering, neon orange tires, Thailand casting ($8-12)

SC-13-A HOG, issued 1989
1. white body, no rocker steering, black tires, Macau casting ($8-12)
2. white body, with rocker steering, black tires, Macau casting ($8-12)
3. white body, with rocker steering, neon orange tires, Macau casting ($8-12)
4. white body, with rocker steering, neon orange tires, Thailand casting ($8-12)
5. white body, with rocker steering, black tires, Thailand casting ($8-12)

SC-14-A MUD MONSTER, issued 1989
1. yellow body, with or without tow slot, black tires, Macau casting ($8-12)
2. yellow body, with tow slot, neon orange tires, Macau casting ($8-12)

SC-15-A BIG PETE, issued 1988
1. lime green body, chrome dump, chrome exhausts, Macau casting ($10-15)
2. lime green body, chrome dump, gray exhausts, Macau casting ($10-15)
3. lime green body, chrome dump, gray exhausts, Thailand casting ($10-15)

SC-16-A DOC CRUSH, issued 1988
1. red body, Macau casting ($15-20)
2. red body, Thailand casting ($30-40)

SC-17-A MUD SLINGER II, issued 1988
1. blue body, black tires, Macau casting ($8-12)
2. blue body, black tires, Thailand casting ($8-12)
3. blue body, neon yellow tires, Thailand casting ($8-12)

SC-18-A '57 CHEVY, issued 1988
1. metallic red body, black tires, Macau casting ($8-12)
2. metallic red body, neon yellow tires, Macau casting ($8-12)
3. metallic red body, neon yellow tires, Thailand casting ($8-12)
4. metallic red body, black tires, Thailand casting ($8-12)

SC-19-A DRAG-ON, issued 1988
1. green body, Macau casting ($8-12)

SC-20-A VOO DOO, issued 1988
1. black body, Macau casting ($8-12)

SC-21-A HOT STUFF, issued 1988
1. red body, Macau casting ($8-12)

SC-22-A SHOWTIME, issued 1988
1. yellow body, Macau casting ($8-12)

SC-23-A CHECKMATE, issued 1988
1. yellow body, Macau casting ($8-12)

SC-24-A 12 PAC, issued 1988
1. orange body, Macau casting ($8-12)

SC-PULLSLEDS, issued 1988
1. powder blue plastic body ($7-10)
2. yellow plastic body ($7-10)

SC-xx WAGON WHEELS, issued 1988
1. red body, "Wagon Wheels" tempa, Macau casting ($75-100)(UK)(OP)

GF-310 GRAFFIC TRAFFIC MONSTER TRUCKS, issued 1993
NOTE: Each model comes with plain white plastic display stand. All models fitted with white tires on chrome wheels.
1. Peterbilt Wrecker body with white booms, green windows ($6-8)(GF)
2. Chevy Blazer body with white interior, amber windows ($6-8)(GF)
3. 4X4 Chevy Van body, purple windows ($6-8)(GF)
4. Flareside Pickup body with white interior, smoke windows ($6-8)(GF)

MW-01 CAROLINA CRUSHER, issued 1994
1. red & yellow body, red plastic grille, lt. amber windows, red roll bar, red chassis, red hubs, "Carolina Crusher" tempa, Thailand casting ($4-5)

MW-02 EQUALIZER, issued 1994
1. metallic blue body, blue metal grille, lt. amber windows, orange roll bar, black chassis, orange hubs, "Equalizer" & clouds tempa, Thailand casting ($4-5)

MW-03 GRAVE DIGGER, issued 1994
1. black body, black grille, clear windows, green chassis, purple hubs, "Grave Digger" tempa, Thailand casting ($4-5)

MW-04 INVADER, issued 1994
1. yellow body, yellow metal grille, lt. amber windows, black roll bar, black chassis, yellow hubs, "Invader" & pink design tempa, Thailand casting ($4-5)

MW-05 PREDATOR, issued 1994
1. black body, black windows, dark orange chassis, black roll bar, yellow hubs, "Predator" tempa, Thailand casting ($4-5)

MW-06 TAURUS, issued 1994
1. black body, black plastic grille, light amber windows, gold roll bar, black chassis, gold hubs, "Taurus" tempa, Thailand casting ($4-5)

NOTE: The four 1/43 scale Monster War trucks include those for Grave Digger, Predator, Invader, & Equalizer. ($9-12 each)

Harley-Davidson

In 1992, Matchbox Toys received a license for Harley-Davidson motorcycles. As Matchbox had molds already at hand, it was a matter of reintroducing an old product in new versions. Models from the Convoy, miniatures, and Superking range were used initially along with a pullback toy from the Kidco range. Those from the Superking, miniature, or Convoy range are listed under their specific categories with an (HD). In 1993, new license tie-ins were added including 1/15 scale motorcycles that were retooled from molds bought from the Italian company Polistil. New castings were made for the Superkings and miniatures range and several play items were included.

73660 HARLEY-DAVIDSON STUNT ACTION BIKES, issued 1993
1. red body, red & black driver ($4-5)
2. blue body, red & white driver ($4-5)
3. orange body, blue & white driver ($4-5)
4. black body, white & orange driver ($4-5)

73375 REAL RIDER, issued 1994
1. revving sound playset with action bike ($25-35)

76210 HARLEY-DAVIDSON STUNT CYCLES, issued 1992
1. blue body, chrome engine ($8-10)
2. turquoise body, chrome engine ($8-10)
3. metallic red body, chrome engine ($8-10)
4. silver-gray body, chrome engine ($8-10)
5. black body, red flames tempa, chrome engine ($8-10)(PS)
6. black body, gold engine ($8-10)(GS)
7. black & red body, red flames tempa, chrome engine ($8-10)(from Radio Control set)
8. purple body, chrome engine ($8-10)
9. red body, chrome engine ($8-10)

76220 MOTORIZED STUNT SET, issued 1992
1. with one stunt cycle ($15-18)

76230 COLLECTORS EDITION, issued 1992
1. with 1 orange stunt cycle, 2 plastic badges & patch ($10-15)

76260 HARLEY-DAVIDSON PLAYSETS, issued 1994
1. Harley-Davidson Custom Shop with one miniature (varies)($6-8)
2. Harley-Davidson Service Center with one miniature (varies)($6-8)

76270 COLLECTORS SET, issued 1992
1. contains silver-gray stunt cycle, CY-8 Kenworth Truck, 2X MB50-D Motorcycles (orange & blue), K-83 Motorcycle in black, patch & poster ($35-50)

76272 HARLEY-DAVIDSON 5 PIECE GIFT SET, issued 1994
1. includes 2 Superkings, 2 miniatures & one Superking truck ($25-35)

76300 HARLEY-DAVIDSON ELECTRAGLIDE, issued 1993
1. metallic blue body, China casting ($18-25)
2. metallic red body, China casting ($18-25)

76310 HARLEY-DAVIDSON ELECTRAGLIDE WITH SIDECAR, issued 1993
1. black body, black sidecar with red painted top, China casting ($45-60)

76320 HARLEY-DAVIDSON CAFE RACER, issued 1993
1. black body, China casting ($18-25)

76330 HARLEY-DAVIDSON SPORTSTER, issued 1993
1. metallic blue body, China casting ($18-25)
2. metallic red body, China casting ($18-25)

877/700 HARLEY-DAVIDSON GIFT SET, issued 1994
1. includes one 24 cycle carry case & four miniatures (sold only in Target stores) ($15-20)(US)

HARLEY-DAVIDSON FAT BOY, issued 1995 (1/9 scale)
1. yellow body, China casting ($35-50)(HD)
2. silver-gray body, China casting ($35-50)(HD)

Matchbox Collectibles

Other than the Yesteryear and Dinky series, Matchbox Collectibles issues several other items that fit into other categories or don't fit into any other category. Since 1995, Matchbox Collectibles issued several Superkings or Miniatures and these are found in their respective categories with a (CL). Items that don't fit into any other specific category are listed here.

Ultimate Dream Machines (CDC Cars)

The original versions of these five 1/43 scale models were secured inside a plexi box. The bases did not include "Matchbox." Only the box featured a "Matchbox Collectibles" sticker. Second runs had the bases retooled to include the "Matchbox Collectibles" name.

ART 112 LAMBORGHINI DIABLO, issued 1995
1. yellow body, issued in plexibox ($20-25)
2. yellow body, "Matchbox" on base ($25-40)

ART 150 FERRARI F40, issued 1995
1. red body, issued in plexibox ($20-25)
2. red body, "Matchbox" on base ($25-40)

ART 173 JAGUAR XJ220, issued 1995
1. purplish body, issued in plexibox ($20-25)
2. purplish body, "Matchbox" on base ($25-40)

ART 213 1993 CORVETTE, issued 1995
1. blue body, issued in plexibox ($20-25)
2. blue body, "Corvettes Unlimited" label, issued in plexibox ($50-75)(C2)
3. blue body, "Matchbox" on base ($25-40)

ART 232 MERCEDES 320SL SOFT TOP, issued 1995
1. silver green body, issued in plexibox ($20-25)
2. silver green body, "Matchbox" on base ($25-40)

YSTS01 HOLIDAY EXPRESS TRAIN, issued 1995
1. set consists of five train pieces in green & red- an engine, box car, tanker, flatbed & caboose. The flatbed features two limited edition MB44-H Model T Vans ($150-200)(CL)

YSTS02 MATCHBOX RAILROAD, issued 1996
1. set consists of five train pieces in black & silver- an engine, box car, tanker, flatbed & caboose. The flatbed features two limited editions-MB4-D Chevy & MB42-D T-Bird in Premiere Collection versions ($150-200)

MBW01 YESTERYEAR WATCH, issued 1994 ($50-75)
MBW02 MATCHBOX EAGLE WATCH, issued 1995 ($85-90)

YM92088 1957 CHEVY NOMAD, issued 1995
1. yellow 1/16 scale model made by Yatming for Matchbox Collectibles and secured to a plastic stand ($35-40)

YCL01 THE LEGACY OF AHRENS-FOX CLOCK, issued 1996
1. black laminated wall click ($90-110)

Matchbox Ultra

In 1997, Matchbox Collectibles developed a new brand name to go along with the Yesteryear and Dinky Brands. This brand became Matchbox Ultra. The original Ultras were 12 miniature size vehicles with premiere wheels. These are listed separately under their specific miniature numbers. Then came the two Matchbox military pieces and these are listed below. A series of six 1/43 scale Corvettes were also called Ultra. Other Ultra brands not included here but are in their associated sections are some Superking and Convoy rigs.

VMM01 MILITARY HUMVEE, issued 1996
1. olive green body with two-tone camouflage ($25-30)

VMM02 MILITARY JEEP 4 X 4, issued 1996
1. olive green body & roof, white star on hood tempa ($25-30)

CCV01 1969 CHEVROLET CORVETTE, issued 1997
1. yellow body, black interior, clear windshield, chrome wheels, black base ($30-35)

CCV02 1993 40ᵗʰ Anniversary Corvette, issued 1997
NOTE: Model is a reissue of ART213.
1. purplish maroon body, black & gray interior, chrome wheels, black base ($30-35)

CCV03 1957 CHEVROLET CORVETTE, issued 1997
1. light turquoise body, white interior, white wall tires, white side flash tempa, includes two separate roofs- one white smooth hardtop & one white convertible type, black base ($30-35)
2. cream body & removable roof, red interior, white wall tires, silver side flash tempa, black base ($30-35)

CCV04 1997 CHEVROLET CORVETTE, issued 1998
1. red body, green tinted windows, black & gray interior, black base ($30-35)

CCV05 1962 CORVETTE STINGRAY, issued 1998
1. silver blue body, slate blue interior, white wall tires, black base ($30-35)

CCV06 1953 CORVETTE, issued 1998
1. cream body, orange-red interior, no tempa, black base ($30-35)
2. red body, red & yellow seats, yellow stripe & "Dependable as Sunshine Coca Cola" tempa, black base (imprinted "Dinky") ($30-35)

Premiums

This series includes models that were once based on Yesteryear or Dinky series but have had those trademark names removed from their baseplates.

JC PENNEY PROMOTIONALS :

YJC01 1930 MODEL A FORD VAN, issued 1996
1. lavender body, black roof & chassis, chrome wheels, "Penney's" tempa ($20-25)(JC)

YJC08 1937 GMC VAN, issued 1996
1. maroon body, black chassis, gold wheels, "JC Penney" tempa ($20-25)(JC)

YJC09 1920 MACK AC TRUCK, issued 1996
1. blue body & chassis, white container roof, chrome wheels, "Penney's" tempa ($20-25)(JC)

YJC13 MODEL FORD TT VAN, issued 1996
1. yellow body, black roof & chassis, gold wheels, "JC Penney & Co." tempa ($20-25)

OLYMPIC SERIES:

OL001 FODEN STEAM LORRY, issued 1996
1. blue body & canopy, brown chassis, "Athens 1896" tempa ($35-50)(based on Y-27-A)

OL002 WALKER ELECTRIC VAN, issued 1996
1. blue body, rose canopy, "Paris 1900" tempa ($35-50) (based on Y-29-A)

OL003 ATKINSON LORRY, issued 1996
1. dark blue body, black base, "St. Louis 1904" tempa ($35-50) (Based on Y-18-B)

OL004 PRESTON TRAM, issued 1996
1. rose body, dark blue window area, mustard base, "London 1908" tempa ($35-50)(based on Y-15-C)

OL005 1912 MODEL T FORD VAN, issued 1996
1. blue-green body, roof & chassis, "Stockholm 1912" tempa ($35-50)(based on Y-12-D)

OL006 1918 CROSSLEY LORRY, issued 1996
1. mint green body & chassis, rose canopies, "Antwerp 1920" tempa ($35-50)(based on Y-13-C)

OL007 1907 UNIC TAXI, issued 1996
1. dark blue body, roof & chassis, "Paris 1924" tempa ($35-50)(based on Y-28-A)

OL008 1927 TALBOT VAN, issued 1996
1. dark blue body & chassis, mustard roof, "Amsterdam 1928" tempa ($35-50)(based on Y-5-D)

OL009 1930 MODEL A FORD VAN, issued 1996
1. rose body, black roof & chassis, "Los Angeles 1932" tempa ($35-50)(based on Y-22-A)

OL010 MERCEDES BENZ LORRY, issued 1996
1. dull rose body, chassis & canopy, "Berlin 1936" tempa ($35-50)(based on Y-6-E)

OL011 BEDFORD PICKUP, issued 1996
1. rose body, dark blue fenders & bed, "London 1948" tempa ($35-50)(based on Y-63-A)

OL012 1948 COMMER VAN, issued 1996
1. blue-green body with mustard roof, black base, "Helsinki 1952" tempa ($35-50)(based on DY-8-A)

OL013 1952 AUSTIN VAN, issued 1996
1. blue-green body with yellow roof, black base, "Melbourne 1956" tempa ($35-50)(based on DY-15-A)

YY-69 STAGE COACH, issued 1995
1. red-brown roof, black roof, light brown undercarriage, pale yellow wheels, 2 different colored brown horses (4), no figures, "Cobb & Co. Royal Mail" tempa, China casting ($75-100)(AU) (*NOTE: Based on YHS03 casting- no "Yesteryear" cast*)

1960 JAGUAR XK150, issued 1996
1. black body, red interior, black tonneau, black base, "AFL Centenary 1897-1996" tempa ($100-150)(AU) (*based on DY-36- note no number or "Dinky" cast*)

Thunderbirds and Stingray

Possibly one of the biggest licensing winners ever made by Matchbox Toys, Thunderbirds, became an instant sellout during their fall 1992 debut. Thunderbirds, based on a 1960s TV show, were originally modeled by Dinky back at the show's original inception. In the spring and fall of 1992, the BBC network in England resurrected the show. Only four models were released in 1992. By 1993, action figures and larger playsets were added. Dolls were added by 1994.

TB-001 THUNDERBIRD 1, issued 1992
1. metallic blue body, gray wings & red nose cone ($7-10)

TB-002 THUNDERBIRD 2 & 4, issued 1992
1. large green #2 with red retractable legs and removable pod. Comes with small Thunderbird #4 in yellow ($15-20)

TB-003 THUNDERBIRD 3, issued 1992
1. red body, white rocket pads ($7-10)

TB-005 PENELOPE'S FAB 1, issued 1992
1. light pink body, clear windows, cream interior, chrome base, China casting ($8-12)

RESCUE GIFT SET, issued 1992
1. standard packaging ($35-50)
2. "Radio Times" packaging ($75-100)

THUNDERBIRDS DOLLS, issued 1994
1. Virgil Tracy ($25-40)
2. Alan Tracy ($25-40)
3. Scott Tracy ($25-40)
4. Gordon Tracy ($25-40)

THUNDERBIRDS ANNIVERSARY SET, issued 1996
1. includes Thunderbird 1, Thunderbird 2, Thunderbird 3, Thunderbird 4 & Penelope's Fab 1 with pin badge, all in gold plate in gift box presentation ($100-150)

PEWTER THUNDERBIRD 2
1. pewter edition on black stand (removable) ($75-100)

41720 Tracey Island Playset ($85-110)
41720 Thunderbird 2 Playset ($50-75)
41775 Electronic Thunderbird 1 ($20-25)
41780 Pd Vehicles Set (set of 3) ($8-12)
41785 The Mole ($12-15)
41790 Pullback Action Vehicles ($12-15)
41750 Figures Assortment ($5-8 each)
Figures include: Parker, John Tracey, Virgil Tracey, Jeff Tracey, Brains, Lady Penelope, Hood, Alan Tracey, Scott Tracey Gordon Tracey.
Thunderbirds Are Go! Bandai Set ($75-100)(JP) includes Matchbox TB-1, TB-3 & Fab 1 with Bandai versions of TB-2, TB-4 & TB-5.

STINGRAY
Following on the heels of the success of Thunderbirds, Matchbox introduced another Gerry Anderson promotion- Stingray.

43200 Stingray & Terrorfish ($10-15)
43210 Marineville Playset ($50-75)
43220 Stingray Action Playset ($30-45)
43250 Figures: includes Commander Shore, Titan, Marina, Troy Tempest, Phones ($5-8 each)

Master Class

Introduced for the German market in 1993 was a new series of 1/24 scale model. Only three models were introduced and no new models were introduced for 1994. The models are highly detailed with opening doors and engine compartments. Interiors even have a textured fuzzy appearance. The models were introduced on the U.S. market in November 1994 by Matchbox Collectibles division in Portland, Oregon.

LS001 LAMBORGHINI DIABLO, issued 1993
1. red body, tan interior, clear windows, chrome wheels, black base, China casting ($35-50)

LS002 PORSCHE 911 CABRIOLET, issued 1993
1. metallic blue body, gray interior, clear windshield, gray wheels, black base, China casting ($35-50)

LS003 JAGUAR XJ220, issued 1993
1. silver-gray body, gray interior, clear windows, gray wheels, black base, China casting ($35-50)

Superfast Minis

Introduced for Europe in 1990, Superfast Minis were 1/90 scale miniatures. Original versions made in Macau had a fifth wheel in the center of the base. Six versions were later issued with Triple Heat sets (a World's Smallest, Superfast Mini, and Miniature). Two Convoy style transporters were also released. The trailers to these opened up into launchers. and are designated MD-250. Superfast Minis are either issued in two packs with a launcher or four-model sets or with the transporter.

MD-200 CARS ASSORTMENT, issued 1990 through 1992
Two Packs ($5-8), Four Packs ($10-15)

1957 CHEVY, issued 1990
1. red body, Macau casting
2. black body, Macau casting
3. yellow body, China casting (TH)

PORSCHE 959, issued 1990
1. silver-gray body, "Porsche" logo, Macau casting (MD250)
2. silver-gray body, stripes design, China casting (TH)

LAMBORGHINI COUNTACH, issued 1990
1. yellow body, Macau casting
2. dark orange body, Macau casting
3. white body, China casting (TH)

CHEVY CAMARO, issued 1990
1. silver-gray body, Macau casting
2. yellow body, Macau casting
3. metallic blue body, China casting (TH)

FERRARI F40, issued 1990
1. red body, "Ferrari" logo, Macau casting (MD250)
2. red body, "F40" design, China casting (TH)

BMW M1, issued 1990
1. silver-gray body, Macau casting
2. white body, Macau casting

JAGUAR XJS, issued 1990
1. silver-gray body, Macau casting
2. metallic green body, Macau casting

T-BIRD TURBO COUPE, issued 1990
1. black body, Macau casting
2. metallic blue body, Macau casting

CORVETTE GRAND SPORT, issued 1990
1. light metallic blue body, Macau casting
2. metallic red body, Macau casting

PORSCHE TURBO, issued 1990
1. red body, "Porsche" tempa, Macau casting (MD250)

CHEVY LUMINA, issued 1990
1. white & orange body, "Matchbox Motorsports" tempa, Macau casting (MD250)

FORD LTD POLICE CAR, issued 1992
1. dark blue body, "Police" tempa, China casting (TH)

MD-250 KENWORTH TRANSPORTERS, issued 1990
1. red MB41-D cab with yellow & orange stripes; gray trailer with red, orange & yellow label. Comes with red Porsche & white/orange Lumina ($25-45)
2. black MB41-D cab with flames tempa; black trailer with flames labels. Comes with silver Porsche 959 & red Ferrari F40 ($25-45)

Real Talkin' Matchbox

This was a new line developed in 1998 and improves upon Matchbox's previous Light and Sound series cars which took existing vehicles and gave them flashing lights and sirens. This product goes on step further by making better sound and complimenting with voice messages. In order to do this, new tools were made. The models are cast slightly larger than the miniatures range to accommodate the sophisticated internal mechanism. Most of the vehicles have been released with Spanish speaking voice mechanisms. These were reported in Puerto Rico and Mexico.

POLICE CAR, issued 1998
1. white & blue body, black windows, blue base, red bar light, "Sheriff C-51" tempa, 5 spoke concave star wheels ($4-5)
2. white body, black windows, black base, red bar light, "Metro Police 8" tempa, 5 spoke concave star wheels ($4-5)
3. white body, black windows, white base, red bar light, "State Trooper/Police 34" 5 spoke concave star wheels ($4-5)(AP)

ROCKET LAUNCHER, issued 1998

1. beige body, black base, brown camouflage tempa, amber dome lights ($4-5)
2. green body, black base, brown & dark green camouflage tempa, amber dome lights ($4-5)
3. olive body, black base, "Unit 5 Stand Clear" tempa, amber dome lights ($4-5)(AP)

UFO, issued 1998
1. olive & brushed black body, green painted lights, green glowing light ($4-5)
2. olive & brushed gold body, orange painted lights, amber glowing light ($4-5)
3. brown & brushed silver body, blue painted lights, red glowing light ($4-5)(AP)

SNACK WAGON, issued 1998
1. peach-pink body, gray base, "Frank's Hot Dogs" & splat designs tempa, 8 spoke wheels ($4-5)
2. white body, blue base, "Mister Softee" tempa, 8 spoke wheels ($4-5)

GARBAGE TRUCK, issued 1998
1. dark blue cab, brushed brown dump, light gray arms, "City Garbage" tempa, 8 spoke wheels ($4-5)
2. red cab, silver-gray dump & arms, "Recycler" tempa, 8 spoke wheels ($4-5)

FIRE TRUCK, issued 1988
1. white & red cab, red body, gray base, red bar light, "Fire Department 14" tempa, 8 spoke wheels ($4-5)
2. lime-yellow cab & body, gray base, red bar light, "Fire Fighter 14" tempa, 8 spoke wheels ($4-5)

RESCUE TRUCK, issued 1998
1. green body, black windows, red bar light, yellow painted rear area & base, "Bear Patrol Forest Service" tempa, 8 spoke wheels ($4-5)
2. orange body, black windows, red bar light, silver painted rear area, black base, "Beach Patrol B-1" tempa, 8 spoke wheels ($4-5)
3. lemon yellow body, black windows, red bar light, red painted rear area, black base, red dome lights, "Lifeguard T-2" tempa, 8 spoke wheels ($4-5)

TOW TRUCK, issued 1998
1. white body, black boom, windows & base, red bar light, "Police" & eagle tempa ($4-5)
2. black body, silver-gray boom, windows & base, amber bar light, "Z Towing- Zaks" tempa ($4-5)

Trax

The Trax line is a series of 1/43 scale models made by the company Trax but distributed by Matchbox Collectibles in Australia. Each model represented a part of Australian motoring history. The line was distributed from the summer of 1992 through late 1993 when the distribution was taken over by a company called Top Gear. The models shown and listed are the only ones distributed by Matchbox. Models in the window boxes do not denote Matchbox, however these were pictured in trade brochures by Matchbox Collectibles. Closed-boxed styles denote Matchbox Collectibles on the package.

TRS1 FJ HOLDEN 40TH ANNIVERSARY GIFT SET, issued 1992
1. includes Holden Sedan in blue with gray interior; Holden Panel Van in cream with red interior, "Cinesound Review" tempa; Holden Pickup in black with red interior & tan rear tonneau ($125-175)

TR2 FJ HOLDEN PANEL VAN, issued 1992
1. red body, gray interior, black painted fenders, "Gilbarco" tempa ($30-45)
2. cream body, red interior, "Vegemite" tempa ($30-45)

TR3 FJ HOLDEN SEDAN, issued 1992
1. green body with light green painted roof, red interior ($30-45)

TR4 FORD FALCON GTHO PHASE 3, issued 1993
1. white body, black interior, black hood stripes ($25-40)

TRS7 FORD SIERRA BATHURST RACING SET, issued 1992
1. includes three Ford Sierras: red body, black interior, "Shell 17/Ultra Hi" tempa; red body, black interior, "35 OXO" tempa; black body, black interior, "Texaco 6" tempa ($35-50)

TR8 TORANA, issued 1993
1. red body, black interior ($25-40)

TRS9 FORD FALCON XRGT 25TH ANNIVERSARY GIFT SET, issued 1993
1. includes Ford Falcon in dark green, black interior, "52D" tempa and Ford Falcon in metallic tan, black interior, hood stripes tempa ($75-100)

TRS10 FORD FALCON XC HARDTOP SET, issued 1993
1. includes two Ford Falcons in white with black interior. One has "1" on roof & doors and other has "2" on roof & doors ($60-85)

TR11 CHARGER, issued 1993
1. metallic green body, gray interior ($25-40)

Other Diecast and Wheeled Vehicles

This section covers all the other wheeled vehicles that Lesney, Universal, and Tyco have made over the years using the "Matchbox" brand. These include entries ranging from Glo Racers to Cap Cars to Parasites and everything-in-between.

Lesney Years 1970-1982

SCORPION CARS
First issued in 1971, these were the answer to Hot Wheels "Sizzlers." The models could be recharged to be run on a special track system. Only two different cars were made and both were available in either purple, orange-gold or green-gold.
SC001 Phantom Scorpion Car ($65-90)
SC002 Tornado Scorpion Car ($65-90)
Mono Circuit Supertrack 1000 ($150-200)
Big Eight Super Track 2000 ($150-200)
Sting Pack 3000 ($100-150)

ZB-1 ZOOMIE BALOONIES
Issued in 1972, these twelve "models" featured plastic bodies with metal baseplates and were run on balloon power. Included are models with names such as Terrible Toad, Hot Foot, Bat Cat, Blood, Bita, Flyn, Rat Racer, Nose Job, etc. Value ($25-50)

PLUG BUGGIES
Issued in 1972, these vegetable racers included either a carrot or a cucumber to which wheels and accessories could be inserted. Value ($50-75)
PB-1 Plug Buggy Carrot
PB-2 Plug Buggy Cucumber

STUNT CARS
These plastic vehicles included four varieties with launchers. Also marketed as Super Stock Rodeo in the United States. Value ($45-60)
XX-1 Bullet Nose
XX-2 Rubber Burner
XX-3 Chop Hopper
XX-4 Buck N Bronc

SCREAMIN DEMONS & CYCLONE CYCLES
Scream'n Demons from 1973 and Cyclone Cycles from 1974 were both based on motorcycles. The Cyclone Cycles were smaller in size. Demons value ($75-100) and Cyclones at ($35-50)
SD-6500 Big Buzzard, SD-6501 Doom Buggy, SD-6502 Tiger Shark, SD-6503 Lunatic Fringe, SD-6504 Crazy Horse, SD-6505 Dirty Devil
Cyclone Cycles-Diamond Back, Copper Head, Bushmaster, and Python

MOBILE ACTION COMMAND (M.A.C.)
First introduced in 1975, M.A.C. included king-size plastic vehicles plus two super large 12" length vehicles and several playsets.
MAC-01-A Fire Fighting Unit, issued 1975 ($10-15)
MAC-02-A Emergency Medical Unit, issued 1975 ($10-15)
MAC-02-B Snow Patrol Unit, issued 1976 ($10-15)
MAC-03-A Air Search Unit, issued 1975 ($10-15)
MAC-03-B Police Patrol Unit, issued 1976 ($10-15)
MAC-04-A All-Terrain Rescue Unit, issued 1975 ($10-15)
MAC-04-B Emergency Repair Unit, issued 1976 ($10-15)
MAC-05-A Military Recon Jeep, issued 1975 ($10-15)
MAC-06-A Sea Rescue Unit, issued 1975 ($10-15)
MAC-06-B Military Medic Unit, issued 1976 ($10-15)
MAC-07-A Military Air Search, issued 1976 ($10-15)
MAC-08-A Frogman Unit, issued 1975 ($10-15)
MAC-200101 Oceana Sea Rescue Unit, issued 1977 ($40-60)
MAC-200501 M.A.C. Rescue Center Playset, issued 1975 ($75-100)
MAC-200701 M.A.C. Command Challenge Playset, issued 1976 ($50-75)
MAC-200802 Mobile Rescue Headquarters, issued 1976 ($40-60)
MAC-200901 Wing Thing Glider, issued 1976 ($25-40)

SENTRON 9
This short-lived 1978 introduction consisted of two different colored Porsche 928's- either gold or red. Each came with a wireless control to make the model run around with battery power.
1. gold body ($150-250)
2. red body ($150-250)

SPEEDTRACK
This series included slot cars. Issued originally in 1979, the series was deleted before Lesney went bankrupt. There were several Speedtrack race sets and accessories available as well. This series was also called "Power track" by 1981.
Vehicles: Renault Alpine, Alpine Racer, Super Vette, Villain's Van, The Hulk Van, Spiderman's Car, VW Scirocco, Triumph TR7, Porsche Turbo, Porsche 935, Monza GT, Pinto Sportsman, Ford Escort, Jaguar XJ, Bandag Bandit, Super Boss, Ferrari Formula 1, Formula 1, Monza Funny Car, Police Car, Porsche 936, BMW 320I, Gremlin Sportsman, Kremer Porsche ($8-12)
Race Sets: RPS2000, RPS4000, LeMans 300, Riverside 500, International 1000, Tyrone Malone's Diesel Race & Chase, Spiderman & The Hulk Race & Chase Set, World Class Racing ($75-100)
Race & Chase set, Monza 200, Trenton 150, Pro-8 Challenge, Jump Cross

Championship, Slipstream Racing ($50-75).
Accessories: 6" Straight Track Pair, 9" Straight track pair, 9" Radius 90 degree curved Track pair, Power Matched Pistol Controller, Battery Eliminator Safety Wall Power Pack plus many others ($8-12)
Also reported in the slot car category are two Tyco brand slot cars with "Matchbox" cast inside the body. These include two Hummer castings. One is the olive green one from the Jurassic Park slot set. The other is a red single release issue. ($15-20 each)

GLO RACERS
Glo Racers were introduced in 1982 as plastic vehicles that glowed in the dark. In 1983, Lesney sold the molds to Lash-Tamaron, who reissued the identical models but with "Lesney Products" deleted from the base and the "Matchbox" removed from the blistercards. All valued ($5-10)
GR-1 Light Beamer
GR-2 Speed Blazer
GR-3 Flamin' Vette
GR-4 Streak Ray
GR-5 Twilight TR
GR-6 Quicksilver
GR-7 Burnin 280
GR-8 Sizzlin ZX
GR-9 Turbo Flash
GR-10 Dark Rider
GR-11 Flash Fire
GR-12 Night Bird

Universal Years 1982-1992

CAP CARS
First introduced in 1983, this series became one of the first new introductions into the diecast category of Universal's new Matchbox Toys. Although not part of the miniatures series, these miniature-sized vehicles featured an opening base hatch in which a small cap could be placed. The model, when shot from a launcher would ignite a sound like a cap gun. Value $8-12 each, except yellow Mazda RX7 at $15-20.
Thunderbolt, Fireball, Atom, Starfire, Bomb, Nitro, Sheriff Patrol, Trail-Tracker, Rocky Mountain Ridge Runner, Mazda RX7, Trail Tramp.

FLASH FORCE 2000
This series is an extension of the Cap Cars series. Introduced in 1984, it includes three Flash Fighters (good guys) and three Rampagers (bad guys). Several larger scale play vehicles were also produced. Standard miniatures valued at ($10-15)
Flash Fighters-Mazda, Corvette, Pickup
Rampagers-Datsun, Pickup, Firebird

650105 Flash Force Base ($35-50)
650106 Rampage Rock ($25-35)
651601 Dark Seeker Battle Van ($35-50)
651602 Cyclone Chopper Helicopter ($50-75)

PARASITES
Introduced in 1985, this set of six vehicles included a fold-up "monster" which, according to Matchbox, "came from the tail of Haley's comet!" Each monster inhabited a model by folding itself up and disguising itself inside the vehicle. Value ($15-25)
Terrorsite (Chevy Van), Extermasite (Dodge Caravan), Nemisite (Corvette), Gammasite (Firebird), Spectersite (Pickup), Destructite (Blazer)

TRICKSHIFTERS
Trickshifters, introduced in 1985, included three paired miniature-sized vehicles for a total of six models. The models performed seven different stunts-wheelies, special turns, and flips based on the positioning of a mounted stick shift which controlled a fifth wheel. Value ($8-10)
Yellow or blue Mazda RX7, red or black Datsun, silver or white Firebird

HOT ROD RACERS
The name "Hot Rod Racers" was used twice by Matchbox. This first entry was introduced in 1986 with a series of four 1/20th scale plastic cars. Each featured a rear stick shift that made the model make revving sounds. Separate label sheets were included to apply to the models. Value ($20-25)
2101 Corvette, issued 1986
2102 1986 Firebird, issued 1986
2103 '57 Chevy, issued 1986
2104 Ferrari, issued 1987

TWINKLETOWN
In 1986, Matchbox Toys introduced a secondary series to their Live-N-Learn preschool range called Twinkletown. The series included six plastic preschool vehicles and four playsets. Each vehicle included a small story book.
Freddy Ready Fire Truck, Tony's Tow Truck, Sheldon's Shoveller, Carrier Camper, Melvin Mail Van, Stevie's School Bus ($12-15)
Gas Station, School House, Fire House, Construction Yard ($20-25)

RADIO CONTROL/L.A. WHEELS
There were two series of Radio Control cars—those marketed through Matchbox Toys USA and those marketed by the Universal Associated Company. U.A.C. was a Matchbox subsidiary that marketed Matchbox Toys not offered through the normal U.S. distributor Matchbox Toys USA. One of the products issued by them was L.A. Wheels radio control vehicles. Radio Control vehicles were first introduced in 1987.
6000 R.C. Radskate, issued 1987 ($75-100)
6010 R.C. Ripskate, issued 1987 ($75-100)
6020 Revvin' 427 Cobra, issued 1987 ($50-75)
6030 Revvin' Pro Street Mustang, issued 1987 ($50-75)
6060 R.C. Snoopy Skateboard, issued 1988 ($75-100)
LA Wheels-various models range ($50-150) depending on size.

TURBO 2
Issued in 1987, Turbo 2s were miniature-sized diecast vehicles with two-speed, friction-powered motors with pullback action. Six styles in two colors each were available. The "AM" prefix refers to Action Matchbox. Value ($10-15)
AM-2601 Pontiac Fiero-yellow
AM-2602 Peugeot 205-pearly silver
AM-2603 Ford Supervan II-dark pink
AM-2604 Racing Porsche-orange
AM-2605 Toyota MR2-red
AM-2606 Group C Racer-blue
AM-2607 Pontiac Fiero-white
AM-2608 Peugeot 205-yellow
AM-2609 Ford Supervan II-white
AM-2610 Racing Porsche-red
AM-2611 Toyota MR2-lime green
AM-2612 Group C Racer-white

BURNIN' KEY CARS
Originally marketed by Kidco and introduced by Matchbox Toys in 1984, 1987 featured all new castings. Models feature plastic bodies and metal bases. A key is inserted into the rear of the vehicle to launch it. Twelve different styles based on six different castings were produced. These include Nissan 300ZX, Porsche 959, Corvette, Firebird, Ferrari, and Ford Mustang. Value ($3-5)

BLAZIN' TURBOS/COLANI CARS
Issued in 1987, this set of four plastic vehicles consisted of pullback friction cars based on designs by the world famous designer Luigi Colani. These were released as Colani Cars in Europe but as Blazin Turbos in the United States. Value ($7-10) each
AM-4050 Colani assortment-gold plated, chrome plated, red plated, blue plated

POCKET ROCKETS/POCKET ROCKET BUGGIES
In 1987, a series of "chunky" pullbacks with friction motors and plastic bodies were issued. "Chunky" versions of cars such as Porsche, Lamborghini, and Mercedes were used amongst the twelve styles available in the colors of red, blue, or yellow—four of each color making up the twelve issues. There were also four dune buggies issued as Pocket Rocket Buggies also featuring friction pullback motors. Four styles were made, with two in black and two in maroon.
AM-4060 Pocket Rocket Assortment ($4-6) each
AM-4080 Pocket Rocket Buggy Assortment ($5-8) each

DUELIN' DRAGSTERS
Eight Duelin Dragsters were introduced in 1987 based on four castings. Each featured a small stubby version of a Corvette, Firebird, Camaro, and Mustang. Each featured pullback motors. Models were issued in pairs with a launcher. Value ($5-8)

POWER LIFTERS
Power Lifters were issued in 1988. These plastic models featured a twin speed pullback motor with a wind back spoiler to create a wheelie. Twelve styles issued based on six castings
AM-4090 Power Lifter Assortment ($8-10) each
Corvette-Vette & Viper
BMW-Mauler & Thunderbolt
Camaro-Snaker & Blackstar
Stingray Vette-Stingray & White Heat
Toyota-Green Demon & Burner
Pickup-Typhoon & Trailblazer

FLASHBACKS
Flashbacks were issued in 1988. The six plastic trucks were actually launchers. Inside each launcher vehicle was a key car. When the launcher impacted a wall, the key car emerged from the rear of the launcher. Many of the Flashbacks proved defective and this resulted in a premature discontinuation of the line.
AM-5010 Flashbacks Assortment ($8-12)
1. Rescue Truck & Porsche 959
2. Desert Camouflage Truck & 300ZX
3. Pickup & Ferrari
4. Off Roader & Porsche 959
5. 4X4 Pickup & Ferrari
6. Forest Camouflage Truck & 300ZX

SPEEDRIDERS
Originally released by LJN, Matchbox modified the base molds to include the Matchbox trademark. Three categories with three models each from this 1986 introduction ran on pen light batteries. Value ($7-10)
Street Bird, Street Vette, Baja Beast, Super Stocker, Racin' rebel, Corvette, Sand Blaster, Street Heat, Go-4-It

BIG MOVERS
Big Movers were introduced in 1989 and discontinued in 1991. This line included Matchbox's only introduction into press steel vehicles. Similar to Tonka and Nylint brand vehicles, these Korean manufactured toys found no favor in the marketplace and were soon discontinued. The line consisted of several size vehicles.
BM-3400 10" Dump Truck ($20-35)
BM-3500 Stubbies Assortment ($10-15 each)
a. Cement Truck
b. Dump Truck
c. Snorkel Truck
d. Tanker
e. Wreck Truck
BM-3550 Stubbie Transporter
a. yellow, "Ipec" livery ($15-20)
b. white, "Matchbox" livery ($15-20)
c. white, "Federal Express" livery ($15-20)
BM-3600 4X4 Road King Pickup ($25-35)
BM-3800 Car Carrier ($50-75)
BM-3810 Container Truck-"Midnight X-Press" ($50-75)
BM-3850 Wreck Truck ($25-35)
BM-3900 14" Super Dump Truck ($40-60)
Models listed as BM-3610, 3620 & 3650 in catalogs may not have been released.

CONNECTABLES
Connectables were first released in 1989. Although discontinued in 1991 in the U.S. market, the European market ran the series through 1995. The models included plastic vehicles which could be split apart and connected to each other making up hundreds of possible models and combinations. Models came in two-, three-, and five-piece multipacks although Europe did issue some Connectables as singles. Although most Connectables are silver-gray, a few releases as singles were in orange plastic.
Two Piece Connectables, issued 1989, 1990 ($3-5)
Chevy Pickup, Racing Porsche 935, VW Dragster, Plane, Flareside pickup, Road Roller, Model A Hot Rod, Chevy Nomad Wagon, Jeep 4X4, Peterbilt wrecker, Racer, Dodge Dragster
Kellogg's Connectables ($15-20)(UK)(OP)
VW Dragster "Snap," Plane "Crackle," Road Roller "Pop"

Three Piece Connectables, issued 1989, 1990 ($4-7)
Kenworth Race Truck, Helicopter, Dragster, Half-Track, Lincoln Limousine, Airplane

Three Piece Connectables Gold Plated Series, issued 1992 ($8-12)
Kenworth Race Truck, Lincoln Limousine, Plane, Dragster

Other Connectable series include:
Micro Connectables, issued 1990 ($8-12)
Convoy Connectables, issued 1990 ($7-10)
5 Piece Theme Connectables, issued 1990 ($12-15)
Motorized Connectables, issued 1990 ($8-12)
Extender Connectables, issued 1991 ($10-12)
Crazy Limos Connectables, issued 1992 ($5-20) (depending on size)
Airport, Custom Gar Garage, Parts Marts & Lube & Tune Playsets, issued 1990 ($10-15) each
CN-380 CFR Kommandos-4 different, issued 1993 ($8-12)
CN-390 Multi Purpose Shuttle-3 different, issued 1993 ($8-12)
CN-400 CRF Transforming-6 different, issued 1993 ($8-12)
CN-800 Large Truck Transport Set, issued 1990 ($50-75)

TUFF WHEELS
In 1989, Matchbox toys introduced the largest Matchbox models ever manufactured-Tuff Wheels. These were manufactured by Mack Plastics for Matchbox. Tuff Wheels were ride-on, battery operated vehicles. Each vehicle supported either one or two small children. Only three Tuff Wheels were ever manufactured although the catalogs depicted many more including different volt sizes as well as non-battery powered versions.
7000 4X4 Pickup, issued 1989 ($350-450)
7010 Turbo Racer, issued 1989 ($350-450)
7020 Ferrari, issued 1990 ($500-750)

SUPERFAST MACHINES
Superfast Machines were a range of four vehicles that were actually plastic snap together kits which included battery powered motors. The series was introduced in 1989 and featured two different style boxes for each vehicle. Four vehicles and a playset were released.
Superfast Machines set ($15-25)
Superfast Machines Tomcat, Speed King, Streaker & Aero-Shot ($8-10)

WORLD'S SMALLEST MATCHBOX
In 1990, Matchbox responded to Galoob's Micro Machines with their own line called World's Smallest Matchbox. These small models were 1/200th scale and were possibly too small as these didn't sell well. The series was canceled the following year but resurrected again in 1992 in England as Micro Motor World.
Introductory Playsets, issued 1990 ($3-5)
sets numbered 1 through 5
35400 Mini Playsets, issued 1990 ($5-8)
1. Fire Station
2. Bank
3. Car Dealership
4. Grocery Store
5. Auto Parts Store
6. Hotel
7. Truck Stop
8. Hospital

9. Airport
10. Car Wash
11. Marina
12. Drag Strip

35320 Deluxe Playsets, issued 1990 ($8-10)
1. Car Rental
2. Restaurant
3. Service station
4. Police station
5. Off-Road
6. Bridge

35370 Magna-Wheel Carry Case, issued 1990 ($8-12)
1. Exotics
2. Emergency
3. Sports
4. Leisure

WD-100 Micro Motorworld Assortments ($8-10)
Car dealership, Marina, Car Wash, Restaurant, Fire Station, Race Track

WD-120 Micro Motorworld Set ($8-10)

WD-130 Air transport Set ($15-20)

WD-196 Micro Motorworld Assortments ($8-10)
City with bridge, City with crossover, City with curve

MATCHBOX 2000
Matchbox 2000 was a new concept toy based on futuristic vehicles that moved by magnetic power. Each small plastic vehicle contained a magnet which interacted with other cars or with two playsets. Models were packaged in three packs and most in two color variations. Value ($7-10)
NA-821 Vertical Service Center, issued 1991 ($15-20)
NA-822 Robotic Positioning Module, issued 1991 ($15-20)

RAILWAYS
In 1991, Matchbox made its first attempt into the train layout world. Although the first train ever represented by a Matchbox model was from the Yesteryear series in the 1950's, no real train sets that operated were issued until this time. Two sets were introduced. A third set was planned for release in 1992 but was never made.
TN-50 Big Boxed Set-issued 1991
Consists of green locomotive, green coach, gray coal tender with two section layout ($75-100)
TN-100 Giant Boxed set, issued 1991
Consists of blue locomotive, red coach, red caboose, red diesel locomotive, and gray coal car with three-section layout ($100-150)

SCREAMIN STOCKS
Introduced in 1992, Screamin Stocks consists of two separately issued miniature sized cars. These include a Chevy Lumina in "Goodwrench" livery and a Ford Thunderbird in "Texaco" livery. A key device could be inserted into the back to launch the car as well as making revving engine sounds. (Value $8-12) each
The models were retooled in 1993 to eliminate the key slot in the rear. The models were double packaged to be used in a playset but this set was never licensed to be produced. Rather than scrap the models, the loose packaging was sold to a jobber who sold them off to toy dealers and close-out stores. (Value $15-20) set

HOT FOOT RACERS
Another 1992 release is Hot Foot Racers. Each of the four styles available comes with a launcher that is strapped to a child's shoe. The model is launched by clicking the launch mechanism on one's foot. Value ($8-12)

Tyco Years 1992-1996

SWOP TOPS
Not a part of the standard miniature line are six miniature-size models called Swop Tops. They feature a swivel design that allows the model's roof section to rotate to make the model either a hardtop or a convertible. The line was introduced in 1993.

FT001 MERCEDES BENZ, issued 1993
1. blue body and roof, dark blue interior, no tempa, Thailand casting ($4-7)

FT002 CORVETTE, issued 1993
1. white body & roof, dull pink interior, "Corvette" & blue design tempa, Thailand casting ($4-7)

FT003 FERRARI TESTAROSSA, issued 1993
1. red body & roof, red interior, small logos tempa, Thailand casting ($4-7)

FT004 NISSAN 300ZX, issued 1993
1. pink body & roof, pink interior, "300ZX" tempa, Thailand casting ($4-7)

FT005 PORSCHE 968, issued 1993
1. silver blue body & roof, light blue interior, small logos tempa, Thailand casting ($15-20)

FT006 FORD MUSTANG, issued 1993
1. fluorescent yellow body & roof, maroon interior, "Mustang" tempa,

Thailand casting ($15-20)

SPARKERS
Another "gimmick" miniature-size line includes Sparkers introduced in 1994. These vehicles feature translucent windows and bases. The bases feature a fifth wheel that, when run on a hard surface, makes a spark to light up the inside of the model. Four body styles are available with two variations of each. All are cast in Thailand.

DODGE DAKOTA, issued 1994
1. white body, lime windows & base, orange & black tempa ($2-4)
2. purple body, rose windows & base, lime & pink tempa ($2-4)

LAMBORGHINI DIABLO, issued 1994
1. dark blue body, orange windows & base, yellow & lime tempa ($2-4)
2. iridescent white body, rose windows & base, black checkers tempa ($2-4)

FERRARI F40, issued 1994
1. black body, orange windows & base, orange & yellow tempa ($2-4)
2. metallic blue body, lime windows & base, yellow & pink tempa ($2-4)

JEEP CHEROKEE, issued 1994
1. black body, lime windows & base, bolts & "Storm" tempa ($2-4)
2. metallic red body, rose windows & base, yellow & black tempa ($2-4)

HOT ROD RACERS
Another novelty miniature line for 1994 includes Hot Rod Racers. Three styles with two variations each. Models are jacked-up and, when pressed down, feature a mechanism that then releases to send the model across a flat surface. Models all cast in Thailand.

DODGE CHALLENGER, issued 1994
1. metallic green body, chrome windows, black interior, "Slammer" & streaks tempa ($4-6)
2. orange & black body, chrome windows, black interior, checkers & "Hemi" tempa ($4-6)

CORVETTE GRAND SPORT, issued 1994
1. fluorescent yellow & black body, chrome windows, spider & web tempa ($4-6)
2. pink & black body, chrome windows, yellow design tempa ($4-6)

FORD MUSTANG GT, issued 1994
1. yellow & pink body, chrome windows, yellow design tempa ($4-6)
2. turquoise & pink body, chrome windows, pink & yellow tempa ($4-6)

POWER CHANGERS
This short-lived 1993 introduction is actually a Tyco toy product marketed with the Matchbox trademark on the blisterpacks as the models are marked "Tyco Toys." The six vehicles consist of a dual vehicle- one model housed inside the shell of another vehicle. The model has two speeds. Once reaching the higher speed, the outer shell of the vehicle splits apart to reveal the second car. Value ($7-10 each)

1490-1 Pace Car & Formula 1
1490-2 Sports Car & Lamborghini
1490-3 Van & Lamborghini
1490-4 Highway Patrol & Ferrari
1490-5 Bandit Pickup & Sports Car
1490-6 Sports Vehicle & Ferrari

CRASH DUMMIES
Tyco holds the license to the Crash Dummies and issued a split-in-half Lumina model. The model exists in two colors with a launcher and a breakaway wall. One set was also issued (see Playsets). The models in the play sets do not come with windshield labels.

43700 CRASH DUMMIES CRASH CARS, issued 1993
1. Black body ($6-8)
2. Red body ($6-8)

ZERO G
A new plastic "anti gravity" racing system includes two-pack issues of models that can race through plastic tube track. All issued in 1995

40100 ZERO G TWIN PACKS, issued 1995
1. Warped Reactor & Formula 1 ($3-5)
2. Air Hammer & Sky Bolter ($3-5)
3. Speed Reaper & Flame Thrower ($3-5)

42200 Zero G Rail Rippers Set, issued 1995 ($12-15)
40300 Zero G Test Track, issued 1995 ($12-15)

CARNIVORES
Issued in 1995 as mechanical monsters from the center of the earth, seven different Carnivores were issued.

37000-1 Chomper ($4-6)
37000-2 Iron Claw ($4-6)
37000-3 Buzz Off ($4-6)
37000-4 Spitfire ($4-6)
37000-5 Skull Shooter ($4-6)
37110-1 Bitewing ($6-8)
37110-2 Venom Spitter ($6-8)

SCX
Introduced in 1995, the Matchbox brand was added to the SCX series from Spain. The models are not made by Matchbox, only marketed by them. These include a large-scale slot car series popular in Europe. ($20-30 each)

83320.20 Toyota Celica "Repsol"
83450.20 Ferrari F40 "Rojo"
83590.20 Porsche 911 "Shell"
83630.20 Audi 90 "Yacco"
83640.20 Mercedes Truck "BP"
83650.20 Mercedes Truck "Antar"
83660.20 Porsche 959 "BP"
83700.20 BMW M3 "Central"
83710.20 Jaguar E "Vintage"
83720.20 Ferrari F1
83790.20 Ferrari F40
83810.20 Porsche 911
83830.20 Mercedes Truck "DEA"
83840.20 Mercedes Truck "Esso"
83880.20 Seat 850 "Vintage"
93140.20 Jaguar XJR-14
93150.20 Mazda 787 "Renown"
93160.20 Mazda 787 "Mazda"

Mattel Years 1997-1998

CAT POWER MACHINES
To supplement the Caterpillar license in the miniature range, Mattel introduced in 1998 larger scale Caterpillar toys made of out plastic.

18901 Power Machines Wheel Loader, issued 1998 ($20-25)
18902 Power Machines Dump Truck, issued 1998 ($20-25)
18903 Power Machine Log Grabber, issued 1998 ($20-25)
65888 Mini Power Machines Off-Highway Truck, issued 1998 ($8-10)
65889 Mini Power Machines Landfill Compactor, issued 1998 ($8-10)
65890 Mini Power Machines Challenger AG Tractor, issued 1998 ($8-10)
65891 Mini Power Machines Track-Type Tractor, issued 1998 ($8-10)
65897 Power Machines Remote Control Bulldozer, issued 1998 ($35-40)

HAUNTED HAULERS
This series was originally devised by Tyco Toys and consisted of six plastic vehicles called Graveyard Runners. The project was shelved for over a year until Mattel, Inc. decided to issue three of the toys in an Avon cosmetic promotion. These were only available through Avon sales representatives through catalog orders and packaged in white boxes. The three models include Neck Wrecker, Ghoul Bus, Drac Bike ($8-10)

MISSION BRAVO, issued 1998
This series was slated as a 1999 introduction but the first vehicles in the series showed up for sale in mid-December 1998. These vehicles include military models in approximately 1/43 scale. They are made more for their play value rather than collectibility. They feature firing rocket mechanisms. Larger models are slated for 1999 introduction.

32514 A-Tak Hornet Helicopter, issued 1998 ($5-6)
32638 LSV Recon Vehicle, issued 1998 ($5-6)
32693 Humvee, issued 1998 ($5-6)
32870 Water Dragon, issued 1998 ($5-6)
35461 Desert Commandos, issued 1998 ($4-5)
35462 Jungle Commandos, issued 1998 ($4-5)
35798 Mountain Commandos, issued 1998 ($4-5)
35799 Sky Commandos, issued 1998 ($4-5)
35977 Sand Tiger, issued 1998 ($10-12)
35978 Sky Scorcher, issued 1998 ($10-12)

Presentation Sets

The first gift sets were known as Presentation Sets and were issued in the United States from 1957 through 1959. These original sets were not based on any "theme" as later gift sets were. Each of the first eight sets' contents were numerically ordered models. That is, PS-1 would contain numbers 1-8, PS-2 would have 9-16 and so on. The sets consisted of mostly first-issue regular wheels, but by 1957 some of them were already discontinued for a larger version of the same model. All presentation sets are now extremely rare. Although the contents of these models may be normal version models, it's the outer cardboard carton that makes these sets so expensive and desirable. Less than a dozen have even been recorded to exist in private collections. Sets are worth in excess of $2,000.

Later sets issued for Europe started "theme" collecting. Army and commercial themes, amongst others, at first these were still termed Presentation sets and can only be identified by an ink stamp on the bottom of the box noted by a number from "PS-2" through "PS-5." Although a PS-1 Private Owner set is listed in catalogs and other literature, there is no record of anyone owning this particular set. Because of the box, contents can be irrelevant when determining the value of these sets, which are usually more than $1,000 each. These sets can be found with normal English text as well as those with German text.

PS-2-B TRANSPORTER & 4 CARS SET, issued 1959
1. contains 30A, 31A, 33A, 36A & A-2A

PS-3-B TRANSPORTER & 6 CARS SET, issued 1959
1. contains 22B, 32A, 33A, 43A, 44A, 45A, A-2-A

PS-4-B COMMERCIAL VEHICLE SET, issued 1959
1. contains 5B, 11B, 21B, 25A, 35A, 40A, 47A, 60A

PS-5-B ARMY TRANSPORT SET, issued 1959
1. contains 49A, 54A, 55A, 61A, 62A, 63A, M-3-A

Gift Sets 1960-1987

It was in 1960 that the name "Gift Set" was first used and continued with themes as a basis for each set. Some sets with the same theme and same number may be issued under a different titled set, but are listed below under the same category for simplicity's sake. Sets from 1960 through 1969 are generally packaged in closed-design boxes without a cellophane front. The boxes themselves, without any contents, have actually commanded higher prices in recent years than the actual models. To determine the value of a 1960s vintage gift, a good rule would be to combine the individual prices of each particular model in the set first. Depending on the age of the set, the higher percent premium gets added to that price. In some instances, a minimum of three to as much as five or more times the contents' value is not unusual. Sets from 1970 to 1987 are generally valued lower—sometimes just double the price of the contents. Post 1982 gift sets are in the next section as the standard "G" denotation ceased to be used . More on this in the next section.

G-1-A COMMERCIAL VEHICLE SET, issued 1960
1. contains 5B, 20B, 37B, 47A, 51A, 59A, 60A, 69A (1960)
2. contains 5C, 10C, 20B, 37B, 46B, 47A, 51A, 69A (1961)
3. contains 5C, 10C, 12B, 13C, 14C, 21C, 46B, 74A (1962)

G-1-B MOTORWAY SET, issued 1964
1. contains 6C, 10C, 13C, 33B, 34B, 38B, 48B, 55B, 71B, R-1-B

G-1-C SERVICE STATION SET, issued 1966
1. contains 13D, 31C, 64B, A-1-B, MG-1-B (1966)
2. contains 13D, 32C, 56B, MG-1-C (1968)

G-1-D SERVICE STATION SUPERSET, issued 1970
1. contains MB13-A, MB15-A, MB32-A, MG-1 Service Station with layout

G-1-E AUTO TRANSPORTER SET, issued 1979
1. contains MB21-C, MB39-B, MB45-B, MB67-A, MB74-C, K-10-C (1979)
2. contains MB6-B, MB21-C, MB39-B, MB55-D, MB67-C, K-10-D (1983)
3. contains MB9-E, MB15-D, MB23-D, MB33-D, MB75-D, K-120-A (1986)

G-2-A CAR TRANSPORTER SET, issued 1960
1. contains 39A, 44A, 45A, 53A, 66A, 75A, A-2-A (1960)
2. contains 22B, 25B, 33A, 39A, 57B, 75A, A-2-A (1961)
3. contains 25B, 30B, 31B, 39B, 48B, 65B, A-2-A (1962)
4. contains 28C, 32B, 44B, 53B, M-8-B (1964)
5. contains 22C, 28C, 36C, 75B, M-8-B or K-8-B (1966)
6. contains 14D, 24C, 31C, 53C, K-8-B (1968)

G-2-B TRANSPORTER SUPERSET/BIG MOVER, issued 1970
1. contains MB8-A, MB14-A, MB24-A, MB53-A, MB67-A, K-11-B (1970)
2. contains MB8-A, MB14-A, MB24-A, MB53-A, MB67-A, K-11-B (1972)
3. contains MB8-B, MB62-B, MB66-B, MB70-B, MB75-B, K-11-B (1973)
4. contains MB9-B, MB32-B, MB41-B, MB44-B, MB51-B, K-11-B (1974)

G-2-C RAILWAY SET, issued 1979
1. contains MB25-C, MB43-C, 2X MB44-C, TP20 Tipper, plastic rail track, etc.

G-2-D STREET RODS/BOLIDES DES RUES, issued 1981 (CN)
1. contains MB15-C, MB25-D, MB26-D, MB72-D

G-2-E CAR TRANSPORTER ACTION PACK, issued 1986
1. contains K-120-A & five assorted Super GT's (contents vary)

G-3-A BUILDING CONSTRUCTOR'S SET, issued 1960
1. contains 2B, 6B, 15B, 16B, 18C, 24B, 28B, M-1-A

G-3-B FARM & AGRICULTURAL SET, issued 1964
1. contains M-5-A, M-7-A, K-8-A (dozer only), K-11-A

G-3-C VACATION SET, issued 1966
1. contains 12C, 23D, 27D, 42B, 45B, 48B, 56B, 68B

G-3-D FARM SET, issued 1968
1. contains 4D, 12C, 37C, 39C, 40C, 43C, 65C, 72B

G-3-E RACING SPECIALS SUPERSET, issued 1970

1. contains MB5-A, MB20-A, MB45-A, MB52-A, MB56-A, MB68-A with extra labels

G-3-F WILD ONES, issued 1973
1. contains MB26-B, MB42-B, MB43-B, MB48-B, MB70-B

G-3-G RACING CAR SET, issued 1979
1. contains MB9-C, MB24-B, MB36-C, MB56-B, K-7-C

G-3-H JCB CONSTRUCTION SET, issued 1987 (UK)
1. contains MB32-D, MB60-G, MB75-D, SB-1-A in "JCB" liveries

G-4-A FARM SET, issued 1960
1. contains 12B, 23B, 31B, 35A, 72A, M-7-A (1960)
2. contains 12B, 23B, 31B, 35A, 50A, 72A, M-7-A (1961)

G-4-B GRAND PRIX RACE TRACK SET, issued 1963
1. contains 13C, 14C, 19C, 32B, 41B, 47B, 52A, 73B, M-1-B, R-4-B (1963)
2. contains 13D, 19D orange & green, 29C, 41C white & yellow, 52B red & blue, 54B, K-5-B or M-6-B, R-4-B (1966-Racetrack Set)
3. contains 3C, 8E, 19D green & orange, 25D, 29C, 41C, 52B red & blue, 67B (1968-Race N Rallye)

G-4-C TRUCK SUPERSET, issued 1970
1. contains MB11-A, 16D, MB21-A, MB47-A, MB49-A, MB51-A, MB58-A, MB63-A

G-4-D TEAM MATCHBOX SUPERFAST CHAMPIONS, issued 1973
1. contains MB24-B in red & green, MB34-A in blue & orange, K-7-C

G-4-E MILITARY ASSAULT, issued 1979
1. contains MB23-A (olive), MB32-C, MB38-C, MB54-C, 61B, MB70-C, plastic ferry & plastic figures ($75-100)

G-4-F CONSTRUCTION SET, issued 1981 (CN)
1. contains MB29-C, MB48-C, MB49-C, MB72-C

G-4-G CONVOY GIFT SET, issued 1982
1. contains CY-3-A, CY-7-A, CY-9-A, MB37-C, MB10-C (1982)
2. contains CY-7-A, CY-9-A, MB59-B, MB61-C, plastic truck stop (1983)
3. contains CY-3-A, CY-5-A, CY-17-A, MB45-C, MB59-B, plastic truck stop (1985)
4. contains CY-17-A, CY-18-A, CY-19-A, MB10-C, MB183 DAF cab (1987)

G-5-A ARMY SET, issued 1960
1. contains 54A, 62A, 63A, 64A, 67A, 68A, M-3-A (1960)
2. contains 12B, 49A, 54A, 61A, 64A, 67A, M-3-A (1964)

G-5-B FIRE STATION SET, issued 1966
1. contains 29C, 54B, 59C, MF-1-A

G-5-C FAMOUS CARS OF YESTERYEAR, issued 1968
1. contains Y-4-B, Y-9-B, Y-12-B, Y-14-B (1969)
2. contains Y-5-C, Y-7-C, Y-8-C, Y-14-B (1970)
3. contains Y-5-C, Y-6-C, Y-7-C, Y-8-C (19740)

G-5-D CONSTRUCTION SET, issued 1979
1. contains MB12-C, MB19-C, MB29-C, MB58-C, MB72-C, plastic load-a-vator (1979)
2. contains MB19-C, MB29-C, MB58-C, MB64-C, MB72-C, plastic load-a-vator (1981)

G-5-E MIDNIGHT HAULERS/POIDS LOURDS DE NUIT, issued 1981 (CN)
1. contains MB11-C, MB14-D, MB23-C, MB42-C

G-5-F FEDERAL EXPRESS ACTION PACK, issued 1987
1. contains MB20-D, MB26-F, MB33-D, MB60-G, SB-1-A in "Federal Express" liveries

G-6-A MODELS OF YESTERYEAR GIFT SET, issued 1961
1. contains Y-1-A, Y-2-A, Y-5-A, Y-10-A, Y-13-A (1961)
2. contains Y-6-B, Y-7-B, Y-10-A, Y-15-A, Y-16-A (1962)
3. contains Y-5-B, Y-6-B, Y-7-B, Y-15-A, Y-16-A (1963)

G-6-B COMMERCIAL TRUCK SET, issued 1964
1. contains 6C, 15C, 16C, 17D, 26B, 30B, 58B, 62B (1964)
2. contains 16C, 17D, 25C, 26B, 30C, 69B, 70B, 71B (1966)
3. contains 1E, 10D, 21D, 26C, 30C, 49B, 60B, 70B (1968)

G-6-C DRAG RACE SET, issued 1972
1. contains MB7-B, MB13-B, MB30-B, MB31-B, MB36-B, MB61-A, thunderbolt launcher

G-6-D FARM SET, issued 1979
1. contains MB40-B, MB46-C, MB51-C, MB71-C, TP19 trailer, plastic farm buildings

G-6-E RESCUE/SAUVETAGE ENSEMBLE, issued 1981 (CN)
1. contains MB13-C, MB22-C, MB41-C, MB59-B

G-6-F VIRGIN ATLANTIC ACTION PACK, issued 1987
1. contains MB15-D, MB65-B, MB68-E, MB75-D, SB-10-A in "Virgin Atlantic" liveries

G-7-A MODELS OF YESTERYEAR GIFT SET, issued 1961
1. contains Y-3-A, Y-8-A, Y-9-A, Y-12-A, Y-14-A (1961)
2. contains Y-3-A, Y-4-B, Y-11-A, Y-12-A, Y-13-A (1962)
3. contains Y-2-B, Y-5-B, Y-10-B, Y-15-A, Y-16-A (1964)
4. contains Y-1-B, Y-3-B, Y-11-B, Y-14-B (1966)

G-7-B CAR FERRY, issued 1972
1. contains blue & yellow plastic ferry with 4 assorted miniatures ($75-100)

G-7-C EMERGENCY SET, issued 1979
1. contains MB10-C, MB13-C, MB22-C, MB41-C, SB-25-A, plastic buildings (1979)
2. contains MB8-D, MB12-D, MB22-C, MB57-D, MB75-D, plastic buildings (1983)

G-8-A CONSTRUCTION SET, issued 1962
1. contains K-1-A, K-2-A, K-3-A, K-5-A, K-6-A (1962)
2. contains K-1-B, K-7-A, K-10-A, K-13-A, K-14-A (1964)
3. contains K-1-B, K-11-A, K-12-A, K-15-A (1966)

G-8-B THUNDER JETS, issued 1979
1. contains SB-5-A, SB-21-A, SB-22-A, SB-24-A

G-8-C TURBO CHARGED ACTION PACK, issued 1984
1. contains MB6-C, MB17-D, MB39-C, MB44-D, MB52-D, plastic launcher

G-9-A MAJOR PACK SET, issued 1962
1. contains M-1-B, M-2-B, M-4-A, M-6-A

G-9-B SERVICE STATION SET, issued 1964
1. contains 13C, 33B, 71B, A-1-B, MG-1-B (1964)
2. contains 13D, 33B, 71B, A-1-B, MG-1-B (1965)

G-9-C COMMANDO TASK FORCE, issued 1976
1. MB16-A, MB28-B, MB73-B, gray plastic ferry & plastic figures ($75-100)

G-10-A GARAGE GIFT SET, issued 1962
1. contains 13C, 25B, 31B, A-1-A, MG-1-A
2. contains 13C, 25B, 31B, A-1-B, MG-1-B

G-10-B FIRE STATION SET, issued 1964
1. contains 2X 9C, 14C, 59B, MF-1-A

G-10-C THUNDER JETS, issued 1976
1. includes SB-2-A, SB-4-A, SB-5-A, SB-12-A

G-10-D PAN AM ACTION PACK, issued 1986
1. contains MB10-C, MB54-F, MB65-B, MB68-E, SB-10-A in "Pan Am" liveries

G-11-A STRIKE FORCE, issued 1976
1. contains MB1-A, MB2-A, MB16-A, MB28-B, MB38-C, MB73-B in military colors

G-11-B LUFTHANSA ACTION PACK, issued 1986
1. contains MB30-E, MB54-F, MB59-D, MB65-B, SB-28-A in "Lufthansa" liveries

G-12-A RESCUE SET, issued 1976
1. contains MB16-A, MB20-B, MB22-C, MB46-B, MB62-C, MB74-B (1976)
2. contains MB16-A, MB20-B, MB22-C, MB46-B, MB64-C, MB74-B (1978)

G-13-A CONSTRUCTION SET, issued 1976
1. contains MB12-C, MB20-B (orange), MB21-B, MB23-B, MB50-B, plastic load-a-vator

G-14-A GRAND PRIX SET, issued 1976
1. contains MB7-B, MB24-B, MB36-C, MB56-B, K-7-C (1976)
2. contains MB7-B, MB24-B, MB27-B, MB36-C, K-7-C (1977)

G-15-A TRANSPORTER SET, issued 1976
1. contains MB1-C, MB4-C, MB6-B, MB8-C, MB45-B, K-10-C

G-16-A SKY GIANTS, issued 1977
1. contains 2X SB-3-A (Lufthansa & Air France), SB-10-A, SB-13-A

G-17-A CAR FERRY, issued 1977
1. contains red plastic car ferry with four assorted miniatures ($75-100)

G-18-A SKY GIANTS, issued 1979
1. contains. SB-3-A, SB-10-A, SB-13-A, SB-23-A

G-25-A COLLECTASET, issued 1984
1. contains 25 assorted miniatures (contents vary)

G-100-A TWIN THUNDERBOLT LAUNCHER SET, issued 1976

1. contains MB7-B, MB61-A, with thunderbolt launcher

Gift Sets 1983- 1996

Although a "G" prefix for gift sets ended in 1987, new prefixes for gifts started being used around 1983–1984. Different prefixes started being used such as (C) Japanese sets, (CY) Convoy sets, (MB) Matchbox sets, (SB) Skybuster sets, (CS) Construction sets, (EM) Emergency sets, and (MC) for Motorcity sets. Motorcity includes gift sets as well as other related items and these are in a further section of this book. For values on this vintage, add 10-20 percent of contents value.

C-1 Sports Car, issued 1984 (JP)
1. contains MB24-D, MB35-C, MB39-C (red), MB40-C

C-2 4WD OFF-ROAD, issued 1984 (JP)
1. contains MB7-D, MB13-D, MB44-D, MB49-D (1984)
2. contains MB5-D, MB7-D, MB13-D, MB22-D (1987)

C-3 EUROPEAN CARS (JP)
1. contains MB7-D, MB43-E, MB66-F, MB75-D

C-4 CONSTRUCTION VEHICLES, issued 1984 (JP)
1. contains MB19-D, MB29-C, MB32-D, MB64-D

C-6 EMERGENCY SET, issued 1987 (JP)
1. contains MB18-C, MB44-F, MB63-E, MB75-D in Japanese liveries

C-7 POLICE SET, issued 1984 (JP)
1. contains MB10-C, MB33-C, MB61-C, MB75-D
2. contains MB10-C, MB33-C, MB44-F, MB57-D

C-8 CAR TRANSPORTER SET, issued 1984 (JP)
1. contains MB3-C (white), MB24-D (white), MB39-C, CY-1-A

C-9 NASA SET, issued 1984 (JP)
1. contains MB54-F, CY-2-A, SB-3-B

C-10 CONSTRUCTION SET, issued 1987 (JP)
1. contains MB29-C, MB30-E, MB32-D, CY-203-A

C-11 AIRPORT SET, issued 1987 (JP)
1. contains MB54-F, MB67-F, SB10-A, SB-28-A in Japanese liveries

C-15 CAR TRANSPORTER SET, issued 1987
1. contains MB7-F, MB9-E, MB23-D, MB31-E, MB33-D, K-120-A

CY-201-A FIRE RESCUE SET, issued 1985
1. contains MB54-F, MB75-D, CY-13-A

CY-202-A POLICE SET, issued 1985
1. contains MB10-C, MB61-C, CY-11-A

CY-203-A CONSTRUCTION SET, issued 1985
1. contains MB29-C, MB30-E, MB32-D, CY-203-A

CY-204-A NASA SET, issued 1986
1. contains MB54-F, MB75-D, CY-2-A

CY-205-A FARM SET, issued 1987
1. contains MB46-C, MB51-C, CY-20-A

CY-206-A TELECOM SET, issued 1987
1. contains MB48-F, MB60-G, CY-15-A in "British Telecom" liveries

MB-824 BUY 5 GET 5 FREE, issued 1991 (UK)
1. includes assortment of 10 models (contents vary)

MB-828 STAR CARS, issued 1990 (DU/GR/AS)
1. includes assortment of 5 cars mounted on star shaped blistercards. Blistercard can be broken down into five single packs at perforations in the cardboard

MB-830 RALLY PACK, issued 1991
1. includes 2 Super GT's, 2 launchers & stop watch (contents vary)

MB-835 CHRISTMAS WORLD RALLYE, issued 1991
1. contains four cars in solid colors of blue, green, yellow and red with playmat (3 different sets available)

SP-20 JAPANESE ISSUE GIFT SET, issued 1977
1. MB5-A (black), MB15-A, MB24-A (gold), MB27-A (yellow) (blue box)
2. No. 2 & 5 Japanese miniatures, J-21 & J-22 (green box)

SB-801 SKYBUSTERS VALUE PACK, issued 1991
1. contains three assorted Skybusters (contents vary)

EM-75 ACTION FIRE, issued 1992
1. contains MB16-E, MB18-C, MB30-E, MB75-D, CY-13-A, TP-110-A raft

EM-90 30 PIECE CARRY PACK, issued 1992

1. contains assortment of miniatures & plastic accessories

CS-75 HEAVY DUTY SQUAD, issued 1992
1. contains MB19-D, MB29-C, MB30-E, MB64-D, MB7-E, CY-30-A

CS-90 30 PIECE CARRY PACK, issued 1992
1. contains assortment of miniatures & plastic accessories

0115 15 PACK GIFT SET, issued 1996 (US)
1. contains assortment of 15 miniatures

0138 SUPER GT 38 PIECE GIFT SET, issued 1989
1. contains assortment of 38 different Super GT's

76270 HARLEY-DAVIDSON COLLECTOR'S EDITION, issued 1992
1. contains 2X MB50-D (blue & orange), CY-8-A, K-83-A (black), Stunt Cycle

030653 THREE PIECE YESTERYEAR SET, issued 1984
1. contains three Yesteryears (contents vary)

DRAGSTER SET, issued 1984 (JP)
1. contains MB4-D, MB46-D, MB69-D, MB74-D

CLASSICS SET, issued 1984 (JP)
1. contains MB4-D, MB42-D, MB69-D, MB71-D

BOOT'S FARM PLAYPACK, issued 1991 (UK-Boot's stores)
1. contains MB35-F, MB43-A, MB46-C, MB51-C, TP-103-A with playmat

BOOT'S ROUND TOWN PLAYPACK, issued 1991 (UK-Boot's stores)
1. contains MB17-C, MB21-E, MB26-F, MB48-F, MB60-G, MB67-F with playmat

JAMES BOND 007 LICENSE TO KILL, issued 1989 (UK)
1. contains MB58-D, SB-25-A, SB-26-A, CY-105-A in special liveries

McDONALD'S HAPPY MEAL SET, issued 1987
1. contains 16 different Super GT's
NOTE: This set was never offered to the consumer. It was a display unit used by selected McDonald's restaurants in the Southwest USA. VERY RARE! ($250-300) intact.

CONNOISSEUR SET, issued 1985
1. contains Y-1-B, Y-3-B, Y-4-C, Y-11-B, Y-13-B, Y-14-B in special colors with special wooden display unit ($175-225)

CLASSIC SPORTS CARS OF THE THIRTIES, issued 1983 (AU)
1. contains Y-14-C, Y-16-B, Y-19-A, Y-20-A

STARTER KIT 5 FOR 4 OFFER, issued 1983
1. contains five assorted Yesteryears (contents vary)

YY-50 FIVE PACK GIFT SET, issued 1982
1. contains Y-3-D, Y-5-D, Y-10-C, Y-12-D, Y-13-C

WINROSS-MATCHBOX GOODWRENCH, issued 1992
1. two "Goodwrench" Matchbox cars-one in full livery & the other in matt black with minimal livery with Winross transporter in cardboard outer box ($150-250)(WR)
2. same as above but in a wooden outer box ($200-300)(WR)

ERTL-MATCHBOX BUDWEISER, issued 1994
1. two Matchbox cars-one in red with full "Budweiser" graphics & the other in black with minimal livery with Ertl transporter in wooden outer box ($200-250)(WR)

PC-18 VIEWMASTER PROMOTION, issued 1996
1. includes MB60-G Ford Transit in red with "Viewmaster" livery, red Viewmaster viewer, special Matchbox viewing reel of 7 regular wheel models with certificate of authenticity in wooden display box ($80-90)(US)

236312 20 CAR GIFT SET, issued 1998
1. includes 20 assorted blisterpacked cars mounted on a cardboard sleeve (sold at Costco)

32835 CHRYSLER CORPORATION GIFT SET, issued 1998
1. includes Viper, Atlantic & Prowler & Convoy

32839 STARTER COLLECTION 10 PACK, issued 1998
1. includes 10 vehicles each from one the 1998 "series" (contents vary)

36105 STARTER COLLECTION 20 PACK, issued 1998
1. includes 20 vehicles, two cars from each one of the 1998 "series"

34359-1 through 34359-6 CORVETTE PREMIERE COLLECTION, issued 1997
1. includes five models of Corvettes in five different sets ($20-25)

34726 TOYS R US 50 YEARS OF FUN FOREVER GIFT SET, issued 1998

1. includes three specially colored miniatures and special "Toys R Us" convoy ($25-30)(TRU)

Supersets/Highway Express Sets

Special gift sets under the Superset and Highway Express names were issued for the U.S. market in 1981-1982. For values add 10 percent to contents' total.

06-00-21 THUNDER ROAD, issued 1981
1. includes MB15-C, MB25-D, MB37-D, MB66-B, MB74-D

06-00-22 SUNDOWN DRIVE, issued 1981
1. includes MB14-C, MB23-C, MB24-D, MB48-D, MB63-D

06-00-23 MIDNIGHT BOULEVARD, issued 1981
1. includes MB8-C, MB26-D, MB31-D, MB46-D, MB72-D

06-00-24 WORKIN' WHEELS, issued 1982
1. includes MB19-D, MB29-C, MB30-E, MB49-C, MB64-D (1982)
2. includes MB19-D, MB29-C, MB30-E, MB32-D, MB64-D (1985)

06-00-25 OFF ROAD RIDERS, issued 1982
1. includes MB5-D, MB7-D, MB13-D, MB22-D, MB44-D (1982)
2. includes MB5-D, MB13-D, MB20-C, MB53-E, MB57-D (1985)

06-00-26 CLASSY CLASSICS, issued 1982
1. includes MB4-D, MB38-E, MB42-D, MB69-D, MB71-D (1982)
2. includes MB42-D, MB47-D, MB69-D, MB71-D, MB73-C (1985)

06-00-27 PACE SETTERS, issued 1982
1. includes MB9-D, MB11-D, MB23-C, MB25-D, MB37-D (1982)
2. includes MB3-C, MB8-E, MB11-E, MB17-D, MB55-F (1985-Turbo Racers)

06-00-61 TRUCKIN' SPEED TRAP, issued 1982
1. contains MB10-C, MB35-C, CY-3-A, CY-8-A

06-00-62 18 WHEELERS, issued 1982
1. contains CY-4-A, CY-7-A, CY-9-A

06-00-63 HIGHWAY HAULERS, issued 1982
1. contains MB19-D, MB30-E, MB56-D, MB61-C, CY-6-A

06-00-64 NASA COUNTDOWN, issued 1982
1. contains MB54-D, 2X CY-2-A, one with rocket & other with SB-3-B

Car Carry Case Gift Sets

Also on the U.S. market were gift set combinations in which the models were placed in a twelve-compartment carry case with clear front. Add $10 to total price of contents for value. Carry cases and play cases are covered in a separate section of this book.

06-10-01/GC-1 ROLAMATICS CAR CASE, issued 1974
1. contains MB10-B, MB39-A, MB57-B, MB67-B, MB69-B (1974)
2. contains MB35-B, MB39-A, MB47-B, MB57-B, MB67-B, MB69-B (1976)

06-10-02/GC-2 RESCUE CAR CARRY CASE, issued 1974
1. contains MB35-A, MB46-B, MB55-B, MB59-B, MB74-B (1974)
2. contains MB2-C, MB20-B, MB22-C, MB46-B, MB62-C, MB74-C (1976)
3. contains MB2-C, MB20-B, MB22-C, MB33-C, MB74-B, MB75-C (1977)

06-10-03 CROSS COUNTRY CARRY CASE
GC-3 KEEP ON TRUCKING CARRY CASE, issued 1974
1. contains MB2-B, MB13-B, MB18-A, MB71-B, MB73-A (1974)
2. contains MB16-A, 2X MB23-B, MB50-B, MB57-B, MB63-B (1976)
3. contains MB11-C, MB37-C, MB42-C, MB50-B, MB63-B, MB71-C (1977)

06-10-10 STREAKERS CARRY CASE, issued 1975
1. contains MB33-B, MB41-B, MB51-B, MB53-B, MB60-B

GC-4 MILITARY CARRY CASE, issued 1977
1. contains MB16-A, MB30-C, MB38-C, MB54-C, MB70-C, MB73-B

GC-6 STREET CLASSICS, issued 1980
1. contains MB3-C, MB8-C, MB21-C, MB62-C, MB67-C

GC-8 EMERGENCY SERVICES, issued 1980
1. contains MB13-C, MB22-C, MB41-C, MB64-C, MB75-C

GC-9 KEEP ON TRUCKIN, issued 1980

1. contains MB11-C, MB19-C, MB49-C, MB63-B, MB69-C

GC-10 OFF THE ROAD, issued 1980
1. contains MB31-C, MB38-C (yellow), MB53-C, MB60-C, TP-7 Glider Trailer

Motorcity

Motorcity, designated as "MC," was devised in 1986 with the release of six mini-play environments based on molds purchased from the Tomy company of Japan. Motorcity includes playsets, play environments, and gift sets. For the value of gift sets, add the prices of the contents together plus 10 percent of the total.

MC-1-A CAR WASH, issued 1986
1. white & blue with "Car wash" labels ($7-10)
2. gray & blue with "Matchbox" labels ($7-10)

MC-2-A PETROL STATION, issued 1986
1. white & gray with "Gasoline" labels ($7-10)
2. gray & white with "Matchbox" labels ($7-10)

MC-3-A PIT STOP, issued 1986
1. white & gray ($7-10)
2. gray & red with "Matchbox" labels ($7-10)

MC-4-A GARAGE, issued 1986
1. white with "Garage" labels ($7-10)
2. gray with "Matchbox" labels ($7-10)

MC-5-A CONSTRUCTION CRANE, issued 1986
1. white & orange ($7-10)
2. gray & orange ($7-10)

MC-6-A CONVEYOR LOADER, issued 1986
1. white & orange with "Matchbox" labels ($7-10)
2. gray & orange with "Matchbox" labels ($7-10)

MC-7-A FARM SET, issued 1988
1. contains MB35-F, 40C, MB43-A, MB46-C, MB51-C, TP-103-A, CY-20-A

MC-8-A CONSTRUCTION SET, issued 1988
1. contains MB19-D, MB29-C, MB30-E, MB42-E, MB64-D, MB70-E, CY-203-A

MC-9-A RACING SET, issued 1989
1. contains MB6-E, MB7-F, MB30-F, MB58-D, MB65-D, CY-111-A

MC-10-A 10 MATCHBOX MINIATURES, issued 1988
1. contains 10 assorted miniatures (contents vary)

MC-11-A CAR TRANSPORTER SET, issued 1988
1. contains MB17-F, MB39-D, CY-1-A

MC-12-A AEROBATIC TEAM SET, issued 1988
1. contains MB46-F, MB75-D, CY-21-A in "Red Rebels" liveries
2. contains MB46-F, MB75-D, CY-21-A in "Flying Aces" liveries

MC-13-A POLICE SET, issued 1988
1. contains MB10-C, MB61-C, CY-11-A

MC-15-A FIRE SET, issued 1990
1. contains MB16-E, MB30-F, MB54-F, MB63-E, SB-26-A, CY-13-A

MC-16-A MOTORCITY PLAYPACK, issued 1989 (UK)
1. contains assortment of eight miniatures & Super GT's with playmat (contents vary)

MC-17-A BRITISH AIRWAYS SET, issued 1991 (UK)
1. contains MB35-F, MB68-E, MB72-E, SB-23-A, SB-31-A in "British Airways" liveries

MC-18-A FERRARI SET, issued 1991
1. contains MB24-H, MB70-D, MB74-H, MB75-D, CY-24-A

MC-19-A SUPER PLAY PACK, issued 1993
1. contains 12 miniatures & playmat (contents vary) ($15-18)

MC-20-A MOTORCITY PLAYTRACK, issued 1987
1. playtrack with bridge, petrol station & signs ($15-20)

MC-20-B GIFT PACK, issued 1988
1. contains assortment of 20 miniatures (contents vary)

MC-23-A PORSCHE SET, issued 1991
1. contains MB3-C (yellow), MB7-F (white), MB55-F (red), MB71-F (black), CY-25-A

MC-24-A RED ARROWS SET, issued 1992 (UK)
1. contains MB35-F, MB68-E, MB75-D, 2X SB-37-A in Royal Air Force liveries

MC-30-A MOTORCITY PLAYTRACK, issued 1987
1. playtrack with bridge, petrol station, car park & signs ($20-25)

MC-40-A MOTORCITY PLAYTRACK, issued 1987
1. playtrack with garage, car hoist, bridges, car park, signs ($20-25)

MC-50-A MOTORCITY CARRY PACK, issued 1991
1. contains assortment of miniatures, Super GT's & plastic accessories

MC-75-A MINI FOLD N GO ASSORTMENT, issued 1991
1. plastic Garage ($8-10)
2. plastic Police Station ($8-10)
3. plastic Rescue Station ($8-10)
4. plastic Fire Station ($8-10)

MC-100-A MOTORCITY PLAYSET, issued 1988
1. playtrack with built-in street of shops & accessories ($12-15)

MC-150-A MOTORCITY AIRPORT, issued 1990
1. aircraft hangar, runway, carpark & playmat ($15-20)

MC-200-A MOTORCITY PLAYTRACK, issued 1988
1. reissue of MC-20 ($20-25)

MC-300-A MOTORCITY PLAYTRACK, issued 1988
1. reissue of MC-30 ($20-25)

MC-400-A MOTORCITY PLAYTRACK, issued 1988
1. reissue of MC-40 ($20-25)

MC-410-A DELUXE PLAYTRACK SET, issued 1993
1. includes playtrack & bridge ($35-50)

MC-500-A MOTORCITY 500 SUPERSET, issued 1991
1. playtrack with multi-level parking garage & accessories ($25-30)

MC-510-A SUPER TRANSPORT SET, issued 1991
1. playtrack with roadway, airport, railway track & accessories ($30-40)

MC-520-A MOTORCITY BUILDING ZONE, issued 1992
1. playtrack with multi-story site & accessories ($30-40)

MC-550 MOTORCITY ELECTRONIC SERVICE CENTER, issued 1991
1. garage with playmat. With 7 working features each with sound effects ($40-50)

MC-560 INTERCOM CITY, issued 1992
1. city environment with "talk-a-tronic" system ($90-110)

MC-580 INTERCOM CITY GRAND PRIX SET, issued 1993
1. includes MB7-F, MB24-H, MB67-F with plastic unit ($125-175)

MC-590 INTERCOM CITY AIRPORT, issued 1993
1. includes MB8-I, MB68-D, SB-31-A with plastic unit ($100-150)

MC-610 CONTAINER PORT, issued 1991
1. playmat with container ship, crane rail track, models ($20-25)

MC-620 CONSTRUCTION YARD, issued 1991
1. playmat with multi-story site, crane, lift ($20-25)

MC-630 FOLD N GO GARAGE, issued 1991
1. fold-up garage with accessories ($18-25)

MC-640 FOLD N GO CAR PARK, issued 1991
1. fold up car park with accessories ($18-25)

MC-660 ELECTRONIC RESCUE STATION, issued 1992
1. playmat with rescue station featuring electronic sounds ($40-50)

MC-700 MINITRONICS ASSORTMENT, issued 1992
1. electronic sound Car Wash ($10-15)
2. electronic sound Tune-Up Center ($10-15)
3. electronic sound Gravel Pit ($10-15)
4. electronic sound Crane ($10-15)

MC-801 GARAGE PLAYPACK, issued 1991 (UK)
1. contains MB21-E, 2 Super GT's, CY-105 (Shell) & plastic garage
2. contains MB21-E, 2 Super GT's, CY-17-A (Shell) & plastic garage

MC-803-A CIRCUS SET, issued 1992
1. contains MB31-B, MB35-F, MB72-K, CY-25-A

MC-804-A CIRCUS SET, issued 1992
1. contains MB31-C, MB35-F, MB40-B, MB72-K, MB73-C, CY-25-A, SB39-A

MC-805-A AROUND LONDON TOUR, issued 1992
1. contains MB4-E, MB8-G, MB17-C, MB31-G, MB63-E & playmat

MC-963-A 30 PIECE SPECIAL COLLECTION, issued 1992 (US)
1. includes assortment of 30 vehicles in which 15 are specially colored
2. includes assortment of 30 pieces in standard colors
NOTE: Both sets contain the same 30 pieces. Issued only at "Sam's Club".

Action System

Formerly known as Motor City, the playset section was revamped and renamed in 1995 as "Action System." Each Action System contains plastic play environments but no models.

AC-1 Police Chase Set, issued 1996 ($6-8)
AC-2 Car Wash, issued 1996 ($6-8)
AC-3 Service Station, issued 1996 ($6-8)
AC-4 Lift Bridge, issued 1996
1. yellow & orange ($9-11)
2. orange & yellow ($9-11)
AC-4 Boat Bridge, issued 1996
1. yellow & orange ($9-11)
2. orange & yellow ($9-11)
AC-5 Police Station, issued 1996 ($9-11)
AC-6 Hospital, issued 1996 ($9-11)
AC-7 Super Spin Car Wash, issued 1996 ($12-18)
AC-8 Fire & Rescue Center, issued 1996 ($12-18)
AC-9 Road Track Set, issued 1996 ($15-20)
AC-10 Super Service Center, issued 1996 ($20-30)

Playsets

This section covers miscellaneous playsets that don't fit into any special categories. Most are identified only with serial numbers. The playsets will be listed chronologically by decade.

PLAYSETS (1969-1979)
M-2 Motorway, issued 1969 ($50-75)
Motorway No. 12, issued 1969 ($60-75)
ST-30 Switch-A-Track, issued 1969 ($50-75)
BR-1 Build-A-Road (50 pieces), issued 1969 ($25-40)
BR-2 Super Build-A-Road (90 pieces), issued 1969 ($35-50)
BR-3 Deluxe Build-A-Road (130 pieces), issued 1969 ($50-75)
AC-1 Magnetic Action Repair Center, issued 1970 ($50-75)
AC-2 Magnetic Action Freight Center, issued 1970 ($50-75)
AC-3 Magnetic Action Farm Center, issued 1970 ($50-75)
DDL-1 Daredevil Drivers, issued 1970 ($35-50)
SNG-1 Steer-N-Go Dune Buggy Roadway, issued 1970 ($75-100)
SNG-2 Steer-N-Go Grand Prix Roadway, issued 1970 ($75-100)
SNG-3 Steer-N-Go Pikes Peak Rally Roadway, issued 1970 ($75-100)
SNG-4 Steer-N-Go Village Roadway, issued 1970 ($75-100)
SNG-5 Steer-N-Go Monte Carlo Roadway, issued 1970 ($75-100)
SM-1 Station Maker, issued 1971 ($50-75)
P-1 Matchbox Stunt Cars Action Playset, issued 1973 ($75-100)
P-2 Matchbox Skybusters Action Playset, issued 1973 ($75-100)
P-3 Matchbox Load-A-Vator Action Playset, issued 1973 ($75-100)
ZR-1 Matchbox Zoom-Around, issued 1973 ($50-75)
PD-1 Power Driver Remote Control, issued 1973 ($50-75)
CH-1 Chopper Chase, issued 1973 ($50-75)
590101 Rev' N Roar, issued 1974 ($40-60)
PM-1 Airport Playmat, issued 1978 ($15-20)
PM-2 Seaport Playmat, issued 1978 ($15-20)
PM-3 Roadway Playmat, issued 1978 ($15-20)

PLAYSETS (1980-1989)
500101 Play & Pack Hat Construction Yard, issued 1984 ($20-25)
500102 Play & Pack Hat Rescue Center ($20-25)
500103 Play & Pack Hat 4X4 Test Center, issued 1984 ($20-25)
550105 City Garage, issued 1981 ($35-50)
550107 Super Spin Car Wash, issued 1981 ($15-25)
550108 Highway Express Truck Stop, issued 1982 ($20-30)
550112 Matchbox Motors, issued 1983 ($15-20)
550117 Super Spin Car Wash, reissued 1983 ($15-20)
560109 Speed Shooter, issued 1984 ($35-50)
600101 Sounds of Service, issued 1981 ($15-25)
1050 Laser Wheels Speed of Light Stunt set, issued 1988 ($12-15)
1310 Competition Arena, issued 1988 ($15-20)

PLAYSETS (1990-1996)
0950 Commando Playset, issued 1990 ($15-20)
1402 Play track, issued 1994 ($12-15)
1403 Deluxe Play Track, issued 1994 ($15-18)
1494 Ring of Fire Stunt Set, issued 1993 ($15-18)
40200 Zero G Rail Rippers, issued 1995 ($12-15)
40300 Zero G Test Track, issued 1995 ($12-15)
42710 Turbo Stunt Set, issued 1993 ($10-15)
42715 Superfast Stunt Set, issued 1994 ($10-15)
42716 Super Duper Double Looper, issued 1996 ($8-12)
42720 Rapid Shot Slam Set, issued 1994 ($15-18)
42722-A Smash & Crash, issued 1995 ($10-12)
42722-B Super Fast Crash, issued 1996 ($10-12)
42725 Rapid Shot Cross Over Crash, issued 1994 ($15-18)
50670 Travel Playsets (Garage, Rescue, Police, Fire), issued 1994 ($5-8) each
50679 Dream Machines Playsets
1. Malibu Beach Shop, issued 1993 ($8-12)
2. Rainbow Stables, issued 1993 ($8-12)
50680 Stackems (Service Station, Emergency Station, Truck Center), issued 1992 ($10-15)

50690 Emergency City, issued 1995 ($25-35)
50695 Car Crusher, issued 1994 ($12-15)
50957 Jeep Jamboree, issued 1991 ($25-40)
LR-730 Lightning Flipout Drag Strip, issued 1991 ($15-25)
LR-740 Electronic Drag Strip, issued 1991 ($15-25)
S710 Crash Dummies Crash Alley, issued 1993 ($18-25)
S720 Double Looper, issued 1993 ($45-60)
Top Circuit Blocks by Trol, issued 1993 ($75-100)(BR)

PLAYSETS (1997-1998)

15440 Mega Rig Rescue Squad Helicopter, issued 1998 ($15-20)
15717 Mega Rig Rescue Squad Speedboat, issued 1998 ($15-20)
15718 Mega Rig Rescue Off Road Truck, issued 1998 ($15-20)
32115 Meg Rig Caterpillar Transporter, issued 1998 ($25-30)
32422 Mega Rig Space Shuttle Transporter, issued 1998 ($25-30)
32974 Military Hangar Outpost, issued 1998 ($5-8)
32975 Police Headquarters, issued 1998 ($5-8)
32976 Battle Zone Hospital, issued 1997 ($5-8)
32986 Caterpillar Quarry Action Set, issued 1998 ($12-15)
32987 Caterpillar Wrecking Zone, issued 1998 ($12-15)
34380-1 Tundra Defense Force, issued 1997 ($20-25)
34380-2 Desert Command Post, issued 1997 ($20-25)
34497 Mega Rig Police Command Center, issued 1998 ($25-30)
35369 Real Talkin' Airport, issued 1998 ($35-40)
35438 Kaybee Toys Double Play Caterpillar Set, issued 1998 ($25-30)
35361 Mega Rig Space Alien Quest, issued 1998 ($8-10)
35362 Mega Rig Rescue Shark Patrol, issued 1998 ($8-10)
35364 Mega Rig Rescue Rhino Safari, issued 1998 ($8-10)
35515 Caterpillar Boulder Blastin' Bridge, issued 1998 ($15-18)
50721-1 "The Lost World" Site B Fuel Depot, issued 1997 ($15-20)(JR)
50721-2 "The Lost World" Site B Garage, issued 1997 ($15-20)(JR)
50732 Super Light & Sound Airport, issued 1997 ($25-35)
67210-1 Hangar Outpost #22, issued 1997 ($5-8)
67210-2 Military Police Headquarters, issued 1997 ($5-8)
67210-3 Military Hospital, issued 1997 ($5-8)

Toys & Games

London to Brighton Veteran Car Game ($250-350)
FB-5 Traffic Game, issued 1969 ($75-100)
JA-196 Jigsaw Puzzles (set of 8), issued 1969 ($150-250)set
CG-1 Crash Game, issued 1970 ($50-75)
CP-1 Car Pow, issued 1970 ($60-75)
CA-1 Cascade Game, issued 1972 ($50-75)
Popsters (suction cup toys), issued 1972 ($100-150)
8450 Boola Ball, issued 1987 ($18-25)
Uri Geller game, issued 1991 ($75-100)
Race For The Cup game, issued 1987 ($75-100)(AU)
Who's Scared? Scaredy Monsters game, issue date unknown ($75-100)(AU)
Go Away Dinosaurs game, issue date unknown ($75-100)(AU)
WH-75 Woosh Ring, issued 1989 ($15-25)

Superfast Race Tracks

In the 1970s, Lesney Products produced race track in yellow similar to the orange track that Hot Wheels uses for their vehicles. Many different sets were issued, all with "SF", "S", "T" or "TA" prefix identifications.

SF-1 Speed Set, issued 1970 ($20-25)
SF-2 Loop Set, issued 1970 ($25-30)
SF-3 Curve and Space Leap Set, issued 1970 ($30-45)
SF-4 Double Super Loop Race Set, issued 1970 ($30-45)
SF-5 Double Super Curve Race Set, issued 1970 ($30-45)
SF-11 Track Pack, issued 1970 ($10-12)
SF-12 Loop Pack, issued 1970 ($10-12)
SF-13 Jump Thru Hoop Pack, issued 1970 ($10-15)
SF-14 180 Degree Curve Pack, issued 1970 ($10-12)
SF-15 Double Track Race Pack, issued 1970 ($10-12)
SF-16 Grand Prix Pack, issued 1970 ($10-15)
SF-18 Lap Counter, issued 1970 ($10-15)
SF-19 Automatic Garage, issued 1970 ($10-15)
SF-20 Superfast Super Booster, issued 1970 ($35-50)
SF-21 Mass Start Grid, issued 1970 ($10-12)
SF-22 Tune Up Kit, issued 1970 ($15-20)

T-100 Devil's Leap Speed Set, issued 1973($20-30)
T-200 Loop Set, issued 1973 ($25-35)
T-400 Double Loop Racing Set, issued 1973 ($30-40)
T-500 Booster Speed Circuit, issued 1973 ($35-45)
T-600 Double Booster Speed Circuit, issued 1973 ($35-45)
T-800 Twin Booster Racing Circuit with Rattlesnake Bends, issued 1973 ($35-45)
T-900 Matchbox Alpine, issued 1973 ($25-40)

TA-00 Track Joiners, issued 1973 ($5-8)
TA-3 Rattlesnake Bend, issued 1973 ($10-12)
TA-4 Pacemaker Hand Booster, issued 1973 ($10-15)
TA-5 Whiplash Chicane, issued 1973 ($10-12)
TA-6 Catapult Pass, issued 1973 ($10-12)
TA-7 Dare Devil Switch, issued 1973 ($10-12)

TA-9 Sky-Jack, issued 1973 ($12-15)
TA-11 Track Pack, issued 1973 ($10-15)
TA-12 Stunt Loop, issued 1973 ($10-12)
TA-17 Slipstream Curve & Trestles, issued 1973 ($15-18)
TA-20 Power Booster, issued 1973 ($35-50)
TA-29 "G" Clamp, issued 1973 ($5-8)
TA-30 Track Extension Pack, issued 1975 ($10-15)
TA-40 Track Extension Pack, issued 1978 ($10-15)
TA-41 New Bend, issued 1978 ($8-12)

S-100 Streak Hit-N-Miss, issued 1979 ($20-25)
S-200 Streak Loop, issued 1975 ($20-25)
S-250 Streak Racing, issued 1983 ($20-25)
S-300 Streak Drag, issued 1975 ($20-25)
S-400 Streak Racing, issued 1975 ($20-25)
S-450 Streak Racing, issued 1983 ($20-25)
S-500 Streak Circuit, issued 1975 ($20-25)
S-700 Streak Count Down, issued 1978 ($20-25)
S-800 Stunt Jump, issued 1979 ($20-25)
S-900 Streak Around, issued 1975 ($20-25)

Matchbox Garages
(and other play buildings)

MG-1-A MATCHBOX ONE STORY GARAGE, issued 1959
1. one story building-yellow building, red base & clock ($175-225)
2. one story building-red building, yellow base & clock ($175-225)

MG-1-B MATCHBOX TWO STORY GARAGE, issued 1961
1. yellow building, red base, "Esso" decals ($350-500)
2. white building, green base, "BP" decals ($100-150)

MG-1-C MATCHBOX SERVICE STATION, issued 1968
1. one story white building with separate plastic pumps & "BP" sign ($75-100)

MG-2-A SERVICE STATION, issued 1979 ($50-75)
MG-3-A TEXACO GARAGE, issued 1979 ($50-75)
MG-4-A SUPER GARAGE, issued 1981 ($45-65)
MG-6-A DELUXE GARAGE, issued 1984 ($20-30)
MG-7-A COMPACT GARAGE, issued 1984 ($20-30)
MG-9-A GEARSHIFT GARAGE, issued 1987 ($20-30)

AP-1 AUTO PARK, issued 1971 ($125-175)

MF-1-A MATCHBOX FIRE STATION, issued 1963
1. cream building with brick face, green roof ($150-200)
2. white building with brick face, red roof ($75-100)
3. white building with plain face, red roof ($125-150)

580101 EMERGENCY STATION, issued 1974 ($50-75)

AUTO SALES, issued 1970 ($250-300)

Roadways and Painting Books

The paper roadways series was first conceived in 1960 and ran through 1969. The series consisted of paper fold-out roadways. Paper and cardboard matter have soared in price in recent years as many of these kinds of items were physically destroyed when played with, unlike plastic or diecast that can survive some heavy play.

Lesney Products also ran a series of four painting books. These are referred to on the U.S. market as coloring books. A paint set was also issued.

R-1-A ROADWAY LAYOUT, issued 1960
1. Lesney Moko and full color picture on outer wrapper ($75-100)

R-1-B ROADWAY, issued 1962
1. Lesney with black & white picture on outer wrapper ($75-100) (1962)
2. full color picture with pasture on outer wrapper ($50-75)(1964)
3. full color picture with "R-1" in blue rectangle in corner of outer wrapper ($15-20)(1968)

R-2-A LAYOUT (HEART OF LONDON), issued 1961
1. Big Ben, Tower Bridge & angel depicted on outer wrapper ($200-250)

R-2-B CONSTRUCTION ROADWAY, issued 1968
1. full color picture depicted with constructed buildings on outer wrapper ($30-40)(1968)
2. full color picture depicting site off water's edge on outer wrapper ($15-20)(1969)

R-3-A ROADWAY LAYOUT (ROYAL LONDON), issued 1961
1. Royal London sites shown on outer wrapper ($200-250)

R-3-B FARM ROADWAY, issued 1968
1. full color picture of farm scene on outer wrapper ($15-20)

R-4-A RACETRACK SPEEDWAY, issued 1961
1. black & white racetrack shown on outer wrapper ($60-75)

R-4-B GRAND PRIX RACE TRACK, issued 1964
1. full color picture of four large race cars on outer wrapper ($50-65)

PAINTING BOOKS, issued 1960
4 different numbered as No. 1, No. 2, No. 3 & No. 4 ($500+ each)

PC-1 PAINT & CRAYON SET, issued 1960
includes paint & crayons in a metal holder ($500+)

Heritage Series Gifts and Souvenirs

Plated versions of models from the miniature, Superking, and Yesteryear ranges that are affixed to trinket boxes, ashtrays, and the like are part of this category, but are listed separately under their respective categories. Other series from this section include British Inn Signs, Pips, Regimental Badges, magnetic board games, and souvenir items. Some of the British Inn Signs can be found in various finishes such as silver plated, gold plated, and light gold plated with the original six in antique silver plating.

BRITISH INN SIGNS, issued 1976 ($10-15)
701 The Lion, 702 Pig & Whistle, 703 The Cock, 704 Elephant & Castle, 705 George & Dragon, 706 Unicorn, 707 The Swan, 708 Sherlock Holmes, 709 Rose & Crown, 710 The Bull, 711 Dick Turpin, 712 The Volunteer, 713 The Mermaid, 714 Spread Eagle, 715 Britannia, 716 Prince of Wales, 717 The Smugglers, 718 The Dolphin

PIPS, issued 1976 ($10-15)
601 Labrador Retriever, 602 French Poodle, 603 Alsatian, 604 Scottie, 605 Rough Collie, 606 Cocker Spaniel

REGIMENTAL BADGES, issued 1976 ($8-12)
551 Royal Marines, 552 Coldstream Guards, 553 17th/21st Lancers, 554 Black Watch, 555 Royal Artillery, 556 Argyll & Sutherland Highlanders

MAGNETIC BOARD GAMES, issued 1976 ($15-20)
801 Draughts, 802 Chess, 803 Solitaire, 804 Nine Men's Morris, 805 Noughts & Crosses, 806 Backgammon, 807 Mini Chinese Checkers

SOUVENIRS, issued (various)
007 Occasional Tray Double Pack ($15-18)
105 stainless steel box with antique pistol ($45-60)
106 stainless steel box with Concorde decoration ($35-50)
107 stainless steel box with "Tower Bridge" decoration ($35-50)
124 deluxe wood box with antique pistol ($45-60)
126 deluxe soft top box with George Washington pistol ($45-60)
127 deluxe wood box with half-cast 1922 London bus ($50-75)
224 simulated onyx double pen stand with George Washington pistol ($45-60)
453 single wood bookend with antique pistol ($35-45)
Onyx pen stand with Jubilee Crest and "Queen's Award" mark (not issued to public) ($75-100)

LANDMARK PAPERWEIGHTS, issued 1978 ($10-15)
501 City of London Coat of Arms, 502 Tower Bridge London scene, 503 Big Ben scene, 504 St. Paul's Cathedral London scene, Silver Jubilee Royal Coat of Arms, Gold figurines-London Guard, Royal Policeman, Volunteer, Beefeater, Drummer, Windsor Castle

FIGURINES ON PEN STANDS, issued 1978 ($35-45)
footballer, golfer, fisherman

Plastic Kits

Lesney Products entered the plastic model kit area in 1973 with twelve plastic airplanes. The line extended each year and in 1980 Lesney Products bought the AMT brand as a secondary kit line to its own brand. Due to the extent of the AMT line, only Matchbox brand kits are listed. When Lesney went bankrupt in 1982, the AMT brand was sold to the Ertl company, which still continues with this brand. The kit division was sold off to Revell in 1990. In 1992, Revell started making "Matchbox" brand kits using older castings of the original kits plus new tooling. These were issued using serial numbers rather than the traditional "PK."

Kit Values: PK-1 to PK-48, 61-64, 71-89 ($10-15)
PK-100 series planes, PK-160 series ships, PK-300 series automobiles ($15-20)
PK-451, PK-400 series planes, PK-450 series planes ($20-25)
PK-500 series planes, PK-550 series planes, PK-600 series planes, PK-650 series planes, PK-700 series Motorcycles ($25-35)
PK-901 ($75-100), PK-1001 ($50-75), PK-5000 & 6000 series ($10-15)
Serial numbered Revell kits based on size and equivalent price range to "PK" kits.

AIRPLANE KITS

1973—PK-1 Hawker Fury, PK-2 Spitfire Mk.1X, PK-3 Boeing P-12E, PK-4 Mitsubishi Zero, PK-5 Dornier Alpha Jet, PK-6 Focke Wulf FW 190, PK-7 Westland Lysander, PK-8 Gloster Gladiator, PK-9 Huey Cobra, PK-10 Strikemaster, PK-11 Hawker Hurricane, PK-12 Northrop F5-A
1974—PK-13 Mustang P51-D, PK-14 Corsair F4U-4, PK-15 Folland Gnat, PK-16 Hawker Harrier, PK-17 Messerschmitt 109E, PK-18 Grumman Hellcat, PK-19 Mikoyan MIG-21, PK-20 Mirage 111C Dassault, PK-21 Messerschmitt 262, PK-22 P-47 Thunderbolt, PK-23 Hawker Tempest, PK-24 Brewster Buffalo, PK-25 Armstrong Whitworth Siskin, PK-26 Henschel 126, PK-101 Corsair Jet, PK-102 Jaguar, PK-103 Beaufighter, PK-104 Curtiss Helldiver, PK-105 Walrus, PK-106 Buccaneer, PK-107 Sky Servant, PK-108 Lynx Helicopter, PK-109 Junkers 188, PK-110 H.S. 125/600 Exec Jet
1975—PK-27 Hawker Siddeley Hawk, PK-28 Lockheed Starfighter, PK-29 Skyhawk
1976—PK-30 Percival Provost, PK-111 Stuka 87B, PK-112 Fairey Swordfish, PK-113 ME 410, PK-114 BAC Lightning, PK-115 Messerschmitt BF110, PK-116 D.H. Mosquito, PK-117 Hawker Hunter, PK-118 Lockheed Lightning, PK-401 Heinkel 115, PK-402 Wellington Mk X, PK-403 Heinkel 111, PK-404 Phantom F4, PK-405 Mitchell B25, PK-406 Tomcat
1977—PK-119 Saab Viggen, PK-120 Boston Havoc, PK-121 Fairchild A10A, PK-501 Spitfire, PK-502 ME 109 E, PK-503 Dauntless
1978—PK-504 Westland Lysander
1979—PK-122 General Dynamics F16A, PK-123 Vickers Wellesley, PK-407 Martin Marauder, PK-408 Canberra Bomber, PK-409 Dornier Do 18, PK-410 Grumman Prowler, PK-505 Tiger Moth, PK-601 Supermarine Stranraer, PK-602 Avro Lancaster, PK-603 Fortress Boeing B-17, PK-604 Handley Page Halifax
1980—PK-31 Curtiss P40N, PK-32 North American F86 Sabre, PK-33 Saab J.29F, PK-34 Aeritalia G91Y, PK-35 Curtiss SBC4, PK-124 Grumman Panther, PK-411 McDonnell Voodoo, PK-506 DeHavilland Venom, PK-651 Douglas Skyraider AD-5, PK-652 FJ4 Fury, PK-653 Kaman Seasprite
1981—PK-507 Puma SA330, PK-605 Handley Page Heyford, PK-606 Consolidated Privateer
1982- PK-36 Fairey Seafox, PK-37 Sea Harrier
1983—PK-551 Victor K.2
1984- PK-38 Dauphin Aerospace, PK-125 Norseman
1985—PK-126 BAC Lightning, PK-127 Twin Otter
1986—PK-39 Northrop F-5B, PK-40 Starfighter TF-104 G, PK-41 Mikoyan MiG-21 MF, PK-128 Jaguar T.MK2, PK-412 Phantom FG1/FGR2
1987—PK-42 T-2C Buckeye, PK-43 Bell OH-58D, PK-44 Mirage IIIB, PK-45 Bae Harrier GR Mk.3, PK-46 Bae Hawk 200, PK-47 Mystere IV.A, PK-129 Armstrong Whitworth Meteor, PK-130 Panavia Tornado F.Mk.3, PK-413 Boeing Vertol Chinook
1988—PK-48 MBB BK.117, PK-131 Saab SK-37 Viggen, PK-132 Heinkel He 70, PK-133 Westland Wessex, PK-134 Douglas Skynight
1989- PK-49 Hawker Hurricane, PK-50 Spitfire Mk IX, PK-51 Focke-Wulf FW190 A-3, PK-52 Se Harrier FRS1

MILITARY KITS
1974—PK-71 Sherman Firefly Tank, PK-72 Comet Tank, PK-73 Panther Tank, PK-74 Panzer III Tank, PK-75 Humber Armored Car, PK-76 Puma Armored Car, PK-77 Wespe Self-Propelled Cannon, PK-78 Half Track M16, PK-79 Chaffee M24 Tank, PK-80 Jagdpanther Tank
1975—PK-81 Panzer II Tank, PK-82 Russian T-34 Tank, PK-83 Hanomag German Half Track
1977—PK-171 PAK & Personnel Carrier & Motorcycle, PK-172 171b Gun & Morris 4X4 & Willys Jeep, PK-1001 Counter Attack
1978—PK-84 Honey Stewart, PK-85 German Radio Car, PK-86 M-40 155mm. Gun, PK-87 Panzer 4/70
1979—PK-88 Krupp Protz KfZ 69, PK-89 Priest 105mm. H.M.C.M7, PK-173 L.R.D.G. 30 cwt. Chevrolet & Jeep, PK-174 M19 45 ton Tank Transporter M90 Diamond 'T' & M9 Rogers Trailer
1980—PK-175 Monty's Caravan, PK-176 Char Bis & Char FT17 Renault
1983—PK-177 Churchill Bridgelayer
1988—PK-178 Challenger

AUTOMOBILE KITS
1975—PK-301 Aston Martin Ulster, PK-302 Bugatti Type 59, PK-303 Porsche 917-10
1976—PK-304 Jaguar SS100, PK-305 Surtees TS.16,
NOTE: original numbers to PK-301 to PK-305 were PK-181 to PK-185 in the 1975 & 1976 catalogs, but renumbered in 1977
1978- PK-306 MG-TC
1979- PK-307 Mercedes SSKL
1980- PK-308 Martini Porsche 935, PK-309 Tyrrell-Ford P34/2
1981- PK-310 Citroen 11CV Legere, PK-451 Packard Victoria
1982- PK-311 Liqui Moli Porsche 935, PK-452 Rolls Royce Phantom I
1985—PK-312 Auto Union Type D

MOTORCYCLE KITS
1980—PK-701 Suzuki RG500, PK-702 Harley-Davidson Electraglide, PK-703 Vincent Blackshadow
1981- PK-704 BMW R100S
SHIP KITS
1977—PK-61 Ariadne, PK-62 "NARVIK" Class Destroyer, PK-161 Graf Spee, PK-162 Exeter
1978—PK-63 Fletcher Destroyer, , PK-163 San Diego
1980—PK-64 H.M.S. Kelley, PK-164 H.M.S. Tiger, PK-165 USS Indianapolis, PK-351 Bismarck, PK-352 Duke of York, PK-901 Flower Class Corvette

PLASTIC FIGURES
1977—PK-5001 British Infantry, PK-5002 US Infantry, PK-5003 German Infantry, PK-5004 Afrika Corps, FK—6001 German Infantry, PK-6002 British Infantry, PK-6003 US Infantry
1978—PK-5005 8th Army, PK-5006 Commandos, PK-6004 Afrika Corps, PK-6005 8th Army
1979—PK-5007 Japanese Infantry, PK-5008 Anzacs, PK-6006 Commandos,
1984—PK-5009 NATO Troops

REVELL MADE KITS
NOTE: This is only a small portion of the Matchbox kits produced by Revell. Most were reissues of earlier Matchbox kits with the "PK" prefix removed from and 4000 added to the numbers.
40011 TF-104G Starfighter
40070 Sd-Kfz 124 Wespe
40141 F 16B Fighting Falcon
40145 Bell AH-IJ Sea Cobra
40146 F.16B RNAF "Tigermeet 1992"
40167 U.S.S. Arizona
40179 M-1 Abrams
40353 Admiral Hipper
40380 Ferrari Testarossa
40381 Ford Escort XR-3
40382 Austin Healey 100-Six
40383 Porsche Speedster
40415 AH-64A Apache
40416 Avado Ar 234 Blitz
40803 Boeing 737
40991 M-41 Walker Tank

Live-N-Learn (Preschool)

Lesney Products entered the preschool toy market in 1972 with six toys. Those original six pieces are now quite rare. By 1973, the Live-N-Learn line extended and was still being produced up to 1997 by Tyco Toys, which merged a few of their products into their own preschool range. By 1998, much of the range was absorbed as Mattel Toys. The toys are similar to those made by Fisher Price and Playskool. Some preschool items may exist in several different color plastic combinations as well as being made in England, China, Thailand, or Singapore

510101 Busy Playground, issued 1972 ($75-100)
510102 Busy Ball, issued 1972 ($75-100)
510103 Busy Buddies, issued 1972 ($75-100)
510104 Busy Marble Mover, issued 1972 ($75-100)
510105 Busy Jump Rope, issued 1972 ($75-100)
510106 Super Mart, issued 1972 ($100-150)
LL-100 Play Boot, issued 1977 ($45-60)
LL-101 Town Set, issued 1991 ($25-30)
LL-102 Farm Set, issued 1991 ($25-30)
LL-103 Railway Set, issued 1991 ($25-30)
LL-120 Mushroom Playhouse, issued 1987 ($35-50)
LL-150 Playboot Playhouse, issued 1984 ($45-60)
LL-170 Key Ringer Garage, issued 1993 ($18-25)
LL-190 Key Ring Runners Assortment (wrecker, fire truck, police car, issued 1993 ($8-12 each)
LL-200 Chuggy Chuffer Train, issued 1977 ($25-35)
LL-210 Activity Bear Cot Bumper, issued 1989 ($25-35)
LL-220 Rock-A-Bear Buggy, issued 1989 ($25-35)
LL-230 Fold & Play Garage, issued 1989 ($35-45)
LL-240 Mr. Plumb Fun, issued 1993 ($25-35)
LL-300 Peg-A-Picture, issued 1983 ($25-35)
LL-310 Jigsaw Puzzle Playmat, issued 1989 ($20-25)
LL-330 My Soft Story Books, issued 1991 ($12-15)
LL-410 Cuddly Activity Bear, issued 1991 ($25-30)
LL-440 Light Up Lullaby Puppy, issued 1993 ($25-35)
LL-500-A Press-A-Print, issued 1980 ($40-50)
LL-500-B Activity Quilt, issued 1987 ($35-50)
LL-600-A Pop-Up Picture Phone, issued 1980 ($35-45)
LL-600-B Snap-A-Tune, issued 1987 ($25-35)
LL-700 Take-A-Part Truck, issued 1980 ($30-35)
LL-800 Tell Time Clock, issued 1974 ($20-25)
LL-801 Giant Play Mat set, issued 1993 ($20-30)
LL-900-A Pull-A-Long Dog, issued 1974 ($75-100)
LL-900-B Drawing Set, issued 1980 ($20-25)
LL-910 Smart Bear, issued 1987 ($20-30)
LL-1000-A Matchbox Family, issued 1974 ($10-15)
LL-1000-B Natter Phone, issued 1987 ($25-35)
LL-1100-A Billy Brick Stacker, issued 1974 ($75-100)
LL-1100-B Money Box, issued 1980 ($15-18)
LL-1200 Tape Measure, issued 1980 ($15-18)
LL-1300-A Family Ferry Boat, issued 1974 ($25-35)
LL-1300-B Squeak-N-Seek, issued 1987 ($20-25)
LL-1400-A Family Camper, issued 1974 ($25-35)
LL-1400-B Build-A-Plane, issued 1982 ($30-35)
LL-1500-A Stack-A-Cake, issued 1974 ($75-100)
LL-1500-B Tubby Tooter Penguin, issued 1980 ($15-18)
LL-1600 Play Slide, issued 1974 ($45-60)
LL-1700-A Play Ball, issued 1974 ($45-60)
LL-1700-B Tubby Tooter Sailor, issued 1980 ($25-30)
LL-1800 Fire Engine, issued 1976 ($20-30)
LL-1900 Big Tap, issued 1980 ($20-30)
LL-2000 Diver Dan issued 1980 ($25-35)
LL-2100 Funny Flyer, issued 1974 ($10-15)
LL-2200 Hoppy Copter, issued 1974 ($10-15)
LL-2300 Tricky Truck, issued 1974 ($10-15)
LL-2400 Chuggy Chuffer, issued 1976 ($10-15)
LL-2500 Hovercraft, issued 1976 ($15-18)
LL-2700 Tractor, issued 1976 ($10-15)
LL-2800 Road Digger, issued 1976 ($10-15)
LL-2900 Dumper, issued 1976 ($10-15)
LL-3000 Shufflie Zoo, issued 1976 ($50-75)
LL-3100 Shufflie Farm, issued 1976 ($50-75)
LL-3200 Shufflie Police, issued 1976 ($50-75)
LL-3300 Shufflie Hospital, issued 1976 ($50-75)
LL-3400 Shufflie Castle, issued 1980 ($75-100)
LL-4000 Activity Bear, issued 1982 ($30-40)
LL-4100 Pull-A-Long Ladybird, issued 1981 ($20-30)
LL-4200 Rock-A-Bye Birdie, issued 1982 ($15-20)
LL-4500 Activity Bear Play Center, issued 1988 ($100-125)
LL-4510 Big Band Bear, issued 1988 ($35-45)
LL-4520 Bathtime Bear, issued 1988 ($35-45)
LL-4600 Activity Rattle, issued 1983 ($15-18)
LL-4700 Stacking Anchor, issued 1984 ($18-25)
LL-4800 Cloud, issued 1984 ($18-25)
LL-4900 Dozey Daisy, issued 1984 ($15-25)
LL-5000 Mini-Mate issued 1984 ($25-40)
LL-5100 Pop-Up Till, issued 1984 ($35-45)
LL-5200 Baby Bear Rattle, issued 1985 ($10-15)
LL-5300 Elephount, issued 1985 ($20-25)
LL-5400 Squeeze-N-Go Sam, issued 1985 ($15-25)
LL-5500 Squeeze-N-Go Froggy, issued 1985 ($12-15)
LL-5800 Pop Up Peter, issued 1986 ($10-15)
LL-5900 Squeeze-N-Go Racer, issued 1986 ($15-25)
LL-6000 Learning Bear, issued 1986 ($35-40)
LL-6100 Vanity Bear, issued 1986 ($20-25)
LL-6200 Squeaky Bear, issued 1986 ($20-25)
LL-6300 Tick Tock Bear, issued 1986 ($20-25)
LL-6400 Trumpet Teether, issued 1986 ($10-15)
LL-6500 Squeaky Star, issued 1986 ($8-12)
LL-6600 Sing Song Shell, issued 1986 ($8-12)
LL-8000 Baggie Bunnie, issued 1988 ($12-15)
LL-8010 Baggie Bunnie Activity Bunnie, issued 1988 ($15-20)
LL-8020 Baggie Bunnie Activity Blanket, issued 1988 ($12-15)
LL-8030 Baggie Bunnie Activity Soft Blocks, issued 1988 ($12-15)
LL-8040 Baggie Bunnie Activity Chime Ball, issued 1988 ($10-15)
LL-8050 Baggie Bunnie Activity Soft Rattle, issued 1988 ($10-15)
LL-8060 Baggie Bunnie Activity Soft Touch Book, issued 1988 ($10-15)
NOTE: In 1994, Tyco eliminated most of the "LL" numbers and replaced them with serial numbers for identification.
1485 Walkie Talkies, issued 1995 ($35-40)
2576 Real Sounds Engine, issued 1994 ($45-50)
2577 Real Sounds Work Bench, issued 1994 ($45-50)
7036 Bubble Fire truck, issued 1994 ($25-35)
51101 Roly Poly Playhouse, issued 1995 ($35-40)
51102 Sort N Go Cement Mixer, issued 1995 ($30-40)
61403 Sing-A-Long Cassette Player, issued 1994 ($45-50)
62510 Big Big Playquilt, issued 1994 ($45-60)
62520 Activity Playnest, issued 1994 ($45-60)
65570 Little Lighthouse, issued 1995 ($25-35)
65577 Wacky Water Wheel, issued 1995 ($25-30)

Dolls

Lesney Products entered the doll market in 1974 with several offerings. In early 1979, they purchased the Vogue Doll company and expanded in this category. As Lesney Products was a toy company, it chose not to restrict itself to only diecast vehicles. To commemorate the introduction of the Vogue Doll line, a special 250-piece edition K-17 Container Truck was produced and given out to special accounts (see "Superkings"). Matchbox Toys sold the Vogue Doll line in 1981, but continued to dabble in the doll category with little success. Some items were issued by the Universal Associated Company and two dolls were marketed in Europe—Michael Jackson and Boy George—under the LJN banner. In 1987, they were the European distributor of the Cricket Doll made by Playmates. Once Tyco Toys bought the Matchbox brand in 1993, all doll categories remained under the Tyco name.

DISCO GIRLS, issued 1974
DG-100 Dee, DG-101 Britt, DG-102 Domino, DG-103 Tia, DG-120 Tony, DG-150 Disco Bride, DG-151 Disco Date, DG-152 Disco Deb, DG-153 Disco Darling ($25-40)

FIGHTING FURIES, issued 1974
FF-100 Captain Peg Leg, FF-101 Hook, FF-102 Ghost of Capt. Kidd, FF-103 Black McCoy, FF-104 Crazy Horse, FF-105 Kid Cortez ($35-50)

FIGHTING FURIES ACCESSORIES, issued 1974
Capt. Blood Adventure, Spanish Main Adventure, One-Eyed Sailor Adventure, Redcoat Adventure, Kung Fu warrior Adventure, Hooded Falcon Adventure, Pirate Ship Carrying Case ($20-30)

MISS MATCHBOX, issued 1974
NOTE: Not all numbers were allocated. Packaged individually on pink blistercards or with a small box on a larger purple blistercard. ($15-18)
M01 Alice in Wonderland, M02 Sailor Sue, M04 Calamity Jane, M05

Polly Painter, M07 Cosy Cathy, M08 Jilly Jodhpur, M09 Cookie Kate, M11 Blue Belle, M13 Party Patti, M14 Mod Millie, M15 Sally Stewardess, M16 Penny Playmate

SUKY/SUSY DOLLS, issued 1976
S01 Ballerina, S02 Nurse, S03 Tennis Pro, S04 Horse Rider, S05 Skater, S06 Shopper, S07 Bedtime, S08 Swimmer, plus accessories ($12-15)

ABBA DOLLS, issued 1978
Based on the Swedish singing quartet from the late 1970s. ($75-100)
AB-101 Anna, AB-102 Frida, AB-103 Bennie, AB-104 Bjorn

CRACKER JACK, issued 1980
NOTE: Boxed in large Cracker Jack box with his little dog ($75-100)

CRACKER JACK, issued 1981 Smaller blistercard version ($50-75)

VOGUE DOLLS
FARAWAY LANDS, issued 1981
English girl, Norway girl, Pioneer girl, German girl, Italy girl, Poland girl, Jamaican girl, Ireland girl, Scotland girl, Austrian girl, Austrian boy ($15-20)

FARAWAY LANDS, issued 1982
Girl dolls from Japan, Germany, England, Holland, Ireland, Poland, Scotland, Austria, Greece, Italy, Spain, Norway ($18-25)

INTERNATIONAL BRIDES, issued 1982
Ireland, Poland, Israel, America, Turkey, Mexico, China, Egypt, France, Germany, England, Brazil ($20-25)

GLITTER GIRLS, issued 1982
Sapphire, Ruby, Crystal, Jade, Amber, Pearl. Also accessory items ($10-15)

GINNY DOLLS, issued 1981
Includes a variety of dolls and accessories too numerous to list. Includes Sassoon license Ginny. (Various prices)

SWEET TREATS, issued 1989
Raspberry Sherbet, Blueberry Cheesecake, Banana Split, Sugar Plum Pudding, Coconut Cupcake, Cotton Candy, Cocoa Pop ($12-15)
Treatmaker Trike ($25-35)

REAL MODELS, issued 1990
Beverly Johnson, Christie Brinkley, Cheryl Tiegs ($18-25)

POPSICLE KIDS, issued 1990
Berry Blue, Merry Cherry, Grape Cakes, La De Lime, Lotta Lime, Ooh La Orange ($10-15)

OTHER DOLLS
Baby Secrets, issued 1989 ($25-35)
Baby Cheer-Up, issued 1990 ($20-25)
Butterfly Princess Single Pack, issued 1990 ($3-5)
Butterfly Princess Four Pack, issued 1990 ($10-15)
Baby Baby, issued 1991 ($35-45)
Hush-A-Bye Baby, issued 1991 ($25-35)

MAXX F-X/FREDDY KRUEGER
Maxx F-X was to have been a series of 12-inch figures which featured a normal male doll that could be dressed up into famous monsters. These were to include Dracula, Frankenstein, the Mummy, Wolfman, the Creature, Alien, Jason, and Freddy Krueger. Only the Freddy Krueger doll was ever released and was almost immediately discontinued when its larger, talking counterpart received so much bad publicity from religious protesters. Both Freddy dolls were withdrawn the same year they were introduced.

Maxx F-X Freddy Kreuger, issued 1989 ($25-35)
Talking Freddy Kreuger Doll, issued 1989 ($65-75)

Voltron

The Voltron series, based on a cartoon TV series, featured a series of robots. The robots came in sets which could be combined to make up larger robots. These were manufactured by a Japanese company, Bandai, for Matchbox Toys. The series was launched in 1985.

700001 Voltron III Miniature Lion Space Robot ($30-50)
700002 Voltron I Miniature Space Warrior Robot ($30-50)
700100 Voltron II Miniature Red Gladiator Space Robot ($30-50)
700110 Voltron II Miniature Blue Gladiator Space Robot ($30-50)
700120 Voltron II Miniature Black Gladiator Space Robot ($30-50)
700200 Voltron III The Deluxe Lion Set ($125-175)
700201 Voltron III Giant Black Lion Robot ($30-50)
700202 Voltron III Yellow & Green Mighty Lion Robots Set ($30-50)
700203 Voltron III Blue & Red Mighty Lion Robots Set ($30-50)
700210 Voltron I The Deluxe Warrior Set ($125-175)
700211 Voltron I Air Warrior Set ($30-50)
700212 Voltron I Space Warrior Set ($30-50)
700213 Voltron I Land Warrior Set ($30-50)
700220 Voltron II The Deluxe Gladiator Set ($90-150)
700401 Voltron Blazing Sword Set ($18-25)
700402 Voltron Miniature Blazing Sword Set ($10-15)

Robotech

In the not-too-distant future, the Earth becomes a final refuge for a damaged alien space vessel, the SDF-1, containing the secrets of an amazing technology advanced far beyond that of humans. Unbeknownst to the people of Earth, a vast armada of warships manned by the evil Zentraedi have been combing the galaxies in search of the lost battle fortress. When the Zentraedi discover the SDF-1, the Earth's Robotech defense force is called upon to defend their planet against the attacks of these merciless aliens.

This is how Matchbox Toys described the Robotech story. Robotech was a cartoon show with eighty-five TV episodes. Matchbox Toys received the license to market and produce much of the Robotech line. Although most of the items were manufactured by Matchbox, a few products were made by Bandai and Godaken and marketed in Matchbox packaging.

7100 MECHA LAUNCHER WITH ROBOTECH VEHICLES, issued 1986
RDF Rescue Ship, RDF Destroyer, Zentraedi Cruiser, Zentraedi Officer's Attack Ship ($8-10)

7110 MONSTER DESTROID CANNON, issued 1986 ($15-20)

7120 MINIATURE SDF-1, issued 1986 ($15-20)

7130 ALPHA FIGHTERS, issued 1986
green & cream, blue & white or maroon & cream ($20-25)

7131 MINI ALPHA FIGHTERS, issued 1986
green & cream, blue & white or maroon & cream ($15-18)

7201 3-3/4" ACTION FIGURES, issued 1986
Rick Hunter, Corg, Zor Prime, Lisa Hayes, Dana Sterling, Rand, Robotech Master, Roy Fokker, Lunk, Max Sterling, Micronized Zentraedi Warrior, Bioroid Terminator, Miriya ($5-8). Scott Bernard ($10-15), Rook Bartley ($18-25), Lynn Minmei ($75-100)
NOTE: Lynn Minmei only comes in a "Harmony Gold" package.

7203 GIANT ZENTRAEDI ACTION FIGURES, issued 1986
Breetai, Exedore, Khyron, Dolza, Armored Zentraedi Warrior ($8-10) & Miriya ($15-25)

7301 ATTACK MECHA ASSORTMENT, issued 1986
Excalibar Mk.IV, Gladiator, Zentraedi Power Armor Botoru Battalion, Zentraedi Powered Armor Quadrono Battalion, Spartan, Raidar X, Invid Scout Ship, Bioroid Invid Fighter ($18-25)

7351 ARMORED CYCLE, issued 1986 ($12-18)
7352 BIOROID HOVERCRAFT, issued 1986 ($10-15)
7353 OFFICER'S BATTLEPOD, issued 1986 ($20-25)
7354 TACTICAL BATTLEPOD, issued 1986 ($20-25)
7355 INVID SHOCK TROOPER, issued 1986 ($20-25)
7356 VERITECH HOVER TANK, issued 1986 ($20-25)
7357 VERITECH FIGHTER, issued 1986 ($50-75)
7395 SDF-1 ACTION PLAYSET, issued 1986 ($75-100)
7700 ROBOTECH WARS VIDEO PLAYSET, issued 1986 ($95-125)

850001 SDF-1, issued 1986 ($40-50)

850100 VERITECH FIGHTER, issued 1986
1. Max Sterling's blue fighter ($15-18)
2. Miriya's red fighter ($15-18)
3. Rick Hunter's white fighter ($15-18)

850201 BATTLOIDS, issued 1986
Civil Defense Unit Spartan Battloid, Tactical Corps Spartan Battloid, Civil Defense Unit Gladiator, Tactical Corps Gladiator, Civil Defense Unit Raidar X, Tactical Corps Raidar X, Civil Defense Unit Excalibar Mk.IV, Tactical Corps Excalibar Mk.IV ($10-15)

11-1/2" FASHION DOLLS, issued 1986
5101 Lynn Minmei, 5102 Lisa Hayes, 5103 Dana Sterling, 5104 Rick Hunter ($20-30)

FASHION DOLL CLOTHES, issued 1986
5201 Exercise Outfit, 5202 Star Disguise Outfit, 5203 Street Clothes, 5204 Party Dress, 5205 Night Gown, 5251 Stage Dress, 5252 Fancy Dress Clothes, 5253 Miss Macross Outfit, 5254 Evening Gown, 5255 Fashion Accessories ($5-8)
5410 DANA'S HOVER CYCLE, issued 1986 ($50-75)

Pee Wee Herman

Matchbox Toys hit a licensing winner with Pee Wee Herman when the Saturday morning TV show, Pee Wee's Playhouse, was very popular in 1989 and 1990. The series was introduced in 1989 with further introductions in 1990. The movie, "Big Top Pee Wee," was supposed to have spawned a series of action figures but only one item, Vance the Talking Pig, was issued.

ACTION FIGURES, issued 1989
Pee Wee Herman ($8-12), King of Kartoons ($10-15), Chairry ($10-15), Cowboy Curtis ($8-12), Miss Yvonne ($8-12), Jambi & Puppet Band ($15-20), Globey & Randi ($12-15), Conkey ($12-15), Pterri ($12-15), Magic Screen ($8-12)

ACTION FIGURES, issued 1990
Ricardo ($15-20), Reba ($20-25)

LARGE TOYS
3500 Talking Pee Wee Herman, issued 1989 ($35-50)
3510 Non-Talking Pee Wee Herman, issued 1989 ($35-50)
3520 Pterri, issued 1989 ($35-50)
3530 Chairry, issued 1989 ($35-50)
3540 Billy Baloney, issued 1989 ($35-50)
3550 Playhouse Playset, issued 1989 ($75-100)
3568 Miniature Pee Wee Herman & Scooter, issued 1989 ($25-35)
3590 Pee Wee's Scooter (ride-on), issued 1989 ($250-350)
3710 Vance the Talking Pig, issued 1990 ($35-50)
Ventriloquist Pee Wee Herman, issued 1990 ($75-100)

Ring Raiders

In 1989, Matchbox Toys obtained a license from "Those Characters from Cleveland" and introduced Ring Raiders. These were small aircraft that attached to a ring to fit upon your finger. The series included a number of aircraft in multi-packs with additional playsets. The line was supposed to have been supported by a TV series, but this never materialized.

8100 4 AIRCRAFT ASSORTMENT, issued 1989
Freedom Wing, Rescue Wing, Rebel Wing, Victory Wing, Valor Wing, Bandit Wing, Bravery Wing, Havoc Wing, Vicious Wing, Hero Wing, Ambush Wing, Vulture Wing ($10-15)

8120 AIR MEDAL AWARD SERIES, issued 1989 ($8-12)
8130 SKY BASE COURAGE, issued 1989 ($12-15)
8140 SKY BASE FREEDOM, issued 1989 ($12-15)
8150 BATTLE BLASTER, issued 1989 ($8-12)
8160 SKULL SQUADRON MOBILE BASE, issued 1989 ($15-20)
8170 RING OF FIRE VIDEO, issued 1989 ($12-18)
8190 WING COMMAND DISPLAY STAND, issued 1989 ($8-12)
RG570 ELECTRONIC FREEDOM FIGHTER, issued 1990 ($35-50)

Other Toy Categories

BABYCISE
Babycise was introduced in 1986 as a Shared Development System, a specially designed infant exercise program developed by a board of certified pediatricians and therapists. The series lasted only one year and was discontinued.

4100 Baby Bells ($10-15)
4110 Clutch Ball ($8-12)
4120 Balance Beam ($15-20)
4130 Bolster ($18-25)
4140 Triangle Play Block ($15-20)
4150 Mirror ($10-15)
4200 Video Gift Set ($25-40)
4225 Starter Kit ($25-40)

LINKITS
Linkits were introduced in 1986 and 1987. Linkits were a type of building system which linked sections together to form different toys. Value $5-15 for smaller sets; up to $35 for larger sets.

LK-1 Good Robug, LK-2 Bad Robug, LK-3 Radions, LK-4 Stridants, LK-5 Espions, LK-6 Terratrek, LK-7 Artillius Unit, LK-8 Robugs on blistercard, LK-9 Expander Pack, LK-10 Cube, LK-11 Likon, LK-22 Agrobot, LK-23 Micro Robot, LK-25 Terratrek, LK-26 Megadrom, LK-27 Maxar, LK-28 Vector & Agrobot, LK-29 QT-40, LK-30 Astromil, LK-31 Kraniodome, LK-34 Workshop II, LK-37 Assortment, LK-50 Frog, LK-51 Agrippa, LK-52 Lizzod, LK-53 Retropods, LK-54 Cranio Jet, LK-56 Mercurion, LK-57 Battloid, LK-58 Ballistix, LK-16/101 Shark, LK-16/102 Dragon, LK-32/101 Green Beast, LK-32/102 Robot, LK-32/103 Space Monkey, LK-32/104 Star Warriors, LK-64/102 Trans Mission Team, LK-64/103 Robot Racers, LK-64/104 Space Walkers, LK-64/105 Chicken Monsters, LK-64/201 Puzzle, LK-128/101 Transport Team, LK-128/102 Space Creatures, LK-128/103 Insects
LK-192/102 Dinosaurs, LK-192/103 Master Robots

RUBIK'S
Back in the early 1980s, the Rubik's Cube became one of the greatest toy phenomena the world had ever seen. More than half a billion cubes were sold. There were competitions to see who could solve the cube the fastest. There was even a Guinness Book entry. In 1987, Erno Rubik signed a license with Matchbox Toys to bring his new puzzle on the market. Although it never attained the cube's sales records, "Link the Rings" began a license partnership with other Rubik's toy puzzles.

MA-012 Rubik's Magic Puzzle- Unlink The Rings, issued 1987 ($10-15)
MA-016 Rubik's Magic Strategy Game, issued 1987 ($18-25)
MA-018 Rubik's Clock, issued 1989 ($15-18)
MA-040 Rubik's Magic Picture Games (includes Monster Sports, Octopus's Garden, Dinosaur Days & Crazy Orchestra), issued 1988 ($5-8) each
MA-080 Link The Rings, issued 1987 ($10-15)
MA-400 Rubik's Cube, issued 1989 ($8-12)
MA-650 Rubik's Illusion Game, issued 1989 ($15-20)
MA-660 Rubik's Dice, issued 1990 ($15-20)
MA-670 Rubik's Triamid, issued 1990 ($15-20)
MA-680 Rubik's Fifteen, issued 1990 ($15-20)
MA-690 Rubik's Tangle #1, #2, #3, & #4 ($15-20 each)

MY PRECIOUS PUFFS

My Precious Puffs, modeled after a dandelion puff, was a series of toys for girls. There were three themes—Beauty, Music, and Party. Each theme included eight different Puffs. These were introduced in 1987 and discontinued the following year. ($5-8)

ZILLION

Although originally introduced in 1987 in answer to the Laser Tag phenomena, the United States market canceled the release of "Laser Flash." The series received limited release in England under the name "Zillion." The product was actually made by Sega for Matchbox Toys. The only item in the series seen by this author is the Pistol & Electronic Target Set. The original price was $35 in 1987; today it is $50-75.

HEAD GAMES

An interesting concept "game" for 1988 was the release of Head Games. The toy is strapped to your head like a hat. Head movement puts a ball in a cup or basket. ($12-18)
86001 Basketball, 86002 Golf, 86003 Tennis, 86004 Football

W.A.C.K.O.

Another game from 1988 is W.A.C.K.O., the acronym of Wild and Crazy Kids Only. These are skill games based on arcade-type fun. Two assortments of four each were produced. ($10-15)

8650 Sports Assortment- Baseball, Hoops, BMX Racer, Gobblers
8660 Action Assortment- Shoot the Rapids, Alligator Alley, Jungle Safari, Escape From Devil's Castle

OH JENNY

Oh Jenny was a licensed product actually made by another company. The other company sold the product in England under its own brand but called it "Oh Penny." The series includes playsets and figures. Introduced in 1989, the packaging exists in Spanish as well as the standard English text.

4300 Complete Play Set (includes 4301-4304), issued 1989 ($85-100)
4301 Family Home, issued 1989 ($30-40)
4302 Stable, issued 1989 ($20-30)
4303 Swimming Pool, issued 1989 ($10-15)
4304 Tree House, issued 1989 ($15-18)
4305 Figures Assortment, issued 1989- Farm Animals, Treehouse Kids, Jenny's Pets, Poolside Family, Sweet Stables Family, House Family ($4-6)
4306 Play Assortment, issued 1989- Pony & Cart Set, Wagon Set, Car & Family ($8-10)
4340 Camper, issued 1990 ($25-40)
4350 Shopping Mall, issued 1990 ($40-50)

WIZZZER TOPS

In 1989, Matchbox Toys received the license to produce Wizzzer Tops. At one time Wizzzers were made by Mattel and are still produced by Tyco Toys. The popular toy celebrates its 25th anniversary in 1996. The top assortment is designated WX-8470. With different decorations and combinations of different-colored top and bottom halves, there were more than one hundred different Wizzzers produced by Matchbox in 1989.

CAROUSEL

In 1989, Matchbox Toys introduced a line of girls' toys known as Carousel. The line included mostly horses and several other animals. The series lasted through 1991.

4450 Carousel Musical Playset, issued 1989 ($50-75)
4480 Carousel Display Stand, issued 1989 ($15-20)
The figures were classified under series such as Classic Horses, Bright Beauties, Fancy Trotters, Fashion Parade, Classic Animals and Rocking Horses.
Included are Hopper, Royal, Ribbon, Frisco, Goodie, Sunset, Starry, Snowflake, Starbright, Wild Flower, Sunshine, Twilight, Sunbeam, Raindrop, Daydream, Silver Dawn, Misty Meadow, Lavender, Jazma, Rosette, Rosegay, Damasque, Finesse, Diamond, Misty, Moonbeam, Rudy, Frosty, Cameo, and Camelot ($15-20)
NOTE: Diamond (the lion) is quite rare ($50-75)

BUBBLEHEADS

This was another product made by someone else but marketed by Matchbox. Bubbleheads, introduced in 1991, included three sets of two balls with faces on them. The balls were constructed in such a way that the face on the ball always stayed upright. ($5-10)
Four different pairs from Silly Sports, Mad Monsters, Funny Faces

MONSTER IN MY POCKET

In 1991, Matchbox Toys was one of the many companies to receive a license to produce Monster In My Pocket. Matchbox got to do the figures, which included dozens of monsters in assorted colors. Contents vary by set. The series continued through 1996 in Europe, although it only had a brief two-year success in the United States.

MT-250 12 Pack Scary Monsters, issued 1992 ($12-15)
MT-260 6 Pack Scary Monsters, issued 1992 ($7-10)
MT-270 Howlers- 4 different, issued 1992 ($6-8) each
MT-310 Super Creepies 6 Pack, issued 1993 ($7-10)
MT-320 Super Creepies 12 Pack, issued 1993 ($12-15)
MT-340 Dinosaur Fact Cards, issued 1993 ($5-8)
MT-350 Secret Single Dinosaur, issued 1993 ($1-3)
MT-360 Dinosaur 6 Pack, issued 1993 ($7-10)
MT-810 4 Pack Monsters, issued 1991 ($4-6)
MT-820 12 Pack Monsters, issued 1991 ($10-15)
MT-850 Monster Mountain Display, issued 1991 ($10-15)
MT-860 Monster In My Pocket Battle Card Game, issued 1991 ($5-7)
MT-900 Monster Clash Game, issued 1992 ($15-20)
73245 Space Alien Pack, issued 1993 ($1-3)
73252 Monster Wrestlers 12 Pack, issued 1995 ($12-15)
73257 Monster Wrestlers Grappling Ring Set, issued 1995 ($10-12)
73263 Monster Wrestlers Training Set, issued 1995 ($10-12)
73264 Monster Wrestlers Physio Terrorist Set, issued 1995 ($8-12)

TROLLS

In 1993, Matchbox distributed Troll figures for the company Arlenco. Value ($6-8)
Cutee Fruiti Trolls, Cuti Rocko, Cuti Rollo, Cuti Rappo

MICRO FOLD N GO, issued 1994

1. Race Park ($8-12)
2. Micro City ($8-12)
3. World Airport ($8-12)

SKYFIGHTERS

These are "slot-car" airplanes. One set was released under the Matchbox brand in England. In the United States the same set is marketed by a company called Marchon. A very limited quantity of "loose" airplanes were available by mail order from Matchbox Toys in England at about $8 each.

NX-410 Electronic Skyfighter Freedom ($85-100)

PLUSH TOYS

Matchbox experimented in plush toys several times starting in 1986 with Need-A-Littles. Matchbox also marketed toys for the Amtoy company in Europe for My Pet Monster, Brush-A-Loves, Little Brush-A-Loves, Kiss-A-Loves, and Hello Colour.

Need-A-Littles, issued 1986
Lamb, Puppy, Bunny, Teddy Bear, Kitten ($30-40)

Pooch Troop, issued 1989
Colonel Ollie Collie, Top Dog, Sergeant Barker, Doc Bernard ($20-30)

Razzcals, issued 1987
four different, also called "Grumples" in the UK ($10-15)

Denver The Dinosaur, issued 1989 ($20-30)
The Noid, issued 1989 ($20-25)

Miscellaneous

This wraps up the rest of the toys made by Lesney Products, Matchbox Toys, and Tyco that don't fit into any other category.
Matchbox cardboard bridge, date unknown ($200+)

Cardboard Carry Case (depicts boy playing with toys), circa 1967 ($75-100)(CN)
1960 World Class Collectors Display Stand, issued 1990 ($10-15)
6010 Sonic Splash Zoom Ball, issued 1995 ($15-20)
8050 Aircraft Carrier Case, issued 1988 ($15-20)
GM-240 Splash Out, issued 1994 ($10-15)
Watch in white with white wristband, issued late 1980's ($50-75)(AU)
"Get In The Fast Lane" Watch, issued 1996 ($50-75)(AU)
Home Display Unit- 5 compartment display in clear plastic, issued 1969 ($10-15)
Skypark Display Unit- 5 compartment display in brown plastic, issued 1983 ($3-5)
PC-1 Model A Ford Van- glass cabinet with parts displayed, issued 1991 ($200-250)(C2)
Flying Hi (Styrofoam toys)- Zeppelin, Bi-Plane & Helicopter, issued 1971 ($35-50) each
Mike & The Modelmakers by M. Sasek (book), issued 1970 ($50-75)
GL-2 Matchbox Glue, issued 1976 ($10-15)
Matchbox Umbrella (toy fair give away), issued mid 1980's ($75-125)
Rutter's Dairy Gift Set (includes milk bottle, tin, cap & MB38-E), issued 1989 ($150-250)
"Direct Line Insurance" miniature phone, issued 1993 ($15-25)
"Direct Line Insurance" phone bank, issued 1996 ($20-30)
Great Beers of The World mug pair, issued 1994 ($15-20)
Lledo brand bus with "Matchbox Toys" labels, issued 1994 ($20-25)
Aguti brand toy truck with "Matchbox" labels, issued 1980's ($25-40)
27-5 Isuzu Hipac Van by Tomica with "Matchbox" logo (from "Miniature Car" gift set), issued 1985 ($25-50)
SUTC Rickshaws- maroon or orange, come blisterpacked with small "Matchbox" paper inside package ($50-75)(CHI)
55415 Action System Emergency City Walkie Talkies, issued 1997 ($35-50)
Burger King "Car of The Week" stand store display, issued 1989 ($50-75)
Kentucky Fried Chicken store display, issued 1995 ($100-150)
Taco Bell store display, issued 1995 (US West coast issue)
Matchbox Taco Bell store display, issued 1998 ($75-100)
Matchbox Beach Ball, issued 1996? ($25-40)(HK)

Carry Cases and Play Cases

The first Matchbox carry case was made by Ideal Toys for Lesney Products in 1966. The first case was only sold at Sears department stores. Carry cases usually have plastic trays that hold 12 cars in each tray, although the earliest carry cases have cardboard inserts. Most carry cases were made to carry 24, 48 or 72 miniatures. One carry case was made for Yesteryears and several for the Convoy series. Play cases look like carry cases from the outside but when opened feature play environments and usually plastic accessories. The earliest of these were also made by Ideal and sold through Sears. Many of these have problems with the plastic hardening and becoming brittle with age.

12 COMPARTMENT CARRY CASES

1. blue vinyl- depicts #56 Hi Tailer, #24 Team, #59 Planet Scout, etc., issued 1976 ($15-18)
2. blue vinyl- clear front (issued with models), issued 1979 ($10-12)
3. blue vinyl- clear front with "Matchbox" in red lettering, issued (unknown) ($10-12)

24 COMPARTMENT CARRY CASES

1. blue vinyl depicts #14 Iso Grifo, #6 Pickup & #62 Cougar, issued 1969 ($35-40)
2. blue vinyl depicts #14 Iso Grifo, #51 8-Wheel Tipper & #53 Zodiac, issued 1969 ($35-50)
3. blue vinyl depicts #68 Porsche 910 & #45 Ford Group 6, issued 1970 ($35-50)
4. blue vinyl- depicts #5 Lotus & #33 Lamborghini, issued 1971 ($20-25)
5. blue vinyl- depicts #61 Blue Shark & #62 Mercury Cougar, issued 1971 ($15-20)
6. blue vinyl- depicts #56 Hi-Tailer, #24 Team Matchbox, #59 Planet Scout, etc., issued 1976 ($15-20)
7. blue vinyl- depicts models in a bridge scene, issued 1979 ($15-18)
8. blue vinyl- depicts generic dump truck & rally car, issued 1979 ($20-30)
9. blue vinyl- depicts #62 Corvette & 22 other models, issued 1980 ($15-20)
10. blue plastic- tool box design "Trage Koffer/ Mallette" labels, issued 1981 ($15-20)
11. blue vinyl- depicts rows of miniatures from 1982 series, issued 1982 ($15-18)
12. blue or black vinyl- depicts #3 Porsche & #24 Datsun 280Z, issued 1983 ($15-18)
13. black vinyl- depicts hand drawn Peterbilt & Racer, issued 1989 ($10-12)
14. yellow vinyl- depicts van, jeep & race cars, issued 1993 ($7-10)
15. yellow vinyl depicts Harley-Davidson Motorcycle, issued 1994 ($10-15)

48 COMPARTMENT CARRY CASE

1. blue vinyl- depicts #32 Jaguar & #19 Lotus, issued 1966 ($125-15)
2. blue vinyl- depicts #41 Ford GT (cardboard or plastic trays), issued 1966 ($75-80)
3. blue vinyl- depicts #20 Lamborghini & #56 BMC Pininfarina, issued 1970 ($20-30)
4. blue vinyl- depicts #19 Road Dragster, #1 Mod Rod & #70 Dodge Dragster, issued 1971 ($35-50)
5. red vinyl- depicts #20 Lamborghini & #56 Pininfarina, issued 1972 ($35-50)
6. blue vinyl- depicts #56 Hi Tailer, #24 Team, #59 Planet Scout, etc. issued 1976 ($20-25)
7. blue vinyl- clear plastic front, easel back, issued 1976 ($35-40)
8. blue vinyl- depicts models in bridge scene, issued 1979 ($15-20)
9. blue vinyl- depicts generic dump truck & rally car, issued 1979 ($25-35)
10. blue vinyl- depicts road scene with bridge overpass, issued 1982 ($20-25)
11. blue vinyl- depicts #62 Corvette & 22 other models, issued 1980 ($15-20)
12. blue vinyl- depicts rows of miniatures from 1982 line, issued 1982 ($15-20)
13. blue vinyl- depicts #32 Sunburner, #40 Vette, #6 Mazda, issued 1983 ($20-25)
14. black vinyl- depicts #32 Sunburner, #40 Vette, #6 Mazda, issued 1983 ($18-20)
15. blue vinyl- shape of Formula 1 Car, issued 1985 ($35-40)
16. red vinyl- shape of Formula 1 Car, issued 1985 ($35-40)
17. yellow vinyl- shape of Formula 1 Car, issued 1985 ($35-40)
18. black vinyl- depicts Countach, Ford Pickup, Race Car & Ambulance, issued 1988 ($25-35)
19. black vinyl- depicts 4 hand drawn vehicles, issued 1989 ($15-18)
20. yellow vinyl- scene of assorted miniatures, issued 1993 ($10-12)
21. yellow vinyl- "Get In The Fast Lane" livery, issued 1994 ($8-12)
22. yellow vinyl- depicts the 1997 range based on the poster design, issued 1997 ($8-12)
23. yellow vinyl (with clear plastic coating)- depicts Viper with "75 Collection", issued 1998 ($8-12)

72 CAR CARRY CASES
1. blue vinyl- depicts #75 Ferrari Berlinetta, issued 1968 ($75-80)
2. blue vinyl- depicts #33 Lamborghini & #41 Ford GT, issued 1972 ($50-60)

MISC. SIZE CARRY CASES
1. blue vinyl- depicts #6 Quarry Truck on one side, #53 Mercedes on the other, holds 40, issued 1965 ($75-100)
2. blue vinyl- depicts #8 Mustang, holds 18, issued 1967 ($50-75)
3. blue plastic- labeled showing #16 Badger, #57 Wildlife Truck & #10 Piston Popper, holds 18, issued 1976 ($15-20)
4. black plastic- steering wheel shape, holds 20, issued 1983 ($15-20)
5. white vinyl in cabover design, holds 36, issued 1983 ($25-30)
6. red plastic, holds 18, issued 1985 ($20-25)
7. blue plastic- tool box sticker with top views, holds 18, issued 1986 ($15-18)
8. CC-1500 Carguantua, issued 1986 ($60-85)
9. yellow plastic- "Securicar" car-like side view shape, holds 14, issued 1989 ($25-30)
10. plastic bucket, holds 30, issued 1990 ($8-10)

CONVOY CARRY CASES
1. black vinyl- "Highway Express," holds 24, issued 1982 ($25-35)
2. blue vinyl- "Convoy" long style truck, holds 8, issued 1984 ($25-35)
3. black vinyl- depicts CY-9, CY-8, CY-5, holds 24, issued 1984 ($25-35)
4. black vinyl- depicts one Peterbilt Truck, holds 10, issued 1989 ($20-25)

YESTERYEAR CARRY CASE
1. blue vinyl- depicts Y-6 Cadillac, holds 16, issued 1969 ($20-35)

PLAY CASES
1. "Garage & Service Station"- Sears by Ideal, issued 1966 ($100-125)
2. blue vinyl- "Matchbox USA Play & Game Case," issued 1970 ($100-125)
3. light blue & orange vinyl- "Matchbox City" (Sears), issued 1972 ($100-125)
4. "Matchbox Construction Site" (Sears), issued 1973 ($100-125)
5. blue vinyl- "Matchbox Airport," issued 1973 ($60-75)
6. red vinyl with roll out mat, "Matchbox Mall" (JC Penney), issued 1973 ($100-150)
7. blue vinyl- "Skybusters Airport Playcase," issued 1975 ($60-75)
8. blue vinyl- "Matchbox City," issued 1976 ($40-50)
9. green vinyl- "Combat Zone," issued 1976 ($40-50)
10. blue vinyl- "Matchbox Town," issued 1977 ($40-50)
11. blue vinyl- "Matchbox Country," issued 1977 ($40-50)
12. blue vinyl- depicts Tonka Trucks (Lesney), issued 1977 ($75-90)
13. yellow vinyl- "Walt Disney Playcase," issued 1979 ($45-60)
14. blue vinyl- "Matchbox Race Case," issued 1977 ($40-50)
15. blue vinyl, "Airport Playcase," issued 1979 ($40-50)
16. blue vinyl, "Paramedic Playcase," issued 1980 ($40-50)
17. blue vinyl, "Off Road Playcase', issued 1980 ($40-50)
18. Garage Carry Case, also holds 18, issued 1983 ($25-30)
19. "Aircraft Carrier" carry case, issued 1988 ($20-25)

Display Cases

The majority of the display cases that were issued by Lesney Products, Universal Toys, and Tyco Toys were all generally available only to those who were dealers. They were never intended as collectibles as they were never offered to the collectors market. Those that have reached collectors are generally those obtained from stores who updated their displays or went out of business. The earliest displays were cardboard. The models were attached to the display by an elastic band. Generally the displays were far from being dust-free units. Later on, the cardboard displays gave way to vacuum-formed plastic displays which are still in use today. Some of these later displays have incorporated wood, glass, or metal in their design. The section will be categorized according to chronological release.

1955: the earliest known display stand was only recently discovered to exist. Seen in early printed literature it held the first 12 miniatures plus the Covered Wagon . Made from silver-gray cardboard
($1000+)
1956: stepped cardboard, holds 24 models & the covered wagon. Depicts 6A Quarry Truck on the header board ($650-1000)
1957: same as above but holds 36 models ($650-1000)
1958: stepped cardboard, holds 55 models plus A-1 & A-2. 6A depicted on header ($650-1000)
1959: stepped cardboard, holds 60 models plus A-1, A-2, A-3, M-1 & M-2. 6A on header ($650-1000)
1960: displays entire 1-75 range; depicts No. 6-A Quarry Truck emerging from its box at the upper left; yellow with red trim, blue header ($500-750)
1963: 1. displays 10 Major Packs and 5 Accessory Packs; depicts M-4-A Ruston Bucyrus emerging from its box at top; yellow with red trim & blue header ($450-600)
2.. displays 16 Yesteryear; depicts Y-15-A Rolls Royce emerging from its box at top; yellow with red trim & blue header ($450-600)
3. displays 13 King-Size; depicts K-7-A Curtiss Wright Dump emerging from its box; yellow with red trim & blue header ($450-600)
1965:
1. displays all 75 miniatures; depicts 53-B Mercedes emerging from its box at upper left. yellow with red border & blue header ($350-450)
2. displays 25 miniatures; depicts 53-B Mercedes emerging from its box with "Authentic Matchies" on blue header; yellow with red border ($450-600)
3. displays 3 miniatures; header reads "New This Month From Matchbox"; yellow steps for 3 models ($150-250)
4. displays 10 Major Packs & A-1 Pumps; depicts M-9 Cooper Jarrett box at upper left with "Matchbox Series Major Packs" at right; yellow inner with red outer border ($450-600)
5. displays 14 King-Size with K-15 compartment at top; depicts K-15 Fire Engine box at upper right; yellow inner with red outer border ($450-600)
6. "M-26" display- metal display with sliding glass doors. Holds all 75 miniatures as well as 15 King-Size in stair step manner ($500-750)
7. "W-20" display- glass covered wood display in yellow with "Matchbox Series Nos. 1 to 75 49 cents" header. Holds 75 miniatures in stair step manner ($150-250)
8. "W-33" display- glass covered wood display in yellow with "Matchbox" headboard. Holds 16 Yesteryear, 10 Major Packs, 15 King-Size and A-1 Pumps in stair step manner ($200-300)
9. "SR-375" Wire dispensing rack- holds 225 boxed miniatures ($15-25)
1966:
1. holds 15 King-Size in yellow cardboard area with insert in blue header to hold the K-16 Twin Tippers; red header reads "Matchbox King Size"; red border ($350-500)
2. V-75 Vacuum Formed Counter Display- white plastic with clear cover; large "Matchbox" in center at 55 cents each; holds 77 miniatures (7 across & 11 down); flat ($175-225)
3. VR-75 Vacuum Formed Revolving Display- white plastic with clear cover & red top; "Matchbox" on yellow background around top at 55 cents; holds 77 miniatures ($100-150)
1967:
1. holds 25 miniatures; depicts MB53-B Mercedes Benz emerging from its box; blue header reads "Matchless Matchbox Series"; yellow with blue header & red border ($250-350)
2. holds 18 King-Size; "Matchbox King-Size" at top on blue header & border; yellow inner ($250-350)
3. VY Yesteryear Vacuum Formed Display; holds 16 Yesteryear; white plastic with clear front & picture frame border in gold ($125-175)
1968:
1. BCM-1 holds 75 miniatures; depicts No. 48 Dump Truck emerging from its box at left; yellow cardboard with blue border ($250-350)
2. BCM-2 holds 25 miniatures; depicts No. 48 Dump truck emerging from its box at top; yellow cardboard with blue border ($175-250)
3. LR-75 Illuminated Motorized Revolving Display- same as VR-75 but with electrical hookup ($150-200)
4. VL-75 Plastic Counter Display- white plastic with "Matchbox" and "55 cents" at center; 77 models run 11 across and 7 down ($175-225)
5. DB-2 Counter Dispenser- blue and yellow cardboard stands at an angle. Holds36 boxed models as a dispenser unit ($75-100)
6. BCK- holds 20 King-Size; yellow cardboard with blue border; header reads "Matchbox King Size" with curved top ($250-300)
7. VK King-Size Vacuum Formed Display- holds 21 King-Size. White plastic with "Matchbox King Size" across center ($175-250)
8. BCY- holds 16 Yesteryear; header reads "Matchbox Models of Yesteryear" in an arc with Y-4 Opel Coupe below; yellow cardboard with blue border ($175-225)
9. VY-2 Yesteryear Plastic Display- white plastic with "Matchbox Models of Yesteryear" at bottom; holds 16 Yesteryear ($150-225)
10. FGD- Fancy Goods Display cardboard in maroon with striped lower tier. Header features car horn with "Models of Yesteryear"; holds 2 Yesteryear (ashtray, box, etc.)
1969:
1. DS-2 largest display ever made is 50" X 10-1/2" X 38-1/2" and weighs 150 pounds! Glass front and sides with gold metal trim. Either side will hold 21 King Size and 16 Yesteryear. Three turnstiles in the center hold 75 miniatures ($1000+)
1971:
SQ-75 Counter Display- four sided turning displaying holds 75 miniatures. White plastic with yellow edges and red top. Top graphics depict 62 Cougar Dragster and 52 Dodge Charger. ($100-150)
VR-759 Revolving Display- wider and shorter version of the VR-75 ($50-75)
1976:
1. 95 01 03 Models of Yesteryear Display. Holds 16 Yesteryear in white vacuum form. Clear front secured by gold radiator design. ($200-25)
1977:
1. SQ-75 Counter Display- white plastic holds 75 models in a four sided turning unit, red top and edges. This same design still exists through 1996! This version depicts 1970s vintage vehicles on four different top panels ($50-75)
2. SQ-75 Counter Display has been revised for 1983 with yellow grid pattern, in 1995 with clear top panel "Get In The Fast Lane" logo with yellow edges and in 1996 with solid color top panel "Get In The Fast Lane" with neon orange top & edging ($35-50)each
1978:
1. 95 01 15 Yesteryear Counter Display- holds 20 Yesteryear; white plastic inner with clear cover with wood-like outer finish. Header attachment with "Matchbox" & "Models of Yesteryear" ($125-175)
1979:
1. 01 06 02 Matchbox Counter Display- holds 81 miniatures. Back holds 450 boxed models. White inner with clear slide up front. Wood-like finish ($100-150)
2. 01 06 02 Matchbox Counter Display- as above but with white laminated finish ($100-150) Issued a few years later
1998:
1. large glass display from "Matchbox Collectibles used for retail operations ($1200-1500)(CL)

Kidco and LJN

Kidco and LJN were independent toy companies, separate from Matchbox Toys. In 1984, Matchbox Toys bought Kidco in a merger agreement. In the United States, the Kidco products were still packaged as "Kidco" but in Europe they were packaged as "Matchbox." Castings were never modified and retained the Kidco on the baseplates.

LJN used Matchbox in Europe to market some of their products. The packaging retained the "LJN" logo and the "Matchbox" logo was added as a sticker to the packaging. The extent of Kidco and LJN Matchbox products is too broad to be fully covered. The following were offered under the Matchbox brand:

KIDCO: Key Cars, Key Car trucks, Burnin' Key Cars, Demolition Key Cars, Key Car motorcycles, Glowin' Burnin' Key Cars, Lock-Up Cars, Gold Key Lock-Ups

LJN: Dungeons & Dragons, Stunt Riders, Dune, Tri-Ex Rough Riders 4X4, Michael Jackson doll, Power Blaster Cycles, Omni Force Rough Riders 4X4, A-Team Rough Riders, Rough Riders 4X4, Boy George soft sculpture doll

Other companies have also used "Matchbox" to market their products including Sanrio with "Hello Colour." Popular toys like Skip It, Koosh Balls, and Moon Shoes to name but a few. These were made by Odd-Zon, Tiger Toys, and Wilson Sports with a "Matchbox" tie-in.

Catalogs

The first pocket catalog for the Matchbox series was produced by the U.S. distributor Fred Bronner. American and English catalogs are always the easiest to obtain. 1983 was the last year for an American edition catalog until Tyco Toys revived the catalog in 1993! Most catalogs after 1983 are International editions which included two to five languages each. Completely different catalogs were made for the first time for Australia, but this was short-lived. Japan also had their own edition for several years that had a different cover and contents than other editions. For values of foreign editions add 5-20 percent depending on the country.

POCKET CATALOGS

1957—depicts No. 1 Road Roller Moko Lesney box
England, USA ($125-150)
1958—depicts No. 44A Rolls Royce emerging from box
USA ($125-150)
1959—1ST EDITION- depicts same as 1958 catalog but with "1959 Edition" in upper right
USA ($90-125)
1959—2nd Edition- depicts A-2 Car Transporter, #43 Hillman Minx & Y-9 Fowler
England ($90-125)
1960—1st Edition- depicts group of regular wheels on top of their boxes in a semi-circle
England, USA ($80-100)
1960—2nd Edition- same cover as 1st edition, contents different. Most obvious is #4 Triumph Cycle & #27 Cadillac Sedan depicted
England, USA ($80-95)
1961—depicts No. 5 Bus
USA, England, International, Canada ($75-80)
1962—depicts No. 65 Jaguar Sedan
USA, English, International, Canada, Germany, French, Italian ($70-80)
1963—depicts No. 53 Mercedes Benz
USA, English, French ($50-60)
1964—depicts No. 28 Jaguar Mk.10
USA, English, International, German, French ($35-50)
1965—depicts racing scene
USA, English, International, German, French ($35-50)
1966—depicts models in a London scene
USA, English, International, Canada, German, French, Japanese ($20-35)
1967—depicts models with different flags
USA, English, International, German, Japanese, French ($10-15)
1968—shows groups of models with "1968" in large type
USA, English, International, German, Japanese, French ($10-15)
1969—shows traffic scene from driver's perspective
USA, English, International, German, Japanese, French, Italian ($5-10)
1969 2nd Edition—shows traffic scene from driver's perspective with "Second Edition" in yellow circle
USA, English, German, French, International, Italian ($5-10)
1970—shows a grouping of assorted models on an orange background
USA, English, German, French, International, Japanese, Italian, Spanish ($5-8)
1971—shows two scorpion cars with "Scorpion" emblem
USA, English, German, French, International, Japanese,. Italian, Spanish, Dutch ($5-8)
1972—shows assorted models on a red cover with race car driver's head
USA, English, German, French, International, Japanese, Italian, Dutch, Norwegian ($5-8)
1973—shows five models in different colored scenes
USA, English, German, French, International, Japanese, Italian, Dutch, Norwegian ($5-8)
1974—shows four models in different scenes

USA, English, German, French, International, Japanese, Italian, Dutch, Swedish ($5-8)

1975—depicts large "1975" with models
USA, English, German, French, International, Japanese, Italian, Dutch, Swedish, East German ($5-8)

1976—depicts large "1976" with model inside each number
USA, English, German, French, Japanese, Italian, Dutch, Swedish, East German ($5-8)

1977—"1977" in upper right with four depictions of toys
USA, English, German, French, Japanese, Italian, Dutch, Swedish, East German ($5-8)

1978—depicts K-66 Jaguar Police set
USA, English, German, French, Italian, Dutch, Swedish, East German ($5-8)

1979—depicts K-21, MB3 & SB3 with "1979/80"
USA, English, German, French, International, Italian, Dutch, Spanish, Swedish, East German, Danish, Farsic, Greek ($5-8)

1979—depicts "Matchbox" logo in Japanese text with selection of different models
Japanese ($15-20)

1980—depicts fire rescue scene
USA, English, German, French, International, Italian, Spanish, Dutch, Swedish, Danish ($3-5)

1981—depicts K-44 Bridge Layer and K-4 Big Tipper
USA, English, German, French, International, Italian, Dutch, Swedish, Danish ($3-5)

1982—depicts Peterbilt & Kenworth models
USA, English, German, French, Italian, Spanish, Dutch, Swedish, Farsic, Finnish ($3-5)

1983—depicts blue cover with yellow & red band
USA, International ($3-5)

1983—depicts young boy in front of rows of Matchbox
Australia ($5-8)

1984—depicts six cars & trucks from miniatures & Superkings range
International (English/German/French text), International (English/ Italian/ Spanish text) ($3-5)

1984—depicts four different London Bus miniatures
Australia ($5-8)

1984—rows of Matchbox with Japanese text in upper left
Japanese ($5-8)

1985—checkered flag design
International, German, French (5-3/4" x 8-1/4") ($5-8)

1985—boy clutching toys
Australia, Australia "Special Edition" ($5-8)

1986—depicts small Live N Learn helicopter towing "1986" with several "Matchbox" logos at the bottom
International (English), German (5-3/4" X 8-1/4"), French, Dutch ($3-5)

1986—depicts construction scene with six vehicles
Australian ($5-8)

1986—depicts Porsche 959 & Toyota MR2 (foldout-small)
Japanese ($5-8)

1987—depicts black upper cover with striped lower with array of models
English, German(two sizes), French (5-3/4" x 8-1/4") ($3-5)

1987—depicts boy playing with Carguantua playset
Australia ($5-8)

1987—depicts row of models running diagonally (fold-out)
Japanese ($5-8)

1988—depicts blue grid design with close-up of K-70 Porsche
English, German, French (5-3/4" X 8-1/4") ($3-5)

1988—fold-out growth chart
Australia ($5-8)

1989—depicts white cover with small inset of playset
English, German, French/ Dutch, Italian/ Spanish ($2-4)

1990—same design as 1989 version with "1990" date
English/ German ($2-4)

1991—depicts large playset
English/German ($2-4)

1992—depicts 8 "Matchbox" logos from top to bottom with five vehicles on front
English/ German, English/ German (Toys R Us edition) ($2-4)

1993—"Matchbox 1993" on yellow background
USA ($1-2)

1993—"Matchbox" with no date on yellow background
Canada ($3-5)

1993 blue cover with child and an assortment of miniatures
English ($2-4)

1993—depicts Motor City setup
German ($2-4)

1994—"Get In The Fast Lane" on orange background (foldout)
USA, Australian (each have different contents) ($1-2)

1994—"Get In The Fast Lane" on orange background (stapled)
English, Toys R Us, Dutch/French ($2-4)

1994—"Collectors Choice"
USA ($2-4)

1995—"Get In The Fast Lane" on orange background
USA, English, Dutch/French ($2-4)

1996—"Get In The Fast Lane" on orange background (foldout)
USA ($1-2)

1996—"Action System" and layout on cover (larger size)
English, German, Dutch/French ($2-4)

1997—1-75 Collection poster
USA ($1-2)

1998- 1-75 Collection poster USA ($2-3) & poster Australia , Czech/ Slovak, Poland ($4-6)

DEALER CATALOGS

Dealer or trade catalogs were given out at toy fairs and were never intended to be given out to collectors. The first trade catalog was made in 1960. Mostly U.S. or English editions were made for the 1960s. Few foreign editions from the 1970s exist. In the 1980s, different trade catalogs were made for the United States and European countries. Japanese editions were also entirely different. When Tyco Toys took over in 1993, U.S. editions covered the entire Tyco product line. Spring trade catalogs were first issued for 1993 by Tyco Toys. For foreign editions, add 10-20 percent.

1960 ($250-350)
1961 ($250-350)
1962 ($250-350)
1963 ($150-250)
1964 ($150-250)
1965 ($125-175)
1966 ($75-100)
1967 ($50-75)
1968 ($35-50)
1969 ($35-50)
1970 ($20-25)
1971 ($20-25)
1972 ($20-25)
1973 ($20-25)
1974 ($20-25)
1975 ($20-25)
1976 ($18-20)
1977 ($18-20)
1978 ($18-20)
1979 ($12-15)
1980 ($8-12)
1981 ($8-12)
1982 ($8-12)
1983 ($5-10)
1984 ($5-10)
1985 ($5-10)
1986 ($5-10)
1987 ($5-10)
1988 ($5-10)
1989 ($5-10)
1990 ($5-10)
1991 ($5-10)
1992 ($5-10)
1993 ($10-15)
1993 spring ($10-15)
1994 ($10-15)
1994 spring ($10-15)
1995 ($10-15)
1995 spring ($10-15)
1996 ($10-15)
1996 spring ($10-15)
1997 spring ($10-15)
1997 ($10-15)
1998 Mattel with CD-ROM ($30-35)

SPECIALTY CATALOGS

There were numerous specialty catalogs produced, especially in the early 1990s, for the Dinky and Yesteryear series, which each had separate catalogs. Matchbox Collectibles has issued Christmas gift catalogs. The Czechoslovakian distributor of Matchbox, Tuzek, produced its own Matchbox catalog, which also contains Burago brand models. The rarest of all specialty catalogs is a 1959 edition catalog that shows the first fourteen Yesteryear models ($175-225)

The Box

The box is where Matchbox got its name. The idea of a matchbox to put a toy in was thought of before, but it wasn't until Lesney put a trademark on the word that a 50-year tradition got its start. Box styles have changed over the years—some designs lasted several years, others a brief year. This section will describe each box type and alert collectors to "rare" boxes. When grading your collection for value, check the box rarity guide below as some boxes have far outreached the contents inside. Sometimes hundreds of dollars have been paid for really rare examples.

Regular Wheel Boxes

TYPE A—MOKO LESNEY WITH SCRIPT LETTERING (1953-1954)
Only the first seven models were ever issued with this box. The word "MOKO" appears in script lettering, while "Lesney" is in block letters. All are quite rare to find.

TYPE B—MOKO LESNEY WITH BLOCK LETTERING (1954-1960)
Basically the same as the type A box, but the word "MOKO" is now in block letters along with the "Lesney" name. No real rare versions stand out, so each box is worth as much as any other.

TYPE C—LESNEY LINE DRAWING BOX (1961)
Issued only in 1961, the box is still basically the same as the type before it. The scroll though now omits the "Moko" name leaving only "A Lesney Product." Most boxes from this type can be quite difficult to obtain

especially because of the short period of time in which they were made.

TYPE D—"MATCHBOX SERIES" IN ARC (1962-1963)
These are the first regular wheel boxes to have full color pictures of the model on the box. Some first-issue models made it to this series and some of the rarest of all regular wheel boxes fall into this vintage. Difficult boxes to obtain include 6B Quarry Truck, 25 Volkswagen, 62 Military Lorry and 71 Army Water Truck. Very rare boxes include 33 Ford Zodiac, 47 Trojan Tea Van, 51 Albion Chieftan, 53 Aston Martin, 55 DUKW, 58 BEA Coach and 66 Citroen DS. ·

TYPE E—"MATCHBOX" IN ARC (1964-1968)
Similar in design to the type before it, the word "Series" now moves from next to the word "Matchbox" to directly below it in much smaller type. Many of the boxes show preproduction colored models, so that the color on the outer box will never match its contents. Difficult to obtain are 22 Pontiac (blue), 36 Opel Diplomat (both green ones), and 44 Rolls Royce (tan). Very rare boxes include the 34 Volkswagen (green), 46 Pickfords Van and 65 Jaguar Sedan.

TYPE F—NUMBER IN BLUE SQUARE (1969)
This was the final style of regular wheel boxes. The box features the word "Matchbox" across the top in red. The number appears in a blue square in the upper right corner. Difficult boxes include 3 Ambulance, 8 Mustang (with Superfast picture) and 12 Safari Land Rover. Very rare boxes include those for the 14 Iso Grifo,22 Pontiac & 62 (with Superfast picture). Four numbers never made it into this series—20, 30, 35 & 69.

Superfast Boxes

TYPE A—NUMBER IN BLUE SQUARE (1969)
The design of the first Superfast box is basically a carry over from the last style Regular Wheel box. Some boxes that have regular wheel model art have red "Superfast" lettering while those with a Superfast model depicted have black "Superfast" lettering. Most of the boxes with regular wheels pictured can be difficult to find with the 14 Iso Grifo probably being the rarest.

TYPE B—"MATCHBOX SUPERFAST" WITH BLUE SQUARE (1970)
Still using the blue square as the identification point, the model now incorporates the words "Matchbox Superfast" across the top. A few models—16 Bulldozer, 39 Ford Tractor, 40 Hay Trailer, 61 Alvis Stalwart, and 65 Combine are regular wheel holdovers that have the same box design but "Superfast" is omitted from the artwork. Most of these five seem to be the harder to find. Most others are equally available except the MB32 Leyland Tanker "Aral" version. The style was used while Type C was being introduced.

TYPE C—"MATCHBOX" WITH WHEEL (1971)
While most of the models continued with the style B box in 1971, new releases for 1971 started being released in a box that featured a Superfast wheel behind the word "Matchbox." Less than 20 models were ever even used for this particular style. The toughest one is the 70 Dodge Dragster with an inset picture in the upper right. Another difficult box is the Japanese edition of the Volkswagen boxed as #30.

TYPE D—"MATCHBOX" WITH STREAKING BACKGROUND (1972-1974)
Like many of the Superfast boxes, not all model numbers are found for any particular box type. The box features a yellow background with a streaking effect background. "Matchbox" appears in the upper left. Models with Rolamatic features have "Rolamatics" added at the upper right. The rarest boxes appears to be that for the 28 Mack Dump Truck and 48 Dodge Dump Truck. Some difficult to obtain boxes include the Japanese edition with the Lotus Europa as #18.

TYPE E-COLORED BACKGROUND WITH "MATCHBOX" LOGO (1975-1976)
Not all model numbers followed through to this style even though it was used for five years. The box depicts the "Matchbox" logo in the upper left. The model number is to the center left. Below this it reads either "Superfast," "Streakers," or "Rolamatics." Background colors vary from number to number. Variations occur with the word "New" appearing or not appearing above the model number on many of the numbers. The rarest one appears to be the 70 Dodge Dragster. Most others appear to be readily available.

TYPE F—BRAZILIAN BOX (1977-1978)
There are five different models depicted on the Brazilian boxes. The model contents are identified by a sticker on the end flaps. The most readily found box has the #41 Siva Spyder. Less common, and quite rare, are those showing the 1 Dodge Challenger, 4 Firebird, 58 Faun Dump and 36 Formula 5000.

TYPE G—LAST PICTURE BOX (1977-1982)
By 1975 up until 1982, almost every model number was represented by this style. Only the 20 & 29 were never issued in this type box. The box features the "Matchbox" logo at the upper left. These are designated as the "last" picture box in 1982, all boxes began as generic editions. Difficult boxes to obtain include 1 Dodge Challenger, 6 Mercedes (blue), 19 Peterbilt Mixer, 61 Peterbilt Wrecker, and 66 Super Boss.

TYPE H—CLEAR PLASTIC (1977)
In 1977, the German market had a test market box produced in clear

plastic with the "Matchbox" logo added to each of the six sides.

TYPE I—BLACK JAPANESE BOX (1977)
A series of nine models were numbered J-1 through J-9 and packaged in black boxes with gray and red stripes and white line drawn pictures.

TYPE J—JAPANESE WHITE BOX (1978-1979)
A short series of boxes were made for Japan with full color pictures with a plain white background. Model numbers used were J-8, J-10, J-11, J-12, J-14, J-21, J-22, J-25, J-31, J-38, J-75, 25, 31, 47, 70 and 75 only. A prototype was issued for a J-19 Mazda RX500 and this is quite rare.

TYPE K—JAPANESE COLORED BACKGROUND (1979)
A handful of models were issued which depicted a full color model on colored background. The only numbers known to exist are 2, 5, and 38.

TYPE L—PICTURE GENERIC (1982)
When the picture box was gone, the Worldwide market opted to go with a generic blue window box. The United States market opted for a yellow generic box. Three of the side panels depicted either a Jeep, Corvette, or Peterbilt. The boxes were poorly printed by an ink stamp on the ends, which made it difficult to read the contents.

TYPE M—YELLOW WITH RED GRID—YELLOW LOGO (1983-1993)
The generic box was improved upon in 1983 as a plain yellow box with red grid lines. The "Matchbox" logo featured a yellow background. Early boxes were ink stamped on the flaps but this was changed to normally printed boxes.

TYPE N—YELLOW WITH RED GRID—WHITE LOGO (1994-1996)
This generic box is essentially the same as the previous box, but the logo now has a white background.

TYPE O—RETRO 1950'S (1986-1996)
These specially designed boxes are privately produced and designed by the M.I.C.A. club to use especially for their convention cars. The box style is based on a late 1950's style line drawn box. The Junior Matchbox Club of Canada issued the entire 1987 and 1988 new model range in these boxes to their members.

TYPE P—GENERIC WHITE & YELLOW PROMO BOX (1994-1996)
Matchbox started making special white generic boxes in 1994 to use with their promotional business. The same style box in yellow was used for the Hershey Convention promotional models.

TYPE Q—SPECIALTY BOXES (1985-1996)
This category covers all boxes that don't fit into any other category as many are one-of-a-kind designs. Promotional models are boxed in this manner. Some promotional models using special boxes include Silvo, Lion, Continental Aero, Chubbies and Matchbox Collectors Club amongst others.

TYPE R—PREMIERE COLLECTION BOX (1996-1998)
When the premiere series was developed for 1996, it was decided to present the model with its box in a blisterpack. Basically a generic box, the box is overall dark gray. Series 1-6 all have this style box. For 1997, the premiere boxes will be changed to colors like red and blue for each individual series issued.

TYPE S—75 CHALLENGE BOX (1996-1997)
Intended for 1997 release, the 75 Challenge series debuted in November 1996. These specially painted metallic gold models each come with a purple and yellow generic box each sporting the model's name and number on three sides and clearly identifying the "75 Challenge."

TYPE T—ORANGE GENERIC BOX (1997)
Released in January 1997, a new generic box will start replacing the grid line box. The box sports the Fast Lane car but without the "Fast Lane" words. The end flaps denote that the model is part of a series of 75 models.

TYPE U— PREMIERE COLLECTION BOX (1998)
The Premiere Collection box was redesigned to have what appears to be a three sided front panel. This type box only appears so far on Series #21.

TYPE V— STAR COLLECTION BOX (1998)
This was a specialty box issued exclusively for the Star Car series in which each box has specially colored design to represent the TV show or movie represented.

Yesteryear Boxes

Yesteryear boxes have had their changes of style over the years since their inception in 1956. Only the closed style boxes are shown in this book and the window style will be briefly mentioned here.

TYPE A—LINE DRAWING STYLE (1956-1959)
The first style box for Yesteryears feature a line drawing of the model on a yellow background. The end flaps features three different numbering styles in which these are termed in England as types A, B & C.

TYPE B—COLOR PICTURE WITH PLAIN YELLOW BACKGROUND (1960-1964)
This is the first color photo box for Yesteryears. The color of the background is plain yellow. "Models of Yesteryear" appears in an arc across the top This is referred to in England as a D1 type box. Most are of equal rarity.

TYPE C—"MODELS OF YESTERYEAR" BANNER WITH BACKGROUND (1964-1966)
Similar in design to the previous type box with "Models of Yesteryear" in an arc across the top, this is referred to in England as a D2 type box. The box now features background scenery in the artwork. Virtually every box in this category could be considered difficult to obtain. The two rarest ones by far are those far the Y-2 London Bus, Y-3 London Tramcar and the Y-13 General Locomotive.

TYPE D—"MATCHBOX" BANNER (1967-1968)
The final picture box for Yesteryear features the color picture with background scenery. The arc at the top features the word "Matchbox." "Models of Yesteryear" goes to a straight line at the bottom of the panel. Some models feature both color variations to match its contents, such as the lilac and yellow Y-7 Mercer and the Y-6 blue and red Bugatti. Many flap variations are indicated as England breaks this box into two categories—D3 and E. Notable rarity includes the Y-8 Sunbeam Motorcycle box.

OTHER YESTERYEAR BOXES
In 1969 the closed in style box gave way to the cellophane front style box. Styles include Type E pink & yellow, Type F purple & yellow, Type G woodgrain style, Type H straw colored and Type I maroon style. Several other styles were made which are too numerous to discuss here.

MAJOR PACK & KING-SIZE BOXES
There are generally four styles used for Major Pack boxes and three for King-Size not including cellophane front style boxes.
MAJOR PACK—A. Moko Lesney, B. Lesney line drawing, C. full color with plain background, D. full color with background scenery
KING-SIZE—A. Line drawing, B. full color with plain background, C. full color with background scenery. Cellophane front boxes are introduced for 1969.

The Blisterpack

Collectors often wonder whether their model in a blisterpack should be left intact or ripped out of its package and the model put on its shelf. That depends on two things—age of the package and rarity of the package. Any model from the 1960s in a blisterpack will definitely have enhanced value because a box is also enclosed with the model. The first blisterpack from 1963 is extremely rare. The first Superfast boxes through early-1971 also enclosed the box with the blistercard. From 1972 through 1996, there are literally dozens of different blisterpacks, far too numerous to cover. Blisterpack designs from the 1970s are generally more difficult to obtain than newer ones, of course. Current blisterpacks that were produced by the millions don't enhance the price by any great percentage if at all. Blisterpacks are generally a U.S. marketing tool. European markets generally used window boxes to market the brand. Only since 1994 did Europe even really start mass marketing the blisterpack.

Pins & Badges

There are dozens of pins and badges with Matchbox-related subject matter. Many have been produced by collector clubs or for toy show events. As these are of a private nature, only those issued and made specifically by Lesney Products or Matchbox Toys are listed.

1. 1-1/4" "Matchbox Collector" with No. 1 Road Roller box (issued with 71A), 1959 ($20-25)
2. "Matchbox Models" with 28C blue Jaguar, 1964 ($25-35)(DU)
3. "Matchbox Models" with 53B red Mercedes, 1964 ($25-35)(DU)
4. 1-1/2" "Matchbox Collector" with 41C Ford GT, full metal, 1969 ($4-6)(US)
5. 1-1/2" "Matchbox Collector" with 41C Ford GT, laminated, 1970 ($4-6)(US)
6. 1-1/2" "Matchbox Collector" with MB56-B & K-51-A (red & white), 1973 ($3-5)(US)
7. 1-1/2" "Matchbox Collector" with MB56-B & K-51-A (pink & white), 1973 ($3-5)
8. 2" "Matchbox Japan Collectors Club" in solid gold metal, 1976 ($35-50)(JP)
9. 1-7/8" "I'm A Matchbox Collector" with MB59-D Porsche, 1979 ($3-5)(US)
10. 2-1/2" "Eat My Dust! Tyrone Speedtrack" (orange or yellow letters), 1982 ($2-4)(US)
11. 2" "Building New Roads To Success," 1983 ($2-4)(US)
12. 2" "Matchbox" with teddy bear, 1983 ($3-5)(UK)
13. 2" "Get Your Hands On a Matchbox," 1983 ($3-5)(UK)
14. 1-3/4" "I'm A Matchbox Collectors Club Member," 1983 ($3-5)(UK)
15. 2" "Matchbox On The Move in 84," issued 1984 ($3-5)(UK)
16. 1-1/2" "Rubik's Magic," issued 1987 ($1-2)(UK)
17. 2" "Junior Matchbox Club," issued 1987 ($2-4)(CN)
18. 2" "JMC Gang Member Year 3," issued 1989 ($2-4)(CN)
19. 1-1/2" "Connectables—What's Yours Called?," issued 1989 ($2-4)(US)
20. 2—7/8" "Days of Thunder," issued 1989 ($5-8)(US)
21. 1-1/4" "Monster In My Pocket" (several designs), issued 1989 ($1-2)(US)
22. 2-7/8" "Big Top Pee Wee," issued 1990 ($2-4)(US)
23. 2" "Get Your Free Mighty Matchbox Truck—Tandy," issued 1990 ($5-8)(AU)
24. 2-1/4" "Casper—Haunting Season Begins May 26th," issued 1995 ($3-5)(US)

The Code System

A code system was originally developed in 1977 by Ray Bush, editor of UK Matchbox at the time. The code system was redeveloped over time down to three codes. The code system was developed to distinguish models that were made or approved by Matchbox or altered by a third party. With the advent of the ASAP company involved in the mix (see "Superfast/Miniatures" text), the code system was slightly revised at the end of 1996 to include these. A Code 4 was added in 1995.

CODE 1—Any model wholly manufactured by Matchbox. These models can be partially manufactured in one factory and altered later in a Matchbox owned or leased facility.
CODE 2—Any model altered in part or in whole by relabeling, repainting or both by a second party not associated with Matchbox but with Matchbox's full written approval. This includes models manufactured as blanks in a Matchbox owned or leased facility and then tampoed or labeled by a second party with either specific or blanket approval.
CODE 3—Any model repainted, relabeled or altered in any manner without Matchbox's consent. A "private" issue model.
CODE 4—Any model wholly manufactured by Matchbox but is usually a one-of-a-kind that is used as an auction item or an awards presentation model.

Only Code 1 and Code 2 models are noted in this book. Code 3s are collected by some individuals but the value of a Code 3 is at what anyone is willing to pay for one. The M.I.C.A. club has a further addition to the Code 2 definition which includes "Code 1 models not available to the general public." This added definition is not generally recognized by all, including this author and is an "excuse" to lump some really rare Code 1 models into a category so that collectors wouldn't be disappointed at not trying to have a complete Code 1 collection. Examples of these "Code 2" models include the Y-1 black Model T, Y-12 blue Hoover, Y-21 Australian art set and the Y-21 & Y-47 Antiques Road Show models. Code 4 models, although quite rare as they are actually Code 1 issues are not listed as they are in most cases one-ofs that no one could hope to own in their collection.

Preproductions and Prototypes

A "preproduction" model is any model that is made by Matchbox before the model is mass produced. The beginnings of a preproduction usually include a wooden or resin blank, followed by a painted resin model. Once the model is tooled, a blank casting is made and assembled. These may have blank cast bases or include partial- or full-base text. Many times—especially when models used to be numbered—unnumbered or incorrectly numbered castings were made. Once a casting is approved, paint trials follow. The first trial is usually white as white paint is cheaper and defects in the painting can be detected at this time. Different color trials follow. Sometimes decal or label trials are done including full decal mockups of the production version.

A "prototype" is a model that made it to the drawing board or is actually a hand-built model. Some prototypes almost make it to full production, but due to unforeseen problems, such as licensing agreements, the project is canceled.

Although some examples of preproductions and prototypes are included in this book, it's literally impossible to catalog such items.

Price valuations cannot be determined to any exact pricing. Values are usually determined by what the market will bear. These are brought to market by Matchbox employees or factory workers. Others are donated by the company for club auctions.

Pirates and Copies

A copy of a Matchbox is any model casting made to look like or resemble a Matchbox casting. They can be of any size, from smaller to larger than the actual Matchbox model. Many are very well done while some are very crude attempts.

A pirate model is any model that actually attempts to steal the "Matchbox" brand name. The model may or may not look like a Matchbox model.

Early "pirate" models were actually manufactured *before* Lesney Products even existed. These prewar or postwar toys were made in Japan and packaged in a match box. The earliest known use of the word "matchbox" for a toy was by Louis Marx in the 1930s for a miniature steel erector set. Later pirate models include a set of plastic road signs—sets A & B were produced in the 1950s. These were illegally produced and taken off the market. An enterprising Hong Kong company issued both convoy style and three-pack miniature models and packaged them in window boxes in 1983, about the same time Universal Toys began ownership of Matchbox. These were changed to include a "Speedburners" logo when legal battles ensued. A plastic building was also done in the 1960s using the Matchbox name, as was a wooden horse cart.

The earliest known copies of Matchbox were called "Shadow Box" and are replicas of early regular wheels. Other enterprising companies used Matchbox-style packaging without actually calling them Matchbox. Clifford Toys are one of these. Polish and Hungarian toy companies are known to have taken Matchbox models apart and to make molds from them. Many are very crude, to the point of brush painting on some models. The entire range of Matchbox has been copied especially the miniatures. Lesser known companies like Guisval and Mira of Spain are known for the Yesteryear and miniature replicas respectively. The current company called Maisto makes some very close looking castings. Maisto is the successor to MC Toys.

One serious violation included the marketing of stolen goods in generic packaging. This included Yesteryear and Dinky models in either purple-and-yellow or white-grid pattern boxes. Some miniatures were packaged in purple-and-yellow blisterpacks. Other brands such as Racing Champions and Corgi were also stolen and packaged the same way. An investigation in 1991 stopped this practice.

Fakes

A fake or a forgery is any Matchbox model that has been altered into a Code 3 version of an existing model, especially of a rare model. These models are worthless in value. A fake includes restored, touched-up, and repainted vehicles. These could be used as "fillers" for your collection but no inherent value can ever be placed on these items. Hints for discovering whether your model is a fake is to check for rivet tampering, fingerprints, brush marks, peeling labels, etc.

Licensed Items

This section has been added because there are many items out there with the "Matchbox" brand on them that are not manufactured by Lesney Products or any successors of Matchbox Toys. Matchbox has licensed out their name on a number of items and this section will cover them in a broad manner and will list the manufacturer if known. No values are listed.

Soap by Oh Dawn & Savon
Pyramids of Ra & Motor City Games by Nintendo
Sleeping Bag by Slumberland
Party Supplies (cups, plates, napkins, etc.) by Gibson
Caps & hats (assorted manufacturers)
Shirts, pants & jackets (assorted manufacturers)
Chocolate eggs by Terry's
Martini glasses
False bottom glasses by Howw
Bubble bath, shampoo & body wash by Kid's Choice
Playing cards by Piatnik
Greeting cards by Gibson
Styrofoam cups
Flying disc (Matchbox USA club)
Neck ties by UK Matchbox & MICA
Beach & bath towels (assorted manufacturers)
Christmas ornament by Carlton Cards
Cup plates by Wilkes Barre Matchbox club
Stay-On picture soap by Norton
Sticker Labels by Gibson
Wrist watches
Bubble bath by Grosvenor
Refrigerator magnets
Inverted Yesteryear goblets
Yesteryears in a bottle by Leland
Loving cups
Matchbooks by AIM
Pewter belt buckles & medallion by AIM
Pin badges from various clubs & events
Back packs & pocket sacks
Bedsheets & curtains
Framed mirrors by Steve Glick
Leslie Smith figurine by MICA
Cameras by Hanimex & Woolworth's
Pens & pencils
Chocolate & candies by Kinnerton
Cuff links by Stratton
Iron on patches
Bumper stickers
Plus others too numerous to mention.

Places To Visit—Sources

Many persons have requested contacts on places to visit or places to purchase their models. The places to visit include Matchbox Toy museums with perhaps the largest collections in the world. Sources include both mail order and shops in which to purchase your models.

Museums

Matchbox & Lesney Toy Museum
home of Charles Mack
62 Saw Mill Road
Durham, Connecticut 06422

Matchbox Road Museum
Pearl Street
Newfield, New Jersey 08344

Chester Toy Museum (Matchbox Room)
13A Lower Bridge Street
Chester, England

Main Sources

Aldrich-Svadeba Toy Company
622 Chenango St.
Binghamton, N.Y. 13901
(mail order only)

Harold's Place
532 Chestnut Street
Lynn, Massachusetts 01904
(store & mail order)

Diecast Toy Exchange
401 Carlisle Ave./P.O. Box 268
York, Pennsylvania 17405
(store & mail order)

Kiddie Kar Kollectibles
1161 Perry Street
Reading, Pennsylvania 19604
(store & mail order)

Midwest Die-Cast Miniatures
681 Paxton Place
Carol Stream IL 60188
(mail order only)

Neil's Wheels Inc.
P.O. Box 354
Old Bethpage, New York 11804
(store & mail order)

Clubs and Newsletters

For those who would like more information on models covered in this book or would like information on newer models as well, a collectors club can be an additional source of information for the Matchbox enthusiast. The following clubs can help you through their newsletters which are published either quarterly, bi-monthly or monthly. Please send a self-addressed stamped envelope when writing to the clubs for information.

Matchbox USA
Founded in 1977, this club offers a monthly publication with the editor being the author of this book. Write to: Matchbox USA, 62 Saw Mill Rd., Durham, CT 06422. On the web at www.mbww.com or email MTCHBOXUSA@aol.com

Matchbox International Collectors Association
Founded in 1985, this club offers a bi-monthly publication. Editors are Stewart Orr and Kevin McGimpsey. For North America write to: MICA NA, P.O. Box 28072, Waterloo, Ontario N2L 6J8, Canada.

American International Matchbox
Founded in 1970 by Harold Colpitts, this monthly newsletter is now being edited by Ms. Jean Conner. Contact: AIM, 532 Chestnut Street, Lynn, MA 01904

Pennsylvania Matchbox Collectors Club
Founded in 1980, this monthly newsletter and club offers to those basically in the Pennsylvania area, but membership is open to all Matchbox collectors. Write to: Mike Appnel, 1161 Perry St., Reading, PA 19604

Bay Area Matchbox Collectors Club
Founded in 1971, this club is open to Bay area, California collectors. Contact: BAMCA, Box 1534, San Jose, CA 95109

Chesapeake Miniature Vehicle Collectors Club
Founded in 1978. This club is devoted to the collecting of all miniature cars. Contact: Win Hurley, 709 Murdock Rd., Baltimore, MD 21212

Matchbox Collectors Guild
Founded in 1997 as an in-house newsletter called "Matchbox Collector" it is published by Matchbox Collectibles. Write to: Matchbox Collectibles, P.O. Box 10490, Glendale, AZ 85318

Illinois Matchbox Collectors Club
Founded in 1996 mainly for collectors in state of Illinois. Contact: Tom Sarlitto, 681 Paxton Place, Carol Stream, IL 60188. On the web at http://hometown.aol.com/jstmtchbx/mdm.html

Matchbox Forum
Founded in 1998 as mainly an internet club although a printed newsletter is also available. Contact: John Yanouzas, 7 North Bigelow Rd., Hampton, CT 06247. On the web at http://www.mtchbxforum.com

Matchbox Northwest Collectors Club
Founded at the end of 1998, this club is mainly directed at collectors in the Pacific Northwest USA. Contact: Tom Larson, 1832 NE 25th Place, Renton, WA 98056

UK Matchbox
Founded in 1977, this club folded in 1985. The club newsletters, if you are able to get copies, are a wealth of information. The editor was Ray Bush.

BIBLIOGRAPHY

Mack, Charles, Matchbox 1-75 Catalog 1969 to Date, 2nd Edition, Matchbox USA Publications, 62 Saw Mill Road, Durham, CT 06422, 1990-1996

_____, "Matchbox Toys- The Regular Wheel Years 1947-1969", Schiffer Publishing Ltd., 4880 Lower Valley Rd., Atglen, PA 19310, 1992

_____, "Matchbox Toys- The Superfast Years 1969-1982", Schiffer Publishing Ltd., 4880 Lower Valley Rd., Atglen, PA 19310, 1992

_____, "Matchbox Toys- The Universal Years 1982-1992", Schiffer Publishing Ltd., 4880 Lower Valley Rd., Atglen, PA 19310, 1993

_____, "Matchbox Toys—The Tyco Years 1993-1994," Schiffer Publishing Ltd., 4880 Lower Valley Rd., Atglen, PA 19310, 1995

McGimpsey, Kevin & Orr, Stewart, "The Yesteryear Book 1956—1996," Major Products Ltd., 13A Lower Bridge St., Chester, CH1 1RS, England, 1996

_____, "Collecting Matchbox Toys—The First Forty Years," Major Productions Ltd., 13A Lower Bridge St., Chester, CH1 1RS, England, 1989